A Programmer's Guide to Java™ SCJP Certification

Third Edition

A Programmer's Guide to Java™ SCJP Certification
A Comprehensive Primer

Third Edition

Khalid A. Mughal
Rolf W. Rasmussen

✦✦Addison-Wesley

Upper Saddle River, New Jersey • Boston • Indianapolis • San Francisco
New York • Toronto • Montreal • London • Munich • Paris • Madrid
Capetown • Sidney • Tokyo • Singapore • Mexico City

Many of the designations used by manufacturers and sellers to distinguish their products are claimed as trademarks. Where those designations appear in this book, and the publisher was aware of a trademark claim, the designations have been printed with initial capital letters or in all capitals.

The authors and publisher have taken care in the preparation of this book, but make no expressed or implied warranty of any kind and assume no responsibility for errors or omissions. No liability is assumed for incidental or consequential damages in connection with or arising out of the use of the information or programs contained herein.

The publisher offers excellent discounts on this book when ordered in quantity for bulk purchases or special sales, which may include electronic versions and/or custom covers and content particular to your business, training goals, marketing focus, and branding interests. For more information, please contact:

U.S. Corporate and Government Sales
(800) 382-3419
corpsales@pearsontechgroup.com

For sales outside the United States please contact:

International Sales
international@pearson.com

Visit us on the Web: informit.com/aw

Library of Congress Cataloging-in-Publication Data

Mughal, Khalid Azim.
  A programmer's guide to Java SCJP certification : a comprehensive primer / Khalid A. Mughal, Rolf W. Rasmussen.—3rd ed.
      p. cm.
  Previously published under title: A programmer's guide to Java certification.
  Includes bibliographical references and index.
  ISBN 0-321-55605-4 (pbk. : alk. paper)
  1. Electronic data processing personnel--Certification. 2. Operating systems (Computers)—Examinations--Study guides. 3. Java (Computer program language)--Examinations--Study guides. I. Rasmussen, Rolf (Rolf W.) II. Mughal, Khalid Azim. Programmer's guide to Java certification. III. Title.

QA76.3.M846 2008
005.2'762--dc22   2008048822

ISBN-13: 978-0-321-55605-9
ISBN-10:   0-321-55605-4
Text printed in the United States on recycled paper at Courier in Stoughton, Massachusetts.
First printing, December 2008

*To the loving memory of my mother, Zubaida Begum,
and my father, Mohammed Azim.*

—K.A.M.

*For Olivia E. Rasmussen and
Louise J. Dahlmo.*

—R.W.R.

Contents Overview

Contents

List of Figures

List of Tables

List of Examples

Foreword

●●●

Consider the following observations:

- Software continues to become ever more pervasive, ever more ubiquitous in our lives.

- Incompetence seems to be the only thing we can count on in today's world and, especially, in the domain of software.

- The Java programming language has become a lingua franca for programmers all over the world.

One can draw varied conclusions from these comments. One of them is that it is of great importance that programmers working with the Java programming language should be as competent as possible.

The Java certification program is an important effort aimed at precisely this goal. Practitioners looking to obtain such certification need good quality training materials, which brings us to this book.

Programming is still more of an art than a science, and will continue to be so for the foreseeable future. Mastering the intricacies of a large and complex programming language is a challenging task that requires time and effort, and above all experience.

Real programming requires more than just mastery of a programming language. It requires mastery of a computing platform, with a rich set of libraries. These libraries are designed to simplify the task of building realistic applications, and they do. Again, the practitioner is faced with a daunting task.

To address the clear need for professional training material, a plethora of books have been written purporting to tutor programmers in the programming language and platform skills they require.

The choice is as mind boggling as the material within the books themselves. Should one try *Java for Frontally Lobotomized Simians* or *Postmodern Java Dialectics*? The readership for these books is largely self selecting. I trust that if you, the reader, have gotten this far, you are looking for something that is intelligent, yet practical. This book is one of the finest efforts in this crowded arena. It brings a necessary level of academic rigor to an area much in need of it, while retaining an essentially pragmatic flavor.

The material in this book is probably all you need to pass the Java certification exam. It certainly isn't all you need to be a good software engineer. You must continue learning about new technologies. The hardest part of this is dealing with things that are completely different from what you are familiar with. Yet this is what distinguishes the top flight engineer from the mediocre one. Keep an open mind; it pays.

Gilad Bracha
Computational Theologist
Sun Java Software
http://java.sun.com/people/gbracha/

Preface

●●●

Writing the Third Edition

The exam for the Sun Certified Programmer for Java Platform, Standard Edition 6, has changed considerably since the second edition of this book was published. The most noticeable change in the current version of the Sun Certified Java Programmer (SCJP) 1.6 exam is the inclusion of the features of Java 5, and the shifting of emphasis towards analyzing code scenarios, rather than individual language constructs. In our opinion, the new exam demands an even greater understanding and actual experience of the language, rather than mere recitation of facts. Proficiency in the language is the key to success.

Since the emphasis of the SCJP 1.6 exam is on the core features of Java, the third edition provides even greater in-depth coverage of the relevant topics. The book covers not just the exam objectives, but also supplementary topics that aid in mastering the exam topics.

The third edition is still a one-source guide for the SCJP 1.6 exam: it provides a mixture of theory and practice for the exam. Use the book to learn Java, pass the SCJP 1.6 exam, and afterwards, use it as a handy language guide. The book also has an appendix devoted to the SCJP 1.6 Upgrade exam.

We have taken into consideration the feedback we have received from readers. The many hours spent in handling the deluge of e-mail have not been in vain. Every single e-mail is appreciated and is hereby acknowledged.

Preparing the third edition dispelled our illusions about newer editions being, to put it colloquially, a piece of cake. Every sentence from the second edition has been weighed carefully, and not many paragraphs have escaped rewriting. UML (Unified Modeling Language) is also extensively employed in this edition. Numerous new review questions have been added. In covering the new topics and expanding the existing ones, new examples, figures, and tables were also specifically created for the third edition.

About This Book

This book provides extensive coverage of the Java programming language and its core Application Programming Interfaces (APIs), with particular emphasis on its syntax and usage. The book is primarily intended for professionals who want to prepare for the SCJP 1.6 exam, but it is readily accessible to any programmer who wants to master the language. For both purposes, it provides in-depth coverage of essential features of the language and its core APIs.

There is a great and increasing demand for certified Java programmers. Sun Microsystems has defined the SCJP 1.6 exam as one that professionals can take to validate their skills. The certification provides the IT industry with a standard to use for hiring such professionals, and allows the professionals to turn their Java skills into credentials that are important for career advancement.

The book provides extensive coverage of all the objectives defined for the exam by Sun. But the exam objectives are selective and do not include many of the essential features of Java. This book covers many additional topics that every Java programmer should master in order to be proficient. In this regard, the book is a comprehensive primer for learning the Java programming language. After mastering the language by working through this book, the reader can confidently sit for the exam.

This book is *not* a complete reference for Java, as it does not attempt to list every member of every class from the Java Development Kit (JDK) API documentation. The purpose is not to document the JDK APIs. This book does not teach programming techniques. The emphasis is on the Java programming language features, their syntax and correct usage through code examples.

The book assumes little background in programming. We believe the exam is accessible to any programmer who works through the book. A Java programmer can easily skip over material that is well understood and concentrate on parts that need reinforcing, whereas a programmer new to Java will find the concepts explained from basic principles.

Each topic is explained and discussed thoroughly with examples, and backed by review questions and exercises to reinforce the concepts. The book is not biased toward any particular platform, but provides platform-specific details where necessary.

Using the Book

The reader can choose a linear or a non-linear route through the book, depending on her programming background. Non-Java programmers wishing to migrate to Java can read Chapter 1, which provides a short introduction to object-oriented programming concepts, and the procedure for compiling and running Java applications. For those preparing for the SCJP 1.6 exam, the book has a separate appendix providing all the pertinent information on taking the exam.

The table of contents; listings of tables, examples, and figures; and a comprehensive index facilitate locating topics discussed in the book.

In particular, we draw attention to the following features:

Exam Objectives

0.1 Exam objectives are stated clearly at the start of every chapter.
0.2 The number in front of the objective identfies the objective as defined by Sun.
0.3 The objectives are organized into major sections, detailing the curriculum for the exam.
0.4 The exam objectives are reproduced in Appendix B where, for each section of the syllabus, references are included to point the reader to relevant topics for the exam.

Supplementary Objectives

- Supplementary objectives cover topics that are *not* on the exam, but which we believe are important for mastering the topics that *are* on the exam.
- Any supplementary objectives are listed as bullets at the beginning of a chapter.

 ## Review Questions

Review questions are provided after every major topic, in order to test and reinforce the material. These review questions reflect the kinds of questions that can be asked on the actual exam. Annotated answers to the review questions are provided in a separate appendix.

Example 0.1 *Example Source Code*

We encourage experimenting with the code examples in order to reinforce the material from the book. These can be downloaded from the book Web site (see p. xli).

Java code is written in a `mono-spaced` font. Lines of code in the examples or in code snippets are referenced in the text by a number, which is specified by using a single-line comment in the code. For example, in the following code snippet, the call to the method `doSomethingInteresting()` hopefully does something interesting at (1).

```
// ...
doSomethingInteresting();                                          // (1)
// ...
```

Names of classes and interfaces start with an uppercase letter. Names of packages, variables, and methods start with a lowercase letter. Constants are all in uppercase letters. Interface names begin with the prefix 'I'. Coding conventions are followed, except when we have had to deviate in the interest of space or clarity.

Chapter Summary

Each chapter concludes with a summary of the topics, pointing out the major concepts discussed in the chapter.

Programming Exercises

Programming exercises at the end of each chapter provide the opportunity to put concepts into practice. Solutions to the programming exercises are provided in a separate appendix.

Mock Exam

A complete mock exam is provided in a separate appendix, which the reader can try when she is ready.

Java SE API Documentation

A vertical gray bar is used to highlight methods and fields found in the classes of the core Java APIs.

Any explanation following the API information is also similarly highlighted.

In order to obtain optimal benefit from using this book in preparing for the SCJP 1.6 exam, we strongly recommend installing the latest version (1.6 or newer) of the JDK and its accompanying API documentation. The book focuses solely on Java, and does not acknowledge previous versions.

Java Platform Upgrade Exam

For those who have taken the Sun Certified Programmer for Java Platform 1.5 Exam, and would like to prepare for the Sun Certified Programmer for Java Platform 1.6 Upgrade Exam, we have provided an appendix with details of the upgrade exam. The appendix contains the upgrade exam objectives, and for each section of the syllabus, references are included to point the reader to topics essential for the upgrade exam.

Book Web Site

This book is backed by a Web site providing auxiliary material:

```
http://www.ii.uib.no/~khalid/pgjc3e/
```

The contents of the Web site include the following:

- source code for all the examples and programming exercises in the book
- mock exam engine
- errata
- links to miscellaneous Java resources (certification, discussion groups, tools, etc.)

Information about the Java Standard Edition and its documentation can be found at the following Web site:

```
http://java.sun.com/javase/
```

The current authoritative technical reference for the Java programming language, *The Java Language Specification, Third Edition* (also published by Addison-Wesley), can be found at this Web site:

```
http://java.sun.com/docs/books/jls/
```

Request for Feedback

Considerable effort has been made to ensure the accuracy of the contents of this book. Several Java professionals have proofread the manuscript. All code examples (including code fragments) have been compiled and tested on various platforms. In the final analysis, any errors remaining are the sole responsibility of the authors.

Any questions, comments, suggestions, and corrections are welcome. Let us know whether the book was helpful or detrimental for your purposes. Any feedback is valuable. The authors can be reached by the following e-mail alias:

```
pgjc3e@ii.uib.no
```

About the Authors

Khalid A. Mughal

Khalid A. Mughal is an Associate Professor at the Department of Informatics at the University of Bergen, Norway. Professor Mughal is responsible for designing and implementing various courses, which use Java, at the Department of Informatics. Over the years, he has taught Programming Languages (Java, C/C++, Pascal), Software Engineering (Object-Oriented System Development), Databases (Data Modeling and Database Management Systems), and Compiler Techniques. He has also given numerous courses and seminars at various levels in object-oriented programming and system development, using Java and Java-related technology, both at the University and for the IT industry. He is the principal author of the book, responsible for writing the material covering the Java topics.

Professor Mughal is also the principal author of an introductory Norwegian textbook on programming in Java (*Java som første programmeringsspråk/Java as First Programming Language, Third Edition*, Cappelen Akademisk Forlag, ISBN-10: 82-02-24554-0, 2006), which he co-authored with Torill Hamre and Rolf W. Rasmussen. Together they have also published another textbook for a 2-semester course in programming (*Java Actually: A Comprehensive Primer in Programming*, Cengage Learning, ISBN-10: 1844809331, 2008).

His current work involves applying Object Technology in the development of content management systems for publication on the Web, and security issues related to web applications. For the past seven years he has been responsible for developing and running web-based programming courses in Java, which are offered to off-campus students.

He is also a member of the Association for Computing Machinery (ACM).

Rolf W. Rasmussen

Rolf W. Rasmussen is the System Development Manager at vizrt, a company that develops solutions for the TV broadcast industry, including real-time 3D graphic renderers, and content and control systems.

Rasmussen works mainly on control and automation systems, video processing, typography, and real-time visualization. He has worked on clean room implementations of the Java class libraries in the past, and is a contributor to the Free Software Foundation.

Over the years, Rasmussen has worked both academically and professionally with numerous programming languages, including Java. He is primarily responsible for developing the review questions and answers, the programming exercises and their solutions, the mock exam, and all the practical aspects related to taking the SCJP exam presented in this book.

As mentioned above, he is also a co-author of two introductory textbooks on programming in Java.

Acknowledgments (First Edition)

A small application for drawing simple shapes is used in the book to illustrate various aspects of GUI building. The idea for this application, as far as we know, first appeared in Appendix D of *Data Structures and Problem Solving Using Java* (M.A. Weiss, Addison-Wesley, 1998).

At Addison-Wesley-Longman (AWL), we would like to thank Emma Mitchell for the support and the guidance she provided us right from the start of this project, Martin Klopstock at AWL for accommodating the non-standard procedure involved in getting the book to the printing press, Clive Birks at CRB Associates for providing the professional look to the contents of this book, and finally, Sally Mortimore at AWL for seeing us over the finishing line. The efforts of other professionals behind the scenes at AWL are also acknowledged.

Many reviewers have been involved during the course of writing this book. First of all, we would like to thank the five anonymous reviewers commissioned by AWL to review the initial draft. Their input was useful in the subsequent writing of this book.

Several people have provided us with feedback on different parts of the material at various stages: Jon Christian Lønningdal, Tord Kålsrud, Kjetil Iversen, Roy Oma, and Arne Løkketangen. Their help is hereby sincerely acknowledged.

We are also very grateful to Laurence Vanhelsuwé, Kris Laporte, Anita Jacob, and Torill Hamre for taking on the daunting task of reviewing the final draft, and providing us with extensive feedback at such short notice. We would like to thank Marit Mughal for reading the manuscript with the trained eye of a veteran English schoolteacher.

We now understand why family members are invariably mentioned in a preface. Without our families' love, support, and understanding this book would have remained a virtual commodity. Khalid would like to thank Marit, Nina, and Laila for their love, and for being his pillars of support, during the writing of this book. Thanks also to the folks in Birmingham for cheering us on. Rolf would like to thank Liv, Rolf V., Knut, and Elisabeth for enduring the strange working hours producing this book has entailed. A special thanks to Marit for providing us with scrumptious dinners for consumption at the midnight hour.

Acknowledgments (Second Edition)

Feedback from many readers helped us to improve the first edition. We would like to thank the following readers for their input in this effort:

Michael F. Adolf, Tony Alicea, Kåre Auglænd, Jorge L. Barroso, Andre Beland, Darren Bruning, Paul Campbell, Roger Chang, Joanna Chappel, Laurian M Chirica, Arkadi Choufrine, Barry Colston, John Cotter, Frédéric Demers, Arthur De Souza, djc, William Ekiel, Darryl Failla, John Finlay, Christopher R. Gardner, Marco Garcia, Peter Gieser, George, Paul Graf, Shyamsundar Gururaj, Ray Ho, Leonardo Holanda, Zhu Hongjun, Kara Van Horn, Peter Horst, Nain Hwu, Kent Johnson, Samir Kanparia, Oleksiy Karpenko, Jeffrey Kenyon, Young Jin Kim, Kenneth

Kisser, Billy Kutulas, Yi-Ming Lai, Robert M. Languedoc, Steve Lasley, Winser Lo, Naga Madipalli, Craig Main, Avinash Mandsaurwale, Thomas Mathai, S. Mehra, Yuan Meng, Simon Miller, William Moore, Anders Morch, George A. Murakami, Sandy Nemecek, Chun Pan, Abigail García Patiño, Anil Philip, Alfred Raouf, Peter Rorden, Christian Seifert, Gurpreet Singh, Christopher Stanwood, Swaminathan Subramanian, Siva Sundaram, Manju Swamy, John Sweeney, Harmon Taylor, Andrew Tolopko, Ravi Verma, Per J. Walstrøm, Chun Wang, James Ward, Winky, Chun Wang, Jimmy Yang, Jennie Yip, Yanqu Zhou, and Yingting Zhou.

At the UK office of Addison-Wesley/Pearson Education, we would like to thank our former editor Simon Plumtree for his unceasing support and patience while we slogged on with the second edition. We would also like to acknowledge the help and support of the following professionals, past and present, at the London office: Alison Birtwell, Sally Carter, Karen Sellwood and Katherin Ekstrom. A special thanks to Karen Mosman (who has since moved on to another job) for her encouragement and advice.

During the last lap of getting the book to the printing press, we were in the capable hands of Ann Sellers at the US office of Addison-Wesley/Pearson Education. We would like to acknowledge her efforts and that of other professionals—in particular, Greg Doench, Jacquelyn Doucette, Amy Fleischer, Michael Mullen, and Dianne Russell—who helped to get this book through the door and on to the bookshelf. Thanks also to Mike Hendrickson for always lending an ear when we met at the OOPSLA conferences, and pointing us in the right direction with our book plans.

We would like to thank the folks at Whizlabs Software for their collaboration in producing the contents for the CD accompanying this book. Those guys certainly know the business of developing exam simulators for certification in Java technology.

We were fortunate in having two Java gurus—Laurence Vanhelsuwé and Marcus Green—to do the technical review of the second edition. As he did for the first edition, Laurence came through and provided us with invaluable feedback, from the minutiae of writing technical books to many technical issues relating to the Java programming language. Marcus put the manuscript through his severe certification scrutiny regarding the specifics of the SCJP exam. We are sorry to have upset their plans for Easter holidays, and hasten to thank them most profusely for taking on the task.

We cannot thank enough our own in-house, private copy-editor: Marit Seljeflot Mughal. She diligently and relentlessly read numerous drafts of the manuscript, usually at very short notice. Marit claims that if she understood what we had written, then a computer-literate person should have no problem whatsoever. This claim remains to be substantiated. If any commas are not used correctly, then it is entirely our fault, in spite of being repeatedly shown how to use them.

We are also indebted to many Java-enabled individuals for providing us valuable feedback on parts of the manuscript for the second edition. This includes Pradeep Chopra, Seema R., and Gaurav Kohli at Whizlabs Software. Unfortunately for us, they only had time to read part of the manuscript. Thanks also to Torill Hamre at the Nansen Environmental and Remote Sensing Center, Bergen, for her useful comments and suggestions. We also thank the following Master students at the Department of Informatics, University of Bergen, for providing useful feedback: Mikal Carlsen, Yngve Espelid, Yngve A. Aas, Sigmund Nysæter, Torkel Holm, and Eskil Saatvedt.

Family support saw us through this writing project as well. Our families have put up with our odd and long working hours, endured our preoccupation and our absence at the dining table. Khalid would like to acknowledge the love and support of his wife, Marit, and daughters, Nina and Laila, while working on this book. Rolf would like to thank Liv, Rolf V., Knut, and Elisabeth for their love, patience and support.

Acknowledgments (Third Edition)

Many readers have sent us e-mails testifying that the Programmer's Guide contributed toward their success on the exam. That is the best advertisement we can hope for. The feedback we have received since the publication of the second edition has had an impact on improving the third edition. In particular, we would like to thank the following diligent readers for their contributions:

Bret ABMac, Einar Andresen, Brian Bradshaw, Nicola Cammillini, Juan Carlos Castro, Sweta Doshi, David Featherstone, Danish Halim, Niels Harremoës, John Holcroft, Leong Jern-Kuan, Rajesh Kesarwani, Ken Kisser, Shampa Kumar, Tony LaPaso, Kaydell Leavitt, Luba Leyzerenok, Adam Lorentzon, Chuck Meier, Philip Mitchell, Sigmund Nysæter, Pat Owens, Sanket Reddy, Raul Saavedra, Oliver Schoettler, Wayne Schroeter, Mark Sullivan, Myoung Son, Bob Souther, Anthony Tang, Frederik Uyttersprot.

Erik Ernst was kind enough to review the chapter on Java generics, for which we are very grateful. The generics chapter was also reviewed by Erik Andreas Brandstadmoen and Kristian Berg. Our sincere thanks to all of you. The pages of feedback we received helped to clarify many subtleties, and made us realize that some dark corners of Java generics are best avoided by mere mortals.

Selected chapters for the third edition were also vetted by the following Java developers in the Bergen area: Olve Hansen, David J.M. Karlsen and Lars Søraas. Many thanks for taking time out from your busy schedule to provide us with your feedback. Our thanks also to Helge W. Johnsen and Amund Trovåg for feedback on review questions regarding new features in Java 1.5.

Our award for Reviewer Par Excellence goes to Jennie Yip. The meticulous notes she provided for the ten chapters of the second edition have had a profound effect on shaping the third edition. Any chance that the feat can be repeated with the third edition? Please name your price.

This time around we were again fortunate enough to have Marcus Green as our technical reviewer. We have heeded his feedback that has kept us, we hope, on the straight and narrow as far as the exam is concerned, and curbed our enthusiasm for including every Java topic that we fancied. Our sincere thanks for the review you provided us.

At Pearson, we would like to thank Greg Doench and Michelle Housley for managing the publication of this edition. We are also grateful to the people behind the scenes at Pearson who helped get the book to the printing press.

Khalid would like to thank the Computer Science Department at Cornell University, where he spent a significant part of his sabbatical (Fall 2007/Spring 2008) working on the third edition. A better place for such an endeavour would be hard to come by.

We cannot thank enough Marit Seljeflot Mughal who has been our personal quality controller, acting as an amalgamated draft reader, copy editor, and proofreader. What she sanctioned we could confidently allow to be seen by the light of day, saving us many embarrassing mistakes, both technical and non-technical. We don't know if it is for us or for the love of Java that you scrutinize the endless drafts that we lay in your path.

Any mistakes or errors remaining are an oversight on our part. Rest assured that every possible effort has been made to get the facts straight.

Without family support this edition would still be wishful thinking. Khalid would like to thank Marit, Laila, Nina and Kenneth for their love, support and understanding—particularly, while working on this book.

—Khalid A. Mughal
Rolf W. Rasmussen

September 2008
Ithaca, New York, USA
Bergen, Norway

Basics of Java Programming

1

●●

Supplementary Objectives

- Introduce the basic terminology and concepts in object-oriented programming: classes, objects, references, fields, methods, members, inheritance, aggregation.
- Identify the essential elements of a Java program.
- Learn how to compile and run a Java program.

1.1 Introduction

Before embarking on the road to Java programmer certification, it is important to understand the basic terminology and concepts in object-oriented programming (OOP). In this chapter, the emphasis is on providing an introduction rather than exhaustive coverage. In-depth coverage of the concepts follows in subsequent chapters of the book.

Java supports the writing of many different kinds of executables: applications, applets, and servlets. The basic elements of a Java application are introduced in this chapter. The old adage that practice makes perfect is certainly true when learning a programming language. To encourage programming on the computer, the mechanics of compiling and running a Java application are outlined.

1.2 Classes

One of the fundamental ways in which we handle complexity is in *abstractions*. An abstraction denotes the essential properties and behaviors of an object that differentiate it from other objects. The essence of OOP is modelling abstractions, using classes and objects. The hard part in this endeavor is finding the right abstraction.

A *class* denotes a category of objects, and acts as a blueprint for creating such objects. A class models an abstraction by defining the properties and behaviors for the objects representing the abstraction. An *object* exhibits the properties and behaviors defined by its class. The properties of an object of a class are also called *attributes*, and are defined by *fields* in Java. A *field* in a class is a variable which can store a value that represents a particular property of an object. The behaviors of an object of a class are also known as *operations*, and are defined using *methods* in Java. Fields and methods in a class declaration are collectively called *members*.

An important distinction is made between the *contract* and the *implementation* that a class provides for its objects. The contract defines *what* services, and the implementation defines *how* these services are provided by the class. Clients (i.e., other objects) only need to know the contract of an object, and not its implementation, in order to avail themselves of the object's services.

As an example, we will implement different versions of a class that models the abstraction of a stack that can push and pop characters. The stack will use an array of characters to store the characters, and a field to indicate the top element in the stack. Using Unified Modeling Language (UML) notation, a class called CharStack is graphically depicted in Figure 1.1, which models the abstraction. Both fields and method names are shown in Figure 1.1a.

Figure 1.1 *UML Notation for Classes*

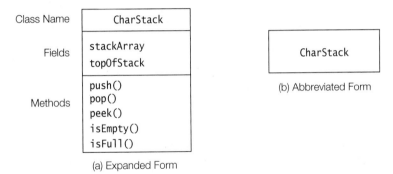

(a) Expanded Form

(b) Abbreviated Form

Declaring Members: Fields and Methods

Example 1.1 shows the declaration of the class CharStack depicted in Figure 1.1. Its intention is to illustrate the salient features of a class declaration in Java, and not the effective implementation of stacks.

A class declaration consists of a series of member declarations. In the case of the class CharStack, it has two fields declared at (1):

- stackArray, which is an array to hold the elements of the stack (in this case, characters)
- topOfStack, which denotes the top element of the stack (i.e., the index of the last character stored in the array)

The class CharStack has five methods, declared at (3), that implement the essential operations on a stack:

- push() pushes a character on to the stack
- pop() removes and returns the top element of the stack
- peek() returns the top element of the stack for inspection
- isEmpty() determines whether the stack is empty
- isFull() determines whether the stack is full

The class declaration also has a method-like declaration with the same name as the class, (2). Such declarations are called *constructors*. As we shall see, a constructor is executed when an object is created from the class. However, the implementation details in the example are not important for the present discussion.

Example 1.1 *Basic Elements of a Class Declaration*

```
//Source Filename: CharStack.java
public class CharStack {          // Class name
  // Class Declarations:
```

```
// Fields:                                                        (1)
private char[] stackArray;    // The array implementing the stack.
private int    topOfStack;    // The top of the stack.

// Constructor:                                                   (2)
public CharStack(int capacity) {
  stackArray = new char[capacity];
  topOfStack = -1;
}

// Methods:                                                       (3)
public void push(char element) { stackArray[++topOfStack] = element; }
public char pop()              { return stackArray[topOfStack--]; }
public char peek()             { return stackArray[topOfStack]; }
public boolean isEmpty()       { return topOfStack < 0; }
public boolean isFull()        { return topOfStack == stackArray.length - 1; }
}
```

1.3 Objects

Class Instantiation, Reference Values, and References

The process of creating objects from a class is called *instantiation*. An *object* is an instance of a class. The object is constructed using the class as a blueprint and is a concrete instance of the abstraction that the class represents. An object must be created before it can be used in a program.

A *reference value* is returned when an object is created. A reference value denotes a particular object. An *object reference* (or simply *reference*) is a variable that can store a reference value. A reference thus provides a handle to an object, as it can indirectly denote an object whose reference value it holds. In Java, an object can only be manipulated via its reference value, or equivalently by a reference that holds its reference value.

The process of creating objects usually involves the following steps:

1. Declaration of a variable to store the reference value of an object.
    This involves declaring a *reference variable* of the appropriate class to store the reference value of the object.

    ```
    // Declaration of two reference variables that will refer to
    // two distinct objects, namely two stacks of characters, respectively.
    CharStack stack1, stack2;
    ```

2. Creating an object.
    This involves using the new operator in conjunction with a call to a constructor, to create an instance of the class.

    ```
    // Create two distinct stacks of chars.
    ```

```
stack1 = new CharStack(10); // Stack length: 10 chars
stack2 = new CharStack(5);  // Stack length: 5 chars
```

The new operator creates an instance of the CharStack class and returns the reference value of this instance. The reference value can be assigned to a reference variable of the appropriate class. The reference variable can then be used to manipulate the object whose reference value is stored in the reference variable.

Each object has its own copy of the fields declared in the class declaration. The two stacks, referenced by stack1 and stack2, will have their own stackArray and topOfStack fields.

The purpose of the constructor call on the right side of the new operator is to initialize the newly created object. In this particular case, for each new CharStack instance created using the new operator, the constructor creates an array of characters. The length of this array is given by the value of the argument to the constructor. The constructor also initializes the topOfStack field.

The declaration of a reference and the instantiation of the class can also be combined, as in the following declaration statement:

```
CharStack stack1 = new CharStack(10),
          stack2 = new CharStack(5);
```

Figure 1.2 shows the UML notation for objects. The graphical representation of an object is very similar to that of a class. Figure 1.2 shows the canonical notation, where the name of the reference variable denoting the object is prefixed to the class name with a colon (':'). If the name of the reference variable is omitted, as in Figure 1.2b, this denotes an anonymous object. Since objects in Java do not have names, but are denoted by references, a more elaborate notation is shown in Figure 1.2c, where objects representing references of the CharStack class explicitly refer to CharStack objects. In most cases, the more compact notation will suffice.

Figure 1.2   *UML Notation for Objects*

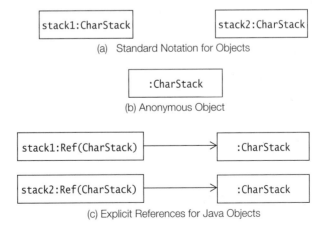

(a)   Standard Notation for Objects

(b) Anonymous Object

(c) Explicit References for Java Objects

Object Aliases

An object can be referred by several references, meaning that they store the reference value of the same object. Such references are called *aliases*. The object can be manipulated via any one of its aliases, as each one refers to the same object.

```
// Create two distinct stacks of chars.
CharStack stackA = new CharStack(12); // Stack length: 12 chars
CharStack stackB = new CharStack(6);  // Stack length: 6 chars

stackB = stackA;                      // (1) aliases after assignment
// The stack previously referenced by stackB can now be garbage collected.
```

Two stacks are created in the code above. Before the assignment at (1), the situation is as depicted in Figure 1.3a. After the assignment at (1), the reference variables stackA and stackB will denote the same stack, as depicted in Figure 1.3b. The *reference value* in stackA is assigned to stackB. The reference variables stackA and stackB are aliases after the assignment, as they refer to the same object. What happens to the stack object that was denoted by the reference variable stackB before the assignment? When objects are no longer in use, their memory is, if necessary, reclaimed and reallocated for other objects. This is called *automatic garbage collection*. Garbage collection in Java is taken care of by the runtime system.

Figure 1.3 *Aliases*

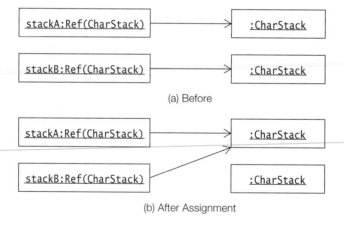

(a) Before

(b) After Assignment

1.4 Instance Members

Each object created will have its own copies of the fields defined in its class. The fields of an object are called *instance variables*. The values of the instance variables in an object comprise its *state*. Two distinct objects can have the same state, if their instance variables have the same values. The methods of an object define its behavior. These methods are called *instance methods*. It is important to note that these methods pertain to each object of the class. This should not be confused with the *implementation* of the methods, which is shared by all instances of the class. Instance variables and instance methods, which belong to objects, are collectively called *instance members*, to distinguish them from *static members*, which belong to the class only. Static members are discussed in Section 1.5.

Invoking Methods

Objects communicate by message passing. This means that an object can be made to exhibit a particular behavior by sending the appropriate message to the object. In Java, this is done by *calling* a method on the object using the binary infix dot ('.') operator. A *method call* spells out the complete message: the object that is the receiver of the message, the method to be invoked, and the arguments to the method, if any. The method invoked on the receiver can also send information back to the sender, via a single return value. The method called must be one that is defined for the object, otherwise the compiler reports an error.

```
CharStack stack = new CharStack(5);      // Create a stack
stack.push('J');                // (1) Character 'J' pushed
char c = stack.pop();           // (2) One character popped and returned: 'J'
stack.printStackElements(); // (3) Compile-time error: No such method in CharStack
```

The sample code above invokes methods on the object denoted by the reference variable stack. The method call at (1) pushes one character on the stack, and the method call at (2) pops one character off the stack. Both push() and pop() methods are defined in the class CharStack. The push() method does not return any value, but the pop() method returns the character popped. Trying to invoke a method named printStackElements on the stack results in a compile-time error, as no such method is defined in the class CharStack.

The dot ('.') notation can also be used with a reference to access the fields of an object. The use of the dot notation is governed by the *accessibility* of the member. The fields in the class CharStack have private accessibility, indicating that they are not accessible from outside the class:

```
stack.topOfStack++;      // Compile-time error: topOfStack is a private field.
```

1.5 Static Members

In some cases, certain members should only belong to the class, and not be part of any object created from the class. An example of such a situation is when a class wants to keep track of how many objects of the class have been created. Defining a counter as an instance variable in the class declaration for tracking the number of objects created does not solve the problem. Each object created will have its own counter field. Which counter should then be updated? The solution is to declare the counter field as being static. Such a field is called a *static variable*. It belongs to the class, and not to any object of the class. A static variable is initialized when the class is loaded at runtime. Similarly, a class can have *static methods* that belong to the class, and not to any specific objects of the class. Static variables and static methods are collectively known as *static members*, and are declared with the keyword static.

Figure 1.4 shows the class diagram for the class CharStack. It has been augmented by two static members that are shown underlined. The augmented definition of the CharStack class is given in Example 1.2. The field counter is a static variable declared at (1). It will be allocated and initialized to the default value 0 when the class is loaded. Each time an object of the CharStack class is created, the constructor at (2) is executed. The constructor explicitly increments the counter in the class. The method getInstanceCount() at (3) is a static method belonging to the class. It returns the counter value when called.

Figure 1.4   *Class Diagram Showing Static Members of a Class*

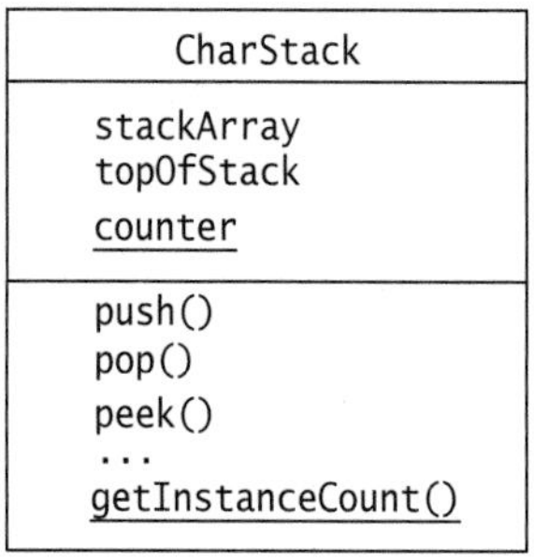

Example 1.2   *Static Members in Class Declaration*

```
//Filename CharStack.java
public class CharStack {
  // Instance variables:
  private char[] stackArray;      // The array implementing the stack.
  private int    topOfStack;      // The top of the stack.

  // Static variable
  private static int counter;                                    // (1)

  // Constructor now increments the counter for each object created.
  public CharStack(int capacity) {                               // (2)
    stackArray = new char[capacity];
    topOfStack = -1;
    counter++;
  }

  // Instance methods:
  public void push(char element) { stackArray[++topOfStack] = element; }
  public char pop()              { return stackArray[topOfStack--]; }
  public char peek()             { return stackArray[topOfStack]; }
  public boolean isEmpty()       { return topOfStack < 0; }
  public boolean isFull()        { return topOfStack == stackArray.length - 1; }
```

```
            // Static method                                              (3)
            public static int getInstanceCount() { return counter; }
        }
```

Figure 1.5 shows the classification of the members in the class CharStack using the terminology we have introduced so far. Table 1.1 at the end of this section, provides a summary of the terminology used in defining members of a class.

Clients can access static members in the class by using the class name. The following code invokes the getInstanceCount() method in the class CharStack:

```
    int count = CharStack.getInstanceCount(); // Class name to invoke static method
```

Figure 1.5   *Members of a Class*

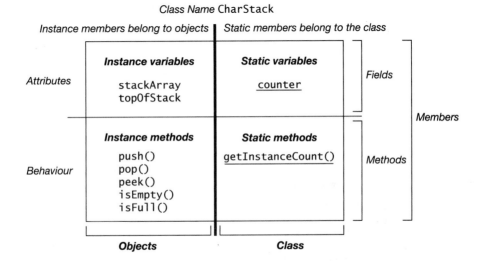

Static members can also be accessed via object references, but this is considered bad style:

```
    CharStack stack1;
    int count1 = stack1.getInstanceCount();    // Reference invokes static method
```

Static members in a class can be accessed both by the class name and via object references, but instance members can only be accessed by object references.

Table 1.1 *Terminology for Class Members*

Instance Members	These are instance variables and instance methods of an object. They can only be accessed or invoked through an object reference.
Instance Variable	A field that is allocated when the class is instantiated, i.e., when an object of the class is created. Also called *non-static field*.
Instance Method	A method that belongs to an instance of the class. Objects of the same class share its implementation.
Static Members	These are static variables and static methods of a class. They can be accessed or invoked either by using the class name or through an object reference.
Static Variable	A field that is allocated when the class is loaded. It belongs to the class and not to any specific object of the class. Also called *static field* or *class variable*.
Static Method	A method which belongs to the class and not to any object of the class. Also called *class method*.

1.6 Inheritance

There are two fundamental mechanisms for building new classes from existing ones: *inheritance* and *aggregation*. It makes sense to *inherit* from an existing class Vehicle to define a class Car, since a car is a vehicle. The class Vehicle has several *parts*; therefore, it makes sense to define a *composite object* of the class Vehicle that has *constituent objects* of such classes as Motor, Axle, and GearBox, which make up a vehicle.

Inheritance is illustrated by an example that implements a stack of characters that can print its elements on the terminal. This new stack has all the properties and behaviors of the CharStack class, but it also has the additional capability of printing its elements. Given that this printable stack is a stack of characters, it can be derived from the CharStack class. This relationship is shown in Figure 1.6. The class PrintableCharStack is called the *subclass*, and the class CharStack is called the *super-class*. The CharStack class is a *generalization* for all stacks of characters, whereas the

Figure 1.6 *Class Diagram Depicting Inheritance Relationship*

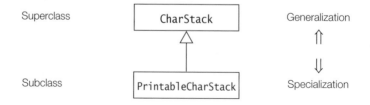

class `PrintableCharStack` is a *specialization* of stacks of characters that can also print their elements.

In Java, deriving a new class from an existing class requires the use of the extends clause in the subclass declaration. A subclass can *extend* only one superclass. The subclass can inherit members of the superclass. The following code fragment implements the `PrintableCharStack` class:

```
class PrintableCharStack extends CharStack {                    // (1)
  // Instance method
  public void printStackElements() {                           // (2)
    // ... implementation of the method...
  }

  // The constructor calls the constructor of the superclass explicitly.
  public PrintableCharStack(int capacity) { super(capacity); }   // (3)
}
```

The `PrintableCharStack` class extends the `CharStack` class at (1). Implementing the `printStackElements()` method in the `PrintableCharStack` class requires access to the field `stackArray` from the superclass `CharStack`. However, this field is *private* and therefore not accessible in the subclass. The subclass can access these fields if the accessibility of the fields is changed to *protected* in the `CharStack` class. Example 1.3 uses a version of the class `CharStack`, which has been modified accordingly. Implementation of the `printStackElements()` method is shown at (2). The constructor of the `PrintableCharStack` class at (3) calls the constructor of the superclass `CharStack` in order to initialize the stack properly.

- -

Example 1.3   *Defining a Subclass*

```
// Source Filename: CharStack.java
public class CharStack {
  // Instance variables
  protected char[] stackArray;  // The array that implements the stack.
  protected int    topOfStack;  // The top of the stack.

  // The rest of the definition is the same as in Example 1.2.
}
```

- -

```
//Filename: PrintableCharStack.java
public class PrintableCharStack extends CharStack {              // (1)

  // Instance method
  public void printStackElements() {                            // (2)
    for (int i = 0; i <= topOfStack; i++)
      System.out.print(stackArray[i]); // print each char on terminal
    System.out.println();
  }

  // Constructor calls the constructor of the superclass explicitly.
  PrintableCharStack(int capacity) { super(capacity); }          // (3)
}
```

- -

Objects of the `PrintableCharStack` class will respond just like the objects of the `Char-Stack` class, but they will also have the additional functionality defined in the subclass:

```
PrintableCharStack pcStack = new PrintableCharStack(3);
pcStack.push('H');
pcStack.push('i');
pcStack.push('!');
pcStack.printStackElements();     // Prints "Hi!" on the terminal
```

1.7 Aggregation

When building new classes from existing classes using *aggregation*, a composite object is built from the constituent objects that are its parts.

Java supports aggregation of objects by reference, since objects cannot contain other objects explicitly. The fields can only contain values of primitive data types or reference values to other objects. Each object of the CharStack class has a field to store the reference value of an array object that holds the characters. Each stack object also has a field of primitive data type int to store the index value that denotes the top of stack. This is reflected in the definition of the CharStack class, which contains an instance variable for each of these parts. In contrast to the constituent objects whose reference values are stored in fields, the values of primitive data types are themselves stored in the fields of the composite object. The *aggregation* relationship is depicted by the UML diagram in Figure 1.7, showing that each object of the CharStack class will have one array object of type char associated with it.

Figure 1.7 *Class Diagram Depicting Aggregation*

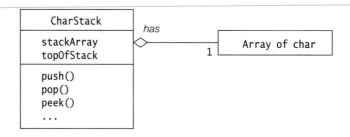

1.8 Tenets of Java

- Code in Java must be encapsulated in classes.
- There are two kinds of values in Java: there are objects that are instances of classes or arrays, and there are *atomic* values of primitive data types.
- References denote objects and are used to manipulate objects.
- Objects in Java cannot contain other objects; they can only contain references to other objects.
- During execution, reclamation of objects that are no longer in use is managed by the runtime system.

 Review Questions

1.1 Which statement about methods is true?

Select the one correct answer.

(a) A method is an implementation of an abstraction.
(b) A method is an attribute defining the property of a particular abstraction.
(c) A method is a category of objects.
(d) A method is an operation defining the behavior for a particular abstraction.
(e) A method is a blueprint for making operations.

1.2 Which statement about objects is true?

Select the one correct answer.

(a) An object is what classes are instantiated from.
(b) An object is an instance of a class.
(c) An object is a blueprint for creating concrete realization of abstractions.
(d) An object is a reference.
(e) An object is a variable.

1.3 Which is the first line of a constructor declaration in the following code?

```
public class Counter {                                   // (1)
  int current, step;
  public Counter(int startValue, int stepValue) {        // (2)
    setCurrent(startValue);
    setStep(stepValue);
  }
  public int  getCurrent()          { return current; }  // (3)
  public void setCurrent(int value) { current = value; } // (4)
  public void setStep(int stepValue) { step = stepValue; } // (5)
}
```

Select the one correct answer.

(a) (1)
(b) (2)
(c) (3)
(d) (4)
(e) (5)

1.4 Given that Thing is a class, how many objects and how many reference variables are created by the following code?

```
Thing item, stuff;
item = new Thing();
Thing entity = new Thing();
```

Select the two correct answers.

(a) One object is created.
(b) Two objects are created.
(c) Three objects are created.
(d) One reference variable is created.
(e) Two reference variables are created.
(f) Three reference variables are created.

1.5 Which statement about instance members is true?

Select the one correct answer.

(a) An instance member is also called a static member.
(b) An instance member is always a field.
(c) An instance member is never a method.
(d) An instance member belongs to an instance, not to the class as a whole.
(e) An instance member always represents an operation.

1.6 How do objects communicate in Java?

Select the one correct answer.

(a) They communicate by modifying each other's fields.
(b) They communicate by modifying the static variables of each other's classes.
(c) They communicate by calling each other's instance methods.
(d) They communicate by calling static methods of each other's classes.

1.7 Given the following code, which statements are true?

```
class A {
  int value1;
}

class B extends A {
  int value2;
}
```

Select the two correct answers.

(a) Class A extends class B.
(b) Class B is the superclass of class A.
(c) Class A inherits from class B.
(d) Class B is a subclass of class A.
(e) Objects of class A have a field named value2.
(f) Objects of class B have a field named value1.

1.9 Java Programs

A Java *source file* can contain more than one class declaration. Each source file name has the extension .java. The JDK enforces the rule that any class in the source file that has public accessibility must be declared in its own file; meaning that such a public class must be declared in a source file whose file name comprises the name of this public class with .java as its extension. The above rule implies that a source file can only contain at the most one public class. If the source file contains a public class, the file naming rule must be obeyed.

Each class declaration in a source file is compiled into a separate *class file*, containing *Java byte code*. The name of this file comprises the name of the class with .class as its extension. The JDK provides tools for compiling and running programs, as explained in the next section. The classes in the Java standard library are already compiled, and the JDK tools know where to find them.

1.10 Sample Java Application

An *application* is just a synonym for a *program*: source code that is compiled and directly executed. In order to create an application in Java, the program must have a class that defines a method named main, which is the starting point for the execution of any application.

Essential Elements of a Java Application

Example 1.4 is an example of an application in which a client uses the CharStack class to reverse a string of characters.

Example 1.4 *An Application*

```
// Source Filename: CharStack.java
public class CharStack {
  // Same as in Example 1.2.
}
```

```
//Filename: Client.java
public class Client {

  public static void main(String[] args) {

    // Create a stack.
    CharStack stack = new CharStack(40);

    // Create a string to push on the stack:
    String str = "!no tis ot nuf era skcatS";
    int length = str.length();
    System.out.println("Original string: " + str);

    // Push the string char by char onto the stack:
    for (int i = 0; i < length; i++) {
      stack.push(str.charAt(i));
    }

    System.out.print("Reversed string: ");
    // Pop and print each char from the stack:
    while (!stack.isEmpty()) { // Check if the stack is not empty.
      System.out.print(stack.pop());
    }
    System.out.println();
  }
}
```

Output from the program:

```
Original string: !no tis ot nuf era skcatS
Reversed string: Stacks are fun to sit on!
```

The public class Client defines a method with the name main. To start the application, the main() method in this public class is invoked by the Java interpreter, also called the Java Virtual Machine (JVM). The *method header* of this main() method should be declared as shown in the following method stub:

```
public static void main(String[] args)    // Method header
{ /* Implementation */ }
```

The main() method has public accessibility, i.e., it is accessible from any class. The keyword static means the method belongs to the class. The keyword void means the method does not return any value. The parameter list, (String[] args), is an array of strings that can be used to pass information to the main() method when the application is started.

Compiling and Running an Application

Java source files can be compiled using the Java compiler tool javac, which is part of the JDK.

The source file `Client.java` contains the declaration of the `Client` class. The source file can be compiled by giving the following command at the command line. (The character > is the command prompt.)

```
>javac Client.java
```

This creates the class file `Client.class` containing the Java byte code for the `Client` class. The `Client` class uses the `CharStack` class, and if the file `CharStack.class` does not already exist, the compiler will also compile the source file `CharStack.java`.

Compiled classes can be executed by the Java interpreter java, which is also part of the JDK. Example 1.4 can be run by giving the following command in the command line:

```
>java Client
```

Note that only the name of the class is specified, resulting in the execution starting in the `main()` method of the specified class. The application in Example 1.4 terminates when the execution of the `main()` method is completed.

 ## Review Questions

1.8   Which command from the JDK should be used to compile the following source code contained in a file named `SmallProg.java`?

```
public class SmallProg {
    public static void main(String[] args) { System.out.println("Good luck!"); }
}
```

Select the one correct answer.

(a) java SmallProg
(b) javac SmallProg
(c) java SmallProg.java
(d) javac SmallProg.java
(e) java SmallProg main

1.9   Which command from the JDK should be used to execute the `main()` method of a class named `SmallProg`?

Select the one correct answer.

(a) java SmallProg
(b) javac SmallProg
(c) java SmallProg.java
(d) java SmallProg.class
(e) java SmallProg.main()

Chapter Summary

The following information was included in this chapter:

- basic concepts in OOP, and how they are supported in Java
- essential elements of a Java application
- compiling and running Java applications

 Programming Exercise

1.1 Modify the program from Example 1.4 to use the `PrintableCharStack` class, rather than the `CharStack` class from Example 1.2. Utilize the `printStackEle-ments()` method from the `PrintableCharStack` class. Is the new program behavior-wise any different from Example 1.4?

Language Fundamentals

2

●●●

Exam Objectives

1.3 Develop code that declares, initializes, and uses primitives, arrays, enums, and objects as static, instance, and local variables. Also, use legal identifiers for variable names.

- ○ *For arrays, see Section 3.6, p. 69.*
- ○ *For enums, see Section 3.5, p. 54.*
- ○ *For initializers, see Section 9.7, p. 406.*

Supplementary Objectives

- Be able to identify the basic elements of the Java programming language: keywords, identifiers, literals and primitive data types.
- Understand the scope of variables.
- Understand initializing variables with default values.

2.1 Basic Language Elements

Like any other programming language, the Java programming language is defined by *grammar rules* that specify how *syntactically* legal constructs can be formed using the language elements, and by a *semantic definition* that specifies the *meaning* of syntactically legal constructs.

Lexical Tokens

The low-level language elements are called *lexical tokens* (or just *tokens*) and are the building blocks for more complex constructs. Identifiers, numbers, operators, and special characters are all examples of tokens that can be used to build high-level constructs like expressions, statements, methods, and classes.

Identifiers

A name in a program is called an *identifier*. Identifiers can be used to denote classes, methods, variables, and labels.

In Java, an *identifier* is composed of a sequence of characters, where each character can be either a *letter* or a *digit*. However, the first character in an identifier must be a letter. Since Java programs are written in the Unicode character set (see p. 23), the definitions of letter and digit are interpreted according to this character set. Note that *connecting punctuation* (such as *underscore* _) and any *currency symbol* (such as $, ¢, ¥, or £) are allowed as letters, but should be avoided in identifier names.

Identifiers in Java are *case sensitive*, for example, `price` and `Price` are two different identifiers.

Examples of Legal Identifiers

```
number, Number, sum_$, bingo, $$_100, mål, grüß
```

Examples of Illegal Identifiers

```
48chevy, all@hands, grand-sum
```

The name 48chevy is not a legal identifier as it starts with a digit. The character @ is not a legal character in an identifier. It is also not a legal operator, so that all@hands cannot be interpreted as a legal expression with two operands. The character - is also not a legal character in an identifier. However, it is a legal operator so grand-sum could be interpreted as a legal expression with two operands.

Keywords

Keywords are reserved words that are predefined in the language and cannot be used to denote other entities. All the keywords are in lowercase, and incorrect usage results in compilation errors.

Keywords currently defined in the language are listed in Table 2.1. In addition, three identifiers are reserved as predefined *literals* in the language: the `null` reference, and the boolean literals `true` and `false` (see Table 2.2). Keywords currently reserved, but not in use, are listed in Table 2.3. A reserved word cannot be used as an identifier. The index contains references to relevant sections where currently used keywords are explained.

Table 2.1 *Keywords in Java*

abstract	default	if	private	this
assert	do	implements	protected	throw
boolean	double	import	public	throws
break	else	instanceof	return	transient
byte	enum	int	short	try
case	extends	interface	static	void
catch	final	long	strictfp	volatile
char	finally	native	super	while
class	float	new	switch	
continue	for	package	synchronized	

Table 2.2 *Reserved Literals in Java*

null	true	false

Table 2.3 *Reserved Keywords not Currently in Use*

const	goto

Literals

A *literal* denotes a constant value, i.e., the value that a literal represents remains unchanged in the program. Literals represent numerical (integer or floating-point), character, boolean or string values. In addition, there is the literal `null` that represents the null reference.

Table 2.4 *Examples of Literals*

Integer	2000	0	-7			
Floating-point	3.14	-3.14	.5	0.5		
Character	'a'	'A'	'0'	':'	'-'	')'
Boolean	true	false				
String	"abba"	"3.14"	"for"	"a piece of the action"		

Integer Literals

Integer data types comprise the following primitive data types: int, long, byte, and short (see Section 2.2, p. 28).

The default data type of an integer literal is always int, but it can be specified as long by appending the suffix L (or l) to the integer value. Without the suffix, the long literals 2000L and 0l will be interpreted as int literals. There is no direct way to specify a short or a byte literal.

In addition to the decimal number system, integer literals can also be specified in octal (*base* 8) and hexadecimal (*base* 16) number systems. Octal and hexadecimal numbers are specified with a 0 and 0x (or 0X) prefix respectively. Examples of decimal, octal and hexadecimal literals are shown in Table 2.5. Note that the leading 0 (zero) digit is not the uppercase letter 0. The hexadecimal digits from a to f can also be specified with the corresponding uppercase forms (A to F). Negative integers (e.g. -90) can be specified by prefixing the minus sign (-) to the magnitude of the integer regardless of number system (e.g., -0132 or -0X5A). Number systems and number representation are discussed in Appendix G. Java does not support literals in binary notation.

Table 2.5 *Examples of Decimal, Octal, and Hexadecimal Literals*

Decimal	Octal	Hexadecimal
8	010	0x8
10L	012L	0xaL
16	020	0x10
27	033	0x1B
90L	0132L	0x5aL
-90	-0132	-0x5A
2147483647 (i.e., $2^{31}-1$)	017777777777	0x7fffffff
-2147483648 (i.e., -2^{31})	-020000000000	-0x80000000
1125899906842624L (i.e., 2^{50})	040000000000000000L	0x4000000000000L

Floating-Point Literals

Floating-point data types come in two flavors: float or double.

The default data type of a floating-point literal is double, but it can be explicitly designated by appending the suffix D (or d) to the value. A floating-point literal can also be specified to be a float by appending the suffix F (or f).

Floating-point literals can also be specified in scientific notation, where E (or e) stands for *Exponent*. For example, the double literal 194.9E-2 in scientific notation is interpreted as 194.9×10^{-2} (i.e., 1.949).

Examples of double *Literals*

```
0.0       0.0d     0D
0.49      .49      .49D
49.0      49.      49D
4.9E+1    4.9E+1D  4.9e1d    4900e-2   .49E2
```

Examples of float *Literals*

```
0.0F      0f
0.49F     .49F
49.0F     49.F     49F
4.9E+1F   4900e-2f  .49E2F
```

Note that the decimal point and the exponent are optional and that at least one digit must be specified.

Boolean Literals

The primitive data type boolean represents the truth-values *true* or *false* that are denoted by the reserved literals true or false, respectively.

Character Literals

A character literal is quoted in single-quotes ('). All character literals have the primitive data type char.

A character literal is represented according to the 16-bit Unicode character set, which subsumes the 8-bit ISO-Latin-1 and the 7-bit ASCII characters. In Table 2.6, note that digits (0 to 9), upper-case letters (A to Z), and lower-case letters (a to z) have contiguous Unicode values. A Unicode character can always be specified as a four-digit hexadecimal number (i.e., 16 bits) with the prefix \u.

Table 2.6   *Examples of Character Literals*

Character Literal	Character Literal using Unicode value	Character
' '	'\u0020'	Space
'0'	'\u0030'	0
'1'	'\u0031'	1
'9'	'\u0039'	9
'A'	'\u0041'	A
'B'	'\u0042'	B
'Z'	'\u005a'	Z
'a'	'\u0061'	a
'b'	'\u0062'	b

Continues

Table 2.6   *Examples of Character Literals (Continued)*

Character Literal	Character Literal using Unicode value	Character
'z'	'\u007a'	z
'Ñ'	'\u0084'	Ñ
'å'	'\u008c'	å
'ß'	'\u00a7'	ß

Escape Sequences

Certain *escape sequences* define special characters, as shown in Table 2.7. These escape sequences can be single-quoted to define character literals. For example, the character literals '\t' and '\u0009' are equivalent. However, the character literals '\u000a' and '\u000d' should not be used to represent newline and carriage return in the source code. These values are interpreted as line-terminator characters by the compiler, and will cause compile time errors. You should use the escape sequences '\n' and '\r', respectively, for correct interpretation of these characters in the source code.

Table 2.7   *Escape Sequences*

Escape Sequence	Unicode Value	Character
\b	\u0008	Backspace (BS)
\t	\u0009	Horizontal tab (HT or TAB)
\n	\u000a	Linefeed (LF) a.k.a. Newline (NL)
\f	\u000c	Form feed (FF)
\r	\u000d	Carriage return (CR)
\'	\u0027	Apostrophe-quote, a.k.a. single quote
\"	\u0022	Quotation mark, a.k.a. double quote
\\	\u005c	Backslash

We can also use the escape sequence \ddd to specify a character literal as an octal value, where each digit d can be any octal digit (0–7), as shown in Table 2.8. The number of digits must be three or fewer, and the octal value cannot exceed \377, i.e., only the first 256 characters can be specified with this notation.

Table 2.8 *Examples of Escape Sequence \ddd*

Escape Sequence \ddd	Character Literal
'\141'	'a'
'\46'	'&'
'\60'	'0'

String Literals

A *string literal* is a sequence of characters which must be enclosed in double quotes
and must occur on a single line. All string literals are objects of the class String (see
Section 10.4, p. 439).

Escape sequences as well as Unicode values can appear in string literals:

```
"Here comes a tab.\t And here comes another one\u0009!"        (1)
"What's on the menu?"                                          (2)
"\"String literals are double-quoted.\""                      (3)
"Left!\nRight!"                                                (4)
"Don't split                                                   (5)
me up!"
```

In (1), the tab character is specified using the escape sequence and the Unicode
value, respectively. In (2), the single apostrophe need not be escaped in strings, but
it would be if specified as a character literal ('\''). In (3), the double quotes in the
string must be escaped. In (4), we use the escape sequence \n to insert a newline.
(5) generates a compile time error, as the string literal is split over several lines.
Printing the strings from (1) to (4) will give the following result:

```
Here comes a tab.    And here comes another one    !
What's on the menu?
"String literals are double-quoted."
Left!
Right!
```

One should also use the escape sequences \n and \r, respectively, for correct interpretation of the characters \u000a (newline) and \u000d (form feed) in string literals.

White Spaces

A *white space* is a sequence of spaces, tabs, form feeds, and line terminator characters in a Java source file. Line terminators can be newline, carriage return, or a carriage return-newline sequence.

A Java program is a free-format sequence of characters that is *tokenized* by the compiler, i.e., broken into a stream of tokens for further analysis. Separators and operators help to distinguish tokens, but sometimes white space has to be inserted

explicitly as a separator. For example, the identifier `classRoom` will be interpreted as a single token, unless white space is inserted to distinguish the keyword `class` from the identifier `Room`.

White space aids not only in separating tokens, but also in formatting the program so that it is easy to read. The compiler ignores the white spaces once the tokens are identified.

Comments

A program can be documented by inserting comments at relevant places in the source code. These comments are for documentation purposes only and are ignored by the compiler.

Java provides three types of comments to document a program:

* A single-line comment: `// ... to the end of the line`
* A multiple-line comment: `/* ... */`
* A documentation (Javadoc) comment: `/** ... */`

Single-Line Comment

All characters after the comment-start sequence `//` through to the end of the line constitute a *single-line comment*.

```
// This comment ends at the end of this line.
int age;        // From comment-start sequence to the end of the line is a comment.
```

Multiple-Line Comment

A *multiple-line comment*, as the name suggests, can span several lines. Such a comment starts with the sequence `/*` and ends with the sequence `*/`.

```
/* A comment
   on several
   lines.
*/
```

The comment-start sequences (`//`, `/*`, `/**`) are not treated differently from other characters when occurring within comments, and are thus ignored. This means that trying to nest multiple-line comments will result in a compile time error:

```
/* Formula for alchemy.
   gold = wizard.makeGold(stone);
   /* But it only works on Sundays. */
*/
```

The second occurrence of the comment-start sequence `/*` is ignored. The last occurrence of the sequence `*/` in the code is now unmatched, resulting in a syntax error.

Documentation Comment

A *documentation comment* is a special-purpose comment that is used by the javadoc tool to generate HTML documentation for the program. Documentation comments are usually placed in front of classes, interfaces, methods, and field definitions. Special tags can be used inside a documentation comment to provide more specific information. Such a comment starts with the sequence /** and ends with the sequence */:

```
/**
 *  This class implements a gizmo.
 *  @author K.A.M.
 *  @version 3.0
 */
```

For details on the javadoc tool, see the tools documentation provided by the JDK.

 ## Review Questions

2.1 Which of the following is not a legal identifier?

Select the one correct answer.

(a) a2z
(b) ödipus
(c) 52pickup
(d) _class
(e) ca$h

2.2 Which statement is true?

Select the one correct answer.

(a) new and delete are keywords in the Java language.
(b) try, catch, and thrown are keywords in the Java language.
(c) static, unsigned, and long are keywords in the Java language.
(d) exit, class, and while are keywords in the Java language.
(e) return, goto, and default are keywords in the Java language.
(f) for, while, and next are keywords in the Java language.

2.3 Which statement about the following comment is true?

```
/* // */
```

Select the one correct answer.

(a) The comment is not valid. The multiple-line comment (/* ... */) does not end correctly, since the comment-end sequence */ is a part of the single-line comment (// ...).
(b) It is a completely valid comment. The // part is ignored by the compiler.
(c) This combination of comments is illegal, and will result in a compile time error.

2.2 Primitive Data Types

Figure 2.1 gives an overview of the primitive data types in Java.

Primitive data types in Java can be divided into three main categories:

- *integral types*—represent signed integers (byte, short, int, long) and unsigned character values (char)
- *floating-point types* (float, double)—represent fractional signed numbers
- *boolean type* (boolean)—represents logical values

Figure 2.1   *Primitive Data Types in Java*

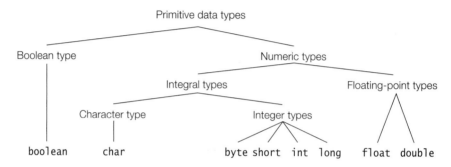

Primitive data values are not objects. Each primitive data type defines the range of values in the data type, and operations on these values are defined by special operators in the language (see Chapter 5).

Each primitive data type also has a corresponding *wrapper* class that can be used to represent a primitive value as an object. Wrapper classes are discussed in Section 10.3, p. 428.

Integer Types

Table 2.9   *Range of Integer Values*

Data Type	Width (bits)	Minimum value MIN_VALUE	Maximum value MAX_VALUE
byte	8	-2^7 (-128)	2^7-1 (+127)
short	16	-2^{15} (-32768)	$2^{15}-1$ (+32767)
int	32	-2^{31} (-2147483648)	$2^{31}-1$ (+2147483647)
long	64	-2^{63} (-9223372036854775808L)	$2^{63}-1$ (+9223372036854775807L)

Integer data types are byte, short, int, and long (see Table 2.9). Their values are signed integers represented by 2's complement (see Section G.4, p. 1010).

The char Type

Table 2.10 *Range of Character Values*

Data Type	Width (bits)	Minimum Unicode value	Maximum Unicode value
char	16	0x0 (\u0000)	0xffff (\uffff)

The data type char represents characters (see Table 2.10). Their values are unsigned integers that denote all the 65536 (2^{16}) characters in the 16-bit Unicode character set. This set includes letters, digits, and special characters.

The first 128 characters of the Unicode set are the same as the 128 characters of the 7-bit ASCII character set, and the first 256 characters of the Unicode set correspond to the 256 characters of the 8-bit ISO Latin-1 character set.

The integer types and the char type are collectively called *integral types*.

The Floating-Point Types

Table 2.11 *Range of Floating-Point Values*

Data Type	Width (bits)	Minimum Positive Value MIN_VALUE	Maximum Positive Value MAX_VALUE
float	32	1.401298464324817E-45f	3.402823476638528860e+38f
double	64	4.94065645841246544e-324	1.79769313486231570e+308

Floating-point numbers are represented by the float and double data types.

Floating-point numbers conform to the IEEE 754-1985 binary floating-point standard. Table 2.11 shows the range of values for positive floating-point numbers, but these apply equally to negative floating-point numbers with the '-' sign as a prefix. Zero can be either 0.0 or -0.0.

Since the size for representation is a finite number of bits, certain floating-point numbers can only be represented as approximations. For example, the value of the expression (1.0/3.0) is represented as an approximation due to the finite number of bits used.

The boolean Type

Table 2.12 *Boolean Values*

Data Type	Width	True Value Literal	False Value Literal
boolean	not applicable	true	false

The data type boolean represents the two logical values denoted by the literals true and false (see Table 2.12).

Boolean values are produced by all *relational* (see Section 5.10, p. 190), *conditional* (see Section 5.13, p. 196) and *boolean logical operators* (see Section 5.12, p. 194), and are primarily used to govern the flow of control during program execution.

Table 2.13 summarizes the pertinent facts about the primitive data types: their width or size, which indicates the number of the bits required to store a primitive value; their range of legal values, which is specified by the minimum and the maximum values permissible; and the name of the corresponding wrapper class (see Section 10.3, p. 428).

Table 2.13 *Summary of Primitive Data Types*

Data Type	Width (bits)	Minimum Value, Maximum Value	Wrapper Class
boolean	not applicable	true, false	Boolean
byte	8	-2^7, 2^7-1	Byte
short	16	-2^{15}, $2^{15}-1$	Short
char	16	0x0, 0xffff	Character
int	32	-2^{31}, $2^{31}-1$	Integer
long	64	-2^{63}, $2^{63}-1$	Long
float	32	$\pm$1.40129846432481707e-45f, $\pm$3.402823476638528860e+38f	Float
double	64	$\pm$4.94065645841246544e-324, $\pm$1.79769313486231570e+308	Double

Review Questions

2.4 Which of the following do not denote a primitive data value in Java?

Select the two correct answers.
(a) "t"
(b) 'k'
(c) 50.5F
(d) "hello"
(e) false

2.5 Which of the following primitive data types are not integer types?

Select the three correct answers.
(a) boolean
(b) byte
(c) float
(d) short
(e) double

2.6 Which integral type in Java has the exact range from -2147483648 (-2^{31}) to 2147483647 ($2^{31}-1$), inclusive?

Select the one correct answer.
(a) byte
(b) short
(c) int
(d) long
(e) char

2.3 Variable Declarations

A *variable* stores a value of a particular type. A variable has a name, a type, and a value associated with it. In Java, variables can only store values of primitive data types and reference values of objects. Variables that store reference values of objects are called *reference variables* (or *object references* or simply *references*).

Declaring and Initializing Variables

Variable declarations are used to specify the type and the name of variables. This implicitly determines their memory allocation and the values that can be stored in them. Examples of declaring variables that can store primitive values:

```
char a, b, c;        // a, b and c are character variables.
double area;         // area is a floating-point variable.
boolean flag;        // flag is a boolean variable.
```

The first declaration above is equivalent to the following three declarations:

```
char a;
char b;
char c;
```

A declaration can also include an initialization expression to specify an appropriate initial value for the variable:

```
int i = 10,            // i is an int variable with initial value 10.
    j = 101;           // j is an int variable with initial value 101.
long big = 2147483648L;  // big is a long variable with specified initial value.
```

Reference Variables

An *reference variable* can store the reference value of an object, and can be used to manipulate the object denoted by the reference value.

A variable declaration that specifies a *reference type* (i.e., a class, an array, or an interface name) declares a reference variable. Analogous to the declaration of variables of primitive data types, the simplest form of reference variable declaration only specifies the name and the reference type. The declaration determines what objects can be referenced by a reference variable. Before we can use a reference variable to manipulate an object, it must be declared and initialized with the reference value of the object.

```
Pizza yummyPizza;    // Variable yummyPizza can reference objects of class Pizza.
Hamburger bigOne,    // Variable bigOne can reference objects of class Hamburger,
         smallOne;   // and so can variable smallOne.
```

It is important to note that the declarations above do not create any objects of class Pizza or Hamburger. The above declarations only create variables that can store references of objects of the specified classes.

A declaration can also include an initializer expression to create an object whose reference value can be assigned to the reference variable:

```
Pizza yummyPizza = new Pizza("Hot&Spicy"); // Declaration with initializer.
```

The reference variable yummyPizza can reference objects of class Pizza. The keyword new, together with the *constructor call* Pizza("Hot&Spicy"), creates an object of the class Pizza. The reference value of this object is assigned to the variable yummyPizza. The newly created object of class Pizza can now be manipulated through the reference variable yummyPizza.

Initializers for initializing fields in objects, and static variables in classes and interfaces are discussed in Section 9.7, p. 406.

Reference variables for arrays are discussed in Section 3.6, p. 69.

2.4 Initial Values for Variables

Default Values for Fields

Default values for fields of primitive data types and reference types are listed in Table 2.14. The value assigned depends on the type of the field.

Table 2.14 *Default Values*

Data Type	Default Value
boolean	false
char	'\u0000'
Integer (byte, short, int, long)	0L for long, 0 for others
Floating-point (float, double)	0.0F or 0.0D
Reference types	null

If no initialization is provided for a static variable either in the declaration or in a static initializer block (see Section 9.9, p. 410), it is initialized with the default value of its type when the class is loaded.

Similarly, if no initialization is provided for an instance variable either in the declaration or in an instance initializer block (see Section 9.10, p. 413), it is initialized with the default value of its type when the class is instantiated.

The fields of reference types are always initialized with the null reference value if no initialization is provided.

Example 2.1 illustrates default initialization of fields. Note that static variables are initialized when the class is loaded the first time, and instance variables are initialized accordingly in *every* object created from the class Light.

Example 2.1 *Default Values for Fields*

```java
public class Light {
  // Static variable
  static int counter;      // Default value 0 when class is loaded.

  // Instance variables:
  int    noOfWatts = 100; // Explicitly set to 100.
  boolean indicator;       // Implicitly set to default value false.
  String  location;        // Implicitly set to default value null.

  public static void main(String[] args) {
    Light bulb = new Light();
    System.out.println("Static variable counter: "    + Light.counter);
    System.out.println("Instance variable noOfWatts: " + bulb.noOfWatts);
```

```
      System.out.println("Instance variable indicator: " + bulb.indicator);
      System.out.println("Instance variable location: "  + bulb.location);
      return;
    }
  }
```

Output from the program:

```
Static variable counter: 0
Instance variable noOfWatts: 100
Instance variable indicator: false
Instance variable location: null
```

Initializing Local Variables of Primitive Data Types

Local variables are variables that are declared in methods, constructors, and blocks (see Chapter 3, p. 39). Local variables are *not* initialized when they are created at method invocation, that is, when the execution of a method is started. The same applies in constructors and blocks. Local variables must be explicitly initialized before being used. The compiler will report as errors any attempts to use uninitialized local variables.

Example 2.2   *Flagging Uninitialized Local Variables of Primitive Data Types*

```
public class TooSmartClass {
  public static void main(String[] args) {
    int weight = 10, thePrice;                        // (1) Local variables

    if (weight <  10) thePrice = 1000;
    if (weight >  50) thePrice = 5000;
    if (weight >= 10) thePrice = weight*10;           // (2) Always executed.
    System.out.println("The price is: " + thePrice);  // (3)
  }
}
```

In Example 2.2, the compiler complains that the local variable thePrice used in the println statement at (3) may not be initialized. However, it can be seen that at runtime, the local variable thePrice will get the value 100 in the last if-statement at (2), before it is used in the println statement. The compiler does not perform a rigorous analysis of the program in this regard. It only compiles the body of a conditional statement if it can deduce the condition to be true. The program will compile correctly if the variable is initialized in the declaration, or if an unconditional assignment is made to the variable.

Replacing the declaration of the local variables at (1) in Example 2.2 with the following declaration solves the problem:

```
int weight = 10, thePrice = 0;           // (1') Both local variables initialized.
```

Initializing Local Reference Variables

Local reference variables are bound by the same initialization rules as local variables of primitive data types.

Example 2.3   *Flagging Uninitialized Local Reference Variables*

```java
public class VerySmartClass {
  public static void main(String[] args) {
    String importantMessage;       // Local reference variable

    System.out.println("The message length is: " + importantMessage.length());
  }
}
```

In Example 2.3, the compiler complains that the local variable `importantMessage` used in the `println` statement may not be initialized. If the variable `importantMessage` is set to the value `null`, the program will compile. However, a runtime error (`NullPointerException`) will occur when the code is executed, since the variable `importantMessage` will not denote any object. The golden rule is to ensure that a reference variable, whether local or not, is assigned a reference to an object before it is used, that is, ensure that it does not have the value `null`.

The program compiles and runs if we replace the declaration with the following declaration of the local variable, which creates a string literal and assigns its reference value to the local reference variable `importantMessage`:

```java
String importantMessage = "Initialize before use!";
```

Arrays and their default values are discussed in Section 3.6, p. 69.

Lifetime of Variables

The lifetime of a variable, that is, the time a variable is accessible during execution, is determined by the context in which it is declared. The lifetime of a variable is also called *scope,* and is discussed in more detail in Section 4.6, p. 129. We distinguish between lifetime of variables in three contexts:

- *Instance variables*—members of a class, and created for each object of the class. In other words, every object of the class will have its own copies of these variables, which are local to the object. The values of these variables at any given time constitute the *state* of the object. Instance variables exist as long as the object they belong to is in use at runtime.

- *Static variables*—also members of a class, but not created for any specific object of the class and, therefore, belong only to the class (see Section 4.6, p. 129). They are created when the class is loaded at runtime, and exist as long as the class is available at runtime.

- *Local variables* (also called *method automatic variables*)—declared in methods, constructors, and blocks; and created for each execution of the method, constructor, or block. After the execution of the method, constructor, or block completes, local (non-final) variables are no longer accessible.

 Review Questions

2.7 Which declarations are valid?

Select the three correct answers.
(a) `char a = '\u0061';`
(b) `char 'a' = 'a';`
(c) `char \u0061 = 'a';`
(d) `ch\u0061r a = 'a';`
(e) `ch'a'r a = 'a';`

2.8 Given the following code within a method, which statement is true?

```
int a, b;
b = 5;
```

Select the one correct answer.
(a) Local variable a is not declared.
(b) Local variable b is not declared.
(c) Local variable a is declared but not initialized.
(d) Local variable b is declared but not initialized.
(e) Local variable b is initialized but not declared.

2.9 In which of these variable declarations will the variable remain uninitialized unless it is explicitly initialized?

Select the one correct answer.
(a) Declaration of an instance variable of type int.
(b) Declaration of a static variable of type float.
(c) Declaration of a local variable of type float.
(d) Declaration of a static variable of type Object.
(e) Declaration of an instance variable of type int[].

2.10 What will be the result of compiling and running the following program?

```
public class Init {

    String title;
    boolean published;

    static int total;
    static double maxPrice;
```

```java
public static void main(String[] args) {
  Init initMe = new Init();
  double price;
  if (true)
    price = 100.00;
  System.out.println("|" + initMe.title + "|" + initMe.published + "|" +
                   Init.total + "|" + Init.maxPrice + "|" + price+ "|");
  }
}
```

Select the one correct answer.

(a) The program will fail to compile.
(b) The program will compile, and print |null|false|0|0.0|0.0|, when run.
(c) The program will compile, and print |null|true|0|0.0|100.0|, when run.
(d) The program will compile, and print | |false|0|0.0|0.0|, when run.
(e) The program will compile, and print |null|false|0|0.0|100.0|, when run.

Chapter Summary

The following information was included in this chapter:

- basic language elements: identifiers, keywords, literals, white space, and comments
- primitive data types: integral, floating-point, and boolean
- notational representation of numbers in decimal, octal, and hexadecimal systems
- declaration and initialization of variables, including reference variables
- usage of default values for instance variables and static variables
- lifetime of instance variables, static variables, and local variables

Programming Exercise

2.1 The following program has several errors. Modify the program so that it will compile and run without errors.

```java
// Filename: Temperature.java
PUBLIC CLASS temperature {
  PUBLIC void main(string args) {
    double fahrenheit = 62.5;
    */ Convert /*
    double celsius = f2c(fahrenheit);
    System.out.println(fahrenheit + 'F' + " = " + Celsius + 'C');
  }

  double f2c(float fahr) {
    RETURN (fahr - 32) * 5 / 9;
  }
}
```

Declarations

3

1.3 Develop code that declares, initializes, and uses primitives, arrays, enums, and objects as static, instance, and local variables. Also, use legal identifiers for variable names.

- *Enums and arrays are covered in this chapter.*
- *For primitive types, see Section 2.2, p. 28.*
- *For initialization of static, instance, and local variables, see Section 2.3, p. 31.*
- *For initializers, see Section 9.7, p. 406.*

1.4 Develop code that declares both static and non-static methods, and—if appropriate—use method names that adhere to the JavaBeans naming standards. Also develop code that declares and uses a variable-length argument list.

1.5 Given a code example, determine if a method is correctly overriding or overloading another method, and identify legal return values (including covariant returns), for the method.

- *For overloaded method resolution, see Section 7.10, p. 324.*
- *For overriding methods, see Section 7.2, p. 288.*
- *For return values, see Section 6.4, p. 228.*
- *For covariant return, see Section 7.2, p. 290.*

1.6 Given a set of classes and superclasses, develop constructors for one or more of the classes. Given a class declaration, determine if a default constructor will be created and, if so, determine the behavior of that constructor. Given a nested or non-nested class listing, write code to instantiate the class.

- *For constructor chaining, see Section 7.5, p. 302, and Section 9.11, p. 416.*
- *For instantiating nested classes, see Chapter 8.*

7.2 Given an example of a class and a command-line, determine the expected runtime behavior.

7.3 Determine the effect upon object references and primitive values when they are passed into methods that perform assignments or other modifying operations on the parameters.

- *For conversions in assignment and method invocation contexts, see Section 5.2, p. 163.*

3.1 Class Declarations

A class declaration introduces a new reference type. It has the following general syntax:

```
<class modifiers> class <class name><formal type parameter list>
                  <extends clause> <implements clause>   // Class header
{ // Class body
    <field declarations>
    <method declarations>
    <nested class declarations>
    <nested interface declarations>
    <nested enum declarations>
    <constructor declarations>
    <initializer blocks>
}
```

In the class header, the name of the class is preceded by the keyword `class`. In addition, the class header can specify the following information:

- *accessibility modifier* (see Section 4.7, p. 132)
- additional *class modifiers* (see Section 4.8, p. 135)
- a *formal type parameter list*, if the class is generic (see Section 14.2, p. 663)
- any class it *extends* (see Section 7.1, p. 284)
- any interfaces it *implements* (see Section 7.6, p. 309)

The class body can contain *member declarations* which comprise:

- *field declarations* (see Section 2.3, p. 31)
- *method declarations* (see Section 3.3, p. 44)
- *nested class, enum, and interface declarations* (see Section 8.1, p. 352)

Members declared `static` belong to the class and are called *static members*. Non-static members belong to the objects of the class and are called *instance members*. In addition, the following can be declared in a class body:

- *constructor declarations* (see Section 3.4, p. 48)
- *static and instance initializer blocks* (see Section 9.7, p. 406)

The member declarations, constructor declarations, and initializer blocks can appear in any order in the class body.

In order to understand what code can be legally declared in a class, we distinguish between *static context* and *non-static context*. A static context is defined by static methods, static field initializers, and static initializer blocks. A non-static context is defined by instance methods, constructors, non-static field initializers, and instance initializer blocks. By *static code* we mean expressions and statements in a static context, and similarly by *non-static code* we mean expressions and statements in a non-static context. One crucial difference between the two contexts is that static code can only refer to other static members.

3.2   JavaBeans Standard

The JavaBeans Standard allows reusable software components to be modelled in Java so that these components can be assembled to create sophisticated applications. In particular, *builder tools* can take advantage of how these components are specified, in order to build new applications based on these components. The JavaBeans specification specifies the rules for defining such components (called *JavaBeans*). The interested reader is encouraged to consult this documentation (see `http://java.sun.com/javase/technologies/desktop/javabeans/docs/spec.html`) for details since we only cover the basic fundamentals for creating JavaBeans .

Naming Patterns for Properties

The rules of the JavaBean specification stipulate *naming patterns* for declaring *properties* of JavaBeans. A naming pattern defines a standard naming convention. A property of an object is normally defined as a field in the object, which is usually not directly accessible by clients (see Example 3.1). A JavaBean should adhere to the following naming patterns when specifying its properties:

- The properties are assumed to be `private`, and their names start with a lowercase letter. Example 3.1 shows that the JavaBean class `Light` has three properties.

- In order to retrieve and change values of its properties, a JavaBean provides *getter* and *setter* methods for them. Example 3.1 shows a JavaBean with three getter and three setter methods for its properties.

- For a property, the setter method starts with the prefix `set`. The rest of the method name is assumed to be a property name, where the first letter of the property name has been converted to uppercase. In Example 3.1, the value of the property `noOfWatts` can be changed by the setter method `setNoOfWatts()`.

  Setter methods are `public` and `void`, having a parameter of the same type as that of the property.

- For a property, the getter method starts with the prefix `get`. The rest of the method name is assumed to be a property name, where the first letter of the property name has been converted to uppercase. In Example 3.1, the value of the property `noOfWatts` can be retrieved by the getter method `getNoOfWatts()`.

  For a `boolean` property, the getter method can start with the prefix `get` or `is`. In Example 3.1, the value of the `boolean` property `indicator` can be retrieved by the getter method `isIndicator()`.

  Getter methods are no-argument `public` methods that return a value of the same type as the parameter of the corresponding setter method.

Example 3.1   *A JavaBean*

```
public class Light {
  // Properties:
  private int      noOfWatts;      // wattage
  private String   location;       // placement
  private boolean  indicator;      // on or off

  // Setters
  public void setNoOfWatts(int noOfWatts)    { this.noOfWatts = noOfWatts; }
  public void setLocation(String location)   { this.location = location; }
  public void setIndicator(boolean indicator) { this.indicator = indicator; }

  // Getters
  public int      getNoOfWatts() { return noOfWatts; }
  public String   getLocation()  { return location; }
  public boolean  isIndicator()  { return indicator; }
}
```

Naming Patterns for the Event Model

A *listener* is an object that is interested in being notified when a particular *event* takes place. The origin of this event is usually an object called the *source*, which notifies interested listeners when the event occurs. In this setup, a listener can be added to or removed from the list of listeners notified by a source about the occurrence of a particular event. This setup is the basis of the *event model* which is depicted in Figure 3.1.

The JavaBean specification stipulates naming patterns for the event model to facilitate its use by builder tools to assemble event-based applications. Figure 3.1 shows where the naming patterns for handling events of type X are applied:

- An event class with the name XEvent, that extends the java.util.EventObject class.

  ```
  public class XEvent extends java.util.EventObject {
    public XEvent(Object source) {
      super(source);
    }
  }
  ```

- A listener interface with the name XListener, that specifies the specific method to be called in a listener when an event of the type XEvent occurs. The listener interface extends the java.util.EventListener interface.

  ```
  public interface XListener extends java.util.EventListener {
    public void methodAInXListener(XEvent ev);
  }
  ```

  A listener interested in XEvents must implement the XListener interface, and must be registered with the source in order to be informed about XEvents.

Figure 3.1 *The Event Model*

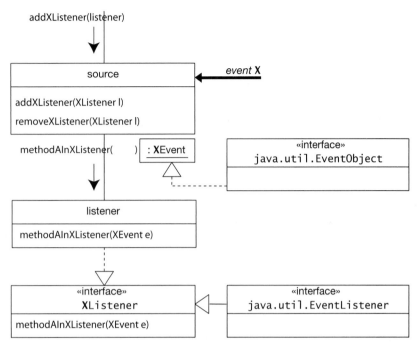

A listener interested in XEvent events is registered with the source using the addXListener() method.
The listener must implement the XListener interface in order to recieve events of type **XEvent**.
The listener is informed about events of type XEvent via the methodAInXListener()
in the XListener interface.

```
public class ListenerObject implements XListener {
  public void methodAInXListener(XEvent e) { /* ... */ }
}
```

- A source for XEvent, that implements the methods addXListener() and remove-
  XListener(). These methods are used to add or remove a listener interested in
  XEvents, respectively. The parameter of these methods is of the type XListener.

```
public class SourceObject {
  public synchronized void addXListener(XListener listener) { /* ... */ }
  public synchronized void removeXListener(XListener listener) { /* ... */ }
}
```

Note that there are no naming patterns defined for the names of the source and the
listener classes. Neither is there any standard convention for naming the methods
specified in the listener interface.

3.3 Method Declarations

The general syntax of a method declaration is

> *<method modifiers> <formal type parameter list> <return type> <method name>*
> *(<formal parameter list>) <throws clause>* // Method header

```
{ // Method body
    <local variable declarations>
    <nested local class declarations>
    <statements>
}
```

In addition to the name of the method, the method header can specify the following information:

- scope or *accessibility modifier* (see Section 4.9, p. 138)
- additional *method modifiers* (see Section 4.10, p. 146)
- a *formal type parameter list*, if the declaration is for a generic method (see Section 14.8, p. 697)
- the *type* of the *return value*, or void if the method does not return any value (see Section 6.4, p. 228)
- a *formal parameter list* (see below)
- *checked exceptions* thrown by the method are specified in a throws clause (see Section 6.9, p. 257)

The *formal parameter list* is a comma-separated list of parameters for passing information to the method when the method is invoked by a *method call* (see Section 3.7, p. 81). An empty parameter list must be specified by ( ). Each parameter is a simple variable declaration consisting of its type and name:

> *<parameter modifier> <type> <parameter name>*

The parameter names are local to the method (see Section 4.6, p. 131). The parameter modifier final is discussed in Section 3.7 on page 89.

The *signature* of a method comprises the method name and the formal parameter list only.

The method body is a *block* containing the *local declarations* and the *statements* of the method. *Local variable declarations* are discussed in Section 2.3 on page 31, and *nested local class declarations* in Section 8.4 on page 371.

Like member variables, member methods can be characterized as:

- *instance methods*
- *static methods*, which are discussed in Section 4.10, p. 148.

Statements

Statements in Java can be grouped into various categories. Variable declarations with explicit initialization of the variables are called *declaration statements* (see Section 2.3, p. 31, and Section 3.6, p. 71). Other basic forms of statements are *control flow statements* (see Section 6.1, p. 204) and *expression statements*.

An *expression statement* is an expression terminated by a semicolon. The expression is evaluated for its side effect and its value discarded. Only certain types of expressions have meaning as statements. They include the following:

- assignments (see Section 5.5, p. 169)
- increment and decrement operators (see Section 5.8, p. 186)
- method calls (see Section 3.7, p. 81)
- object creation expressions with the new operator (see Section 5.15, p. 201)

A solitary semicolon denotes the *empty statement* that does nothing.

A block, {}, is a *compound* statement which can be used to group zero or more local declarations and statements (see Section 4.6, p. 131). Blocks can be nested, since a block is a statement that can contain other statements. A block can be used in any context where a simple statement is permitted. The compound statement which is embodied in a block, begins at the left brace, {, and ends with a matching right brace, }. Such a block must not be confused with an array initialization block in declaration statements (see Section 3.6, p. 71).

Labeled statements are discussed in Section 6.4 on page 223.

Instance Methods and the Object Reference this

Instance methods belong to every object of the class and can only be invoked on objects. All members defined in the class, both static and non-static, are accessible in the context of an instance method. The reason is that all instance methods are passed an implicit reference to the *current object*, that is, the object on which the method is being invoked. The current object can be referenced in the body of the instance method by the keyword this. In the body of the method, the this reference can be used like any other object reference to access members of the object. In fact, the keyword this can be used in any non-static context. The this reference can be used as a normal reference to reference the current object, but the reference cannot be modified—it is a final reference (Section 4.10, p. 148).

The this reference to the current object is useful in situations where a local variable hides, or *shadows*, a field with the same name. In Example 3.2, the two parameters noOfWatts and indicator in the constructor of the Light class have the same names as the fields in the class. The example also declares a local variable location, which has the same name as one of the fields. The reference this can be used to distinguish the fields from the local variables. At (1), the this reference is used to identify the field noOfWatts, which is assigned the value of the parameter noOfWatts. Without the this reference at (2), the value of the parameter indicator is assigned back to this parameter, and not to the field by the same name, resulting in a logical error. Similarly at (3), without the this reference, it is the local variable location that is assigned the value of the parameter site, and not the field by the same name.

. . . .

Example 3.2   *Using the* this *Reference*

```java
public class Light {
  // Fields:
  int     noOfWatts;      // wattage
  boolean indicator;      // on or off
  String  location;       // placement

  // Constructor
  public Light(int noOfWatts, boolean indicator, String site) {
    String location;

    this.noOfWatts = noOfWatts;    // (1) Assignment to field.
    indicator = indicator;         // (2) Assignment to parameter.
    location = site;               // (3) Assignment to local variable.
    this.superfluous();            // (4)
    superfluous();                 // equivalent to call at (4)
  }

  public void superfluous() { System.out.println(this); }  // (5)

  public static void main(String[] args) {
    Light light = new Light(100, true, "loft");
    System.out.println("No. of watts: " + light.noOfWatts);
    System.out.println("Indicator: "    + light.indicator);
    System.out.println("Location: "     + light.location);
  }
}
```

Output from the program:

```
Light@df6ccd
Light@df6ccd
No. of watts: 100
Indicator: false
Location: null
```

. . . .

If a member is not shadowed by a local declaration, the simple name member is considered a short-hand notation for this.member. In particular, the this reference can be used explicitly to invoke other methods in the class. This is illustrated at (4) in Example 3.2, where the method superfluous() is called.

If, for some reason, a method needs to pass the current object to another method, it can do so using the this reference. This is illustrated at (5) in Example 3.2, where the current object is passed to the println() method.

Note that the this reference cannot be used in a static context, as static code is not executed in the context of any object.

Method Overloading

Each method has a *signature*, which comprises the name of the method, and the types and order of the parameters in the formal parameter list. Several method implementations may have the same name, as long as the method signatures differ. This is called *method overloading*. Since overloaded methods have the same name, their parameter lists must be different.

Rather than inventing new method names, method overloading can be used when the same logical operation requires multiple implementations. The Java standard library makes heavy use of method overloading. For example, the class java.lang.Math contains an overloaded method min(), which returns the minimum of two numeric values.

```
public static double min(double a, double b)
public static float min(float a, float b)
public static int min(int a, int b)
public static long min(long a, long b)
```

In the following examples, five implementations of the method methodA are shown:

```
void methodA(int a, double b) { /* ... */ }      // (1)
int  methodA(int a)           { return a; }      // (2)
int  methodA()                { return 1; }      // (3)
long methodA(double a, int b) { return b; }      // (4)
long methodA(int x, double y) { return x; }      // (5) Not OK.
```

The corresponding signatures of the five methods are as follows:

```
methodA(int, double)          1'
methodA(int)                  2': Number of parameters.
methodA()                     3': Number of parameters.
methodA(double, int)          4': Order of parameters.
methodA(int, double)          5': Same as 1'.
```

The first four implementations of the method named methodA are overloaded correctly, each time with a different parameter list and, therefore, different signatures. The declaration at (5) has the same signature methodA(int, double) as the declaration at (1) and is, therefore, not a valid overloading of this method.

```
void bake(Cake k)  { /* ... */ }                 // (1)
void bake(Pizza p) { /* ... */ }                 // (2)

int    halfIt(int a) { return a/2; }             // (3)
double halfIt(int a) { return a/2.0; }           // (4) Not OK. Same signature.
```

The method named bake is correctly overloaded at (1) and (2), with two different signatures. In the implementation, changing just the return type (as shown at (3) and (4) above), is not enough to overload a method, and will be flagged as a compile-time error. The parameter list in the declarations must be different.

Only methods declared in the same class and those that are inherited by the class can be overloaded. Overloaded methods should be considered as individual methods that just happen to have the same name. Methods with the same name are allowed, since methods are identified by their signature. At compile time, the right implementation of an overloaded method is chosen based on the signature of the method call. Details of method overloading resolution can be found in Section 7.10 on page 324. Method overloading should not be confused with *method overriding* (see Section 7.2, p. 288).

3.4 Constructors

The main purpose of constructors is to set the initial state of an object, when the object is created by using the `new` operator.

A constructor has the following general syntax:

> *<accessibility modifier> <class name>* (*<formal parameter list>*)
>   *<throws clause>* // Constructor header
>
>   { // Constructor body
>   *<local variable declarations>*
>   *<nested local class declarations>*
>   *<statements>*
>   }

Constructor declarations are very much like method declarations. However, the following restrictions on constructors should be noted:

- Modifiers other than an accessibility modifier are not permitted in the constructor header. For accessibility modifiers for constructors, see Section 4.9 on page 138.

- Constructors cannot return a value and, therefore, do not specify a return type, not even `void`, in the constructor header. But their declaration can use the `return` statement that does not return a value in the constructor body (Section 6.4, p. 228).

- The constructor name must be the same as the class name.

Class names and method names exist in different *namespaces*. Thus, there are no name conflicts in Example 3.3, where a method declared at (2) has the same name as the constructor declared at (1). However, using such naming schemes is strongly discouraged.

Example 3.3 *Namespaces*

```
public class Name {

  Name() {                          // (1)
    System.out.println("Constructor");
  }

  void Name() {                     // (2)
    System.out.println("Method");
  }

  public static void main(String[] args) {
    new Name().Name();              // (3) Constructor call followed by method call.
  }
}
```

Output from the program:

```
Constructor
Method
```

The Default Constructor

A *default constructor* is a constructor without any parameters, i.e., it is a no-parameter constructor. It has the following signature:

<class name>()

If a class does not specify *any* constructors, then an *implicit* default constructor is generated for the class by the compiler. The implicit default constructor is equivalent to the following implementation:

<class name>() { super(); }   // No parameters. Calls superclass constructor.

The only action taken by the implicit default constructor is to call the superclass constructor. This ensures that the inherited state of the object is initialized properly (see Section 7.5, p. 302). In addition, all instance variables in the object are set to the default value of their type, barring those that are initialized by an initialization expression in their declaration.

In the following code, the class Light does not specify any constructors.

```
class Light {
  // Fields:
  int     noOfWatts;      // wattage
  boolean indicator;      // on or off
  String  location;       // placement

  // No constructors
  //...
}
```

```
class Greenhouse {
  // ...
  Light oneLight = new Light();      // (1) Call to implicit default constructor.
}
```

In the code above, the following implicit default constructor is called when a Light object is created by the object creation expression at (1):

```
Light() { super(); }
```

Creating an object using the new operator with the implicit default constructor, as at (1), will initialize the fields of the object to their default values (that is, the fields noOfWatts, indicator, and location in a Light object will be initialized to 0, false, and null, respectively).

A class can choose to provide an implementation of the default constructor. In the following example, the class Light provides an explicit default constructor at (1). Note that it has the same name as the class, and that it does not specify any parameters.

```
class Light {
  // ...
  // Explicit Default Constructor:
  Light() {                         // (1)
    noOfWatts = 50;
    indicator = true;
    location  = "X";
  }
  //...
}

class Greenhouse {
  // ...
  Light extraLight = new Light();    // (2) Call of explicit default constructor.
}
```

The explicit default constructor ensures that any object created with the object creation expression new Light(), as at (2), will have its fields noOfWatts, indicator and location initialized to 50, true and "X", respectively.

If a class defines any explicit constructors, it can no longer rely on the implicit default constructor to set the state of its objects. If such a class requires a default constructor, its implementation must be provided. In the example below, the class Light only provides a non-default constructor at (1). It is called at (2) when an object of the class Light is created with the new operator. Any attempt to call the default constructor will be flagged as a compile-time error, as shown at (3).

```
class Light {
  // ...
  // Only non-default Constructor:
  Light(int noOfWatts, boolean indicator, String location) {      // (1)
    this.noOfWatts = noOfWatts;
    this.indicator = indicator;
    this.location  = location;
  }
```

```
    //...
  }
class Greenhouse {
  // ...
  Light moreLight  = new Light(100, true, "Greenhouse");  // (2) OK.
//Light firstLight = new Light();                         // (3) Compile-time
error.
  }
```

Overloaded Constructors

Like methods, constructors can also be overloaded. Since the constructors in a class all have the same name as the class, their signatures are differentiated by their parameter lists. In the following example, the class Light now provides both an explicit implementation of the default constructor at (1) and a non-default constructor at (2). The constructors are overloaded, as is evident by their signatures. The non-default constructor is called when an object of the class Light is created at (3), and the default constructor is likewise called at (4). Overloading of constructors allows appropriate initialization of objects on creation, depending on the constructor invoked (see also chaining of constructors in Section 7.5, p. 302.)

```
class Light {
  // ...
  // Explicit Default Constructor:
  Light() {                                               // (1)
    noOfWatts = 50;
    indicator = true;
    location  = "X";
  }

  // Non-default Constructor:
  Light(int noOfWatts, boolean indicator, String location) { // (2)
    this.noOfWatts = noOfWatts;
    this.indicator = indicator;
    this.location  = location;
  }
  //...
}
class Greenhouse {
  // ...
  Light moreLight  = new Light(100, true, "Greenhouse");  // (3) OK.
  Light firstLight = new Light();                         // (4) OK.
}
```

Review Questions

3.1 Which one of these declarations is a valid method declaration?

Select the one correct answer.
(a) `void method1          { /* ... */ }`
(b) `void method2()        { /* ... */ }`
(c) `void method3(void)    { /* ... */ }`
(d) `method4()             { /* ... */ }`
(e) `method5(void)         { /* ... */ }`

3.2 Which statements, when inserted at (1), will not result in compile-time errors?

```
public class ThisUsage {
  int planets;
  static int suns;

  public void gaze() {
    int i;
    // (1) INSERT STATEMENT HERE
  }
}
```

Select the three correct answers.
(a) `i = this.planets;`
(b) `i = this.suns;`
(c) `this = new ThisUsage();`
(d) `this.i = 4;`
(e) `this.suns = planets;`

3.3 Given the following pairs of method declarations, which statements are true?

```
void fly(int distance) {}
int  fly(int time, int speed) { return time*speed; }
```

```
void fall(int time) {}
int  fall(int distance) { return distance; }
```

```
void glide(int time) {}
void Glide(int time) {}
```

Select the two correct answers.
(a) The first pair of methods will compile, and overload the method name `fly`.
(b) The second pair of methods will compile, and overload the method name `fall`.
(c) The third pair of methods will compile, and overload the method name `glide`.
(d) The second pair of methods will not compile.
(e) The third pair of methods will not compile.

3.4   Given a class named Book, which one of these constructor declarations is valid for the class Book?

Select the one correct answer.

(a) `Book(Book b) {}`
(b) `Book Book() {}`
(c) `private final Book() {}`
(d) `void Book() {}`
(e) `public static void Book(String[] args) {}`
(f) `abstract Book() {}`

3.5   Which statements are true?

Select the two correct answers.

(a) A class must define a constructor.
(b) A constructor can be declared `private`.
(c) A constructor can return a value.
(d) A constructor must initialize all fields when a class is instantiated.
(e) A constructor can access the non-static members of a class.

3.6   What will be the result of compiling the following program?

```
public class MyClass {
  long var;

  public void MyClass(long param) { var = param; }  // (1)

  public static void main(String[] args) {
    MyClass a, b;
    a = new MyClass();                        // (2)
    b = new MyClass(5);                       // (3)
  }
}
```

Select the one correct answer.

(a) A compilation error will occur at (1), since constructors cannot specify a return value.
(b) A compilation error will occur at (2), since the class does not have a default constructor.
(c) A compilation error will occur at (3), since the class does not have a constructor that takes one argument of type `int`.
(d) The program will compile without errors.

3.5   Enumerated Types

An *enumerated type* defines *a finite set of symbolic names and their values*. These symbolic names are usually called *enum constants* or *named constants*. One way to define such constants is to declare them as final, static variables in a class (or interface) declaration:

```
public class MachineState {
  public static final int BUSY = 1;
  public static final int IDLE = 0;
  public static final int BLOCKED = -1;
}
```

Such constants are not typesafe, as *any* int value can be used where we need to use a constant declared in the MachineState class. Such a constant must be qualified by the class (or interface) name, unless the class is extended (or the interface is implemented). When such a constant is printed, only its value (for example, 0), and not its name (for example, IDLE) is printed. A constant also needs recompiling if its value is changed, as the values of such constants are compiled into the client code.

An enumerated type in Java is much more powerful than the approach outlined above. It is certainly more convenient to use than implementing one from scratch using the *typesafe enum pattern* (see *Effective Java* by Josh Bloch, ISBN-10: 0321356683).

Declaring Typesafe Enums

The canonical form of declaring an enum *type* is shown below.

```
enum MachineState { BUSY, IDLE, BLOCKED } // Canonical form
```

The keyword enum is used to declare an enum type. The basic notation requires the *type name* and *a comma-separated list of enum constants*. In this case, the name of the enum type is MachineState. It defines three enum constants. An enum constant can be any legal Java identifier, but the convention is to use uppercase letters in the name. Essentially, an enum declaration defines a *reference type* that has a *finite number of permissible values* referenced by the enum constants, and the compiler ensures they are used in a typesafe manner.

Using Typesafe Enums

Example 3.4 illustrates using enum constants. An enum type is essentially used as any other reference type, and the restrictions are noted later in this section. Enum constants are in fact final, static variables of the enum type, and they are implicitly initialized with objects of the enum type when the enum type is loaded at runtime. Since the enum constants are static members, they can be accessed using the name of the enum type—analogous to accessing static members in a class.

Example 3.4 shows a machine client that uses a machine whose state is an enum constant. From Example 3.4, we see that an enum constant can be passed as an argument, as shown as (1), and we can declare references whose type is an enum type, as shown as (3), but we can*not* create new constants (that is, objects) of the enum type MachineState. An attempt to do so at (5), results in a compile-time error.

The string representation of an enum constant is its name, as shown at (4). Note that it is not possible to pass a type of value other than a MachineState enum constant in the call to the method setState() of the Machine class, as shown at (2).

Example 3.4 *Using Enums*

```
// Filename: MachineState.java
public enum MachineState { BUSY, IDLE, BLOCKED }
```

```
// Filename: Machine.java
public class Machine {

  private MachineState state;

  public void setState(MachineState state) { this.state = state; }
  public MachineState getState() { return this.state; }
}
```

```
// Filename: MachineClient.java
public class MachineClient {
  public static void main(String[] args) {

    Machine machine = new Machine();
    machine.setState(MachineState.IDLE);        // (1) Passed as a value.
    // machine.setState(1);                      // (2) Compile-time error!

    MachineState state = machine.getState();     // (3) Declaring a reference.
    System.out.println(
        "The machine state is: " + state         // (4) Printing the enum name.
    );
    // MachineState newState = new MachineState();// (5) Compile-time error!
  }
}
```

Output from the program:

```
The machine state is: IDLE
```

Declaring Enum Constructors and Members

An enum type declaration is a special kind of reference type declaration. It can declare constructors and other members as in an ordinary class, but the enum constants must be declared before any other declarations (see the declaration of the enum type `Meal` in Example 3.5). The list of enum constants must be terminated by a semi-colon (;). Each enum constant name can be followed by an argument list that is passed to the constructor of the enum type having the matching parameter signature.

In Example 3.5, the enum type `Meal` contains a constructor declaration at (1) with the following signature:

```
Meal(int, int)
```

Each enum constant is specified with an argument list with the signature (`int`, `int`) that matches the constructor signature. In addition, the enum declaration declares two fields for the meal time at (3), and two instance methods to retrieve the meal time at (4).

When the enum type is loaded at runtime, the constructor is run for each enum constant, passing the argument values specified for the enum constant. For the `Meal` enum type, three objects are created that are initialized with the specified argument values, and are referenced by the three enum constants, respectively. Note that each enum constant is a `final`, `static` reference that stores the reference value of an object of the enum type, and methods of the enum type can be called on this object by using the enum constant name. This is illustrated at (5) in Example 3.5 by calling methods on the object referenced by the enum constant `Meal.BREAKFAST`.

An implicit standard constructor is created if no constructors are provided for the enum type. As mentioned earlier, an enum type cannot be instantiated using the `new` operator. The constructors cannot be called explicitly. The only accessibility modifier allowed for a constructor is `private`.

Example 3.5 *Declaring Enum Constructors and Members*

```
// Filename: Meal.java
public enum Meal {
    BREAKFAST(7,30), LUNCH(12,15), DINNER(19,45);           // (1)

    // Non-default constructor                               (2)
    Meal(int hh, int mm) {
        assert (hh >= 0 && hh <= 23): "Illegal hour.";
        assert (mm >= 0 && mm <= 59): "Illegal mins.";
        this.hh = hh;
        this.mm = mm;
    }

    // Fields for the meal time:                             (3)
    private int hh;
    private int mm;

    // Instance methods:                                     (4)
    public int getHour() { return this.hh; }
    public int getMins() { return this.mm; }
}
```

```
// Filename: MealAdministrator.java
public class MealAdministrator {
  public static void main(String[] args) {

    System.out.printf(                                    // (5)
        "Please note that no eggs will be served at %s, %02d:%02d.%n",
        Meal.BREAKFAST, Meal.BREAKFAST.getHour(), Meal.BREAKFAST.getMins()
    );

    System.out.println("Meal times are as follows:");
    Meal[] meals = Meal.values();                         // (6)
    for (Meal meal : meals)                               // (7)
      System.out.printf("%s served at %02d:%02d%n",
                meal, meal.getHour(), meal.getMins()
      );

    Meal formalDinner = Meal.valueOf("DINNER");           // (8)
    System.out.printf("Formal dress is required for %s at %02d:%02d.%n",
        formalDinner, formalDinner.getHour(), formalDinner.getMins()
    );
  }
}
```

Output from the program:

```
Please note that no eggs will be served at BREAKFAST, 07:30.
Meal times are as follows:
BREAKFAST served at 07:30
LUNCH served at 12:15
DINNER served at 19:45
Formal dress is required for DINNER at 19:45.
```

Implicit Static Methods for Enum Types

All enum types implicitly have the following static methods, and methods with these names cannot be declared in an enum type declaration:

static *EnumTypeName*[] values()

Returns an array containing the enum constants of this enum type, *in the order they are specified.*

static *EnumTypeName* valueOf(String name)

Returns the enum constant with the specified name. An IllegalArgumentException is thrown if the specified name does not match the name of an enum constant. The specified name is *not* qualified with the enum type name.

The static method values() is called at (6) in Example 3.5 to create an array of enum constants. This array is traversed in the for(:) loop at (7), printing the information about each meal. The for(:) loop is discussed in Section 6.3, p. 220.

The static method valueOf() is called at (8) in Example 3.5 to retrieve the enum constant that has the specified name "DINNER". A printf statement is used to print the information about the meal denoted by this enum constant.

Inherited Methods from the Enum Class

All enum types are subtypes of the java.lang.Enum class which provides the default behavior. All enum types are comparable (Section 15.1, p. 765) and serializable (Section 11.6, p. 510).

All enum types inherit the following final methods from the java.lang.Enum class, and these methods can therefore not be overridden by an enum type:

```
protected final Object clone()
```

An instance of an enum type cannot be cloned (see Section 10.2, p. 424). The method throws an CloneNotSupportedException.

```
final int compareTo(E o)
```

The *natural order* of the enum constants in an enum type is according to their *ordinal values* (see the ordinal() method below). The compareTo() method in the Comparable interface is discussed in Section 15.1, p. 765.

```
final boolean equals(Object other)
```

This method returns true if the specified object is equal to this enum constant (Section 15.1, p. 751).

```
protected final void finalize()
```

An enum constant cannot be finalized, because this final method effectively prevents enum types from implementing their own finalize() method (see Section 9.4, p. 396).

```
final Class<E> getDeclaringClass()
```

This method returns the Class object corresponding to this enum constant's enum type (see Section 10.2, p. 424).

```
final int hashCode()
```

This method returns a hash code for this enum constant (see Section 15.1, p. 760).

```
final String name()
```

This method returns the name of this enum constant, exactly as declared in its enum declaration.

```
final int ordinal()
```

This method returns the *ordinal value* of this enum constant (that is, its position in its enum type declaration). The first enum constant is assigned an ordinal value of zero. If the ordinal value of an enum constant is less than the ordinal value of another enum constant of the same enum type, the former occurs before the latter in the enum type declaration.

Note that the equality test implemented by the equals() method is based on reference equality (==) of the enum constants, not on value equality (Section 5.11, p. 193). An enum type has a finite number of distinct objects. Comparing two enum references for equality means determining whether they store the reference value of the same enum contant, i.e., whether the references are aliases. Thus, for any two enum references meal1 and meal2, the expression meal1.equals(meal2) and meal1 == meal2 are equivalent.

The Enum class also overrides the toString() method from the Object class (see Section 10.2, p. 424). The toString() method returns the name of the enum constant, but it is *not* final, and can be overridden by an enum type. Example 3.6 uses some of the methods mentioned in this subsection.

Extending Enum Types: Constant-Specific Class Bodies

A review of *subtyping* (Section 7.1, p. 284), *overriding* (Section 7.2, p. 288), and *anonymous classes* (Section 8.5, p. 377) can be helpful before diving into this subsection.

Constant-specific class bodies define anonymous classes inside an enum type, i.e., they implicitly extend the enclosing enum type. The enum type Meal in Example 3.6 declares constant-specific class bodies for its constants. The following skeletal code declares the constant-specific class body for the enum constant BREAKFAST:

```
BREAKFAST(7,30) {                    // (1) Start of constant-specific class body
  public double mealPrice(Day day) {  // (2) Overriding abstract method
    ...
  }
  public String toString() {          // (3) Overriding method from the Enum
class
    ...
  }
}                                     // (4) End of constant-specific class body
```

The constant-specific class body, as the name implies, is a class body that is specific to a particular enum constant. As any class body, it is enclosed in braces, { }. It is declared immediately after the enum constant and any constructor arguments. In the code above, it starts at (1) and ends at (4). Like any class body, it can contain member declarations. In the above case, the body contains two method declarations: an implementation of the method mealPrice() at (2) that overrides the abstract method declaration at (7) in the enclosing enum supertype, and an implementation of the toString() method at (3) that overrides the one inherited by the Meal enum type from the superclass java.lang.Enum.

The constant-specific class body is an anonymous class, i.e., a class with no name. Each constant-specific class body defines a distinct, albeit anonymous, subtype of the enclosing enum type. In the code above, the constant-specific class body defines a subtype of the Meal enum type. It inherits members of the enclosing enum supertype, that are not private, overridden, or hidden. When the enum type Meal is loaded at runtime, this constant-specific class body is instantiated, and the reference value of the instance is assigned to the enum constant BREAKFAST. Note that the type of the enum constant is Meal, which is the supertype of the anonymous sub-type represented by the constant-specific class body. Since supertype references can refer to subtype objects, the above assignment is legal.

Each enum constant overrides the abstract method mealPrice() declared in the enclosing enum supertype, i.e., provides an implementation for the method. The compiler will report an error if this is not the case. Although the enum type decla-ration specifies an abstract method, the enum type declaration is *not* declared abstract—contrary to an abstract class. Given that the references meal and day are of the enum types Meal and Day from Example 3.6, respectively, the method call

```
meal.mealPrice(day)
```

will execute the mealPrice() method from the constant-specific body of the enum constant denoted by the reference meal.

Two constant-specific class bodies, associated with the enum constants BREAKFAST and LUNCH, override the toString() method from the Enum class. Note that the toString() method is not overridden in the Meal enum type, but in the anonymous classes represented by two constant-specific class bodies. The third enum constant, DINNER, relies on the toString() method inherited from the Enum class.

Constructors, abstract methods, and static methods cannot be declared in a constant-specific class body. Instance methods declared in constant-specific class bodies are only accessible if they override methods in the enclosing enum supertype.

Example 3.6 *Declaring Constant-Specific Class Bodies*

```
// Filename: Day.java
public enum Day {
  MONDAY, TUESDAY, WEDNESDAY, THURSDAY, FRIDAY, SATURDAY, SUNDAY
}
```

```
// Filename: Meal.java
public enum Meal {
  // Each enum constant defines a constant-specific class body
  BREAKFAST(7,30) {                                               // (1)
    public double mealPrice(Day day) {                            // (2)
      double breakfastPrice = 10.50;
      if (day.equals(Day.SATURDAY) || day == Day.SUNDAY)
        breakfastPrice *= 1.5;
      return breakfastPrice;
    }
    public String toString() {                                    // (3)
      return "Breakfast";
    }
  },                                                              // (4)
  LUNCH(12,15) {
    public double mealPrice(Day day) {                            // (5)
      double lunchPrice = 20.50;
      switch (day) {
        case SATURDAY: case SUNDAY:
```

```java
          lunchPrice *= 2.0;
      }
      return lunchPrice;
    }
    public String toString() {
      return "Lunch";
    }
  },
  DINNER(19,45) {
    public double mealPrice(Day day) {                              // (6)
      double dinnerPrice = 25.50;
      if (day.compareTo(Day.SATURDAY) >= 0 && day.compareTo(Day.SUNDAY) <= 0)
        dinnerPrice *= 2.5;
      return dinnerPrice;
    }
  };

  // Abstract method implemented in constant-specific class bodies.
  abstract double mealPrice(Day day);                              // (7)

  // Enum constructor:
  Meal(int hh, int mm) {
    assert (hh >= 0 && hh <= 23): "Illegal hour.";
    assert (mm >= 0 && mm <= 59): "Illegal mins.";
    this.hh = hh;
    this.mm = mm;
  }

  // Instance fields: Time for the meal.
  private int hh;
  private int mm;

  // Instance methods:
  public int getHour() { return this.hh; }
  public int getMins() { return this.mm; }

}

// Filename: MealPrices.java
public class MealPrices {

  public static void main(String[] args) {                         // (8)
    System.out.printf(
        "Please note that %s, %02d:%02d, on %s costs $%.2f.%n",
        Meal.BREAKFAST.name(),                                     // (9)
        Meal.BREAKFAST.getHour(), Meal.BREAKFAST.getMins(),
        Day.MONDAY,
        Meal.BREAKFAST.mealPrice(Day.MONDAY)                       // (10)
    );

    System.out.println("Meal prices on " + Day.SATURDAY + " are as follows:");
    Meal[] meals = Meal.values();
    for (Meal meal : meals)
      System.out.printf(
          "%s costs $%.2f.%n", meal, meal.mealPrice(Day.SATURDAY)   // (11)
```

```
      );
    }
  }
```

Output from the program:

```
Please note that BREAKFAST, 07:30, on MONDAY costs $10.50.
Meal prices on SATURDAY are as follows:
Breakfast costs $15.75.
Lunch costs $41.00.
DINNER costs $63.75.
```

In Example 3.6, the `mealPrice()` method declaration at (2) uses both the `equals()` method and the `==` operator to compare enum constants for equality. The `meal-Price()` method declaration at (5) uses enum constants in a `switch` statement (Section 6.2, p. 207). Note that the case labels in the `switch` statement are enum constant names, without the enum type name. The `mealPrice()` method declaration at (6) uses the `compareTo()` method to compare enum constants.

The `main()` method at (8) in Example 3.6 demonstrates calling the `mealPrice()` method in the constant-specific class bodies. The `mealPrice()` method is called at (10) and (11). Example 3.6 also illustrates the difference between the `name()` and the `toString()` methods of the enum types. The `name()` method is called at (9), and the `toString()` method is called at (10) and (11). The `name()` method always prints the enum constant name exactly as it was declared. Which `toString()` method is executed depends on whether the `toString()` method in the `Enum` class is overridden. Only the constant-specific class bodies of the enum constants BREAKFAST and LUNCH override this method. The output from the program confirms this to be the case.

Declaring Typesafe Enums Revisited

An enum type can be declared as a top-level type. Enum types can also be nested, but only within other `static` members, or other top-level type declarations (Section 8.2, p. 355). When nested, it is implicitly `static`, and can be declared with the keyword `static`. The following skeletal code shows the two enum types `Day` and `Meal` declared as static members in the class `MealPrices`:

```
public class MealPrices {
  public enum Day { /* ... */ }                        // Static member

  public static enum Meal { /* ... */ }                // Static member

  public static void main(String[] args) { /* ... */ }   // Static method
}
```

An enum type cannot be explicitly extended using the extends clause. An enum type is implicitly `final`, unless it contains constant-specific class bodies. If it declares constant-specific class bodies, it is implicitly extended. No matter what, it cannot be explicitly declared `final`.

An enum type cannot be declared abstract, regardless of whether each abstract method is overridden in the constant-specific class body of every enum constant.

Like a class, an enum can implement interfaces.

```
public interface ITimeInfo {
  public int getHour();
  public int getMins();
}

public enum Meal implements ITimeInfo {
  // ...
  public int getHour() { return this.hh; }
  public int getMins() { return this.mm; }
}
```

The Java Collections Framework provides a special purpose *set* implementation (java.util.EnumSet) and a special purpose *map* implementation (java.util.EnumMap) for use with enum types. These special purpose implementations provide better performance for enum types than the general purpose counterparts, and are worth checking out.

 ## Review Questions

3.7 Which statements about the enum type are true?

Select the three correct answers.

(a) An enum type is a subclass of the abstract class java.lang.Enum, hence it is Comparable and Serializable.
(b) An enum type can implement interfaces.
(c) We can instantiate an enum type using the new operator.
(d) An enum type can define constructors.
(e) We can explicitly use the extend clause to extend an enum type.
(f) Enum types do not inherit members from the Object class.

3.8 What will be the result of attempting to compile and run the following code?

```
public enum Drill {
  ATTENTION("Attention!"), EYES_RIGHT("Eyes right!"),
  EYES_LEFT("Eyes left!"), AT_EASE("At ease!");

  private String command;

  Drill(String command) {
    this.command = command;
  }

  public static void main(String[] args) {
    System.out.println(ATTENTION);           // (1)
    System.out.println(AT_EASE);             // (2)
  }
}
```

Select the one correct answer.

(a) The code compiles, but reports a ClassNotFoundException when run, since an enum type cannot be run as a standalone application.

(b) The compiler reports errors in (1) and (2), as the constants must be qualified by the enum type name Drill.

(c) The compiler reports errors in (1) and (2), as the constants cannot be accessed in a static context.

(d) The code compiles and prints:

```
ATTENTION
AT_EASE
```

(e) The code compiles and prints:

```
Attention!
At ease!
```

(f) None of the above.

3.9 What will be the result of compiling and running the following code?

```java
import java.util.Arrays;

public enum Priority {
  ONE(1) { public String toString() { return "LOW"; } },       // (1)
  TWO(2),
  THREE(3) { public String toString() { return "NORMAL"; } },   // (2)
  FOUR(4),
  FIVE(5) { public String toString() { return "HIGH"; } };      // (3)

  private int pValue;

  Priority(int pValue) {
    this.pValue = pValue;
  }

  public static void main(String[] args) {
    System.out.println(Arrays.toString(Priority.values()));
  }
}
```

Select the one correct answer.

(a) The code compiles, but reports a ClassNotFoundException when run, since an enum type cannot be run as a standalone application.

(b) The compiler reports syntax errors in (1), (2), and (3).

(c) The code compiles and prints:

```
[LOW, TWO, NORMAL, FOUR, HIGH]
```

(d) The code compiles and prints:

```
[ONE, TWO, THREE, FOUR, HIGH]
```

(e) None of the above.

3.10   Which statement about the following program is true?

```
public enum Scale {
  GOOD('C'), BETTER('B'), BEST('A');

  private char grade;

  Scale(char grade) {
    this.grade = grade;
  }
  abstract public char getGrade();

  public static void main (String[] args) {
    System.out.println (GOOD.getGrade());     // (1)
  }
}
```

Select the one correct answer.

(a) Since the enum type declares an abstract method, the enum type must be declared as abstract.

(b) The method call GOOD.getGrade() in (1) can be written without the enum type name.

(c) An enum type cannot declare an abstract method.

(d) An enum type can declare an abstract method, but each enum constant must provide an implementation.

3.11   What will be the result of compiling and running the following code?

```
public enum TrafficLight {
  RED("Stop"), YELLOW("Caution"), GREEN("Go");

  private String action;

  TrafficLight(String action) {
    this.action = action;
  }

  public static void main(String[] args) {
    TrafficLight green = new TrafficLight("Go");
    System.out.println(GREEN.equals(green));
  }
}
```

Select the one correct answer.

(a) The code will compile and print: true.

(b) The code will compile and print: false.

(c) The code will not compile, as an enum type cannot be instantiated.

(d) An enum type does not have the equals() method.

3.12   Given the following program:

```
public enum Scale2 {
  GOOD('C')   { public char getGrade() { return grade; } },
  BETTER('B') { public char getGrade() { return grade; } },
  BEST('A')   { public char getGrade() { return grade; } };

  private char grade;

  Scale2(char grade) {
    this.grade = grade;
  }
  // (1) INSERT CODE HERE

  public static void main (String[] args) {
    System.out.println(GOOD.getGrade());
  }
}
```

Which code, when inserted at (1), will make the program print C?

Select the two correct answers.

(a) `public char getGrade() { return grade; }`
(b) `public int getGrade() { return grade; }`
(c) `abstract public int getGrade();`
(d) `abstract public char getGrade();`

3.13   Given the following program:

```
enum Scale3 {
  GOOD(Grade.C), BETTER(Grade.B), BEST(Grade.A);

  enum Grade {A, B, C}
  private Grade grade;

  Scale3(Grade grade) {
    this.grade = grade;
  }

  public Grade getGrade() { return grade; }
}

public class Scale3Client {
  public static void main (String[] args) {
    System.out.println(/* (1) INSERT CODE HERE */);
  }
}
```

Which code, when inserted at (1), will make the program print true?

Select the four correct answers.

(a) `Scale3.GOOD.getGrade() != Scale3.Grade.C`
(b) `Scale3.GOOD.getGrade().compareTo(Scale3.Grade.C) != 0`
(c) `Scale3.GOOD.getGrade().compareTo(Scale3.Grade.A) > 0`

(d) Scale3.GOOD.compareTo(Scale3.BEST) > 0

(e) Scale3.GOOD.getGrade() instanceof Scale3.Grade

(f) Scale3.GOOD instanceof Scale3

(g) Scale3.GOOD.getGrade().toString().equals(Scale3.Grade.C.toString())

3.14 What will be the result of compiling and running the following code?

```
public enum Scale5 {
  GOOD, BETTER, BEST;

  public char getGrade() {
    char grade = '\u0000';
    switch(this){
      case GOOD:   grade = 'C'; break;
      case BETTER: grade = 'B'; break;
      case BEST:   grade = 'A'; break;
    }
    return grade;
  }

  public static void main (String[] args) {
    System.out.println(GOOD.getGrade());
  }
}
```

Select the one correct answer.

(a) The program will not compile, as the switch expression is not compatible with the case labels.

(b) The program will not compile, as enum constants cannot be used as case labels.

(c) The case labels must be qualified with the enum type name.

(d) The program compiles, and when run, prints: C

(e) The program compiles, and when run, prints: GOOD

(f) None of the above.

3.15 Given the following code:

```
package p1;
enum March {LEFT, RIGHT}                    // (1)
public class Defence {
  enum March {LEFT, RIGHT}                  // (2)
  static enum Military {
    INFANTRY, AIRFORCE;
    enum March {LEFT, RIGHT}                // (3)
  }
  class Secret {
    enum March {LEFT, RIGHT}               // (4)
  }
  static class Open {
    enum March {LEFT, RIGHT}               // (5)
  }
  public static void declareWar() {
```

```
    enum March {LEFT, RIGHT}                          // (6)
  }
  public void declarePeace() {
    enum March {LEFT, RIGHT}                          // (7)
  }
}
```

Which enum declarations are not legal?

Select the three correct answers.

(a) The enum declaration at (1) is not legal.
(b) The enum declaration at (2) is not legal.
(c) The enum declaration at (3) is not legal.
(d) The enum declaration at (4) is not legal.
(e) The enum declaration at (5) is not legal.
(f) The enum declaration at (6) is not legal.
(g) The enum declaration at (7) is not legal.

3.16   Given the following code:

```
public enum Direction {
  EAST, WEST, NORTH, SOUTH;

  public static void main (String[] args) {
    // (1) INSERT LOOP HERE
  }
}
```

Which loops, when inserted independently at (1), will give the following output:

```
EAST
WEST
NORTH
SOUTH
```

Select the three correct answers.

(a) for (Direction d : Direction.values()) {
        System.out.println(d);
    }

(b) for (Direction d : Direction.values()) {
        System.out.println(d.name());
    }

(c) for (String name : Direction.names()) {
        System.out.println(name);
    }

(d) for (Direction d : java.util.Arrays.asList(Direction.values())) {
        System.out.println(d);
    }

(e) for (Direction d : java.util.Arrays.asList(Direction.class)) {
        System.out.println(d);
    };
```
```

3.17   What will be the result of compiling and running the following code?

```
enum Rank {
  FIRST(20), SECOND(0), THIRD(8);
  Rank(int value) {
    System.out.print(value);
  }
}
public class EnumCreation {
  public static void main (String[] args) {
    System.out.println("\n" + Rank.values().length);
  }
}
```

Select the one correct answer.

(a) The program will compile and print:

3

(b) The program will compile and print:

2008
3

(c) The program will compile. When run, it will print:

2008

and throw an exception.

(d) None of the above.

3.6 Arrays

An *array* is a data structure that defines an indexed collection of a fixed number of homogeneous data elements. This means that all elements in the array have the same data type. A position in the array is indicated by a non-negative integer value called the *index*. An element at a given position in the array is accessed using the index. The size of an array is fixed and cannot be changed.

In Java, arrays are objects. Arrays can be of primitive data types or reference types. In the former case, all elements in the array are of a specific primitive data type. In the latter case, all elements are references of a specific reference type. References in the array can then denote objects of this reference type or its subtypes. Each array object has a final field called length, which specifies the array size, i.e., the number of elements the array can accommodate. The first element is always at index 0 and the last element at index *n*-1, where *n* is the value of the length field in the array.

Simple arrays are *one-dimensional arrays*, that is, a simple list of values. Since arrays can store reference values, the objects referenced can also be array objects. Thus, multi-dimensional arrays are implemented as *array of arrays*.

Passing array references as parameters is discussed in Section 3.7. Type conversions for array references on assignment and on method invocation are discussed in Section 7.7, p. 317.

Declaring Array Variables

A one-dimensional array variable declaration has either the following syntax:

   <element type>[] *<array name>*;

or

   <element type> *<array name>*[];

where *<element type>* can be a primitive data type or a reference type. The array variable *<array name>* has the type *<element type>*[]. Note that the array size is not specified. This means that the array variable *<array name>* can be assigned the reference value of an array of any length, as long as its elements have *<element type>*.

It is important to understand that the declaration does not actually create an array. It only declares a reference that can refer to an array object.

```
int anIntArray[], oneInteger;
Pizza[] mediumPizzas, largePizzas;
```

The two declarations above declare anIntArray and mediumPizzas to be reference variables that can refer to arrays of int values and arrays of Pizza objects, respectively. The variable largePizzas can denote an array of pizzas, but the variable oneInteger cannot denote an array of int values—it is a simple variable of the type int .

The [] notation can also be specified after a variable name to declare it as an array variable, but then it only applies to this variable.

An array variable that is declared as a member of a class, but is not initialized to any array, will be initialized to the default reference value null. This default initialization does *not* apply to local reference variables and, therefore, does not apply to local array variables either (see Section 2.4, p. 33). This should not be confused with initialization of the elements of an array during array construction.

Constructing an Array

An array can be constructed for a fixed number of elements of a specific type, using the new operator. The reference value of the resulting array can be assigned to an array variable of the corresponding type. The syntax of the *array creation expression* is shown on the right-hand side of the following assignment statement:

   <array name> = new *<element type>* [*<array size>*];

The minimum value of *<array size>* is 0, in other words, zero-length arrays can be constructed in Java. If the array size is negative, a `NegativeArraySizeException` is thrown.

Given the following array declarations:

```
int anIntArray[], oneInteger;
Pizza[] mediumPizzas, largePizzas;
```

the arrays can be constructed as follows:

```
anIntArray   = new int[10];       // array for 10 integers
mediumPizzas = new Pizza[5];      // array of 5 pizzas
largePizzas  = new Pizza[3];      // array of 3 pizzas
```

The array declaration and construction can be combined.

<element type₁>[] *<array name>* = new *<element type₂>*[*<array size>*];

Here the array type *<element type₂>*[] must be *assignable* to the array type *<element type₁>*[] (Section 7.7, p. 317). When the array is constructed, all its elements are initialized to the default value for *<element type₂>*. This is true for both member and local arrays when they are constructed.

In all examples below, the code constructs the array, and the array elements are implicitly initialized to their default value. For example, all elements of the array `anIntArray` get the value 0, and all element of the array `mediumPizzas` get the value `null` when the arrays are constructed.

```
int[] anIntArray = new int[10];                   // Default element value: 0.

Pizza[] mediumPizzas = new Pizza[5];              // Default element value: null.

// Pizza class extends Object class
Object[] objArray = new Pizza[3];                 // Default element value: null.

// Pizza class implements Eatable interface
Eatable[] eatables = new Pizza[2];                // Default element value: null.
```

The value of the field `length` in each array is set to the number of elements specified during the construction of the array; for example, `mediumPizzas.length` has the value 5.

Once an array has been constructed, its elements can also be explicitly initialized individually; for example, in a loop. The examples in the rest of this section make use of a loop to traverse the elements of an array for various purposes.

Initializing an Array

Java provides the means of declaring, constructing, and explicitly initializing an array in one declaration statement:

<element type>[] *<array name>* = { *<array initialize list>* };

This form of initialization applies to member as well as local arrays. The *<array initialize list>* is a comma-separated list of zero or more expressions. Such an array initialization block results in the construction and initialization of the array.

```
int[] anIntArray = {13, 49, 267, 15, 215};
```

The array anIntArray is declared as an array of ints. It is constructed to hold 5 elements (equal to the length of the list of expressions in the block), where the first element is initialized to the value of the first expression (13), the second element to the value of the second expression (49), and so on.

```
// Pizza class extends Object class
Object[] objArray = { new Pizza(), new Pizza(), null };
```

The array objArray is declared as an array of the Object class, constructed to hold three elements. The initialization code sets the first two elements of the array to refer to two Pizza objects, while the last element is initialized to the null reference. Note that the number of objects created in the above declaration statement is actually *three*: the array object with three references and the two Pizza objects.

The expressions in the *<array initialize list>* are evaluated from left to right, and the array name obviously cannot occur in any of the expressions in the list. In the examples above, the *<array initialize list>* is terminated by the right curly bracket, }, of the block. The list can also be legally terminated by a comma. The following array has length two, and not three:

```
Topping[] pizzaToppings = { new Topping("cheese"), new Topping("tomato"), };
```

The declaration statement at (1) in the following code defines an array of four String objects, while the declaration statement at (2) shows that a String object is not the same as an array of char.

```
// Array with 4 String objects:
String[] pets = {"crocodiles", "elephants", "crocophants", "elediles"}; // (1)

// Array of 3 characters:
char[] charArray = {'a', 'h', 'a'};      // (2) Not the same as "aha".
```

Using an Array

The array object is referenced by the array name, but individual array elements are accessed by specifying an index with the [] operator. The array element access expression has the following syntax:

<array name> [*<index expression>*]

Each individual element is treated as a simple variable of the element type. The *index* is specified by the *<index expression>*, which can be any expression that evaluates to a non-negative int value. Since the lower bound of an array is always 0, the upper bound is one less than the array size, that is, *<array name>*.length-1. The ith element in the array has index (i-1). At runtime, the index value is automatically checked to ensure that it is within the array index bounds. If the index value is less than 0, or greater than or equal to *<array name>*.length, an ArrayIndexOutOf-BoundsException is thrown. A program can either check the index explicitly or catch the exception (see Section 6.5, p. 235), but an illegal index is typically an indication of a program bug.

In the array element access expression, the *<array name>* can be any expression that returns a reference to an array. For example, the following expression returns the character 'H' at index 1 in the character array returned by a call to the toCharArray() method of the String class: "AHA".toCharArray()[1].

The array operator [] is used to declare array types (Topping[]), specify array size (new Topping[3]), and to access array elements (toppings[1]). This operator is not used when the array reference is manipulated, for example, in an array reference assignment (see Section 7.9, p. 320), or when the array reference is passed as an actual parameter in a method call (see Section 3.7, p. 86).

Example 3.7 shows traversal of arrays. The loop at (3) initializes the local array trialArray declared at (2) five times with pseudo-random numbers (from 0.0 to 100.0), by calling the method randomize() declared at (5). The minimum value in the array is found by calling the method findMinimum() declared at (6), and is stored in the array storeMinimum declared at (1). The loop at (4) prints the minimum values from the trials. The start value of the loop variable is initially set to 0. The loop condition tests whether the loop variable is less than the length of the array; this guarantees that the index will not go out of bounds.

Example 3.7   *Using Arrays*

```java
public class Trials {
  public static void main(String[] args) {
    // Declare and construct the local arrays:
    double[] storeMinimum = new double[5];              // (1)
    double[] trialArray = new double[15];              // (2)
    for (int i = 0; i < storeMinimum.length; ++i) {    // (3)

      // Initialize the array.
      randomize(trialArray);

      // Find and store the minimum value.
      storeMinimum[i] = findMinimum(trialArray);
    }

    // Print the minimum values:                        (4)
    for (int i = 0; i < storeMinimum.length; ++i)
      System.out.printf("%.4f%n", storeMinimum[i]);
  }

  public static void randomize(double[] valArray) {    // (5)
    for (int i = 0; i < valArray.length; ++i)
      valArray[i] = Math.random() * 100.0;
  }
```

```
public static double findMinimum(double[] valArray) {  // (6)
  // Assume the array has at least one element.
  double minValue = valArray[0];
  for (int i = 1; i < valArray.length; ++i)
    minValue = Math.min(minValue, valArray[i]);
  return minValue;
  }
}
```

Possible output from the program:

```
6.9330
2.7819
6.7427
18.0849
26.2462
```

Anonymous Arrays

As shown earlier in this section, the following declaration statement

<element type₁>[] *<array name>* = new *<element type₂>*[*<array size>*]; // (1)

```
int[] intArray = new int[5];
```

can be used to construct arrays using an array creation expression. The size of the array is specified in the array creation expression, which creates the array and initializes the array elements to their default values. On the other hand, the following declaration statement

<element type>[] *<array name>* = { *<array initialize list>* };   // (2)

```
int[] intArray = {3, 5, 2, 8, 6};
```

both creates the array and initializes the array elements to specific values given in the array initializer block. However, the array initialization block is *not* an expression.

Java has another array creation expression, called *anonymous array*, which allows the concept of the array creation expression from (1) and the array initializer block from (2) to be combined, to create and initialize an array object:

new *<element type>*[] { *<array initialize list>* }

```
new int[] {3, 5, 2, 8, 6}
```

The construct has enough information to create a nameless array of a specific type. Neither the name of the array nor the size of the array is specified. The construct returns the reference value of the newly-created array, which can be assigned to references and passed as argument in method calls. In particular, the following two examples of declaration statements are equivalent.

```
int[] intArray = {3, 5, 2, 8, 6};           // (1)

int[] intArray = new int[] {3, 5, 2, 8, 6}; // (2)
```

In (1), an array initializer block is used to create and initialize the elements. In (2), an anonymous array expression is used. It is tempting to use the array initialization block as an expression; for example, in an assignment statement, as a short cut for assigning values to array elements in one go. However, this is illegal—instead, an anonymous array expression should be used.

```
int[] daysInMonth;
daysInMonth = {31, 28, 31, 30, 31, 30, 31, 31, 30, 31, 30, 31}; // Not ok.
daysInMonth = new int[] {31, 28, 31, 30, 31, 30, 31, 31, 30, 31, 30, 31}; // ok.
```

The concept of anonymous arrays is similar to that of *anonymous classes* (see Section 8.5, p. 377): they both combine the definition and the creation of objects into one operation.

In Example 3.8, an anonymous array is constructed at (1), and passed as a parameter to the static method findMinimum() defined at (2). Note that no array name or array size is specified for the anonymous array.

Example 3.8 *Using Anonymous Arrays*

```
public class AnonArray {
  public static void main(String[] args) {
    System.out.println("Minimum value: " +
        findMinimum(new int[] {3, 5, 2, 8, 6}));          // (1)
  }

  public static int findMinimum(int[] dataSeq) {          // (2)
    // Assume the array has at least one element.
    int min = dataSeq[0];
    for (int index = 1; index < dataSeq.length; ++index)
      if (dataSeq[index] < min)
        min = dataSeq[index];
    return min;
  }
}
```

Output from the program:

```
Minimum value: 2
```

Multidimensional Arrays

Since an array element can be an object reference and arrays are objects, array elements can themselves reference other arrays. In Java, an array of arrays can be defined as follows:

<element type>[][]...[] *<array name>*;

or

<element type> <array name>[][]...[];

In fact, the sequence of square bracket pairs, [], indicating the number of dimensions, can be distributed as a postfix to both the element type and the array name. Arrays of arrays are also often called *multidimensional arrays*.

The following declarations are all equivalent:

```
int[][] mXnArray;      // 2-dimensional array
int[]   mXnArray[];    // 2-dimensional array
int     mXnArray[][];  // 2-dimensional array
```

It is customary to combine the declaration with the construction of the multidimensional array.

```
int[][] mXnArray = new int[4][5];    // 4 x 5 matrix of ints
```

The previous declaration constructs an array mXnArray of four elements, where each element is an array (row) of 5 int values. The concept of rows and columns is often used to describe the dimensions of a 2-dimensional array, which is often called a *matrix*. However, such an interpretation is not dictated by the Java language.

Each row in the previous matrix is denoted by mXnArray[i], where $0 \leq i < 4$. Each element in the ith row, mXnArray[i], is accessed by mXnArray[i][j], where $0 \leq j < 5$. The number of rows is given by mXnArray.length, in this case 4, and the number of values in the ith row is given by mXnArray[i].length, in this case 5 for all the rows, where $0 \leq i < 4$.

Multidimensional arrays can also be constructed and explicitly initialized using array initializer blocks discussed for simple arrays. Note that each row is an array which uses an array initializer block to specify its values:

```
double[][] identityMatrix = {
  {1.0, 0.0, 0.0, 0.0 }, // 1. row
  {0.0, 1.0, 0.0, 0.0 }, // 2. row
  {0.0, 0.0, 1.0, 0.0 }, // 3. row
  {0.0, 0.0, 0.0, 1.0 }  // 4. row
}; // 4 x 4 Floating-point matrix
```

Arrays in a multidimensional array need not have the same length, and are often called *ragged arrays*. The array of arrays pizzaGalore in the code below will have five rows, the first four rows have different lengths but the fifth row is left unconstructed.

```
Pizza[][] pizzaGalore = {
  { new Pizza(), null, new Pizza() },    // 1. row is an array of 3 elements.
  { null, new Pizza()},                  // 2. row is an array of 2 elements.
  new Pizza[1],                          // 3. row is an array of 1 element.
  {},                                    // 4. row is an array of 0 elements.
  null                                   // 5. row is not constructed.
};
```

When constructing multidimensional arrays with the new operator, the length of the deeply nested arrays may be omitted. In which case, these arrays are left unconstructed. For example, an array of arrays to represent a room on a floor in a hotel on a street in a city can have the type HotelRoom[][][][]. From left to right, the square brackets represent indices for street, hotel, floor, and room, respectively. This 4-dimensional array of arrays can be constructed piecemeal, starting with the leftmost dimension and proceeding to the rightmost.

```
HotelRoom[][][][] rooms = new HotelRoom[10][5][][];  // Just streets and hotels.
```

The above declaration constructs the array of arrays rooms partially with ten streets, where each street has five hotels. Floors and rooms can be added to a particular hotel on a particular street:

```
rooms[0][0]       = new HotelRoom[3][]; // 3 floors in 1st. hotel on 1st. street.
rooms[0][0][0]    = new HotelRoom[8];   // 8 rooms on 1st. floor in this hotel.
rooms[0][0][0][0] = new HotelRoom();    // Initializes 1st. room on this floor.
```

The code below constructs an array of arrays matrix, where the first row has one element, the second row has two elements, and the third row has three elements. Note that the outer array is constructed first. The second dimension is constructed in a loop that constructs the array in each row. The elements in the multidimensional array will be implicitly initialized to the default double value (0.0D). In Figure 3.2, the array of arrays matrix is depicted after the elements have been explicitly initialized.

```
double[][] matrix = new double[3][];       // No. of rows.

for (int i = 0; i < matrix.length; ++i)
   matrix[i] = new double[i + 1];          // Construct a row.
```

Two other ways of initializing such an array of arrays are shown below. The first one uses array initializer blocks, and the second one uses an anonymous array of arrays.

```
double[][] matrix2 = {     // Using array initializer blocks.
  {0.0},                   // 1. row
  {0.0, 0.0},              // 2. row
  {0.0, 0.0, 0.0}          // 3. row
}

double[][] matrix3 = new double[][] { // Using an anonymous array of arrays.
  {0.0},                   // 1. row
  {0.0, 0.0},              // 2. row
  {0.0, 0.0, 0.0}          // 3. row
}
```

The type of the variable matrix is double[][], i.e., a two-dimensional array of double values. The type of the variable matrix[i] (where $0 \leq i < $ matrix.length) is double[], i.e., a one-dimensional array of double values. The type of the variable matrix[i][j] (where $0 \leq i < $ matrix.length and $0 \leq j < $ matrix[i].length) is double, i.e., a simple variable of type double.

Nested loops are a natural match for manipulating multidimensional arrays. In Example 3.9, a rectangular 4×3 int matrix is declared and constructed at (1). The program finds the minimum value in the matrix. The outer loop at (2) traverses the rows (mXnArray[i], where $0 \leq i < $ mXnArray.length), and the inner loop at (3) traverses

Figure 3.2 *Array of Arrays*

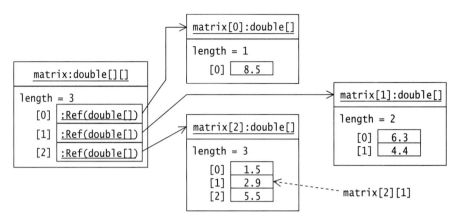

the elements in each row in turn (mXnArray[i][j], where $0 \le j <$ mXnArray[i].length). The outer loop is executed mXnArray.length times, or 4 times, and the inner loop is executed (mXnArray.length) × (mXnArray[i].length), or 12 times, since all rows have the same length, 3.

The for(:) loop also provides a safe and convenient way of traversing an array, and ample examples are provided in Section 6.3, p. 220.

The Java standard library also provides the class java.util.Arrays that contains various static methods for manipulating arrays, such as sorting and searching (see Section 15.11, p. 842).

Example 3.9 *Using Multidimensional Arrays*

```java
public class MultiArrays {

    public static void main(String[] args) {
        // Declare and construct the M X N matrix.
        int[][] mXnArray = {                                         // (1)
            {16,  7, 12}, // 1. row
            { 9, 20, 18}, // 2. row
            {14, 11,  5}, // 3. row
            { 8,  5, 10}  // 4. row
        }; // 4 x 3 int matrix

        // Find the minimum value in a M X N matrix:
        int min = mXnArray[0][0];
        for (int i = 0; i < mXnArray.length; ++i)                    // (2)
            // Find min in mXnArray[i], i.e. in the row given by index i:
            for (int j = 0; j < mXnArray[i].length; ++j)             // (3)
                min = Math.min(min, mXnArray[i][j]);

        System.out.println("Minimum value: " + min);
    }
}
```

Output from the program:

```
Minimum value: 5
```

 Review Questions

3.18 Given the following declaration, which expression returns the size of the array, assuming the array has been initialized?

```
int[] array;
```

Select the one correct answer.
(a) `array[].length()`
(b) `array.length()`
(c) `array[].length`
(d) `array.length`
(e) `array[].size()`
(f) `array.size()`

3.19 Is it possible to create arrays of length zero?

Select the one correct answer.
(a) Yes, you can create arrays of any type with length zero.
(b) Yes, but only for primitive data types.
(c) Yes, but only for arrays of reference types.
(d) No, you cannot create zero-length arrays, but the `main()` method may be passed a zero-length array of `Strings` when no program arguments are specified.
(e) No, it is not possible to create arrays of length zero in Java.

3.20 Which one of the following array declaration statements is not legal?

Select the one correct answer.
(a) `int []a[] = new int [4][4];`
(b) `int a[][] = new int [4][4];`
(c) `int a[][] = new int [][4];`
(d) `int []a[] = new int [4][];`
(e) `int [][]a = new int [4][4];`

3.21 Which of these array declaration statements are not legal?

Select the two correct answers.
(a) `int[] i[] = { { 1, 2 }, { 1 }, {}, { 1, 2, 3 } };`
(b) `int i[] = new int[2] {1, 2};`
(c) `int i[][] = new int[][] { {1, 2, 3}, {4, 5, 6} };`
(d) `int i[][] = { { 1, 2 }, new int[ 2 ] };`
(e) `int i[4] = { 1, 2, 3, 4 };`

3.22 What would be the result of compiling and running the following program?

```java
// Filename: MyClass.java
class MyClass {
  public static void main(String[] args) {
    int size = 20;
    int[] arr = new int[ size ];

    for (int i = 0; i < size; ++i) {
      System.out.println(arr[i]);
    }
  }
}
```

Select the one correct answer.

(a) The code will not compile, because the array type `int[]` is incorrect.
(b) The program will compile, but will throw an `ArrayIndexOutOfBoundsException` when run.
(c) The program will compile and run without error, but will produce no output.
(d) The program will compile and run without error, and will print the numbers 0 through 19.
(e) The program will compile and run without error, and will print 0 twenty times.
(f) The program will compile and run without error, and will print `null` twenty times.

3.23 What would be the result of compiling and running the following program?

```java
public class DefaultValuesTest {
  int[] ia = new int[1];
  boolean b;
  int i;
  Object o;

  public static void main(String[] args) {
    DefaultValuesTest instance = new DefaultValuesTest();
    instance.print();
  }

  public void print() {
    System.out.println(ia[0] + " " + b + " " + i + " " + o);
  }
}
```

Select the one correct answer.

(a) The program will fail to compile because of uninitialized variables.
(b) The program will throw a `java.lang.NullPointerException` when run.
(c) The program will print: 0 false NaN null.
(d) The program will print: 0 false 0 null.
(e) The program will print: null 0 0 null.
(f) The program will print: null false 0 null.

3.7 Parameter Passing

Objects communicate by calling methods on each other. A *method call* is used to invoke a method on an object. Parameters in the method call provide one way of exchanging information between the caller object and the callee object (which need not be different).

Defining methods is discussed in Section 3.3, p. 44. Invoking static methods on classes is discussed in Section 4.10, p. 147.

The syntax of a method call can be any one of the following:

<object reference>.*<method name>* (*<actual parameter list>*)

<class name>.*<static method name>* (*<actual parameter list>*)

<method name> (*<actual parameter list>*)

The *<object reference>* must be an expression that evaluates to a reference value denoting the object on which the method is called. If the caller and the callee are the same, *<object reference>* can be omitted (see discussion on the this reference in Section 3.3, p. 45). The *<class name>* can be the *fully qualified name* (see Section 4.2, p. 105) of the class. The *<actual parameter list>* is *comma-separated* if there is more than one parameter. The parentheses are mandatory even if the actual parameter list is empty. This distinguishes the method call from field access. One can specify fully qualified names for classes and packages using the dot operator.

```
objRef.doIt(time, place);          // Explicit object reference
int i = java.lang.Math.abs(-1);    // Fully qualified class name
int j = Math.abs(-1);              // Simple class name
someMethod(ofValue);               // Object or class implicitly implied
someObjRef.make().make().make();   // make() returns a reference value
```

The dot operator ('.') has left associativity. In the last code line, the first call of the make() method returns a reference value that denotes the object on which to execute the next call, and so on. This is an example of *call chaining*.

Each *actual parameter* (also called an *argument*) is an expression that is evaluated, and whose value is passed to the method when the method is invoked. Its value can vary from invocation to invocation. *Formal parameters* are parameters defined in the *method declaration* (see Section 3.3, p. 44) and are local to the method (see Section 2.4, p. 36).

In Java, all parameters are *passed by value*, that is, an actual parameter is evaluated and its value is assigned to the corresponding formal parameter. Table 3.1 summarizes the value that is passed depending on the type of the formal parameter. In the case of primitive data types, the data value of the actual parameter is passed. If the actual parameter is a reference to an object (i.e., instantiation of a class, enum, or array), the reference value is passed and not the object itself. If the actual parameter is an array element of a primitive data type, its data value is passed, and if the array element is a reference to an object, then its reference value is passed.

Table 3.1   *Parameter Passing By Value*

Data Type of the Formal Parameters	Value Passed
Primitive data types	Primitive data value
Class or enum type	Reference value
Array type	Reference value

It should also be stressed that each invocation of a method has its own copies of the formal parameters, as is the case for any local variables in the method (Section 6.5, p. 235).

The order of evaluation in the actual parameter list is always *from left to right*. The evaluation of an actual parameter can be influenced by an earlier evaluation of an actual parameter. Given the following declaration:

```
int i = 4;
```

the method call

```
leftRight(i++, i);
```

is effectively the same as

```
leftRight(4, 5);
```

and not as

```
leftRight(4, 4);
```

Section 5.2, p. 164, provides an overview of conversions that can take place in a method invocation context. Method invocation conversions for primitive values are discussed in the next subsection (p. 82), and those for reference types are discussed in Section 7.10, p. 323. Calling variable arity methods and generic methods is discussed in Section 3.8, p. 90, and in Section 14.8, p. 697, respectively.

For the sake of simplicity, the examples in subsequent sections primarily show method invocation on the same object or the same class. The parameter passing mechanism is no different when different objects or classes are involved.

Passing Primitive Data Values

An actual parameter is an expression that is evaluated first and the resulting value is then assigned to the corresponding formal parameter at method invocation. The use of this value in the method has no influence on the actual parameter. In particular, when the actual parameter is a variable of a primitive data type, the value of the variable is copied to the formal parameter at method invocation. Since formal parameters are local to the method, any changes made to the formal parameter will not be reflected in the actual parameter after the call completes.

Legal type conversions between actual parameters and formal parameters of *primitive data types* are summarized here from Table 5.1, p. 163:

- widening primitive conversion
- unboxing conversion, followed by an optional widening primitive conversion

These conversions are illustrated by invoking the following method

```
static void doIt(long i) { /* ... */ }
```

with the following code:

```
Integer intRef = 34;
Long longRef = 34L;
doIt(34);          // (1) Primitive widening conversion: long <-- int
doIt(longRef);     // (2) Unboxing: long <-- Long
doIt(intRef);      // (3) Unboxing, followed by primitive widening conversion:
                   //     long <-- int <-- Integer
```

However, for parameter passing, there are no implicit narrowing conversions for integer constant expressions (see Section 5.2, p. 164).

Example 3.10 *Passing Primitive Values*

```
public class CustomerOne {
  public static void main (String[] args) {
    PizzaFactory pizzaHouse = new PizzaFactory();
    int pricePrPizza = 15;
    double totPrice = pizzaHouse.calcPrice(4, pricePrPizza);      // (1)
    System.out.println("Value of pricePrPizza: " + pricePrPizza); // Unchanged.
  }
}

class PizzaFactory {
  public double calcPrice(int numberOfPizzas, double pizzaPrice) {  // (2)
    pizzaPrice = pizzaPrice/2.0;       // Changes price.
    return numberOfPizzas * pizzaPrice;
  }
}
```

Output from the program:

```
Value of pricePrPizza: 15
```

In Example 3.10, the method calcPrice() is defined in the class PizzaFactory at (2). It is called from the CustomerOne.main() method at (1). The value of the first actual parameter, 4, is copied to the int formal parameter numberOfPizzas. Note that the second actual parameter pricePrPizza is of the type int, while the corresponding formal parameter pizzaPrice is of the type double. Before the value of the actual parameter pricePrPizza is copied to the formal parameter pizzaPrice, it is implicitly widened to a double. The passing of primitive values is illustrated in Figure 3.3.

The value of the formal parameter pizzaPrice is changed in the calcPrice() method, but this does not affect the value of the actual parameter pricePrPizza on

Figure 3.3   *Parameter Passing: Primitive Data Values*

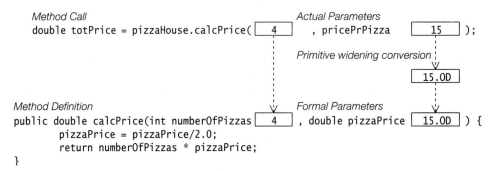

return. It still has the value 15. The bottom line is that the formal parameter is a local variable, and changing its value does not affect the value of the actual parameter.

Passing Reference Values

If the actual parameter expression evaluates to a reference value, the resulting reference value is assigned to the corresponding formal parameter reference at method invocation. In particular, if an actual parameter is a reference to an object, the reference value stored in the actual parameter is passed. This means that both the actual parameter and the formal parameter are aliases to the object denoted by this reference value during the invocation of the method. In particular, this implies that changes made to the object via the formal parameter *will* be apparent after the call returns.

Type conversions between actual and formal parameters of reference types are discussed in Section 7.10, p. 323.

Example 3.11   *Passing Reference Values*

```
public class CustomerTwo {
  public static void main (String[] args) {
    Pizza favoritePizza = new Pizza();              // (1)
    System.out.println("Meat on pizza before baking: " + favoritePizza.meat);
    bake(favoritePizza);                            // (2)
    System.out.println("Meat on pizza after baking: " + favoritePizza.meat);
  }
  public static void bake(Pizza pizzaToBeBaked) {   // (3)
    pizzaToBeBaked.meat = "chicken";  // Change the meat on the pizza.
    pizzaToBeBaked = null;                          // (4)
  }
}

class Pizza {                                       // (5)
  String meat = "beef";
}
```

Output from the program:

```
Meat on pizza before baking: beef
Meat on pizza after baking: chicken
```

In Example 3.11, a `Pizza` object is created at (1). Any object of the class `Pizza` created using the class declaration at (5) always results in a beef pizza. In the call to the `bake()` method at (2), the reference value of the object referenced by the actual parameter `favoritePizza` is assigned to the formal parameter `pizzaToBeBaked` in the declaration of the `bake()` method at (3).

One particular consequence of passing reference values to formal parameters is that any changes made to the object via formal parameters will be reflected back in the calling method when the call returns. In this case, the reference `favoritePizza` will show that chicken has been substituted for beef on the pizza. Setting the formal parameter `pizzaToBeBaked` to `null` at (4) does not change the reference value in the actual parameter `favoritePizza`. The situation at method invocation, and just before return from method `bake()`, is illustrated in Figure 3.4.

Figure 3.4   *Parameter Passing: Reference Values*

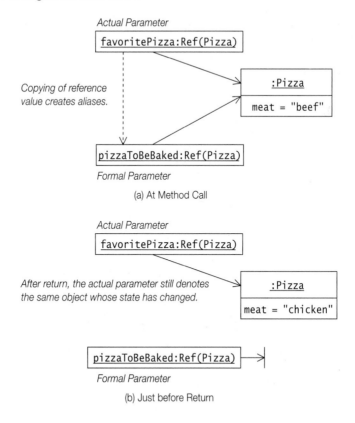

(a) At Method Call

(b) Just before Return

In summary, the formal parameter can only change the *state* of the object whose reference value was passed to the method.

The parameter passing strategy in Java is *call-by-value* and not *call-by-reference*, regardless of the type of the parameter. Call-by-reference would have allowed values in the actual parameters to be changed via formal parameters; that is, the value in `pricePrPizza` to be halved in Example 3.10 and `favoritePizza` to be set to `null` in Example 3.11. However, this cannot be directly implemented in Java.

Passing Arrays

The discussion on passing reference values in the previous section is equally valid for arrays, as arrays are objects in Java. Method invocation conversions for array types are discussed along with those for other reference types in Section 7.10, p. 323.

Example 3.12 *Passing Arrays*

```java
public class Percolate {

  public static void main (String[] args) {
    int[] dataSeq = {6,4,8,2,1};     // Create and initialize an array.

    // Write array before percolation:
    printIntArray(dataSeq);

    // Percolate:
    for (int index = 1; index < dataSeq.length; ++index)
      if (dataSeq[index-1] > dataSeq[index])
        swap(dataSeq, index-1, index);                              // (1)

    // Write array after percolation:
    printIntArray(dataSeq);
  }

  public static void swap(int[] intArray, int i, int j) {          // (2)
    int tmp = intArray[i]; intArray[i] = intArray[j]; intArray[j] = tmp;
  }

  public static void swap(int v1, int v2) {                        // (3)
    int tmp = v1; v1 = v2; v2 = tmp;
  }

  public static void printIntArray(int[] array) {                  // (4)
    for (int value : array)
      System.out.print(" " + value);
    System.out.println();
  }
}
```

Output from the program:

```
6 4 8 2 1
4 6 2 1 8
```

In Example 3.12, the idea is to repeatedly swap neighboring elements in an integer array until the largest element in the array *percolates* to the last position in the array.

Note that in the declaration of the method swap() at (2), the formal parameter intArray is of the array type int[]. The swap() method is called in the main() method at (1), where one of the actual parameters is the array variable dataSeq. The reference value of the array variable dataSeq is assigned to the array variable intArray at method invocation. After return from the call to the swap() method, the array variable dataSeq will reflect the changes made to the array via the corresponding formal parameter. This situation is depicted in Figure 3.5 at the first call and return from the swap() method, indicating how values of elements at indices 0 and 1 in the array have been swapped.

However, the declaration of the swap() method at (3) will *not* swap two values. The method call

```
swap(dataSeq[index-1], dataSeq[index]);
```

will have no effect on the array elements, as the swapping is done on the values of the formal parameters.

Figure 3.5 *Parameter Passing: Arrays*

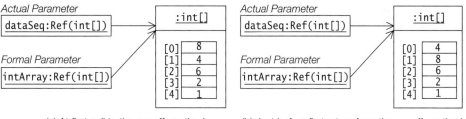

(a) At first call to the swap() method   (b) Just before first return from the swap() method

The method printIntArray() at (4) also has a formal parameter of array type int[]. Note that the formal parameter is specified as an array reference using the [] notation, but this notation is not used when an array is passed as an actual parameter.

Array Elements as Actual Parameters

Array elements, like other variables, can store values of primitive data types or reference values of objects. In the latter case, it means they can also be arrays, i.e., arrays of arrays (see Section 3.6, p. 74). If an array element is of a primitive data type, its data value is passed, and if it is a reference to an object, the reference value is passed. The method invocation conversions apply to the values of array elements as well.

Example 3.13 *Array Elements as Primitive Data Values*

```
public class FindMinimum {

  public static void main(String[] args) {
    int[] dataSeq = {6,4,8,2,1};

    int minValue = dataSeq[0];
    for (int index = 1; index < dataSeq.length; ++index)
      minValue = minimum(minValue, dataSeq[index]);            // (1)

    System.out.println("Minimum value: " + minValue);
  }

  public static int minimum(int i, int j) {                    // (2)
    return (i <= j) ? i : j;
  }
}
```

Output from the program:

```
Minimum value: 1
```

In Example 3.13, note that the value of all but one element of the array `dataSeq` is retrieved and passed consecutively at (1) to the formal parameter j of the `minimum()` method defined at (2). The discussion in Section 3.7 on call-by-value also applies to array elements that have primitive values.

Example 3.14 *Array Elements as Reference Values*

```
public class FindMinimumMxN {

  public static void main(String[] args) {
    int[][] matrix = { {8,4},{6,3,2},{7} };                    // (1)

    int min = findMinimum(matrix[0]);                          // (2)
    for (int i = 1; i < matrix.length; ++i) {
      int minInRow = findMinimum(matrix[i]);                   // (3)
      if (min > minInRow) min = minInRow;
    }
    System.out.println("Minimum value in matrix: " + min);
  }

  public static int findMinimum(int[] seq) {                   // (4)
    int min = seq[0];
    for (int i = 1; i < seq.length; ++i)
```

```
            min = Math.min(min, seq[i]);
        return min;
    }
}
```

Output from the program:

```
Minimum value in matrix: 2
```

- -

In Example 3.14, note that the formal parameter seq of the findMinimum() method defined at (4) is an array variable. The variable matrix denotes an array of arrays declared at (1) simulating a multidimensional array, which has three rows, where each row is a simple array. The first row, denoted by matrix[0], is passed to the findMinimum() method in the call at (2). Each remaining row is passed by its reference value in the call to the findMinimum() method at (3).

final **Parameters**

A formal parameter can be declared with the keyword final preceding the parameter declaration in the method declaration. A final parameter is also known as a *blank final variable*; that is, it is blank (uninitialized) until a value is assigned to it, (e.g., at method invocation) and then the value in the variable cannot be changed during the lifetime of the variable (see also the discussion in Section 4.10, p. 148). The compiler can treat final variables as constants for code optimization purposes. Declaring parameters as final prevents their values from being changed inadvertently. Whether a formal parameter is declared as final, does not affect the caller's code.

The declaration of the method calcPrice() from Example 3.10 is shown below, with the formal parameter pizzaPrice declared as final.

```
public double calcPrice(int numberOfPizzas, final double pizzaPrice) {  // (2')
    pizzaPrice = pizzaPrice/2.0;                        // (3) Not allowed.
    return numberOfPizzas * pizzaPrice;
}
```

If this declaration of the calcPrice() method is compiled, the compiler will not allow the value of the final parameter pizzaPrice to be changed at (3) in the body of the method.

As another example, the declaration of the method bake() from Example 3.11 is shown below, with the formal parameter pizzaToBeBaked declared as final.

```
public static void bake(final Pizza pizzaToBeBaked) { // (3)
    pizzaToBeBaked.meat = "chicken";                   // (3a) Allowed.
    pizzaToBeBaked = null;                             // (4) Not allowed.
}
```

If this declaration of the bake() method is compiled, the compiler will not allow the reference value of the final parameter pizzaToBeBaked to be changed at (4) in the body of the method. Note that this applies to the reference value in the `final` parameter, not the object denoted by this parameter. The state of the object can be changed as before, as shown at (3a).

3.8 Variable Arity Methods

A *fixed arity* method must be called with the same number of actual parameters (also called *arguments*) as the number of formal parameters specified in its declaration. If the method declaration specifies two formal parameters, every call of this method must specify exactly two arguments. We say that the arity of this method is 2. In other words, the arity of such a method is fixed, and it is equal to the number of formal parameters specified in the method declaration.

Java also allows declaration of *variable arity* methods; meaning that the number of arguments in its call can be *varied*. As we shall see, invocations of such a method may contain more actual parameters than formal parameters. Variable arity methods are heavily employed in formatting text representation of values (see Section 12.7, p. 593). The variable arity method `System.out.printf()` is used in many examples for this purpose.

The *last* formal parameter in a variable arity method declaration is declared as follows:

> *<type>*... *<formal parameter name>*

The ellipsis (...) is specified between the *<type>* and the *<formal parameter name>*. The *<type>* can be a primitive type, a reference type, or a type parameter. Whitespace can be specified on both sides of the ellipsis. Such a parameter is usually called a *varargs parameter*.

Apart from the varargs parameter, a variable arity method is identical to a fixed arity method. The method `publish()` below is a variable arity method:

```
public static void publish(int n, String... data) {        // (int, String[])
   System.out.println("n: " + n + ", data size: " + data.length);
}
```

The varargs parameter in a variable arity method is always interpreted as having the type:

> *<type>*[]

In the body of the `publish()` method, the varargs parameter data has the type `String[]`, i.e., a simple array of `Strings`.

Only *one* varargs parameter is permitted in the formal parameter list, and it is always the *last* parameter in the formal parameter list. Given that the method declaration has n formal parameters, and the method call has k actual parameters, k must be equal to or greater than n-1. The last k-n+1 actual parameters are evaluated and stored in an array whose reference value is passed as the value of the actual parameter. In the case of the `publish()` method, *n* is equal to 2, so *k* can be 1, 2, 3, and so on. The following invocations of the `publish()` method show what arguments are passed in each method call:

```
publish(1);                // (1, new String[] {})
publish(2, "two");         // (2, new String[] {"two"})
publish(3, "two", "three"); // (3, new String[] {"two", "three"})
```

Each method call results in an implicit array being created, and passed as argument. This array can contain zero or more argument values that do *not* correspond to the formal parameters preceding the varargs parameter. This array is referenced by the varargs parameter data in the method declaration. The calls above would result in the `publish()` method printing:

```
n: 1, data size: 0
n: 2, data size: 1
n: 3, data size: 2
```

Calling a Varargs Method

Example 3.15 illustrates various aspects of calling a varargs method. The method `flexiPrint()` in the VarargsDemo class has a varargs parameter:

```
public static void flexiPrint(Object... data) { // Object[]
  //...
}
```

The varargs method prints the name of the Class object representing the *actual array* that is passed. It prints the number of elements in this array, and also the text representation of each element in the array.

The method `flexiPrint()` is called in the `main()` method. First with the values of primitive types and Strings ((1) to (8)), then it is called with the program arguments supplied in the command line, ((9) to (11)).

Compiling the program results in a *warning*, which we ignore for the time being. The program can still be run, as shown in Example 3.15. The numbers at the end of the lines in the output relate to numbers in the code, and are not printed by the program.

- -

Example 3.15 *Calling a Varargs Method*

```
public class VarargsDemo {

  public static void flexiPrint(Object... data) { // Object[]
    // Print the name of the Class object for the varargs parameter.
    System.out.print("\nType: " + data.getClass().getName());

    System.out.println("  No. of elements: " + data.length);

    for(int i = 0; i < data.length; i++)
```

```
      System.out.print(data[i] + " ");
    if (data.length != 0)
      System.out.println();
  }

  public static void main(String... args) {
    int    day   = 1;
    String month = "March";
    int    year  = 2009;

    // Passing primitives and non-array types.
    flexiPrint();                         // (1) new Object[] {}
    flexiPrint(day);                      // (2) new Object[] {new Integer(day)}
    flexiPrint(day, month);               // (3) new Object[] {new Integer(day),
                                          //                  month}
    flexiPrint(day, month, year);         // (4) new Object[] {new Integer(day),
                                          //                  month,
                                          //                  new Integer(year)}

    // Passing an array type.
    Object[] dateInfo = {day,             // (5) new Object[] {new Integer(day),
                         month,           //                  month,
                         year};           //                  new Integer(year)}
    flexiPrint(dateInfo);                 // (6) Non-varargs call
    flexiPrint((Object) dateInfo);        // (7) new Object[] {(Object) dateInfo}
    flexiPrint(new Object[] {dateInfo});  // (8) Non-varargs call

    // Explicit varargs or non-varargs call.
    flexiPrint(args);                     // (9) Warning!
    flexiPrint((Object) args);            // (10) Explicit varargs call.
    flexiPrint((Object[]) args);          // (11) Explicit non-varargs call
  }
}
```

Compiling the program:

```
>javac VarargsDemo.java
VarargsDemo.java:39: warning: non-varargs call of varargs method with inexact
argument type for last parameter;
cast to java.lang.Object for a varargs call
cast to java.lang.Object[] for a non-varargs call and to suppress this warning
    flexiPrint(args);                     // (10) Warning!
              ^
1 warning
```

Running the program:

```
>java VarargsDemo To arg or not to arg

Type: [Ljava.lang.Object;  No. of elements: 0            (1)

Type: [Ljava.lang.Object;  No. of elements: 1            (2)
1

Type: [Ljava.lang.Object;  No. of elements: 2            (3)
1 March
```

```
Type: [Ljava.lang.Object;  No. of elements: 3            (4)
1 March 2009

Type: [Ljava.lang.Object;  No. of elements: 3            (6)
1 March 2009

Type: [Ljava.lang.Object;  No. of elements: 1            (7)
[Ljava.lang.Object;@1eed786

Type: [Ljava.lang.Object;  No. of elements: 1            (8)
[Ljava.lang.Object;@1eed786

Type: [Ljava.lang.String;  No. of elements: 6            (9)
To arg or not to arg

Type: [Ljava.lang.Object;  No. of elements: 1            (10)
[Ljava.lang.String;@187aeca

Type: [Ljava.lang.String;  No. of elements: 6            (11)
To arg or not to arg
```

Varargs and Non-Varargs Method Calls

The calls in (1) to (4) are all *varargs calls*, as an implicit Object array is created, in which the values of the actual parameters are stored. The reference value of this array is passed to the method. The printout shows that the type of the parameter is actually an array of Objects ([Ljava.lang.Object;).

The call at (6) is different from the previous calls, in that the actual parameter is an array that has the *same* type (Object[]) as the varargs parameter, without having to create an implicit array. In such a case, *no* implicit array is created, and the reference value of the array dateInfo is passed to the method. See also the result from this call at (6) in the output. The call at (6) is a *non-varargs call*, where no implicit array is created:

```
    flexiPrint(dateInfo);            // (6) Non-varargs call
```

However, if the actual parameter is cast to the type Object as in (7), a *varargs* call is executed:

```
    flexiPrint((Object) dateInfo);   // (7) new Object[] {(Object) dateInfo}
```

The type of the actual argument is now *not* the same as that of the varargs parameter, resulting in an array of the type Object[] being created, in which the array dateInfo is stored as an element. The printout at (7) shows that only the text representation of the dateInfo array is printed, and not its elements, as it is the sole element of the implicit array.

The call at (8) is a *non-varargs* call, for the same reason as the call in (6), but now the array dateInfo is explicitly stored as an element in an array of the type Object[] that matches the type of the varargs parameter:

```
flexiPrint(new Object[] {dateInfo}); // (8) Non-varargs call
```

The compiler issues a *warning* for the call at (9):

```
flexiPrint(args);                    // (9) Warning!
```

The actual parameter args is an array of the type String[], which is a *subtype* of Object[]—the type of the varargs parameter. The array args can be passed in a non-varargs call as an array of the type String[], or in a varargs call as *an element* in an implicitly created array of the type Object[]. *Both* calls are feasible and valid in this case. Note that the compiler chooses a non-varargs call rather than a varargs call, but also issues a warning. The result at (9) confirms this course of action.

The array args of the type String[] is explicitly passed as an Object in a varargs call at (10), similar to the call at (7):

```
flexiPrint((Object) args);           // (10) Explicit varargs call.
```

The array args of type String[] is explicitly passed as an array of the type Object[] in a non-varargs call at (11). This call is equivalent to the call at (9), where the widening reference conversion is implicit, but now without a warning at compile time. The two calls print the same information, as evident from the output at (9) and (11):

```
flexiPrint((Object[]) args);         // (11) Explicit non-varargs call
```

The compiler will complain if an attempt is made to overload the method flexi-Print() in the class VarargsDemo, as shown in the following code:

```
public static void flexiPrint(Object... data) { }  // Compile-time error!
public static void flexiPrint(Object[] data) { }   // Compile-time error!
```

These declarations would result in two methods with equivalent signatures in the same class, if this was permitted. Overloading and overriding of methods with varargs is discussed in Section 7.10, p. 324. The implications that generics have for varargs are discussed in Section 14.13, p. 729.

3.9 The main() Method

The mechanics of compiling and running Java applications using the JDK are outlined in Section 1.10. The java command executes a method called main in the class specified on the command line. Any class can have a main() method, but only the main() method of the class specified in the java command is executed to start a Java application.

The main() method must have public accessibility so that the interpreter can call this method (see Section 4.9, p. 138). It is a static method belonging to the class, so that no object of the class is required to start the execution (see Section 4.10, p. 147).

It does not return a value, that is, it is declared void (see Section 6.4, p. 228). It always has an array of String objects as its only formal parameter. This array contains any arguments passed to the program on the command line (see p. 95). The following method header declarations fit the bill, and any one of them can be used for the main() method:

```
public static void main(String[] args)     // Method header
public static void main(String... args)     // Method header
```

The above requirements do not exclude specification of additional modifiers (see Section 4.10, p. 146) or any throws clause (see Section 6.9, p. 257). The main() method can also be overloaded like any other method (see Section 3.3, p. 47). The JVM ensures that the main() method having the above method header is the starting point of program execution.

Program Arguments

Any arguments passed to the program on the command line can be accessed in the main() method of the class specified on the command line:

```
>java Colors red green blue
```

These arguments are called *program arguments*. Note that the command name, java, and the class name Colors are not passed to the main() method of the class Colors, nor are any other options that are specified in the command line.

Since the formal parameter of the main() method is an array of String objects, individual String elements in the array can be accessed by using the [] operator.

In Example 3.16, the three arguments "red", "green", and "blue" can be accessed in the main() method of the Colors class as args[0], args[1], and args[2], respectively. The total number of arguments is given by the field length of the String array args. Note that program arguments can only be passed as strings, and must be explicitly converted to other values by the program, if necessary.

When no arguments are specified on the command line, an array of zero String elements is created and passed to the main() method. This means that the reference value of the formal parameter in the main() method is never null.

Program arguments supply information to the application, which can be used to tailor the runtime behavior of the application according to user requirements.

Example 3.16 *Passing Program Arguments*

```
public class Colors {
  public static void main(String[] args) {
    System.out.println("No. of program arguments: " + args.length);
    for (int i = 0; i < args.length; i++)
      System.out.println("Argument no. " + i + " (" + args[i] + ") has " +
                          args[i].length() + " characters.");
  }
}
```

Running the program:

```
>java Colors red green blue
No. of program arguments: 3
Argument no. 0 (red) has 3 characters.
Argument no. 1 (green) has 5 characters.
Argument no. 2 (blue) has 4 characters.
```

 ## Review Questions

3.24   What will be printed when the following program is run?

```
public class ParameterPass {
  public static void main(String[] args) {
    int i = 0;
    addTwo(i++);
    System.out.println(i);
  }

  static void addTwo(int i) {
    i += 2;
  }
}
```

Select the one correct answer.

(a) 0
(b) 1
(c) 2
(d) 3

3.25   What will be the result of compiling and running the following program?

```
public class Passing {
  public static void main(String[] args) {
    int a = 0; int b = 0;
    int[] bArr = new int[1]; bArr[0] = b;

    inc1(a); inc2(bArr);

    System.out.println("a=" + a + " b=" + b + " bArr[0]=" + bArr[0]);
  }

  public static void inc1(int x) { x++; }

  public static void inc2(int[] x) { x[0]++; }
}
```

Select the one correct answer.

(a) The code will fail to compile, since x[0]++; is not a legal statement.
(b) The code will compile and will print "a=1 b=1 bArr[0]=1", when run.
(c) The code will compile and will print "a=0 b=1 bArr[0]=1", when run.
(d) The code will compile and will print "a=0 b=0 bArr[0]=1", when run.
(e) The code will compile and will print "a=0 b=0 bArr[0]=0", when run.

3.26 Which statements, when inserted at (1), will cause a compilation error?

```java
public class ParameterUse {
  static void main(String[] args) {
    int a = 0;
    final int b = 1;
    int[] c = { 2 };
    final int[] d = { 3 };
    useArgs(a, b, c, d);
  }

  static void useArgs(final int a, int b, final int[] c, int[] d) {
    // (1) INSERT STATEMENT HERE.
  }
}
```

Select the two correct answers.

(a) a++;

(b) b++;

(c) b = a;

(d) c[0]++;

(e) d[0]++;

(f) c = d;

3.27 Which method declarations are valid declarations?

Select the three correct answers.

(a) `void compute(int... is) { }`

(b) `void compute(int is...) { }`

(c) `void compute(int... is, int i, String... ss) { }`

(d) `void compute(String... ds) { }`

(e) `void compute(String... ss, int len) { }`

(f) `void compute(char[] ca, int... is) { }`

3.28 Given the following code:

```java
public class RQ800_40 {
  static void print(Object... obj) {
    System.out.println("Object...: " + obj[0]);
  }
  public static void main(String[] args) {
    // (1) INSERT METHOD CALL HERE.
  }
}
```

Which method call, when inserted at (1), will not result in the following output from the program:

```
Object...: 9
```

Select the one correct answer.

(a) `print("9", "1", "1");`

(b) `print(9, 1, 1);`

(c) `print(new int[] {9, 1, 1});`
(d) `print(new Integer[] {9, 1, 1});`
(e) `print(new String[] {"9", "1", "1"});`
(f) `print(new Object[] {"9", "1", "1"});`

3.29 What will be the result of compiling and running the following program?

```
public class RQ800_20 {
  static void compute(int... is) {                              // (1)
    System.out.print("|");
    for(int i : is) {
      System.out.print(i + "|");
    }
    System.out.println();
  }
  static void compute(int[] ia, int... is) {                    // (2)
    compute(ia);
    compute(is);
  }
  static void compute(int[] inta, int[]... is) {                // (3)
    for(int[] ia : is) {
      compute(ia);
    }
  }
  public static void main(String[] args) {
    compute(new int[] {10, 11}, new int[] {12, 13, 14});        // (4)
    compute(15, 16);                                            // (5)
    compute(new int[] {17, 18}, new int[][] {{19}, {20}});      // (6)
    compute(null, new int[][] {{21}, {22}});                    // (7)
  }
}
```

Select the one correct answer.

(a) The program does not compile because of errors in one or more calls to the compute() method.

(b) The program compiles, but throws a `NullPointerException` when run.

(c) The program compiles and prints:

```
|10|11|
|12|13|14|
|15|16|
|19|
|20|
|21|
|22|
```

(d) The program compiles and prints:

```
|12|13|14|
|15|16|
|10|11|
|19|
|20|
|21|
|22|
```

3.30 Which of these method declarations are valid declarations of the main() method that would be called by the JVM in order to start the execution of a Java application?

Select the three correct answers.
(a) static void main(String[] args) { /* ... */ }
(b) public static int main(String[] args) { /* ... */ }
(c) public static void main(String args) { /* ... */ }
(d) final public static void main(String[] arguments) { /* ... */ }
(e) public int main(Strings[] args, int argc) { /* ... */ }
(f) static public void main(String args[]) { /* ... */ }
(g) static public void main(String... args) { /* ... */ }

3.31 Which of the following are reserved keywords?

Select the three correct answers.
(a) public
(b) static
(c) void
(d) main
(e) String
(f) args

3.32 Given the class

```
// File name: Args.java
public class Args {
  public static void main(String[] args) {
    System.out.println(args[0] + " " + args[args.length-1]);
  }
}
```

what would be the result of executing the following command line?

```
>java Args In politics stupidity is not a handicap
```

Select the one correct answer.
(a) The program will throw an ArrayIndexOutOfBoundsException.
(b) The program will print "java handicap".
(c) The program will print "Args handicap".
(d) The program will print "In handicap".
(e) The program will print "Args a".
(f) The program will print "In a".

3.33 Which statement about the following program is true?

```
class MyClass {
  public static void main(String[] args) {
    String[] numbers = { "one", "two", "three", "four" };

    if (args.length == 0) {
```

```
        System.out.println("no arguments");
      } else {
        System.out.println(numbers[ args.length ] + " arguments");
      }
    }
  }
```

Select the one correct answer.

(a) The program will fail to compile.

(b) The program will throw a NullPointerException when run with no program arguments.

(c) The program will print "no arguments" and "two arguments" when called with zero and three program arguments, respectively.

(d) The program will print "no arguments" and "three arguments" when called with zero and three program arguments, respectively.

(e) The program will print "no arguments" and "four arguments" when called with zero and three program arguments, respectively.

(f) The program will print "one arguments" and "four arguments" when called with zero and three program arguments, respectively.

 Chapter Summary

The following information was included in this chapter:

- overview of declarations that can be specified in a class

- understanding pattern names for properties and the event model in the JavaBeans standard

- defining methods, usage of the this reference in an instance method, and method overloading

- defining constructors, usage of the default constructor, and overloading of constructors

- declaring and using enum types, and extending them implicitly

- explanation of declaration, construction, initialization, and usage of both one- and multi-dimensional arrays, including anonymous arrays

- parameter passing, both primitive values and object references, including arrays and array elements; and declaring final parameters

- declaring and calling methods with varargs

- declaration of the main() method whose execution starts the application

- passing program arguments to the main() method

Programming Exercises

3.1 Imagine you are creating an application that has a number of different tools a user may invoke. These tools need a special context to work in. The context describes the current active selection in the application. The selection consists of a reference to an arbitrary object. We wish to create a JavaBean representing an editing context that the tools may use. The JavaBean should contain the aforementioned selection reference. We do not want to allow direct manipulation of the reference, but want to have methods in the editing context that allow anyone to get and set the current selection.

Write such a JavaBean. Be sure to get the accessibility right.

3.2 Write a program to grade a short multiple-choice quiz. The correct answers for the quiz are:

```
1. C    5. B
2. A    6. C
3. B    7. C
4. D    8. A
```

Assume that the pass marks are 5 out of 8. The program stores the correct answers in an array. The submitted answers are specified as program arguments. Let X represent a question that was not answered on the quiz. Use an enum type to represent the result of answering a question.

The program calculates and prints a report along the following lines:

```
Question  Submitted Ans. Correct Ans.  Result
   1            C              C        CORRECT
   2            B              A          WRONG
   3            B              B        CORRECT
   4            D              D        CORRECT
   5            B              B        CORRECT
   6            C              C        CORRECT
   7            A              C          WRONG
   8            X              A     UNANSWERED
No. of correct answers:       5
No. of wrong answers:         2
No. of questions unanswered: 1
The candidate PASSED.
```

Access Control

4

Exam Objectives

1.1 Develop code that declares classes (including abstract and all forms of nested classes), interfaces, and enums, and includes the appropriate use of `package` and `import` statements (including static imports).

- ○ *The package and import statements are covered in this chapter.*
- ○ *For class declarations, see Section 3.1, p. 40.*
- ○ *For abstract classes, see Section 4.8, p. 135.*
- ○ *For nested classes, see Chapter 8, p. 351.*
- ○ *For interfaces, see Section 7.6, p. 309.*
- ○ *For enums, see Section 3.5, p. 54.*

7.1 Given a code example and a scenario, write code that uses the appropriate access modifiers, package declarations, and import statements to interact with (through access or inheritance) the code in the example.

7.5 Given the fully-qualified name of a class that is deployed inside and/or outside a JAR file, construct the appropriate directory structure for that class. Given a code example and a classpath, determine whether the classpath will allow the code to compile successfully.

Supplementary Objectives

- Creating JAR files.
- Using system properties.

4.1 Java Source File Structure

The structure of a skeletal Java source file is depicted in Figure 4.1. A Java source file can have the following elements that, if present, must be specified in the following order:

1. An optional package declaration to specify a package name. Packages are discussed in Section 4.2.

2. Zero or more import declarations. Since import declarations introduce type or static member names in the source code, they must be placed before any type declarations. Both type and static `import` statements are discussed in Section 4.2.

3. Any number of *top-level* type declarations. Class, enum, and interface declarations are collectively known as *type declarations*. Since these declarations belong to the same package, they are said to be defined at the *top level*, which is the package level.

   The type declarations can be defined in any order. Technically, a source file need not have any such declaration, but that is hardly useful.

   The JDK imposes the restriction that at the most one `public` class declaration per source file can be defined. If a `public` class is defined, the file name must match this `public` class. If the `public` class name is `NewApp`, the file name must be `NewApp.java`.

   Classes are discussed in Section 3.1, p. 40, and interfaces are discussed in Section 7.6, p. 309.

Note that except for the `package` and the `import` statements, all code is encapsulated in classes and interfaces. No such restriction applies to comments and white space.

Figure 4.1   *Java Source File Structure*

```
// Filename: NewApp.java
```
```
// PART 1: (OPTIONAL) package declaration
package com.company.project.fragilePackage;
```
```
// PART 2: (ZERO OR MORE) import declarations
import java.io.*;
import java.util.*;
import static java.lang.Math.*;
```
```
// PART 3: (ZERO OR MORE) top-level class and interface declarations
public class NewApp { }

class A { }

interface IX { }

class B { }

interface IY { }

enum C { FIRST, SECOND, THIRD }

// end of file
```

4.2 Packages

A package in Java is an encapsulation mechanism that can be used to group related classes, interfaces, enums, and subpackages.

Figure 4.2 shows an example of a package hierarchy, comprising a package called wizard that contains two other packages: pandorasBox and spells. The package pandorasBox has a class called Clown that implements an interface called Magic, also found in the same package. In addition, the package pandorasBox has a class called LovePotion and a subpackage called artifacts containing a class called Ailment. The package spells has two classes: Baldness and LovePotion. The class Baldness is a subclass of class Ailment found in the subpackage artifacts in the package pandorasBox.

The dot (.) notation is used to uniquely identify package members in the package hierarchy. The class wizard.pandorasBox.LovePotion is different from the class wizard.spells.LovePotion. The Ailment class can be easily identified by the name wizard.pandorasBox.artifacts.Ailment. This is called the *fully qualified name* of the type. Note that the fully qualified name of the type in a named package comprises the fully qualified name of the package and the simple name of the type. The *simple type name* Ailment and the *fully qualified package name* wizard.pandorasBox.artifacts together define the *fully qualified type name* wizard.pandorasBox.artifacts.Ailment. Analogously, the fully qualified name of a *subpackage* comprises the fully qualified name of the parent package and the simple name of the subpackage.

Java programming environments usually map the fully qualified name of packages to the underlying (hierarchical) file system. For example, on a Unix system, the class file LovePotion.class corresponding to the fully qualified name wizard.pandoras-Box.LovePotion would be found under the directory wizard/pandorasBox.

Figure 4.2 *Package Hierarchy*

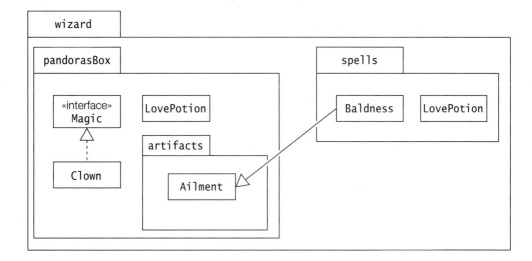

Conventionally, a global naming scheme based on the Internet domain names is used to uniquely identify packages. If the above package wizard was implemented by a company called Sorcerers Limited that owns the domain sorcerersltd.com, its fully qualified name would be:

```
com.sorcerersltd.wizard
```

Because domain names are unique, packages with this naming scheme are globally identifiable. It is not advisable to use the top-level package names java and sun, as these are reserved for the Java designers.

The subpackage wizard.pandorasBox.artifacts could easily have been placed elsewhere, as long as it was uniquely identified. Subpackages in a package do not affect the accessibility of the other package members. For all intents and purposes, subpackages are more an *organizational* feature rather than a language feature. Accessibility of members in a package is discussed in Section 4.6. Accessibility of members defined in type declarations is discussed in Section 4.9.

Defining Packages

A package hierarchy represents an organization of the Java classes and interfaces. It does *not* represent the source code organization of the classes and interfaces. The source code is of no consequence in this regard. Each Java source file (also called *compilation unit*) can contain zero or more type declarations, but the compiler produces a separate *class* file containing the Java byte code for each of them. A type declaration can indicate that its Java byte code be placed in a particular package, using a package declaration.

The package statement has the following syntax:

package *<fully qualified package name>*;

At most one package declaration can appear in a source file, and it must be the first statement in the source file. The package name is saved in the Java byte code for the types contained in the package.

Note that this scheme has two consequences. First, all the classes and interfaces in a source file will be placed in the same package. Second, several source files can be used to specify the contents of a package.

If a package declaration is omitted in a compilation unit, the Java byte code for the declarations in the compilation unit will belong to an *unnamed package* (also called the *default package*), which is typically synonymous with the current working directory on the host system.

Example 4.1 illustrates how the packages in Figure 4.2 can be defined using the package declaration. There are four compilation units. Each compilation unit has a package declaration, ensuring that the type declarations are compiled into the correct package. The complete code can be found in Example 4.10 on page 133.

Example 4.1   *Defining Packages and Using Type Import*

```
//File: Clown.java
package wizard.pandorasBox;                    // (1) Package declaration

import wizard.pandorasBox.artifacts.Ailment;   // (2) Importing class

public class Clown implements Magic { /* ... */ }

interface Magic { /* ... */ }
```

```
//File: LovePotion.java
package wizard.pandorasBox;                    // (1) Package declaration

public class LovePotion { /* ... */ }
```

```
//File: Ailment.java
package wizard.pandorasBox.artifacts;          // (1) Package declaration

public class Ailment { /* ... */ }
```

```
//File: Baldness.java
package wizard.spells;                         // (1)Package declaration

import wizard.pandorasBox.*;                    // (2) Type-import-on-demand
import wizard.pandorasBox.artifacts.*;          // (3) Import from subpackage

public class Baldness extends Ailment {         // (4) Abbreviated name for Ailment
  wizard.pandorasBox.LovePotion tlcOne;        // (5) Fully qualified name
  LovePotion tlcTwo;                            // (6) Class in same package
  // ...
}

class LovePotion { /* ... */ }
```

Using Packages

The import facility in Java makes it easier to use the contents of packages. This subsection discusses importing *reference types* and *static members of reference types* from packages.

Importing Reference Types

The accessibility of types (classes and interfaces) in a package determines their access from other packages. Given a reference type that is accessible from outside a package, the reference type can be accessed in two ways. One way is to use the fully qualified name of the type. However, writing long names can become tedious. The second way is to use the `import` declaration that provides a shorthand notation for specifying the name of the type, often called *type import*.

The `import` declarations must be the first statement after any package declaration in a source file. The simple form of the `import` declaration has the following syntax:

  `import` *<fully qualified type name>*;

This is called *single-type-import*. As the name implies, such an `import` declaration provides a shorthand notation for a single type. The *simple* name of the type (that is, its identifier) can now be used to access this particular type. Given the following `import` declaration:

  `import wizard.pandorasBox.Clown;`

the simple name `Clown` can be used in the source file to refer to this class.

Alternatively, the following form of the `import` declaration can be used:

  `import` *<fully qualified package name>*`.*`;

This is called *type-import-on-demand*. It allows any type from the specified package to be accessed by its simple name.

An `import` declaration does not recursively import subpackages. The declaration also does not result in inclusion of the source code of the types. The declaration only imports type names (that is, it makes type names available to the code in a compilation unit).

All compilation units implicitly import the `java.lang` package (see Section 10.1, p. 424). This is the reason why we can refer to the class `String` by its simple name, and need not use its fully qualified name `java.lang.String` all the time.

Example 4.1 shows several usages of the `import` statement. Here we will draw attention to the class `Baldness` in the file `Baldness.java`. This class relies on two classes that have the same simple name `LovePotion` but are in different packages: `wizard.pandorasBox` and `wizard.spells`, respectively. To distinguish between the two classes, we can use their fully qualified names. However, since one of them is in the same package as the class `Baldness`, it is enough to fully qualify the class from the other package. This solution is used in Example 4.1 at (5). Such name conflicts can usually be resolved by using variations of the `import` statement together with fully qualified names.

The class `Baldness` extends the class `Ailment`, which is in the subpackage `artifacts` of the `wizard.pandorasBox` package. The `import` declaration at (3) is used to import the types from the subpackage `artifacts`.

The following example shows how a single-type-import declaration can be used to disambiguate a type name when access to the type is ambiguous by its simple name. The following `import` statement allows the simple name `List` as shorthand for the `java.awt.List` type as expected:

  `import java.awt.*;          // imports all reference types from java.awt`

Given the following two `import` declarations:

```
import java.awt.*;        // imports all type names from java.awt
import java.util.*;       // imports all type names from java.util
```

the simple name `List` is now ambiguous as both the types `java.util.List` and `java.awt.List` match.

Adding a single-type-import declaration for the `java.awt.List` type last allows the simple name `List` as a shorthand notation for this type:

```
import java.awt.*;        // imports all type names from java.awt
import java.util.*;       // imports all type names from java.util
import java.awt.List;     // imports the type List from java.awt explicitly
```

Importing Static Members of Reference Types

Analogous to the type import facility, Java also allows import of static members of reference types from packages, often called *static import*.

Static import allows accessible static members (static fields, static methods, static member classes, enum, and interfaces) declared in a type to be imported, so that they can be used by their simple name, and therefore need not be qualified. The import applies to the whole compilation unit, and importing from the unnamed package is not permissible.

The two forms of static import are shown below:

```
// Single-static-import: imports a specific static member from the designated type
import static <fully qualified type name>.<static member name>;
```

```
// Static-import-on-demand: imports all static members in the designated type
import static <fully qualified type name>.*;
```

Both forms require the use of the keyword `static`. In both cases, the *fully qualified name of the reference type* we are importing from is required.

The first form allows *single static import* of individual static members, and is demonstrated in Example 4.2. The constant `PI`, which is a static field in the class `java.lang.Math`, is imported at (1). Note the use of the fully qualified name of the type in the static import statement. The static method named `sqrt` from the class `java.lang.Math` is imported at (2). Only the *name* of the static method is specified in the static import statement. No parameters are listed. Use of any other static member from the `Math` class requires that the fully qualifying name of the class be specified. Since types from the `java.lang` package are imported implicitly, the fully qualified name of the `Math` class is not necessary, as shown at (3).

Static import on demand is easily demonstrated by replacing the two `import` statements in Example 4.2 by the following `import` statement:

```
import static java.lang.Math.*;
```

We can also dispense with the use of the class name `Math` in (3), as all static members from the `Math` class are now imported:

```
double hypotenuse = hypot(x, y);   // (3') Type name can now be omitted.
```

Example 4.2   *Single Static Import*

```java
import static java.lang.Math.PI;         // (1) Static field
import static java.lang.Math.sqrt;       // (2) Static method
// Only specified static members are imported.

public class CalculateI {
  public static void main(String[] args) {
    double x = 3.0, y = 4.0;
    double squareroot = sqrt(y);            // Simple name of static method
    double hypotenuse = Math.hypot(x, y);   // (3) Requires type name.
    double area = PI * y * y;               // Simple name of static field
    System.out.printf("Square root: %.2f, hypotenuse: %.2f, area: %.2f%n",
                      squareroot, hypotenuse, area);
  }
}
```

Output from the program:

```
Square root: 2.00, hypotenuse: 5.00, area: 50.27
```

Using static import avoids the *interface constant antipattern,* as illustrated in Example 4.3. The static import statement at (1) allows the interface constants in the package mypkg to be accessed by their simple names. The static import facility avoids the MyFactory class having to *implement* the interface in order to access the constants by their simple name:

```java
public class MyFactory implements mypkg.IMachineState {
  // ...
}
```

Example 4.3   *Avoiding the Interface Constant Antipattern*

```java
package mypkg;

public interface IMachineState {
  // Fields are public, static and final.
  int BUSY = 1;
  int IDLE = 0;
  int BLOCKED = -1;
}
```

```java
import static mypkg.IMachineState.*;      // (1) Static import interface constants

public class MyFactory {
  public static void main(String[] args) {
    int[] states = { IDLE, BUSY, IDLE, BLOCKED };
    for (int s : states)
      System.out.print(s + " ");
  }
}
```

Output from the program:

```
0 1 0 -1
```

Static import is ideal for importing enum constants from packages, as such constants are static members of an enum type. Example 4.4 combines type and static import. The enum constants can be accessed at (4) using their simple names because of the static import statement at (2). The type import at (1) is required to access the enum type State by its simple name at (5).

Example 4.4   *Importing Enum Constants*

```
package mypkg;

public enum State { BUSY, IDLE, BLOCKED }
```

```
import mypkg.State;                    // (1) Single type import

import static mypkg.State.*;           // (2) Static import on demand
import static java.lang.System.out;    // (3) Single static import

public class Factory {
  public static void main(String[] args) {
    State[] states = {
        IDLE, BUSY, IDLE, BLOCKED        // (4) Using static import implied by (2).
    };
    for (State s : states)              // (5) Using type import implied by (1).
      out.print(s + " ");              // (6) Using static import implied by (3).
  }
}
```

Output from the program:

```
IDLE BUSY IDLE BLOCKED
```

Identifiers in a class can *shadow* static members that are imported. Example 4.5 illustrates the case where the parameter out of the method writeInfo() has the same name as the statically imported field java.lang.System.out. The type of the parameter is PrintWriter, and that of the statically imported field is PrintStream. Both classes PrintStream and PrintWriter define the method println() that is called in the program. The only way to access the imported field in the method writeInfo() is to use its fully qualified name.

Example 4.5   *Shadowing by Importing*

```
import static java.lang.System.out;        // (1) Static import

import java.io.FileNotFoundException;
import java.io.PrintWriter;                // (2) Single type import

public class ShadowingByImporting {

  public static void main(String[] args) throws FileNotFoundException {
    out.println("Calling println() in java.lang.System.out");
    PrintWriter pw = new PrintWriter("log.txt");
    writeInfo(pw);
    pw.flush();
    pw.close();
  }

  public static void writeInfo(PrintWriter out) { // Shadows java.lang.System.out
    out.println("Calling println() in the parameter out");
    System.out.println("Calling println() in java.lang.System.out"); // Qualify
  }
}
```

Output from the program:

```
Calling println() in java.lang.System.out
Calling println() in java.lang.System.out
```

Contents of the file `log.txt`:

```
Calling println() in the parameter out
```

Conflicts can also occur when a static method with the same signature is imported by *several* static import statements. In Example 4.6, a method named binarySearch is imported 21 times by the static import statements. This method is overloaded twice in the java.util.Collections class and 18 times in the java.util.Arrays class, in addition to one declaration in the mypkg.Auxiliary class. The classes java.util.Arrays and mypkg.Auxiliary have a declaration of this method with the *same signature* that matches the method call at (2), resulting in a signature conflict. The conflict can again be resolved by specifying the fully qualified name of the method.

If the static import statement at (1) is removed, there is no conflict, as only the class java.util.Arrays has a method that matches the method call at (2). If the declaration of the method binarySearch() at (3) is allowed, there is also *no* conflict, as this method declaration will *shadow* the imported method whose signature it matches.

Example 4.6   *Conflict in Importing Static Method with the Same Signature*

```
package mypkg;

public class Auxiliary {
  public static int binarySearch(int[] a, int key) { // Same in java.util.Arrays.
    // Implementation is omitted.
    return -1;
  }
}
```

```
import static java.util.Collections.binarySearch;  //    2 overloaded methods
import static java.util.Arrays.binarySearch;        // + 18 overloaded methods
import static mypkg.Auxiliary.binarySearch; // (1) Causes signature conflict.

class MultipleStaticImport {
  public static void main(String[] args) {
    int index = binarySearch(new int[] {10, 50, 100}, 50); // (2) Not ok!
    System.out.println(index);
  }

//  public static int binarySearch(int[] a, int key) {     // (3)
//     return -1;
//  }
}
```

Example 4.6 illustrates importing nested static types (Section 8.2, p. 355). The class
yap.Machine declares three static members, which all are *types*. Since these nested
members are types that are static, they can be imported both as types *and* as static
members. The class MachineClient uses the static types declared in the yap.Machine
class. The program shows how the import statements influence which types and
members are accessible. The following statement in the main() method declared at
(10) does not compile:

```
String s1 = IDLE;                        // Ambiguous because of (3) and (6)
```

because the constant IDLE is imported from both the static class StateConstant and
the enum type MachineState by the following import statements:

```
import static yap.Machine.StateConstant.*;    // (3)
...
import static yap.Machine.MachineState.*;     // (6)
```

Similarly, the following statement in the main() method is also not permitted:

```
MachineState ms1 = BLOCKED;               // Ambiguous because of (3) and (6)
```

The conflicts are resolved by qualifying the member just enough to make the
names unambiguous.

Example 4.7   *Importing Nested Static Types*

```
package yap;                                  // yet another package

public class Machine {                        // Class with 3 nested types

  public static class StateConstant {         // A static member class
    public static final String BUSY = "Busy";
    public static final String IDLE = "Idle";
    public static final String BLOCKED = "Blocked";
  }

  public enum MachineState {                   // A nested enum is static.
    BUSY, IDLE, BLOCKED
  }

  public enum AuxMachineState {                // Another static enum
    UNDER_REPAIR, WRITE_OFF, HIRED, AVAILABLE;
  }
}
```

```
import yap.Machine;                           // (0)

import yap.Machine.StateConstant;             // (1)
import static yap.Machine.StateConstant;      // (2) Superfluous because of (1)
import static yap.Machine.StateConstant.*;    // (3)

import yap.Machine.MachineState;              // (4)
import static yap.Machine.MachineState;       // (5) Superfluous because of (4)
import static yap.Machine.MachineState.*;     // (6)

import yap.Machine.AuxMachineState;           // (7)
import static yap.Machine.AuxMachineState;    // (8) Superfluous because of (7)
import static yap.Machine.AuxMachineState.*;  // (9)
import static yap.Machine.AuxMachineState.WRITE_OFF;  // (10)
```

```
public class MachineClient {
  public static void main(String[] args) {    // (10)

    StateConstant msc = new StateConstant();  // Requires (1) or (2)
    //String s1 = IDLE;                        // Ambiguous because of (3) and (6)
    String s2 = StateConstant.IDLE;           // Explicit disambiguation necessary.

    //MachineState ms1 = BLOCKED;              // Ambiguous because of (3) and (6)
    MachineState ms2 = MachineState.BLOCKED;  // Requires (4) or (5)
    MachineState ms3 = MachineState.IDLE;     // Explicit disambiguation necessary.

    AuxMachineState[] states = {              // Requires (7) or (8)
        AVAILABLE, HIRED, UNDER_REPAIR,       // Requires (9)
        WRITE_OFF,                            // Requires (9) or (10)
        AuxMachineState.WRITE_OFF,            // Requires (7) or (8)
        Machine.AuxMachineState.WRITE_OFF,    // Requires (0)
        yap.Machine.AuxMachineState.WRITE_OFF // Does not require any import
    };
```

```
        for (AuxMachineState s : states)
          System.out.print(s + " ");
    }
  }
```

Output from the program:

```
AVAILABLE HIRED UNDER_REPAIR WRITE_OFF WRITE_OFF WRITE_OFF WRITE_OFF
```

Compiling Code into Packages

In this chapter, we will use pathname conventions used on a Unix platform. See Section 11.2, p. 468, for a discussion on pathnames and conventions for specifying pathnames on different platforms. While trying out the examples in this section, attention should be paid to platform-dependencies in this regard. Particularly, the fact that the *separator character* in a *file path* for the Unix and Windows platform is '/' and '\', respectively.

As mentioned earlier, a package can be mapped on a hierarchical file system. We can think of a package name as a pathname in the file system. Referring to Example 4.1, the package name wizard.pandorasBox corresponds to the pathname wizard/pandorasBox. The Java byte code for all types declared in the source files Clown.java and LovePotion.java will be placed in the *package directory* with the pathname wizard/pandorasBox, as these source files have the following package declaration:

```
package wizard.pandorasBox;
```

The *location* in the file system where the package directory should be created is specified using the -d option (d for *destination*) of the javac command. The term *destination directory* is a synonym for this location in the file system. The compiler will create the package directory with the pathname wizard/pandorasBox (including any subdirectories required) *under* the specified location, and place the Java byte code for the types declared in the source files Clown.java and LovePotion.java inside the package directory.

Assuming that the current directory (.) is the directory /pgjc/work, and the four source files in Example 4.1 are to be found in this directory, the command

```
>javac -d . Clown.java LovePotion.java Ailment.java Baldness.java
```

issued in the current directory will create a file hierarchy under this directory, that mirrors the package hierarchy in Figure 4.2 (see also Figure 4.3). Note the subdirectories that are created for a fully qualified package name, and where the class files are located. In the command line above, space between the -d option and its argument is mandatory.

We can specify any *relative* pathname that designates the destination directory, or its *absolute* pathname:

```
>javac -d /pgjc/work Clown.java LovePotion.java Ailment.java Baldness.java
```

We can, of course, specify other destinations than the current directory where the class files with the byte code should be stored. The following command

```
>javac -d ../myapp Clown.java LovePotion.java Ailment.java Baldness.java
```

in the current directory /pgjc/work will create the necessary packages with the class files under the destination directory /pgjc/myapp.

Without the -d option, the default behavior of the javac compiler is to place all class files directly under the current directory (where the source files are located), rather than in the appropriate subdirectories corresponding to the packages.

Figure 4.3   *File Hierarchy*

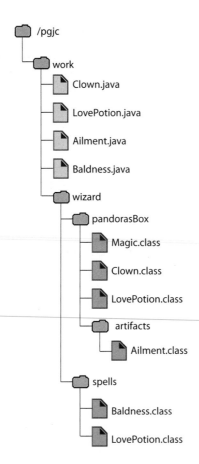

The compiler will report an error if there is any problem with the destination directory specified with the -d option (e.g., if it does not exist or does not have the right file permissions).

Running Code from Packages

Referring to Example 4.1, if the current directory has the absolute pathname /pgjc/ work and we want to run Clown.class in the directory with the pathname ./wizard/ pandorasBox, the *fully qualified name* of the Clown class *must* be specified in the java command

```
>java wizard.pandorasBox.Clown
```

This will load the class Clown from the byte code in the file with the pathname ./ wizard/pandorasBox/Clown.class, and start the execution of its main() method.

4.3 Searching for Classes

The documentation for the JDK tools explains how to organize packages in more elaborate schemes. In particular, the CLASSPATH environment variable can be used to specify the *class search path* (usually abbreviated to just *class path*), which are *pathnames* or *locations* in the file system where JDK tools should look when searching for classes and other resource files. Alternatively, the -classpath option (often abbreviated to -cp) of the JDK tool commands can be used for the same purpose. The CLASSPATH environment variable is not recommended for this purpose, as its class path value affects *all* Java applications on the host platform, and any application can modify it. However, the -cp option can be used to set the class path for each application individually. This way, an application cannot modify the class path for other applications. The class path specified in the -cp option supersedes the path or paths set by the CLASSPATH environment variable while the JDK tool command is running. We will not discuss the CLASSPATH environment variable here, and assume it to be undefined.

Basically, the JDK tools first look in the directories where the Java standard libraries are installed. If the class is not found in the standard libraries, the tool searches in the class path. When no class path is defined, the default value of the class path is assumed to be the current directory. If the -cp option is used and the current directory should be searched by the JDK tool, the current directory must be specified as an entry in the class path, just like any other directory that should be searched. This is most conveniently done by including '.' as one of the entries in the class path.

We will use the file hierarchies shown in Figure 4.4 to illustrate some of the intricacies involved when searching for classes. The current directory has the absolute pathname /top/src, where the source files are stored. The package pkg is stored under the directory with the absolute pathname /top/bin. The source code in the two source files A.java and B.java is also shown in Figure 4.4.

The file hierarchy before any files are compiled is shown in Figure 4.4a. Since the class B does not use any other classes, we compile it first with the following command, resulting in the file hierarchy shown in Figure 4.4b:

Figure 4.4   *Searching for Classes*

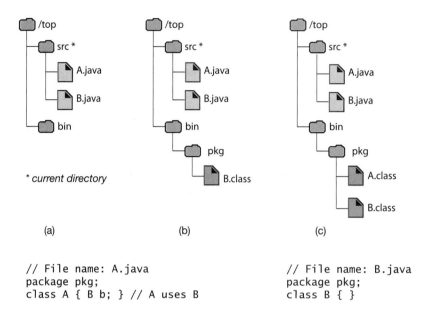

```
// File name: A.java            // File name: B.java
package pkg;                    package pkg;
class A { B b; } // A uses B    class B { }
```

```
>javac -d ../bin B.java
```

Next, we try to compile the file A.java, and get the following results:

```
>javac -d ../bin A.java
A.java:3: cannot find symbol
symbol  : class B
location: class pkg.A
public class A { B b; }
                 ^
1 error
```

The compiler cannot find the class B, i.e., the file B.class containing the Java byte code for the class B. From Figure 4.4b we can see that it is in the package pkg under the directory bin, but the compiler cannot find it. This is hardly surprising, as there is no byte code file for the class B in the current directory, which is the default value of the class path. The command below sets the value of the class path to be /top/ bin, and compilation is successful (see Figure 4.4c):

```
>javac -cp /top/bin -d ../bin A.java
```

It is very important to understand that when we want the JDK tool to search in a *named package*, it is the *location* of the package that is specified, i.e., the class path indicates the directory that *contains* the first element of the fully qualified package name. In Figure 4.4c, the package pkg is contained under the directory whose absolute path is /top/bin. The following command will *not* work, as the directory /top/ bin/pkg does *not* contain a package with the name pkg that has a class B:

```
>javac -cp /top/bin/pkg -d ../bin A.java
```

Also, the compiler is not using the class path to find the source file(s) that are specified in the command line. In the command above, the source file has the relative pathname ./A.java. So the compiler looks for the source file in the current directory. The class path is used to find classes used by the class A.

Given the file hierarchy in Figure 4.3, the following -cp option sets the class path so that *all* packages (wizard.pandorasBox, wizard.pandorasBox.artifacts, wizard.spells) in Figure 4.3 will be searched, as all packages are located under the specified directory:

```
-cp /pgjc/work
```

However, the following -cp option will not help in finding *any* of the packages in Figure 4.3, as none of the *packages* are located under the specified directory:

```
>java -cp /pgjc/work/wizard pandorasBox.Clown
```

The command above also illustrates an important point about package names: the *fully qualified package name* should not be split. The package name for the class wizard.pandorasBox.Clown is wizard.pandorasBox, and must be specified fully. The following command will search all packages in Figure 4.3 for classes that are used by the class wizard.pandorasBox.Clown:

```
>java -cp /pgjc/work wizard.pandorasBox.Clown
```

The class path can specify several *entries*, i.e., several locations, and the JDK tool searches them in the order they are specified, from left to right.

```
-cp /pgjc/work:/top/bin/pkg:.
```

We have used the path-separator character ':' for Unix platforms to separate the entries, and also included the current directory (.) as an entry. There should be no white space on either side of the path-separator character.

The search in the class path entries stops once the required class file is found. Therefore, the order in which entries are specified can be significant. If a class B is found in a package pkg located under the directory /ext/lib1, and also in a package pkg located under the directory /ext/lib2, the order in which the entries are specified in the two -cp options shown below is significant. They will result in the class pkg.B being found under /ext/lib1 and /ext/lib2, respectively.

```
-cp /ext/lib1:/ext/lib2
-cp /ext/lib2:/ext/lib1
```

The examples so far have used absolute pathnames for class path entries. We can of course use relative pathnames as well. If the current directory has the absolute pathname /pgjc/work in Figure 4.3, the following command will search the packages under the current directory:

```
>java -cp . wizard.pandorasBox.Clown
```

If the current directory has the absolute pathname /top/src in Figure 4.4, the following command will compile the file ./A.java:

```
>javac -cp ../bin/pkg -d ../bin A.java
```

If the name of an entry in the class path includes white space, the name should be double quoted in order to be interpreted correctly:

```
-cp "../new bin/large pkg"
```

4.4 The JAR Utility

The JAR (Java ARchive) utility provides a convenient way of bundling and deploying Java programs. A JAR file is created by using the jar tool. A typical JAR file for an application will contain the class files and any other resources needed by the application (for example image and audio files). In addition, a special *manifest file* is also created and included in the archive. The manifest file can contain pertinent information, such as which class contains the main() method for starting the application.

The jar command has many options (akin to the Unix tar command). A typical command for making a JAR file for an application (for example, Example 4.10) has the following syntax:

```
>jar cmf whereismain.txt bundledApp.jar wizard
```

Option c tells the jar tool to create an archive. Option m is used to create and include a manifest file. Information to be included in the manifest file comes from a text file specified on the command line (whereismain.txt). Option f specifies the name of the archive to be created (bundledApp.jar). The JAR file name can be any valid file name. Files to be included in the archive are listed on the command line after the JAR file name. In the command line above, the contents under the wizard directory will be archived. If the order of the options m and f is switched in the command line, the order of the respective file names for these options must also be switched.

Information to be included in the manifest file is specified as name-value pairs. In Example 4.10, program execution should start in the main() method of the wizard.pandorasBox.Clown class. The file whereismain.txt has the following single text line:

```
Main-Class: wizard.pandorasBox.Clown
```

The value of the predefined header named Main-Class specifies the execution entry point of the application. The last text line in the file must be terminated by a newline as well, in order to be processed by the jar tool. This is also true even if the file only has a single line.

The application in an archive can be run by issuing the following command:

```
>java -jar bundledApp.jar
```

Program arguments can be specified after the JAR file name.

Another typical use of a JAR file is bundling packages as libraries so that other Java programs can use them. Such JAR files can be made available centrally, e.g., in the jre/lib/ext directory under Unix, where the jre directory contains the Java runtime environment. The *pathname* of such a JAR file can also be specified in the CLASS-PATH environment variable. Clients can also use the -cp option to specify the pathname of the JAR file in order to utilize its contents. In all cases, the Java tools will be able to find the packages contained in the JAR file. The compiler can search the JAR file for classes when compiling the program, and the JVM can search the JAR file for classes to load in order to run the program.

As an example, we consider the file organization in Figure 4.5, where the class MyApp uses the class org.graphics.draw3d.Menu, and also classes from packages in the JAR file gui.jar in the directory /top/lib. We can compile the file MyApp.java in the current directory /top/src with the following command:

```
>javac -cp /top/lib/gui.jar:/top/lib -d /top/bin MyApp.java
```

Note that we need to specify *pathnames* of JAR files, but we specify *locations* where to search for particular packages.

We can also use the class path wildcard * to include all JAR files contained in a directory. Referring to Figure 4.5, the following -cp option will set the class path to include both the JAR files gui.jar and db.jar:

```
>javac -cp /top/lib/*:/top/lib -d /top/bin MyApp.java
```

Figure 4.5 *Searching in JAR files*

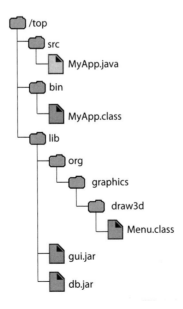

It may be necessary to quote the wildcard, depending on the configuration of the command line environment:

```
>javac -cp "/top/lib/*":/top/lib -d /top/bin MyApp.java
```

The wildcard * only expands to *JAR* files under the directory designated by the class path entry. It does *not* expand to any *class* files. Neither does it expand recursively to any JAR files contained in any subdirectories under the directory designated by the class path entry. The order in which the JAR files are searched depends on how the wildcard is expanded, and should not be relied upon when using the JDK tools.

4.5 System Properties

The Java runtime environment maintains persistent information like the operating system (OS) name, the JDK version, and various platform-dependent conventions (e.g., file separator, path separator, line terminator). This information is stored as a collection of *properties* on the platform on which the Java runtime environment is installed. Each property is defined as a *name-value* pair. For example, the name of the OS is stored as a property with the name "os.name" and the value "Windows Vista" on a platform running this OS. Properties are stored in a hash table, and applications can access them through the class java.util.Properties, which is a subclass of the java.util.Hashtable class (Section 15.8, p. 821).

Example 4.8 provides a basic introduction to using system properties. The System. getProperties() method returns a Properties hashtable containing all the properties stored on the host platform, (1). An application-defined property can be added to the Properties hashtable by calling the setProperty() method, with the appropriate name and value of the property. At (2), a property with the name "appName" and the value "BigKahuna" is put into the Properties hashtable. A property with a particular name can be retrieved from the Properties hashtable by calling the getProperties() method with the property name as argument, (3). Note that the type of both property name and value is String.

The program in Example 4.8 is run with the following command line:

```
>java SysProp os.name java.version appName FontSize
```

The program arguments are property names. The program looks them up in the Properties hashtable, and prints their values. We see that the value of the application-defined property with the name "appNam" is retrieved correctly. However, no property with the name "FontSize" is found, there null is printed as its value.

Another way of adding a property is by specifying it with the -D option (D for *Define*) in the java command. Running the program with the following command line

```
>java SysProp -DFontSize=18 os.name java.version appName FontSize
```

produces the following result:

```
os.name=Windows Vista
java.version=1.6.0_05
appName=BigKahuna
FontSize=18
```

The name and the value of the property are separated by the character = when specified using the -D option. The property is added by the JVM, and made available to the application.

There is also no white space on either side of the separator = in the -D option syntax, and the value can be double quoted, if necessary.

Example 4.8   *Using Properties*

```java
import java.util.Properties;

public class SysProp {
  public static void main(String[] args) {
    Properties props = System.getProperties();      // (1)
    props.setProperty("appName", "BigKahuna");       // (2)
    for (String prop : args) {
      String value = props.getProperty(prop);        // (3)
      System.out.printf("%s=%s%n", prop, value);
    }
  }
}
```

Output from the program:

```
>javac SysProp.java
>java SysProp os.name java.version appName FontSize
os.name=Windows Vista
java.version=1.6.0_05
appName=BigKahuna
FontSize=null
```

 Review Questions

4.1   What will be the result of attempting to compile this code?

```java
import java.util.*;

package com.acme.toolkit;

public class AClass {
  public Other anInstance;
}

class Other {
  int value;
}
```

Select the one correct answer.

(a) The code will fail to compile, since the class Other has not yet been declared when referenced in the class AClass.
(b) The code will fail to compile, since an import statement cannot occur as the first statement in a source file.
(c) The code will fail to compile, since the package declaration cannot occur after an import statement.
(d) The code will fail to compile, since the class Other must be defined in a file called Other.java.
(e) The code will fail to compile, since the class Other must be declared public.
(f) The class will compile without errors.

4.2 Given the following code:

```
// (1) INSERT ONE IMPORT STATEMENT HERE
public class RQ700_20 {
  public static void main(String[] args) {
    System.out.println(sqrt(49));
  }
}
```

Which statements, when inserted at (1), will result in a program that prints 7, when compiled and run?

Select the two correct answers.

(a) import static Math.*;
(b) import static Math.sqrt;
(c) import static java.lang.Math.sqrt;
(d) import static java.lang.Math.sqrt();
(e) import static java.lang.Math.*;

4.3 Given the following code:

```
// (1) INSERT ONE IMPORT STATEMENT HERE
public class RQ700_10 {
  public static void main(String[] args) {
    System.out.println(Locale.UK);      // Locale string for UK is "en_GB".
  }
}
```

Which statements, when inserted at (1), will result in a program that prints en_GB, when compiled and run?

Select the two correct answers.

(a) import java.util.*;
(b) import java.util.Locale;
(c) import java.util.Locale.UK;
(d) import java.util.Locale.*;
(e) import static java.util.*;
(f) import static java.util.Locale;
(g) import static java.util.Locale.UK;
(h) import static java.util.Locale.*;

4.4 Given the following code:

```
package p1;
enum Signal {
  GET_SET, ON_YOUR_MARKS, GO;
}
-------------------------------------------------------------
package p2;
// (1) INSERT IMPORT STATEMENT(S) HERE
public class RQ700_50 {
  public static void main(String[] args) {
    for(Signal sign : Signal.values()) {
      System.out.println(sign);
    }
  }
}
```

Which import statement(s), when inserted at (1), will result in a program that prints the constants of the enum type Signal, when compiled and run?

Select the one correct answer.

(a) `import static p1.Signal.*;`

(b) `import p1.Signal;`

(c) `import p1.*;`

(d) `import p1.Signal;`
    `import static p1.Signal.*;`

(e) `import p1.*;`
    `import static p1.*;`

(f) None of the above.

4.5 Given the following code:

```
package p3;
public class Util {
  public enum Format {
    JPEG { public String toString() {return "Jpeggy"; }},
    GIF  { public String toString() {return "Giffy"; }},
    TIFF { public String toString() {return "Tiffy"; }};
  }
  public static <T> void print(T t) {
    System.out.print("|" + t + "|");
  }
}
-------------------------------------------------------------
// (1) INSERT IMPORT STATEMENTS HERE
public class NestedImportsA {
  public static void main(String[] args) {
    Util u = new Util();
    Format[] formats = {
        GIF, TIFF,
        JPEG,
        Format.JPEG,
        Util.Format.JPEG,
        p3.Util.Format.JPEG
```

```
      };
      for (Format fmt : formats)
        print(fmt);
  }
 }
```

Which sequence of import statements, when inserted at (1), will result in the code compiling, and the execution of the main() method printing:

|Giffy||Tiffy||Jpeggy||Jpeggy||Jpeggy||Jpeggy|

Select the three correct answers.

(a) `import p3.Util;`
    `import p3.Util.Format;`
    `import static p3.Util.print;`
    `import static p3.Util.Format.*;`

(b) `import p3.Util;`
    `import static p3.Util.Format;`
    `import static p3.Util.print;`
    `import static p3.Util.Format.*;`

(c) `import p3.*;`
    `import static p3.Util.*;`
    `import static p3.Util.Format.*;`

(d) `import p3.*;`
    `import p3.Util.*;`
    `import static p3.Util.Format.*;`

4.6   Which statements are true about the import statement?

Select the two correct answers.

(a) Static import from a class automatically imports names of static members of any nested types declared in that class.
(b) Static members of the default package cannot be imported.
(c) Static import statements must be specified after any type import statements.
(d) In the case of a name conflict, the name in the last static import statement is chosen.
(e) A declaration of a name in a compilation unit can shadow a name that is imported.

4.7   Given the source file A.java:

```
package top.sub;
public class A {}
```

And the following directory hierarchy:

```
/proj
  |--- src
  |      |--- top
  |             |--- sub
  |                     |--- A.java
  |--- bin
```

Assuming that the current directory is /proj/src, which of the following statements are true?

Select the three correct answers.

(a) The following command will compile, and place the ~~file A.class~~ under /proj/
bin:

^byte code of the class top.sub.A

```
javac -d . top/sub/A.java
```

(b) The following command will compile, and place the file A.class under /proj/
bin:

```
javac -d /proj/bin top/sub/A.java
```

(c) The following command will compile, and place the file A.class under /proj/
bin:

```
javac -D /proj/bin ./top/sub/A.java
```

(d) The following command will compile, and place the file A.class under /proj/
bin:

```
javac -d ../bin top/sub/A.java
```

(e) After successful compilation, the absolute pathname of the file A.class will be:
/proj/bin/A.class

(f) After successful compilation, the absolute pathname of the file A.class will be:
/proj/bin/top/sub/A.class

4.8 Given the following directory structure:

```
/top
 |--- wrk
        |--- pkg
               |--- A.java
               |--- B.java
```

Assume that the two files A.java and B.java contain the following code, respectively:

```
// Filename: A.java
package pkg;
class A { B b; }
```

```
// Filename: B.java
package pkg;
class B {...}
```

For which combinations of current directory and command is the compilation successful?

Select the two correct answers.

(a) Current directory: /top/wrk
    Command: javac -cp .:pkg A.java

(b) Current directory: /top/wrk
    Command: javac -cp . pkg/A.java

(c) Current directory: /top/wrk
    Command: javac -cp pkg A.java

(d) Current directory: /top/wrk
    Command: javac -cp .:pkg pkg/A.java

(e) Current directory: /top/wrk/pkg
    Command: javac A.java

(f) Current directory: /top/wrk/pkg
    Command: javac -cp . A.java

4.9 Given the following directory structure:

```
/proj
  |--- src
  |     |--- A.class
  |
  |
  |--- bin
        |--- top
              |--- sub
                    |--- A.class
```

Assume that the current directory is /proj/src. Which classpath specifications will find the file A.class for the class top.sub.A?

Select the two correct answers.

(a) -cp /proj/bin/top

(b) -cp /proj/bin/top/sub

(c) -cp /proj/bin/top/sub/A.class

(d) -cp ../bin;.

(e) -cp /proj

(f) -cp /proj/bin

4.10 Given that the name of the class MyClass is specified correctly, which commands are syntactically valid:

Select the two correct answers.

(a) java -Ddebug=true MyClass

(b) java -ddebug=true MyClass

(c) java -Ddebug="true" MyClass

(d) java -D debug=true MyClass

4.11 Which statement is true?

Select the one correct answer.

(a) A JAR file can only contain one package.

(b) A JAR file can only be specified for use with the java command, in order to run a program.

(c) The classpath definition of the platform overrides any entries specified in the classpath option.

(d) The -d option is used with the java command, and the -D is used with the javac command.

(e) None of the above statements are true.

4.6 Scope Rules

Java provides explicit accessibility modifiers to control the accessibility of members in a class by external clients (see Section 4.9, p. 138), but in two areas access is governed by specific scope rules:

- Class scope for members: how member declarations are accessed within the class.

- Block scope for local variables: how local variable declarations are accessed within a block.

Class Scope for Members

Class scope concerns accessing members (including inherited ones) from code within a class. Table 4.1 gives an overview of how static and non-static code in a class can access members of the class, including those that are inherited. Table 4.1 assumes the following declarations:

```
class SuperName {
  int instanceVarInSuper;
  static int staticVarInSuper;

  void instanceMethodInSuper()    { /* ... */ }
  static void staticMethodInSuper() { /* ... */ }
  // ...
}

class ClassName extends SuperName {
  int instanceVar;
  static int staticVar;

  void instanceMethod()      { /* ... */ }
  static void staticMethod() { /* ... */ }
  // ...
}
```

The golden rule is that static code can only access other static members by their simple names. Static code is not executed in the context of an object, therefore the references this and super are not available. An object has knowledge of its class, therefore, static members are always accessible in a non-static context.

Note that using the class name to access static members within the class is no different from how external clients access these static members.

Some factors that can influence the scope of a member declaration are:

- shadowing of a field declaration, either by local variables (see Section 4.6, p. 131) or by declarations in the subclass (see Section 7.3, p. 294)
- initializers preceding the field declaration (see Section 9.7, p. 406)
- overriding an instance method from a superclass (see Section 7.2, p. 288)
- hiding a static method declared in a superclass (see Section 7.3, p. 294)

Accessing members within nested classes is discussed in Chapter 8.

Table 4.1 *Accessing Members within a Class*

Member declarations	Non-static Code in the Class ClassName Can Refer to the Member as	Static Code in the Class ClassName Can Refer to the Member as

Instance variables	`instanceVar`
	`this.instanceVar`
	`instanceVarInSuper`
	`this.instanceVarInSuper`
	`super.instanceVarInSuper`
		Not possible

Instance methods	`instanceMethod()`
	`this.instanceMethod()`
	`instanceMethodInSuper()`
	`this.instanceMethodInSuper()`
	`super.instanceMethodInSuper()`
		Not possible

Static variables	`staticVar`
	`this.staticVar`
	`ClassName.staticVar`
	`staticVarInSuper`
	`this.staticVarInSuper`
	`super.staticVarInSuper`
	`ClassName.staticVarInSuper`
	`SuperName.staticVarInSuper`
		`staticVar`
		
		`ClassName.staticVar`
		`staticVarInSuper`
		
		`ClassName.staticVarInSuper`
		`SuperName.staticVarInSuper`

Static methods	`staticMethod()`
	`this.staticMethod()`
	`ClassName.staticMethod()`
	`staticMethodInSuper()`
	`this.staticMethodInSuper()`
	`super.staticMethodInSuper()`
	`ClassName.staticMethodInSuper()`
	`SuperName.staticMethodInSuper()`
		`staticMethod()`
		
		`ClassName.staticMethod()`
		`staticMethodInSuper()`
		
		`ClassName.staticMethodInSuper()`
		`SuperName.staticMethodInSuper()`

Within a class C, references of type C can be used to access *all* members in the class C, regardless of their accessibility modifiers. In Example 4.9, the method duplicate-Light at (1) in the class Light has the parameter oldLight and the local variable new-Light that are references of the class Light. Even though the fields of the class are private, they are accessible through the two references (oldLight and newLight) in the method duplicateLight() as shown at (2), (3), and (4).

Example 4.9   *Class Scope*

```
class Light {
  // Instance variables:
  private int     noOfWatts;      // wattage
  private boolean indicator;      // on or off
  private String  location;       // placement

  // Instance methods:
  public void switchOn()  { indicator = true; }
  public void switchOff() { indicator = false; }
  public boolean isOn()   { return indicator; }

  public static Light duplicateLight(Light oldLight) {      // (1)
    Light newLight = new Light();
    newLight.noOfWatts = oldLight.noOfWatts;                // (2)
    newLight.indicator = oldLight.indicator;               // (3)
    newLight.location  = oldLight.location;                // (4)
    return newLight;
  }
}
```

Block Scope for Local Variables

Declarations and statements can be grouped into a *block* using braces, {}. Blocks can be nested, and scope rules apply to local variable declarations in such blocks. A local declaration can appear anywhere in a block. The general rule is that a variable declared in a block is *in scope* inside the block in which it is declared, but it is not accessible outside of this block. It is not possible to redeclare a variable if a local variable of the same name is already declared in the current scope.

Local variables of a method include the formal parameters of the method and variables that are declared in the method body. The local variables in a method are created each time the method is invoked, and are therefore distinct from local variables in other invocations of the same method that might be executing (see Section 6.5, p. 235).

Figure 4.6 illustrates block scope for local variables. A method body is a block. Parameters cannot be redeclared in the method body, as shown at (1) in Block 1.

A local variable—already declared in an enclosing block and, therefore, visible in a nested block—cannot be redeclared in the nested block. These cases are shown at (3), (5), and (6).

A local variable in a block can be redeclared in another block if the blocks are *disjoint*, that is, they do not overlap. This is the case for variable i at (2) in Block 3 and at (4) in Block 4, as these two blocks are disjoint.

The scope of a local variable declaration begins from where it is declared in the block and ends where this block terminates. The scope of the loop variable index is the entire Block 2. Even though Block 2 is nested in Block 1, the declaration of the variable index at (7) in Block 1 is valid. The scope of the variable index at (7) spans from its declaration to the end of Block 1, and it does not overlap with that of the loop variable index in Block 2.

Figure 4.6 *Block Scope*

```
public static void main(String args[]) {              // Block 1
//   String args = "";       // (1) Cannot redeclare parameters.
     char digit = 'z';

     for (int index = 0; index < 10; ++index) {       // Block 2
         switch(digit) {                               // Block 3
             case 'a':
                 int i;      // (2)
             default:
//               int i;      // (3) Already declared in the same block.
         } // switch

         if (true) {                                   // Block 4
             int i;          // (4) OK
//           int digit;      // (5) Already declared in enclosing block 1.
//           int index;      // (6) Already declared in enclosing block 2.
         } //if
     } // for
     int index;              // (7) OK
} // main
```

4.7 Accessibility Modifiers for Top-Level Type Declarations

The accessibility modifier public can be used to declare top-level types (that is, classes, enums, and interfaces) in a package to be accessible from everywhere, both inside their own package and other packages. If the accessibility modifier is omitted, they are only accessible in their own package and not in any other packages or subpackages. This is called *package* or *default accessibility*.

Accessibility modifiers for nested reference types are discussed in Section 8.1 on page 352.

Example 4.10 *Accessibility Modifiers for Classes and Interfaces*

```java
//File: Clown.java
package wizard.pandorasBox;                       // (1) Package declaration

import wizard.pandorasBox.artifacts.Ailment;      // (2) Importing class

public class Clown implements Magic {
  LovePotion tlc;                                 // (3) Class in same package
  wizard.pandorasBox.artifacts.Ailment problem;   // (4) Fully qualified class name
  Clown() {
    tlc = new LovePotion("passion");
    problem = new Ailment("flu");                 // (5) Simple class name
  }
  public void levitate()  { System.out.println("Levitating"); }
  public void mixPotion() { System.out.println("Mixing " + tlc); }
  public void healAilment() { System.out.println("Healing " + problem); }

  public static void main(String[] args) {        // (6)
    Clown joker = new Clown();
    joker.levitate();
    joker.mixPotion();
    joker.healAilment();
  }
}

interface Magic { void levitate(); }              // (7)
```

```java
//File: LovePotion.java
package wizard.pandorasBox;              // (1) Package declaration

public class LovePotion {               // (2) Accessible outside package
  String potionName;
  public LovePotion(String name) { potionName = name; }
  public String toString() { return potionName; }
}
```

```java
//File: Ailment.java
package wizard.pandorasBox.artifacts;   // (1) Package declaration

public class Ailment {                  // (2) Accessible outside package
  String ailmentName;
  public Ailment(String name) { ailmentName = name; }
  public String toString() { return ailmentName; }
}
```

```java
//File: Baldness.java
package wizard.spells;                  // (1)Package declaration
```

```
import wizard.pandorasBox.*;              // (2) Type import on demand
import wizard.pandorasBox.artifacts.*;   // (3) Import of subpackage

public class Baldness extends Ailment {   // (4) Simple name for Ailment
  wizard.pandorasBox.LovePotion tlcOne;   // (5) Fully qualified name
  LovePotion tlcTwo;                      // (6) Class in same package
  Baldness(String name) {
    super(name);
    tlcOne = new wizard.pandorasBox.      // (7) Fully qualified name
    LovePotion("romance");
    tlcTwo = new LovePotion();            // (8) Class in same package
  }
}

class LovePotion // implements Magic       // (9) Not accessible
{ public void levitate(){} }
```

Compiling and running the program from the current directory gives the following results:

```
>javac -d . Clown.java LovePotion.java Ailment.java Baldness.java
>java wizard.pandorasBox.Clown
Levitating
Mixing passion
Healing flu
```

In Example 4.10, the class Clown and the interface Magic are placed in a package called wizard.pandorasBox. The public class Clown is accessible from everywhere. The Magic interface has default accessibility, and can only be accessed within the package wizard.pandorasBox. It is not accessible from other packages, not even from its subpackages.

The class LovePotion is also placed in the package called wizard.pandorasBox. The class has public accessibility and is, therefore, accessible from other packages. The two files Clown.java and LovePotion.java demonstrate how several compilation units can be used to group classes in the same package.

The class Clown, from the file Clown.java, uses the class Ailment. The example shows two ways in which a class can access classes from other packages:

1. Denote the class by its fully qualified class name, as shown at (4) (wizard. pandorasBox.artifacts.Ailment).

2. Import the class explicitly from the package wizard.pandorasBox.artifacts as shown at (2), and use the simple class name Ailment, as shown at (5).

In the file Baldness.java at (9), the class LovePotion wishes to implement the interface Magic from the package wizard.pandorasBox, but cannot do so, although the source file imports from this package. The reason is that the interface Magic has default accessibility and can, therefore, only be accessed within the package wizard.pandorasBox.

Just because a type is accessible does not necessarily mean that members of the type are also accessible. Member accessibility is governed separately from type accessibility, as explained in Section 4.6.

Table 4.2   *Summary of Accessibility Modifiers for Top-Level Types*

Modifiers	Top-Level Types
default (no modifier)	Accessible in its own package (*package accessibility*)
public	Accessible anywhere

4.8   Other Modifiers for Classes

The modifiers abstract and final can be applied to top-level and nested classes.

abstract **Classes**

A class can be declared with the keyword abstract to indicate that it cannot be instantiated. A class might choose to do this if the abstraction it represents is so general that it needs to be specialized in order to be of practical use. The class Vehicle might be specified as abstract to represent the general abstraction of a vehicle, as creating instances of the class would not make much sense. Creating instances of non-abstract subclasses, like Car and Bus, would make more sense, as this would make the abstraction more concrete.

Any *normal class* (that is, a class declared with the keyword class) can be declared abstract. However, if such a class that has one or more abstract methods (see Section 4.10, p. 150), it must be declared abstract. Obviously such classes cannot be instantiated, as their implementation might only be partial. A class might choose this strategy to dictate certain behavior, but allow its subclasses the freedom to provide the relevant implementation. In other words, subclasses of the abstract class have to take a stand and provide implementations of any inherited abstract methods before instances can be created. A subclass that does not provide an implementation of its inherited abstract methods, must also be declared abstract.

In Example 4.11, the declaration of the abstract class Light has an abstract method named kwhPrice at (1). This forces its subclasses to provide an implementation for this method. The subclass TubeLight provides an implementation for the method kwhPrice() at (2). The class Factory creates an instance of the class TubeLight at (3). References of an abstract class can be declared, as shown at (4), but an abstract class cannot be instantiated, as shown at (5). References of an abstract class can refer to objects of the subclasses, as shown at (6).

Interfaces just specify abstract methods and not any implementation; they are, by their nature, implicitly abstract (that is, they cannot be instantiated). Though it is legal, it is redundant to declare an interface with the keyword abstract (see Section 7.6, p. 309).

Enum types *cannot* be declared abstract, because of the way they are implemented in Java (see Section 3.5, p. 54).

Example 4.11   *Abstract Classes*

```
abstract class Light {
  // Fields:
  int     noOfWatts;      // wattage
  boolean indicator;      // on or off
  String  location;       // placement

  // Instance methods:
  public void switchOn()  { indicator = true; }
  public void switchOff() { indicator = false; }
  public boolean isOn()   { return indicator; }

  // Abstract instance method
  abstract public double kwhPrice();                // (1) No method body
}
//_____
class TubeLight extends Light {
  // Field
  int tubeLength;

  // Implementation of inherited abstract method.
  public double kwhPrice() { return 2.75; }         // (2)
}
//_____
public class Factory {
  public static void main(String[] args) {
    TubeLight cellarLight = new TubeLight();        // (3) OK
    Light nightLight;                               // (4) OK
//  Light tableLight = new Light();                 // (5) Compile-time error
    nightLight = cellarLight;                       // (6) OK
    System.out.println("KWH price: " + nightLight.kwhPrice());
  }
}
```

Output from the program:

```
KWH price: 2.75
```

final **Classes**

A class can be declared final to indicate that it cannot be extended; that is, one cannot declare subclasses of a final class. This implies that one cannot override any methods declared in such a class. In other words, the class behavior cannot be changed by extending the class. A final class marks the lower boundary of its *implementation inheritance hierarchy* (see Section 7.1, p. 284). Only a class whose definition is *complete* (that is, provides implementations of all its methods) can be declared final.

A final class must be complete, whereas an abstract class is considered incomplete. Classes, therefore, cannot be both final and abstract at the same time. Interfaces are inherently abstract, as they can only specify methods that are abstract, and therefore cannot be declared final. A final class and an interface represent two extremes when it comes to providing an implementation. An abstract class represents a compromise between these two extremes. An enum type is also implicitly final, and cannot be explicitly declared with the keyword final.

The Java standard library includes many final classes; for example, the java.lang.String class and the wrapper classes for primitive values.

If it is decided that the class TubeLight in Example 4.11 may not be extended, it can be declared final:

```
final class TubeLight extends Light {
  // ...
}
```

Discussion of final methods, fields, and local variables can be found in Section 4.10, p. 148.

Table 4.3 *Summary of Other Modifiers for Types*

Modifiers	Classes	Interfaces	Enum types
abstract	A non-final class can be declared abstract. A class with an abstract method must be declared abstract. An abstract class cannot be instantiated.	Permitted, but redundant.	Not permitted.
final	A non-abstract class can be declared final. A class with a final method need not be declared final. A final class cannot be extended.	Not permitted.	Not permitted.

4.12 Given the following class, which of these alternatives are valid ways of referring to the class from outside of the package `net.basemaster`?

```
package net.basemaster;

public class Base {
  // ...
}
```

Select the two correct answers.

(a) By simply referring to the class as `Base`.
(b) By simply referring to the class as `basemaster.Base`.
(c) By simply referring to the class as `net.basemaster.Base`.
(d) By importing with `net.basemaster.*`, and referring to the class as `Base`.
(e) By importing with `net.*`, and referring to the class as `basemaster.Base`.

4.13 Which one of the following class declarations is a valid declaration of a class that cannot be instantiated?

Select the one correct answer.

(a) `class Ghost        { abstract void haunt(); }`
(b) `abstract class Ghost { void haunt(); }`
(c) `abstract class Ghost { void haunt() {}; }`
(d) `abstract Ghost        { abstract void haunt(); }`
(e) `static class Ghost   { abstract haunt(); }`

4.14 Which one of the following class declarations is a valid declaration of a class that cannot be extended?

Select the one correct answer.

(a) `class Link { }`
(b) `abstract class Link { }`
(c) `native class Link { }`
(d) `static class Link { }`
(e) `final class Link { }`
(f) `private class Link { }`
(g) `abstract final class Link { }`

4.9 Member Accessibility Modifiers

By specifying member accessibility modifiers, a class can control what information is accessible to clients (that is, other classes). These modifiers help a class to define a *contract* so that clients know exactly what services are offered by the class.

The accessibility of members can be one of the following:

- ○ `public`
- ○ `protected`
- ○ default (also called *package accessibility*)
- ○ `private`

If an accessibility modifier is not specified, the member has package or default accessibility.

In the following discussion on accessibility modifiers for members of a class, keep in mind that the member accessibility modifier only has meaning if the class (or one of its subclasses) is accessible to the client. Also, note that only one accessibility modifier can be specified for a member. The discussion in this section applies to both instance and static members of top-level classes. It applies equally to *constructors* as well. Discussion of member accessibility for nested classes is deferred to Chapter 8.

In UML notation, the prefixes +, #, and -, when applied to a member name, indicate `public`, `protected`, and `private` member accessibility, respectively. No prefix indicates default or package accessibility.

`public` **Members**

Public accessibility is the least restrictive of all the accessibility modifiers. A `public` member is accessible from anywhere, both in the package containing its class and in other packages where this class is visible. This is true for both instance and static members.

Example 4.12 contains two source files, shown at (1) and (6). The package hierarchy defined by the source files is depicted in Figure 4.7, showing the two packages, packageA and packageB, containing their respective classes. The classes in packageB use classes from packageA. The class SuperclassA in packageA has two subclasses: SubclassA in packageA and SubclassB in packageB.

Example 4.12 *Public Accessibility of Members*

```
//Filename: SuperclassA.java                     (1)
package packageA;

public class SuperclassA {
  public int superclassVarA;                     // (2)
  public void superclassMethodA() {/*...*/}       // (3)
}

class SubclassA extends SuperclassA {
  void subclassMethodA() { superclassVarA = 10; }   // (4) OK.
}
```

```java
class AnyClassA {
  SuperclassA obj = new SuperclassA();
  void anyClassMethodA() {
    obj.superclassMethodA();                          // (5) OK.
  }
}
```

```java
//Filename: SubclassB.java                            (6)
package packageB;
import packageA.*;

public class SubclassB extends SuperclassA {
  void subclassMethodB() { superclassMethodA(); }    // (7) OK.
}

class AnyClassB {
  SuperclassA obj = new SuperclassA();
  void anyClassMethodB() {
    obj.superclassVarA = 20;                          // (8) OK.
  }
}
```

Accessibility is illustrated in Example 4.12 by the accessibility modifiers for the field superclassVarA and the method superclassMethodA() at (2) and (3), respectively, defined in the class SuperclassA. These members are accessed from four different clients in Example 4.12.

- Client 1: From a subclass in the same package, which accesses an inherited field. SubclassA is such a client, and does this at (4).

- Client 2: From a non-subclass in the same package, which invokes a method on an instance of the class. AnyClassA is such a client, and does this at (5).

- Client 3: From a subclass in another package, which invokes an inherited method. SubclassB is such a client, and does this at (7).

- Client 4: From a non-subclass in another package, which accesses a field in an instance of the class. AnyClassB is such a client, and does this at (8).

In Example 4.12, the field superclassVarA and the method superclassMethodA() have public accessibility, and are accessible by all four clients listed above. Subclasses can access their inherited public members by their simple name, and all clients can access public members through an instance of the class. Public accessibility is depicted in Figure 4.7.

Figure 4.7 *Public Accessibility*

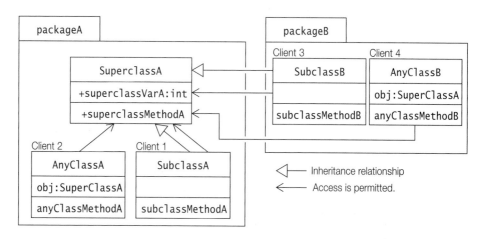

protected **Members**

A protected member is accessible in all classes in the same package, and by all sub-classes of its class in any package where this class is visible. In other words, non-subclasses in other packages cannot access protected members from other packages. It is more restrictive than public member accessibility.

In Example 4.12, if the field superclassVarA and the method superclassMethodA() have protected accessibility, they are accessible within packageA, and only accessible by subclasses in any other packages.

```
public class SuperclassA {
  protected int superclassVarA;                    // (2) Protected member
  protected void superclassMethodA() {/*...*/}      // (3) Protected member
}
```

Client 4 in packageB cannot access these members, as shown in Figure 4.8.

A subclass in another package can only access protected members in the superclass via references of its own type or its subtypes. The following new declaration of SubclassB in packageB from Example 4.12 illustrates the point:

```
// Filename: SubclassB.java
package packageB;
import packageA.*;
public class SubclassB extends SuperclassA {      // In packageB.
  SuperclassA objRefA = new SuperclassA();        // (1)
  void subclassMethodB(SubclassB objRefB) {
    objRefB.superclassMethodA();                  // (2) OK.
    objRefB.superclassVarA = 5;                   // (3) OK.
    objRefA.superclassMethodA();                  // (4) Not OK.
    objRefA.superclassVarA = 10;                  // (5) Not OK.
  }
}
```

Figure 4.8 *Protected Accessibility*

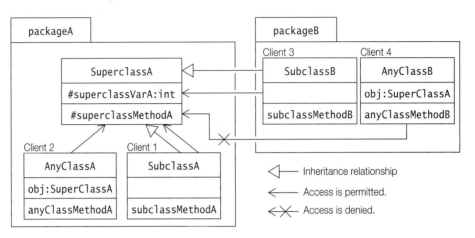

The class SubclassB declares the field objRefA of type SuperclassA at (1). The method subclassMethodB() has the formal parameter objRefB of type SubclassB. Access is permitted to a protected member of SuperclassA in packageA by a reference of the subclass, as shown at (2) and (3), but not by a reference of its superclass, as shown at (4) and (5). Access to the field superclassVarA and the call to the method superclassMethodA() occur in SubclassB. These members are declared in SuperclassA. SubclassB is not involved in the implementation of SuperclassA, which is the type of the reference objRefA. Hence, access to protected members at (4) and (5) is not permitted as these are not members of an object that can be guaranteed to be implemented by the code accessing them.

Accessibility to protected members of the superclass would also be permitted via any reference whose type is a subclass of SubclassB. The above restriction helps to ensure that subclasses in packages different from their superclass can only access protected members of the superclass in their part of the implementation inheritance hierarchy. In other words, a protected member of a superclass is only accessible in a subclass that is in another package if the member is inherited by an object of the subclass (or by an object of a subclass of this subclass).

Default Accessibility for Members

When no member accessibility modifier is specified, the member is only accessible by other classes in its own class's package. Even if its class is visible in another (possibly nested) package, the member is not accessible elsewhere. Default member accessibility is more restrictive than protected member accessibility.

In Example 4.12, if the field `superclassVarA` and the method `superclassMethodA()` are defined with no accessibility modifier, they are only accessible within `packageA`, but not in any other packages.

```
public class SuperclassA {
  int superclassVarA;                        // (2)
  void superclassMethodA() {/*...*/}         // (3)
}
```

The clients in `packageB` (that is, Clients 3 and 4) cannot access these members. This situation is depicted in Figure 4.9.

Figure 4.9 *Default Accessibility*

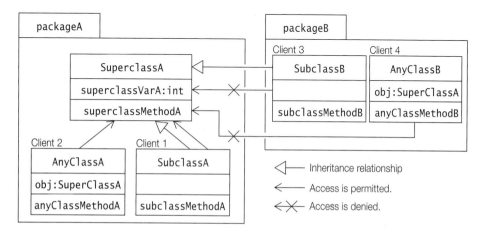

private **Members**

This is the most restrictive of all the accessibility modifiers. Private members are not accessible from any other classes. This also applies to subclasses, whether they are in the same package or not. Since they are not accessible by their simple name in a subclass, they are also not inherited by the subclass. This is not to be confused with the existence of such a member in the state of an object of the subclass (see Section 9.11, p. 416). A standard design strategy for JavaBeans is to make all fields private and provide public accessor methods for them. Auxiliary methods are often declared private, as they do not concern any client.

In Example 4.12, if the field `superclassVarA` and the method `superclassMethodA()` have private accessibility, they are not accessible by any other clients.

```
public class SuperclassA {
  private int superclassVarA;                    // (2) Private member
  private void superclassMethodA() {/*...*/}     // (3) Private member
}
```

None of the clients in Figure 4.10 can access these members.

Figure 4.10 *Private Accessibility*

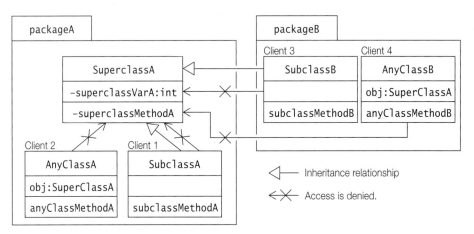

Table 4.4 *Summary of Accessibility Modifiers for Members*

Modifiers	Members
`public`	Accessible everywhere.
`protected`	Accessible by any class in the same package as its class, and accessible only by subclasses of its class in other packages.
`default` (no modifier)	Only accessible by classes, including subclasses, in the same package as its class (package accessibility).
`private`	Only accessible in its own class and not anywhere else.

 Review Questions

4.15 Given the following declaration of a class, which fields are accessible from outside the package `com.corporation.project`?

```
package com.corporation.project;

public class MyClass {
            int i;
    public   int j;
    protected int k;
    private  int l;
}
```

Select the two correct answers.

(a) Field i is accessible in all classes in other packages.
(b) Field j is accessible in all classes in other packages.
(c) Field k is accessible in all classes in other packages.
(d) Field k is accessible in subclasses only in other packages.
(e) Field l is accessible in all classes in other packages.
(f) Field l is accessible in subclasses only in other packages.

4.16 How restrictive is the default accessibility compared to `public`, `protected`, and `private` accessibility?

Select the one correct answer.

(a) Less restrictive than `public`.
(b) More restrictive than `public`, but less restrictive than `protected`.
(c) More restrictive than `protected`, but less restrictive than `private`.
(d) More restrictive than `private`.
(e) Less restrictive than `protected` from within a package, and more restrictive than `protected` from outside a package.

4.17 Which statement is true about the accessibility of members?

Select the one correct answer.

(a) A private member is always accessible within the same package.
(b) A private member can only be accessed within the class of the member.
(c) A member with default accessibility can be accessed by any subclass of the class in which it is declared.
(d) A private member cannot be accessed at all.
(e) Package/default accessibility for a member can be declared using the keyword `default`.

4.18 Which lines that are marked will compile in the following code?

```
//Filename: A.java
package packageA;

public class A {
  protected int pf;
}
```

```
//Filename: B.java
package packageB;
import packageA.A;

public class B extends A {
  void action(A obj1, B obj2, C obj3) {
    pf = 10;                 // (1)
    obj1.pf = 10;            // (2)
    obj2.pf = 10;            // (3)
    obj3.pf = 10;            // (4)
```

```
    }
  }

  class C extends B {
    void action(A obj1, B obj2, C obj3) {
      pf = 10;                  // (5)
      obj1.pf = 10;             // (6)
      obj2.pf = 10;             // (7)
      obj3.pf = 10;             // (8)
    }
  }

  class D {
    void action(A obj1, B obj2, C obj3) {
      pf = 10;                  // (9)
      obj1.pf = 10;             // (10)
      obj2.pf = 10;             // (11)
      obj3.pf = 10;             // (12)
    }
  }
```

Select the five correct answers.

(a) (1)
(b) (2)
(c) (3)
(d) (4)
(e) (5)
(f) (6)
(g) (7)
(h) (8)
(i) (9)
(j) (10)
(k) (11)
(l) (12)

4.10 Other Modifiers for Members

The following keywords can be used to specify certain characteristics of members in a type declaration:

- static
- final
- abstract
- synchronized
- native
- transient
- volatile

static **Members**

Static members belong to the class in which they are declared and are not part of any instance of the class. The declaration of static members is prefixed by the keyword static to distinguish them from instance members. Depending on the accessibility modifiers of the static members in a class, clients can access these by using the class name or through object references of the class. The class need not be instantiated to access its static members.

Static variables (also called *class variables*) exist in the class they are defined in only. They are not instantiated when an instance of the class is created. In other words, the values of these variables are not a part of the state of any object. When the class is loaded, static variables are initialized to their default values if no explicit initialization expression is specified (see Section 9.9, p. 410).

Static methods are also known as *class methods*. A static method in a class can directly access other static members in the class. It cannot access instance (i.e., non-static) members of the class, as there is no notion of an object associated with a static method.

A typical static method might perform some task on behalf of the whole class and/or for objects of the class. In Example 4.13, the static variable counter keeps track of the number of instances of the Light class that have been created. The example shows that the static method writeCount can only access static members directly, as shown at (2), but not non-static members, as shown at (3). The static variable counter will be initialized to the value 0 when the class is loaded at runtime. The main() method at (4) in the class Warehouse shows how static members of the class Light can be accessed using the class name and via object references of the type Light.

A summary of how static members are accessed in static and non-static code is given in Table 4.1, p. 130.

Example 4.13 *Accessing Static Members*

```
class Light {
  // Fields:
  int     noOfWatts;      // wattage
  boolean indicator;      // on or off
  String  location;       // placement

  // Static variable
  static int counter;     // No. of Light objects created.       (1)

  // Explicit default constructor
  Light(int noOfWatts, boolean indicator, String location) {
    this.noOfWatts = noOfWatts;
    this.indicator = indicator;
    this.location  = location;
    ++counter;          // Increment counter.
  }
```

```
    // Static method
    public static void writeCount() {
      System.out.println("Number of lights: " + counter);        // (2)
      // Compile-time error. Field noOfWatts is not accessible:
      // System.out.println("Number of Watts: " + noOfWatts);    // (3)
    }
  }
  //_____
  public class Warehouse {
    public static void main(String[] args) {                     // (4)

      Light.writeCount();                                  // Invoked using class name
      Light light1 = new Light(100, true, "basement"); // Create an object
      System.out.println(
          "Value of counter: " + Light.counter           // Accessed via class name
      );
      Light light2 = new Light(200, false, "garage");  // Create another object
      light2.writeCount();                                 // Invoked using reference
      Light light3 = new Light(300, true, "kitchen");  // Create another object
      System.out.println(
          "Value of counter: " + light3.counter          // Accessed via reference
      );
      final int i;
    }
  }
```

Output from the program:

```
Number of lights: 0
Value of counter: 1
Number of lights: 2
Value of counter: 3
```

final **Members**

A final variable is a constant despite being called a variable. Its value cannot be changed once it has been initialized. Instance and static variables can be declared final. Note that the keyword final can also be applied to local variables, including method parameters. Declaring a variable final has the following implications:

- A final variable of a primitive data type cannot change its value once it has been initialized.

- A final variable of a reference type cannot change its reference value once it has been initialized. This effectively means that a final reference will always refer to the same object. However, the keyword final has no bearing on whether the *state of the object* denoted by the reference can be changed or not.

Final static variables are commonly used to define *manifest constants* (also called *named constants*), e.g., Integer.MAX_VALUE, which is the maximum int value. Variables defined in an interface are implicitly final (see Section 7.6, p. 309). Note that a final variable need not be initialized in its declaration, but it must be initialized in the code once before it is used. These variables are also known as *blank final varia-bles*. For a discussion on `final` parameters, see Section 3.7, p. 89.

A `final` method in a class is *complete* (that is, has an implementation) and cannot be overridden in any subclass (see Section 7.2, p. 288).

Final variables ensure that values cannot be changed and `final` methods ensure that behavior cannot be changed. Final classes are discussed in Section 4.8, p. 136.

The compiler may be able to perform code optimizations for `final` members, because certain assumptions can be made about such members.

In Example 4.14, the class `Light` defines a `final` static variable at (1) and a `final` method at (2). An attempt to change the value of the `final` variable at (3) results in a compile-time error. The subclass `TubeLight` attempts to override the `final` method `setWatts()` from the superclass `Light` at (4), which is not permitted. The class `Warehouse` defines a `final` local reference `aLight` at (5). The state of the object denoted by the reference `tableLight` is changed at (6), but its reference value cannot be changed as attempted at (7). Another `final` local reference `streetLight` is declared at (8), but it is not initialized. The compiler reports an error when an attempt is made to use this reference at (9).

Example 4.14 *Accessing Final Members*

```
class Light {
  // Final static variable                    (1)
  final public static double KWH_PRICE = 3.25;

  int noOfWatts;

  // Final instance method                    (2)
  final public void setWatts(int watt) {
    noOfWatts = watt;
  }

  public void setKWH() {
    // KWH_PRICE = 4.10;                       // (3) Not OK. Cannot be changed.
  }
}
//_____
class TubeLight extends Light {
  // Final method in superclass cannot be overridden.
  // This method will not compile.
  /*
    public void setWatts(int watt) {    // (4) Attempt to override.
        noOfWatts = 2*watt;
    }
  */
}
//_____
```

```
public class Warehouse {
  public static void main(String[] args) {

    final Light tableLight = new Light();// (5) Final local variable.
    tableLight.noOfWatts = 100;          // (6) OK. Changing object state.
//  tableLight = new Light();            // (7) Not OK. Changing final reference.

    final Light streetLight;             // (8) Not initialized.
//  streetLight.noOfWatts = 2000;        // (9) Not OK.
  }
}
```

abstract **Methods**

An abstract method has the following syntax:

> abstract *<accessibility modifier> <return type> <method name>* (*<parameter list>*)
>   *<throws clause>*;

An abstract method does not have an implementation; i.e., no method body is
defined for an abstract method, only the *method header* is provided in the class declaration. The keyword abstract is mandatory in the header of an abstract method
declared in a class. Its class is then incomplete and must be explicitly declared
abstract (see Section 4.8, p. 135). Subclasses of an abstract class must then provide
the method implementation; otherwise, they must also be declared abstract. The
accessibility of an abstract method declared in a class cannot be private, as subclasses would not be able to override the method and provide an implementation.
See Section 4.8, where Example 4.11 also illustrates the use of abstract methods.

Only an instance method can be declared abstract. Since static methods cannot be
overridden, declaring an abstract static method makes no sense. A final method
cannot be abstract (i.e., cannot be incomplete) and vice versa. The keyword
abstract can only be combined with accessibility modifiers public or private.

Methods specified in an interface are implicitly abstract (see Section 7.6, p. 309),
and the keyword abstract is seldom specified in their method headers. These
methods can only have public or package accessibility.

synchronized **Methods**

Several threads can be executing in a program (see Section 13.5, p. 626). They might
try to execute several methods on the same object simultaneously. Methods can be
declared synchronized if it is desirable that only one thread at a time can execute a
method of the object. Their execution is then mutually exclusive among all threads.
At any given time, at most one thread can be executing a synchronized method on
an object. This discussion also applies to static synchronized methods of a class.

In Example 4.15, both the push() method, declared at (1), and the pop() method,
declared at (2), are synchronized in the class StackImpl. Only one thread at a time can

execute a synchronized method in an object of the class StackImpl. This means that it is not possible for the state of an object of the class StackImpl to be corrupted, for example, while one thread is pushing an element and another is attempting to pop the stack.

Example 4.15 *Synchronized Methods*

```
class StackImpl {                        // Non-generic partial implementation
  private Object[] stackArray;
  private int topOfStack;
  // ...
  synchronized public void push(Object elem) { // (1)
    stackArray[++topOfStack] = elem;
  }

  synchronized public Object pop() {            // (2)
    Object obj = stackArray[topOfStack];
    stackArray[topOfStack] = null;
    topOfStack--;
    return obj;
  }

  // Other methods, etc.
  public Object peek() { return stackArray[topOfStack]; }
}
```

native **Methods**

Native methods are methods whose implementation is not defined in Java but in another programming language, for example, C or C++. Such a method can be declared as a member in a Java class declaration. Since its implementation appears elsewhere, only the method header is specified in the class declaration. The keyword native is mandatory in the method header. A native method can also specify checked exceptions in a throws clause (Section 6.9, p. 257), but the compiler cannot check them, since the method is not implemented in Java.

In the following example, a native method in the class Native is declared at (2). The class also uses a static initializer block (see Section 9.9, p. 410) at (1) to load the native library when the class is loaded. Clients of the Native class can call the native method like any another method, as at (3).

```
class Native {

  /*
   * The static block ensures that the native method library
   * is loaded before the native method is called.
   */
  static {
    System.loadLibrary("NativeMethodLib"); // (1) Load native library.
  }
```

```
    native void nativeMethod();              // (2) Native method header.
    // ...

  }

  class Client {
    //...
    public static void main(String[] args) {
      Native trueNative = new Native();
      trueNative.nativeMethod();             // (3) Native method call.
    }
    //...
  }
```

The Java Native Interface (JNI) is a special API that allows Java methods to invoke native functions implemented in C.

transient **Fields**

Often it is desirable to save the state of an object. Such objects are said to be *persistent*. In Java, the state of an object can be stored using serialization (see Section 11.6, p. 510). Serialization transforms objects into an output format that is conducive for storing objects. Objects can later be retrieved in the same state as when they were serialized, meaning that all fields included in the serialization will have the same values as at the time of serialization.

Sometimes the value of a field in an object should not be saved, in which case, the field can be specified as transient in the class declaration. This implies that its value should not be saved when objects of the class are written to persistent storage. In the following example, the field currentTemperature is declared transient at (1), because the current temperature is most likely to have changed when the object is restored at a later date. However, the value of the field mass, declared at (2), is likely to remain unchanged. When objects of the class Experiment are serialized, the value of the field currentTemperature will not be saved, but that of the field mass will be, as part of the state of the serialized object.

```
  class Experiment implements Serializable {
    // ...

    // The value of currentTemperature will not persist.
    transient int currentTemperature;     // (1) Transient value.

    double mass;                          // (2) Persistent value.

  }
```

Specifying the transient modifier for static variables is redundant and, therefore, discouraged. Static variables are not part of the persistent state of a serialized object.

volatile **Fields**

During execution, compiled code might cache the values of fields for efficiency reasons. Since multiple threads can access the same field, it is vital that caching is not allowed to cause inconsistencies when reading and writing the value in the field. The volatile modifier can be used to inform the compiler that it should not attempt to perform optimizations on the field, which could cause unpredictable results when the field is accessed by multiple threads (see also Example 13.5, p. 644).

In the simple example below, the value of the field clockReading might be changed unexpectedly by another thread while one thread is performing a task that involves always using the current value of the field clockReading. Declaring the field as volatile ensures that a write operation will always be performed on the master field variable, and a read operation will always return the correct current value.

```
class VitalControl {
  // ...
  volatile long clockReading;
  // Two successive reads might give different results.

}
```

Table 4.5 *Summary of Other Modifiers for Members*

Modifiers	Fields	Methods
static	Defines a class variable.	Defines a class method.
final	Defines a constant.	The method cannot be overridden.
abstract	Not applicable.	No method body is defined. Its class must also be designated abstract.
synchronized	Not applicable.	Only one thread at a time can execute the method.
native	Not applicable.	Declares that the method is implemented in another language.
transient	The value in the field will not be included when the object is serialized.	Not applicable.
volatile	The compiler will not attempt to optimize access to the value in the field.	Not applicable.

Review Questions

4.19 Which statements about the use of modifiers are true?

Select the two correct answers.

(a) If no accessibility modifier (public, protected, or private) is specified for a member declaration, the member is only accessible by classes in the package of its class and by subclasses of its class in any package.

(b) You cannot specify accessibility of local variables. They are only accessible within the block in which they are declared.

(c) Subclasses of a class must reside in the same package as the class they extend.

(d) Local variables can be declared static.

(e) The objects themselves do not have any accessibility modifiers, only the object references do.

4.20 Given the following source code, which comment line can be uncommented without introducing errors?

```
abstract class MyClass {
  abstract void f();
  final     void g() {}
//final     void h() {}                           // (1)

  protected static int i;
  private           int j;
}
final class MyOtherClass extends MyClass {
//MyOtherClass(int n) { m = n; }                  // (2)

  public static void main(String[] args) {
    MyClass mc = new MyOtherClass();
  }

  void f() {}
  void h() {}
//void k() { i++; }                               // (3)
//void l() { j++; }                               // (4)

  int m;
}
```

Select the one correct answer.

(a) (1)

(b) (2)

(c) (3)

(d) (4)

4.21 What would be the result of compiling and running the following program?

```
class MyClass {
  static MyClass ref;
  String[] arguments;

  public static void main(String[] args) {
    ref = new MyClass();
    ref.func(args);
  }

  public void func(String[] args) {
    ref.arguments = args;
  }
}
```

Select the one correct answer.

(a) The program will fail to compile, since the static method main() cannot have a call to the non-static method func().

(b) The program will fail to compile, since the non-static method func() cannot access the static variable ref.

(c) The program will fail to compile, since the argument args passed to the static method main() cannot be passed to the non-static method func().

(d) The program will compile, but will throw an exception when run.

(e) The program will compile and run successfully.

4.22 Given the following member declarations, which statement is true?

```
int a;                         // (1)
static int a;                  // (2)
int f() { return a; }          // (3)
static int f() { return a; }   // (4)
```

Select the one correct answer.

(a) Declarations (1) and (3) cannot occur in the same class declaration.

(b) Declarations (2) and (4) cannot occur in the same class declaration.

(c) Declarations (1) and (4) cannot occur in the same class declaration.

(d) Declarations (2) and (3) cannot occur in the same class declaration.

4.23 Which statement is true?

Select the one correct answer.

(a) A static method can call other non-static methods in the same class by using the this keyword.

(b) A class may contain both static and non-static variables, and both static and non-static methods.

(c) Each object of a class has its own instance of the static variables declared in the class.

(d) Instance methods may access local variables of static methods.

(e) All methods in a class are implicitly passed the this reference as argument, when invoked.

4.24   What, if anything, is wrong with the following code?

```
abstract class MyClass {
  transient int j;
  synchronized int k;

  final void MyClass() {}

  static void f() {}
}
```

Select the one correct answer.

(a) The class `MyClass` cannot be declared `abstract`.
(b) The field `j` cannot be declared `transient`.
(c) The field `k` cannot be declared `synchronized`.
(d) The method `MyClass()` cannot be declared `final`.
(e) The method `f()` cannot be declared `static`.
(f) Nothing is wrong with the code; it will compile successfully.

4.25   Which one of these is not a legal member declaration within a class?

Select the one correct answer.

(a) `static int a;`
(b) `final Object[] fudge = { null };`
(c) `abstract int t;`
(d) `native void sneeze();`
(e) `final static private double PI = 3.14159265358979323846;`

4.26   Which statements about modifiers are true?

Select the two correct answers.

(a) Abstract classes can declare `final` methods.
(b) Fields can be declared `native`.
(c) Non-abstract methods can be declared in `abstract` classes.
(d) Classes can be declared `native`.
(e) Abstract classes can be declared `final`.

4.27   Which statement is true?

Select the one correct answer.

(a) The values of `transient` fields will not be saved during serialization.
(b) Constructors can be declared `abstract`.
(c) The initial state of an array object constructed with the statement `int[] a = new int[10]` will depend on whether the array variable a is a local variable or a field.
(d) A subclass of a class with an `abstract` method must provide an implementation for the abstract method.
(e) Only static methods can access static members.

Chapter Summary

The following information was included in this chapter:

- the structure of a Java source file
- defining, using, and deploying packages
- explanation of class scope for members, and block scope for local variables
- discussion of accessibility (default, public) and other modifiers (abstract, final) for reference types
- applicability of member accessibility (default, public, protected, private) and other member modifiers (static, final, abstract, synchronized, native, transient, volatile)

Programming Exercise

4.1 Design a class for a bank database. The database should support the following operations:

- o deposit a certain amount into an account
- o withdraw a certain amount from an account
- o get the balance (i.e., the current amount) in an account
- o transfer an amount from one account to another

The amount in the transactions is a value of type double. The accounts are identified by instances of the class Account that is in the package com.megabankcorp.records. The database class should be placed in a package called com.megabankcorp.system.

The deposit, withdraw, and balance operations should not have any implementation, but allow subclasses to provide the implementation. The transfer operation should use the deposit and withdraw operations to implement the transfer. It should not be possible to alter this operation in any subclass, and only classes within the package com.megabankcorp.system should be allowed to use this operation. The deposit and withdraw operations should be accessible in all packages. The balance operation should only be accessible in subclasses and classes within the package com.megabankcorp.system.

Operators and Expressions

5

Exam Objectives

3.1 Develop code that uses the primitive wrapper classes (such as `Boolean`, `Character`, `Double`, `Integer`, etc.), and/or autoboxing & unboxing. Discuss the differences between the `String`, `StringBuilder`, and `StringBuffer` classes.

  ○ *Boxing/unboxing are covered in this chapter.*

  ○ *For primitive wrapper classes and string handling classes, see Chapter 10, p. 423.*

7.6 Write code that correctly applies the appropriate operators including assignment operators (limited to: =, +=, -=), arithmetic operators (limited to: +, -, *, /, %, ++, --), relational operators (limited to: <, <=, >, >=, ==, !=), the instanceof operator, logical operators (limited to: &, |, ^, !, &&, ||), and the conditional operator (? :), to produce a desired result. Write code that determines the equality of two objects or two primitives.

  ○ *For the instanceof operator, see Section 7.11, p. 328.*

  ○ *For object equality, see also Section 15.1, p. 751.*

Supplementary Objectives

- Distinguish between conversion categories and conversion contexts, and understand which conversions are permissible in each conversion context.
- Understand the order in which operands and operators are evaluated, including the precedence and associativity rules.

5.1 Conversions

In this section we first discuss the different kinds of type conversions that can be applied to values, and in the next section we discuss the contexts in which these conversions are permitted. Some type conversions must be explicitly stated in the program, while others are performed implicitly. Some type conversions can be checked at compile time to guarantee their validity at runtime, while others will require an extra check at runtime.

Widening and Narrowing Primitive Conversions

For the primitive data types, the value of a *narrower* data type can be converted to a value of a *wider* data type. This is called a *widening primitive conversion*. Widening conversions from one primitive type to the next wider primitive type are summarized in Figure 5.1. The conversions shown are transitive. For example, an int can be directly converted to a double without first having to convert it to a long and a float.

Note that the target type of a widening primitive conversion has a *wider range* of values than the source type, e.g., the range of the long type subsumes the range of the int type. In widening conversions between *integral* types, the source value remains intact, with no loss of magnitude information. However, a widening conversion from an int or a long value to a float value, or from a long value to a double value, may result in a *loss of precision*. The floating-point value in the target type is then a correctly rounded approximation of the integer value. Note that precision relates to the number of significant bits in the value, and must not be confused with *magnitude*, which relates how big a value can be represented.

Figure 5.1 *Widening Primitive Conversions*

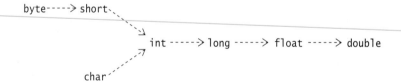

Converting from a wider primitive type to a narrower primitive type is called a *narrowing primitive conversion*, which can result in loss of magnitude information, and possibly in precision as well. Any conversion which is not a widening primitive conversion according to Figure 5.1 is a narrowing primitive conversion. The target type of a narrowing primitive conversion has a *narrower range* of values than the source type, for example, the range of the int type does not include all the values in the range of the long type.

Note that all conversions between char and the two integer types byte and short are considered narrowing primitive conversions: the reason being that the conversions between the unsigned type char and the signed types byte or short can result in loss of information. These narrowing conversions are done in two steps, first converting the source value to the int type, and then converting the int value to the target type.

Widening primitive conversions are usually done implicitly, whereas narrowing primitive conversions usually require a *cast* (Section 5.2, p. 164). It is not illegal to use a cast for a widening conversion. However, the compiler will flag any conversion that require a cast if none has been specified. Regardless of any loss of magnitude or precision, widening and narrowing primitive conversions *never* result in a runtime exception.

Ample examples of widening and narrowing primitive conversions can be found in this chapter and also in Section 3.7, p. 81.

Widening and Narrowing Reference Conversions

The *subtype-supertype* relationship between reference types determines which conversions are permissible between them. Conversions *up* the *type hierarchy* are called *widening reference conversions* (also called *upcasting*), i.e., such a conversion converts from a subtype to a supertype.

```
Object obj = "upcast me";  // Widening: Object <----- String
```

Conversions *down* the type hierarchy represent *narrowing reference conversions* (also called *downcasting*).

```
String str = (String) obj; // Narrowing requires cast: String <----- Object
```

A subtype is a *narrower* type than its supertype in the sense that it has no relationship with other subtypes of its supertype, i.e., a supertype can be the supertype of types that a subtype is not supertype of. For example, given that A is the supertype of immediate subtypes B, C, and D, each subtype is narrower than the supertype A, as any one of the subtypes cannot represent the other two subtypes. Contexts under which reference conversions can occur are discussed in Section 7.8, p. 319.

Widening reference conversions are usually done implicitly, whereas narrowing reference conversions usually require a cast (Section 5.2, p. 164). The compiler will reject casts that are not legal or issue an *unchecked warning* under certain circumstances if type safety cannot be guaranteed (Section 14.2, p. 670).

Widening reference conversions do not require any runtime checks and never result in an exception during execution. This is not the case for narrowing reference conversions, which require a runtime check and can throw a ClassCastException if the conversion is not legal.

Boxing and Unboxing Conversions

For an overview of the primitive types and their wrapper types, see Table 2.13, p. 30. For an overview of the methods provided by the wrapper types, see Section 10.3, p. 428.

A *boxing conversion* converts the value of a primitive type to a corresponding value of its wrapper type. If p is a value of a *primitiveType,* boxing conversion converts p into a reference r of corresponding *WrapperType,* such that r.*primitiveType*Value() == p. In the code below, the int value 10 results in an object of the type Integer implicitly being created that contains the int value 10. We say that the int value 10 has been *boxed* in an object of the wrapper type Integer.

```
Integer iRef = 10;                          // Boxing: Integer <----- int
System.out.println(iRef.intValue() == 10);  // true
```

An *unboxing conversion* converts the value of a wrapper type to a value of its corresponding primitive type. If r is a reference of a *WrapperType,* unboxing conversion converts the reference r into r.*primitiveType*Value(), where *primitiveType* is the primitive type corresponding to the *WrapperType.* In the code below, the value in the Integer object referenced by iRef is implicitly converted to the int type. We say that the wrapper object has been *unboxed* to its corresponding primitive type.

```
int i = iRef;                               // Unboxing: int <----- Integer
System.out.println(iRef.intValue() == i);   // true
```

Note that both boxing and unboxing are done implicitly in the right context. Boxing allows primitive values to be used where an object of their wrapper type is expected, and unboxing allows the converse. Unboxing makes it possible to use a Boolean wrapper object in a boolean expression and as an integral wrapper object in an arithmetic expression. Unboxing a wrapper reference that has the null value results in a NullPointerException. Ample examples of boxing and unboxing can be found in this chapter and in Section 7.8, p. 319.

Other Conversions

We briefly mention some other conversions and where they are covered in this book.

- *Identity conversions* are always permitted, as they allow conversions from a type to that same type. An identity conversion is always permitted.

```
int i = (int) 10;                   // int <---- int
String str = (String) "Hi";         // String <---- String
```

- *String conversions* allow a value of any other type to be converted to a String type in the context of the string concatenation operator + (Section 5.7, p. 185).

- *Unchecked conversions* are permitted to facilitate operability between legacy and generic code (Section 14.2, p. 670).

- *Capture conversions* aid in increasing the usefulness of wildcards in generic code (Section 14.9, p. 703).

5.2 Type Conversion Contexts

Selected conversion contexts and the conversions that are applicable in these contexts are summarized in Table 5.1. The conversions shown in each context occur *implicitly*, without the program having to take any special action. For other conversion contexts, see the sections mentioned in the subsection **Other Conversions**, p. 162.

Table 5.1 *Selected Conversion Contexts and Conversion Categories*

Conversion Categories	Conversion Contexts			
	Assignment	Method Invocation	Casting	Numeric Promotion
Widening/ Narrowing *Primitive* Conversions	widening narrowing for *constant expressions* of non-long integer type, with optional boxing	widening	both	widening
Widening/ Narrowing *Reference* Conversions	widening	widening	both, followed by optional unchecked conversion	Not applicable
Boxing/ Unboxing Conversions	unboxing, followed by optional widening *primitive* conversion boxing, followed by optional widening *reference* conversion	unboxing, followed by optional widening *primitive* conversion boxing, followed by optional widening *reference* conversion	both	unboxing, followed by optional widening *primitive* conversion

Assignment Context

Assignment conversions that can occur in an assignment context are shown in the second column of Table 5.1. An assignment conversion converts the type of an expression to the type of a target variable.

An expression (or its value) is *assignable* to the target variable, if the type of the expression can be converted to the type of the target variable by an assignment conversion. Equivalently, the type of the expression is *assignment compatible* with the type of the target variable.

For assignment conversion involving primitive data types, see Section 5.5, p. 169. Note the special case where a narrowing conversion occurs when assigning a non-long integer constant expression:

```
byte b = 10;   // Narrowing conversion: byte <--- int
```

For assignment conversions involving reference types, see Section 7.8, p. 319.

Method Invocation Context

Method invocation conversions that can occur in a method invocation context are shown in the third column of Table 5.1. Note that method invocation and assignment conversions differ in one respect: method invocation conversions do not include the implicit narrowing conversion performed for integer constant expressions.

A method invocation conversion involves converting each argument value in a method or constructor call to the type of the corresponding formal parameter in the method or constructor declaration.

Method invocation conversions involving parameters of primitive data types are discussed in Section 3.7, p. 82, and those involving reference types are discussed in Section 7.8, p. 319.

Casting Context of the Unary Type Cast Operator: (*type*)

Java, being a *strongly typed* language, checks for *type compatibility* (i.e., checks if a type can substitute for another type in a given context) at compile time. However, some checks are only possible at runtime (for example, which type of object a reference actually denotes during execution). In cases where an operator would have incompatible operands (e.g., assigning a double to an int), Java demands that a *type cast* be used to *explicitly* indicate the type conversion. The type cast construct has the following syntax:

(*<type>*) *<expression>*

The *cast operator* (*<type>*) is applied to the value of the *<expression>*. At runtime, a cast results in a new value of *<type>*, which best represents the value of the *<expression>* in the old type. We use the term *casting* to mean applying the cast operator for *explicit* type conversion.

However, in the context of casting, *implicit* casting conversions can take place. These casting conversions are shown in the fourth column of Table 5.1. Casting conversions include more conversion categories than the assignment or the method invocation conversions. In the code below, the comments indicate the category of the conversion that takes place because of the cast operator on the right-hand side of each assignment—although some casts are not necessary for the sake of the assignment.

```
long l = (long) 10;    // Widening primitive conversion: long <--- int
int i = (int) l;       // Narrowing primitive conversion: int <--- long
Object obj = (Object) "Upcast me"; // Widening ref conversion: Object <--- String
String str = (String) obj;         // Narrowing ref conversion: String <--- Object
Integer iRef = (Integer) i;        // Boxing: Integer <--- int
i = (int) iRef;                    // Unboxing: int <--- Integer
```

A casting conversion is applied to the value of the operand *<expression>* of a cast operator. Casting can be applied to primitive values as well as references. Casting between primitive data types and reference types is not permitted, except where boxing and unboxing is applicable. Boolean values cannot be cast to other data values, and vice versa. The reference literal null can be cast to any reference type.

Examples of casting between primitive data types are provided in this chapter. Casting reference values is discussed in Section 7.11, p. 327. Implications that generics have on casting are discussed in Section 14.13, p. 724.

Numeric Promotion Context

Numeric operators only allow operands of certain types. Numeric promotion results in conversions being applied to the operands to convert them to permissible types. *Numeric promotion conversions* that can occur in a numeric promotion context are shown in the fifth column of Table 5.1. Permissible conversion categories are: widening primitive conversions and unboxing conversions. A distinction is made between unary and binary numeric promotion.

Unary Numeric Promotion

Unary numeric promotion proceeds as follows:

- If the single operand is of type Byte, Short, Character, or Integer, it is unboxed. If the resulting value is narrower than int, it is promoted to a value of type int by a widening conversion.

- Otherwise, if the single operand is of type Long, Float, or Double, it is unboxed.

- Otherwise, if the single operand is of a type narrower than int, its value is promoted to a value of type int by a widening conversion.

- Otherwise, the operand remains unchanged.

In other words, unary numeric promotion results in an operand value that is either int or wider.

Unary numeric promotion is applied in the following expressions:

- operand of the unary arithmetic operators + and - (see Section 5.6, p. 174)

- array creation expression; e.g., `new int[20]`, where the dimension expression (in this case 20) must evaluate to an `int` value (see Section 3.6, p. 70)

- indexing array elements; e.g., `objArray['a']`, where the index expression (in this case `'a'`) must evaluate to an `int` value (see Section 3.6, p. 72)

Binary Numeric Promotion

Binary numeric promotion implicitly applies appropriate widening primitive conversions so that a pair of operands have the widest numeric type of the two, which is always at least `int`. Given T to be the widest numeric type of the two operands after any unboxing conversions have been performed, the operands are promoted as follows during binary numeric promotion:

> If T is wider than `int`, both operands are converted to T; otherwise, both operands are converted to `int`.

This means that the resulting type of the operands is at least `int`.

Binary numeric promotion is applied in the following expressions:

- operands of the arithmetic operators *, /, %, +, and - (see Section 5.6, p. 174)

- operands of the relational operators <, <=, >, and >= (see Section 5.10, p. 190)

- operands of the numerical equality operators == and != (see Section 5.11, p. 191)

- operands of the conditional operator ? :, under certain circumstances (see Section 5.14, p. 201)

5.3 Precedence and Associativity Rules for Operators

Precedence and associativity rules are necessary for deterministic evaluation of expressions. The operators are summarized in Table 5.2. The majority of them are discussed in subsequent sections in this chapter.

The following remarks apply to Table 5.2:

- The operators are shown with decreasing precedence from the top of the table.

- Operators within the same row have the same precedence.

- Parentheses, ( ), can be used to override precedence and associativity.

- The *unary operators*, which require one operand, include the following: the postfix increment (++) and decrement (--) operators from the first row, all the prefix operators (+, -, ++, --, ~, !) in the second row, and the prefix operators (object creation operator `new`, cast operator (*type*)) in the third row.

- The conditional operator (? :) is *ternary*, that is, requires three operands.

- All operators not listed above as unary or ternary, are *binary,* that is, require two operands.
- All binary operators, except for the relational and assignment operators, associate from left to right. The relational operators are nonassociative.
- Except for unary postfix increment and decrement operators, all unary operators, all assignment operators, and the ternary conditional operator associate from right to left.

Table 5.2 *Operator Summary*

Postfix operators	`[] . (parameters) expression++ expression--`
Unary prefix operators	`++expression --expression +expression -expression ~ !`
Unary prefix creation and cast	`new (type)`
Multiplicative	`* / %`
Additive	`+ -`
Shift	`<< >> >>>`
Relational	`< <= > >= instanceof`
Equality	`== !=`
Bitwise/logical AND	`&`
Bitwise/logical XOR	`^`
Bitwise/logical OR	`|`
Conditional AND	`&&`
Conditional OR	`||`
Conditional	`?:`
Assignment	`= += -= *= /= %= <<= >>= >>>= &= ^= |=`

Precedence rules are used to determine which operator should be applied first if there are two operators with different precedence, and these follow each other in the expression. In such a case, the operator with the highest precedence is applied first.

2 + 3 * 4 is evaluated as 2 + (3 * 4) (with the result 14) since * has higher precedence than +.

Associativity rules are used to determine which operator should be applied first if there are two operators with the same precedence, and these follow each other in the expression.

Left associativity implies grouping from left to right:

1 + 2 - 3 is interpreted as ((1 + 2) - 3), since the binary operators + and - both have same precedence and left associativity.

Right associativity implies grouping from right to left:

- - 4 is interpreted as (- (- 4)) (with the result 4), since the unary operator - has right associativity.

The precedence and associativity rules together determine the *evaluation order of the operators*.

5.4 Evaluation Order of Operands

In order to understand the result returned by an operator, it is important to understand the *evaluation order of its operands*. In general, the operands of operators are evaluated from left to right.

The evaluation order also respects any parentheses, and the precedence and associativity rules of operators.

Examples illustrating how the operand evaluation order influences the result returned by an operator, can be found in Sections 5.5 and 5.8.

Left-Hand Operand Evaluation First

The left-hand operand of a binary operator is fully evaluated before the right-hand operand is evaluated.

The evaluation of the left-hand operand can have side effects that can influence the value of the right-hand operand. For example, in the following code:

```
int b = 10;
System.out.println((b=3) + b);
```

the value printed will be 6 and not 13. The evaluation proceeds as follows:

```
(b=3) + b
 3   + b      b is assigned the value 3
 3   + 3
 6
```

If evaluation of the left-hand operand of a binary operator raises an exception (see Section 6.5, p. 235), we cannot rely on the presumption that the right-hand operand has been evaluated.

Operand Evaluation before Operation Execution

Java guarantees that *all* operands of an operator are fully evaluated *before* the actual operation is performed. This rule does not apply to the short-circuit conditional operators &&, ||, and ?:.

This rule also applies to operators that throw an exception (the integer division operator / and the integer remainder operate %). The operation is only performed if the operands evaluate normally. Any side-effects of the right-hand operand will have been effectuated before the operator throws an exception.

Left to Right Evaluation of Argument Lists

In a method or constructor invocation, each argument expression in the argument list is fully evaluated before any argument expression to its right.

If evaluation of an argument expression does not complete normally, we cannot presume that any argument expression to its right has been evaluated.

5.5 The Simple Assignment Operator =

The assignment statement has the following syntax:

> *<variable>* = *<expression>*

which can be read as *"the target, <variable>, gets the value of the source, <expression>"*. The previous value of the target variable is overwritten by the assignment operator =.

The target *<variable>* and the source *<expression>* must be assignment compatible. The target variable must also have been declared. Since variables can store either primitive values or reference values, *<expression>* evaluates to either a primitive value or a reference value.

Assigning Primitive Values

The following examples illustrate assignment of primitive values:

```
int j, k;
j = 10;           // j gets the value 10.
j = 5;            // j gets the value 5. Previous value is overwritten.
k = j;            // k gets the value 5.
```

The assignment operator has the lowest precedence allowing the expression on the right-hand side to be evaluated before assignment.

```
int i;
i = 5;            // i gets the value 5.
i = i + 1;        // i gets the value 6. + has higher precedence than =.
i = 20 - i * 2;   // i gets the value 8: (20 - (i * 2))
```

Assigning References

Copying reference values by assignment creates aliases, which is discussed in Section 1.3, p. 6. The following example recapitulates that discussion:

```
Pizza pizza1 = new Pizza("Hot&Spicy");
Pizza pizza2 = new Pizza("Sweet&Sour");

pizza2 = pizza1;
```

Variable `pizza1` is a reference to a pizza that is hot and spicy, and `pizza2` is a reference to a pizza which is sweet and sour. Assigning `pizza1` to `pizza2` means that `pizza2` now refers to the same pizza as `pizza1`, i.e., the hot and spicy one. After the assignment, these variables are aliases and either one can be used to manipulate the hot and spicy `Pizza` object.

Assigning a reference value does *not* create a copy of the source object denoted by the reference variable on the right-hand side. It merely assigns the reference value to the variable on the right-hand side to the variable on the left-hand side, so that they denote the same object. Reference assignment also does not copy the *state* of the source object to any object denoted by the reference variable on the left-hand side.

A more detailed discussion of reference assignment can be found in Section 7.8, p. 319.

Multiple Assignments

The assignment statement is an *expression statement*, which means that application of the binary assignment operator returns the value of the expression on the *right-hand* side.

```
int j, k;
j = 10;          // j gets the value 10 which is returned
k = j;           // k gets the value of j, which is 10, and this value is returned
```

The last two assignments can be written as multiple assignments, illustrating the right associativity of the assignment operator.

```
k = j = 10;      // (k = (j = 10))
```

Multiple assignments are equally valid with references.

```
Pizza pizzaOne, pizzaTwo;
pizzaOne = pizzaTwo = new Pizza("Supreme"); // Aliases.
```

The following example shows the effect of operand evaluation order:

```
int[] a = {10, 20, 30, 40, 50}; // an array of int
int index = 4;
a[index] = index = 2;           // (1)
```

What is the value of `index`, and which array element `a[index]` is assigned a value in the multiple assignment statement at (1)? The evaluation proceeds as follows:

```
a[index] = index = 2;
a[4]     = index = 2;
a[4]     = (index = 2);     // index gets the value 2. = is right associative.
a[4]     =      2;          // The value of a[4] is changed from 50 to 2.
```

Type Conversions in Assignment Context

If the target and source have the same type in an assignment, then, obviously, the source and the target are assignment compatible and the source value need not be converted. Otherwise, if a widening primitive conversion is permissible, then the widening conversion is applied implicitly, i.e., the source type is converted to the target type in an assignment context.

```
// Widening Primitive Conversions
int    smallOne = 1234;
long   bigOne   = 2000;        // Widening: int to long.
double largeOne = bigOne;      // Widening: long to double.
double hugeOne  = (double) bigOne;  // Cast redundant but allowed.
```

A widening primitive conversion can result in loss of *precision*. In the next example, the precision of the least significant bits of the long value may be lost when converting to a float value.

```
long bigInteger = 98765432112345678L;
float fpNum = bigInteger;  // Widening but loss of precision: 9.8765436E16
```

Additionally, implicit narrowing primitive conversions on assignment can occur in cases where *all* of the following conditions are fulfilled:

- the source is a *constant expression* of either byte, short, char, or int type
- the target type is either byte, short, or char type
- the value of the source is determined to be in the range of the target type at compile time

Here are some examples to illustrate how these conditions effect narrowing primitive conversions:

```
// Above conditions fulfilled for implicit narrowing primitive conversions.
short s1 = 10;        // int value in range.
short s2 = 'a';       // char value in range.
char c1 = 32;         // int value in range.
char c2 = (byte)35;   // byte value in range. (int value in range, without cast.)
byte b1 = 40;         // int value in range.
byte b2 = (short)40;  // short value in range. (int value in range, without cast.)
final int i1 = 20;
byte b3 = i1;         // final value of i1 in range.
```

All other narrowing primitive conversions will produce a compile-time error on assignment and will explicitly require a cast. Here are some examples:

```
// Above conditions not fulfilled for implicit narrowing primitive conversions.
// A cast is required.
int i2 = -20;
final int i3 = i2;
final int i4 = 200;
short s3 = (short) i2; // Not constant expression.
char c3 = (char) i3;   // final value of i3 not determinable.
char c4 = (char) i2;   // Not constant expression.
```

```
byte b4 = (byte) 128;   // int value not in range.
byte b5 = (byte) i4;    // final value of i4 not in range.
```

Floating-point values are truncated when cast to integral values.

```
// The value is truncated to fit the size of the target type.
float huge   = (float) 1.7976931348623157d; // double to float.
long  giant  = (long) 4415961481999.03D;    // (1) double to long.
int   big    = (int) giant;                 // (2) long to int.
short small  = (short) big;                 // (3) int to short.
byte  minute = (byte) small;                // (4) short to byte.
char  symbol = (char) 112.5F;               // (5) float to char.
```

Table 5.3 shows how the values are truncated for assignments from (1) to (5).

Table 5.3 *Examples of Truncated Values*

Binary	Decimal	
0000000000000000000001000000010000101011110100001100001100001111	4415961481999	(1)
00101011110100001100001100001111	735101711	(2)
1100001100001111	-15601	(3)
00001111	15	(4)
0000000001110000	'p'	(5)

The discussion on numeric assignment conversions also applies to numeric parameter values at method invocation (see Section 3.7, p. 82), except for the narrowing conversions, which always require a cast.

The following examples illustrate boxing and unboxing in assignment context:

```
Boolean  boolRef = true;  // boxing
Byte     bRef    = 2;     // constant in range: narrowing to byte, then boxing
// Byte  bRef2   = 257;   // constant not in range: cast required
Integer iRef3 = (short)10; // constant in range: casting by narrowing to short,
                           // widening to int, then boxing

short s = 10;             // narrowing
// Integer   iRef1 = s;   // short not assignable to Integer

boolean bv1 = boolRef;    // unboxing
byte b1 = bRef;           // unboxing

Integer iRefVal = null;           // Always allowed.
int     j = iRefVal;              // NullPointerException!
if (iRefVal != null) j = iRefVal; // Avoids the exception
```

Review Questions

5.1 Given the following declaration:

```
char c = 'A';
```

What is the simplest way to convert the character value in c into an int?

Select the one correct answer.

(a) `int i = c;`
(b) `int i = (int) c;`
(c) `int i = Character.getNumericValue(c);`

5.2 What will be the result of compiling and running the following program?

```
public class Assignment {
  public static void main(String[] args) {
    int a, b, c;
    b = 10;
    a = b = c = 20;
    System.out.println(a);
  }
}
```

Select the one correct answer.

(a) The program will fail to compile since the compiler will report that the variable c in the multiple assignment statement a = b = c = 20; has not been initialized.
(b) The program will fail to compile, because the multiple assignment statement a = b = c = 20; is illegal.
(c) The code will compile and print 10, when run.
(d) The code will compile and print 20, when run.

5.3 What will be the result of compiling and running the following program?

```
public class MyClass {
  public static void main(String[] args) {
    String a, b, c;
    c = new String("mouse");
    a = new String("cat");
    b = a;
    a = new String("dog");
    c = b;

    System.out.println(c);
  }
}
```

Select the one correct answer.

(a) The program will fail to compile.
(b) The program will print mouse, when run.

(c) The program will print cat, when run.
(d) The program will print dog, when run.
(e) The program will randomly print either cat or dog, when run.

5.6 Arithmetic Operators: *, /, %, +, -

Arithmetic operators are used to construct mathematical expressions as in algebra. Their operands are of numeric type (which includes the char type).

Arithmetic Operator Precedence and Associativity

In Table 5.4, the precedence of the operators is in decreasing order, starting from the top row, which has the highest precedence. Unary subtraction has higher precedence than multiplication. The operators in the same row have the same precedence. Binary multiplication, division, and remainder operators have the same precedence. The unary operators have right associativity, and the binary operators have left associativity.

Table 5.4 *Arithmetic Operators*

Unary	+ *Addition*	- *Subtraction*	
Binary	* *Multiplication*	/ *Division*	% *Remainder*
	+ *Addition*	- *Subtraction*	

Evaluation Order in Arithmetic Expressions

Java guarantees that the operands are fully evaluated from left to right before an arithmetic binary operator is applied. If evaluation of an operand results in an error, the subsequent operands will not be evaluated.

In the expression a + b * c, the operand a will always be fully evaluated before the operand b, which will always be fully evaluated before the operand c. However, the multiplication operator * will be applied before the addition operator +, respecting the precedence rules. Note that a, b, and c are arbitrary arithmetic expressions that have been determined to be the operands of the operators.

The evaluation order and precedence rules for arithmetic expressions are illustrated in Example 5.1. The evaluation of each operand in the expression at (1) results in a call of the operandEval() method declared at (2). The first argument to this method is a number to identify the operand and the second argument is the operand value which is returned by the method. The output from the program shows that all three operands were evaluated from left to right and the value of the variable i shows that the precedence rules were applied in the evaluation.

Example 5.1 *Operand Evaluation Order*

```
public class OperandEvaluationOrder {
  public static void main(String[] args) {
    // Evaluate: 4 + 5 * 6
    int i = operandEval(1, 4) + operandEval(2, 5) * operandEval(3, 6);  // (1)
    System.out.println();
    System.out.println("Value of i: " + i);
  }

  static int operandEval(int opNum, int operand) {                       // (2)
    System.out.print(opNum);
    return operand;
  }
}
```

Output from the program:

```
123
Value of i: 34
```

Range of Numeric Values

As we have seen, all numeric types have a range of valid values (Section 2.2, p. 28). This range is given by the constants named MAX_VALUE and MIN_VALUE, which are defined in each numeric wrapper class.

The arithmetic operators are overloaded, meaning that the operation of an operator varies depending on the type of its operands. Floating-point arithmetic is performed if any operand of an operator is of floating-point type, otherwise, integer arithmetic is performed.

Values that are out-of-range or are the results of invalid expressions are handled differently depending on whether integer or floating-point arithmetic is performed.

Integer Arithmetic

Integer arithmetic always returns a value that is in range, except in the case of integer division by zero and remainder by zero, which causes an ArithmeticException (see the division operator / and the remainder operator % below). A valid value does not necessarily mean that the result is correct, as demonstrated by the following examples:

```
int tooBig   = Integer.MAX_VALUE + 1;   // -2147483648 which is Integer.MIN_VALUE.
int tooSmall = Integer.MIN_VALUE - 1;   //  2147483647 which is Integer.MAX_VALUE.
```

The results above should be values that are out-of-range. However, integer arithmetic *wraps* if the result is out-of-range, i.e., the result is reduced modulo in the range of the result type. In order to avoid wrapping of out-of-range values, programs should either use explicit checks or a wider type. If the type `long` is used in the examples above, the results would be correct in the `long` range:

```
long notTooBig   = Integer.MAX_VALUE + 1L;   //  2147483648L in range.
long notTooSmall = Integer.MIN_VALUE - 1L;   // -2147483649L in range.
```

Floating-Point Arithmetic

Certain floating-point operations result in values that are out-of-range. Typically, adding or multiplying two very large floating-point numbers can result in an out-of-range value which is represented by *Infinity* (see Figure 5.2). Attempting floating-point division by zero also returns infinity. The examples below show how this value is printed as signed infinity.

```
System.out.println( 4.0 / 0.0);        // Prints:  Infinity
System.out.println(-4.0 / 0.0);        // Prints: -Infinity
```

Both positive and negative infinity represent *overflow* to infinity, that is, the value is too large to be represented as a `double` or `float` (see Figure 5.2). Signed infinity is represented by named constants `POSITIVE_INFINITY` and `NEGATIVE_INFINITY` in the wrapper classes java.lang.Float and java.lang.Double. A value can be compared with these constants to detect overflow.

Figure 5.2   *Overflow and Underflow in Floating-point Arithmetic*

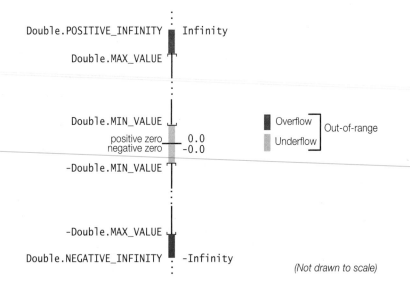

Floating-point arithmetic can also result in *underflow* to zero, i.e., the value is too small to be represented as a `double` or `float` (see Figure 5.2). Underflow occurs in the following situations:

- the result is between `Double.MIN_VALUE` (or `Float.MIN_VALUE`) and zero; e.g., the result of (`5.1E-324 - 4.9E-324`). Underflow then returns positive zero `0.0` (or `0.0F`).

- the result is between `-Double.MIN_VALUE` (or `-Float.MIN_VALUE`) and zero; e.g., the result of (`-Double.MIN_VALUE * 1E-1`). Underflow then returns negative zero `-0.0` (or `-0.0F`).

Negative zero compares equal to positive zero, i.e., (`-0.0 == 0.0`) is `true`.

Certain operations have no mathematical result, and are represented by *NaN* (*Not a Number*). For example, calculating the square root of -1. Another example is (floating-point) dividing zero by zero:

```
System.out.println(0.0 / 0.0);        // Prints: NaN
```

NaN is represented by the constant named `NaN` in the wrapper classes `java.lang.Float` and `java.lang.Double`. Any operation involving NaN produces NaN. Any comparison (except inequality `!=`) involving NaN and any other value (including NaN) returns `false`. An inequality comparison of NaN with another value (including NaN) always returns `true`. However, the recommended way of checking a value for NaN is to use the static method `isNaN()` defined in both wrapper classes, `java.lang.Float` and `java.lang.Double`.

Strict Floating-Point Arithmetic: `strictfp`

Although floating-point arithmetic in Java is defined in accordance with the IEEE-754 32-bit (`float`) and 64-bit (`double`) standard formats, the language does allow JVM implementations to use other extended formats for intermediate results. This means that floating-point arithmetic can give different results on such JVMs, with possible loss of precision. Such a behavior is termed *non-strict*, in contrast to being *strict* and adhering to the standard formats.

To ensure that identical results are produced on all JVMs, the keyword `strictfp` can be used to enforce strict behavior for floating-point arithmetic. The modifier `strictfp` can be applied to classes, interfaces, and methods. A `strictfp` method ensures that all code in the method is executed strictly. If a class or interface is declared to be `strictfp`, then all code (in methods, initializers, and nested classes and interfaces) is executed strictly. If the expression is determined to be in a `strictfp` construct, it is executed strictly. However, note that strictness is not inherited by the subclasses or subinterfaces. Constant expressions are always evaluated strictly at compile time.

Unary Arithmetic Operators: –, +

The unary operators have the highest precedence of all the arithmetic operators. The unary operator – negates the numeric value of its operand. The following example illustrates the right associativity of the unary operators:

```
int value = - -10;              // (-(-10)) is 10
```

Notice the blank needed to separate the unary operators; otherwise, these would be interpreted as the decrement operator -- (see Section 5.8, p. 186). The unary operator + has no effect on the evaluation of the operand value.

Section G.4 on page 1010 discusses how negative integers are represented using 2's complement.

Multiplicative Binary Operators: *, /, %

Multiplication Operator: *

The multiplication operator * multiplies two numbers.

```
int    sameSigns     = -4   * -8;      // result:  32
double oppositeSigns =  4.0 * -8.0;    // result: -32.0
int    zero          =  0   * -0;      // result:   0
```

Division Operator: /

The division operator / is overloaded. If its operands are integral, the operation results in *integer division*.

```
int    i1 = 4  / 5;    // result: 0
int    i2 = 8  / 8;    // result: 1
double d1 = 12 / 8;    // result: 1.0, integer division, then widening conversion.
```

Integer division always returns the quotient as an integer value, i.e., the result is truncated toward zero. Note that the division performed is integer division if the operands have integral values, even if the result will be stored in a floating-point type. The integer value is subjected to a widening conversion in the assignment context.

An ArithmeticException is thrown when attempting integer division with zero, meaning that integer division by zero is an illegal operation.

If any of the operands is a floating-point type, the operation performs *floating-point division*, where relevant operand values undergo binary numeric promotion:

```
double d2 = 4.0 / 8;       // result: 0.5
double d3 = 8 / 8.0;       // result: 1.0
double d4 = 12.0F / 8;     // result: 1.5F

double result1 = 12.0 / 4.0 * 3.0;    // ((12.0 / 4.0) * 3.0) which is 9.0
double result2 = 12.0 * 3.0 / 4.0;    // ((12.0 * 3.0) / 4.0) which is 9.0
```

Remainder Operator: %

In mathematics, when we divide a number (the *dividend*) by another number (the *divisor*), the result can be expressed in terms of a *quotient* and a *remainder*. For example, dividing 7 by 5, the quotient is 1 and the remainder is 2. The remainder operator % returns the remainder of the division performed on the operands.

```
int quotient  = 7 / 5;    // Integer division operation: 1
int remainder = 7 % 5;    // Integer remainder operation: 2
```

For *integer remainder operation*, where only integer operands are involved, evaluation of the expression (x % y) always satisfies the following relation:

$$x == (x \, / \, y) * y + (x \, \% \, y)$$

In other words, the right-hand side yields a value that is always equal to the value of the dividend. The following examples show how we can calculate the remainder so that the above relation is satisfied:

Calculating (7 % 5):
```
 7 == (7 / 5) * 5 + (7 % 5)
   == ( 1  ) * 5 + (7 % 5)
   ==             5 + (7 % 5)
 2 ==               (7 % 5)        i.e., (7 % 5) is equal to 2
```

Calculating (7 % -5):
```
 7 == (7 / -5) * -5 + (7 % -5)
   == ( -1  ) * -5 + (7 % -5)
   ==            5 + (7 % -5)
 2 ==              (7 % -5)        i.e., (7 % -5) is equal to 2
```

Calculating (-7 % 5):
```
-7 == (-7 / 5) * 5 + (-7 % 5)
   == ( -1  ) * 5 + (-7 % 5)
   ==           -5 + (-7 % 5)
-2 ==              (-7 % 5)        i.e., (-7 % 5) is equal to -2
```

Calculating (-7 % -5):
```
-7 == (-7 / -5) * -5 + (-7 % -5)
   == ( 1  ) * -5 + (-7 % -5)
   ==           -5 + (-7 % -5)
-2 ==              (-7 % -5)       i.e., (-7 % -5) is equal to -2
```

The above relation shows that the remainder can only be negative if the dividend is negative, and the sign of the divisor is irrelevant. A shortcut to evaluating the remainder involving negative operands is the following: ignore the signs of the operands, calculate the remainder, and negate the remainder if the dividend is negative.

```
int  r0 =  7 % 7;     // 0
int  r1 =  7 % 5;     // 2
long r2 =  7L % -5L;  // 2L
int  r3 = -7 % 5;     // -2
long r4 = -7L % -5L;  // -2L
boolean relation = -7L == (-7L / -5L) * -5L + r4;  // true
```

An `ArithmeticException` is thrown if the divisor evaluates to zero.

Note that the remainder operator not only accepts integral operands, but floating-point operands as well. The *floating-point remainder* r is defined by the relation:

$$r == a - (b * q)$$

where a and b are the dividend and the divisor, respectively, and q is the integer quotient of (a/b). The following examples illustrate a floating-point remainder operation:

```
double  dr0 =  7.0 % 7.0;    //  0.0
float   fr1 =  7.0F % 5.0F;   //  2.0F
double  dr1 =  7.0 % -5.0;    //  2.0
float   fr2 = -7.0F % 5.0F;   // -2.0F
double  dr2 = -7.0 % -5.0;    // -2.0
boolean fpRelation = dr2 == (-7.0) - (-5.0) * (long)(-7.0 / -5.0);  // true
float   fr3 = -7.0F % 0.0F;   // NaN
```

Additive Binary Operators: +, -

The addition operator + and the subtraction operator - behave as their names imply: add or subtract values. The binary operator + also acts as *string concatenation* if any of its operands is a string (see Section 5.7, p. 185).

Additive operators have lower precedence than all the other arithmetic operators. Table 5.5 includes examples that show how precedence and associativity are used in arithmetic expression evaluation.

Table 5.5 *Examples of Arithmetic Expression Evaluation*

Arithmetic Expression	Evaluation	Result When Printed
3 + 2 - 1	((3 + 2) - 1)	4
2 + 6 * 7	(2 + (6 * 7))	44
-5+7- -6	(((-5)+7)-(-6))	8
2+4/5	(2+(4/5))	2
13 % 5	(13 % 5)	3
11.5 % 2.5	(11.5 % 2.5)	1.5
10 / 0	ArithmeticException	
2+4.0/5	(2.0+(4.0/5.0))	2.8
4.0 / 0.0	(4.0 / 0.0)	Infinity
-4.0 / 0.0	((-4.0) / 0.0)	-Infinity
0.0 / 0.0	(0.0 / 0.0)	NaN

Numeric Promotions in Arithmetic Expressions

Unary numeric promotion is applied to the single operand of the unary arithmetic operators - and +. When a unary arithmetic operator is applied to an operand whose type is narrower than int, the operand is promoted to a value of type int, with the operation resulting in an int value. If the conditions for implicit narrowing conversion are not fulfilled (p. 171), assigning the int result to a variable of a narrower type will require a cast. This is demonstrated by the following example, where the byte operand b is promoted to an int in the expression (-b):

```
byte b = 3;          // int literal in range. Narrowing conversion.
b = (byte) -b;       // Cast required on assignment.
```

Binary numeric promotion is applied to operands of binary arithmetic operators. Its application leads to type promotion for the operands, as explained in Section 5.2, p. 165. The result is of the promoted type, which is always type int or wider. For the expression at (1) in Example 5.2, numeric promotions proceed as shown in Figure 5.3. Note the integer division performed in evaluating the subexpression (c / s).

Example 5.2   *Numeric Promotion in Arithmetic Expressions*

```java
public class NumPromotion {
  public static void main(String[] args) {
    byte   b = 32;
    char   c = 'z';                    // Unicode value 122 (\u007a)
    short  s = 256;
    int    i = 10000;
    float  f = 3.5F;
    double d = 0.5;
    double v = (d * i) + (f * - b) - (c / s);    // (1) 4888.0D
    System.out.println("Value of v: " + v);
  }
}
```

Output from the program:

```
Value of v: 4888.0
```

Figure 5.3   *Numeric Promotion in Arithmetic Expressions*

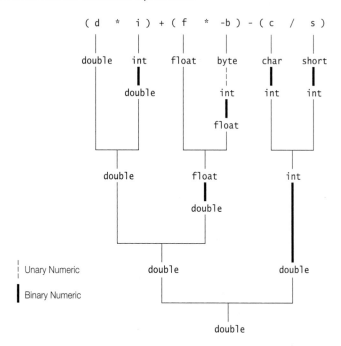

In addition to the binary numeric promotions in arithmetic expression evaluation, the resulting value can undergo an implicit widening conversion if assigned to a variable. In the first two declaration statements below, only assignment conversions take place. Numeric promotions take place in the evaluation of the right-hand expression in the other declaration statements.

```
Byte   b = 10;        // constant in range: narrowing and boxing on assignment.
Short  s = 20;        // constant in range: narrowing and boxing on assignment.
char   c = 'z';       // 122 (\u007a)
int    i = s * b;     // Values in s and b promoted to int: unboxing, widening
long   n = 20L + s;   // Value in s promoted to long: unboxing, widening
float  r = s + c;     // Values in s and c promoted to int, followed by implicit
                      // widening conversion of int to float on assignment.
double d = r + i;     // value in i promoted to float, followed by implicit
                      // widening conversion of float to double on assignment.
```

Binary numeric promotion for operands of binary operators implies that each operand of a binary operator is promoted to type int or a broader numeric type, if necessary. As with unary operators, care must be exercised in assigning the value resulting from applying a binary operator to operands of these types.

```
short h = 40;         // OK: int converted to short. Implicit narrowing.
h = h + 2;            // Error: cannot assign an int to short.
```

The value of expression h + 2 is of type int. Although the result of the expression is in the range of short, this cannot be determined at compile time. The assignment requires a cast.

```
h = (short) (h + 2);    // OK
```

Notice that applying the cast operator (short) to the individual operands does not work:

```
h = (short) h + (short) 2;      // The resulting value should be cast.
```

In this case, binary numeric promotion leads to an int value as the result of evaluating the expression on the right-hand side and, therefore, requires an additional cast to narrow it to a short value.

Arithmetic Compound Assignment Operators: *=, /=, %=, +=, -=

A compound assignment operator has the following syntax:

<variable> <op>= <expression>

and the following semantics:

<variable> = (<type>) ((<variable>) <op> (<expression>))

The type of the *<variable>* is *<type>* and the *<variable>* is evaluated only once. Note the cast and the parentheses implied in the semantics. Here *<op>*= can be any of the compound assignment operators specified in Table 5.2. The compound assignment operators have the lowest precedence of all the operators in Java, allowing the expression on the right-hand side to be evaluated before the assignment. Table 5.4 defines the arithmetic compound assignment operators.

Table 5.6 *Arithmetic Compound Assignment Operators*

Expression:	Given T as the Numeric Type of x, the Expression Is Evaluated as:
x *= a	x = (T) ((x) * (a))
x /= a	x = (T) ((x) / (a))
x %= a	x = (T) ((x) % (a))
x += a	x = (T) ((x) + (a))
x -= a	x = (T) ((x) - (a))

The implied cast operator, (T), in the compound assignments becomes necessary when the result must be narrowed to the target type. This is illustrated by the following examples:

```
int i = 2;
i *= i + 4;              // (1) Evaluated as i = (int) ((i) * (i + 4)).

Integer iRef = 2;
iRef *= iRef + 4;        // (2) Evaluated as iRef = (Integer) ((iRef) * (iRef + 4)).

byte b = 2;
b += 10;                 // (3) Evaluated as b = (byte) (b + 10).
b = b + 10;              // (4) Will not compile. Cast is required.
```

At (1) the source int value is assigned to the target int variable, and the cast operator (int) in this case is an *identity conversion* (i.e., conversion from a type to the same type). Such casts are permitted. The assignment at (2) entails unboxing to evaluate the expression on the right-hand side, followed by boxing to assign the int value. However, at (3), as the source value is an int value because the byte value in b is promoted to int to carry out the addition, assigning it to a target byte variable requires an implicit narrowing conversion. The situation at (4) with simple assignment will not compile, because implicit narrowing conversion is not applicable.

The *<variable>* is only evaluated once in the expression, not twice, as one might infer from the definition of the compound assignment operator. In the following assignment, a[i] is only evaluated once:

```
int[] a = new int[] { 2008, 2009, 2010 };
int i = 2;
a[i] += 1;       // evaluates as a[2] = a[2] + 1, and a[2] gets the value 2011.
```

Implicit narrowing conversions are also applied for increment and decrement operators (see Section 5.8, p. 186).

Other compound assignment operators include boolean logical, bitwise, and shift operators—of which, only the boolean logical operators are discussed in this book (see Section 5.12, p. 194).

Review Questions

5.4   Which of the following expressions will be evaluated using floating-point arithmetic?

Select the three correct answers.
(a) 2.0 * 3.0
(b) 2 * 3
(c) 2/3 + 5/7
(d) 2.4 + 1.6
(e) 0x10 * 1L * 300.0

5.5   What is the value of the expression (1 / 2 + 3 / 2 + 0.1)?

Select the one correct answer.
(a) 1
(b) 1.1
(c) 1.6
(d) 2
(e) 2.1

5.6   What will be the result of compiling and running the following program?

```
public class Integers {
  public static void main(String[] args) {
    System.out.println(0x10 + 10 + 010);
  }
}
```

Select the one correct answer.
(a) The program will not compile because of errors in the expression 0x10 + 10 + 010.
(b) When run, the program will print 28.
(c) When run, the program will print 30.
(d) When run, the program will print 34.
(e) When run, the program will print 36.
(f) When run, the program will print 101010.

5.7   Which of the following expressions are valid?

Select the three correct answers.
(a) (- 1 -)
(b) (+ + 1)
(c) (+-+-+-1)
(d) (--1)
(e) (1 * * 1)
(f) (- -1)

5.8 What is the value of evaluating the following expression (- -1-3 * 10 / 5-1)?

Select the one correct answer.
(a) –8
(b) –6
(c) 7
(d) 8
(e) 10
(f) None of the above.

5.9 Which of these assignments are valid?

Select the four correct answers.
(a) `short s = 12;`
(b) `long l = 012;`
(c) `int other = (int) true;`
(d) `float f = -123;`
(e) `double d = 0x12345678;`

5.7 The Binary String Concatenation Operator +

The binary operator + is overloaded in the sense that the operation performed is determined by the type of the operands. When one of the operands is a String object, a string conversion is performed on the other operand, implicitly converting it to its string representation, before the string concatenation is performed. Non-String operands are converted as follows:

• For an operand of a primitive data type, its value is first converted to a reference value using the object creation expression. A string representation of the reference value is obtained as explained below for reference types.

• Values like true, false, and null are represented by string representations of these literals. A reference variable with the value null also has the string representation "null" in this context.

• For all reference value operands, a string representation is constructed by calling the toString() method on the referred object. Most classes override this method from the Object class in order to provide a more meaningful string representation of their objects. Discussion of the toString() method can be found in Section 10.2, p. 424.

The string concatenation operator + is left associative, and the result of the concatenation is always a new String object. The String class is discussed in Section 10.4, p. 439.

```
String theName = " Uranium";
theName = " Pure" + theName;              // " Pure Uranium"
String trademark1 = 100 + "%" + theName;  // "100% Pure Uranium"      (1)
```

The integer literal 100 is implicitly converted to the string "100" before concatenation. This conversion corresponds to first creating an object of the wrapper class Integer, which boxes the integer 100, and then creating a string from this object by using the toString() method supplied by this class:

```
new Integer(100).toString();
```

Note that using the character literal '%', instead of the string literal "%" in line (1) above, does not give the same result:

```
String trademark2 = 100 + '%' + theName;      // "137 Pure Uranium"
```

Integer addition is performed by the first + operator: 100 + '%', that is, (100 + 37). Caution should be exercised as the + operator might not be applied as intended, as shown by the following example:

```
System.out.println("We put two and two together and get " + 2 + 2);
```

The above statement prints "We put two and two together and get 22" and not "We put two and two together and get 4". The first integer literal 2 is promoted to a String literal "2" for the first concatenation, resulting in the String literal "We put two and two together and get 2". This result is then concatenated with the String literal "2". The whole process proceeds as follows:

```
"We put two and two together and get "   +  2  +  2
"We put two and two together and get "   + "2" +  2
"We put two and two together and get 2"      +  2
"We put two and two together and get 2"      + "2"
"We put two and two together and get 22"
```

Both occurrences of the + operator are treated as string concatenation. To convey the intended meaning of the sentence, parentheses are highly recommended:

```
System.out.println("We put two and two together and get " + (2 + 2));
```

The compiler uses a *string builder* to avoid the overhead of temporary String objects when applying the string concatenation operator (+), as explained in Section 10.5, p. 460.

5.8 Variable Increment and Decrement Operators: ++, --

Variable increment (++) and decrement (--) operators come in two flavors: *prefix* and *postfix*. These unary operators have the side effect of changing the value of the arithmetic operand which must evaluate to a variable. Depending on the operator used, the variable is either incremented or decremented by 1.

These operators cannot be applied to a variable that is declared final and which has been initialized, as the side effect would change the value in such a variable.

These operators are very useful for updating variables in loops where only the side effect of the operator is of interest.

The Increment Operator ++

Prefix increment operator has the following semantics:

++i adds 1 to the value in i, and stores the new value in i. It returns the *new* value as the value of the expression. It is equivalent to the following statements:

```
i += 1;
result = i;
return result;
```

Postfix increment operator has the following semantics:

j++ adds 1 to the value in j, and stores the new value in j. It returns the *old* value in j *before* the new value is stored in j, as the value of the expression. It is equivalent to the following statements:

```
result = j;
j += 1;
return result;
```

The Decrement Operator --

Prefix decrement operator has the following semantics:

--i subtracts 1 from the value of i, and stores the new value in i. It returns the *new* value as the value of the expression.

Postfix decrement operator has the following semantics:

j-- subtracts 1 from the value of j, and stores the new value in j. It returns the *old* value in j before the new value is stored in j as the value of the expression.

The above discussion on decrement and increment operators applies to any variable whose type is a numeric primitive type or its corresponding numeric wrapper type. Necessary numeric promotions are performed on the value 1 and the value of the variable. Before assigning the new value to the variable, it is subjected to any narrowing primitive conversion and/or boxing that might be necessary.

Here are some examples to illustrate the behavior of increment and decrement operators:

```
// (1) Prefix order: increment/decrement operand before use.
int i = 10;
int k = ++i + --i;  // ((++i) + (--i)). k gets the value 21 and i becomes 10.
--i;                // Only side effect utilized. i is 9. (expression statement)

Integer iRef = 10;  // Boxing on assignment
k = ++iRef + --iRef;// ((++iRef) + (--iRef)). k gets the value 21 and
                    // iRef refers to an Integer object with the value 10.
--iRef;             // Only side effect utilized. iRef refers to an Integer
                    // object with the value 9. (expression statement)

// (2) Postfix order: increment/decrement operand after use.
long i = 10;
```

```
long k = i++ + i--;   // ((i++) + (i--)). k gets the value 21L and i becomes 10L.
i++;                  // Only side effect utilized. i is 11L. (expression statement)
```

An increment or decrement operator, together with its operand, can be used as an *expression statement* (see Section 3.3, p. 45).

Execution of the assignment in the second declaration statement under (1) proceeds as follows:

```
k = ((++i) + (--i))        Operands are evaluated from left to right.
k = ( 11   + (--i))        Side-effect: i += 1, i gets the value 11.
k = ( 11   +  10)          Side-effect: i -= 1, i gets the value 10.
k = 21
```

Expressions where variables are modified multiple times during the evaluation should be avoided, because the order of evaluation is not always immediately apparent.

We cannot associate increment and decrement operators. Given that a is a variable, we cannot write (++(++a)). The reason is that any operand to ++ must evaluate to a variable, but the evaluation of (++a) results in a value.

In the example below, both binary numeric promotion and an implicit narrowing conversion are performed to achieve the side effect of modifying the value of the operand. The int value of the expression (++b) (that is, 11), is assigned to the int variable i. The side effect of incrementing the value of the byte variable b requires binary numeric promotion to perform int addition, followed by an implicit narrowing conversion of the int value to byte to perform the assignment.

```
byte b = 10;
int  i = ++b;       // i is 11, and so is b.
```

The example below illustrates applying the increment operator to a floating-point operand. The side effect of the ++ operator is overwritten by the assignment.

```
double x = 4.5;
x = x + ++x;        // x gets the value 10.0.
```

Review Questions

5.10   Which statements are true?

Select the three correct answers.

(a) The expression (1 + 2 + "3") evaluates to the string "33".
(b) The expression ("1" + 2 + 3) evaluates to the string "15".
(c) The expression (4 + 1.0f) evaluates to the float value 5.0f.
(d) The expression (10/9) evaluates to the int value 1.
(e) The expression ('a' + 1) evaluates to the char value 'b'.

5.11 What happens when you try to compile and run the following program?

```
public class Prog1 {
  public static void main(String[] args) {
    int k = 1;
    int i = ++k + k++ + + k;      // (1)
    System.out.println(i);
  }
}
```

Select the one correct answer.

(a) The program will not compile, because of errors in the expression at (1).
(b) The program will compile and print the value 3, when run.
(c) The program will compile and print the value 4, when run.
(d) The program will compile and print the value 7, when run.
(e) The program will compile and print the value 8, when run.

5.12 What is the label of the first line that will cause a compile time error in the following program?

```
public class MyClass {
  public static void main(String[] args) {
    char c;
    int i;
    c = 'a'; // (1)
    i = c;   // (2)
    i++;     // (3)
    c = i;   // (4)
    c++;     // (5)
  }
}
```

Select the one correct answer.

(a) (1)
(b) (2)
(c) (3)
(d) (4)
(e) (5)
(f) None of the above. The compiler will not report any errors.

5.13 What is the result of compiling and running the following program?

```
public class Cast {
  public static void main(String[] args) {
    byte b = 128;
    int  i = b;
    System.out.println(i);
  }
}
```

Select the one correct answer.

(a) The program will not compile because a byte value cannot be assigned to an int variable without using a cast.
(b) The program will compile and print 128, when run.
(c) The program will not compile because the value 128 is not in the range of values for the byte type.
(d) The program will compile but will throw a ClassCastException when run.
(e) The program will compile and print 255, when run.

5.14   What will be the result of compiling and running the following program?

```java
public class EvaluationOrder {
  public static void main(String[] args) {
    int[] array = { 4, 8, 16 };
    int i=1;
    array[++i] = --i;
    System.out.println(array[0] + array[1] + array[2]);
  }
}
```

Select the one correct answer.

(a) 13
(b) 14
(c) 20
(d) 21
(e) 24

5.9 Boolean Expressions

As the name implies, a boolean expression has the boolean data type and can only evaluate to the values true or false.

Boolean expressions, when used as conditionals in control statements, allow the program flow to be controlled during execution.

Boolean expressions can be formed using *relational operators* (Section 5.10, p. 190), *equality operators* (Section 5.11, p. 191), *bitwise operators* (which are not covered in this book), *boolean logical operators* (Section 5.12, p. 194), *conditional operators* (Section 5.13, p. 196), the *assignment operator* (Section 5.5, p. 169), and the instanceof operator (Section 7.11, p. 328).

5.10 Relational Operators: <, <=, >, >=

Given that a and b represent numeric expressions, the relational (also called *comparison*) operators are defined as shown in Table 5.7.

Table 5.7 *Relational Operators*

a < b	a less than b?
a <= b	a less than or equal to b?
a > b	a greater than b?
a >= b	a greater than or equal to b?

All relational operators are binary operators and their operands are numeric expressions. Binary numeric promotion is applied to the operands of these operators. The evaluation results in a `boolean` value. Relational operators have precedence lower than arithmetic operators, but higher than that of the assignment operators.

```
double  hours = 45.5;
boolean overtime = hours >= 35.0;    // true.
boolean order = 'A' < 'a';           // true. Binary numeric promotion applied.
Double time = 18.0;
boolean beforeMidnight = time < 24.0;// true. Binary numeric promotion applied.
```

Relational operators are nonassociative. Mathematical expressions like $a \le b \le c$ must be written using relational and boolean logical/conditional operators.

```
int a = 1, b = 7, c = 10;
boolean valid1 = a <= b <= c;        // (1) Illegal.
boolean valid2 = a <= b && b <= c;   // (2) OK.
```

Since relational operators have left associativity, the evaluation of the expression a <= b <= c at (1) in the examples above would proceed as follows: ((a <= b) <= c). Evaluation of (a <= b) would yield a `boolean` value that is not permitted as an operand of a relational operator, i.e., (*<boolean value>* <= c) would be illegal.

5.11 Equality

We distinguish between primitive data equality, object reference equality, and object value equality.

The equality operators have lower precedence than the relational operators, but higher than that of the assignment operators.

Primitive Data Value Equality: ==, !=

Given that a and b represent operands of primitive data types, the primitive data value equality operators are defined as shown in Table 5.8.

The equality operator == and the inequality operator != can be used to compare primitive data values, including `boolean` values. Binary numeric promotion is applied to the nonboolean operands of these equality operators.

Table 5.8 *Primitive Data Value Equality Operators*

a == b	Determines whether a and b are equal, i.e., have the same primitive value. (Equality)
a != b	Determines whether a and b are not equal, i.e., do not have the same primitive value. (Inequality)

```
int year = 2002;
boolean isEven  = year % 2 == 0;     // true.
boolean compare = '1' == 1;          // false. Binary numeric promotion applied.
boolean test    = compare == false;  // true.
```

Care must be exercised in comparing floating-point numbers for equality, as an infinite number of floating-point values can be stored in a finite number of bits only as approximations. For example, the expression (1.0 - 2.0/3.0 == 1.0/3.0) returns false, although mathematically the result should be true.

Analogous to the discussion for relational operators, mathematical expressions like $a = b = c$ must be written using relational and logical/conditional operators. Since equality operators have left associativity, the evaluation of the expression a == b == c would proceed as follows: ((a == b) == c). Evaluation of (a == b) would yield a boolean value that *is* permitted as an operand of a data value equality operator, but (*<boolean value>* == c) would be illegal if c had a numeric type. This problem is illustrated in the examples below. The expression at (1) is illegal, but those at (2) and (3) are legal.

```
int a, b, c;
a = b = c = 5;
boolean valid1 = a == b == c;        // (1) Illegal.
boolean valid2 = a == b && b == c;   // (2) Legal.
boolean valid3 = a == b == true;     // (3) Legal.
```

Object Reference Equality: ==, !=

The equality operator == and the inequality operator != can be applied to reference variables to test whether they refer to the same object. Given that r and s are reference variables, the reference equality operators are defined as shown in Table 5.9.

Table 5.9 *Reference Equality Operators*

r == s	Determines whether r and s are equal, i.e., have the same reference value and therefore refer to the same object (also called *aliases*). (Equality)
r != s	Determines whether r and s are not equal, i.e., do not have the same reference value and therefore refer to different objects. (Inequality)

The operands must be cast compatible: it must be possible to cast the reference value of the one into the other's type; otherwise, it is a compile-time error. Casting of references is discussed in Section 7.8, p. 319.

```
Pizza pizza_A = new Pizza("Sweet&Sour");        // new object
Pizza pizza_B = new Pizza("Sweet&Sour");        // new object
Pizza pizza_C = new Pizza("Hot&Spicy");         // new object

String banner = "Come and get it!";             // new object

boolean test  = banner  == pizza_A;             // (1) Compile-time error.
boolean test1 = pizza_A == pizza_B;             // false
boolean test2 = pizza_A == pizza_C;             // false

pizza_A = pizza_B;                              // Denote the same object, are aliases.
boolean test3 = pizza_A == pizza_B;             // true
```

The comparison banner == pizza_A in (1) is illegal, because the String and Pizza types are not related and therefore the reference value of one type cannot be cast to the other type. The values of test1 and test2 are false because the three references denote different objects, regardless of the fact that pizza_A and pizza_B are both sweet and sour pizzas. The value of test3 is true because now both pizza_A and pizza_B denote the same object.

The equality and inequality operators are applied to object references to check whether two references denote the same object or not. The state of the objects that the references denote is not compared. This is the same as testing whether the references are aliases, i.e., denoting the same object.

The null literal can be assigned to any reference variable, and the reference value in a reference variable can be compared for equality with the null literal. The comparison can be used to avoid inadvertent use of a reference variable that does not denote any object.

```
if (objRef != null) {
    // ... use objRef ...
}
```

Note that only when the type of *both* operands is either a reference type or the null type, do these operators test for object reference equality. Otherwise, they test for primitive data equality (see also Section 10.3, p. 432). In (2) below, binary numeric promotion involving unboxing is performed.

```
Integer iRef = 10;
boolean b1 = iRef == null;        // (1) object reference equality
boolean b2 = iRef == 10;          // (2) primitive data equality
```

Object Value Equality

The Object class provides the method public boolean equals(Object obj), which can be *overridden* (see Section 7.2, p. 288) to give the right semantics of *object value equality*. The default implementation of this method in the Object class returns true only if the object is compared with itself, i.e., as if the equality operator == had been used to compare aliases of an object. This means that if a class does not override the semantics of the equals() method from the Object class, object value equality is the same as object reference equality. For a detailed discussion on implementing the equals() method, see Section 15.1, p. 751.

Certain classes in the standard API override the equals() method, e.g., java.lang.String, java.util.Date, java.io.File and the wrapper classes for the primitive data types. For two String objects, value equality means they contain identical character sequences. For the wrapper classes, value equality means that the primitive values in the two wrapper objects are equal (see also Section 10.3, p. 432).

```
// Equality for String objects means identical character sequences.
String movie1 = new String("The Revenge of the Exception Handler");
String movie2 = new String("High Noon at the Java Corral");
String movie3 = new String("The Revenge of the Exception Handler");
boolean test0 = movie1.equals(movie2);          // false
boolean test1 = movie1.equals(movie3);          // true

// Equality for Boolean objects means same primitive value
Boolean flag1 = true;
Boolean flag2 = false;
boolean test2 = flag1.equals(flag2);            // false

// The Pizza class does not override the equals() method,
// can use either equals() inherited from Object or ==.
Pizza pizza1 = new Pizza("VeggiesDelight");
Pizza pizza2 = new Pizza("VeggiesDelight");
Pizza pizza3 = new Pizza("CheeseDelight");
boolean test3 = pizza1.equals(pizza2);          // false
boolean test4 = pizza1.equals(pizza3);          // false
boolean test5 = pizza1 == pizza2;               // false
pizza1 = pizza2;                                // Creates aliases
boolean test7 = pizza1.equals(pizza2);          // true
boolean test6 = pizza1 == pizza2;               // true
```

5.12 Boolean Logical Operators: !, ∧, &, |

Boolean logical operators include the unary operator ! (*logical complement*) and the binary operators & (*logical* AND), | (*logical inclusive* OR), and ∧ (*logical exclusive* OR, also called *logical* XOR). Boolean logical operators can be applied to boolean or Boolean operands, returning a boolean value. The operators &, |, and ∧ can also be applied to integral operands to perform *bitwise* logical operations (which are not covered in this book).

Given that x and y represent boolean expressions, the boolean logical operators are defined in Table 5.10.

These operators always evaluate both the operands, unlike their counterpart conditional operators && and || (see Section 5.13, p. 196). Unboxing is applied to the operand values, if necessary. Truth-values for boolean logical operators are shown in Table 5.10.

Table 5.10 *Truth-Values for Boolean Logical Operators*

x	y	!x	x & y	x | y	x ^ y
true	true	false	true	true	false
true	false	false	false	true	true
false	true	true	false	true	true
false	false	true	false	false	false

Operand Evaluation for Boolean Logical Operators

In the evaluation of boolean expressions involving boolean logical AND, XOR, and OR operators, both the operands are evaluated. The order of operand evaluation is always from left to right.

```
if (i > 0 & i++ < 10) {/*...*/} // i will be incremented, regardless of value in i.
```

The binary boolean logical operators have precedence lower than arithmetic and relational operators, but higher than assignment, conditional AND, and OR operators (see Section 5.13, p. 196). This is illustrated in the following examples:

```
boolean b1, b2, b3 = false, b4 = false;
Boolean b5 = true;
b1 = 4 == 2 & 1 < 4;          // false, evaluated as (b1 = ((4 == 2) & (1 < 4)))
b2 = b1 | !(2.5 >= 8);        // true
b3 = b3 ^ b5;                 // true, unboxing conversion on b5
b4 = b4 | b1 & b2;            // false
```

Order of evaluation is illustrated for the last example:

```
    (b4 = (b4 | (b1 & b2)))
 ⟹ (b4 = (false | (b1 & b2)))
 ⟹ (b4 = (false | (false & b2)))
 ⟹ (b4 = (false | (false & true)))
 ⟹ (b4 = (false | false))
 ⟹ (b4 = false)
```

Note that b2 was evaluated although, strictly speaking, it was not necessary. This behavior is guaranteed for boolean logical operators.

Boolean Logical Compound Assignment Operators: &=, ^=, |=

Compound assignment operators for the boolean logical operators are defined in Table 5.11. The left-hand operand must be a boolean variable, and the right-hand operand must be a boolean expression. An identity conversion is applied implicitly on assignment.

Table 5.11 *Boolean Logical Compound Assignment Operators*

Expression:	Given b and a Are of Type Boolean, the Expression Is Evaluated as:
b &= a	b = (b & (a))
b ^= a	b = (b ^ (a))
b |= a	b = (b | (a))

See also the discussion on arithmetic compound assignment operators in Section 5.6, p. 182. Here are some examples to illustrate the behavior of boolean logical compound assignment operators:

```
boolean b1 = false, b2 = false, b3 = false;
Boolean b4 = false;
b1 |= true;            // true
b4 ^= b1;              // (1) true, unboxing in (b4 ^ b1), boxing on assignment
b3 &= b1 | b2;         // (2) false. b3 = (b3 & (b1 | b2)).
b3 = b3 & b1 | b2;     // (3) true.  b3 = ((b3 & b1) | b2).
```

The assignment at (1) entails unboxing to evaluate the expression on the right-hand side, followed by boxing to assign the boolean result. It is also instructive to compare how the assignments at (2) and (3) above are performed, giving different results for the same value of the operands, showing how the precedence affects the evaluation.

5.13 Conditional Operators: &&, ||

The conditional operators && and || are similar to their counterpart logical operators & and |, except that their evaluation is *short-circuited*. Given that x and y represent values of boolean or Boolean expressions, the conditional operators are defined in Table 5.12. In the table, the operators are listed in decreasing precedence order.

Table 5.12 *Conditional Operators*

Conditional AND	x && y	true if both operands are true; otherwise, false.
Conditional OR	x || y	true if either or both operands are true; otherwise, false.

Unlike their logical counterparts & and |, which can also be applied to integral operands for bitwise operations, the conditional operators && and || can only be applied to boolean operands. Their evaluation results in a boolean value. Truth-values for conditional operators are shown in Table 5.13. Not surprisingly, they have the same truth-values as their counterpart logical operators.

Note that, unlike their logical counterparts, there are no compound assignment operators for the conditional operators.

Table 5.13 *Truth-values for Conditional Operators*

x	y	x && y	x || y
true	true	true	true
true	false	false	true
false	true	false	true
false	false	false	false

Short-Circuit Evaluation

In evaluation of boolean expressions involving conditional AND and OR, the left-hand operand is evaluated before the right one, and the evaluation is short-circuited (i.e., if the result of the boolean expression can be determined from the left-hand operand, the right-hand operand is not evaluated). In other words, the right-hand operand is evaluated conditionally.

The binary conditional operators have precedence lower than either arithmetic, relational, or logical operators, but higher than assignment operators. Unboxing of the operand value takes place when necessary, before the operation is performed. The following examples illustrate usage of conditional operators:

```
Boolean b1 = 4 == 2 && 1 < 4;    // false, short-circuit evaluated as
                                 // (b1 = ((4 == 2) && (1 < 4)))
boolean b2 = !b1 || 2.5 > 8;     // true, short-circuit evaluated as
                                 // (b2 = ((!b1) || (2.5 > 8)))
Boolean b3 = !(b1 && b2);        // true
boolean b4 = b1 || !b3 && b2;    // false, short-circuit evaluated as
                                 // (b4 = (b1 || ((!b3) && b2)))
```

The order of evaluation for computing the value of boolean variable b4 proceeds as follows:

```
    (b4 = (b1 || ((!b3) && b2)))
 ⟹ (b4 = (false || ((!b3) && b2)))
 ⟹ (b4 = (false || ((!true) && b2)))
 ⟹ (b4 = (false || ((false) && b2)))
 ⟹ (b4 = (false || false))
 ⟹ (b4 = false)
```

Note that b2 is not evaluated, short-circuiting the evaluation. Example 5.3 illustrates the short-circuit evaluation of the initialization expressions in the declaration statements above. In addition, it shows an evaluation (see the declaration of b5) involving boolean logical operators that always evaluate both operands. See also Example 5.1 that uses a similar approach to illustrate the order of operand evaluation in arithmetic expressions.

Example 5.3   *Short-Circuit Evaluation Involving Conditional Operators*

```java
public class ShortCircuit {
  public static void main(String[] args) {
    // Boolean b1 = 4 == 2 && 1 < 4;
    Boolean b1 = operandEval(1, 4 == 2) && operandEval(2, 1 < 4);
    System.out.println();
    System.out.println("Value of b1: " + b1);

    // boolean b2 = !b1 || 2.5 > 8;
    boolean b2 = !operandEval(1, b1) || operandEval(2, 2.5 > 8);
    System.out.println();
    System.out.println("Value of b2: " + b2);

    // Boolean b3 = !(b1 && b2);
    Boolean b3 = !(operandEval(1, b1) && operandEval(2, b2));
    System.out.println();
    System.out.println("Value of b3: " + b3);

    // boolean b4 = b1 || !b3 && b2;
    boolean b4 = operandEval(1, b1) || !operandEval(2, b3) && operandEval(3, b2);
    System.out.println();
    System.out.println("Value of b4: " + b4);

    // boolean b5 = b1 | !b3 & b2;     // Using boolean logical operators
    boolean b5 = operandEval(1, b1) | !operandEval(2, b3) & operandEval(3, b2);
    System.out.println();
    System.out.println("Value of b5: " + b5);
  }

  static boolean operandEval(int opNum, boolean operand) {         // (1)
    System.out.print(opNum);
    return operand;
  }
}
```

Output from the program:

```
1
Value of b1: false
1
Value of b2: true
1
Value of b3: true
12
Value of b4: false
123
Value of b5: false
```

Short-circuit evaluation can be used to ensure that a reference variable denotes an object before it is used.

```java
if (objRef != null && objRef.doIt()) { /*...*/ }
```

The method call is now conditionally dependent on the left-hand operand and will not be executed if the variable objRef has the null reference. If we use the logical & operator and the variable objRef has the null reference, evaluation of the right-hand operand will result in a NullPointerException.

In summary, we employ the conditional operators && and | | if the evaluation of the right-hand operand is conditionally dependent on the left-hand operand. We use the boolean logical operators & and | if both operands must be evaluated. The subtlety of conditional operators is illustrated by the following examples:

```
if (i > 0 && i++ < 10) {/*...*/}   // i is not incremented if i > 0 is false.
if (i > 0 || i++ < 10) {/*...*/}   // i is not incremented if i > 0 is true.
```

 ## Review Questions

5.15   Which of the following expressions evaluate to true?

Select the two correct answers.

(a) (false | true)
(b) (null != null)
(c) (4 <= 4)
(d) (!true)
(e) (true & false)

5.16   Which statements are true?

Select the two correct answers.

(a) The remainder operator % can only be used with integral operands.
(b) Short-circuit evaluation occurs with boolean logical operators.
(c) The arithmetic operators *, /, and % have the same level of precedence.
(d) A short value ranges from -128 to +127, inclusive.
(e) (+15) is a legal expression.

5.17   Which statements are true about the lines of output printed by the following program?

```
public class BoolOp {
  static void op(boolean a, boolean b) {
    boolean c = a != b;
    boolean d = a ^ b;
    boolean e = c == d;
    System.out.println(e);
  }

  public static void main(String[] args) {
    op(false, false);
    op(true, false);
    op(false, true);
    op(true, true);
  }
}
```

Select the three correct answers.

(a) All lines printed are the same.
(b) At least one line contains false.
(c) At least one line contains true.
(d) The first line contains false.
(e) The last line contains true.

5.18   What is the result of running the following program?

```
public class OperandOrder {
  public static void main(String[] args) {
    int i = 0;
    int[] a = {3,6};
    a[i] = i = 9;
    System.out.println(i + " " + a[0] + " " + a[1]);
  }
}
```

Select the one correct answer.

(a) When run, the program throws an exception of type ArrayIndexOutOfBoundsEx-
     ception.
(b) When run, the program will print "9 9 6".
(c) When run, the program will print "9 0 6".
(d) When run, the program will print "9 3 6".
(e) When run, the program will print "9 3 9".

5.19   Which statements are true about the output from the following program?

```
public class Logic {
  public static void main(String[] args) {
    int i = 0;
    int j = 0;

    boolean t = true;
    boolean r;

    r = (t &  0 < (i+=1));
    r = (t && 0 < (i+=2));
    r = (t |  0 < (j+=1));
    r = (t || 0 < (j+=2));
    System.out.println(i + " " + j);
  }
}
```

Select the two correct answers.

(a) The first digit printed is 1.
(b) The first digit printed is 2.
(c) The first digit printed is 3.
(d) The second digit printed is 1.
(e) The second digit printed is 2.
(f) The second digit printed is 3.

5.14 The Conditional Operator: ?:

The ternary conditional operator allows conditional expressions to be defined. The operator has the following syntax:

> *<condition>* ? *<expression₁>* : *<expression₂>*

If the boolean expression *<condition>* is true then *<expression₁>* is evaluated; otherwise, *<expression₂>* is evaluated. Of course, *<expression₁>* and *<expression₂>* must evaluate to values of compatible types. The value of the expression evaluated is returned by the conditional expression.

```
boolean leapYear = false;
int daysInFebruary = leapYear ? 29 : 28;   // 28
```

The conditional operator is the expression equivalent of the if-else statement (Section 6.2, p. 205). The conditional expression can be nested and the conditional operator associates from right to left:

```
(a?b?c?d:e:f:g) evaluates as (a?(b?(c?d:e):f):g)
```

5.15 Other Operators: new, [], instanceof

The new operator is used to create objects, i.e., instances of classes and arrays. It is used with a constructor call to instantiate classes (see Section 3.4, p. 48), and with the [] notation to create arrays (see Section 3.6, p. 70). It is also used to instantiate anonymous arrays (see Section 3.6, p. 74), and anonymous classes (see Section 8.5, p. 377).

```
Pizza onePizza = new Pizza();       // Create an instance of the Pizza class.
```

The [] notation is used to declare and construct arrays and also to access array elements (see Section 3.6, p. 69).

```
int[] anArray = new int[5];// Declare and construct an int array of 5 elements.
anArray[4] = anArray[3];   // Element at index 4 gets value of element at index 3.
```

The boolean, binary, and infix operator instanceof is used to test the type of an object (see Section 7.11, p. 327).

```
Pizza myPizza = new Pizza();
boolean test1 = myPizza instanceof Pizza; // True.
boolean test2 = "Pizza" instanceof Pizza; // Compile error. String is not Pizza.
boolean test3 = null instanceof Pizza;    // Always false. null is not an instance.
```

Chapter Summary

The following information was included in this chapter:

- type conversion categories and conversion contexts, and which conversions are permissible in each conversion context.

- operators in Java, including precedence and associativity rules.

- defining and evaluating arithmetic and boolean expressions, and the order in which operands and operators are evaluated.

Programming Exercise

5.1   The program below is supposed to calculate and print the time it takes for light to travel from the sun to the earth. It contains some logical errors. Fix the program so that it will compile and print the correct result when run.

```java
//Filename: Sunlight.java
public class Sunlight {
  public static void main(String[] args) {
    // Distance from sun (150 million kilometers)
    int kmFromSun = 150000000;

    int lightSpeed = 299792458; // meters per second

    // Convert distance to meters.
    int mFromSun = kmFromSun * 1000;

    int seconds = mFromSun / lightSpeed;

    System.out.print("Light will use ");
    printTime(seconds);
    System.out.println(" to travel from the sun to the earth.");
  }

  public static void printTime(int sec) {
    int min = sec / 60;
    sec = sec - (min * 60);
    System.out.print(min + " minute(s) and " + sec + " second(s)");
  }
}
```

Control Flow

6

Exam Objectives

2.1 Develop code that implements an `if` or `switch` statement; and identify legal argument types for these statements.

2.2 Develop code that implements all forms of loops and iterators, including the use of `for`, the enhanced `for` loop (for-each), `do`, `while`, labels, `break`, and `continue`; and explain the values taken by loop counter variables during and after loop execution.

2.3 Develop code that makes use of assertions, and distinguish appropriate from inappropriate uses of assertions.

2.4 Develop code that makes use of exceptions and exception handling clauses (`try`, `catch`, `finally`), and declares methods and overriding methods that throw exceptions.

2.5 Recognize the effect of an exception arising at a specified point in a code fragment. Note that the exception may be a runtime exception, a checked exception, or an error.

2.6 Recognize situations that will result in any of the following being thrown: `ArrayIndexOutOfBoundsException`, `ClassCastException`, `IllegalArgumentException`, `IllegalStateException`, `NullPointerException`, `NumberFormatException`, `AssertionError`, `ExceptionInInitializerError`, `StackOverflowError`, or `NoClassDefFoundError`. Understand which of these are thrown by the virtual machine and recognize situations in which others should be thrown programmatically.

Supplementary Objectives

- Understand method execution.
- Understand exception propagation through the runtime stack.

6.1 Overview of Control Flow Statements

Control flow statements govern *the flow of control* in a program during execution, i.e., the order in which statements are executed in a running program. There are three main categories of control flow statements:

- *Selection* statements: if, if-else, and switch.
- *Iteration* statements: while, do-while, basic for, and enhanced for.
- *Transfer* statements: break, continue, return, try-catch-finally, throw, and assert.

6.2 Selection Statements

Java provides selection statements that allow the program to choose between alternative actions during execution. The choice is based on criteria specified in the selection statement. These selection statements are

- simple if statement
- if-else statement
- switch statement

The Simple if Statement

The simple if statement has the following syntax:

```
if (<conditional expression>)
    <statement>
```

It is used to decide whether an action is to be performed or not, based on a condition. The condition is specified by *<conditional expression>* and the action to be performed is specified by *<statement>*, which can be a single statement or a code block. The *<conditional expression>* must evaluate to a boolean or a Boolean value. In the latter case, the Boolean value is unboxed to the corresponding boolean value.

The semantics of the simple if statement are straightforward. The *<conditional expression>* is evaluated first. If its value is true, *<statement>* (called the if block) is executed and execution continues with the rest of the program. If the value is false, the if block is skipped and execution continues with the rest of the program. The semantics are illustrated by the activity diagram in Figure 6.1a.

In the following examples of the if statement, it is assumed that the variables and the methods have been appropriately defined:

```
if (emergency)              // emergency is a boolean variable
    operate();

if (temperature > critical)
    soundAlarm();
```

Figure 6.1   *Activity Diagram for* if *Statements*

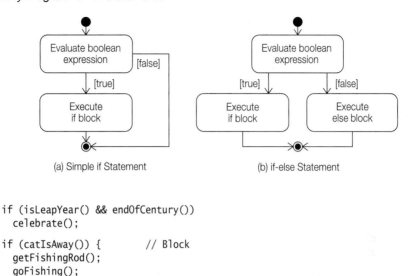

(a) Simple if Statement   (b) if-else Statement

```
if (isLeapYear() && endOfCentury())
   celebrate();

if (catIsAway()) {          // Block
   getFishingRod();
   goFishing();
}
```

Note that *<statement>* can be a *block*, and the block notation is necessary if more than one statement is to be executed when the *<conditional expression>* is true.

Since the *<conditional expression>* evaluates to a boolean value, it avoids a common programming error: using an expression of the form (a=b) as the condition, where inadvertently an assignment operator is used instead of a relational operator. The compiler will flag this as an error, unless both a and b are boolean.

Note that the if block can be any valid statement. In particular, it can be the empty statement (;) or the empty block ({}). A common programming error is an inadvertent use of the empty statement.

```
if (emergency); // Empty if block
   operate();    // Executed regardless of whether it was an emergency or not.
```

The if-else **Statement**

The if-else statement is used to decide between two actions, based on a condition. It has the following syntax:

```
if (<conditional expression>)
   <statement₁>
else
   <statement₂>
```

The *<conditional expression>* is evaluated first. If its value is true (or unboxed to true), *<statement₁>* (the if block) is executed and execution continues with the rest of the program. If the value is false (or unboxed to false), *<statement₂>* (the else block) is executed and execution continues with the rest of the program. In other words, one of two mutually exclusive actions is performed. The else clause is optional; if omitted, the construct is equivalent to the simple if statement. The semantics are illustrated by the activity diagram in Figure 6.1b.

In the following examples of the if-else statement, it is assumed that all variables and methods have been appropriately defined:

```
if (emergency)
  operate();
else
  joinQueue();

if (temperature > critical)
  soundAlarm();
else
  businessAsUsual();

if (catIsAway()) {
  getFishingRod();
  goFishing();
} else
  playWithCat();
```

Since actions can be arbitrary statements, the if statements can be nested.

```
if (temperature >= upperLimit) {     // (1)
  if (danger)                        // (2) Simple if.
    soundAlarm();
  if (critical)                      // (3)
    evacuate();
  else                               // Goes with if at (3).
    turnHeaterOff();
} else                               // Goes with if at (1).
    turnHeaterOn();
```

The use of the block notation, {}, can be critical to the execution of if statements. The if statements (A) and (B) in the following examples do *not* have the same meaning. The if statements (B) and (C) are the same, with extra indentation used in (C) to make the meaning evident. Leaving out the block notation in this case could have catastrophic consequences: the heater could be turned on when the temperature is above the upper limit.

```
// (A):
if (temperature > upperLimit) {      // (1) Block notation.
  if (danger) soundAlarm();          // (2)
} else                               // Goes with if at (1).
  turnHeaterOn();

// (B):
if (temperature > upperLimit)        // (1) Without block notation.
  if (danger) soundAlarm();          // (2)
else turnHeaterOn();                 // Goes with if at (2).

// (C):
if (temperature > upperLimit)        // (1)
  if (danger)                        // (2)
    soundAlarm();
  else                               // Goes with if at (2).
    turnHeaterOn();
```

The rule for matching an else clause is that an else clause always refers to the nearest if that is not already associated with another else clause. Block notation and proper indentation can be used to make the meaning obvious.

Cascading if-else statements are a sequence of nested if-else statements where the if of the next if-else statement is joined to the else clause of the previous one. The decision to execute a block is then based on all the conditions evaluated so far.

```
if (temperature >= upperLimit) {                                 // (1)
  soundAlarm();
  turnHeaterOff();
} else if (temperature < lowerLimit) {                           // (2)
  soundAlarm();
  turnHeaterOn();
} else if (temperature == (upperLimit-lowerLimit)/2) {           // (3)
  doingFine();
} else                                                           // (4)
  noCauseToWorry();
```

The block corresponding to the first if condition that evaluates to true is executed, and the remaining ifs are skipped. In the example given above, the block at (3) will execute only if the conditions at (1) and (2) are false and the condition at (3) is true. If none of the conditions are true, the block associated with the last else clause is executed. If there is no last else clause, no actions are performed.

The switch **Statement**

Conceptually, the switch statement can be used to choose one among many alternative actions, based on the value of an expression. Its general form is as follows:

```
switch (<switch expression>) {
  case label₁: <statement₁>
  case label₂: <statement₂>
  ...
  case labelₙ: <statementₙ>
  default:    <statement>
} // end switch
```

The syntax of the switch statement comprises a switch expression followed by the switch body, which is a block of statements. The type of the switch expression is either an enumerated type or one of the following types: char, byte, short, int, or the corresponding wrapper type for these primitive types. The statements in the switch body can be labeled, this defines entry points in the switch body where control can be transferred depending on the value of the switch expression. The execution of the switch statement is as follows:

- The switch expression is evaluated first. If the value is a wrapper type, an unboxing conversion is performed.

- The value of the switch expression is compared with the case labels. Control is transferred to the <statement₁> associated with the case label that is equal to the value of the switch expression. After execution of the associated statement, control *falls through* to the *next* statement unless appropriate action is taken.

• If no case label is equal to the value of the switch expression, the statement associated with the default label is executed.

Figure 6.2 illustrates the flow of control through a switch statement where the default label is declared last.

All labels (including the default label) are optional, and can be defined in any order in the switch body. There can be at the most one default label in a switch statement. If no valid case labels are found and the default label is left out, the whole switch statement is skipped.

The case labels are constant expressions whose values must be unique, meaning no duplicate values are allowed. As a matter of fact, a case label must be a compile-time constant expression whose value must be *assignable* to the type of the switch expression (see Section 5.2, p. 163). In particular, all the case label values must be in the range of the type of the switch expression. Note that the type of the case label cannot be boolean, long, or floating-point.

Figure 6.2   *Activity Diagram for a* switch *Statement*

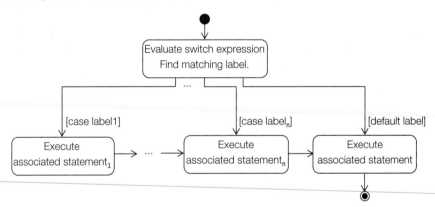

Example 6.1   *Fall Through in a* switch *Statement*

```java
public class Advice {

    public final static int LITTLE_ADVICE   = 0;
    public final static int MORE_ADVICE     = 1;
    public final static int LOTS_OF_ADVICE  = 2;

    public static void main(String[] args) {
        dispenseAdvice(LOTS_OF_ADVICE);
    }
```

```
    public static void dispenseAdvice(int howMuchAdvice) {
      switch(howMuchAdvice) {                              // (1)
        case LOTS_OF_ADVICE:
          System.out.println("See no evil.");             // (2)
        case MORE_ADVICE:
          System.out.println("Speak no evil.");           // (3)
        case LITTLE_ADVICE:
          System.out.println("Hear no evil.");            // (4)
          break;                                          // (5)
        default:
          System.out.println("No advice.");               // (6)
      }
    }
  }
```

Output from the program:

```
See no evil.
Speak no evil.
Hear no evil.
```

In Example 6.1, depending on the value of the howMuchAdvice parameter, different advice is printed in the switch statement at (1) in the method dispenseAdvice(). The example shows the output when the value of the howMuchAdvice parameter is LOTS_OF_ADVICE. In the switch statement, the associated statement at (2) is executed, giving one advice. Control then falls through to the statement at (3), giving the second advice. Control falls through to (4), dispensing the third advice, and finally, executing the break statement at (5) causes control to exit the switch statement. Without the break statement at (5), control would continue to fall through the remaining statements, if there were any. Execution of the break statement in a switch body transfers control out of the switch statement (see Section 6.4, p. 224). If the parameter howMuchAdvice has the value MORE_ADVICE, then the advice at (3) and (4) are given. The value LITTLE_ADVICE results in only one advice at (4) being given. Any other value results in the default action, which announces that there is no advice.

The associated statement of a case label can be a *list* of statements (which need *not* be a statement block). The case label is prefixed to the first statement in each case. This is illustrated by the associated statement for the case label LITTLE_ADVICE in Example 6.1, which comprises statements (4) and (5).

Example 6.2 makes use of a break statement inside a switch statement to convert a char value representing a digit to its corresponding word in English. Note that the break statement is the last statement in the list of statements associated with each case label. It is easy to think that the break statement is a part of the switch statement syntax, but technically it is not.

Example 6.2   *Using* break *in a* switch *Statement*

```java
public class Digits {

  public static void main(String[] args) {
    System.out.println(digitToString('7') + " " + digitToString('8') + " " +
                       digitToString('6'));
  }

  public static String digitToString(char digit) {
    String str = "";
    switch(digit) {
      case '1': str = "one";   break;
      case '2': str = "two";   break;
      case '3': str = "three"; break;
      case '4': str = "four";  break;
      case '5': str = "five";  break;
      case '6': str = "six";   break;
      case '7': str = "seven"; break;
      case '8': str = "eight"; break;
      case '9': str = "nine";  break;
      case '0': str = "zero";  break;
      default:  System.out.println(digit + " is not a digit!");
    }
    return str;
  }
}
```

Output from the program:

```
seven eight six
```

Several case labels can prefix the same statement. They will all result in the associated statement being executed. This is illustrated in Example 6.3 for the switch statement at (1).

The first statement in the switch body must have a case or default label, otherwise it is unreachable. This statement will never be executed, since control can never be transferred to it. The compiler will flag this as an error.

Since each action associated with a case label can be an arbitrary statement, it can be another switch statement. In other words, switch statements can be nested. Since a switch statement defines its own local block, the case labels in an inner block do not conflict with any case labels in an outer block. Labels can be redefined in nested blocks, unlike variables which cannot be redeclared in nested blocks (see Section 4.6, p. 131). In Example 6.3, an inner switch statement is defined at (2). This allows further refinement of the action to take on the value of the switch expression, in cases where multiple labels are used in the outer switch statement. A break statement terminates the innermost switch statement in which it is executed.

Example 6.3 *Nested* switch *Statement*

```
public class Seasons {

  public static void main(String[] args) {
    int monthNumber = 11;
    switch(monthNumber) {                                  // (1) Outer
      case 12: case 1: case 2:
        System.out.println("Snow in the winter.");
        break;
      case 3: case 4: case 5:
        System.out.println("Green grass in the spring.");
        break;
      case 6: case 7: case 8:
        System.out.println("Sunshine in the summer.");
        break;
      case 9: case 10: case 11:                            // (2)
        switch(monthNumber) { // Nested switch                (3) Inner
          case 10:
            System.out.println("Halloween.");
            break;
          case 11:
            System.out.println("Thanksgiving.");
            break;
        } // end nested switch
        // Always printed for case labels 9, 10, 11
        System.out.println("Yellow leaves in the fall.");    // (4)
        break;
      default:
        System.out.println(monthNumber + " is not a valid month.");
    }
  }
}
```

Output from the program:

```
Thanksgiving.
Yellow leaves in the fall.
```

Example 6.4 illustrates using enum types in a switch statement. The enum type SPICE_DEGREE is defined at (1). The type of the switch expression is SPICE_DEGREE. Note that the enum constants are *not* specified with their fully qualified name (see (2a). Using the fully qualified name results in a compile-time error, as shown at (2b). Only enum constants that have the same enum type as the switch expression can be specified as case label values. The semantics of the switch statement are the same as described earlier.

Example 6.4   *Enums in* switch *Statement*

```
public class SwitchingFun {

  enum SPICE_DEGREE {                                  // (1)
    MILD, MEDIUM, HOT, SUICIDE;
  }

  public static void main(String[] args) {
    SPICE_DEGREE spiceDegree = SPICE_DEGREE.HOT;
    switch (spiceDegree) {
      case HOT:                                        // (2a) OK!
//    case SPICE_LEVEL.HOT:                             // (2b) COMPILE-TIME ERROR!
        System.out.println("Have fun!");
        break;
      case SUICIDE:
        System.out.println("Good luck!");
        break;
      default:
        System.out.println("Enjoy!");
    }
  }
}
```

Output from the program:

```
Have fun!
```

Review Questions

6.1   What will be the result of attempting to compile and run the following class?

```
public class IfTest {
  public static void main(String[] args) {
    if (true)
    if (false)
    System.out.println("a");
    else
    System.out.println("b");
  }
}
```

Select the one correct answer.

(a) The code will fail to compile because the syntax of the if statement is incorrect.

(b) The code will fail to compile because the compiler will not be able to determine which if statement the else clause belongs to.

(c) The code will compile correctly and display the letter a, when run.

(d) The code will compile correctly and display the letter b, when run.

(e) The code will compile correctly, but will not display any output.

6.2 Which statements are true?

Select the three correct answers.

(a) The conditional expression in an if statement can have method calls.
(b) If a and b are of type boolean, the expression (a = b) can be the conditional expression of an if statement.
(c) An if statement can have either an if clause or an else clause.
(d) The statement if (false) ; else ; is illegal.
(e) Only expressions which evaluate to a boolean value can be used as the condition in an if statement.

6.3 What, if anything, is wrong with the following code?

```
void test(int x) {
  switch (x) {
    case 1:
    case 2:
    case 0:
    default:
    case 4:
  }
}
```

Select the one correct answer.

(a) The variable x does not have the right type for a switch expression.
(b) The case label 0 must precede case label 1.
(c) Each case section must end with a break statement.
(d) The default label must be the last label in the switch statement.
(e) The body of the switch statement must contain at least one statement.
(f) There is nothing wrong with the code.

6.4 Which of these combinations of switch expression types and case label value types are legal within a switch statement?

Select the two correct answers.

(a) switch expression of type int and case label value of type char.
(b) switch expression of type float and case label value of type int.
(c) switch expression of type byte and case label value of type float.
(d) switch expression of type char and case label value of type long.
(e) switch expression of type boolean and case label value of type boolean.
(f) switch expression of type Byte and case label value of type byte.
(g) switch expression of type byte and case label value of type Byte.

6.5 What will be the result of attempting to compile and run the following program?

```
public class Switching {
  public static void main(String[] args) {
    final int iLoc = 3;
    switch (6) {
      case 1:
```

```
      case iLoc:
      case 2 * iLoc:
        System.out.println("I am not OK.");
      default:
        System.out.println("You are OK.");
      case 4:
        System.out.println("It's OK.");
    }
  }
}
```

Select the one correct answer.

(a) The code will fail to compile because of the case label value 2 * iLoc.
(b) The code will fail to compile because the default label is not specified last in the switch statement.
(c) The code will compile correctly and will only print the following, when run:
```
I am not OK.
You are OK.
It's OK.
```
(d) The code will compile correctly and will only print the following, when run:
```
You are OK.
It's OK.
```
(e) The code will compile correctly and will only print the following, when run:
```
It's OK.
```

6.6 What will be the result of attempting to compile and run the following program?

```
public class MoreSwitching {
  public static void main(String[] args) {
    final int iLoc = 3;
    Integer iRef = 5;
    switch (iRef) {
      default:
        System.out.println("You are OK.");
      case 1:
      case iLoc:
      case 2 * iLoc:
        System.out.println("I am not OK.");
        break;
      case 4:
        System.out.println("It's OK.");
    }
  }
}
```

Select the one correct answer.

(a) The code will fail to compile because the type of the switch expression is not valid.
(b) The code will compile correctly and will only print the following, when run:
```
You are OK.
I am not OK.
```

(c) The code will compile correctly and will only print the following, when run:
```
You are OK.
I am not OK.
It's OK.
```
(d) The code will compile correctly and will only print the following, when run:
```
It's OK.
```

6.7   What will be the result of attempting to compile and run the following program?
```
public class KeepOnSwitching {
  public static void main(String[] args) {
    final int iLoc = 3;
    final Integer iFour = 4;
    Integer iRef = 4;
    switch (iRef) {
      case 1:
      case iLoc:
      case 2 * iLoc:
        System.out.println("I am not OK.");
      default:
        System.out.println("You are OK.");
      case iFour:
        System.out.println("It's OK.");
    }
  }
}
```

Select the one correct answer.
(a) The code will fail to compile because of the value of one of the case labels.
(b) The code will fail to compile because of the type of the switch expression.
(c) The code will compile correctly and will only print the following, when run:
```
You are OK.
It's OK.
```
(d) The code will compile correctly and will only print the following, when run:
```
It's OK.
```

6.8   What will be the result of attempting to compile and run the following code?
```
public enum Scale5 {
  GOOD, BETTER, BEST;

  public char getGrade() {
    char grade = '\u0000';
    switch(this){
      case GOOD:
        grade = 'C';
        break;
      case BETTER:
        grade = 'B';
        break;
      case BEST:
        grade = 'A';
```

```
        break;
    }
    return grade;
}

public static void main (String[] args) {
  System.out.println(GOOD.getGrade());
}
}
```

Select the one correct answer.

(a) The program will not compile because of the switch expression.

(b) The program will not compile, as enum constants cannot be used as case labels.

(c) The case labels must be qualified with the enum type name.

(d) The program compiles and only prints the following, when run:

C

(e) The program compiles and only prints the following, when run:

GOOD

(f) None of the above.

6.3 Iteration Statements

Loops allow a block of statements to be executed repeatedly (that is, iterated). A boolean condition (called the *loop condition*) is commonly used to determine when to terminate the loop. The statements executed in the loop constitute the *loop body*. The loop body can be a single statement or a block.

Java provides three language constructs for loop construction:

• the while statement

• the do-while statement

• the basic for statement

These loops differ in the order in which they execute the loop body and test the loop condition. The while loop and the basic for loop test the loop condition *before* executing the loop body, while the do-while loop tests the loop condition *after* execution of the loop body.

In addition to the basic for loop, there is a specialized one called the *enhanced* for loop (also called the *for-each* loop) that simplifies iterating over arrays and collections. We will use the notations for(;;) and for(:) to designate the basic for loop and the enhanced for loop, respectively.

The while **Statement**

The syntax of the while loop is

```
while (<loop condition>)
    <loop body>
```

The *<loop condition>* is evaluated before executing the *<loop body>*. The while state-ment executes the *<loop body>* as long as the *<loop condition>* is true. When the *<loop condition>* becomes false, the loop is terminated and execution continues with the statement immediately following the loop. If the *<loop condition>* is false to begin with, the *<loop body>* is not executed at all. In other words, a while loop can execute zero or more times. The *<loop condition>* must evaluate to a boolean or a Boolean value. In the latter case, the reference value is unboxed to a boolean value. The flow of control in a while statement is shown in Figure 6.3.

Figure 6.3   *Activity Diagram for the* while *Statement*

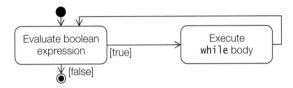

The while statement is normally used when the number of iterations is not known.

```
while (noSignOfLife())
    keepLooking();
```

Since the *<loop body>* can be any valid statement, inadvertently terminating each line with the empty statement (;) can give unintended results. Always using a block statement, { ... }, as the *<loop body>* helps to avoid such problems.

```
while (noSignOfLife());        // Empty statement as loop body!
    keepLooking();             // Statement not in the loop body.
```

The do-while **Statement**

The syntax of the do-while loop is

```
do
    <loop body>
while (<loop condition>);
```

The *<loop condition>* is evaluated *after* executing the *<loop body>*. The value of the *<loop condition>* is subjected to unboxing if it is of the type Boolean. The do-while statement executes the *<loop body>* until the *<loop condition>* becomes false. When the *<loop condition>* becomes false, the loop is terminated and execution continues with the statement immediately following the loop. Note that the *<loop body>* is exe-cuted at least once. Figure 6.4 illustrates the flow of control in a do-while statement.

Figure 6.4 *Activity Diagram for the* do-while *Statement*

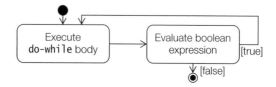

The *<loop body>* in a do-while loop is invariably a statement block. It is instructive to compare the while and the do-while loops. In the examples below, the mice might never get to play if the cat is not away, as in the loop at (1). The mice do get to play at least once (at the peril of losing their life) in the loop at (2).

```
while (cat.isAway()) {        // (1)
   mice.play();
}

do {                          // (2)
   mice.play();
} while (cat.isAway());
```

The for(;;) Statement

The for(;;) loop is the most general of all the loops. It is mostly used for counter-controlled loops, i.e., when the number of iterations is known beforehand.

The syntax of the loop is as follows:

```
for (<initialization>; <loop condition>; <increment expression>)
    <loop body>
```

The *<initialization>* usually declares and initializes a loop variable that controls the execution of the *<loop body>*. The *<loop condition>* must evaluate to a boolean or a Boolean value. In the latter case, the reference value is converted to a boolean value by unboxing. The *<loop condition>* usually involves the loop variable, and if the loop condition is true, the loop body is executed; otherwise, execution continues with the statement following the for(;;) loop. After each iteration (that is, execution of the loop body), the *<increment expression>* is executed. This usually modifies the value of the loop variable to ensure eventual loop termination. The loop condition is then tested to determine whether the loop body should be executed again. Note that the *<initialization>* is only executed once on entry to the loop. The semantics of the for(;;) loop are illustrated in Figure 6.5, and can be summarized by the following equivalent while loop code template:

```
<initialization>
while (<loop condition>) {
    <loop body>
    <increment expression>
}
```

Figure 6.5 *Activity Diagram for the* for *Statement*

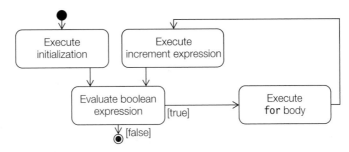

The following code creates an int array and sums the elements in the array.

```
int sum = 0;
int[] array = {12, 23, 5, 7, 19};
for (int index = 0; index < array.length; index++)    // (1)
  sum += array[index];
```

The loop variable index is declared and initialized in the *<initialization>* section of the loop. It is incremented in the *<increment expression>* section.

The for(;;) loop defines a local block so that the *scope* of this declaration is the for(;;) block, which comprises the *<initialization>*, the *<loop condition>*, the *<loop body>* and the *<increment expression>* sections. Any variable declared in the for(;;) block is thus not accessible after the for(;;) loop terminates. The loop at (1) showed how a declaration statement can be specified in the *<initialization>* section. Such a declaration statement can also specify a comma-separated list of variables.

```
for (int i = 0, j = 1, k = 2; ... ; ...) ...;      // (2)
```

The variables i, j, and k in the declaration statement all have type int. All variables declared in the *<initialization>* section are local variables in the for(;;) block and obey the scope rules for local blocks. However, note that the following code will not compile, as variable declarations of different types (in this case, int and String) require declaration statements that are terminated by semicolons:

```
for (int i = 0, String str = "@"; ... ; ...) ...;  // (3) Compile time error.
```

The *<initialization>* section can also be a comma-separated list of *expression* statements (see Section 3.3, p. 45). For example, the loop at (2) can be rewritten by factoring out the variable declaration.

```
int i, j, k;  // Variable declaration
for (i = 0, j = 1, k = 2; ... ; ...) ...;          // (4) Only initialization
```

The *<initialization>* section is now a comma-separated list of three expressions. The expressions in such a list are always evaluated from left to right. Note that the variables i, j, and k at (4) are not local to the loop.

Declaration statements cannot be mixed with expression statements in the *<initialization>* section, as is the case at (5) in the following example. Factoring out the variable declaration, as at (6), leaves a legal comma-separated list of expression statements only.

```java
// (5) Not legal and ugly:
for (int i = 0, System.out.println("This won't do!"); flag; i++) { // Error!
  // loop body
}

// (6) Legal, but still ugly:
int i;                                         // declaration factored out.
for (i = 0, System.out.println("This is legal!"); flag; i++) {    // OK.
  // loop body
}
```

The *<increment expression>* can also be a comma-separated list of expression statements. The following code specifies a for(;;) loop that has a comma-separated list of three variables in the *<initialization>* section, and a comma-separated list of two expressions in the *<increment expression>* section:

```java
// Legal usage but not recommended.
int[][] sqMatrix = { {3, 4, 6}, {5, 7, 4}, {5, 8, 9} };
for (int i = 0, j = sqMatrix[0].length - 1, asymDiagonal = 0;  // initialization
     i < sqMatrix.length;                                       // loop condition
     i++, j--)                                       // increment expression
  asymDiagonal += sqMatrix[i][j];                    // loop body
```

All sections in the for(;;) header are optional. Any or all of them can be left empty, but the two semicolons are mandatory. In particular, leaving out the *<loop condition>* signifies that the loop condition is true. The "crab", (;;), is commonly used to construct an infinite loop, where termination is presumably achieved through code in the loop body (see next section on transfer statements):

```java
for (;;) Java.programming();       // Infinite loop
```

The for(:) Statement

The enhanced for loop is convenient when we need to iterate over an array or a collection, especially when some operation needs to be performed on each element of the array or collection. In this section we discuss iterating over arrays, and in Chapter 15 we take a closer look at the for(:) loop for iterating over collections.

Earlier in this chapter we used a for(;;) loop to sum the values of elements in an int array:

```java
int sum = 0;
int[] intArray = {12, 23, 5, 7, 19};
for (int index = 0; index < intArray.length; index++) {    // (1) using for(;;) loop
  sum += intArray[index];
}
```

The for(;;) loop at (1) above is rewritten using the for(:) loop in Figure 6.6. The body of the loop is executed for each element in the array, where the variable element successively denotes the current element in the array intArray. When the loop terminates, the variable sum will contain the sum of all elements in the array. We do not care

Figure 6.6   *Enhanced* for *Statement*

element declaration   expression

```
         for (int element : intArray)
         {
loop body    sum += element;
         }
```

about the *position* of the elements in the array, just that the loop iterates over *all* elements of the array.

From Figure 6.6 we see that the for(:) loop header has two parts. The *expression* must evaluate to a reference value that refers to an array, i.e., the array we want to iterate over. The array can be an array of primitive values or objects, or even an array of arrays. The *expression* is only evaluated once. The *element declaration* specifies a local variable that can be assigned a value of the element type of the array. This assignment might require either a boxing or an unboxing conversion. The type of the array in the code snippet is int[], and the element type is int. Therefore, the element variable is declared to be of type int. The element variable is local to the loop block and is not accessible after the loop terminates. Also, changing the value of the current variable does *not* change any value in the array. The *loop body*, which can be a simple statement or a statement block, is executed for each element in the array and there is no danger of any out-of-bounds errors.

The for(:) loop has its limitations. We cannot change element values and it does not provide any provision for positional access using an index. The for(:) loop only increments by one and always in a forward direction. It does not allow iterations over several arrays simultaneously. Under such circumstances the for(;;) loop can be more convenient.

Here are some code examples of for(:) loops that are legal:

```
// Some 1-dim arrays:
int[] intArray = {10, 20, 30};
Integer[] intObjArray = {10, 20, 30};
String[] strArray = {"one", "two"};

// Some 2-dim arrays:
Object[][] objArrayOfArrays = {intObjArray, strArray};
Number[][] numArrayOfArrays = {{1.5, 2.5}, intObjArray, {100L, 200L}};
int[][] intArrayOfArrays = {{20}, intArray, {40}};

// Iterate over an array of Strings.
// Expression type is String[], and element type is String.
// String is assignable to Object.
for (Object obj : strArray) {}

// Iterate over an array of ints.
// Expression type is int[], and element type is int.
// int is assignable to Integer (boxing conversion)
for (Integer iRef : intArrayOfArrays[0]){}
```

```
// Iterate over an array of Integers.
// Expression type is Integer[], and element type is Integer.
// Integer is assignable to int (unboxing conversion)
for (int i : intObjArray){}

// Iterate over a 2-dim array of ints.
// Outer loop: expression type is int[][], and element type is int[].
// Inner loop: expression type is int[], element type is int.
for (int[] row : intArrayOfArrays)
  for (int val : row) {}

// Iterate over a 2-dim array of Numbers.
// Outer loop: expression type is Number[][], and element type is Number[].
// Outer loop: Number[] is assignable to Object[].
// Inner loop: expression type is Object[], element type is Object.
for (Object[] row : numArrayOfArrays)
  for (Object obj : row) {}

// Outer loop: expression type is Integer[][], and element type is Integer[].
// Outer loop: Integer[] is assignable to Number[].
// Inner loop: expression type is int[], and element type is int.
// Inner loop: int is assignable to double.
for (Number[] row : new Integer[][] {intObjArray, intObjArray, intObjArray})
  for (double num : new int[] {}) {}
```

Here are some code examples of for(:) loops that are not legal:

```
// Expression type is Number[][], element type is Number[].
// Number[] is not assignable to Number.
for (Number num : numArrayOfArrays) {}          // Compile-time error.

// Expression type is Number[], element type is Number.
// Number is not assignable to int.
for (int row : numArrayOfArrays[0]) {}           // Compile-time error.

// Outer loop: expression type is int[][], and element type is int[].
// int[] is not assignable to Integer[].
for (Integer[] row : intArrayOfArrays)           // Compile-time error.
  for (int val : row) {}

// Expression type is Object[][], and element type is Object[].
// Object[] is not assignable to Integer[].
for (Integer[] row : objArrayOfArrays) {}        // Compile-time error.

// Outer loop: expression type is String[], and element type is String.
// Inner loop: expression type is String which is not legal here.
for (String str : strArray)
  for (char val : str) {}                        // Compile-time error.
```

When using the for(:) loop to iterate over an array, the two main causes of errors are: the expression in the loop header does not represent an array and/or the element type of the array is not assignable to the local variable declared in the loop header.

6.4 Transfer Statements

Java provides six language constructs for transferring control in a program:

- break
- continue
- return
- try-catch-finally
- throw
- assert

This section discusses the first three statements, and the remaining statements are discussed in subsequent sections.

Note that Java does not have a goto statement, although goto is a reserved word.

Labeled Statements

A statement may have a *label*.

> *<label>* : *<statement>*

A label is any valid identifier and it always immediately precedes the statement. Label names exist in their own name space, so that they do not conflict with names of packages, classes, interfaces, methods, fields, and local variables. The scope of a label is the statement prefixed by the label, meaning that it cannot be redeclared as a label inside the labeled statement—analogous to the scope of local variables.

```
L1: if (i > 0) {
  L1: System.out.println(i);    // (1) Not OK. Label redeclared.
}

L1: while (i < 0) {             // (2) OK.
  L2: System.out.println(i);
}

L1: {                           // (3) OK. Labeled block.
  int j = 10;
  System.out.println(j);
}

L1: try {                       // (4) OK. Labeled try-catch-finally block.
  int j = 10, k = 0;
  L2: System.out.println(j/k);
} catch (ArithmeticException ae) {
  L3: ae.printStackTrace();
} finally {
  L4: System.out.println("Finally done.");
}
```

A statement can have multiple labels:

```
LabelA: LabelB: System.out.println("Mutliple labels. Use judiciously.");
```

A declaration statement cannot have a label:

```
L0: int i = 0;                     // Compile time error.
```

A labeled statement is executed as if it was unlabeled, unless it is the break or continue statement. This is discussed in the next two subsections.

The break **Statement**

The break statement comes in two forms: the *unlabeled* and the *labeled* form.

```
break;             // the unlabeled form
break <label>;     // the labeled form
```

The unlabeled break statement terminates loops (for(;;), for(:), while, do-while) and switch statements, and transfers control out of the current context (i.e., the closest enclosing block). The rest of the statement body is skipped, and execution continues after the enclosing statement.

In Example 6.5, the break statement at (1) is used to terminate a for loop. Control is transferred to (2) when the value of i is equal to 4 at (1), skipping the rest of the loop body and terminating the loop.

Example 6.5 also shows that the unlabeled break statement only terminates the innermost loop or switch statement that contains the break statement. The break statement at (3) terminates the inner for loop when j is equal to 2, and execution continues in the outer switch statement at (4) after the for loop.

Example 6.5   *The* break *Statement*

```
class BreakOut {

  public static void main(String[] args) {

    for (int i = 1; i <= 5; ++i) {
      if (i == 4)
        break; // (1) Terminate loop. Control to (2).
      // Rest of loop body skipped when i gets the value 4.
      System.out.printf("%d     %.2f%n", i, Math.sqrt(i));
    } // end for
    // (2) Continue here.

    int n = 2;
    switch (n) {
      case 1:
        System.out.println(n);
        break;
      case 2:
        System.out.println("Inner for loop: ");
```

```
                    for (int j = 0; j <= n; j++)
                       if (j == 2)
                          break; // (3) Terminate loop. Control to (4).
                       else
                          System.out.println(j);
                default:
                    System.out.println("default: " + n); // (4) Continue here.
            }
        }
    }
```

Output from the program:

```
1    1.00
2    1.41
3    1.73
Inner for loop:
0
1
default: 2
```

A labeled break statement can be used to terminate *any* labeled statement that contains the break statement. Control is then transferred to the statement following the enclosing labeled statement. In the case of a labeled block, the rest of the block is skipped and execution continues with the statement following the block:

```
out:
{                                    // (1) Labeled block
    // ...
    if (j == 10) break out;          // (2) Terminate block. Control to (3).
    System.out.println(j);           // Rest of the block not executed if j == 10.
    // ...
}
// (3) Continue here.
```

In Example 6.6, the program continues to add the elements below the diagonal of a square matrix until the sum is greater than 10. Two nested for loops are defined at (1) and (2). The outer loop is labeled outer at (1). The unlabeled break statement at (3) transfers control to (5) when it is executed, that is, it terminates the inner loop and control is transferred to the statement after the inner loop. The labeled break statement at (4) transfers control to (6) when it is executed (i.e., it terminates both the inner and the outer loop, transferring control to the statement after the loop labeled outer).

Example 6.6   *Labeled* break *Statement*

```
class LabeledBreakOut {
  public static void main(String[] args) {
    int[][] squareMatrix = {{4, 3, 5}, {2, 1, 6}, {9, 7, 8}};
    int sum = 0;
    outer:                                        // label
      for (int i = 0; i < squareMatrix.length; ++i){    // (1)
```

```
        for (int j = 0; j < squareMatrix[i].length; ++j) {  // (2)
            if (j == i) break;          // (3) Terminate this loop.
            //      Control to (5).
            System.out.println("Element[" + i + ", " + j + "]: " +
                                    squareMatrix[i][j]);
            sum += squareMatrix[i][j];
            if (sum > 10) break outer;// (4) Terminate both loops.
            // Control to (6).
        } // end inner loop
        // (5) Continue with outer loop.
    } // end outer loop
    // (6) Continue here.
    System.out.println("sum: " + sum);
  }
}
```

Output from the program:

```
Element[1, 0]: 2
Element[2, 0]: 9
sum: 11
```

The continue Statement

Like the break statement, the continue statement also comes in two forms: the *unlabeled* and the *labeled* form.

```
continue;              // the unlabeled form
continue <label>;      // the labeled form
```

The continue statement can only be used in a for(;;), for(:), while, or do-while loop to prematurely stop the current iteration of the loop body and proceed with the next iteration, if possible. In the case of the while and do-while loops, the rest of the loop body is skipped, that is, stopping the current iteration, with execution continuing with the *<loop condition>*. In the case of the for(;;) loop, the rest of the loop body is skipped, with execution continuing with the *<increment expression>*.

In Example 6.7, an unlabeled continue statement is used to skip an iteration in a for(;;) loop. Control is transferred to (2) when the value of i is equal to 4 at (1), skipping the rest of the loop body and continuing with the *<increment expression>* in the for statement.

Example 6.7   continue *Statement*

```
class Skip {
  public static void main(String[] args) {
    for (int i = 1; i <= 5; ++i) {
      if (i == 4) continue;              // (1) Control to (2).
      // Rest of loop body skipped when i has the value 4.
      System.out.printf("%d     %.2f%n", i, Math.sqrt(i));
      // (2) Continue with increment expression.
```

```
        } // end for
      }
    }
```

Output from the program:

```
    1    1.00
    2    1.41
    3    1.73
    5    2.24
```

A labeled continue statement must occur within a labeled loop that has the same label. Execution of the labeled continue statement then transfers control to the end of that enclosing labeled loop. In Example 6.8, the unlabeled continue statement at (3) transfers control to (5) when it is executed; i.e., the rest of the loop body is skipped and execution continues with the next iteration of the inner loop. The labeled continue statement at (4) transfers control to (6) when it is executed (i.e., it terminates the inner loop but execution continues with the next iteration of the loop labeled outer). It is instructive to compare the output from Example 6.6 (labeled break) and Example 6.8 (labeled continue).

Example 6.8 *Labeled* continue *Statement*

```
class LabeledSkip {
  public static void main(String[] args) {
    int[][] squareMatrix = {{4, 3, 5}, {2, 1, 6}, {9, 7, 8}};
    int sum = 0;
    outer:                                        // label
      for (int i = 0; i < squareMatrix.length; ++i){      // (1)
        for (int j = 0; j < squareMatrix[i].length; ++j) {  // (2)
          if (j == i) continue;                   // (3) Control to (5).
          System.out.println("Element[" + i + ", " + j + "]: " +
            squareMatrix[i][j]);
          sum += squareMatrix[i][j];
          if (sum > 10) continue outer;           // (4) Control to (6).
          // (5) Continue with inner loop.
        } // end inner loop
        // (6) Continue with outer loop.
      } // end outer loop
    System.out.println("sum: " + sum);
  }
}
```

Output from the program:

```
Element[0, 1]: 3
Element[0, 2]: 5
Element[1, 0]: 2
Element[1, 2]: 6
Element[2, 0]: 9
sum: 25
```

The return **Statement**

The return statement is used to stop execution of a method and transfer control back to the calling code (also called the *caller*). The usage of the two forms of the return statement is dictated by whether it is used in a void or a non-void method (see Table 6.1). The first form does not return any value to the calling code, but the second form does. Note that the keyword void does not represent any type.

In Table 6.1, the *<expression>* must evaluate to a primitive value or a reference value, and its type must be *assignable* to the *return type* specified in the method header (see Section 5.5, p. 169 and Section 7.9, p. 320). See also the discussion on covariant return in connection with method overriding in Section 7.2.

As can be seen from Table 6.1, a void method need not have a return statement—in which case the control normally returns to the caller after the last statement in the method's body has been executed. However, a void method can only specify the first form of the return statement. This form of the return statement can also be used in constructors, as these also do not return a value.

Table 6.1 also shows that the first form of the return statement is not allowed in a non-void method. The second form of the return statement is mandatory in a non-void method, if the method execution is not terminated programmatically, for example, by throwing an exception. Example 6.9 illustrates the use of the return statement summarized in Table 6.1.

Table 6.1 *The return Statement*

Form of return Statement	In void **Method**	In Non-void **Method**
return;	optional	not allowed
return *<expression>*;	not allowed	mandatory, if the method is not terminated explicitly

Example 6.9 *The return Statement*

```
public class ReturnDemo {

  public static void main (String[] args) { // (1) void method can use return.
    if (args.length == 0) return;
    output(checkValue(args.length));
  }

  static void output(int value) {  // (2) void method need not use return.
    System.out.println(value);
    return 'a';                      // Not OK. Can not return a value.
  }
```

```
      static int checkValue(int i) {    // (3) Non-void method: Any return statement
                                        //     must return a value.
        if (i > 3)
          return i;                     // OK.
        else
          return 2.0;                   // Not OK. double not assignable to int.
      }

      static int AbsentMinded() {       // (4) Non-void method
        throw new RuntimeException();    // OK: No return statement provided, but
                                        // method terminates by throwing an exception.
      }
    }
```

 Review Questions

6.9 What will be the result of attempting to compile and run the following code?

```
class MyClass {
  public static void main(String[] args) {
    boolean b = false;
    int i = 1;
    do {
      i++;
      b = ! b;
    } while (b);
    System.out.println(i);
  }
}
```

Select the one correct answer.

(a) The code will fail to compile because b is an invalid conditional expression for the do-while statement.
(b) The code will fail to compile because the assignment b = ! b is not allowed.
(c) The code will compile without error and will print 1, when run.
(d) The code will compile without error and will print 2, when run.
(e) The code will compile without error and will print 3, when run.

6.10 What will be the output when running the following program?

```
public class MyClass {
  public static void main(String[] args) {
    int i=0;
    int j;
    for (j=0; j<10; ++j) { i++; }
    System.out.println(i + " " + j);
  }
}
```

Select the two correct answers.

(a) The first number printed will be 9.
(b) The first number printed will be 10.
(c) The first number printed will be 11.
(d) The second number printed will be 9.
(e) The second number printed will be 10.
(f) The second number printed will be 11.

6.11   Which one of these for statements is valid?

Select the one correct answer.

(a) `int j=10; for (int i=0, j+=90; i<j; i++) { j--; }`
(b) `for (int i=10; i=0; i--) {}`
(c) `for (int i=0, j=100; i<j; i++, --j) {;}`
(d) `int i, j; for (j=100; i<j; j--) { i += 2; }`
(e) `int i=100; for ((i>0); i--) {}`

6.12   What will be the result of attempting to compile and run the following program?

```
class MyClass {
  public static void main(String[] args) {
    int i = 0;
    for (   ; i<10; i++) ;       // (1)
    for (i=0;      ; i++) break; // (2)
    for (i=0; i<10;   ) i++;     // (3)
    for (  ;     ;   ) ;         // (4)
  }
}
```

Select the one correct answer.

(a) The code will fail to compile because the expression in the first section of the for statement (1) is empty.
(b) The code will fail to compile because the expression in the middle section of the for statement (2) is empty.
(c) The code will fail to compile because the expression in the last section of the for statement (3) is empty.
(d) The code will fail to compile because the for statement (4) is invalid.
(e) The code will compile without error, and the program will run and terminate without any output.
(f) The code will compile without error, but will never terminate when run.

6.13   Which statements are valid when occurring on their own?

Select the three correct answers.

(a) `while () break;`
(b) `do { break; } while (true);`
(c) `if (true) { break; }`
(d) `switch (1) { default: break; }`
(e) `for (;true;) break;`

6.14 Given the following code fragment, which of the following lines will be a part of the output?

```
outer:
for (int i = 0; i < 3; i++) {
  for (int j = 0; j < 2; j++) {
    if (i == j) {
      continue outer;
    }
    System.out.println("i=" + i + ", j=" + j);
  }
}
```

Select the two correct answers.

(a) i=1, j=0
(b) i=0, j=1
(c) i=1, j=2
(d) i=2, j=1
(e) i=2, j=2
(f) i=3, j=3
(g) i=3, j=2

6.15 What will be the result of attempting to compile and run the following code?

```
class MyClass {
  public static void main(String[] args) {
    for (int i = 0; i<10; i++) {
      switch(i) {
        case 0:
          System.out.println(i);
      }
      if (i) {
        System.out.println(i);
      }
    }
  }
}
```

Select the one correct answer.

(a) The code will fail to compile because of an illegal switch expression in the switch statement.
(b) The code will fail to compile because of an illegal conditional expression in the if statement.
(c) The code will compile without error and will print the numbers 0 through 10, when run.
(d) The code will compile without error and will print the number 0, when run.
(e) The code will compile without error and will print the number 0 twice, when run.
(f) The code will compile without error and will print the numbers 1 through 10, when run.

6.16 Which of the following implementations of a max() method will correctly return the largest value?

```
// (1)
int max(int x, int y) {
  return (if (x > y) { x; } else { y; });
}

// (2)
int max(int x, int y) {
  return (if (x > y) { return x; } else { return y; });
}

// (3)
int max(int x, int y) {
  switch (x < y) {
    case true:
      return y;
    default:
      return x;
  };
}

// (4)
int max(int x, int y) {
  if (x>y) return x;
  return y;
}
```

Select the one correct answer.

(a) Implementation labeled (1).
(b) Implementation labeled (2).
(c) Implementation labeled (3).
(d) Implementation labeled (4).

6.17 Given the following code, which statement is true?

```
class MyClass {
  public static void main(String[] args) {
    int k=0;
    int l=0;
    for (int i=0; i <= 3; i++) {
      k++;
      if (i == 2) break;
      l++;
    }
    System.out.println(k + ", " + l);
  }
}
```

Select the one correct answer.

(a) The program will fail to compile.
(b) The program will print 3, 3, when run.
(c) The program will print 4, 3, when run, if break is replaced by continue.
(d) The program will fail to compile if break is replaced by return.
(e) The program will fail to compile if break is by an empty statement.

6.18 Which statements are true?

Select the two correct answers.

(a) `{{}}` is a valid statement block.
(b) `{ continue; }` is a valid statement block.
(c) `block: { break block; }` is a valid statement block.
(d) `block: { continue block; }` is a valid statement block.
(e) The break statement can only be used in a loop (`while`, `do-while` or `for`) or a `switch` statement.

6.19 Which declaration will result in the program compiling and printing 90, when run?

```
public class RQ400_10 {
  public static void main(String[] args) {
    // (1) INSERT DECLARATION HERE
    int sum = 0;
    for (int i : nums)
      sum += i;
    System.out.println(sum);
  }
}
```

Select the two correct answers.

(a) `Object[] nums = {20, 30, 40};`
(b) `Number[] nums = {20, 30, 40};`
(c) `Integer[] nums = {20, 30, 40};`
(d) `int[] nums = {20, 30, 40};`
(e) None of the above.

6.20 Which method declarations, when inserted at (1), will result in the program compiling and printing 90 when run?

```
public class RQ400_30 {
  public static void main(String[] args) {
    doIt();
  }
  // (1) INSERT METHOD DECLARATION HERE.
}
```

Select the two correct answers.

(a) ```
    public static void doIt() {
      int[] nums = {20, 30, 40};
      for (int sum = 0, i : nums)
        sum += i;
      System.out.println(sum);
    }
    ```
(b) ```
    public static void doIt() {
      for (int sum = 0, i : {20, 30, 40})
        sum += i;
      System.out.println(sum);
    }
    ```

(c)
```java
public static void doIt() {
    int sum = 0;
    for (int i : {20, 30, 40})
        sum += i;
    System.out.println(sum);
}
```
(d)
```java
public static void doIt() {
    int sum = 0;
    for (int i : new int[] {20, 30, 40})
        sum += i;
    System.out.println(sum);
}
```
(e)
```java
public static void doIt() {
    int[] nums = {20, 30, 40};
    int sum = 0;
    for (int i : nums)
        sum += i;
    System.out.println(sum);
}
```

6.21 Given the declaration:

```java
int[][] nums = {{20}, {30}, {40}};
```

Which code will compile and print 90, when run?

Select the one correct answer.

(a)
```java
{
    int sum = 0;
    for (int[] row : nums[])
        for (int val : nums[row])
            sum += val;
    System.out.println(sum);
}
```
(b)
```java
{
    int sum = 0;
    for (int[] row : nums[][])
        for (int val : nums[row])
            sum += val;
    System.out.println(sum);
}
```
(c)
```java
{
    int sum = 0;
    for (int[] row : nums)
        for (int val : nums[row])
            sum += val;
    System.out.println(sum);
}
```
(d)
```java
{
    int sum = 0;
    for (int[] row : nums)
        for (int val : row)
```

```
          sum += val;
       System.out.println(sum);
    }
(e) {
       int sum = 0;
       for (Integer[] row : nums)
         for (int val : row)
           sum += val;
       System.out.println(sum);
    }
```

6.22   What will be the result of compiling and running the following program?

```
public class RQ200_150 {
  public static void main(String[] args) {
    for (Character cRef = 'A'; cRef < 'F'; cRef++)
      switch(cRef) {
        default: System.out.print((char)('a' + cRef - 'A')); break;
        case 'B': System.out.print(cRef); break;
        case 68: System.out.print(cRef);  // 68 == 'D'
      }
  }
}
```

Select the one correct answer.

(a) The code will fail to compile because of errors in the for loop header.
(b) The code will fail to compile because of errors in the switch statement.
(c) The code will compile, but throws a NullPointerException.
(d) The code will compile and print: aBcDe

6.5 Stack-Based Execution and Exception Propagation

An exception in Java signals the occurrence of some unexpected error situation during execution, e.g., a requested file cannot be found, an array index is out of bounds, or a network link failed. Explicit checks in the code for such situations can easily result in incomprehensible code. Java provides an exception handling mechanism for dealing with such error situations systematically.

The exception mechanism is built around the *throw-and-catch* paradigm. To *throw* an exception is to signal that an unexpected condition has occurred. To *catch* an exception is to take appropriate action to deal with the exception. An exception is caught by an *exception handler,* and the exception need not be caught in the same context that it was thrown in. The runtime behavior of the program determines which exceptions are thrown and how they are caught. The throw-and-catch principle is embedded in the try-catch-finally construct.

Several threads can be executing in the JVM (see Chapter 13). Each thread has its own *runtime stack* (also called the *call stack* or the *invocation stack*) that is used to handle execution of methods. Each element on the stack (called an *activation record* or a *stack frame*) corresponds to a method call. Each new call results in a new activation record being pushed on the stack, which stores all the pertinent information such as storage for the local variables. The method with the activation record on the top of the stack is the one currently executing. When this method finishes executing, its record is popped from the stack. Execution then continues in the method corresponding to the activation record which is now uncovered on the top of the stack. The methods on the stack are said to be *active*, as their execution has not completed. At any given time, the active methods on a runtime stack comprise what is called the *stack trace* of a thread's execution.

Example 6.10 is a simple program to illustrate method execution. It calculates the average for a list of integers, given the sum of all the integers and the number of integers. It uses three methods:

- The method main() which calls the method printAverage() with parameters giving the total sum of the integers and the total number of integers, (1a).

- The method printAverage() which in turn calls the method computeAverage(), (3).

- The method computeAverage() which uses integer division to calculate the average and returns the result, (7).

Example 6.10 *Method Execution*

```
public class Average1 {

  public static void main(String[] args) {
    printAverage(100, 20);                          // (1a)
    System.out.println("Exit main().");             // (2)
  }

  public static void printAverage(int totalSum, int totalNumber) {
    int average = computeAverage(totalSum, totalNumber);  // (3)
    System.out.println("Average = " +                     // (4)
      totalSum + " / " + totalNumber + " = " + average);
    System.out.println("Exit printAverage().");           // (5)
  }

  public static int computeAverage(int sum, int number) {
    System.out.println("Computing average.");       // (6)
    return sum/number;                              // (7)
  }
}
```

Output of program execution:
```
Computing average.
Average = 100 / 20 = 5
Exit printAverage().
Exit main().
```

Execution of Example 6.10 is illustrated in Figure 6.7. Each method execution is shown as a box with the local variables declared in the method. The height of the box indicates how long a method is active. Before the call to the method System.out.println() at (6) in Figure 6.7, the stack trace comprises the three active methods: main(), printAverage() and computeAverage(). The result 5 from the method computeAverage() is returned at (7) in Figure 6.7. The output from the program is in correspondence with the sequence of method calls in Figure 6.7. The program terminates normally, therefore this program behavior is called *normal execution*.

If the method call at (1) in Example 6.10

```
    printAverage(100, 20);                            // (1a)
```

is replaced with

```
    printAverage(100,  0);                            // (1b)
```

and the program is run again, the output is as follows:

```
Computing average.
Exception in thread "main" java.lang.ArithmeticException: / by zero
        at Average1.computeAverage(Average1.java:18)
        at Average1.printAverage(Average1.java:10)
        at Average1.main(Average1.java:5)
```

Figure 6.7 *Method Execution*

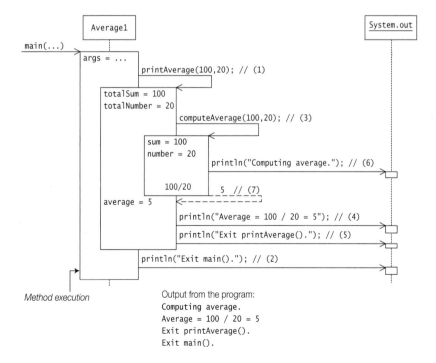

Figure 6.8 illustrates the program execution. All goes well until the return statement at (7) in the method computeAverage() is executed. An error condition occurs in calculating the expression sum/number, because integer division by 0 is an illegal operation. This error condition is signaled by the JVM by *throwing* an Arithmetic-Exception (see "Exception Types" on page 239). This exception is *propagated* by the JVM through the runtime stack as explained next.

Figure 6.8 illustrates the case where an exception is thrown and the program does not take any explicit action to deal with the exception. In Figure 6.8, execution of the computeAverage() method is suspended at the point where the exception is thrown. The execution of the return statement at (7) never gets completed. Since this method does not have any code to deal with the exception, its execution is likewise terminated abruptly and its activation record popped. We say that the method *completes abruptly*. The exception is then offered to the method whose activation is now on the top of the stack (method printAverage()). This method does not have any code to deal with the exception either, so its execution completes abruptly. The statements at (4) and (5) in the method printAverage() never get executed. The exception now propagates to the last active method (method main()). This does not deal with the exception either. The main() method also completes abruptly. The

Figure 6.8   *Exception Propagation*

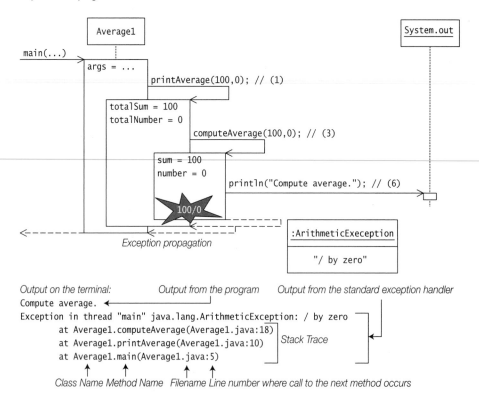

statement at (2) in the `main()` method never gets executed. Since the exception is not *caught* by any of the active methods, it is dealt with by the main thread's *default exception handler*. The default exception handler usually prints the name of the exception, with an explanatory message, followed by a printout of the stack trace at the time the exception was thrown. An uncaught exception results in the death of the thread in which the exception occurred.

If an exception is thrown during the evaluation of the left-hand operand of a binary expression, then the right-hand operand is not evaluated. Similarly, if an exception is thrown during the evaluation of a list of expressions (e.g., a list of actual parameters in a method call), evaluation of the rest of the list is skipped.

If the line numbers in the stack trace are not printed in the output as shown previously, use the following command to run the program:

```
>java -Djava.compiler=NONE Average1
```

6.6 Exception Types

Exceptions in Java are objects. All exceptions are derived from the `java.lang.Throwable` class. Figure 6.9 shows a partial hierarchy of classes derived from the `Throwable` class. The two main subclasses `Exception` and `Error` constitute the main categories of *throwables*, the term used to refer to both exceptions and errors. Figure 6.9 also shows that not all exception classes are found in the same package.

The `Throwable` class provides a `String` variable that can be set by the subclasses to provide a *detail message*. The purpose of the detail message is to provide more information about the actual exception. All classes of throwables define a one-parameter constructor that takes a string as the detail message.

The class `Throwable` provides the following common methods to query an exception:

`String getMessage()`

Returns the detail message.

`void printStackTrace()`

Prints the stack trace on the standard error stream. The stack trace comprises the method invocation sequence on the runtime stack when the exception was thrown. The stack trace can also be written to a `PrintStream` or a `PrintWriter` by supplying such a destination as an argument to one of the two overloaded `printStackTrace()` methods.

`String toString()`

Returns a short description of the exception, which typically comprises the class name of the exception together with the string returned by the `getMessage()` method.

Figure 6.9 *Partial Exception Inheritance Hierarchy*

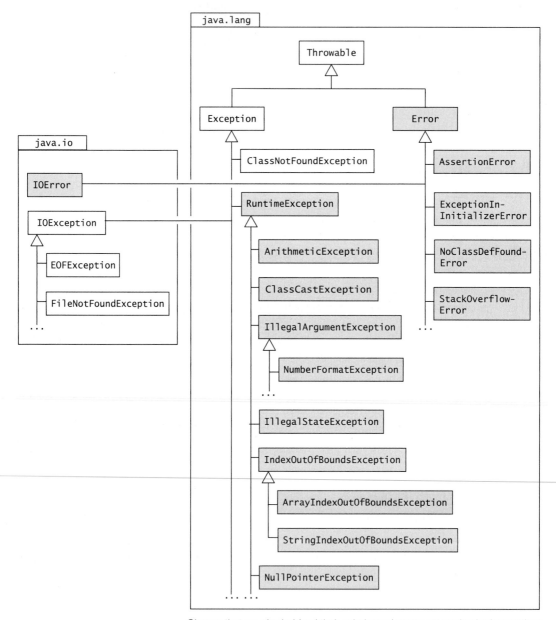

Classes that are shaded (and their subclasses) represent unchecked exceptions.

In dealing with throwables, it is important to recognize *situations* under which particular throwables can occur, and the *source* that is responsible for throwing them. By *source* here we mean:

- either it is the *JVM* that is responsible for throwing the throwable, or

- that the throwable is explicitly thrown *programmatically* by the code in the application or any API used by the application.

In further discussion on exception types, we provide an overview of situations under which selected throwables can occur and the source responsible for throwing them.

The Exception **Class**

The class Exception represents exceptions that a program would normally want to catch. Its subclass RuntimeException represents many common programming errors that can manifest at runtime (see the next subsection). Other subclasses of the Exception class define other categories of exceptions, e.g., I/O-related exceptions in the java.io package (IOException, FileNotFoundException, EOFException, IOError). Usage of I/O-related exceptions can be found in Chapter 11 on files and streams.

ClassNotFoundException

The subclass ClassNotFoundException signals that the JVM tried to load a class by its string name, but the class could not be found. A typical example of this situation is when the class name is misspelled while starting program execution with the java command. The source in this case is the JVM throwing the exception to signal that the class cannot be found and therefore execution cannot be started.

The RuntimeException **Class**

Runtime exceptions are all subclasses of the java.lang.RuntimeException class, which is a subclass of the Exception class. As these runtime exceptions are usually caused by program bugs that should not occur in the first place, it is usually more appropriate to treat them as faults in the program design and let them be handled by the default exception handler.

ArithmeticException

This exception represents situations where an illegal arithmetic operation is attempted, e.g., integer division by 0. It is typically thrown by the JVM. See Chapter 5 on operators for more details.

ArrayIndexOutOfBoundsException

Java provides runtime checking of the array index value, i.e., out-of-bounds array indices. The subclass ArrayIndexOutOfBoundsException represents exceptions thrown by the JVM that signal out-of-bound errors specifically for arrays, i.e., an invalid index is used to access an element in the array. The index value must satisfy the relation $0 \leq$ *index value* $<$ *length of the array*. See Section 3.6, p. 69, covering arrays.

ClassCastException

This exception is thrown by the JVM to signal that an attempt was made to cast a reference value to a type that was not legal, e.g., casting the reference value of an Integer object to the Long type. Casting reference values is discussed in Section 7.11, p. 327.

IllegalArgumentException and NumberFormatException

The IllegalArgumentException is thrown programmatically to indicate that a method was called with an illegal or inappropriate argument. For example, the classes Pattern and Matcher in the java.util.regex package and the Scanner class in the java.util package have methods that throw this exception. See Chapter 12 on locales, regular expressions, and formatting for more details.

The class NumberFormatException is a subclass of the IllegalArgumentException class, and is specialized to signal problems when converting a string to a numeric value if the format of the characters in the string is not appropriate for the conversion. This exception is also thrown programmatically. The numeric wrapper classes all have methods that throw this exception if things go wrong when converting a string to a numeric value. See Section 10.3, p. 428, on wrapper classes, for more details.

IllegalStateException

This exception is thrown programmatically when an operation is attempted, but the runtime environment or the application is not in an appropriate state for the requested operation. The Scanner class in the java.util package has methods that throw this exception if they are called and the scanner has been closed. See Section 12.7, p. 593, on formatting, for more details.

NullPointerException

This exception is typically thrown by the JVM when an attempt is made to use the null value as a reference value to refer to an object. This might involve calling an instance method using a reference that has the null value, or accessing a field using a reference that has the null value. This programming error has made this exception one of the most profusely thrown by the JVM.

The Error Class

The class Error and its subclasses define errors that are invariably never explicitly caught and are usually irrecoverable. Not surprisingly, most such errors are signalled by the JVM. Apart from the subclasses mentioned below, other subclasses of the java.lang.Error class define errors that indicate class linkage (LinkageError), thread (ThreadDeath), and virtual machine (VirtualMachineError) problems.

AssertionError

The subclass `AssertionError` of the `java.lang.Error` class is used by the Java assertion facility. This error is thrown by the JVM in response to the condition in the assert statement evaluating to `false`. Section 6.10 discusses the assertion facility.

ExceptionInInitializerError

The JVM throws this error to signal that an unexpected problem occurred during the evaluation of a static initializer block or an initializer expression in a static variable declaration (see Section 9.7, p. 406).

IOError

This error in the `java.io` package is thrown programmatically by the methods of the `java.io.Console` class to indicate that a serious, irrecoverable I/O error has occurred (see Section 11.5, p. 500).

NoClassDefFoundError

This error is thrown by the JVM when an application needs a class, but no definition of the class could be found. For instance, the application might want to use the class as part of a method call or create a new instance. The class existed when the application was compiled, but it cannot be found at runtime. The reason for this problem might be that the name of the class might be misspelled in the command line, the CLASSPATH might not specify the correct path, or the class file with the byte code is no longer available.

StackOverflowError

This error occurs when the runtime stack has no more room for new method activation records. We say that the stack has *overflowed*. This situation can occur when method execution in an application recurses too deeply. Here is a *recursive method* to illustrate stack overflow:

```
public void callMe() {
  System.out.println("Don't do this at home!");
  callMe();
}
```

Once this method is called, it will keep on calling itself until the runtime stack is full, resulting in the `StackOverflowError` being thrown by the JVM.

Checked and Unchecked Exceptions

Except for `RuntimeException`, `Error`, and their subclasses, all exceptions are called *checked* exceptions. The compiler ensures that if a method can throw a checked exception, directly or indirectly, the method must explicitly deal with it. The method must either catch the exception and take the appropriate action, or pass the exception on to its caller (see Section 6.9, p. 257).

Exceptions defined by `Error` and `RuntimeException` classes and their subclasses are known as *unchecked* exceptions, meaning that a method is not obliged to deal with these kinds of exceptions (shown with grey color in Figure 6.9). They are either irrecoverable (exemplified by the `Error` class) and the program should not attempt to deal with them, or they are programming errors (exemplified by the `RuntimeException` class) and should usually be dealt with as such, and not as exceptions.

Defining New Exceptions

New exceptions are usually defined to provide fine-grained categorization of error situations, instead of using existing exception classes with descriptive detail messages to differentiate between the situations. New exceptions can either extend the `Exception` class directly or one of its checked subclasses, thereby making the new exceptions checked, or the `RuntimeException` class to create new unchecked exceptions.

As exceptions are defined by classes, they can declare fields and methods, thus providing more information as to their cause and remedy when they are thrown and caught. The `super()` call can be used to set the detail message for the exception. Note that the exception class must be instantiated to create an exception object that can be thrown and subsequently caught and dealt with. The code below sketches a class declaration for an exception that can include all pertinent information about the exception.

```
public class EvacuateException extends Exception {
  // Data
  Date date;
  Zone zone;
  TransportMode transport;

  // Constructor
  public EvacuateException(Date d, Zone z, TransportMode t) {
    // Call the constructor of the superclass
    super("Evacuation of zone " + z);
    // ...
  }
  // Methods
  // ...
}
```

Several examples illustrate exception handling in the subsequent sections.

6.7 Exception Handling: try, catch, and finally

The mechanism for handling exceptions is embedded in the try-catch-finally construct, which has the following general form:

```
try {                                    // try block
  <statements>
} catch (<exception type₁> <parameter₁>) { // catch block
  <statements>
}
...
  catch (<exception typeₙ> <parameterₙ>) { // catch block
  <statements>
} finally {                              // finally block
  <statements>
}
```

Exceptions thrown during execution of the try block can be caught and handled in a catch block. A finally block is guaranteed to be executed, regardless of the cause of exit from the try block, or whether any catch block was executed. Figure 6.10 shows three typical scenarios of control flow through the try-catch-finally construct.

A few aspects about the syntax of this construct should be noted. The block notation is mandatory. For each try block there can be zero or more catch blocks, but only one finally block. The catch blocks and the finally block must always appear in conjunction with a try block, and in the right order. A try block must be followed by at least one catch block or a finally block must be specified. Each catch block defines an exception handler. The header of the catch block takes exactly one argument, which is the exception the block is willing to handle. The exception must be of the Throwable class or one of its subclasses.

Each block (try, catch, or finally) of a try-catch-finally construct can contain arbitrary code, which means that a try-catch-finally construct can also be nested in any such block. However, such nesting can easily make the code difficult to read and is best avoided.

The try Block

The try block establishes a context for exception handling. Termination of a try block occurs as a result of encountering an exception, or from successful execution of the code in the try block.

The catch blocks are skipped for all normal exits from the try block where no exceptions were raised, and control is transferred to the finally block if one is specified (see (1) in Figure 6.10).

For all exits from the try block resulting from exceptions, control is transferred to the catch blocks—if any such blocks are specified—to find a matching catch block

Figure 6.10   *The* `try-catch-finally` *Construct*

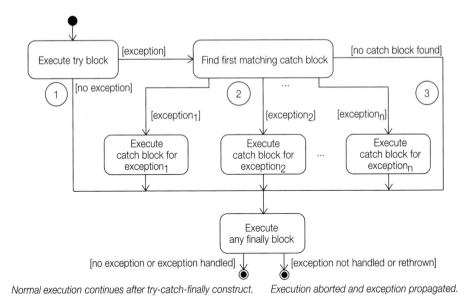

Normal execution continues after try-catch-finally construct.   Execution aborted and exception propagated.

((2) in Figure 6.10). If no catch block matches the thrown exception, control is transferred to the `finally` block if one is specified (see (3) in Figure 6.10).

The catch **Block**

Only an exit from a `try` block resulting from an exception can transfer control to a catch block. A catch block can only catch the thrown exception if the exception is assignable to the parameter in the catch block (see Section 7.8, p. 319). The code of the first such catch block is executed and all other catch blocks are ignored.

On exit from a catch block, normal execution continues unless there is any pending exception that has been thrown and not handled. If this is the case, the method is aborted and the exception is propagated up the runtime stack as explained earlier.

After a catch block has been executed, control is always transferred to the `finally` block if one is specified. This is always true as long as there is a `finally` block, regardless of whether the catch block itself throws an exception.

In Example 6.11, the method `printAverage()` calls the method `computeAverage()` in a try-catch construct at (4). The catch block is declared to catch exceptions of type `ArithmeticException`. The catch block handles the exception by printing the stack trace and some additional information at (7) and (8), respectively. Normal execution of the program is illustrated in Figure 6.11, which shows that the try block is executed but no exceptions are thrown, with normal execution continuing after the try-catch construct. This corresponds to Scenario 1 in Figure 6.10.

Example 6.11   *The* try-catch *Construct*

```java
public class Average2 {

  public static void main(String[] args) {
    printAverage(100, 20);                              // (1)
    System.out.println("Exit main().");                // (2)
  }

  public static void printAverage(int totalSum, int totalNumber) {
    try {                                              // (3)
      int average = computeAverage(totalSum, totalNumber);// (4)
      System.out.println("Average = " +               // (5)
          totalSum + " / " + totalNumber + " = " + average);
    } catch (ArithmeticException ae) {                 // (6)
      ae.printStackTrace();                            // (7)
      System.out.println("Exception handled in " +
                         "printAverage().");           // (8)
    }
    System.out.println("Exit printAverage().");        // (9)
  }

  public static int computeAverage(int sum, int number) {
    System.out.println("Computing average.");          // (10)
    return sum/number;                                 // (11)
  }
}
```

Output from the program, with call printAverage(100, 20) at (1):

```
Computing average.
Average = 100 / 20 = 5
Exit printAverage().
Exit main().
```

Output from the program, with call printAverage(100, 0) at (1):

```
Computing average.
java.lang.ArithmeticException: / by zero
        at Average2.computeAverage(Average2.java:24)
        at Average2.printAverage(Average2.java:11)
        at Average2.main(Average2.java:5)
Exception handled in printAverage().
Exit printAverage().
Exit main().
```

Figure 6.11 *Exception Handling (Scenario 1)*

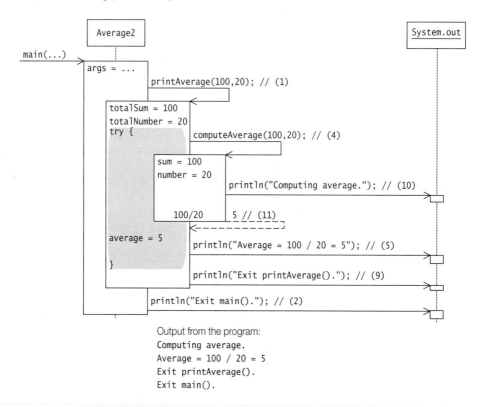

Output from the program:
Computing average.
Average = 100 / 20 = 5
Exit printAverage().
Exit main().

However, if we run the program in Example 6.11 with the following call in (1):

```
printAverage(100, 0)
```

an ArithmeticException is thrown by the integer division in the method compute-Average(). From Figure 6.12 we see that the execution of the method computeAverage() is stopped and the exception propagated to method printAverage(), where it is handled by the catch block at (6). Normal execution of the method continues at (9) after the try-catch construct, as witnessed by the output from the statements at (9) and (2). This corresponds to Scenario 2 in Figure 6.10.

In Example 6.12, the main() method calls the printAverage() method in a try-catch construct at (1). The catch block at (3) is declared to catch exceptions of type ArithmeticException. The printAverage() method calls the computeAverage() method in a try-catch construct at (7), but here the catch block is declared to catch exceptions of type IllegalArgumentException. Execution of the program is illustrated in Figure 6.13, which shows that the ArithmeticException is first propagated to the catch block in the printAverage() method. But since this catch block cannot handle this exception, it is propagated further to the catch block in the main() method, where it is caught and handled. Normal execution continues at (6) after the exception is handled.

Figure 6.12 *Exception Handling (Scenario 2)*

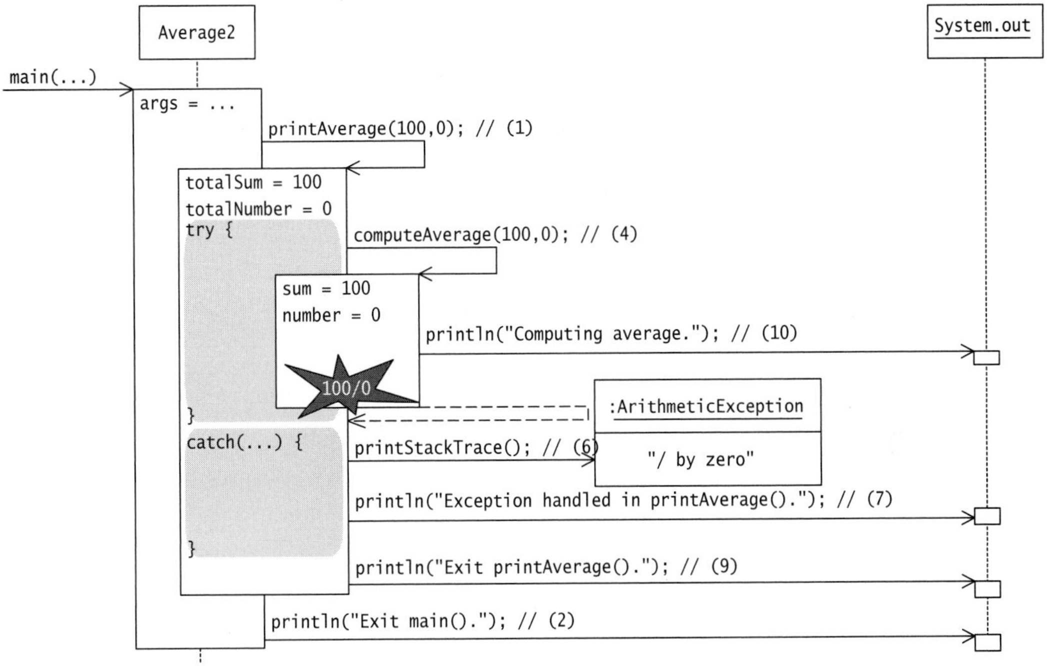

Note that the execution of the try block at (7) in the printAverage() method is never completed: the statement at (9) is never executed. The catch block at (10) is skipped. The execution of the printAverage() method is aborted: the statement at (13) is never executed, and the exception is propagated. This corresponds to Scenario 3 in Figure 6.10.

Figure 6.13   *Exception Handling (Scenario 3)*

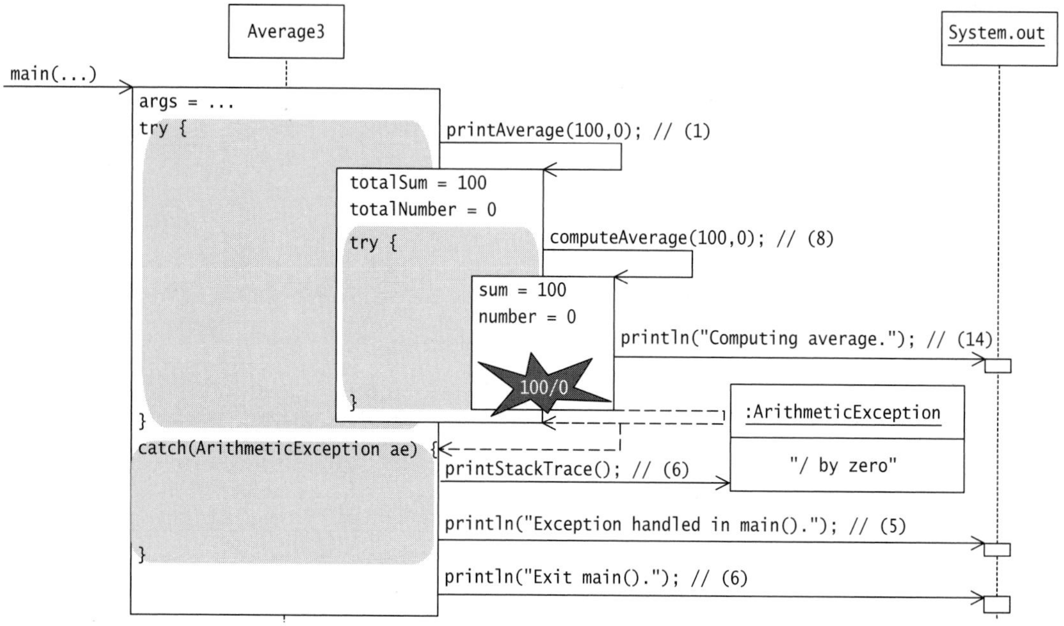

Output from the program:
```
Computing average.
java.lang.ArithmeticException: / by zero
        at Average3.computeAverage(Average3.java:30)
        at Average3.printAverage(Average3.java:17)
        at Average3.main(Average3.java:6)
Exception handled in main().
Exit main().
```

Example 6.12   *Exception Propagation*

```java
public class Average3 {

  public static void main(String[] args) {
    try {                                        // (1)
      printAverage(100, 0);                      // (2)
    } catch (ArithmeticException ae) {           // (3)
      ae.printStackTrace();                      // (4)
      System.out.println("Exception handled in " +
      "main().");                      // (5)
    }
    System.out.println("Exit main().");          // (6)
  }
```

```
    public static void printAverage(int totalSum, int totalNumber) {
      try {                                                    // (7)
        int average = computeAverage(totalSum, totalNumber);// (8)
        System.out.println("Average = " +                    // (9)
           totalSum + " / " + totalNumber + " = " + average);
      } catch (IllegalArgumentException iae) {                // (10)
        iae.printStackTrace();                                // (11)
        System.out.println("Exception handled in " +
        "printAverage().");            // (12)
      }
      System.out.println("Exit printAverage().");            // (13)
    }

    public static int computeAverage(int sum, int number) {
      System.out.println("Computing average.");              // (14)
      return sum/number;                                     // (15)
    }
  }
```

Output from the program:

```
Computing average.
java.lang.ArithmeticException: / by zero
        at Average3.computeAverage(Average3.java:30)
        at Average3.printAverage(Average3.java:17)
        at Average3.main(Average3.java:6)
Exception handled in main().
Exit main().
```

The scope of the argument name in the catch block is the block itself. As mentioned earlier, the type of the exception object must be *assignable* to the type of the argument in the catch block (see Section 7.8, p. 319). In the body of the catch block, the exception object can be queried like any other object by using the argument name. The javac compiler also complains if a catch block for a superclass exception shadows the catch block for a subclass exception, as the catch block of the subclass exception will never be executed. The following example shows incorrect order of the catch blocks at (1) and (2), which will result in a compile time error: the superclass Exception will shadow the subclass ArithmeticException.

```
...
// Compiler complains
catch (Exception e) {                    // (1) superclass
  System.out.println(e);
} catch (ArithmeticException e) {        // (2) subclass
  System.out.println(e);
}
...
```

The finally **Block**

If the try block is executed, then the finally block is guaranteed to be executed, regardless of whether any catch block was executed. Since the finally block is always executed before control transfers to its final destination, the finally block can be used to specify any clean-up code (e.g., to free resources such as files and net connections).

A try-finally construct can be used to control the interplay between two actions that must be executed in the correct order, possibly with other intervening actions. In the following code, the operation in the calculateAverage() method is dependent on the success of the sumNumbers() method, this is checked by the value of the sum variable before calling the calculateAverage() method.

```
int sum = -1;
try {
  sum = sumNumbers();
  // other actions
} finally {
  if (sum >= 0) calculateAverage();
}
```

The code above guarantees that if the try block is entered, the sumNumbers()method will be executed first, and later the calculateAverage() method will be executed in the finally block, regardless of how execution proceeds in the try block. We can, if desired, include any catch blocks to handle any exceptions.

If the finally block neither throws an exception nor executes a control transfer statement like a return or a labeled break, the execution of the try block or any catch block determines how execution proceeds after the finally block (see Figure 6.10, p. 246).

- If there is no exception thrown during execution of the try block or the exception has been handled in a catch block, normal execution continues after the finally block.

- If there is any pending exception that has been thrown and not handled (either due to the fact that no catch block was found or the catch block threw an exception), the method is aborted and the exception is propagated after the execution of the finally block.

If the finally block throws an exception, this exception is propagated with all its ramifications—regardless of how the try block or any catch block were executed. In particular, the new exception overrules any previously unhandled exception.

If the finally block executes a control transfer statement, such as a return or a labeled break, this control transfer statement determines how the execution will proceed—regardless of how the try block or any catch block were executed. In particular, a value returned by a return statement in the finally block will supercede any value returned by a return statement in the try block or a catch block.

The output of Example 6.13 shows that the finally block at (9) is executed, regardless of whether an exception is thrown in the try block at (3) or not. If an exception is thrown, it is caught and handled by the catch block at (6). After the execution of the finally block at (9), normal execution continues at (10).

Example 6.13 *The* try-catch-finally *Construct*

```java
public class Average4 {

  public static void main(String[] args) {
    printAverage(100, 20);                              // (1)
    System.out.println("Exit main().");                // (2)
  }

  public static void printAverage(int totalSum, int totalNumber) {
    try {                                              // (3)
      int average = computeAverage(totalSum, totalNumber);// (4)
      System.out.println("Average = " +                // (5)
        totalSum + " / " + totalNumber + " = " + average);
    } catch (ArithmeticException ae) {                 // (6)
      ae.printStackTrace();                            // (7)
      System.out.println("Exception handled in " +
        "printAverage().");          // (8)
    } finally {                                        // (9)
      System.out.println("Finally done.");
    }
    System.out.println("Exit printAverage().");        // (10)
  }

  public static int computeAverage(int sum, int number) {
    System.out.println("Computing average.");          // (11)
    return sum/number;                                 // (12)
  }
}
```

Output from the program, with the call printAverage(100, 20) at (1):

```
Computing average.
Average = 100 / 20 = 5
Finally done.
Exit printAverage().
Exit main().
```

Output from the program, with the call printAverage(100, 0) at (1):

```
Computing average.
java.lang.ArithmeticException: / by zero
        at Average4.computeAverage(Average4.java:26)
        at Average4.printAverage(Average4.java:11)
        at Average4.main(Average4.java:5)
Exception handled in printAverage().
Finally done.
Exit printAverage().
Exit main().
```

On exiting from the finally block, if there is any pending exception, the method is aborted and the exception propagated as explained earlier. This is illustrated in Example 6.14. The method printAverage() is aborted after the finally block at (6) has been executed, as the ArithmeticException thrown at (9) is not handled by any method. In this case, the exception is handled by the default exception handler. Notice the difference in the output from Example 6.13 and Example 6.14.

Example 6.14 *The* try-finally *Construct*

```java
public class Average5 {

    public static void main(String[] args) {
        printAverage(100, 0);                                    // (1)
        System.out.println("Exit main().");                      // (2)
    }

    public static void printAverage(int totalSum, int totalNumber) {
        try {                                                    // (3)
            int average = computeAverage(totalSum, totalNumber);// (4)
            System.out.println("Average = " +                   // (5)
                totalSum + " / " + totalNumber + " = " + average);
        } finally {                                              // (6)
            System.out.println("Finally done.");
        }
        System.out.println("Exit printAverage().");              // (7)
    }

    public static int computeAverage(int sum, int number) {
        System.out.println("Computing average.");                // (8)
        return sum/number;                                       // (9)
    }
}
```

Output from the program:

```
Computing average.
Finally done.
Exception in thread "main" java.lang.ArithmeticException: / by zero
        at Average5.computeAverage(Average5.java:21)
        at Average5.printAverage(Average5.java:10)
        at Average5.main(Average5.java:4)
```

Example 6.15 shows how the execution of a control transfer statement such as a return in the finally block affects the program execution. The first output from the program shows that the average is computed but the value returned is from the return statement at (8) in the finally block, not from the return statement at (6) in the try block. The second output shows that the ArithmeticException thrown in the computeAverage() method and propagated to the printAverage() method is nullified by the return statement in the finally block. Normal execution continues after the return statement at (8), with the value 0 being returned from the printAverage() method.

Example 6.15 *The* finally *Block and the* return *Statement*

```java
public class Average6 {

  public static void main(String[] args) {
    System.out.println("Average: " + printAverage(100, 20));  // (1)
    System.out.println("Exit main().");                       // (2)
  }

  public static int printAverage(int totalSum, int totalNumber) {
    int average = 0;
    try {                                                     // (3)
      average = computeAverage(totalSum, totalNumber);        // (4)
      System.out.println("Average = " +                       // (5)
          totalSum + " / " + totalNumber + " = " + average);
      return average;                                         // (6)
    } finally {                                               // (7)
      System.out.println("Finally done.");
      return average*2;                                       // (8)
    }
  }

  public static int computeAverage(int sum, int number) {
    System.out.println("Computing average.");                 // (9)
    return sum/number;                                        // (10)
  }
}
```

Output from the program, with call printAverage(100, 20) in (1):

```
Computing average.
Average = 100 / 20 = 5
Finally done.
Average: 10
Exit main().
```

Output from the program, with call printAverage(100, 0) in (1):

```
Computing average.
Finally done.
Average: 0
Exit main().
```

6.8 The throw Statement

Earlier examples in this chapter have shown how an exception can be thrown implicitly by the JVM during execution. Now we look at how an application can programmatically throw an exception using the throw statement. The general format of the throw statement is as follows:

throw *<object reference expression>*;

The compiler ensures that the *<object reference expression>* is of the type Throwable class or one of its subclasses. At runtime a NullPointerException is thrown by the JVM if the *<object reference expression>* is null. This ensures that a Throwable will always be propagated. A detail message is often passed to the constructor when the exception object is created.

```
throw new ArithmeticException("Integer division by 0");
```

When an exception is thrown, normal execution is suspended. The runtime system proceeds to find a catch block that can handle the exception. The search starts in the context of the current try block, propagating to any enclosing try blocks and through the runtime stack to find a handler for the exception. Any associated finally block of a try block encountered along the search path is executed. If no handler is found, then the exception is dealt with by the default exception handler at the top level. If a handler is found, normal execution resumes after the code in its catch block has been executed, barring any rethrowing of an exception.

In Example 6.16, an exception is thrown using a throw statement at (17). This exception is propagated to the main() method where it is caught and handled by the catch block at (3). Note that the finally blocks at (6) and (14) are executed. Execution continues normally from (7).

- -

Example 6.16   *Throwing Exceptions*

```
public class Average7 {

    public static void main(String[] args) {
        try {                                               // (1)
            printAverage(100, 0);                           // (2)
        } catch (ArithmeticException ae) {                  // (3)
            ae.printStackTrace();                           // (4)
            System.out.println("Exception handled in " +    // (5)
                "main().");
        } finally {
            System.out.println("Finally in main().");       // (6)
        }
        System.out.println("Exit main().");                 // (7)
    }

    public static void printAverage(int totalSum, int totalNumber) {
        try {                                               // (8)
            int average = computeAverage(totalSum, totalNumber); // (9)
            System.out.println("Average = " +               // (10)
                totalSum + " / " + totalNumber + " = " + average);
        } catch (IllegalArgumentException iae) {            // (11)
            iae.printStackTrace();                          // (12)
            System.out.println("Exception handled in " +    // (13)
                "printAverage().");
        } finally {
            System.out.println("Finally in printAverage()."); // (14)
        }
```

```
        System.out.println("Exit printAverage().");              // (15)
    }

    public static int computeAverage(int sum, int number) {
        System.out.println("Computing average.");
        if (number == 0)                                         // (16)
            throw new ArithmeticException("Integer division by 0");  // (17)
        return sum/number;                                       // (18)
    }
}
```

Output from the program:

```
Computing average.
Finally in printAverage().
java.lang.ArithmeticException: Integer division by 0
        at Average7.computeAverage(Average7.java:35)
        at Average7.printAverage(Average7.java:19)
        at Average7.main(Average7.java:6)
Exception handled in main().
Finally in main().
Exit main().
```

6.9 The throws **Clause**

A throws clause can be specified in the method header.

```
... someMethod(...)
    throws <ExceptionType₁>, <ExceptionType₂>,..., <ExceptionTypeₙ> { ... }
```

Each $<ExceptionType_i>$ declares an exception, normally only checked exceptions are declared. The compiler enforces that the checked exceptions thrown by a method are limited to those specified in its throws clause. Of course, the method can throw exceptions that are subclasses of the checked exceptions in the throws clause. This is permissible since exceptions are objects and a subclass object can polymorphically act as an object of its superclass (see Section 7.1, p. 284). The throws clause can specify unchecked exceptions, but this is seldom done and the compiler does not verify them.

In a method, a checked exception can be thrown directly by using the throw statement, or indirectly by calling other methods that can throw a checked exception. If a checked exception is thrown in a method, it must be handled in one of three ways:

- By using a try block and catching the exception in a handler and dealing with it
- By using a try block and catching the exception in a handler, but throwing another exception that is either unchecked or declared in its throws clause
- By explicitly allowing propagation of the exception to its caller by declaring it in the throws clause of its method header

This mechanism ensures that a checked exception will be dealt with, regardless of the path of execution. This aids development of robust programs, as allowance can be made for many contingencies. Native methods can also declare checked exceptions in their throws clause, but the compiler is not able to check them for consistency.

In Example 6.17, a new checked exception is defined. The checked exception class IntegerDivisionByZero is defined at (11) by extending the Exception class. The method main() calls the method printAverage() in a try block at (1). In the if statement at (9), the method computeAverage() throws the checked exception Integer-DivisionByZero defined at (11). Neither the computeAverage() method nor the printAverage() method catch the exception, but instead throw it to their caller, as declared in the throws clause in their headers at (6) and (8). The exception propagates to the main() method. Since the printAverage() method was called from the context of the try block at (1) in the main() method, the exception is successfully matched with its catch block at (3). The exception is handled and the finally block at (4) executed, with normal execution proceeding at (5). If the method main() did not catch the exception, it would have to declare this exception in a throws clause. In that case, the exception would end up being taken care of by the default exception handler.

Example 6.17   *The* throws *Clause*

```java
public class Average8 {
  public static void main(String[] args) {
    try {                                         // (1)
      printAverage(100, 0);                       // (2)
    } catch (IntegerDivisionByZero idbze) {       // (3)
      idbze.printStackTrace();
      System.out.println("Exception handled in " +
      "main().");
    } finally {                                   // (4)
      System.out.println("Finally done in main().");
    }

    System.out.println("Exit main().");           // (5)
  }

  public static void printAverage(int totalSum, int totalNumber)
  throws IntegerDivisionByZero {                  // (6)

    int average = computeAverage(totalSum, totalNumber);
    System.out.println("Average = " +
      totalSum + " / " + totalNumber + " = " + average);
    System.out.println("Exit printAverage().");   // (7)
  }
```

```
   public static int computeAverage(int sum, int number)
   throws IntegerDivisionByZero {                              // (8)

      System.out.println("Computing average.");
      if (number == 0)                                         // (9)
        throw new IntegerDivisionByZero("Integer Division By Zero");
      return sum/number;                                       // (10)
   }
}

class IntegerDivisionByZero extends Exception {                // (11)
   IntegerDivisionByZero(String str) { super(str); }          // (12)
}
```

Output from the program:

```
Computing average.
IntegerDivisionByZero: Integer Division By Zero
        at Average8.computeAverage(Average8.java:33)
        at Average8.printAverage(Average8.java:22)
        at Average8.main(Average8.java:7)
Exception handled in main().
Finally done in main().
Exit main().
```

The exception type specified in the throws clause in the method header can be a superclass type of the actual exceptions thrown, i.e., the exceptions thrown must be assignable to the type of the exceptions specified in the throws clause. If a method can throw exceptions of the type A, B, and C where these are subclasses of type D, then the throws clause can either specify A, B, and C or just specify D. In the printAverage() method, the method header could specify the superclass Exception of the subclass IntegerDivisionByZero in a throws clause.

```
   public static void printAverage(int totalSum, int totalNumber) throws Exception {
      /* ... */
   }
```

It is generally considered bad programming style to specify exception superclasses in the throws clause of the method header when the actual exceptions thrown in the method are instances of their subclasses. Programmers will be deprived of information about which specific subclass exceptions can be thrown in, unless they have access to the source code.

A subclass can *override* a method defined in its superclass by providing a new implementation (see Section 7.2, p. 288). What happens when an inherited method with a list of exceptions in its throws clause is overridden in a subclass? The method definition in the subclass can omit the throws clause, or it can specify *checked* exception classes in a throws clause that covers the checked exceptions from the throws clause of the inherited method. This means that an overriding method *cannot* allow more checked exceptions in its throws clause than the inherited method does. Allowing more checked exceptions in the overriding method would create problems for clients who already deal with the exceptions specified in the inherited method. Such clients would be ill prepared if an object of the subclass (under the guise of polymorphism) threw a checked exception they were not prepared for.

In the following code, the method `superclassMethodX` in superclass A is overridden in subclass B. The `throws` clause of the method in subclass B at (2) is a subset of the exceptions specified for the method in the superclass at (1). However, there are no restrictions on specifying *unchecked* exceptions in the `throws` clause of the overriding method.

```
class A {
  // ...
  protected void superclassMethodX()
    throws FirstException, SecondException, ThirdException {/* ... */} // (1)
  // ...
}

class B extends A {
  // ...
  protected void superclassMethodX()
    throws FirstException, ThirdException { /* ... */ }                // (2)
  // ...

}
```

Handling of checked exceptions in initializers is covered in Section 9.7 on page 406.

 ## Review Questions

6.23 Which digits, and in what order, will be printed when the following program is run?

```
public class MyClass {
  public static void main(String[] args) {
    int k=0;
    try {
      int i = 5/k;
    } catch (ArithmeticException e) {
      System.out.println("1");
    } catch (RuntimeException e) {
      System.out.println("2");
      return;
    } catch (Exception e) {
      System.out.println("3");
    } finally {
      System.out.println("4");
    }
    System.out.println("5");
  }
}
```

Select the one correct answer.

(a) The program will only print 5.
(b) The program will only print 1 and 4, in that order.
(c) The program will only print 1, 2, and 4, in that order.
(d) The program will only print 1, 4, and 5, in that order.

(e) The program will only print 1, 2, 4, and 5, in that order.

(f) The program will only print 3 and 5, in that order.

6.24   Given the following program, which statements are true?

```
public class Exceptions {
  public static void main(String[] args) {
    try {
      if (args.length == 0) return;
      System.out.println(args[0]);
    } finally {
      System.out.println("The end");
    }
  }
}
```

Select the two correct answers.

(a) If run with no arguments, the program will produce no output.

(b) If run with no arguments, the program will print "The end".

(c) The program will throw an ArrayIndexOutOfBoundsException.

(d) If run with one argument, the program will simply print the given argument.

(e) If run with one argument, the program will print the given argument followed by "The end".

6.25   What will be the result of attempting to compile and run the following program?

```
public class MyClass {
  public static void main(String[] args) {
    RuntimeException re = null;
    throw re;
  }
}
```

Select the one correct answer.

(a) The code will fail to compile because the main() method does not declare that it throws RuntimeException in its declaration.

(b) The program will fail to compile because it cannot throw re.

(c) The program will compile without error and will throw java.lang.Runtime-Exception when run.

(d) The program will compile without error and will throw java.lang.Null-PointerException when run.

(e) The program will compile without error and will run and terminate without any output.

6.26   Which statements are true?

Select the two correct answers.

(a) If an exception is not caught in a method, the method will terminate and normal execution will resume.

(b) An overriding method must declare that it throws the same exception classes as the method it overrides.

(c) The main() method of a program can declare that it throws checked exceptions.

(d) A method declaring that it throws a certain exception class may throw instances of any subclass of that exception class.

(e) finally blocks are executed if, and only if, an exception gets thrown while inside the corresponding try block.

6.27 Which digits, and in what order, will be printed when the following program is compiled and run?

```java
public class MyClass {
  public static void main(String[] args) {
    try {
      f();
    } catch (InterruptedException e) {
      System.out.println("1");
      throw new RuntimeException();
    } catch (RuntimeException e) {
      System.out.println("2");
      return;
    } catch (Exception e) {
      System.out.println("3");
    } finally {
      System.out.println("4");
    }
    System.out.println("5");
  }

  // InterruptedException is a direct subclass of Exception.
  static void f() throws InterruptedException {
    throw new InterruptedException("Time for lunch.");
  }
}
```

Select the one correct answer.

(a) The program will print 5.

(b) The program will print 1 and 4, in that order.

(c) The program will print 1, 2, and 4, in that order.

(d) The program will print 1, 4, and 5, in that order.

(e) The program will print 1, 2, 4, and 5, in that order.

(f) The program will print 3 and 5, in that order.

6.28 Which digits, and in what order, will be printed when the following program is run?

```java
public class MyClass {
  public static void main(String[] args) throws InterruptedException {
    try {
      f();
      System.out.println("1");
    } finally {
      System.out.println("2");
    }
```

```
      System.out.println("3");
    }

    // InterruptedException is a direct subclass of Exception.
    static void f() throws InterruptedException {
      throw new InterruptedException("Time to go home.");
    }
  }
```

Select the one correct answer.

(a) The program will print 2 and throw `InterruptedException`.
(b) The program will print 1 and 2, in that order.
(c) The program will print 1, 2, and 3, in that order.
(d) The program will print 2 and 3, in that order.
(e) The program will print 3 and 2, in that order.
(f) The program will print 1 and 3, in that order.

6.29 What is wrong with the following code?

```
public class MyClass {
  public static void main(String[] args) throws A {
    try {
      f();
    } finally {
      System.out.println("Done.");
    } catch (A e) {
      throw e;
    }
  }

  public static void f() throws B {
    throw new B();
  }
}

class A extends Throwable {}

class B extends A {}
```

Select the one correct answer.

(a) The `main()` method must declare that it throws B.
(b) The `finally` block must follow the `catch` block in the `main()` method.
(c) The catch block in the `main()` method must declare that it catches B rather than A.
(d) A single try block cannot be followed by both a `finally` and a `catch` block.
(e) The declaration of class A is illegal.

6.30 What is the minimal list of exception classes that the overriding method f() in the following code must declare in its throws clause before the code will compile correctly?

```
class A {
  // InterruptedException is a direct subclass of Exception.
  void f() throws ArithmeticException, InterruptedException {
```

```
      div(5, 5);
    }
    int div(int i, int j) throws ArithmeticException {
      return i/j;
    }
  }
  public class MyClass extends A {
    void f() /* throws [...list of exceptions...] */ {
      try {
        div(5, 0);
      } catch (ArithmeticException e) {
        return;
      }
      throw new RuntimeException("ArithmeticException was expected.");
    }
  }
```

Select the one correct answer.

(a) Does not need to specify any exceptions.
(b) Needs to specify that it throws ArithmeticException.
(c) Needs to specify that it throws InterruptedException.
(d) Needs to specify that it throws RuntimeException.
(e) Needs to specify that it throws both ArithmeticException and Interrupted-
    Exception.

6.31   What, if anything, would cause the following code not to compile?

```
class A {
  void f() throws ArithmeticException {
    //...
  }
}

public class MyClass extends A {
  public static void main(String[] args) {
    A obj = new MyClass();

    try {
      obj.f();
    } catch (ArithmeticException e) {
      return;
    } catch (Exception e) {
      System.out.println(e);
      throw new RuntimeException("Something wrong here");
    }
  }

  // InterruptedException is a direct subclass of Exception.
  void f() throws InterruptedException {
    //...
  }
}
```

Select the one correct answer.

(a) The `main()` method must declare that it throws `RuntimeException`.

(b) The overriding `f()` method in `MyClass` must declare that it throws `Arithmetic-Exception`, since the `f()` method in class `A` declares that it does.

(c) The overriding `f()` method in `MyClass` is not allowed to throw `Interrupted-Exception`, since the `f()` method in class `A` does not throw this exception.

(d) The compiler will complain that the `catch(ArithmeticException)` block shadows the `catch(Exception)` block.

(e) You cannot throw exceptions from a `catch` block.

(f) Nothing is wrong with the code, it will compile without errors.

6.10 Assertions

In Java, assertions can be used to document and validate assumptions made about the state of the program at designated locations in the code. Each assertion contains a boolean expression that is expected to be `true` when the assertion is executed. If this assumption is `false`, the JVM throws a special error represented by the `AssertionError` class. The assertion facility uses the exception handling mechanism to propagate the error. Since the assertion error signals failure in program behavior, it should *not* be caught programmatically, but allowed to propagate to the top level. As we shall see later in this section, the assertion facility can be enabled or disabled at runtime, i.e., we can choose whether assertions should be executed or not at runtime.

The assertion facility is an invaluable aid in implementing *correct* programs (i.e., programs that adhere to their specifications). It should not be confused with the exception handling mechanism that aids in developing *robust* programs (i.e., programs that handle unexpected situations gracefully). Used judiciously, the two mechanisms facilitate programs that are *reliable*.

The `assert` Statement and the `AssertionError` Class

The following two forms of the assert statement can be used to specify assertions:

```
assert <boolean expression> ;                    // the simple form

assert <boolean expression> : <message expression> ;     // the augmented form
```

The *<boolean expression>* can be a `boolean` or a `Boolean` expression. In the latter case, its value is unboxed to a `boolean` value. If assertions are enabled (see p. 269), the execution of an assert statement proceeds as shown in Figure 6.14. The two forms are essentially equivalent to the following code, respectively:

```
if (<assertions enabled> && !<boolean expression>)     // the simple form
  throw new AssertionError();

if (<assertions enabled> && !<boolean expression>)     // the augmented form
  throw new AssertionError(<message expression>);
```

If assertions are enabled, then the *<boolean expression>* is evaluated. If its value is true, execution continues normally after the `assert` statement. However, if it is `false`, an `AssertionError` is thrown and propagated. In the simple form, the `AssertionError` does not provide any detailed message about the assertion failure.

Figure 6.14 *Execution of the Simple* assert *Statement (with Assertions Enabled)*

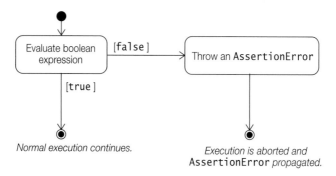

The augmented form specifies a *<message expression>* that can be used to provide a detailed error message. In the augmented form, if the assertion is `false`, the *<message expression>* is evaluated and its value passed to the appropriate `AssertionError` constructor. The *<message expression>* must evaluate to a value (i.e., either a primitive or a reference value). The `AssertionError` constructor invoked converts the value to a textual representation. In particular, the *<message expression>* cannot call a method that is declared `void`. The compiler will flag this as an error. The augmented form is recommended, as it allows a detailed error message to be included in reporting the assertion failure.

Example 6.18 illustrates using assertions. Statements at (2), (3), and (4) in class Speed are all `assert` statements. In this particular context of calculating the speed, it is required that the values satisfy the assumptions at (2), (3), and (4) in the private method `calcSpeed()`. The simple form of the `assert` statement is used at (2) and (4).

```
assert distance >= 0.0;                                    // (2)
...
assert speed >= 0.0;                                       // (4)
```

The augmented form is used at (3).

```
assert time > 0.0 : "Time is not a positive value: " + time; // (3)
```

The augmented form at (3) is equivalent to the following line of code, assuming assertions have been enabled at runtime:

```
if (time <= 0.0) throw new AssertionError("Time is not a positive value: " + time);
```

The `java.lang.AssertionError` class is a subclass of `java.lang.Error` (see Figure 6.9). Thus `AssertionError`s are unchecked. They can be explicitly caught and handled using the try-catch construct, and the execution continues normally, as one would expect. However, Errors are seldom caught and handled by the program, and the same applies to AssertionErrors. Catching these errors would defeat the whole purpose of the assertion facility.

In addition to the default constructor (invoked by the simple assert form), the AssertionError class provides seven single-parameter constructors: six for the primitive data types (byte and short being promoted to int) and one for object references (type Object). The type of the *<message expression>* used in the augmented assertion statement determines which of the overloaded constructors is invoked. It is not possible to query the AssertionError object for the actual value passed to the constructor. However, the method getMessage() will return the textual representation of the value.

Example 6.18 *Using Assertions*

```
public class Speed {

  public static void main(String[] args) {
    Speed objRef = new Speed();
    double speed = objRef.calcSpeed(-12.0, 3.0);                // (1a)
//    double speed = objRef.calcSpeed(12.0, -3.0);              // (1b)
    // double speed = objRef.calcSpeed(12.0, 2.0);              // (1c)
    // double speed = objRef.calcSpeed(12.0, 0.0);              // (1d)
    System.out.println("Speed (km/h): " + speed);
  }

  /** Requires distance >= 0.0 and time > 0.0 */
  private double calcSpeed(double distance, double time) {
    assert distance >= 0.0;                                      // (2)
    assert time > 0.0 : "Time is not a positive value: " + time; // (3)
    double speed = distance / time;
    assert speed >= 0.0;                                         // (4)
    return speed;
  }
}
```

Compiling Assertions

The assertion facility was introduced in Java 1.4. Prior to Java 1.4, assert was an identifier and not a keyword. Starting with Java 1.4, it could only be used as a keyword in the source code. Also starting with Java 1.5, the javac compiler will compile assertions *by default*. This means that incorrect use of the keyword assert will be flagged as a compile time error, e.g., if assert is used as an identifier.

Option -source 1.3

Source code that uses assert as an identifier can still be compiled, but then it cannot use assert as a keyword. The option -source 1.3 must be specified with the javac command. This option instructs the compiler that the source code is compatible to the Java release 1.3. (Other Java releases from 1.3 onwards can be specified with this option.)

The following program uses assert as an identifier:

```
// File: Legacy.java
public class Legacy {
 public static void main(String[] args) {
    double assert = 1.3;
    System.out.println("Not assertive enough with " + assert);
 }
}
```

Compiling the file Legacy.java and running the Legacy class above gives the following results:

```
>javac -source 1.3 Legacy.java
Legacy.java:4: warning: as of release 1.4, 'assert' is a keyword, and may not be
 used as an identifier
(use -source 1.4 or higher to use 'assert' as a keyword)
    double assert = 1.3;
         ^
Legacy.java:5: warning: as of release 1.4, 'assert' is a keyword, and may not be
 used as an identifier
(use -source 1.4 or higher to use 'assert' as a keyword)
    System.out.println("Not assertive enough with " + assert);
                                                        ^
2 warnings
>java Legacy
Not assertive enough with 1.3
```

The class Legacy compiles with warnings, but the code runs without any problem. However, compiling the file Speed.java (Example 6.18, p. 267) gives the following result:

```
>javac -source 1.3 Speed.java
Speed.java:15: warning: as of release 1.4, 'assert' is a keyword, and may not be
 used as an identifier
(use -source 1.4 or higher to use 'assert' as a keyword)
    assert distance >= 0.0;                                          // (2)
      ^
Speed.java:15: ';' expected
    assert distance >= 0.0;                                          // (2)
            ^
...
4 errors
3 warnings
```

The compiler rejects assert statements in the source. It will also warn about the use of the keyword assert as an identifier. In other words, source code that contains the keyword `assert` as an identifier will compile (barring any other errors), but it will also result in a *warning*.

Runtime Enabling and Disabling of Assertions

Enabling assertions means they will be executed at runtime. By default, assertions are disabled. Their execution is then effectively equivalent to empty statements. This means that disabled assertions carry an insignificant performance penalty, although they add storage overhead to the byte code of a class. Typically, assertions are enabled during development and left disabled once the program is deployed. Since assertions are already in the compiled code, they can be turned on whenever needed.

Two options are provided by the `java` command to enable and disable assertions with various granularities. The option `-enableassertions`, or its short form `-ea`, enables assertions, and the option `-disableassertions`, or its short form `-da`, disables assertions at various granularities. The granularities that can be specified are shown in Table 6.2.

Table 6.2   *Granularities for Enabling and Disabling Assertions at Runtime*

Option	Granularity
`-ea` `-da`	Applies to all non-system classes.
`-ea:<package name>...` `-da:<package name>...`	Applies to the named package and its subpackages.
`-ea:...` `-da:...`	Applies to the unnamed package in the current working directory.
`-ea:<class name>` `-da:<class name>`	Applies to the named class.

Assertion Execution for All Non-System Classes

The `-ea` option means that *all non-system* classes loaded during the execution of the program have their assertions enabled. A *system class* is a class that is in the Java platform libraries. For example, classes in the `java.*` packages are system classes. A system class is loaded directly by the JVM.

Note that class files not compiled with an assertion-aware compiler are not affected, whether assertions are enabled or disabled. Also, once a class has been loaded and initialized at runtime, its assertion status cannot be changed.

Assuming that the file Speed.java (Example 6.18, p. 267) has been compiled, all assertions in non-system classes required for execution (of which Speed class is one) can be enabled, and the program run as follows:

```
>java -ea Speed
Exception in thread "main" java.lang.AssertionError
        at Speed.calcSpeed(Speed.java:15)
        at Speed.main(Speed.java:6)
```

Since the distance is negative at (1a), the assertion at (2) fails in Example 6.18. An AssertionError is thrown, which is propagated, being finally caught by the default exception handler and resulting in the stack trace being printed on the console.

All assertions (in all non-system classes) can be disabled during the execution of the Speed class.

```
>java -da Speed
Speed (km/h): -4.0
```

In this case, this is effectively equivalent to running the program with neither the -ea nor the -da options.

```
>java Speed
Speed (km/h): -4.0
```

If we comment-out (1a) and uncomment (1b) in Example 6.18 and run the program with the options enabled, we get the following behavior from the program.

```
>java -ea Speed
Exception in thread "main" java.lang.AssertionError: Time is not a positive value:
-3.0
        at Speed.calcSpeed(Speed.java:16)
        at Speed.main(Speed.java:7)
```

We see that the value of the *<message expression>* in the augmented assertion at (3) is written on the console, together with the stack trace, because this assertion failed.

Assertion Execution at the Package Level

Assume that we have a program called Trickster in the *unnamed package*, that uses the wizard package shown in Figure 6.15 (same as Figure 4.2 on page 105).

The following command line will only enable assertions for all classes in the package wizard.pandorasBox and its subpackage wizard.pandorasBox.artifacts. The assertions in the class Trickster are not enabled.

```
>java -ea:wizard.pandorasBox... Trickster
```

Without the ... notation, the package name will be interpreted as a class name. Non-existent package names specified in the command line are silently accepted, but simply have no consequences during execution.

Figure 6.15 *Package Hierarchy*

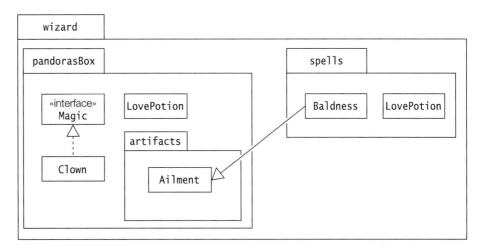

The following command line will only enable assertions in the unnamed package and, thereby, the assertions in the class `Trickster`, since this class resides in the unnamed package.

```
>java -ea:... Trickster
```

Note that the package option applies to the package specified and all its subpackages, recursively.

Assertion Execution at the Class Level

The following command line will only enable assertions in the `Trickster` class.

```
>java -ea:Trickster Trickster
```

The following command line will only enable assertions in the specified class `wizard.pandorasBox.artifacts.Ailment`, and no other class.

```
>java -ea:wizard.pandorasBox.artifacts.Ailment Trickster
```

The java command can contain multiple instances of the options, each specifying its own granularity. The options are then processed in order of their specification from left to right, before any classes are loaded. The latter options take priority over former options. This allows a fine-grained control of what assertions are enabled at runtime. The following command line will enable assertions for all classes in the package `wizard.pandorasBox` and its subpackage `wizard.pandorasBox.artifacts`, but disable them in the class `wizard.pandorasBox.artifacts.Ailment`.

```
>java -ea:wizard.pandorasBox... -da:wizard.pandorasBox.artifacts.Ailment Trickster
```

The following commands all enable assertions in the class wizard.spells.Baldness.

```
>java -ea                        Trickster
>java -ea:wizard...              Trickster
>java -ea:wizard.spells...       Trickster
>java -ea:wizard.spells.Baldness Trickster
```

It is worth noting that inheritance (see Section 7.1, p. 284) has no affect on the execution of assertions. Assertions are enabled or disabled on a per-class basis. Whether assertions in the superclass will be executed through code inherited by the subclass depends entirely on the superclass. In the following command line, assertions from the superclass wizard.pandorasBox.artifacts.Ailment will not be executed, although assertions for the subclass wizard.spells.Baldness are enabled:

```
>java -ea -da:wizard.pandorasBox.artifacts.Ailment Trickster
```

Assertion Execution for All System Classes

In order to enable or disable assertions in *all system classes*, we can use the options shown in Table 6.3. Enabling assertions in system classes can be useful to shed light on internal errors reported by the JVM. In the following command line, the first option -esa will enable assertions for all system classes. The second option -ea:wizard... will enable assertions in the package wizard and its subpackages wizard.pandorasBox, wizard.pandorasBox.artifacts and wizard.spells, but the third option -da:wizard.pandorasBox.artifacts... will disable them in the package wizard.pandorasBox.artifacts.

```
>java -esa -ea:wizard... -da:wizard.pandorasBox.artifacts... Trickster
```

Table 6.3 *Enabling and Disabling Assertions in All System Classes at Runtime*

Option	Short Form	Description
-enablesystemassertions	-esa	Enable assertions in *all* system classes.
-disablesystemassertions	-dsa	Disable assertions in *all* system classes.

Using Assertions

Assertions should have no side effects that can produce adverse behavior in the code, whether enabled or not. The assertion facility is a defensive mechanism, meaning that it should only be used to test the code, and should not be employed after the code is delivered. The program should exhibit the same behavior whether assertions are enabled or disabled. The program should not rely on any computations done within an assertion statement. With assertions enabled, the following statement would be executed, but if assertions were disabled, it could have dire consequences.

```
assert reactor.controlCoreTemperature();
```

Assertions should also not be used to validate information supplied by a client. A typical example is argument checking in public methods. Argument checking is part of such a method's contract, which could be violated if the assertions were disabled. A special case is program arguments on the command line. Their validation should be enforced by exception handling, and not by assertions. Another drawback is that assertion failures can only provide limited information about the cause of any failure, in the form of an AssertionError. Appropriate argument checking can provide more suitable information about erroneous arguments, in the form of specific exceptions such as IllegalArgumentException, IndexOutOfBoundsException, or NullPointerException.

The rest of this section illustrates useful idioms that employ assertions.

Internal Invariants

Very often assumptions about the program are documented as comments in the code. The following code at (1) makes the assumption that the variable status must be negative for the last else clause to be executed.

```
int status = ref1.compareTo(ref2);
if (status == 0) {
  ...
} else if (status > 0) {
  ...
} else { // (1) status must be negative.
  ...
}
```

This assumption is an *internal invariant* and can be verified using an assertion, as shown at (2) below.

```
int status = ref1.compareTo(ref2);
if (status == 0) {
  ...
} else if (status > 0) {
  ...
} else {
  assert status < 0 : status; // (2)
  ...
}
```

Often an alternative action is chosen, based on a value that is guaranteed to be one of a small set of predefined values. A switch statement with no default clause is a typical example. The value of the switch expression is guaranteed to be one of the case labels and the default case is omitted, as the following code shows.

```
switch (trinityMember) {
  case THE_FATHER:
    ...
    break;
  case THE_SON:
    ...
    break;
```

```
  case THE_HOLY_GHOST:
    ...
    break;
}
```

A default clause that executes an assertion can be used to formulate this invariant.

```
default:
  assert false : trinityMember;
```

If assertions are enabled, an AssertionError will signal the failure in case the trinity no longer holds. Note that using enum constants in the switch statement above makes the default clause unnecessary.

However, the previous code causes a compile-time error in a non-void method if all case labels return a value and no return statement follows the switch statement.

```
switch (trinityMember) {
  case THE_FATHER:
    return psalm101;
  case THE_SON:
    return psalm102;
  case THE_HOLY_GHOST:
    return psalm103;
  default:
    assert false: trinityMember;
}
return psalm100;        // (3) Compile time error if omitted.
```

Without the return statement at (3) and with assertions disabled, the method could return without a value, violating the fact that it is a non-void method. Explicitly throwing an AssertionError rather than using an assert statement in the default clause, would be a better option in this case.

```
default:
  throw new AssertionError(trinityMember);
```

Control Flow Invariants

Control flow invariants can be used to test assumptions about the flow of control in the program. The following idiom can be employed to explicitly test that certain locations in the code will never be reached.

```
assert false : "This line should never be reached.";
```

If program control does reach this statement, assertion failure will detect it.

In the following code, the assumption is that execution never reaches the end of the method declaration indicated by (1).

```
private void securityMonitor() {
  // ...
  while (alwaysOnDuty) {
    // ...
    if (needMaintenance)
      return;
```

```
    // ...
  }
  // (1) This line should never be reached.
}
```

The previous assertion can be inserted after (1) to check the assumption.

Care should be taken in using this idiom, as the compiler can flag the assert statement at this location as being unreachable. For example, if the compiler can deduce that the `while` condition will always be `true`, it will flag the assert statement as being unreachable.

Preconditions and Postconditions

The assertion facility can be used to practice a limited form of *programming-by-contract*. For example, the assertion facility can be used to check that methods comply with their contract.

Preconditions define assumptions for the proper execution of a method when it is invoked. As discussed earlier, assertions should not be used to check arguments in public methods. For non-public methods, preconditions can be checked at the start of method execution.

```
private void adjustReactorThroughput(int increment) {
  // Precondition:
  assert isValid(increment) : "Throughput increment invalid.";
  // Proceed with the adjustment.
  // ...
}
```

Postconditions define assumptions about the successful completion of a method. Postconditions in any method can be checked by assertions executed just before returning from the method. For example, if the method `adjustReactorThroughPut()` guarantees that the reactor core is in a stable state after its completion, we can check this postcondition using an assertion.

```
private void adjustReactorThroughput(int increment) {
  // Precondition:
  assert isValid(increment) : "Throughput increment invalid.";
  // Proceed with the adjustment.
  // ...
  // Postcondition -- the last action performed before returning.
  assert isCoreStable() : "Reactor core not stable.";
}
```

Section 8.4 (p. 371) provides an example using a *local class* where data can be saved before doing a computation, so that it can later be used to check a postcondition.

Other Uses

If minimizing the size of the class file is crucial, then the following conditional compilation idiom should be used to insert assertions in the source code:

```
final static boolean COMPILE_ASSERTS = false;
...
if (COMPILE_ASSERTS)
  assert whatEverYouWant;        // Not compiled if COMPILE_ASSERTS is false.
...
```

It is possible to enforce that a class be loaded and initialized only if its assertions are enabled. The idiom for this purpose uses a *static initializer block* (see Section 9.7, p. 406).

```
static {  // Static initializer
  boolean assertsAreEnabled = false;  // (1)
  assert assertsAreEnabled = true;    // (2) utilizing side effect
  if (!assertsAreEnabled)             // (3)
    throw new AssertionError("Enable assertions!");
}
```

The declaration statement at (1) sets the local variable assertsAreEnabled to false. If assertions are enabled, the assert statement at (2) is executed. The assignment operator sets the variable assertsAreEnabled to true as a side effect of evaluating the boolean expression that has the value true. The assertion at (2) is, of course, true. No exception is thrown by the if statement at (3). However, if assertions are disabled, the assert statement at (2) is never executed. As the variable assertsAreEnabled is false, the if statement at (3) throws an exception. The static initializer is placed first in the class declaration, so that it is executed first during class initialization.

 ## Review Questions

6.32 Assuming assertions are enabled, which of these assertion statements will throw an error?

Select the two correct answers.

(a) `assert true : true;`
(b) `assert true : false;`
(c) `assert false : true;`
(d) `assert false : false;`

6.33 Which of the following are valid runtime options?

Select the two correct answers.

(a) `-ae`
(b) `-enableassertions`
(c) `-source 1.6`
(d) `-disablesystemassertions`
(e) `-dea`

6.34 What is the class name of the exception thrown by an assertion statement?

Select the one correct answer.

(a) Depends on the assertion statement.
(b) `FailedAssertion`
(c) `AssertionException`
(d) `RuntimeException`
(e) `AssertionError`
(f) `Error`

6.35 What can cause an assertion statement to be ignored?

Select the one correct answer.

(a) Nothing.
(b) Using appropriate compiler options.
(c) Using appropriate runtime options.
(d) Using both appropriate compiler and runtime options.

6.36 Given the following method, which statements will throw an exception, assuming assertions are enabled?

```
static int inv(int value) {
  assert value > -50 : value < 100;
  return 100/value;
}
```

Select the two correct answers.

(a) `inv(-50);`
(b) `inv(0);`
(c) `inv(50);`
(d) `inv(100);`
(e) `inv(150);`

6.37 Which runtime options would cause assertions to be enabled for the class `org.example.ttp.Bottle`?

Select the two correct answers.

(a) `-ea`
(b) `-ea:Bottle`
(c) `-ea:org.example`
(d) `-ea:org...`
(e) `-enableexceptions:org.example.ttp.Bottle`
(f) `-ea:org.example.ttp`

6.38 What will be the result of compiling and running the following code with assertions enabled?

```
public class TernaryAssertion {
  public static void assertBounds(int low, int high, int value) {
```

```
      assert ( value > low ? value < high : false )
          : (value < high ? "too low" : "too high" );
    }
    public static void main(String[] args) {
      assertBounds(100, 200, 150);
    }
  }
```

Select the one correct answer.

(a) The compilation fails because the method name assertBounds cannot begin with the keyword assert.

(b) The compilation fails because the assert statement is invalid.

(c) The compilation succeeds and the program runs without errors.

(d) The compilation succeeds and an AssertionError with the error message "too low" is thrown.

(e) The compilation succeeds and an AssertionError with the error message "too high" is thrown.

6.39   Which statements are true about the AssertionError class?

Select the two correct answers.

(a) It is a checked exception.

(b) It has a method named toString.

(c) It has a method named getErrorMessage.

(d) It can be caught by a try-catch construct.

6.40   Which of these classes is the direct superclass of AssertionError?

Select the one correct answer.

(a) Object

(b) Throwable

(c) Exception

(d) Error

(e) RuntimeError

6.41   Given the following command, which classes would have assertions enabled?

```
    java -ea -da:com... net.example.LaunchTranslator
```

Select the two correct answers.

(a) com.example.Translator

(b) java.lang.String

(c) dot.com.Boom

(d) net.example.LaunchTranslator

(e) java.lang.AssertionError

Chapter Summary

The following information was included in this chapter:

- discussion of the selection statements: `if`, `if-else`, `switch`
- discussion of the iteration statements: `for(;;)`, `for(:)`, `while`, `do-while`
- discussion of the transfer statements: `break`, `continue`, `return`
- discussion of exception handling and exception classes in the core APIs
- defining new exception types
- discussion of the `try-catch-finally` construct and control flow paths through the construct
- throwing exceptions programmatically with the `throw` statement
- using the `throws` clause to specify checked exceptions
- discussion of the `assert` statement
- using, compiling, and executing assertions

Programming Exercises

6.1   Create different versions of a program that finds all the primes below 100. Create one version that only uses the `for(;;)` loop (i.e., no `while` or `do-while`). Create another version that only uses the `while` loop.

6.2   Here is a skeleton of a system for simulating a nuclear power plant. Implement the methods in the class named `Control`. Modify the method declarations if necessary. The Javadoc comments for each method give a description of what the implementation should do. Some of the methods in the other classes have unspecified implementations. Assume that these methods have been properly implemented and provide hooks to the rest of the system.

```
package energy;
/** A PowerPlant with a reactor core. */
public class PowerPlant {
  /** Each power plant has a reactor core. This has package
      accessibility so that the Control class that is defined in
      the same package can access it. */
  Reactor core;

  /** Initializes the power plant, creates a reactor core. */
  PowerPlant() {
    core = new Reactor();
  }

  /** Sound the alarm to evacuate the power plant. */
```

```java
    public void soundEvacuateAlarm() {
      // ... implementation unspecified ...
    }

    /** Get the level of reactor output that is most desirable at this time.
        (Units are unspecified.) */
    public int getOptimalThroughput() {
      // ... implementation unspecified ...
      return 0;
    }

    /** The main entry point of the program: sets up a PowerPlant
        object and a Control object and lets the Control object run the
        power plant. */
    public static void main(String[] args) {
      PowerPlant plant = new PowerPlant();
      Control ctrl = new Control(plant);
      ctrl.runSystem();
    }
}

/** A reactor core that has a throughput that can be either decreased or
    increased. */
class Reactor {
  /** Get the current throughput of the reactor. (Units are unspecified.) */
  public int getThroughput() {
    // ... implementation unspecified ...
    return 0;
  }

  /** @returns true if the reactor status is critical, false otherwise. */
  public boolean isCritical() {
    // ... implementation unspecified ...
    return false;
  }

  /** Ask the reactor to increase throughput. */
  void increaseThroughput() throws ReactorCritical {
    // ... implementation unspecified ...
  }

  /** Ask the reactor to decrease throughput. */
  void decreaseThroughput() {
    // ... implementation unspecified ...
  }
}

/** This exception class should be used to report that the reactor status is
    critical. */
class ReactorCritical extends Exception {}

/** A controller that will manage the power plant and make sure that the reactor
    runs with optimal throughput. */
class Control {
```

```java
    PowerPlant thePlant;

    final static int TOLERANCE = 10;

    public Control(PowerPlant p) {
      thePlant = p;
    }

    /** Run the power plant by continuously monitoring the
        optimalThroughput and the actual throughput of the reactor. If
        the throughputs differ by more than 10 units, i.e. tolerance,
        adjust the reactor throughput.
        If the reactor status becomes critical, the evacuate alarm is
        sounded and the reactor is shut down.
        <p>The runSystem() method can handle the reactor core directly
        but calls methods needAdjustment(), adjustThroughput(), and shutdown()
        instead. */
    public void runSystem() {
      // ... provide implementation here ...
    }

    /** Reports whether the throughput of the reactor needs adjusting,
        given the target throughput.
        This method should also monitor and report if the reactor status becomes
        critical.
        @return true if the optimal and actual throughput values
        differ by more than 10 units. */
    public boolean needAdjustment(int target) {
      // ... provide implementation here ...
      return true;
    }

    /** Adjust the throughput of the reactor by calling increaseThroughput() and
        decreaseThroughput() methods until the actual throughput is within 10
        units of the target throughput. */
    public void adjustThroughput(int target) {
      // ... provide implementation here ...
    }

    /** Shut down the reactor by lowering the throughput to 0. */
    public void shutdown() {
      // ... provide implementation here ...
    }
}
```

Object-Oriented Programming

7

●●●

> **Supplementary Objectives**
>
> - Understand the concepts single implementation inheritance, multiple interface inheritance, subtype-supertype relationship, and their implications for object-oriented programming (OOP).
> - Understand the contexts in which widening and narrowing reference conversions are applied.

7.1 Single Implementation Inheritance

Inheritance is one of the fundamental mechanisms for code reuse in OOP. It allows new classes to be derived from an existing class. The new class (also called *subclass, subtype, derived class, child class*) can inherit members from the old class (also called *superclass, supertype, base class, parent class*). The subclass can add new behavior and properties and, under certain circumstances, modify its inherited behavior.

In Java, *implementation inheritance* is achieved by extending classes (i.e., adding new fields and methods) and modifying inherited members (see Section 7.2, p. 288). Inheritance of members is closely tied to their declared accessibility. If a superclass member is accessible by its simple name in the subclass (without the use of any extra syntax like super), that member is considered inherited. This means that private, overridden, and hidden members of the superclass are *not* inherited (see Section 7.2, p. 288). Inheritance should not be confused with the *existence* of such members in the state of a subclass object (see Example 7.1).

The superclass is specified using the extends clause in the header of the subclass declaration. The subclass only specifies the additional new and modified members in its class body. The rest of its declaration is made up of its inherited members. If no extends clause is specified in the header of a class declaration, the class implicitly inherits from the java.lang.Object class (see Section 10.2, p. 424). This implicit inheritance is assumed in the declaration of the Light class at (1) in Example 7.1. Also in Example 7.1, the subclass TubeLight at (2) explicitly uses the extends clause and only specifies additional members to what it already inherits from the superclass Light (which, in turn, inherits from the Object class). Members of the superclass Light that are accessible by their simple names in the subclass TubeLight, are inherited by the subclass.

Private members of the superclass are not inherited by the subclass and can only be indirectly accessed. The private field indicator of the superclass Light is not inherited, but exists in the subclass object and is indirectly accessible.

Using appropriate accessibility modifiers, the superclass can limit which members can be accessed directly and, thereby, inherited by its subclasses (see Section 4.9, p. 138). As shown in Example 7.1, the subclass can use the inherited members as if they were declared in its own class body. This is not the case for members that are declared private in the superclass. Members that have package accessibility in the superclass are also not inherited by subclasses in other packages, as these members are accessible by their simple names only in subclasses within the same package as the superclass.

Since constructors (see Section 7.5, p. 302) and initializer blocks (see Section 9.7, p. 406) are *not* members of a class, they are *not* inherited by a subclass.

Extending generic classes is discussed in Section 14.2, p. 668.

Example 7.1 *Extending Classes: Inheritance and Accessibility*

```java
class Light {                              // (1)
  // Instance fields:
              int     noOfWatts;           // wattage
  private   boolean indicator;             // on or off
  protected String  location;              // placement

  // Static field:
  private static int counter;              // no. of Light objects created

  // Constructor:
  Light() {
    noOfWatts = 50;
    indicator = true;
    location  = "X";
    counter++;
  }

  // Instance methods:
  public  void    switchOn()  { indicator = true; }
  public  void    switchOff() { indicator = false; }
  public  boolean isOn()      { return indicator; }
  private void    printLocation() {
    System.out.println("Location: " + location);
  }

  // Static methods:
  public static void writeCount() {
    System.out.println("Number of lights: " + counter);
  }
  //...
}
//_____
class TubeLight extends Light {            // (2) Subclass uses the extends clause.
  // Instance fields:
  private int tubeLength = 54;
  private int colorNo    = 10;

  // Instance methods:
  public int getTubeLength() { return tubeLength; }

  public void printInfo() {
    System.out.println("Tube length: "  + getTubeLength());
```

```
      System.out.println("Color number: " + colorNo);
      System.out.println("Wattage: "      + noOfWatts);     // Inherited.
 //   System.out.println("Indicator: "    + indicator);     // Not Inherited.
      System.out.println("Indicator: "    + isOn());         // Inherited.
      System.out.println("Location: "     + location);       // Inherited.
 //   printLocation();                                        // Not Inherited.
 //   System.out.println("Counter: "   + counter);          // Not Inherited.
      writeCount();                                           // Inherited.
    }
    // ...
  }
 //_____
  public class Utility {                    // (3)
    public static void main(String[] args) {
      new TubeLight().printInfo();
    }
  }
```

Output from the program:

```
Tube length: 54
Color number: 10
Wattage: 50
Indicator: true
Location: X
Number of lights: 1
```

Inheritance Hierarchy

In Java, a class can only extend *one* other class; i.e., it can only have one immediate superclass. This kind of inheritance is sometimes called *single* or *linear implementation inheritance*. The name is appropriate, as the subclass inherits the *implementations* of its superclass members. The inheritance relationship can be depicted as an *inheritance hierarchy* (also called *class hierarchy*). Classes higher up in the hierarchy are more *generalized*, as they abstract the class behavior. Classes lower down in the hierarchy are more *specialized*, as they customize the inherited behavior by additional properties and behavior. Figure 7.1 illustrates the inheritance relationship between the class Light, which represents the more general abstraction, and its more specialized subclasses. The java.lang.Object class is always at the top of any Java inheritance hierarchy, as all classes, with the exception of the Object class itself, inherit (either directly or indirectly) from this class.

Relationships: is-a and has-a

Inheritance defines the relationship *is-a* (also called the *superclass–subclass* relationship) between a superclass and its subclasses. This means that an object of a subclass *is-a* superclass object, and can be used wherever an object of the superclass can be used. This is often employed as a litmus test for choosing inheritance in object-oriented design. It has particular consequences on how objects can be used.

Figure 7.1 *Inheritance Hierarchy*

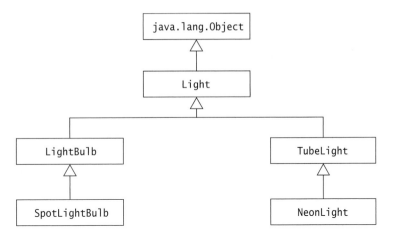

An object of the TubeLight class *is-an* object of the superclass Light. Referring to Figure 7.1, an object of the TubeLight class can be used wherever an object of the superclass Light can be used. The inheritance relationship is transitive: if class B extends class A, then a class C, which extends class B, will also inherit from class A via class B. An object of the SpotLightBulb class *is-an* object of the class Light. The *is-a* relationship does not hold between peer classes: an object of the LightBulb class is not an object of the class TubeLight and vice versa.

Whereas inheritance defines the relationship *is-a* between a superclass and its subclasses, *aggregation* defines the relationship *has-a* (also called the *whole–part* relationship) between an instance of a class and its constituents (also called *parts*). Aggregation comprises the *usage* of objects. An instance of class Light *has* (or *uses*) the following parts: a field to store its wattage (noOfWatts), a field to store whether it is on or off (indicator), and a String object to store its location (denoted by the field reference location). In Java, a composite object cannot contain other objects. It can only store *reference values* of its constituent objects in its fields. This relationship defines an *aggregation hierarchy* (also called *object hierarchy*) that embodies the *has-a* relationship. Constituent objects can be shared between objects, and their lifetimes can be dependent or independent of the lifetime of the composite object. Inheritance and aggregation are compared in Section 7.13, p. 342.

The Supertype-Subtype Relationship

A class defines a reference type. Therefore the inheritance hierarchy can be regarded as a *type hierarchy*, embodying the *supertype-subtype relationship* between reference types. In the context of Java, the supertype-subtype relationship implies that the reference value of a subtype object can be assigned to a supertype reference, because a subtype object can be substituted for a supertype object. This assignment involves a *widening reference conversion* (see Section 5.1, p. 161), as references are assigned *up* the inheritance hierarchy. Using the reference types in Example 7.1, the following code assigns the reference value of an object of the subtype TubeLight to the reference light of the supertype Light:

```
    Light light = new TubeLight();              // (1) widening reference conversion
```

We can now use the reference light to invoke those methods on the subtype object that are inherited from the supertype Light:

```
    light.switchOn();                           // (2)
```

Note that the compiler only knows about the *declared type* of the reference light, which is Light, and ensures that only methods from this type can be called using the reference light. However, at runtime, the reference light will refer to an object of the subtype TubeLight when the call to the method switchOn() is executed. It is the *type of the object* that the reference is referring to at runtime that determines which method is executed. The subtype object inherits the switchOn() method from its supertype Light, and it is this method that is executed. The type of the object that the reference refers to at runtime is often called the *dynamic type* of the reference.

One might be tempted to invoke methods exclusive to the TubeLight subtype via the supertype reference light:

```
    light.getTubeLength();                      // (3) Not OK.
```

However, this will not work, as the compiler does not know what object the reference light is denoting. It only knows the declared type of the reference. As the declaration of the class Light does not have a method called getTubeLength(), this method call at (3) results in a compile-time error. As we shall see later in this chapter, eliciting subtype-specific behavior using a supertype reference requires a narrowing reference conversion with an explicit cast (Section 7.11, p. 327).

The rest of this chapter will elaborate on various aspects of OOP, and understanding them is founded in understanding the consequences of the subtype-supertype relationship.

7.2 Overriding Methods

Instance Method Overriding

Under certain circumstances, a subclass may *override* instance methods that it would otherwise inherit from a superclass. Overriding such a method allows the subclass to provide its *own* implementation of the method. When the method is invoked on an object of the subclass, it is the method implementation in the subclass that is executed. The overridden method in the superclass is *not* inherited by the subclass, and the new method in the subclass must abide by the following rules of method overriding:

- The new method definition must have the same *method signature*, i.e., the method name, and the types and the number of parameters, including their order, are the same as in the overridden method.

  Whether parameters in the overriding method should be final is at the discretion of the subclass (see Section 3.9, p. 95). A method's signature does not comprise the final modifier of parameters, only their types and order.

- The return type of the overriding method can be a *subtype* of the return type of the overridden method (called *covariant return*).

- The new method definition cannot *narrow* the accessibility of the method, but it can *widen* it (see Section 4.9, p. 138).

- The new method definition can only throw all or none, or a subset of the checked exceptions (including their subclasses) that are specified in the throws clause of the overridden method in the superclass (see Section 6.9, p. 259).

These requirements also apply to interfaces, where a subinterface can override abstract method declarations from its superinterfaces (see Section 7.6, p. 309). The implications of generics on overriding methods is discussed in Section 14.12, p. 718.

In Example 7.2, the new definition of the getBill() method at (6) in the subclass TubeLight has the same signature and the same return type as the method at (2) in the superclass Light. The new definition specifies a subset of the exceptions (ZeroHoursException) thrown by the overridden method (the exception class Invalid HoursException is a superclass of NegativeHoursException and ZeroHoursException). The new definition also widens the accessibility (public) from what it was in the overridden definition (protected). The overriding method also declares the parameter to be final, but this has no bearing in overriding the method.

The astute reader will have noticed the @Override annotation preceding the method definition at (6). The compiler will now report an error if the method definition does *not* override an inherited method. The annotation helps to ensure that the method definition overrides, and not overloads another method silently (see Section 14.12, p. 718).

Invocation of the method getBill() on an object of subclass TubeLight using references of the subclass and the superclass at (14) and (15), results in the new definition at (6) being executed, since both references are aliases of the TubeLight object created at (11).

```
tubeLight.getBill(5);                 // (14) Invokes method at (6).
light1.getBill(5);                    // (15) Invokes method at (6).
```

Not surprisingly, the invocation of the method getBill() on an object of superclass Light using a reference of the superclass at (16), results in the overridden definition at (2) being executed:

```
light2.getBill(5);                    // (16) Invokes method at (2).
```

Covariant return in Overriding Methods

In Example 7.2, the definition of the method makeInstance() at (8) overrides the method definition at (3). Note that the method signatures are the same, but the return type at (8) is a subtype of the return type at (3). The method at (8) returns an object of the subtype TubeLight, whereas the method at (3) returns an object of the supertype Light. This is an example of *covariant return*.

Depending on whether we call the method makeInstance() on an object of the subtype TubeLight or that of the supertype Light, the respective method definition will be executed. The code at (17) and (18) illustrates what object is returned by the method, depending on which method definition is executed.

Note that covariant return only applies to *reference* types, not to primitive types. For example, changing the return type of the getBill() method at (6) to float, will result in a compile-time error. There is no subtype relationship between primitive types.

Example 7.2 *Overriding, Overloading, and Hiding*

```java
//Exceptions
class InvalidHoursException extends Exception {}
class NegativeHoursException extends InvalidHoursException {}
class ZeroHoursException extends InvalidHoursException {}

class Light {

  protected String billType = "Small bill";        // (1) Instance field

  protected double getBill(int noOfHours)
                    throws InvalidHoursException { // (2) Instance method
    if (noOfHours < 0)
      throw new NegativeHoursException();
    double smallAmount = 10.0, smallBill = smallAmount * noOfHours;
    System.out.println(billType + ": " + smallBill);
    return smallBill;
  }

  public Light makeInstance() {                     // (3) Instance method
    return new Light();
  }

  public static void printBillType() {              // (4) Static method
    System.out.println("Small bill");
  }
}
//_____
class TubeLight extends Light {

  public static String billType = "Large bill";  // (5) Hiding field at (1).

  @Override
  public double getBill(final int noOfHours)
```

```
                       throws ZeroHoursException {     // (6) Overriding instance method at (2).
        if (noOfHours == 0)
          throw new ZeroHoursException();
        double largeAmount = 100.0, largeBill = largeAmount * noOfHours;
        System.out.println(billType + ": " + largeBill);
        return largeBill;
      }

      public double getBill() {                 // (7) Overloading method at (6).
        System.out.println("No bill");
        return 0.0;
      }

      @Override
      public TubeLight makeInstance() {     // (8) Overriding instance method at (3).
        return new TubeLight();
      }

      public static void printBillType() { // (9) Hiding static method at (4).
        System.out.println(billType);
      }
    }
    //_____
    public class Client {
      public static void main(String[] args) throws InvalidHoursException { // (10)

        TubeLight tubeLight = new TubeLight();      // (11)
        Light     light1    = tubeLight;            // (12) Aliases.
        Light     light2    = new Light();          // (13)

        System.out.println("Invoke overridden instance method:");
        tubeLight.getBill(5);                       // (14) Invokes method at (6).
        light1.getBill(5);                          // (15) Invokes method at (6).
        light2.getBill(5);                          // (16) Invokes method at (2).

        System.out.println(
                "Invoke overridden instance method with covariant return:");
        System.out.println(
                light2.makeInstance().getClass()); // (17) Invokes method at (3).
        System.out.println(
            tubeLight.makeInstance().getClass()); // (18) Invokes method at (8).

        System.out.println("Access hidden field:");
        System.out.println(tubeLight.billType);   // (19) Accesses field at (5).
        System.out.println(light1.billType);      // (20) Accesses field at (1).
        System.out.println(light2.billType);      // (21) Accesses field at (1).

        System.out.println("Invoke hidden static method:");
        tubeLight.printBillType();                 // (22) Invokes method at (9).
        light1.printBillType();                    // (23) Invokes method at (4).
        light2.printBillType();                    // (24) Invokes method at (4).

        System.out.println("Invoke overloaded method:");
        tubeLight.getBill();                       // (25) Invokes method at (7).
      }
    }
```

Output from the program:

```
Invoke overridden instance method:
Large bill: 500.0
Large bill: 500.0
Small bill: 50.0
Invoke overridden instance method with covariant return:
class Light
class TubeLight
Access hidden field:
Large bill
Small bill
Small bill
Invoke hidden static method:
Large bill
Small bill
Small bill
Invoke overloaded method:
No bill
```

Here are a few more facts to note about overriding. A subclass must use the keyword super in order to invoke an overridden method in the superclass (see p. 295).

An instance method in a subclass cannot override a static method in the superclass. The compiler will flag this as an error. A static method is class-specific and not part of any object, while overriding methods are invoked on behalf of objects of the subclass. However, a static method in a subclass can *hide* a static method in the superclass (see below).

A final method cannot be overridden, because the modifier final prevents method overriding. An attempt to override a final method will result in a compile-time error. An abstract method, on the other hand, requires the non-abstract subclasses to override the method, in order to provide an implementation.

The accessibility modifier private for a method means that the method is not accessible outside the class in which it is defined; therefore, a subclass cannot override it. However, a subclass can give its own definition of such a method, which may have the same signature as the method in its superclass.

Overriding vs. Overloading

Method overriding should not be confused with *method overloading* (see Section 3.3, p. 47).

Method overriding always requires the same method signature (name and parameter types) and the same or covariant return types. Overloading occurs when the method names are the same, but the parameter lists differ. Therefore, to overload methods, the parameters must differ either in type, order, or number. As the return type is not a part of the method signature, just having different return types is not enough to overload methods.

Only non-final instance methods in the superclass that are directly accessible from the subclass can be overridden. Both instance and static methods can be overloaded in the class they are defined in or in a subclass of their class.

Invoking an overridden method in the superclass from a subclass requires a special syntax (e.g., the keyword super). This is not necessary for invoking an overloaded method in the superclass from a subclass. If the right kinds of arguments are passed in the method call occurring in the subclass, the overloaded method in the superclass will be invoked. In Example 7.2, the method getBill() at (2) in class Light is overridden in class TubeLight at (6) and overloaded at (7). When invoked at (25), the definition at (7) is executed.

For overloaded methods, which method implementation will be executed at runtime is determined at *compile time* (see Section 7.10, p. 324), but for overridden methods, the method implementation to be executed is determined at *runtime* (see Section 7.12, p. 340). Table 7.1 provides a comparison between overriding and overloading.

Table 7.1 *Overriding vs. Overloading*

Comparison Criteria	Overriding	Overloading
Method name	Must be the same.	Must be the same.
Argument list	Must be the same.	Must be different.
Return type	Can be the same type or a covariant type.	Can be different.
throws clause	Must not throw new checked exceptions. Can narrow exceptions thrown.	Can be different.
Accessibility	Can make it less restrictive, but not more restrictive.	Can be different.
Declaration context	A method can only be overridden in a subclass.	A method can be overloaded in the same class or in a subclass.
Method call resolution	The *runtime type* of the reference, i.e., the type of the object referenced at *runtime*, determines which method is selected for execution.	At compile time, the *declared type* of the reference is used to determine which method will be executed at runtime.

7.3 Hiding Members

Field Hiding

A subclass cannot override fields of the superclass, but it can *hide* them. The sub-class can define fields with the same name as in the superclass. If this is the case, the fields in the superclass cannot be accessed in the subclass by their simple names; therefore, they are not inherited by the subclass. Code in the subclass can use the keyword super to access such members, including hidden fields. A client can use a reference of the *superclass* to access members that are hidden in the sub-class, as explained below. Of course, if the hidden field is static, it can also be accessed by the superclass name.

The following distinction between invoking instance methods on an object and accessing fields of an object must be noted. When an instance method is invoked on an object using a reference, it is the *class of the current object* denoted by the reference, not the type of reference, that determines which method implementation will be executed. In Example 7.2 at (14), (15), and (16), this is evident from invoking the overridden method getBill(): the method from the class corresponding to the current object is executed, regardless of the reference type. When a field of an object is accessed using a reference, it is the *type of the reference*, not the class of the current object denoted by the reference, that determines which field will actually be accessed. In Example 7.2 at (19), (20), and (21), this is evident from accessing the hidden field billType: the field accessed is declared in the class corresponding to the reference type, regardless of the object denoted by the reference.

In contrast to method overriding, where an instance method cannot override a static method, there are no such restrictions on the hiding of fields. The field bill-Type is static in the subclass, but not in the superclass. The type of the fields need not be the same either, it is only the field name that matters in the hiding of fields.

Static Method Hiding

A static method *cannot* override an inherited instance method, but it can *hide* a static method if the exact requirements for overriding instance methods are ful-filled (see Section 7.2, p. 288). A hidden superclass static method is not inherited. The compiler will flag an error if the signatures are the same, but the other require-ments regarding return type, throws clause, and accessibility are not met. If the sig-natures are different, the method name is overloaded, not hidden.

A call to a static or final method is bound to a method implementation at compile time (private methods are implicitly final). Example 7.2 illustrates invocation of static methods. Analogous to accessing fields, the method invoked in (22), (23), and (24) is determined by the *class* of the reference. In (22) the class type is Tube-Light, therefore, the static method printBillType() at (9) in this class is invoked. In (23) and (24), the class type is Light and the hidden static method printBillType() at (4) in that class is invoked. This is borne out by the output from the program.

A hidden static method can always be invoked by using the superclass name in the subclass declaration. Additionally, the keyword super can be used in non-static code in the subclass declaration to invoke hidden static methods.

7.4 **The Object Reference** super

The this reference is available in non-static code and refers to the current object. When an instance method is invoked, the this reference denotes the object on which the method is called (see Section 3.3, p. 45). The keyword super can also be used in non-static code (e.g., in the body of an instance method), but only in a subclass, to access fields and invoke methods from the superclass (see Table 4.1, p.130). The keyword super provides a reference to the current object as an instance of its superclass. In method invocations with super, the method from the superclass is invoked regardless of the actual type of the object or whether the current class overrides the method. It is typically used to invoke methods that are overridden and to access members that are hidden in the subclass. Unlike the this keyword, the super keyword cannot be used as an ordinary reference. For example, it cannot be assigned to other references or cast to other reference types.

In Example 7.3, the declaration of the method demonstrate() at (9) in the class Neon-Light makes use of the super keyword to access members higher up in its inheritance hierarchy. This is the case when the banner() method is invoked at (10). This method is defined at (4) in the class Light and not in the immediate superclass Tube-Light of the subclass NeonLight. The overridden method getBill() and its overloaded version at (6) and (8) in the class TubeLight are invoked, using super at (11) and (12), respectively.

The class NeonLight is a subclass of the class TubeLight, which is a subclass of the class Light, which has a field named billType and a method named getBill defined at (1) and (2), respectively. One might be tempted to use the syntax super.super.getBill(20) in the subclass NeonLight to invoke this method, but this is not a valid construct. One might also be tempted to cast the this reference to the class Light and try again as shown at (13). The output shows that the method getBill() at (6) in the class TubeLight was executed, not the one from the class Light. The reason is that a cast only changes the type of the reference (in this case to Light), not the class of the object (which is still NeonLight). Method invocation is determined by the class of the current object, resulting in the inherited method getBill() in the class TubeLight being executed. There is no way to invoke the method getBill() in the class Light from the subclass NeonLight.

At (14) the keyword super is used to access the field billType at (5) in the class Tube-Light. At (15) the field billType from the class Light is accessed successfully by casting the this reference, because it is the type of the reference that determines which field is accessed. From non-static code in a subclass, it is possible to directly access fields in a class higher up the inheritance hierarchy by casting the this reference. However, it is futile to cast the this reference to invoke instance methods in a class higher up the inheritance hierarchy, as illustrated above in the case of the overridden method getBill().

Finally, the calls to the static methods at (16) and (17) using the super and this references, exhibit runtime behavior analogous to accessing fields, as discussed earlier.

Example 7.3   *Using the* super *Keyword*

```java
//Exceptions
class InvalidHoursException extends Exception {}
class NegativeHoursException extends InvalidHoursException {}
class ZeroHoursException extends InvalidHoursException {}

class Light {

  protected String billType  = "Small bill";        // (1)

  protected double getBill(int noOfHours)
  throws InvalidHoursException {                     // (2)
    if (noOfHours < 0)
      throw new NegativeHoursException();
    double smallAmount = 10.0, smallBill = smallAmount * noOfHours;
    System.out.println(billType + ": " + smallBill);
    return smallBill;
  }

  public static void printBillType() {              // (3)
    System.out.println("Small bill");
  }

  public void banner() {                            // (4)
    System.out.println("Let there be light!");
  }
}
//_____
class TubeLight extends Light {

  public static String billType = "Large bill"; // (5) Hiding static field at (1).

  @Override
  public double getBill(final int noOfHours)
        throws ZeroHoursException {      // (6) Overriding instance method at (2).
    if (noOfHours == 0)
      throw new ZeroHoursException();
    double largeAmount = 100.0, largeBill = largeAmount * noOfHours;
    System.out.println(billType + ": " + largeBill);
    return largeBill;
  }

  public static void printBillType() {    // (7) Hiding static method at (3).
    System.out.println(billType);
  }
```

```
  public double getBill() {                    // (8) Overloading method at (6).
    System.out.println("No bill");
    return 0.0;
  }
}
//_____
class NeonLight extends TubeLight {
  // ...
  public void demonstrate() throws InvalidHoursException {    // (9)
    super.banner();                                    // (10) Invokes method at (4)
    super.getBill(20);                                 // (11) Invokes method at (6)
    super.getBill();                                   // (12) Invokes method at (8)
    ((Light) this).getBill(20);                        // (13) Invokes method at (6)
    System.out.println(super.billType);                // (14) Accesses field at (5)
    System.out.println(((Light) this).billType);       // (15) Accesses field at (1)
    super.printBillType();                             // (16) Invokes method at (7)
    ((Light) this).printBillType();                    // (17) Invokes method at (3)
  }
}
//_____
public class Client {
  public static void main(String[] args)
  throws InvalidHoursException {
    NeonLight neonRef = new NeonLight();
    neonRef.demonstrate();
  }
}
```

Output from the program:

```
Let there be light!
No bill
Large bill: 2000.0
Large bill: 2000.0
Large bill
Small bill
Large bill
Small bill
```

 Review Questions

7.1   Which statements are true?

Select the two correct answers.

(a) In Java, the extends clause is used to specify the inheritance relationship.
(b) The subclass of a non-abstract class can be declared abstract.
(c) All members of the superclass are inherited by the subclass.
(d) A final class can be abstract.
(e) A class in which all the members are declared private, cannot be declared public.

7.2   Which statements are true?

Select the two correct answers.

(a) A class can only be extended by one class.
(b) Every Java object has a `public` method named `equals`.
(c) Every Java object has a `public` method named `length`.
(d) A class can extend any number of classes.
(e) A non-`final` class can be extended by any number of classes.

7.3   Which statements are true?

Select the two correct answers.

(a) A subclass must define all the methods from the superclass.
(b) It is possible for a subclass to define a method with the same name and parameters as a method defined by the superclass.
(c) It is possible for a subclass to define a field with the same name as a field defined by the superclass.
(d) It is possible for two classes to be the superclass of each other.

7.4   Given the following classes and declarations, which statements are true?

```
// Classes
class Foo {
  private int i;
  public void f() { /* ... */ }
  public void g() { /* ... */ }
}

class Bar extends Foo {
  public int j;
  public void g() { /* ... */ }
}

// Declarations:
  Foo a = new Foo();
  Bar b = new Bar();
```

Select the three correct answers.

(a) The `Bar` class is a subclass of `Foo`.
(b) The statement `b.f();` is legal.
(c) The statement `a.j = 5;` is legal.
(d) The statement `a.g();` is legal.
(e) The statement `b.i = 3;` is legal.

7.5   Which statement is true?

Select the one correct answer.

(a) Private methods cannot be overridden in subclasses.
(b) A subclass can override any method in a superclass.
(c) An overriding method can declare that it throws checked exceptions that are not thrown by the method it is overriding.

(d) The parameter list of an overriding method can be a subset of the parameter list of the method that it is overriding.

(e) The overriding method must have the same return type as the overridden method.

7.6 Given classes A, B, and C, where B extends A, and C extends B, and where all classes implement the instance method void doIt(). How can the doIt() method in A be called from an instance method in C?

Select the one correct answer.

(a) doIt();

(b) super.doIt();

(c) super.super.doIt();

(d) this.super.doIt();

(e) A.this.doIt();

(f) ((A) this).doIt();

(g) It is not possible.

7.7 What would be the result of compiling and running the following program?

```java
// Filename: MyClass.java
public class MyClass {
  public static void main(String[] args) {
    C c = new C();
    System.out.println(c.max(13, 29));
  }
}

class A {
  int max(int x, int y) { if (x>y) return x; else return y; }
}

class B extends A{
  int max(int x, int y) { return super.max(y, x) - 10; }
}

class C extends B {
  int max(int x, int y) { return super.max(x+10, y+10); }
}
```

Select the one correct answer.

(a) The code will fail to compile because the max() method in B passes the arguments in the call super.max(y, x) in the wrong order.

(b) The code will fail to compile because a call to a max() method is ambiguous.

(c) The code will compile and print 13, when run.

(d) The code will compile and print 23, when run.

(e) The code will compile and print 29, when run.

(f) The code will compile and print 39, when run.

7.8   Which is the simplest expression that can be inserted at (1), so that the program prints the value of the text field from the Message class?

```
// Filename: MyClass.java
class Message {
  // The message that should be printed:
  String text = "Hello, world!";
}

class MySuperclass {
  Message msg = new Message();
}

public class MyClass extends MySuperclass {
  public static void main(String[] args) {
    MyClass object = new MyClass();
    object.print();
  }

  public void print() {
    System.out.println( /* (1) INSERT THE SIMPLEST EXPRESSION HERE */ );
  }
}
```

Select the one correct answer.

(a) `text`
(b) `Message.text`
(c) `msg.text`
(d) `object.msg.text`
(e) `super.msg.text`
(f) `object.super.msg.text`

7.9   Which method declarations, when inserted at (7), will not result in a compile-time error?

```
class MySuperclass {
  public        Integer step1(int i)                        { return 1; }    // (1)
  protected     String  step2(String str1, String str2) { return str1; }  // (2)
  public        String  step2(String str1)                  { return str1; }  // (3)
  public static String  step2()                             { return "Hi"; }  // (4)

  public MyClass        makeIt()  { return new MyClass(); }                   // (5)
  public MySuperclass makeIt2() { return new MyClass(); }                   // (6)
}

public class MyClass extends MySuperclass {
  // (7) INSERT METHOD DECLARATION HERE
}
```

Select the two correct answers.

(a) `public int step1(int i) { return 1; }`
(b) `public String step2(String str2, String str1) { return str1; }`
(c) `private void step2() { }`

(d) `private static void step2() { }`
(e) `private static String step2(String str) { return str; }`
(f) `public MySuperclass makeIt() { return new MySuperclass(); }`
(g) `public MyClass makeIt2() { return new MyClass(); }`

7.10 What would be the result of compiling and running the following program?

```
class Vehicle {
  static public String getModelName() { return "Volvo"; }
  public long getRegNo() { return 12345; }
}

class Car extends Vehicle {
  static public String getModelName() { return "Toyota"; }
  public long getRegNo() { return 54321; }
}

public class TakeARide {
  public static void main(String args[]) {
    Car c = new Car();
    Vehicle v = c;

    System.out.println("|" + v.getModelName() + "|" + c.getModelName() +
                       "|" + v.getRegNo()     + "|" + c.getRegNo() + "|");
  }
}
```

Select the one correct answer.

(a) The code will fail to compile.
(b) The code will compile and print |Toyota|Volvo|12345|54321|, when run.
(c) The code will compile and print |Volvo|Toyota|12345|54321|, when run.
(d) The code will compile and print |Toyota|Toyota|12345|12345|, when run.
(e) The code will compile and print |Volvo|Volvo|12345|54321|, when run.
(f) The code will compile and print |Toyota|Toyota|12345|12345|, when run.
(g) The code will compile and print |Volvo|Toyota|54321|54321|, when run.

7.11 What would be the result of compiling and running the following program?

```
final class Item {
  Integer size;
  Item(Integer size) { this.size = size; }
  public boolean equals(Item item2) {
    if (this == item2) return true;
    return this.size.equals(item2.size);
  }
}

public class SkepticRide {
  public static void main(String[] args) {
    Item itemA = new Item(10);
    Item itemB = new Item(10);
    Object itemC = itemA;
    System.out.println("|" + itemA.equals(itemB) +
                       "|" + itemC.equals(itemB) + "|");
  }
}
```

Select the one correct answer.

(a) The code will fail to compile.
(b) The code will compile and print |false|false|, when run.
(c) The code will compile and print |false|true|, when run.
(d) The code will compile and print |true|false|, when run.
(e) The code will compile and print |true|true|, when run.

7.5 Chaining Constructors Using `this()` and `super()`

Constructors are discussed in Section 3.4, p. 48. Other uses of the keywords `this` and `super` can be found in Section 7.2, p. 288, and Section 8.3, p. 360.

The `this()` Constructor Call

Constructors cannot be inherited or overridden. They can be overloaded, but only in the same class. Since a constructor always has the same name as the class, each parameter list must be different when defining more than one constructor for a class. In Example 7.4, the class `Light` has three overloaded constructors. In the non-default constructor at (3), the `this` reference is used to access the fields shadowed by the parameters. In the `main()` method at (4), the appropriate constructor is invoked depending on the arguments in the constructor call, as illustrated by the program output.

Example 7.4 *Constructor Overloading*

```
class Light {

  // Fields:
  private int     noOfWatts;     // wattage
  private boolean indicator;     // on or off
  private String  location;      // placement

  // Constructors:
  Light() {                                      // (1) Explicit default constructor
    noOfWatts = 0;
    indicator = false;
    location  = "X";
    System.out.println("Returning from default constructor no. 1.");
  }
  Light(int watts, boolean onOffState) {                    // (2) Non-default
    noOfWatts = watts;
    indicator = onOffState;
    location  = "X";
    System.out.println("Returning from non-default constructor no. 2.");
  }
  Light(int noOfWatts, boolean indicator, String location) {  // (3) Non-default
    this.noOfWatts = noOfWatts;
```

```
        this.indicator = indicator;
        this.location  = location;
        System.out.println("Returning from non-default constructor no. 3.");
    }
}
//_____
public class DemoConstructorCall {
    public static void main(String[] args) {                        // (4)
        System.out.println("Creating Light object no. 1.");
        Light light1 = new Light();
        System.out.println("Creating Light object no. 2.");
        Light light2 = new Light(250, true);
        System.out.println("Creating Light object no. 3.");
        Light light3 = new Light(250, true, "attic");
    }
}
Output from the program:

Creating Light object no. 1.
Returning from default constructor no. 1.
Creating Light object no. 2.
Returning from non-default constructor no. 2.
Creating Light object no. 3.
Returning from non-default constructor no. 3.
```

Example 7.5 illustrates the use of the this() construct, which is used to implement *local chaining* of constructors in the class when an instance of the class is created. The first two constructors at (1) and (2) from Example 7.4 have been rewritten using the this() construct in Example 7.5 at (1) and (2), respectively. The this() construct can be regarded as being locally overloaded, since its parameters (and hence its signature) can vary, as shown in the body of the constructors at (1) and (2). The this() call invokes the local constructor with the corresponding parameter list. In the main() method at (4), the appropriate constructor is invoked depending on the arguments in the constructor call when each of the three Light objects are created. Calling the default constructor to create a Light object results in the second and third constructors being executed as well. This is confirmed by the output from the program. In this case, the output shows that the third constructor completed first, followed by the second, and finally the default constructor that was called first. Bearing in mind the definition of the constructors, the constructors are invoked in the *reverse* order; i.e., invocation of the default constructor immediately leads to invocation of the second constructor by the call this(0, false), and its invocation leads to the third constructor being called immediately by the call this(watt, ind, "X"), with the completion of the execution in the reverse order of their invocation. Similarly, calling the second constructor to create an instance of the Light class results in the third constructor being executed as well.

Java requires that any this() call must occur as the *first* statement in a constructor. The this() call can be followed by any other relevant code. This restriction is due to Java's handling of constructor invocation in the superclass when an object of the subclass is created. This mechanism is explained in the next subsection.

Example 7.5 *The* this() *Constructor Call*

```java
class Light {
  // Fields:
  private int     noOfWatts;
  private boolean indicator;
  private String  location;

  // Constructors:
  Light() {                                    // (1) Explicit default constructor
    this(0, false);
    System.out.println("Returning from default constructor no. 1.");
  }
  Light(int watt, boolean ind) {               // (2) Non-default
    this(watt, ind, "X");
    System.out.println("Returning from non-default constructor no. 2.");
  }
  Light(int noOfWatts, boolean indicator, String location) { // (3) Non-default
    this.noOfWatts = noOfWatts;
    this.indicator = indicator;
    this.location  = location;
    System.out.println("Returning from non-default constructor no. 3.");
  }
}
//_____
public class DemoThisCall {
  public static void main(String[] args) {                 // (4)
    System.out.println("Creating Light object no. 1.");
    Light light1 = new Light();                             // (5)
    System.out.println("Creating Light object no. 2.");
    Light light2 = new Light(250, true);                    // (6)
    System.out.println("Creating Light object no. 3.");
    Light light3 = new Light(250, true, "attic");           // (7)
  }
}
```

Output from the program:

```
Creating Light object no. 1.
Returning from non-default constructor no. 3.
Returning from non-default constructor no. 2.
Returning from default constructor no. 1.
Creating Light object no. 2.
Returning from non-default constructor no. 3.
Returning from non-default constructor no. 2.
Creating Light object no. 3.
Returning from non-default constructor no. 3.
```

The super() **Constructor Call**

The super() construct is used in a subclass constructor to invoke a constructor in the *immediate* superclass. This allows the subclass to influence the initialization of its inherited state when an object of the subclass is created. A super() call in the constructor of a subclass will result in the execution of the relevant constructor from the superclass, based on the signature of the call. Since the superclass name is known in the subclass declaration, the compiler can determine the superclass constructor invoked from the signature of the parameter list.

A constructor in a subclass can access the class's inherited members by their simple names. The keyword super can also be used in a subclass constructor to access inherited members via its superclass. One might be tempted to use the super keyword in a constructor to specify initial values of inherited fields. However, the super() construct provides a better solution to initialize the inherited state.

In Example 7.6, the non-default constructor at (3) of the class Light has a super() call (with no arguments) at (4). Although the constructor is not strictly necessary, as the compiler will insert one—as explained below—it is included for expositional purposes. The non-default constructor at (6) of the class TubeLight has a super() call (with three arguments) at (7). This super() call will match the non-default constructor at (3) of the superclass Light. This is evident from the program output.

Example 7.6   *The* super() *Constructor Call*

```
class Light {
  // Fields:
  private int     noOfWatts;
  private boolean indicator;
  private String  location;

  // Constructors:
  Light() {                                      // (1) Explicit default constructor
    this(0, false);
    System.out.println(
    "Returning from default constructor no. 1 in class Light");
  }
  Light(int watt, boolean ind) {                           // (2) Non-default
    this(watt, ind, "X");
    System.out.println(
    "Returning from non-default constructor no. 2 in class Light");
  }
  Light(int noOfWatts, boolean indicator, String location) {   // (3) Non-default
    super();                                     // (4)
    this.noOfWatts = noOfWatts;
    this.indicator = indicator;
    this.location  = location;
    System.out.println(
        "Returning from non-default constructor no. 3 in class Light");
  }
```

```
}
//_____
class TubeLight extends Light {
  // Instance variables:
  private int tubeLength;
  private int colorNo;

  // Constructors:
  TubeLight(int tubeLength, int colorNo) {                    // (5) Non-default
    this(tubeLength, colorNo, 100, true, "Unknown");
    System.out.println(
        "Returning from non-default constructor no. 1 in class TubeLight");
  }
  TubeLight(int tubeLength, int colorNo, int noOfWatts,
            boolean indicator, String location) {            // (6) Non-default
    super(noOfWatts, indicator, location);                   // (7)
    this.tubeLength = tubeLength;
    this.colorNo    = colorNo;
    System.out.println(
        "Returning from non-default constructor no. 2 in class TubeLight");
  }
}
//_____
public class Chaining {
  public static void main(String[] args) {
    System.out.println("Creating a TubeLight object.");
    TubeLight tubeLightRef = new TubeLight(20, 5);            // (8)
  }
}
```

Output from the program:

```
Creating a TubeLight object.
Returning from non-default constructor no. 3 in class Light
Returning from non-default constructor no. 2 in class TubeLight
Returning from non-default constructor no. 1 in class TubeLight
```

The super() construct has the same restrictions as the this() construct: if used, the super() call must occur as the *first* statement in a constructor, and it can only be used in a constructor declaration. This implies that this() and super() calls cannot both occur in the same constructor. The this() construct is used to *chain* constructors in the *same* class. The constructor at the end of such a chain can invoke a superclass constructor using the super() construct. Just as the this() construct leads to chaining of constructors in the same class, the super() construct leads to chaining of subclass constructors to superclass constructors. This chaining behavior guarantees that all superclass constructors are called, starting with the constructor of the class being instantiated, all the way to the top of the inheritance hierarchy, which is always the Object class. Note that the body of the constructor is executed in the reverse order to the call order, as super() can only occur as the first statement in a constructor. This ensures that the constructor from the Object class is completed first, followed by the constructors in the other classes down to the class being instantiated in the inheritance hierarchy. This is called (subclass–superclass) *constructor chaining*. The output from Example 7.6 clearly illustrates this chain of events when an object of the class TubeLight is created.

If a constructor at the end of a this()-chain (which may not be a chain at all if no this() call is invoked) does not have an explicit call to super(), the call super() (without the parameters) is implicitly inserted by the compiler to invoke the default constructor of the superclass. In other words, if a constructor has neither a this() nor a super() call as its first statement, the compiler inserts a super() call to the default constructor in the superclass. The code

```
class A {
  public A() {}
  // ...
}
class B extends A {
  // no constructors
  // ...
}
```

is equivalent to

```
class A {
  public A() { super(); }      // (1)
  // ...
}
class B extends A {
  public B() { super(); }      // (2)
  // ...
}
```

where the default constructors with calls to the default superclass constructor are inserted in the code.

If a superclass only defines non-default constructors (i.e., only constructors with parameters), its subclasses cannot rely on the implicit super() call being inserted. This will be flagged as a compile-time error. The subclasses must then explicitly call a superclass constructor, using the super() construct with the right arguments.

```
class NeonLight extends TubeLight {
  // Field
  String sign;

  NeonLight() {                                // (1)
    super(10, 2, 100, true, "Roof-top");       // (2) Cannot be commented out.
    sign = "All will be revealed!";
  }
  // ...
}
```

The above declaration of the subclass NeonLight provides a constructor at (1). The call of the constructor at (2) in the superclass TubeLight cannot be omitted. If it is omitted, any insertion of a super() call (with no arguments) in this constructor will try to match a default constructor in the superclass TubeLight, which only provides non-default constructors. The class NeonLight will not compile unless an explicit valid super() call is inserted at (2).

If the superclass provides only non-default constructors (that is, does not have a default constructor), this has implications for its subclasses. A subclass that relies on its own implicit default constructor will fail to compile. This is because the implicit default constructor of the subclass will attempt to call the (non-existent) default constructor in the superclass. A constructor in a subclass must explicitly use the super() call, with the appropriate arguments, to invoke a non-default constructor in the superclass. This is because the constructor in the subclass cannot rely on an implicit super() call to the default constructor in the superclass.

 ## Review Questions

7.12   Which constructors can be inserted at (1) in MySub without causing a compile-time error?

```java
class MySuper {
  int number;
  MySuper(int i) { number = i; }
}

class MySub extends MySuper {
  int count;
  MySub(int count, int num) {
    super(num);
    this.count = count;
  }

  // (1) INSERT CONSTRUCTOR HERE
}
```

Select the one correct answer.

(a) MySub() {}
(b) MySub(int count) { this.count = count; }
(c) MySub(int count) { super(); this.count = count; }
(d) MySub(int count) { this.count = count; super(count); }
(e) MySub(int count) { this(count, count); }
(f) MySub(int count) { super(count); this(count, 0); }

7.13   Which statement is true?

Select the one correct answer.

(a) A super() or this() call must always be provided explicitly as the first statement in the body of a constructor.
(b) If both a subclass and its superclass do not have any declared constructors, the implicit default constructor of the subclass will call super() when run.
(c) If neither super() nor this() is declared as the first statement in the body of a constructor, this() will implicitly be inserted as the first statement.

(d) If super() is the first statement in the body of a constructor, this() can be declared as the second statement.
(e) Calling super() as the first statement in the body of a constructor of a subclass will always work, since all superclasses have a default constructor.

7.14   What will the following program print when run?

```
// Filename: MyClass.java
public class MyClass {
  public static void main(String[] args) {
    B b = new B("Test");
  }
}
class A {
  A() { this("1", "2"); }

  A(String s, String t) { this(s + t); }

  A(String s) { System.out.println(s); }
}
class B extends A {
  B(String s) { System.out.println(s); }

  B(String s, String t) { this(t + s + "3"); }

  B() { super("4"); };
}
```

Select the one correct answer.

(a) It will just print Test.
(b) It will print Test followed by Test.
(c) It will print 123 followed by Test.
(d) It will print 12 followed by Test.
(e) It will print 4 followed by Test.

7.6 Interfaces

Extending classes using *single implementation inheritance* creates new class types. A superclass reference can refer to objects of its own type and its subclasses strictly according to the inheritance hierarchy. Because this relationship is linear, it rules out *multiple implementation inheritance*, i.e., a subclass inheriting from more than one superclass. Instead Java provides *interfaces*, which not only allow new named reference types to be introduced, but also permit *multiple interface inheritance*.

Generic interfaces are discussed in Section 14.2, p. 666.

Defining Interfaces

A top-level interface has the following general syntax:

```
<accessibility modifier> interface <interface name>
                        <extends interface clause> // Interface header
    { // Interface body
      <constant declarations>
      <abstract method declarations>
      <nested class declarations>
      <nested interface declarations>
    }
```

In the interface header, the name of the interface is preceded by the keyword `inter-face`. The interface name can also include a list of *formal type parameters* (see Section 14.2, p. 666). In addition, the interface header can specify the following information:

- scope or *accessibility modifier* (see Section 4.6, p. 129)

- any interfaces it *extends* (see Section 7.6, p. 313)

The interface body can contain *member declarations* which comprise:

- *constant declarations* (see Section 7.6, p. 314)

- *abstract method declarations* (see Section 7.6, p. 313)

- *nested class and interface declarations* (see Section 8.1, p. 352)

An interface does not provide any implementation and is, therefore, `abstract` by definition. This means that it cannot be instantiated. Declaring an interface `abstract` is superfluous and seldom done.

The member declarations can appear in any order in the interface body. Since interfaces are meant to be implemented by classes, interface members implicitly have `public` accessibility and the `public` modifier can be omitted.

Interfaces with empty bodies can be used as *markers* to *tag* classes as having a certain property or behavior. Such interfaces are also called *ability* interfaces. Java APIs provide several examples of such marker interfaces: `java.lang.Cloneable`, `java.io.Serializable`, `java.util.EventListener`.

Abstract Method Declarations

An interface defines a *contract* by specifying a set of abstract method declarations, but provides no implementations (see Section 4.10, p. 150). The methods in an interface are all implicitly `abstract` and `public` by virtue of their definition. Only the modifiers `abstract` and `public` are allowed, but these are invariably omitted. An abstract method declaration has the following form:

```
<optional type parameter list> <return type> <method name> (<parameter list>)
    <throws clause>;
```

The optional list of formal type parameters is specified for generic method declarations (see Section 14.8, p. 697).

Example 7.7 declares two interfaces: IStack at (1) and ISafeStack at (5). These interfaces are discussed in the subsequent subsections.

Example 7.7 *Interfaces*

```
interface IStack {                                           // (1)
  void    push(Object item);
  Object pop();
}
//_____
class StackImpl implements IStack {                          // (2)
  protected Object[] stackArray;
  protected int      tos;  // top of stack

  public StackImpl(int capacity) {
    stackArray = new Object[capacity];
    tos        = -1;
  }

  public void push(Object item) { stackArray[++tos] = item; }  // (3)

  public Object pop() {                                       // (4)
    Object objRef = stackArray[tos];
    stackArray[tos] = null;
    tos--;
    return objRef;
  }

  public Object peek() { return stackArray[tos]; }
}
//_____
interface ISafeStack extends IStack {                        // (5)
  boolean isEmpty();
  boolean isFull();
}
//_____
class SafeStackImpl extends StackImpl implements ISafeStack {  // (6)

  public SafeStackImpl(int capacity) { super(capacity); }
  public boolean isEmpty() { return tos < 0; }               // (7)
  public boolean isFull()  { return tos >= stackArray.length-1; }  // (8)
}
//_____
public class StackUser {

  public static void main(String[] args) {                   // (9)
    SafeStackImpl safeStackRef  = new SafeStackImpl(10);
    StackImpl     stackRef      = safeStackRef;
    ISafeStack    isafeStackRef = safeStackRef;
    IStack        istackRef     = safeStackRef;
```

```
    Object          objRef       = safeStackRef;

    safeStackRef.push("Dollars");                                        // (10)
    stackRef.push("Kroner");
    System.out.println(isafeStackRef.pop());
    System.out.println(istackRef.pop());
    System.out.println(objRef.getClass());
  }
}
```

Output from the program:

```
Kroner
Dollars
class SafeStackImpl
```

Implementing Interfaces

Any class can elect to implement, wholly or partially, zero or more interfaces. A class specifies the interfaces it implements as a comma-separated list of unique interface names in an implements clause in the class header. The interface methods must all have public accessibility when implemented in the class (or its subclasses). A class can neither narrow the accessibility of an interface method nor specify new exceptions in the method's throws clause, as attempting to do so would amount to altering the interface's contract, which is illegal. The criteria for overriding methods also apply when implementing interface methods (see Section 7.2, p. 288).

A class can provide implementations of methods declared in an interface, but to reap the benefits of interfaces, the class must also specify the interface name in its implements clause.

In Example 7.7, the class StackImpl implements the interface IStack. It both specifies the interface name using the implements clause in its class header at (2) and provides the implementation for the methods in the interface at (3) and (4). Changing the public accessibility of these methods in the class will result in a compile-time error, as this would narrow their accessibility.

A class can choose to implement only some of the methods of its interfaces (i.e., give a partial implementation of its interfaces). The class must then be declared as abstract (see Section 4.8, p. 135). Note that interface methods cannot be declared static, because they comprise the contract fulfilled by the *objects* of the class implementing the interface. Interface methods are always implemented as instance methods.

The interfaces a class implements and the classes it extends (directly or indirectly) are called *supertypes* of the class. Conversely, the class is a *subtype* of its supertypes. Classes implementing interfaces introduce multiple interface inheritance into their implementation inheritance hierarchy. However, note that regardless of how many interfaces a class implements directly or indirectly, it only provides a single implementation of a member that might have been declared in multiple interfaces.

Extending Interfaces

An interface can extend other interfaces, using the extends clause. Unlike extending classes, an interface can extend several interfaces. The interfaces extended by an interface (directly or indirectly) are called *superinterfaces*. Conversely, the interface is a *subinterface* of its superinterfaces. Since interfaces define new reference types, superinterfaces and subinterfaces are also supertypes and subtypes, respectively.

A subinterface inherits all methods from its superinterfaces, as their method declarations are all implicitly `public`. A subinterface can override abstract method declarations from its superinterfaces. Overridden methods are not inherited. Abstract method declarations can also be overloaded, analogous to method overloading in classes.

Example 7.7 provides an example of multiple interface inheritance. In Example 7.7, the interface `ISafeStack` extends the interface `IStack` at (5). The class `SafeStackImpl` both extends the `StackImpl` class and implements the `ISafeStack` interface at (6). Both the implementation and the interface inheritance hierarchies for classes and interfaces defined in Example 7.7 are shown in Figure 7.2.

In UML, an interface resembles a class. One way to differentiate between them is to use an «*interface*» stereotype as in Figure 7.2. Interface inheritance is depicted in a similar manner to implementation inheritance, but uses an unbroken inheritance arrow. Thinking in terms of types, every reference type in Java is a subtype of the `Object` type. This means that any interface type is also a subtype of the `Object` type. We have augmented Figure 7.2 with an extra inheritance arrow to show this subtype relation.

It is instructive to note how the class `SafeStackImpl` implements the `ISafeStack` interface: it inherits implementations of the push() and pop() methods from its superclass `StackImpl`, and provides its own implementation of the isFull() and isEmpty() methods from the `ISafeStack` interface. The interface `ISafeStack` inherits two abstract method declarations from its superinterface `IStack`. All its methods are implemented by the `SafeStackImpl` class. The class `SafeStackImpl` implicitly implements the `IStack` interface: it implements the `ISafeStack` interface that it inherits from the `IStack` interface. This is readily evident from the diamond shape of the inheritance hierarchy in Figure 7.2. There is only one single *implementation* inheritance into the class `SafeStackImpl`, namely from its superclass `StackImpl`.

Note that there are three different inheritance relations at work when defining inheritance among classes and interfaces:

1. Single implementation inheritance hierarchy between classes: a class extends another class (subclasses–superclasses).
2. Multiple inheritance hierarchy between interfaces: an interface extends other interfaces (subinterfaces–superinterfaces).

Figure 7.2   *Inheritance Relations*

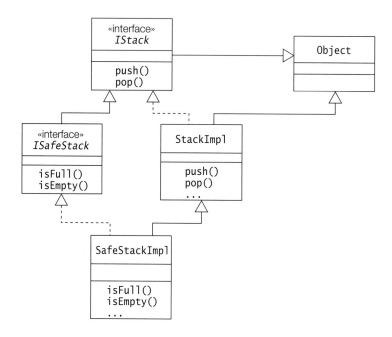

3. Multiple interface inheritance hierarchy between interfaces and classes: a class implements interfaces.

Interface References

Although interfaces cannot be instantiated, references of an interface type can be declared. The reference value of an object can be assigned to references of the object's supertypes. In Example 7.7, an object of the class SafeStackImpl is created in the main() method of the class StackUser at (9). The reference value of the object is assigned to references of all the object's supertypes, which are used to manipulate the object. Polymorphic behavior of supertype references is discussed in Section 7.12, p. 340.

Constants in Interfaces

An interface can also define named constants. Such constants are defined by field declarations and are considered to be public, static, and final. These modifiers can be omitted from the declaration. Such a constant must be initialized with an initializer expression (see Section 9.8, p. 406).

An interface constant can be accessed by any client (a class or interface) using its fully qualified name, regardless of whether the client extends or implements its interface. However, if a client is a class that implements this interface or an interface that extends this interface, then the client can also access such constants directly by their simple names, without resorting to the fully qualified name. Such a client inherits the interface constants. Typical usage of constants in interfaces is illustrated in Example 7.8, showing both direct access and use of fully qualified names in the print statements at (1) and (2), respectively.

Extending an interface that has constants is analogous to extending a class having static variables. In particular, these constants can be hidden by the subinterfaces. In the case of multiple inheritance of interface constants, any name conflicts can be resolved by using fully qualified names for the constants involved.

When defining a *set of related constants*, the recommended practice is to use an enumerated type (Section 3.5, p. 54), rather than named constants in an interface.

Example 7.8 *Variables in Interfaces*

```
interface Constants {
  double PI_APPROXIMATION = 3.14;
  String AREA_UNITS        = "sq.cm.";
  String LENGTH_UNITS      = "cm.";
}
//_____
public class Client implements Constants {
  public static void main(String[] args) {
    double radius = 1.5;

    // (1) Using direct access:
    System.out.printf("Area of circle is %.2f %s%n",
            PI_APPROXIMATION * radius*radius, AREA_UNITS);

    // (2) Using fully qualified name:
    System.out.printf("Circumference of circle is %.2f %s%n",
            2.0 * Constants.PI_APPROXIMATION * radius, Constants.LENGTH_UNITS);
  }
}
```

Output from the program:

```
Area of circle is 7.06 sq.cm.
Circumference of circle is 9.42 cm.
```

 Review Questions

7.15 Which statements about interfaces are true?

Select the two correct answers.

(a) Interfaces allow multiple implementation inheritance.
(b) Interfaces can be extended by any number of interfaces.
(c) Interfaces can extend any number of interfaces.
(d) Members of an interface are never static.
(e) Members of an interface can always be declared static.

7.16   Which of these field declarations are legal within the body of an interface?

Select the three correct answers.

(a) `public static int answer = 42;`
(b) `int answer;`
(c) `final static int answer = 42;`
(d) `public int answer = 42;`
(e) `private final static int answer = 42;`

7.17   Which statements about the keywords `extends` and `implements` are true?

Select the two correct answers.

(a) The keyword `extends` is used to specify that an interface inherits from another interface.
(b) The keyword `extends` is used to specify that a class implements an interface.
(c) The keyword `implements` is used to specify that an interface inherits from another interface.
(d) The keyword `implements` is used to specify that a class inherits from an interface.
(e) The keyword `implements` is used to specify that a class inherits from another class.

7.18   Which statement is true about the following code?

```
// Filename: MyClass.java
abstract class MyClass implements Interface1, Interface2 {
  public void f() { }
  public void g() { }
}

interface Interface1 {
  int VAL_A = 1;
  int VAL_B = 2;

  void f();
  void g();
}

interface Interface2 {
  int VAL_B = 3;
  int VAL_C = 4;

  void g();
  void h();
}
```

Select the one correct answer.

(a) `MyClass` only implements `Interface1`. Implementation for `void h()` from `Interface2` is missing.
(b) The declarations of `void g()` in the two interfaces conflict, therefore, the code will not compile.

(c) The declarations of int VAL_B in the two interfaces conflict, therefore, the code will not compile.

(d) Nothing is wrong with the code, it will compile without errors.

7.19 Which declaration can be inserted at (1) without causing a compilation error?

```
interface MyConstants {
  int r = 42;
  int s = 69;
  // (1) INSERT CODE HERE
}
```

Select the two correct answers.

(a) `final double circumference = 2 * Math.PI * r;`
(b) `int total = total + r + s;`
(c) `int AREA = r * s;`
(d) `public static MAIN = 15;`
(e) `protected int CODE = 31337;`

7.7 Arrays and Subtyping

Table 7.2 summarizes the types found in Java. Only primitive data and reference values can be stored in variables. Only class and array types can be explicitly instantiated to create objects.

Table 7.2 *Types and Values*

Types	Values
Primitive data types	Primitive data values
Class, interface, enum, and array types (*reference types*)	Reference values

Arrays and Subtype Covariance

Arrays are objects in Java. Array types (`boolean[]`, `Object[]`, `StackImpl[]`) implicitly augment the inheritance hierarchy. The inheritance hierarchy depicted in Figure 7.2 can be augmented by the corresponding array types. The resulting *type hierarchy* is shown in Figure 7.3. An array type is shown as a "class" with the [] notation appended to the name of the element type. The class `SafeStackImpl` is a subclass of the class `StackImpl`. The corresponding array types, `SafeStackImpl[]` and `StackImpl[]`, are shown as subtype and supertype, respectively, in the type hierarchy. Figure 7.3 also shows array types corresponding to some of the primitive data types.

Figure 7.3   *Reference Type Hierarchy: Arrays and Subtype Covariance*

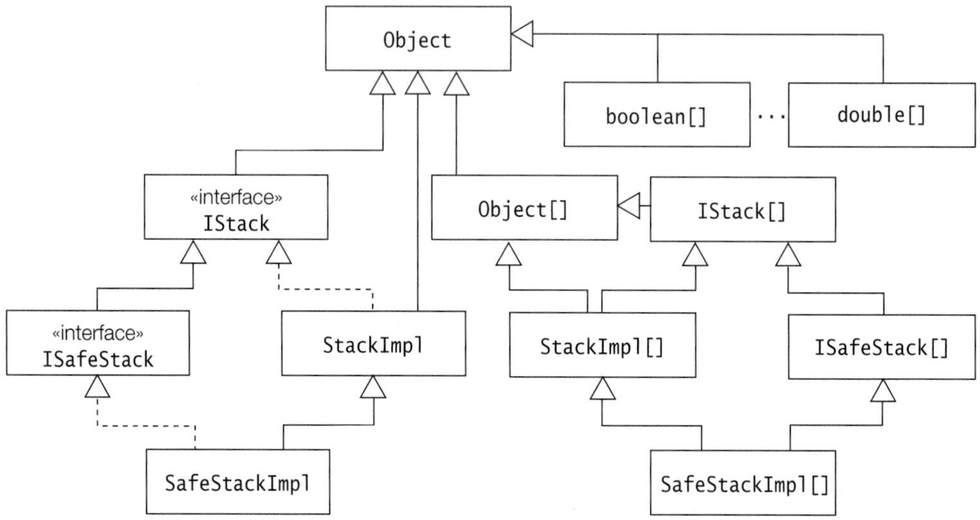

From the type hierarchy in Figure 7.3, we can summarize the following:

- *All* reference types are subtypes of the Object type. This applies to classes, interfaces, enum, and array types, as these are all reference types.

- All arrays of reference types are also subtypes of the array type Object[], but arrays of primitive data types are not. Note that the array type Object[] is also a subtype of the Object type.

- If a non-generic reference type is a subtype of another non-generic reference type, the corresponding array types also have an analogous subtype-supertype relationship. This is called the *subtype covariance relationship*. This relationship however does *not* hold for parameterized types (see Section 14.4, p. 673).

- There is no subtype-supertype relationship between a type and its corresponding array type.

We can create an array of an interface type, but we cannot instantiate an interface (as is the case with abstract classes). In the declaration statement below, the reference iSafeStackArray has type ISafeStack[] (i.e., an array of the interface type ISafeStack).

```
ISafeStack[] iSafeStackArray = new ISafeStack[5];
```

The array creation expression creates an array whose element type is ISafeStack. The array object can accommodate five references of the type ISafeStack. However, the declaration statement does not initialize these references to refer to any objects, but they are initialized to the default value null.

Array Store Check

An array reference exhibits polymorphic behavior like any other reference, subject to its location in the type hierarchy (see Section 7.12, p. 340). However, a runtime check is necessary when objects are inserted in an array, as the following example illustrates.

The following assignment is valid, as a supertype reference (StackImpl[]) can refer to objects of its subtype (SafeStackImpl[]):

```
StackImpl[] stackImplArray = new SafeStackImpl[2];     // (1)
```

Since StackImpl is a supertype of SafeStackImpl, the following assignment is also valid:

```
stackImplArray[0] = new SafeStackImpl(10);              // (2)
```

The assignment at (2) inserts a SafeStackImpl object in the SafeStackImpl[] object (i.e., the array of SafeStackImpl) created at (1).

Since the type of stackImplArray[i], (0 ≤ i < 2), is StackImpl, it should be possible to do the following assignment as well:

```
stackImplArray[1] = new StackImpl(20);                 // (3) ArrayStoreException
```

At compile time there are no problems, as the compiler cannot deduce that the array variable stackImplArray will actually denote a SafeStackImpl[] object at runtime. However, the assignment at (3) results in an ArrayStoreException to be thrown at runtime, as a SafeStackImpl[] object cannot possibly contain objects of type StackImpl.

In order to make the array store check feasible at runtime, an array retains information about its declared element type at runtime.

7.8 Reference Values and Conversions

A review of Section 5.1, p. 160, on conversions is recommended before proceeding with this section.

Reference values, like primitive values, can be assigned, cast, and passed as arguments. Conversions can occur in the following contexts:

* assignment
* method invocation
* casting

The rule of thumb for the primitive data types is that widening conversions are permitted, but narrowing conversions require an explicit cast. The rule of thumb for reference values is that widening conversions up the type hierarchy are permitted, but narrowing conversions down the hierarchy require an explicit cast. In other words, conversions that are from a subtype to its supertypes are allowed, other conversions require an explicit cast or are otherwise illegal. There is no notion of promotion for reference values.

Unchecked conversions involving generic and raw types are discussed in Section 14.2, p. 670.

7.9 Reference Value Assignment Conversions

In the context of assignments, the following conversions are permitted (Table 5.1, p. 163):

*   widening primitive and reference conversions (long ← int, Object ← String)
*   boxing conversion of primitive values, followed by optional widening reference conversion (Integer ← int, Number ← Integer ← int)
*   unboxing conversion of a primitive value wrapper object, followed by optional widening primitive conversion (long ← int ← Integer)

And only for assigment conversions, we have the following:

*   narrowing conversion for constant expressions of non-long integer type, with optional boxing (Byte ← byte ← int)

Note that the above rules imply that a widening conversion cannot be followed by any boxing conversion, but the converse is permitted.

Widening reference conversions typically occur during assignment *up* the type hierarchy, with implicit conversion of the source reference value to that of the destination reference type:

```
Object obj = "Up the tree";    // Widening reference conversion: Object <-- String
String str1 = obj;        // Not ok. Narrowing reference conversion requires a cast.
String str2 = new Integer(10); // Illegal. No relation between String and Integer.
```

The source value can be a primitive value, in which case the value is boxed in a wrapper object corresponding to the primitive type. If the destination reference type is a supertype of the wrapper type, a widening reference conversion can occur:

```
Integer iRef = 10;  // Only boxing
Number num = 10L;   // Boxing, followed by widening: Number <--- Long <--- long
Object obj = 100;   // Boxing, followed by widening: Object <--- Integer <--- int
```

More examples of boxing during assignment can be found in Section 5.1, p. 162.

. . . .

Example 7.9 *Assigning and Passing Reference Values*

```
interface IStack                { /* From Example 7.7 */ }
interface ISafeStack extends IStack { /* From Example 7.7 */ }
class StackImpl implements IStack  { /* From Example 7.7 */ }
```

```java
class SafeStackImpl extends StackImpl
            implements ISafeStack   { /* From Example 7.7 */ }

public class ReferenceConversion {

  public static void main(String[] args) {
    // Reference declarations:
    Object        objRef;
    StackImpl     stackRef;
    SafeStackImpl safeStackRef;
    IStack        iStackRef;
    ISafeStack    iSafeStackRef;

    // SourceType is a class type:
    safeStackRef = new SafeStackImpl(10);
    objRef       = safeStackRef;    // (1) Always possible
    stackRef     = safeStackRef;    // (2) Subclass to superclass assignment
    iStackRef    = stackRef;        // (3) StackImpl implements IStack
    iSafeStackRef = safeStackRef;   // (4) SafeStackImpl implements ISafeStack

    // SourceType is an interface type:
    objRef    = iStackRef;          // (5) Always possible
    iStackRef = iSafeStackRef;      // (6) Sub- to super-interface assignment

    // SourceType is an array type:
    Object[]        objArray       = new Object[3];
    StackImpl[]     stackArray     = new StackImpl[3];
    SafeStackImpl[] safeStackArray = new SafeStackImpl[5];
    ISafeStack[]    iSafeStackArray = new ISafeStack[5];
    int[]           intArray       = new int[10];

    // Reference value assignments:
    objRef     = objArray;          // (7) Always possible
    objRef     = stackArray;        // (8) Always possible
    objArray   = stackArray;        // (9) Always possible
    objArray   = iSafeStackArray;   // (10) Always possible
    objRef     = intArray;          // (11) Always possible
    // objArray   = intArray;       // (12) Compile-time error
    stackArray = safeStackArray;    // (13) Subclass array to superclass array
    iSafeStackArray = safeStackArray;// (14) SafeStackImpl implements ISafeStack

    // Method Invocation Conversions:
    System.out.println("First call:");
    sendParams(stackRef, safeStackRef, iStackRef,
            safeStackArray, iSafeStackArray);                    // (15)
    //  Call Signature: sendParams(StackImpl, SafeStackImpl, IStack,
    //                       SafeStackImpl[], ISafeStack[]);

    System.out.println("Second call:");
    sendParams(iSafeStackArray, stackRef, iSafeStackRef,
            stackArray, safeStackArray);                         // (16)
    //  Call Signature: sendParams(ISafeStack[], StackImpl, ISafeStack,
    //                       StackImpl[], SafeStackImpl[]);
  }
```

```
public static void sendParams(Object objRefParam, StackImpl stackRefParam,
    IStack iStackRefParam, StackImpl[] stackArrayParam,
    final IStack[] iStackArrayParam) {                              // (17)
  //  Signature: sendParams(Object, StackImpl, IStack, StackImpl[], IStack[])
  //  Print class name of object denoted by the reference at runtime.
  System.out.println(objRefParam.getClass());
  System.out.println(stackRefParam.getClass());
  System.out.println(iStackRefParam.getClass());
  System.out.println(stackArrayParam.getClass());
  System.out.println(iStackArrayParam.getClass());
  }
}
```

Output from the program:

```
First call:
class SafeStackImpl
class SafeStackImpl
class SafeStackImpl
class [LSafeStackImpl;
class [LSafeStackImpl;
Second call:
class [LSafeStackImpl;
class SafeStackImpl
class SafeStackImpl
class [LSafeStackImpl;
class [LSafeStackImpl;
```

The rules for reference value assignment are stated, based on the following code:

```
SourceType srcRef;
// srcRef is appropriately initialized.
DestinationType destRef = srcRef;
```

If an assignment is legal, the reference value of srcRef is said to be *assignable* (or *assignment compatible*) to the reference of DestinationType. The rules are illustrated by concrete cases from Example 7.9. Note that the code in Example 7.9 uses reference types from Example 7.7, p. 311.

- If the SourceType is a *class type*, the reference value in srcRef may be assigned to the destRef reference, provided the DestinationType is one of the following:
  - ○ DestinationType is a superclass of the subclass SourceType.
  - ○ DestinationType is an interface type that is implemented by the class SourceType.

```
objRef        = safeStackRef;   // (1) Always possible
stackRef      = safeStackRef;   // (2) Subclass to superclass assignment
iStackRef     = stackRef;       // (3) StackImpl implements IStack
iSafeStackRef = safeStackRef;   // (4) SafeStackImpl implements ISafeStack
```

- If the SourceType is an *interface type*, the reference value in srcRef may be assigned to the destRef reference, provided the DestinationType is one of the following:

  ○ DestinationType is Object.
  ○ DestinationType is a superinterface of subinterface SourceType.

  ```
  objRef    = iStackRef;      // (5) Always possible
  iStackRef = iSafeStackRef; // (6) Subinterface to superinterface assignment
  ```

- If the SourceType is an *array type*, the reference value in srcRef may be assigned to the destRef reference, provided the DestinationType is one of the following:

  ○ DestinationType is Object.
  ○ DestinationType is an array type, where the element type of the SourceType is assignable to the element type of the DestinationType.

  ```
  objRef     = objArray;            // (7) Always possible
  objRef     = stackArray;          // (8) Always possible
  objArray   = stackArray;          // (9) Always possible
  objArray   = iSafeStackArray;     // (10) Always possible
  objRef     = intArray;            // (11) Always possible
  // objArray  = intArray;          // (12) Compile-time error
  stackArray = safeStackArray;      // (13) Subclass array to superclass array
  iSafeStackArray = safeStackArray;// (14) SafeStackImpl implements ISafeStack
  ```

The rules for assignment are enforced at compile time, guaranteeing that no type conversion error will occur during assignment at runtime. Such conversions are *type safe*. The reason the rules can be enforced at compile time is that they concern the *declared type* of the reference (which is always known at compile time) rather than the actual type of the object being referenced (which is known at runtime).

7.10 Method Invocation Conversions Involving References

The conversions for reference value assignment are also applicable for *method invocation conversions*, except for the narrowing conversion for constant expressions of non-long integer type (Table 5.1, p. 163). This is reasonable, as parameters in Java are passed by value (see Section 3.7, p. 81), requiring that values of actual parameters must be assignable to formal parameters of compatible types.

In Example 7.9, the method sendParams() at (17) has the following signature, showing the types of the formal parameters:

```
sendParams(Object, StackImpl, IStack, StackImpl[], IStack[])
```

The method call at (15) has the following signature, showing the types of the actual parameters:

```
sendParams(StackImpl, SafeStackImpl, IStack, SafeStackImpl[], ISafeStack[]);
```

Note that the assignment of the values of the actual parameters to the corresponding formal parameters is legal, according to the rules for assignment discussed earlier.

The method call at (16) provides another example of the parameter passing conversion. It has the following signature:

```
sendParams(ISafeStack[], StackImpl, ISafeStack, StackImpl[], SafeStackImpl[]);
```

Analogous to assignment, the rules for parameter passing conversions are based on the reference type of the parameters and are enforced at compile time. The output in Example 7.9 shows the class of the actual objects referenced by the formal parameters at runtime, which in this case turns out to be either SafeStackImpl or SafeStackImpl[]. The characters [L in the output indicate a one-dimensional array of a class or interface type (see the Class.getName() method in the Java API documentation).

Overloaded Method Resolution

In this subsection, we take a look at some aspects regarding *overloaded method resolution*, i.e., how the compiler determines which overloaded method will be invoked by a given method call at runtime.

Resolution of overloaded methods selects the *most specific* method for execution. One method is more specific than another method if all actual parameters that can be accepted by the one can be accepted by the other. If there is more than one such method, the call is *ambiguous*. The following overloaded methods illustrate this situation.

```
private static void flipFlop(String str, int i, Integer iRef) { // (1)
    out.println(str + " ==> (String, int, Integer)");
}
private static void flipFlop(String str, int i, int j) {        // (2)
    out.println(str + " ==> (String, int, int)");
}
```

Their method signatures are, as follows:

```
flipFlop(String, int, Integer)                        // See (1) above
flipFlop(String, int, int)                            // See (2) above
```

The following method call is ambiguous:

```
flipFlop("(String, Integer, int)", new Integer(4), 2004);  // (3) Ambiguous call.
```

It has the call signature:

```
flipFlop(String, Integer, int)                        // See (3) above
```

The method at (1) can be called with the second argument unboxed and the third argument boxed, as can the method at (2) with only the second argument unboxed. In other words, for the call at (3), none of the methods is more specific than the other one. Example 7.10 illustrates a simple case of how method resolution is done to choose the most specific one of the overloaded methods. The method testIfOn() is overloaded at (1) and (2) in the class Overload. The call client.testIfOn(tubeLight) at (3) *satisfies* the parameter lists in both implementations given at (1) and (2), as the reference tubeLight, which denotes an object of the class TubeLight, can also be assigned to a reference of its superclass Light. The *most specific* method, (2), is chosen, resulting in false being written on the terminal. The call client.test-IfOn(light) at (4) only satisfies the parameter list in the implementation given at (1), resulting in true being written on the terminal.

- -

Example 7.10 *Choosing the Most Specific Method (Simple Case)*

```
class Light { /* ... */ }

class TubeLight extends Light { /* ... */ }

public class Overload {
    boolean testIfOn(Light aLight)         { return true; }    // (1)
    boolean testIfOn(TubeLight aTubeLight) { return false; }   // (2)

    public static void main(String[] args) {

        TubeLight tubeLight = new TubeLight();
        Light     light     = new Light();

        Overload client = new Overload();
        System.out.println(client.testIfOn(tubeLight));// (3) ==> method at (2)
        System.out.println(client.testIfOn(light));    // (4) ==> method at (1)

    }
}
```

Output from the program:

```
false
true
```

- -

The algorithm used by the compiler for the resolution of overloaded methods incorporates the following phases:

1. It first performs overload resolution without permitting boxing, unboxing, or the use of a varargs call.

2. If phase (1) fails, it performs overload resolution allowing boxing and unboxing, but excluding the use of a varargs call.

3. If phase (2) fails, it performs overload resolution combining a varargs call, boxing, and unboxing.

Example 7.11 provides some insight into how the compiler determines the most specific overloaded method using the phases outlined above. The example has six overloaded declarations of the method action(). The signature of each method is given by the local variable signature in each method. The first formal parameter of each method is the *signature of the call* that invoked the method. The printout from each method thus allows us to see which method call resolved to which method.

The `main()` method contains ten calls, (8) to (17), of the `action()` method. In each call, the first argument is the signature of that method call.

An important thing to note is that the compiler chooses a *non-varargs* call over a varargs call, as seen in the calls from (8) to (12).

```
(String) => (String)                          (8) calls (1)
(String, int) => (String, int)                (9) calls (2)
(String, Integer) => (String, int)            (10) calls (2)
(String, int, byte) => (String, int, int)     (11) calls (3)
(String, int, int) => (String, int, int)      (12) calls (3)
```

An unboxing conversion (`Integer` to `int`) takes place for the call at (10). A widening primitive conversion (`byte` to `int`) takes place for the call at (11).

Varargs calls are chosen from (13) to (17):

```
(String, int, long) => (String, Number[])         (13) calls (5)
(String, int, int, int) => (String, Integer[])    (14) calls (4)
(String, int, double) => (String, Number[])       (15) calls (5)
(String, int, String) => (String, Object[])       (16) calls (6)
(String, boolean) => (String, Object[])           (17) calls (6)
```

When a varargs call is chosen, the method determined has the most specific varargs parameter that is applicable for the actual argument. For example, in the method call at (14), the type `Integer[]` is more specific than `Number[]` or `Object[]`. Note also the boxing of the elements of the implicitly created array in the calls from (13) to (17).

- -

Example 7.11   *Overloaded Method Resolution*

```java
import static java.lang.System.out;

class OverloadResolution {

  public void action(String str) {                  // (1)
    String signature = "(String)";
    out.println(str + " => " + signature);
  }

  public void action(String str, int m) {           // (2)
    String signature = "(String, int)";
    out.println(str + " => " + signature);
  }

  public void action(String str, int m, int n) {    // (3)
    String signature = "(String, int, int)";
    out.println(str + " => " + signature);
  }

  public void action(String str, Integer... data) { // (4)
    String signature = "(String, Integer[])";
    out.println(str + " => " + signature);
```

```
    }

    public void action(String str, Number... data) {  // (5)
      String signature = "(String, Number[])";
      out.println(str + " => " + signature);
    }

    public void action(String str, Object... data) {  // (6)
      String signature = "(String, Object[])";
      out.println(str + " => " + signature);
    }

    public static void main(String[] args) {
      OverloadResolution ref = new OverloadResolution();
      ref.action("(String)");                               // (8)   calls (1)
      ref.action("(String, int)",             10);          // (9)   calls (2)
      ref.action("(String, Integer)",         new Integer(10));  // (10)  calls (2)
      ref.action("(String, int, byte)",       10, (byte)20);     // (11)  calls (3)
      ref.action("(String, int, int)",        10,  20);    // (12)  calls (3)
      ref.action("(String, int, long)",       10,  20L);   // (13)  calls (5)
      ref.action("(String, int, int, int)",   10,  20,  30);  // (14)  calls (4)
      ref.action("(String, int, double)",     10,  20.0);  // (15)  calls (5)
      ref.action("(String, int, String)",     10,  "what?");  // (16)  calls (6)
      ref.action("(String, boolean)",         false);      // (17)  calls (6)
    }
  }
```

Output from the program:

(String) => (String)	(8) calls (1)
(String, int) => (String, int)	(9) calls (2)
(String, Integer) => (String, int)	(10) calls (2)
(String, int, byte) => (String, int, int)	(11) calls (3)
(String, int, int) => (String, int, int)	(12) calls (3)
(String, int, long) => (String, Number[])	(13) calls (5)
(String, int, int, int) => (String, Integer[])	(14) calls (4)
(String, int, double) => (String, Number[])	(15) calls (5)
(String, int, String) => (String, Object[])	(16) calls (6)
(String, boolean) => (String, Object[])	(17) calls (6)

7.11 Reference Casting and the instanceof Operator

The Cast Operator

The type cast expression for reference types has the following syntax:

(<destination type>) <reference expression>

where the *<reference expression>* evaluates to a reference value of an object of some reference type. A type cast expression checks that the reference value refers to an object whose type is compatible with the *<destination type>*, i.e. its type is a subtype of the *<destination type>*. If this is not the case, a `ClassCastException` is thrown. The literal `null` can be cast to any reference type. The construct (*<destination type>*) is usually called the *cast operator*.

The following conversions can be applied to the operand of a cast operator:

- both widening and narrowing reference conversions, followed optionally by an unchecked conversion
- both boxing and unboxing conversions

The implications that generics have for the cast operator, and the unchecked conversions that can occur, are discussed in Section 14.13, p. 724.

Boxing and unboxing conversions that can occur during casting is illustrated by the following code:

```
// (1) Boxing and casting: Number <-- Integer <-- int:
Number num = (Number) 100;
// (2) Casting, boxing, casting: Object <-- Integer <-- int <-- double:
Object obj = (Object) (int) 10.5;
// (3) Casting, unboxing, casting: double <--- int <-- Integer <-- Object:
double d = (double) (Integer) obj;
```

Note that the resulting object from the cast expressions in (1) and (2) is an `Integer`. The boxing conversions from `int` to `Integer` in (1) and (2) are implicit, and the unboxing conversion from `Integer` to `int` in (3) is also implicit.

The `instanceof` Operator

The binary `instanceof` operator can be used for comparing *types*. It has the following syntax (note that the keyword is composed of only lowercase letters):

<reference expression> `instanceof` *<destination type>*

The `instanceof` operator returns `true` if the left-hand operand (that is, the reference value that results from the evaluation of *<reference expression>*) can be a *subtype* of the right-hand operand (*<destination type>*). It always returns `false` if the left-hand operand is `null`. If the `instanceof` operator returns `true`, the corresponding type cast expression will always be valid. Both the type cast expression and the `instanceof` operators require a compile-time check and a runtime check, as explained below.

The compile-time check determines whether there is a subclass-superclass relationship between the source and the destination types. Given that the type of the *<reference expression>* is *<source type>*, the compiler determines whether a reference of *<source type>* and a reference of *<destination type>* can refer to objects of a reference type that are a common subtype of both *<source type>* and *<destination type>* in the type hierarchy. If this is not the case, then obviously there is no relationship between the types, and neither the cast nor the `instanceof` operator application would be valid. At runtime, the *<reference expression>* evaluates to a reference value of an object. It is the type of the actual object that determines the outcome of the operation, as explained earlier.

What implications generics has for the instanceof operator is discussed in Section 14.13, p. 723.

With the classes Light and String as *<source type>* and *<destination type>*, respectively, there is no subtype-supertype relationship between the *<source type>* and *<destination type>*. The compiler would reject casting a reference of type Light to type String or applying the instanceof operator, as shown at (2) and (3) in Example 7.12. References of the classes Light and TubeLight can refer to objects of the class TubeLight (or its subclasses) in the inheritance hierarchy depicted in Figure 7.2. Therefore, it makes sense to apply the instanceof operator or cast a reference of the type Light to the type TubeLight as shown at (4) and (5), respectively, in Example 7.12.

At runtime, the result of applying the instanceof operator at (4) is false, because the reference light1 of the class Light will actually denote an object of the subclass LightBulb, and this object cannot be denoted by a reference of the peer class TubeLight. Applying the cast at (5) results in a ClassCastException for the same reason. This is the reason why cast conversions are said to be *unsafe*, as they may throw a ClassCastException at runtime. Note that if the result of the instanceof operator is false, the cast involving the operands will also throw a ClassCastException.

In Example 7.12, the result of applying the instanceof operator at (6) is also false, because the reference light1 will still denote an object of the class LightBulb, whose objects cannot be denoted by a reference of its subclass SpotLightBulb. Thus applying the cast at (7) causes a ClassCastException to be thrown at runtime.

The situation shown at (8), (9), and (10) illustrates typical usage of the instanceof operator to determine what object a reference is denoting so that it can be cast for the purpose of carrying out some specific action. The reference light1 of the class Light is initialized to an object of the subclass NeonLight at (8). The result of the instanceof operator at (9) is true, because the reference light1 will denote an object of the subclass NeonLight, whose objects can also be denoted by a reference of its superclass TubeLight. By the same token, the cast at (10) is also valid. If the result of the instanceof operator is true, the cast involving the operands will also be valid.

Example 7.12 *The* instanceof *and Cast Operators*

```
class Light { /* ... */ }
class LightBulb extends Light { /* ... */ }
class SpotLightBulb extends LightBulb { /* ... */ }
class TubeLight extends Light { /* ... */ }
class NeonLight extends TubeLight { /* ... */ }

public class WhoAmI {
  public static void main(String[] args) {
    boolean result1, result2, result3, result4, result5;
```

```
      Light light1 = new LightBulb();                    // (1)
      //  String str = (String) light1;                  // (2) Compile-time error.
      //  result1 = light1 instanceof String;            // (3) Compile-time error.

      result2 = light1 instanceof TubeLight;             // (4) false. Peer class.
      //  TubeLight tubeLight1 = (TubeLight) light1;      // (5) ClassCastException.

      result3 = light1 instanceof SpotLightBulb;         // (6) false: Superclass
      //  SpotLightBulb spotRef = (SpotLightBulb) light1;// (7) ClassCastException

      light1 = new NeonLight();                           // (8)
      if (light1 instanceof TubeLight) {                  // (9) true
        TubeLight tubeLight2 = (TubeLight) light1;        // (10) OK
        // Can now use tubeLight2 to access an object of the class NeonLight,
        // but only those members that the object inherits or overrides
        // from the class TubeLight.
      }
    }
  }
}
```

As we have seen, the instanceof operator effectively determines whether the reference value in the reference on the left-hand side refers to an object whose class is a
subtype of the type of the reference specified on the right-hand side. At runtime, it
is the type of the actual object denoted by the reference on the left-hand side that
is compared with the type specified on the right-hand side. In other words, what
matters at runtime is the type of the actual object denoted by the reference, not the
declared type of the reference.

Example 7.13 provides more examples of the instanceof operator. It is instructive
to go through the print statements and understand the results printed out. The
literal null is not an instance of any reference type, as shown in the print statements
(1), (2), and (16). An instance of a superclass is not an instance of its subclass, as
shown in the print statement (4). An instance of a class is not an instance of a totally
unrelated class, as shown in the print statement (10). An instance of a class is not
an instance of an interface type that the class does not implement, as shown in the
print statement (6). Any array of non-primitive type is an instance of both Object
and Object[] types, as shown in the print statements (14) and (15), respectively.

Example 7.13 *Using the* instanceof *Operator*

```
interface IStack                        { /* From Example 7.7 */ }
interface ISafeStack extends IStack     { /* From Example 7.7 */ }
class StackImpl implements IStack        { /* From Example 7.7 */ }
class SafeStackImpl extends StackImpl
              implements ISafeStack      { /* From Example 7.7 */ }

public class Identification {
  public static void main(String[] args) {
    Object obj = new Object();
    StackImpl stack = new StackImpl(10);
```

```
        SafeStackImpl safeStack = new SafeStackImpl(5);
        IStack iStack;

        System.out.println("(1): " +
            (null instanceof Object));      // Always false.
        System.out.println("(2): " +
            (null instanceof IStack));      // Always false.

        System.out.println("(3): " +
            (stack instanceof Object));     // true: instance of subclass of Object.
        System.out.println("(4): " +
            (obj instanceof StackImpl));    // false: Object not subtype of StackImpl.
        System.out.println("(5): " +
            (stack instanceof StackImpl)); // true: instance of StackImpl.

        System.out.println("(6): " +
            (obj instanceof IStack));       // false: Object does not implement IStack.
        System.out.println("(7): " +
            (safeStack instanceof IStack));// true: SafeStackImpl implements IStack.

        obj = stack;                        // Assigning subclass to superclass.
        System.out.println("(8): " +
            (obj instanceof StackImpl));    // true: instance of StackImpl.
        System.out.println("(9): " +
            (obj instanceof IStack));       // true: StackImpl implements IStack.
        System.out.println("(10): " +
            (obj instanceof String));       // false: No relationship.

        iStack = (IStack) obj;          // Cast required: superclass assigned subclass.
        System.out.println("(11): " +
            (iStack instanceof Object));     // true: instance of subclass of Object.
        System.out.println("(12): " +
            (iStack instanceof StackImpl)); // true: instance of StackImpl.

        String[] strArray = new String[10];
        //  System.out.println("(13): " +
        //      (strArray instanceof String);// Compile-time error, no relationship.
        System.out.println("(14): " +
            (strArray instanceof Object));   // true: array subclass of Object.
        System.out.println("(15): " +
            (strArray instanceof Object[])); // true: array subclass of Object[].
        System.out.println("(16): " +
            (strArray[0] instanceof Object));// false: strArray[0] is null.
        System.out.println("(17): " +
            (strArray instanceof String[])); // true: array of String.

        strArray[0] = "Amoeba strip";
        System.out.println("(18): " +
            (strArray[0] instanceof String));// true: instance of String.
    }
}
```

Output from the program:

```
    (1): false
    (2): false
```

```
(3): true
(4): false
(5): true
(6): false
(7): true
(8): true
(9): true
(10): false
(11): true
(12): true
(14): true
(15): true
(16): false
(17): true
(18): true
```

 ## Review Questions

7.20   Which statement about the program is true?

```java
// Filename: MyClass.java
public class MyClass {
  public static void main(String[] args) {
    A[] arrA;
    B[] arrB;

    arrA = new A[10];
    arrB = new B[20];
    arrA = arrB;        // (1)
    arrB = (B[]) arrA;  // (2)
    arrA = new A[10];
    arrB = (B[]) arrA;  // (3)
  }
}

class A {}

class B extends A {}
```

Select the one correct answer.

(a) The program will fail to compile because of the assignment at (1).

(b) The program will throw a java.lang.ClassCastException in the assignment at (2), when run.

(c) The program will throw a java.lang.ClassCastException in the assignment at (3), when run.

(d) The program will compile and run without errors, even if the cast operator (B[]) in the statements at (2) and (3) is removed.

(e) The program will compile and run without errors, but will not do so if the cast operator (B[]) in statements at (2) and (3) is removed.

7.21 What is the label of the first line that will cause compilation to fail in the following program?

```
// Filename: MyClass.java
class MyClass {
  public static void main(String[] args) {
    MyClass a;
    MySubclass b;

    a = new MyClass();           // (1)
    b = new MySubclass();        // (2)

    a = b;                       // (3)
    b = a;                       // (4)

    a = new MySubclass();        // (5)
    b = new MyClass();           // (6)
  }
}

class MySubclass extends MyClass {}
```

Select the one correct answer.

(a) (1)
(b) (2)
(c) (3)
(d) (4)
(e) (5)
(f) (6)

7.22 Given the following type and reference declarations, which assignment is legal?

```
// Type declarations:
interface I1 {}
interface I2 {}
class C1 implements I1 {}
class C2 implements I2 {}
class C3 extends C1 implements I2 {}

// Reference declarations:
  C1 obj1;
  C2 obj2;
  C3 obj3;
```

Select the one correct answer.

(a) obj2 = obj1;
(b) obj3 = obj1;
(c) obj3 = obj2;
(d) I1 a = obj2;
(e) I1 b = obj3;
(f) I2 c = obj1;

7.23 Given the following class and reference declarations, what can be said about the statement `y = (Sub) x`?

```
// Class declarations:
class Super {}
class Sub extends Super {}

// Reference declarations:
  Super x;
  Sub y;
```

Select the one correct answer.

(a) Illegal at compile time.
(b) Legal at compile time, but might be illegal at runtime.
(c) Definitely legal at runtime, but the cast operator (Sub) is not strictly needed.
(d) Definitely legal at runtime, and the cast operator (Sub) is needed.

7.24 Given the following class declarations and declaration statements, which assignment is legal at compile time?

```
// Class declarations:
interface A {}
class B {}
class C extends B implements A {}
class D implements A {}

// Declaration statements:
  B b = new B();
  C c = new C();
  D d = new D();
```

Select the one correct answer.

(a) c = d;
(b) d = c;
(c) A a = d;
(d) d = (D) c;
(e) c = b;

7.25 Which letters will be printed when the following program is run?

```
// Filename: MyClass.java
public class MyClass {
  public static void main(String[] args) {
    B b = new C();
    A a = b;
    if (a instanceof A) System.out.println("A");
    if (a instanceof B) System.out.println("B");
    if (a instanceof C) System.out.println("C");
    if (a instanceof D) System.out.println("D");
  }
}

class A {}
class B extends A {}
```

```
class C extends B {}
class D extends C {}
```

Select the three correct answers.

(a) A will be printed.
(b) B will be printed.
(c) C will be printed.
(d) D will be printed.

7.26 Given three classes A, B, and C, where B is a subclass of A, and C is a subclass of B, which one of these boolean expressions is true only when an object denoted by reference o has actually been instantiated from class B, as opposed to from A or C?

Select the one correct answer.

(a) `(o instanceof B) && (!(o instanceof A))`
(b) `(o instanceof B) && (!(o instanceof C))`
(c) `!((o instanceof A) || (o instanceof B))`
(d) `(o instanceof B)`
(e) `(o instanceof B) && !((o instanceof A) || (o instanceof C))`

7.27 When run, the following program will print all the letters I, J, C, and D. True or false?

```
public class MyClass {
  public static void main(String[] args) {
    I x = new D();
    if (x instanceof I) System.out.println("I");
    if (x instanceof J) System.out.println("J");
    if (x instanceof C) System.out.println("C");
    if (x instanceof D) System.out.println("D");
  }
}

interface I{}
interface J{}
class C implements I {}
class D extends C implements J {}
```

Select the one correct answer.

(a) True.
(b) False.

7.28 What will be the result of compiling and running the following program?

```
public class RQ200_10 {
  public static void main(String[] args) {
    Integer iRef;
    iRef = 786;                        //(1)
    iRef = (Integer)(2007 - 786);      //(2)
    iRef = (int)3.14;                  //(3)
    iRef = (Integer)3.14;              //(4)
    iRef = (Integer)(int)3.14;         //(5)
```

```
       }
     }
```

Select the one correct answer.

(a) The code will fail to compile because of errors in at least one of the lines (1), (2), and (3).
(b) The code will fail to compile because of errors in both the lines (4) and (5).
(c) The code will fail to compile because of error in line (4).
(d) The code will fail to compile because of error in line (5).
(e) The code will compile, but throw a ClassCastException.
(f) The code will compile and execute normally.

7.29   What will the program print when compiled and run?

```
public class RQ200_60 {
  public static void main(String[] args) {
    Integer i = -10;
    Integer j = -10;
    System.out.print(i==j);
    System.out.print(i.equals(j));
    Integer n = 128;
    Integer m = 128;
    System.out.print(n==m);
    System.out.print(n.equals(m));
  }
}
```

Select the one correct answer.

(a) falsetruefalsetrue
(b) truetruetruetrue
(c) falsetruetruetrue
(d) truetruefalsetrue
(e) None of the above.

7.30   What will the program print when compiled and run?

```
public class RQ200_70 {
  public static void main(String[] args) {
    Integer i = new Integer(-10);
    Integer j = new Integer(-10);
    Integer k = -10;
    System.out.print(i==j);
    System.out.print(i.equals(j));
    System.out.print(i==k);
    System.out.print(i.equals(k));
  }
}
```

Select the one correct answer.

(a) falsetruefalsetrue
(b) truetruetruetrue
(c) falsetruetruetrue

(d) truetruefalsetrue

(e) None of the above.

7.31 Given:

```java
public class RQ200_20 {
  private Map<String, Integer> accounts = new HashMap<String, Integer>();
  public int getBalance(String accountName) {
    Integer total = (Integer) accounts.get(accountName);      // (1)
    if (total == null) total = new Integer(0);                // (2)
    return total.intValue();                                   // (3)
  }
  public void setBalance(String accountName, int amount) {
    accounts.put(accountName, new Integer(amount));            // (4)
  }
}
```

Which statements can be replaced so that the program still compiles and runs without errors?

Select the three correct answers.

(a) Replace (1)–(3) with:

```java
int total = accounts.get(accountName);
if (total == null) total = 0;
return total;
```

(b) Replace (1)–(3) with:

```java
int total = accounts.get(accountName);
return total == null ? 0 : total;
```

(c) Replace (1)–(3) with:

```java
return accounts.get(accountName);
```

(d) Replace (4) with:

```java
accounts.put(accountName, amount);
```

(e) Replace (4) with:

```java
accounts.put(accountName, amount.intValue());
```

7.32 What is the result of compiling and running the following program?

```java
class YingYang {
  void yingyang(Integer i) {
    System.out.println("Integer: " + i);
  }

  void yingyang(Integer[] ints) {
    System.out.println("Integer[]: " + ints[0]);
  }

  void yingyang(Integer... ints) {
    System.out.println("Integer...: " + ints[0]);
  }
}
```

```
public class RQ800_50 {
  public static void main(String[] args) {
    YingYang yy = new YingYang();
    yy.yingyang(10);
    yy.yingyang(10,12);
    yy.yingyang(new Integer[] {10, 20});
    yy.yingyang(new Integer(10), new Integer(20));
  }
}
```

Select the one correct answer.

(a) The class YingYang does not compile because of errors.

(b) The program compiles and prints:

```
Integer: 10
Integer...: 10
Integer...: 10
Integer...: 10
```

(c) The program compiles and prints:

```
Integer: 10
Integer...: 10
Integer[]: 10
Integer...: 10
```

7.33   What is the result of compiling and running the following program?

```
public class RQ800_60 {
  static void printFirst(Integer... ints) {
    System.out.println("Integer...: " + ints[0]);
  }

  static void printFirst(Number... nums) {
    System.out.println("Number...: " + nums[0]);
  }

  static void printFirst(Object... objs) {
    System.out.println("Object...: " + objs[0]);
  }

  public static void main(String[] args) {
    printFirst(10);
    printFirst((byte)20);
    printFirst('3', '0');
    printFirst("40");
    printFirst((short)50, 55);
    printFirst((Number[])new Integer[] {70, 75});
  }
}
```

Select the one correct answer.

(a) The program does not compile because of ambiguous method calls.

(b) The program compiles and prints:

```
Integer...: 10
Integer...: 20
Integer...: 3
Object...: 40
Integer...: 50
Number...: 70
```

(c) The program compiles and prints:

```
Integer...: 10
Number...: 20
Object...: 3
Object...: 40
Number...: 50
Number...: 70
```

(d) The program compiles and prints:

```
Integer...: 10
Integer...: 20
Integer...: 3
Object...: 40
Number...: 50
Number...: 70
```

7.34 What is the result of compiling and running the following program?

```java
public class RQ800_80 {
    static String compute(long... ls)              { return "ONE"; }
    static String compute(Long... ls)              { return "TWO"; }
    static String compute(Integer i1, Integer i2)  { return "THREE"; }
    static String compute(Long l1, Long l2)        { return "FOUR"; }
    static String compute(Number n1, Number n2)    { return "FIVE"; }

    public static void main(String[] args) {
        System.out.println(compute((byte)5, (byte)10) + ", " + compute(5, 10));
        System.out.println(compute(5L, 10) + ", " + compute(5L, 10L));
    }
}
```

Select the one correct answer.

(a) The program does not compile because of errors.

(b) The program compiles and prints:

```
THREE, THREE
FOUR, FOUR
```

(c) The program compiles and prints:

```
FIVE, THREE
FIVE, FOUR
```

(d) The program compiles and prints:

```
FIVE, THREE
ONE, TWO
```

(e) The program compiles and prints:

```
ONE, THREE
ONE, ONE
```

7.12 Polymorphism and Dynamic Method Lookup

Which object a reference will actually denote during runtime cannot always be determined at compile time. Polymorphism allows a reference to denote objects of different types at different times during execution. A supertype reference exhibits polymorphic behavior since it can denote objects of its subtypes.

When a non-private instance method is invoked on an object, the method definition actually executed is determined both by the type of the object at runtime and the method signature. Dynamic method lookup is the process of determining which method definition a method signature denotes during runtime, based on the type of the object. However, a call to a private instance method is not polymorphic. Such a call can only occur within the class and gets bound to the private method implementation at compile time.

The inheritance hierarchy depicted in Figure 7.4 is implemented in Example 7.14. The implementation of the method draw() is overridden in all subclasses of the class Shape. The invocation of the draw() method in the two loops at (3) and (4) in Example 7.14 relies on the polymorphic behavior of references and dynamic method lookup. The array shapes holds Shape references denoting a Circle, a Rectangle and a Square, as shown at (1). At runtime, dynamic lookup determines the draw() implementation to execute, based on the type of the object denoted by each element in the array. This is also the case for the elements of the array drawables at (2), which holds IDrawable references that can be assigned the reference value of any object of a class that imple-

Figure 7.4 *Type Hierarchy to Illustrate Polymorphism*

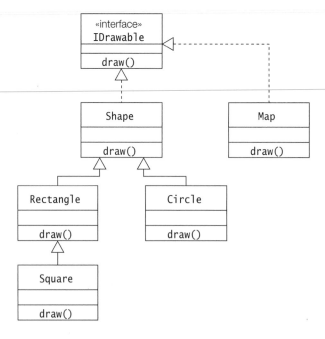

ments the IDrawable interface. The first loop will still work without any change if objects of new subclasses of the class Shape are added to the array shapes. If they did not override the draw() method, an inherited version of the method would be executed. This polymorphic behavior applies to the array drawables, where the subtype objects are guaranteed to have implemented the IDrawable interface.

Polymorphism and dynamic method lookup form a powerful programming paradigm that simplifies client definitions, encourages object decoupling, and supports dynamically changing relationships between objects at runtime.

Example 7.14 *Polymorphism and Dynamic Method Lookup*

```java
interface IDrawable {
  void draw();
}

class Shape implements IDrawable {
  public void draw() { System.out.println("Drawing a Shape."); }
}

class Circle extends Shape {
  public void draw() { System.out.println("Drawing a Circle."); }
}

class Rectangle extends Shape {
  public void draw() { System.out.println("Drawing a Rectangle."); }
}

class Square extends Rectangle {
  public void draw() { System.out.println("Drawing a Square."); }
}

class Map implements IDrawable {
  public void draw() { System.out.println("Drawing a Map."); }
}

public class PolymorphRefs {
  public static void main(String[] args) {
    Shape[] shapes = {new Circle(), new Rectangle(), new Square()};      // (1)
    IDrawable[] drawables = {new Shape(), new Rectangle(), new Map()};  // (2)

    System.out.println("Draw shapes:");
    for (Shape shape : shapes)                                           // (3)
      shape.draw();

    System.out.println("Draw drawables:");
    for (IDrawable drawable : drawables)                                 // (4)
      drawable.draw();
  }
}
```

Output from the program:

```
Draw shapes:
```

```
Drawing a Circle.
Drawing a Rectangle.
Drawing a Square.
Draw drawables:
Drawing a Shape.
Drawing a Rectangle.
Drawing a Map.
```

7.13 Inheritance Versus Aggregation

Figure 7.5 is a UML class diagram showing several aggregation relationships and one inheritance relationship. The class diagram shows a queue defined by aggregation and a stack defined by inheritance. Both are based on linked lists. A linked list is defined by aggregation. A non-generic implementation of these data structures is shown in Example 7.15. The purpose of the example is to illustrate inheritance and aggregation, not industrial-strength implementation of queues and stacks. The class Node at (1) is straightforward, defining two fields: one denoting the data and the other denoting the next node in the list. The class LinkedList at (2) keeps track of the list by managing a head and a tail reference. Nodes can be inserted in the front or back, but deleted only from the front of the list.

Figure 7.5 *Implementing Data Structures by Inheritance and Aggregation*

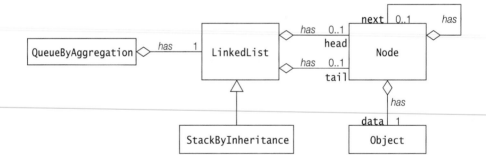

Example 7.15 *Implementing Data Structures by Inheritance and Aggregation*

```
class Node {                                             // (1)
  private Object data;    // Data
  private Node    next;   // Next node

  // Constructor for initializing data and reference to the next node.
  Node(Object data, Node next) {
    this.data = data;
    this.next = next;
  }
}
```

```java
  // Methods:
  public void   setData(Object obj) { data = obj; }
  public Object getData()           { return data; }
  public void   setNext(Node node)  { next = node; }
  public Node   getNext()           { return next; }
}
//_____
class LinkedList {                                            // (2)
  protected Node head = null;
  protected Node tail = null;

  // Methods:
  public boolean isEmpty() { return head == null; }
  public void insertInFront(Object dataObj) {
    if (isEmpty()) head = tail = new Node(dataObj, null);
    else head = new Node(dataObj, head);
  }
  public void insertAtBack(Object dataObj) {
    if (isEmpty())
      head = tail = new Node(dataObj, null);
    else {
      tail.setNext(new Node(dataObj, null));
      tail = tail.getNext();
    }
  }
  public Object deleteFromFront() {
    if (isEmpty()) return null;
    Node removed = head;
    if (head == tail) head = tail = null;
    else head = head.getNext();
    return removed.getData();
  }
}
//_____
class QueueByAggregation {                                    // (3)
  private LinkedList qList;

  // Constructor
  QueueByAggregation() {
    qList = new LinkedList();
  }

  // Methods:
  public boolean isEmpty() { return qList.isEmpty(); }
  public void enqueue(Object item) { qList.insertAtBack(item); }
  public Object dequeue() {
    if (qList.isEmpty()) return null;
    return qList.deleteFromFront();
  }
  public Object peek() {
    return (qList.isEmpty() ? null : qList.head.getData());
  }
}
//_____
```

```
class StackByInheritance extends LinkedList {                    // (4)
  public void push(Object item) { insertInFront(item); }
  public Object pop() {
    if (isEmpty()) return null;
    return deleteFromFront();
  }
  public Object peek() {
    return (isEmpty() ? null : head.getData());
  }
}
//_____
public class Client {                                           // (5)
  public static void main(String[] args) {
    String string1 = "Queues are boring to stand in!";
    int length1 = string1.length();
    QueueByAggregation queue = new QueueByAggregation();
    for (int i = 0; i<length1; i++)
      queue.enqueue(new Character(string1.charAt(i)));
    while (!queue.isEmpty())
      System.out.print(queue.dequeue());
    System.out.println();

    String string2 = "!no tis ot nuf era skcatS";
    int length2 = string2.length();
    StackByInheritance stack = new StackByInheritance();
    for (int i = 0; i<length2; i++)
      stack.push(new Character(string2.charAt(i)));
    stack.insertAtBack(new Character('!'));                      // (6)
    while (!stack.isEmpty())
      System.out.print(stack.pop());
    System.out.println();
  }
}
```

Output from the program:

```
Queues are boring to stand in!
Stacks are fun to sit on!!
```

Choosing between inheritance and aggregation to model relationships can be a crucial design decision. A good design strategy advocates that inheritance should be used only if the relationship *is-a* is unequivocally maintained throughout the lifetime of the objects involved; otherwise, aggregation is the best choice. A *role* is often confused with an *is-a* relationship. For example, given the class Employee, it would not be a good idea to model the roles an employee can play (such as a manager or a cashier) by inheritance if these roles change intermittently. Changing roles would involve a new object to represent the new role every time this happens.

Code reuse is also best achieved by aggregation when there is no *is-a* relationship. Enforcing an artificial *is-a* relationship that is not naturally present is usually not a good idea. This is illustrated in Example 7.15 at (6). Since the class StackByInheritance at (4) is a subclass of the class LinkedList at (2), any inherited method from the superclass can be invoked on an instance of the subclass. Also, methods that contradict the abstraction represented by the subclass can be invoked, as shown at (6). Using aggregation in such a case results in a better solution, as demonstrated by the class `QueueByAggregation` at (3). The class defines the operations of a queue by *delegating* such requests to the underlying class `LinkedList`. Clients implementing a queue in this manner do not have access to the underlying class and, therefore, cannot break the abstraction.

Both inheritance and aggregation promote encapsulation of *implementation*, as changes to the implementation are localized to the class. Changing the *contract* of a superclass can have consequences for the subclasses (called the *ripple effect*) and also for clients who are dependent on a particular behavior of the subclasses.

Polymorphism is achieved through inheritance and interface implementation. Code relying on polymorphic behavior will still work without any change if new subclasses or new classes implementing the interface are added. If no obvious *is-a* relationship is present, polymorphism is best achieved by using aggregation with interface implementation.

7.14 Basic Concepts in Object-Oriented Design

In this section, we provide a brief explanation of some basic concepts in object-oriented (OO) design. The reader is encouraged to consult the vast body of literature that is readily available on this subject.

Encapsulation

An object has properties and behaviors that are *encapsulated* inside the object. The services it offers to its clients comprises its *contract*, or public interface. Only the contract defined by the object is available to the clients. The *implementation* of its properties and behavior is not a concern of the clients. Encapsulation helps to make clear the distinction between an object's contract and implementation. This has major consequences for program development. The implementation of an object can change without implications for the clients. Encapsulation also reduces complexity, as the internals of an object are hidden from the clients who cannot alter its implementation.

Encapsulation is achieved through *information hiding*, by making judicious use of language features provided for this purpose. Information hiding in Java can be achieved at different levels of granularity:

- method or block level

  Localizing information in a method hides it from the outside.

- class level

  The accessibility of members declared in a class can be controlled through member accessibility modifiers. One much-advocated information-hiding technique is to prevent direct access by clients to data maintained by an object. The fields of the object are private and its contract defines public methods for the services provided by the object. Such tight encapsulation helps to separate the use from the implementation of a class.

- package level

  Classes that belong together can be grouped into relevant packages by using the package statement. Inter-package accessibility of classes can be controlled by class accessibility modifiers.

Cohesion

Cohesion is an *inter-class* measure of how well-structured and closely-related the functionality is in a class. The objective is to design classes with *high* cohesion, that perform well-defined and related tasks (also called *functional cohesion*). The public methods of a highly cohesive class typically implement a single specific task that is related to the purpose of the class. For example, in an MVC-based application, the respective classes for the Model, the View, and the Controller should be focused on providing functionality that only relates to their individual purpose. A method in one class should not perform a task that should actually be implemented by one of the other two classes.

Lack of cohesion in a class means that the purpose of the class is not focused, and unrelated functionality is ending up in the class (also called *coincidental cohesion*)—which will eventually impact the maintainability of the application.

Coupling

Coupling is a measure of *intra-class dependencies*. Objects need to interact with each other, therefore dependencies between classes are inherent in OO design. However, these dependencies should be minimized in order to achieve *loose* coupling, which aids in creating extensible applications.

One major source of intra-class dependencies is the exposure of implementation details of an object. Such details can be utilized by other objects, and this dependency can impede changes in the implementation, resulting in less extensible applications.

High cohesion and loose coupling help to achieve the main goals of OO design: maintainability, reusability, extensibility, and reliability.

Review Questions

7.35 What will be the result of compiling and running the following program?

```java
public class Polymorphism {
  public static void main(String[] args) {
    A ref1 = new C();
    B ref2 = (B) ref1;
    System.out.println(ref2.f());
  }
}

class A           { int f() { return 0; } }
class B extends A { int f() { return 1; } }
class C extends B { int f() { return 2; } }
```

Select the one correct answer.

(a) The program will fail to compile.
(b) The program will compile but will throw a ClassCastException, when run.
(c) The program will compile and print 0, when run.
(d) The program will compile and print 1, when run.
(e) The program will compile and print 2, when run.

7.36 What will be the result of compiling and running the following program?

```java
public class Polymorphism2 {
  public static void main(String[] args) {
    A ref1 = new C();
    B ref2 = (B) ref1;
    System.out.println(ref2.g());
  }
}

class A {
  private int f() { return 0; }
  public int g() { return 3; }
}
class B extends A {
  private int f() { return 1; }
  public int g() { return f(); }
}
class C extends B {
  public int f() { return 2; }
}
```

Select the one correct answer.

(a) The program will fail to compile.
(b) The program will compile and print 0, when run.
(c) The program will compile and print 1, when run.
(d) The program will compile and print 2, when run.
(e) The program will compile and print 3, when run.

7.37   Which statements about the program are true?

```
public interface HeavenlyBody { String describe(); }

class Star {
  String starName;
  public String describe() { return "star " + starName; }
}

class Planet extends Star {
  String name;
  public String describe() {
    return "planet " + name + " orbiting star " + starName;
  }
}
```

Select the two correct answers:

(a) The code will fail to compile.
(b) The code defines a Planet *is-a* Star relationship.
(c) The code will fail to compile if the name starName is replaced with the name bodyName throughout the declaration of the Star class.
(d) The code will fail to compile if the name starName is replaced with the name name throughout the declaration of the Star class.
(e) An instance of Planet is a valid instance of HeavenlyBody.

7.38   Given the following code, which statement is true?

```
public interface HeavenlyBody { String describe(); }

class Star implements HeavenlyBody {
  String starName;
  public String describe() { return "star " + starName; }
}

class Planet {
  String name;
  Star orbiting;
  public String describe() {
    return "planet " + name + " orbiting " + orbiting.describe();
  }
}
```

Select the one correct answer:

(a) The code will fail to compile.
(b) The code defines a Planet *has-a* Star relationship.
(c) The code will fail to compile if the name starName is replaced with the name bodyName throughout the declaration of the Star class.
(d) The code will fail to compile if the name starName is replaced with the name name throughout the declaration of the Star class.
(e) An instance of Planet is a valid instance of a HeavenlyBody.

7.39 Which statement is not true?

Select the one correct answer.

(a) Maximizing cohesion and minimizing coupling are the hallmarks of a well-designed application.
(b) Coupling is an inherent property of any non-trivial OO design.
(c) Adhering to the JavaBeans naming standard can aid in achieving encapsulation.
(d) Dependencies between classes can be minimized by hiding implementation details.
(e) Each method implementing a single task will result in a class that has high cohesion.
(f) None of the above.

Chapter Summary

The following information was included in this chapter:

- inheritance and its implications in OOP
- overriding and hiding of superclass members
- method overriding versus method overloading
- usage of the `super` reference to access superclass members
- usage of `this()` and `super()` calls, including constructor chaining
- interfaces and multiple interface inheritance
- subtype-supertype relationship
- conversions when assigning, casting, and passing reference values
- identifying the type of objects using the `instanceof` operator
- polymorphism and dynamic method lookup
- inheritance (*is-a*) versus aggregation (*has-a*)
- best practices for OO design: tight encapsulation, loose coupling, and high cohesion in classes.

Programming Exercises

7.1 Declare an interface called `Function` that has a method named `evaluate` that takes an `int` parameter and returns an `int` value.

Create a class called `Half` that implements the `Function` interface. The implementation of the method `evaluate()` should return the value obtained by dividing the `int` argument by 2.

In a client, create a method that takes an arbitrary array of int values as a parameter, and returns an array that has the same length, but the value of an element in the new array is half that of the value in the corresponding element in the array passed as the parameter. Let the implementation of this method create an instance of Half, and use this instance to calculate values for the array that is returned.

7.2   Rewrite the method that operated on arrays from the previous exercise: the method should now also accept a Function reference as an argument, and use this argument instead of an instance of the Half class.

Create a class called Print that implements the method evaluate() in the Function interface. This method simply prints the int value passed as argument, and returns this value.

Now, write a program that creates an array of int values from 1 to 10, and does the following:

o Prints the array using an instance of the Print class and the method described earlier.

o Halves the values in the array and prints the values again, using the Half and Print classes, and the method described above.

Nested Type Declarations

●●●

1.1 Develop code that declares classes (including abstract and all forms of nested classes), interfaces, and enums, and includes the appropriate use of **package** and **import** statements (including static imports).

  ○ *For class declrations, see Section 3.1, p. 40.*

  ○ *For abstract classes, see Section 4.8, p. 135.*

  ○ *For interfaces, see Section 7.6, p. 309.*

  ○ *For enums, see Section 3.5, p. 54.*

  ○ *For package and import statements, see Section 4.2, p. 105.*

1.6 Given a set of classes and superclasses, develop constructors for one or more of the classes. Given a class declaration, determine if a default constructor will be created and, if so, determine the behavior of that constructor. Given a nested or non-nested class listing, write code to instantiate the class.

  ○ *For constructors, see Section 3.4, p. 48.*

  ○ *For default constructors, see Section 3.4, p. 49.*

  ○ *For constructor chaining, see Section 7.5, p. 302, and Section 9.11, p. 416.*

- State which nested classes create instances that are associated with instances of the enclosing context.

- State the access rules that govern accessing entities in the enclosing context of nested classes and write code that uses the augmented syntax involving the this keyword for this purpose.

- State whether a definition of a nested class can contain static and non-static members.

- Distinguish between the inheritance hierarchy and the enclosing context of any nested class or interface.

8.1 Overview of Nested Type Declarations

A class that is declared within another type declaration is called a *nested class*. Similarly, an interface or an enum type that is declared within another type declaration is called a *nested interface* or a *nested enum type*, respectively. A *top-level class, enum type*, or *interface* is one that is not nested. By a *nested type* we mean either a nested class, a nested enum, or a nested interface.

In addition to the top-level types, there are four categories of *nested classes*, one of *nested enum types*, and one of *nested interfaces*, defined by the context these nested types are declared in:

- static member classes, enums, and interfaces
- non-static member classes
- local classes
- anonymous classes

The last three categories are collectively known as *inner classes*. They differ from non-inner classes in one important aspect: that an instance of an inner class may be associated with an instance of the enclosing class. The instance of the enclosing class is called the *immediately enclosing instance*. An instance of an inner class can access the members of its immediately enclosing instance by their simple names.

A *static member class, enum, or interface* can be declared either at the top-level, or in a nested `static` type. A `static` class can be instantiated like any ordinary top-level class, using its full name. No enclosing instance is required to instantiate a static member class. An enum or an interface cannot be instantiated with the new operator. Note that there are no non-static member, local, or anonymous interfaces. This is also true for enum types.

Non-static member classes are defined as instance members of other classes, just as fields and instance methods are defined in a class. An instance of a non-static member class always has an enclosing instance associated with it.

Local classes can be defined in the context of a block as in a method body or a local block, just as local variables can be defined in a method body or a local block.

Anonymous classes can be defined as expressions and instantiated *on the fly*. An instance of a local (or an anonymous) class has an enclosing instance associated with it, if the local (or anonymous) class is declared in a non-static context.

A nested type cannot have the same name as any of its enclosing types.

Locks on nested classes are discussed in Section 13.5, p. 629.

Generic nested classes and interfaces are discussed in Section 14.13, p. 731. It is not possible to declare a generic enum type (Section 14.13, p. 733).

Skeletal code for nested types is shown in Example 8.1. Table 8.1 presents a summary of various aspects relating to nested types. The *Type* column lists the different kinds of types that can be declared. The *Declaration Context* column lists the lexical context in which a type can be declared. The *Accessibility Modifiers* column indicates what accessibility can be specified for the type. The *Enclosing Instance* column specifies whether an enclosing instance is associated with an instance of the type. The *Direct Access to Enclosing Context* column lists what is directly accessible in the enclosing context from within the type. The *Declarations in Type Body* column refers to what can be declared in the body of the type. Subsequent sections on each nested type elaborate on the summary presented in Table 8.1. (*N/A* in the table means "not applicable".)

Example 8.1 *Overview of Type Declarations*

```
class TLC {                    // (1) Top level class

  static class SMC {/*...*/}   // (2) Static member class

  interface SMI {/*...*/}      // (3) Static member interface

  class NSMC {/*...*/}         // (4) Non-static member (inner) class

  void nsm() {
    class NSLC {/*...*/}       // (5) Local (inner) class in non-static context
  }

  static void sm() {
    class SLC {/*...*/}        // (6) Local (inner) class in static context
  }

  SMC nsf = new SMC() {        // (7) Anonymous (inner) class in non-static context
    /*...*/
  };

  static SMI sf = new SMI() {  // (8) Anonymous (inner) class in static context
    /*...*/
  };

  enum SME {/*...*/}           // (9) Static member enum
}
```

Nested types can be regarded as a form of encapsulation, enforcing relationships between types by greater proximity. They allow structuring of types and a special binding relationship between a nested object and its enclosing instance. Used judiciously, they can be beneficial, but unrestrained use of nested types can easily result in unreadable code.

Table 8.1 *Overview of Type Declarations*

Type	Declaration Context	Accessibility Modifiers	Enclosing Instance	Direct Access to Enclosing Context	Declarations in Type Body
Top-level Class, Enum, or Interface	Package	public or default	No	N/A	All that are valid in a class, enum, or interface body, respectively
Static Member Class, Enum, or Interface	As member of a top-level type or a nested static type	All	No	Static members in enclosing context	All that are valid in a class, enum, or interface body, respectively
Non-static Member Class	As non-static member of enclosing type	All	Yes	All members in enclosing context	Only non-static declarations + final static fields
Local Class	In block with non-static context	None	Yes	All members in enclosing context + final local variables	Only non-static declarations + final static fields
	In block with static context	None	No	Static members in enclosing context + final local variables	Only non-static declarations + final static fields
Anonymous Class	As expression in non-static context	None	Yes	All members in enclosing context + final local variables	Only non-static declarations + final static fields
	As expression in static context	None	No	Static members in enclosing context + final local variables	Only non-static declarations + final static fields

8.2 Static Member Types

Declaring and Using Static Member Types

A static member class, enum type, or *interface* comprises the same declarations as those allowed in an ordinary top-level class, enum type, or interface, respectively. A static member class must be declared explicitly with the keyword static, as a static member of an enclosing type. Nested interfaces are considered implicitly static, the keyword static can, therefore, be omitted. Nested enum types are treated analogously to nested interface in this regard: they are static members.

The accessibility modifiers allowed for members in an enclosing type declaration can naturally be used for nested types. Static member classes, enum types and interfaces can only be declared in top-level type declarations, or within other nested static members.

As regards nesting of types, any further discussion on nested classes and interfaces is also applicable to nested enum types.

In Example 8.2, the top-level class ListPool at (1) contains a static member class MyLinkedList at (2), which in turn defines a static member interface ILink at (3) and a static member class BiNode at (4). The static member class BiNode at (4) implements the static member interface IBiLink at (5). Note that each static member class is defined as static, just like static variables and methods in a top-level class.

Example 8.2   *Static Member Types*

```
//Filename: ListPool.java
package smc;

public class ListPool {                          // (1) Top-level class

  public static class MyLinkedList {             // (2) Static member class

    private interface ILink { }                  // (3) Static member interface

    public static class BiNode
              implements IBiLink { }             // (4) Static member class
  }

  interface IBiLink
          extends MyLinkedList.ILink { }         // (5) Static member interface
}
```

```
//Filename: MyBiLinkedList.java
package smc;

public class MyBiLinkedList implements ListPool.IBiLink { // (6)
```

```
    ListPool.MyLinkedList.BiNode objRef1
            = new ListPool.MyLinkedList.BiNode();      // (7)

  //ListPool.MyLinkedList.ILink ref;                   // (8) Compile-time error!
  }
```

The *full name* of a (static or non-static) member class or interface includes the names of the classes and interfaces it is lexically nested in. For example, the full name of the member class BiNode at (4) is ListPool.MyLinkedList.BiNode. The full name of the member interface IBiLink at (5) is ListPool.IBiLink. Each member class or interface is uniquely identified by this naming syntax, which is a generalization of the naming scheme for packages. The full name can be used in exactly the same way as any other top-level class or interface name, as shown at (6) and (7). Such a member's fully qualified name is its full name prefixed by the name of its package. For example, the fully qualified name of the member class at (4) is smc.ListPool.MyLinkedList.BiNode. Note that a nested member type cannot have the same name as an enclosing type.

For all intents and purposes, a static member class or interface is very much like any other top-level class or interface. Static variables and methods belong to a class, and not to instances of the class. The same is true for static member classes and interfaces.

Within the scope of its top-level class or interface, a member class or interface can be referenced regardless of its accessibility modifier and lexical nesting, as shown at (5) in Example 8.2. Its accessibility modifier (and that of the types making up its full name) come into play when it is referenced by an external client. The declaration at (8) in Example 8.2 will not compile because the member interface ListPool.MyLinkedList.ILink has private accessibility.

A static member class can be instantiated without any reference to any instance of the enclosing context, as is the case for instantiating top-level classes. An example of creating an instance of a static member class is shown at (7) in Example 8.2 using the new operator.

If the file ListPool.java containing the declarations in Example 8.2 is compiled, it will result in the generation of the following class files in the package smc, where each file corresponds to either a class or an interface declaration:

```
ListPool$MyLinkedList$BiNode.class
ListPool$MyLinkedList$ILink.class
ListPool$MyLinkedList.class
ListPool$IBiLink.class
ListPool.class
```

Note how the full class name corresponds to the class file name (minus the extension), with the dollar sign ($) replaced by the dot sign (.).

There is seldom any reason to import nested types from packages. It would undermine the encapsulation achieved by such types. However, a compilation unit can use the import facility to provide a shortcut for the names of member classes and interfaces. Note that type import and static import of nested static types is equivalent: in both cases, a type name is imported. Some variations on usage of the (static) import declaration for static member classes are shown in Example 8.3.

Example 8.3 *Importing Static Member Types*

```
//Filename: Client1.java
import smc.ListPool.MyLinkedList;                          // (1) Type import

public class Client1 {
   MyLinkedList.BiNode objRef1 = new MyLinkedList.BiNode();// (2)
}
```

```
//Filename: Client2.java
import static smc.ListPool.MyLinkedList.BiNode;            // (3) Static import

public class Client2 {
   BiNode objRef2 = new BiNode();                          // (4)
}

class BiListPool implements smc.ListPool.IBiLink { }       // (5) Not accessible!
```

In the file `Client1.java`, the import statement at (1) allows the static member class `BiNode` to be referenced as `MyLinkedList.BiNode` in (2), whereas in the file `Client2.java`, the static import at (3) will allow the same class to be referenced using its simple name, as at (4). At (5), the fully qualified name of the static member interface is used in an `implements` clause. However, the interface `smc.ListPool.IBiLink` is declared with package accessibility in its enclosing class `ListPool` in the package `smc`, and therefore not visible in other packages, including the default package.

Accessing Members in Enclosing Context

Static code does not have a `this` reference and can, therefore, only directly access other members that are declared `static` within the same class. Since static member classes are `static`, they do not have any notion of an enclosing instance. This means that any code in a static member class can only directly access static members, but not instance members, in its enclosing context.

Figure 8.1 is a class diagram that illustrates static member classes and interfaces. These are shown as members of the enclosing context, with the {static} tag to indicate that they are static, i.e., they can be instantiated without regard to any object of the enclosing context. Since they are members of a class or an interface, their accessibility can be specified exactly like that of any other member of a class or interface. The classes from the diagram are implemented in Example 8.4.

Figure 8.1   *Static Member Classes and Interfaces*

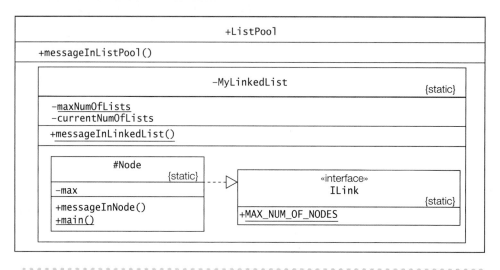

· ·

Example 8.4   *Accessing Members in Enclosing Context (Static Member Classes)*

```
//Filename: ListPool.java
public class ListPool {                             // Top-level class

  public void messageInListPool() {                 // Instance method
    System.out.println("This is a ListPool object.");
  }

  private static class MyLinkedList {               // (1) Static class
    private static int maxNumOfLists = 100;         // Static variable
    private int currentNumOfLists;                  // Instance variable

    public static void messageInLinkedList() {      // Static method
      System.out.println("This is MyLinkedList class.");
    }

    interface ILink { int MAX_NUM_OF_NODES = 2000; }  // (2) Static interface

    protected static class Node implements ILink {  // (3) Static class

      private int max = MAX_NUM_OF_NODES;           // (4) Instance variable

      public void messageInNode() {                 // Instance method
        //   int currentLists = currentNumOfLists;  // (5) Not OK.
        int maxLists = maxNumOfLists;
        int maxNodes = max;

        //   messageInListPool();                   // (6) Not OK.
        messageInLinkedList();                      // (7) Call static method
      }

      public static void main (String[] args) {
        int maxLists = maxNumOfLists;               // (8)
```

```
            // int maxNodes = max;                    // (9) Not OK.
            messageInLinkedList();                    // (10) Call static method
        }
    }  // Node
  }  // MyLinkedList
} // ListPool
```

Compiling the program:

```
>javac ListPool.java
```

Running the program:

```
>java ListPool$MyLinkedList$Node
This is MyLinkedList class.
```

- -

Example 8.4 demonstrates accessing members directly in the enclosing context of class Node defined at (3). The initialization of the field max at (4) is valid, since the field MAX_NUM_OF_NODES, defined in the outer interface ILink at (2), is implicitly static. The compiler will flag an error at (5) and (6) in the method messageInNode() because direct access to non-static members in the enclosing class is not permitted by *any* method in a static member class. It will also flag an error at (9) in the method main() because a static method cannot access directly other non-static fields in its own class. The statements at (8) and (10) access static members only in the enclosing context. The references in these statements can also be specified using full names.

```
int maxLists = ListPool.MyLinkedList.maxNumOfLists;    // (8')
ListPool.MyLinkedList.messageInLinkedList();           // (10')
```

Note that a static member class can define both static and instance members, like any other top-level class. However, its code can only directly access static members in its enclosing context.

A static member class, being a member of the enclosing class or interface, can have any accessibility (public, protected, package/default, private), like any other member of a class. The class MyLinkedList at (1) has private accessibility, whereas its nested class Node at (3) has protected accessibility. The class Node defines the method main() which can be executed by the command

```
>java ListPool$MyLinkedList$Node
```

Note that the class Node is specified using the full name of the class file minus the extension.

8.3 Non-Static Member Classes

Non-static member classes are inner classes that are defined without the keyword static as members of an enclosing class or interface. Non-static member classes are on par with other non-static members defined in a class. The following aspects about non-static member classes should be noted:

- An instance of a non-static member class can only exist with an instance of its enclosing class. This means that an instance of a non-static member class must be created in the context of an instance of the enclosing class. This also means that a non-static member class cannot have static members. In other words, the non-static member class does not provide any services, only instances of the class do. However, final static variables are allowed, as these are constants.

- Code in a non-static member class can directly refer to any member (including nested) of any enclosing class or interface, including private members. No fully qualified reference is required.

- Since a non-static member class is a member of an enclosing class, it can have any accessibility: public, package/default, protected, or private.

A typical application of non-static member classes is implementing data structures. For example, a class for linked lists could define the nodes in the list with the help of a non-static member class which could be declared private so that it was not accessible outside of the top-level class. Nesting promotes encapsulation, and the close proximity allows classes to exploit each other's capabilities.

Instantiating Non-Static Member Classes

In Example 8.5, the class MyLinkedList at (1) defines a non-static member class Node at (5). The example is in no way a complete implementation for linked lists. Its main purpose is to illustrate nesting and use of non-static member classes.

Example 8.5 *Defining and Instantiating Non-static Member Classes*

```java
class MyLinkedList {                                         // (1)
  private String message = "Shine the light";               // (2)

  public Node makeInstance(String info, Node next) {        // (3)
    return new Node(info, next);                            // (4)
  }

  public class Node {                                        // (5) NSMC
    //   static int maxNumOfNodes = 100;                     // (6) Not OK.
    final static int maxNumOfNodes = 100;                    // (7) OK.
    private String nodeInfo;                                 // (8)
    private Node next;

    public Node(String nodeInfo, Node next) {               // (9)
      this.nodeInfo = nodeInfo;
      this.next = next;
    }

    public String toString() {
      return message + " in " + nodeInfo + " (" + maxNumOfNodes + ")"; // (10)
    }
  }
}
```

```
        public class ListClient {                                          // (11)
          public static void main(String[] args) {                         // (12)
            MyLinkedList list = new MyLinkedList();                        // (13)
            MyLinkedList.Node node1 = list.makeInstance("node1", null);    // (14)
            System.out.println(node1);                                     // (15)
    //      MyLinkedList.Node nodeX
    //            = new MyLinkedList.Node("nodeX", node1);                  // (16) Not OK.
            MyLinkedList.Node node2 = list.new Node("node2", node1);       // (17)
            System.out.println(node2);                                     // (18)
          }
        }
```

Output from the program:

```
    Shine the light in node1 (100)
    Shine the light in node2 (100)
```

First, note that in Example 8.5, the declaration of a static variable at (6) in class Node is flagged as a compile-time error, but defining a final static variable at (7) is allowed.

A special form of the new operator is used to instantiate a non-static member class:

<enclosing object reference>.new *<non-static member class constructor call>*

The *<enclosing object reference>* in the object creation expression evaluates to an instance of the enclosing class in which the designated non-static member class is defined. A new instance of the non-static member class is created and associated with the indicated instance of the enclosing class. Note that the expression returns a reference value that denotes a new instance of the non-static member class. It is illegal to specify the full name of the non-static member class in the constructor call, as the enclosing context is already given by the *<enclosing object reference>*.

The non-static method makeInstance() at (3) in the class MyLinkedList creates an instance of the Node using the new operator, as shown at (4):

```
    return new Node(info, next);                    // (4)
```

This creates an instance of a non-static member class in the context of the instance of the enclosing class on which the makeInstance() method is invoked. The new operator in the statement at (4) has an implicit this reference as the *<enclosing object reference>*, since the non-static member class is directly defined in the context of the object denoted by the this reference:

```
    return this.new Node(info, next);               // (4')
```

The makeInstance() method is called at (14). This method call associates an inner object of the Node class with the object denoted by the reference list. This inner object is denoted by the reference node1. This reference can then be used in the normal way to access members of the inner object. An example of such a use is shown at (15) in the print statement where this reference is used to call the toString() method implicitly on the inner object.

An attempt to create an instance of the non-static member class without an outer instance, using the new operator with the full name of the inner class, as shown at (16), results in a compile-time error.

The special form of the new operator is also used in the object creation expression at (17).

```
MyLinkedList.Node node2 = list.new Node("node2", node1);          // (17)
```

The reference list denotes an object of the class MyLinkedList. After the execution of the statement at (17), the MyLinkedList object has two instances of the non-static member class Node associated with it. This is depicted in Figure 8.2, where the outer object (denoted by list) of class MyLinkedList is shown with its two associated inner objects (denoted by the references node1 and node2, respectively) right after the execution of the statement at (17). In other words, multiple objects of the non-static member classes can be associated with an object of an enclosing class at runtime.

Figure 8.2   *Outer Object with Associated Inner Objects*

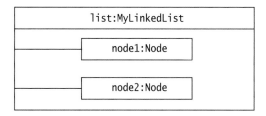

Accessing Members in Enclosing Context

An implicit reference to the enclosing object is always available in every method and constructor of a non-static member class. A method can explicitly use this reference with a special form of the this construct, as explained in the next example.

From within a non-static member class, it is possible to refer to all members in the enclosing class directly. An example is shown at (10) in Example 8.5, where the field message from the enclosing class is accessed in the non-static member class. It is also possible to explicitly refer to members in the enclosing class, but this requires special usage of the this reference. One might be tempted to write the statement at (10) as follows:

```
return this.message + " in " + this.nodeInfo +
                      " (" + this.maxNumOfNodes + ")"; // (10a)
```

The reference this.nodeInfo is correct, because the field nodeInfo certainly belongs to the current object (denoted by this) of the Node class, but this.message can*not* possibly work, as the current object (indicated by this) of the Node class has no field named message. The correct syntax is the following:

```
return MyLinkedList.this.message + " in " + this.nodeInfo +
                      " (" + this.maxNumOfNodes + ")"; // (10b)
```

The expression

<*enclosing class name*>.this

evaluates to a reference that denotes the enclosing object (of the class <*enclosing class name*>) of the current instance of a non-static member class.

Accessing Hidden Members

Fields and methods in the enclosing context can be *hidden* by fields and methods with the same names in the non-static member class. The special form of the this syntax can be used to access members in the enclosing context, somewhat analogous to using the keyword super in subclasses to access hidden superclass members.

Example 8.6 *Special Form of* this *and* new *Constructs in Non-static Member Classes*

```
//Filename: Client2.java
class TLClass {                                          // (1)  TLC
  private String id = "TLClass ";                        // (2)
  public TLClass(String objId) { id = id + objId; }      // (3)
  public void printId() {                                // (4)
    System.out.println(id);
  }

  class InnerB {                                         // (5)  NSMC
    private String id = "InnerB ";                       // (6)
    public InnerB(String objId) { id = id + objId; }     // (7)
    public void printId() {                              // (8)
      System.out.print(TLClass.this.id + " : ");         // (9)  Refers to (2)
      System.out.println(id);                            // (10) Refers to (6)
    }

    class InnerC {                                       // (11) NSMC
      private String id = "InnerC ";                     // (12)
      public InnerC(String objId) { id = id + objId; }   // (13)
      public void printId() {                            // (14)
        System.out.print(TLClass.this.id + " : ");       // (15) Refers to (2)
        System.out.print(InnerB.this.id + " : ");        // (16) Refers to (6)
        System.out.println(id);                          // (17) Refers to (12)
      }
      public void printIndividualIds() {                 // (18)
        TLClass.this.printId();                          // (19) Calls (4)
        InnerB.this.printId();                           // (20) Calls (8)
        printId();                                       // (21) Calls (14)
      }
    } // InnerC
  } // InnerB
} // TLClass
//_____
public class OuterInstances {                            // (22)
  public static void main(String[] args) {               // (23)
    TLClass a = new TLClass("a");                        // (24)
    TLClass.InnerB b = a.new InnerB("b");                // (25)
```

```
TLClass.InnerB.InnerC c1 = b.new InnerC("c1");           // (26)
TLClass.InnerB.InnerC c2 = b.new InnerC("c2");           // (27)
b.printId();                                             // (28)
c1.printId();                                            // (29)
c2.printId();                                            // (30)
TLClass.InnerB bb = new TLClass("aa").new InnerB("bb");  // (31)
TLClass.InnerB.InnerC cc = bb.new InnerC("cc");          // (32)
bb.printId();                                            // (33)
cc.printId();                                            // (34)
TLClass.InnerB.InnerC ccc =
  new TLClass("aaa").new InnerB("bbb").new InnerC("ccc");// (35)
ccc.printId();                                           // (36)
System.out.println("------------");
ccc.printIndividualIds();                                // (37)
    }
}
```

Output from the program:

```
TLClass a : InnerB b
TLClass a : InnerB b : InnerC c1
TLClass a : InnerB b : InnerC c2
TLClass aa : InnerB bb
TLClass aa : InnerB bb : InnerC cc
TLClass aaa : InnerB bbb : InnerC ccc
------------
TLClass aaa
TLClass aaa : InnerB bbb
TLClass aaa : InnerB bbb : InnerC ccc
```

Example 8.6 illustrates the special form of the this construct employed to access members in the enclosing context, and also demonstrates the special form of the new construct employed to create instances of non-static member classes. The example shows the non-static member class InnerC at (11), which is nested in the non-static member class InnerB at (5), which in turn is nested in the top-level class TLClass at (1). All three classes have a private non-static String field named id and a non-static method named printId. The member name in the nested class *hides* the name in the enclosing context. These members are *not* overridden in the nested classes because no inheritance is involved. In order to refer to the hidden members, the nested class can use the special this construct, as shown at (9), (15), (16), (19), and (20). Within the nested class InnerC, the three forms used in the following statements to access its field id are equivalent:

```
System.out.println(id);              // (17)
System.out.println(this.id);         // (17a)
System.out.println(InnerC.this.id);  // (17b)
```

The main() method at (23) uses the special syntax of the new operator to create objects of non-static member classes and associate them with enclosing objects. An instance of class InnerC (denoted by c) is created at (26) in the context of an instance of class InnerB (denoted by b), which was created at (25) in the context of an instance of class TLClass (denoted by a), which in turn was created at (24). The reference c1 is used at (29) to invoke the method `printId()` declared at (14) in the nested class `InnerC`. This method prints the field `id` from all the objects associated with an instance of the nested class `InnerC`.

When the intervening references to an instance of a non-static member class are of no interest (i.e., if the reference values need not be stored in variables), the new operator can be chained as shown at (31) and (35).

Note that the (outer) objects associated with the instances denoted by the references c1, cc, and ccc are distinct, as evident from the program output. However, the instances denoted by references c1 and c2 have the same outer objects associated with them.

Inheritance Hierarchy and Enclosing Context

Inner classes can extend other classes, and vice versa. An inherited field (or method) in an inner subclass can hide a field (or method) with the same name in the enclosing context. Using the simple name to access this member will access the inherited member, not the one in the enclosing context.

Example 8.7 illustrates the situation outlined earlier. The standard form of the this reference is used to access the inherited member, as shown at (4). The keyword super would be another alternative. To access the member from the enclosing context, the special form of the this reference together with the enclosing class name is used, as shown at (5).

Example 8.7 *Inheritance Hierarchy and Enclosing Context*

```
class Superclass {
  protected double x = 3.0e+8;
}
//_____
class TopLevelClass {                         // (1) Top-level Class
  private double x = 3.14;

  class Inner extends Superclass {            // (2) Non-static member Class
    public void printHidden() {               // (3)

      // (4) x from superclass:
      System.out.println("this.x: " + this.x);

      // (5) x from enclosing context:
      System.out.println("TopLevelClass.this.x: " + TopLevelClass.this.x);
    }
  } // Inner
} // TopLevelClass
//_____
public class HiddenAndInheritedAccess {
  public static void main(String[] args) {
    TopLevelClass.Inner ref = new TopLevelClass().new Inner();
```

```
      ref.printHidden();
    }
  }
```

Output from the program:

```
this.x: 3.0E8
TopLevelClass.this.x: 3.14
```

Some caution should be exercised when extending an inner class. Some of the subtleties involved are illustrated by Example 8.8. The nesting and the inheritance hierarchy of the classes involved is shown in Figure 8.3. The question that arises is how do we provide an *outer instance* when creating a *subclass instance* of a non-static member class, e.g., when creating objects of the classes SubclassC and OuterB in Figure 8.3.

Figure 8.3   *Nested Classes and Inheritance*

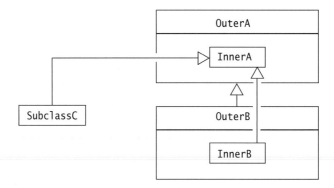

The non-static member class InnerA, declared at (2) in the class OuterA, is extended by SubclassC at (3). Note that SubclassC and the class OuterA are not related in any way, and that the subclass OuterB inherits the class InnerA from its superclass OuterA. An instance of SubclassC is created at (8). An instance of the class OuterA is explicitly passed as argument in the constructor call to SubclassC. The constructor at (4) for SubclassC has a special super() call in its body at (5). This call ensures that the constructor of the superclass InnerA has an outer object (denoted by the reference outerRef) to bind to. Using the standard super() call in the subclass constructor is not adequate, because it does not provide an outer instance for the superclass constructor to bind to. The non-default constructor at (4) and the outerRef.super() expression at (5) are mandatory to set up the proper relationships between the objects involved.

The outer object problem mentioned above does not arise if the subclass that extends an inner class is also declared within an outer class that extends the outer class of the superclass. This situation is illustrated at (6) and (7): the classes InnerB and OuterB extend the classes InnerA and OuterA, respectively. The type InnerA is inherited by the class OuterB from its superclass OuterA. Thus, an object of class OuterB can act as an outer object for an instance of class InnerA. The object creation expression at (9)

```
new OuterB().new InnerB();
```

creates an OuterB object and implicitly passes its reference to the default constructor of class InnerB. The default constructor of class InnerB invokes the default constructor of its superclass InnerA by calling super() and passing it the reference of the OuterB object, which the superclass constructor can readily bind to.

Example 8.8 *Extending Inner Classes*

```
class OuterA {                                // (1)
  class InnerA { }                            // (2)
}
//_____
class SubclassC extends OuterA.InnerA {       // (3) Extends NSMC at (2)

  // (4) Mandatory non-default constructor:
  SubclassC(OuterA outerRef) {
    outerRef.super();                         // (5) Explicit super() call
  }
}
//_____
class OuterB extends OuterA {                 // (6) Extends class at (1)
  class InnerB extends OuterB.InnerA { }      // (7) Extends NSMC at (2)
}
//_____
public class Extending {
  public static void main(String[] args) {

    // (8) Outer instance passed explicitly in constructor call:
    new SubclassC(new OuterA());

    // (9) No outer instance passed explicitly in constructor call to InnerB:
    new OuterB().new InnerB();
  }
}
```

 Review Questions

8.1   What will be the result of compiling and running the following program?

```
public class MyClass {
  public static void main(String[] args) {
    Outer objRef = new Outer();
    System.out.println(objRef.createInner().getSecret());
  }
}
```

```
class Outer {
  private int secret;
  Outer() { secret = 123; }

  class Inner {
    int getSecret() { return secret; }
  }

  Inner createInner() { return new Inner(); }
}
```

Select the one correct answer.

(a) The program will fail to compile because the class Inner cannot be declared within the class Outer.

(b) The program will fail to compile because the method createInner() cannot be allowed to pass objects of the class Inner to methods outside of the class Outer.

(c) The program will fail to compile because the field secret is not accessible from the method getSecret().

(d) The program will fail to compile because the method getSecret() is not visible from the main() method in the class MyClass.

(e) The code will compile and print 123, when run.

8.2   Which statements about nested classes are true?

Select the two correct answers.

(a) An instance of a static member class has an inherent outer instance.

(b) A static member class can contain non-static fields.

(c) A static member interface can contain non-static fields.

(d) A static member interface has an inherent outer instance.

(e) An instance of the outer class can be associated with many instances of a non-static member class.

8.3   What will be the result of compiling and running the following program?

```
public class MyClass {
  public static void main(String[] args) {
    State st = new State();
    System.out.println(st.getValue());
    State.Memento mem = st.memento();
    st.alterValue();
    System.out.println(st.getValue());
    mem.restore();
    System.out.println(st.getValue());
  }

  public static class State {
    protected int val = 11;

    int getValue() { return val; }
    void alterValue() { val = (val + 7) % 31; }
    Memento memento() { return new Memento(); }

    class Memento {
```

```
      int val;

      Memento() { this.val = State.this.val; }
      void restore() { ((State) this).val = this.val; }
    }
  }
}
```

Select the one correct answer.

(a) The program will fail to compile because the static main() method attempts to create a new instance of the static member class State.

(b) The program will fail to compile because the class State.Memento is not accessible from the main() method.

(c) The program will fail to compile because the non-static member class Memento declares a field with the same name as a field in the outer class State.

(d) The program will fail to compile because the State.this.val expression in the Memento constructor is invalid.

(e) The program will fail to compile because the ((State) this).val expression in the method restore() of the class Memento is invalid.

(f) The program will compile and print 11, 18, and 11, when run.

8.4 What will be the result of compiling and running the following program?

```
public class Nesting {
  public static void main(String[] args) {
    B.C obj = new B().new C();
  }
}

class A {
  int val;
  A(int v) { val = v; }
}

class B extends A {
  int val = 1;
  B() { super(2); }

  class C extends A {
    int val = 3;
    C() {
      super(4);
      System.out.println(B.this.val);
      System.out.println(C.this.val);
      System.out.println(super.val);
    }
  }
}
```

Select the one correct answer.

(a) The program will fail to compile.

(b) The program will compile and print 2, 3, and 4, in that order, when run.

(c) The program will compile and print 1, 4, and 2, in that order, when run.

(d) The program will compile and print 1, 3, and 4, in that order, when run.

(e) The program will compile and print 3, 2, and 1, in that order, when run.

8.5 Which statements about the following program are true?

```
public class Outer {
  public void doIt() {
  }
  public class Inner {
    public void doIt() {
    }
  }

  public static void main(String[] args) {
    new Outer().new Inner().doIt();
  }
}
```

Select the two correct answers.

(a) The doIt() method in the Inner class overrides the doIt() method in the Outer class.

(b) The doIt() method in the Inner class overloads the doIt() method in the Outer class.

(c) The doIt() method in the Inner class hides the doIt() method in the Outer class.

(d) The full name of the Inner class is Outer.Inner.

(e) The program will fail to compile.

8.6 What will be the result of compiling and running the following program?

```
public class Outer {
  private int innerCounter;

  class Inner {
    Inner() {innerCounter++;}
    public String toString() {
      return String.valueOf(innerCounter);
    }
  }

  private void multiply() {
    Inner inner = new Inner();
    this.new Inner();
    System.out.print(inner);
    inner = new Outer().new Inner();
    System.out.println(inner);
  }

  public static void main(String[] args) {
    new Outer().multiply();
  }
}
```

Select the one correct answer.

(a) The program will fail to compile.
(b) The program will compile but throw an exception when run.
(c) The program will compile and print 22, when run.
(d) The program will compile and print 11, when run.
(e) The program will compile and print 12, when run
(f) The program will compile and print 21, when run.

8.4 Local Classes

A local class is an inner class that is defined in a block. This could be a method body, a constructor body, a local block, a static initializer, or an instance initializer.

Blocks in a non-static context have a `this` reference available, which refers to an instance of the class containing the block. An instance of a local class, which is declared in such a non-static block, has an instance of the enclosing class associated with it. This gives such a non-static local class much of the same capability as a non-static member class.

However, if the block containing a local class declaration is defined in a static context (that is, a static method or a static initializer), the local class is implicitly static in the sense that its instantiation does not require any outer object. This aspect of local classes is reminiscent of static member classes. However, note that a local class cannot be specified with the keyword `static`.

Some restrictions that apply to local classes are

- Local classes cannot have static members, as they cannot provide class-specific services. However, `final` static fields are allowed, as these are constants. This is illustrated in Example 8.9 at (1) and (2) in the `NonStaticLocal` class, and also by the `StaticLocal` class at (11) and (12).

- Local classes cannot have any accessibility modifier. The declaration of the class is only accessible in the context of the block in which it is defined, subject to the same scope rules as for local variable declarations.

- -

Example 8.9   *Access in Enclosing Context (Local Classes)*

```
class Base {
  protected int nsf1;
}

class TLCWithLocalClasses {    // Top level Class
  private double nsf1;         // Non-static field
  private int    nsf2;         // Non-static field
  private static int sf;       // Static field
```

```
    void nonStaticMethod(final int fp) { // Non-static Method
      final int flv  = 10;        // final local variable
      final int hlv  = 30;        // final (hidden) local variable
      int nflv = 20;              // non-final local variable

      class NonStaticLocal extends Base { // Non-static local class
      //static int f1;            // (1) Not OK. Static members not allowed.
        final static int f2 = 10;// (2) final static members allowed.
        int     f3  = fp;         // (3) final param from enclosing method.
        int     f4  = flv;        // (4) final local var from enclosing method.
      //double f5 = nflv;         // (5) Not OK. Only finals from enclosing method.
        double f6 = nsf1;         // (6) Inherited from superclass.
        double f6a = this.nsf1;   // (6a) Inherited from superclass.
        double f6b = super.nsf1;  // (6b) Inherited from superclass.
        double f7  = TLCWithLocalClasses.this.nsf1;// (7) In enclosing object.
        int     f8  = nsf2;       // (8)  In enclosing object.
        int     f9  = sf;         // (9)  static from enclosing class.
        int     hlv;              // (10) Hides local variable.
      }
    }

    static void staticMethod(final int fp) { // Static Method
      final int flv  = 10;        // final local variable
      final int hlv  = 30;        // final (hidden) local variable
      int nflv = 20;              // non-final local variable

      class StaticLocal extends Base { // Static local class
      //static int f1;            // (11) Not OK. Static members not allowed.
        final static int f2 = 10;// (12) final static members allowed.
        int     f3  = fp;         // (13) final param from enclosing method.
        int     f4  = flv;        // (14) final local var from enclosing method.
      //double f5 = nflv;         // (15) Not OK. Only finals from enclosing method.
        double f6 = nsf1;         // (16) Inherited from superclass.
        double f6a = this.nsf1;   // (16a) Inherited from superclass.
        double f6b = super.nsf1;  // (16b) Inherited from superclass.
      //double f7  = TLCWithLocalClasses.this.nsf1; //(17) No enclosing object.
      //int     f8  = nsf2;       // (18)  No enclosing object.
        int     f9  = sf;         // (19)  static from enclosing class.
        int     hlv;              // (20) Hides local variable.
      }
    }
  }
```

Accessing Declarations in Enclosing Context

Example 8.9 illustrates how a local class can access declarations in its enclosing context. Declaring a local class in a static or a non-static block influences what the class can access in the enclosing context.

Accessing Local Declarations in the Enclosing Block

A local class can access `final` local variables, `final` method parameters, and `final` catch-block parameters in the scope of the local context. Such `final` variables are also read-only in the local class. This situation is shown at (3) and (4), where the `final` parameter fp and the `final` local variable flv of the method nonStaticMethod() in the NonStaticLocal class are accessed. This also applies to static local classes, as shown at (13) and (14) in the StaticLocal class.

Access to non-`final` local variables is not permitted from local classes, as shown at (5) and (15).

Declarations in the enclosing block of a local class can be hidden by declarations in the local class. At (10) and (20), the field hlv hides the local variable by the same name in the enclosing method. There is no way for the local class to refer to such hidden declarations.

Accessing Members in the Enclosing Class

A local class can access members inherited from its superclass in the usual way. The field nsf1 in the superclass Base is inherited by the local subclass NonStatic-Local. This inherited field is accessed in the NonStaticLocal class, as shown at (6), (6a), and (6b), by using the field's simple name, the standard this reference, and the super keyword, respectively. This also applies for static local classes, as shown at (16), (16a), and (16b).

Fields and methods in the enclosing class can be hidden by member declarations in the local class. The non-static field nsf1, inherited by the local classes, hides the field by the same name in the class TLCWithLocalClasses. The special form of the this construct can be used in non-static local classes for *explicit* referencing of members in the enclosing class, regardless of whether these members are hidden or not.

```
double f7 = TLCWithLocalClasses.this.nsf1; // (7)
```

However, the special form of the this construct cannot be used in a static local class, as shown at (17), since it does not have any notion of an outer object. The static local class cannot refer to such hidden declarations.

A non-static local class can access both static and non-static members defined in the enclosing class. The non-static field nsf2 and static field sf are defined in the enclosing class TLCWithLocalClasses. They are accessed in the NonStaticLocal class at (8) and (9), respectively. The special form of the this construct can also be used in non-static local classes, as previously mentioned.

However, a static local class can only directly access members defined in the enclosing class that are static. The static field sf in the class TLCWithLocalClasses is accessed in the StaticLocal class at (19), but the non-static field nsf1 cannot be accessed, as shown at (17).

Instantiating Local Classes

Clients outside the scope of a local class cannot instantiate the class directly because such classes are, after all, local. A local class can be instantiated in the block in which it is defined. Like a local variable, a local class must be declared before being used in the block.

A method can return instances of any local class it declares. The local class type must then be assignable to the return type of the method. The return type cannot be the same as the local class type, since this type is not accessible outside of the method. A supertype of the local class must be specified as the return type. This also means that, in order for the objects of the local class to be useful outside the method, a local class should implement an interface or override the behavior of its supertypes.

Example 8.10 illustrates how clients can instantiate local classes. The nesting and the inheritance hierarchy of the classes involved is shown in Figure 8.4. The non-static local class Circle at (5) is defined in the non-static method createCircle() at (4), which has the return type Shape. The static local class Map at (8) is defined in the static method createMap() at (7), which has the return type IDrawable. The main() method creates a polymorphic array drawables of type IDrawable[] at (10), which is initialized at lines (10) through (13) with instances of the local classes.

Figure 8.4 *Local Classes and Inheritance Hierarchy*

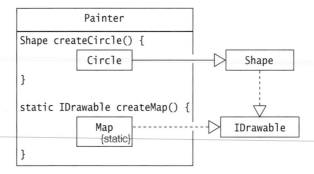

Example 8.10 *Instantiating Local Classes*

```
interface IDrawable {                    // (1)
  void draw();
}
//_____
class Shape implements IDrawable {       // (2)
  public void draw() { System.out.println("Drawing a Shape."); }
}
//_____
class Painter {                          // (3) Top-level Class
  public Shape createCircle(final double radius) { // (4) Non-static Method
```

```
      class Circle extends Shape {        // (5) Non-static local class
        public void draw() {
          System.out.println("Drawing a Circle of radius: " + radius);
        }
      }
      return new Circle();                // (6) Object of non-static local class
    }

    public static IDrawable createMap() { // (7) Static Method
      class Map implements IDrawable {    // (8) Static local class
        public void draw() { System.out.println("Drawing a Map."); }
      }
      return new Map();                   // (9) Object of static local class
    }
  }
//_____
  public class LocalClassClient {
    public static void main(String[] args) {
      IDrawable[] drawables = {                // (10)
          new Painter().createCircle(5),  // (11) Object of non-static local class
          Painter.createMap(),            // (12) Object of static local class
          new Painter().createMap()       // (13) Object of static local class
      };
      for (int i = 0; i < drawables.length; i++)    // (14)
        drawables[i].draw();

      System.out.println("Local Class Names:");
      System.out.println(drawables[0].getClass());   // (15)
      System.out.println(drawables[1].getClass());   // (16)
    }
  }
```

Output from the program:

```
Drawing a Circle of radius: 5.0
Drawing a Map.
Drawing a Map.
Local Class Names:
class Painter$1$Circle
class Painter$1$Map
```

Creating an instance of a non-static local class requires an instance of the enclosing class. In Example 8.10, the non-static method createCircle() is invoked on the instance of the enclosing class to create an instance of the non-static local class, as shown at (11). In the non-static method, the reference to the instance of the enclosing context is passed implicitly in the constructor call of the non-static local class at (6).

A static method can be invoked either through the class name or through a reference of the class type. An instance of a static local class can be created either way by calling the createMap() method, as shown at (12) and (13). As might be expected, no outer object is involved.

As references to a local class cannot be declared outside of the local context, the functionality of the class is only available through supertype references. The method draw() is invoked on objects in the array at (14). The program output indicates which objects were created. In particular, note that the final parameter radius of the method createCircle() at (4) is accessed by the draw() method of the local class Circle at (5). An instance of the local class Circle is created at (11) by a call to the method createCircle(). The draw() method is invoked on this instance of the local class Circle in the loop at (14). The value of the final parameter radius is still accessible to the draw() method invoked on this instance, although the call to the method createCircle(), which created the instance in the first place, has completed. Values of final local variables continue to be available to instances of local classes whenever these values are needed.

The output in Example 8.10 also shows the actual names of the local classes. In fact, the local class names are reflected in the class file names.

Another use of local classes is shown in Example 8.11. The code shows how local classes can be used, together with assertions, to implement certain kinds of postconditions (see Section 6.10, p. 275). The basic idea is that a computation wants to save or cache some data that is later required when checking a postconditon. For example, a deposit is made into an account, and we want to check that the transaction is valid after it is done. The computation can save the old balance before the transaction, so that the new balance can be correlated with the old balance after the transaction.

The local class Auditor at (2) acts as a repository for data that needs to be retrieved later to check the postcondition. Note that it accesses the final parameter, but declarations that follow its declaration would not be accessible. The assertion in the method check() at (4) ensures that the postcondition is checked, utilizing the data that was saved when the Auditor object was constructed at (5).

- -

Example 8.11   *Objects of Local Classes as Caches*

```
class Account {
  int balance;

  /** (1) Method makes a deposit into an account. */
  void deposit(final int amount) {

    /** (2) Local class to save the necessary data and to check
        that the transaction was valid. */
    class Auditor {

      /** (3) Stores the old balance. */
      private int balanceAtStartOfTransaction = balance;

      /** (4) Checks the postcondition. */
      void check() {
        assert balance - balanceAtStartOfTransaction == amount;
      }
    }
```

```
            Auditor auditor = new Auditor();  // (5) Save the data.
            balance += amount;                // (6) Do the transaction.
            auditor.check();                  // (7) Check the postcondition.
        }

    public static void main(String[] args) {
        Account ac = new Account();
        ac.deposit(250);
    }
}
```

8.5 Anonymous Classes

Classes are usually first defined and then instantiated using the new operator. Anonymous classes combine the process of definition and instantiation into a single step. Anonymous classes are defined at the location they are instantiated, using additional syntax with the new operator. As these classes do not have a name, an instance of the class can only be created together with the definition.

An anonymous class can be defined and instantiated in contexts where a reference value can be used (i.e., as expressions that evaluate to a reference value denoting an object). Anonymous classes are typically used for creating objects *on the fly* in contexts such as the value in a return statement, an argument in a method call, or in initialization of variables. Typical uses of anonymous classes are to implement *event listeners* in GUI-based applications, threads for simple tasks (see examples in Chapter 13, p. 613), and comparators for providing a total ordering of objects (see Example 15.11, p. 774).

Like local classes, anonymous classes can be defined in static or non-static context. The keyword static is never used.

Extending an Existing Class

The following syntax can be used for defining and instantiating an anonymous class that extends an existing class specified by *<superclass name>*:

new *<superclass name>* (*<optional argument list>*) { *<member declarations>* }

Optional arguments can be specified, which are passed to the superclass constructor. Thus, the superclass must provide a constructor corresponding to the arguments passed. No extends clause is used in the construct. Since an anonymous class cannot define constructors (as it does not have a name), an instance initializer can be used to achieve the same effect as a constructor. Only non-static members and final static fields can be declared in the class body.

Example 8.12   *Defining Anonymous Classes*

```
interface IDrawable {                              // (1)
  void draw();
}
//_____
class Shape implements IDrawable {                 // (2)
  public void draw() { System.out.println("Drawing a Shape."); }
}
//_____
class Painter {                                    // (3) Top-level Class

  public Shape createShape() {                     // (4) Non-static Method
    return new Shape(){                            // (5) Extends superclass at (2)
      public void draw() { System.out.println("Drawing a new Shape."); }
    };
  }
  public static IDrawable createIDrawable() {   // (7) Static Method
    return new IDrawable(){                        // (8) Implements interface at (1)
      public void draw() {
        System.out.println("Drawing a new IDrawable.");
      }
    };
  }
}
//_____
public class AnonClassClient {
  public static void main(String[] args) {      // (9)
    IDrawable[] drawables = {                    // (10)
      new Painter().createShape(),               // (11) non-static anonymous class
      Painter.createIDrawable(),                 // (12) static anonymous class
      new Painter().createIDrawable()            // (13) static anonymous class
    };
    for (int i = 0; i < drawables.length; i++)   // (14)
      drawables[i].draw();

    System.out.println("Anonymous Class Names:");
    System.out.println(drawables[0].getClass());// (15)
    System.out.println(drawables[1].getClass());// (16)
  }
}
```

Output from the program:

```
Drawing a new Shape.
Drawing a new IDrawable.
Drawing a new IDrawable.
Anonymous Class Names:
class Painter$1
class Painter$2
```

Class declarations from Example 8.10 are adapted to use anonymous classes in Example 8.12. The non-static method createShape() at (4) defines a non-static anonymous class at (5), which extends the superclass Shape. The anonymous class over-rides the inherited method draw().

```
// ...
class Shape implements IDrawable {            // (2)
  public void draw() { System.out.println("Drawing a Shape."); }
}

class Painter {                               // (3) Top-level Class

  public Shape createShape() {                // (4) Non-static Method
    return new Shape() {                       // (5) Extends superclass at (2)
        public void draw() { System.out.println("Drawing a new Shape."); }
    };
  }
  // ...

}
// ...
```

As we cannot declare references of an anonymous class, the functionality of the class is only available through superclass references. Usually it makes sense to override methods from the superclass. Any other members declared in an anonymous class cannot be accessed directly by an external client.

Implementing an Interface

The following syntax can be used for defining and instantiating an anonymous class that implements an interface specified by *<interface name>*:

new *<interface name>*() { *<member declarations>* }

An anonymous class provides a single interface implementation, and no arguments are passed. The anonymous class implicitly extends the Object class. Note that no implements clause is used in the construct. The class body has the same restrictions as previously noted for anonymous classes extending an existing class.

An anonymous class implementing an interface is shown below. Details can be found in Example 8.12. The static method createIDrawable() at (7) defines a static anonymous class at (8), which implements the interface IDrawable, by providing an implementation of the method draw(). The functionality of objects of an anonymous class that implements an interface is available through references of the interface type and the Object type (i.e., the supertypes).

```
interface IDrawable {                         // (1) Interface
  void draw();
}
// ...
class Painter {                               // (3) Top-level Class
  // ...
  public static IDrawable createIDrawable() { // (7) Static Method
    return new IDrawable(){                    // (8) Implements interface at (1)
      public void draw() {
```

```
        System.out.println("Drawing a new IDrawable.");
      }
    };
  }
}
// ...
```

The following code is an example of a typical use of anonymous classes in building GUI-applications. The anonymous class at (1) implements the ActionListener interface that has the method actionPerformed(). When the addActionListener() method is called on the GUI-button denoted by the reference quitButton, the anonymous class is instantiated and the reference value of the object is passed as a parameter to the method. The method addActionListener() of the GUI-button can use the reference value to invoke the method actionPerformed() in the ActionListener object.

```
quitButton.addActionListener(
    new ActionListener() {      // (1) Anonymous class implements an interface.
      // Invoked when the user clicks the quit button.
      public void actionPerformed(ActionEvent evt) {
        System.exit(0);         // (2) Terminates the program.
      }
    }
);
```

Instantiating Anonymous Classes

The discussion on instantiating local classes (see Example 8.10) is also valid for instantiating anonymous classes. The class AnonClassClient in Example 8.12 creates one instance at (11) of the non-static anonymous class defined at (5), and two instances at (12) and (13) of the static anonymous class defined at (8). The program output shows the polymorphic behavior and the runtime types of the objects. Similar to a non-static local class, an instance of a non-static anonymous class has an instance of its enclosing class at (11). An enclosing instance is not mandatory for creating objects of a static anonymous class, as shown at (12).

The names of the anonymous classes at runtime are also shown in the program output in Example 8.12. They are also the names used to designate their respective class files. Anonymous classes are not so anonymous after all.

Accessing Declarations in Enclosing Context

Access rules for local classes (see Section 8.4, p. 372) also apply to anonymous classes. Example 8.13 is an adaptation of Example 8.9 and illustrates the access rules for anonymous classes. The local classes in Example 8.9 have been adapted to anonymous classes in Example 8.13. The TLCWithAnonClasses class has two methods, one non-static and the other static, which return an instance of a non-static and a static anonymous class, respectively. Both anonymous classes extend the Base class.

Anonymous classes can access final variables only in the enclosing context. Inside the definition of a non-static anonymous class, members of the enclosing context can be referenced using the *<enclosing class name>*.this construct. Non-static anonymous classes can also access any non-hidden members in the enclosing context by their simple names, whereas static anonymous classes can only access non-hidden static members.

Example 8.13   *Accessing Declarations in Enclosing Context (Anonymous Classes)*

```
class Base {
  protected int nsf1;
}
//_____
class TLCWithAnonClasses {      // Top level Class
  private double nsf1;          // Non-static field
  private int    nsf2;          // Non-static field
  private static int sf;        // Static field

  Base nonStaticMethod(final int fp) { // Non-static Method
    final int flv  = 10;        // final local variable
    final int hlv  = 30;        // final (hidden) local variable
    int nflv = 20;              // non-final local variable

    return new Base() {         // Non-static anonymous class
    //static int f1;            // (1) Not OK. Static members not allowed.
      final static int f2 = 10; // (2) final static members allowed.
      int    f3  = fp;          // (3) final param from enclosing method.
      int    f4  = flv;         // (4) final local var from enclosing method.
    //double f5  = nflv;        // (5) Not OK. Only finals from enclosing method.
      double f6  = nsf1;        // (6) Inherited from superclass.
      double f6a = this.nsf1;   // (6a) Inherited from superclass.
      double f6b = super.nsf1;  // (6b) Inherited from superclass.
      double f7  = TLCWithAnonClasses.this.nsf1; // (7) In enclosing object.
      int    f8  = nsf2;        // (8)  In enclosing object.
      int    f9  = sf;          // (9)  static from enclosing class.
      int    hlv;               // (10) Hides local variable.
    };
  }

  static Base staticMethod(final int fp) { // Static Method
    final int flv  = 10;        // final local variable
    final int hlv  = 30;        // final (hidden) local variable
    int nflv = 20;              // non-final local variable

    return new Base() {         // Static anonymous class
    //static int f1;            // (11) Not OK. Static members not allowed.
      final static int f2 = 10; // (12) final static members allowed.
      int    f3  = fp;          // (13) final param from enclosing method.
      int    f4  = flv;         // (14) final local var from enclosing method.
    //double f5  = nflv;        // (15) Not OK. Only finals from enclosing method.
      double f6  = nsf1;        // (16 ) Inherited from superclass.
      double f6a = this.nsf1;   // (16a) Inherited from superclass.
      double f6b = super.nsf1;  // (16b) Inherited from superclass.
```

```
    //double f7 = TLCWithAnonClasses.this.nsf1;  //(17) No enclosing object.
    //int    f8 = nsf2;              // (18)  No enclosing object.
      int    f9 = sf;               // (19)  static from enclosing class.
      int    hlv;                   // (20) Hides local variable.
    };
  }
}
```

 ## Review Questions

8.7   Which statement is true?

Select the one correct answer.

(a) Non-static member classes must have either default or `public` accessibility.
(b) All nested classes can declare static member classes.
(c) Methods in all nested classes can be declared `static`.
(d) All nested classes can be declared `static`.
(e) Static member classes can contain non-static methods.

8.8   Given the declaration

```
interface IntHolder { int getInt(); }
```

which of the following methods are valid?

```
//----(1)----
  IntHolder makeIntHolder(int i) {
    return new IntHolder() {
      public int getInt() { return i; }
    };
  }
//----(2)----
  IntHolder makeIntHolder(final int i) {
    return new IntHolder {
      public int getInt() { return i; }
    };
  }
//----(3)----
  IntHolder makeIntHolder(int i) {
    class MyIH implements IntHolder {
      public int getInt() { return i; }
    }
    return new MyIH();
  }
//----(4)----
  IntHolder makeIntHolder(final int i) {
    class MyIH implements IntHolder {
      public int getInt() { return i; }
    }
    return new MyIH();
  }
//----(5)----
```

```
    IntHolder makeIntHolder(int i) {
      return new MyIH(i);
    }
    static class MyIH implements IntHolder {
      final int j;
      MyIH(int i) { j = i; }
      public int getInt() { return j; }
    }
```

Select the two correct answers.

(a) The method labeled (1).
(b) The method labeled (2).
(c) The method labeled (3).
(d) The method labeled (4).
(e) The method labeled (5).

8.9 Which statements are true?

Select the two correct answers.

(a) No other static members, except `final` static fields, can be declared within a non-static member class.
(b) If a non-static member class is nested within a class named `Outer`, methods within the non-static member class must use the prefix `Outer.this` to access the members of the class `Outer`.
(c) All fields in any nested class must be declared `final`.
(d) Anonymous classes cannot have constructors.
(e) If `objRef` is an instance of any nested class within the class `Outer`, the expression `(objRef instanceof Outer)` will evaluate to `true`.

8.10 What will be the result of compiling and running the following program?

```
import java.util.Iterator;
class ReverseArrayIterator<T> implements Iterable<T>{

  private T[] array;
  public ReverseArrayIterator(T[] array) { this.array = array; }

  public Iterator<T> iterator() {
    return new Iterator<T>() {
      private int next = array.length - 1;

      public boolean hasNext() { return (next >= 0); }
      public T next() {
        T element = array[next];
        next--;
        return element;
      }
      public void remove() { throw new UnsupportedOperationException(); }
    };
  }
```

```
public static void main(String[] args) {
  String[] array = { "Hi", "Howdy", "Hello" };
  ReverseArrayIterator<String> ra = new ReverseArrayIterator<String>(array);
  for (String str : ra) {
    System.out.print("|" + str + "|");
  }
}
}
```

Select the one correct answer.

(a) The program will fail to compile.
(b) The program will compile but throw an exception when run.
(c) The program will compile and print |Hi||Howdy||Hello|, when run.
(d) The program will compile and print |Hello||Howdy||Hi|, when run.
(e) The program will compile and print the strings in an unpredictable order, when run.

8.11   Which statement is true?

Select the one correct answer.

(a) Top-level classes can be declared static.
(b) Classes declared as members of top-level classes can be declared static.
(c) Local classes can be declared static.
(d) Anonymous classes can be declared static.
(e) No classes can be declared static.

8.12   Which expression can be inserted at (1) so that compiling and running the program will print LocalVar.str1?

```
public class Access {
  final String str1 = "Access.str1";

  public static void main(final String args[]) {
    final String str1 = "LocalVar.str1";

    class Helper { String getStr1() { return str1; } }
    class Inner {
      String str1 = "Inner.str1";
      Inner() {
        System.out.println( /* (1) INSERT EXPRESSION HERE */ );
      }
    }
    Inner inner = new Inner();
  }
}
```

Select the one correct answer.

(a) str1
(b) this.str1
(c) Access.this.str1
(d) new Helper().getStr1()
(e) this.new Helper().getStr1()

(f) `Access.new Helper().getStr1()`
(g) `new Access.Helper().getStr1()`
(h) `new Access().new Helper().getStr1()`

8.13 What will be the result of compiling and running the following program?

```java
public class TipTop {
  static final Integer i1 = 1;
  final Integer i2 = 2;
  Integer i3 = 3;

  public static void main(String[] args) {
    final Integer i4 = 4;
    Integer i5 = 5;

    class Inner {
      final Integer i6 = 6;
      Integer i7 = 7;

      Inner () {
        System.out.print(i6 + i7);
      }
    }
  }
}
```

Select the one correct answer.

(a) The program will fail to compile.
(b) The program will compile but throw an exception when run.
(c) The program will compile and print 67, when run.
(d) The program will compile and print 13, when run.
(e) The program will compile but will not print anything, when run.

8.14 Which expressions, when inserted at (1), will result in compile-time errors?

```java
public class TopLevel {
  static final Integer i1 = 1;
  final Integer i2 = 2;
  Integer i3 = 3;

  public static void main(String[] args) {
    final Integer i4 = 4;
    Integer i5 = 5;

    class Inner {
      final Integer i6 = 6;
      Integer i7 = 7;
      Inner (final Integer i8, Integer i9) {
        System.out.println(/* (1) INSERT EXPRESSION HERE */);
      }
    }
    new Inner(8, 9);
  }
}
```

Select the three correct answers.
(a) i1
(b) i2
(c) i3
(d) i4
(e) i5
(f) i6
(g) i7
(h) i8
(i) i9

 ## Chapter Summary

The following information was included in this chapter:

- categories of nested classes: static member classes and interfaces, non-static member classes, local classes, anonymous classes

- discussion of salient aspects of nested classes and interfaces:
  - the context in which they can be defined
  - which accessibility modifiers are valid for such classes and interfaces
  - whether an instance of the enclosing context is associated with an instance of the nested class
  - which entities a nested class or interface can access in its enclosing contexts
  - whether both static and non-static members can be defined in a nested class

- importing and using nested classes and interfaces

- instantiating non-static member classes using *<enclosing object reference>*.new syntax

- accessing members in the enclosing context of inner classes using *<enclosing class name>*.this syntax

- accessing members both in the inheritance hierarchy and the enclosing context of nested classes

- implementing anonymous classes by extending an existing class or by implementing an interface

 ## Programming Exercise

8.1   Create a new program with a nested class named PrintFunc that extends class Print from Exercise 7.2, p. 350. In addition to just printing the value, class Print-

Func should first apply a Function object on the value. The class PrintFunc should have a constructor that takes an instance of Function type as a parameter. The evaluate() method of the class PrintFunc should use the Function object on its argument. The evaluate() method should print and return the result. The evaluate() method in superclass Print should be used to print the value.

The program should behave like the one in Exercise 7.2, p. 350, but this time use the nested class PrintFunc instead of class Print.

Object Lifetime

9

●●

9.1 Garbage Collection

Efficient memory management is essential in a runtime system. Storage for objects is allocated in a designated part of the memory called the *heap* which has a finite size. Garbage collection is a process of managing the heap efficiently; i.e., reclaiming memory occupied by objects that are no longer needed and making it available for new objects. Java provides automatic garbage collection, meaning that the runtime environment can take care of memory management without the program having to take any special action. Objects allocated on the heap (through the new operator) are administered by the automatic garbage collector. The automatic garbage collection scheme guarantees that a reference to an object is always valid while the object is needed by the program. The object will not be reclaimed, leaving the reference dangling.

Having an automatic garbage collector frees the programmer from the responsibility of writing code for deleting objects. By relying on the automatic garbage collector, a Java program also forfeits any significant influence on the garbage collection of its objects (see p. 398). However, this price is insignificant when compared to the cost of putting the code for object management in place and plugging all the memory leaks. Time-critical applications should bear in mind that the automatic garbage collector runs as a background task and may have a negative impact on their performance.

9.2 Reachable Objects

An automatic garbage collector essentially performs two tasks:

- decides if and when memory needs to be reclaimed
- finds objects that are no longer needed by the program and reclaims their storage

A program has no guarantees that the automatic garbage collector will be run during its execution. A program should not rely on the scheduling of the automatic garbage collector for its behavior (see p. 398).

In order to understand how the automatic garbage collector finds objects whose storage should be reclaimed, we need to look at the activity going on in the JVM. Java provides thread-based multitasking, meaning that there can be several threads executing in the JVM, each doing its own task (see Chapter 13). A thread is an independent path of execution through the program code. A thread is alive if it has not completed its execution. Each live thread has its own runtime stack, as explained in Section 6.5 on page 235. The runtime stack contains activation records of methods that are currently active. Local references declared in a method can always be found in the method's activation record, stored on the runtime stack associated with the thread in which the method is called. Objects, on the other hand, are always created on the heap. If an object has a field reference, the field is to be found inside the object in the heap, and the object denoted by the field reference is also to be found in the heap.

An example of how memory is organized during execution is depicted in Figure 9.1. It shows two live threads (t_1 and t_2) and their respective runtime stacks with the activation records. The diagram shows which objects in the heap are referenced by local references in the method activation records. The diagram also shows field references in objects, which refer to other objects in the heap. Some objects have several aliases.

An object in the heap is said to be *reachable* if it is referenced by any *local* reference in a runtime stack. Additionally, any object that is denoted by a reference in a reachable object is also said to be reachable. Reachability is a transitive relation. Thus, a reachable object has at least one chain of reachable references from the runtime stack. Any reference that makes an object reachable is called a *reachable reference*. An object that is not reachable is said to be *unreachable*.

A reachable object is *alive*, and is *accessible* by a live thread. Note that an object can be accessible by more than one thread. Any object that is *not* accessible by a live thread is a candidate for garbage collection. When an object becomes unreachable and is waiting for its memory to be reclaimed, it is said to be *eligible* for garbage collection. An object is eligible for garbage collection if all references denoting it are in eligible objects. Eligible objects do not affect the future course of program execution. When the garbage collector runs, it finds and reclaims the storage of eligible objects. However, garbage collection does not necessarily occur as soon as an object becomes unreachable.

From Figure 9.1 we see that objects o4, o5, o11, o12, o14, and o15 all have reachable references. Objects o13 and o16 have no reachable references and are, therefore, eligible for garbage collection.

From the discussion above we can conclude that if a composite object becomes unreachable, its constituent objects also become unreachable, barring any reachable references to the constituent objects. Although the objects o1, o2, and o3 form a circular list, they do not have any reachable references. Thus, these objects are all eligible for garbage collection. On the other hand, the objects o5, o6, and o7 form a linear list, but they are all reachable, as the first object in the list, o5, is reachable. The objects o8, o10, o11, and o9 also form a linear list (in that order), but not all objects in the list are reachable. Only the objects o9 and o11 are reachable, as object o11 has a reachable reference. The objects o8 and o10 are eligible for garbage collection.

The *lifetime* of an object is the time from its creation to the time it is garbage collected. Under normal circumstances, an object is accessible from the time when it is created to the time when it is unreachable. The lifetime of an object can also include a period when it is eligible for garbage collection, waiting for its storage to be reclaimed. The finalization mechanism (see p. 396) in Java does provide a means for *resurrecting* an object after it is eligible for garbage collection, but the finalization mechanism is rarely used for this purpose.

Figure 9.1   *Memory Organization at Runtime*

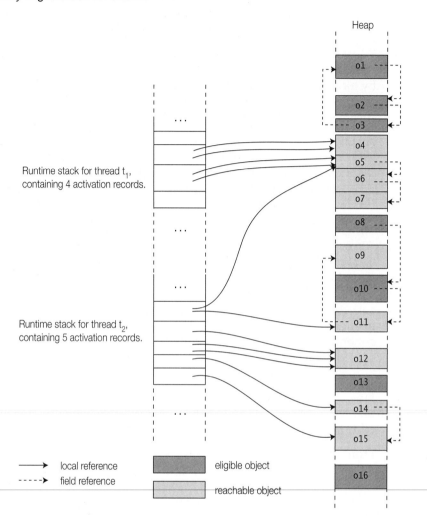

9.3   Facilitating Garbage Collection

The automatic garbage collector determines which objects are not reachable and, therefore, eligible for garbage collection. It will certainly go to work if there is an imminent memory shortage. Automatic garbage collection should not be perceived as a license for uninhibited creation of objects and then forgetting about them. However, certain programming practices can nevertheless help in minimizing the overhead associated with garbage collection during program execution.

Certain objects, such as files and network connections, can tie up resources and should be disposed of properly when they are no longer needed. In most cases, the finally block in the try-catch-finally construct (see Section 6.7, p. 245) provides a convenient facility for such purposes, as it will always be executed, thereby ensuring proper disposal of any unwanted resources.

To optimize its memory footprint, a live thread should only retain access to an object as long as the object is needed for its execution. The program can allow objects to become eligible for garbage collection as early as possible by removing all references to the object when it is no longer needed.

Objects that are created and accessed by local references in a method are eligible for garbage collection when the method terminates unless reference values to these objects are exported out of the method. This can occur if a reference value is returned from the method, passed as argument to another method that records the reference value, or thrown as an exception. However, a method need not always leave objects to be garbage collected after its termination. It can facilitate garbage collection by taking suitable action, for example, by nulling references.

```
import java.io.*;

class WellBehavedClass {
  // ...
  void wellBehavedMethod() {
    File aFile;
    long[] bigArray = new long[20000];
    // ... uses local variables ...
    // Does cleanup (before starting something extensive)
    aFile = null;                     // (1)
    bigArray = null;                  // (2)

    // Start some other extensive activity
    // ...
  }
  // ...
}
```

In the previous code, the local variables are set to null after use at (1) and (2), before starting some other extensive activity. This makes the objects denoted by the local variables eligible for garbage collection from this point onward, rather than after the method terminates. This optimization technique of nulling references need only be used as a last resort when resources are scarce.

Here are some other techniques to facilitate garbage collection:

- When a method returns a reference value and the object denoted by the value is not needed, not assigning this value to a reference also facilitates garbage collection.

- If a reference is assigned a new value, the object that was previously denoted by the reference prior to the assignment can become eligible for garbage collection.

- Removing reachable references to a composite object can make the constituent objects become eligible for garbage collection, as explained earlier.

Example 9.1 illustrates how a program can influence garbage collection eligibility. Class `HeavyItem` represents objects with a large memory footprint, on which we want to monitor garbage collection. Each composite `HeavyItem` object has a reference to a large array. The class overrides the `finalize()` method from the `Object` class to print out an ID when the object is finalized. This method is always called on an eligible object before it is destroyed (see finalizers, p. 396). We use it to indicate in the output if and when a `HeavyItem` is reclaimed. To illustrate the effect of garbage collection on object hierarchies, each `HeavyItem` object may also have a reference to another `HeavyItem`.

In Example 9.1, the class `RecyclingBin` defines a method `createHeavyItem()` at (4). In this method, the `HeavyItem` created at (5) is eligible for garbage collection after the reassignment of reference `itemA` at (6), as this object will have no references. The `HeavyItem` created at (6) is accessible on return from the method. Its fate depends on the code that calls this method.

In Example 9.1, the class `RecyclingBin` also defines a method `createList()` at (8). It returns the reference value in the reference `item1`, which denotes the first item in a list of three `HeavyItems`. Because of the list structure, none of the `HeavyItems` in the list are eligible for garbage collection on return from the method. Again, the fate of the objects in the list is decided by the code that calls this method. It is enough for the first item in the list to become unreachable, in order for all objects in the list to become eligible for garbage collection (barring any reachable references).

Example 9.1 *Garbage Collection Eligibility*

```
class HeavyItem {                                     // (1)
  int[]     itemBody;
  String    itemID;
  HeavyItem nextItem;

  HeavyItem(String ID, HeavyItem itemRef) {           // (2)
    itemBody = new int[100000];
    itemID   = ID;
    nextItem = itemRef;
  }
  protected void finalize() throws Throwable {         // (3)
    System.out.println(itemID + ": recycled.");
    super.finalize();
  }
}
//_____
public class RecyclingBin {

  public static HeavyItem createHeavyItem(String itemID) {          // (4)
    HeavyItem itemA = new HeavyItem(itemID + " local item", null);  // (5)
    itemA = new HeavyItem(itemID, null);                            // (6)
    System.out.println("Return from creating HeavyItem " + itemID);
    return itemA;                                                   // (7)
  }
```

```
public static HeavyItem createList(String listID) {        // (8)
  HeavyItem item3 = new HeavyItem(listID + ": item3", null);    // (9)
  HeavyItem item2 = new HeavyItem(listID + ": item2", item3);   // (10)
  HeavyItem item1 = new HeavyItem(listID + ": item1", item2);   // (11)
  System.out.println("Return from creating list " + listID);
  return item1;                                              // (12)
}

public static void main(String[] args) {                   // (13)
  HeavyItem list = createList("X");                         // (14)
  list = createList("Y");                                   // (15)

  HeavyItem itemOne = createHeavyItem("One");               // (16)
  HeavyItem itemTwo = createHeavyItem("Two");               // (17)
  itemOne = null;                                           // (18)
  createHeavyItem("Three");                                 // (19)
  createHeavyItem("Four");                                  // (20)
  System.out.println("Return from main().");
}
}
```

Possible output from the program:

```
Return from creating list X
Return from creating list Y
X: item3: recycled.
X: item2: recycled.
X: item1: recycled.
Return from creating HeavyItem One
Return from creating HeavyItem Two
Return from creating HeavyItem Three
Three local item: recycled.
Three: recycled.
Two local item: recycled.
Return from creating HeavyItem Four
One local item: recycled.
One: recycled.
Return from main().
```

In Example 9.1, the main() method at (13) in the class RecyclingBin uses the methods createHeavyItem() and createList(). It creates a list X at (14), but the reference to its first item is reassigned at (15), making objects in list X eligible for garbage collection after (15). The first item of list Y is stored in the reference list, making this list non-eligible for garbage collection during the execution of the main() method.

The main() method creates two items at (16) and (17), storing their reference values in the references itemOne and itemTwo, respectively. The reference itemOne is nulled at (18), making HeavyItem with identity One eligible for garbage collection. The two calls to the createHeavyItem() method at (19) and (20) return reference values to HeavyItems, which are not stored, making each object eligible for garbage collection right after the respective method call returns.

The output from the program bears out the observations made above. Objects in list Y (accessible through the reference list) and HeavyItem with identity Two (accessible through the reference itemTwo) remain non-eligible while the main() method executes. Although the output shows that HeavyItems with identity Four was never garbage collected, it is not accessible once it becomes eligible for garbage collection at (20). Any objects in the heap after the program terminates are reclaimed by the operating system.

9.4 Object Finalization

Object finalization provides an object with a last resort to undertake any action before its storage is reclaimed. The automatic garbage collector calls the finalize() method in an object that is eligible for garbage collection before actually destroying the object. The finalize() method is defined in the Object class.

```
protected void finalize() throws Throwable
```

An implementation of the finalize() method is called a *finalizer*. A subclass can override the finalizer from the Object class in order to take more specific and appropriate action before an object of the subclass is destroyed. Note that the overridden method cannot narrow the visibility of the method and it must be declared either protected or public.

A finalizer can, like any other method, catch and throw exceptions (see Section 6.7, p. 245). However, any exception thrown but not caught by a finalizer that is called by the garbage collector is ignored, and the finalization of this object is terminated. The finalizer is only called once on an object, regardless of whether any exception is thrown during its execution. In case of finalization failure, the object still remains eligible for disposal at the discretion of the garbage collector (unless it has been resurrected, as explained in the next subsection). Since there is no guarantee that the garbage collector will ever run, there is also no guarantee that the finalizer will ever be called.

In the following code, the finalizer at (1) will take appropriate action if and when called on objects of the class before they are garbage collected, ensuring that the resource is freed. Since it is not guaranteed that the finalizer will ever be called at all, a program should not rely on the finalization to do any critical operations.

```
public class AnotherWellBehavedClass {
  SomeResource objRef;
  // ...
  protected void finalize() throws Throwable {      // (1)
    try {                                           // (2)
      if (objRef != null) objRef.close();
    } finally {                                     // (3)
      super.finalize();                             // (4)
    }
  }
}
```

Note that an *enum type* cannot declare a finalizer. Therefore, an enum constant may never be finalized.

9.5 Finalizer Chaining

Unlike subclass constructors, overridden finalizers are not implicitly chained (see Section 7.5, p. 302). Therefore, the finalizer in a subclass should explicitly call the finalizer in its superclass as its last action, as shown at (4) in the previous code. The call to the finalizer of the superclass is in a `finally` block at (3), guaranteed to be executed regardless of any exceptions thrown by the code in the `try` block at (2).

Example 9.2 illustrates chaining of finalizers. It creates a user-specified number of large objects of a user-specified size. The number and size are provided through command-line program arguments. The loop at (7) in the `main()` method creates `Blob` objects, but does not store any references to them. Objects created are instances of the class `Blob` defined at (3). The `Blob` constructor at (4) initializes the field `size` by constructing a large array of integers. The `Blob` class extends the `BasicBlob` class that assigns each blob a unique number (`blobId`) and keeps track of the number of blobs (`population`) not yet garbage collected. Creation of each `Blob` object by the constructor at (4) prints the ID number of the object and the message `"Hello"`. The `finalize()` method at (5) is called before a `Blob` object is garbage collected. It prints the message `"Bye"` and calls the `finalize()` method in the class `BasicBlob` at (2), which decrements the population count. The program output shows that two blobs were not garbage collected at the time the print statement at (8) was executed. It is evident from the number of `"Bye"` messages that three blobs were garbage collected before all the five blobs had been created in the loop at (7).

- -

Example 9.2   *Using Finalizers*

```
class BasicBlob {                                          // (1)
  static    int idCounter;
  static    int population;
  protected int blobId;

  BasicBlob() {
    blobId = idCounter++;
    ++population;
  }
  protected void finalize() throws Throwable {             // (2)
    --population;
    super.finalize();
  }
}
//_____
class Blob extends BasicBlob {                             // (3)
  int[] size;
```

```
  Blob(int bloatedness) {                                    // (4)
    size = new int[bloatedness];
    System.out.println(blobId + ": Hello");
  }

  protected void finalize() throws Throwable {               // (5)
    System.out.println(blobId + ": Bye");
    super.finalize();
  }
}
//_____
public class Finalizers {
  public static void main(String[] args) {                   // (6)
    int blobsRequired, blobSize;
    try {
      blobsRequired = Integer.parseInt(args[0]);
      blobSize      = Integer.parseInt(args[1]);
    } catch(IndexOutOfBoundsException e) {
      System.err.println("Usage: Finalizers <number of blobs> <blob size>");
      return;
    }
    for (int i=0; i<blobsRequired; ++i) {                    // (7)
      new Blob(blobSize);
    }
    System.out.println(BasicBlob.population + " blobs alive"); // (8)
  }
}
```

Running the program with the command

```
>java Finalizers 5 500000
```

resulted in the following output:

```
0: Hello
1: Hello
2: Hello
0: Bye
1: Bye
2: Bye
3: Hello
4: Hello
2 blobs alive
```

9.6 Invoking Garbage Collection Programmatically

Although Java provides facilities to invoke the garbage collection explicitly, there are no guarantees that it will be run. The program can only request that garbage collection be performed, but there is no way that garbage collection can be forced.

The System.gc() method can be used to request garbage collection, and the System.runFinalization() method can be called to suggest that any pending finalizers be run for objects eligible for garbage collection.

```
static void gc()
```

Requests that garbage collection be run.

```
static void runFinalization()
```

Requests that any pending finalizers be run for objects eligible for garbage collection.

Alternatively, corresponding methods in the `Runtime` class can be used. A Java application has a unique `Runtime` object that can be used by the application to interact with the JVM. An application can obtain this object by calling the method `Runtime.getRuntime()`. The `Runtime` class provides various methods related to memory issues.

```
static Runtime getRuntime()
```

Returns the `Runtime` object associated with the current application.

```
void gc()
```

Requests that garbage collection be run. However, it is recommended to use the more convenient static method `System.gc()`.

```
void runFinalization()
```

Requests that any pending finalizers be run for objects eligible for garbage collection. Again, it is more convenient to use the static method `System.runFinalization()`.

```
long freeMemory()
```

Returns the amount of free memory (bytes) in the JVM that is available for new objects.

```
long totalMemory()
```

Returns the total amount of memory (bytes) available in the JVM. This includes both memory occupied by current objects and that which is available for new objects.

Example 9.3 illustrates invoking garbage collection. The class `MemoryCheck` is an adaptation of the class `Finalizers` from Example 9.2. The `RunTime` object for the application is obtained at (7). This object is used to get information regarding total memory and free memory in the JVM at (8) and (9), respectively. Blobs are created in the loop at (10). The amount of free memory after blob creation is printed at (11). We see from the program output that some blobs were already garbage collected before the execution got to (11). A request for garbage collection is made at (12). Checking free memory after the request shows that more memory has become available, indicating that the request was honored. It is instructive to run the program without the method call `System.gc()` at (12), in order to compare the results.

Example 9.3   *Invoking Garbage Collection*

```
class BasicBlob {  /* See Example 9.2. */ }
class Blob extends BasicBlob { /* See Example 9.2.*/ }
//_____
public class MemoryCheck {
  public static void main(String[] args) {                          // (6)
    int blobsRequired, blobSize;
    try {
      blobsRequired = Integer.parseInt(args[0]);
      blobSize      = Integer.parseInt(args[1]);
    } catch(IndexOutOfBoundsException e) {
      System.err.println("Usage: MemoryCheck <number of blobs> <blob size>");
      return;
    }
    Runtime environment = Runtime.getRuntime();                     // (7)
    System.out.println("Total memory: " + environment.totalMemory());// (8)
    System.out.println("Free memory before blob creation: " +
                    environment.freeMemory());                      // (9)
    for (int i=0; i<blobsRequired; ++i) {                          // (10)
      new Blob(blobSize);
    }
    System.out.println("Free memory after blob creation: " +
                    environment.freeMemory());                      // (11)
    System.gc();                                                    // (12)
    System.out.println("Free memory after requesting GC: " +
                    environment.freeMemory());                      // (13)
    System.out.println(BasicBlob.population + " blobs alive");       // (14)
  }
}
```

Running the program with the command

```
>java MemoryCheck 5 100000
```

resulted in the following output:

```
Total memory: 2031616
Free memory before blob creation: 1773192
0: Hello
1: Hello
2: Hello
1: Bye
2: Bye
3: Hello
0: Bye
3: Bye
4: Hello
Free memory after blob creation: 818760
4: Bye
Free memory after requesting GC: 1619656
0 blobs alive
```

Certain aspects regarding automatic garbage collection should be noted:

- There are no guarantees that objects that are eligible for garbage collection will have their finalizers executed. Garbage collection might not even be run if the program execution does not warrant it. Thus, any memory allocated during program execution might remain allocated after program termination, but will be reclaimed by the operating system.
- There are also no guarantees about the order in which the objects will be garbage collected, or the order in which their finalizers will be executed. Therefore, the program should not make any assumptions based on these aspects.
- Garbage collection does not guarantee that there is enough memory for the program to run. A program can rely on the garbage collector to run when memory gets very low and it can expect an OutOfMemoryException to be thrown if its memory demands cannot be met.

 Review Questions

9.1 Which statement is true?

Select the one correct answer.

(a) Objects can be explicitly destroyed using the keyword delete.
(b) An object will be garbage collected immediately after it becomes unreachable.
(c) If object obj1 is accessible from object obj2, and object obj2 is accessible from obj1, then obj1 and obj2 are not eligible for garbage collection.
(d) Once an object has become eligible for garbage collection, it will remain eligible until it is destroyed.
(e) If object obj1 can access object obj2 that is eligible for garbage collection, then obj1 is also eligible for garbage collection.

9.2 Identify the location in the following program where the object, initially referenced with arg1, is eligible for garbage collection.

```
public class MyClass {
  public static void main(String[] args) {
    String msg;
    String pre = "This program was called with ";
    String post = " as first argument.";
    String arg1 = new String((args.length > 0) ? "'" + args[0] + "'" :
                             "<no argument>");
    msg = arg1;
    arg1 = null;              // (1)
    msg = pre + msg + post;   // (2)
    pre = null;               // (3)
    System.out.println(msg);
    msg = null;               // (4)
    post = null;              // (5)
    args = null;              // (6)
  }
}
```

Select the one correct answer.

(a) After the line labeled (1).
(b) After the line labeled (2).
(c) After the line labeled (3).
(d) After the line labeled (4).
(e) After the line labeled (5).
(f) After the line labeled (6).

9.3   How many objects are eligible for garbage collection when control reaches (1)?

```
public class Eligible {
  public static void main(String[] args) {
    for (int i = 0; i < 5; i++) {
      Eligible obj = new Eligible();
      new Eligible();
    }
    System.gc();       // (1);
  }
}
```

Select the one correct answer.

(a) 0.
(b) 5.
(c) 10.
(d) Hard to say.

9.4   How many objects are eligible for garbage collection when control reaches (1)?

```
public class Link {
  private Link next;
  Link(Link next) { this.next = next; }
  public void finalize() { System.out.print("X"); }

  public static void main(String[] args) {
    Link p = null;
    for (int i = 0; i < 5; i++) {
      p = new Link(p);
    }
    System.gc();                          // (1);
  }
}
```

Select the one correct answer.

(a) 0
(b) 5
(c) 10
(d) Hard to say.

9.5 How many objects are eligible for garbage collection when control reaches (1)?

```
public class Elements {
  public static void main(String[] args) {
    int[] array = new int[4];
    for (int i = 0; i < 4; i++) {
      array[i] = i;
    }
    array[0] = array[1] = array[2] = array[3] = 0;
    System.gc();                          // (1);
  }
}
```

Select the one correct answer.

(a) 0
(b) 1
(c) 4
(d) Hard to say.

9.6 How many objects are reachable when control reaches (1)?

```
public class Nullify {

  private static void nullify(Integer[] array) { array = null; }

  public static void main(String[] args) {
    Integer[] array = new Integer[4];
    for (int i = 0; i < 4; i++) {
      array[i] = i;
    }
    nullify(array);
    System.gc();                          // (1);
  }
}
```

Select the one correct answer.

(a) 0
(b) 1
(c) 4
(d) 5
(e) Hard to say.

9.7 Which statement is true?

Select the one correct answer.

(a) If an exception is thrown during the execution of the finalize() method of an eligible object, the exception is ignored and the object is destroyed.
(b) All objects have a finalize() method.
(c) Objects can be destroyed by explicitly calling the finalize() method.
(d) The finalize() method can be declared with any accessibility.
(e) The compiler will fail to compile code that defines an overriding finalize() method that does not explicitly call the overridden finalize() method from the superclass.

9.8   Which statement is true?

Select the one correct answer.

(a) The compiler will fail to compile code that explicitly tries to call the `finalize()` method.
(b) The `finalize()` method must be declared with `protected` accessibility.
(c) An overriding `finalize()` method in any class can always throw checked exceptions.
(d) The `finalize()` method can be overloaded.
(e) The body of the `finalize()` method can only access other objects that are eligible for garbage collection.

9.9   Which statement describes guaranteed behavior of the garbage collection and finalization mechanisms?

Select the one correct answer.

(a) Objects will not be destroyed until they have no references to them.
(b) The `finalize()` method will never be called more than once on an object.
(c) An object eligible for garbage collection will eventually be destroyed by the garbage collector.
(d) If object A became eligible for garbage collection before object B, then object A will be destroyed before object B.
(e) An object, once eligible for garbage collection, can never become accessible by a live thread.

9.10   Which method headers will result in a correct implementation of a finalizer for the following class?

```
public class Curtain {
  // (1) INSERT METHOD HEADER HERE ...
  {
    System.out.println("Final curtain");
    super.finalize();
  }
}
```

Select the two correct answers.

(a) `void finalize() throws Throwable`
(b) `void finalize() throws Exception`
(c) `void finalize()`
(d) `protected void finalize() throws Throwable`
(e) `protected void finalize() throws Exception`
(f) `protected void finalize()`
(g) `public void finalize() throws Throwable`
(h) `public void finalize() throws Exception`
(i) `public void finalize()`
(j) `private void finalize() throws Throwable`
(k) `private void finalize() throws Exception`
(l) `private void finalize()`

9.11 Which scenario cannot definitely be the result of compiling and running the following program?

```java
public class Grade {
  private char grade;
  Grade(char grade) { this.grade = grade; }

  public void finalize() throws Throwable {
    System.out.print(grade);
    super.finalize();
  }
  public static void main(String[] args) {
    new Grade('A'); new Grade('F');
    System.gc();
  }
}
```

Select the one correct answer.

(a) The program may print AF.
(b) The program may print FA.
(c) The program may print A.
(d) The program may print F.
(e) The program may print AFA.
(f) The program may not print anything.

9.12 Which scenario can be the result of compiling and running the following program?

```java
public class MyString {
  private String str;
  MyString(String str) { this.str = str; }

  public void finalize() throws Throwable {
    System.out.print(str);
    super.finalize();
  }

  public void concat(String str2) {
    this.str.concat(str2);
  }

  public static void main(String[] args) {
    new MyString("A").concat("B");
    System.gc();
  }
}
```

Select the two correct answers.

(a) The program may print AB.
(b) The program may print BA.
(c) The program may print A.
(d) The program may print B.
(e) The program may not print anything.

9.7 Initializers

Initializers can be used to set initial values for fields in objects and classes. There are three different types of initializers:

- *field initializer expressions*
- *static initializer blocks*
- *instance initializer blocks*

The rest of this section provides details on these initializers, concluding with a discussion on the procedure involved in constructing the state of an object when the object is created by using the new operator.

9.8 Field Initializer Expressions

Initialization of fields can be specified in field declaration statements using initializer expressions. The value of the initializer expression must be assignment compatible to the declared field (see Section 5.5, p. 169 and Section 7.9, p. 320). We distinguish between static and non-static field initializers.

```
class ConstantInitializers {
  int minAge = 12;                    // (1) Non-static
  static double pensionPoints = 10.5; // (2) Static
  // ...
}
```

The fields of an object are initialized with the values of initializer expressions when the object is created by using the new operator. In the previous example, the declaration at (1) will result in the field minAge being initialized to 12 in every object of the class ConstantInitializers created with the new operator. If no explicit initializer expressions are specified, default values (see Section 2.4, p. 33) are assigned to the fields.

When a class is loaded, it is initialized, i.e., its static fields are initialized with the values of the initializer expressions. The declaration at (2) will result in the static field pensionPoints being initialized to 10.5 when the class is loaded by the JVM. Again, if no explicit initializers are specified, default values are assigned to the static fields.

An initializer expression for a static field cannot refer to non-static members by their simple names. The keywords this and super cannot occur in a static initializer expression.

Since a class is always initialized before it can be instantiated, an instance initializer expression can always refer to any static member of a class, regardless of the member declaration order. In the following code, the instance initializer expression at (1) refers to the static field NO_OF_WEEKS declared and initialized at (2). Such a *forward reference* is legal. More examples of forward references are given in the next subsection.

```
class MoreInitializers {
        int noOfDays    = 7 * NO_OF_WEEKS;    // (1) Non-static
    static int NO_OF_WEEKS = 52;              // (2) Static
    // ...
}
```

Initializer expressions can also be used to define constants in interfaces (see Section 7.6, p. 309). Such initializer expressions are implicitly static, as they define values of final static fields.

Initializer expressions are also used to initialize local variables (see Section 2.3, p. 31). A local variable is initialized with the value of the initializer expression every time the local variable declaration is executed.

Forward References and Declaration Order of Initializer Expressions

When an object is created using the new operator, instance initializer expressions are executed in the order in which the instance fields are declared in the class.

Java requires that the declaration of a field must occur before its usage in any initializer expression if the field is *used on the right-hand side of an assignment* in the initializer expression. This essentially means that the declaration of a field must occur before the value of the field is *read* in an initializer expression. Using the field on the left-hand side of an assignment in the initializer expression does not violate the declaration-before-reading rule, as this constitutes a write operation. This rule applies when the usage of the field is by its simple name.

There is one caveat to the declaration-before-reading rule: it does not apply if the initializer expression defines an anonymous class, as the usage then occurs in a different class which has its own accessibility rules in the enclosing context. Restrictions outlined earlier help to detect initialization anomalies at compile time.

In the next example, the initialization at (2) generates a compile-time error, because the field width in the initializer expression violates the declaration-before-reading rule. The usage of the field width in the initializer expression at (2) does not occur on the left-hand side of the assignment. This is an illegal forward reference. To remedy the situation, the declaration of the field width at (4) can be moved in front of the declaration at (2). In any case, we can use the keyword this as shown at (3), but this will read the default value 0 in the field width.

```
class NonStaticInitializers {
    int length  = 10;              // (1)
//double area = length * width;     // (2) Not Ok. Illegal forward reference.
    double area = length * this.width;  // (3) Ok, but width has default value 0.
    int width   = 10;              // (4)

    int sqSide = height = 20;      // (5) OK. Legal forward reference.
    int height;                    // (6)
}
```

The forward reference at (5) is legal. The usage of the field height in the initializer expression at (5) occurs on the left-hand side of the assignment. The initializer expression at (5) is evaluated as (sqSide = (height = 20)). Every object of the class NonStaticInitializers will have the field height set to the value 20.

The declaration-before-reading rule is equally applicable to static initializer expressions when static fields are referenced by their simple names.

Example 9.4 shows why the order of field initializer expressions can be important. The initializer expressions in Example 9.4 are calls to methods defined in the class. Methods are not subject to the same access rules as initializer expressions. The call at (2) to the method initMaxGuests() defined at (4) is expected to return the maximum number of guests. However, the field occupancyPerRoom at (3) will not have been explicitly initialized; therefore, its default value 0 will be used in the method initMaxGuests(), which will return an incorrect value. The program output shows that after object creation, the occupancy per room is correct, but the maximum number of guests is wrong.

Example 9.4   *Initializer Expression Order and Method Calls*

```
class Hotel {
    private int noOfRooms        = 12;                         // (1)
    private int maxNoOfGuests    = initMaxGuests();            // (2) Bug
    private int occupancyPerRoom = 2;                          // (3)

    public int initMaxGuests() {                              // (4)
        System.out.println("occupancyPerRoom: " + occupancyPerRoom);
        System.out.println("maxNoOfGuests:    " + noOfRooms * occupancyPerRoom);
        return noOfRooms * occupancyPerRoom;
    }

    public int getMaxGuests() { return maxNoOfGuests; }        // (5)

    public int getOccupancy() { return occupancyPerRoom; }     // (6)
}
//_____
public class TestOrder {
    public static void main(String[] args) {
        Hotel hotel = new Hotel();                            // (7)
        System.out.println("After object creation: ");
        System.out.println("occupancyPerRoom: " + hotel.getOccupancy()); // (8)
        System.out.println("maxNoOfGuests:    " + hotel.getMaxGuests()); // (9)
    }
}
```

Output from the program:

```
occupancyPerRoom: 0
maxNoOfGuests:    0
After object creation:
occupancyPerRoom: 2
maxNoOfGuests:    0
```

Exception Handling and Initializer Expressions

Initializer expressions in named classes and interfaces must not result in any uncaught checked exception (see Section 6.6, p. 243). If any checked exception is thrown during execution of an initializer expression, it must be caught and handled by code called from the initializer expression. This restriction does not apply to instance initializer expressions in anonymous classes.

Example 9.5 illustrates exception handling for initializer expressions in named classes. The static initializer expression at (3) calls the static method createHotel-Pool() at (4), which catches and handles the checked TooManyHotelsException defined at (2). If the method createHotelPool() were to use the throws clause to specify the checked exception, instead of catching and handling it within a try-catch block, the initializer expression at (3), which called the method, would have to handle the exception. However, the initializer expression cannot specify any exception handling, as the compiler would complain.

The instance initializer expression at (5) calls the method initMaxGuests() at (6), which can throw the unchecked RoomOccupancyTooHighException. If thrown, this exception will be caught and handled in the main() method. Program output confirms that an unchecked RoomOccupancyTooHighException was thrown during program execution.

Example 9.5 *Exceptions in Initializer Expressions*

```
class RoomOccupancyTooHighException
      extends RuntimeException {}                    // (1) Unchecked Exception
class TooManyHotelsException
      extends Exception {}                           // (2) Checked Exception
//_____
class Hotel {
  // Static Members
  private static int noOfHotels = 12;
  private static Hotel[] hotelPool = createHotelPool();   // (3)

  private static Hotel[] createHotelPool() {              // (4)
    try {
      if (noOfHotels > 10)
        throw new TooManyHotelsException();
    } catch (TooManyHotelsException e) {
      noOfHotels = 10;
      System.out.println("No. of hotels adjusted to " + noOfHotels);
    }
    return new Hotel[noOfHotels];
  }
  // Instance Members
  private int noOfRooms      = 215;
  private int occupancyPerRoom = 5;
  private int maxNoOfGuests  = initMaxGuests();           // (5)
```

```
    private int initMaxGuests() {                            // (6)
      if (occupancyPerRoom > 4)
        throw new RoomOccupancyTooHighException();
      return noOfRooms * occupancyPerRoom;
    }
}
//_____
public class ExceptionsInInitializers {
  public static void main(String[] args) {
    try { new Hotel(); }
    catch (RoomOccupancyTooHighException exception) {
      exception.printStackTrace();
    }
  }
}
```

Output from the program:

```
No. of hotels adjusted to 10
RoomOccupancyTooHighException
        at Hotel.initMaxGuests(ExceptionsInInitializers.java:28)
        at Hotel.<init>(ExceptionsInInitializers.java:24)
        at ExceptionsInInitializers.main(ExceptionsInInitializers.java:35)
```

9.9 Static Initializer Blocks

Java allows static initializer blocks to be defined in a class. Although such blocks can include arbitrary code, they are primarily used for initializing static fields. The code in a static initializer block is executed only once, when the class is initialized.

The syntax of a static initializer block comprises the keyword static followed by a local block that can contain arbitrary code, as shown at (3).

```
class StaticInitializers {
  final static int ROWS = 12, COLUMNS = 10;           // (1)
  static long[][] matrix = new long[ROWS][COLUMNS];   // (2)
  // ...
  static {                                            // (3) Static Initializer
    for (int i = 0; i < matrix.length; i++)
      for (int j = 0; j < matrix[i].length; j++)
        matrix[i][j] = 2*i + j;
  }
  // ...
}
```

When the class StaticInitializers is first loaded in the previous example, the final static fields at (1) are initialized. Then the array of arrays matrix of specified size is created at (2), followed by the execution of the static block at (3).

If a class relies on native method implementations, a static initializer can be used to load any external libraries that the class needs (see Section 4.10, p. 151).

Note that the static initializer block is not contained in any method. A class can have more than one static initializer block. Initializer blocks are *not* members of a class nor can they have a `return` statement because they cannot be called directly.

When a class is initialized, the initializer expressions in static field declarations and static initializer blocks are executed in the order they are specified in the class. In the previous example, the initializer expressions at (1) and (2) are executed before the static initializer block at (3).

Similar restrictions apply to static initializer blocks as for static initializer expressions: the keywords `this` and `super` cannot occur in a static initializer block because such a block defines a static context.

Forward References and Declaration Order of Static Initializers

When making forward references using simple names, code in a static initializer block is also subject to the declaration-before-reading rule discussed in the previous subsection. Example 9.6 illustrates forward references and the order of execution for static initializer expressions and static initializer blocks. An illegal forward reference occurs at (4), where an attempt is made to read the value of the field `sf1` before its declaration. At (11) the read operation is after the declaration and, therefore, allowed. Forward reference made on the left-hand side of the assignment is always allowed, as shown at (2), (5), and (7). The initializers are executed in their declaration order. A static field has the value it was last assigned in an initializer. If there is no explicit assignment, the field has the default value of its type.

Example 9.6 *Static Initializers and Forward References*

```java
// Demonstrates forward references.
public class StaticForwardReferences {

    static {                    // (1) Static initializer block
      sf1 = 10;                 // (2) OK. Assignment to sf1 allowed
      // sf1 = if1;             // (3) Not OK. Non-static field access in static context
      // int a = 2 * sf1;       // (4) Not OK. Read operation before declaration
      int b = sf1 = 20;         // (5) OK. Assignment to sf1 allowed
      int c = StaticForwardReferences.sf1;// (6) OK. Not accessed by simple name
    }

    static int sf1 = sf2 = 30;  // (7) Static field. Assignment to sf2 allowed
    static int sf2;             // (8) Static field
    int if1 = 5;                // (9) Non-static field

    static {                    // (10) Static initializer block
      int d = 2 * sf1;          // (11) OK. Read operation after declaration
      int e = sf1 = 50;         // (12)
    }

    public static void main(String[] args) {
      System.out.println("sf1: " + StaticForwardReferences.sf1);
      System.out.println("sf2: " + StaticForwardReferences.sf2);
    }
}
```

Output from the program:

```
sf1: 50
sf2: 30
```

Exception Handling and Static Initializer Blocks

Exception handling in static initializer blocks is no different from that in static initializer expressions: uncaught checked exceptions cannot be thrown. A static initializer block cannot be called directly, therefore, any checked exceptions must be caught and handled in the body of the static initializer block. Example 9.7 shows a static initializer block at (3) that catches and handles a checked exception in the try-catch block at (4).

Example 9.7 also shows a static initializer block at (5) that throws an unchecked exception at (6) during class initialization. As the program output shows, this exception is handled by the default exception handler, resulting in termination of the program.

Example 9.7   *Static Initializer Blocks and Exceptions*

```
class BankrupcyException
      extends RuntimeException {}            // (1) Unchecked Exception
class TooManyHotelsException
      extends Exception {}                   // (2) Checked Exception

class Hotel {
  // Static Members
  private static boolean bankrupt  = true;
  private static int     noOfHotels = 11;
  private static Hotel[] hotelPool;

  static {                                   // (3) Static block
    try {                                    // (4) Handles checked exception
      if (noOfHotels > 10)
        throw new TooManyHotelsException();
    } catch (TooManyHotelsException e) {
      noOfHotels = 10;
      System.out.println("No. of hotels adjusted to " + noOfHotels);
    }
    hotelPool = new Hotel[noOfHotels];
  }

  static {                                   // (5) Static block
    if (bankrupt)
      throw new BankrupcyException();        // (6) Throws unchecked exception
  }
  // ...
}
```

```
public class ExceptionInStaticInitBlocks {
  public static void main(String[] args) {
    new Hotel();
  }
}
```

Output from the program:

```
No. of hotels adjusted to 10
Exception in thread "main" java.lang.ExceptionInInitializerError
        at ExceptionInStaticInitBlocks.main(ExceptionInStaticInitBlocks.java:32)
Caused by: BankrupcyException
        at Hotel.<clinit>(ExceptionInStaticInitBlocks.java:25)
```

9.10 Instance Initializer Blocks

Just as static initializer blocks can be used to initialize static fields in a named class, Java provides the ability to initialize fields during object creation using instance initializer blocks. In this respect, such blocks serve the same purpose as constructors during object creation. The syntax of an instance initializer block is the same as that of a local block, as shown at (2) in the following code. The code in the local block is executed every time an instance of the class is created.

```
class InstanceInitializers {

  long[] squares = new long[10];    // (1)
  // ...
  {                                  // (2) Instance Initializer
    for (int i = 0; i < squares.length; i++)
      squares[i] = i*i;
  }
  // ...
}
```

The array squares of specified size is created first at (1), followed by the execution of the instance initializer block at (2) every time an instance of the class Instance-Initializers is created. Note that the instance initializer block is not contained in any method. A class can have more than one instance initializer block, and these (and any instance initializer expressions in instance field declarations) are executed in the order they are specified in the class.

Forward References and Declaration Order of Instance Initializers

Analogous to other initializers discussed so far, an instance initializer block cannot make a forward reference to a field that violates the declaration-before-reading rule. In Example 9.8, an illegal forward reference occurs in the code at (4), which attempts to read the value of the field nsf1 before it is declared. The read operation at (11) is after the declaration and is, therefore, allowed. Forward reference made on the left-hand side of the assignment is always allowed, as shown at (2), (3), (5), and (7).

Example 9.8 *Instance Initializers and Forward References*

```
class NonStaticForwardReferences {

    {                          // (1) Instance initializer block
      nsf1 = 10;               // (2) OK. Assignment to nsf1 allowed
      nsf1 = sf1;              // (3) OK. Static field access in non-static context
      // int a = 2 * nsf1;     // (4) Not OK. Read operation before declaration
      int b = nsf1 = 20;       // (5) OK. Assignment to nsf1 allowed
      int c = this.nsf1;       // (6) OK. Not accessed by simple name
    }

    int nsf1 = nsf2 = 30;      // (7) Non-static field. Assignment to nsf2 allowed
    int nsf2;                  // (8) Non-static field
    static int sf1 = 5;        // (9) Static field

    {                          // (10) Instance initializer block
      int d = 2 * nsf1;        // (11) OK. Read operation after declaration
      int e = nsf1 = 50;       // (12)
    }

    public static void main(String[] args) {
      NonStaticForwardReferences objRef = new NonStaticForwardReferences();
      System.out.println("nsf1: " + objRef.nsf1);
      System.out.println("nsf2: " + objRef.nsf2);
    }
}
```

Output from the program:

```
nsf1: 50
nsf2: 30
```

As in a instance initializer expression, the keywords this and super can be used to refer to the current object in an instance initializer block. As in a static initializer block, the return statement is also not allowed in instance initializer blocks.

An instance initializer block can be used to factor out common initialization code that will be executed regardless of which constructor is invoked. A typical usage of an instance initializer block is in anonymous classes (see Section 8.5, p. 377), which cannot declare constructors, but can instead use instance initializer blocks to initialize fields. In Example 9.9, the anonymous class defined at (1) uses an instance initializer block defined at (2) to initialize its fields.

Example 9.9 *Instance Initializer Block in Anonymous Class*

```
class Base {
  protected int a;
  protected int b;
  void print() { System.out.println("a: " + a); }
}
```

```
//_____
class AnonymousClassMaker {
  Base createAnonymous() {
    return new Base() {              // (1) Anonymous class
      {                             // (2) Instance initializer
        a = 5; b = 10;
      }
      void print() {
        super.print();
        System.out.println("b: " + b);
      }
    }; // end anonymous class
  }
}
//_____
public class InstanceInitBlock {
  public static void main(String[] args) {
    new AnonymousClassMaker().createAnonymous().print();
  }
}
```

Output from the program:

```
a: 5
b: 10
```

Exception Handling and Instance Initializer Blocks

Exception handling in instance initializer blocks is similar to that in static initializer blocks. Example 9.10 shows an instance initializer block at (3) that catches and handles a checked exception in the try-catch block at (4). Another instance initializer block at (5) throws an unchecked exception at (6). The runtime system handles the exception, printing the stack trace and terminating the program.

Exception handling in instance initializer blocks differs from that in static initializer blocks in the following aspect: the execution of an instance initializer block can result in an uncaught checked exception, provided the exception is declared in the throws clause of *every* constructor in the class. Static initializer blocks cannot allow this, since no constructors are involved in class initialization. Instance initializer blocks in anonymous classes have even greater freedom: they can throw any exception.

Example 9.10 *Exception Handling in Instance Initializer Blocks*

```
class RoomOccupancyTooHighException
      extends Exception {}              // (1) Checked exception
class BankrupcyException
      extends RuntimeException {}       // (2) Unchecked exception
//_____
```

```
class Hotel {
  // Instance Members
  private boolean bankrupt        = true;
  private int     noOfRooms       = 215;
  private int     occupancyPerRoom = 5;
  private int     maxNoOfGuests;

  {                                           // (3) Instance initializer block
    try {                                     // (4) Handles checked exception
      if (occupancyPerRoom > 4)
        throw new RoomOccupancyTooHighException();
    } catch (RoomOccupancyTooHighException exception) {
      System.out.println("ROOM OCCUPANCY TOO HIGH: " + occupancyPerRoom);
      occupancyPerRoom = 4;
    }
    maxNoOfGuests = noOfRooms * occupancyPerRoom;
  }

  {                                           // (5) Instance initializer block
    if (bankrupt)
      throw new BankrupcyException();         // (6) Throws unchecked exception
  }   // ...
}
//_____
public class ExceptionsInInstBlocks {
  public static void main(String[] args) {
    new Hotel();
  }
}
```

Output from the program:

```
ROOM OCCUPANCY TOO HIGH: 5
Exception in thread "main" BankrupcyException
        at Hotel.<init>(ExceptionsInInstBlocks.java:26)
        at ExceptionsInInstBlocks.main(ExceptionsInInstBlocks.java:32)
```

9.11 Constructing Initial Object State

Object initialization involves constructing the initial state of an object when it is created by using the new operator. First, the fields are initialized to their default values (see Section 2.4, p. 33)—whether they are subsequently given non-default initial values or not—then the constructor is invoked. This can lead to *local* chaining of constructors. The invocation of the constructor at the end of the local chain of constructor invocations results in the following actions, before the constructor's execution resumes:

- Implicit or explicit invocation of the superclass constructor. Constructor chaining ensures that the inherited state of the object is constructed first (see Section 7.5, p. 302).

- Initialization of the instance fields by executing their instance initializer expressions and any instance initializer blocks, in the order they are specified in the class declaration.

Example 9.11 illustrates object initialization. The new operator is used at (8) to create an object of class SubclassB. The default constructor SubclassB() at (2) uses the this() construct to locally chain to the non-default constructor at (3). It is this constructor that leads to an implicit call of the superclass constructor. As can be seen from the program output, the execution of the superclass's constructor at (1) reaches completion first. This is followed by the execution of the instance initializer block at (4) and instance initializer expression at (6). Then the execution of the body of the non-default constructor at (3) is resumed. Finally, the default constructor completes its execution, thereby completing the construction of the object state.

Note that the instance initializers are executed in the order they are specified in the class declaration. The forward reference to the field value at (5) is legal because the usage of the field value is on the left-hand side of the assignment (it does not violate the declaration-before-reading rule. The default value of the field value is overwritten by the instance initializer block at (5). The field value is again overwritten by the instance initializer expression at (6), and finally by the non-default constructor at (3).

Example 9.11   *Object State Construction*

```java
class SuperclassA {
  public SuperclassA() {                              // (1)
    System.out.println("Constructor in SuperclassA");
  }
}
//_____
class SubclassB extends SuperclassA {

  SubclassB() {                                       // (2) Default constructor
    this(3);
    System.out.println("Default constructor in SubclassB");
  }

  SubclassB(int i) {                                  // (3) Non-default constructor
    System.out.println("Non-default constructor in SubclassB");
    value = i;
  }

  {                                                   // (4) Instance initializer block
    System.out.println("Instance initializer block in SubclassB");
    value = 2;                                        // (5)
  }

  int value = initializerExpression();                // (6)

  private int initializerExpression() {               // (7)
    System.out.println("Instance initializer expression in SubclassB");
```

```
        return 1;
      }
    }
//_____
public class ObjectConstruction {
  public static void main(String[] args) {
    SubclassB objRef = new SubclassB();            // (8)
    System.out.println("value: " + objRef.value);
  }
}
```

Output from the program:

```
Constructor in SuperclassA
Instance initializer block in SubclassB
Instance initializer expression in SubclassB
Non-default constructor in SubclassB
Default constructor in SubclassB
value: 3
```

Some care should be exercised when writing constructors for non-final classes, since the object that is constructed might be a subclass instance. Example 9.12 shows a situation where use of overridden methods in *superclass* initializers and constructors can give unexpected results. The example intentionally uses the this reference to underline the fact that the instance methods and constructors are invoked on the current object, and that the constructor call results in the initialization of the object state, as expected.

The program output shows that the field superValue at (1) in class SuperclassA never gets initialized explicitly when an object of the SubclassB is created at (8). The SuperclassA constructor at (2) does have a call to a method that has the name doValue at (3). A method with such a name is defined in the class SuperclassA at (4), but is also overridden in SubclassB at (7). The program output indicates that the method doValue() from the SubclassB is called at (3) in the SuperclassA constructor. The implementation of the method doValue() at (4) never gets executed when an object of the SubclassB is created. Method invocation always determines the implementation of the method to be executed, based on the *actual* type of the object. Keeping in mind that it is an object of SubclassB that is being initialized, the call to the method named doValue at (3) results in the method from SubclassB being executed. This can lead to unintended results. The overriding method doValue() at (7) in the class SubclassB can access the field value declared at (5) before its initializer expression has been executed; i.e., the method invoked can access the state of the object *before* this has been completely initialized.

Example 9.12 *Initialization under Object State Construction*

```java
class SuperclassA {
  protected int superValue;                                    // (1)
  SuperclassA() {                                              // (2)
    System.out.println("Constructor in SuperclassA");
    this.doValue();                                            // (3)
  }
  void doValue() {                                             // (4)
    this.superValue = 911;
    System.out.println("superValue: " + this.superValue);
  }
}
//_____
class SubclassB extends SuperclassA {
  private int value = 800;                                     // (5)
  SubclassB() {                                                // (6)
    System.out.println("Constructor in SubclassB");
    this.doValue();
    System.out.println("superValue: " + this.superValue);
  }
  void doValue() {                                             // (7)
    System.out.println("value: " + this.value);
  }
}
//_____
public class ObjectInitialization {
  public static void main(String[] args) {
    System.out.println("Creating an object of SubclassB.");
    new SubclassB();                                           // (8)
  }
}
```

Output from the program:

```
Creating an object of SubclassB.
Constructor in SuperclassA
value: 0
Constructor in SubclassB
value: 800
superValue: 0
```

Class initialization takes place before any instance of the class can be created or a static method of the class can be invoked. A superclass is initialized before its subclasses are initialized. Initializing a class involves initialization of the static fields by executing their static initializer expressions and any static initializer blocks.

Initialization of an interface only involves execution of any static initializer expressions for the static fields declared in the interface. An interface cannot specify instance initializer expressions as it has no instance fields, nor can it specify instance initializer blocks as it cannot be instantiated.

Review Questions

9.13 Given the following class, which of these static initializer blocks can be inserted at (1)?

```
public class MyClass {
  private static int count = 5;
  final static int STEP = 10;
  boolean alive;

  // (1) INSERT STATIC INITIALIZER BLOCK HERE
}
```

Select the three correct answers.

(a) static { alive = true; count = 0; }
(b) static { STEP = count; }
(c) static { count += STEP; }
(d) static ;
(e) static {;}
(f) static { count = 1; }

9.14 What will be the result of compiling and running the following program?

```
public class MyClass {
  public static void main(String[] args) {
    MyClass obj = new MyClass(n);
  }

  static int i = 5;
  static int n;
  int j = 7;
  int k;

  public MyClass(int m) {
    System.out.println(i + ", " + j + ", " + k + ", " + n + ", " + m);
  }

  { j = 70; n = 20; } // Instance Initializer Block

  static { i = 50; }  // Static Initializer Block
}
```

Select the one correct answer.

(a) The code will fail to compile because the instance initializer block tries to assign a value to a static field.
(b) The code will fail to compile because the field k will be uninitialized when it is used.
(c) The code will compile and print 50, 70, 0, 20, 0, when run.
(d) The code will compile and print 50, 70, 0, 20, 20, when run.
(e) The code will compile and print 5, 70, 0, 20, 0, when run.
(f) The code will compile and print 5, 7, 0, 20, 0, when run.

9.15 Given the following class, which instance initializer block inserted at (1) will allow the class to be compiled?

```java
public class MyClass {
  static int gap = 10;
  double length;
  final boolean active;

  // (1) INSERT CODE HERE
}
```

Select the one correct answer.

(a) `instance { active = true; }`
(b) `MyClass { gap += 5; }`
(c) `{ gap = 5; length = (active ? 100 : 200) + gap; }`
(d) `{ ; }`
(e) `{ length = 4.2; }`
(f) `{ active = (gap > 5); length = 5.5 + gap;}`

9.16 What will be the result of compiling and running the following program?

```java
public class Initialization {
  private static String msg(String msg) {
    System.out.println(msg); return msg;
  }

  public Initialization() { m = msg("1"); }

  { m = msg("2"); }

  String m = msg("3");

  public static void main(String[] args) {
    Object obj = new Initialization();
  }
}
```

Select the one correct answer.

(a) The program will fail to compile.
(b) The program will compile, and print 1, 2, and 3, when run.
(c) The program will compile, and print 2, 3, and 1, when run.
(d) The program will compile, and print 3, 1, and 2, when run.
(e) The program will compile, and print 1, 3, and 2, when run.

9.17 What will be the result of compiling and running the following program?

```java
public class Initialization {
  private static String msg(String msg) {
    System.out.println(msg); return msg;
  }

  static String m = msg("1");

  { m = msg("2"); }

  static { m = msg("3"); }
```

```
    public static void main(String[] args) {
      Object obj = new Initialization();
    }
  }
```

Select the one correct answer.

(a) The program will fail to compile.
(b) The program will compile and print 1, 2, and 3, when run.
(c) The program will compile and print 2, 3, and 1, when run.
(d) The program will compile and print 3, 1, and 2, when run.
(e) The program will compile and print 1, 3, and 2, when run.

9.18   Which of the labeled lines in the following code can be *uncommented* by removing
        the // characters and still allow the code to compile correctly?

```
class GeomInit {
//int width = 14;              /* Line A */
  {
//   area = width * height;    /* Line B */
  }
  int width = 37;
  {
//   height = 11;              /* Line C */
  }
  int height, area;
//area = width * height;       /* Line D */
  {
//   int width = 15;           /* Line E */
    area = 100;
  }
};
```

Select the two correct answers.

(a) Line A
(b) Line B
(c) Line C
(d) Line D
(e) Line E

Chapter Summary

The following information was included in this chapter:

- discussion of automatic garbage collection, including the workings of the garbage collector and guidelines for facilitating garbage collection
- discussion of object finalization and chaining as part of garbage collection
- discussion of static and instance initializers, both as initializer expressions and as initializer blocks
- discussion of the role played by initializers in initializing objects, classes, and interfaces

Fundamental Classes

10

3.1 Develop code that uses the primitive wrapper classes (such as `Boolean`, `Character`, `Double`, `Integer`, etc.), and/or autoboxing & unboxing. Discuss the differences between the `String`, `StringBuilder`, and `StringBuffer` classes.

  o *For boxing and unboxing, see Section 5.1, p. 162.*

* Understand the functionality inherited by all classes from the `Object` class.
* Understand the significance of immutability of `String` objects.

10.1   Overview of the `java.lang` Package

The `java.lang` package is indispensable when programming in Java. It is automatically imported into every source file at compile time. The package contains the `Object` class that is the superclass of all classes, and the wrapper classes (`Boolean`, `Character`, `Byte`, `Short`, `Integer`, `Long`, `Float`, `Double`) used to handle primitive values as objects. It provides classes essential for interacting with the JVM (`Runtime`), for security (`SecurityManager`), for loading classes (`ClassLoader`), for dealing with threads (`Thread`), and for exceptions (`Throwable`). The `java.lang` package also contains classes that provide the standard input, output, and error streams (`System`), string handling (`String`, `StringBuilder`, `StringBuffer`), and mathematical functions (`Math`).

Figure 10.1 shows the important classes that are discussed in detail in this chapter.

Figure 10.1   *Partial Inheritance Hierarchy in the* `java.lang` *Package*

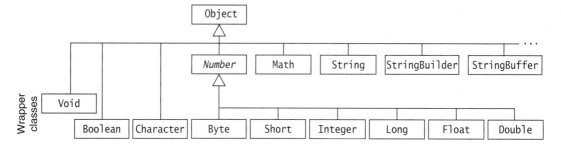

10.2   The `Object` Class

All classes extend the `Object` class, either directly or indirectly. A class declaration, without the `extends` clause, implicitly extends the `Object` class (see Section 7.1, p. 284). Thus, the `Object` class is always at the root of any inheritance hierarchy. The `Object` class defines the basic functionality that all objects exhibit and all classes inherit. Note that this also applies to arrays, since these are genuine objects in Java.

The `Object` class provides the following general utility methods (see Example 10.1 for usage of some of these methods):

> `int hashCode()`
>
> When storing objects in hash tables, this method can be used to get a hash value for an object. This value is guaranteed to be consistent during the execution of the program. This method returns the memory address of the object as the default hash value of the object. For a detailed discussion of the `hashCode()` method, see Section 15.1 on page 748.

```
boolean equals(Object obj)
```

Object reference and value equality are discussed together with the == and != operators (see Section 5.11, p. 191). The equals() method in the Object class returns true only if the two references compared denote the same object. The equals() method is usually overridden to provide the semantics of object value equality, as is the case for the wrapper classes and the String class. For a detailed discussion of the equals() method, see Section 15.1 on page 748.

```
final Class<?> getClass()
```

Returns the *runtime class* of the object, which is represented by an object of the class java.lang.Class at runtime.

```
protected Object clone() throws CloneNotSupportedException
```

New objects that are exactly the same (i.e., have identical states) as the current object can be created by using the clone() method, i.e., primitive values and reference values are copied. This is called *shallow copying*. A class can override this method to provide its own notion of cloning. For example, cloning a composite object by recursively cloning the constituent objects is called *deep copying*.

When overridden, the method in the subclass is usually declared public to allow any client to clone objects of the class. If the overriding clone() method in the subclass relies on the clone() method in the Object class (i.e., a shallow copy), the subclass must implement the Cloneable marker interface to indicate that its objects can be safely cloned. Otherwise, the clone() method in the Object class will throw a checked CloneNotSupportedException.

```
String toString()
```

If a subclass does not override this method, it returns a textual representation of the object, which has the following format:

"*<name of the class>*@*<hash code value of object>*"

Since the default hash value of an object is its memory address, this value is printed as a hexadecimal number, e.g., 3e25a5. This method is usually overridden and used for debugging purposes. The method call System.out.println(objRef) will implicitly convert its argument to a textual representation by calling the toString() method on the argument. See also the binary string concatenation operator +, discussed in Section 5.6 on page 180.

```
protected void finalize() throws Throwable
```

This method is discussed in connection with garbage collection (see Section 9.4, p. 396). It is called on an object just before it is garbage collected, so that any cleaning up can be done. However, the default finalize() method in the Object class does not do anything useful.

In addition, the Object class provides support for thread communication in synchronized code, through the following methods, which are discussed in Section 13.6 on page 634:

```
final void wait(long timeout) throws InterruptedException
final void wait(long timeout, int nanos) throws InterruptedException
final void wait() throws InterruptedException
final void notify()
final void notifyAll()
```

A thread invokes these methods on the object whose lock it holds. A thread waits for notification by another thread.

Example 10.1 *Methods in the* Object *class*

```
class MyClass implements Cloneable {

  public Object clone() {
    Object obj = null;
    try { obj = super.clone();}            // Calls overridden method.
    catch (CloneNotSupportedException e) { System.out.println(e);}
    return obj;
  }
}
//_____
public class ObjectMethods {
  public static void main(String[] args) {
    // Two objects of MyClass.
    MyClass obj1 = new MyClass();
    MyClass obj2 = new MyClass();

    // Two strings.
    String str1 = new String("WhoAmI");
    String str2 = new String("WhoAmI");

    // Method hashCode() overridden in String class.
    // Strings that are equal have the same hash code.
    System.out.println("hash code for str1: " + str1.hashCode());
    System.out.println("hash code for str2: " + str2.hashCode() + "\n");

    // Hash codes are different for different MyClass objects.
    System.out.println("hash code for MyClass obj1: " + obj1.hashCode());
    System.out.println("hash code for MyClass obj2: " + obj2.hashCode()+"\n");

    // Method equals() overridden in the String class.
    System.out.println("str1.equals(str2): " + str1.equals(str2));
    System.out.println("str1 == str2:      " + (str1 == str2) + "\n");

    // Method equals() from the Object class called.
    System.out.println("obj1.equals(obj2): " + obj1.equals(obj2));
    System.out.println("obj1 == obj2:      " + (obj1 == obj2) + "\n");
```

```
        // The runtime object that represents the class of an object.
        Class rtStringClass  = str1.getClass();
        Class rtMyClassClass = obj1.getClass();
        // The name of the class represented by the runtime object.
        System.out.println("Class for str1: " + rtStringClass);
        System.out.println("Class for obj1: " + rtMyClassClass + "\n");

        // The toString() method is overridden in the String class.
        String textRepStr = str1.toString();
        String textRepObj = obj1.toString();
        System.out.println("Text representation of str1: " + textRepStr);
        System.out.println("Text representation of obj1: " + textRepObj + "\n");

        // Shallow copying of arrays.
        MyClass[] array1 = {new MyClass(), new MyClass(), new MyClass()};
        MyClass[] array2 = array1.clone();
        // Array objects are different, but share the element objects.
        System.out.println("array1 == array2:        " + (array1 == array2));
        for(int i = 0; i < array1.length; i++) {
          System.out.println("array1[" + i + "] == array2[" + i + "] : " +
                             (array1[i] == array2[i]));
        }
        System.out.println();

        // Clone an object of MyClass.
        MyClass obj3 = (MyClass) obj1.clone(); // Cast required.
        System.out.println("hash code for MyClass obj3: " + obj3.hashCode());
        System.out.println("obj1 == obj3: " + (obj1 == obj3));
    }
}
```

Output from the program:

```
hash code for str1: -1704812257
hash code for str2: -1704812257

hash code for MyClass obj1: 25669322
hash code for MyClass obj2: 14978587

str1.equals(str2): true
str1 == str2:      false

obj1.equals(obj2): false
obj1 == obj2:      false

Class for str1: class java.lang.String
Class for obj1: class MyClass

Text representation of str1: WhoAmI
Text representation of obj1: MyClass@187aeca

array1 == array2:        false
array1[0] == array2[0] : true
array1[1] == array2[1] : true
array1[2] == array2[2] : true
```

```
hash code for MyClass obj3: 19770577
obj1 == obj3: false
```

 Review Questions

10.1   What is the return type of the `hashCode()` method in the `Object` class?

Select the one correct answer.
(a) `String`
(b) `int`
(c) `long`
(d) `Object`
(e) `Class`

10.2   Which statement is true?

Select the one correct answer.
(a) If the references `x` and `y` denote two different objects, the expression `x.equals(y)` is always `false`.
(b) If the references `x` and `y` denote two different objects, the expression `(x.hashCode() == y.hashCode())` is always `false`.
(c) The `hashCode()` method in the `Object` class is declared `final`.
(d) The `equals()` method in the `Object` class is declared `final`.
(e) All arrays have a method named `clone`.

10.3   Which exception can the `clone()` method of the `Object` class throw?

Select the one correct answer.
(a) `CloneNotSupportedException`
(b) `NotCloneableException`
(c) `IllegalCloneException`
(d) `NoClonesAllowedException`

10.3 The Wrapper Classes

Wrapper classes were introduced with the discussion of the primitive data types (see Section 2.2, p. 28), and also in connection with boxing and unboxing of primitive values (see Section 5.1, p. 162). Primitive values in Java are not objects. In order to manipulate these values as objects, the java.lang package provides a *wrapper* class for each of the primitive data types. All wrapper classes are `final`. The objects of all wrapper classes that can be instantiated are *immutable*, i.e., the value in the wrapper object cannot be changed.

Although the `Void` class is considered a wrapper class, it does not wrap any primitive value and is not instantiable (i.e., has no `public` constructors). It just denotes the Class object representing the keyword void. The Void class will not be discussed further in this section.

In addition to the methods defined for constructing and manipulating objects of primitive values, the wrapper classes also define useful constants, fields, and conversion methods.

Figure 10.2 *Converting Values Between Primitive, Wrapper, and* String *Types*

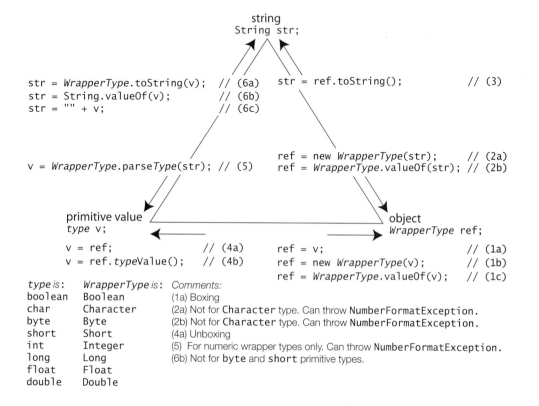

Common Wrapper Class Constructors

The Character class has only one public constructor, taking a char value as parameter. The other wrapper classes all have two public one-argument constructors: one takes a primitive value and the other takes a string.

```
WrapperType(type v)
WrapperType(String str)
```

The *type* is a primitive data type. The string argument is converted to a primitive value that corresponds to the *WrapperType*. Otherwise a NumberFormat-Exception is thrown if the string is not parsable.

Wrapping Primitive Values in Objects

Boxing is a convenient way to wrap a primitive value in an object (see (1a) in Figure 10.2 and Section 5.1, p. 162).

```
Character charObj1   = '\n';
Boolean   boolObj1   = true;
Integer   intObj1    = 2008;
Double    doubleObj1 = 3.14;
```

A constructor that takes a primitive value can be used to create wrapper objects (see (1b) in Figure 10.2).

```
Character charObj1   = new Character('\n');
Boolean   boolObj1   = new Boolean(true);
Integer   intObj1    = new Integer(2008);
Double    doubleObj1 = new Double(3.14);
```

We can also use the valueOf() method that takes the primitive value to wrap as an argument (see (1c) in Figure 10.2).

```
Character charObj1   = Character.valueOf('\n');
Boolean   boolObj1   = Boolean.valueOf(true);
Integer   intObj1    = Integer.valueOf(2008);
Double    doubleObj1 = Double.valueOf(3.14);
```

Converting Strings to Wrapper Objects

A constructor that takes a String object representing the primitive value can also be used to create wrapper objects. The constructors for the numeric wrapper types throw an unchecked NumberFormatException if the String parameter does not parse to a valid number (see (2a) in Figure 10.2).

```
Boolean boolObj2   = new Boolean("TrUe");     // case ignored: true
Boolean boolObj3   = new Boolean("XX");       // false
Integer intObj2    = new Integer("2008");
Double  doubleObj2 = new Double("3.14");
Long    longObj1   = new Long("3.14");        // NumberFormatException
```

Common Wrapper Class Utility Methods

Converting Strings to Wrapper Objects

Each wrapper class (except Character) defines the static method valueOf(String str) that returns the wrapper object corresponding to the primitive value represented by the String object passed as argument (see (6b) in Figure 10.2). This method for the numeric wrapper types also throws a NumberFormatException if the String parameter is not a valid number.

```
    static WrapperType valueOf(String str)
```

```
Boolean boolObj4   = Boolean.valueOf("false");
Integer intObj3    = Integer.valueOf("1949");
Double  doubleObj3 = Double.valueOf("-3.0");
```

In addition to the one-argument valueOf() method, the integer wrapper classes define an overloaded static valueOf() method that can take a second argument. This argument specifies the base (or *radix*) in which to interpret the string representing the signed integer in the first argument:

```
static WrapperType valueOf(String str, int base)
```

```
Byte    byteObj1  = Byte.valueOf("1010", 2);    // Decimal value 10
Short   shortObj2 = Short.valueOf("012", 8);    // Not "\012". Decimal value 10.
Integer intObj4   = Integer.valueOf("-a", 16);  // Not "-0xa". Decimal value -10.
Long    longObj2  = Long.valueOf("-a", 16);     // Not "-0xa". Decimal value -10L.
```

Converting Wrapper Objects to Strings

Each wrapper class overrides the toString() method from the Object class. The overriding method returns a String object containing the string representation of the primitive value in the wrapper object (see (3) in Figure 10.2).

```
String toString()
```

```
String charStr   = charObj1.toString();    // "\n"
String boolStr   = boolObj2.toString();    // "true"
String intStr    = intObj1.toString();     // "2008"
String doubleStr = doubleObj1.toString();  // "3.14"
```

Converting Primitive Values to Strings

Each wrapper class defines a static method toString(*type* v) that returns the string corresponding to the primitive value of *type*, passed as argument (see (6a) in Figure 10.2).

```
static String toString(type v)
```

```
String charStr2   = Character.toString('\n'); // "\n"
String boolStr2   = Boolean.toString(true);   // "true"
String intStr2    = Integer.toString(2008);   // Base 10. "2008"
String doubleStr2 = Double.toString(3.14);    // "3.14"
```

For integer primitive types, the base is assumed to be 10. For floating-point numbers, the textual representation (decimal form or scientific notation) depends on the sign and the magnitude (absolute value) of the number. The NaN value, positive infinity, and negative infinity will result in the strings "NaN", "Infinity", and "-Infinity", respectively.

In addition, the wrapper classes Integer and Long define overloaded toString() methods for converting integers to string representation in decimal, binary, octal, and hexadecimal notation (see p. 435).

Converting Wrapper Objects to Primitive Values

Unboxing is a convenient way to unwrap the primitive value in a wrapper object (see (4a) in Figure 10.2 and Section 5.1, p. 162).

```
char    c = charObj1;          // '\n'
boolean b = boolObj2;          // true
int     i = intObj1;           // 2008
double  d = doubleObj1;        // 3.14
```

Each wrapper class defines a *type*Value() method which returns the primitive value in the wrapper object (see (4b) in Figure 10.2).

```
type typeValue()
```

```
char    c = charObj1.charValue();       // '\n'
boolean b = boolObj2.booleanValue();    // true
int     i = intObj1.intValue();         // 2008
double  d = doubleObj1.doubleValue();   // 3.14
```

In addition, each numeric wrapper class defines *type*Value() methods for converting the primitive value in the wrapper object to a value of any numeric primitive data type. These methods are discussed below.

Wrapper Comparison, Equality, and Hashcode

Each wrapper class also implements the Comparable<*Type*> interface (see Section 15.1, p. 765), which defines the following method:

```
int compareTo(Type obj2)
```

This method returns a value which is less than, equal to, or greater than zero, depending on whether the primitive value in the current wrapper *Type* object is less than, equal to, or greater than the primitive value in the wrapper *Type* object denoted by argument obj2.

```
// Comparisons based on objects created above
Character charObj2   = 'a';
int result1 = charObj1.compareTo(charObj2);       // < 0
int result2 = intObj1.compareTo(intObj3);         // > 0
int result3 = doubleObj1.compareTo(doubleObj2);   // == 0
int result4 = doubleObj1.compareTo(intObj1);      // ClassCastException
```

Each wrapper class overrides the equals() method from the Object class (see Section 15.1, p. 751). The overriding method compares two wrapper objects for object value equality.

```
boolean equals(Object obj2)
```

```
// Comparisons based on objects created above
boolean charTest   = charObj1.equals(charObj2);       // false
boolean boolTest   = boolObj2.equals(Boolean.FALSE);  // false
boolean intTest    = intObj1.equals(intObj2);         // true
boolean doubleTest = doubleObj1.equals(doubleObj2);   // true
```

The following values are *interned* when they are wrapped during boxing, i.e., only *one* wrapper object exists in the program for these primitive values when boxing is applied:

- `boolean` values `true` or `false`,
- a `byte`,
- a `char` in the range `\u0000` to `\u007f`,
- an `int` or `short` value in the range -128 and 127

If references `w1` and `w2` refer to two wrapper objects that box the *same* value which is among the ones mentioned above, then `w1 == w2` is always true. In other words, for the values listed above, object equality and reference equality give the same result.

```
// Reference and object equality
Byte bRef1 = (byte)10;
Byte bRef2 = (byte)10;
System.out.println(bRef1 == bRef2);           // true
System.out.println(bRef1.equals(bRef2));      // true

Integer iRef1 = 1000;
Integer iRef2 = 1000;
System.out.println(iRef1 == iRef2);           // false
System.out.println(iRef1.equals(iRef2));      // true
```

Each wrapper class also overrides the `hashCode()` method in the `Object` class (see Section 15.1, p. 760). The overriding method returns a hash value based on the primitive value in the wrapper object.

```
int hashCode()
```

```
int index = charObj1.hashCode();
```

Numeric Wrapper Classes

The numeric wrapper classes `Byte`, `Short`, `Integer`, `Long`, `Float`, and `Double` are all subclasses of the abstract class `Number` (see Figure 10.1).

Each numeric wrapper class defines an assortment of constants, including the minimum and maximum value of the corresponding primitive data type:

```
NumericWrapperType.MIN_VALUE
NumericWrapperType.MAX_VALUE
```

The following code retrieves the minimum and maximum values of various numeric types:

```
byte   minByte   = Byte.MIN_VALUE;     // -128
int    maxInt    = Integer.MAX_VALUE;  // 2147483647
double maxDouble = Double.MAX_VALUE;   // 1.7976931348623157e+308
```

Converting Numeric Wrapper Objects to Numeric Primitive Types

Each numeric wrapper class defines the following set of *type*`Value()` methods for converting the primitive value in the wrapper object to a value of any numeric primitive type:

```
byte    byteValue()
short   shortValue()
int     intValue()
long    longValue()
float   floatValue()
double  doubleValue()
```

See also (4b) in Figure 10.2.

The following code shows conversion of values in numeric wrapper objects to any numeric primitive type.

```
Byte    byteObj2   = new Byte((byte) 16);      // Cast mandatory
Integer intObj5    = new Integer(42030);
Double  doubleObj4 = new Double(Math.PI);

short  shortVal  = intObj5.shortValue();       // (1)
long   longVal   = byteObj2.longValue();
int    intVal    = doubleObj4.intValue();      // (2) Truncation
double doubleVal = intObj5.doubleValue();
```

Notice the potential for loss of information at (1) and (2) above, when the primitive value in a wrapper object is converted to a narrower primitive data type.

Converting Strings to Numeric Values

Each numeric wrapper class defines a static method parse*Type*(String str), which returns the primitive numeric value represented by the String object passed as argument. The *Type* in the method name parse*Type* stands for the name of a numeric wrapper class, except for the name of the Integer class which is abbreviated to Int. These methods throw a NumberFormatException if the String parameter is not a valid argument (see (5) in Figure 10.2.)

```
type parseType(String str)

byte   value1 = Byte.parseByte("16");
int    value2 = Integer.parseInt("2010");      // parseInt, not parseInteger.
int    value3 = Integer.parseInt("7UP");       // NumberFormatException
double value4 = Double.parseDouble("3.14");
```

For the integer wrapper types, the overloaded static method parse*Type*() can additionally take a second argument, which can specify the base in which to interpret the string representing the signed integer in the first argument:

```
type parseType(String str, int base)

byte   value6 = Byte.parseByte("1010", 2);     // Decimal value 10
short  value7 = Short.parseShort("012", 8);    // Not "\012". Decimal value 10.
int    value8 = Integer.parseInt("-a", 16);    // Not "-0xa". Decimal value -10.
long   value9 = Long.parseLong("-a", 16);      // Not "-0xa". Decimal value -10L.
```

Converting Integer Values to Strings in Different Notations

The wrapper classes Integer and Long provide static methods for converting integers to string representation in decimal, binary, octal, and hexadecimal notation. Some of these methods from the Integer class are listed here, but analogous methods are also defined in the Long class. Example 10.2 demonstrates use of these methods.

```
static String toBinaryString(int i)
static String toHexString(int i)
static String toOctalString(int i)
```

These three methods return a string representation of the integer argument as an *unsigned* integer in base 2, 16, and 8, respectively, with no extra leading zeroes.

```
static String toString(int i, int base)
static String toString(int i)
```

The first method returns the minus sign '-' as the first character if the integer i is negative. In all cases, it returns the string representation of the *magnitude* of the integer i in the specified base.

The last method is equivalent to the method toString(int i, int base), where the base has the value 10, that returns the string representation as a signed decimal (see also (6a) in Figure 10.2).

Example 10.2 *String Representation of Integers*

```
public class IntegerRepresentation {
  public static void main(String[] args) {
    int positiveInt = +41;    // 051, 0x29
    int negativeInt = -41;    // 037777777727, -051, 0xffffffd7, -0x29

    System.out.println("String representation for decimal value: " + positiveInt);
    integerStringRepresentation(positiveInt);
    System.out.println("String representation for decimal value: " + negativeInt);
    integerStringRepresentation(negativeInt);
  }

  public static void integerStringRepresentation(int i) {
    System.out.println("    Binary:\t" + Integer.toBinaryString(i));
    System.out.println("    Octal:\t"  + Integer.toOctalString(i));
    System.out.println("    Hex:\t"    + Integer.toHexString(i));
    System.out.println("    Decimal:\t"  + Integer.toString(i));

    System.out.println("    Using toString(int i, int base) method:");
    System.out.println("    Base 2:\t" + Integer.toString(i, 2));
    System.out.println("    Base 8:\t" + Integer.toString(i, 8));
    System.out.println("    Base 16:\t"  + Integer.toString(i, 16));
    System.out.println("    Base 10:\t"  + Integer.toString(i, 10));
  }
}
```

Output from the program:

```
String representation for decimal value: 41
    Binary:101001
    Octal:51
    Hex:29
    Decimal:41
    Using toString(int i, int base) method:
    Base 2:101001
    Base 8:51
    Base 16:29
    Base 10:41
String representation for decimal value: -41
    Binary:11111111111111111111111111010111
    Octal:37777777727
    Hex:ffffffd7
    Decimal:-41
    Using toString(int i, int base) method:
    Base 2:-101001
    Base 8:-51
    Base 16:-29
    Base 10:-41
```

The Character Class

The Character class defines a myriad of constants, including the following which represent the minimum and the maximum value of the char type (see Section 2.2, p. 29):

```
Character.MIN_VALUE
Character.MAX_VALUE
```

The Character class also defines a plethora of static methods for handling various attributes of a character, and case issues relating to characters, as defined by the Unicode standard, version 4.0:

```
static int     getNumericValue(char ch)
static boolean isLowerCase(char ch)
static boolean isUpperCase(char ch)
static boolean isTitleCase(char ch)
static boolean isDigit(char ch)
static boolean isLetter(char ch)
static boolean isLetterOrDigit(char ch)
static char    toUpperCase(char ch)
static char    toLowerCase(char ch)
static char    toTitleCase(char ch)
```

The following code converts a lowercase character to an uppercase character:

```
char ch = 'a';
if (Character.isLowerCase(ch)) ch = Character.toUpperCase(ch);
```

The `Boolean` **Class**

The `Boolean` class defines the following wrapper objects to represent the primitive values `true` and `false`, respectively:

```
Boolean.TRUE
Boolean.FALSE
```

 Review Questions

10.4 Which of the following are wrapper classes?

Select the three correct answers.
(a) `java.lang.Void`
(b) `java.lang.Int`
(c) `java.lang.Boolean`
(d) `java.lang.Long`
(e) `java.lang.String`

10.5 Which of the following classes do not extend the `java.lang.Number` class?

Select the two correct answers.
(a) `java.lang.Float`
(b) `java.lang.Byte`
(c) `java.lang.Character`
(d) `java.lang.Boolean`
(e) `java.lang.Short`

10.6 Which of these classes define immutable objects?

Select the three correct answers.
(a) `Character`
(b) `Byte`
(c) `Number`
(d) `Short`
(e) `Object`

10.7 Which of these classes have a one-parameter constructor taking a string?

Select the two correct answers.
(a) `Void`
(b) `Integer`
(c) `Boolean`
(d) `Character`
(e) `Object`

10.8 Which of the wrapper classes have a booleanValue() method?

Select the one correct answer.

(a) All wrapper classes.
(b) All wrapper classes except Void.
(c) All wrapper classes that also implement the compareTo() method.
(d) All wrapper classes extending Number.
(e) Only the class Boolean.

10.9 Which statements are true about wrapper classes?

Select the two correct answers.

(a) String is a wrapper class.
(b) Double has a compareTo() method.
(c) Character has a intValue() method.
(d) Byte extends Number.

10.10 What will the program print when compiled and run?

```java
public class RQ200_60 {
  public static void main(String[] args) {
    Integer i = -10;
    Integer j = -10;
    System.out.print(i==j);
    System.out.print(i.equals(j));
    Integer n = 128;
    Integer m = 128;
    System.out.print(n==m);
    System.out.print(n.equals(m));
  }
}
```

Select the one correct answer.

(a) falsetruefalsetrue
(b) truetruetruetrue
(c) falsetruetruetrue
(d) truetruefalsetrue
(e) None of the above.

10.11 What will the program print when compiled and run?

```java
public class RQ200_70 {
  public static void main(String[] args) {
    Integer i = new Integer(-10);
    Integer j = new Integer(-10);
    Integer k = -10;
    System.out.print(i==j);
    System.out.print(i.equals(j));
    System.out.print(i==k);
    System.out.print(i.equals(k));
  }
}
```

Select the one correct answer.

(a) `falsetruefalsetrue`

(b) `truetruetruetrue`

(c) `falsetruetruetrue`

(d) `truetruefalsetrue`

(e) None of the above.

10.4 The `String` Class

Handling character sequences is supported through three `final` classes: `String`, `StringBuilder` and `StringBuffer`. The Java 2 platform uses the variable-length UTF-16 encoding to store characters in `char` arrays and in the string handling classes. The UTF-16 encoding allows characters whose Unicode values are in the range 0000 to 10FFFF. The `char` type only represents Unicode values in the range 0000 to FFFF, i.e. characters that can be represented in a single 16-bit word. This means that the *supplementary characters* are represented by multiple `char` values, i.e. multiple 16-bit words, when these are stored in a string or a `char` array. The string handling classes provide methods to handle the full range of characters in the UTF-16 encoding, but we will not dwell on the subject in this book.

Immutability

The `String` class implements immutable character strings, which are read-only once the string has been created and initialized, whereas the `StringBuilder` class implements dynamic character strings. The `StringBuffer` class is a *thread-safe* version of the `StringBuilder` class.

This section discusses the class `String` that provides facilities for creating, initializing, and manipulating character strings. The next section discusses the `StringBuilder` and `StringBuffer` classes.

Creating and Initializing Strings

String Literals Revisited

The easiest way of creating a `String` object is using a string literal:

```
String str1 = "You cannot change me!";
```

A string literal is a reference to a `String` object. The value in the `String` object is the character sequence enclosed in the double quotes of the string literal. Since a string literal is a reference, it can be manipulated like any other `String` reference. The reference value of a string literal can be assigned to another `String` reference: the reference `str1` will denote the `String` object with the value `"You cannot change me!"` after the assignment above. A string literal can be used to invoke methods on its `String` object:

```
int strLength = "You cannot change me!".length();  // 21
```

The compiler optimizes handling of string literals (and compile-time constant expressions that evaluate to strings): only one String object is shared by all string-valued constant expressions with the same character sequence. Such strings are said to be *interned*, meaning that they share a unique String object if they have the same content. The String class maintains a private pool where such strings are interned.

```
String str2 = "You cannot change me!";
```

Both String references str1 and str2 denote the same String object, initialized with the character string: "You cannot change me!". So does the reference str3 in the following code. The compile-time evaluation of the constant expression involving the two string literals, results in a string that is already interned:

```
String str3 = "You cannot" + " change me!";  // Compile-time constant expression
```

In the following code, both the references can1 and can2 denote the same String object that contains the string "7Up":

```
String can1 = 7 + "Up";   // Value of compile-time constant expression: "7Up"
String can2 = "7Up";      // "7Up"
```

However, in the code below, the reference can4 will denote a *new* String object that will have the value "7Up" at runtime:

```
String word = "Up";
String can4 = 7 + word;  // Not a compile-time constant expression.
```

The sharing of String objects between string-valued constant expressions poses no problem, since the String objects are immutable. Any operation performed on one String reference will never have any effect on the usage of other references denoting the same object. The String class is also declared final, so that no subclass can override this behavior.

String Constructors

The String class has numerous constructors to create and initialize String objects based on various types of arguments. Here we present a few selected constructors:

Note that using a constructor creates a brand new String object, i.e., using a constructor does not intern the string. A reference to an interned string can be obtained by calling the intern() method in the String class—in practice, there is usually no reason to do so.

In the following code, the String object denoted by str4 is different from the String object passed as argument:

```
String str4 = new String("You cannot change me!");
```

Constructing String objects can also be done from arrays of bytes, arrays of characters, or string builders:

```
byte[] bytes = {97, 98, 98, 97};
```

```
String()
```

This constructor creates a new String object, whose content is the empty string, "".

```
String(String str)
```

This constructor creates a new String object, whose contents are the same as those of the String object passed as argument.

```
String(char[] value)
String(char[] value, int offset, int count)
```

These constructors create a new String object whose contents are copied from a char array. The second constructor allows extraction of a certain number of characters (count) from a given offset in the array.

```
String(StringBuilder builder)
String(StringBuffer buffer)
```

These constructors allow interoperability with the StringBuilder and the StringBuffer class, respectively.

```
char[] characters = {'a', 'b', 'b', 'a'};
StringBuilder strBuilder = new StringBuilder("abba");
//...
String byteStr  = new String(bytes);       // Using array of bytes: "abba"
String charStr  = new String(characters); // Using array of chars: "abba"
String buildStr = new String(strBuilder); // Using string builder: "abba"
```

In Example 10.3, note that the reference str1 does not denote the same String object as the references str4 and str5. Using the new operator with a String constructor always creates a new String object. The expression "You cannot" + words is not a constant expression and, therefore, results in a new String object. The local references str2 and str3 in the main() method and the static reference str1 in the Auxiliary class all denote the same interned string. Object value equality is hardly surprising between these references. It might be tempting to use the operator == for object value equality of string literals, but this is not advisable.

. . . .

Example 10.3   *String Construction and Equality*

```
public class StringConstruction {

    static String str1 = "You cannot change me!";          // Interned

    public static void main(String[] args) {
        String emptyStr = new String();                     // ""
        System.out.println("emptyStr: \"" + emptyStr + "\"");

        String str2 = "You cannot change me!";              // Interned
        String str3 = "You cannot" + " change me!";         // Interned
        String str4 = new String("You cannot change me!");  // New String object
```

```
        String words = " change me!";
        String str5 = "You cannot" + words;                    // New String object

        System.out.println("str1 == str2:      " + (str1 == str2));    // (1) true
        System.out.println("str1.equals(str2): " + str1.equals(str2)); // (2) true

        System.out.println("str1 == str3:      " + (str1 == str3));    // (3) true
        System.out.println("str1.equals(str3): " + str1.equals(str3)); // (4) true

        System.out.println("str1 == str4:      " + (str1 == str4));    // (5) false
        System.out.println("str1.equals(str4): " + str1.equals(str4)); // (6) true

        System.out.println("str1 == str5:      " + (str1 == str5));    // (7) false
        System.out.println("str1.equals(str5): " + str1.equals(str5)); // (8) true

        System.out.println("str1 == Auxiliary.str1:      " +
                      (str1 == Auxiliary.str1));       // (9) true
        System.out.println("str1.equals(Auxiliary.str1): " +
                      str1.equals(Auxiliary.str1));    // (10) true

        System.out.println("\"You cannot change me!\".length(): " +
            "You cannot change me!".length());// (11) 21
    }
}

class Auxiliary {
    static String str1 = "You cannot change me!";        // Interned
}
```

Output from the program:

```
emptyStr: ""
str1 == str2:      true
str1.equals(str2): true
str1 == str3:      true
str1.equals(str3): true
str1 == str4:      false
str1.equals(str4): true
str1 == str5:      false
str1.equals(str5): true
str1 == Auxiliary.str1:      true
str1.equals(Auxiliary.str1): true
"You cannot change me!".length(): 21
```

The CharSequence Interface

This interface is implemented by all three classes: String, StringBuilder and String-Buffer. Many methods in these classes accept arguments of this interface type, and specify it as their return type. This facilitates interoperability between these classes. This interface defines the following methods:

`char charAt(int index)`

A character at a particular index in a sequence can be read using the charAt() method. The first character is at index 0 and the last one at index one less than the number of characters in the string. If the index value is not valid, an Index-OutOfBoundsException is thrown.

`int length()`

This method returns the number of char values in this sequence.

`CharSequence subSequence(int start, int end)`

This method returns a new CharSequence that is a subsequence of this sequence. Characters from the current sequence are read from index start to the index end-1, inclusive.

`String toString()`

This method returns a string containing the characters in this sequence in the same order as this sequence.

Reading Characters from a String

`char charAt(int index)`

This method is defined in the CharSequence interface which the String class implements (p. 442).

`void getChars(int srcBegin, int srcEnd, char[] dst, int dstBegin)`

This method copies characters from the current string into the destination character array. Characters from the current string are read from index srcBegin to the index srcEnd-1, inclusive. They are copied into the destination array (dst), starting at index dstBegin and ending at index dstbegin+(srcEnd-srcBegin)-1. The number of characters copied is (srcEnd-srcBegin). An IndexOutOfBounds-Exception is thrown if the indices do not meet the criteria for the operation.

`int length()`

This method is defined in the CharSequence interface which the String class implements (p. 442).

`boolean isEmpty()`

This method returns true if the length of the string is 0, otherwise false.

Example 10.4 uses some of these methods at (3), (4), (5), and (6). The program prints the frequency of a character in a string and illustrates copying from a string into a character array.

Example 10.4 *Reading Characters from a String*

```
public class ReadingCharsFromString {
  public static void main(String[] args) {
    int[] frequencyData = new int [Character.MAX_VALUE];      // (1)
    String str = "You cannot change me!";                     // (2)

    // Count the frequency of each character in the string.
    for (int i = 0; i < str.length(); i++)                    // (3)
      try {
        frequencyData[str.charAt(i)]++;                        // (4)
      } catch(StringIndexOutOfBoundsException e) {
        System.out.println("Index error detected: "+ i +" not in range.");
      }

    // Print the character frequency.
    System.out.println("Character frequency for string: \"" + str + "\"");
    for (int i = 0; i < frequencyData.length; i++)
      if (frequencyData[i] != 0)
        System.out.println((char)i + " (code "+ i +"): " +
            frequencyData[i]);

    System.out.println("Copying into a char array:");
    char[] destination = new char [str.length()];
    str.getChars( 0,           7, destination, 0);             // (5) "You can"
    str.getChars(10, str.length(), destination, 7);           // (6) " change me!"

    // Print the character array.
    for (int i = 0; i < 7 + (str.length() - 10); i++)
      System.out.print(destination[i]);
    System.out.println();
  }
}
```

Output from the program:

```
Character Frequency for string: "You cannot change me!"
  (code 32): 3
! (code 33): 1
Y (code 89): 1
a (code 97): 2
c (code 99): 2
e (code 101): 2
g (code 103): 1
h (code 104): 1
m (code 109): 1
n (code 110): 3
o (code 111): 2
t (code 116): 1
u (code 117): 1
Copying into a char array:
You can change me!
```

In Example 10.4, the frequencyData array at (1) stores the frequency of each character that can occur in a string. The string in question is declared at (2). Since a char value is promoted to an int value in arithmetic expressions, it can be used as an index in an array. Each element in the frequencyData array functions as a frequency counter for the character corresponding to the index value of the element:

```
frequencyData[str.charAt(i)]++;                    // (4)
```

The calls to the getChars() method at (5) and (6) copy particular substrings from the string into designated places in the destination array, before printing the whole character array.

We leave it as an exercise for the reader to implement a solution for character frequencies using a Map (see Section 15.8, p. 821).

Comparing Strings

Characters are compared based on their Unicode values.

```
boolean test = 'a' < 'b';     // true since 0x61 < 0x62
```

Two strings are compared *lexicographically,* as in a dictionary or telephone directory, by successively comparing their corresponding characters at each position in the two strings, starting with the characters in the first position. The string "abba" is less than "aha", since the second character 'b' in the string "abba" is less than the second character 'h' in the string "aha". The characters in the first position in each of these strings are equal. See also *The Comparator<E> Interface*, p. 771.

The following public methods can be used for comparing strings:

```
boolean equals(Object obj)
boolean equalsIgnoreCase(String str2)
```

The String class overrides the equals() method from the Object class. The String class equals() method implements String object value equality as two String objects having the same sequence of characters. The equalsIgnoreCase() method does the same, but ignores the case of the characters.

```
int compareTo(String str2)
```

The String class implements the Comparable<String> interface. The compareTo() method compares the two strings and returns a value based on the outcome of the comparison:

- the value 0, if this string is equal to the string argument
- a value less than 0, if this string is lexicographically less than the string argument
- a value greater than 0, if this string is lexicographically greater than the string argument

Here are some examples of string comparisons:

```
String strA = new String("The Case was thrown out of Court");
String strB = new String("the case was thrown out of court");

boolean b1 = strA.equals(strB);              // false
boolean b2 = strA.equalsIgnoreCase(strB);    // true

String str1 = new String("abba");
String str2 = new String("aha");

int compVal1 = str1.compareTo(str2);         // negative value => str1 < str2
```

Character Case in a String

```
String toUpperCase()
String toUpperCase(Locale locale)
String toLowerCase()
String toLowerCase(Locale locale)
```

Note that the original string is returned if none of the characters need their case changed, but a new String object is returned if any of the characters need their case changed. These methods delegate the character-by-character case conversion to corresponding methods from the Character class.

These methods use the rules of the (default) *locale* (returned by the method Locale.getDefault()), which embodies the idiosyncrasies of a specific geographical, political, or cultural region regarding number/date/currency formats, character classification, alphabet (including case idiosyncrasies), and other localizations (see Section 12.1, p. 532).

Example of case in strings:

```
String strA = new String("The Case was thrown out of Court");
String strB = new String("the case was thrown out of court");

String strC = strA.toLowerCase();  // Case conversion => New String object:
                                   // "the case was thrown out of court"
String strD = strB.toLowerCase();  // No case conversion => Same String object
String strE = strA.toUpperCase();  // Case conversion => New String object:
                                   // "THE CASE WAS THROWN OUT OF COURT"

boolean test1 = strC == strA;      // false
boolean test2 = strD == strB;      // true
boolean test3 = strE == strA;      // false
```

Concatenation of Strings

Concatenation of two strings results in a string that consists of the characters of the first string followed by the characters of the second string. The overloaded operator + for string concatenation is discussed in Section 5.6 on page 180. In addition, the following method can be used to concatenate two strings:

```
String concat(String str)
```

The concat() method does not modify the String object on which it is invoked, as String objects are immutable. Instead the concat() method returns a reference to a brand new String object:

```
String billboard = "Just";
billboard.concat(" lost in space.");  // (1) Returned reference value not stored.
System.out.println(billboard);         // (2) "Just"
billboard = billboard.concat(" advertise").concat(" here.");  // (3) Chaining.
System.out.println(billboard);         // (4) "Just advertise here."
```

At (1), the reference value of the String object returned by the method concat() is not stored. This String object becomes inaccessible after (1). We see that the reference billboard still denotes the string literal "Just" at (2).

At (3), two method calls to the concat() method are *chained*. The first call returns a reference value to a new String object whose content is "Just advertise". The second method call is invoked on this String object using the reference value that was returned in the first method call. The second call results in yet another String object whose content is "Just advertise here.". The reference value of this String object is assigned to the reference billboard. Because String objects are immutable, the creation of the temporary String object with the content "Just advertise" is inevitable at (3).

The compiler uses a string builder to avoid this overhead of temporary String objects when applying the string concatenation operator (p. 460).

A simple way to convert any primitive value to its string representation is by concatenating it with the empty string (""), using the string concatenation operator (+) (see also (6c) in Figure 10.2):

```
String strRepresentation = "" + 2008;  // String conversion: "2008" <---- 2008
```

Application of the concatenation operator may result in string conversion being performed on one of the operands, as shown above. The string concatenation operator (+) is discussed in Section 5.7, p. 185. Some more examples of string concatenation follow:

```
String motto = new String("Program once");    // (1)
motto += ", execute everywhere.";             // (2)
motto = motto.concat(" Don't bet on it!");    // (3)
```

Note that a new String object is assigned to the reference motto each time in the assignment at (1), (2), and (3). The String object with the contents "Program once" becomes inaccessible after the assignment at (2). The String object with the contents "Program once, execute everywhere." becomes inaccessible after (3). The reference motto denotes the String object with the following contents after execution of the assignment at (3):

```
"Program once, execute everywhere. Don't bet on it!"
```

Searching for Characters and Substrings

The following overloaded methods can be used to find the index of a character or the start index of a substring in a string. These methods search *forward* toward the end of the string. In other words, the index of the *first* occurrence of the character or substring is found. If the search is unsuccessful, the value –1 is returned.

```
int indexOf(int ch)
int indexOf(int ch, int fromIndex)
```

The first method finds the index of the first occurrence of the argument character in a string. The second method finds the index of the first occurrence of the argument character in a string, starting at the index specified in the second argument. If the index argument is negative, the index is assumed to be 0. If the index argument is greater than the length of the string, it is effectively considered to be equal to the length of the string; resulting in the value -1 being returned.

```
int indexOf(String str)
int indexOf(String str, int fromIndex)
```

The first method finds the start index of the first occurrence of the substring argument in a string. The second method finds the start index of the first occurrence of the substring argument in a string, starting at the index specified in the second argument.

The String class also defines a set of methods that search for a character or a substring, but the search is *backwards* toward the start of the string. In other words, the index of the *last* occurrence of the character or substring is found.

```
int lastIndexOf(int ch)
int lastIndexOf(int ch, int fromIndex)
int lastIndexOf(String str)
int lastIndexOf(String str, int fromIndex)
```

The following methods can be used to create a string in which all occurrences of a character or a subsequence in a string have been replaced with another character or subsequence:

```
String replace(char oldChar, char newChar)
String replace(CharSequence target, CharSequence replacement)
```

The first method returns a new String object that is a result of replacing all occurrences of the oldChar in the current string with the newChar. The current string is returned if no occurrences of the oldChar can be found.

The second method returns a new String object that is a result of replacing all occurrences of the character sequence target in the current string with the character sequence replacement. The current string is returned if no occurrences of the target can be found.

```
boolean contains(CharSequence cs)
```

This method returns true if the current string contains the specified character sequence, otherwise false.

Examples of search methods:

```
String funStr = "Java Jives";
//                  0123456789

int jInd1a = funStr.indexOf('J');           // 0
int jInd1b = funStr.indexOf('J', 1);        // 5
int jInd2a = funStr.lastIndexOf('J');       // 5
int jInd2b = funStr.lastIndexOf('J', 4);    // 0

String banner = "One man, One vote";
//               01234567890123456

int subInd1a = banner.indexOf("One");          // 0
int subInd1b = banner.indexOf("One", 3);       // 9
int subInd2a = banner.lastIndexOf("One");      // 9
int subInd2b = banner.lastIndexOf("One", 10);  // 9
int subInd2c = banner.lastIndexOf("One", 8);   // 0
int subInd2d = banner.lastIndexOf("One", 2);   // 0

String newStr = funStr.replace('J', 'W');          // "Wava Wives"
String newBanner = banner.replace("One", "No");    // "No man, No vote"
boolean found1 = banner.contains("One");           // true
boolean found2 = newBanner.contains("One");        // false
```

Extracting Substrings

> `String trim()`

This method can be used to create a string where white space (in fact all characters with values less than or equal to the space character '\u0020') from the front (leading) and the end (trailing) of a string has been removed.

> `String substring(int startIndex)`
> `String substring(int startIndex, int endIndex)`

The String class provides these overloaded methods to extract substrings from a string. A new String object containing the substring is created and returned. The first method extracts the string that starts at the given index startIndex and extends to the end of the string. The end of the substring can be specified by using a second argument endIndex that is the index of the first character *after* the substring, i.e., the last character in the substring is at index endIndex-1. If the index value is not valid, a StringIndexOutOfBoundsException is thrown.

Examples of extracting substrings:

```
String utopia = "\t\n  Java Nation \n\t  ";
utopia = utopia.trim();                    // "Java Nation"
utopia = utopia.substring(5);              // "Nation"
String radioactive = utopia.substring(3,6); // "ion"
```

Converting Primitive Values and Objects to Strings

The String class overrides the toString() method in the Object class and returns the String object itself:

```
String toString()
```

This method is defined in the CharSequence interface which the String class implements (p. 442).

The String class also defines a set of static overloaded valueOf() methods to convert objects and primitive values into strings.

```
static String valueOf(Object obj)
static String valueOf(char[] charArray)
static String valueOf(boolean b)
static String valueOf(char c)
```

All these methods return a string representing the given parameter value. A call to the method with the parameter obj is equivalent to obj.toString(). The boolean values true and false are converted into the strings "true" and "false". The char parameter is converted to a string consisting of a single character.

```
static String valueOf(int i)
static String valueOf(long l)
static String valueOf(float f)
static String valueOf(double d)
```

The static valueOf() method that accepts a primitive value as argument is equivalent to the static toString() method in the corresponding wrapper class for each of the primitive data types (see also (6a) and (6b) in Figure 10.2 on p. 393).

Note that there are no valueOf() methods that accept a byte or a short.

Examples of string conversions:

```
String anonStr   = String.valueOf("Make me a string.");    // "Make me a string."
String charStr   = String.valueOf(new char[] {'a', 'h', 'a'});// "aha"
String boolTrue  = String.valueOf(true);                   // "true"
String doubleStr = String.valueOf(Math.PI);                // "3.141592653589793"
```

Formatting Values

The String class provides support for *formatted text representation* of primitive values and objects through its overloaded format() methods. Formatting of values is covered extensively in Section 12.7, p. 593.

```
static String format(String format, Object... args)
static String format(Locale l, String format, Object... args)
```

These methods return a string that is a result of applying the specified format string to the values in the vararg array args.

Pattern Matching

Methods for string pattern matching take an argument that specifies a regular expression (see Section 12.6, p. 554).

Matching

The following method attempts to match the current string against the specified regular expression. The call

```
str.matches(regexStr);
```

is equivalent to the call

```
Pattern.matches(regexStr, str);
```

See *The* `java.util.regex.Pattern` *Class*, p. 562, for details.

> `boolean matches(String regexStr)`
>
> The method only returns `true` if the *entire* string matches the regular expression.

Matching and Replacing

The following methods can be used to replace substrings that match a given regular expression. The call

```
str.replaceFirst(regexStr, replacement);
```

is equivalent to the call

```
Pattern.compile(regexStr).matcher(str).replaceFirst(replacement);
```

See *The* `java.util.regex.Matcher` *Class*, p. 570, for details.

> `String replaceFirst(String regexStr, String replacement)`
> `String replaceAll(String regexStr, String replacement)`
>
> The first method returns a new `String` by replacing the *first* substring of this string that matches the given regular expression with the given replacement.
>
> The second method returns a new `String` by replacing *each* substring of this string that matches the given regular expression with the given replacement.

Splitting

The `split()` method can be called on a string to create an array by splitting the string according to a regular expression pattern (see Section 12.6, p. 554). Given that the reference `input` is of type `String`, the call

```
input.split(regexStr, limit);
```

is equivalent to the call

```
Pattern.compile(regexStr).split(input, limit);
```

Splitting is covered in *The java.util.regex.Pattern Class*, p. 563.

```
String[] split(String regexStr)
String[] split(String regexStr, int limit)
```

The method splits the current string around matches of the specified pattern. The limit determines how many times the pattern will be applied to the string to create the array.

Other miscellaneous methods exist for reading the string characters into an array of characters (toCharArray()), converting the string into an array of bytes (getBytes()), and searching for prefixes (startsWith()) and suffixes (endsWith()) of the string. The method hashCode() can be used to compute a hash value based on the characters in the string.

Review Questions

10.12   Which of the following operators cannot have an operand of type String?

Select the two correct answers.
(a) +
(b) -
(c) +=
(d) .
(e) &

10.13   Which expression will extract the substring "kap", given the following declaration:

```
String str = "kakapo";
```

Select the one correct answer.
(a) str.substring(2, 2)
(b) str.substring(2, 3)
(c) str.substring(2, 4)
(d) str.substring(2, 5)
(e) str.substring(3, 3)

10.14   What will be the result of attempting to compile and run the following code?

```
class MyClass {
  public static void main(String[] args) {
    String str1 = "str1";
    String str2 = "str2";
    String str3 = "str3";

    str1.concat(str2);
    System.out.println(str3.concat(str1));
  }
}
```

Select the one correct answer.

(a) The code will fail to compile because the expression str3.concat(str1) will not result in a valid argument for the println() method.
(b) The program will print str3str1str2, when run.
(c) The program will print str3, when run.
(d) The program will print str3str1, when run.
(e) The program will print str3str2, when run.

10.15 Which statement about the trim() method of the String class is true?

Select the one correct answer.

(a) It returns a string where the leading white space of the original string has been removed.
(b) It returns a string where the trailing white space of the original string has been removed.
(c) It returns a string where both the leading and trailing white space of the original string has been removed.
(d) It returns a string where all the white space of the original string has been removed.
(e) None of the above.

10.16 Which statements are true?

Select the two correct answers.

(a) String objects are immutable.
(b) Subclasses of the String class can be mutable.
(c) All wrapper classes are declared final.
(d) All objects have a public method named clone.
(e) The expression ((new StringBuilder()) instanceof String) is always true.

10.17 Which of these expressions are legal?

Select the four correct answers.
(a) "co".concat("ol")
(b) ("co" + "ol")
(c) ('c' + 'o' + 'o' + 'l')
(d) ("co" + new String('o' + 'l'))
(e) ("co" + new String("co"))

10.18 What will be the result of attempting to compile and run the following program?

```
public class RefEq {
  public static void main(String[] args) {
    String s = "ab" + "12";
    String t = "ab" + 12;
    String u = new String("ab12");
    System.out.println((s==t) + " " + (s==u));
  }
}
```

Select the one correct answer.

(a) The program will fail to compile.
(b) The program will print false false, when run.
(c) The program will print false true, when run.
(d) The program will print true false, when run.
(e) The program will print true true, when run.

10.19   Which of these parameter lists can be found in a constructor of the String class?

Select the three correct answers.

(a) ()
(b) (int capacity)
(c) (char[] data)
(d) (String str)

10.20   Which method is not defined in the String class?

Select the one correct answer.

(a) trim()
(b) length()
(c) concat(String)
(d) hashCode()
(e) reverse()

10.21   Which statement about the charAt() method of the String class is true?

Select the one correct answer.

(a) The charAt() method takes a char value as an argument.
(b) The charAt() method returns a Character object.
(c) The expression ("abcdef").charAt(3) is illegal.
(d) The expression "abcdef".charAt(3) evaluates to the character 'd'.
(e) The index of the first character is 1.

10.22   Which expression will evaluate to true?

Select the one correct answer.

(a) "hello: there!".equals("hello there")
(b) "HELLO THERE".equals("hello there")
(c) ("hello".concat("there")).equals("hello there")
(d) "Hello There".compareTo("hello there") == 0
(e) "Hello there".toLowerCase().equals("hello there")

10.23   What will the following program print when run?

```
public class Search {
  public static void main(String[] args) {
    String s = "Contentment!";
    int middle = s.length()/2;
```

```
        String nt = s.substring(middle-1, middle+1);
        System.out.println(s.lastIndexOf(nt, middle));
    }
}
```

Select the one correct answer.

(a) 2

(b) 4

(c) 5

(d) 7

(e) 9

(f) 11

10.24 What will the following program print when run?

```
public class Uppity {
  public static void main(String[] args) {
    String str1 = "lower", str2 = "LOWER", str3 = "UPPER";
    str1.toUpperCase();
    str1.replace("LOWER","UPPER");
    System.out.println((str1.equals(str2)) + " " + (str1.equals(str3)));
  }
}
```

Select the one correct answer.

(a) The program will print false true.

(b) The program will print false false.

(c) The program will print true false.

(d) The program will print true true.

(e) The program will fail to compile.

(f) The program will compile, but throw an exception at runtime.

10.25 What will the following program print when run?

```
public class FunCharSeq {
  private static void putO(String s1) {
    s1 = s1.trim();
    s1 += "O";
  }

  public static void main(String[] args) {
    String s1 = " W ";
    putO(s1);
    s1.concat("W");
    System.out.println("|" + s1 + "|");
  }
}
```

Select the one correct answer.

(a) |WOW|

(b) | WW |

(c) | WO |

(d) | W |

(e) The program will fail to compile.

(f) The program will compile, but throw an exception at runtime.

10.5 The `StringBuilder` and the `StringBuffer` Classes

Thread-Safety

The classes `StringBuilder` and `StringBuffer` implement *mutable* sequences of characters. Both classes support the same operations. However, the `StringBuffer` class is the *thread-safe* analog of the `StringBuilder` class. Certain operations on a string buffer are synchronized, so that when used by multiple threads, these operations are performed in an orderly way (see Section 13.5, p. 626). Note that a `String` object is also thread-safe—because it is immutable, a thread cannot change its state. String builders are preferred when heavy modification of character sequences is involved and synchronization of operations is not important.

Although the rest of this section is about string builders, it is equally applicable to string buffers.

Mutability

In contrast to the `String` class, which implements immutable character sequences, the `StringBuilder` class implements mutable character sequences. Not only can the character sequences in a string builder be changed, but the capacity of the string builder can also change dynamically. The *capacity* of a string builder is the maximum number of characters that a string builder can accommodate before its size is automatically augmented.

Although there is a close relationship between objects of the `String` and `StringBuilder` classes, these are two independent `final` classes, both directly extending the `Object` class. Hence, `String` references cannot be stored (or cast) to `StringBuilder` references, and vice versa.

The `StringBuilder` class provides various facilities for manipulating string builders:

- constructing string builders
- changing, deleting, and reading characters in string builders
- constructing strings from string builders
- appending, inserting, and deleting in string builders
- controlling string builder capacity

Constructing String Builders

The `final` class `StringBuilder` provides four constructors that create and initialize `StringBuilder` objects and set their initial capacity.

```
StringBuilder(String str)
StringBuilder(CharSequence charSeq)
```

The contents of the new `StringBuilder` object are the same as the contents of the `String` object or the character sequence passed as argument. The initial capacity of the string builder is set to the length of the argument sequence, plus room for 16 more characters.

```
StringBuilder(int length)
```

The new `StringBuilder` object has no content. The initial capacity of the string builder is set to the value of the argument `length`, which cannot be less than 0.

```
StringBuilder()
```

This constructor also creates a new `StringBuilder` object with no content. The initial capacity of the string builder is set for 16 characters.

Examples of `StringBuilder` object creation and initialization:

```
StringBuilder strBuilder1 = new StringBuilder("Phew!");  // "Phew!", capacity 21
StringBuilder strBuilder2 = new StringBuilder(10);       // "", capacity 10
StringBuilder strBuilder3 = new StringBuilder();         // "", capacity 16
```

Reading and Changing Characters in String Builders

```
int length()
```
                        From the `CharSequence` interface (p. 442).

Returns the number of characters in the string builder.

```
char charAt(int index)
void setCharAt(int index, char ch)
```
                        From the `CharSequence` interface (p. 442).

These methods read and change the character at a specified index in the string builder, respectively. The first character is at index 0 and the last one at index one less than the number of characters in the string builder. A `StringIndexOutOfBoundsException` is thrown if the index is not valid.

```
CharSequence subSequence(int start, int end)
```

This method is implemented as part of the `CharSequence` interface (p. 442).

The following is an example of reading and changing string builder contents:

```
StringBuilder strBuilder = new StringBuilder("Javv");      // "Javv", capacity 20
strBuilder.setCharAt(strBuilder.length()-1, strBuilder.charAt(1)); // "Java"
```

Constructing Strings from String Builders

The StringBuilder class overrides the toString() method from the Object class (see also the CharSequence interface, p. 442). It returns the contents of a string builder in a String object.

```
String fromBuilder = strBuilder.toString();                          // "Java"
```

Differences between the String and StringBuilder Classes

Since the StringBuilder class does not override the equals() method from the Object class, nor does it implement the Comparable interface, the contents of string builders should be converted to String objects for string comparison.

The StringBuilder class also does not override the hashCode() method from the Object class. Again, a string builder can be converted to a String object in order to obtain a hash value.

Appending, Inserting, and Deleting Characters in String Builders

Appending, inserting, and deleting characters automatically results in adjustment of the string builder's capacity, if necessary. The indices passed as arguments in the methods must be equal to or greater than 0. A StringIndexOutOfBoundsException is thrown if an index is not valid.

Note that the methods in this subsection return the reference value of the modified stringbuilder, making it convenient to chain calls to these methods.

Appending Characters to a String Builder

The overloaded method append() can be used to *append* characters at the *end* of a string builder.

```
StringBuilder append(Object obj)
```

The obj argument is converted to a string as if by the static method call String.valueOf(obj), and this string is appended to the current string builder.

```
StringBuilder append(String str)
StringBuilder append(CharSequence charSeq)
StringBuilder append(CharSequence charSeq, int start, int end)
StringBuilder append(char[] charArray)
StringBuilder append(char[] charArray, int offset, int length)
StringBuilder append(char c)
```

These methods allow characters from various sources to be appended to the end of the current string builder.

```
StringBuilder append(boolean b)
StringBuilder append(int i)
StringBuilder append(long l)
StringBuilder append(float f)
StringBuilder append(double d)
```

These methods convert the primitive value of the argument to a string by applying the static method String.valueOf() to the argument, before appending the result to the string builder.

Inserting Characters in a String Builder

The overloaded method `insert()` can be used to *insert* characters at a *given position* in a string builder.

```
StringBuilder insert(int offset, Object obj)
StringBuilder insert(int dstOffset, CharSequence seq)
StringBuilder insert(int dstOffset, CharSequence seq, int start, int end)
StringBuilder insert(int offset, String str)
StringBuilder insert(int offset, char[] charArray)
StringBuilder insert(int offset, char c)
StringBuilder insert(int offset, boolean b)
StringBuilder insert(int offset, int i)
StringBuilder insert(int offset, long l)
StringBuilder insert(int offset, float f)
StringBuilder insert(int offset, double d)
```

The argument is converted, if necessary, by applying the static method `String.valueOf()`. The offset argument specifies where the characters are to be inserted and must be greater than or equal to 0.

Deleting Characters in a String Builder

The following methods can be used to delete characters from *specific positions* in a string builder:

```
StringBuilder deleteCharAt(int index)
StringBuilder delete(int start, int end)
```

The first method deletes a character at a specified index in the string builder, contracting the string builder by one character. The second method deletes a substring, which is specified by the start index (inclusive) and the end index (exclusive).

Among other miscellaneous methods included in the class `StringBuilder` is the following method, which reverses the contents of a string builder:

```
StringBuilder reverse()
```

Examples of appending, inserting, and deleting in string builders:

```
StringBuilder builder = new StringBuilder("banana split");   // "banana split"
builder.delete(4,12);                                        // "bana"
builder.append(42);                                          // "bana42"
builder.insert(4,"na");                                      // "banana42"
builder.reverse();                                           // "24ananab"
builder.deleteCharAt(builder.length()-1);                    // "24anana"
builder.append('s');                                         // "24ananas"
```

All the previous methods modify the contents of the string builder and also return a reference value denoting the string builder. This allows *chaining* of method calls. The method calls invoked on the string builder denoted by the reference `builder` can be chained as follows, giving the same result:

```
builder.delete(4,12).append(42).insert(4,"na").reverse().
    deleteCharAt(builder.length()-1).append('s');        // "24ananas"
```

The method calls in the chain are evaluated from left to right, so that the previous chain of calls is interpreted as follows:

```
(((((builder.delete(4,12)).append(42)).insert(4,"na")).reverse()).
    deleteCharAt(builder.length()-1)).append('s');       // "24ananas"
```

Each method call returns the reference value of the modified string builder. This value is used to invoke the next method. The string builder remains denoted by the reference builder.

The compiler uses string builders to implement the string concatenation, +. The following example code of string concatenation

```
String str1 = 4 + "U" + "Only";                          // (1) "4UOnly"
```

is equivalent to the following code using one string builder:

```
String str2 = new StringBuilder().
              append(4).append("U").append("Only").toString(); // (2)
```

The code at (2) does not create any temporary String objects when concatenating several strings, since a single StringBuilder object is modified and finally converted to a String object.

Controlling String Builder Capacity

```
int capacity()
```

Returns the current capacity of the string builder, i.e., the number of characters the current builder can accommodate without allocating a new, larger array to hold characters.

```
void ensureCapacity(int minCapacity)
```

Ensures that there is room for at least a minCapacity number of characters. It expands the string builder, depending on the current capacity of the builder.

```
void trimToSize()
```

Attempts to reduce the storage used for the character sequence. It may affect the capacity of the string builder.

```
void setLength(int newLength)
```

This method ensures that the actual number of characters, i.e., the length of the string builder, is exactly equal to the value of the newLength argument, which must be greater than or equal to 0. This operation can result in the string being truncated or padded with null characters ('\u0000').

This method only affects the capacity of the string builder if the value of the parameter newLength is greater than current capacity.

One use of this method is to clear the string builder:

```
builder.setLength(0);       // Empty the builder.
```

Review Questions

10.26   What will be the result of attempting to compile and run the following program?

```java
public class MyClass {
  public static void main(String[] args) {
    String s = "hello";
    StringBuilder sb = new StringBuilder(s);
    sb.reverse();
    if (s == sb) System.out.println("a");
    if (s.equals(sb)) System.out.println("b");
    if (sb.equals(s)) System.out.println("c");
  }
}
```

Select the one correct answer.

(a) The code will fail to compile because the constructor of the String class is not called properly.
(b) The code will fail to compile because the expression (s == sb) is illegal.
(c) The code will fail to compile because the expression (s.equals(sb)) is illegal.
(d) The program will print c, when run.
(e) The program will throw a ClassCastException, when run.

10.27   What will be the result of attempting to compile and run the following program?

```java
public class MyClass {
  public static void main(String[] args) {
    StringBuilder sb = new StringBuilder("have a nice day");
    sb.setLength(6);
    System.out.println(sb);
  }
}
```

Select the one correct answer.

(a) The code will fail to compile because there is no method named setLength in the StringBuilder class.
(b) The code will fail to compile because the StringBuilder reference sb is not a legal argument to the println() method.
(c) The program will throw a StringIndexOutOfBoundsException, when run.
(d) The program will print have a nice day, when run.
(e) The program will print have a, when run.
(f) The program will print ce day, when run.

10.28   Which of these parameter lists can be found in a constructor of the StringBuilder class?

Select the three correct answers.

(a) ()
(b) (int capacity)

    (c) `(char[] data)`
    (d) `(String str)`

10.29   Which method is not defined in the `StringBuilder` class?

Select the one correct answer.
    (a) `trim()`
    (b) `length()`
    (c) `append(String)`
    (d) `reverse()`
    (e) `setLength(int)`

10.30   What will be the result of attempting to compile and run the following program?

```java
public class StringMethods {
  public static void main(String[] args) {
    String str = new String("eeny");
    str.concat(" meeny");
    StringBuilder strBuilder = new StringBuilder(" miny");
    strBuilder.append(" mo");
    System.out.println(str + strBuilder);
  }
}
```

Select the one correct answer.
    (a) The program will fail to compile.
    (b) The program will print eeny meeny miny mo, when run.
    (c) The program will print meeny miny mo, when run.
    (d) The program will print eeny miny mo, when run.
    (e) The program will print eeny meeny miny, when run.

10.31   What will the following program print when run?

```java
public class PeskyCharSeq {
  public static void main (String[] args) {
    StringBuilder sb1 = new StringBuilder("WOW");
    StringBuilder sb2 = new StringBuilder(sb1);
    System.out.println((sb1==sb2) + " " + sb1.equals(sb2));
  }
}
```

Select the one correct answer.
    (a) The program will print false true.
    (b) The program will print false false.
    (c) The program will print true false.
    (d) The program will print true true.
    (e) The program will fail to compile.
    (f) The program will compile, but throws an exception at runtime.

10.32 What will the following program print when run?

```java
public class MoreCharSeq {
  public static void main (String[] args) {
    String s1 = "WOW";
    StringBuilder s2 = new StringBuilder(s1);
    String s3 = new String(s2);
    System.out.println((s1.hashCode() == s2.hashCode()) + " " +
                       (s1.hashCode() == s3.hashCode()));
  }
}
```

Select the one correct answer.

(a) The program will print `false true`.
(b) The program will print `false false`.
(c) The program will print `true false`.
(d) The program will print `true true`.
(e) The program will fail to compile.
(f) The program will compile, but throw an exception at runtime.

10.33 What will the following program print when run?

```java
public class CharSeq {
  public static void main (String[] args) {
    String cs1 = "JAVA";
    StringBuilder cs2 = new StringBuilder(cs1);
    System.out.println(cs1.compareTo(cs2) == cs2.compareTo(cs1));
  }
}
```

Select the one correct answer.

(a) The program will print `false`.
(b) The program will print `true`.
(c) The program will fail to compile.
(d) The program will compile, but throw an exception at runtime.

10.34 What will the following program print when run?

```java
public class Appendage {
  private static void putO(StringBuilder s1) {
    s1 = s1.append("O");
  }

  public static void main(String[] args) {
    StringBuilder s1 = new StringBuilder("W");
    putO(s1);
    s1.append("W!");
    System.out.println(s1);
  }
}
```

Select the one correct answer.

(a) The program will print `WW!`.

(b) The program will print WOW!.
(c) The program will print W.
(d) The program will fail to compile.
(e) The program will compile, but throw an exception at runtime.

10.35 What will the following program print when run?

```java
public class Chains {
  private static StringBuilder putO(StringBuilder s1) {
    s1.append("O");
    return s1;
  }

  public static void main(String[] args) {
    StringBuilder s1 = new StringBuilder("W");
    boolean status = putO(s1).append("W!").toString().compareTo("WOW!") != 0;
    System.out.println(s1 + " " + status);
  }
}
```

Select the one correct answer.

(a) The program will print WOW! false.
(b) The program will print WOW! true.
(c) The program will print WW! true.
(d) The program will fail to compile.
(e) The program will compile, but throw an exception at runtime.

 Chapter Summary

The following information was included in this chapter:

- discussion of the Object class, which is the most fundamental class in Java
- discussion of the wrapper classes, which not only allow primitive values to be treated as objects, but also contain useful methods for converting values
- discussion of the String class, showing how immutable strings are created and used
- discussion of the StringBuilder class, showing how dynamic strings are created and manipulated
- comparison of the String, StringBuilder, and StringBuffer classes

Programming Exercises

10.1 Create a class named `Pair`, which aggregates two arbitrary objects. Implement the `equals()` and `hashCode()` methods in such a way that a `Pair` object is identical to another `Pair` object if, and only if, the pair of constituent objects are identical. Make the `toString()` implementation return the textual representation of both the constituent objects in a `Pair` object. Objects of the `Pair` class should be immutable.

10.2 A palindrome is a text phrase that is spelled the same backward and forward. The word *redivider* is a palindrome, since the word would be spelled the same even if the character sequence were reversed. Write a program that takes a string as an argument and reports whether the string is a palindrome.

Files and Streams

●●

Exam Objectives

3.2 Given a scenario involving navigating file systems, reading from files, or writing to files, or interacting with the user, develop the correct solution using the following classes (sometimes in combination), from `java.io`: `BufferedReader`, `BufferedWriter`, `File`, `FileReader`, `FileWriter`, `PrintWriter`, and `Console`.

3.3 Develop code that serializes and/or de-serializes objects using the following APIs from `java.io`: `DataInputStream`, `DataOutputStream`, `FileInputStream`, `FileOutputStream`, `ObjectInputStream`, `ObjectOutputStream` and `Serializable`.

Supplementary Objectives

- Distinguish between byte and character streams, and identify the roots of their inheritance hierarchies.
- Write code to use specific character encodings.

11.1   Input and Output

The java.io package provides an extensive library of classes for dealing with input and output. Java provides *streams* as a general mechanism for dealing with data I/O. Streams implement *sequential access* of data. There are two kinds of streams: *byte streams* and *character streams* (a.k.a. *binary streams* and *text streams*, respectively). An *input stream* is an object that an application can use to read a sequence of data, and an *output stream* is an object that an application can use to write a sequence of data. An *input stream* acts as a *source* of data, and an *output stream* acts as a *destination* of data. The following entities can act as both input and output streams:

- an array of bytes or characters
- a file
- a *pipe* (a mechanism by which a program can communicate data to another program during execution)
- a network connection

Streams can be *chained* with *filters* to provide new functionality. In addition to dealing with bytes and characters, streams are provided for input and output of Java primitive values and objects. The java.io package also provides a general interface to interact with the file system of the host platform.

11.2   The File Class

The File class provides a general machine-independent interface for the file system of the underlying platform. A File object represents the pathname of a file or directory in the host file system. An application can use the functionality provided by the File class for handling files and directories in the file system. The File class is *not* meant for handling the contents of files. For that purpose, there are the FileInput-Stream and FileOutputStream classes, which are discussed later in this chapter.

The pathname for a file or directory is specified using the naming conventions of the host system. However, the File class defines platform-dependent constants that can be used to handle file and directory names in a platform-independent way:

```
public static final char separatorChar
public static final String separator
```

Defines the character or string that separates the directory and the file components in a pathname. This separator is '/', '\' or ':' for Unix, Windows, and Macintosh, respectively.

```
public static final char pathSeparatorChar
public static final String pathSeparator
```

Defines the character or string that separates the file or directory names in a "path list." This character is ':' or ';' for Unix and Windows, respectively.

Some examples of pathnames are:

```
/book/chapter1                    on Unix
C:\book\chapter1                  on Windows
HD:book:chapter1                  on Macintosh
```

Some examples of path lists are:

```
/book:/manual:/draft              on Unix
C:\book;D:\manual;A:\draft        on Windows
```

Files and directories can be referenced using both *absolute* and *relative* pathnames, but the pathname must follow the conventions of the host platform. On Unix platforms, a pathname is absolute if its first character is the separator character. On Windows platforms, a path is absolute if the ASCII '\' is the first character, or follows the volume name (e.g., C:), in a pathname. On the Macintosh, a pathname is absolute if it begins with a name followed by a colon. Java programs should not rely on system-specific pathname conventions. The File class provides facilities to construct pathnames in a platform-independent way.

The File class has various constructors for associating a file or a directory pathname to an object of the File class. Creating a File object does not mean creation of any file or directory based on the pathname specified. A File instance, called the *abstract pathname,* is a representation of the pathname of a file and directory. The pathname cannot be changed once the File object is created.

File(String pathname)

The pathname (of a file or a directory) can be an absolute pathname or a pathname relative to the *current directory.* An *empty string* as argument results in an abstract pathname for the current directory.

```
// "/book/chapter1" - absolute pathname of a file
File chap1 = new File(File.separator + "book" + File.separator + "chapter1");
// "draft/chapters" - relative pathname of a directory
File draftChapters = new File("draft" + File.separator + "chapters");
```

File(String directoryPathname, String fileName)

This creates a File object whose pathname is as follows: directoryPathname + separator + fileName.

```
// "/book/chapter1" - absolute pathname of a file
File updatedChap1 = new File(File.separator + "book", "chapter1");
```

File(File directory, String fileName)

If the directory argument is null, the resulting File object represents a file in the current directory. If the directory argument is not null, it creates a File object that represents a file in the given directory. The pathname of the file is then the pathname of the directory File object + separator + fileName.

```
// "chapter13" - relative pathname of a file
File parent = null;
File chap13 = new File(parent, "chapter13");

// "draft/chapters/chapter13" - relative pathname of a file
File draftChapters = new File("draft" + File.separator + "chapters");
File updatedChap13 = new File(draftChapters, "chapter13");
```

An object of the File class provides a handle to a file or directory in the file system, and can be used to create, rename, and delete the entry.

A File object can also be used to query the file system for information about a file or directory:

- whether the entry exists
- whether the File object represents a file or directory
- get and set read, write, or execute permissions for the entry
- get pathname information about the file or directory
- list all entries under a directory in the file system

Many methods of the File class throw a SecurityException in the case of a security violation, for example if read or write access is denied. Some methods also return a boolean value to indicate whether the operation was successful.

Querying the File System

The File class provides a number of methods for obtaining the platform-dependent representation of a pathname and its components.

```
String getName()
```

Returns the name of the file entry, excluding the specification of the directory in which it resides.

On Unix, the name part of "/book/chapters/one" is "one".

On Windows platforms, the name part of "c:\java\bin\javac" is "javac".

On the Macintosh, the name part of "HD:java-tools:javac" is "javac".

The strings "." and ".." generally designate the current directory and the parent directory in pathnames, respectively.

```
String getPath()
```

The method returns the (absolute or relative) pathname of the file represented by the File object.

```
String getAbsolutePath()
```

If the File object represents an absolute pathname, this pathname is returned, otherwise the returned pathname is constructed by concatenating the current directory pathname, the separator character and the pathname of the File object.

`String getCanonicalPath() throws IOException`

Also platform-dependent, the canonical path usually specifies an absolute pathname in which all relative references have been completely resolved.

For example, if the `File` object represented the absolute pathname "c:\book\ chapter1" on Windows, this pathname would be returned by these methods. On the other hand, if the `File` object represented the relative pathname "..\book\chapter1" and the current directory had the absolute pathname "c:\documents", the pathname returned by the getPath(), getAbsolutePath(), and getCanonicalPath() methods would be "..\book\chapter1", "c:\documents\..\book\chapter1" and "c:\book\chapter1", respectively.

`String getParent()`

The parent part of the pathname of this `File` object is returned if one exists, otherwise the `null` value is returned. The parent part is generally the prefix obtained from the pathname after deleting the file or directory name component found after the last occurrence of the separator character. However, this is not true for all platforms.

On Unix, the parent part of "/book/chapter1" is "/book", whose parent part is "/", which in turn has no parent.

On Windows platforms, the parent part of "c:\java-tools" is "c:\", which in turn has no parent.

On the Macintosh, the parent part of "HD:java-tools" is "HD:", which in turn has no parent.

`boolean isAbsolute()`

Whether a `File` object represents an absolute pathname can be determined using this method.

The following three methods can be used to query the file system about the modification time of a file or directory, determine the size (in bytes) of a file, and ascertain whether two pathnames are identical.

`long lastModified()`

The modification time returned is encoded as a `long` value, and should only be compared with other values returned by this method.

`long length()`

Returns the size (in bytes) of the file represented by the `File` object.

`boolean equals(Object obj)`

This method just compares the pathnames of the `File` objects, and returns true if they are identical. On Unix systems, alphabetic case is significant in comparing pathnames; on Windows systems it is not.

File or Directory Existence

A File object is created using a pathname. Whether this pathname denotes an entry that actually exists in the file system can be checked using the exists() method:

```
boolean exists()
```

Since a File object can represent a file or a directory, the following methods can be used to distinguish whether a given File object represents a file or a directory, respectively:

```
boolean isFile()
boolean isDirectory()
```

File and Directory Permissions

Write, read and execute permissions can be set by calling the following methods. If the first argument is true, the operation permission is set; otherwise it is cleared. If the second argument is true, the permission only affects the owner; otherwise it affects all users. These methods throw a SecurityException if permission cannot be changed. It should be noted that the exact interpretation of these permissions is platform dependent.

```
boolean setReadable(boolean readable)
boolean setReadable(boolean readable, boolean owner)

boolean setWritable(boolean writable)
boolean setWritable(boolean writable, boolean owner)

boolean setExecutable(boolean executable)
boolean setExecutable(boolean executable, boolean owner)
```

To check whether the specified file has write, read, or execute permissions, the following methods can be used. They throw a SecurityException if general access is not allowed, i.e., the application is not even allowed to check whether it can read, write or execute a file.

```
boolean canWrite()
boolean canRead()
boolean canExecute()
```

Listing Directory Entries

The entries in a specified directory can be obtained as an array of file names or abstract pathnames using the following list() methods. The current directory and the parent directory are excluded from the list.

```
String[] list()
String[] list(FilenameFilter filter)
File[]   listFiles()
File[]   listFiles(FilenameFilter filter)
File[]   listFiles(FileFilter filter)
```

The filter argument can be used to specify a *filter* that determines whether an entry should be included in the list. These methods return null if the abstract pathname does not denote a directory, or if an I/O error occurs. A filter is an object of a class that implements either of these two interfaces:

```
interface FilenameFilter {
    boolean accept(File currentDirectory, String entryName);
}
interface FileFilter {
    boolean accept(File pathname);
}
```

The list() methods call the accept() methods of the filter for each entry to determine whether the entry should be included in the list.

Creating New Files and Directories

The File class can be used to create files and directories. A file can be created whose pathname is specified in a File object using the following method:

```
boolean createNewFile() throws IOException
```

It creates a new, empty file named by the abstract pathname if, and only if, a file with this name does not already exist. The returned value is true if the file was successfully created, false if the file already exists. Any I/O error results in an IOException.

A directory whose pathname is specified in a File object can be created using the following methods:

```
boolean mkdir()
boolean mkdirs()
```

The mkdirs() method creates any intervening parent directories in the pathname of the directory to be created.

Renaming Files and Directories

A file or a directory can be renamed, using the following method which takes the new pathname from its argument. It throws a SecurityException if access is denied.

▢ boolean renameTo(File dest)

Deleting Files and Directories

A file or a directory can be deleted using the following method. In the case of a directory, it must be empty before it can be deleted. It throws a SecurityException if access is denied.

▢ boolean delete()

Example 11.1 *Listing Files Under a Directory*

```
import java.io.File;
import java.io.IOException;

public class DirectoryLister {
  public static void main(String[] args) {
    if (args.length == 0) {                                      // (1)
      System.err.println("Please specify a directory name.");
      return;
    }
    File entry = new File(args[0]);                              // (2)
    listDirectory(entry);
  }

  public static void listDirectory(File entry) {
    try {
      if (!entry.exists()) {                                     // (3)
        System.out.println(entry.getName() + " not found.");
        return;
      }
      if (entry.isFile()) {
        // Write the pathname of the entry:
        System.out.println(entry.getCanonicalPath());           // (4)
      } else if (entry.isDirectory()) {
        // Create list of entries for this directory:
        String[] entryNames = entry.list();                     // (5)
        for (String entryName : entryNames) {
          // Create a File object for each entry name:
          File thisEntry = new File(entry.getPath(), entryName); // (6)
          // List this entry by a recursive call:
          listDirectory(thisEntry);                             // (7)
        }
      }
    } catch(IOException e) { System.out.println("Error: " + e); }
  }
}
```

Running the program on a Windows platform:

```
java DirectoryLister D:\docs\JC-Book\special
```

produces the following output:

```
D:\docs\JC-Book\special\book19990308\JC-14-applets.fm
D:\docs\JC-Book\special\book19990308\JC-16-swing.fm
D:\docs\JC-Book\special\JC-11-awtlayout.fm
```

The class DirectoryLister in Example 11.1 lists all entries in a directory specified in the command line. If no directory is given, an error message is printed; either by the print statement at (1) or as a result of an exception at (2). In the method list-Directory(), each entry is tested to see if it exists, as shown at (3). The entry could be an alias (*symbolic link* in Unix or *shortcut* in Windows terminology) and its destination might not exist. The method determines whether the entry is a file, in which case the absolute pathname is listed, as shown at (4). In the case of a directory, an array of entry names is created, as shown at (5). For each entry in the directory, a File object is created, as shown at (6). The method listDirectory() is called recursively for each entry, as shown at (7).

11.3 Byte Streams: Input Streams and Output Streams

The abstract classes InputStream and OutputStream are the root of the inheritance hierarchies for handling the reading and writing of *bytes* (Figure 11.1). Their subclasses, implementing different kinds of input and output streams, override the following methods from the InputStream and OutputStream classes to customize the reading and writing of bytes, respectively:

The InputStream class:
```
int read() throws IOException
int read(byte[] b) throws IOException
int read(byte[] b, int off, int len) throws IOException
```

Note that the first read() method reads a *byte*, but returns an int value. The byte read resides in the eight least significant bits of the int value, while the remaining bits in the int value are zeroed out. The read() methods return the value –1 when the end of the stream is reached.

The OutputStream class:
```
void write(int b) throws IOException
void write(byte[] b) throws IOException
void write(byte[] b, int off, int len) throws IOException
```

The first write() method takes an int as argument, but truncates it down to the eight least significant bits before writing it out as a byte.

Figure 11.1 *Partial Byte Stream Inheritance Hierarchies*

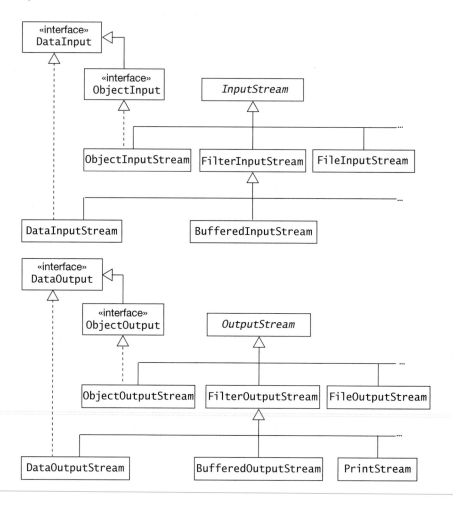

```
void close() throws IOException
void flush() throws IOException                    Only for OutputStream
```

A stream should be *closed* when no longer needed, to free system resources. Closing an output stream automatically *flushes* the stream, meaning that any data in its internal buffer is written out. An output stream can also be manually flushed by calling the second method.

Read and write operations on streams are synchronous (*blocking*) operations, i.e., a call to a read or write method does not return before a byte has been read or written.

Many methods in the classes contained in the java.io package throw the checked IOException. A calling method must therefore either catch the exception explicitly, or specify it in a throws clause.

Table 11.1 and Table 11.2 give an overview of the byte streams. Usually an output stream has a corresponding input stream of the same type.

Table 11.1 *Selected Input Streams*

`FileInputStream`	Data is read as bytes from a file. The file acting as the input stream can be specified by a `File` object, a `FileDescriptor` or a `String` file name.
`FilterInputStream`	Superclass of all input stream filters. An input filter must be chained to an underlying input stream.
`DataInputStream`	A filter that allows the binary representation of Java primitive values to be read from an underlying input stream. The underlying input stream must be specified.
`ObjectInputStream`	Allows binary representations of Java objects and Java primitive values to be read from a specified input stream.

Table 11.2 *Selected Output Streams*

`FileOutputStream`	Data is written as bytes to a file. The file acting as the output stream can be specified by a `File` object, a `FileDescriptor` or a `String` file name.
`FilterOutputStream`	Superclass of all output stream filters. An output filter must be chained to an underlying output stream.
`DataOutputStream`	A filter that allows the binary representation of Java primitive values to be written to an underlying output stream. The underlying output stream must be specified.
`ObjectOutputStream`	Allows the binary representation of Java objects and Java primitive values to be written to a specified underlying output stream.

File Streams

The classes `FileInputStream` and `FileOutputStream` define byte input and output streams that are connected to files. Data can only be read or written as a sequence of bytes.

An input stream for reading bytes can be created using the following constructors:

```
FileInputStream(String name) throws FileNotFoundException
FileInputStream(File file) throws FileNotFoundException
FileInputStream(FileDescriptor fdObj)
```

The file can be specified by its name, through a `File` object, or using a `FileDe-`
`scriptor` object.

If the file does not exist, a `FileNotFoundException` is thrown. If it exists, it is set to be read from the beginning. A `SecurityException` is thrown if the file does not have read access.

An output stream for writing bytes can be created using the following constructors:

```
FileOutputStream(String name) throws FileNotFoundException
FileOutputStream(String name, boolean append) throws FileNotFoundException
FileOutputStream(File file) throws IOException
FileOutputStream(FileDescriptor fdObj)
```

The file can be specified by its name, through a File object, or using a File Descriptor object.

If the file does not exist, it is created. If it exists, its contents are reset, unless the appropriate constructor is used to indicate that output should be appended to the file. A SecurityException is thrown if the file does not have write access or it cannot be created.

The FileInputStream class provides an implementation for the read() methods in its superclass InputStream. Similarly, the FileOutputStream class provides an implementation for the write() methods in its superclass OutputStream.

Example 11.2 demonstrates usage of writing and reading bytes to and from file streams. It copies the contents of one file to another file. The input and the output file names are specified on the command line. The streams are created at (1) and (2). The input file is read one byte at a time and written straight to the output file, as shown in the try block at (3). The end of file is reached when the read() method returns the value -1. The streams are explicitly closed, as shown at (4). Note that most of the code consists of try-catch constructs to handle the various exceptions. The example could be optimized by using buffering for reading and writing several bytes at a time.

Example 11.2   *Copy a File*

```
/* Copy a file.
   Command syntax: java CopyFile <from_file> <to_file>
*/
import java.io.FileInputStream;
import java.io.FileNotFoundException;
import java.io.FileOutputStream;
import java.io.IOException;

class CopyFile {
  public static void main(String[] args) {
    FileInputStream fromFile;
    FileOutputStream toFile;

    // Assign the files
    try {
      fromFile = new FileInputStream(args[0]);         // (1)
      toFile = new FileOutputStream(args[1]);          // (2)
    } catch(FileNotFoundException e) {
      System.err.println("File could not be copied: " + e);
```

```
        return;
    } catch(ArrayIndexOutOfBoundsException e) {
        System.err.println("Usage: CopyFile <from_file> <to_file>");
        return;
    }

    // Copy bytes
    try {                                           // (3)
        while (true) {
            int i = fromFile.read();
            if(i == -1) break;          // check end of file
            toFile.write(i);
        }
    } catch(IOException e) {
        System.err.println("Error reading/writing.");
    }

    // Close the files
    try {                                           // (4)
        fromFile.close();
        toFile.close();
    } catch(IOException e) {
        System.err.println("Error closing file.");
    }
  }
}
```

Filter Streams

A *filter* is a high-level stream that provides additional functionality to an under-lying stream to which it is chained. The data from the underlying stream is mani-pulated in some way by the filter. The FilterInputStream and FilterOutputStream classes, together with their subclasses, define input and output filter streams. The subclasses BufferedInputStream and BufferedOutputStream implement filters that buffer input from and output to the underlying stream, respectively. The sub-classes DataInputStream and DataOutputStream implement filters that allow binary representation of Java primitive values to be read and written, respectively, to and from an underlying stream.

Reading and Writing Binary Values

The java.io package contains the two interfaces DataInput and DataOutput, that streams can implement to allow reading and writing of binary representations of Java primitive values (boolean, char, byte, short, int, long, float, double). The meth-ods for writing binary representations of Java primitive values are named writeX, where X is any Java primitive data type. The methods for reading binary represen-tations of Java primitive values are similarly named readX. Table 11.3 gives an overview of the readX() and writeX() methods found in these two interfaces. A file containing *binary values* (i.e., binary representation of Java primitive vales) is usually called a *binary file*.

Note the methods provided for reading and writing strings. Whereas the methods readChar() and writeChar() handle a single character, the methods readLine() and writeChars() handle a string of characters. The methods readUTF() and writeUTF() also read and write characters, but use the UTF-8 character encoding. However, the recommended practice for reading and writing characters is to use *character streams*, called *readers* and *writers*, that are discussed in Section 11.4.

The filter streams DataOutputStream and DataInputStream implement DataOutput and DataInput interfaces, respectively, and can be used to read and write binary representations of Java primitive values to and from an underlying stream. Both the writeX() and readX() methods throw an IOException in the event of an I/O error. In particular, the readX() methods throw an EOFException (a subclass of IOEXception) if the input stream does not contain the correct number of bytes to read. Bytes can also be skipped from a DataInput stream, using the skipBytes(int n) method which skips n bytes. The following constructors can be used to set up filters for reading and writing Java primitive values, respectively, from an underlying stream:

```
DataInputStream(InputStream in)
DataOutputStream(OutputStream out)
```

Table 11.3 *The* DataInput *and* DataOutput *Interfaces*

Type	Methods in the *DataInput* Interface	Methods in the *DataOutput* interface
boolean	readBoolean()	writeBoolean(boolean b)
char	readChar()	writeChar(int c)
byte	readByte()	writeByte(int b)
short	readShort()	writeShort(int s)
int	readInt()	writeInt(int i)
long	readLong()	writeLong(long l)
float	readFloat()	writeFloat(float f)
double	readDouble()	writeDouble(double d)
String	readLine()	writeChars(String str)
String	readUTF()	writeUTF(String str)

Writing Binary Values to a File

To write the binary representation of Java primitive values to a *binary file*, the following procedure can be used, which is also depicted in Figure 11.2.

1. Create a FileOutputStream:

   ```
   FileOutputStream outputFile = new FileOutputStream("primitives.data");
   ```

2. Create a DataOutputStream which is chained to the FileOutputStream:

   ```
   DataOutputStream outputStream = new DataOutputStream(outputFile);
   ```

3. Write Java primitive values using relevant writeX() methods:

   ```
   outputStream.writeBoolean(true);
   outputStream.writeChar('A');                    // int written as Unicode char
   outputStream.writeByte(Byte.MAX_VALUE);         // int written as 8-bits byte
   outputStream.writeShort(Short.MIN_VALUE);       // int written as 16-bits short
   outputStream.writeInt(Integer.MAX_VALUE);
   outputStream.writeLong(Long.MIN_VALUE);
   outputStream.writeFloat(Float.MAX_VALUE);
   outputStream.writeDouble(Math.PI);
   ```

   Note that in the case of char, byte, and short data types, the int argument to the writeX() method is converted to the corresponding type, before it is written (see Table 11.3).

4. Close the filter stream, which also closes the underlying stream:

   ```
   outputStream.close();
   ```

Figure 11.2 *Stream Chaining for Reading and Writing Binary Values to a File*

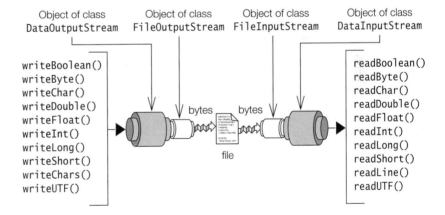

Reading Binary Values From a File

To read the binary representation of Java primitive values from a *binary file* the following procedure can be used, which is also depicted in Figure 11.2.

1. Create a FileInputStream:

   ```
   FileInputStream inputFile = new FileInputStream("primitives.data");
   ```

2. Create a `DataInputStream` which is chained to the `FileInputStream`:

```
DataInputStream inputStream = new DataInputStream(inputFile);
```

3. Read the (exact number of) Java primitive values in the *same order* they were written out, using relevant readX() methods:

```
boolean v = inputStream.readBoolean();
char    c = inputStream.readChar();
byte    b = inputStream.readByte();
short   s = inputStream.readShort();
int     i = inputStream.readInt();
long    l = inputStream.readLong();
float   f = inputStream.readFloat();
double  d = inputStream.readDouble();
```

4. Close the filter stream, which also closes the underlying stream:

```
inputStream.close();
```

Example 11.3 uses both procedures described above: first to write and then to read some Java primitive values to and from a file. It also checks to see if the end of the stream has been reached, signalled by an `EOFException`. The values are also written to the standard input stream.

- -

Example 11.3   *Reading and Writing Binary Values*

```java
import java.io.DataInputStream;
import java.io.DataOutputStream;
import java.io.EOFException;
import java.io.FileInputStream;
import java.io.FileOutputStream;
import java.io.IOException;

public class BinaryValuesIO {
  public static void main(String[] args) throws IOException {
    // Create a FileOutputStream.
    FileOutputStream outputFile = new FileOutputStream("primitives.data");

    // Create a DataOutputStream which is chained to the FileOutputStream.
    DataOutputStream outputStream = new DataOutputStream(outputFile);

    // Write Java primitive values in binary representation:
    outputStream.writeBoolean(true);
    outputStream.writeChar('A');                   // int written as Unicode char
    outputStream.writeByte(Byte.MAX_VALUE);        // int written as 8-bits byte
    outputStream.writeShort(Short.MIN_VALUE);      // int written as 16-bits short
    outputStream.writeInt(Integer.MAX_VALUE);
    outputStream.writeLong(Long.MIN_VALUE);
    outputStream.writeFloat(Float.MAX_VALUE);
    outputStream.writeDouble(Math.PI);

    // Close the output stream, which also closes the underlying stream.
    outputStream.flush();
    outputStream.close();
```

```
// Create a FileInputStream.
FileInputStream inputFile = new FileInputStream("primitives.data");

// Create a DataInputStream which is chained to the FileInputStream.
DataInputStream inputStream = new DataInputStream(inputFile);

// Read the binary representation of Java primitive values
// in the same order they were written out:
boolean v = inputStream.readBoolean();
char    c = inputStream.readChar();
byte    b = inputStream.readByte();
short   s = inputStream.readShort();
int     i = inputStream.readInt();
long    l = inputStream.readLong();
float   f = inputStream.readFloat();
double  d = inputStream.readDouble();

// Check for end of stream:
try {
  int value = inputStream.readByte();
  System.out.println("More input: " + value);
} catch (EOFException eofe) {
  System.out.println("End of stream");
} finally {
  // Close the input stream, which also closes the underlying stream.
  inputStream.close();
}

// Write the values read to the standard input stream:
System.out.println("Values read:");
System.out.println(v);
System.out.println(c);
System.out.println(b);
System.out.println(s);
System.out.println(i);
System.out.println(l);
System.out.println(f);
System.out.println(d);
  }
}
```

Output from the program:

```
End of stream
Values read:
true
A
127
-32768
2147483647
-9223372036854775808
3.4028235E38
3.141592653589793
```

Review Questions

11.1 Which of these can act both as the source of an input stream and as the destination of an output stream, based on the classes provided by the java.io package?

Select the four correct answers.

(a) A file
(b) A network connection
(c) A pipe
(d) A string
(e) An array of chars

11.2 Which of these statements about the constant named separator of the File class are true?

Select the two correct answers.

(a) The variable is of type char.
(b) The variable is of type String.
(c) It can be assumed that the value of the variable always is the character '/'.
(d) It can be assumed that the value of the variable always is one of '/', '\' or ':'.
(e) The separator can consist of more than one character.

11.3 Which one of these methods in the File class will return the name of the entry, excluding the specification of the directory in which it resides?

Select the one correct answer.

(a) getAbsolutePath()
(b) getName()
(c) getParent()
(d) getPath()
(e) None of the above.

11.4 What will the method length() in the class File return?

Select the one correct answer.

(a) The number of characters in the file.
(b) The number of kilobytes in the file.
(c) The number of lines in the file.
(d) The number of words in the file.
(e) None of the above.

11.5 Given the following program:

```
import java.io.File;
import java.io.IOException;

public final class Filing {
```

```java
public static void main (String[] args) throws IOException {
  File file = new File("./documents","../book/../chapter1");
  System.out.println(file.getPath());
  System.out.println(file.getAbsolutePath());
  System.out.println(file.getCanonicalPath());
  System.out.println(file.getName());
  System.out.println(file.getParent());
  }
}
```

Assume that the current or working directory has the absolute path "/wrk". Which lines below will not be included in the output from the program?

Select the two correct answers.

(a) ./documents/../book/../chapter1
(b) ./documents/book/chapter1
(c) /wrk/./documents/../book/../chapter1
(d) /wrk/documents/book/chapter1
(e) /wrk/chapter1
(f) chapter1
(g) ./documents/../book/..

11.6 Given the following program:

```java
import java.io.File;
public class ListingFiles {
  public static void main(String[] args) {
    File currentDirectory = new File(".");
    printFiles1(currentDirectory);
    printFiles2(currentDirectory);
    printFiles3(currentDirectory);
  }

  public static void printFiles1(File currentDirectory) {
    String[] entryNames = currentDirectory.list();
    for (String entryName : entryNames) {
      System.out.println(entryName);
    }
  }

  public static void printFiles2(File currentDirectory) {
    File[] entries = currentDirectory.listFiles();
    for (File entry : entries) {
      System.out.println(entry);
    }
  }

  public static void printFiles3(File currentDirectory) {
    File[] entries = currentDirectory.listFiles();
    for (File entry : entries) {
      System.out.println(entry.getPath());
    }
  }
}
```

Assume that the current or working directory has the absolute path "/wrk" and contains only one file with the name "ListingFiles.class".

Which statement is true about the program?

Select the one correct answer.

(a) All three methods printFiles1(), printFiles2(), and printFiles3() will produce the same output.
(b) Only the methods printFiles1() and printFiles2(), will produce the same output.
(c) Only the methods printFiles2() and printFiles3(), will produce the same output.
(d) Only the methods printFiles1() and printFiles3(), will produce the same output.
(e) The program does not compile because the list() method does not exist in the File class.

11.7   A file is readable but not writable on the file system of the host platform. What will be the result of calling the method canWrite() on a File object representing this file?

Select the one correct answer.

(a) A SecurityException is thrown.
(b) The boolean value false is returned.
(c) The boolean value true is returned.
(d) The file is modified from being unwritable to being writable.
(e) None of the above.

11.8   What is the type of the parameter given to the method renameTo() in the class File?

Select the one correct answer.

(a) File
(b) FileDescriptor
(c) FileNameFilter
(d) String
(e) char[]

11.9   If write(0x01234567) is called on an instance of OutputStream, what will be written to the destination of the stream?

Select the one correct answer.

(a) The bytes 0x01, 0x23, 0x34, 0x45, and 0x67, in that order.
(b) The bytes 0x67, 0x45, 0x34, 0x23, and 0x01, in that order.
(c) The byte 0x01.
(d) The byte 0x67.
(e) None of the above.

11.10   Given the following code, under which circumstances will the method return false?

```java
public static boolean test(InputStream is) throws IOException {
  int value = is.read();
  return value >= 0;
}
```

Select the one correct answer.

(a) A character of more than 8 bits was read from the input stream.
(b) An I/O error occurred.
(c) Never.
(d) The end of the stream was reached in the input stream.

11.11   Which of these classes provides methods for writing binary representations of Java primitive values?

Select the two correct answers.

(a) `DataOutputStream`
(b) `FileOutputStream`
(c) `ObjectOutputStream`
(d) `PrintStream`
(e) `BufferedOutputStream`

11.12   Given the following program:

```java
import java.io.DataInputStream;
import java.io.EOFException;
import java.io.FileInputStream;
import java.io.FileNotFoundException;
import java.io.IOException;

public class Endings {
  public static void main(String[] args) {
    try {
      FileInputStream fos = new FileInputStream("info.dat");
      DataInputStream dis = new DataInputStream(fos);
      int i = dis.readByte();
      while (i != -1) {
        System.out.print((byte)i + "|");
        i = dis.readByte();
      }
    } catch (FileNotFoundException fnf) {
      System.out.println("File not found");
    } catch (EOFException eofe) {
      System.out.println("End of stream");
    } catch (IOException ioe) {
      System.out.println("Input error");
    }
  }
}
```

Assume that the file "info.dat" exits in the current directory and has only the byte values 10, 20 and 30, stored in that order.

Which statement is true about the program?

Select the one correct answer.

(a) The program will not compile because a certain unchecked exception is not caught.
(b) The program will compile and print 10|20|30|Input error.
(c) The program will compile and print 10|20|30|End of stream.
(d) The program will compile and print 10|20|30|, and then block in order to read from the file.
(e) The program will compile and print 10|20|30|, and terminate because of an uncaught exception.

11.4 Character Streams: Readers and Writers

A *character encoding* is a scheme for representing characters. Java programs represent values of the char type internally in the 16-bit Unicode character encoding, but the host platform might use another character encoding to represent and store characters externally. For example, the ASCII (American Standard Code for Information Interchange) character encoding is widely used to represent characters on many platforms. However, it is only one small subset of the Unicode standard.

The abstract classes Reader and Writer are the roots of the inheritance hierarchies for streams that read and write *Unicode characters* using a specific character encoding (as shown in Figure 11.3). A *reader* is an input character stream that reads a sequence of Unicode characters, and a *writer* is an output character stream that writes a sequence of Unicode characters. Character encodings are used by readers and writers to convert between external encoding and internal Unicode characters. Table 11.4 and Table 11.5 give an overview of some selected character streams found in the java.io package.

Table 11.4 *Selected Readers*

BufferedReader	A reader that buffers the characters read from an underlying reader. The underlying reader must be specified and an optional buffer size can be given.
InputStreamReader	Characters are read from a byte input stream which must be specified. The default character encoding is used if no character encoding is explicitly specified.
FileReader	Reads characters from a file, using the default character encoding. The file can be specified by a File object, a FileDescriptor, or a String file name. It automatically creates a FileInputStream that is associated with the file.

Figure 11.3 *Partial Character Stream Inheritance Hierarchies*

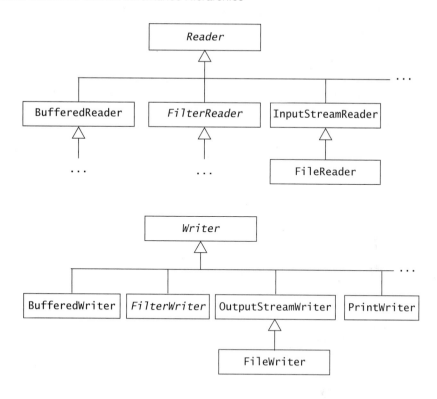

Readers use the following methods for reading Unicode characters:

```
int read() throws IOException
int read(char cbuf[]) throws IOException
int read(char cbuf[], int off, int len) throws IOException
```

Note that the read() methods read the character as an int in the range 0 to 65535 (0x0000–0xFFFF). The value –1 is returned if the end of the stream has been reached.

```
long skip(long n) throws IOException
```

A reader can skip over characters using the skip() method.

Table 11.5 *Selected Writers*

BufferedWriter	A writer that buffers the characters before writing them to an underlying writer. The underlying writer must be specified, and an optional buffer size can be specified.
OutputStreamWriter	Characters are written to a byte output stream which must be specified. The default character encoding is used if no explicit character encoding is specified.
FileWriter	Writes characters to a file, using the default character encoding. The file can be specified by a File object, a FileDescriptor, or a String file name. It automatically creates a FileOutputStream that is associated with the file.
PrintWriter	A filter that allows *text* representation of Java objects and Java primitive values to be written to an underlying output stream or writer. The underlying output stream or writer must be specified.

Writers use the following methods for writing Unicode characters:

```
void write(int c) throws IOException
```

The write() method takes an int as argument, but writes only the least significant 16 bits.

```
void write(char[] cbuf) throws IOException
void write(String str) throws IOException
void write(char[] cbuf, int off, int length) throws IOException
void write(String str, int off, int length) throws IOException
```

These methods write the characters from an array of characters or a string.

```
void close() throws IOException
void flush() throws IOException
```

Like byte streams, a character stream should be closed when no longer needed to free system resources. Closing a character output stream automatically *flushes* the stream. A character output stream can also be manually flushed.

Like byte streams, many methods of the character stream classes throw an IOException that a calling method must either catch explicitly or specify in a throws clause.

Print Writers

The capabilities of the OutputStreamWriter and the InputStreamReader classes are limited, as they primarily write and read characters.

In order to write a text representation of Java primitive values and objects, a PrintWriter should be chained to either a writer, a byte output stream, a File, or a String file name, using one of the following constructors:

```
PrintWriter(Writer out)
PrintWriter(Writer out, boolean autoFlush)
PrintWriter(OutputStream out)
PrintWriter(OutputStream out, boolean autoFlush)
PrintWriter(File file)
PrintWriter(File file, String charsetName)
PrintWriter(String fileName)
PrintWriter(String fileName, String charsetName)
```

The autoFlush argument specifies whether the PrintWriter should be flushed when any println() method of the PrintWriter class is called.

When the underlying writer is specified, the character encoding supplied by the underlying writer is used. However, an OutputStream has no notion of any character encoding, so the necessary intermediate OutputStreamWriter is automatically created, which will convert characters into bytes, using the default character encoding.

When supplying the File object or the file name, the character encoding can be specified explicitly.

The PrintWriter class provides the following methods for writing text representation of Java primitive values and objects (Table 11.6):

Table 11.6 *Print Methods of the* PrintWriter *Class*

print()-methods	*println*-methods
	println()
print(boolean b)	println(boolean b)
print(char c)	println(char c)
print(int i)	println(int i)
print(long l)	println(long l)
print(float f)	println(float f)
print(double d)	println(double d)
print(char[] s)	println(char[] ca)
print(String s)	println(String str)
print(Object obj)	println(Object obj)

The println() methods write the text representation of their argument to the underlying stream, and then append a *line-separator*. The println() methods use the correct platform-dependent line-separator. For example, on Unix platforms the line-separator is '\n' (newline), while on Windows platforms it is "\r\n" (carriage return + newline) and on the Macintosh it is '\r' (carriage return).

The print() methods create a text representation of an object by calling the toString() method on the object. The print() methods do not throw any IOException.

Instead, the checkError() method of the PrintWriter class must be called to check for errors.

In addition, the PrintWriter class provides the format() method and the convenient printf() method to write *formatted* values. Details on formatting values can be found in Section 12.7, p. 593.

Writing Text Files

When writing text to a file using the default character encoding, the following four procedures for setting up a PrintWriter can be used.

Setting up a PrintWriter based on an OutputStreamWriter which is chained to a FileOutputStream (Figure 11.4a):

1. Create a FileOutputStream:

   ```
   FileOutputStream outputFile = new FileOutputStream("info.txt");
   ```

2. Create an OutputStreamWriter which is chained to the FileOutputStream:

   ```
   OutputStreamWriter outputStream = new OutputStreamWriter(outputFile);
   ```

   The OutputStreamWriter uses the default character encoding for writing the characters to the file.

3. Create a PrintWriter which is chained to the OutputStreamWriter:

   ```
   PrintWriter printWriter1 = new PrintWriter(outputStream, true);
   ```

Setting up a PrintWriter based on a FileOutputStream (Figure 11.4b):

1. Create a FileOutputStream:

   ```
   FileOutputStream outputFile = new FileOutputStream("info.txt");
   ```

2. Create a PrintWriter which is chained to the FileOutputStream:

   ```
   PrintWriter printWriter2 = new PrintWriter(outputFile, true);
   ```

   The intermediate OutputStreamWriter to convert the characters using the default encoding is automatically supplied.

Setting up a PrintWriter based on a FileWriter (Figure 11.4c):

1. Create a FileWriter which is a subclass of OutputStreamWriter:

   ```
   FileWriter fileWriter = new FileWriter("info.txt");
   ```

   This is equivalent to having an OutputStreamWriter chained to a FileOutput-Stream for writing the characters to the file, as shown in Figure 11.4a.

2. Create a PrintWriter which is chained to the FileWriter:

   ```
   PrintWriter printWriter3 = new PrintWriter(fileWriter, true);
   ```

Setting up a PrintWriter, given the file name (Figure 11.4d):

1. Create a PrintWriter, supplying the file name:

   ```
   PrintWriter printWriter3 = new PrintWriter("info.txt");
   ```

Figure 11.4 *Setting up a* PrintWriter *to Write to a File*

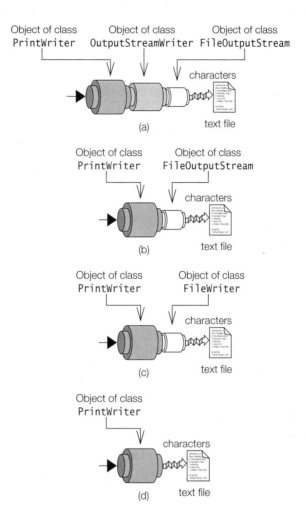

The underlying OutputStreamWriter is created to write the characters to the file in the default encoding, as shown in Figure 11.4d. In this case, there is no automatic flushing.

If a specific character encoding is desired for the writer, the first procedure (Figure 11.4a) can be used, the encoding being specified for the OutputStreamWriter:

```
FileOutputStream    outputFile   = new FileOutputStream("info.txt");
OutputStreamWriter outputStream = new OutputStreamWriter(outputFile, "8859_1");
PrintWriter         printWriter4 = new PrintWriter(outputStream, true);
```

This writer will use the 8859_1 character encoding to write the characters to the file. Alternatively, we can use one of the two PrintWriter constructors that accept a character encoding:

```
PrintWriter printWriter5 = new PrintWriter("info.txt", "8859_1");
```

A BufferedWriter can be also used to improve the efficiency of writing characters to the underlying stream (*explained later in this subsection*).

Reading Text Files

Java primitive values and objects cannot be read directly from their text representation. Characters must be read and converted to the relevant values explicitly. One common strategy is to write *lines of text* and tokenize the characters as they are read, a line at a time (see the subsection *The java.util.Scanner Class*, p. 571). Such files are usually called *text files*.

When reading *characters* from a file using the default character encoding, the following two procedures for setting up an InputStreamReader can be used.

Setting up an InputStreamReader which is chained to a FileInputStream (Figure 11.5a):

1.   Create a FileInputStream:

```
FileInputStream inputFile = new FileInputStream("info.txt");
```

2.   Create an InputStreamReader which is chained to the FileInputStream:

```
InputStreamReader reader = new InputStreamReader(inputFile);
```

The InputStreamReader uses the default character encoding for reading the characters from the file.

Figure 11.5   *Setting up Readers to read Characters*

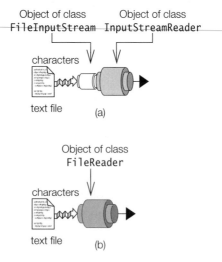

Setting up a `FileReader` which is a subclass of `InputStreamReader` (Figure 11.5b):

1. Create a `FileReader`:

    ```
    FileReader fileReader = new FileReader("info.txt");
    ```

    This is equivalent to having an `InputStreamReader` chained to a `FileInputStream` for reading the characters from the file, using the default character encoding. Other constructors of the `FileReader` class accept a `File` or a `FileDescriptor`.

If a specific character encoding is desired for the reader, the first procedure must be used (Figure 11.5a), the encoding being specified for the `InputStreamReader`:

```
FileInputStream inputFile = new FileInputStream("info.txt");
InputStreamReader reader = new InputStreamReader(inputFile, "8859_1");
```

This reader will use the 8859_1 character encoding to read the characters from the file. A `BufferedReader` can also be used to improve the efficiency of reading characters from the underlying stream, as explained later in this section.

Using Buffered Writers

A `BufferedWriter` can be chained to the underlying writer by using one of the following constructors:

```
BufferedWriter(Writer out)
BufferedWriter(Writer out, int size)
```

The default buffer size is used, unless the buffer size is explicitly specified.

Characters, strings, and arrays of characters can be written using the methods for a `Writer`, but these now use buffering to provide efficient writing of characters. In addition, the `BufferedWriter` class provides the method `newLine()` for writing the platform-dependent line-separator.

The following code creates a `PrintWriter` whose output is buffered and the characters are written using the 8859_1 character encoding (Figure 11.6a):

```
FileOutputStream    outputFile    = new FileOutputStream("info.txt");
OutputStreamWriter outputStream  = new OutputStreamWriter(outputFile, "8859_1");
BufferedWriter     bufferedWriter1 = new BufferedWriter(outputStream);
PrintWriter        printWriter1  = new PrintWriter(bufferedWriter1, true);
```

The following code creates a `PrintWriter` whose output is buffered, and the characters are written using the default character encoding (Figure 11.6b):

```
FileWriter     fileWriter    = new FileWriter("info.txt");
BufferedWriter bufferedWriter2 = new BufferedWriter(fileWriter);
PrintWriter    printWriter2  = new PrintWriter(bufferedWriter2, true);
```

Note that in both cases, the `PrintWriter` is used to write the characters. The `Buffered Writer` is sandwiched between the `PrintWriter` and the underlying `OutputStream Writer`.

Figure 11.6 *Buffered Writers*

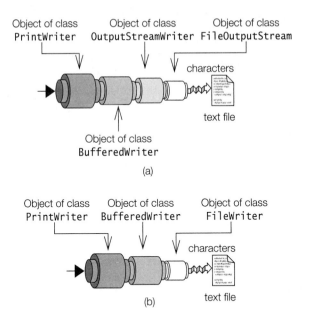

Using Buffered Readers

A BufferedReader can be chained to the underlying reader by using one of the following constructors:

```
BufferedReader(Reader in)
BufferedReader(Reader in, int size)
```

The default buffer size is used, unless the buffer size is explicitly specified.

In addition to the methods of the Reader class, the BufferedReader class provides the method readLine() to read a line of text from the underlying reader:

```
String readLine() throws IOException
```

The null value is returned when the end of the stream is reached. The returned string must explicitly be converted to other values.

The following code creates a BufferedReader that can be used to read text lines from a file, using the 8859_1 character encoding (Figure 11.7a):

```
FileInputStream   inputFile      = new FileInputStream("info.txt");
InputStreamReader reader         = new InputStreamReader(inputFile, "8859_1");
BufferedReader    bufferedReader1 = new BufferedReader(reader);
```

The following code creates a BufferedReader that can be used to read text lines from a file, using the default character encoding (Figure 11.7b):

```
FileReader     fileReader      = new FileReader("lines.txt");
BufferedReader bufferedReader2 = new BufferedReader(fileReader);
```

Note that in both cases the `BufferedReader` object is used to read the text lines.

Figure 11.7 *Buffered Readers*

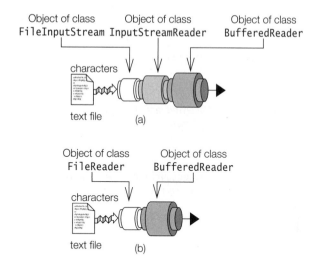

In contrast to Example 11.3, which demonstrated the reading and writing of binary representations of primitive data values, Example 11.4 illustrates the reading and writing of text representations of primitive data values.

The `CharEncodingDemo` class in Example 11.4 writes text representations of Java primitive values, using the 8859_1 character encoding (Figure 11.6a). The `PrintWriter` is buffered. Its underlying writer uses the specified encoding, as shown at (1). Values are written out with the text representation of one value on each line, as shown at (2), and the writer is closed, as shown at (3). The example uses the same character encoding to read the text file. A `BufferedReader` is created (Figure 11.7a). Its underlying reader uses the specified encoding, as shown at (4). The text representation of the values is read in the same order the values were written out, one value per line. The characters in the line are explicitly converted to an appropriate type of value, as shown at (5). An alternate approach to extracting values from a text line is to use a scanner (p. 571).

We check for the end of the stream at (6), which is signalled by the `null` value returned by the `readLine()` method of the `BufferedReader` class. The `BufferedReader` is closed, as shown at (7), and the values are echoed on the standard output stream, as shown at (8). Note the exceptions that are specified in the `throws` clause of the `main()` method.

Example 11.4 *Demonstrating Readers and Writers, and Character Encoding*

```java
import java.io.BufferedReader;
import java.io.BufferedWriter;
import java.io.FileInputStream;
import java.io.FileOutputStream;
import java.io.IOException;
import java.io.InputStreamReader;
import java.io.OutputStreamWriter;
import java.io.PrintWriter;

public class CharEncodingDemo {
  public static void main(String[] args)
                   throws IOException, NumberFormatException {

    // Character encoding.                                          (1)
    FileOutputStream outputFile = new FileOutputStream("info.txt");
    OutputStreamWriter writer = new OutputStreamWriter(outputFile, "8859_1");
    BufferedWriter bufferedWriter1 = new BufferedWriter(writer);
    PrintWriter printWriter = new PrintWriter(bufferedWriter1, true);
    System.out.println("Writing using encoding: " + writer.getEncoding());

    // Print Java primitive values, one on each line.               (2)
    printWriter.println(true);
    printWriter.println('A');
    printWriter.println(Byte.MAX_VALUE);
    printWriter.println(Short.MIN_VALUE);
    printWriter.println(Integer.MAX_VALUE);
    printWriter.println(Long.MIN_VALUE);
    printWriter.println(Float.MAX_VALUE);
    printWriter.println(Math.PI);

    // Close the writer, which also closes the underlying stream     (3)
    printWriter.flush();
    printWriter.close();

    // Create a BufferedReader which uses 8859_1 character encoding  (4)
    FileInputStream inputFile = new FileInputStream("info.txt");
    InputStreamReader reader = new InputStreamReader(inputFile, "8859_1");
    BufferedReader bufferedReader = new BufferedReader(reader);
    System.out.println("Reading using encoding: " + reader.getEncoding());

    // Read the (exact number of) Java primitive values             (5)
    // in the same order they were written out, one on each line
    boolean v = bufferedReader.readLine().equals("true")? true : false;
    char    c = bufferedReader.readLine().charAt(0);
    byte    b = (byte) Integer.parseInt(bufferedReader.readLine());
    short   s = (short) Integer.parseInt(bufferedReader.readLine());
    int     i = Integer.parseInt(bufferedReader.readLine());
    long    l = Long.parseLong(bufferedReader.readLine());
    float   f = Float.parseFloat(bufferedReader.readLine());
    double  d = Double.parseDouble(bufferedReader.readLine());
```

```
    // Check for end of stream:                                          (6)
    String line = bufferedReader.readLine();
    if (line != null ) {
      System.out.println("More input: " + line);
    } else {
      System.out.println("End of stream");
    }

    // Close the reader, which also closes the underlying stream         (7)
    bufferedReader.close();

    // Write the values read on the terminal                             (8)
    System.out.println("Values read:");
    System.out.println(v);
    System.out.println(c);
    System.out.println(b);
    System.out.println(s);
    System.out.println(i);
    System.out.println(l);
    System.out.println(f);
    System.out.println(d);
  }
}
```

Output from the program:

```
Writing using encoding: ISO8859_1
Reading using encoding: ISO8859_1
End of stream
Values read:
true
A
127
-32768
2147483647
-9223372036854775808
3.4028235E38
3.141592653589793
```

The Standard Input, Output, and Error Streams

The *standard output* stream (usually the display) is represented by the `PrintStream` object `System.out`. The *standard input* stream (usually the keyboard) is represented by the `InputStream` object `System.in`. In other words, it is a byte input stream. The *standard error* stream (also usually the display) is represented by `System.err` which is another object of the `PrintStream` class. The `PrintStream` class offers `print()` methods which act as corresponding `print()` methods from the `PrintWriter` class. These methods can be used to write output to `System.out` and `System.err`. In other words, both `System.out` and `System.err` act like `PrintWriter`, but in addition they have `write()` methods for writing bytes.

In order to read *characters* typed by the user, the `Console` class is recommended (*see the next section*).

Comparison of Byte Streams and Character Streams

It is instructive to see which byte streams correspond to which character streams. Table 11.7 shows the correspondence between byte and character streams. Note that not all classes have a corresponding counterpart.

Table 11.7 *Correspondence Between Selected Byte and Character Streams*

Byte Streams	Character Streams
`OutputStream`	`Writer`
`InputStream`	`Reader`
No counterpart	`OutputStreamWriter`
No counterpart	`InputStreamReader`
`FileOutputStream`	`FileWriter`
`FileInputStream`	`FileReader`
`BufferedOutputStream`	`BufferedWriter`
`BufferedInputStream`	`BufferedReader`
`PrintStream`	`PrintWriter`
`DataOutputStream`	*No counterpart*
`DataInputStream`	*No counterpart*
`ObjectOutputStream`	*No counterpart*
`ObjectInputStream`	*No counterpart*

11.5 The `Console` Class

A *console* is a unique *character-based* device associated with a JVM. Whether a JVM has a console depends on the platform, and also on the manner in which the JVM is invoked. When the JVM is started from a command line, and the standard input and output streams have not been redirected, the console will normally correspond to the keyboard and the display (Figure 11.8). In any case, the console will be represented by an instance of the class `Console`. This `Console` instance is obtained by calling the static method `console()` of the `System` class. If there is no console associated with the JVM, the `null` value is returned by this method.

```
// Obtaining the console:
Console console = System.console();
```

```
        if (console == null) {
          System.err.println("No console available.");
          return;
        }
        // Continue ...
```

Figure 11.8 *Keyboard and Display as Console*

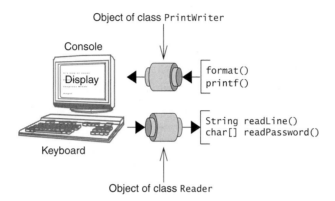

For creating dialog for console-based applications, the Console class provides the following functionality:

- Prompt and read a line of character-based response.

```
        String username = console.readLine("Enter the user name (%d chars): ", 4);
```

  The readLine() method first prints the formatted prompt on the console, and then returns the characters typed at the console when the line is terminated by the ENTER key.

- Prompt and read passwords without echoing the characters on the console.

```
        char[] password;
        do {
            password = console.readPassword("Enter password (min. %d chars): ", 6);
        } while (password.length < 6);
```

  The readPassword() method first prints the formatted prompt, and returns the password characters typed by the user in an array of char when the line is terminated by the ENTER key. The password characters are not echoed on the display.

  Since a password is sensitive data, the recommended practice is to have it stored in memory only as long as it is necessary and to zero-fill the char array as soon as possible in order to overwrite the password characters.

- Print formatted strings to the console.

  The Console class provides the format() and the printf() methods for this purpose. Using these methods and creating formatted strings are covered in Section 12.7, p. 593.

Note that the console only returns character-based input. For reading other types of values from the standard input stream, the Scanner class (p. 571) can be considered.

The Console class provides methods for *formatted prompting* and *reading* from the console, and obtaining the reader associated with it.

```
String readLine()
String readLine(String format, Object... args)
```

The first method reads a single line of text from the console. The second method prints a formatted prompt first, then reads a single line of text from the console. The prompt is constructed by formatting the specified args according to the specified format.

```
char[] readPassword()
char[] readPassword(String format, Object... args)
```

The first method reads a password or a password phrase from the console with echoing disabled. The second method does the same, but first prints a formatted prompt.

```
Reader reader()
```

This retrieves the unique Reader object associated with this console.

The Console class provides the following methods for *writing* formatted strings to the console, and obtaining the writer associated with it:

```
Console format(String format, Object... args)
Console printf(String format, Object... args)
```

These methods write a formatted string to this console's output stream using the specified format string and arguments, according to the default locale.

```
PrintWriter writer()
```

The method retrieves the unique PrintWriter object associated with this console.

```
void flush()
```

This method flushes the console and forces any buffered output to be written immediately.

Example 11.5 illustrates a typical use of the Console class to change the password of a user. A password file can first be generated by running the program in the class MakePasswordFile. Each user name (String) and the hash value (int) of the corresponding password are stored on a single line in a text file, separated by a space. At the start of the program, this information is read into a map declared at (1) by the method readPWStore() declared at (9). This method uses a BufferedReader chained to a FileReader to read the lines in the text file. The login name and the password hash values are extracted using a Scanner and put into the password map.

At the end of the program, the updated password map is written back to the file at (6) by the method writePWStore() declared at (10). This method uses a PrintWriter chained to a FileWriter to write the information. It uses the printf() method of the PrintWriter to format the login/password information on each line that is written to the file.

The console is obtained at (2). The login name and the current password are read at (4) by calling the readLine() and the readPassword() methods, respectively:

```
...
login = console.readLine("Enter your login: ");
oldPassword = console.readPassword("Enter your current password: ");
...
```

User verification is done by the verifyPassword() method at (7). The char array is first converted to a string by calling the String.copyValueOf() method. The hash value of this string is compared with the hash code of the password for the user looked up in the password map.

The code at (5) implements the procedure for changing the password. The user is asked to submit the new password, and then asked to confirm it. Note the password characters are not echoed. The respective char arrays returned with this input are compared for equality by the static method equals() in the java.util.Arrays class, that compares two arrays. The password is changed by the changePassword() method at (8). This puts a new entry in the password map, whose value is the hash value of the new password.

The char arrays with the passwords are zero-filled by calling the Arrays.fill() method when they are no longer needed.

Example 11.5   *Changing Passwords*

```
import java.io.FileWriter;
import java.io.IOException;
import java.io.PrintWriter;
import java.util.Map;
import java.util.Set;
import java.util.TreeMap;

/** Class to create a password file */
public final class MakePasswordFile {

  public static void main (String[] args) throws IOException {
    Map<String, Integer> pwStore = new TreeMap<String, Integer>();
    pwStore.put("tom", "123".hashCode());
    pwStore.put("dick", "456".hashCode());
    pwStore.put("harry", "789".hashCode());

    PrintWriter destination = new PrintWriter(new FileWriter("pws.txt"));
    Set<Map.Entry<String, Integer>> pwSet = pwStore.entrySet();
    for (Map.Entry<String, Integer> entry : pwSet) {
      // Format: login password
```

```
          destination.printf("%s %s%n", entry.getKey(), entry.getValue());
        }
      destination.flush();
      destination.close();
    }
}
```

```
import java.io.BufferedReader;
import java.io.Console;
import java.io.FileReader;
import java.io.FileWriter;
import java.io.IOException;
import java.io.PrintWriter;
import java.util.Arrays;
import java.util.Map;
import java.util.Scanner;
import java.util.Set;
import java.util.TreeMap;

/** Class to change the password of a user */
public class ChangePassword {

  // Map for storing login/password info.                          (1)
  private static Map<String, Integer> pwStore;

  public static void main (String[] args) throws IOException  {

    // Obtain the console:                                          (2)
    Console console = System.console();
    if (console == null) {
      System.err.println("No console available.");
      return;
    }

    // Read the login/password info from a file:                   (3)
    readPWStore();

    // Verify user:                                                 (4)
    String login;
    char[] oldPassword;
    do {
      login = console.readLine("Enter your login: ");
      oldPassword = console.readPassword("Enter your current password: ");
    } while (login.length() == 0 || oldPassword.length == 0 ||
             !verifyPassword(login, oldPassword));
    Arrays.fill(oldPassword, '0');

    // Changing the password:                                       (5)
    boolean noMatch = false;
    do {
      // Read the new password and its confirmation:
      char[] newPasswordSelected
             = console.readPassword("Enter your new password: ");
      char[] newPasswordConfirmed
```

```
                             = console.readPassword("Confirm your new password: ");

          // Compare the supplied passwords:
          noMatch = newPasswordSelected.length == 0  ||
                    newPasswordConfirmed.length == 0 ||
                    !Arrays.equals(newPasswordSelected, newPasswordConfirmed);
          if (noMatch) {
            console.format("Passwords don't match. Please try again.%n");
          } else {
            changePassword(login, newPasswordSelected);
            console.format("Password changed for %s.%n", login);
          }
          // Zero-fill the password arrays:
          Arrays.fill(newPasswordSelected, '0');
          Arrays.fill(newPasswordConfirmed, '0');
        } while (noMatch);

        // Save the login/password info to a file:                     (6)
        writePWStore();
      }

      /** Verifies the password. */                                   // (7)
      private static boolean verifyPassword(String login, char[] password) {
        Integer suppliedPassword = String.copyValueOf(password).hashCode();
        Integer storedPassword = pwStore.get(login);
        return storedPassword != null && storedPassword.equals(suppliedPassword);
      }

      /** Changes the password for the user. */                       // (8)
      private static void changePassword(String login, char[] password) {
        Integer newPassword = String.copyValueOf(password).hashCode();
        pwStore.put(login, newPassword);
      }

      /** Reads login/password from a file */                         // (9)
      private static void readPWStore() throws IOException {
        pwStore = new TreeMap<String, Integer>();
        BufferedReader source = new BufferedReader(new FileReader("pws.txt"));
        while (true) {
          String txtLine = source.readLine();
          if (txtLine == null) break;              // EOF?
          Scanner scanner = new Scanner(txtLine);
          // Format: <login string> <password int hash value>
          String login = scanner.next();
          Integer password = scanner.nextInt();
          pwStore.put(login, password);
        }
        source.close();
      }

      /** Writes login/password to a file */                         // (10)
      private static void writePWStore() throws IOException {
        PrintWriter destination = new PrintWriter(new FileWriter("pws.txt"));
        Set<Map.Entry<String, Integer>> pwSet = pwStore.entrySet();
        for (Map.Entry<String, Integer> entry : pwSet) {
```

```
        // Format: <login string> <password int hash value>
        destination.printf("%s %s%n", entry.getKey(), entry.getValue());
      }
      destination.close();
    }
  }
```

Running the program:

```
>java ChangePassword
Enter your login: tom
Enter your current password:
Enter your new password:
Confirm your new password:
Password changed for tom
```

 Review Questions

11.13   Which of these are valid parameter types for the `write()` methods of the `Writer` class?

Select the three correct answers.
(a) `String`
(b) `char`
(c) `char[]`
(d) `int`

11.14   What is the default encoding for an `OutputStreamWriter`?

Select the one correct answer.

(a) 8859_1
(b) UTF8
(c) Unicode
(d) The default is system-dependent.
(e) The default is not system-dependent, but is none of the above.

11.15   Which of these integer types do not have their own `print()` method in the `PrintWriter` class?

Select the one correct answer.
(a) `byte`
(b) `char`
(c) `int`
(d) `long`
(e) All have their own `print()` method.

11.16   How can one access the standard error stream?

Select the one correct answer.

(a) It is accessed via a member of the `System.err` class.

(b) It is accessed via the static variable named out in the System class.
(c) It is accessed via the static variable named err in the System class.
(d) It is accessed via the static variable named err in the Runtime class.
(e) It is returned by a method in the System class.

11.17 How can we programmatically guarantee that a call to a print() method of the PrintWriter class was successful or not?

Select the one correct answer.

(a) Check if the return value from the call is -1.
(b) Check if the return value from the call is null.
(c) Catch the IOException that is thrown when an I/O error occurs.
(d) Call the checkError() method of the PrinterWriter class immediately after the print() method call returns to see if an IOException was thrown.

11.18 Given the following program:

```java
import java.io.EOFException;
import java.io.FileInputStream;
import java.io.FileNotFoundException;
import java.io.IOException;
import java.io.InputStreamReader;

public class MoreEndings {
  public static void main(String[] args) {
    try {
      FileInputStream fis = new FileInputStream("seq.txt");
      InputStreamReader isr = new InputStreamReader(fis);
      int i = isr.read();
      while (i != -1) {
        System.out.print((char)i + "|");
        i = isr.read();
      }
    } catch (FileNotFoundException fnf) {
      System.out.println("File not found");
    } catch (EOFException eofe) {
      System.out.println("End of stream");
    } catch (IOException ioe) {
      System.out.println("Input error");
    }
  }
}
```

Assume that the file "seq.txt" exists in the current directory, has the required access permissions, and contains the string "Hello".

Which statement about the program is true?

Select the one correct answer.

(a) The program will not compile because a certain unchecked exception is not caught.
(b) The program will compile and print H|e|l|l|o|Input error.

(c) The program will compile and print H|e|l|l|o|End of stream.

(d) The program will compile, print H|e|l|l|o|, and then terminate normally.

(e) The program will compile, print H|e|l|l|o|, and then block in order to read from the file.

(f) The program will compile, print H|e|l|l|o|, and terminate because of an uncaught exception.

11.19 Which code, when inserted at (1), will result in the program compiling and running without errors?

```java
import java.io.*;

public class MakeLines {
  public static void main(String[] args) {
    try {
      String fileName = "greetings.txt";
      // (1) INSERT CODE HERE ...
      writeGreetings(stream);
      stream.close();
    } catch (IOException ioe) {
      System.out.println("I/O error");
    }
  }

  private static void writeGreetings(Writer writer) {
    try {
      BufferedWriter bw = new BufferedWriter(writer);
      bw.write("Hello");
      bw.newLine();
      bw.write("Howdy");
      bw.newLine();
      bw.flush();
    } catch (IOException ioe) {
      System.out.println("I/O error");
    }
  }
}
```

Select the three correct answers.

(a) `FileOutputStream fos = new FileOutputStream(fileName);`

(b) `OutputStreamWriter stream = new OutputStreamWriter(fos);`

(c) `FileOutputStream fos = new FileOutputStream(fileName);`

(d) `InputStreamWriter stream = new InputStreamWriter(fos);`

(e) `FileOutputStream stream = new FileOutputStream(fileName);`

(f) `PrintWriter stream = new PrintWriter(fileName);`

(g) `FileWriter stream = new FileWriter(fileName);`

11.20 Given the following program:

```java
import java.io.BufferedReader;
import java.io.EOFException;
import java.io.FileNotFoundException;
```

```
import java.io.FileReader;
import java.io.IOException;

public class NoEndings {
  public static void main(String[] args) {
    try {
      FileReader fr = new FileReader("greetings.txt");
      BufferedReader br = new BufferedReader(fr);
      System.out.print(br.readLine() + "|");
      System.out.print(br.readLine() + "|");
      System.out.print(br.readLine() + "|");
    } catch (EOFException eofe) {
      System.out.println("End of stream");
    } catch (IOException ioe) {
      System.out.println("Input error");
    }
  }
}
```

Assume that the file "greeting.txt" exists in the current directory, has the required access permissions, and contains the following two lines of text:

```
Hello
Howdy
```

Which statement is true about the program?

Select the one correct answer.

(a) The program will not compile because the `FileNotFoundException` is not caught.
(b) The program will compile, print `Hello|Howdy|null|`, and then terminate normally.
(c) The program will compile and print `Hello|Howdy|Input error`.
(d) The program will compile and print `Hello|Howdy|End of stream`.
(e) The program will compile, print `Hello|Howdy|`, and then block in order to read from the file.
(f) The program will compile, print `Hello|Howdy|`, and terminate because of an uncaught exception.

11.21   Given the following program:

```
import java.io.Console;

public class ConsoleInput {

  public static void main(String[] args){
    Console console = System.console();
    if (console == null) {
      System.err.println("No console available.");
      return;
    }
    String username = console.readLine("Enter user name (%d chars): ", 4);
    char[] password = console.readPassword("Enter password (%d chars): ", 4);

    System.out.println("Username: " + username);
```

```
        System.out.println("Password: " + String.valueOf(password));
    }
}
```

Assume that the user types the strings "java dude" and "fort knox" when prompted for the user name and the password, respectively.

Which statement about the program is true?

Select the one correct answer.

(a) The program will print:
```
Username: java
Password: fort knox
```

(b) The program will print:
```
Username: java dude
Password: fort
```

(c) The program will print:
```
Username: java dude
Password: fort knox
```

(d) The program will print:
```
Username: java
Password: fort
```

11.6 Object Serialization

Object serialization allows an object to be transformed into a sequence of bytes that can later be re-created (*deserialized*) into the original object. After deserialization, the object has the same state as it had when it was serialized, barring any data members that were not serializable. This mechanism is generally known as *persistence*. Java provides this facility through the ObjectInput and ObjectOutput interfaces, which allow the reading and writing of objects from and to streams. These two interfaces extend the DataInput and DataOutput interfaces, respectively (see Figure 11.1, p. 476).

The ObjectOutputStream class and the ObjectInputStream class implement the ObjectOutput interface and the ObjectInput interface, respectively, providing methods to write and read binary representation of objects as well as Java primitive values. Figure 11.9 gives an overview of how these classes can be chained to underlying streams and some selected methods they provide. The figure does not show the methods inherited from the abstract OutputStream and InputStream superclasses.

The read and write methods in the two classes can throw an IOException, and the read methods will throw an EOFException if the end of the stream has been reached.

Figure 11.9   *Object Stream Chaining*

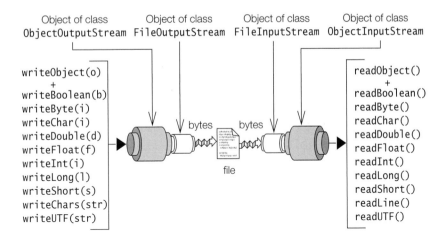

The `ObjectOutputStream` **Class**

The class `ObjectOutputStream` can write objects to any stream that is a subclass of the `OutputStream`, e.g., to a file or a network connection (socket). An `Object OutputStream` must be chained to an `OutputStream` using the following constructor:

```
ObjectOutputStream(OutputStream out) throws IOException
```

For example, in order to store objects in a file and thus provide persistent storage for objects, an `ObjectOutputStream` can be chained to a `FileOutputStream`:

```
FileOutputStream outputFile = new FileOutputStream("obj-storage.dat");
ObjectOutputStream outputStream = new ObjectOutputStream(outputFile);
```

Objects can be written to the stream using the `writeObject()` method of the `ObjectOutputStream` class:

```
final void writeObject(Object obj) throws IOException
```

The `writeObject()` method can be used to write *any* object to a stream, including strings and arrays, as long as the object implements the `java.io.Serializable` interface, which is a marker interface with no methods. The `String` class, the primitive wrapper classes and all array types implement the `Serializable` interface. A serializable object can be any compound object containing references to other objects, and all constituent objects that are serializable are serialized recursively when the compound object is written out. This is true even if there are cyclic references between the objects. Each object is written out only once during serialization. The following information is included when an object is serialized:

• the class information needed to reconstruct the object.

- the values of all serializable non-transient and non-static members, including those that are inherited.

An exception of the type java.io.NotSerializableException is thrown if a non-serializable object is encountered during the serialization process. Note also that objects of subclasses that extend a serializable class are always serializable.

The ObjectInputStream Class

An ObjectInputStream is used to restore (*deserialize*) objects that have previously been serialized using an ObjectOutputStream. An ObjectInputStream must be chained to an InputStream, using the following constructor:

```
ObjectInputStream(InputStream in)
        throws IOException, StreamCorruptedException
```

For example, in order to restore objects from a file, an ObjectInputStream can be chained to a FileInputStream:

```
FileInputStream inputFile = new FileInputStream("obj-storage.dat");
ObjectInputStream inputStream = new ObjectInputStream(inputFile);
```

The method readObject() of the ObjectInputStream class is used to read an object from the stream:

```
final Object readObject()
        throws OptionalDataException, ClassNotFoundException, IOException
```

Note that the reference returned is of type Object regardless of the actual type of the retrieved object, and can be cast to the desired type. Objects and values must be read in the same order as when they were serialized.

Serializable, non-transient data members of an object, including those data members that are inherited, are restored to the values they had at the time of serialization. For compound objects containing references to other objects, the constituent objects are read to re-create the whole object structure. In order to deserialize objects, the appropriate classes must be available at runtime. Note that new objects are created during deserialization, so that no existing objects are overwritten.

The class ObjectSerializationDemo in Example 11.6 serializes some objects in the writeData() method at (1), and then deserializes them in the readData() method at (2). The readData() method also writes the data to the standard output stream.

The writeData() method writes the following values to the output stream: an array of strings (strArray), a long value (num), an array of int values (intArray), and lastly a String object (commonStr) which is shared with the array of strings, strArray. However, this shared String object is actually only serialized once. Duplication is automatically avoided when the same object is serialized several times. Note that the array elements and the characters in a String object are not written out explicitly one by one. It is enough to pass the object reference in the writeObject() method call. The method also recursively goes through the array of strings, strArray, serializing each String object in the array.

The method readData() deserializes the data in the order in which it was written. An explicit cast is needed to convert the reference of a deserialized object to a subtype. Note that new objects are created by the readObject() method, and that an object created during the deserialization process has the same state as the object that was serialized.

Example 11.6   *Object Serialization*

```java
//Reading and Writing Objects
import java.io.EOFException;
import java.io.FileInputStream;
import java.io.FileNotFoundException;
import java.io.FileOutputStream;
import java.io.IOException;
import java.io.ObjectInputStream;
import java.io.ObjectOutputStream;
import java.util.Arrays;

public class ObjectSerializationDemo {
  void writeData() {                                     // (1)
    try {
      // Set up the output stream:
      FileOutputStream outputFile = new FileOutputStream("obj-storage.dat");
      ObjectOutputStream outputStream = new ObjectOutputStream(outputFile);

      // Write data:
      String[] strArray = {"Seven", "Eight", "Six"};
      long num = 2008;
      int[] intArray = {1, 3, 1949};
      String commonStr = strArray[2];                    // "Six"
      outputStream.writeObject(strArray);
      outputStream.writeLong(num);
      outputStream.writeObject(intArray);
      outputStream.writeObject(commonStr);

      // Flush and close the output stream:
      outputStream.flush();
      outputStream.close();
    } catch (FileNotFoundException e) {
      System.err.println("File not found: " + e);
    } catch (IOException e) {
      System.err.println("Write error: " + e);
    }
  }

  void readData() {                                      // (2)
    try {
      // Set up the input stream:
      FileInputStream inputFile = new FileInputStream("obj-storage.dat");
      ObjectInputStream inputStream = new ObjectInputStream(inputFile);
```

```java
            // Read the data:
            String[] strArray = (String[]) inputStream.readObject();
            long num = inputStream.readLong();
            int[] intArray = (int[]) inputStream.readObject();
            String commonStr = (String) inputStream.readObject();

            // Write data to the standard output stream:
            System.out.println(Arrays.toString(strArray));
            System.out.println(Arrays.toString(intArray));
            System.out.println(commonStr);

            // Close the stream:
            inputStream.close();
        } catch (FileNotFoundException e) {
            System.err.println("File not found: " + e);
        } catch (EOFException e) {
            System.err.println("End of stream: " + e);
        } catch (IOException e) {
            System.err.println("Read error: " + e);
        } catch (ClassNotFoundException e) {
            System.err.println("Class not found: " + e);
        }
    }

    public static void main(String[] args) {
        ObjectSerializationDemo demo = new ObjectSerializationDemo();
        demo.writeData();
        demo.readData();
    }
}
```

Output from the program:

```
[Seven, Eight, Six]
[1, 3, 1949]
Six
```

Example 11.7 illustrates some salient aspects of serialization. The setup comprises the classes Wheel and Unicycle, and their client class SerialClient. The class Unicycle has a field of type Wheel, and the class Wheel has a field of type int. The class Serial-Client provides two methods, writeData() and readData(), declared at (4) and (5), respectively. The writeData() method serializes a unicycle with a wheel of size 65 to a file. The readData() method deserializes the bytes on the file. The state of the objects is printed to the standard output stream before serialization, and so is the state of the object created by deserialization.

If we run the program with the following declarations for the Wheel and the Unicycle classes, where both classes are serializable:

```java
class Wheel implements Serializable {                              // (1)
    private int wheelSize;
    ...
}
```

```
class Unicycle implements Serializable {                        // (2)
  private Wheel wheel;                                          // (3)
  ...
}
```

we get the following output, showing that both serialization and deserialization were successful:

```
Before writing: Unicycle with wheel size: 65
After reading: Unicycle with wheel size: 65
```

Example 11.7 *Non-Serializable Objects*

```
import java.io.Serializable;

//public class Wheel implements Serializable {                 // (1)
public class Wheel {                                           // (1a)
  private int wheelSize;

  Wheel(int ws) { wheelSize = ws; }

  public String toString() { return "wheel size: " + wheelSize; }
}
```

```
import java.io.Serializable;

public class Unicycle implements Serializable {                // (2)
  private Wheel wheel;                                         // (3)
//transient private Wheel wheel;                               // (3a)

  Unicycle (Wheel wheel) { this.wheel = wheel; }

  public String toString() { return "Unicycle with " + wheel; }
}
```

```
import java.io.FileInputStream;
import java.io.FileOutputStream;
import java.io.IOException;
import java.io.ObjectInputStream;
import java.io.ObjectOutputStream;

public class SerialClient {

  public static void main(String args[])
                    throws IOException, ClassNotFoundException {
    SerialClient demo = new SerialClient();
    demo.writeData();
    demo.readData();
  }

  void writeData() throws IOException {                        // (4)
    // Set up the output stream:
    FileOutputStream outputFile = new FileOutputStream("storage.dat");
    ObjectOutputStream outputStream = new ObjectOutputStream(outputFile);
```

```
        // Write the data:
        Wheel wheel = new Wheel(65);
        Unicycle uc = new Unicycle(wheel);
        System.out.println("Before writing: " + uc);
        outputStream.writeObject(uc);

        // Close the stream:
        outputStream.flush();
        outputStream.close();
    }

    void readData() throws IOException, ClassNotFoundException {       // (5)
        // Set up the input streams:
        FileInputStream inputFile = new FileInputStream("storage.dat");
        ObjectInputStream inputStream = new ObjectInputStream(inputFile);

        // Read data.
        Unicycle uc = (Unicycle) inputStream.readObject();

        // Write data on standard output stream.
        System.out.println("After reading: " + uc);

        // Close the stream.
        inputStream.close();
    }
}
```

If we make the wheel field of the Unicycle class *transient*, (3a):

```
class Wheel implements Serializable {                                 // (1)
    private int wheelSize;
    ...
}

class Unicycle implements Serializable {                             // (2)
    transient private Wheel wheel;                                    // (3a)
    ...
}
```

we get the following output, showing that the wheel field of the Unicycle object was not serialized:

```
Before writing: Unicycle with wheel size: 65
After reading: Unicycle with null
```

As noted earlier, static fields are not serialized, as these are not part of the state of an object.

If the class Wheel in Example 11.7 is *not* serializable, (1a):

```
class Wheel {                                                         // (1a)
    private int wheelSize;
    ...
}
```

```
class Unicycle implements Serializable {                    // (2)
  private Wheel wheel;                                      // (3)
  ...
}
```

we get the following output when we run the program, i.e., a Unicycle object can*not* be serialized because its constituent Wheel object is not serializable:

```
>java SerialClient
Before writing: Unicycle with wheel size: 65
Exception in thread "main" java.io.NotSerializableException: Wheel
  at java.io.ObjectOutputStream.writeObject0(ObjectOutputStream.java:1156)
  at java.io.ObjectOutputStream.defaultWriteFields(ObjectOutputStream.java:1509)
  at java.io.ObjectOutputStream.writeSerialData(ObjectOutputStream.java:1474)
  at java.io.ObjectOutputStream.writeOrdinaryObject(ObjectOutputStream.java:1392)
  at java.io.ObjectOutputStream.writeObject0(ObjectOutputStream.java:1150)
  at java.io.ObjectOutputStream.writeObject(ObjectOutputStream.java:326)
  at SerialClient.writeData(SerialClient.java:25)
  at SerialClient.main(SerialClient.java:12)
```

Customizing Object Serialization

As we have seen, the class of the object must implement the Serializable interface if we want the object to be serialized. If this object is a compound object, then all its constituent objects must also be serializable, and so on.

It is not always possible for a client to declare that a class is Serializable. It might be declared final, and therefore not extendable. The client might not have access to the code, or extending this class with a serializable subclass might not be an option. Java provides a customizable solution for serializing objects in such cases.

The basic idea behind the scheme is to use default serialization as much as possible, and provide "hooks" in the code for the serialization mechanism to call specific methods to deal with objects or values that should not or cannot be serialized by the default methods of the object streams.

Customizing serialization is illustrated in Example 11.8. The serializable class Unicycle would like to use the Wheel class, but this class is not serializable. If the wheel field in the Unicycle class is declared to be transient, it will be ignored by the default serialization procedure. This is not a viable option, as the unicycle will be missing the wheel size when a serialized unicycle is deserialized, as was illustrated in Example 11.7.

Any serializable object has the option of customizing its own serialization if it implements the following pair of methods:

```
private void writeObject(ObjectOutputStream) throws IOException;
private void readObject(ObjectInputStream)
                throws IOException, ClassNotFoundException;
```

These methods are *not* part of any interface. Although private, these methods can be called by the JVM. The first method is called on the object when its serialization starts. The serialization procedure uses the reference value of the object passed in

the ObjectOutputStream.writeObject() method to call the first method on this object.
The second method is called on the object created when the deserialization procedure is initiated by the call to the ObjectInputStream.readObject() method.

Customizing serialization for objects of the class Unicycle in Example 11.8 is
achieved by the methods at (3b) and (3c). Note that the field wheel is declared transient at (3a) and excluded by the normal serialization process.

In the method writeObject() at (3b), the pertinent lines of code are the following:

```
oos.defaultWriteObject();
oos.writeInt(wheel.getWheelSize());
```

The call to the defaultWriteObject() method of the ObjectOutputStream does what its
name implies: normal serialization of the current object. The second line of code
does the customization: it writes the binary int value of the wheel size to the
ObjectOutputStream. Code for customization can be called both before and after the
call to the defaultWriteObject() method, as long as the same order is used during
deserialization.

In the method readObject() at (3c), the pertinent lines of code are the following:

```
ois.defaultReadObject();
int wheelSize = ois.readInt();
wheel = new Wheel(wheelSize);
```

The call to the defaultReadObject() method of the ObjectInputStream does what its
name implies: normal deserialization of the current object. The second line of
code reads the binary int value of the wheel size from the ObjectInputStream. The
third line of code creates a Wheel object passing this value in the constructor call,
and assigns its reference value to the wheel field of the current object. Again, code
for customization can be called both before and after the call to the defaultRead-
Object() method, as long as it is in correspondence with the customization code
in the writeObject() method.

The client class SerialClient in Example 11.8 is the same as the one in Example 11.7.
The output from the program confirms that the object state prior to serialization is
identical to the object state after deserialization.

- -

Example 11.8 *Customized Serialization*

```
public class Wheel {                                                    // (1a)
  private int wheelSize;

  Wheel(int ws) { wheelSize = ws; }

  int getWheelSize() { return wheelSize; }

  public String toString() { return "wheel size: " + wheelSize; }
}
```

```java
import java.io.IOException;
import java.io.ObjectInputStream;
import java.io.ObjectOutputStream;
import java.io.Serializable;

public class Unicycle implements Serializable {                  // (2)
  transient private Wheel wheel;                                 // (3a)

  Unicycle(Wheel wheel) { this.wheel = wheel; }

  public String toString() { return "Unicycle with " + wheel; }

  private void writeObject(ObjectOutputStream oos) {             // (3b)
    try {
      oos.defaultWriteObject();
      oos.writeInt(wheel.getWheelSize());
    } catch (IOException e) {
      e.printStackTrace();
    }
  }

  private void readObject(ObjectInputStream ois) {               // (3c)
    try {
      ois.defaultReadObject();
      int wheelSize = ois.readInt();
      wheel = new Wheel(wheelSize);
    } catch (IOException e) {
      e.printStackTrace();
    } catch (ClassNotFoundException e) {
      e.printStackTrace();
    }
  }
}
```

```java
public class SerialClient { // Same as in Example 11.7 }
```

Output from the program:

```
Before writing: Unicycle with wheel size: 65
After reading: Unicycle with wheel size: 65
```

Serialization and Inheritance

The inheritance hierarchy of an object also determines what its state will be after it is deserialized. An object will have the same state at deserialization as it had at the time it was serialized if *all* its superclasses are also serializable. This is because the normal object creation procedure using constructors is *not* run during deserialization (see Section 9.11, p. 416, on constructing the initial object state).

However, if any superclass of an object is *not* serializable, then the normal creation procedure using constructors *is* run, starting at the first non-serializable superclass, all the way up to the Object class. This means that the state at deserialization might

not be the same as at the time the object was serialized, because superconstructors
run during deserialization may have initialized the object's state.

Example 11.9 illustrates how inheritance affects serialization. The Student class is a
subclass of the Person class. Whether the superclass Person is serializable or not has
implications for serializing objects of the Student subclass, in particular, when their
byte representation is deserialized.

The following code in the method writeData() declared at (1) in the class Serial-
Inheritance serializes a Student object:

```
Student student = new Student("Pendu", 1007);
System.out.println("Before writing: " + student);
outputStream.writeObject(student);
```

The corresponding code for deserialization is in the method readData() declared at
(2) in the class SerialInheritance:

```
Student student = (Student) inputStream.readObject();
System.out.println("After reading: " + student);
```

We get the following output from the program in Example 11.9 when it is run with
(1a) in the Person class and the Student class, i.e., when the superclass is serializable
and so is the subclass, by virtue of inheritance. The results show that the object
state prior to serialization is identical to the object state after deserialization. In this
case, no superclass constructors were run during deserialization.

```
Before writing: Student state(Pendu, 1007)
After reading: Student state(Pendu, 1007)
```

However, this is not the case when the superclass Person is not serializable. We get
the following output from the program in Example 11.9 when it is run with (1b) in
the Person class and the Student class, i.e. when only the subclass is serializable, but
not the superclass. The output shows that the object state prior to serialization is
not identical to the object state after deserialization.

```
Before writing: Student state(Pendu, 1007)
After reading: Student state(null, 1007)
```

During deserialization, the *default* constructor of the Person superclass at (2) is run.
As we can see from the declaration of the Person class in Example 11.9, this default
constructor does not initialize the name field, which remains initialized with the
default value for reference types, i.e., null.

. . . .

Example 11.9   *Serialization and Inheritance*

```
// A superclass
// public class Person implements Serializable {           // (1a)
public class Person  {                                      // (1b)
  private String name;

  Person() {}                                               // (2)
  Person(String name) { this.name = name; }
```

```java
  public String getName() { return name; }
}
```

```java
import java.io.Serializable;

//public class Student extends Person {                          // (1a)
public class Student extends Person implements Serializable {  // (1b)

  private long studNum;

  Student(String name, long studNum) {
    super(name);
    this.studNum = studNum;
  }

  public String toString() {
    return "Student state(" + getName() + ", " + studNum + ")";
  }
}
```

```java
import java.io.FileInputStream;
import java.io.FileOutputStream;
import java.io.IOException;
import java.io.ObjectInputStream;
import java.io.ObjectOutputStream;

public class SerialInheritance {
  public static void main(String[] args)
                    throws IOException, ClassNotFoundException {
    SerialInheritance demo = new SerialInheritance();
    demo.writeData();
    demo.readData();
  }

  void writeData() throws IOException {                         // (1)
    // Set up the output stream:
    FileOutputStream outputFile = new FileOutputStream("storage.dat");
    ObjectOutputStream outputStream = new ObjectOutputStream(outputFile);

    // Write the data:
    Student student = new Student("Pendu", 1007);
    System.out.println("Before writing: " + student);
    outputStream.writeObject(student);

    // Close the stream:
    outputStream.flush();
    outputStream.close();
  }

  void readData() throws IOException, ClassNotFoundException {   // (2)
    // Set up the input stream:
    FileInputStream inputFile = new FileInputStream("storage.dat");
    ObjectInputStream inputStream = new ObjectInputStream(inputFile);
```

```
      // Read data.
      Student student = (Student) inputStream.readObject();

      // Write data on standard output stream.
      System.out.println("After reading: " + student);

      // Close the stream.
      inputStream.close();
   }
}
```

 ## Review Questions

11.22 How many methods are defined in the `Serializable` interface?

Select the one correct answer.

(a) None
(b) One
(c) Two
(d) Three
(e) None of the above.

11.23 Which of the following best describes the data written by an `ObjectOutputStream`?

Select the one correct answer.

(a) Bytes and other Java primitive types.
(b) Object hierarchies.
(c) Object hierarchies and Java primitive types.
(d) Single objects.
(e) Single objects and Java primitive types.

11.24 Given the following code:

```
public class Person {
  protected String name;
  Person() { }
  Person(String name) { this.name = name; }
}
```

```
import java.io.Serializable;
public class Student extends Person implements Serializable {
  private long studNum;
  Student(String name, long studNum) {
    super(name);
    this.studNum = studNum;
  }
  public String toString() { return "(" + name + ", " + studNum + ")"; }
}
```

```
import java.io.*;
public class RQ800_10 {
```

```
    public static void main(String args[])
                    throws IOException, ClassNotFoundException {
      FileOutputStream outputFile = new FileOutputStream("storage.dat");
      ObjectOutputStream outputStream = new ObjectOutputStream(outputFile);
      Student stud1 = new Student("Aesop", 100);
      System.out.print(stud1);
      outputStream.writeObject(stud1);
      outputStream.flush();
      outputStream.close();

      FileInputStream inputFile = new FileInputStream("storage.dat");
      ObjectInputStream inputStream = new ObjectInputStream(inputFile);
      Student stud2 = (Student) inputStream.readObject();
      System.out.println(stud2);
      inputStream.close();
    }
  }
```

Which statement about the program is true?

Select the one correct answer.

(a) It fails to compile.
(b) It compiles, but throws an exception at runtime.
(c) It prints (Aesop, 100)(Aesop, 100).
(d) It prints (Aesop, 100)(null, 100).
(e) It prints (Aesop, 100)(, 100).

11.25 Given the following code:

```
public class Person  {
  protected String name;
  Person() { this.name = "NoName"; }
  Person(String name) { this.name = name; }
}
```

```
import java.io.Serializable;
public class Student extends Person implements Serializable {
  private long studNum;
  Student(String name, long studNum) {
    super(name);
    this.studNum = studNum;
  }
  public String toString() { return "(" + name + ", " + studNum + ")"; }
}
```

```
import java.io.*;
public class RQ800_20 {

  public static void main(String args[])
                    throws IOException, ClassNotFoundException {
    FileOutputStream outputFile = new FileOutputStream("storage.dat");
    ObjectOutputStream outputStream = new ObjectOutputStream(outputFile);
    Student stud1 = new Student("Aesop", 100);
    System.out.print(stud1);
```

```
        outputStream.writeObject(stud1);
        outputStream.flush();
        outputStream.close();

        FileInputStream inputFile = new FileInputStream("storage.dat");
        ObjectInputStream inputStream = new ObjectInputStream(inputFile);
        Student stud2 = (Student) inputStream.readObject();
        System.out.println(stud2);
        inputStream.close();
    }
}
```

Which statement about the program is true?

Select the one correct answer.

(a) It fails to compile.
(b) It compiles, but throws an exception at runtime.
(c) It prints (Aesop, 100)(Aesop, 100).
(d) It prints (Aesop, 100)(null, 100).
(e) It prints (Aesop, 100)(NoName, 100).

11.26   Given the following code:

```
import java.io.Serializable;
public class Person implements Serializable {
  protected String name;
  Person() { this.name = "NoName"; }
  Person(String name) { this.name = name; }
}
```

```
public class Student extends Person {
  private long studNum;
  Student(String name, long studNum) {
    super(name);
    this.studNum = studNum;
  }
  public String toString() { return "(" + name + ", " + studNum + ")"; }
}
```

```
import java.io.*;
public class RQ800_30 {

  public static void main(String args[])
                    throws IOException, ClassNotFoundException {
    FileOutputStream outputFile = new FileOutputStream("storage.dat");
    ObjectOutputStream outputStream = new ObjectOutputStream(outputFile);
    Student stud1 = new Student("Aesop", 100);
    System.out.print(stud1);
    outputStream.writeObject(stud1);
    outputStream.flush();
    outputStream.close();

    FileInputStream inputFile = new FileInputStream("storage.dat");
    ObjectInputStream inputStream = new ObjectInputStream(inputFile);
```

```
        Student stud2 = (Student) inputStream.readObject();
        System.out.println(stud2);
        inputStream.close();
    }
}
```

Which statement about the program is true?

Select the one correct answer.

(a) It fails to compile.
(b) It compiles, but throws an exception at runtime.
(c) It prints (Aesop, 100)(Aesop, 100).
(d) It prints (Aesop, 100)(null, 100).
(e) It prints (Aesop, 100)(NoName, 100).

11.27 Given the following code:

```
import java.io.Serializable;
public class Person implements Serializable {
  protected transient String name;
  Person(String name) { this.name = name; }
}
```

```
public class Student extends Person {
  private long studNum;
  Student(String name, long studNum) {
    super(name);
    this.studNum = studNum;
  }
  public String toString() { return "(" + name + ", " + studNum + ")"; }
}
```

```
import java.io.*;
public class RQ800_40 {

  public static void main(String args[])
                  throws IOException, ClassNotFoundException {
    FileOutputStream outputFile = new FileOutputStream("storage.dat");
    ObjectOutputStream outputStream = new ObjectOutputStream(outputFile);
    Student stud1 = new Student("Aesop", 100);
    System.out.print(stud1);
    outputStream.writeObject(stud1);
    outputStream.flush();
    outputStream.close();

    FileInputStream inputFile = new FileInputStream("storage.dat");
    ObjectInputStream inputStream = new ObjectInputStream(inputFile);
    Student stud2 = (Student) inputStream.readObject();
    System.out.println(stud2);
    inputStream.close();
  }
}
```

Which statement about the program is true?

Select the one correct answer.

(a) It fails to compile.
(b) It compiles, but throws an exception at runtime.
(c) It prints (Aesop, 100)(Aesop, 100).
(d) It prints (Aesop, 100)(null, 100).
(e) It prints (Aesop, 100)(NoName, 100).

11.28   Given the following code:

```
import java.io.Serializable;
public class Person implements Serializable {
  protected transient String name;
  Person() { this.name = "NoName"; }
  Person(String name) { this.name = name; }
}
```

```
import java.io.*;
public class Student extends Person {
  private long studNum;
  Student(String name, long studNum) {
    super(name);
    this.studNum = studNum;
  }

  public String toString() { return "(" + name + ", " + studNum + ")"; }

  private void writeObject(ObjectOutputStream oos) throws IOException {
      oos.defaultWriteObject();
      oos.writeObject("NewName");
  }

  private void readObject(ObjectInputStream ois)
              throws IOException, ClassNotFoundException {
      ois.defaultReadObject();
      name = (String) ois.readObject();
  }
}
```

```
import java.io.*;
public class RQ800_50 {

  public static void main(String args[])
                  throws IOException, ClassNotFoundException {
    FileOutputStream outputFile = new FileOutputStream("storage.dat");
    ObjectOutputStream outputStream = new ObjectOutputStream(outputFile);
    Student stud1 = new Student("Aesop", 100);
    System.out.print(stud1);
    outputStream.writeObject(stud1);
    outputStream.flush();
    outputStream.close();

    FileInputStream inputFile = new FileInputStream("storage.dat");
    ObjectInputStream inputStream = new ObjectInputStream(inputFile);
```

```
        Student stud2 = (Student) inputStream.readObject();
        System.out.println(stud2);
        inputStream.close();
    }
}
```

Which statement about the program is true?

Select the one correct answer.

(a) It fails to compile.
(b) It compiles, but throws an exception at runtime.
(c) It prints (Aesop, 100)(Aesop, 100).
(d) It prints (Aesop, 100)(NewName, 100).
(e) It prints (Aesop, 100)(NoName, 100).

11.29   Given the following code:

```
public class Person {
  protected transient String name;
  Person() { this.name = "NoName"; }
  Person(String name) { this.name = name; }
}
```

```
public class Student extends Person {
  protected long studNum;
  Student() { }
  Student(String name, long studNum) {
    super(name);
    this.studNum = studNum;
  }
}
```

```
import java.io.*;

public class GraduateStudent extends Student implements Serializable {
  private int year;
  GraduateStudent(String name, long studNum, int year) {
    super(name, studNum);
    this.year = year;
  }

  public String toString() {
    return "(" + name + ", " + studNum + ", " + year  + ")";
  }

  private void readObject(ObjectInputStream ois)
              throws IOException, ClassNotFoundException {
    ois.defaultReadObject();
    name = "NewName";
    studNum = 200;
    year =2;
  }
}
```

```java
import java.io.*;
public class RQ800_70 {

  public static void main(String args[])
                     throws IOException, ClassNotFoundException {
    FileOutputStream outputFile = new FileOutputStream("storage.dat");
    ObjectOutputStream outputStream = new ObjectOutputStream(outputFile);
    GraduateStudent stud1 = new GraduateStudent("Aesop", 100, 1);
    System.out.print(stud1);
    outputStream.writeObject(stud1);
    outputStream.flush();
    outputStream.close();

    FileInputStream inputFile = new FileInputStream("storage.dat");
    ObjectInputStream inputStream = new ObjectInputStream(inputFile);
    GraduateStudent stud2 = (GraduateStudent) inputStream.readObject();
    System.out.println(stud2);
    inputStream.close();
  }
}
```

Which statement about the program is true?

Select the one correct answer.

(a) It fails to compile.
(b) It compiles, but throws an exception at runtime.
(c) It prints (Aesop, 100, 1)(Aesop, 100, 1).
(d) It prints (Aesop, 100, 1)(NewName, 0, 1).
(e) It prints (Aesop, 100, 1)(NewName, 200, 2).

11.30   Given the following code:

```java
import java.io.Serializable;
public class Person implements Serializable {
  protected transient String name;
  Person(String name) { this.name = name; }
}
```

```java
public class Student extends Person {
  private static int numOfStudents;
  private long studNum;
  Student(String name, long studNum) {
    super(name);
    this.studNum = studNum;
    ++numOfStudents;
  }
  public String toString() {
    return "(" + name + ", " + studNum + ", " + numOfStudents + ")";
  }
}
```

```java
import java.io.*;
public class RQ800_80 {
```

```
public static void main(String args[])
                    throws IOException, ClassNotFoundException {
    FileOutputStream outputFile = new FileOutputStream("storage.dat");
    ObjectOutputStream outputStream = new ObjectOutputStream(outputFile);
    Student stud1 = new Student("Aesop", 100);
    System.out.print(stud1);
    outputStream.writeObject(stud1);
    outputStream.flush();
    outputStream.close();

    Student student = new Student("Mowgli", 300);

    FileInputStream inputFile = new FileInputStream("storage.dat");
    ObjectInputStream inputStream = new ObjectInputStream(inputFile);
    Student stud2 = (Student) inputStream.readObject();
    System.out.println(stud2);
    inputStream.close();
  }
}
```

Which statement about the program is true?

Select the one correct answer.

(a) It fails to compile.
(b) It compiles, but throws an exception at runtime.
(c) It prints (Aesop, 100, 1)(Aesop, 100, 1).
(d) It prints (Aesop, 100, 1)(null, 100, 2).
(e) It prints (Aesop, 100, 1)(null, 100, 1).

 ## Chapter Summary

The following information was included in this chapter:

- Discussion of the File class, which provides an interface to the host file system.

- Byte streams, as represented by the InputStream and OutputStream classes.

- File streams, as represented by the FileInputStream and FileOutputStream classes.

- Reading and writing binary files using the DataInputStream and DataOutputStream classes.

- Character streams, as represented by the Reader and Writer classes.

- Usage of character encodings, including Unicode and UTF8, by the InputStreamReader and OutputStreamWriter classes.

- Reading and writing text files.

- Buffered character streams, as represented by the BufferedReader and BufferedWriter classes.

- Standard input, output, and error streams represented by the fields System.in, System.out and System.err, respectively.

- Object serialization: reading and writing objects.

Programming Exercise

11.1   Write a program that reads text from a source using one encoding, and writes the text to a destination using another encoding. The program should have four optional arguments:

- The first argument, if present, should specify the encoding of the source. The default source encoding should be "8859_1".

- The second argument, if present, should specify the encoding of the destination. The default destination encoding should be "UTF8".

- The third argument, if present, should specify a source file. If no argument is given, the standard input should be used.

- The fourth argument, if present, should specify a destination file. If no argument is given, the standard output should be used.

Use buffering, and read and write 512 bytes at a time to make the program efficient.

Errors should be written to the standard error stream.

Localization, Pattern Matching, and Formatting

12

Exam Objectives

3.4 Use standard J2SE APIs in the `java.text` package to correctly format or parse dates, numbers, and currency values for a specific locale; and, given a scenario, determine the appropriate methods to use if you want to use the default locale or a specific locale. Describe the purpose and use of the `java.util.Locale` class.

3.5 Write code that uses standard J2SE APIs in the `java.util` and `java.util.regex` packages to format or parse strings or streams. For strings, write code that uses the `Pattern` and `Matcher` classes and the `String.split` method. Recognize and use regular expression patterns for matching (limited to: . (dot), * (star), + (plus), ?, \d, \s, \w, [], ()). The use of *, +, and ? will be limited to greedy quantifiers, and the parenthesis operator will only be used as a grouping mechanism, not for capturing content during matching. For streams, write code using the `Formatter` and `Scanner` classes and the `PrintWriter.format/printf` methods. Recognize and use formatting parameters (limited to: %b, %c, %d, %f, %s) in format strings.

Supplementary Objectives

- Write regular expressions using boundary matchers and logical operators.
- Write code to use a matcher in the match-and-replace mode.
- Write code to use a scanner with delimiters and patterns.
- Write code to use a scanner in multi-line mode.
- Format time/date values using time/date conversions with the `printf()` and `format()` methods.

12.1 The `java.util.Locale` Class

An accounting system for the US market is obviously not going to function well, for example, in the Norwegian market. For one thing, the formatting of date, number and currency are not the same—not to mention that the languages in the two markets are different. Adapting programs so that they have global awareness of such differences is called *internationalization* (a.k.a., "in8ln"). A *locale* represents a specific geographical, political, or cultural region. Its two most important attributes are *language* and *country*. Certain classes in the Java Standard Library provide *locale-sensitive* operations. For example, they provide methods to format values that represent *dates*, *currency* and *numbers* according to a specific locale. Developing programs that are responsive to a specific locale is called *localization*.

A locale is represented by an instance of the class `java.util.Locale`. Many locale-sensitive methods require such an instance for their operation. A locale object can be created using the following constructors:

```
Locale(String language)
Locale(String language, String country)
```

The language argument is an ISO-639-1 Language Code (which uses two lower-case letters), and the country argument is an ISO-3166 Country Code (which uses two uppercase letters).

Examples of selected language codes and country codes are given in Table 12.1 and Table 12.2, respectively.

Table 12.1 *Selected Language Codes*

Language Code	Language
"en"	English
"no"	Norwegian
"fr"	French

Table 12.2 *Selected Country Codes*

Country Code	Country
"US"	United States (US)
"GB"	Great Britain (GB)
"NO"	Norway
"FR"	France

The Locale class also has predefined locales for certain *languages,* irrespective of the region where they are spoken (see Table 12.3).

Table 12.3   *Selected Predefined Locales for Languages*

Constant	Language
Locale.ENGLISH	Locale with English (new Locale("en",""))
Locale.FRENCH	Locale with French (new Locale("fr",""))
Locale.GERMAN	Locale with German (new Locale("de","")), i.e., Deutsch.

The Locale class also has predefined locales for certain *combinations of countries and languages* (see Table 12.4).

Table 12.4   *Selected Predefined Locales for Countries*

Constant	Country
Locale.US	Locale for US (new Locale("en","US"))
Locale.UK	Locale for United Kingdom/Great Britain (new Locale("en","GB"))
Locale.CANADA_FRENCH	Locale for Canada with French language (new Locale("fr","CA"))

Normally a program uses the *default locale* on the platform to provide localization. The Locale class provides a get and set method to manipulate the default locale.

```
static Locale getDefault()
static void setDefault(Locale newLocale)
```

The first method returns the current value of the default locale, and the second one sets a specific locale as the default locale.

```
String getDisplayCountry()
String getDisplayCountry(Locale inLocale)
```

Returns a name for the locale's country that is appropriate for display to the user, depending on the default locale in the first method or the inLocale argument in the second method.

```
String getDisplayLanguage()
String getDisplayLanguage(Locale inLocale)
```

Returns a name for the locale's language that is appropriate for display to the user, depending on the default locale in the first method or the inLocale argument in the second method.

```
String getDisplayName()
String getDisplayName(Locale inLocale)
```

Returns a name for the locale that is appropriate for display.

A locale is an immutable object, having *two sets* of *get* methods to return the *display name* of the country and the language in the locale. The first set returns the display name of the current locale according to the default locale, while the second set returns the display name of the current locale according to the locale specified as argument in the method call.

Example 12.1 illustrates the use of the get methods in the Locale class. The method call locNO.getDisplayCountry() returns the country display name (Norwegian) of the Norwegian locale according to the default locale (which is the United Kingdom), whereas the method call locNO.getDisplayCountry(locFR) returns the country display name (Norvège) of the Norwegian locale according to the French locale.

Example 12.1 *Understanding Locales*

```java
import java.util.Locale;
public class LocalesEverywhere {

  public static void main(String[] args) {

    Locale locDF = Locale.getDefault();
    Locale locNO =  new Locale("no", "NO");     // Locale: Norwegian/Norway
    Locale locFR =  new Locale("fr", "FR");     // Locale: French/France

    // Display country name for Norwegian locale:
    System.out.println("In " + locDF.getDisplayCountry() + "(default)" +
                        ": " + locNO.getDisplayCountry());
    System.out.println("In " + locNO.getDisplayCountry() +
                        ": " + locNO.getDisplayCountry(locNO));
    System.out.println("In " + locFR.getDisplayCountry() +
                        ": " + locNO.getDisplayCountry(locFR));

    // Display language name for Norwegian locale:
    System.out.println("In " + locDF.getDisplayCountry() +  "(default)" +
                        ": " + locNO.getDisplayLanguage());
    System.out.println("In " + locNO.getDisplayCountry() +
                        ": " + locNO.getDisplayLanguage(locNO));
    System.out.println("In " + locFR.getDisplayCountry() +
                        ": " + locNO.getDisplayLanguage(locFR));
  }
}
```

Output from the program:

```
In United Kingdom(default): Norway
In Norway: Norge
In France: Norvège
In United Kingdom(default): Norwegian
In Norway: norsk
In France: norvégien
```

12.2 The `java.util.Date` **Class**

The Date class represents time as a `long` integer which is the number of milliseconds measured from January 1, 1970 00:00:00.000 GMT. This starting point is called the *epoch*. The `long` value used to represent a point in time comprises both the *date* and the *time of day*. The Date class provides the following constructors:

```
Date()
Date(long milliseconds)
```

The default constructor returns the *current date and time of day*. The second constructor returns the date/time corresponding to the specified `milliseconds` after the *epoch*.

Some selected methods from the date class are shown below. The Date class has mostly deprecated methods, and provides date operations in terms of milliseconds only. However, it is useful for printing the date value in a standardized long format, as the following example shows:

```
Tue Mar 04 17:22:37 EST 2008
```

The Date class is not locale-sensitive, and has been replaced by the Calendar and DateFormat classes. The class overrides the methods clone(), equals(), hashCode(), and toString() from the Object class, and implements the Comparable<Date> interface.

```
public String toString()
```

Returns the value of the current Date object in a standardized long format and, if necessary, adjusted to the default time zone.

```
long getTime()
void setTime(long milliseconds)
```

The first method returns the value of the current Date object as the number of milliseconds after the epoch. The second method sets the date in the current Date object, measured in `milliseconds` after the epoch.

```
boolean after(Date date)
boolean before(Date date)
```

The methods determine whether the current date is strictly after or before a specified date, respectively.

Example 12.2 illustrates using the Date class. The toString() method (called implicitly in the print statements) prints the date value in a long format. The date value can be manipulated as a `long` integer, and a negative `long` value can be used to represent a date *before* the epoch.

Example 12.2 *Using the* Date *class*

```java
import java.util.Date;
public class UpToDate {

  public static void main(String[] args) {

    // Get the current date:
    Date currentDate = new Date();
    System.out.println("Date formatted: " + currentDate);
    System.out.println("Date value in milliseconds: " + currentDate.getTime());

    // Create a Date object with a specific value of time measured
    // in milliseconds from the epoch:
    Date date1 = new Date(1200000000000L);

    // Change the date in the Date object:
    System.out.println("Date before adjustment: " + date1);
    date1.setTime(date1.getTime() + 1000000000L);
    System.out.println("Date after adjustment: " + date1);

    // Compare two dates:
    String compareStatus = currentDate.after(date1) ? "after" : "before";
    System.out.println(currentDate + " is " + compareStatus + " " + date1);

    // Set a date before epoch:
    date1.setTime(-1200000000000L);
    System.out.println("Date before epoch: " + date1);
  }
}
```

Output from the program:

```
Date formatted: Wed Mar 05 00:37:28 EST 2008
Date value in milliseconds: 1204695448609
Date before adjustment: Thu Jan 10 16:20:00 EST 2008
Date after adjustment: Tue Jan 22 06:06:40 EST 2008
Wed Mar 05 00:37:28 EST 2008 is after Tue Jan 22 06:06:40 EST 2008
Date before epoch: Tue Dec 22 21:40:00 EST 1931
```

12.3 The `java.util.Calendar` Class

A calendar represents a specific instant in time that comprises *a date and a time of day*. The abstract class `java.util.Calendar` provides a rich set of date operations to represent and manipulate many variations on date/time representation. However, the locale-sensitive formatting of the calendar is delegated to the `DateFormat` class (see Section 12.4).

Static Factory Methods to Create a Calendar

The following factory methods of the `Calendar` class create and return an instance of the `GregorianCalendar` class that represents the current date/time.

```
static Calendar getInstance()
static Calendar getInstance(Locale loc)
```

The first method returns a calendar with the *current* date/time using the default time zone and default locale. The second returns a calendar with the *current* date/time using the default time zone and specified locale.

Interoperability with the `Date` Class

Interoperability with the `Date` class is provided by the following two methods:

```
Date getTime()
```

Returns the date/time of the calendar in a `Date` object, as an offset in milliseconds from the epoch.

```
void setTime(Date date)
```

Sets the current calendar's date/time from the value of the specified date.

Selected get and set Methods

Information in a calendar is accessed via a *field number*. The `Calendar` class defines field numbers for the various fields (e.g., year, month, day, hour, minutes, seconds) in a calendar. Selected field numbers are shown in Table 12.5. For example, the constant `Calendar.Year` is the field number that indicates the field with the value of the year in a calendar.

Table 12.5 *Selected Field Numbers to Indicate Information in a Calendar*

Constant	Field Number that indicates:
`Calendar.WEEK_OF_YEAR` `Calendar.WEEK_OF_MONTH`	The week number within the current year and within the current month, respectively.

`Calendar.DAY_OF_YEAR`
`Calendar.DAY_OF_MONTH`
`Calendar.DATE`
`Calendar.DAY_OF_WEEK`
	The day number within the current year, the current month, the current date (same as `DAY_OF_MONTH`) and the current week, respectively.

`Calendar.YEAR`
`Calendar.MONTH`
`Calendar.HOUR`
`Calendar.HOUR_OF_DAY`
`Calendar.MINUTE`
`Calendar.SECOND`
`Calendar.MILLISECOND`
	The year within the calendar.
	The month within the year.
	The hour within the day (12-hour clock).
	The hour within the day (24-hour clock).
	The minutes within the hour.
	The seconds within the minute.
	The milliseconds within the second.

The get() method returns the value of the field designated by the field number passed as argument. The return value of a field is an int. Table 12.6 shows some selected *field values* that are represented as constants. The first day of the month or year has the value 1. The value of the first day of the week depends on the locale. However, the first month of the year, i.e., Calendar.JANUARY, has the value 0.

```
Calendar calendar = Calendar.getInstance();
out.println(calendar.getTime());           // Wed Mar 05 16:20:36 EST 2008
int year = calendar.get(Calendar.YEAR);
int month = calendar.get(Calendar.MONTH);
int dayOfMonth = calendar.get(Calendar.DAY_OF_MONTH);
out.printf("%4d-%02d-%02d%n", year, month + 1, dayOfMonth);  // 2008-03-05
```

We have added 1 to the month in the last statement, before printing the date.

Table 12.6 *Selected Constants that Represent Values in a Calendar*

Constant	Description
Calendar.SUNDAY Calendar.MONDAY ... Calendar.SATURDAY	Integer values that indicate the days in a week.
Calendar.JANUARY Calendar.FEBRUARY ... Calendar.DECEMBER	Integer values that represent the months in a year.

Particular fields in a calendar can be set to a specific value, or they can be cleared. Many set operations can be done without recomputing and normalizing the values in a calendar. In the code below, the values in the calendar are first recomputed and normalized when the get operation is performed in (3). Note how the day and the month has changed from the values in (1).

```
out.println(calendar.getTime());                  // (1) Wed Mar 05 21:51:57 EST 2008
calendar.set(Calendar.DAY_OF_MONTH, 33);          // (2) Set day of month to 33
calendar.set(Calendar.MONTH, Calendar.OCTOBER);   // (3) Set month to October.
out.println(calendar.getTime());                  // (4) Sun Nov 02 21:51:57 EST 2008
```

Since not all locales start the week on the same day of the week, the Calendar class provides methods to set and get the first day of the week in a calendar.

```
out.println(calendar.getFirstDayOfWeek());        // 1
```

```
int get(int fieldNumber)
```

Returns the value of the given calendar field. See Table 12.5 for fields that can be specified.

```
void set(int fieldNUmber, int fieldValue)
void set(int year, int month, int dayOfMonth)
void set(int year, int month, int dayOfMonth, int hourOfDay, int minute)
void set(int year, int month, int dayOfMonth, int hourOfDay,
         int minute, int second)
```

The first method sets the specified calendar field to the given value. See Table 12.5 for fields that can be specified. See Table 12.6 for values that can be specified for certain fields. The other methods set particular fields. The calendar's date/time value in milliseconds is not recomputed until the next get operation is performed.

```
void clear()
void clear(int fieldNumber)
```

Clear all fields or designated field in the calendar, i.e., sets the field(s) as undefined.

```
int getFirstDayOfWeek()
void setFirstDayOfWeek(int value)
```

The first method returns which day of the week is the first day of the week in the calendar. The second method sets a particular day as the first day of the week (see Table 12.6 for valid values).

Manipulating a Calendar

The following code illustrates how the add() method works. Note how, when we added 13 months to the calendar, the number of months is normalized *and* the year has been incremented, as 13 months is 1 year and 1 month.

```
out.println(calendar.getTime());      // Wed Mar 05 22:03:29 EST 2008
calendar.add(Calendar.MONTH, 13);     // Add 13 more months
out.println(calendar.getTime());      // Sun Apr 05 22:03:29 EDT 2009
```

The following code illustrates how the roll() method is different from the add() method. Note how, when we added 13 months to the calendar now, only the number of months is normalized but the year is *not* incremented, i.e., the roll() method does *not* recompute larger fields as a consequence of normalizing smaller fields.

```
out.println(calendar.getTime());      // Wed Mar 05 22:03:29 EST 2008
calendar.roll(Calendar.MONTH, 13);    // Add 13 more months
out.println(calendar.getTime());      // Sat Apr 05 22:03:29 EDT 2008
```

```
void add(int field, int amount)
```

This is equivalent to calling set(field, get(field) + amount). All fields are recomputed.

```
void roll(int field, int amount)
```

This is equivalent to calling add(field,amount), but *larger* fields are unchanged. A positive amount means rolling up, a negative amount means rolling down.

Comparing Calendars

   int compareTo(Calendar anotherCalendar)

Implements Comparable<Calendar>, thus calendars can be compared (as offsets in milliseconds from the epoch).

Example 12.3 shows further examples of using the methods in the Calendar class. It is instructive to compare the code with the output from the program.

Example 12.3   *Using the* Calendar *Class*

```
import java.util.Calendar;
import java.util.Date;
public class UsingCalendar {
  public static void main(String[] args) {

    // Get a calendar with current time and print its date:
    Calendar calendar = Calendar.getInstance();
    printDate("The date in the calendar: ", calendar);

    // Convert to Date:
    Date date1 = calendar.getTime();
    System.out.println("The date in the calendar: " + date1);

    // Set calendar according to a Date:
    Date date2 = new Date(1200000000000L);
    System.out.println("The date is " + date2);
    calendar.setTime(date2);
    printDate("The date in the calendar: ", calendar);

    // Set values in a calendar
    calendar.set(Calendar.DAY_OF_MONTH, 33);
    calendar.set(Calendar.MONTH, 13);
    calendar.set(Calendar.YEAR, 2010);
    printDate("After setting: ", calendar);

    // Adding to a calendar
    calendar.add(Calendar.MONTH, 13);
    printDate("After adding: ", calendar);

    // Rolling a calendar
    calendar.roll(Calendar.MONTH, 13);
    printDate("After rolling: ", calendar);

    // First day of the week.
    System.out.println((calendar.SUNDAY == calendar.getFirstDayOfWeek() ?
                "Sunday is" : "Sunday is not" ) +
                " the first day of the week.");
  }

  static private void printDate(String prompt, Calendar calendar) {
    System.out.print(prompt);
```

```
        System.out.printf("%4d/%02d/%02d%n",
                        calendar.get(Calendar.YEAR),
                        (calendar.get(Calendar.MONTH) + 1),  // Adjust for month
                        calendar.get(Calendar.DAY_OF_MONTH));
    }
}
```

Output from the program:

```
The date in the calendar: 2008/03/05
The date in the calendar: Wed Mar 05 21:31:26 EST 2008
The date is Thu Jan 10 16:20:00 EST 2008
The date in the calendar: 2008/01/10
After setting: 2011/02/10
After adding: 2012/03/10
After rolling: 2012/04/10
Sunday is not the first day of the week.
```

12.4 The `java.text.DateFormat` Class

For dealing with text issues like formatting and parsing dates, time, currency and numbers, the Java Standard Library provides the java.text package. The abstract class DateFormat in this package provides methods for formatting and parsing dates and time.

See also the discussion in Section 12.7, Formatting Values, p. 593.

Static Factory Methods to Create a Date/Time Formatter

The class DateFormat provides formatters for dates, time of day, and combinations of date and time for the default locale or for a specified locale. The factory methods provide a high degree of flexibility when it comes to mixing and matching different formatting styles and locales. However, the formatting style and the locale cannot be changed after the formatter is created. The factory methods generally return an instance of the concrete class SimpleDateFormat, which is a subclass of DateFormat.

```
static DateFormat getInstance()
```

Returns a default date/time formatter that uses the DateFormat.SHORT style for both the date and the time (see also See Table 12.7).

```
static DateFormat getDateInstance()
static DateFormat getDateInstance(int dateStyle)
static DateFormat getDateInstance(int dateStyle, Locale loc)

static DateFormat getTimeInstance()
static DateFormat getTimeInstance(int timeStyle)
static DateFormat getTimeInstance(int timeStyle, Locale loc)

static DateFormat getDateTimeInstance()
static DateFormat getDateTimeInstance(int dateStyle, int timeStyle)
static DateFormat getDateTimeInstance(int dateStyle, int timeStyle,
                            Locale loc)
```

The first three methods return a formatter for dates. The next three methods return a formatter for time of day. The last three methods return a formatter for date and time. The no-argument methods return a formatter in default style(s) and in default locale.

The arguments dateStyle and timeStyle specify the style that should be used for formatting. See Table 12.7 for formatting styles. The styles DateFormat.DEFAULT and DateFormat.MEDIUM are equivalent.

Table 12.7 *Formatting Styles for Date and Time*

Style for Date/Time	Description	Examples (Locale: US)
DateFormat.DEFAULT	Default style pattern.	Mar 6, 2008 6:08:39 PM
DateFormat.FULL	Full style pattern.	Thursday, March 6, 2008 6:08:39 PM EST
DateFormat.LONG	Long style pattern.	March 6, 2008 6:08:39 PM EST
DateFormat.MEDIUM	Medium style pattern.	Mar 6, 2008 6:08:39 PM
DateFormat.SHORT	Short style pattern.	3/6/08 6:08 PM

Formatting Dates

A date/time formatter can be applied to a Date object by calling the format() method. The value of the Date object is formatted according to the formatter used.

Example 12.4 shows the result of formatting the current date/time with the same formatting style for both the date and the time, according to the US locale.

```
String format(Date date)
```

Formats the specified date/time and returns the resulting string.

Example 12.4 *Formatting Date/Time*

```java
import java.text.DateFormat;
import java.util.Date;
import java.util.Locale;

class UsingDateFormat {
  public static void main(String[] args) {

    // Create some date/time formatters:
    DateFormat[] dateTimeFormatters = new DateFormat[] {
        DateFormat.getDateTimeInstance(DateFormat.FULL, DateFormat.FULL,
                                    Locale.US),
        DateFormat.getDateTimeInstance(DateFormat.LONG, DateFormat.LONG,
                                    Locale.US),
        DateFormat.getDateTimeInstance(DateFormat.MEDIUM, DateFormat.MEDIUM,
                                    Locale.US),
        DateFormat.getDateTimeInstance(DateFormat.SHORT, DateFormat.SHORT,
                                    Locale.US)
    };
    // Style names:
    String[] styles = { "FULL", "LONG", "MEDIUM", "SHORT" };

    // Format current date/time using different date formatters:
    Date date = new Date();
    int i = 0;
    for(DateFormat dtf : dateTimeFormatters)
      System.out.printf("%-6s: %s%n", styles[i++], dtf.format(date));
  }
}
```

Output from the program:

```
FULL  : Thursday, March 6, 2008 6:08:39 PM EST
LONG  : March 6, 2008 6:08:39 PM EST
MEDIUM: Mar 6, 2008 6:08:39 PM
SHORT : 3/6/08 6:08 PM
```

Parsing Strings to Date/Time

Although we have called it a date/time formatter, the instance returned by the factory methods mentioned earlier is also a *parser* that converts strings into date/time values. Example 12.5 illustrates the parsing of strings to date/time values. It uses the Norwegian locale defined at (1). Four locale-specific *date* formatters are created at (2). Each one is used to format the current date and the resulting string is parsed back to a Date object:

```java
String strDate = df.format(date);                      // (4)
Date parsedDate = df.parse(strDate);                   // (5)
```

The string is parsed according to the locale associated with the formatter. Being *lenient* during parsing means allowing values that are incorrect or incomplete. Lenient parsing is illustrated at (6):

```
System.out.println("32.01.08|" + dateFormatters[0].parse("32.01.08|"));
```

The string "32.01.08|" is parsed by the date formatter according to the Norwegian locale. Although the value 32 is invalid for the number of days in a month, the output shows that it was normalized correctly. A *strict* formatter would have thrown a ParseException. Since the string was parsed to a *date*, default values for the *time* are set in the Date object. Also, trailing characters in the string after the date are ignored. The formatting style in the date formatter (in this case, DateFormat.SHORT) and the contents of the input string (in this case, "32.01.08") must be compatible with each other. Note that in the print statement, the Date object from the parsing is converted to a string according to the *default* locale:

```
32.01.08|Fri Feb 01 00:00:00 EST 2008
```

Date parse(String str) throws ParseException

Parses the specified string for date/time. No leading white space is allowed. Trailing characters after the date are ignored. Throws java.text.ParseException if unsuccessful.

void setLenient(boolean lenient)
boolean isLenient()

Sets or gets the status whether parsing should be lenient or strict. Default behavior is lenient parsing.

Example 12.5 *Using the* DateFormat *class*

```
import java.text.DateFormat;
import java.text.ParseException;
import java.util.Date;
import java.util.Locale;
class FormattingDates {
  public static void main(String[] args) throws ParseException {
    // Locale to use:
    Locale localeNOR = new Locale("no", "NO");            //  (1) Norway

    // Create some date formatters:                                  (2)
    DateFormat[] dateFormatters = new DateFormat[] {
        DateFormat.getDateInstance(DateFormat.SHORT, localeNOR),
        DateFormat.getDateInstance(DateFormat.MEDIUM,localeNOR),
        DateFormat.getDateInstance(DateFormat.LONG,  localeNOR),
        DateFormat.getDateInstance(DateFormat.FULL,  localeNOR)
    };

    // Parsing the date:                                             (3)
    System.out.println("Parsing:");
    Date date = new Date();
    for(DateFormat df : dateFormatters)
```

```
        try {
          String strDate = df.format(date);                        // (4)
          Date parsedDate = df.parse(strDate);                     // (5)
          System.out.println(strDate + "|" + df.format(parsedDate));
        } catch (ParseException pe) {
          System.out.println(pe);
        }

      // Leniency:                                                   (6)
      System.out.println("Leniency:");
      System.out.println("32.01.08|" + dateFormatters[0].parse("32.01.08|"));
    }
  }
```

Output from the program:

```
Parsing:
07.03.08|07.03.08
07.mar.2008|07.mar.2008
7. mars 2008|7. mars 2008
7. mars 2008|7. mars 2008
Leniency:
32.01.08|Fri Feb 01 00:00:00 EST 2008
```

Managing the Calendar and the Number Formatter

Each date/time formatter has a Calendar that is used to produce the date/time values from the Date object. In addition, a formatter has a number formatter (NumberFormat, Section 12.5) that is used to format the date/time values. The calendar and the number formatter are associated when the date/time formatter is created, but they can also be set programmatically by using the methods shown below.

void setCalendar(Calendar calendar)

Set the calendar to use for values of date and time. Otherwise, the default calendar for the default or specified locale is used.

Calendar getCalendar()

Get the calendar associated with this date/time formatter.

void setNumberFormat(NumberFormat numberFormatter)

Set the number formatter to use for values of date and time.

NumberFormat getNumberFormat()

Get the number formatter associated with the date/time formatter.

12.5 The `java.text.NumberFormat` Class

The abstract class `NumberFormat` provides methods for formatting and parsing *numbers* and *currency* values. Using a `NumberFormat` is in many ways similar to using a `DateFormat`.

See also the discussion in Section 12.7, Formatting Values, p. 593.

Static Factory Methods to Create a Number Formatter

The `NumberFormat` class provides factory methods for creating locale-sensitive formatters for numbers and currency values. However, the locale cannot be changed after the formatter is created. The factory methods return an instance of the concrete class `java.text.DecimalFormat` or an instance of the final class `java.util.Currency` for formatting numbers or currency values, respectively. Although we have called the instance a formatter, it is also a parser—analogous to using a date/time formatter.

```
static NumberFormat getNumberInstance()
static NumberFormat getNumberInstance(Locale loc)

static NumberFormat getCurrencyInstance()
static NumberFormat getCurrencyInstance(Locale loc)
```

The first two methods return a general formatter for numbers, i.e., a number formatter. The next two methods return a formatter for currency amounts, i.e., a currency formatter.

Formatting Numbers and Currency

A number formatter can be used to format a `double` or a `long` value. Depending on the number formatter, the formatting is locale-sensitive: either default or specific.

The following code shows how we can create a *number* formatter for the Norwegian locale and use it to format numbers according to this locale. Note the grouping of the digits and the decimal sign used in formatting according to this locale.

```
Double num = 12345.6789;
Locale locNOR = new Locale("no", "NO");                    // Norway
NumberFormat nfNOR = NumberFormat.getNumberInstance(locNOR);
String formattedNumStr = nfNOR.format(num);
System.out.println(formattedNumStr);                       // 12 345,679
```

The following code shows how we can create a *currency* formatter for the Norwegian locale, and use it to format currency values according to this locale. Note the currency symbol and the grouping of the digits, with the amount being rounded to two decimal places.

```
NumberFormat cfNOR = NumberFormat.getCurrencyInstance(locNOR);
String formattedCurrStr = cfNOR.format(num);
System.out.println(formattedCurrStr);                      // kr 12 345,68
```

```
String format(double d)
String format(long l)
```

Formats the specified number and returns the resulting string.

```
Currency getCurrency()
void setCurrency(Currency currency)
```

The first method returns the currency object used by the formatter. The last method allows the currency symbol to be set explicitly in the currency formatter, according to the ISO 4217 currency codes. For example, we can set the Euro symbol in a fr_France currency formatter with this method.

Parsing Strings to Numbers

A *number* formatter can be used to parse strings that are textual representations of *numeric* values. The following code shows the Norwegian number formatter from above being used to parse strings. In (1), the result is a long value because the dot (.) in the input string is not a legal character according to the number format used in the Norwegian locale. In (2), the result is a double value because the comma (,) in the input string is the decimal sign in the Norwegian locale. Note that the print statement prints the resulting number according to the *default* locale.

```
out.println(nfNOR.parse("9876.598"));     // (1)  9876
out.println(nfNOR.parse("9876,598"));     // (2)  9876.598
```

The following code demonstrates using a *currency* formatter as a parser. Note that the currency symbol is interpreted according to the locale in the currency parser. In (3), although a space is a grouping character in the Norwegian locale when formatting currency values, it is a *delimiter* in the input string.

```
out.println(cfNOR.parse("kr 9876.598"));  // 9876
out.println(cfNOR.parse("kr 9876,598"));  // 9876.598
out.println(cfNOR.parse("kr 9 876,59"));  // (3)  9
```

```
Number parse(String str) throws ParseException
```

Parses the specified string either to a Double or Long. No leading white space is allowed. Trailing characters after the number are ignored. Throws java.text.ParseException if unsuccessful.

```
void setParseIntegerOnly(boolean intOnly)
boolean isParseIntegerOnly()
```

Sets or gets the status whether this formatter should only parse integers.

Specifying the Number of Digits

The following methods allow the formatting of numbers to be further refined by setting the number of digits to be allowed in the integer and the decimal part of a number. However, a concrete number formatter can enforce certain limitations on these bounds.

```
void setMinimumIntegerDigits(int n)
int getMinimumIntegerDigits()

void setMaximumIntegerDigits(int n)
int getMaximumIntegerDigits()

void setMinimumFractionDigits(int n)
int getMinimumFractionDigits()

void setMaximumFractionDigits(int n)
int getMaximumFractionDigits()
```

Sets or gets the minimum or maximum number of digits to be allowed in the integer or decimal part of a number.

Example 12.6 further demonstrates the usage of number/currency formatters/ parsers. It uses two methods: runFormatters() and runParsers() declared at (1) and (2), respectively. The first one runs formatters supplied in an array on a specified numeric value, and the second one runs the formatters supplied in an array as parsers on an input string. Since the NumberFormat class does not provide a method for determining the locale of a formatter, an array of locales is used to supply this information. Note that the parsing succeeds if the input string is conducive to the locale used by the parser.

Example 12.6 *Using the* NumberFormat *class*

```
import java.text.NumberFormat;
import java.text.ParseException;
import java.util.Locale;
import static java.lang.System.out;

public class FormattingNumbers {
  public static void main(String[] args) {

    // Create an array of locales:
    Locale[] locales = {
        Locale.getDefault(),                              // Default: GB/UK
        new Locale("no", "NO"),                           // Norway
        Locale.JAPAN                                      // Japan
    };

    // Create an array of number formatters:
    NumberFormat[] numFormatters = new NumberFormat[] {
        NumberFormat.getNumberInstance(),                 // Default: GB/UK
        NumberFormat.getNumberInstance(locales[1]),       // Norway
        NumberFormat.getNumberInstance(locales[2])        // Japan
    };

    // Create an array of currency formatters:
    NumberFormat[] currFormatters = new NumberFormat[] {
        NumberFormat.getCurrencyInstance(),               // Default: GB/UK
        NumberFormat.getCurrencyInstance(locales[1]),     // Norway
        NumberFormat.getCurrencyInstance(locales[2])      // Japan
```

```
        };

        // Number to format:
        double number = 9876.598;

        // Format a number by different number formatters:
        out.println("Formatting the number: " + number);
        runFormatters(number, numFormatters, locales);

        // Set the max decimal digits to 2 for number formatters:
        for (NumberFormat nf : numFormatters) {
          nf.setMaximumFractionDigits(2);
        }
        out.println("\nFormatting the number " + number + " (to 2 dec. places):");
        runFormatters(number, numFormatters, locales);

        // Format a currency amount by different currency formatters:
        out.println("\nFormatting the currency amount: " + number);
        runFormatters(number, currFormatters, locales);

        // Parsing a number:
        runParsers("9876.598", numFormatters, locales);
        runParsers("9876,598", numFormatters, locales);
        runParsers("9876@598", numFormatters, locales);
        runParsers("@9876598", numFormatters, locales);    // Input error

        // Parsing a currency amount:
        runParsers("£9876.598", currFormatters, locales);
        runParsers("kr 9876,598", currFormatters, locales);
        runParsers("JPY 98@76598", currFormatters, locales);
        runParsers("@9876598", currFormatters, locales);  // Input error
      }

      /** Runs the formatters on the value. */
      static void runFormatters(double value, NumberFormat[] formatters,    // (1)
                                Locale[] locales) {
        for(int i = 0; i < formatters.length; i++)
          out.printf("%-24s: %s%n", locales[i].getDisplayName(),
                                    formatters[i].format(value));
      }

      /** Runs the parsers on the input string. */
      static void runParsers(String inputString, NumberFormat[] formatters, // (2)
                             Locale[] locales) {
        out.println("\nParsing: " + inputString);
        for(int i = 0; i < formatters.length; i++)
          try {
            out.printf("%-24s: %s%n", locales[i].getDisplayName(),
                                      formatters[i].parse(inputString));
          } catch (ParseException pe) {
            out.println(pe);
          }
      }
    }
```

Output from the program:

```
Formatting the number: 9876.598
English (United Kingdom): 9,876.598
Norwegian (Norway)    : 9 876,598
Japanese (Japan)      : 9,876.598

Formatting the number 9876.598 (to 2 dec. places):
English (United Kingdom): 9,876.6
Norwegian (Norway)    : 9 876,6
Japanese (Japan)      : 9,876.6

Formatting the currency amount: 9876.598
English (United Kingdom): £9,876.60
Norwegian (Norway)    : kr 9 876,60
Japanese (Japan)      : JPY 9,877

Parsing: 9876.598
English (United Kingdom): 9876.598
Norwegian (Norway)    : 9876
Japanese (Japan)      : 9876.598

Parsing: 9876,598
English (United Kingdom): 9876598
Norwegian (Norway)    : 9876.598
Japanese (Japan)      : 9876598

Parsing: 9876@598
English (United Kingdom): 9876
Norwegian (Norway)    : 9876
Japanese (Japan)      : 9876

Parsing: @9876598
java.text.ParseException: Unparseable number: "@9876598"
java.text.ParseException: Unparseable number: "@9876598"
java.text.ParseException: Unparseable number: "@9876598"

Parsing: £9876.598
English (United Kingdom): 9876.598
java.text.ParseException: Unparseable number: "£9876.598"
java.text.ParseException: Unparseable number: "£9876.598"

Parsing: kr 9876,598
java.text.ParseException: Unparseable number: "kr 9876,598"
Norwegian (Norway)    : 9876.598
java.text.ParseException: Unparseable number: "kr 9876,598"

Parsing: JPY 98@76598
java.text.ParseException: Unparseable number: "JPY 98@76598"
java.text.ParseException: Unparseable number: "JPY 98@76598"
Japanese (Japan)      : 98

Parsing: @9876598
java.text.ParseException: Unparseable number: "@9876598"
java.text.ParseException: Unparseable number: "@9876598"
java.text.ParseException: Unparseable number: "@9876598"
```

Review Questions

12.1   The language and the country of the UK locale are "anglais" and "Royaume-Uni" in
the France locale, respectively, and the language and the country of the France
locale are "French" and "France" in the UK locale, respectively. What will the following program print when compiled and run?

```java
public class LocaleInfo {
  public static void main(String[] args) {
    printLocaleInfo(Locale.UK, Locale.FRANCE);
    printLocaleInfo(Locale.FRANCE, Locale.UK);
  }
  public static void printLocaleInfo(Locale loc1, Locale loc2) {
    System.out.println(loc1.getDisplayLanguage(loc2) + ", " +
                       loc2.getDisplayCountry(loc1));
  }
}
```

Select the one correct answer.

(a) French, Royaume-Uni
     anglais, France

(b) anglais, Royaume-Uni
     French, France

(c) anglais, France
     French, Royaume-Uni

(d) French, France
     anglais, Royaume-Uniint i = 0;

12.2   Which statements are not true about the java.util.Date class?

Select the two correct answers.

(a) The java.util.Date class implements the Comparable<Date> interface.
(b) The java.util.Date class is locale-sensitive.
(c) The default constructor of the java.util.Date class returns the current date/
     time.
(d) The non-default constructor of the java.util.Date class throws an IllegalArgu-
     mentException if the argument value is negative.

12.3   Which code, when inserted at (1), will not set the date to *1. January 2009*?

```java
public class ChangingDate {
  public static void main(String[] args) {

    // Create a calendar that is set to 31. December 2008:
    Calendar calendar = Calendar.getInstance();
    calendar.set(Calendar.DAY_OF_MONTH, 31);
    calendar.set(Calendar.MONTH, Calendar.DECEMBER);
    calendar.set(Calendar.YEAR, 2008);
    calendar.set(Calendar.SECOND, 0);
```

```
      calendar.set(Calendar.MINUTE, 0);
      calendar.set(Calendar.HOUR_OF_DAY, 0);

      // (1) INSERT CODE HERE ...
      System.out.println(calendar.getTime());
    }
  }
```

Select the two correct answers.

(a) `calendar.set(Calendar.DAY_OF_MONTH, 1);`

(b) `calendar.set(Calendar.MONTH, Calendar.JANUARY);`

(c) `calendar.set(Calendar.YEAR, 2009);`

(d) `calendar.set(Calendar.DAY_OF_MONTH, 1);`

(e) `calendar.set(Calendar.MONTH, 12);`

(f) `calendar.add(Calendar.DAY_OF_MONTH, 1);`

(g) `calendar.roll(Calendar.DAY_OF_MONTH, 1);`

(h) `calendar.set(2009, 0, 1);`

(i) `calendar.set(2009, 1, 1);`

12.4 Which code, when inserted at (1), will make the program compile and execute normally?

```
public class Dating {
  public static void main(String[] args) {
    Date date = new Date();
    // (1) INSERT CODE HERE ...
  }
}
```

Select the one correct answer.

(a) `DateFormat df = new DateFormat(Locale.US);`
    `System.out.println(df.format(date));`

(b) `DateFormat df = new DateFormat(DateFormat.FULL, Locale.US);`
    `System.out.println(df.format(date));`

(c) `DateFormat df = DateFormat.getDateTimeInstance(DateFormat.FULL, Locale.US);`
    `System.out.println(df.format(date));`

(d) `DateFormat df = DateFormat.getDateTimeInstance(date);`
    `System.out.println(df.format(DateFormat.FULL, Locale.US));`

(e) `DateFormat df = DateFormat.getDateInstance(DateFormat.FULL, Locale.US);`
    `System.out.println(df.format(date));`

12.5 Which code, when inserted at (1), will not make the program compile and execute normally? Assume that the order of the values in a date is according to the US locale: month, day of month, and year, respectively.

```
public class ParsingDates {
  public static void main(String[] args) throws ParseException {
    // (1) INSERT DECLARATION HERE ...
    System.out.println(parseDate(inputStr));
  }
```

```
      public static Date parseDate(String inputString) throws ParseException {
        DateFormat dfUS = DateFormat.getDateInstance(DateFormat.SHORT, Locale.US);
        return dfUS.parse(inputString);
      }

  }
```

Select the one correct answer.

(a) `String inputStr = "3/7/08";`
(b) `String inputStr = "03/07/08";`
(c) `String inputStr = "3/37/08";`
(d) `String inputStr = "13/07/08";`
(e) `String inputStr = "3/07/08/2008";`
(f) `String inputStr = "  3/07/08    ";`
(g) `String inputStr = "Mar 7, 2008";`

12.6   Which statement is true about the program? Assume that the decimal sign is a dot (.) and the grouping character is a comma (,) for the US locale.

```
  public class ParsingNumbers {
    public static void main(String[] args) {
      // (1) DECLARATION INSERTED HERE ...
      System.out.println(parseNumber(inputStr));
    }

    public static Number parseNumber(String inputString) {
      NumberFormat nfUS = NumberFormat.getNumberInstance(Locale.US);
      Double num = nfUS.parse(inputString);
      return num;
    }
  }
```

Select the one correct answer.

(a) The following declaration, when inserted at (1), will result in the program compiling without errors and executing normally:

   `String inputStr = "1234.567";`

(b) The following declaration, when inserted at (1), will result in the program compiling without errors and executing normally:

   `String inputStr = "0.567";`

(c) The following declaration, when inserted at (1), will result in the program compiling without errors and executing normally:

   `String inputStr = "1234..";`

(d) The following declaration, when inserted at (1), will result in the program compiling without errors and executing normally:

   `String inputStr = "1,234.567";`

(e) The following declaration, when inserted at (1), will result in the program compiling without errors and executing normally:

   `String inputStr = "1 234.567";`

(f) Regardless of which declaration from (a) to (e) is inserted for the input reference at (1), the program will not compile.

(g) Regardless of which declaration from (a) to (e) is inserted for the input reference at (1), the program will compile, but result in an exception at runtime.

12.6 String Pattern Matching Using Regular Expressions

Using *patterns* to search for sequences of characters (i.e., strings) in the input is a powerful technique that can be used to search, modify, and maintain text-based data (e.g., XML data, log files, comma-separated values (CSV)). The java.util.regex package in the Java Standard Library provides support for *string pattern matching* that is based on *regular expressions*. Such an expression is specified using a special notation, which is precisely defined. A regular expression thus defines a pattern that represents *a set of strings* that we are interested in *matching* against characters in the input. We will use the term *regular expression* and *pattern* synonymously.

Before we can do string pattern matching with a regular expression, we have to *compile* it, i.e., turn it into a representation that can be used with an *engine* (also called an *automaton*) that can read the characters in the input and match them against the pattern. As we shall see, the java.util.Pattern class allows us to compile a regular expression, and the java.util.Matcher class allows us to create an engine for string pattern matching with the compiled regular expression.

The description of regular expressions presented here is by no means exhaustive. It should be regarded as a basic introduction, providing the fundamentals to go forth and explore the exciting world of regular expressions.

Regular Expression Fundamentals

The simplest form of a pattern is a *character* or a *sequence of characters* that matches itself. The pattern o, comprising the character o, will only match itself in the target string (i.e., the input).

```
Index:   012345678901234567890123456789012345678
Target:  All good things come to those who wait
Pattern: o
Match:   (5,5:o)(6,6:o)(17,17:o)(22,22:o)(26,26:o)(32,32:o)
```

The characters in the target are read from left to right sequentially and matched against the pattern. A *match* is announced when the pattern matches a particular occurrence of (zero or more) characters in the target. Six matches were found for the pattern o in the given target. A match is shown in the following notation:

(*start_index*,*end_index*:*group*)

where *start_index* and *end_index* are indices in the target indicating *where* a pattern match was found, and *group* comprises the character(s) delineated by the two indices in the target, that matched the pattern. (Example 12.8, p. 568, was used to generate all regular expression examples presented in this subsection.)

The example below searches for the pattern who in the given target, showing that three matches were found:

```
Index:   012345678901234567890123456789012345678
Target:  Interrogation with who, whose and whom.
Pattern: who
Match:   (19,21:who)(24,26:who)(34,36:who)
```

The regular expression notation uses a number of *metacharacters* (\, [], -, ^, $, ., ?, *, +, (), |) to define its constructs, i.e., these characters have a special meaning when used in a regular expression. A character is often called a *non-metacharacter* when it is not supposed to have any special meaning.

Characters

Table 12.8 shows regular expressions for matching a *single* character in the input. Examples of regular expressions with non-metacharacters were shown earlier. Such regular expressions match themselves in the input.

The pattern \t will match a tab character in the input, and the pattern \n will match a newline in the input. Since the backslash (\) is a metacharacter, we need to *escape* it (\\) in order to use it as a non-metacharacter in a pattern. Any metacharacter in a pattern can be escaped with a backslash (\). Note the similarity with escape sequences in Java strings, which also use the \ character as the escape character.

Table 12.8   *Selected Characters*

Character	Matches
x	The non-metacharacter x
\\	The backslash as non-metacharacter
\t	The tab character ('\u0009')
\n	The newline (line feed) character ('\u000A')
\r	The carriage-return character ('\u000D')
\f	The form-feed character ('\u000C')

Character Classes

The notation [] can be used to define a pattern that represents a *set of characters*, called a *character class*. Table 12.9 shows examples of such patterns. A ^ character is interpreted as a metacharacter when specified immediately after the [character. In this context, it *negates* all the characters in the set. Anywhere else in the [] construct, it is a non-metacharacter. The pattern [^aeiouAEIOU] represents the set of all characters that excludes all vowels, i.e., it matches any character that is not a vowel.

```
Index:    012345678901
Target:   I said I am.
Pattern:  [^aeiouAEIOU]
Match:    (1,1: )(2,2:s)(5,5:d)(6,6: )(8,8: )(10,10:m)(11,11:.)
```

The - character is used to specify *intervals* inside the [] notation. If the interval cannot be determined for a - character, it is treated as a non-metacharacter. For example, in the pattern [-A-Z], the first - character is interpreted as a non-metacharacter, but the second occurrence is interpreted as a metacharacter that represents an interval.

```
Index:    0123456789012
Target:   I-love-REGEX.
Pattern:  [-A-Z]
Match:    (0,0:I)(1,1:-)(6,6:-)(7,7:R)(8,8:E)(9,9:G)(10,10:E)(11,11:X)
```

Except for the \ metacharacter which retains its meaning, the other metacharacters $, ., ?, *, +, (,) and | are recognized as non-metacharacters in a [] construct.

Table 12.9   *Selected Character Classes*

Character Classes	Matches
[abc]	a, b, or c (*simple class*)
[^abc]	Any character except a, b, or c (*negation*)
[a-zA-Z]	a through z or A through Z, inclusive (*range*)
[a-d[m-p]]	a through d, or m through p, i.e., [a-dm-p] (*union*)
[a-z&&[def]]	d, e, or f (*intersection*)
[a-z&&[^bc]]	a through z, except for b and c, i.e., [ad-z] (*subtraction*)
[a-z&&[^m-p]]	a through z, and not m through p, i.e., [a-lq-z] (*subtraction*)

Predefined Character Classes

Table 12.10 shows a shorthand for writing some selected character classes. Note that a character class matches *one single character* at a time in the output, and not a sequence of characters (unless it has only one character). The metacharacter . should be paid special attention to, as it will match one occurrence of any single character.

```
Index:    012345678901234567890123456789012345678901234567890123456789
Target:   Who is who? Whose is it? To whom it may concern. How are you?
Pattern:  .[Hh]o
Match:    (0,2:Who)(7,9:who)(12,14:Who)(28,30:who)(48,50: Ho)
```

Here is another example, using a predefined character class in a pattern to recognize a date or time format:

```
Index:   012345678901234567890
Target:  01-03-49 786 09-09-09
Pattern: \d\d-\d\d-\d\d
Match:   (0,7:01-03-49)(13,20:09-09-09)
```

Table 12.10 *Selected Predefined Character Classes*

Pre-defined Character Classes	Matches
.	Any character (may also match a line terminator)
\d	A digit, i.e., [^0-9]
\D	A non-digit, i.e., [^\d]
\s	A whitespace character, i.e., [\t\n\x0B\f\r]
\S	A non-whitespace character, i.e., [^\s]
\w	A word character, i.e., [a-zA-Z_0-9]
\W	A non-word character: [^\w]

Boundary Matchers

Sometimes we are interested in finding a pattern match at either the beginning or the end of a string/line. This can be achieved by using *boundary matchers* (also called *anchors*), as shown in Table 12.11. Here is an example of a simple pattern to determine if the input ends in a ? character. We have to escape the ? character in order to use it as a non-metacharacter in the pattern. Note that, except for the ? character at the end of the input, the other ? characters in the input are not recognized.

```
Index:   012345678901234567890123456789012345678
Target:  Who is who? Who me? Who else?
Pattern: \?$
Match:   (28,28:?)
```

Table 12.11 *Boundary Matchers*

Boundary Matcher	Matches (R *is a regular expression.*)
^R	*Anchoring* at the beginning of a string/line
R$	*Anchoring* at the end of a string/line

Logical Operators

Table 12.12 shows *logical operators* that we can use to create more complex regular expressions. The logical operators are shown in *increasing order of precedence,* analogous to the logical operators in boolean expressions. Here is an example that uses all three logical operators for recognizing any case-insensitive occurrence of Java or C++ in the input:

```
Index:   012345678901234567890123456789012345678901
Target:  JaVA jAvA C++ jAv c+++1 javan C+
Pattern: ([Jj][aA][vV][aA])|([Cc]\+\+)
Match:   (0,3:JaVA)(5,8:jAvA)(10,12:C++)(18,20:c++)(24,27:java)
```

Table 12.12   *Selected Logical Operators*

Logical Operator	(R *and* U *are regular expressions)* Matches	Example
R | U	Either R or U. (*Logical OR*)	^[a-z]|\?$, a lowercase letter at the beginning or a ? at the end of the line.
RU	R followed by U. (*Logical AND, concatenation*)	[Jj][aA][vV][aA], any occurrence of Java in upper or lowercase letters.
(R)	R as a *group.*	(^[a-z])|(\?$)

Quantifiers

Quantifiers are powerful operators that *repeatedly* try to match a regular expression with the remaining characters in the input. These quantifiers (also called *repetition operators*) are defined as follows:

- R?, that matches the regular expression R zero or one time.
- R*, that matches the regular expression R zero or more times.
- R+, that matches the regular expression R one or more times.

The pattern a? is matched with a target string in the following example:

```
Index:   012345
Target:  banana
Pattern: a?
Match:   (0,0:)(1,1:a)(2,2:)(3,3:a)(4,4:)(5,5:a)(6,6:)
```

The pattern a? is interpreted as an a or as the *empty string.* There is a match with the pattern a? at *every* character in the target. When the current character is not an a in the target, the *empty string* is returned as the match. We can regard this as the engine inserting empty strings in the input to match the pattern a?. This behavior does not alter the target.

The pattern \d\d?-\d\d?-\d\d? is used as a simplified date format in the following example. The regular expression \d\d? represents any one or any two digits.

```
Index:   01234567890123456789012345678901
Target:  01-3-49 23-12 9-09-09 01-01-2010
Pattern: \d\d?-\d\d?-\d\d?
Match:   (0,6:01-3-49)(14,20:9-09-09)(22,29:01-01-20)
```

The pattern a* is interpreted as a non-zero sequence of a's or as the empty string (meaning no a's). The engine returns an empty string as the match, when the character in the input cannot be a part of a sequence of a's.

```
Index:   01234567
Target:  baananaa
Pattern: a*
Match:   (0,0:)(1,2:aa)(3,3:)(4,4:a)(5,5:)(6,7:aa)(8,8:)
```

The pattern (0|[1-9]\d*)\.\d\d recognizes all non-zero-leading, positive floating-point numbers that have at least one digit in the integral part and exactly two decimal places. Note that the regular expression \d* is equivalent to the regular expression [0-9]*.

```
Index:   012345678901234567890123456789 0
Target:  .50 1.50 0.50 10.50 00.50 1.555
Pattern: (0|[1-9]\d*)\.\d\d
Match:   (4,7:1.50)(9,12:0.50)(14,18:10.50)(21,24:0.50)(26,29:1.55)
```

The regular expression \d* used in the above pattern represents a sequence of digits or the empty string. A sequence of digits is some *permutation* of the digits from 0 to 9. In other words, the regular expression \d* represents *all* permutations of digits, which is also all non-negative integers, plus the empty string.

The pattern a+ is interpreted as a non-zero sequence of a's, i.e., at least one a. Compare the results below with the results for using the pattern a* above on the same target. No empty strings are returned when an a cannot be matched in the target.

```
Index:   01234567
Target:  baananaa
Pattern: a+
Match:   (1,2:aa)(4,4:a)(6,7:aa)
```

The regular expression \d+ represents *all* permutations of digits. The pattern \d+.\d+ represents all positive floating-point numbers that have at least one digit in the integral part and at least one digit in the fraction part. Note that \d+ is equivalent to [0-9]+.

```
Index:   0123456789012345678901234 5678
Target:  .50 1.50 0. 10.50 00.50 1.555
Pattern: \d+\.\d+
Match:   (4,7:1.50)(12,16:10.50)(18,22:00.50)(24,28:1.555)
```

The quantifiers presented above are called *greedy quantifiers*. Such a quantifier reads as much input as possible, and *backtracks* if necessary, to match as much of the input as possible. In other words, it will return the *longest possible match*. An engine for a greedy quantifier is eager to return a match. If it backtracks, it will do so until it finds the first valid match.

The example below illustrates greediness. The pattern `<.+>` is supposed to recognize a tag, i.e., a non-zero sequence of characters enclosed in angle brackets (< >). The example below shows that only *one* tag is found in the target. The greedy quantifier + returns the longest possible match in the input.

```
Index:   012345678901234567890123456789012345678901234
Target:  My <>very<> <emphasis>greedy</emphasis> regex
Pattern: <.+>
Match:   (3,38:<>very<> <emphasis>greedy</emphasis>)
```

There are counterparts to the greedy quantifiers called the *reluctant* and the *possessive* quantifiers (see Table 12.13). A *reluctant quantifier* (also called *lazy quantifier*) only reads enough of the input to match the pattern. Such a quantifier will apply its regular expression as few times as possible, only expanding the match as the engine backtracks to find a match for the overall regular expression. In other words, it will return the *shortest possible match*.

The example below illustrates *reluctantness/laziness*. The pattern `<.+?>` uses the reluctant quantifier +?, and is supposed to recognize a tag as before. The example below shows the result of applying the pattern to a target. The reluctant quantifier +? returns the shortest possible match for each tag recognized in the input.

```
Index:   0123456789012345678901234567890123456789012345678901234567
Target:  My <>very<> <emphasis>reluctant</emphasis> regex
Pattern: <.+?>
Match:   (3,10:<>very<>)(12,21:<emphasis>)(31,41:</emphasis>)
```

The result is certainly better with the reluctant quantifier. We can improve the matching by using the trick shown in this pattern: `<[^>]+>`. Since the match has two enclosing angle brackets, the pattern negates the end angle bracket, creating a character class that excludes the end angle bracket. The engine can keep expanding the tag name as long as no end angle bracket is found in the input. When this bracket is found in the input, a match can be announced, without incurring the penalty of backtracking. Note that the pattern below is using the greedy quantifier +.

```
Index:   01234567890123456789012345678901234567890123456
Target:  My <>very<> <emphasis>powerful</emphasis> regex
Pattern: <[^>]+>
Match:   (12,21:<emphasis>)(30,40:</emphasis>)
```

Lastly, there are the *possessive quantifiers* that always consume the entire input, and then go for one make-or-break attempt to find a match. A possessive quantifier never backtracks, even if doing so would succeed in finding a match. There are certain situations where possessive quantifiers can outperform the other types of quantifiers, but we will not pursue the subject any further in this book.

Table 12.13   *Quantifier Classification*

Greedy	Reluctant	Possessive	Matches (R *is a regular expression*)
R?	R??	R?+	R zero or one time, i.e., R is optional.
R*	R*?	R*+	R zero or more times.
R+	R+?	R++	R one or more times.

Escaping Metacharacters

A regular expression can be specified as a string expression in a Java program. In the declaration below, the string literal "who" contains the pattern who.

```
String p1 = "who";     // regex: who
```

The pattern \d represents a single digit character. If we are not careful in how we specify this pattern in a string literal, we run into trouble.

```
String p2 = "\d";     // Java compiler: Invalid escape sequence!
```

The escape sequence \d is invalid in the string literal above. Both string literals and regular expressions use a backslash (\) to escape metacharacters. For every backslash in a regular expression, we need to escape it in the string literal, i.e. specify it as a backslash pair (\\). This ensures that the Java compiler accepts the string literal, and the string will contain only *one* backslash for every backslash pair that is specified in the string literal. A backslash contained in the string is thus interpreted correctly as a backslash in the regular expression.

```
String p3 = "\\d";     // regex: \d
String p4 = "\\.";     // regex: \.  (i.e. the . non-metacharacter)
String p5 = ".";       // regex: .   (i.e. the . metacharacter)
```

If we want to use a backslash as a non-metacharacter in a regular expression, we have to escape the backslash (\), i.e use the pattern \\. In order to escape these two backslashes in a string literal, we need to specify *two* consecutive backslash pairs (\\\\). Each backslash pair becomes a single backslash inside the string, resulting in the two pairs becoming a single backslash pair, which is interpreted correctly in the regular expression, as the two backslash characters represent a backslash non-metacharacter.

```
String nonMetaBackslash = "\\\\";   // regex: \\ (i.e. the \ non-metacharacter)
```

Below are examples of string literals for some of the regular expressions we have seen earlier. Each backslash in the regular expression is escaped in the string literal.

```
String p6 = "\\d\\d-\\d\\d-\\d\\d";   // regex: \d\d-\d\d-\d\d
String p7 = "\\d+\\.\\d+";             // regex: \d+\.\d+
String p8 = "(^[a-z])|(\\?$)";         // regex: (^[a-z])|(\?$)
```

The `java.util.regex.Pattern` Class

The two classes `Pattern` and `Matcher` in the `java.util.regex` package embody the paradigm for working efficiently with regular expressions in Java. It consists of the following steps:

1. Compiling the regular expression string into a `Pattern` object which constitutes the compiled representation of the regular expression (i.e., a pattern) mentioned earlier:

   ```
   Pattern pattern = Pattern.compile(regexStr);
   ```

2. Using the `Pattern` object to obtain a `Matcher` (i.e., an engine) for applying the pattern to a specified input of type `java.lang.CharSequence`:

   ```
   Matcher matcher = pattern.matcher(input);
   ```

3. Using the operations of the matcher to apply the pattern to the input:

   ```
   boolean eureka = matcher.matches();
   ```

The approach outlined above is recommended, as it avoids compiling the regular expression string repeatedly, and it is specially optimized for using the same pattern multiple times on the same input or different inputs. When used on the same input repeatedly, the pattern can be used to find multiple matches.

As mentioned above, the input must be of type `CharSequence`, which is a readable sequence of char values. The interface `CharSequence` is implemented by such classes as `String` and `StringBuilder`.

With the setup outlined above, it is possible to use the *same pattern* with *different engines*. The bookkeeping for doing the actual pattern matching against some input is localized in the matcher, not in the pattern.

Compiling a Pattern

The two methods below can be used to compile a regular expression string into a pattern and to retrieve the regular expression string from the pattern, respectively.

```
String regexStr = "\\d\\d-\\d\\d-\\d\\d";  // regex: \d\d-\d\d-\d\d
Pattern datePattern = Pattern.compile(regexStr);
```

`static Pattern compile(String regexStr)`

Compiles the specified regular expression string into a pattern. Throws the unchecked `PatternSyntaxException` if the regular expression is invalid. When the source is *line-oriented*, it is recommended to use the overloaded `compile()` method that additionally takes the argument `Pattern.MULTILINE`.

`String pattern()`

Returns the regular expression string from which this pattern was compiled.

Creating a Matcher

The `matcher()` method returns a `Matcher`, which is the engine that does the actual pattern matching. This method does *not* apply the underlying pattern to the specified input. The matcher provides special operations to actually do the pattern matching.

```
Matcher dateMatcher = datePattern.matcher("01-03-49 786 09-09-09");
```

The `Pattern` class also provides a static convenience method that executes all the steps outlined above for pattern matching. The regular expression string and the input are passed to the static method `matches()`, which does the pattern matching on the entire input. The regular expression string is compiled and the matcher is created each time the method is called. Calling the `matches()` method is not recommended if the pattern is to be used multiple times.

```
boolean dateFound = Pattern.matches("\\d\\d-\\d\\d-\\d\\d", "01-03-49"); // true
```

`Matcher matcher(CharSequence input)`

Creates a matcher that will match the specified input against this pattern.

`static boolean matches(String regexStr, CharSequence input)`

Compiles the specified regular expression string and attempts to match the specified input against it. The method only returns true if the *entire* input matches the pattern.

Splitting

The normal mode of pattern matching is to find *matches* for the pattern in the input. In other words, the *result* of pattern matching is the sequences of characters (i.e., the matches, also called *groups*) that match the pattern. *Splitting* returns sequences of characters that do *not* match the pattern. In other words, the matches are spliced out and the sequences of non-matching characters thus formed from the input are returned in an array of type `String`. The pattern is used as a *delimiter* to *tokenize* the input. The *token* in this case is a sequence of non-matching characters, possibly the empty string. The classes `StringTokenizer` and `Scanner` in the `java.util` package also provide the functionality for tokenizing text-based input. See the subsection *The java.util.Scanner Class*, p. 571.

The example below shows the results from splitting an input on a given pattern. The input is a '|'-separated list of names. The regular expression string is `"\\|"`, where the metacharacter | is escaped in order to use it as a non-metacharacter. Splitting the given input according to the specified regular expression, results in the array of `String` shown below.

```
Input: "tom|dick|harry"    Split: "\\|"
Results: { "tom", "dick", "harry" }
```

The `split()` method can be called on a pattern to create an array by splitting the input according to the pattern. Each successful *application* of the pattern, meaning each match of the pattern delimiter in the input, results in a split of the input, with the non-matched characters before the match resulting in a *new* element in the array, and any remaining input being returned as the *last* element of the array.

```
String[] split(CharSequence input, int limit)
```

Splits the specified input around matches of this pattern. The limit determines how many times this pattern will be applied to the input to create the array.

The number of applications of the pattern is controlled by the *limit* value passed to the method, as explained in Table 12.14. The code below will result in the array shown earlier:

```
String input = "tom|dick|harry";
String splitRegex = "\\|";                          // regex: \|
Pattern splitPattern = Pattern.compile(splitRegex);
String[] results = splitPattern.split(input, 4); // { "tom", "dick", "harry" }
```

Table 12.14 *Implications of the Limit Value in the* split() *Method*

Limit n	No. of Applications	Array Length	Other Remarks
n > 0	At the most n-1 times, meaning it can also be fewer if the input was exhausted	No greater than n, meaning it can also be smaller if the input was exhausted	Any remaining input is returned in the last element of the array
n == 0	As many times as possible to split the entire input	Any length required to split the entire input	Trailing empty strings are discarded
n < 0	As many times as possible to split the entire input	Any length required to split the entire input	Trailing empty strings are *not* discarded

Using the split() method is illustrated in Example 12.7. The doPatSplits() method at (1) creates a Pattern at (2) and calls the split() method at (3) on this pattern. Partial output from Example 12.7 is shown below. Limit value 1 does not split the input, limit value 2 splits the input once, and so on. Limit value greater than 3 does not change the results, as the input is exhausted at limit value 3. A non-positive limit value splits the input on the pattern as many times as necessary, until the input is exhausted.

```
Input: tom|dick|harry     Split: \|
Limit Length Results
   3      3    { "tom", "dick", "harry" }
   2      2    { "tom", "dick|harry" }
   1      1    { "tom|dick|harry" }
   0      3    { "tom", "dick", "harry" }
  -1      3    { "tom", "dick", "harry" }
```

If we change the input above to the input shown below, we see how empty strings come into the picture. The empty string is returned as a token to "mark" the split when the delimiter is found at the head of any remaining input, or at the end of the input. Five applications of the pattern were necessary to exhaust the input. Note that the limit value 0 does not return trailing empty strings.

```
Input: |tom||dick|harry|     Split: \|
Limit Length Results
   6     6    { "", "tom", "", "dick", "harry", "" }
   5     5    { "", "tom", "", "dick", "harry|" }
   4     4    { "", "tom", "", "dick|harry|" }
   3     3    { "", "tom", "|dick|harry|" }
   2     2    { "", "tom||dick|harry|" }
   1     1    { "|tom||dick|harry|" }
   0     5    { "", "tom", "", "dick", "harry" }
  -1     6    { "", "tom", "", "dick", "harry", "" }
```

Example 12.7 *Splitting*

```java
import java.util.regex.Pattern;

public class Splitting {
  public static void main(String[] args) {

    System.out.println("===Using the Pattern.split() method===");
    doPatSplits("tom|dick|harry", "\\|", -1, 3);
    doPatSplits("|tom||dick|harry|", "\\|", -1, 6);

    System.out.println("===Using the String.split() method===");
    doStrSplits("tom|dick|harry", "\\|", -1, 3);
  }

  public static void doPatSplits(String input, String splitRegex,
                            int lowerLimit, int upperLimit) {     // (1)
    System.out.print("Input: " + input);
    System.out.println("     Split: " + splitRegex);
    System.out.println("Limit Length Results");
    Pattern splitPattern = Pattern.compile(splitRegex);           // (2)
    for (int limit = upperLimit; limit >= lowerLimit; limit--) {
      String[] results = splitPattern.split(input, limit);        // (3)
      System.out.printf("%3d%6d     ", limit, results.length);
      printCharSeqArray(results);
    }
  }

  public static void doStrSplits(String input, String splitRegex,
                            int lowerLimit, int upperLimit) {     // (4)
    System.out.print("Input: " + input);
    System.out.println("     Split: " + splitRegex);
    System.out.println("Limit Length Results");
    for (int limit = upperLimit; limit >= lowerLimit; limit--) {
      String[] results = input.split(splitRegex, limit);          // (5)
      System.out.printf("%3d%6d     ", limit, results.length);
```

```
      printCharSeqArray(results);
    }
  }

  static void printCharSeqArray(CharSequence[] array) {                // (6)
    System.out.print("{ ");
    for (int i = 0; i < array.length; i++) {
      System.out.print("\"" + array[i] + "\"");
      System.out.print((i != array.length -1) ? ", " : " ");
    }
    System.out.println("}");
  }
}
```

The String class also has a split() method that takes the *regular expression string* and
the *limit* as parameters. Given that the reference input is of type String, the call
input.split(regexStr,limit) is equivalent to the call Pattern.compile(regexStr).
split(input, limit). The doStrSplits() method at (4) in Example 12.7 uses the split()
method in the String class. Here is another example of using the split() method
from the String class:

```
String[] results = "tom|dick|harry".split("\\|", 0); // { "tom", "dick", "harry" }
```

We will not split hairs here any more, but encourage experimenting with splitting
various input on different patterns using the code in Example 12.7.

The java.util.regex.Matcher **Class**

A Matcher is an engine that performs match operations on a character sequence by
interpreting a Pattern. A matcher is created from a pattern by invoking the Pattern.
matcher() method. Here we will explore the following three modes of operation for
a matcher:

1. *One-Shot Matching*: Using the matches() method in the Matcher class to match
   the *entire* input sequence against the pattern.

   ```
   Pattern pattern = Pattern.compile("\\d\\d-\\d\\d-\\d\\d");
   Matcher matcher = pattern.matcher("01-03-49");
   boolean isMatch = matcher.matches();       // true

   matcher = pattern.matcher("1-3-49");
   isMatch = matcher.matches();               // false
   ```

   The convenience method matches() in the Pattern class in the last subsection
   calls the matches() method in the Matcher class implicitly.

   boolean matches()

   Attempts to match the entire input sequence against the pattern. The method
   returns true only if the *entire* input matches the pattern.

2. *Successive Matching*: Using the find() method in the Matcher class to successively apply the pattern on the input sequence to look for the next match (*discussed further in this subsection*).

3. *Match-and-Replace Mode*: Using the matcher to find matches in the input sequence and replace them (*discussed further in this subsection*).

Successive Matching

The main steps of *successive matching* using a matcher are somewhat analogous to using an iterator to traverse a collection (p. 786). These steps are embodied in the code below, which is extracted from Example 12.8.

```
...
Pattern pattern = Pattern.compile(regexStr);      // (2)
Matcher matcher = pattern.matcher(target);        // (3)
while(matcher.find()) {                            // (4)
  ...
  String matchedStr = matcher.group();            // (7)
  ...
}
...
```

Once a matcher has been obtained, the find() method of the Matcher class can be used to find the *next* match in the input (called target in the code). The find() returns true if a match was found.

If the previous call to the find() method returned true, and the matcher has not been *reset* since then, the next call to the find() method will advance the search in the target for the next match from the first character not matched by the previous match. If the previous call to the find() returned false, no match was found, and the entire input has been exhausted.

The call to the find() method is usually made in a loop condition, so that any match found can be dealt with successively in the body of the loop. A match found by the find() method is called the *previous match* (as opposed to the *next match* which is yet to be found). The characters comprising the previous match are called a *group*, and can be retrieved by calling the group() method of the Matcher class. The group's location in the target can be retrieved by calling the start() and the end() methods of the Matcher class, as explained below. The two methods find() and group() are called successively in *lockstep* to find all matches/groups in the input.

Once pattern matching has commenced, the matcher can be reset. Its target and pattern can also be changed by passing the new target to the reset() method and by passing the new pattern to the usePattern() method, respectively. The reset() method resets the search to start from the beginning of the input, but the usePattern() method does not.

```
boolean find()
```

Attempts to find the *next* match in the input that matches the pattern. The first call to this method, or a call to this method after the matcher is reset, always starts the search for a match at the beginning of the input.

```
String group()
```

Returns the characters (substring) in the input that comprise the previous match.

```
int start()
int end()
```

The first method returns the *start index* of the previous match. The second method returns the *index of the last character matched, plus one*. The values returned by these two methods define a *substring* in the input.

```
Matcher reset()
Matcher reset(CharSequence input)
```

The method resets this matcher, so that the next call to the find() method will begin the search for a match from the *start* of the *current* input. The second method resets this matcher, so that the next call to the find() method will begin the search for a match from the *start* of the *new* input.

```
Matcher usePattern(Pattern newPattern)
```

Replaces the pattern used by this matcher with another pattern. This change does not affect the search position in the input.

```
Pattern pattern()
```

Returns the pattern that is interpreted by this matcher.

Example 12.8 is a complete program that illustrates successive matching. In fact, the program in Example 12.8 was used to generate all examples of regular expressions in the subsection *Regular Expression Fundamentals*, p. 554. Again, we recommend experimenting with successive matching on various inputs and patterns to better understand regular expressions.

Example 12.8 *String Pattern Matching*

```java
import java.util.regex.Matcher;
import java.util.regex.Pattern;

public class MatchMaker {
  public static void main(String[] args) {
    // All examples from the subsection "Regular Expression Fundamentals".
    matchMaker("o",              "All good things come to those who wait");
    matchMaker("who",            "Interrogation with who, whose and whom.");
    matchMaker("[^aeiouAEIOU]", "I said I am.");
    matchMaker("[-A-Z]",        "I-love-REGEX.");
```

```
            matchMaker(".[Hh]o",
                       "Who is who? Whose is it? To whom it may concern. How are you?");
            matchMaker("\\d\\d-\\d\\d-\\d\\d", "01-03-49 786 09-09-09");
            matchMaker("\\?$",                 "Who is who? Who me? Who else?");
            matchMaker("([Jj][aA][vV][aA])|([Cc]\\+\\+)",
                       "JaVA jAvA C++ jAv c+++1 javan C+");
            matchMaker("a?",                   "banana");
            matchMaker("\\d\\d?-\\d\\d?-\\d\\d?", "01-3-49 23-12 9-09-09 01-01-2010");
            matchMaker("a*",                   "baananaa");
            matchMaker("(0|[1-9]\\d*)\\.\\d\\d", ".50 1.50 0.50 10.50 00.50 1.555");
            matchMaker("a+",                   "baananaa");
            matchMaker("\\d+\\.\\d+",          ".50 1.50 0. 10.50 00.50 1.555");
            matchMaker("<.+>",    "My <>very> <emphasis>greedy</emphasis> regex");
            matchMaker("<.+?>",   "My <>very> <emphasis>reluctant</emphasis> regex");
            matchMaker("<[^>]+>", "My <>very> <emphasis>powerful</emphasis> regex");
            // Some more regular expression examples.
            matchMaker("(^[a-z])|(\\?$)",      "who is who? Who me? Who else?");
            matchMaker("[\\\\-^$.?*+()|]",     "\\-^$.?*+()|");
            matchMaker("[-+]?[0-9]+",          "+123 -34 567 2.3435");
            matchMaker("[a-zA-Z][a-zA-Z0-9]+", "+a123 -X34 567 m2.3mm435");
            matchMaker("[^,]+",                "+a123, -X34, 567, m2,3mm435");
            matchMaker("\\\\",                 "book\\\\chapter\\section\\");
            matchMaker("[^\\\\]+",             "book\\\\chapter\\section\\");
        }

        public static void matchMaker(String regexStr, String target) {      // (1)
            System.out.print("Index:   ");
            for (int i = 0; i < target.length(); i++) {
                System.out.print(i%10);
            }
            System.out.println();
            System.out.println("Target:  " + target);
            System.out.println("Pattern: " + regexStr);
            System.out.print( "Match:   ");
            Pattern pattern = Pattern.compile(regexStr);                      // (2)
            Matcher matcher = pattern.matcher(target);                       // (3)
            while(matcher.find()) {                                          // (4)
                int startCharIndex = matcher.start();                        // (5)
                int lastPlus1Index = matcher.end();                          // (6)
                int lastCharIndex = startCharIndex == lastPlus1Index ?
                                    lastPlus1Index : lastPlus1Index-1;
                String matchedStr = matcher.group();                         // (7)
                System.out.print("(" + startCharIndex + "," + lastCharIndex + ":" +
                                 matchedStr + ")");
            }
            System.out.println();
        }
    }
```

Output from the program:

```
    ...
    Index:   0123456789012345678901
    Target:  book\\chapter\section\
    Pattern: [^\\]+
    Match:   (0,3:book)(6,12:chapter)(14,20:section)
```

Match-and-Replace Mode

In this mode, the matcher allows the matched characters in the input to be replaced with new ones. Details of the methods used for this purpose are given below. The find() and the appendReplacement() methods comprise the *match-and-replace loop*, with the appendReplacement() method completing the operation when the loop finishes.

Note that these methods use a StringBuffer, and have *not* been updated to work with a StringBuilder.

`Matcher appendReplacement(StringBuffer sb, String replacement)`

Implements a *non-terminal append-and-replace step*, i.e., it successively adds the non-matched characters in the input, followed by the replacement of the match, to the string buffer.

The find() method and the appendReplacement() method are used in *lockstep* to successively replace all matches, and the appendTail() method is called as the last step to complete the match-and-replace operation.

`StringBuffer appendTail(StringBuffer sb)`

Implements a *terminal append-and-replace step*, i.e., it copies the remaining characters from the input to the string buffer, which is then returned. It should be called after appendReplacement() operations have completed.

`String replaceAll(String replacement)`

Replaces every subsequence of the input that matches the pattern with the specified replacement string. The method resets the matcher first and returns the result after the replacement.

`String replaceFirst(String replacement)`

Replaces the first subsequence of the input that matches the pattern with the specified replacement string. The method resets the matcher first and returns the result after the replacement.

Example 12.9 illustrates the match-and-replace loop. Non-matching characters in the input and the replacements of the matches are successively added to the string buffer in the loop at (1), with the call to the appendTail() method at (3) completing the operation. The same operation is repeated using the replaceAll() method at (4).

Using the replaceAll() method replaces *all* matches with the *same* replacement, but the match-and-replace loop offers greater flexibility in this regard, as each replacement can be tailored when a match is found.

Example 12.9 *Match and Replace*

```java
import java.util.regex.Matcher;
import java.util.regex.Pattern;

public class MatchAndReplace {
  public static void main(String[] args) {

    // Match and replace loop:
    Pattern pattern = Pattern.compile("be");
    String input = "What will be will be.";
    System.out.println(input);
    Matcher matcher = pattern.matcher(input);
    StringBuffer strBuf = new StringBuffer();
    while (matcher.find()) {                            // (1)
        matcher.appendReplacement(strBuf, "happen");   // (2)
    }
    matcher.appendTail(strBuf);                         // (3)
    System.out.println(strBuf);

    // Match and replace all:
    matcher.reset();
    String result = matcher.replaceAll("happen");      // (4)
    System.out.println(result);
  }
}
```

Output from the program:

```
What will be will be.
What will happen will happen.
What will happen will happen.
```

The `java.util.Scanner` Class

A *scanner* reads *characters* from a *source* and converts them into *tokens*. The source is usually a text-based input stream containing *formatted* data. The formatted values in the source are separated by *delimiters*, usually whitespace. A *token* is a sequence of characters in the source that comprises a formatted value. A scanner generally uses regular expressions to recognize tokens in the source input. A point to note is that a scanner can also use regular expressions to recognize delimiters, which are normally discarded. Such a scanner is also called a *tokenizer* (also called a *lexical analyzer*), and the process is called *tokenization*. Some scanners also convert the tokens into values of appropriate types for further processing. Scanners with this additional functionality are usually called *parsers*.

The class Scanner in the java.util package provides powerful tools to implement text scanners which use regular expressions to tokenize and parse formatted data into primitive types and strings. The Pattern.split() method (and the String.split() method that uses this method) also provide tokenizing capabilities (p. 563), but these are not as versatile as the Scanner class.

We will discuss two modes of operation for a scanner:

- *Tokenizing Mode*, for tokenizing a stream of formatted data values.

- *Multi-Line Mode*, for searching or finding matches in line-oriented input.

Basics of Tokenizing

Tokenizing is analogous to successive matching (p. 567), involving reading of the characters in the source, and recognizing tokens in the source. Example 12.10 shows a bare-bones tokenizer that tokenizes a string, but it embodies the paradigm for constructing more sophisticated scanners. The rest of the subsection will present variations on this tokenizer.

1. The source for the input to the scanner must be identified. The example shows a String as the source, but we can also use other sources, such as a File, an InputStream or a BufferedReader.

2. A scanner is created and associated with the source that is passed as argument in the constructor call. The Scanner class provides constructors for various kinds of sources.

3. The bulk of the work of a scanner is done in a *lookahead-and-parse loop*.

    The condition of the loop is a call to a *lookahead* method to see if an appropriate token can be identified in the remaining source. The Scanner class provides lookahead methods named hasNext*Type* to determine whether the next token in the source is of the appropriate primitive *Type*. Note that the scanner reads the characters from the source *sequentially.*

    The call to the hasNext() method at (3) returns true if there is a (String) token in the source. The loop terminates when the hasNext() method returns false, meaning that the source string has been exhausted, i.e., there are no more tokens.

    Each successive call to a lookahead method causes the scanner to advance and look for the *next* token in the source.

4. If a lookahead method determines that there is a token in the source, the token can be parsed in the loop body. The Scanner class provides *parse* methods named next*Type* to parse the next token in the source to the appropriate primitive type. The call to the next() method at (4) parses the next token to a String. In the example, the parsed value is printed, but it can be stored and used as desired. Also in the example, the scanner uses the default delimiters (whitespace) to tokenize the string.

    A lookahead method and its corresponding parse method are used in *lockstep* to ensure that characters in the source are matched and parsed to a token of an appropriate type.

5. A scanner whose source has been explicitly associated in the code, should be closed when it is no longer needed. This also closes the source, if that is necessary.

Example 12.10 *Tokenizing Mode*

```java
import static java.lang.System.out;

import java.util.Scanner;

class BareBonesTokenizer {
  public static void main(String[] args) {
    String input = "The world will end today -- not!";// (1) String as source
    Scanner lexer = new Scanner(input);            // (2) Create a scanner
    while (lexer.hasNext()) {                       // (3) Processing loop
      out.println(lexer.next());                   // (4) Parsing
    }
    lexer.close();                                 // (5) Close the scanner
  }
}
```

Output from the program:

```
The
world
will
end
today
--
not!
```

Constructing a Scanner

A scanner must be constructed and associated with a source before it can be used to parse text-based data. The source of a scanner is passed as an argument in the appropriate constructor call. Once a source is associated with a scanner it cannot be changed. If the source is a byte stream (e.g., an InputStream), the bytes are converted to characters using the default character encoding. A character encoding can also be specified as an additional argument in an overloaded constructor, except when the source is a String.

Scanner(*SourceType* source)

Returns an appropriate scanner. *SourceType* can be a String, a File, an Input-Stream, a ReadableByteChannel, or a Readable (implemented by various Readers).

Lookahead Methods

The Scanner class provides two overloaded hasNext() methods that accept a regular expression specified as a string expression or as a Pattern, respectively. The next token is matched against this pattern. All primitive types and string literals have a pre-defined format which is used by the appropriate lookahead method.

All lookahead methods return true if the match with the next token is successful. This means that we can safely call the corresponding parse method to parse the token to an appropriate type. Note that a lookahead method does *not* advance past any input character, regardless of whether the lookahead was successful. It only determines whether appropriate input is available at the current position in the input.

```
boolean hasNext()
boolean hasNext(Pattern pattern)
boolean hasNext(String pattern)
```

The first method returns true if this scanner has another (string) token in its input. The last two methods return true if the next token matches the specified pattern or the pattern constructed from the specified string, respectively.

```
boolean hasNextIntegralType()
boolean hasNextIntegralType(int radix)
```

Returns true if the next token in this scanner's input can be interpreted as a value of the integral type corresponding to *IntegralType* in the default or specified radix. The name *IntegralType* can be Byte, Short, Int or Long, corresponding to the primitive types byte, short, int, or long, respectively.

```
boolean hasNextFPType()
```

Returns true if the next token in this scanner's input can be interpreted as a value of the floating-point type corresponding to *FPType*. The name *FPType* can be Float or Double, corresponding to the types float or double, respectively.

```
boolean hasNextBoolean()
```

Returns true if the next token in this scanner's input can be interpreted as a boolean value using a case insensitive pattern created from the string "true|false".

```
boolean hasNextLine()
```

Returns true if there is another line in the input of this scanner.

A scanner uses white space as its default delimiter pattern to identify tokens. The useDelimiters() method of the Scanner class can be used to set a different delimiter pattern for the scanner during parsing. Note that a scanner uses regular expressions for two purposes: a *delimiter pattern* to identify delimiter characters and a *token pattern* to find a token in the input.

A scanner is able to read and parse any value that has been formatted by a printf method, provided the *same* locale is used. The useLocale() method of the Scanner class can be used to change the locale used by a scanner.

The delimiters, the locale, and the radix can be changed any time during the tokenizing process.

```
Pattern delimiter()
Scanner useDelimiter(Pattern pattern)
Scanner useDelimiter(String pattern)
```

The first method returns the pattern this scanner is currently using to match delimiters. The last two methods set its delimiting pattern to the specified pattern or to the pattern constructed from the specified pattern string, respectively.

```
Locale locale()
Scanner useLocale(Locale locale)
```

These methods return this scanner's locale or set its locale to the specified locale, respectively.

```
int radix()
Scanner useRadix(int radix)
```

These methods return this scanner's default radix or set its radix to the specified radix, respectively.

Parsing the Next Token

The Scanner class provides methods to parse strings and values of all primitive types, except the char type.

Corresponding to the hasNext() methods, the Scanner class provides two overloaded next() methods that accept a regular expression as a string expression or as a Pattern, respectively. This pattern is used to find the next token.

It is important to understand how a parse method works. A call to a parse method first skips over any delimiters at the current position in the source, and then reads characters up to the *next delimiter*. The scanner attempts to match the *non-delimiter* characters that have been read against the pattern associated with the parse method. If the match succeeds, a token has been found, which can be parsed accordingly. The current position is advanced to the new delimiter character after the token. The upshot of this behavior is that if a parse method is *not* called when a lookahead method reports there is a token, the scanner will *not* advance in the input. In other words, tokenizing will not proceed unless the next token is "cleared."

A scanner will throw an InputMismatchException when it cannot parse the input, and the current position will remain unchanged.

```
String next()
String next(Pattern pattern)
String next(String pattern)
```

The first method scans and returns the next token as a String. The last two methods return the next string in the input that matches the specified pattern or the pattern constructed from the specified string, respectively.

```
ReturnIntegralType nextIntegralType()
ReturnIntegralType nextIntegralType(int radix)
```

Returns the next token in the input as a value of primitive type corresponding to *IntegralType*. The name *IntegralType* can be Byte, Short, Int, or Long, corresponding to the primitive types byte, short, int, or long, respectively. The name *ReturnIntegralType* is the primitive type corresponding to the name *Integral-Type*.

```
ReturnFPType nextFPType()
```

Returns the next token in the input as a value of the primitive type corresponding to *FPType*. The name *FPType* can be Float or Double, corresponding to the primitive types float or double, respectively. The name *ReturnFPType* is the primitive type corresponding to the name *FPType*.

```
boolean nextBoolean()
```

Returns the next token in the input as a boolean value.

```
String nextLine()
```

Advances this scanner past the current line and returns the input that was skipped.

Parsing Primitive Values

Example 12.11 illustrates parsing of primitive values (and strings) from formatted data. To parse such values, we need to know what *type* of values occur in what *order* in the input so that an appropriate lookahead and a corresponding parse method can be used. We also need to know what *locale* was used to format them and which *delimiters* separate the individual values in the input. This is exactly the information accepted by the parse() method at (1).

The order in which the different type of values occur in the input is specified by the vararg parameter tokenTypes, whose element type is the enum type TokenType. A call to the method parse(), such as the one shown below, thus indicates the order, the type and the number of values to expect in the input.

```
parse(locale, input, delimiters,
      TokenType.INT, TokenType.DOUBLE, TokenType.BOOL,
      TokenType.INT, TokenType.LONG,   TokenType.STR);
```

Example 12.11 can be used as the basis for experimenting with a scanner for parsing primitive values in the formatted input.

- -

Example 12.11 *Parsing Primitive Values and Strings*

```
import static java.lang.System.out;

import java.util.Locale;
import java.util.Scanner;
```

```
                  public class ParsingPrimitiveValues {

                    /** Types of tokens to parse */
                    enum TokenType { INT, LONG, FLOAT, DOUBLE, BOOL, STR }

                    public static void main(String[] args) {

                      // Using default delimiters (i.e. whitespace).
                      // Note Norwegian locale format for floating-point numbers.
                      String input = "123 45,56 false 567 722 blahblah";
                      String delimiters = "default";
                      Locale locale = new Locale("no", "NO");
                      parse(locale, input, delimiters,
                            TokenType.INT, TokenType.DOUBLE, TokenType.BOOL,
                            TokenType.INT, TokenType.LONG,   TokenType.STR);

                      // Note the use of backslash to escape characters in regex.
                      input = "2008 | 2 | true";
                      delimiters = "\\s*\\|\\s*";
                      parse(null, input, delimiters,
                            TokenType.INT, TokenType.INT, TokenType.BOOL);

                      // Another example of a regex to specify delimiters.
                      input = "Always = true | 2 $ U";
                      delimiters = "\\s*(\\||\\$|=)\\s*";
                      parse(null, input, delimiters,
                            TokenType.STR, TokenType.BOOL, TokenType.INT, TokenType.STR);
                    }

                    /**
                     * Parses the input using the locale, the delimiters and
                     * expected sequence of tokens.
                     */
                    public static void parse(Locale locale, String input, String delimiters,
                                             TokenType... tokenTypes) { // (1) Vararg
                      Scanner lexer = new Scanner(input);              // (2) Create a scanner.
                      if (!delimiters.equalsIgnoreCase("default")) { // (3) Change delimiters?
                        lexer.useDelimiter(delimiters);
                      }
                      if (locale != null) {                           // (4) Change locale?
                        lexer.useLocale(locale);
                      }
                      out.println("Locale: " + lexer.locale());
                      out.println("Delim:  " + delimiters);
                      out.println("Input:  " + input);
                      out.print("Tokens: ");

                      // (5) Iterate through the tokens:
                      for (TokenType tType : tokenTypes) {
                        if (!lexer.hasNext()) break;       // (6) Handle premature end of input.
                        switch(tType) {
                          case INT:    out.print("<" + lexer.nextInt() + ">"); break;
                          case LONG:   out.print("<" + lexer.nextLong() + ">"); break;
                          case FLOAT:  out.print("<" + lexer.nextFloat() + ">"); break;
                          case DOUBLE: out.print("<" + lexer.nextDouble() + ">"); break;
```

```
            case BOOL:    out.print("<" + lexer.nextBoolean() + ">"); break;
            case STR:     out.print("<" + lexer.next() + ">"); break;
            default:      assert false;
        }
    }
    System.out.println("\n");
    lexer.close();                              // (7) Close the scanner.
  }
}
```

Output from the program:

```
Locale: no_NO
Delim:  default
Input:  123 45,56 false 567 722 blahblah
Tokens: <123><45.56><false><567><722><blahblah>

Locale: en_GB
Delim:  \s*\|\s*
Input:  2008 | 2 | true
Tokens: <2008><2><true>

Locale: en_GB
Delim:  \s*(\||\$|=)\s*
Input:  Always = true | 2 $ U
Tokens: <Always><true><2><U>
```

Miscellaneous Scanner Methods

The skip() method can be used to skip characters in the input during the course of tokenizing. This operation *ignores* delimiters and will only skip input that matches the specified pattern. If no such input is found, it throws a NoSuchElementException.

The match() method can be called after the value of a token has been returned. The MatchResult interface provides methods to retrieve the start index, the end index, and the group of the token. For example, after parsing a floating-point number in the input, a MatchResult can be obtained by calling the match() method, which can then be queried about the location of the characters comprising the value, etc.

When the source is an input stream (e.g., a File, an InputStream, a Reader), a read operation can throw an IOException. If this exception is thrown in the course of a lookahead method call, it is not propagated by the scanner and the scanner assumes that the end of the input has been reached. Subsequent calls to a lookahead method will throw a NoSuchElementException. To determine whether processing terminated because of a genuine end of input or an IOException, the ioException() method can be called to verify the situation.

Closing a scanner is recommended when the client code has explicit control over the assigning of the source. Calling a scanning method on a closed scanner results in an IllegalStateException.

```
Scanner skip(Pattern pattern)
Scanner skip(String pattern)
```

These methods skip input that matches the specified pattern or the pattern constructed from the specified string, respectively, *ignoring any delimiters*. If no match is found at the current position, no input is skipped and a NoSuchElement-Exception is thrown.

```
MatchResult match()
```

Returns the match result of the last scanning operation performed by this scanner.

```
IOException ioException()
```

Returns the IOException last thrown by this scanner's underlying Readable object.

```
Scanner reset()
```

Resets this scanner to the default state with regard to delimiters, locale, and radix.

```
void close()
```

Closes this scanner. When a scanner is closed, it will close its input source if the source implements the Closeable interface (implemented by various Channels, InputStreams, Readers).

Using Delimiters and Patterns with a Scanner

Example 12.12 is the analog of Example 12.8 that uses a scanner instead of a matcher. The thing to note about Example 12.12 is the loop at (4). The method call hasNext() looks ahead to see if there is any input. The method call hasNext(pattern) attempts to match the pattern with the next token (found using the delimiters). If the attempt is not successful, the method call next() returns the token, which is ignored, but advances the scanner.

The split() method (p. 563) in the Pattern and the String classes can also tokenize, but is not as versatile as a scanner. The example below shows the difference between a scanner and a matcher. In the tokenizing mode, a scanner tokenizes and then attempts to match the token with the pattern. A matcher does not tokenize, but searches for the pattern in the input. The results below make this difference quite apparent in the number of matches the two approaches find in the same input.

Results from a scanner (see Example 12.12):

```
Index:   01234567890123456789012345678901
Target:  JaVA jAvA C++ jAv c+++1 javan C+
Delimit: default
Pattern: ([Jj][aA][vV][aA])|([Cc]\+\+)
Match:   (0,3:JaVA)(5,8:jAvA)(10,12:C++)
```

Results from a matcher (see Example 12.8):

```
Index:   01234567890123456789012345678901
Target:  JaVA jAvA C++ jAv c+++1 javan C+
Pattern: ([Jj][aA][vV][aA])|([Cc]\+\+)
Match:   (0,3:JaVA)(5,8:jAvA)(10,12:C++)(18,20:c++)(24,27:java)
```

Example 12.12 *Using Delimiters and Patterns with a Scanner*

```java
import static java.lang.System.out;

import java.util.Scanner;
import java.util.regex.MatchResult;
import java.util.regex.Pattern;

public class Tokenizer {
  public static void main(String[] args) {
    tokenize("([Jj][aA][vV][aA])|([Cc]\\+\\+)",
             "JaVA jAvA C++ jAv c+++1 javan C+", "default");
    tokenize("[a-z[A-Z]]+", "C:\\Program Files\\3MM\\MSN2Lite\\Help", "\\\\");
  }

  public static void tokenize(String regexStr, String source,
                              String delimiters) {              // (1)
    System.out.print("Index:   ");
    for (int i = 0; i < source.length(); i++) {
      System.out.print(i%10);
    }
    System.out.println();
    System.out.println("Target:  " + source);
    System.out.println("Delimit: " + delimiters);
    System.out.println("Pattern: " + regexStr);
    System.out.print(  "Match:   ");
    Pattern pattern = Pattern.compile(regexStr);                // (2)
    Scanner lexer = new Scanner(source);                        // (3)
    if (!delimiters.equalsIgnoreCase("default"))
      lexer.useDelimiter(delimiters);                           // (5)
    while(lexer.hasNext()) {                                    // (4)
      if (lexer.hasNext(pattern)) {                             // (5)
        String matchedStr = lexer.next(pattern);               // (5)
        MatchResult matchResult = lexer.match();               // (6)
        int startCharIndex = matchResult.start();
        int lastPlus1Index = matchResult.end();
        int lastCharIndex = startCharIndex == lastPlus1Index ?
            lastPlus1Index : lastPlus1Index-1;
        out.print("(" + startCharIndex + "," + lastCharIndex + ":" +
            matchedStr + ")");
      } else {
        lexer.next();                                           // (7)
      }
    }
    System.out.println();
  }
}
```

Output from the program:

```
...
Index:   0123456789012345678901234567890123
Target:  C:\Program Files\3MM\MSN2Lite\Help
Delimit: \\
Pattern: [a-z[A-Z]]+
Match:   (30,33:Help)
```

Multi-Line Mode

If the input is *line-oriented*, the scanner can be used to perform search in the input one line at a time. The methods hasNextLine(), findInLine(), and nextLine() form the trinity that implements the multi-line mode of searching the input with a pattern.

Example 12.13 illustrates the basics of the multi-line use of a scanner. The program processes a text file line by line, printing the names found in each line. The program essentially comprises *two nested loops*: an *outer* loop to access the input one line at a time, and an *inner* loop to search for all names in this line. The name of the source file is specified as a program argument at (1). The pattern that defines a name is specified at (2), and a scanner with the text file as the source is created at (3).

The call to the lookahead method hasNextLine() at (4) checks to see if there is another line of input. If that is the case, the findInLine() method is called at (5) to find the first match. All characters in the line are treated as being significant by the findInLine() method, including the delimiters that are set for the scanner. If a call to the findInLine() method results in a match, it advances the search past the matched input in the line and returns the matched input. The value returned by the findInLine() method can be used as a condition in an inner loop to successively find remaining occurrences of the pattern in the line at (8).

If no match is found in the line, the findInLine() method returns the value null and the search position remains unchanged. The findInLine() method never reads past a line separator. This means that the scanner does not budge if a match cannot be found in the line or if it has reached the end of the line. A call to the nextLine() method at (9) reads the rest of the line, i.e., any characters from the current position to the end of the line, *including the line separator*. The scanner is thus poised to process the next line.

Since the findInLine() method only recognizes the line separator as a delimiter, absence of line separators in the input may result in buffering of the input while the scanner tries to match the search pattern.

```
String findInLine(Pattern pattern)
String findInLine(String pattern)
```

These methods attempt to find the next occurrence of the specified pattern or the pattern constructed from the specified string, respectively, *ignoring any delimiters*.

Example 12.13 *Multi-Line Mode*

```
import static java.lang.System.out;

import java.io.File;
import java.io.IOException;
import java.util.Scanner;
import java.util.regex.Pattern;

class MultiLineMode {
  public static void main(String[] args) throws IOException {
    String source = args[0];                    // (1) Filename from program args
    Pattern pattern = Pattern.compile("[a-zA-Z]+",
                                  Pattern.MULTILINE);// (2) Search pattern
    Scanner lexer = new Scanner(new File(source));// (3) Create a scanner
    // Outer loop:
    while (lexer.hasNextLine()) {                // (4) Lookahead for next line
      String match = lexer.findInLine(pattern);  // (5) Find the first match
      // Inner loop:
      while (match != null) {                    // (6) Parse rest of the line
        out.println(match);                      // (7) Process the match
        match = lexer.findInLine(pattern);       // (8) Get the next match
      }
      lexer.nextLine();                          // (9) Clear rest of the line
    }
    IOException ioe = lexer.ioException();
    if (ioe != null)                             // (10) Check for read problem
      throw ioe;
    lexer.close();                               // (11) Close the scanner
  }
}
```

Running the program:

```
>java MultiLineMode MultiLineMode.java
import
static
...
scanner
```

 ## Review Questions

12.7   Which statements are true about the following target string?

"oblaada oblaadi"

Select the three correct answers.

(a) The regular expression a+ will match two substrings of the target string.
(b) The regular expression aa+ will match two substrings of the target string.
(c) The regular expression (aa)+ will match two substrings of the target string.
(d) The regular expressions aa+ and (aa)+ will match the same two substrings of
     the target string.

12.8 Which statements are true about the following target string?

```
"oblaada oblaadi"
```

Select the three correct answers.

(a) The regular expression a? will match five non-empty substrings of the target string.

(b) The regular expression aa? will match two non-empty substrings of the target string.

(c) The regular expression (aa)? will match two non-empty substrings of the target string.

(d) The regular expressions aa? and (aa)? will not match the same non-empty substrings of the target string.

12.9 Which statement is true about the following target string?

```
"oblaada oblaadi"
```

Select the one correct answer.

(a) The regular expression a* will match three non-empty substrings of the target string.

(b) The regular expression aa* will match at least two non-empty substrings of the target string.

(c) The regular expression (aa)* will match two non-empty substrings of the target string.

(d) The regular expressions a* and aa* will match the same non-empty substrings of the target string.

(e) All of the above.

12.10 Which statement is true about the following target string?

```
"0.5 7UP _4me"
```

Select the one correct answer.

(a) The pattern \d will match 0.5, 7, and 4 in the target string.

(b) The pattern \d will match 0, ., 5, 7, and 4 in the target string.

(c) The pattern \w will match UP and me in the target string.

(d) The pattern \s will match 0.5, 7UP, and _4me in the target string.

(e) The pattern . will match the . character in the target string.

(f) The regular expression [meUP] will match UP and me in the target string.

(g) None of the above.

12.11 Which statements are true about the following program?

```java
import java.util.regex.Pattern;
public class RQ500_10 {
  public static void main(String[] args) {
    System.out.println(Pattern.matches("+?\d", "+2007"));      // (1)
    System.out.println(Pattern.matches("+?\\d+","+2007"));     // (2)
    System.out.println(Pattern.matches("\+?\\d+", "+2007"));   // (3)
```

```
    System.out.println(Pattern.matches("\\+?\\d+", "+2007"));   // (4)
  }
}
```

Select the two correct answers.

(a) Only in the statements at (1) and (2) will the compiler report an invalid escape sequence.

(b) Only in the statements at (3) and (4) will the compiler report an invalid escape sequence.

(c) Only in the statements at (1) and (3) will the compiler report an invalid escape sequence.

(d) The statements at (2) and (4) will compile but will throw an exception at runtime.

(e) After any compile-time errors have been eliminated, only one of the statements will print true when executed.

(f) None of the above.

12.12   Given the following code:

```
import java.util.regex.Pattern;
public class RQ500_20 {
  public static void main(String[] args) {
    String[] regexes = {
      "(-|+)\\d+",      "(-|+)?\\d+", "(-|\\+)\\d+",    // 0, 1, 2
      "(-|\\+)?\\d+", "[-+]?\\d+",  "[-+]?[0-9]+",    // 3, 4, 5
      "[-\\+]?\\d+" };                               // 6
    // (1) INSERT DECLARATION STATEMENT HERE

    System.out.println(Pattern.matches(regexes[i], "2007"));
    System.out.println(Pattern.matches(regexes[i], "-2007"));
    System.out.println(Pattern.matches(regexes[i], "+2007"));
  }
}
```

Which declarations, when inserted independently at (1), will make the program print:

```
true
true
true
```

Select the four correct answers.

(a) `int i = 0;`
(b) `int i = 1;`
(c) `int i = 2;`
(d) `int i = 3;`
(e) `int i = 4;`
(f) `int i = 5;`
(g) `int i = 6;`

12.13 Given the following code:

```
import java.util.regex.Pattern;
import java.util.regex.Matcher;
public class RQ500_40 {
  public static void main(String[] args) {
    String regex  = "ja[^java]*va";
    String index  = "01234567890123456789 0123456";
    String target = "jambo valued jam vacationer";
    Pattern pattern = _____.compile(_____);
    Matcher matcher = _____.matcher(_____);
    while(matcher._____()) {
      int startIndex = matcher._____();
      int endIndex   = matcher._____();
      int lastIndex  = startIndex == endIndex ? endIndex : endIndex-1;
      String matchedStr = matcher._____();
      System.out.print("(" + startIndex + "," + lastIndex + ":" +
                       matchedStr + ")");
    }
    System.out.println();
  }
}
```

Which identifiers, when filled in the blanks in the order they are specified, will make the program print:

```
(0,7:jambo va)(13,18:jam va)
```

Select the one correct answer.

(a) Pattern, pattern, target, regex, find, start, end, group
(b) Matcher, pattern, regex, target, hasMore, start, end, element
(c) Matcher, pattern, regex, target, hasNext, start, end, next
(d) Pattern, regex, pattern, target, find, start, end, group
(e) Pattern, regex, pattern, target, hasNext, start, end, next
(f) Pattern, regex, pattern, target, find, start, end, result

12.14 What will the program print when compiled and run?

```
public class RQ500_60 {
  public static void main(String[] args) {
    String regex   = "[Jj].?[Aa].?[Vv].?[Aa]";
    String target1 = "JAVA JaVa java jaVA";
    String target2 = "JAAAVA JaVVa jjaavvaa ja VA";
    Pattern pattern = Pattern.compile(regex);
    Matcher matcher = pattern.matcher(target1);
    makeMatch(matcher);
    matcher.reset();
    makeMatch(matcher);
    matcher.reset(target2);
    makeMatch(matcher);
  }

  public static void makeMatch(Matcher matcher) {
    System.out.print("|");
```

```java
      while(matcher.find()) {
        System.out.print(matcher.group() + "|");
      }
      System.out.println();
    }
  }
```

Select the one correct answer.

(a) |JAVA|JaVa|java|jaVA|
    |JAAAVA|JaVVa|jjaavva|ja VA|

(b) |JAVA|JaVa|java|jaVA|
    |
    |JAAAVA|JaVVa|jjaavva|ja VA|

(c) |JAVA|JaVa|java|jaVA|
    |JAVA|JaVa|java|jaVA|
    |JAAAVA|JaVVa|jjaavva|ja VA|

(d) |JAVA|JaVa|java|jaVA|
    |JAVA|JaVa|java|jaVA|
    |JaVVa|jjaavva|ja VA|

(e) The program will throw an exception when run.

12.15   What will the program print when compiled and run?

```java
public class RQ500_70 {
  public static void main(String[] args) {
    System.out.print(Pattern.compile("\\s+")
                  .matcher("|     To be     |\n|or \tnot \t\t\tto be|")
                  .replaceAll(" "));
  }
}
```

Select the one correct answer.

(a) | To be |
    |or not to be|

(b) | To be |
    |or   not   to be|

(c) | To be |
    |or \tnot \t\t\tto be|

(d) | To be | |or not to be|

(e) | To be ||or not to be|

(f) | To be ||or \tnot \tto be|

(g) The program will not compile.

(h) The program will throw an exception when run.

12.16   What will the program print when compiled and run?

```java
public class RQ500_80 {
  public static void main(String[] args) {
    matchMaker("X.*z", "XyzXyz Xz");   // (1)
    matchMaker("X.+z", "XyzXyz Xz");   // (2)
    matchMaker("X.*?z", "XyzXyz Xz");  // (3)
```

```
      matchMaker("X.+?z", "XyzXyz Xz");   // (4)
    }

    public static void matchMaker(String regStr, String target) {
      Matcher matcher = Pattern.compile(regStr).matcher(target);
      System.out.print("|");
      while(matcher.find()) {
        System.out.print(matcher.group() + "|");
      }
      System.out.println();
    }
  }
```

Select the one correct answer.

(a) |Xyz|Xyz|Xz|
     |XyzXyz|Xz|
     |Xyz|Xyz|Xz|
     |Xyz|Xyz|

(b) |XyzXyz Xz|
     |XyzXyz Xz|
     |Xyz|Xyz|Xz|
     |Xyz|Xyz|

(c) |XyzXyz Xz|
     |XyzXyz|Xz|
     |XyzXyz Xz|
     |XyzXyz|Xz|

(d) The program will throw an exception when run.

12.17   What will the program print when compiled and run?

```
public class RQ500_90 {
  public static void main(String[] args) {
    CharSequence inputStr = "no 7up 4 _u too!";
    String patternStr = "[a-zA-Z0-9_]+";
    Matcher matcher = Pattern.compile(patternStr).matcher(inputStr);
    StringBuffer buf = new StringBuffer();
    while (matcher.find()) {
      String matchedStr = matcher.group();
      matchedStr =  Character.toUpperCase(matchedStr.charAt(0)) +
                    matchedStr.substring(1);
      matcher.appendReplacement(buf, matchedStr);
    }
    matcher.appendTail(buf);
    System.out.println(buf);
  }
}
```

Select the one correct answer.

(a) No 7Up 4 _U Too!

(b) No 7up 4 _u Too!

(c) No 7Up 4 _u Too!

(d) No 7up 4 _U Too!

(e) The program will throw an exception when run.

12.18 What will the program print when compiled and run?

```java
public class RQ500_110 {
  public static void main(String[] args) {
    printArray("Smile:-)and:)the:-(world.-)smiles:o)with-you".
               split("[.:\\-()o]+"));
  }

  private static <T> void printArray(T[] array) {
    System.out.print("|");
    for (T element : array)
      System.out.print(element + "|");
    System.out.println();
  }
}
```

Select the one correct answer.

(a) |Smile|and|the|world|smiles|with-you|

(b) |Smile|and|the|world|smiles|with-y|u|

(c) |Smile|and|the|world|smiles|with|you|

(d) |Smile|and|the|w|r1d|smiles|with|y|u|

(e) The program will not compile.

(f) The program will compile and will throw an exception when run.

(g) The program will compile and will execute normally without printing anything.

12.19 Which statements are true about the Scanner class?

Select the 3 correct answers.

(a) The Scanner class has constructors that can accept the following as an argument: a String, a StringBuffer, a StringBuilder, a File, an InputStream, a Reader.

(b) The Scanner class provides a method called hasNextBoolean, but not a method called hasNextChar.

(c) The methods hasNext(), next(), skip(), findInLine(), and useDelimiters() of the Scanner class can take a Pattern or a String as an argument.

(d) The situation where the scanner cannot match the next token or where the input is exhausted, can be detected by catching an unchecked NoSuchElement-Exception in the program.

12.20 Given the following code:

```java
public class RQ600_10 {
  public static void main(String[] args)  {
    Scanner lexer = new Scanner(System.in);
    // (1) INSERT PRINT STATEMENT HERE.
  }
}
```

Which print statements, when inserted independently at (1), will not make the program run as follows (with user input shown in bold):

```
>java RQ600_10
99 20.07 true 786
99
>
```

Select the three correct answers.

(a) `System.out.println(lexer.nextByte());`

(b) `System.out.println(lexer.nextShort());`

(c) `System.out.println(lexer.nextInt());`

(d) `System.out.println(lexer.nextLong());`

(e) `System.out.println(lexer.nextDouble());`

(f) `System.out.println(lexer.nextBoolean());`

(g) `System.out.println(lexer.next());`

(h) `System.out.println(lexer.nextLine());`

12.21 Given the following code:

```
public class RQ600_30 {
  public static void main(String[] args) {
    String input = "A00.20BCDE0.0060.0F0.800";
    Scanner lexer = new Scanner(input).useDelimiter(____(1)____);
    System.out.print("|");
    while (lexer.hasNext()) {
      System.out.print(lexer.next() + "|");
      System.out.print(lexer.nextInt() + "|");
    }
    lexer.close();
  }
}
```

Which pattern strings, when inserted at (1), will not give the following output:

```
|A|2|BCDE|6|F|8|
```

Select the two correct answers.

(a) `"[0\\.]+"`

(b) `"[0.]+"`

(c) `"(0|.)+"`

(d) `"(0|\\.)+"`

(e) `"0+(\\.)*"`

(f) `"0+\\.*0*"`

12.22 What will the program print when compiled and run?

```
public class RQ600_40 {
  public static void main(String[] args) {
    String input = "_AB..0C.-12.),DEF0..-34G.(H.";
    Scanner lexer = new Scanner(input).useDelimiter("\\w+\\.");
    while (lexer.hasNext())
      System.out.print(lexer.next());
```

```
      lexer.close();
    }
  }
```

Select the one correct answer.

(a) `.-.),.-.(`

(b) `-),-(`

(c) `.-),-(.`

(d) `.-),.-(`

(e) The program will not compile.

(f) The program will compile and will throw an exception when run.

12.23   Given the following code:

```
public class RQ600_50 {
  public static void main(String[] args) {
    String input = "1234||567.|12.34|.56||78.|.";
    String delimiters = "\\|+";
    // (1) INSERT DECLARATION HERE

    lexIt(regex, delimiters, input);
  }

  public static void lexIt(String regex, String delimiters, String input) {
    Scanner lexer = new Scanner(input).useDelimiter(delimiters);
    while (lexer.hasNext()) {
      if (lexer.hasNext(regex))
        System.out.printf("%7s", lexer.next(regex) + ",");
      else
        System.out.printf("%7s", "X" + lexer.next() + ",");
    }
    System.out.println();
    lexer.close();
  }
}
```

Which declaration statements, when inserted at (1), will give the following output:

```
   1234,   567.,  12.34,    .56,    78.,     X.,
```

Select the one correct answer.

(a) `String regex = "\\d+\\.?";`

(b) `String regex = "\\.?\\d+";`

(c) `String regex = "\\d+\\.\\d+";`

(d) `String regex = "\\d*\\.?\\d*";`

(e) `String regex = "\\d+\\.?\\d*";`

(f) `String regex = "(\\d+\\.?|\\.?\\d+|\\d+\\.\\d+)";`

(g) The program will not compile regardless of which declaration from above is inserted at (1).

(h) The program will compile and run, but will throw an exception regardless of which declaration from above is inserted at (1).

12.24 What will the program print when compiled and run?

```java
public class RQ600_70 {
  public static void main(String[] args) {
    Scanner lexer = new Scanner("B4, we were||m8s & :-) 2C,1 THR,");

    lexer.useDelimiter("[|,]");
    System.out.print("<" + lexer.next("\\w*") + "><" + lexer.next() + ">");

    lexer.useDelimiter("[a-z|& ]+");
    System.out.print("<" + lexer.nextInt() + "><" + lexer.next() + ">");

    lexer.useDelimiter("[ ,]");
    System.out.print("<" + lexer.next("\\w+") + "><" + lexer.next("\\d+") + ">");
    lexer.next();

    lexer.close();
  }
}
```

Select the one correct answer.

(a) `<B4>< we were><8><:-)><2C><1>`
(b) `<B4>< we were><m8s><:-)><2C><THR>`
(c) `<B4><we were><8><:-)><2C,><1>`
(d) `<B4>< we were><8s><2C1><><THR>`
(e) The program will not compile.
(f) The program will compile and will throw an exception when run.

12.25 What will the program print when compiled and run?

```java
public class RQ600_80 {
  public static void main(String[] args) {
    Scanner lexer = new Scanner("Trick or treat");
    while(lexer.hasNext()) {
      if(lexer.hasNext("[kcirTtea]+"))
        System.out.print("Trick!");
      lexer.next();
    }
    lexer.close();
  }
}
```

Select the one correct answer.

(a) The program will not compile.
(b) The program will compile and will throw an exception when run.
(c) The program will compile and will go into an infinite loop when run.
(d) The program will compile, run, and terminate normally, without any output.
(e) The program will compile, run, and terminate normally, with the output Trick!.
(f) The program will compile, run, and terminate normally, with the output Trick!Trick!.
(g) The program will compile, run, and terminate normally, with the output Trick!treat!.

12.26   Given the following code:

```
public class RQ600_20 {
  public static void main(String[] args) {
    System.out.print("|");
    // (1) INSERT CODE HERE

    System.out.println();
    lexer.close();
  }
}
```

Which code, when inserted independently at (1), will not print one of the lines shown below:

```
|2007| -25.0|mp3 4 u | true| after8|
|mp|u|true|after|
|2007.0|25.0|0.0|mp3|4.0|u|true|after8|
|4|
|2007|25|0|3|4|8|
|2007.0|-25.0|
```

Select the three correct answers.

(a)   `Scanner lexer = new Scanner("2007, -25.0,mp3 4 u , true, after8");`
     `lexer.useDelimiter(",");`
     `while(lexer.hasNext())`
       `System.out.print(lexer.next() + "|");`

(b)   `Scanner lexer = new Scanner("2007, -25.0,mp3 4 u , true, after8");`
     `lexer.useDelimiter("\\s*,\\s*");`
     `while(lexer.hasNext())`
       `if(lexer.hasNextDouble())`
         `System.out.print(lexer.nextDouble() + "|");`
       `else`
         `lexer.next();`

(c)   `Scanner lexer = new Scanner("2007, -25.0,mp3 4 u , true, after8");`
     `lexer.useDelimiter("\\s*,\\s*");`
     `while(lexer.hasNext())`
       `if(lexer.hasNextDouble())`
         `System.out.print(lexer.nextDouble() + "|");`

(d)   `Scanner lexer = new Scanner("2007, -25.0,mp3 4 u , true, after8");`
     `lexer.useDelimiter("[,\\- .a-z]+");`
     `while(lexer.hasNext())`
       `if(lexer.hasNextInt())`
         `System.out.print(lexer.nextInt() + "|");`
       `else`
         `lexer.next();`

(e)   `Scanner lexer = new Scanner("2007, -25.0,mp3 4 u , true, after8");`
     `lexer.useDelimiter("[,\\- .\\d]+");`
     `while(lexer.hasNext())`
       `if(lexer.hasNextBoolean())`
         `System.out.print(lexer.nextInt() + "|");`
       `else`
         `lexer.next();`

(f) Scanner lexer = new Scanner("2007, -25.0,mp3 4 u , true, after8");
```
    lexer.useDelimiter("[,\\- .\\d]+");
    while(lexer.hasNext())
      if(lexer.hasNextBoolean())
        System.out.print(lexer.nextBoolean() + "|");
      else
        System.out.print(lexer.next() + "|");
```

(g) Scanner lexer = new Scanner("2007, -25.0,mp3 4 u , true, after8");
```
    lexer.useDelimiter("[,\\- .]+");
    while(lexer.hasNext())
      if(lexer.hasNextDouble())
        System.out.print(lexer.nextDouble() + "|");
      else
        System.out.print(lexer.next() + "|");
```

(h) Scanner lexer = new Scanner("2007, -25.0,mp3 4 u , true, after8");
```
    lexer.useDelimiter("[,\\- .]+");
    do {
      if(lexer.hasNextInt())
        System.out.print(lexer.nextInt() + "|");
    } while(lexer.hasNext());
```

(i) Scanner lexer = new Scanner("2007, -25.0,mp3 4 u , true, after8");
```
    lexer.reset();
    do {
      if(lexer.hasNextInt())
        System.out.print(lexer.nextInt() + "|");
      else
        lexer.next();
    } while(lexer.hasNext());
```

12.7 Formatting Values

Overview

The class java.util.Formatter provides the core support for *formatted text representation* of primitive values and objects through its overloaded format() methods:

```
format(String format, Object... args)
format(Locale l, String format, Object... args)
```

Writes a string that is a result of applying the specified format string to the values in the vararg array args. The resulting string is written to the *destination object* that is associated with the formatter.

The destination object of a formatter is specified when the formatter is created. The destination object can, for example, be a String, a StringBuilder, a file, or any OutputStream.

The classes java.io.PrintStream and java.io.PrintWriter also provide an overloaded format() method with the same signature for formatted output. These streams use an associated Formatter that sends the output to the PrintStream or the PrintWriter, respectively. However, the format() method returns the current Formatter, Print-Stream, or PrintWriter, respectively, for these classes, allowing method calls to be chained.

The String class also provides an analogous format() method, but it is static. Unlike the format() method of the classes mentioned earlier, this static method returns the resulting string after formatting the values.

In addition, the classes PrintStream and PrintWriter provide the following convenience methods:

```
printf(String format, Object... args)
printf(Locale l, String format, Object... args)
```

These methods delegate the formatting to the format() method in the respective classes.

The java.io.Console only provides the first form of the format() and the printf() methods (without the locale specification), writing the resulting string to the console's output stream, and returning the current console.

The syntax of the *format string* provides support for layout justification and alignment, common formats for numeric, string, and date/time values, and some locale-specific formatting. The format string can specify *fixed text* and embedded *format specifiers*. The fixed text is copied to the output verbatim, and the format specifiers are replaced by the textual representation of the corresponding argument values. The mechanics of formatting values is illustrated below by using the PrintStream that is associated with the System.out field, i.e., the standard output stream. The following call to the printf() method of this PrintStream formats three values:

```
System.out.printf("Formatted output|%6d|%8.3f|%10s|%n", // Format string
                  2008, Math.PI, "Hello");               // Values to format
```

At runtime, the following characters are printed to the standard output stream, according to the default locale (in this case, Norwegian):

```
Formatted output|  2008|   3,142|     Hello|
```

The format string is the first actual parameter in the method call. It contains four *format specifiers*. The first three are %6d, %8.3f, and %10s, which specify how the three arguments should be processed. Their location in the format string specifies where the textual representation of the arguments should be inserted. The fourth format specifier %n is special, and stands for a platform-specific line separator. All other text in the format string is fixed, including any other spaces or punctuation, and is printed unchanged.

An implicit vararg array is created for the values of the three arguments specified in the call, and passed to the method. In the above example, the first value is formatted according to the first format specifier, the second value is formatted according to the second format specifier, and so on. The '|' character has been used in the format string to show how many character positions are taken up by the text representation of each value. The output shows that the int value was written right-justified, spanning six character positions using the format specifier %6d, the double value of Math.PI took up eight character positions and was rounded to three decimal places using the format specifier %8.3f, and the String value was written right-justified spanning ten character positions using the format specifier %10s. Since the default locale is Norwegian, the decimal sign is a comma (,) in the output. We now turn to the details of defining format specifiers.

Defining Format Specifiers

The general syntax of a format specifier is as follows:

%[argument_index][flags][width][precision]conversion

Only the special character % and the formatting *conversion* are not optional. Table 12.15 provides an overview of the formatting conversions. The occurrence of the character % in a format string marks the start of a format specifier, and the associated formatting conversion marks the end of the format specifier. A format specifier in the format string is replaced either by the textual representation of the corresponding value or by the specifier's special meaning. The compiler does not provide much help regarding the validity of the format specifier. Depending on the error in the format specifier, a corresponding exception is thrown at runtime (see *Selected Format Exceptions*, p. 601).

The optional *argument_index* has the format i$, or it is the < character. In the format i$, i is a decimal integer indicating the *position* of the argument in the vararg array, starting with position 1. The first argument is referenced by 1$, the second by 2$, and so on. The < character indicates the same argument that was used in the preceding format specifier in the format string, and cannot therefore occur in the first format specifier. The following printf() statements illustrate argument indexing:

```
String fmtYMD = "Year-Month-Day: %3$s-%2$s-%1$s%n";
String fmtDMY = "Day-Month-Year: %1$s-%2$s-%3$s%n";
out.printf(fmtYMD, 1, "March", 2008);  // Year-Month-Day: 2008-March-1
out.printf(fmtDMY, 1, "March", 2008);  // Day-Month-Year: 1-March-2008
out.printf("|%s|%<s|%<s|%n", "March"); // |March|March|March|
```

The optional *flag* is a character that specifies the layout of the output format. Table 12.16 provides an overview of the permissible flags, where an entry is either marked *ok* or ×, meaning the flag is applicable or not applicable for the conversion, respectively. The combination of valid flags in a format specifier depends on the conversion.

The optional *width* is a decimal integer indicating the *minimum* number of characters to be written to the output.

The optional *precision* has the format .n, where n is a decimal integer and is used usually to restrict the number of characters. The specific behavior depends on the conversion.

The order of the various components of a format specifier is important. More details and examples are provided in the next subsection on formatting conversions.

Table 12.15   *Formatting Conversions*

Conversion Specification	Conversion Category	Description
'b', 'B'	general	If the argument *arg* is null, the result is "false". If *arg* is a boolean or Boolean, the result is string returned by String.valueOf(). Otherwise, the result is "true".
'h', 'H'	general	If the argument *arg* is null, the result is "null". Otherwise, the result is obtained by invoking Integer.toHexString(arg.hashCode()).
's', 'S'	general	If the argument *arg* is null, the result is "null". If *arg* implements Formattable, arg.formatTo() is invoked. Otherwise, the result is obtained by invoking arg.toString().
'c', 'C'	character	The result is a Unicode character.
'd'	integral	The result is formatted as a decimal integer.
'o'	integral	The result is formatted as an octal integer.
'x', 'X'	integral	The result is formatted as a hexadecimal integer.
'e', 'E'	floating point	The result is formatted as a decimal number in computerized scientific notation.
'f'	floating point	The result is formatted as a decimal number.
'g', 'G'	floating point	The result is formatted using computerized scientific notation for large exponents and decimal format for small exponents.
'a', 'A'	floating point	The result is formatted as a hexadecimal floating-point number with a significand and an exponent.
't', 'T'	date/time	Prefix for date and time conversion characters.
'%'	percent	The result is the character %, i.e., "%%" escapes the % metacharacter.
'n'	line separator	The result is the platform-specific line separator, i.e., "%n"

Table 12.16 *Flags*

Flag	Integrals			Floating-point				Description
	d	**o**	**x** **X**	**e** **E**	**f**	**g** **G**	**a** **A**	
`'-'`	*ok*	*ok*	*ok*	*ok*	*ok*	*ok*	*ok*	Left-justified, requires a positive width. (Also *ok* for general, character, and date/time categories.)
`'#'`	×	*ok*	*ok*	*ok*	*ok*	×	*ok*	Include radix for integrals. Include decimal point for floating-point.
`'+'`	*ok*	×	×	*ok*	*ok*	*ok*	*ok*	Include the sign.
`' '`	*ok*	×	×	*ok*	*ok*	*ok*	*ok*	Leading space for positive values.
`'0'`	*ok*	*ok*	*ok*	*ok*	*ok*	*ok*	*ok*	Zero-padded, requires a positive width.
`','`	*ok*	×	×	×	*ok*	*ok*	×	Use locale-specific grouping separator.
`'('`	*ok*	×	×	*ok*	*ok*	*ok*	×	Negative numbers in parentheses.

Conversion Categories and Formatting Conversions

The required conversion in a format specifier is a character indicating how the argument should be formatted. The set of valid conversions for a given argument depends on the argument's data type. The different conversions can be grouped into categories depending on the data types they can be applied to. These conversion categories are shown in Table 12.15, together with information about each conversion. An uppercase conversion converts any non-digit characters in the result to uppercase according to the default or a specific locale. We will not always mention the uppercase conversion explicitly, but it is understood that any discussion about the lowercase conversion also applies to the uppercase conversion.

General Conversions: 'b', 'B', 'h', 'H', 's', 'S'

These *general conversions* may be applied to any argument type.

The width indicates the *minimum* number of characters to output. The precision specifies the *maximum* number of characters to output, and takes precedence over the width, resulting in truncating the output if the precision is smaller than the width. Padding is only done to fulfill the minimum requirement.

Only the '-' flag is applicable for left-justifying the output, requiring a positive width.

The conversions 'b' and 'B' represent *boolean conversions*. The following printf statement illustrates using boolean conversions. Note how null and non-boolean values are formatted and the effect of precision on the output.

```
out.printf("|%7b|%-7b|%7.3b|%2.3b|%b|%n",
    null, true, false, "false", "Kaboom"); // |  false|true   |  fal|tru|true|
```

The conversions 'h' and 'H' represent *hash code conversions*. The output is the hash code of the object:

```
out.printf("|%7h|%-7h|%n", null, "Kaboom"); // |   null|85809961|
```

The conversions 's' and 'S' represent *string conversions*. The following printf calls illustrates using string conversions. An array is passed as argument in the method call. Note how we can access the elements of this array in the format specifier with and without argument indices. Note also how the precision and the width affect the output.

```
Object[] arguments = {null, 2008, "Kaboom"};
out.printf("1|%.1s|%.2s|%.3s|%n", arguments);             // 1|n|20|Kab|
out.printf("2|%6.1s|%4.2s|%2.3s|%n", arguments);          // 2|     n|  20|Kab|
out.printf("3|%2$s|%3$s|%1$s|%n", arguments);             // 3|2008|Kaboom|null|
out.printf("4|%2$-4.2s|%3$2.3s|%1$-6.1s|%n", arguments);  // 4|20  |Kab|n     |
```

Character Conversion: 'c', 'C'

These *character conversions* may be applied to primitive types which represent Unicode characters, including char, byte, short, and the corresponding object wrapper types.

The '-' flag is only applicable for left-justifying the output, requiring a positive width.

The width specifies the *minimum* number of characters to output, padded with spaces if necessary.

The precision is not applicable for the character conversions.

Some examples of using the character conversions are shown below, together with the output:

```
out.printf("1|%c|%-6c|%6c|%c|%n",
    null, (byte) 58, ':', 'a'); // 1|null|:     |     :|a|
```

Integral Conversions: 'd', 'o', 'x', 'X'

The 'd', 'o', and 'x' conversions format an argument in *decimal, octal* or *hexadecimal formats*, respectively. These integral conversions may be applied to the integral types: byte, short, int, long, and to the corresponding object wrapper types.

Table 12.16 shows which flags are allowed for the integral conversions. The following flag combinations are not permitted: "+ " (sign/space) or "-0" (left-justified/zero-padded). Both '-' and '0' require a positive width.

The width indicates the *minimum* number of characters to output, including any characters because of the flag that are specified. It is overridden if the argument actually requires a greater number of characters than the width.

For integral conversions, the precision is *not* applicable. If a precision is provided, an exception will be thrown.

Some examples of using the integral conversions are shown below, together with the output:

```
out.printf("1|%d|%o|%x|%n", (byte) 63, 63, 63L);      // 1|63|77|3f|
out.printf("2|%d|%o|%x|%n",
           (byte) -63, -63, -63L);        // 2|-63|37777777701|ffffffffffffffc1|
out.printf("3|%+05d|%-+5d|%+d|%n", -63, 63, 63);   // 3|-0063|+63  |+63|
out.printf("4|% d|% d|%(d|%n", -63, 63, -63);      // 4|-63| 63|(63)|
out.printf("5|%-, 10d|%, 10d|%,(010d|%n",
           -654321, 654321, -654321);      // 5|-654,321  |   654,321|(0654,321)|
// out.printf("6|%+ d|%-0d|%n", 123, 123);     // Illegal flag combinations!
// out.printf("7|%+2.3d|%n", 123, 123);        // Precision not permitted!
```

See also Section 12.5, The `java.text.NumberFormat` Class, p. 546, where formatting of numbers is discussed.

Floating-Point Conversions: 'e', 'E', 'f', 'g', 'G', 'a', 'A'

These *floating-point conversions* may be applied to floating-point types: float, double, and the corresponding object wrapper types.

The conversions 'e' and 'E' use *computerized scientific notation* (e.g., 1234.6e+00). The conversion 'f' uses *decimal format* (for example, 1234.6). The conversions 'g' and 'G' use *general scientific notation*, i.e. computerized scientific notation for large exponents and decimal format for small exponents. The conversions 'a' and 'A' use *hexadecimal exponential format* (e.g., 0x1.5bfp1, where the exponent p1 is 2^1).

Table 12.16 shows which flags are allowed for the integral conversions. As for the integral conversions, the following flag combinations are not permitted: "+ " (sign/space) or "-0" (left-justified/zero-padded). Both '-' and '0' require a positive width.

The width indicates the *minimum* number of characters to output, with padding if necessary.

If the conversion is 'e', 'E', 'f', 'a' or 'A', the precision is the number of *decimal places*. If the conversion is 'g' or 'G', the precision is the number of *significant digits*. If no precision is given, it defaults to 6. In any case, the value is rounded if necessary.

Some examples of using the floating-point conversions are shown below, together with the output in the UK locale (the default locale in this case).

```
out.printf("1|%1$e|%1$f|%n", Math.E);      // 1|2.718282e+00|2.718282|
out.printf("2|% .3f|%-+10.3f|%1$+10f|%n",
           Math.PI, -Math.PI);             // 2| 3.142|-3.142    | +3.141593|
out.printf("3|%-12.2f|%12.2f|%n",
           1.0/0, 0.0/0.0);                // 3|Infinity     |          NaN|
```

Here is an example of a table of aligned numerical values:

```
for(int i = 0; i < 4; ++i) {
  for(int j = 0; j < 3; ++j)
    out.printf("%,10.2f", Math.random()*10000.0);
  out.println();
}
```

Output (default locale is UK):

```
  548.35  3,944.18  1,963.84
7,357.72  9,764.11    209.10
4,897.17  6,026.72  3,133.10
6,109.59  6,591.39  4,872.63
```

See also Section 12.5, The `java.text.NumberFormat` Class, p. 546,where formatting of numbers is discussed.

Date/Time Conversions: 't', 'T'

These *date/time conversions* may be applied to types which are capable of encoding a date and/or time: long, Long, Calendar, and Date. The general syntax for the string specifier for these conversions is the following:

> %[argument_index][flags][width]conversion

The optional argument index, flags, and width are defined as for general, character and numeric types. No precision can be specified.

The required conversion is a *two* character sequence. The first character is 't' or 'T'. The second character indicates the format to be used. Here we will only present an overview of date/time conversions that are called *date/time composition conversions* (shown in Table 12.17). The following printf calls use these formats to output the values in the current calendar according to the US locale:

```
Calendar myCalendar = Calendar.getInstance();
out.printf(Locale.US, "1|%tR%n", myCalendar); // 1|15:50
out.printf(Locale.US, "2|%tT%n", myCalendar); // 2|15:50:45
out.printf(Locale.US, "3|%tr%n", myCalendar); // 3|03:50:45 PM
out.printf(Locale.US, "4|%tD%n", myCalendar); // 4|03/11/08
out.printf(Locale.US, "5|%tF%n", myCalendar); // 5|2008-03-11
out.printf(Locale.US, "6|%tc%n", myCalendar); // 6|Tue Mar 11 15:50:45 EDT 2008
```

See also Section 12.4, The `java.text.DateFormat` Class, p. 541,where formatting of date/time values is discussed.

Table 12.17 *Selected Time/Date Composition Conversions*

Conversion Specification	Description
'R'	Time formatted for the 24-hour clock as "%tH:%tM"
'T'	Time formatted for the 24-hour clock as "%tH:%tM:%tS".
'r'	Time formatted for the 12-hour clock as "%tI:%tM:%tS %tP". The location of the morning or afternoon marker ('%tp') may be locale-dependent.
'D'	Date formatted as "%tm/%td/%ty".
'F'	ISO 8601 complete date formatted as "%tY-%tm-%td".
'c'	Date and time formatted as "%ta %tb %td %tT %tZ %tY", e.g., Tue Mar 04 17:22:37 EST 2008.

Selected Format Exceptions

Table 12.18 shows some selected *unchecked* exceptions in the java.util package that can be thrown because of errors in a format string. These exceptions are subclasses of the IllegalFormatException class.

Table 12.18 *Selected Format Exceptions*

Format Exception	Meaning
DuplicateFormatFlagsException	Flag used more than once.
FormatFlagsConversionMismatchException	Flag and conversion not compatible.
IllegalFormatConversionException	Type of argument not compatible with the conversion.
IllegalFormatFlagsException	Invalid flag combination.
IllegalFormatPrecisionException	Precision invalid or not permissible.
IllegalFormatWidthException	Width invalid or not permissible.
MissingFormatArgumentException	A conversion has no corresponding argument.
MissingFormatWidthException	A positive width was not specified.
UnknownFormatConversionException	Conversion is unknown.
UnknownFormatFlagsException	A flag is unknown.

Using the `format()` Method

The destination object of a `Formatter`, mentioned earlier, can be any one of the following:

- a `StringBuilder`, by default
- an `Appendable`, e.g., a `String` that implements this interface
- a file specified either by its name or by a `File` object
- a `PrintStream`, or another `OutputStream`

The `Formatter` class provides various constructors that allow mixing and matching of a destination object, a character encoding (i.e., a `Charset`) and a locale. Where no destination object is specified, the default destination object is a `StringBuilder`. The formatted output can be retrieved by calling the `toString()` method of the `Formatter` class. When no character encoding or locale is specified, the default character encoding or the default locale is used, respectively. The `Formatter` class also provides the `flush()` and the `close()` methods, analogous to those of an output stream, that also affect the destination object. Once a formatter is closed, calling the format() method throws a `FormatterClosedException`.

Various constructors in the `Formatter` class:

```
Formatter()
Formatter(Locale l)

Formatter(Appendable a)
Formatter(Appendable a, Locale l)

Formatter(File file)
Formatter(File file, String charset)
Formatter(File file, String charset, Locale l)

Formatter(OutputStream os)
Formatter(OutputStream os, String charset)
Formatter(OutputStream os, String charset, Locale l)

Formatter(String fileName)
Formatter(String fileName, String charset)
Formatter(String fileName, String charset, Locale l)

Formatter(PrintStream ps)
```

Example 12.14 illustrates the use of the `format()` method from different classes. Using the static `String.format()` method is shown at (1). The output is printed to the standard output stream, using the default character encoding and the default locale. The `PrintWriter.format()` method is used at (2). The formatted output is written to the specified file, using the default character encoding and the locale passed to the `format()` method. The `format()` method of the `System.out` field is used to write the output directly to the standard output stream at (3), i.e., the same as using the `printf()` method.

The `Formatter.format()` method is used at (4). The formatted output is written to the specified `StringBuilder`, using the default character encoding and the specified locale. The `Formatter.format()` method is used at (5) to write to an `OutputStream`. The formatted output is written to the specified file using the default character encoding and the locale passed to the `format()` method. The program flushes and closes any streams or formatters that were created explicitly.

Example 12.14 *Using the* `format()` *Method*

```java
import java.io.FileNotFoundException;
import java.io.FileOutputStream;
import java.io.PrintWriter;
import java.util.Formatter;
import java.util.Locale;

/* Using the format() method */
class UsingFormatMethod {

  public static void main(String[] args) throws FileNotFoundException {
    // String.format() returns a string with the formatted text.        (1)
    String output = String.format("1:Formatted output|%6d|%8.2f|%-10s|%n",
                          2008, 12345.678, "Hello");
    System.out.print(output);

    // PrintWriter.format() writes to the specified file,                (2)
    // using the specified locale.
    PrintWriter pw = new PrintWriter("output2.txt");
    pw.format(new Locale("no", "NO"),
              "2:Formatted output|%6d|%8.2f|%-10s|%n",
               2008, 12345.678, "Hello");
    pw.flush();
    pw.close();

    // PrintStream.format() writes to the standard output stream.        (3)
    System.out.format("3:Formatted output|%6d|%8.2f|%-10s|%n",
                      2008, 12345.678, "Hello");

    // Formatter.format() writes to the string builder,                 (4)
    // using specified locale.
    StringBuilder stb = new StringBuilder();
    Formatter fmt = new Formatter(stb, new Locale("no", "NO"));
    fmt.format("4:Formatted output|%6d|%8.2f|%-10s|%n",
               2008, 12345.678, "Hello");
    System.out.print(stb);
    fmt.flush();
    fmt.close();

    // Formatter.format() writes to the specified file,                 (5)
    // using the specified locale.
    Formatter fmt2 = new Formatter(new FileOutputStream("output5.txt"));
    fmt2.format(new Locale("no", "NO"),
                "5:Formatted output|%6d|%8.2f|%-10s|%n",
                 2008, 12345.678, "Hello");
```

```
        fmt2.flush();
        fmt2.close();
      }
    }
```

Output from the program:

```
    1:Formatted output|   2008|12345.68|Hello      |
    3:Formatted output|   2008|12345.68|Hello      |
    4:Formatted output|   2008|12345,68|Hello      |
```

Contents of the file output2.txt after program execution:

```
    2:Formatted output|   2008|12345,68|Hello      |
```

Contents of the file output5.txt after program execution:

```
    5:Formatted output|   2008|12345,68|Hello      |
```

Review Questions

12.27   Which classes in the Java API provide both forms of the format() method?

```
    format(String formatStr, Object... args)
    format(java.util.Locale l, String formatStr, Object... args)
```

Select the four correct answers.

(a) java.lang.String
(b) java.util.StringBuilder
(c) java.io.PrintStream
(d) java.io.PrintWriter
(e) java.util.Scanner
(f) java.util.Formatter
(g) java.util.Console

12.28   Which classes in the Java API provide both forms of the printf() method?

```
    printf(String formatStr, Object... args)
    printf(java.util.Locale l, String formatStr, Object... args)
```

Select the two correct answers.

(a) java.lang.String
(b) java.util.StringBuilder
(c) java.io.PrintStream
(d) java.io.PrintWriter
(e) java.util.Scanner
(f) java.util.Formatter
(g) java.util.Console

12.29 Which statements are not true about formatting values?

Select the two correct answers.

(a) The method call `out.printf(formatStr,args)` gives the same results as the method call `out.format(formatStr,args)`, where `out` is a reference to either a `java.io.PrintStream` or a `java.io.PrintWriter`.

(b) The conversions `'s'` and `'b'` can be applied to any argument type.

(c) The conversion `'d'` can only be applied to integers, including `char` values.

(d) The flag combination `'+-'` is valid, but `'(+-'` is not.

(e) The flag `'-'` cannot be used without specifying a positive width.

(f) The flags `' '` and `'0'` can be combined if a positive width is specified.

(g) The argument index is always specified before any flags.

12.30 Given the following code:

```
public class RQ600_20 {
  public static void main(String[] args) {
    // (1) INSERT CODE HERE
  }
}
```

Which code, when inserted at (1), will print the following in the terminal window:

```
Formatted output: 1234.04
```

Select the one correct answer.

(a) `String output = String.format("Formatted output: %.2f%n", 1234.0354);`
   `System.out.print(output);`

(b) `System.out.format("Formatted output: %.2f%n", 1234.0354);`

(c) `StringBuilder stb = new StringBuilder();`
   `Formatter fmt = new Formatter(stb);`
   `fmt.format("Formatted output: %.2f%n", 1234.0354);`
   `System.out.print(stb);`

(d) `Formatter fmt2 = new Formatter(System.out);`
   `fmt2.format("Formatted output: %.2f%n", 1234.0354);`

(e) All of the above

12.31 Given the following code:

```
public class RQ600_10 {

  public static void main(String[] args) throws FileNotFoundException {
    // (1) INSERT CODE HERE
  }
}
```

Which code, when inserted at (1), will print the following to the file named `"output.txt"`:

```
Formatted output: 1234.04
```

Select the one correct answer.

(a)
```java
PrintWriter pw = new PrintWriter("output.txt");
pw.format("Formatted output: %.2f%n", 1234.0354);
pw.flush();
pw.close();
```

(b)
```java
PrintStream ps = new PrintStream("output.txt");
ps.format("Formatted output: %.2f%n", 1234.0354);
ps.flush();
ps.close();
```

(c)
```java
Formatter fmt1 = new Formatter(new FileOutputStream("output.txt"));
fmt1.format("Formatted output: %.2f%n", 1234.0354);
fmt1.flush();
fmt1.close();
```

(d)
```java
Formatter fmt2 = new Formatter("output.txt");
fmt2.format("Formatted output: %.2f%n", 1234.0354);
fmt2.flush();
fmt2.close();
```

(e) All of the above

12.32   Given the following code:

```java
public class RQ600_110 {
  public static void main(String[] args) {
    Object[][] twoDimArray = {
        {"Tom",  -100.678,    44, 'X', true},
        {"Dick",    50.88,   777, 'Y', false},
        {"Harry", -20.4455, 5151, 'Z', false}
    };
    // (1) INSERT DECLARATION HERE
    for (Object[] oneDimArray : twoDimArray) {
      System.out.format(formatStr, oneDimArray);
    }
  }
}
```

Which declarations, when inserted at (1), will print the following:

```
|X|  Tom|t|(100.68)|    44|
|Y| Dick|f|  +50.88|   777|
|Z|Harry|f| (20.45)|  5151|
```

Select the two correct answers.

(a) `String formatStr = "|%4$-1c|%5s|%5$1.1b|%(+8.2f|%6d|%n";`
(b) `String formatStr = "|%4$c|%5s|%5$.1b|%(+8.2f|%6s|%n";`
(c) `String formatStr = "|%4$c|%5s|%5$.1b|%2$(+-8.2f|%3$6s|%n";`
(d) `String formatStr = "|%4$c|%1$5s|%5$.1b|%2$(+8.2f|%3$,6d|%n";`

12.33   What will the following print when compiled and run?

```java
public class RQ600_100 {
  public static void main(String[] args) {
    Double[] dArray = {10.987, -100.678, 1000.345};
```

```
      System.out.format("|");
      for (int i = 0; i < dArray.length; i++) {
        System.out.format("%(,+-" + (i+1) + "." + (i+1) + "f|", dArray[i]);
      }
    }
  }
```

Select the one correct answer.

(a) `|(11.0)|(-100.68)|(+1,000.345)|`

(b) `|+11.0|-100.68|+1,000.345|`

(c) `|+11.0|(100.68)|+1,000.345|`

(d) The program will not compile.

(e) The program will compile, but throw a `java.util.IllegalFormatFlagsException` when run.

12.34   What will the following print when compiled and run?

```
public class RQ600_120 {
  public static void main(String[] args) {
    System.out.printf("|%0.0f|", 12.5);
    System.out.printf("|%0.s|", 12.5);
    System.out.printf("|%( +-10.2f|", -12.5);
    System.out.format("|%10.2f|%d", 12.5 );
    System.out.format("|%!10.2f|", 12.5 );
  }
}
```

Select the one correct answer.

(a) `|12|12.|(12.50)    |    12.50|    -12.50|`

(b) `|13|13.|(-12.50)   |    12.50|    -12.50|`

(c) The program will not compile.

(d) The program will compile, but throw an exception when run.

12.35   Which statements, when inserted at (1), will result in the program throwing an exception when run?

```
public class RQ600_40 {
  public static void main(String[] args) {
    // (1) INSERT STATEMENT HERE
  }
}
```

Select the two correct answers.

(a) `System.out.printf("|%-10c|", 'L');`

(b) `System.out.printf("|%5.1c|", 125);`

(c) `System.out.printf("|%c|", 33);`

(d) `System.out.printf("|%+c|", 33);`

(e) `System.out.printf("|%c|", new Character('h'));`

(f) `System.out.printf("|%-4c|", new Integer("33"));`

(g) `System.out.printf("|%c|", null);`

(h) `System.out.printf("|%2$2c|", 123, 'V', true);`

12.36   Which statement, when inserted at (1), will format and print either the value -123 or 123 in the terminal window?

```
public class RQ600_50 {
  public static void main(String[] args) {
    // (1) INSERT STATEMENT HERE
  }
}
```

Select the one correct answer.

(a) `System.out.printf("|%(d|", -123);`
(b) `System.out.printf("|%-+5d|", 123);`
(c) `System.out.printf("|%(07d|", -123);`
(d) `System.out.printf("|%(-+7d|", -123);`
(e) `System.out.printf("|%-5d|", -123);`
(f) `System.out.printf("|%3d|", new Integer("-123"));`
(g) `System.out.printf("|%2$4d|", null, 123, true);`
(h) All of the above

12.37   Which statement, when inserted at (1), will result in the program throwing an exception when run?

```
public class RQ600_55 {
  public static void main(String[] args) {
    // (1) INSERT STATEMENT HERE
  }
}
```

Select the one correct answer.

(a) `System.out.printf("|%-d|", -123);`
(b) `System.out.printf("|%3.0d|", 123);`
(c) `System.out.printf("|%d|", "false");`
(d) `System.out.printf("|%3d|", 123.45);`
(e) `System.out.printf("|%-5d|", 'a');`
(f) `System.out.printf("|%d|", new Character('h'));`
(g) `System.out.printf("|%d|", new Boolean("911"));`
(h) `System.out.printf("|%d|", false);`
(i) All of the above.

12.38   Given the following code:

```
public class RQ600_60 {
  public static void main(String[] args) {
    System.out.format("|");
    // (1) INSERT LOOP HERE
    System.out.format("%n");
  }
}
```

Which loops, when inserted at (1), will result in the program printing:

```
| t| tr| tru|   true|
```

Select the three correct answers.

```
(a) for (int i = 1; i < 5; i++) {
        System.out.format("%" + i*2 + "." + i + "b|", 2007);
    }
(b) for (int i = 0; i < 5; i++) {
        System.out.format("%" + (i==0 ? "" : i*2) + "." + i + "b|", 2007);
    }
(c) for (int i = 0; i < 4; i++) {
        System.out.format("%" + (i+1)*2 + "." + i + "b|", 2007);
    }
(d) for (int i = 0; i < 4; i++) {
        System.out.format("%" + (i+1)*2 + "." + (i+1) + "b|", 2007);
    }
(e) for (int i = 4; i > 0; i--) {
        System.out.format("%" + (5-i)*2 + "." + (5-i) + "b|", 2007);
    }
```

12.39   Given the following code:

```
public class RQ600_90 {
    public static void main(String[] args) {
        Integer[] integerArray = {10, 100, 1000, 10000};
        int[] intArray = {10, 100, 1000, 10000};
        // (1) INSERT STATEMENT HERE
    }
}
```

Which statement, when inserted at (1), will result in the program printing:

```
|1000|+10 |  100|
```

Select the one correct answer.

(a) `System.out.printf("|%3$4d|%4d|%2$04d|%n", integerArray);`
(b) `System.out.printf("|%3$4d|%-+4d|%2$4d|%n", integerArray);`
(c) `System.out.printf("|%+4d|%4d|%4d|%n", integerArray);`
(d) `System.out.printf("|%4d|%4d|%4d|%n", intArray);`
(e) None of the above.

12.40   Given the following code:

```
public class RQ600_80 {
    public static void main(String[] args) {
        for (int i = 5; i < 10; i++) {
            System.out.format("|");
            for (int j = 0; j < 3; j++) {
                System.out.format("%" + i + "." + j + "f|", 123.456);
            }
            System.out.format("%n");
        }
    }
}
```

Which of the following lines will occur in the output of the program?

Select the one correct answer.

(a) | 123|123.5|123.46|
(b) | 123| 123.5|123.46|
(c) | 123| 123.5| 123.46|
(d) | 123| 123.5| 123.46|
(e) | 123| 123.5| 123.46|
(f) All of the above.

 ## Chapter Summary

The following information was included in this chapter:

- using the Locale class in various contexts for localization.

- relationships between the Date, Calendar, and DateFormat classes for managing and formatting time/date values.

- the functionality provided by the NumberFormat class for formatting numbers and currency values.

- fundamentals for writing regular expressions.

- the relationship between the Pattern and the Matcher to provide functionality for successive matching, and the match-and-replace mode of a Matcher.

- splitting input using the split() method of the Pattern and String class.

- the functionality provided by the Scanner for parsing primitive values and strings in text-based input.

- string pattern matching with a Scanner using delimiters and patterns.

- using a Scanner in multi-line mode.

- using formatting specifiers in the printf() and format() methods for formatting strings, primitive values, and time/date values.

 ## Programming Exercises

12.1 Write a program to *grep* a text file, i.e. find all matches for the given regular expression in the text file. The program provides a test file, but ideally the file name and the regular expression should be specified on the command line. Given the test data below, the program prints:

```
1: [(3,4:be), (16,17:be)]
3: [(2,3:be)]
4: [(0,1:Be), (12,13:be), (22,23:be), (35,36:Be)]
```

A skeleton for the program is given below.

```java
import java.io.BufferedReader;
import java.io.FileReader;
import java.io.FileWriter;
import java.io.IOException;
import java.util.ArrayList;
import java.util.List;
import java.util.regex.Matcher;
import java.util.regex.Pattern;

public class VerySimpleGrep {
  public static void main(String[] args) throws IOException {
    // Test file
    FileWriter fw = new FileWriter("test.txt");
    fw.write("To be or not to be.\n");
    fw.write("Only A's, no B's.\n");
    fw.write("A bee movie is not funny.\n");
    fw.write("Bessy was a beautiful beatnik from Bern.\n");
    fw.close();
    String fileName = "test.txt";
    String regexStr = "[bB]e";
    grepFile(fileName, regexStr);
  }

  /**
   * Finds and prints matches for the regex in the text file.
   * @param fileName
   * @param regex
   * @throws IOException
   */
  public static void grepFile(String fileName, String regex)
                              throws IOException {
    // ...
  }

  /**
   * Finds the matches for the pattern in the target.
   * @param pattern
   * @param target
   * @return List<String> with the matches found in the target
   */
  public static List<String> grepLine(Pattern pattern, String target) {
    // ...
  }
}
```

12.2 Write a method that reads input specified in Comma-Separated-Value (CSV) format. Each line represents a *record* with a fixed number of *fields*. The fields in each record are separated by a comma. The last field of the record is terminated by a line separator.

The method reads the input one line at a time, and extracts the field values. The program must ensure that the correct number of fields are specified in each record.

Given the test data below, the program prints:

```
[2.5, 25, 250]
[Hi, Hello, Howdy]
[2008, 2009, 2010]
[one, two, three]
```

A skeleton for the program is given below.

```java
import static java.lang.System.out;
import java.io.BufferedReader;
import java.io.FileReader;
import java.io.FileWriter;
import java.io.IOException;
import java.util.Arrays;
import java.util.Scanner;
import java.util.regex.Pattern;

public class CSVReader {

  public static void main(String[] args) throws IOException {
    FileWriter fw = new FileWriter("csv.txt");
    fw.write("2.5,25,250\n");
    fw.write("Hi,Hello,Howdy\n");
    fw.write("2008,2009,2010\n");
    fw.write("one,two,three\n");
    fw.close();
    BufferedReader source = new BufferedReader(new FileReader("csv.txt"));
    readCSV(source, 3);
    source.close();
  }

  /**
   * Reads values in CSV format.
   * @param source
   * @param numOfFields
   * @throws IOException
   */
  public static void readCSV(Readable source,
                        int numOfFields)throws IOException {
    // ...
  }

  /**
   * Creates a pattern that corresponds to the number of fields
   * specified in CSV format on each line/record.
   * @param numOfFields
   * @return Pattern
   */
  public static Pattern compileCSVPattern(int numOfFields) {
    // ...
  }
}
```

Threads 13

●●●

Exam Objectives
4.1 Write code to define, instantiate, and start new threads using both `java.lang.Thread` and `java.lang.Runnable`.
4.2 Recognize the states in which a thread can exist, and identify ways in which a thread can transition from one state to another.
4.3 Given a scenario, write code that makes appropriate use of object locking to protect static or instance variables from concurrent access problems.
4.4 Given a scenario, write code that makes appropriate use of `wait`, `notify`, or `notifyAll`.

Supplementary Objectives
• Recognize conditions that might prevent a thread from executing.
• Write code to start and stop a thread.
• Understand aspects of thread behavior that are not guaranteed.

13.1 Multitasking

Multitasking allows several activities to occur concurrently on the computer. A distinction is usually made between:

- Process-based multitasking
- Thread-based multitasking

At the coarse-grain level there is *process-based* multitasking, which allows processes (i.e., programs) to run concurrently on the computer. A familiar example is running the spreadsheet program while also working with the word-processor. At the fine-grain level there is *thread-based* multitasking, which allows parts of the *same* program to run concurrently on the computer. A familiar example is a word-processor that is printing and formatting text at the same time. This is only feasible if the two tasks are performed by two independent paths of execution at runtime. The two tasks would correspond to executing parts of the program concurrently. The sequence of code executed for each task defines a separate path of execution, and is called a *thread* (*of execution*).

In a single-threaded environment only one task at a time can be performed. CPU cycles are wasted, for example, when waiting for user input. Multitasking allows idle CPU time to be put to good use.

Some advantages of thread-based multitasking as compared to process-based multitasking are:

- threads share the same address space
- context switching between threads is usually less expensive than between processes
- the cost of communication between threads is relatively low

Java supports thread-based multitasking and provides high-level facilities for multithreaded programming. *Thread safety* is the term used to describe the design of classes that ensure that the state of their objects is always consistent, even when the objects are used concurrently by multiple threads.

13.2 Overview of Threads

A thread is an independent sequential path of execution within a program. Many threads can run concurrently within a program. At runtime, threads in a program exist in a common memory space and can, therefore, share both data and code (i.e., they are *lightweight* compared to processes). They also share the process running the program.

Every thread in Java is created and controlled by a unique object of the `java.lang.Thread` class. Often the thread and its associated `Thread` object are thought of as being synonymous.

Threads make the runtime environment asynchronous, allowing different tasks to be performed concurrently. Using this powerful paradigm in Java centers around understanding the following aspects of multithreaded programming:

- creating threads and providing the code that gets executed by a thread (see Section 13.4, p. 615)
- accessing common data and code through synchronization (see Section 13.5, p. 626).
- transitioning between thread states (see Section 13.6, p. 634).

13.3 The Main Thread

The runtime environment distinguishes between *user threads* and *daemon threads*. As long as a user thread is alive, the JVM does not terminate. A daemon thread is at the mercy of the runtime system: it is stopped if there are no more user threads running, thus terminating the program. Daemon threads exist only to serve user threads.

When a standalone application is run, a user thread is automatically created to execute the main() method of the application. This thread is called the *main thread*. If no other user threads are spawned, the program terminates when the main() method finishes executing. All other threads, called *child* threads, are spawned from the main thread, inheriting its user-thread status. The main() method can then finish, but the program will keep running until all user threads have completed. Calling the setDaemon(boolean) method in the Thread class marks the status of the thread as either daemon or user, but this must be done before the thread is *started*. Any attempt to change the status after the thread has been started, throws an IllegalThreadStateException. Marking all spawned threads as daemon threads ensures that the application terminates when the main thread dies.

When a GUI application is started, a special thread is automatically created to monitor the user–GUI interaction. This user thread keeps the program running, allowing interaction between the user and the GUI, even though the main thread might have completed after the main() method finished executing.

13.4 Thread Creation

A thread in Java is represented by an object of the Thread class. Implementing threads is achieved in one of two ways:

- implementing the java.lang.Runnable interface
- extending the java.lang.Thread class

Implementing the Runnable **Interface**

The Runnable interface has the following specification, comprising one abstract method declaration:

```
public interface Runnable {
  void run();
}
```

A thread, which is created based on an object that implements the Runnable interface, will execute the code defined in the public method run(). In other words, the code in the run() method defines an independent path of execution and thereby the entry and the exits for the thread. A thread ends when the run() method ends, either by normal completion or by throwing an uncaught exception.

The procedure for creating threads based on the Runnable interface is as follows:

1. A class implements the Runnable interface, providing the run() method that will be executed by the thread. An object of this class is a Runnable object.

2. An object of the Thread class is created by passing a Runnable object as an argument in the Thread constructor call. The Thread object now has a Runnable object that implements the run() method.

3. The start() method is invoked on the Thread object created in the previous step. The start() method returns immediately after a thread has been spawned. In other words, the call to the start() method is asynchronous.

When the thread, represented by the Thread object on which the start() method was invoked, gets to run, it executes the run() method of the Runnable object. This sequence of events is illustrated in Figure 13.1.

Figure 13.1 *Spawning Threads Using a* Runnable *Object*

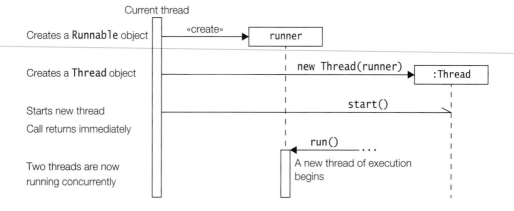

The following is a summary of important constructors and methods from the java.lang.Thread class:

```
Thread(Runnable threadTarget)
Thread(Runnable threadTarget, String threadName)
```

The argument threadTarget is the object whose run() method will be executed when the thread is started. The argument threadName can be specified to give an explicit name for the thread, rather than an automatically generated one. A thread's name can be retrieved by calling the getName() method.

```
static Thread currentThread()
```

This method returns a reference to the Thread object of the currently executing thread.

```
final String getName()
final void setName(String name)
```

The first method returns the name of the thread. The second one sets the thread's name to the specified argument.

```
void run()
```

The Thread class implements the Runnable interface by providing an implementation of the run() method. This implementation in the Thread class does nothing and returns. Subclasses of the Thread class should override this method. If the current thread is created using a separate Runnable object, the run() method of the Runnable object is called.

```
final void setDaemon(boolean flag)
final boolean isDaemon()
```

The first method sets the status of the thread either as a daemon thread or as a user thread, depending on whether the argument is true or false, respectively. The status should be set before the thread is started. The second method returns true if the thread is a daemon thread, otherwise, false.

```
void start()
```

This method spawns a new thread, i.e., the new thread will begin execution as a child thread of the current thread. The spawning is done asynchronously as the call to this method returns immediately. It throws an IllegalThread-StateException if the thread is already started.

In Example 13.1, the class Counter implements the Runnable interface. At (1), the class defines the run() method that constitutes the code to be executed in a thread. In each iteration of the while loop, the current value of the counter is printed and incremented, as shown at (2). Also, in each iteration, the thread will sleep for 250 milliseconds, as shown at (3). While it is sleeping, other threads may run (see Section 13.6, p. 640).

The code in the main() method ensures that the Counter object created at (4) is passed to a new Thread object in the constructor call, as shown at (5). In addition, the thread is enabled for execution by the call to its start() method, as shown at (6).

The static method currentThread() in the Thread class can be used to obtain a reference to the Thread object associated with the current thread. We can call the get-Name() method on the current thread to obtain its name. An example of its usage is shown at (2), that prints the name of the thread executing the run() method. Another example of its usage is shown at (8), that prints the name of the thread executing the main() method.

Example 13.1 *Implementing the* Runnable *Interface*

```
class Counter implements Runnable {
  private int currentValue;
  public Counter() { currentValue = 0; }
  public int getValue() { return currentValue; }

  public void run() {                                // (1) Thread entry point
    try {
      while (currentValue < 5) {
        System.out.println(
            Thread.currentThread().getName()         // (2) Print thread name.
            + ": " + (currentValue++)
        );
        Thread.sleep(250);                           // (3) Current thread sleeps.
      }
    } catch (InterruptedException e) {
      System.out.println(Thread.currentThread().getName() + " interrupted.");
    }
    System.out.println("Exit from thread: " + Thread.currentThread().getName());
  }
}
//_____
public class Client {
  public static void main(String[] args) {
    Counter counterA = new Counter();                    // (4) Create a counter.
    Thread worker = new Thread(counterA, "Counter A");// (5) Create a new thread.
    System.out.println(worker);
    worker.start();                                      // (6) Start the thread.

    try {
      int val;
      do {
        val = counterA.getValue();                       // (7) Access the counter value.
        System.out.println(
            "Counter value read by " +
            Thread.currentThread().getName() +           // (8) Print thread name.
            ": " + val
        );
        Thread.sleep(1000);                              // (9) Current thread sleeps.
      } while (val < 5);
    } catch (InterruptedException e) {
```

```
        System.out.println("The main thread is interrupted.");
    }

    System.out.println("Exit from main() method.");
  }
}
```

Possible output from the program:

```
Thread[Counter A,5,main]
Counter value read by main thread: 0
Counter A: 0
Counter A: 1
Counter A: 2
Counter A: 3
Counter value read by main thread: 4
Counter A: 4
Exit from thread: Counter A
Counter value read by main thread: 5
Exit from main() method.
```

The Client class uses the Counter class. It creates an object of the class Counter at (4) and retrieves its value in a loop at (7). After each retrieval, the main thread sleeps for 1,000 milliseconds at (9), allowing other threads to run.

Note that the main thread executing in the Client class sleeps for a longer time between iterations than the Counter A thread, giving the Counter A thread the opportunity to run as well. The Counter A thread is a *child* thread of the main thread. It inherits the user-thread status from the main thread. If the code after the statement at (6) in the main() method was removed, the main thread would finish executing before the child thread. However, the program would continue running until the child thread completed its execution.

Since thread scheduling is not predictable (Section 13.6, p. 638) and Example 13.1 does not enforce any synchronization between the two threads in accessing the counter value, the output shown may vary. The first line of the output shows the string representation of the Thread object associated with the counter: its name (Counter A), its priority (5), and its parent thread (main). The output from the main thread and the Counter A thread is interspersed. It also shows that the value in the Counter A thread was incremented faster than the main thread could access the counter's value after each increment.

Extending the Thread Class

A class can also extend the Thread class to create a thread. A typical procedure for doing this is as follows (see Figure 13.2):

1. A class extending the Thread class overrides the run() method from the Thread class to define the code executed by the thread.

2. This subclass may call a Thread constructor explicitly in its constructors to initialize the thread, using the super() call.

3. The start() method inherited from the Thread class is invoked on the object of the class to make the thread eligible for running.

Figure 13.2 *Spawning Threads—Extending the* Thread *Class*

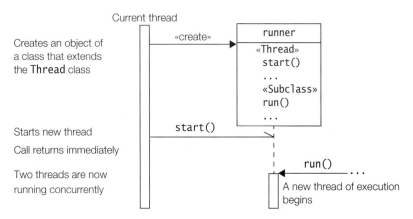

In Example 13.2, the Counter class from Example 13.1 has been modified to illustrate creating a thread by extending the Thread class. Note the call to the constructor of the superclass Thread at (1) and the invocation of the inherited start() method at (2) in the constructor of the Counter class. The program output shows that the Client class creates two threads and exits, but the program continues running until the child threads have completed. The two child threads are independent, each having its own counter and executing its own run() method.

The Thread class implements the Runnable interface, which means that this approach is not much different from implementing the Runnable interface directly. The only difference is that the roles of the Runnable object and the Thread object are combined in a single object.

Adding the following statement before the call to the start() method at (2) in Example 13.2:

```
setDaemon(true);
```

illustrates the daemon nature of threads. The program execution will now terminate after the main thread has completed, without waiting for the daemon Counter threads to finish normally:

```
Method main() runs in thread main
Thread[Counter A,5,main]
Thread[Counter B,5,main]
Counter A: 0
Exit from main() method.
Counter B: 0
```

Example 13.2 *Extending the* Thread *Class*

```
class Counter extends Thread {

  private int currentValue;

  public Counter(String threadName) {
    super(threadName);                             // (1) Initialize thread.
    currentValue = 0;
    System.out.println(this);
//  setDaemon(true);
    start();                                       // (2) Start this thread.
  }

  public int getValue() { return currentValue; }

  public void run() {                              // (3) Override from superclass.
    try {
      while (currentValue < 5) {
        System.out.println(getName() + ": " + (currentValue++));
        Thread.sleep(250);                         // (4) Current thread sleeps.
      }
    } catch (InterruptedException e) {
      System.out.println(getName() + " interrupted.");
    }
    System.out.println("Exit from thread: " + getName());
  }
}
//_____
public class Client {
  public static void main(String[] args) {

    System.out.println("Method main() runs in thread " +
        Thread.currentThread().getName());         // (5) Current thread

    Counter counterA = new Counter("Counter A"); // (6) Create a thread.
    Counter counterB = new Counter("Counter B"); // (7) Create a thread.

    System.out.println("Exit from main() method.");
  }
}
```

Possible output from the program:

```
Method main() runs in thread main
Thread[Counter A,5,main]
Thread[Counter B,5,main]
Exit from main() method.
Counter A: 0
Counter B: 0
Counter A: 1
Counter B: 1
Counter A: 2
Counter B: 2
Counter A: 3
```

```
Counter B: 3
Counter A: 4
Counter B: 4
Exit from thread: Counter A
Exit from thread: Counter B
```

When creating threads, there are two reasons why implementing the Runnable interface may be preferable to extending the Thread class:

- Extending the Thread class means that the subclass cannot extend any other class, whereas a class implementing the Runnable interface has this option.

- A class might only be interested in being runnable and, therefore, inheriting the full overhead of the Thread class would be excessive.

The two previous examples illustrated two different ways to create a thread. In Example 13.1 the code to create the Thread object and call the start() method to initiate the thread execution is in the client code, not in the Counter class. In Example 13.2, this functionality is in the constructor of the Counter class, not in the client code.

Inner classes are useful for implementing threads that do simple tasks. The anonymous class below will create a thread and start it:

```
(new Thread() {
  public void run() {
    for(;;) System.out.println("Stop the world!");
  }
}
).start();
```

 Review Questions

13.1   Which is the correct way to start a new thread?

Select the one correct answer.
(a) Just create a new Thread object. The thread will start automatically.
(b) Create a new Thread object and call the method begin().
(c) Create a new Thread object and call the method start().
(d) Create a new Thread object and call the method run().
(e) Create a new Thread object and call the method resume().

13.2   When extending the Thread class to implement the code executed by a thread, which method should be overridden?

Select the one correct answer.
(a) begin()
(b) start()
(c) run()

    (d) `resume()`

    (e) `behavior()`

13.3 Which statements are true?

Select the two correct answers.

(a) The class `Thread` is abstract.

(b) The class `Thread` implements `Runnable`.

(c) The `Runnable` interface has a single method named `start`.

(d) Calling the method `run()` on an object implementing `Runnable` will create a new thread.

(e) A program terminates when the last user thread finishes.

13.4 What will be the result of attempting to compile and run the following program?

```
public class MyClass extends Thread {
  public MyClass(String s) { msg = s; }
  String msg;
  public void run() {
    System.out.println(msg);
  }

  public static void main(String[] args) {
    new MyClass("Hello");
    new MyClass("World");
  }
}
```

Select the one correct answer.

(a) The program will fail to compile.

(b) The program will compile without errors and will print `Hello` and `World`, in that order, every time the program is run.

(c) The program will compile without errors and will print a never-ending stream of `Hello` and `World`.

(d) The program will compile without errors and will print `Hello` and `World` when run, but the order is unpredictable.

(e) The program will compile without errors and will simply terminate without any output when run.

13.5 What will be the result of attempting to compile and run the following program?

```
class Extender extends Thread {
  public Extender() { }
  public Extender(Runnable runnable) {super(runnable);}
  public void run() {System.out.print("|Extender|");}
}

public class Implementer implements Runnable {
  public void run() {System.out.print("|Implementer|");}
```

```
public static void main(String[] args) {
  new Extender(new Implementer()).start();            // (1)
  new Extender().start();                             // (2)
  new Thread(new Implementer()).start();             // (3)
  }
}
```

Select the one correct answer.

(a) The program will fail to compile.
(b) The program will compile without errors and will print |Extender| twice and |Implementer| once, in some order, every time the program is run.
(c) The program will compile without errors and will print|Extender| once and |Implementer| twice, in some order, every time the program is run.
(d) The program will compile without errors and will print |Extender| once and |Implementer| once, in some order, every time the program is run
(e) The program will compile without errors and will simply terminate without any output when run.
(f) The program will compile without errors, and will print |Extender| once and |Implementer| once, in some order, and terminate because of an runtime error.

13.6   What will be the result of attempting to compile and run the following program?

```
class R1 implements Runnable {
  public void run() {
    System.out.print(Thread.currentThread().getName());
  }
}
public class R2 implements Runnable {
  public void run() {
    new Thread(new R1(),"|R1a|").run();
    new Thread(new R1(),"|R1b|").start();
    System.out.print(Thread.currentThread().getName());
  }

  public static void main(String[] args) {
    new Thread(new R2(),"|R2|").start();
  }
}
```

Select the one correct answer.

(a) The program will fail to compile.
(b) The program will compile without errors and will print |R1a| twice and |R2| once, in some order, every time the program is run.
(c) The program will compile without errors and will print|R1b| twice and |R2| once, in some order, every time the program is run.
(d) The program will compile without errors and will print |R1b| once and |R2| twice, in some order, every time the program is run.
(e) The program will compile without errors and will print |R1a| once, |R1b| once, and |R2| once, in some order, every time the program is run.

13.7   What will be the result of attempting to compile and run the following program?

```java
public class Threader extends Thread {
  Threader(String name) {
    super(name);
  }
  public void run() throws IllegalStateException {
    System.out.println(Thread.currentThread().getName());
    throw new IllegalStateException();
  }
  public static void main(String[] args) {
    new Threader("|T1|").start();
  }
}
```

Select the one correct answer.

(a) The program will fail to compile.

(b) The program will compile without errors, will print |T1|, and terminate nor-mally every time the program is run.

(c) The program will compile without errors, will print |T1|, and throw an Ille-galStateException, every time the program is run.

(d) None of the above.

13.8   What will be the result of attempting to compile and run the following program?

```java
public class Worker extends Thread {
  public void run() {
    System.out.print("|work|");
  }
  public static void main(String[] args) {
    Worker worker = new Worker();
    worker.start();
    worker.run();
    worker.start();
  }
}
```

Select the one correct answer.

(a) The program will fail to compile.

(b) The program will compile without errors, will print |work| twice, and termi-nate normally every time the program is run.

(c) The program will compile without errors, will print |work| three times, and terminate normally every time the program is run.

(d) The program will compile without errors, will print |work| twice, and throw an IllegalStateException, every time the program is run.

(e) None of the above.

13.5 Synchronization

Threads share the same memory space, i.e., they can share resources. However, there are critical situations where it is desirable that only one thread at a time has access to a shared resource. For example, crediting and debiting a shared bank account concurrently among several users without proper discipline, will jeopardize the integrity of the account data. Java provides high-level concepts for *synchronization* in order to control access to shared resources.

Locks

A *lock* (also called a *monitor*) is used to synchronize access to a shared resource. A lock can be associated with a shared resource. Threads gain access to a shared resource by first acquiring the lock associated with the resource. At any given time, at most one thread can hold the lock and thereby have access to the shared resource. A lock thus implements *mutual exclusion* (also known as *mutex*).

In Java, *all* objects have a lock—including arrays. This means that the lock from any Java object can be used to implement mutual exclusion. By associating a shared resource with a Java object and its lock, the object can act as a *guard*, ensuring synchronized access to the resource. Only one thread at a time can access the shared resource guarded by the *object lock*.

The object lock mechanism enforces the following rules of synchronization:

* A thread must *acquire* the object lock associated with a shared resource, before it can *enter* the shared resource. The runtime system ensures that no other thread can enter a shared resource if another thread already holds the object lock associated with it. If a thread cannot immediately acquire the object lock, it is *blocked*, i.e., it must wait for the lock to become available.

* When a thread *exits* a shared resource, the runtime system ensures that the object lock is also relinquished. If another thread is waiting for this object lock, it can try to acquire the lock in order to gain access to the shared resource.

It should be made clear that programs should not make any assumptions about the order in which threads are granted ownership of a lock.

Classes also have a class-specific lock that is analogous to the object lock. Such a lock is actually a lock on the java.lang.Class object associated with the class. Given a class A, the reference A.class denotes this unique Class object. The class lock can be used in much the same way as an object lock to implement mutual exclusion.

The keyword synchronized and the lock mechanism form the basis for implementing synchronized execution of code. There are two ways in which execution of code can be synchronized, by declaring *synchronized methods* or *synchronized code blocks*.

Synchronized Methods

If the methods of an object should only be executed by one thread at a time, then the declaration of all such methods should be specified with the keyword synchronized. A thread wishing to execute a synchronized method must first obtain the object's lock (i.e., hold the lock) before it can enter the object to execute the method. This is simply achieved by calling the method. If the lock is already held by another thread, the calling thread waits. No particular action on the part of the program is necessary. A thread relinquishes the lock simply by returning from the synchronized method, allowing the next thread waiting for this lock to proceed.

Synchronized methods are useful in situations where methods can manipulate the state of an object in ways that can corrupt the state if executed concurrently. A stack implementation usually defines the two operations push and pop as synchronized, ensuring that pushing and popping of elements are mutually exclusive operations. If several threads were to share a stack, then one thread would, for example, not be able to push an element on the stack while another thread was popping the stack. The integrity of the stack is maintained in the face of several threads accessing the state of the same stack. This situation is illustrated by Example 13.3.

The code in Example 13.3 is intentionally non-generic in order to avoid generic considerations getting in the way. The main() method in class Mutex creates a stack at (6), which is used by the two threads created at (7) and (8). The two threads continually push and pop the stack. The non-synchronized push() and pop() methods at (2a) and (4a) intentionally sleep at (3) and (5), respectively, between an update and the use of the value in the field topOfStack. This setup increases the chances for the state of the stack being corrupted by one of the threads, while the other one is sleeping. The output from the program in Example 13.3 bears this out when the methods are not declared synchronized. Non-synchronized updating of the value in the field topOfStack between the two threads is a disaster waiting to happen. This is an example of what is called a *race condition*. It occurs when two or more threads simultaneously update the same value and, as a consequence, leave the value in an undefined or inconsistent state.

From the output shown in Example 13.3, we can see that the main thread exits right after creating and starting the threads. The threads push and pop the stack. The stack state eventually gets corrupted, resulting in an ArrayOutOfBoundsException in the Pusher thread. The uncaught exception results in the demise of the Pusher thread, but the Popper thread continues.

Running the program in Example 13.3 with the synchronized version of the push() and pop() methods at (2b) and (4b), respectively, avoids the race condition. The method sleep() does not relinquish any lock that the thread might have on the current object. It is only relinquished when the synchronized method exits, guaranteeing mutually exclusive push and pop operations on the stack.

Example 13.3 *Mutual Exclusion*

```
class StackImpl {                                        // (1)
  private Object[] stackArray;
  private int topOfStack;

  public StackImpl(int capacity) {
    stackArray = new Object[capacity];
    topOfStack = -1;
  }

  public boolean push(Object element) {                  // (2a) non-synchronized
//public synchronized boolean push(Object element) {     // (2b) synchronized
    if (isFull()) return false;
    ++topOfStack;
    try { Thread.sleep(1000); } catch (Exception e) { } // (3) Sleep a little.
    stackArray[topOfStack] = element;
    return true;
  }

  public Object pop() {                                   // (4a) non-synchronized
//public synchronized Object pop() {                      // (4b) synchronized
    if (isEmpty()) return null;
    Object obj = stackArray[topOfStack];
    stackArray[topOfStack] = null;
    try { Thread.sleep(1000); } catch (Exception e) { } // (5) Sleep a little.
    topOfStack--;
    return obj;
  }

  public boolean isEmpty() { return topOfStack < 0; }
  public boolean isFull()  { return topOfStack >= stackArray.length - 1; }
}
//_____
public class Mutex {
  public static void main(String[] args) {

    final StackImpl stack = new StackImpl(20);         // (6) Shared by the threads.

    (new Thread("Pusher") {                            // (7) Thread no. 1
      public void run() {
        for(;;) {
          System.out.println("Pushed: " + stack.push(2008));
        }
      }
    }).start();

    (new Thread("Popper") {                            // (8) Thread no. 2
      public void run() {
        for(;;) {
          System.out.println("Popped: " + stack.pop());
        }
      }
```

```
        }).start();

        System.out.println("Exit from main().");
    }
}
```

Possible output from the program when run with (2a) and (4a):

```
Exit from main().
...
Pushed: true
Popped: 2008
Popped: 2008
Popped: null
...
Popped: null
java.lang.ArrayIndexOutOfBoundsException: -1
        at StackImpl.push(Mutex.java:15)
        at Mutex$1.run(Mutex.java:41)
Popped: null
Popped: null
...
```

While a thread is inside a synchronized method of an object, all other threads that wish to execute this synchronized method or any other synchronized method of the object will have to wait. This restriction does not apply to the thread that already has the lock and is executing a synchronized method of the object. Such a method can invoke other synchronized methods of the object without being blocked. The non-synchronized methods of the object can always be called at any time by any thread.

Static methods synchronize on the class lock. Acquiring and relinquishing a class lock by a thread in order to execute a static synchronized method is analogous to that of an object lock for a synchronized instance method. A thread acquires the class lock before it can proceed with the execution of any static synchronized method in the class, blocking other threads wishing to execute any static synchronized methods in the same class. This does not apply to static, non-synchronized methods, which can be invoked at any time. A thread acquiring the lock of a class to execute a static synchronized method has no effect on any thread acquiring the lock on any object of the class to execute a synchronized instance method. In other words, synchronization of static methods in a class is independent from the synchronization of instance methods on objects of the class.

A subclass decides whether the new definition of an inherited synchronized method will remain synchronized in the subclass.

Synchronized Blocks

Whereas execution of synchronized methods of an object is synchronized on the lock of the object, the synchronized block allows execution of arbitrary code to be synchronized on the lock of an arbitrary object. The general form of the synchro-nized statement is as follows:

synchronized (*<object reference expression>*) { *<code block>* }

The *<object reference expression>* must evaluate to a non-null reference value, other-wise a NullPointerException is thrown. The code block is usually related to the object on which the synchronization is being done. This is analagous to a synchro-nized method, where the execution of the method is synchronized on the lock of the current object. The following code is equivalent to the synchronized pop() method at (4b) in Example 13.3:

```
public Object pop() {
  synchronized (this) {              // Synchronized block on current object
    // ...
  }
}
```

Once a thread has entered the code block after acquiring the lock on the specified object, no other thread will be able to execute the code block, or any other code requiring the same object lock, until the lock is relinquished. This happens when the execution of the code block completes normally or an uncaught exception is thrown. In contrast to synchronized methods, this mechanism allows fine-grained synchronization of code on arbitrary objects.

Object specification in the synchronized statement is mandatory. A class can choose to synchronize the execution of a part of a method by using the this reference and putting the relevant part of the method in the synchronized block. The braces of the block cannot be left out, even if the code block has just one statement.

```
class SmartClient {
  BankAccount account;
  // ...
  public void updateTransaction() {
    synchronized (account) {         // (1) synchronized block
      account.update();              // (2)
    }
  }
}
```

In the previous example, the code at (2) in the synchronized block at (1) is synchro-nized on the BankAccount object. If several threads were to concurrently execute the method updateTransaction() on an object of SmartClient, the statement at (2) would be executed by one thread at a time only after synchronizing on the BankAccount object associated with this particular instance of SmartClient.

Inner classes can access data in their enclosing context (see Section 8.1, p. 352). An inner object might need to synchronize on its associated outer object in order to ensure integrity of data in the latter. This is illustrated in the following code where the synchronized block at (5) uses the special form of the this reference to synchro-nize on the outer object associated with an object of the inner class. This setup ensures that a thread executing the method setPi() in an inner object can only access the `private double` field `myPi` at (2) in the synchronized block at (5) by first acquiring the lock on the associated outer object. If another thread has the lock of the associated outer object, the thread in the inner object has to wait for the lock to be relinquished before it can proceed with the execution of the synchronized block at (5). However, synchronizing on an inner object and on its associated outer object are independent of each other, unless enforced explicitly, as in the following code:

```
class Outer {                       // (1) Top-level Class
  private double myPi;              // (2)

  protected class Inner {           // (3) Non-static member Class
    public void setPi() {           // (4)
      synchronized(Outer.this) {    // (5) Synchronized block on outer object
        myPi = Math.PI;             // (6)
      }
    }
  }
}
```

Synchronized blocks can also be specified on a class lock:

```
synchronized (<class name>.class) { <code block> }
```

The block synchronizes on the lock of the object denoted by the reference *<class name>*.`class`. This object (of type `Class`) represents the class in the JVM. A `static` synchronized method `classAction()` in class `A` is equivalent to the following declaration:

```
static void classAction() {
  synchronized (A.class) {          // Synchronized block on class A
    // ...
  }
}
```

In summary, a thread can hold a lock on an object

- by executing a synchronized instance method of the object
- by executing the body of a synchronized block that synchronizes on the object
- by executing a synchronized static method of a class (in which case, the object is the `Class` object representing the class in the JVM)

 Review Questions

13.9   Given the following program, which statements are guaranteed to be true?

```
public class ThreadedPrint {
  static Thread makeThread(final String id, boolean daemon) {
    Thread t = new Thread(id) {
      public void run() {
        System.out.println(id);
      }
    };
    t.setDaemon(daemon);
```

```
      t.start();
      return t;
    }

    public static void main(String[] args) {
      Thread a = makeThread("A", false);
      Thread b = makeThread("B", true);
      System.out.print("End\n");
    }
  }
```

Select the two correct answers.

(a) The letter A is always printed.
(b) The letter B is always printed.
(c) The letter A is never printed after End.
(d) The letter B is never printed after End.
(e) The program might print B, End, and A, in that order.

13.10 Given the following program, which alternatives would make good choices to synchronize on at (1)?

```
    public class Preference {
      private int account1;
      private Integer account2;

      public void doIt() {
        final Double account3 = new Double(10e10);
        synchronized(/* ___(1)___ */) {
          System.out.print("doIt");
        }
      }
    }
```

Select the two correct answers.

(a) Synchronize on account1.
(b) Synchronize on account2.
(c) Synchronize on account3.
(d) Synchronize on this.

13.11 Which statements are not true about the synchronized block?

Select the three correct answers.

(a) If the expression in a synchronized block evaluates to null, a NullPointer-Exception will be thrown.
(b) The lock is only released if the execution of the block terminates normally.
(c) A thread cannot hold more than one lock at a time.
(d) Synchronized statements cannot be nested.
(e) The braces cannot be omitted even if there is only a single statement to execute in the block.

13.12 Which statement is true?

Select the one correct answer.

(a) No two threads can concurrently execute synchronized methods on the same object.

(b) Methods declared synchronized should not be recursive, since the object lock will not allow new invocations of the method.

(c) Synchronized methods can only call other synchronized methods directly.

(d) Inside a synchronized method, one can assume that no other threads are currently executing any other methods in the same class.

13.13 Given the following program, which statement is true?

```
public class MyClass extends Thread {
  static Object lock1 = new Object();
  static Object lock2 = new Object();
  static volatile int i1, i2, j1, j2, k1, k2;
  public void run() { while (true) { doIt(); check(); } }
  void doIt() {
    synchronized(lock1) { i1++; }
    j1++;
    synchronized(lock2) { k1++; k2++; }
    j2++;
    synchronized(lock1) { i2++; }
  }
  void check() {
    if (i1 != i2) System.out.println("i");
    if (j1 != j2) System.out.println("j");
    if (k1 != k2) System.out.println("k");
  }
  public static void main(String[] args) {
    new MyClass().start();
    new MyClass().start();
  }
}
```

Select the one correct answer.

(a) The program will fail to compile.

(b) One cannot be certain whether any of the letters i, j, and k will be printed during execution.

(c) One can be certain that none of the letters i, j, and k will ever be printed during execution.

(d) One can be certain that the letters i and k will never be printed during execution.

(e) One can be certain that the letter k will never be printed during execution.

13.14 Given the following program, which code modifications will result in *both* threads being able to participate in printing one smiley (:-)) per line continuously?

```
public class Smiley extends Thread {

  public void run() {                          // (1)
    while(true) {                              // (2)
```

```
      try {                                           // (3)
          System.out.print(":");                      // (4)
          sleep(100);                                 // (5)
          System.out.print("-");                      // (6)
          sleep(100);                                 // (7)
          System.out.println(")");                    // (8)
          sleep(100);                                 // (9)
      } catch (InterruptedException e) {
        e.printStackTrace();
      }
    }
  }

  public static void main(String[] args) {
    new Smiley().start();
    new Smiley().start();
  }
}
```

Select the two correct answers.

(a) Synchronize the run() method with the keyword synchronized, (1).

(b) Synchronize the while loop with a synchronized(Smiley.class) block, (2).

(c) Synchronize the try-catch construct with a synchronized(Smiley.class) block, (3).

(d) Synchronize the statements (4) to (9) with one synchronized(Smiley.class) block.

(e) Synchronize each statement (4), (6), and (8) individually with a synchronized (Smiley.class) block.

(f) None of the above will give the desired result.

13.6 Thread Transitions

Thread States

Understanding the life cycle of a thread is valuable when programming with threads. Threads can exist in different states. Just because a thread's start() method has been called, it does not mean that the thread has access to the CPU and can start executing straight away. Several factors determine how it will proceed.

Figure 13.3 shows the states and the transitions in the life cycle of a thread.

- *New state*
  A thread has been *created*, but it has not yet *started*. A thread is started by calling its start() method, as explained in Section 13.4.

- *Ready-to-run state*
  A thread starts life in the Ready-to-run state (see p. 639).

- *Running state*
  If a thread is in the Running state, it means that the thread is currently executing (see p. 639).

- *Dead state*
  Once in this state, the thread cannot ever run again (see p. 650).

- *Non-runnable states*
  A running thread can transit to one of the non-runnable states, depending on the circumstances. A thread remains in a non-runnable state until a special transition occurs. A thread does not go directly to the Running state from a non-runnable state, but transits first to the Ready-to-run state.
  The non-runnable states can be characterized as follows:

  ○ *Sleeping*: The thread *sleeps* for a specified amount of time (see p. 640).

  ○ *Blocked for I/O*: The thread waits for a *blocking* operation to complete (see p. 649).

  ○ *Blocked for join completion*: The thread awaits *completion* of another thread (see p. 647).

  ○ *Waiting for notification*: The thread awaits *notification* from another thread (see p. 640).

  ○ *Blocked for lock acquisition*: The thread waits to *acquire* the lock of an object (see p. 626).

Figure 13.3   *Thread States*

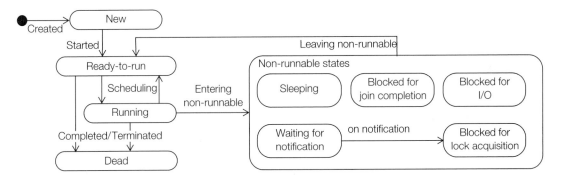

The Thread class provides the getState() method to determine the state of the current thread. The method returns a constant of type Thread.State (i.e., the type State is a static inner enum type declared in the Thread class). The correspondence between the states represented by its constants and the states shown in Figure 13.3 is summarized in Table 13.1.

Table 13.1   *Thread States*

Constant in the Thread.State enum type	State in Figure 13.3	Description of the thread
NEW	*New*	Created but not yet started.
RUNNABLE	*Runnable*	Executing in the JVM.
BLOCKED	*Blocked for lock acquisition*	Blocked while waiting for a lock.
WAITING	*Waiting for notify, Blocked for join completion*	Waiting indefinitely for another thread to perform a particular action.
TIMED_WAITING	*Sleeping, Waiting for notify, Blocked for join completion*	Waiting for another thread to perform an action for up to a specified time.
TERMINATED	*Dead*	Completed execution.

Various methods from the Thread class are presented next. Examples of their usage are presented in subsequent sections.

```
final boolean isAlive()
```

This method can be used to find out if a thread is alive or dead. A thread is *alive* if it has been started but not yet terminated, i.e., it is not in the Dead state.

```
final int getPriority()
final void setPriority(int newPriority)
```

The first method returns the priority of a thread. The second method changes its priority. The priority set will be the minimum of the specified newPriority and the maximum priority permitted for this thread.

```
Thread.State getState()
```

This method returns the state of this thread (see Table 13.1). It should be used for monitoring the state and not for synchronizing control.

```
static void yield()
```

This method causes the current thread to temporarily pause its execution and, thereby, allow other threads to execute. It is up to the JVM to decide if and when this transition will take place.

```
static void sleep (long millisec) throws InterruptedException
```

The current thread sleeps for the specified time before it becomes eligible for running again.

```
final void join() throws InterruptedException
final void join(long millisec) throws InterruptedException
```

A call to any of these two methods invoked on a thread will wait and not return until either the thread has completed or it is timed out after the specified time, respectively.

```
void interrupt()
```

The method interrupts the thread on which it is invoked. In the Waiting-for-notification, Sleeping, or Blocked-for-join-completion states, the thread will receive an InterruptedException.

Example 13.4 illustrates transitions between thread states. A thread at (1) sleeps a little at (2) and then does some computation in a loop at (3), after which the thread terminates. The main() method monitors the thread in a loop at (4), printing the thread state returned by the getState() method. The output shows that the thread goes through the RUNNABLE state when the run() method starts to execute and then transits to the TIMED_WAITING state to sleep. On waking up, it computes the loop in the RUNNABLE state, and transits to the TERMINATED state when the run() method finishes.

Example 13.4 *Thread States*

```
public class ThreadStates {

  private static Thread t1 = new Thread("T1") {     // (1)
    public void run() {
      try {
        sleep(2);                                    // (2)
        for(int i = 10000; i > 0; i--);              // (3)
      } catch (InterruptedException ie){
        ie.printStackTrace();
      }
    }
  };

  public static void main(String[] args) {
    t1.start();
    while(true) {                                    // (4)
      Thread.State state = t1.getState();
      System.out.println(state);
      if (state == Thread.State.TERMINATED) break;
    }
  }
}
```

Possible output from the program:

```
RUNNABLE
TIMED_WAITING
```

```
...
TIMED_WAITING
RUNNABLE
...
RUNNABLE
TERMINATED
```

Thread Priorities

Threads are assigned priorities that the thread scheduler *can* use to determine how the threads will be scheduled. The thread scheduler can use thread priorities to determine which thread gets to run. The thread scheduler favors giving CPU time to the thread with the highest priority in the Ready-to-run state. This is not necessarily the thread that has been the longest time in the Ready-to-run state. Heavy reliance on thread priorities for the behavior of a program can make the program unportable across platforms, as thread scheduling is host platform–dependent.

Priorities are integer values from 1 (lowest priority given by the constant Thread.MIN_PRIORITY) to 10 (highest priority given by the constant Thread.MAX_PRIORITY). The default priority is 5 (Thread.NORM_PRIORITY).

A thread inherits the priority of its parent thread. The priority of a thread can be set using the setPriority() method and read using the getPriority() method, both of which are defined in the Thread class. The following code sets the priority of the thread myThread to the minimum of two values: maximum priority and current priority incremented to the next level:

```
myThread.setPriority(Math.min(Thread.MAX_PRIORITY, myThread.getPriority()+1));
```

The setPriority() method is an *advisory* method, meaning that it provides a hint from the program to the JVM, which the JVM is in no way obliged to honor. The method can be used to fine-tune the *performance* of the program, but should not be relied upon for the *correctness* of the program.

Thread Scheduler

Schedulers in JVM implementations usually employ one of the two following strategies:

- Preemptive scheduling.

  If a thread with a higher priority than the current running thread moves to the Ready-to-run state, the current running thread can be *preempted* (moved to the Ready-to-run state) to let the higher priority thread execute.

- Time-Sliced or Round-Robin scheduling.

  A running thread is allowed to execute for a fixed length of time, after which it moves to the Ready-to-run state to await its turn to run again.

It should be emphasised that thread schedulers are implementation- and platform-dependent; therefore, how threads will be scheduled is unpredictable, at least from platform to platform.

Running and Yielding

After its start() method has been called, the thread starts life in the Ready-to-run state. Once in the Ready-to-run state, the thread is eligible for running, i.e., it waits for its turn to get CPU time. The thread scheduler decides which thread runs and for how long.

Figure 13.4 illustrates the transitions between the Ready-to-Run and Running states. A call to the static method yield(), defined in the Thread class, may cause the current thread in the Running state to transit to the Ready-to-run state, thus relinquishing the CPU. If this happens, the thread is then at the mercy of the thread scheduler as to when it will run again. It is possible that if there are no threads in the Ready-to-run state, this thread can continue executing. If there are other threads in the Ready-to-run state, their priorities can influence which thread gets to execute.

As with the setPriority() method, the yield() method is also an advisory method, and therefore comes with no guarantees that the JVM will carry out the call's bidding. A call to the yield() method does not affect any locks that the thread might hold.

Figure 13.4   *Running and Yielding*

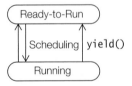

By calling the static method yield(), the running thread gives other threads in the Ready-to-run state a chance to run. A typical example where this can be useful is when a user has given some command to start a CPU-intensive computation, and has the option of cancelling it by clicking on a CANCEL button. If the computation thread hogs the CPU and the user clicks the CANCEL button, chances are that it might take a while before the thread monitoring the user input gets a chance to run and take appropriate action to stop the computation. A thread running such a computation should do the computation in increments, yielding between increments to allow other threads to run. This is illustrated by the following run() method:

```
public void run() {
  try {
    while (!done()) {
      doLittleBitMore();
      Thread.yield();      // Current thread yields
    }
```

```
    } catch (InterruptedException ie) {
      doCleaningUp();
    }
  }
}
```

Sleeping and Waking Up

Transitions by a thread to and from the Sleeping state are illustrated in Figure 13.5.

Figure 13.5   *Sleeping and Waking up*

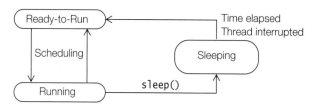

A call to the static method sleep() in the Thread class will cause the currently running thread to temporarily pause its execution and transit to the Sleeping state. This method does not relinquish any lock that the thread might have. The thread will sleep for at least the time specified in its argument, before transitioning to the Ready-to-run state where it takes its turn to run again. If a thread is interrupted while sleeping, it will throw an InterruptedException when it awakes and gets to execute.

There are two overloaded versions of the sleep() method in the Thread class, allowing time to be specified in milliseconds, and additionally in nanoseconds.

Usage of the sleep() method is illustrated in Examples 13.1, 13.2, and 13.3.

Waiting and Notifying

Waiting and notifying provide means of communication between threads that *synchronize on the same object* (see Section 13.5, p. 626). The threads execute wait() and notify() (or notifyAll()) methods on the shared object for this purpose. These final methods are defined in the Object class and, therefore, inherited by all objects. These methods can only be executed on an object whose lock the thread holds (in other words, in synchronized code), otherwise, the call will result in an IllegalMonitorStateException.

```
final void wait(long timeout) throws InterruptedException
final void wait(long timeout, int nanos) throws InterruptedException
final void wait() throws InterruptedException
```

A thread invokes the wait() method on the object whose lock it holds. The thread is added to the *wait set* of the current object.

```
final void notify()
final void notifyAll()
```

A thread invokes a notification method on the current object whose lock it holds to notify thread(s) that are in the wait set of the object.

Communication between threads is facilitated by waiting and notifying, as illustrated by Figures 13.6 and 13.7. A thread usually calls the wait() method on the object whose lock it holds because a condition for its continued execution was not met. The thread leaves the Running state and transits to the Waiting-for-notification state. There it waits for this condition to occur. The thread relinquishes ownership of the object lock.

Figure 13.6 *Waiting and Notifying*

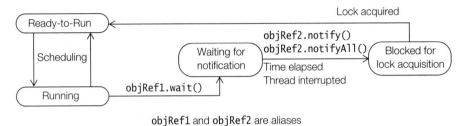

objRef1 and objRef2 are aliases

Transition to the Waiting-for-notification state and relinquishing the object lock are completed as one *atomic* (non-interruptible) operation. The releasing of the lock of the shared object by the thread allows other threads to run and execute synchronized code on the same object after acquiring its lock.

Note that the waiting thread relinquishes only the lock of the object on which the wait() method was invoked. It does not relinquish any other object locks that it might hold, which will remain locked while the thread is waiting.

Each object has a *wait set* containing threads waiting for notification. Threads in the Waiting-for-notification state are grouped according to the object whose wait() method they invoked.

Figure 13.7 shows a thread t_1 that first acquires a lock on the shared object, and afterward invokes the wait() method on the shared object. This relinquishes the object lock and the thread t_1 awaits to be notified. While the thread t_1 is waiting, another thread t_2 can acquire the lock on the shared object for its own purposes.

A thread in the Waiting-for-notification state can be awakened by the occurrence of any one of these three incidents:

1. Another thread invokes the notify() method on the object of the waiting thread, and the waiting thread is selected as the thread to be awakened.

2. The waiting thread times out.

3. Another thread interrupts the waiting thread.

Figure 13.7   *Thread Communication*

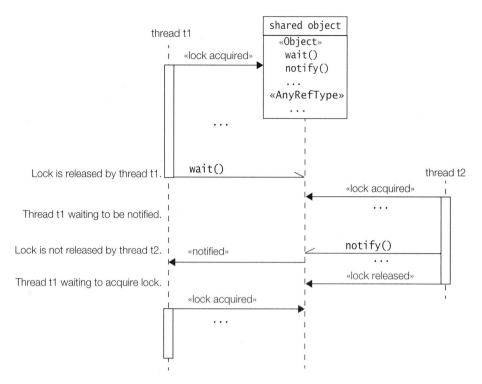

Notified

Invoking the notify() method on an object wakes up a single thread that is waiting for the lock of this object. The selection of a thread to awaken is dependent on the thread policies implemented by the JVM. On being *notified,* a waiting thread first transits to the Blocked-for-lock-acquisition state to acquire the lock on the object, and not directly to the Ready-to-run state. The thread is also removed from the wait set of the object. Note that the object lock is not relinquished when the notifying thread invokes the notify() method. The notifying thread relinquishes the lock at its own discretion, and the awakened thread will not be able to run until the notifying thread relinquishes the object lock.

When the notified thread obtains the object lock, it is enabled for execution, waiting in the Ready-to-run state for its turn to execute again. Finally, when it does execute, the call to the wait() method returns and the thread can continue with its execution.

From Figure 13.7 we see that thread t_2 does not relinquish the object lock when it invokes the notify() method. Thread t_1 is forced to wait in the Blocked-for-lock-acquisition state. It is shown no privileges and must compete with any other threads waiting for lock acquisition.

A call to the notify() method has no effect if there are no threads in the wait set of the object.

In contrast to the notify() method, the notifyAll() method wakes up *all* threads in the wait set of the shared object. They will all transit to the Blocked-for-lock-acquisition state and contend for the object lock as explained earlier.

It should be stressed that a program should not make any assumptions about the order in which threads awaken in response to the notify() or notifyAll() method and transit to the Blocked-for-lock-acquisition state.

Timed-out

The wait() call specified the time the thread should wait before being timed out, if it was not awakened by being notified. The awakened thread competes in the usual manner to execute again. Note that the awakened thread has no way of knowing whether it was timed out or woken up by one of the notification methods.

Interrupted

This means that another thread invoked the interrupt() method on the waiting thread. The awakened thread is enabled as previously explained, but the return from the wait() call will result in an InterruptedException if and when the awakened thread finally gets a chance to run. The code invoking the wait() method must be prepared to handle this checked exception.

Using Wait and Notify

In Example 13.5, three threads are manipulating the same stack. Two of them are pushing elements on the stack, while the third one is popping elements off the stack. The class diagram for Example 13.5 is shown in Figure 13.8. The example comprises the following classes:

- The subclasses StackPopper at (9) and StackPusher at (10) extend the abstract superclass StackUser at (5).
- Class StackUser, which extends the Thread class, creates and starts each thread.
- Class StackImpl implements the synchronized methods pop() and push().

Again, the code in Example 13.5 has not been generified in order to keep things simple.

Figure 13.8 *Stack Users*

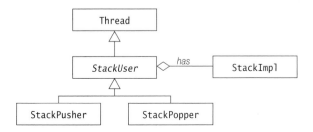

In Example 13.5, the field topOfStack in class StackImpl is declared volatile, so that read and write operations on this variable will access the *master* value of this variable, and not any copies, during runtime (see Section 4.10, p. 153).

Since the threads manipulate the same stack object, and the push() and pop() methods in the class StackImpl are synchronized, it means that the threads synchronize on the same object. In other words, the mutual exclusion of these operations is guaranteed on the same stack object.

Example 13.5   *Waiting and Notifying*

```
class StackImpl {
  private Object[] stackArray;
  private volatile int topOfStack;

  StackImpl (int capacity) {
    stackArray = new Object[capacity];
    topOfStack = -1;
  }

  public synchronized Object pop() {
    System.out.println(Thread.currentThread() + ": popping");
    while (isEmpty())
      try {
        System.out.println(Thread.currentThread() + ": waiting to pop");
        wait();                                        // (1)
      } catch (InterruptedException ie) {
        System.out.println(Thread.currentThread() + " interrupted.");
      }
    Object element = stackArray[topOfStack];
    stackArray[topOfStack--] = null;
    System.out.println(Thread.currentThread() +
                        ": notifying after popping");
    notify();                                          // (2)
    return element;
  }

  public synchronized void push(Object element) {
    System.out.println(Thread.currentThread() + ": pushing");
    while (isFull())
      try {
        System.out.println(Thread.currentThread() + ": waiting to push");
        wait();                                        // (3)
      } catch (InterruptedException ie) {
        System.out.println(Thread.currentThread() + " interrupted.");
      }
    stackArray[++topOfStack] = element;
    System.out.println(Thread.currentThread() +
                        ": notifying after pushing");
    notify();                                          // (4)
  }

  public boolean isFull() { return topOfStack >= stackArray.length -1; }
```

```
                  public boolean isEmpty() { return topOfStack < 0; }
              }
              //_____
              abstract class StackUser implements Runnable {        // (5) Stack user

                  protected StackImpl stack;                        // (6)

                  StackUser(String threadName, StackImpl stack) {
                      this.stack = stack;
                      Thread worker = new Thread(this, threadName);
                      System.out.println(worker);
                      worker.setDaemon(true);                       // (7) Daemon thread status
                      worker.start();                               // (8) Start the thread
                  }
              }
              //_____
              class StackPopper extends StackUser {                 // (9) Popper
                  StackPopper(String threadName, StackImpl stack) {
                      super(threadName, stack);
                  }
                  public void run() { while (true) stack.pop(); }
              }
              //_____
              class StackPusher extends StackUser {                 // (10) Pusher
                  StackPusher(String threadName, StackImpl stack) {
                      super(threadName, stack);
                  }
                  public void run() { while (true) stack.push(2008); }
              }
              //_____
              public class WaitAndNotifyClient {
                  public static void main(String[] args)
                                  throws InterruptedException {     // (11)

                      StackImpl stack = new StackImpl(5);           // Stack of capacity 5.

                      new StackPusher("A", stack);
                      new StackPusher("B", stack);
                      new StackPopper("C", stack);
                      System.out.println("Main Thread sleeping.");
                      Thread.sleep(10);
                      System.out.println("Exit from Main Thread.");
                  }
              }
```

Possible output from the program:

```
Thread[A,5,main]
Thread[B,5,main]
Thread[C,5,main]
Main Thread sleeping.
...
Thread[A,5,main]: pushing
Thread[A,5,main]: waiting to push
Thread[B,5,main]: pushing
Thread[B,5,main]: waiting to push
```

```
Thread[C,5,main]: popping
Thread[C,5,main]: notifying after pop
Thread[A,5,main]: notifying after push
Thread[A,5,main]: pushing
Thread[A,5,main]: waiting to push
Thread[B,5,main]: waiting to push
Thread[C,5,main]: popping
Thread[C,5,main]: notifying after pop
Thread[A,5,main]: notifying after push
...
Thread[B,5,main]: notifying after push
...
Exit from Main Thread.
...
```

Example 13.5 illustrates how a thread waiting as a result of calling the wait() method on an object is notified by another thread calling the notify() method on the same object, in order for the first thread to start running again.

One usage of the wait() call is shown in Example 13.5 at (1) in the synchronized pop() method. When a thread executing this method on the StackImpl object finds that the stack is empty, it invokes the wait() method in order to wait for some thread to push something on this stack first.

Another use of the wait() call is shown at (3) in the synchronized push() method. When a thread executing this method on the StackImpl object finds that the stack is full, it invokes the wait() method to await some thread removing an element first, in order to make room for a push operation on the stack.

When a thread executing the synchronized method push() on the StackImpl object successfully pushes an element on the stack, it calls the notify() method at (4). The wait set of the StackImpl object contains all waiting threads that have earlier called the wait() method at either (1) or (3) on this StackImpl object. A single thread from the wait set is enabled for running. If this thread was executing a pop operation, it now has a chance of being successful because the stack is not empty at the moment. If this thread was executing a push operation, it can try again to see if there is room on the stack.

When a thread executing the synchronized method pop() on the StackImpl object successfully pops an element off the stack, it calls the notify() method at (2). Again assuming that the wait set of the StackImpl object is not empty, one thread from the set is arbitrarily chosen and enabled. If the notified thread was executing a pop operation, it can proceed to see if the stack still has an element to pop. If the notified thread was executing a push operation, it now has a chance of succeeding, because the stack is not full at the moment.

Note that the waiting condition at (1) for the pop operation is executed in a loop. A waiting thread that has been notified is not guaranteed to run right away. Before it gets to run, another thread may synchronize on the stack and empty it. If the notified thread was waiting to pop the stack, it would now incorrectly pop the stack, because the condition was not tested after notification. The loop ensures that the condition is always tested after notification, sending the thread back to the Waiting-on-notification state if the condition is not met. To avert the analogous danger of pushing on a full stack, the waiting condition at (3) for the push operation is also executed in a loop.

The behavior of each thread can be traced in the output from Example 13.5. Each push-and-pop operation can be traced by a sequence consisting of the name of the operation to be performed, followed by zero or more wait messages, and concluding with a notification after the operation is done. For example, thread A performs two pushes as shown in the output from the program:

```
Thread[A,5,main]: pushing
Thread[A,5,main]: waiting to push
...
Thread[A,5,main]: notifying after push
Thread[A,5,main]: pushing
Thread[A,5,main]: waiting to push
...
Thread[A,5,main]: notifying after push
```

Thread B is shown doing one push:

```
Thread[B,5,main]: pushing
Thread[B,5,main]: waiting to push
...
Thread[B,5,main]: notifying after push
```

Whereas thread C pops the stack twice without any waiting:

```
Thread[C,5,main]: popping
Thread[C,5,main]: notifying after pop
...
Thread[C,5,main]: popping
Thread[C,5,main]: notifying after pop
```

When the operations are interweaved, the output clearly shows that the pushers wait when the stack is full, and only push after the stack is popped.

The three threads created are daemon threads. Their status is set at (7). They will be terminated if they have not completed when the main thread dies, thereby stopping the execution of the program.

Joining

A thread can invoke the overloaded method join() on another thread in order to wait for the other thread to complete its execution before continuing, i.e., the first thread waits for the second thread to *join it after completion*. A running thread t_1 invokes the method join() on a thread t_2. The join() call has no effect if thread t_2 has already completed. If thread t_2 is still alive, thread t_1 transits to the Blocked-for-join-completion state. Thread t_1 waits in this state until one of these events occur (see Figure 13.9):

- Thread t_2 completes.

  In this case thread t_1 moves to the Ready-to-run state, and when it gets to run, it will continue normally after the call to the join() method.

- Thread t_1 is timed out.

  The time specified in the argument of the join() method call has elapsed without thread t_2 completing. In this case as well, thread t_1 transits to the Ready-to-run state. When it gets to run, it will continue normally after the call to the join() method.

- Thread t_1 is interrupted.

  Some thread interrupted thread t_1 while thread t_1 was waiting for join completion. Thread t_1 transits to the Ready-to-run state, but when it gets to execute, it will now throw an InterruptedException.

Figure 13.9 *Joining of Threads*

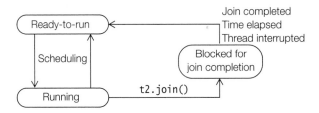

Example 13.6 illustrates joining of threads. The AnotherClient class below uses the Counter class, which extends the Thread class from Example 13.2. It creates two threads that are enabled for execution. The main thread invokes the join() method on the Counter A thread. If the Counter A thread has not already completed, the main thread transits to the Blocked-for-join-completion state. When the Counter A thread completes, the main thread will be enabled for running. Once the main thread is running, it continues with execution after (5). A parent thread can call the isAlive() method to find out whether its child threads are alive before terminating itself. The call to the isAlive() method on the Counter A thread at (6) correctly reports that the Counter A thread is not alive. A similar scenario transpires between the main thread and the Counter B thread. The main thread passes through the Blocked-for-join-completion state twice at the most.

Example 13.6 *Joining of Threads*

```
class Counter extends Thread { /* See Example 13.2. */ }
//_____
public class AnotherClient {
  public static void main(String[] args) {

    Counter counterA = new Counter("Counter A");
```

```
       Counter counterB = new Counter("Counter B");

       try {
         System.out.println("Wait for the child threads to finish.");
         counterA.join();                                      // (5)
         if (!counterA.isAlive())                              // (6)
           System.out.println("Counter A not alive.");
         counterB.join();                                      // (7)
         if (!counterB.isAlive())                              // (8)
           System.out.println("Counter B not alive.");
       } catch (InterruptedException ie) {
         System.out.println("Main Thread interrupted.");
       }
       System.out.println("Exit from Main Thread.");
     }
   }
```

Possible output from the program:

```
Thread[Counter A,5,main]
Thread[Counter B,5,main]
Wait for the child threads to finish.
Counter A: 0
Counter B: 0
Counter A: 1
Counter B: 1
Counter A: 2
Counter B: 2
Counter A: 3
Counter B: 3
Counter A: 4
Counter B: 4
Exit from Counter A.
Counter A not alive.
Exit from Counter B.
Counter B not alive.
Exit from Main Thread.
```

Blocking for I/O

A running thread, on executing a *blocking operation* requiring a resource (like a call
to an I/O method), will transit to the Blocked-for-I/O state. The blocking operation
must complete before the thread can proceed to the Ready-to-run state. An example is a thread reading from the standard input terminal which blocks until input
is provided:

```
int input = System.in.read();
```

Thread Termination

A thread can transit to the Dead state from the Running or the Ready-to-run states. The thread dies when it completes its run() method, either by returning normally or by throwing an exception. Once in this state, the thread cannot be resurrected. There is no way the thread can be enabled for running again, not even by calling the start() method again on the thread object.

Example 13.7 illustrates a typical scenario where a thread can be controlled by one or more threads. Work is performed by a loop body, which the thread executes continually. It should be possible for other threads to start and stop the *worker* thread. This functionality is implemented by the class Worker at (1), which has a private field theThread declared at (2) to keep track of the Thread object executing its run() method.

The kickStart() method at (3) in class Worker creates and starts a thread if one is not already running. It is not enough to just call the start() method on a thread that has terminated. A new Thread object must be created first. The terminate() method at (4) sets the field theThread to null. Note that this does not affect any Thread object that might have been referenced by the reference theThread. The runtime system maintains any such Thread object; therefore, changing one of its references does not affect the object.

The run() method at (5) has a loop whose execution is controlled by a special condition. The condition tests to see whether the Thread object referenced by the reference theThread and the Thread object executing now, are one and the same. This is bound to be the case if the reference theThread has the same reference value that it was assigned when the thread was created and started in the kickStart() method. The condition will then be true, and the body of the loop will execute. However, if the value in the reference theThread has changed, the condition will be false. In that case, the loop will not execute, the run() method will complete and the thread will terminate.

A client can control the thread implemented by the class Worker, using the kickStart() and the terminate() methods. The client is able to terminate the running thread at the start of the next iteration of the loop body by calling the terminate() method that changes the value of the theThread reference to null.

In Example 13.7, a Worker object is first created at (8) and a thread started on this Worker object at (9). The main thread invokes the sleep() method at (10) to temporarily cease its execution for 2 milliseconds giving the thread of the Worker object a chance to run. The main thread, when it is executing again, terminates the thread of the Worker object at (11), as explained earlier. This simple scenario can be generalized where several threads, sharing a single Worker object, could be starting and stopping the thread of the Worker object.

Example 13.7 *Thread Termination*

```
class Worker implements Runnable {                      // (1)
  private volatile Thread theThread;                    // (2)

  public void kickStart() {                             // (3)
    if (theThread == null) {
      theThread = new Thread(this);
      theThread.start();
    }
  }

  public void terminate() {                             // (4)
    theThread = null;
  }

  public void run() {                                   // (5)
    while (theThread == Thread.currentThread()) {       // (6)
      System.out.println("Going around in loops.");
    }
  }
}
//_____
public class Controller {
  public static void main(String[] args) {              // (7)
    Worker worker = new Worker();                       // (8)
    worker.kickStart();                                 // (9)
    try {
      Thread.sleep(2);                                  // (10)
    } catch(InterruptedException ie) {
      ie.printStackTrace();
    }
    worker.terminate();                                 // (11)
  }
}
```

Possible output from the program:

```
Going around in loops.
Going around in loops.
Going around in loops.
Going around in loops.
Going around in loops.
```

Deadlocks

A deadlock is a situation where a thread is waiting for an object lock that another
thread holds, and this second thread is waiting for an object lock that the first
thread holds. Since each thread is waiting for the other thread to relinquish a lock,
they both remain waiting forever in the Blocked-for-lock-acquisition state. The
threads are said to be *deadlocked*.

A deadlock is depicted in Figure 13.10. Thread t_1 has a lock on object o_1, but cannot acquire the lock on object o_2. Thread t_2 has a lock on object o_2, but cannot acquire the lock on object o_1. They can only proceed if one of them relinquishes a lock the other one wants, which is never going to happen.

Figure 13.10   *Deadlock*

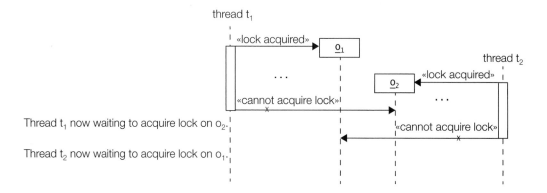

The situation in Figure 13.10 is implemented in Example 13.8. Thread t_1 at (3) tries to synchronize at (4) and (5), first on string o_1 at (1) then on string o_2 at (2), respectively. The thread t_2 at (6) does the opposite. It synchronizes at (7) and (8), first on string o_2 then on string o_1, respectively. A deadlock can occur as explained previously.

However, the potential of deadlock in the situation in Example 13.8 is easy to fix. If the two threads acquire the locks on the objects in the same order, then mutual lock dependency is avoided and a deadlock can never occur. This means having the same locking order at (4) and (5) as at (7) and (8). In general, the cause of a deadlock is not always easy to discover, let alone easy to fix.

Example 13.8   *Deadlock*

```
public class DeadLockDanger {

    String o1 = "Lock " ;                       // (1)
    String o2 = "Step ";                        // (2)

    Thread t1 = (new Thread("Printer1") {       // (3)
        public void run() {
            while(true) {
                synchronized(o1) {               // (4)
                    synchronized(o2) {           // (5)
                        System.out.println(o1 + o2);
                    }
                }
            }
        }
```

```
          }
        }
      });

      Thread t2 = (new Thread("Printer2") {        // (6)
        public void run() {
          while(true) {
            synchronized(o2) {                     // (7)
              synchronized(o1) {                   // (8)
                System.out.println(o2 + o1);
              }
            }
          }
        }
      });

      public static void main(String[] args) {
        DeadLockDanger dld = new DeadLockDanger();
        dld.t1.start();
        dld.t2.start();
      }
    }
```

Possible output from the program:

```
...
Lock Step
Lock Step
Lock Step
Lock Step
Lock Step
−
```

Review Questions

13.15 Which one of these events will cause a thread to die?

Select the one correct answer.
(a) The method sleep() is called.
(b) The method wait() is called.
(c) Execution of the start() method ends.
(d) Execution of the run() method ends.
(e) Execution of the thread's constructor ends.

13.16 Which statements are true about the following code?

```
public class Joining {
  static Thread createThread(final int i, final Thread t1) {
    Thread t2 = new Thread() {
      public void run() {
        System.out.println(i+1);
```

```
      try {
        t1.join();
      } catch (InterruptedException ie) {
      }
      System.out.println(i+2);
    }
  };
  System.out.println(i+3);
  t2.start();
  System.out.println(i+4);
  return t2;
}

public static void main(String[] args) {
  createThread(10, createThread(20, Thread.currentThread()));
}
}
```

Select the two correct answers.

(a) The first number printed is 13.

(b) The number 14 is printed before the number 22.

(c) The number 24 is printed before the number 21.

(d) The last number printed is 12.

(e) The number 11 is printed before the number 23.

13.17   Which statements are true about the following program?

```
public class ThreadAPI {
  private static Thread t1 = new Thread("T1") {
    public void run() {
      try { wait(1000); } catch (InterruptedException ie){}
  }};

  private static Thread t2 = new Thread("T2") {
    public void run() {
      notify();
  }};

  private static Thread t3 = new Thread("T3") {
    public void run() {
      yield();
  }};

  private static Thread t4 = new Thread("T4") {
    public void run() {
      try { sleep(100); } catch (InterruptedException ie){}
  }};

  public static void main(String[] args) {
    t1.start(); t2.start(); t3.start(); t4.start();
    try { t4.join(); } catch (InterruptedException ie){}
  }
}
```

Select the three correct answers.

(a) The program will compile and will run and terminate normally.
(b) The program will compile but thread t1 will throw an exception.
(c) The program will compile but thread t2 will throw an exception.
(d) The program will compile but thread t3 will throw an exception.
(e) Enclosing the call to the sleep() method in a try-catch construct in thread t4 is unnecessary.
(f) Enclosing the call to the join() method in a try-catch construct in the main thread is necessary.

13.18 Which code, when inserted at (1), will result in the program compiling and printing Done on the standard input stream, and then all threads terminating normally?

```
public class RunningThreads {

  private static Thread t1 = new Thread("T1") {
    public void run() {
      synchronized(RunningThreads.class) {
        try {
          // (1) INSERT CODE HERE ...
        } catch (InterruptedException ie){
          ie.printStackTrace();
        }
        System.out.println("Done");
      }}};

  public static void main(String[] args) {
    t1.start();
    try {
      t1.join();
    } catch (InterruptedException ie){
      ie.printStackTrace();
    }
  }
}
```

Select the two correct answers.

(a) wait();
(b) wait(100);
(c) RunningThreads.class.wait();
(d) RunningThreads.class.wait(100);
(e) yield();
(f) sleep(100);

13.19 What can be guaranteed by calling the method yield()?

Select the one correct answer.

(a) All lower priority threads will be granted CPU time.
(b) The current thread will sleep for some time while some other threads run.
(c) The current thread will not continue until other threads have terminated.

(d) The thread will wait until it is notified.

(e) None of the above.

13.20   In which class or interface is the notify() method defined?

Select the one correct answer.

(a) Thread

(b) Object

(c) Appendable

(d) Runnable

13.21   How can the priority of a thread be set?

Select the one correct answer.

(a) By using the setPriority() method in the Thread class.

(b) By passing the priority as an argument to a constructor of the Thread class.

(c) Both of the above.

(d) None of the above.

13.22   Which statements are true about locks?

Select the two correct answers.

(a) A thread can hold more than one lock at a time.

(b) Invoking wait() on a Thread object will relinquish all locks held by the thread.

(c) Invoking wait() on an object whose lock is held by the current thread will relinquish the lock.

(d) Invoking notify() on a object whose lock is held by the current thread will relinquish the lock.

(e) Multiple threads can hold the same lock at the same time.

13.23   What will be the result of invoking the wait() method on an object without ensuring that the current thread holds the lock of the object?

Select the one correct answer.

(a) The code will fail to compile.

(b) Nothing special will happen.

(c) An IllegalMonitorStateException will be thrown if the wait() method is called while the current thread does not hold the lock of the object.

(d) The thread will be blocked until it gains the lock of the object.

13.24   Which of these are plausible reasons why a thread might be alive, but still not be running?

Select the four correct answers.

(a) The thread is waiting for some condition as a result of a wait() call.

(b) The execution has reached the end of the run() method.

(c) The thread is waiting to acquire the lock of an object in order to execute a certain method on that object.

(d) The thread does not have the highest priority and is currently not executing.

(e) The thread is sleeping as a result of a call to the sleep() method.

13.25 What will the following program print when compiled and run?

```java
public class Tank {
  private boolean isEmpty = true;

  public synchronized void emptying() {
    pause(true);
    isEmpty = !isEmpty;
    System.out.println("emptying");
    notify();
  }

  public synchronized void filling() {
    pause(false);
    isEmpty = !isEmpty;
    System.out.println("filling");
    notify();
  }

  private void pause(boolean flag) {
    while(flag ? isEmpty : !isEmpty) {
      try {
        wait();
      } catch (InterruptedException ie) {
        System.out.println(Thread.currentThread() + " interrupted.");
      }
    }
  }

  public static void main(String[] args) {
    final Tank token = new Tank();
    (new Thread("A") { public void run() {for(;;) token.emptying();}}).start();
    (new Thread("B") { public void run() {for(;;) token.filling();}}).start();
  }
}
```

Select the one correct answer.

(a) The program will compile and continue running once started, but will not print anything.

(b) The program will compile and continue running once started, printing only the string "emptying".

(c) The program will compile and continue running once started, printing only the string "filling".

(d) The program will compile and continue running once started, always printing the string "filling" followed by the string "emptying".

(e) The program will compile and continue running once started, printing the strings "filling" and "emptying" in some order.

13.26   What will the following program print when compiled and run?

```java
public class Syncher2 {
  final static int[] intArray = new int[2];

  private static void pause() {
    while(intArray[0] == 0) {
      try { intArray.wait(); }
      catch (InterruptedException ie) {
        System.out.println(Thread.currentThread() + " interrupted.");
      }
    }
  }

  public static void main (String[] args) {

    Thread runner = new Thread() {
      public void run() {
        synchronized (intArray) {
          pause();
          System.out.println(intArray[0] + intArray[1]);
    }}};

    runner.start();
    intArray[0] = intArray[1] = 10;
    synchronized(intArray) {
      intArray.notify();
    }
  }
}
```

Select the one correct answer.

(a) The program will not compile.
(b) The program will compile, but throw an exception when run.
(c) The program will compile and continue running once started, but will not print anything.
(d) The program will compile and print 0 and terminate normally, when run.
(e) The program will compile and print 20 and terminate normally, when run.
(f) The program will compileand print some other number than 0 or 20, and terminate normally, when run.

 Chapter Summary

The following information was included in this chapter:

• creating threads by extending the Thread class or implementing the Runnable interface

• writing synchronized code using synchronized methods and synchronized blocks to achieve mutually exclusive access to shared resources

- understanding thread states, and the transitions between them, and thread communication
- understanding which thread behavior a program must not take as guaranteed

 Programming Exercises

13.1   Implement three classes: Storage, Counter, and Printer. The Storage class should store an integer. The Counter class should create a thread that starts counting from 0 (0, 1, 2, 3, ...) and stores each value in the Storage class. The Printer class should create a thread that keeps reading the value in the Storage class and printing it.

Write a program that creates an instance of the Storage class and sets up a Counter and a Printer object to operate on it.

13.2   Modify the program from the previous exercise to ensure that each number is printed exactly once, by adding suitable synchronization.

Generics

14

Exam Objectives

6.4 Develop code that makes proper use of type parameters in class/interface declarations, instance variables, method arguments, and return types; and write generic methods or methods that make use of wildcard types and understand the similarities and differences between these two approaches.

Supplementary Objectives

- Distinguishing between generic types and parameterized types
- Identifying contexts where unchecked warnings can be issued, and why they signal potential problems with type-safety
- Using bounded type parameters
- Understanding type capture
- Understanding implications of type erasure
- Understanding implications for overloading and overriding
- Understanding reifiable types, and where they are required
- Understanding implications and restrictions for instance tests, casting, arrays, varargs, and exception handling

14.1 Introducing Generics

Generics allow reference types (classes, interfaces, and array types) and methods to be *parameterized* with *type information*. An *abstract data type* (ADT) defines both the *types* of objects and the *operations* that can be performed on these objects. Generics allow us to specify the types used by the ADT, so that the *same* definition of an ADT can be used on *different* types of objects.

Generics in Java are a way of providing type information in ADTs, so that the compiler can guarantee type-safety of operations at runtime. Generics are implemented as compile-time transformations, with negligible impact on the JVM. The generic type declaration is compiled once into a single Java class file, and the use of the generic type is checked against this file. Also, no extraneous Java class files are generated for each use of the generic type.

The primary benefits of generics are increased language expressiveness with improved type safety, resulting in improved robustness and reliability of code. Generics avoid verbosity of using casts in many contexts, thus improving code clarity. Since the compiler guarantees type-safety, this eliminates the necessity of explicit type checking and casting at runtime.

One major goal when introducing generics in Java has been backward compatibility with legacy code (i.e., non-generic code). Interoperability with legacy code and the lack of generic type information at runtime largely determine how generics work in Java. Many of the restrictions on generics in Java can be attributed to these two factors.

Generics are used extensively in implementing the Java Collections Framework. An overview of Chapter 15 on collections and maps is therefore recommended as many of the examples in this chapter make use of generic types from this framework.

Before the introduction of generics in Java, a general implementation of a collection maintained its objects in references of the type Object. The bookkeeping of the actual type of the objects fell on the client code. Example 14.1 illustrates this approach. It implements a *self-referential data structure* called a *node*. Each node holds a data value and a reference to another node. Such data structures form the basis for building *linked data structures*.

Example 14.1 *A Legacy Class*

```java
class LegacyNode {
  private Object    data;    // The value in the node
  private LegacyNode next;    // The reference to the next node.
  LegacyNode(Object data, LegacyNode next) {
    this.data = data;
    this.next = next;
  }
  public void        setData(Object obj)      { this.data = obj; }
```

```
public Object    getData()                  { return this.data; }
public void      setNext(LegacyNode next) { this.next = next; }
public LegacyNode getNext()                 { return this.next; }
public String    toString() {
  return this.data + (this.next == null? "" : ", " + this.next);
}
}
```

The class `LegacyNode` can be used to create a linked list with arbitrary objects:

```
LegacyNode node1 = new LegacyNode(4, null);        // (Integer, null)
LegacyNode node2 = new LegacyNode("July", node1);  // (String, Integer, null)
```

Primitive values are encapsulated in corresponding wrapper objects. If we want to retrieve the data from a node, this object is returned via an `Object` reference:

```
Object obj = node2.getData();
```

In order to access type-specific properties or behavior of the fetched object, the reference value in the `Object` reference must be converted to the right type. To avoid a `ClassCastException` at runtime when applying the cast, we must make sure that the object referred to by the `Object` reference is of the right type:

```
if (obj instanceof String) {         // Is the object of the right type?
  String str = (String) obj;         // Type conversion to the subclass String.
  System.out.println(str.toUpperCase()); // Specific method in the String class.
}
```

The approach outlined above places certain demands on how to use the class Legacy-Node to create and maintain linked structures. For example, it is the responsibility of the client code to ensure that the objects being put in nodes are of the same type. Implementing classes for specific types of objects is not a good solution. First, it can result in code duplication, and second, it is not always known in advance what types of objects will be put in the nodes. Generic types offer a better solution, where one generic class is defined and specific reference types are supplied each time we want to instantiate the class.

14.2 Generic Types and Parameterized Types

We first introduce the basic terminology and concepts relating to generics in Java.

Generic Types

A *generic type* is a reference type that defines a *list of formal type parameters* or *type variables* (T1, T2, ..., Tn) that must be provided before it can be used as a type. Example 14.2 declares a generic type which, in this case, is a *generic class* called Node<E>, that allows nodes of specific types to be maintained. It has only one formal type parameter, E, that represents the type of the data in a node.

```
class Node<E> {
...
}
```

The formal type parameter E does not explicitly specify a type, but serves as a placeholder for a type to be defined in an invocation of the generic type. The formal type parameters of a generic type are specified within angular brackets, <>, immediately after the class name. A type parameter is an unqualified identifier. If a generic class has several formal type parameters, these are specified as a comma-separated list, <T1, T2, ..., Tn>. It is quite common to use one-letter names for formal type parameters; a convention that we will follow in this book. For example, E is used for the type of elements in a collection, K and V are used for the type of the keys and the type of the values in a map, and T is used to represent an arbitrary type.

As a starting point for declaring a generic class, we can begin with a class where the Object type is utilized to generalize the use of the class. In the declaration of the generic class Node<E> we have used E in all the places where the type Object was used in the declaration of the class LegacyNode in Example 14.1. From the declaration of the class Node<E> we can see that the formal type E is used like a reference type in the class body: as a field type (1), as a return type (5), and as a parameter type in the methods (4). Use of the class name in the generic class declaration is parameterized by the type parameter ((2), (6), (7)), with one notable exception: the formal type parameter is *not* specified after the class name in the constructor declaration at (3). Which actual reference type the formal type parameter E represents is not known in the generic class Node<E>. Therefore, we can only call methods that are inherited from the Object class on the field data, as these methods are inherited by all objects, regardless of their object type. One such example is the call to the toString() method in the method declaration at (8).

The scope of the type parameter E of the generic type includes any non-static inner classes, but excludes any static inner classes—the parameter E cannot be accessed in static context. It also excludes any nested generic declarations where the same name is redeclared as a formal type parameter. However, shadowing of type parameter names should be avoided.

Example 14.2 *A Generic Class for Nodes*

```
class Node<E> {
  private E            data;    // Data                          (1)
  private Node<E>      next;    // Reference to next node        (2)
  Node(E data, Node<E> next) {                                // (3)
    this.data = data;
    this.next = next;
  }
  public void    setData(E data)       { this.data = data; }  // (4)
  public E       getData()             { return this.data; }  // (5)
  public void    setNext(Node<E> next) { this.next = next; }  // (6)
  public Node<E> getNext()             { return this.next; }  // (7)
  public String toString() {                                 // (8)
    return this.data.toString() +
```

```
                        (this.next == null ? "" : ", " + this.next.toString());
   }
}
```

Some Restrictions on the Use of Type Parameters in a Generic Type

A constructor declaration in a generic class cannot specify the formal type parameters of the generic class in its constructor header after the class name:

```
class Node<E> {
   ...
   Node<E>() { ... }                         // Compile-time error!
   ...
}
```

A formal type parameter cannot be used to create a new instance, as it is not known which concrete type it represents. The following code in the declaration of the Node<E> class would be illegal:

```
E ref = new E();                           // Compile-time error!
```

A formal type parameter is a *non-static type*. It cannot be used in a static context, for much the same reason as an instance variable cannot be used in a static context: it is associated with objects. The compiler will report errors at (1), (2), and (3) in the code below:

```
class Node<E> {
   public static E e1;                      // (1) Compile-time error!
   public static E oneStaticMethod(E e2) {  // (2) Compile-time error!
      E e3;                                 // (3) Compile-time error!
      System.out.println(e3);
   }
   // ...
}
```

Parameterized Types

A *parameterized type* (also called *type instance*) is an *invocation* or *instantiation* of a generic type, that is a specific usage of the generic type where the formal type parameters are replaced by *actual type parameters*. Analogy with method declarations and method invocations can be helpful in understanding the relationship between generic types and parameterized types. We pass actual parameters in a method invocation to execute a method. In the case of a generic type invocation, we pass actual *type* parameters in order to instantiate a generic type.

We can declare references and create objects of parameterized types, and call methods on these objects, in much the same way as we use non-generic classes.

```
Node<Integer> intNode = new Node<Integer>(2008, null);
```

The actual type parameter Integer, explicitly specified in the declaration statement above, binds to the formal type parameter E in Example 14.2. The compiler treats the parameterized type Node<Integer> as a *new type*. The parameterized type Node<Integer> constrains the generic type Node<E> to Integer objects, thus implementing homogenous nodes with Integers. The reference intNode can only refer to a Node of Integer.

In the object creation expression of the new operator, the actual type parameter is mandatory after the class name, and the node created can only be used to store an object of this concrete type. Methods can be called on objects of parameterized types:

```
Integer iRef = intNode.getData();                       // 2008
```

In the method call above, the actual type parameter is determined from the type of the reference used to make the call. The type of the intNode reference is Node<Integer>, therefore, the actual type parameter is Integer. The method header is Integer getData(), meaning that the method will return a value of type Integer. The compiler checks that the return value can be assigned. As the compiler guarantees that the return value will be an Integer and can be assigned, no explicit cast or runtime check is necessary. Here are some more examples of calling methods of parameterized types:

```
intNode.setData(2010);                         // Ok.
intNode.setData("TwentyTen");                   // (1) Compile-time error!
intNode.setNext(new Node<Integer>(2009, null)); // (2010, (2009, null))
intNode.setNext(new Node<String>("Hi", null));  // (2) Compile-time error!
```

In the method calls shown above, the compiler determines that the actual type parameter is Integer. The method signatures are setData(Integer) and setNext(Node<Integer>). As expected, we get a compile-time error when we try to pass an argument that is not compatible with the parameter types in the method signatures, e.g., at (1) and (2). The parameterized types Node<Integer> and Node<String> are two *unrelated* types. The compiler reports any inconsistent use of a parameterized type, so that errors can be caught earlier at compile-time and use of explicit casts in the source code is minimized, as evident from (3) and (4), respectively.

```
Node<String> strNode = new Node<String>("hi", null);
intNode = strNode;                 // (3) Compile-time error!
String str = strNode.getData();    // (4) No explicit cast necessary.
```

Generic Interfaces

Generic types also include generic interfaces, which are declared analogous to generic classes. The specification of formal type parameters in a generic interface is the same as in a generic class. Example 14.3 declares a generic interface for objects that store a data value of type E and return a reference value of type IMonoLink<E>.

Example 14.3 *A Generic Interface and its Implementation*

```
interface IMonoLink<E> {
  void      setData(E data);
  E         getData();
  void      setNext(IMonoLink<E> next);
  IMonoLink<E> getNext();
}

class MonoNode<E> implements IMonoLink<E> {
  private E              data;    // Data
  private IMonoLink<E>     next;   // Reference to next node    // (1)
  MonoNode(E data, IMonoLink<E> next) {                          // (2)
    this.data = data;
    this.next = next;
  }
  public void     setData(E data)     { this.data = data; }
  public E        getData()           { return this.data; }
  public void     setNext(IMonoLink<E> next) { this.next = next; } // (2)
  public IMonoLink<E> getNext()               { return this.next; } // (3)
  public String toString() {
    return this.data.toString() +
         (this.next == null? "" : ", " + this.next.toString());
  }
}
```

A generic interface can be implemented by a generic (or a non-generic) class:

```
class MonoNode<E> implements IMonoLink<E> {
  // ...
}
```

Note that the construct <E> is used in two different ways in the class header. The first occurrence of <E> *declares* E to be a type parameter, and the second occurrence of <E> *parameterizes* the generic interface with this type parameter. The declare-before-use rule also applies to type parameters. The version of the MonoNode class in Example 14.3 differs from the Node class in Example 14.2 at (1), (2), (3), and (4). These changes were necessary to make the MonoNode<E> class compliant with the IMonoLink<E> interface.

A generic interface can be parameterized in the same way as a generic class. In the code below, the reference strNode has the parameterized type IMonoLink<String>. It is assigned the reference value of a node of type MonoNode<String>. The assignment is legal, since the parameterized type MonoNode<String> is a subtype of the parameterized type IMonoLink<String>:

```
IMonoLink<String> strNode2 = new MonoNode<String>("Bye", null);
System.out.println(strNode2.getData());                    // Prints: Bye
```

As with non-generic interfaces, generic interfaces cannot be instantiated either:

```
IMonoLink<String> strNode3 = new IMonoLink<String>("Bye", null); // Error!
```

Below is an example of a non-generic class implementing a generic interface:

```
class LymphNode implements IMonoLink<Lymph> {
  private Lymph           body;
  private IMonoLink<Lymph> location;
  public  void  setData(Lymph obj) { body = obj; }
  public  Lymph getData()           { return body; }
  public  void  setNext(IMonoLink<Lymph> loc) { this.location = loc; }
  public  IMonoLink<Lymph> getNext()          { return this.location; }
}
class Lymph { /*... */ }
```

The generic interface IMonoLink<E> is parameterized by a concrete type, namely, Lymph. The type LymphNode is a subtype of the parameterized type IMonoLink<Lymph>, as it implements the methods of the generic interface IMonoLink<E> in accordance with the type parameter Lymph.

The Java standard library contains many examples of generic interfaces. Two of these interfaces are discussed in detail in the subsections *The Comparable<E> Interface*, p. 765, and *The Comparator<E> Interface*, p. 771.

Extending Generic Types

A non-final generic type can be extended. Example 14.4 shows that the generic interface IBiLink<E> extends the generic interface IMonoLink<E>, and that the generic class BiNode<E> extends the generic class MonoNode<E> and implements the generic interface IBiLink<E> (see Figure 14.1).

Figure 14.1   *Extending Generic Types*

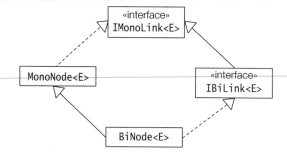

```
interface IBiLink<E> extends IMonoLink<E> {
  // ...
}

class BiNode<E> extends MonoNode<E> implements IBiLink<E> {
  // ...
}
```

The compiler checks that the formal type parameters of the superclass in the extends clause can be resolved. In the case above, the formal type parameter E, that is specified for the subclass, is also used as the type parameter for the superclass and also to constrain the interface to the same type parameter. This dependency ensures that an invocation of the subclass will result in the same actual parameter being used by the superclass and for the interface.

```
BiNode<Integer> intBiNode = new BiNode<Integer>(2020, null, null);
MonoNode<Integer> intMonoNode = intBiNode;           // (1)
Integer iRef = intMonoNode.getData();                // 2020
MonoNode<Number> numMonoNode = intBiNode;            // (2) Compile-time error.
```

The assignment at (1) is type-safe, as the parameterized class BiNode<Integer> is a subtype of the parameterized class MonoNode<Integer>. It is important to note that the superclass and the subclass are parameterized with the *same* type parameter, otherwise the subtype relationship between the superclass and the subclass does not hold. We get a compile-time error at (2) because the parameterized class BiNode<Integer> is *not* a subtype of the parameterized class MonoNode<Number>. Section 14.4 provides more details on subtype relationships for generic types.

Example 14.4   *Extending Generic Types*

```
interface IBiLink<T> extends IMonoLink<T> {
  void    setPrevious(IBiLink<T> previous);
  IBiLink<T> getPrevious();
}

class BiNode<E> extends MonoNode<E> implements IBiLink<E> {
  private IBiLink<E>  previous;    // Reference to previous node
  BiNode(E data, IBiLink<E> next, IBiLink<E> previous) {
    super(data, next);
    this.previous = previous;
  }
  public void setPrevious(IBiLink<E> previous) { this.previous = previous; }
  public IBiLink<E> getPrevious()              { return this.previous; }
  public String toString() {
    return (this.previous == null? "" : this.previous + ", ") +
           this.getData() +
           (this.getNext() == null? "" : ", " + this.getNext());
  }
}
```

Example 14.4 showed examples of generic types being extended to new generic subtypes. We can extend a non-generic type to a generic subtype as well:

```
class AbstractNode { /* ... */ }                    // A non-generic supertype
class SimpleNode<E> extends AbstractNode { /* ... */ }// A generic subtype
```

We can also extend concrete parameterized types to specialized non-generic subtypes:

```
class IntegerBiNode extends BiNode<Integer> {          // A non-generic subtype
  IntegerBiNode(Integer data, IntegerBiNode next, IntegerBiNode previous) {
    super(data, next, previous);
  }
  //...
}
```

Note that a subtype can inherit only one parameterization of the same generic interface supertype. Implementing or extending a parameterized type fixes the parameterization for the base type and any subtypes. In the declaration below, the subtype WeirdNode<E> tries to implement the interface IMonoLink<Integer>, but at the same time, it is a subtype of the interface IMonoLink<E> which the superclass MonoNode<E> implements:

```
class WeirdNode<E> extends MonoNode<E> implements IMonoLink<Integer> { // Error!
  //...
}
```

There is great flexibility in extending reference types, but care must be exercised to achieve the desired result.

Raw Types and Unchecked Warnings

A generic type without its formal type parameters is called a *raw type*. The raw type is the supertype of all parameterized types of the generic class. For example, the raw type Node is the supertype of the parameterized types Node<String>, Node<Integer>, and Node<Node<String>>. The last parameterized type is an example of a *nested parameterization*. It means that a node of this type has a node of type Node<String> as data.

A parameterized type (e.g., Node<String>) is *not* a class. Parameterized types are used by the compiler to check that objects created are used correctly in the program. The parameterized types Node<String>, Node<Integer>, Node<Node<String>> are all represented at runtime by their raw type Node. In other words, the compiler does *not* create a new class for each parameterized type. Only one class (Node) exists that has the name of the generic class (Node<E>), and the compiler generates only one class file (Node.class) with the Java byte code for the generic class.

Only reference types (excluding array creation and enumerations) can be used in invocations of generic types. A primitive type is not permitted as an actual type parameter, the reason being that values of primitive types have different sizes. This would require different code being generated for each primitive type used as an actual type parameter, but there is only one implementation of a generic class in Java.

Generics are implemented in the compiler only. The JVM is oblivious about the use of generic types. It does not differentiate between Node<String> and Node<Integer>, and just knows about the class Node. The compiler translates the generic class by a process known as *type erasure*; meaning that information about type parameters is erased and casts are inserted to make the program type-safe at runtime. The compiler guarantees that casts added at compile time never fail at runtime, when the program compiles without any *unchecked warnings*.

It is possible to use a generic class by its raw type only, like a non-generic class, without specifying actual type parameters for its usage. Example 14.5 illustrates mixing generic and non-generic code. The compiler will issue an unchecked warning if such a use can be a potential problem at runtime. Such usage is permitted for backward compatibility with legacy code, but is strongly advised against when writing new code. The assignment at (5) below shows that it is always possible to assign the reference value of a parameterized type to a reference of the raw type, as the latter is the supertype of the former. However, the raw type reference can be used to violate the type safety of the node at runtime, as shown at (6). Calling a method on a node using the raw type reference results in an *unchecked call warning*. In this particular case, a String is set as the data of an Integer node.

```
Node rawNode = intNode;            // (5) Assigning to raw type always possible.
rawNode.setData("BOOM");           // (6) Unchecked call warning!
Node<Integer> intNode = rawNode;   // (7) Unchecked conversion warning!
iRef = intNode.getData();          // (8) ClassCastException!
```

Assigning the reference value of a raw type to a reference of the parameterized type results in an *unchecked conversion warning*, shown at (7). If the node referenced by the raw type reference is not of the Integer type, using it as a node of Integer could lead to problems at runtime. Note that the assignment at (8) is type compatible, but its type safety is compromised by the corruption of the Integer node at runtime, resulting in a ClassCastException.

The class Preliminaries in Example 14.5 is shown compiled with the non-standard option -Xlint:unchecked. The compiler recommends using this option when non-generic and generic code are mixed this way. The program compiles in spite of the unchecked warnings, and can be executed. But all guarantees of type-safety are off in the face of unchecked warnings.

Example 14.5 *Unchecked Warnings*

```
//A client for the generic class Node<T>.
public class Preliminaries {
  public static void main(String[] args) {
    Node<Integer> intNode = new Node<Integer>(2008, null);
    Integer iRef = intNode.getData();           // 2008
    intNode.setData(2010);                       // Ok.
//  intNode.setData("TwentyTen");                // (1) Compile-time error!
    intNode.setNext(new Node<Integer>(2009, null)); // (2010, (2009, null))
//  intNode.setNext(new Node<String>("Hi", null)); // (2) Compile-time error!

    Node<String> strNode = new Node<String>("hi", null);
//  intNode = strNode;                 // (3) Compile-time error!
    String str = strNode.getData();   // (4) No explicit cast necessary.

    Node rawNode = intNode;            // (5) Assigning to raw type always possible.
    rawNode.setData("BOOM");           // (6) Unchecked call warning!
```

```
        intNode = rawNode;              // (7) Unchecked conversion warning!
        iRef = intNode.getData();       // (8) ClassCastException!
    }
}
```

Compiling the program:

```
>javac -Xlint:unchecked Preliminaries.java
Preliminaries.java:16: warning: [unchecked] unchecked call to setData(E) as a
member of the raw type Node
        rawNode.setData("BOOM");        // (6) Unchecked call warning!
                ^
Preliminaries.java:17: warning: [unchecked] unchecked conversion
found    : Node
required: Node<java.lang.Integer>
        intNode = rawNode;              // (7) Unchecked conversion warning!
                ^
2 warnings
```

Running the program:

```
>java Preliminaries
Exception in thread "main" java.lang.ClassCastException: java.lang.String cannot
  be cast to java.lang.Integer
        at Preliminaries.main(Preliminaries.java:18)
```

14.3 Collections and Generics

Before the introduction of generics in Java 1.5, a collection in the Java Collections
Framework could hold references to objects of any type. For example, any object
which is an instance of the java.lang.Object class or its subclasses could be maintained in an instance of the java.util.ArrayList class, which implements the
java.util.List interface.

```
List wordList = new ArrayList();         // Using non-generic types.
wordList.add("two zero zero eight");     // Can add any object.
wordList.add(2004);
//...
Object element = wordList.get(0);        // Always returns an Object.
//...
if (element instanceof String) {         // Runtime check to avoid ClassCastException
    String strInt = (String) element;    // Cast required.
    //...
}
```

The client of a collection has to do most of the bookkeeping with regard to using
the collection in a type-safe manner: which objects are put in the collection and
how objects retrieved are used. Using the Object class as the element type allows
the implementation of the collection class to be specific, but its use to be generic.

An `ArrayList` is a specific implementation of the `List` interface, but usage of the class `ArrayList` is generic with regard to any object.

Using a generic collection, the compiler provides the type-safety, and the resulting code is less verbose.

```
List<String> wordList = new ArrayList<String>();   // Using a specific type.
wordList.add("two zero zero eight");               // Can add strings only
wordList.add(2004);                                // Compile-time error!
//...
String element = wordList.get(0);                  // Always returns a String.
//...
```

Runtime checks or explicit casts are not necessary now. Generic types allow the implementation of the collection class to be generic, but its use to be specific. The generic type `ArrayList<E>` is a generic implementation of the `List<E>` interface, but now the usage of the parameterized type `ArrayList<String>` is specific, as it constrains the generic type `ArrayList<E>` to strings.

14.4   Wildcards

In this section, we discuss how using wildcards can increase the expressive power of generic types. But first we examine one major difference between array types and parameterized types. The generic class `Node<E>` used in this subsection is defined in Example 14.2, p. 664.

The Subtype Covariance Problem with Parameterized Types

The following three declarations create three nodes of `Integer`, `Double`, and `Number` type, respectively.

```
Node<Integer>  intNode    = new Node<Integer>(2010,null);    // (1)
Node<Double>   doubleNode = new Node<Double>(3.14,null);     // (2)
Node<Number>   numNode    = new Node<Number>(2020, null);    // (3)
```

In the declaration at (3), the formal type parameter `E` is bound to the actual type parameter `Number`, i.e., the signature of the constructor is `Node(Number, Node<Number>)`. The signature of the constructor call is `Node(Integer, null)`. Since the type `Integer` is a subtype of the type `Number`, and `null` can be assigned to any reference, the constructor call succeeds.

In the method calls at (4) and (5) below, the method signature in both cases is `setData(Number)`. The method calls again succeed, since the actual parameters are of types `Double` and `Integer`, that are subtypes of `Number`:

```
numNode.setData(10.5);                                          // (4)
numNode.setData(2009);                                          // (5)
```

However, the following calls do *not* succeed:

```
numNode.setNext(intNode);                    // (6) Compile-time error!
numNode = new Node<Number>(2030, doubleNode);  // (7) Compile-time error!
```

The actual type parameter is determined to be Number at (6). The compiler complains that the method setData(Node<Number>) is *not* applicable for the arguments (Node<Integer>), i.e., the method signature setData(Node<Number>) is *not* compatible with the method call signature setData(Node<Integer>). The compiler also complains at (7): the constructor signature Node(Number, Node<Number>) is *not* applicable for the arguments (Integer, Node<Double>). The problem is with the second argument at (7). We cannot pass an argument of type Node<Integer> or Node<Double> where a parameter of type Node<Number> is expected. The following assignments will also not compile:

```
numNode = intNode;                           // (8) Compile-time error!
numNode = doubleNode;                         // (9) Compile-time error!
```

The reason for the compile-time errors is that Node<Integer> and Node<Double> are *not* subtypes of Node<Number>, although Integer and Double are subtypes of Number. In the case of arrays, the array types Integer[] and Double[] *are* subtypes of the array type Number[]. The subtyping relationship between the individual types carries over to corresponding array types. This type relationship is called *subtype covariance* (see Figure 14.2). This relationship holds for arrays because the element type is available at runtime. If it were allowed for parameterized types at compile-time, it could lead to problems at runtime, since the element type would not be known, as it has been erased by the compiler.

```
numNode = intNode;                  // If this was allowed,
numNode.setData(25.5);              // the data could be corrupted,
Integer iRef = intNode.getData();   // resulting in a ClassCastException!
```

Therefore, the subtype covariance relationship does not hold for parameterized types that are instantiations of the same generic type with different actual type parameters, regardless of any subtyping relationship between the actual type parameters. The actual type parameters are *concrete* types (e.g., Integer, Number), and, therefore, the parameterized types are called *concrete parameterized types*. Such parameterized types are totally unrelated. As an example from the Java Collections Framework, the parameterized type Map<String, Integer> is not a subtype of the parameterized type Map<String, Number>.

Figure 14.2 *No Subtype Covariance for Parameterized Types*

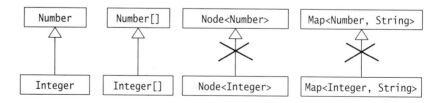

Wildcard Types

Wildcard types are type parameters defined using the *wildcard* symbol ?. The wildcard ? by itself represents *all* types. The parameterized type List<?> represents a list of all types, whereas the concrete parameterized type List<Integer> only represents a list of Integer. In other words, a *wildcard type* can represent *many types*. Therefore a parameterized type that has wildcard card types as actual type parameters can represent a family of types, in contrast to a concrete parameterized type that only represents itself. The wildcard types provided in Java represent different subtype relationships that are summarized in Table 14.1.

Wildcard types provide the solution for increased expressive power to overcome the limitations discussed earlier when using generics in Java, but introduce limitations of their own as to what operations can be carried out on an object using references of wildcard types. We will use the class Node<E> in Example 14.2 as a running example to discuss the use of wildcard types.

Table 14.1 *Summary of Subtyping Relationships for Generic Types*

Name	Syntax	Semantics	Description
Subtype Covariance	? extends Type	Any subtype of Type (including Type)	*Bounded wildcard* with *upper bound*
Subtype Contravariance	? super Type	Any supertype of Type (including Type)	*Bounded wildcard* with *lower bound*
Subtype Bivariance	?	All types	*Unbounded wildcard*
Subtype Invariance	Type	Only type Type	*Type parameter/argument*

Subtype Covariance: ? extends Type

The wildcard type ? extends Type represents all *subtypes* of Type (including Type itself). The wildcard type ? extends Type is called an *upper bounded wildcard* with Type representing its *upper bound*.

The wildcard type ? extends Number denotes all subtypes of Number, and the parameterized type Node<? extends Number> denotes the family of invocations of Node<E> for types that are subtypes of Number. Figure 14.3 shows a partial type hierarchy for the parameterized type Node<? extends Number>. Note that the parameterized type Node<? extends Integer> is a subtype of the parameterized type Node<? extends Number>, since the wildcard type ? extends Integer represents all subtypes of Integer, and these are also subtypes of Number.

Figure 14.3 *Partial Type Hierarchy for* Node<? extends Number>

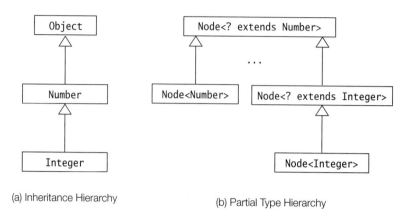

(a) Inheritance Hierarchy   (b) Partial Type Hierarchy

Subtype Contravariance: ? super Type

The wildcard type ? super Type represents all *supertypes* of Type (including Type itself). The wildcard type ? super Type is called a *lower bounded wildcard* with Type representing its *lower bound*.

The wildcard type ? super Integer denotes all supertypes of Integer, and the parameterized type Node<? super Integer> denotes a family of invocations of Node<E> for types that are supertypes of Integer. Figure 14.4 shows a partial type hierarchy for the parameterized type Node<? super Integer>. Note that the parameterized type Node<? super Number> is a *subtype* of the parameterized type Node<? super Integer>, since the wildcard type ? super Number represents all supertypes of Number, and these are also supertypes of Integer.

Figure 14.4 *Partial Type Hierarchy for* Node<? super Integer>

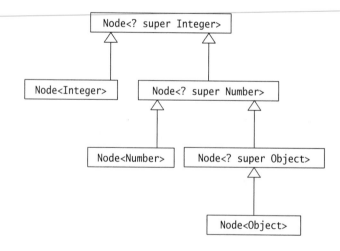

Subtype Bivariance: ?

As mentioned earlier, the wildcard type ? represents *all* types. The wildcard type ? is called the *unbounded wildcard*, since it has no bounds as the other two wildcard types. By definition, it represents both the upper and the lower bounded wildcards for any bound.

The parameterized type Node<?> denotes the family of invocations of Node<E> for any type, i.e., denotes a Node of any kind, and is therefore the supertype of all invocations of Node<E> (see also Figure 14.5, p. 678).

Subtype Invariance: Type

When a concrete type Type is used as an actual type parameter in a parameterized type, it represents Type itself. Since Type can be *any* concrete type, it is called an *unbounded type parameter*. The concrete parameterized type Node<Integer> represents the invocation of Node<E> for the concrete actual type parameter Integer. As we have seen earlier, there is no subtype covariance relationship between concrete parameterized types, but there is such relationship between bounded parameterized types and concrete parameterized types (see also Figure 14.3 and Figure 14.4).

Let us recapitulate the basic terminology before proceeding further. A generic type can specify one or more formal type parameters. A parameterized type is an invocation of a generic type, supplying the required actual type parameters. An actual type parameter can be a wildcard type (possibly bounded) or a concrete type. A concrete type is either a non-generic type or a parameterized type that has concrete types as parameters.

Some Restrictions on Wildcard Types

Wildcards cannot be used in instance creation expressions:

```
Node<?> anyNode = new Node<?>(2006, null);              // Compile-time error!
Node<? extends Integer> extIntNodeA
              = new Node<? extends Integer>(0, null);   // Compile-time error!
Node<? extends Integer> extIntNodeB = new Node<Integer>(0, null);  // OK
```

The actual type parameter in the constructor call must be a concrete type. Creating instances of wildcard parameterized types is analogous to instantiating interface types; neither can be used in instance creation expressions.

Wildcards cannot be used in the header of reference type declarations. Supertypes in the extends and implements clauses cannot have wildcards.

```
class QuestionableNode<?>  { /* ... */ }                       // Not OK.
class SubNode extends Node<?> { /* ... */ }                    // Not OK.
interface INode extends Comparable<? extends Node<?>> { /* ... */ }  // Not OK.
```

However, *nested wildcards* are not a problem in a reference type declaration header or in an object creation expression:

```
class OddNode extends Node<Node<?>> implements Comparable<Node<?>> { /* ... */ }
...
Node<?> nodeOfAnyNode = new Node<Node<?>>(new Node<Integer>(2006, null), null);
```

14.5 Using References of Wildcard Parameterized Types

A wildcard type can be used to declare parameterized references, i.e., references whose type is a wildcard parameterized type. In this section, we look at how such references are used in the following contexts: assignment between such references, and calling methods of generic types using such references. The generic class Node<E> used in this subsection is defined in Example 14.2, p. 664.

Figure 14.5 *Partial Type Hierarchy for Selected Parameterized Types of* Node<E>

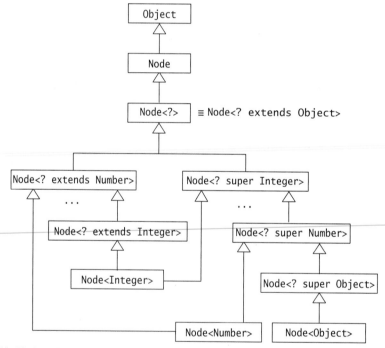

All widening reference conversions are type-safe.
All narrowing reference conversions require an explicit cast, except for the following:
- Narrowing reference conversion from Node to Node<?>,
  or from Node<?> to Node<? extends Object>, is safe.
- Narrowing reference conversion from Node to Node<? extends Object>,
  or to any subtype below Node<?>, results in an unchecked conversion warning.

Generic Reference Assignment

A reference of a supertype can refer to an object of a subtype, and this substitution principle applies to parameterized types as well. Assignment compatibility is according to the type hierarchy of the parameterized types. Figure 14.5 shows partial type hierarchy for selected parameterized types of the generic class Node<E>. It combines the type hierarchies from Figure 14.3 and Figure 14.4. As we would expect, *widening reference conversions* according to the type hierarchy are always type-safe. All but the last assignment statement in the code below are legal. The types Node<Number> and Node<Integer> are unrelated. (The notation B <: A means B is a subtype of A.)

```
Node<Object>  objNode;
Node<Number>  numNode;
Node<Integer> intNode;
Node<? extends Number> extNumNode
                  = intNode; // Node<Integer> <: Node<? extends Number>
Node<? super Integer>  supIntNode
                  = numNode; // Node<Number> <: Node<? super Integer>
supIntNode = objNode;        // Node<Object> <: Node<? super Integer>
numNode    = intNode;        // Compile-time error! Types unrelated.
```

In the following code, we get an error at (1) because the types Node<? extends Number> and Node<? super Number> are unrelated, but that is not the case for the types Node<? extends Object> and Node<? super Object> at (2). The family of types denoted by the type Node<? super Object> has the type Node<Object> only, which is also a subtype of the type Node<? extends Object>.

```
Node<? super Number>   supNumNode;
Node<? extends Object> extObjNode;
Node<? super Object>   supObjNode;
extNumNode = supNumNode; // (1) Compile-time error! Types unrelated.
extObjNode = supObjNode; // (2) Node<? super Object> <: Node<? extends Object>
supObjNode = extObjNode; // (3) Compile-time error!
```

Narrowing reference conversion requires an explicit cast, except for the cases noted below (see also Figure 14.5). The raw type Node and the unbounded wildcard parameterized type Node<?> are essentially equivalent in this regard. Conversion between the two is type-safe:

```
Node    rawNode;
Node<?> anyNode;
rawNode = anyNode;  // Node <-- Node<?> is type-safe.
anyNode = rawNode;  // Node<?> <-- Node is type-safe.
```

The unbounded wildcard parameterized type Node<?> and the upper bounded wildcard parameterized type Node<? extends Object> are also essentially equivalent (see (4)), except when assigned a value of the raw type Node (see (5)).

```
// (4):
anyNode = extObjNode;  // Node<?> <-- Node<? extends Object> is type-safe.
extObjNode = anyNode;  // Node<? extends Object> <-- Node<?> is type-safe.
```

```
// (5):
anyNode    = rawNode;  // Node<?> <-- Node  is type-safe.
extObjNode = rawNode;  // Node<? extends Object> <-- Node: Unchecked Conversion
```

Assigning a value of the raw type Node to a reference of the type Node<? extends Object> results in an *unchecked conversion warning*—which conforms to the general rule when mixing legacy and generic code: assigning the value of a raw type to a reference of a bounded wildcard parameterized type or a concrete parameterized type results in an unchecked conversion warning, as illustrated by the examples below.

```
extNumNode = rawNode; // Node<? extends Number> <-- Node: Unchecked Conversion
intNode    = rawNode; // Node<Integer> <-- Node: Unchecked Conversion Warning
```

For a discussion of explicit casting of parameterized references, see the subsection *Implications for Casting*, p. 724.

Using Parameterized References to Call Set and Get Methods

Generic classes are suitable for implementing ADTs called *collections* (also called *containers*) where the element type is usually specified by a type parameter. The Java Collections Framework is a prime example of such collections. A collection usually provides two basic operations: a *set* operation (also called a *write* or *put* operation) to add an element to the collection, and a *get* operation (also called a *read* operation) to retrieve an element from the collection. The *set* operation takes a parameter of the type T, where T is a type parameter of the generic class. The *get* operation returns a value of the type parameter T. The class Node<E> provides these two basic operations to manipulate the data in a node:

```
class Node<E> {
  private E data;
  // ...
  public void setData(E obj) { data = obj; }      // (1)
  public E    getData()      { return data; }     // (2)
  // ...
}
```

So far we have called these two methods using references of concrete parameterized types:

```
Node<Number> numNode = new Node<Number>(2008, null);
numNode.setData(2010);                      // (3) Can only set a Number.
Number data = numNode.getData();            // (4) Can only get a Number.
```

The actual type parameter in the above method calls is a concrete type, but what happens when we use a reference of a wildcard parameterized type that represents a family of types? For example, what if the type of the reference numNode is Node<? extends Number>. Is the method call in (3) type-safe? Is the assignment in (4) type-safe? Operations that can potentially break the type-safety are either flagged as compile-time errors or warnings. If there are warnings but no errors, the program still compiles. However, type-safety at runtime is not guaranteed.

The key to using generics in Java is understanding the implications of wildcard parameterized types in the language—and why the compiler will not permit certain operations involving wildcards, since these might break the type-safety of the program. To illustrate some of the subtleties, we compile the class in Example 14.6 successively with different headers for the method checkIt(). The parameter type is different in each method header, from (h1) to (h5). The method uses three local variables object, number and integer of type Object, Number, and Integer, respectively ((v1) to (v3)). There are three calls to the setData() method of the generic class Node<E> to set an Object, a Number, and an Integer as the data in the node referenced by the reference s0 ((s1) to (s3)). There are also three calls to the getData() method of the generic class Node<E>, assigning the return value to each of the local variables (s4) to (s6)). And finally, the last statement, (s7), tests whether the data retrieved can be put back in again.

Example 14.6 *Illustrating Get and Set Operations Using Parameterized References*

```
class WildcardAccessRestrictions {

//static void checkIt(Node s0) {                        // (h1)
//static void checkIt(Node<?> s0) {                     // (h2)
//static void checkIt(Node<? extends Number> s0) {      // (h3)
//static void checkIt(Node<? super Number> s0) {        // (h4)
  static void checkIt(Node<Number> s0) {                // (h5)
    // Local variables
    Object  object  = new Object();                     // (v1)
    Number  number  = 1.5;                               // (v2)
    Integer integer = 10;                                // (v3)
    // Method calls
    s0.setData(object);                                  // (s1)
    s0.setData(number);                                  // (s2)
    s0.setData(integer);                                 // (s3)
    object  = s0.getData();                              // (s4)
    number  = s0.getData();                              // (s5)
    integer = s0.getData();                              // (s6)
    s0.setData(s0.getData());                            // (s7)
  }
}
```

Attempts to compile the method in Example 14.6 with different headers are shown in Table 14.2. The rows are statements from (s1) to (s7) from Example 14.6. The columns indicate the type of the parameter s0 in the method headers (h1) to (h5). The reference s0 is used to call the methods. The entry **ok** means the compiler did not report any errors or any unchecked warnings. The entry **!** means the compiler did not report any errors but issued an unchecked call warning. The entry × means the compiler reported an error. In other words, we cannot carry out the operations that are marked with the entry ×.

Table 14.2 *Get and Set Operations Using Parameterized References*

Type of s0 / Operation	Node	Node<?>	Node <? extends Number>	Node <? super Number>	Node<Number>
`s0.setData(object);`	!	×	×	×	×
`s0.setData(number);`	!	×	×	**ok**	**ok**
`s0.setData(integer);`	!	×	×	**ok**	**ok**
`object = s0.getData();`	**ok**	**ok**	**ok**	**ok**	**ok**
`number = s0.getData();`	×	×	**ok**	×	**ok**
`integer = s0.getData();`	×	×	×	×	×
`s0.setData(s0.getData());`	!	×	×	×	**ok**

Raw Type References

The type of the reference `s0` is the raw type `Node`. This case illustrates the non-generic paradigm of using a collection: we can put any object, but we can only get an `Object`. From Table 14.2, we see that we can put any object as data in a node of the raw type `Node`, but the compiler issues *unchecked call warnings*, as we are putting an object into a raw type node whose element type is not known. We can only get an `Object`, as we cannot be more specific about the data type.

Unbounded Wildcard References: ?

The type of the reference `s0` is `Node<?>`. The compiler determines that the actual type parameter for each method call is the wildcard ?, i.e., any type. Obviously, we cannot set any data in a node whose element type cannot be determined. It might not be type-safe. And we cannot guarantee the type of its data either, because the data type can be any type, but we can safely read it as an `Object`. Note that we can always write a `null`, as the `null` value can be assigned to any reference.

Upper Bounded Wildcard References: ? extends Type

The type of the reference `s0` is `Node<? extends Number>`, where *Type* is `Number`. This means that the reference `s0` refers to a node containing an object whose type is either `Number` or a subtype of `Number`, but the specific (sub)type of the object cannot always be determined at compile time. Putting *any* object, except a `null`, into such a node might not be type-safe.

The code below shows what would happen if any object was allowed to be set as data in a `Long` node via its alias `s0`. If (1), (2), or (3) were allowed, we would get a

ClassCastException at (4) because the data could not be assigned to a Long reference, as the type-safety of the node longNode will have been violated, either with a supertype object or an object of an unrelated type.

```
Long longInt = 20L;
Node<Long> longNode = new Node<Long>(longInt, null);  // Node of Long, that is
Node<? extends Number> s0 = longNode;// referenced by a Node<? extends Number> ref.
s0.setData(object);              // If this was allowed, or        (1)
s0.setData(number);              // if this was allowed, or        (2)
s0.setData(integer);             // if this was allowed,           (3)
longInt = longNode.getData();    // we would get an exception here. (4)
```

The following method call will also not compile, as the compiler cannot give any guarantees at compile time that the reference s0 will refer to a node of Long at runtime:

```
s0.setData(longInt);            // Compile-time error!
```

The upper bound in the wildcard type ? extends Number is Number. Therefore, the data of the node with the wildcard type ? extends Number must be a Number (i.e., either an object of type Number or an object of a subtype of Number). Thus, we can only safely assign the reference value returned by the *get* operation to a reference of type Number or a supertype of Number.

Lower Bounded Wildcard References: ? super Type

Using a reference of type Node<? super Number>, where *Type* is Number, we can only put a Number or a subtype object of Number into the node, as such a number would also be a subtype object of any supertype of Number. Since we cannot guarantee which specific supertype of Number the node actually has, we cannot put any supertype object of Number in the node. The code below shows what would happen if an unrelated supertype object was put in as data in a Node<? super Number>. If (1) were allowed, we would get a ClassCastException at (2) because the data value (of a supertype) cannot be assigned to a Number reference (which is a subtype).

```
Node<Number> numNode = new Node<Number>(2008, null);
Node<? super Number> s0 = numNode;
s0.setData(object);           // (1) If this was allowed,
number = numNode.getData();   // (2) we would get an exception here.
```

Since the type of the reference s0 is Node<? super Number>, the reference s0 can refer to a node containing an object whose type is either Number or some supertype of Number. When we *get* the data from such a node, we can only safely assume that it is an Object. Keeping in mind that a supertype of Number can refer to objects that are unrelated to Number (e.g., an Object reference that can refer to a String), if (3) were allowed in the code below, we would get a ClassCastException at (3):

```
Node<Object> objNode = new Node<Object>("Hi", null);       // String as data.
Node<? super Number> s0 = objNode;
number = s0.getData();        // (3) If allowed, we would get an exception here.
object = s0.getData();        // This is always ok.
```

Unbounded Type References: Type

The type of the reference s0 is Node<Number>, where *Type* is Number. The actual type parameter for each method call is determined to be Number. Thus the type of the parameter in the setData() method and the return value of the getData() method is Number. Therefore we can pass the reference value of a Number or a subclass object of Number to the setData() method, and can assign the reference value returned by the getData() method to a reference of the type Number or a supertype of Number. In this case, we can put a Number, and get a Number.

Table 14.3 gives a summary of using parameterized references for set and get operations. If we only want to get an element of type T from a container, we can use the upper bounded wildcard ? extends T. If we only want to put an element of type T into a container, we can use the lower bounded wildcard ? super T. If we want to both get and set elements of type T in a container, we can use the unbounded type T.

Table 14.3   *Summary of Get and Set Operations using Parameterized References*

Type of s0 ──────── Operation	Node	Node<?>	Node<? extends Number>	Node<? super Number>	Node<Number>
set/put/write	*Any object*	*Cannot put anything*	*Cannot put anything*	Number *or* *subtype*	Number *or* *subtype*
get/read	Object *only*	Object *only*	Number *or* *supertype*	Object *only*	Number *or* *supertype*

14.6 Bounded Type Parameters

In the declaration of the generic class Node<E>, the type parameter E is *unbounded*, i.e. it can be any reference type. However, sometimes it may necessary to restrict what type the type parameter E can represent. The canonical example is restricting that the type parameter E is Comparable<E>, so that objects can be compared.

Wildcard types *cannot* be used in the header of a generic class to restrict the type parameter:

```
class CmpNode<? extends Comparable> { ... }          // Compile-time error!
```

However, the type parameter can be bounded by a *constraint* as follows:

```
class CmpNode<E extends Comparable<E>>  {             // E is bounded.
  CmpNode(E data, CmpNode<E> next) {
    super(data, next);
  }
  // ...
}
```

In the constraint `<E extends Comparable<E>>`, E is *bounded* and `Comparable<E>` is the *upper bound*. The declaration above states that the actual type parameter when we parameterize the generic class `CmpNode` must not only implement the `Comparable` interface, but the objects of the actual type parameter must be comparable to each other. This implies that the type, say A, that we can use to parameterize the generic class, must implement the parameterized interface `Comparable<A>`.

If we base the implementation of the `CmpNode` class on the generic class `Node<E>`, we can write the declaration as follows:

```
class CmpNode<E extends Comparable<E>> extends Node<E> {
  // ...
}
```

The extends clause is used in two different ways: for the generic class `CmpNode` to extend the class `Node<E>`, and to constrain the type parameter E of the generic class `CmpNode` to the `Comparable<E>` interface. Although the type parameter E must implement the interface `Comparable<E>`, we do *not* use the keyword `implements` in a constraint. Neither can we use the super clause to constrain the type parameter of a generic class.

If we want `CmpNodes` to have a natural ordering based on the natural ordering of their data values, we can declare the generic class `CmpNode` as follows:

```
class CmpNode<E extends Comparable<E>> extends Node<E>
                              implements Comparable<CmpNode<E>> {
  CmpNode(E data, CmpNode<E> next) {
    super(data, next);
  }
  public int compareTo(CmpNode<E> node2) {
    return this.getData().compareTo(node2.getData());
  }
}
```

Note how the `Comparable` interface is parameterized in the `implements` clause. The constraint `<E extends Comparable<E>>` specifies that the type parameter E is `Comparable`, and the clause `implements Comparable<CmpNode<E>>` specifies that the generic class `CmpNode` is `Comparable`.

Here are some examples of how the generic class `CmpNode` can be parameterized:

```
CmpNode<Integer> intCmpNode  = new CmpNode<Integer>(2020, null);  // (1)
CmpNode<Number>  numCmpNode  = new CmpNode<Number>(2020, null);   // (2) Error!
CmpNode<Integer> intCmpNode2 = new CmpNode<Integer>(2010, null);
int result = intCmpNode.compareTo(intCmpNode2);
```

The actual type parameter `Integer` in (1) implements `Comparable<Integer>`, but the actual type parameter `Number` in (2) is not `Comparable`. In the invocation `CmpNode<A>`, the compiler ensures that A implements `Comparable<A>`.

Multiple Bounds

A bounded type parameter can have *multiple bounds*, B_1 & B_2 & ... & B_n, which must be satisfied by the *actual* type parameter:

```
class CmpNode<T extends Number & Serializable> ...
```

An extra bound, the Serializable interface, has been added using the ampersand (&). The formal type parameter T is a subtype of *both* Number and Serializable, and represents both of these concrete types in the body of the generic class. The constraint above will only allow the generic type to be parameterized by an actual type parameter which is a subtype of *both* Number and Serializable.

We can add as many bounds as necessary. A type parameter E having multiple bounds is a *subtype* of all of the types denoted by the individual bounds. A bound can be a parameterized type, as in the following generic class header:

```
class CmpNode<E extends Comparable<E> & Serializable> ...
```

If the raw type of a bound is a (non-final) superclass of the bounded type parameter, it can only be specified as the first bound and there can only be one such bound (as a subclass can only extend one immediate superclass). The raw type of an individual bound cannot be used with different type arguments, since a type parameter cannot be the subtype of more than one bound having the same raw type. In the class header below, whatever E is, it cannot be a subtype of two parameterizations of the same interface type (i.e., Comparable) at the same time:

```
class CmpNode<E extends Comparable<E> & Serializable & Comparable<String>> //Error
```

If the type parameter has a bound, methods of the bound can be invoked on instances of the type parameter in the generic class. Otherwise, only methods from the Object class can be invoked on instances of the type parameter. In the declaration of the generic class Node<E> in Example 14.2, we cannot call any methods on instances of the type parameter except for those in the Object class, because the type parameter is unbounded. Since the instances of the type parameter E are guaranteed to be Comparable<E> in the generic class CmpNode, we can call the method compareTo() of the Comparable interface on these instances.

Review Questions

14.1   What will be the result of attempting to compile and run the following code?

```
public class RQ100_50 {
  public static void main(String[] args) {
    List<Integer> lst = new ArrayList<Integer>();  // (1)
    lst.add(2007);
    lst.add(2008);
    List<Number> numList = lst;                     // (2)
    for(Number n : numList)                         // (3)
      System.out.println(n + " ");
  }
}
```

Select the one correct answer.

(a) The code will fail to compile because of an error in (1).
(b) The code will fail to compile because of an error in (2).
(c) The code will fail to compile because of an error in (3).
(d) The code will compile, but throw a ClassCastException at runtime in (2).
(e) The code will compile and will print "2007 2008 ", when run.

14.2 What will be the result of attempting to compile and run the following code?

```
class Fruit {}
class Apple extends Fruit {}
class Orange extends Fruit {}

public class RQ100_60 {
  public static void main(String[] args) {
    ArrayList<Apple> aList = new ArrayList<Apple>();
    aList.add(new Apple());
    ArrayList bList = aList;            // (1)
    ArrayList<Orange> oList = bList;    // (2)
    oList.add(new Orange());
    System.out.println(aList);
  }
}
```

Select the one correct answer.

(a) The code will fail to compile because of errors in (1) and (2).
(b) The code will fail to compile because of an error in (1).
(c) The code will fail to compile because of an error in (2).
(d) The code will compile with an unchecked warning in both (1) and (2).
(e) The code will compile with an unchecked warning in (1).
(f) The code will compile with an unchecked warning in (2).
(g) The code will compile without warnings, but throw a ClassCastException at runtime in (2).
(h) The code will compile without warnings and will print "[Apple@hhhhhh, Orange@HHHHHHH]", when run. (hhhhhh and HHHHHHH represent some hash code.)

14.3 What will be the result of attempting to compile and run the following code?

```
public class RQ100_40 {
  public static void main(String[] args) {
    List <? super Integer> sList = new ArrayList<Number>(); //(1)
    int i = 2007;
    sList.add(i);
    sList.add(++i);                              //(2)
    Number num = sList.get(0);                   //(3)
  }
}
```

Select the one correct answer.

(a) The code will fail to compile because of an error in (1).
(b) The code will fail to compile because of an error in (2).

(c) The code will fail to compile because of an error in (3).

(d) The code will compile, but throw a ClassCastException at runtime at (3).

(e) The code will compile and execute normally.

14.4   What will be the result of attempting to compile the following code?

```java
public class RQ100_70 {
  public static void main(String[] args) {
    List<Integer> glst1 = new ArrayList();      //(1)
    List nglst1 = glst1;                        //(2)
    List nglst2 = nglst1;                       //(3)
    List<Integer> glst2 = glst1;                //(4)
  }
}
```

Select the one correct answer.

(a) The code will compile without any warnings.

(b) The code will compile with an unchecked warning in (1).

(c) The code will compile with an unchecked warning in (2).

(d) The code will compile with an unchecked warning in (3).

(e) The code will compile with an unchecked warning in (4).

14.5   Which occurrences of the type parameter T are illegal?

```java
public class Box<T> {
  private T item;                                   // (1)
  private static T[] storage = new T[100];          // (2)

  public Box(T item) { this.item = item; }          // (3)

  public T getItem() { return item; }               // (4)
  public void setItem(T newItem) { item = newItem; } // (5)

  public static void getAllItems(T newItem) {       // (6)
    T temp;                                          // (7)
  }
}
```

Select the three correct answers.

(a) Occurrence of the type parameter T in (1).

(b) Occurrences of the type parameter T in (2).

(c) Occurrence of the type parameter T in (3).

(d) Occurrence of the type parameter T in (4).

(e) Occurrence of the type parameter T in (5).

(f) Occurrence of the type parameter T in (6).

(g) Occurrence of the type parameter T in (7).

14.6   Which statements are true about the following code?

```java
public class RQ100_14 {
  public static void main(String[] args) {
    List legacyList = new ArrayList<Integer>(); // (1)
```

```
        List<?> anyList = legacyList;              // (2)
        legacyList = anyList;                      // (3)
    }
}
```

Select the one correct answer.

(a) The compiler will report errors in the code.

(b) The code will compile with an unchecked warning in (1).

(c) The code will compile with an unchecked warning in (2).

(d) The code will compile with an unchecked warning in (3).

(e) The code will compile without unchecked warnings.

14.7 Which declarations will compile without warnings?

Select the four correct answers.

(a) Map<Integer, Map<Integer, String>> map1
                = new HashMap<Integer, HashMap<Integer, String>>();

(b) Map<Integer, HashMap<Integer, String>> map2
                = new HashMap<Integer, HashMap<Integer, String>>();

(c) Map<Integer, Integer> map3 = new HashMap<Integer, Integer>();

(d) Map<? super Integer, ? super Integer> map4
                = new HashMap<? super Integer, ? super Integer>();

(e) Map<? super Integer, ? super Integer> map5 = new HashMap<Number, Number>();

(f) Map<? extends Number, ? extends Number> map6
                = new HashMap<Number, Number>();

(g) Map <?,?> map7 = new HashMap<?,?>();

14.8 Which statement is true about the following code?

```
class Fruit {}
class Apple extends Fruit {}

public class RQ100_15 {
  public static void main(String[] args) {
    List<? extends Apple> lst1 = new ArrayList<Fruit>(); // (1)
    List<? extends Fruit> lst2 = new ArrayList<Apple>(); // (2)
    List<? super Apple> lst3 = new ArrayList<Fruit>();   // (3)
    List<? super Fruit> lst4 = new ArrayList<Apple>();   // (4)
    List<?> lst5 = lst1;                                 // (5)
    List<?> lst6 = lst3;                                 // (6)
    List lst7 = lst6;                                    // (7)
    List<?> lst8 = lst7;                                 // (8)
  }
}
```

Select the one correct answer.

(a) (1) will compile, but (2) will not.

(b) (3) will compile, but (4) will not.

(c) (5) will compile, but (6) will not.

(d) (7) will compile, but (8) will not.

(e) None of the above.

14.9 Which statements can be inserted at (1) without the compiler reporting any errors?

```
public class RQ100_12 {
  public static void main(String[] args) {
    List lst = new ArrayList<String>();
    // (1) INSERT HERE
  }
}
```

Select the four correct answers.

(a) `lst.add(null);`
(b) `lst.add("OK");`
(c) `lst.add(2007);`
(d) `String v1 = lst.get(0);`
(e) `Object v2 = lst.get(0);`

14.10 Which declaration can be inserted at (1) so that the program compiles without errors?

```
public class RQ100_84 {
  // (1) INSERT DECLARATION HERE...
  public long getNum(String name) {
    Long number = accounts.get(name);
    return number == null ? 0 : number;
  }
  public void setNum(String name, long number) {
    accounts.put(name, number);
  }
}
```

Select the one correct answer.

(a) `private Map<String, long> accounts = new HashMap<String, long>();`
(b) `private Map<String, Long> accounts = new HashMap<String, Long>();`
(c) `private Map<String<Long>> accounts = new HashMap<String<Long>>();`
(d) `private Map<String, Long> accounts = new Map<String, Long>();`
(e) `private Map accounts = new HashMap();`

14.11 What will be the result of attempting to compile and run the following code?

```
public class RQ100_11 {
  public static void main(String[] args) {
    Set set = new TreeSet<String>();
    set.add("one");
    set.add(2);
    set.add("three");
    System.out.println(set);
  }
}
```

Select the one correct answer.

(a) The program does not compile.
(b) The program compiles with unchecked warnings and prints the elements in the set.

(c) The program compiles without unchecked warnings and prints the elements in the set.

(d) The program compiles with unchecked warnings and throws an exception at runtime.

(e) The program compiles without unchecked warnings and throws an exception at runtime.

14.12 What will be the result of attempting to compile the following code?

```
class Vehicle { }
class Car extends Vehicle { }
class Sedan extends Car { }

class Garage<V> {
  private V v;
  public V get() { return this.v; }
  public void put(V v) { this.v = v; }
}

public class GarageAdmin {

  private Object object = new Object();
  private Vehicle vehicle = new Vehicle();
  private Car car = new Car();
  private Sedan sedan = new Sedan();

  public void doA(Garage g) {
    g.put(object);              // (1)
    g.put(vehicle);             // (2)
    g.put(car);                 // (3)
    g.put(sedan);               // (4)
    object  = g.get();          // (5)
    vehicle = g.get();          // (6)
    car     = g.get();          // (7)
    sedan   = g.get();          // (8)
  }
}
```

Select the two correct answers.

(a) The call to the put() method in statements (1) - (4) will compile.

(b) The assignment statement (5) will compile.

(c) The assignment statements (6), (7), and (8) will compile.

14.13 What will be the result of attempting to compile the following code?

```
class Vehicle { }
class Car extends Vehicle { }
class Sedan extends Car { }

class Garage<V> {
  private V v;
  public V get() { return this.v; }
  public void put(V v) { this.v = v; }
```

```
        }

    public class GarageAdmin {

        private Object object = new Object();
        private Vehicle vehicle = new Vehicle();
        private Car car = new Car();
        private Sedan sedan = new Sedan();

        public void doB(Garage<Car> g) {
            g.put(object);                // (1)
            g.put(vehicle);               // (2)
            g.put(car);                   // (3)
            g.put(sedan);                 // (4)
            object  = g.get();            // (5)
            vehicle = g.get();            // (6)
            car     = g.get();            // (7)
            sedan   = g.get();            // (8)
        }
    }
```

Select the two correct answers.

(a) The call to the put() method in statements (1) - (2) will compile.
(b) The call to the put() method in statements (3) - (4) will compile.
(c) The assignment statements (5), (6) and (7) will compile.
(d) The assignment statement (8) will compile.

14.14   What will be the result of attempting to compile the following code?

```
class Vehicle { }
class Car extends Vehicle { }
class Sedan extends Car { }

class Garage<V> {
    private V v;
    public V get() { return this.v; }
    public void put(V v) { this.v = v; }
}

public class GarageAdmin {

    private Object object = new Object();
    private Vehicle vehicle = new Vehicle();
    private Car car = new Car();
    private Sedan sedan = new Sedan();

    public void doC(Garage<?> g) {
        g.put(object);                  // (1)
        g.put(vehicle);                 // (2)
        g.put(car);                     // (3)
        g.put(sedan);                   // (4)
        object  = g.get();              // (5)
        vehicle = g.get();              // (6)
        car     = g.get();              // (7)
```

```
    sedan   = g.get();         // (8)
  }
}
```

Select the one correct answer.

(a) The call to the put() method in statements (1) - (2) will compile.
(b) The call to the put() method in statements (3) - (4) will compile.
(c) The assignment statement (5) will compile.
(d) The assignment statements (6), (7), and (8) will compile.

14.15 What will be the result of attempting to compile the following code?

```
class Vehicle { }
class Car extends Vehicle { }
class Sedan extends Car { }

class Garage<V> {
  private V v;
  public V get() { return this.v; }
  public void put(V v) { this.v = v; }
}

public class GarageAdmin {

  private Object object = new Object();
  private Vehicle vehicle = new Vehicle();
  private Car car = new Car();
  private Sedan sedan = new Sedan();

  public void doD(Garage<? extends Car> g) {
    g.put(object);             // (1)
    g.put(vehicle);            // (2)
    g.put(car);                // (3)
    g.put(sedan);              // (4)
    object  = g.get();         // (5)
    vehicle = g.get();         // (6)
    car     = g.get();         // (7)
    sedan   = g.get();         // (8)
  }
}
```

Select the one correct answer.

(a) The call to the put() method in statements (1) - (2) will compile.
(b) The call to the put() method in statements (3) - (4) will compile.
(c) The assignment statements (5), (6), and (7) will compile.
(d) The assignment statement (8) will compile.

14.16 What will be the result of attempting to compile the following code?

```
class Vehicle { }
class Car extends Vehicle { }
class Sedan extends Car { }
```

```java
class Garage<V> {
  private V v;
  public V get() { return this.v; }
  public void put(V v) { this.v = v; }
}

public class GarageAdmin {

  private Object object = new Object();
  private Vehicle vehicle = new Vehicle();
  private Car car = new Car();
  private Sedan sedan = new Sedan();

  public void doE(Garage<? super Car> g) {
    g.put(object);            // (1)
    g.put(vehicle);           // (2)
    g.put(car);               // (3)
    g.put(sedan);             // (4)
    object  = g.get();        // (5)
    vehicle = g.get();        // (6)
    car     = g.get();        // (7)
    sedan   = g.get();        // (8)
  }
}
```

Select the two correct answers.

(a) The call to the put() method in statements (1) - (2) will compile.
(b) The call to the put() method in statements (3) - (4) will compile.
(c) The assignment statement (5) will compile.
(d) The assignment statements (6), (7), and (8) will compile.

14.17   Given the following class declaration:

```java
class ClassA<U> implements Comparable<U> {
  public int compareTo(U a) { return 0; }
}
```

Which class declarations below will compile without errors?

Select the three correct answers.

(a) class ClassB<U,V> extends ClassA<R> {}
(b) class ClassC<U,V> extends ClassA<U> {}
(c) class ClassD<U,V> extends ClassA<V, U> {}
(d) class ClassE<U> extends ClassA<Comparable<Number>> {}
(e) class ClassF<U extends Comparable<U> & Serializable> extends ClassA<Number> {}
(f) class ClassG<U implements Comparable<U>> extends ClassA<Number> {}
(g) class ClassH<U extends Comparable<U>> extends ClassA<? extends Number> {}
(h) class ClassI<U extends String & Comparable<U>> extends ClassA<U> {}
(i) class ClassJ<U> extends ClassA<Integer> implements Comparable<Number>{}

14.7 Implementing a Simplified Generic Stack

The Node<E> class from Example 14.2, p. 664, can be used to implement linked data structures. Example 14.7 is an implementation of a simplified generic stack. The emphasis is not on how to develop a full-blown, industrial-strength implementation, but on how to present a simple example in the context of this book in order to become familiar with code that utilizes generics. For thread-safety issues concerning a stack, see the subsection *Waiting and Notifying*, p. 640, in Chapter 13, on threads.

The class MyStack<E> implements the interface IStack<E> shown in Example 14.7, and uses the class Node<E> from Example 14.2. The class NodeIterator<E> in Example 14.7 provides an iterator to traverse linked nodes. The class MyStack<E> is Iterable<E>, meaning we can use the for(:) loop to traverse a stack of this class (see (9) and (12)). It is instructive to study the code to see how type parameters are used in various contexts, how the iterator is implemented, and how we can use the for(:) loop to traverse a stack. For details on the Iterable<E> and Iterator<E> interfaces, see the subsection *Iterators*, p. 785, in Chapter 15.

- -

Example 14.7 *Implementing a Simplified Generic Stack*

```java
import java.util.Iterator;

/** Interface of a generic stack */
public interface IStack<E> extends Iterable<E> {
  void push(E element);            // Add the element to the top of the stack
  E pop();                         // Remove the element at the top of the stack.
  E peek();                        // Get the element at the top of the stack.
  int size();                      // No. of elements on the stack.
  boolean isEmpty();               // Determine if the stack is empty.
  boolean isMember(E element);     // Determine if the element is in the stack.
  E[] toArray(E[] toArray);        // Copy elements from stack to array
  String toString();               // Return suitable string representation of
                                   // elements on the stack: (e1, e2, ..., en)
}
```

```java
import java.util.Iterator;
import java.util.NoSuchElementException;

/** Simplified implementation of a generic stack */
public class MyStack<E> implements IStack<E> {            // (1)
  // Top of stack.
  private Node<E> tos;                                     // (2)
  // Size of stack
  private int numOfElements;                               // (3)

  public boolean isEmpty() { return tos == null; }         // (4)
  public int size() { return numOfElements; }              // (5)

  public void push(E element) {                            // (6)
    tos = new Node<E>(element, tos);
```

```java
      ++numOfElements;
    }

    public E pop() {                                          // (7)
      if (!isEmpty()) {
        E data = tos.getData();
        tos = tos.getNext();
        --numOfElements;
        return data;
      }
      throw new NoSuchElementException("No elements.");
    }

    public E peek()  {                                        // (8)
      if (!isEmpty()) return tos.getData();
      throw new NoSuchElementException("No elements.");
    }
    // Membership
    public boolean isMember(E element) {                      // (9)
      for (E data : this)
        if (data.equals(element))
          return true;      // Found.
      return false;         // Not found.
    }
    // Get iterator.
    public Iterator<E> iterator() {                           // (10)
      return new NodeIterator<E>(this.tos);
    }
    // Copy to array as many elements as possible.
    public E[] toArray(E[] toArray) {                         // (11)
      Node<E> thisNode = tos;
      for (int i = 0; thisNode != null && i < toArray.length; i++) {
        toArray[i] = thisNode.getData();
        thisNode = thisNode.getNext();
      }
      return toArray;
    }
    // String representation: (e1, e2, ..., en).
    public String toString() {                               // (12)
      StringBuilder rep = new StringBuilder("(");
      for (E data : this)
        rep.append(data + ", ");
      if (!isEmpty()) {
        int len = rep.length();
        rep.delete(len - 2, len);
      }
      rep.append(")");
      return rep.toString();
    }
}
```

```java
import java.util.Iterator;

/** Iterator for nodes */
public class NodeIterator<E> implements Iterator<E> {
```

```java
  private Node<E> thisNode;

  public NodeIterator(Node<E> first) { thisNode = first;  }

  public boolean hasNext() { return thisNode != null; }

  public E next() {
    E data = thisNode.getData();
    thisNode = thisNode.getNext();
    return data;
  }

  public void remove() { throw new UnsupportedOperationException(); }
}
```

14.8 Generic Methods and Constructors

We first look at how generic methods and constructors are declared, and then at how they can be called—both with and without explicit actual type parameters.

To facilitate experimenting, the code snippets used in this subsection have been collected in Example 14.8.

Example 14.8 *Declaring and Calling Generic Methods*

```java
public class Utilities {

  // The key and the array element type can be any type.
  static boolean containsV1(Object key, Object[] array) { // (1) Non-generic
                                                          //      version
    for(Object element : array)
      if(key.equals(element)) return true;
    return false;
  }

  // The key and the array element type are the same.
  static <E> boolean containsV2(E key, E[] array) {       // (2) Generic version
    for(E element : array)
      if(key.equals(element)) return true;
    return false;
  }

  // The type of the key is a subtype of the array element type.
  static <E, K extends E> boolean containsV3(K key, E[] array) {
    for(E element : array)
      if(key.equals(element)) return true;
    return false;
  }
```

```java
      public static void main(String[] args) {
        Integer[] intArray = {10, 20, 30};

        // (1) E is Integer.
        // Method signature:       containsV2(Integer, Integer[])
        // Method call signature: containsV2(Integer, Integer[])
        assert Utilities.<Integer>containsV2(20, intArray) == true;

        // (2) E is Number.
        // Method signature:       containsV2(Number, Number[])
        // Method call signature: containsV2(Double, Integer[])
        assert Utilities.<Number>containsV2(30.5, intArray) == false;

        // (3) E is Comparable<Integer>.
        // Method signature:       containsV2(Comparable<Integer>,
        //                                    Comparable<Integer>[])
        // Method call signature: containsV2(Integer, Integer[]).
        assert Utilities.<Comparable<Integer>> containsV2(20, intArray) == true;

        // (4) E is Integer.
        // Method signature:       containsV2(Integer, Integer[])
        // Method call signature: containsV2(Double,  Integer[])
//      assert Utilities.<Integer>containsV2(30.5, intArray) == false;  // Error!

//      assert <Integer>containsV2(20, intArray) == true;     // (5) Syntax error

        // (6) E is inferred to be Integer.
        // Method signature:       containsV2(Integer, Integer[])
        // Method call signature: containsV2(Integer, Integer[])
        assert Utilities.containsV2(20, intArray) == true;

        // (7) E is inferred to be ? extends Number.
        // Method signature:       containsV2(? extends Number, ? extends Number[])
        // Method call signature: containsV2(Double, Integer[])
        assert Utilities.containsV2(30.5, intArray) == false;

        // (8) E is inferred to be ? extends Object.
        // Method signature:       containsV2(? extends Object, ? extends Object[])
        // Method call signature: containsV2(String, Integer[])
        assert Utilities.containsV2("Hi", intArray) == false;

        // Method signature:       containsV2(Integer, Integer[])
        // Method call signature: containsV2(String, Integer[])
//      assert Utilities.<Integer>containsV2("Hi", intArray) == false;// (9) Error!

//      assert Utilities.containsV3("Hi", intArray) == false;        // (10) Error!
//      assert Utilities.containsV3(30.5, intArray) == false;        // (11) Error!

        // (12) E is Number. K is Number. The constraint (K extends E) is satisfied.
        // Method signature:       containsV3(Number, Number[])
        // Method call signature: containsV3(Double, Integer[])
        assert Utilities.<Number, Number>containsV3(30.0, intArray) == false;

        // (13) E is Integer. K is Number.
        // The constraint (K extends E) is not satisfied.
```

```
//   assert Utilities.<Integer, Number>
//   containsV3(30.5, intArray) == false;                   // Compile-time Error!

     // (14) E is Number. K is Integer. The constraint (K extends E) is satisfied.
     // Method signature:      containsV3(Integer, Number[])
     // Method call signature: containsV3(Double, Integer[])
//   assert Utilities.<Number, Integer>
//   containsV3(30.5, intArray) == false;                   // Compile-time Error!

     // (15) Incorrect no. of type parameters.
//   assert Utilities.<Number> containsV3(30.5, intArray) == false;      // Error!
  }
}
```

Generic Method Declaration

A generic method (also called *polymorphic method*) is implemented like an ordinary method, except that one or more formal type parameters are specified immediately preceding the return type. In the case of a generic constructor, the formal parameters are specified before the class name in the constructor header. Much of what applies to generic methods in this regard, also applies to generic constructors.

The method containsV1() at (1) below is a non-generic method to determine the membership of an arbitrary key in an arbitrary array of objects. (We will declare all static generic methods in a class called Utilities, unless otherwise stated.)

```
static boolean containsV1(Object key, Object[] array) { // (1) Non-generic version
  for(Object element : array)
    if(key.equals(element)) return true;
  return false;
}
```

The method declaration at (1) is too general in the sense that it does not express any relationship between the key and the array. This kind of type dependency between parameters can be achieved by using generic methods. The method containsV2() at (2) below is a generic method to determine the membership of a key of type E in an array of type E. The type Object in (1) has been replaced by the type parameter E in (2), with the formal type parameter E being specified before the return type, in the same way as for a generic type.

```
static <E> boolean containsV2(E key, E[] array) {        // (2) Generic version
  for(E element : array)
    if(key.equals(element)) return true;
  return false;
}
```

As with the generic types, a formal type parameter can have a bound, which is a type (i.e., not a type parameter). A formal type parameter can be used in the return type, the formal parameter list, and the method body. It can also be used to specify bounds in the formal type parameter list.

A generic method need not be declared in a generic type. If declared in a generic type, a *generic instance method* can also use the type parameters of the generic type, as any other non-generic instance methods of the generic type. A *generic static method* is only able to use it own type parameters.

Calling Generic Methods

Given the following class declaration:

```
public class Utilities {
  static <E_1,..., E_k> void genericMethod(P_1 p_1,..., P_m p_m) { ... }
  // ...
}
```

Note that in the method declaration above, a type P_i may or may not be from the list of type variables E_1, ..., E_k. We can the call the method in various ways. One main difference from calling a non-generic method is that the actual type parameters can be specified before the method name in the call to a generic method. In the method calls shown below, <A_1,..., A_k> are the actual type parameters and (a_1,..., a_m) are the actual arguments. The specification <A_1,..., A_k> of the actual type parameters, if specified, must be in its entirety. If the specification of the actual type parameters is omitted, then the compiler *infers* the actual type parameters.

The following method calls can occur in any static or non-static context where the class Utilities is accessible:

```
Utilities ref;
ref.<A_1,..., A_k>genericMethod(a_1,..., a_m);
Utilities.<A_1,..., A_k>genericMethod(a_1,..., a_m);
```

The following method calls can only occur in a non-static context of the class Utilities:

```
this.<A_1,..., A_k>genericMethod(a_1,..., a_m);          // Non-static context
super.<A_1,..., A_k>genericMethod(a_1,..., a_m);         // Non-static context
Utilities.super.<A_1,..., A_k>genericMethod(a_1,..., a_m); // Non-static context
```

Another difference from calling non-generic methods is that, if the actual type parameters are explicitly specified, the syntax of a generic *static* method call requires an explicit reference, or the raw type. When the actual type parameters are not explicitly specified, the syntax of a generic method call is similar to that of a non-generic method call.

Here are some examples of calls to the containsV2() method (declared above at (2)) where the actual parameter is specified explicitly. We can see from the method signature and the method call signature that the method can be applied to the arguments in (1), (2), and (3), but not in (4). In (5) we must specify a reference or the class name, because the actual type parameter is specified explicitly.

```
Integer[] intArray = {10, 20, 30};

// (1) E is Integer.
```

```
// Method signature:       containsV2(Integer, Integer[])
// Method call signature: containsV2(Integer, Integer[])
assert Utilities.<Integer>containsV2(20, intArray) == true;

// (2) E is Number.
// Method signature:       containsV2(Number, Number[])
// Method call signature: containsV2(Double, Integer[])
assert Utilities.<Number>containsV2(30.5, intArray) == false;

// (3) E is Comparable<Integer>.
// Method signature:       containsV2(Comparable<Integer>, Comparable<Integer>[])
// Method call signature: containsV2(Integer,          Integer[])
assert Utilities.<Comparable<Integer>> containsV2(20, intArray) == true;

// (4) E is Integer.
// Method signature:       containsV2(Integer, Integer[])
// Method call signature: containsV2(Double,  Integer[])
assert Utilities.<Integer>containsV2(30.5, intArray) == false;  // Error!

assert <Integer>containsV2(20, intArray) == true;              // (5) Syntax error
```

Here are some examples of calls where the compiler infers the actual type parameters from the method call. Since both the key and the element type are Integer, the compiler infers that the actual type parameter is Integer at (6). In (7), where the key type is Double and the element type is Integer, the compiler infers the actual type parameter to be some subtype of Number, i.e., the first common supertype of Double and Integer. In (8), the compiler infers the actual type parameter to be some subtype of Object. In all cases below, the method is applicable to the arguments.

```
// (6) E is inferred to be Integer.
// Method signature:       containsV2(Integer, Integer[])
// Method call signature: containsV2(Integer, Integer[])
assert Utilities.containsV2(20, intArray) == true;

// (7) E is inferred to be ? extends Number.
// Method signature:       containsV2(? extends Number, ? extends Number[])
// Method call signature: containsV2(Double, Integer[])
assert Utilities.containsV2(30.5, intArray) == false;

// (8) E is inferred to be ? extends Object.
// Method signature:       containsV2(? extends Object, ? extends Object[])
// Method call signature: containsV2(String, Integer[])
assert Utilities.containsV2("Hi", intArray) == false;
```

In (8), if we had specified the actual type parameter explicitly to be Integer, the compiler would flag an error:

```
// Method signature:       containsV2(Integer, Integer[])
// Method call signature: containsV2(String, Integer[])
assert Utilities.<Integer>containsV2("Hi", intArray) == false; // (9) Error!
```

We can explicitly specify the key type to be a subtype of the element type by introducing a new formal parameter and a bound on the key type:

```
static <E, K extends E> boolean containsV3(K key, E[] array) {
  for(E element : array)
    if(key.equals(element)) return true;
  return false;
}
```

The following calls at (10) and (11) now result in a compile-time error, as the key type is not a subtype of the element type:

```
assert Utilities.containsV3("Hi", intArray) == false; // (10) Compile-time error!
assert Utilities.containsV3(30.5, intArray) == false; // (11) Compile-time error!
```

The examples below illustrate how constraints come into play in method calls. In (12) the constraint is satisfied and the method signature is applicable to the arguments. In (13) the constraint is not satisfied, therefore the call is rejected. In (14) the constraint is satisfied, but the method signature is not applicable to the arguments. The call in (15) is rejected because the number of actual type parameters specified in the call is incorrect.

```
// (12) E is Number. K is Number. The constraint (K extends E) is satisfied.
// Method signature:      containsV3(Number, Number[])
// Method call signature: containsV3(Double, Integer[])
assert Utilities.<Number, Number>containsV3(30.0, intArray) == false;

// (13) E is Integer. K is Number. The constraint (K extends E) is not satisfied.
assert Utilities.<Integer, Number>
                  containsV3(30.5, intArray) == false;     // Compile-time Error!

// (14) E is Number. K is Integer. The constraint (K extends E) is satisfied.
// Method signature:      containsV3(Integer, Number[])
// Method call signature: containsV3(Double, Integer[])
assert Utilities.<Number, Integer>
                  containsV3(30.5, intArray) == false;     // Compile-time Error!

// (15) Incorrect no. of type parameters.
assert Utilities.<Number> containsV3(30.5, intArray) == false;          // Error!
```

We cannot change the order of the formal type parameters in the formal type parameter specification, as shown below. This is an example of an illegal *forward reference* to a formal type parameter. The type parameter E is used in the constraint (K extends E), but has not yet been declared.

```
static <K extends E, E>                         // Illegal forward reference.
       boolean containsV3(K key, E[] array) { ... }
```

Typically, the dependencies among the parameters of a method and its return type are expressed by formal parameters. Here are some examples:

```
public static <K,V> Map<V,List<K>> toMultiMap(Map<K,V> origMap) { ... }   // (16)
public static <N> Set<N> findVerticesOnPath(Map<N,Collection<N>> graph,
                                  N startVertex)      { ... }   // (17)
```

The method header at (16) expresses the dependency that the map returned by the method has the values of the original map as keys, and its values are lists of keys of the original map, i.e. the method creates a *multimap*. In the method header at

(17), the type parameter N specifies that the element type of the set of vertices to be returned, the type of the keys in the map, the element type of the collections that are values of the map, and the type of the start vertex, are the same.

14.9 Wildcard Capture

As we have seen, a wildcard can represent a family of types. However, the compiler needs to have a more concrete notion of a type than a wildcard in order to do the necessary type checking. Internally, the compiler represents the wildcard by some anonymous, but specific, type. Although this type is unknown, it belongs to the family of types represented by the wildcard. This specific, but unknown, type is called the *capture of* the wildcard.

Compiler messages about erroneous usage of wildcards often refer to the capture of a wildcard. Here are some examples of such error messages, based on compiling the following code:

```
// Filename: WildcardCapture.java
...
Node<?>                  anyNode;                    // (1)
Node<? super Number>     supNumNode;                 // (2)

Node<Integer> intNode = anyNode;                     // (3) Compile-time error!
Node<? extends Number> extNumNode = supNumNode;  // (4) Compile-time error!
anyNode.setData("Trash");                            // (5) Compile-time error!
```

The assignment at (3) results in the following error message:

```
WildcardCapture.java:9: incompatible types
found    : Node<capture#10 of ?>
required: Node<java.lang.Integer>
    Node<Integer> intNode = anyNode;                 // (3) Compile-time error!
                            ^
```

The type of the reference anyNode is Node<capture#10 of ?>. The string "capture#10 of ?" is the designation used by the compiler for the type capture of the wildcard (?) at (3). The number 10 in "capture#10 of ?" distinguishes it from the type capture of any other occurrences of wildcards in the statement. The type of the reference intNode is Node<Integer>. The reference value of a Node<capture#10 of ?> cannot be assigned to a Node<Integer> reference. Whatever the type capture of the wildcard is, it cannot be guaranteed to be Integer, and the assignment is rejected. To put it another way, the assignment involves a narrowing reference conversion, requiring an explicit cast which is not provided: Node<?> is the supertype of all invocations of the generic class Node<E>.

The error message below for the assignment at (4) shows the type capture of the lower bounded wildcard at (4) to be "capture#311 of ? super java.lang.Number". Figure 14.5, p. 678, also shows that the Node<capture#311 of ? super java.lang.Number> and Node<? extends java.lang.Number> types are unrelated.

```
WildcardCapture.java:10: incompatible types
found   : Node<capture#311 of ? super java.lang.Number>
required: Node<? extends java.lang.Number>
    Node<? extends Number> extNumNode = supNumNode; // (4) Compile-time error!
                                        ^
```

The method call at (5) results in the following error message:

```
WildcardCapture.java:11: setData(capture#351 of ?) in Node<capture#351 of ?>
cannot be applied to (java.lang.String)
    anyNode.setData("Trash");                       // (5) Compile-time error!
            ^
```

The type of the reference anyNode is Node<capture#351 of ?> and the type of the formal parameter in the method declaration is "capture#351 of ?". The type of the actual parameter in the method call is String, which is not compatible with "capture#351 of ?". The call is not allowed. As we have seen earlier, with a <?> reference we cannot put anything into a data structure.

If we have the following method in the class MyStack:

```
public static <T> void move(MyStack<? super T> dstStack,
                            MyStack<? extends T> srcStack) {
  while (!srcStack.isEmpty())
    dstStack.push(srcStack.pop());
}
```

and we try to compile the following client code:

```
MyStack<?> anyStack;
MyStack.move(anyStack, anyStack);   // Compile-time error!
```

the compiler issues the following error message:

```
MyStackUser.java:67: <T>move(MyStack<? super T>,MyStack<? extends T>) in MyStack
cannot be applied to (MyStack<capture#774 of ?>,MyStack<capture#371 of ?>)
      MyStack.move(anyStack, anyStack);     // Compile-time error!
              ^
```

The error message shows that each occurrence of a wildcard in a statement is represented by a distinct type capture. We see that the signature of the move() method is move(MyStack<? super T>, MyStack<? extends T>). The type of the reference anyStack is MyStack<?>. The static types of the two arguments in the method call are MyStack<capture#774 of ?> and MyStack<capture#371 of ?>. The numbers in the type capture names differentiate between the type captures of different wildcard occurrences. The signature of the argument list is (MyStack<capture#774 of ?>, MyStack<capture#371 of ?>). The type parameter T cannot be inferred from the types of the arguments, as the stacks are considered to be of two different types and, therefore, the call is rejected.

Capture Conversion

Consider the following non-generic method which does not compile:

```
static void fillWithFirstV1(List<?> list) {
  Object firstElement = list.get(0);        // (1)
  for (int i = 1; i < list.size(); i++)
    list.set(i, firstElement);               // (2) Compile-time error
}
```

The method should fill any list passed as argument with the element in its first position. The call to the set() method is not permitted, as a *set* operation is not possible with a <?> reference (see Table 14.3, p. 684). Using the wildcard ? to parameterize the list does not work. We can replace the wild card with a type parameter of a generic method, as follows:

```
static <E> void fillWithFirstOne(List<E> list) {
  E firstElement = list.get(0);            // (3)
  for (int i = 1; i < list.size(); i++)
    list.set(i, firstElement);             // (4)
}
```

Since the type of the argument is List<E>, we can set and get objects of type E from the list. We have also changed the type of the reference firstElement from Object to E in order to set the first element in the list.

It turns out that if the first method fillWithFirstV1() is re-implemented with a call to the generic method fillWithFirstOne(). It all works well:

```
static void fillWithFirstV2(List<?> list) {
  fillWithFirstOne(list);                  // (5) Type conversion
}
```

The wildcard in the argument of the fillWithFirstV1() has a type capture. In the call to the fillWithFirstOne() method at (5), this type capture is converted to the type E. This conversion is called *capture conversion*, and it comes into play under certain conditions, which are beyond the scope of this book.

14.10 Flexibility with Wildcard Parameterized Types

Nested Wildcards

We have seen that the subtype relationship is invariant for the unbounded type parameter <T>:

```
Collection<Number> colNum;
Set<Number> setNum;
Set<Integer> setInt;
colNum = setNum; // (1) Set<Number> <: Collection<Number>
colNum = setInt; // (2) Compile-time error!
```

The same is true when concrete parameterized types are used as actual type parameters, implementing what are called *nested parameterized types*, i.e., using parameterized types as type parameters.

```
Collection<Collection<Number>> colColNum; // Collection of Collections of Number
Set<Collection<Number>>        setColNum; // Set of Collections of Number
Set<Set<Integer>>              setSetInt; // Set of Sets of Integer
colColNum = setColNum;                    // (3) Set<Collection<Number>> <:
                                          //     Collection<Collection<Number>>
colColNum = setSetInt;                    // (4) Compile-time error!
setColNum = setSetInt;                    // (5) Compile-time error!
```

Again, we can use the upper bounded wildcard to induce subtype covariance. The upper bounded wildcard is applied at the *top level* in the code below. The assignment below at (8) is not compatible, because Set<Set<Integer>> is *not* a subtype of Collection<? extends Collection<Number>>.

```
Collection<? extends Collection<Number>> colExtColNum;
colExtColNum = colColNum;        // (6) Collection<Collection<Number>> <:
                                 //     Collection<? extends Collection<Number>>
colExtColNum = setColNum;        // (7) Set<Collection<Number>> <:
                                 //     Collection<? extends Collection<Number>>
colExtColNum = setSetInt;        // (8) Compile-time error!
```

In the code below, the wildcard is applied at the *inner-most* level:

```
Collection<Collection<? extends Number>> colColExtNum;
colColExtNum = colColNum;        // (9)  Compile-time error!
colColExtNum = setColNum;        // (10) Compile-time error!
colColExtNum = setSetInt;        // (11) Compile-time error!
```

The assignments above show that the upper bounded wildcard induces subtype covariance *only* at the top level. In (9), type A (=Collection<Number>) is a subtype of type B (=Collection<? extends Number>), but because subtype covariance relationship does not hold between parameterized types, the type Collection<A> (=Collection<Collection<Number>>) is *not* a subtype of Collection<B> (= Collection<Collection<? extends Number>>).

The above discussion also applies when a parameterized type has more than one type parameter:

```
Map<Number, String>  mapNumStr;
Map<Integer, String> mapIntStr;
mapNumStr = mapIntStr;              // (12) Compile-time error!
```

Again, the upper bounded wildcard can only be used at the top level to induce subtype covariance:

```
Map<Integer, ? extends Collection<String>> mapIntExtColStr;
Map<Integer, Collection<? extends String>> mapIntColExtStr;
Map<Integer, Collection<String>>           mapIntColStr;
Map<Integer, Set<String>>                  mapIntSetStr;
mapIntExtColStr = mapIntColStr;// (13) Map<Integer, Collection<String>> <:
                               //      Map<Integer, ? extends Collection<String>>
mapIntExtColStr = mapIntSetStr;// (14) Map<Integer, Set<String>> <:
                               //      Map<Integer, ? extends Collection<String>>
```

```
mapIntColStr    = mapIntSetStr;    // (15) Compile-time error!
mapIntColExtStr = mapIntColStr;    // (16) Compile-time error!
mapIntColExtStr = mapIntSetStr;    // (17) Compile-time error!
```

Wildcard Parameterized Types as Formal Parameters

We now examine the implications of using wildcard parameterized types as formal parameters of a method.

We want to add a method in the class MyStack<E> (Example 14.7, p. 695) for moving the elements of a source stack to the current stack. Here are three attempts at implementing such a method for the class MyStack<E>:

```
public void moveFromV1(MyStack<E> srcStack) {            // (1)
  while (!srcStack.isEmpty())
    this.push(srcStack.pop());
}

public void moveFromV2(MyStack<? extends E> srcStack) {  // (2)
  while (!srcStack.isEmpty())
    this.push(srcStack.pop());
}

public void moveFromV3(MyStack<? super E> srcStack) {    // (3) Compile-time error!
  while (!srcStack.isEmpty())
    this.push(srcStack.pop());
}
```

Given the following three stacks:

```
MyStack<Number> numStack   = new MyStack<Number>();           // Stack of Number
numStack.push(5.5); numStack.push(10.5); numStack.push(20.5);
MyStack<Integer> intStack1 = new MyStack<Integer>();          // Stack of Integer
intStack1.push(5); intStack1.push(10); intStack1.push(20);
MyStack<Integer> intStack2 = new MyStack<Integer>();          // Stack of Integer
intStack2.push(15); intStack2.push(25); intStack2.push(35);
```

we can only move elements between stacks of the same type with the method at (1):

```
intStack1.moveFromV1(intStack2);
numStack.moveFromV1(intStack2);  // Compile-time error!
```

The compile-time error above is due to the fact that MyStack<Integer> is not a subtype of MyStack<Number>. However, we can move elements from a stack of type MyStack<? extends E> to the current stack using the method at (2). This is possible because a reference of a type MyStack<? extends E> can refer to a stack with objects of type E or its subclass and the *get* operation (i.e., the pop() method) is permissible, returning an object which has an actual type bounded by the upper bound E. The returned object can always be put into a stack of type E or its supertype.

```
intStack1.moveFromV2(intStack2);
numStack.moveFromV2(intStack2);
```

The method at (3) will only allow Objects to be popped from a stack of type MyStack<? super E>, which could only be pushed onto a stack of type Object. Since E cannot be

determined at compile time, the push() operation on the current stack is not permitted. Of the first two methods, the method at (2) is more flexible in permitting the widest range of calls.

Similarly, we can add a method in the class MyStack<E> for moving the elements of
the current stack to a destination stack:

```
public void moveToV1(MyStack<E> dstStack) {                       // (3)
  while (!this.isEmpty())
    dstStack.push(this.pop());
}

public void moveToV2(MyStack<? extends E> dstStack) {      // (4)
  while (!this.isEmpty())
    dstStack.push(this.pop());          // Compile-time error!
}

public void moveToV3(MyStack<? super E> dstStack) {        // (5)
  while (!this.isEmpty())
    dstStack.push(this.pop());
}
```

In the method at (4), the reference of type MyStack<? extends E> does not allow any *set*
operations (in this case, the push() method) on the destination stack. The method at
(5) provides the most flexible solution, as a reference of type MyStack<? super E> permits *set* operations for objects of type E or its subtypes:

```
        intStack1.moveToV1(intStack2);
        intStack1.moveToV1(numStack);       // Compile-time error!

        intStack1.moveToV3(intStack2);
        intStack1.moveToV3(numStack);
```

Based on the discussion above, we can write a *generic method* for moving elements
from a source stack to a destination stack. The following method signature is preferable, where objects of type E or its subtypes can be popped from the source stack
and pushed onto a destination stack of type E or its supertype:

```
public static <T> void move(MyStack<? super T> dstStack,  // (6)
                            MyStack<? extends T> srcStack) {
  while (!srcStack.isEmpty())
    dstStack.push(srcStack.pop());
}

// Client code
MyStack.move(intStack2, intStack1);
MyStack.move(numStack, intStack1);
MyStack.move(intStack2, numStack);       // Compile-time error!
```

It is a common idiom to use wildcards as shown above in the method at (6), as the
upper bounded wildcard (? extends Type) can be used to *get* objects from a data structure, and the lower bounded wildcard (? super Type) can be used to *set* objects in a
data structure. Using wildcards in the method signature can increase the utility of a
method, especially when explicit type parameters are specified in the method call.

Flexible Comparisons with Wildcards

Another common idiom in programming with generics is using the `Comparable<T>` interface as a bound and parameterizing it with the lower bounded wildcard (`? super T`) to allow for greater flexibility in doing comparisons. In the following two method declarations, the `Comparable<T>` interface is used as a bound, but parameterized differently:

```
static <T extends Comparable<T>>        T max     (T obj1, T obj2) { ... } // (1)
static <T extends Comparable<? super T>> T superMax(T obj1, T obj2) { ... } // (2)
```

The two methods are declared at (1) and (2) in Example 14.9, and can be used to find the maximum of two objects that are comparable. Both methods are applied to objects of subclasses of two different superclasses (see Figure 14.6). The superclass `ProgrammerCMP` implements the `Comparable<ProgrammerCMP>` interface, which is inherited by its subclasses `JProgrammerCMP` and `CProgrammerCMP`. The implication being that the objects of *different subclasses* can also be compared with each other. However, the superclass `Programmer` leaves the implementation of the `Comparable<E>` interface to its subclasses `JProgrammer` and `CProgrammer`. The implication in this case being that the objects of different subclasses *cannot* be compared with one another.

Figure 14.6 *Flexible Comparisons with Wildcards*

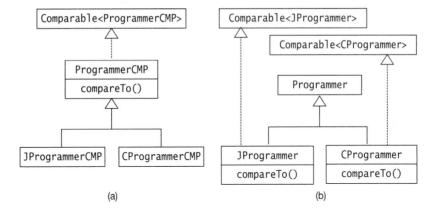

The important thing to note in Example 14.9 is that the method `max()` does *not* allow objects of a subclass to be compared with one another, when no explicit type parameter is specified in the method call. For example, we cannot compare two `JProgrammerCMP`s as shown at (4), because they are *not* `Comparable<JProgrammerCMP>`. They are `Comparable<ProgrammerCMP>`, which is not the same thing. If the actual type parameter is *explicitly* specified as `ProgrammerCMP`, as shown at (5), the comparison is permitted.

```
jProgCMP = max(jProgCMP, jProgCMP);            // (4) Compile-time Error!
progCMP = WhoIsComparble.<ProgrammerCMP>max(jProgCMP, jProgCMP); // (5)
```

If the superMax() method with the lower bounded wildcard (? super T) is used, the situation above does not arise. The constraint is Comparable<? super JProgrammerCMP>, and Comparable<ProgrammerCMP> is a subtype of Comparable<? super JProgrammerCMP>. Since the subclass JProgrammerCMP is a subtype of Comparable<ProgrammerCMP>, the subclass satisfies the constraint and its objects can be compared. In all other respects the two methods are equivalent, but the superMax() method is preferable.

Similarly, the Comparator used by the following method can be parameterized with the lower bounded wildcard for greater flexibility:

```
public static <T> T max(T obj1, T obj2, Comparator<? super T> comp) {  // (3)
  return (comp.compare(obj1, obj2) < 0) ? obj2 : obj1;
}
```

Example 14.9   *Flexible Comparisons*

```
import java.util.Collection;
import java.util.Collections;
import java.util.Comparator;

/** Comparison in superclass */
abstract class ProgrammerCMP implements Comparable<ProgrammerCMP> {
  protected String name;
  protected int loc;        // Lines of code
  ProgrammerCMP(String name, int loc) {
    this.name = name; this.loc = loc;
  }
  public int compareTo(ProgrammerCMP that) {
    return this.loc < that.loc ? - 1 :
      this.loc == that.loc ? 0 : 1 ;
  }
}
class JProgrammerCMP extends ProgrammerCMP {
  JProgrammerCMP (int loc) { super("JProgrammerCMP", loc); }
}
class CProgrammerCMP extends ProgrammerCMP {
  CProgrammerCMP (int loc) { super("CProgrammerCMP", loc); }
}

/** Comparison in subclasses */
abstract class Programmer {
  protected String name;
  protected int loc;        // Lines of code
  Programmer(String name, int loc) { this.name = name; this.loc = loc; }
}
class JProgrammer extends Programmer implements Comparable<JProgrammer>{
  JProgrammer (int loc) { super("JProgrammer", loc); }
  public int compareTo(JProgrammer that) {
    return this.loc < that.loc ? - 1 : this.loc == that.loc ? 0 : 1 ;
  }
}
class CProgrammer extends Programmer implements Comparable<CProgrammer> {
  CProgrammer (int loc) { super("CProgrammer", loc); }
```

```java
    public int compareTo(CProgrammer that) {
      return this.loc < that.loc ? - 1 : this.loc == that.loc ? 0 : 1 ;
    }
  }

  /** Tests generic methods */
  public class WhoIsComparable {
    public static <T extends Comparable<T>> T max(T obj1, T obj2) {    // (1)
      return (obj1.compareTo(obj2) < 0) ? obj2 : obj1;
    }
    public static <T extends Comparable<? super T>> T              // (2)
      superMax(T obj1, T obj2) {
      return (obj1.compareTo(obj2) < 0) ? obj2 : obj1;
    }
    public static <T> T
      max(T obj1, T obj2, Comparator<? super T> comp) {            // (3)
      return (comp.compare(obj1, obj2) < 0) ? obj2 : obj1;
    }

    public static void main(String[] args) {
      JProgrammerCMP jProgCMP = new JProgrammerCMP(1000);
      CProgrammerCMP cProgCMP = new CProgrammerCMP(50);
      JProgrammer jProg = new JProgrammer(1000);
      CProgrammer cProg = new CProgrammer(50);

      ProgrammerCMP  progCMP;
      Programmer  prog;

      /* Using <T extends Comparable<T>> T max(T, T) method */
      // Comparison in superclass
      jProgCMP = max(jProgCMP, jProgCMP);            // (4) Compile-time Error!
      progCMP = WhoIsComparable.<ProgrammerCMP>max(jProgCMP, jProgCMP); // (5)
      progCMP = max(jProgCMP, cProgCMP);
      // Comparison in subclasses
      jProg = max(jProg, jProg);
      jProg = WhoIsComparable.<JProgrammer>max(jProg, jProg);
      prog = max(jProg, cProg);                      // Expected error.

      /* Using <T extends Comparable<? super T>> T superMax(T, T) method */
      // Comparison in superclass
      jProgCMP = superMax(jProgCMP, jProgCMP);       // (6)
      progCMP = WhoIsComparable.<ProgrammerCMP>superMax(jProgCMP, jProgCMP);
      progCMP = superMax(jProgCMP, cProgCMP);
      // Comparison in subclasses
      jProg = superMax(jProg, jProg);
      jProg = WhoIsComparable.<JProgrammer>superMax(jProg, jProg);
      prog = superMax(jProg, cProg);                 // Expected error.
    }
  }
```

Recursive Bounds

The classes MonoNode and BiNode are declared in Example 14.3, p. 667, and Example 14.4, p. 669, respectively:

```
class MonoNode<E> implements IMonoLink<E> {
  private E              data;    // Data
  private IMonoLink<E>   next;    // Reference to next node     // (1)
  // ...
}

class BiNode<E> extends MonoNode<E> implements IBiLink<E> {
  private IBiLink<E> previous;    // Reference to previous node  // (2)
  // ...
}
```

Note that the next field has the type IMonoLink<E>, but the previous field has the type IBiLink<E>. This means that when traversing a linked structure constructed from nodes that implement the IBiLink<E> interface, we have to be careful. The method traverseBinTree() below traverses a binary tree constructed from such nodes. The method prints the data in the nodes. Note that it is necessary to cast the reference value returned by the getNext() method, as shown at (3).

```
public static <T> void traverseBinTree(IBiLink<T> root) {
  if (root.getPrevious() != null)
    traverseBinTree(root.getPrevious());
  System.out.print(root.getData() + ", ");
  if (root.getNext() != null)
    traverseBinTree((IBiLink<T>)root.getNext());  // (3) Cast necessary.
}
```

Example 14.10 declares a class called RecNode. The header of this class at (1) is declared as follows:

```
abstract class RecNode<E, T extends RecNode<E, T>>
```

The class specifies two type parameters: E and T. The type parameter E stands for the type of the data in the node, (2). The type parameter T stands for the type of the next field in the node, (3). It has the bound RecNode<E, T>, meaning that T must be a subtype of the bound, i.e., of RecNode<E, T>. In other words, the class RecNode can only be parameterized by its subclasses. The two parameters E and T are used in the class for their respective purposes.

. . . .

Example 14.10 *Using Recursive Bounds*

```
abstract class RecNode<E, T extends RecNode<E, T>> {      // (1)
  private E data;                                         // (2)
  private T next;                                         // (3)

  RecNode(E data, T next) {
    this.data = data;
    this.next = next;
```

```
        }
        public void setData(E obj)  { data = obj; }
        public E    getData()       { return data; }
        public void setNext(T next) { this.next = next; }
        public T getNext()          { return next; }
        public String toString() {
          return this.data + (this.next == null ? "" : ", " + this.next);
        }
    }


    final class RecBiNode<E> extends RecNode<E, RecBiNode<E>> {            // (4)

      private RecBiNode<E>  previous;     // Reference to previous node   // (5)

      RecBiNode(E data, RecBiNode<E> next, RecBiNode<E> previous) {
        super(data, next);
        this.previous = previous;
      }
      public void setPrevious(RecBiNode<E> previous) { this.previous = previous; }
      public RecBiNode<E> getPrevious()              { return this.previous; }
      public String toString() {
        return (this.previous == null? "" : this.previous + ", ") +
        this.getData() +
       (this.getNext() == null? "" : ", " + this.getNext());
      }
    }
```

Example 14.10 declares another class called RecBiNode. The header of this class at (4) is declared as follows:

```
    final class RecBiNode<E> extends RecNode<E, RecBiNode<E>>
```

Note that the class has only one type parameter, E, that represents the data type in the node. The class extends the RecNode class, which is parameterized with the data type E and the type RecBiNode<E> to represent the type of the next field in the super-class RecNode. The class RecBiNode also declares a previous field of type RecBiNode<E> at (5), and the corresponding get and set methods. The upshot of this class declaration is that, for a node of type RecBiNode<E>, both the next and the previous fields have the same type as a node of this class. The traversal method can now be written without using any casts, passing it a node of the subtype RecBiNode<E>:

```
    public static <T> void traverseBinTree(RecBiNode<T> root) {      // (2)
      if (root.getPrevious() != null)
        traverseBinTree(root.getPrevious());
      System.out.print(root.getData() + ", ");
      if (root.getNext() != null)
        traverseBinTree(root.getNext());                     // No cast necessary!
    }
```

The class declaration at (1) in Example 14.10 uses what is called a *recursive bound* in its constraint T extends RecNode<E,T>. New subtypes of the class RecNode can be implemented using this idiom, and the type of the next field will be the same as the subtype.

Earlier in this chapter we saw the constraint T extends Comparable<T>, which is also a recursive bound. Another example of recursive bounds is the declaration of the Enum<E extends Enum<E>> class in the Java Standard Library.

14.11 Type Erasure

Understanding translation by type erasure helps to understand the restrictions and limitations that arise when using generics in Java. Although the compiler generates generic-free byte code, we can view the process as a source-to-source translation that generates non-generic code from generic code.

The translated code has no information about type parameters, i.e., the type parameters have been *erased*—hence the term, *type erasure*. This involves replacing the usage of the type parameters with concrete types and inserting suitable type conversions to ensure type correctness. In certain situations, bridge methods are also inserted for backward compatibility.

The process of determining the *erasure* of a type, i.e., what a type in the source code should be replaced with, uses the following rules:

1. Drop all type parameter specifications from parameterized types.
2. Replace any type parameter as follows:

   a. Replace it with the erasure of its bound, if it has one.

   b. Replace it with Object, if it has none.

   c. Replace it with the erasure of the *first* bound, if it has multiple bounds.

Table 14.4 shows examples of translation by erasure for some representative types, and the rules that are applied.

Table 14.4   *Examples of Type Erasure*

Type	Erasure	Rule no.
List<E> List<Integer> List<String> List<List<String>> List<? super Integer> List<? extends Number>	List	1
List<Integer>[]	List[]	1
List	List	1
int	int	For any primitive type
Integer	Integer	For any non-generic type

(continues)

Table 14.4 *Examples of Type Erasure (continued)*

Type	Erasure	Rule no.

class Subclass
  extends Superclass
  implements
  Comparable<Subclass> {...}
	class Subclass
	  extends Superclass
	  implements
	  Comparable {...}
		1

public static
  <T extends Comparable<? super T>>
  T
  max(T obj1,
    T obj2)
  { ... }
	public static
	
	  Comparable
	  max(Comparable obj1,
	    Comparable obj2)
	  { ... }
		2a. The first bound is Comparable.

public static <T> T
  doIt(T t)
  { T lv = t; }
	public static Object
	  doIt(Object t)
	  { Object lv = t; }
		2b

T extends MyClass &
  Comparable<T> &
  Serializable
	MyClass	2c. The first bound is MyClass.

The following code mixes legacy and generic code. Note that a ClassCastException is expected at (5) because the type-safety of the stack of String has been compromised.

```
// Pre-erasure code
List<String> strList = new ArrayList<String>(); // (0)
List list = strList;        // (1) Assignment to non-generic reference is ok.
strList = list;             // (2) warning: unchecked conversion
strList.add("aha");         // (3) Method call type-safe.
list.add(23);               // (4) warning: [unchecked] unchecked call to add(E)
                            //     as a member of the raw type java.util.List
System.out.println(strList.get(1).length());  // (5) ClassCastException
```

It is instructive to compare the corresponding lines of code in the pre-erasure code above and the post-erasure results shown below. A cast is inserted to convert from Object type to String type in (5'). This is necessary because post-erasure code can only get an Object from the list, and in order to call the length() method, the reference value of this object must be converted to String. It is this cast that is the cause of the exception at runtime.

```
// Post-erasure code
List strList = new ArrayList();                              // (0')
List list = strList;                                         // (1')
strList = list;                                              // (2')
strList.add("aha");                                          // (3')
list.add(Integer.valueOf(23));                               // (4')
System.out.println(((String)strList.get(1)).length()); // (5')
```

Bridge Methods

Bridge methods are inserted in subclasses by the compiler to ensure that overriding of method works correctly. The canonical example is the implementation of the Comparable interface. The post-erasure code of the class CmpNode<E> from Section 14.6 on page 684 is shown below. A second compareTo() method has been inserted by the compiler at (2), whose method signature is compareTo(Object). This is necessary because, without this method, the class would not implement the Comparable interface, as the compareTo() method of the interface would not be overridden correctly.

```
class CmpNode extends Node implements Comparable {
  CmpNode(Object data, CmpNode next) {
    super(data, next);
  }
  public int compareTo(CmpNode node2) {        // (1)
    return this.getData().compareTo(node2.getData());
  }
  public int compareTo(Object node2) {         // (2)
    return this.compareTo((CmpNode)node2);     // Calls the method at (1).
  }
}
```

Such a bridge method cannot be invoked in the source code, and is provided for backward compatibility with legacy code. There are Java decompilers readily available that can be used to examine the code generated by the compiler.

14.12 Implications for Overloading and Overriding

Method Signature

Method signatures play a crucial role in overloading and overriding of methods. The method signature comprises the method name and the formal parameter list. Two methods (or constructors) have the *same signature* if both of the following conditions are fulfilled:

- they have the *same name*
- they have the *same formal parameter types*

Two methods (or constructors) have the *same formal parameter types* if both of the following conditions are fulfilled:

- they have the *same number* of *formal parameters* and *type parameters*
- the formal parameters and the bounds of the type parameters are the same after the occurrences of formal parameters in one are substituted with the corresponding types from the second.

The signature of a method m() is a *subsignature* of the signature of another method n(), if either one of these two conditions hold:

- Method n() has the *same* signature as method m(), or
- The signature of method m() is the same as the *erasure* of the signature of method n().

The signatures of the two methods m() and n() are *override-equivalent* if either one of these two conditions hold:

- The signature of method m() is a subsignature of the signature of method n(), or
- The signature of method n() is a subsignature of the signature of method m().

Implications for Overloading

Given the definitions above, we can now state that two methods are *overloaded* if they have the same name, but their signatures are *not override-equivalent*. Given the following three generic method declarations in a class:

```
static <T> void merge (MyStack<T> s1, MyStack<T> s2) { /*...*/ }
static <T> void merge (MyStack<T> s1, MyStack<? extends T> s2) { /*...*/ }
static <T> void merge (MyStack<T> s1, MyStack<? super T> s2) { /*...*/ }
```

After erasure, the signature of all three methods is:

```
merge(MyStack, MyStack)
```

i.e., the signatures of the methods are override-equivalent, hence these methods are *not* overloaded. A class cannot contain two methods with override-equivalent signatures, and the compiler will report an error.

These three methods:

```
static <T> void merge (Node<T> s1, MyStack<T> s2)               { /*...*/ }
static <T> void merge (MyStack<T> s1, MyStack<? extends T> s2) { /*...*/ }
static <T> void merge (MyStack<T> s1, Node<? super T> s2)       { /*...*/ }
```

have the following signatures after erasure, respectively:

```
merge (Node, MyStack)
merge (MyStack, MyStack)
merge (MyStack, Node)
```

We can see that no two signatures are override-equivalent. Therefore, the three methods are overloaded.

The declaration of the class Sup below shows some variations on the method signature. The resulting signature of the method header (which includes the method signature) is shown after erasure in the comment corresponding to the method.

```
class Sup<T> {
  void doIt(boolean b) { }                         // (1) void doIt(boolean)

  void doIt(T t) { }                               // (2) void doIt(Object)

  List<StringBuilder> doIt(StringBuilder sb) {     // (3) List doIt(StringBuilder)
    return null;
  }
```

```
<E extends Comparable<E>> void doIt(E element)  // (4) void doIt(Comparable)
  { }

<E> E doIt(MyStack<? extends E> stack) {          // (5) Object doIt(MyStack)
  return null;
}
}
```

Adding any of the following method declarations to the class Sup would be an error, as each one of these method declarations has a method signature that is the same as one of the methods already in the class, i.e., the signatures are override-equivalent.

```
void doIt(Object obj) { }                         // (2') void doIt(Object)

<E extends StringBuilder> List<E> doIt(E sb) {    // (3') List doIt(StringBuilder)
  return null;
}

void doIt(Comparable<T> element) { }              // (4') void doIt(Comparable)

<E> E doIt(MyStack<? super E> stack) {            // (5') Object doIt(MyStack)
  return null;
}
```

Implications for Overriding

The following conditions should be satisfied in order for a subtype method to override a supertype method:

- The signature of the subtype method is a *subsignature* of the signature of the supertype method (which is discussed in this subsection)
- Their *return types* should be compatible (Section 7.2, p. 288)
- Their throws *clauses* should be compatible (Section 6.9, p. 259)

Here we discuss the implication of method signatures for overriding.

The @Override Annotation

We can solicit the aid of the compiler to ensure that a method declaration overrides an inherited method correctly. If a method declaration is preceded by the annotation @Override, the compiler will issue an error if the method does not override an inherited method.

Example 14.11 illustrates the use of this annotation. The intention in the class Cmp-Node is to override the equals() method from the Object class and the compareTo() method from the Comparable interface. The error messages alert us to the fact that the annotated methods do not override any inherited methods. The method signatures are not subsignatures of any method signatures that are inherited. The formal parameters are not correct for overriding in (1) and (2). They should be as shown at (1') and (2').

Example 14.11 *Using the* @Override *Annotation*

```
class CmpNode<E extends Comparable<E>>
                extends Node<E> implements Comparable<CmpNode<E>> {

  CmpNode(E data, CmpNode<E> next) {
    super(data, next);
  }

  @Override
  public boolean equals(CmpNode node2) {          // (1) Compile-time error.
//public boolean equals(Object node2) {           // (1') Correct header.
    return this.compareTo(node2) == 0;
  }

  @Override
  public int compareTo(Object node2) {            // (2) Compile-time error.
//public int compareTo(CmpNode<E> node2) {        // (2') Correct header
    return this.getData().compareTo(node2.getData());
  }
}
```

Compiling the class CmpNode:

```
>javac CmpNode.java
...
CmpNode.java:8: method does not override or implement a method from a supertype
  @Override
  ^
...
CmpNode.java:14: method does not override or implement a method from a supertype
  @Override
  ^
```

Non-Generic Method in Non-Generic Subtype Overrides Method in Non-Generic Supertype

In Example 14.12, the signature at (1') is the same as the signature at (1): set(Integer). The signature at (2') is the same as the *erasure* of the signature at (2): set(List). The method at (2') shows a non-generic subtype method overriding a supertype method that uses generics. This is needed for legacy code: *legacy supertypes* can be generified without it having consequences for any subtypes, as the signature of a subtype method that overrides a supertype method will be the same as the erasure of the signature of this supertype method.

Example 14.12 *Subsignatures*

```
class SupA {
  public void set(Integer ref) {/*...*/}          // (1)
  public void set(List<Integer> list) {/*...*/}   // (2)
}

class SubA extends SupA {
  @Override
  public void set(Integer iRef) {/*...*/} // (1') same as at (1)
  @Override
  public void set(List list) {/*...*/}     // (2') same as the erasure at (2)
}
```

Non-Generic Method in Non-Generic Subtype Overrides Method in Generic Supertype

In Example 14.13, both the subclasses SubB1 and SubB2 are subtypes of the concrete supertype SupB<Number>, i.e., T is Number in SupB<T>. The signatures of the methods in SubB1 are the same as the signatures of the methods in SupB, therefore, the methods are overridden. After erasure, the methods in SupB are equivalent to:

```
public void set(Object t) {/*...*/}       // (1)
public Object get() {return null;}        // (2)
```

The compiler adds the following bridge method in SubB1 in order for overriding to work properly at runtime:

```
public void set(Object t) {set((Number)t);}       // (1')
```

It does not add a bridge method for the get() method in SubB1, because of covariant return: the return type Number for the method get() in SubB1 is a subtype of the return type Object of the method get() in SupB.

Example 14.13 *Overriding from Generic Supertype*

```
class SupB<T> {
  public void set(T t) {/*...*/}         // (1)
  public T get() {return null;}          // (2)
}

class SubB1 extends SupB<Number> {
  @Override
  public void set(Number num) {/*...*/} // (1a) Overrides
  @Override
  public Number get() {return 0;}       // (2a) Overrides
}

class SubB2 extends SupB<Number> {
  public void set(Object obj) {/*...*/} // (1b) Error: same erasure
```

```
        public void set(Long l) {/*...*/}      // (1c) Overloads

        public Object get() {return 0;}        // (2b) Error: incompatible return type
      }
```

We now examine the methods in SubB2. The set() method at (1b) has the *same eras-ure* as the set() method at (1) in the supertype SupB. If overriding were allowed, the bridge method added would result in *two* methods with the same signature set(Object) in SubB2. Two methods with the same signature are not permitted in the same class—called a *name clash*, therefore (1b) is not allowed.

The method set() at (1c) is overloaded because its signature is different from the other set() methods in SubB2 and SupB. The method get() at (2b) has the return type Object, while the get() method in SupB<Number> has the return type Number. The return types are not covariant, and (2b) is rejected.

Example 14.14 shows a typical error where a generic supertype is extended, but its parameterization is missing in the extends clause of the subtype, as shown at (2). The set() method in SubZ neither overrides nor overloads the method at (1). Both methods have the same signature after erasure: set(Object). Adding a bridge method in SubZ would result in a name clash. (1a) is rejected.

Example 14.14 *Missing Supertype Parameterization*

```
      class SupZ<T> {
        public void set(T t) {/*...*/}  // (1)
      }

      class SubZ<E> extends SupZ {      // (2) Supertype not parameterized
        public void set(E e) {/*...*/}  // (1a) Error: same erasure
      }
```

Genericity and Inherited Methods

The subsignature requirement for overriding means that the signature of the sub-type method must either be the *same* as that of the supertype method, or it must be the same as the *erasure* of the signature of the supertype method. Note the implica-tion of the last sentence: the signature of the subtype method must be the same as the *erasure of the supertype method*, *not* the other way around. The converse is neither overloading nor overriding, but a *name clash* and reported as an error.

The subsignature requirement also implies that a *generic subtype method cannot over-ride a non-generic supertype method*. In other words, genericity cannot be added to an inherited method. This case is illustrated in Example 14.15. It is the erasures of the sig-natures of the generic methods in the subtype that are the same as the signatures of the non-generic methods in the supertype. Overriding requires the converse. A name clash is generally the reason why neither overriding nor overloading is permitted.

Example 14.15 *Genericity Cannot Be Added to Inherited Methods*

```
class SupJ {
  public void set(Object obj) {/*...*/}// (1)
  public Object get() {return null;}   // (2)
}

class SubJ extends SupJ {
  public <S> void set(S s) {/*...*/}   // (1a) Error: same erasure
  public <S> S get() {return null;}    // (2a) Error: same erasure
}
```

14.13 Limitations and Restrictions on Generic Types

Reifiable Types

Concrete parameterized types are used by the compiler and then translated by erasure to their raw types, losing information about the parameterization in the process. In other words, only the raw types of these concrete parameterized types are available at runtime. For example, List<Integer> and List<String> are both erased to the raw type List. The same applies to unbounded parameterized types: List<E> is erased to List.

Non-generic types are not affected by type erasure and, therefore, have *not* lost any information and are, therefore, available fully at runtime. For example, the types Integer and String remain intact and are present unchanged at runtime.

Types that are completely available at runtime are known as *reifiable types*, i.e., type erasure has *not* removed any important information about them (see Table 14.5). Types whose information has been affected by erasure are called *non-reifiable types* (see Table 14.6).

Note that unbounded wildcard parameterized types (Node<?>, MyStack<?>) are reifiable, whereas concrete parameterized types (Node<Number>, MyStack<String>) and bounded wildcard parameterized types (Node<? extends Number>, MyStack<? super String>) are non-reifiable.

As we shall see in the rest of this section, certain operations in Java are only permitted on reifiable types (as their type information is fully intact and available at runtime), and not on non-reifiable types (as their type information is not fully available at runtime, since it has been affected by type erasure).

Table 14.5 *Examples of Reifiable Types*

Reifiable Type	Example
A primitive type	`int, double, boolean`
A non-generic type	`Exception, System, Math, Number`
A raw type	`List, ArrayList, Map, HashMap`
A parameterized type in which all type arguments are *unbounded wildcards* (unbounded wildcard parameterized type)	`List<?>, ArrayList<?>, Map<?,?>, HashMap<?,?>`
An *array type* whose component type is reifiable	`double[], Number[], List[], HashMap<?,?>[], Number[][]`

Table 14.6 *Examples of Non-Reifiable Types*

Non-Reifiable Type	Example
A type parameter	`E, T, K, V`
A parameterized type with *concrete or unbounded type parameters* (concrete or unbounded parameterized type)	`List<E>, List<String>, ArrayList<Integer>, HashMap<String, Number> Map<K, V>`
A parameterized type with a *bound* (bounded wildcard parameterized type)	`List<? extends Object>, ArrayList<? extends Number>, Comparable<? super Integer>`
An *array type* whose component type is non-reifiable	`List<E>[], ArrayList<Number>[], Comparable<? super Integer>[], HashMap<K, V>[]`

Implications for instanceof operator

Instance tests require type information at runtime, i.e., these are runtime tests that require *reifiable* types. An instance test against a non-reifiable type is not permitted and *always* generates a *compile-time error*.

In (1) below, we want to determine whether the object referenced by obj is an instance of the concrete parameterized type MyStack<Integer>, i.e., whether it is a stack of Integer:

```
Obj obj;
...
boolean isIntStack = obj instanceof MyStack<Integer>; // (1) Compile-time error!
```

The post-erasure code for (1) is equivalent to the following statement:

```
boolean isIntStack = obj instanceof MyStack;          // (1')
```

The statement in (1') cannot perform the instance test expected in (1), as erasure has removed the information about the concrete type parameter Integer, i.e., the type MyStack<Integer> is non-reifiable. The compiler issues an error, because the JVM will only be able to find a stack of the erasure type (MyStack) and not a stack of a parameterized type (MyStack<Integer>).

Given that T is a formal type parameter, the following code will also not compile, as the arguments of the instanceof operator are non-reifiable types:

```
Object thingy;
...
boolean isT      = thingy instanceof T;               // Compile-time error!
boolean isTStack = obj instanceof MyStack<T>;         // Compile-time error!
```

If we just wanted to determine that an instance was some stack, the instance test can be performed against the raw type or the unbounded wildcard parameterized type, as these types are reifiable:

```
boolean isRawStack = obj instanceof MyStack;
boolean isAnyStack = obj instanceof MyStack<?>;       // Preferable.
```

Implications for Casting

For non-generic code, if the instance test is true, the cast is safe to apply:

```
Number num = 2008;
if (num instanceof Integer) {
  int i = (Integer) num;
}
```

Since it is not possible to test that an object is an instance of a non-reifiable type, it is also not possible to check the cast to such a type at runtime. A non-reifiable type could have lost important type information during erasure and the cast may not have the desired affect at runtime. A cast to a non-reifiable type is *generally* flagged as an *unchecked cast warning,* and the cast is replaced by a cast to its erasure. Again, the compiler permits casts to allow interoperability between legacy code and generic code—usually with a warning.

The following code shows why a warning is necessary. The reference value of a Number node, declared at (1), is assigned to a reference of type Node<?> at (2). This reference is cast to a Node<String> and its reference value is assigned to a reference of type Node<String> at (3). A String is set as data in the node at (4). The data is retrieved from the node via the numNode reference and assigned to a Number reference at (5).

```
Node<Number> numNode = new Node<Number>(20, null); // (1)
Node<?> anyNode = numNode;                          // (2)
Node<String> strNode = (Node<String>) anyNode;      // (3) Unchecked cast
strNode.setData("Peekaboo");                        // (4)
Number num = numNode.getData();                     // (5) ClassCastException
```

The erasure of the assignment at (3) is equivalent to the following assignment, with the cast succeeding at runtime:

```
Node strNode = (Node) anyNode;                      // (3')
```

However, a ClassCastException occurs at (5) because a String cannot be assigned to a Number. The compiler warns of potential problems by issuing an unchecked cast warning at (3).

The types Node<String> and Node<Number> are unrelated. That is the reason why the Number node in the above example was compromised by going through a node of type Node<?>. As we would expect, a cast between unrelated types results in a compile-time error:

```
strNode = (Node<String>) numNode;                   // Compile-time error
```

If we are casting a generic supertype to a generic subtype, where the parameterization is identical, the cast is safe and no warning is issued:

```
// BiNode<E> is a subtype of MonoNode<E>
MonoNode<String> monoStrNode = new BiNode<String>("Hi", null, null);
BiNode<String> biStrNode = (BiNode<String>) monoStrNode; //  Ok. No warning.
```

The method castaway() below shows examples of casting an Object reference that refers to a node of type String, declared at (2).

```
@SuppressWarnings("unchecked") // (1) Suppress warnings in (4),(6),(7).
public static void castaway() {
  Object obj = new Node<String>("one", null);    // (2)
  Node<String> node1 = obj;                       // (3) Compile-time error!
  Node<String> node2 = (Node<String>) obj;        // (4) Unchecked cast
  Node<String> node3 = (Node<?>) obj;             // (5) Compile-time error!
  Node<String> node4 = (Node<String>)(Node<?>) obj;  // (6) Unchecked cast
  Node<String> node5 = (Node) obj;                // (7) Unchecked conversion
  Node<?> node6 = (Node) obj;                     // (8)
  Node<?> node7 = (Node<?>)obj;                   // (9)
}
```

It is instructive to see what warnings and errors are issued by the compiler. The compile-time error at (3) is due to incompatible types: an Object cannot be assigned to a Node<String> reference. The compiler issues an unchecked cast warning at (3) because of the cast from an Object to the concrete parameterized type Node<String>. The compile-time error at (5) is due to incompatible types: a Node<?> cannot be assigned to a Node<String> reference. There are two casts in (6): an Object is cast to Node<?>, which in turn is cast to Node<String>. The cast to Node<?> is permitted, but the second cast results in an unchecked cast warning. Note that an assignment of a Node<?> to a Node<String> is not permitted, but a cast is permitted with a warning. (8) and (9) show that casting to the raw type or to the unbounded wildcard is always permitted, since both types are reifiable.

We have used the annotation @SuppressWarnings("unchecked") at (1) to suppress the unchecked warning in the method castaway(). Use of this annotation is recommended when we *know* that unchecked cast warnings are inevitable in a language construct (a type declaration, a field, a method, a parameter, a constructor, a local variable). Any unchecked warnings reported by the compiler are then those that were *not* documented using this annotation. The use of an unbounded wildcard is recommended in casts, rather than using raw types, as it provides for stricter type checking.

Implications for Arrays

Array store checks are based on the element type being a reifiable type, in order to ensure that subtype covariance between array types is not violated at runtime. In the code below, the element type of the array is String and the array store check at (1) disallows the assignment, resulting in an ArrayStoreException, because the reference value of a Double cannot be stored in a String reference.

```
String[] strArray = new String[] {"Hi", "Hello", "Howdy"};
Object[] objArray = strArray; // String[] is a subtype of Object[]
objArray[0] = 2010.5;         // (1) ArrayStoreException
```

We cannot instantiate a formal type parameter, nor can we create an array of such a type:

```
// T is a formal type parameter.
T t = new T();           // Compile-time error!
T[] anArray = new T[10]; // Compile-time error!
```

It is also not possible to create an array whose element type is a concrete or a bounded wildcard parameterized type:

```
// An array of Lists of String
List<String>[] list1 = {                             // Compile-time error
  Arrays.asList("one", "two"), Arrays.asList("three", "four")
};
```

```
List<String>[] list2 = new List<String>[] {       // Compile-time error
  Arrays.asList("one", "two"), Arrays.asList("three", "four")
};
```

```
// An array of Lists of any subtype of Number
List<? extends Number>[] list3
            = new List<? extends Number>[] {    // Compile-time error
  Arrays.asList(20.20, 60.60), Arrays.asList(2008, 2009)
};
```

Unbounded wildcard parameterized types are allowed as element types, because these types are essentially equivalent to the raw types (see Section 14.5, p. 679):

```
List<?>[] list4 = {
  Arrays.asList("one", "two"), Arrays.asList("three", "four")
};
```

```
List<?>[] list5 = new List<?>[] {
  Arrays.asList(20.20, 60.60), Arrays.asList(2008, 2007)
};
List[] list6 = list5;
```

Note that we can always declare a *reference* of a non-reifiable type. It is creating arrays of these types that is not permitted.

```
class MyIntList extends ArrayList<Integer> { }       // A reifiable subclass.

// Client code
List<Integer>[] arrayOfLists = new MyIntList[5];      // Array of Lists of Integer
List<Integer[]> listOfArrays
                 = new ArrayList<Integer[]>();        // List of Arrays of Integer
```

The class MyStack<E> in Example 14.7, p. 695, implements a method to convert a stack to an array:

```
// Copy to array as many elements as possible.
public E[] toArray(E[] toArray) {                                    // (11)
  Node<E> thisNode = tos;
  for (int i = 0; thisNode != null && i < toArray.length; i++) {
    toArray[i] = thisNode.getData();
    thisNode = thisNode.getNext();
  }
  return toArray;
}
```

Note that the array is passed as parameter, because we cannot create an array of the parameter type, as the following version of the method shows:

```
public E[] toArray2() {
  E[] toArray = new E[numOfElements];                // Compile-time error
  int i = 0;
  for (E data : this) {
    toArray[i++] = data;
  }
  return toArray;
}
```

The third version below uses an array of Object. The cast is necessary in order to be compatible with the return type. However, the cast is to a non-reifiable type, resulting in an unchecked cast warning:

```
public E[] toArray3() {
  E[] toArray = (E[])new Object[numOfElements];     // (1) Unchecked cast warning
  int i = 0;
  for (E data : this) { toArray[i++] = data; }
  return toArray;
}
```

The method implementation above has a serious problem, even though the code compiles. We get a ClassCastException at (2) below, because we cannot assign the reference value of an Object[] to an Integer[] reference:

```
MyStack<Integer> intStack = new MyStack<Integer>();
intStack.push(9); intStack.push(1); intStack.push(1);
Integer[] intArray = intStack.toArray3();           // (2) ClassCastException
```

The final and correct version of this method uses *reflection* to create an array of the right element type:

```
@SuppressWarnings("unchecked")
public E[] toArray4(E[] toArray) {
  if (toArray.length != numOfElements) {

    toArray = (E[])java.lang.reflect.Array.newInstance(  // (3)
                        toArray.getClass().getComponentType(),
                        numOfElements);   // Suppressed unchecked warning
  }
  int i = 0;
  for (E data : this) { toArray[i++] = data; }
  return toArray;
}
```

The method is passed an array whose element type is looked up through reflection, and an array of this element type (and right size) is created at (3). The method new-Instance() of the Array class creates an array of specified element type and size. The element type is looked up through the class literal of the array supplied as argument. The unchecked cast warning is suppressed, because we know it is unavoidable. We will not go into the nitty-gritty details of using reflection here.

The client code now works as expected. We pass an array of zero length, and let the method create the array.

```
MyStack<Integer> intStack = new MyStack<Integer>();
intStack.push(9); intStack.push(1); intStack.push(1);
Integer[] intArray = intStack.toArray4(new Integer[0]);   // (3) OK.
```

The next example demonstrates the danger of casting an array of a reifiable type to an array of non-reifiable type. An array of the raw type List (reifiable type) is created at (1), and cast to an array of List<Double> (non-reifiable type). The cast results in an unchecked cast warning. The first element of the array of List<Double> is initialized with a list of Double at (2). The reference value of this array is assigned to a reference of type List<? extends Number> at (3). Using this reference, the array of Double in the first element of the array is replaced with a list of Integer. Using the alias arrayOf-ListsOfDouble of type List<Double>[], the first element in the first list of the array (an Integer) is assigned to a Double reference. Since the types are incompatible, a Class-CastException is thrown at (5). Note that the array store check at (4) succeeds, because the check is against the reified element type of the array, List, and not List<Double>.

```
List<Double>[] arrayOfListsOfDouble
                = (List<Double>[]) new List[1];    // (1) Unchecked cast warning!
arrayOfListsOfDouble[0] = Arrays.asList(10.10);    // (2) Initialize
List<? extends Number>[] arrayofListsOfExtNums = arrayOfListsOfDouble; // (3)
arrayofListsOfExtNums[0] = Arrays.asList(10);      // (4) Array storage check ok
Double firstOne = arrayOfListsOfDouble[0].get(0);  // (5) ClassCastException!
```

Implications for Varargs

Because varargs are treated as arrays, generics have implications for varargs (Section 3.8, p. 90). Most of the workarounds for arrays are not applicable, as array creation is implicit for varargs. In a method call, implicit creation of a *generic array with the varargs* results in an *unchecked generic array creation warning*—and type-safety is no longer guaranteed.

The method asStack() below has a varargs parameter at (1) whose type is a non-reifiable type T. The method pushes the specified elements on to the specified stack.

```
public static <T> void asStack(MyStack<T> stack, T...elements) {     // (1)
  for (T element : elements) {
    stack.push(element);
  }
}
```

The method above is called by the client code below at (4). The idea is to initialize a stack of stacks of Integer with a stack of Integer. An implicit generic array (new MyStack<Integer>[] { intStack }) is created by the compiler, which is passed in the method call at (4). The compiler also issues an unchecked array creation warning, but the code compiles and runs without any problems.

```
/* Client code */
// (2) Create a stack of stacks of Integer:
MyStack<MyStack<Integer>> stackOfStacks = new MyStack<MyStack<Integer>>();

// (3) Create a stack of Integer:
MyStack<Integer> intStack = new MyStack<Integer>();
intStack.push(2008); intStack.push(2009);

// Initializes the stack of stacks with the stack of Integer.
MyStack.asStack(stackOfStacks, intStack); // (4) Unchecked array creation!
intStack = stackOfStacks.pop();   // (5) Pop the stack of stacks of Integer.
int tos = intStack.pop();         // (6) Pop the stack of Integer.
assert tos == 2008;
```

The implicit array passed as argument is available as an array of a *non-reifiable type* in the body of the method asStack(). The integrity of this array can be compromised by making the array store check report a false positive, i.e., succeed when the store operation should normally fail. This is demonstrated by the method declaration below, in the assignment statement at (1a), where the contents of the elements array are changed before they are copied to the specified stack.

```
public static <T> void asStackMalicious(MyStack<T> stack, T...elements) {
  // Compromise the elements array:
  MyStack<Double> doubleStack = new MyStack<Double>();
  doubleStack.push(20.20);
  elements[0] = (T) doubleStack;// (1a) Array store check can be a false positive.

  // Copy from array:
  for (T element : elements) {
    stack.push(element);
  }
}
```

A partial erasure for the method asStackMalicious() is shown below.

```java
public static void asStackMalicious(MyStack stack, Object...elements) {
  // Compromise the elements array:
  MyStack doubleStack = new MyStack();
  doubleStack.push(Double.valueOf(20.20));
  elements[0] = (Object) doubleStack;  // (1b)
  ...
}
```

Note that the *cast* succeeds for any object at (1b). If we now call the method asStack-Malicious(), instead of the method asStack() at (4) in the client code above, the code compiles with an unchecked cast warning at (1a), plus the generic array creation warning in the client code at (4).

```java
MyStack.asStackMalicious(stackOfStacks, intStack); // (4') Unchecked warning!
```

At runtime, the reference elements in the method asStackMalicious() refers to the implicit array created in the call, i.e., new MyStack[] { intStack }. The signature of the method call at runtime is equivalent to:

```java
asStackMalicious(MyStack, MyStack[])
```

The assignment at (1a) succeeds, as the actual runtime element type of the elements array is MyStack, and the type of the value we want to assign is MyStack. The element type of the stack has been erased. When the code is run, the array store check succeeds at (1a), as does the assignment at (5). The error is only discovered after a ClassCastException is thrown at (6), because a Double cannot be assigned to an Integer. The general rule is to avoid varargs in methods where the parameter is of a non-reifiable type.

Implications for Exception Handling

When an exception is thrown in a try block, it is matched against the parameter of each catch block that is associated with the try block. This test is similar to the instance test, requiring reifiable types. The following restrictions apply:

- The type of the parameter of a catch block must be a reifiable type and it must also be a subtype of Throwable.

- A generic type cannot extend the Throwable class.

- A parameterized type cannot be specified in a throws clause.

The following example illustrates the three restrictions:

```java
// (1) A generic class can not extend Exception:
class MyGenericException<T> extends Exception { }        // Compile-time error!

public class ExceptionErrors {

  // (2) Cannot specify parameterized types in throws clause:
  public static void main(String[] args)
                  throws MyGenericException<String> { // Compile-time error!
    try {
```

```
        throw new MyGenericException<String>();

    // (3) Cannot use parameterized type in catch block:
    } catch (MyGenericException<String> e) {                // Compile-time error!
      e.printStackTrace();
    }
  }
}
```

However, *type parameters* are allowed in the throws clause, as Example 14.16 shows. In the declaration of the MyActionListener interface, the method doAction() can throw an exception of type E. The interface is implemented by the class FileAction, that provides the actual type parameter (FileNotFoundException) and implements the doAction() method with this actual type parameter. All is above board, as only reifiable types are used for exception handling in the class FileAction.

Example 14.16 *Type Parameter in* throws *Clause*

```
public interface MyActionListener<E extends Exception> {
  public void doAction() throws E;        // Type parameter in throws clause
}
```

```
import java.io.FileNotFoundException;

public class FileAction implements MyActionListener<FileNotFoundException> {

  public void doAction() throws FileNotFoundException {
    throw new FileNotFoundException("Does not exist");
  }
  public static void main(String[] args) {
    FileAction fileAction = new FileAction();
    try {
      fileAction.doAction();
    } catch (FileNotFoundException e) {
      e.printStackTrace();
    }
  }
}
```

Implications for Nested Classes

All nested classes and interfaces can be declared as generic types *except* anonymous classes. Anonymous classes do not have a name, and a class name is required for declaring a generic class and specifying its type parameters. An anonymous class can be a parameterized type, where the actual type parameters are supplied in the anonymous class expression.

```
class GenericTLC<A> {               // (1) Top level class

  static class SMC<B> {/*...*/}     // (2) Static member class

  interface SMI<C> {/*...*/}        // (3) Static member interface

  class NSMC<D> {/*...*/}           // (4) Non-static member (inner) class

  void nsm() {
    class NSLC<E> {/*...*/}         // (5) Local (inner) class in non-static context
  }

  static void sm() {
    class SLC<F> {/*...*/}          // (6) Local (inner) class in static context
  }

  // Anonymous classes as parameterized types:
  SMC<Integer> nsf = new SMC<Integer>() {       // (7) In non-static context
    /*...*/
  };
  static SMI<String> sf = new SMI<String>() {  // (8) In static context
    /*...*/
  };
}
```

The type parameter names of a generic nested class can hide type parameter names in the enclosing context (see (2) in Example 14.17). Only a non-static nested class can use the type parameters in its enclosing context, as type parameters cannot be referenced in a static context.

Example 14.17 also illustrates instantiating generic nested classes. As a static member class does not have an outer instance, only its simple name is parameterized, and not the enclosing types, as shown by the code at (6). As a non-static member class requires an outer instance, any generic enclosing types must also be parameterized and instantiated, as shown by the code at (7). See Section 8.3, p. 360, for the syntax used in instantiating nested classes.

Example 14.17 *Generic Nested Classes*

```
public class ListPool<T> {          // (1) Top level class

  static class MyLinkedList<T> {    // (2) Hiding type parameter in enclosing context
    T t;                            // T refers to (2)
  }

  class Node<E> {                   // (4) Non-static member (inner) class
    T t;                            // T refers to (1)
    E e;
  }

  public static void main(String[] args) {
    // (5) Instantiating a generic top-level class:
    ListPool<String> lp = new ListPool<String>();
```

```
                // (6) Instantiating a generic static member class:
                ListPool.MyLinkedList<String> list = new ListPool.MyLinkedList<String>();

                // (7) Instantiating a generic non-static member class:
                ListPool<String>.Node<Integer> node1 = lp.new Node<Integer>();
                ListPool<String>.Node<Double> node2 = lp.new Node<Double>();
                ListPool<Integer>.Node<String> node3
                            = new ListPool<Integer>().new Node<String>();
    }
}
```

Other Implications

Enums

Because of the way enum types are implemented using the java.lang.Enum class, we cannot declare a generic enum type:

```
    enum COIN_TOSS<C> { HEAD, TAIL; }                        // Compile-time error!
```

An enum type can implement a parameterized interface, just like a non-generic class can. The enum type TRIPLE_JUMP implements the interface Comparator<TRIPLE_JUMP>:

```
    enum TRIPLE_JUMP implements Comparator<TRIPLE_JUMP> {
      HOP, STEP, JUMP;

      public int compare(TRIPLE_JUMP a1, TRIPLE_JUMP a2) {
        return a1.compareTo(a2);
      }
    }
```

Class Literals

Objects of the class Class<T> represent classes and interfaces at runtime, i.e., an instance of the Class<T> represents the type T. A class literal expression can only use reifiable types as type parameters, as there is only one class object.

```
                Node<Integer> intNode = new Node<Integer>(2008, null);
                Class<Node> class0 = Node<Integer>.class; // Compile-time error!
                Class<Node> class1 = Node.class;          // OK
```

The getClass() method of the Object class also returns a Class object. The actual result type of this object is Class<? extends |T|> where |T| is the erasure of the static type of the expression on which the getClass() method is called. The following code shows that all invocations of the generic type Node<T> are represented by a single class literal:

```
                Node<String> strNode = new Node<String>("Hi", null);
                Class<?> class2 = strNode.getClass();
                Class<?> class3 = intNode.getClass();
                assert class1 == class2;
                assert class2 == class3;
```

Review Questions

14.18 Which statements can be inserted at (1) without the compiler reporting any errors?

```
public class RQ100_05 {
  public static void main(String[] args) {
    List<?> lst = new ArrayList<String>();
    // (1) INSERT HERE
  }
}
```

Select the two correct answers.

(a) lst.add(null);
(b) lst.add("OK");
(c) lst.add(2007);
(d) String v1 = lst.get(0);
(e) Object v2 = lst.get(0);

14.19 What will the program print when compiled and run?

```
public class RQ100_00 {
  public static void main(String[] args) {
    List<String> lst1 = new ArrayList<String>();
    List<Integer> lst2 = new ArrayList<Integer>();
    List<List<Integer>> lst3 = new ArrayList<List<Integer>>();
    System.out.print(lst1.getClass() + " ");
    System.out.print(lst2.getClass() + " ");
    System.out.println(lst3.getClass());
  }
}
```

Select the one correct answer.

(a) class java.util.ArrayList<String> class java.util.ArrayList<Integer> class
    java.util.ArrayList<List<Integer>>
(b) class java.util.ArrayList class java.util.ArrayList class
    java.util.ArrayList
(c) class java.util.List class java.util.List class java.util.List
(d) class java.util.List<String> class java.util.List<Integer> class
    java.util.List<List<Integer>>
(e) The program will not compile.
(f) The program compiles, but throws an exception when run.

14.20 Which declarations can be inserted at (1) without the compiler reporting any
errors?

```
public class RQ100_01 {
  public static void main(String[] args) {
    //  (1) INSERT DECLARATIONS HERE
  }

  public static <E extends Number> List<E> justDoIt(List<? super E> nums) {
```

```
      return null;
    }
  }
```

Select the three correct answers.

(a) `ArrayList<Integer> inParam = new ArrayList<Integer>();`
    `ArrayList<Integer> returnValue = justDoIt(inParam);`

(b) `ArrayList<Integer> inParam = new ArrayList<Integer>();`
    `List<Integer> returnValue = justDoIt(inParam);`

(c) `ArrayList<Integer> inParam = new ArrayList<Integer>();`
    `List<Number> returnValue = justDoIt(inParam);`

(d) `List<Number> inParam = new ArrayList<Number>();`
    `ArrayList<Integer> returnValue = justDoIt(inParam);`

(e) `List<Number> inParam = new ArrayList<Number>();`
    `List<Number> returnValue = justDoIt(inParam);`

(f) `List<Integer> inParam = new ArrayList<Integer>();`
    `List<Integer> returnValue = justDoIt(inParam);`

14.21 The class java.lang.String implements the interface java.lang.CharSequence. Given
       the following code:

```
public class RQ100_02 {
  public static void main(String[] args) {
    List<String> lst = Arrays.asList("Java", "only", "promotes", "fun");
    Collection<String> resultList = delete4LetterWords(lst);
  }

  // (1) INSERT METHOD HEADER HERE
  {
    Collection<E> permittedWords = new ArrayList<E>();
    for (E word : words) {
      if (word.length() != 4) permittedWords.add(word);
    }
    return permittedWords;
  }
}
```

Which method header can be inserted at (1) so that the program compiles and runs
without errors?

Select the one correct answer.

(a) `static <E extends CharSequence> Collection<? extends CharSequence>`
    `delete4LetterWords(Collection<E> words)`

(b) `static <E extends CharSequence> List<E>`
    `delete4LetterWords(Collection<E> words)`

(c) `static <E extends CharSequence> Collection<E>`
    `delete4LetterWords(Collection<? extends CharSequence> words)`

(d) `static <E extends CharSequence> List<E>`
    `delete4LetterWords(Collection<? extends CharSequence> words)`

(e) static <E extends CharSequence> Collection<E>
     delete4LetterWords(Collection<E> words)

(f) public <E super CharSequence> Collection<E>
     delete4LetterWords(Collection<E> words)

14.22 Which declaration can be inserted at (1) so that the program compiles and runs without errors?

```
public class RQ100_06 {
  public static void main(String[] args) {
    //  (1) INSERT DECLARATION HERE
    for (int i = 0; i <= 5; i++) {
      List<Integer> row = new ArrayList<Integer>();
      for (int j = 0; j <= i; j++)
        row.add(i * j);
      ds.add(row);
    }
    for (List<Integer> row : ds)
      System.out.println(row);
  }
}
```

Select the one correct answer.

(a) List<List<Integer>> ds = new List<List<Integer>>();
(b) List<ArrayList<Integer>> ds = new ArrayList<ArrayList<Integer>>();
(c) List<List<Integer>> ds = new ArrayList<List<Integer>>();
(d) ArrayList<ArrayList<Integer>> ds = new ArrayList<ArrayList<Integer>>();
(e) List<List<Integer>> ds = new ArrayList<ArrayList<Integer>>();
(f) List<List, Integer> ds = new List<List, Integer>();
(g) List<List, Integer> ds = new ArrayList<List, Integer>();
(h) List<List, Integer> ds = new ArrayList<ArrayList, Integer>();

14.23 Which method declarations cannot be inserted independently at (2) to overload the method at (1)?

```
public class RQ_Overloading {

  static <T> void overloadMe(List<T> s1, List<T> s2) { } // (1)
  // (2) INSERT DECLARATION HERE.
}
```

Select the two correct answers.

(a) static <T> void overloadMe(Collection<T> s1, List<T> s2) { }
(b) static <T> void overloadMe(List<T> s1, List<? extends T> s2) { }
(c) static <T> void overloadMe(List<T> s1, Collection<? super T> s2) { }
(d) static <T> void overloadMe(Collection<T> s1, Collection<? super T> s2) { }
(e) static <T> void overloadMe(Collection<T> s1, List<? super T> s2) { }
(f) static <T> void overloadMe(List<? extends T> s1, List<? super T> s2) { }

14.24 Which declarations can be inserted at (1) so that the program compiles and runs without errors?

```java
public class RQ100_07 {
  public static void main(String[] args) {
    // (1) INSERT DECLARATION HERE
    appendAndPrint(lst, "hello");
  }

  static <T> void appendAndPrint(Collection<T> ds, T t) {
    ds.add(t);
    System.out.println(ds);
  }
}
```

Select the two correct answers.

(a) List<?> lst = new LinkedList<Object>();
(b) List<? extends Object> lst = new LinkedList<Object>();
(c) List<? super Object> lst = new LinkedList<Object>();
(d) List<Object> lst = new LinkedList<Object>();

14.25 Which method declaration can be inserted at (1) so that the program compiles without warnings?

```java
public class RQ100_87 {
  public static void main(String[] args) {
    List raw = new ArrayList();
    raw.add("2007");
    raw.add(2008);
    raw.add("2009");
    justDoIt(raw);
  }
  // (1) INSERT METHOD DECLARATION HERE.
}
```

Select the one correct answer.

(a) static void justDoIt(List<Integer> lst) { }
(b) static void justDoIt(List<?> lst) { }
(c) static <T> void justDoIt(List<T> lst) { }
(d) None of the above.

14.26 Which method calls can be inserted at (1) so that the program compiles without warnings?

```java
public class GenParam {
  public static void main(String[] args) {
    List<Number> numList = new ArrayList<Number>();
    List<Integer> intList = new ArrayList<Integer>();
    // (1) INSERT CODE HERE
  }

  static <T> void move(List<? extends T> lst1, List<? super T> lst2) { }
}
```

Select the three correct answers.

(a) GenParam.move(numList, intList);
(b) GenParam.<Number>move(numList, intList);
(c) GenParam.<Integer>move(numList, intList);
(d) GenParam.move(intList, numList);
(e) GenParam.<Number>move(intList, numList);
(f) GenParam.<Integer>move(intList, numList);

14.27 Which statement is true about the following code?

```java
public class RQ100_86 {

    static void print1(List<String> lst) {      // (1)
        for(String element : lst) {
            System.out.print(element + " ");
        }
    }

    static void print2(List<String> lst) {      // (2)
        for(Object element : lst) {
            System.out.print(element + " ");
        }
    }

    static void print3(List<?> lst) {           // (3)
        for(Object element : lst) {
            System.out.print(element + " ");
        }
    }

    static <T> void print4(List<T> lst) {       // (4)
        for(Object element : lst) {
            System.out.print(element + " ");
        }
    }

    static <T> void print5(List<T> lst) {       // (5)
        for(T element : lst) {
            System.out.print(element + " ");
        }
    }
}
```

Select the one correct answer.

(a) The formal type parameter specification for the methods in (1), (2), and (3) is missing.
(b) The generic methods in (4) and (5) should be declared in a generic class.
(c) The element type Object for the local variable element in the for(:) loop header of the method in (3) is inconsistent with the element type of the list.
(d) The element type Object for the local variable element in the for(:) loop header of the method in (4) is inconsistent with the element type of the list.
(e) The program will compile without warnings.
(f) None of the above.

14.28 Which statements are true about the following code?

```
class MyClass<V> {
       MyClass()          {System.out.println(this);}          // (1)
       MyClass(V v)       {System.out.println(v);}             // (2)
   <T> MyClass(T t)       {System.out.println(t);}             // (3)
   <T> MyClass(T t, V v){System.out.println(t + ", " + v);}    // (4)
   }
```

Select the two correct answers.

(a) The class attempts to declare four constructors.
(b) Only one of the two constructors in (2) and (3) can be declared in the class.
(c) A generic class cannot declare generic constructors.
(d) The compiler reports an error in (3), since the type parameter V is not used.
(e) The class compiles without problems.

14.29 Which declaration statement is not valid in the code below?

```
class AClass<V> {
       AClass()          {System.out.println(this);}          // (1)
   <T> AClass(T t)       {System.out.println(t);}             // (2)
   <T> AClass(T t, V v) {System.out.println(t + ", " + v);}   // (3)
   }
```

Select the one correct answer.

(a) AClass<String> ref1 = new AClass<String>();
(b) AClass<String> ref2 = new AClass<String>("one");
(c) AClass<String> ref3 = new AClass<String>(2007);
(d) AClass<String> ref4 = new <Integer>AClass<String>(2007);
(e) AClass<String> ref5 = new <String>AClass<String>("one");
(f) AClass<String> ref6 = new AClass<String>(2007, "one");
(g) AClass<String> ref7 = new <Integer>AClass<String>(2007, "one");
(h) AClass<String> ref8 = new <Integer>AClass<String>("one", 2007);

14.30 Which statements are true about the following code?

```
class SupX {
  public void set(Collection<?> c) {/*...*/} // (1)
}
class SubX extends SupX {
  public void set(List<?> l) {/*...*/}        // (2)
  public void set(Collection c) {/*...*/}     // (3)
}
//-----------------------------------------
class SupY {
  public void set(Collection c) {/*...*/}     // (4)
}

class SubY extends SupY {
  public void set(Collection<?> c) {/*...*/} // (5)
}
```

Select the three correct answers.

(a) The method at (2) overloads the method at (1).
(b) The method at (2) overrides the method at (1).
(c) The method at (2) results in a compile-time error.
(d) The method at (3) overloads the method at (1).
(e) The method at (3) overrides the method at (1).
(f) The method at (3) results in a compile-time error.
(g) The method at (5) overloads the method at (4).
(h) The method at (5) overrides the method at (4).
(i) The method at (5) results in a compile-time error.

14.31   Which statements are true about the following code?

```
class SupC<T> {
  public void set(T t) {/*...*/}        // (1)
  public T get() {return null;}         // (2)
}

class SubC1<M,N> extends SupC<M> {
  public void set(N n) {/*...*/}        // (3)
  public N get() {return null;}         // (4)
}

class SubC2<M,N extends M> extends SupC<M> {
  public void set(N n) {/*...*/}        // (5)
  public N get() {return null;}         // (6)
}
```

Select the four correct answers.

(a) The method at (3) overloads the method at (1).
(b) The method at (3) overrides the method at (1).
(c) The method at (3) results in a compile-time error.
(d) The method at (4) overloads the method at (2).
(e) The method at (4) overrides the method at (2).
(f) The method at (4) results in a compile-time error.
(g) The method at (5) overloads the method at (1).
(h) The method at (5) overrides the method at (1).
(i) The method at (5) results in a compile-time error.
(j) The method at (6) overloads the method at (2).
(k) The method at (6) overrides the method at (2).
(l) The method at (6) results in a compile-time error.

14.32   Which types cannot be declared as generic types?

Select the three correct answers.

(a) Enum types
(b) Static member classes
(c) Any subclass of Throwable, i.e., exception classes
(d) Nested interfaces

(e) Anonymous classes

(f) Non-static member classes

(g) Local classes

14.33 What will be printed when the program is compiled and run?

```
class Tantrum<E extends Exception> {
  public void throwOne(E e) throws E {
    throw e;
  }
}

class TantrumException extends Exception {
  TantrumException(String str) {
    super(str);
  }
}

public class TakeException {
  public static void main(String[] args) {
    Tantrum<TantrumException> tantrum = new Tantrum<TantrumException>();
    try {
      tantrum.throwOne(new TantrumException("Tantrum thrown."));
    } catch (TantrumException te) {
      System.out.println(te.getMessage());
    }
  }
}
```

Select the one correct answer.

(a) The class Tantrum will not compile.

(b) The class TakeException will not compile.

(c) The program will compile, print "Tantrum thrown.", and terminate normally when run.

(d) The program will compile and will throw an exception and abort the execution when run.

14.34 What will be printed when the program is compiled and run?

```
public class CastAway {
  public static void main(String[] args) {
    Object obj = new ArrayList<Integer>();        // (1)
    List<?>       list1 = (List<?>) obj;           // (2)
    List<?>       list2 = (List) obj;              // (3)
    List          list3 = (List<?>) obj;           // (4)
    List<Integer> list4 = (List) obj;              // (5)
    List<Integer> list5 = (List<Integer>) obj;     // (6)
  }
}
```

Select the one correct answer.

(a) The program will not compile.

(b) The program will compile without any unchecked warnings. It will run with no output and terminate normally.

(c) The program will compile without any unchecked warnings. When run, it will throw an exception.

(d) The program will compile, but issue unchecked warnings. It will run with no output and terminate normally.

(e) The program will compile, but issue unchecked warnings. When run, it will throw an exception.

14.35   What will be printed when the program is compiled and run?

```java
public class InstanceTest2 {
  public static void main(String[] args) {
    List<Integer> intList = new ArrayList<Integer>();
    Set<Double> doubleSet = new HashSet<Double>();
    List<?>         list = intList;
    Set<?>          set = doubleSet;

    scuddle(intList);
    scuddle(doubleSet);
    scuddle(list);
    scuddle(set);
  }

  private static void scuddle(Collection<?> col) {
    if (col instanceof List<?>) {
      System.out.println("I am a list.");
    } else if (col instanceof Set<?>) {
      System.out.println("I am a set.");
    }
  }
}
```

Select the one correct answer.

(a) The method scuddle() will not compile.

(b) The method main() will not compile.

(c) The program will compile, but issue an unchecked warning in method scuddle(). It will run and terminate normally with the following output:

```
I am a list.
I am a set.
I am a list.
I am a set.
```

(d) The program will compile, but issue an unchecked warning in the method main(). When run, it will throw an exception.

(e) The program will compile without any unchecked warnings. It will run and terminate normally, with the following output:

```
I am a list.
I am a set.
I am a list.
I am a set.
```

(f) The program will compile without any unchecked warnings. It will run and terminate normally, with the following output:

```
I am a list.
I am a set.
```

(g) None of the above.

14.36 Which statements will compile without errors and unchecked warnings when inserted at (1)?

```java
public class Restrictions<T> {
  public void test() {
    // (1) INSERT ASSIGNMENT HERE.
  }
}
```

Select the four correct answers.

(a) `T ref = new T();`

(b) `T[] arrayRef = new T[10];`

(c) `List<T>[] arrayOfLists0 = { new List<T>(), new List<T>() };`

(d) `List<T>[] arrayOfLists1 = new List<T>[10];`

(e) `List<?>[] arrayOfLists2 = new List<?>[10];`

(f) `List    [] arrayOfLists3 = new List<?>[10];`

(g) `List<?>[] arrayOfLists4 = new List[10];`

(h) `List    [] arrayOfLists5 = new List[10];`

(i) `List<String>[] arrayOfLists6 = new List[10];`

14.37 What will be printed when the program is compiled and run?

```java
public class GenArrays {
  public static <E> E[] copy(E[] srcArray) {
    E[] destArray = (E[]) new Object[srcArray.length];
    int i = 0;
    for (E element : srcArray) {
      destArray[i++] = element;
    }
    return destArray;
  }

  public static void main(String[] args) {
    String[] sa = {"9", "1", "1" };
    String[] da = GenArrays.copy(sa);
    System.out.println(da[0]);
  }
}
```

Select the one correct answer.

(a) The program will not compile.

(b) The program will compile, but issue an unchecked warning. When run, it will print "9".

(c) The program will compile, but issue an unchecked warning. When run, it will throw an exception.

(d) The program will compile without any unchecked warnings. When run, it will print "9".

(e) The program will compile without any unchecked warnings. When run, it will throw an exception.

14.38   What is the result of compiling and running the following program?

```java
import java.util.Arrays;
import java.util.List;

public class GenVarArgs {
  public static <T> void doIt(List<T>... aols) {          // (1)
    for(int i = 0; i < aols.length; i++) {
      System.out.print(aols[i] + " ");
    }
  }

  public static void main(String... args) {               // (2)
    List<String> ls1 = Arrays.asList("one", "two");
    List<String> ls2 = Arrays.asList("three", "four");
    List<String>[] aols = new List[] {ls1, ls2};          // (3)
    doIt(aols);                                           // (4)
  }
}
```

Select the one correct answer.

(a) The program does not compile because of errors in (1).
(b) The program does not compile because of errors in (2).
(c) The program does not compile because of errors in (3).
(d) The program does not compile because of errors in (4).
(e) The program compiles and prints: [one, two] [three, four]

 Chapter Summary

The following information was included in this chapter:

- how generic types, parameterized types, and raw types are related
- declaring generic types (classes and interfaces) and parameterized types
- extending generic types
- mixing generic code and legacy code
- the significance of unchecked warnings on type-safety
- understanding subtype relationships for wildcards
- understanding type hierarchy for wildcard parameterized types
- understanding widening and narrowing reference conversions in type hierarchy of wildcard parameterized types
- understanding restrictions on set and get operations when using references of wildcard parameterized types
- using bounded type parameters
- how to implement a generic class that is also Iterable

- understanding wildcard capture
- programming with wildcard parameterized types
- discussion of type erasure
- how overloading and overriding work with generics
- what reifiable types are and their role in generics
- understanding the limitations and restrictions that generics place on instance tests, casting, arrays, varargs, and exception handling

 Programming Exercises

14.1   Write the generic method toMultiMap() that creates a multimap from a given map, as explained on page 702.

14.2   Write the generic method findVerticesOnPath() of the GraphTraversal class shown below. The method finds all the vertices on a path from a start vertex in a directed graph. (See also the explanation to the method declaration at (17) on page 702). The method uses the stack implementation MyStack<E> from Example 14.7, p. 695.

```java
import java.util.Arrays;
import java.util.Collection;
import java.util.HashMap;
import java.util.HashSet;
import java.util.Map;
import java.util.Set;

public class GraphTraversal {

    public static void main(String[] args) {
        // (1) Given a directed graph with five vertices:
        Integer[][] neighbors = {
            {1, 3},   // Vertex 0
            {2},      // Vertex 1
            {4},      // Vertex 2
            {1, 2},   // Vertex 3
            {}        // Vertex 4
        };
        Map<Integer, Collection<Integer>> graph
                            = new HashMap<Integer, Collection<Integer>>();
        for (int i = 0; i < neighbors.length; i++) {
            graph.put(i, Arrays.asList(neighbors[i]));
        }

        // (2) Get start vertex.
        int startVertex;
        try {
            startVertex = Integer.parseInt(args[0]);
        } catch (ArrayIndexOutOfBoundsException ive) {
```

```java
      System.out.println("Usage: java GraphTraversal [0-4]");
      return;
    } catch (NumberFormatException nfe) {
      System.out.println("Usage: java GraphTraversal [0-4]");
      return;
    }

    Set<Integer> visitedSet = GraphTraversal.findVerticesOnPath(graph,
                                                      startVertex);
    System.out.print("Vertex " + startVertex + " is connected to " + visitedSet);
  }

  /**
   * Finds the vertices on a path from a given vertex in a directed graph.
   * In the map, the key is a vertex, and the value is the collection
   * containing its neighbours.
   */
  public static <N> Set<N> findVerticesOnPath(Map<N,Collection<N>> graph,
                                              N startVertex) {
    // Implement the body of the method.
    // Uses the generic class MyStack from Example 14.7.
  }
}
```

Collections and Maps

15

Exam Objectives

6.1 Given a design scenario, determine which collection classes and/or interfaces should be used to properly implement that design, including the use of the `Comparable` interface.

6.2 Distinguish between correct and incorrect overrides of corresponding `hashCode` and `equals` methods, and explain the difference between == and the `equals` method.

6.3 Write code that uses the generic versions of the Collections API, in particular, the `Set`, `List`, and `Map` interfaces and implementation classes. Recognize the limitations of the non-generic Collections API and how to refactor code to use the generic versions. Write code that uses the `NavigableSet` and `NavigableMap` interfaces.

6.4 Develop code that makes proper use of type parameters in class/interface declarations, instance variables, method arguments, and return types; and write generic methods or methods that make use of wildcard types and understand the similarities and differences between these two approaches.

  ○ *For generics, see Chapter 14, p. 661.*

6.5 Use capabilities in the `java.util` package to write code to manipulate a list by sorting, performing a binary search, or converting the list to an array. Use capabilities in the `java.util` package to write code to manipulate an array by sorting, performing a binary search, or converting the array to a list. Use the `java.util.Comparator` and `java.lang.Comparable` interfaces to affect the sorting of lists and arrays. Furthermore, recognize the effect of the "natural ordering" of primitive wrapper classes and `java.lang.String` on sorting.

Supplementary Objectives

• Write code that uses deques, as defined by the `Deque` interface and implemented by the `ArrayDeque` class.

15.1 Comparing Objects

The majority of the non-final methods of the Object class are meant to be over-ridden. They provide general contracts for objects, which the classes overriding the methods should honor.

It is important to understand how and why a class should override the equals() and hashCode() methods. Implementation of the compareTo() method of the Comparable interface is closely related to the other two methods.

Objects of a class that override the equals() method can be used as elements in a collection. If they override the hashCode() method, they can also be used as elements in a HashSet and as keys in a HashMap. Implementing the Comparable interface allows them to be used as elements in sorted collections and as keys in sorted maps. Table 15.2 on p. 782 summarizes the methods that objects should provide if the objects are to be maintained in collections and maps.

As a running example, we will implement different versions of a class for *version numbers*. A version number (VNO) for a software product comprises three pieces of information:

- a release number
- a revision number
- a patch number

The idea is that releases do not happen very often. Revisions take place more frequently than releases, but less frequently than code patches are issued. We can say that the release number is most *significant*. The revision number is less significant than the release number, and the patch number is the least significant of the three fields. This ranking would also be employed when ordering version numbers chronologically.

We will develop different implementations of the version number in this section and test them using the test() method declared at (1) in the TestCaseVNO class (Example 15.1). This static method is a generic method, with type parameter N representing a version number class.

The test() method in Example 15.1 is passed three references (latest, inShops, older) that denote three different objects of a version number class, as shown at (2a), (2b), and (2c), respectively. It is also passed an array of version numbers, named versions, as shown at (3). The last parameter, shown at (4), is an array of Integers, named downloads, whose elements represent the number of downloads for the version numbers from the corresponding position in the versions array. The method prints the name of the version number class at (5) from one of the version numbers passed as parameter. The method then performs various tests on the version numbers and tries to use them in different ways. This is explained in more detail below.

Example 15.1 *A Test Case for Version Numbers*

```java
import java.util.Arrays;
import java.util.Collections;
import java.util.HashMap;
import java.util.List;
import java.util.Map;
import java.util.TreeMap;
import java.util.TreeSet;
import static java.lang.System.out;

public class TestCaseVNO {
  /** Type parameter N represents a class implementing a version number. */
  public static <N> void test(                                   // (1)
                  N latest,                                       // (2a)
                  N inShops,                                      // (2b)
                  N older,                                        // (2c)
                  N[] versions,                                   // (3)
                  Integer[] downloads) {                          // (4)

    // Print the class name.
    out.println(latest.getClass());                              // (5)

    // Various tests.
    out.println("Test object reference and value equality:");
    out.printf ("     latest: %s, inShops: %s, older: %s%n" ,
                   latest, inShops, older);
    out.println("     latest == inShops:      " + (latest == inShops)); // (6)
    out.println("     latest.equals(inShops): " +
                   (latest.equals(inShops)));                    // (7)
    out.println("     latest == older:        " + (latest == older));   // (8)
    out.println("     latest.equals(older):   " + latest.equals(older));// (9)

    N searchKey = inShops;                                       // (10)
    boolean found = false;
    for (N version : versions) {
      found = searchKey.equals(version);                         // (11)
      if (found) break;
    }
    out.println("Array: " + Arrays.toString(versions));          // (12)
    out.println("     Search key " + searchKey + " found in array: " +
               found);                                           // (13)

    List<N> vnoList = Arrays.asList(versions);                   // (14)
    out.println("List: " + vnoList);
    out.println("     Search key " + searchKey + " contained in list: " +
               vnoList.contains(searchKey));                     // (15)

    Map<N, Integer> versionStatistics = new HashMap<N, Integer>(); // (16)
    for (int i = 0; i < versions.length; i++)                    // (17)
      versionStatistics.put(versions[i], downloads[i]);
    out.println("Map: " + versionStatistics);                    // (18)
    out.println("     Hash code for keys in the map:");
    for (N version : versions)                                   // (19)
```

```
        out.printf("    %10s: %s%n", version, version.hashCode());
        out.println("    Search key " + searchKey + " has hash code: " +
                searchKey.hashCode());                              // (20)
        out.println("    Map contains search key " + searchKey + ": " +
                versionStatistics.containsKey(searchKey));          // (21)

        out.println("Sorted set:\n    " + (new TreeSet<N>(vnoList)));  // (22)
        out.println("Sorted map:\n    " +
                (new TreeMap<N, Integer>(versionStatistics)));      // (23)

        out.println("List before sorting: " + vnoList);
        Collections.sort(vnoList, null);                           // (24)
        out.println("List after sorting:  " + vnoList);

        int resultIndex = Collections.binarySearch(vnoList, searchKey, null);// (25)
        out.println("Binary search in list found key " + searchKey +
                " at index: " + resultIndex);
    }
}
```

Output from running the program in Example 15.9, p. 769, that uses the TestCaseVNO class:

```
class VersionNumber
Test object reference and value equality:
    latest: (9.1.1), inShops: (9.1.1), older: (6.6.6)
    latest == inShops:      false
    latest.equals(inShops): true
    latest == older:        false
    latest.equals(older):   false
Array: [(3.49.1), (8.19.81), (2.48.28), (10.23.78), (9.1.1)]
    Search key (9.1.1) found in array: true
List: [(3.49.1), (8.19.81), (2.48.28), (10.23.78), (9.1.1)]
    Search key (9.1.1) contained in list: true
Map: {(9.1.1)=123, (2.48.28)=54, (8.19.81)=786, (3.49.1)=245, (10.23.78)=1010}
    Hash code for keys in the map:
       (3.49.1): 332104
       (8.19.81): 336059
       (2.48.28): 331139
       (10.23.78): 338102
        (9.1.1): 336382
    Search key (9.1.1) has hash code: 336382
    Map contains search key (9.1.1): true
Sorted set:
    [(2.48.28), (3.49.1), (8.19.81), (9.1.1), (10.23.78)]
Sorted map:
    {(2.48.28)=54, (3.49.1)=245, (8.19.81)=786, (9.1.1)=123, (10.23.78)=1010}
List before sorting: [(3.49.1), (8.19.81), (2.48.28), (10.23.78), (9.1.1)]
List after sorting:  [(2.48.28), (3.49.1), (8.19.81), (9.1.1), (10.23.78)]
Binary search in list found key (9.1.1) at index: 3
```

The workings of the test() method in Example 15.1 are best understood in terms of what it prints. The output shown in Example 15.1 corresponds to running the program in Example 15.9, p. 769. This program calls the test() method with objects of the VersionNumber class from Example 15.8. The VersionNumber class overrides the equals() and the hashCode() methods, and implements the Comparable interface.

The version numbers are tested for both object reference and object value equality. The object referenced by the reference latest is compared with the object referenced by the reference inShops and with the object referenced by the reference older, as shown at (6), (7), (8), and (9). The output from the program shows that the result is false for object reference equality and the result for object value equality is true if the objects have the same state.

Overriding the equals() method appropriately makes it possible to search for objects in arrays, collections, or maps. Searching involves specifying a copy object, called the *search key*, which can be compared with objects in the collection. Searching in an array is illustrated by the code from (10) to (13). As can be seen from the output, searching for the version number (9.1.1) in the versions array is successful.

The versions array is converted to a List at (14), referenced by the reference vnoList, and the contains() method is called at (15) to determine whether the search key is in this list. The contains() method of a List relies on the equals() method provided by its elements. The result is, as expected, true.

An empty HashMap is created at (16) and populated at (17) with version numbers as keys and Integer objects as values, based on the associative arrays versions and downloads. The versionStatistics map is printed at (18). Hash codes for all the map keys are printed at (19), and the hash code for the search key is printed at (20). Since the hashCode() method is overridden by the version number class, the attempt to determine whether the search key is in the map is successful.

A sorted set and a sorted map are created from the vnoList list and the versionStatistics map at (22) and (23), respectively. The program output shows that the version numbers in the TreeSet and the TreeMap are sorted in natural ordering.

The unsorted vnoList is sorted successfully at (24). Finally, a binary search for the key in the sorted list at (25) is also reported to be successful.

At (24) and (25), the null value is passed as a comparator. The method called then assumes natural ordering. This was necessary to avoid compile time errors with some of the implementations of the version number discussed in this section.

The equals() Method

If every object is to be considered unique, then it is not necessary to override the equals() method in the Object class. This method implements object reference equality. It implements the most discriminating equivalence relation possible on objects. Each instance of the class is only equal to itself.

The class SimpleVNO in Example 15.2 does not override the equals() method in the Object class. It only overrides the toString() method to generate a meaningful textual representation for a version number.

Example 15.2 *Not Overriding the* equals() *and the* hashCode() *Methods*

```java
public class SimpleVNO {
  // Does not override equals() or hashCode().

  private int release;
  private int revision;
  private int patch;

  public SimpleVNO(int release, int revision, int patch) {
    this.release  = release;
    this.revision = revision;
    this.patch    = patch;
  }

  public String toString() {
    return "(" + release + "." + revision + "." + patch + ")";
  }
}
```

The class TestSimpleVNO in Example 15.3 creates objects of the class SimpleVNO to test with the test() method of the TestCaseVNO class in Example 15.1, passing the relevant objects to this method as explained earlier. Successive implementations of the version number will also be tested in the same way.

Example 15.3 *Testing the* equals() *and the* hashCode() *Methods*

```java
public class TestSimpleVNO {
  public static void main(String[] args) {
    // Three individual version numbers.
    SimpleVNO latest  = new SimpleVNO(9,1,1);               // (1)
    SimpleVNO inShops = new SimpleVNO(9,1,1);               // (2)
    SimpleVNO older   = new SimpleVNO(6,6,6);               // (3)

    // An array of version numbers.
    SimpleVNO[] versions =  new SimpleVNO[] {               // (4)
        new SimpleVNO( 3,49, 1), new SimpleVNO( 8,19,81),
        new SimpleVNO( 2,48,28), new SimpleVNO(10,23,78),
        new SimpleVNO( 9, 1, 1)};

    // An array with number of downloads.
    Integer[] downloads = {245, 786, 54,1010, 123};        // (5)

    TestCaseVNO.test(latest, inShops, older, versions, downloads); // (6)
  }
}
```

Output from the program:

```
class SimpleVNO
Test object reference and value equality:
    latest: (9.1.1), inShops: (9.1.1), older: (6.6.6)
    latest == inShops:      false
    latest.equals(inShops): false
    latest == older:        false
    latest.equals(older):   false
Array: [(3.49.1), (8.19.81), (2.48.28), (10.23.78), (9.1.1)]
    Search key (9.1.1) found in array: false
List: [(3.49.1), (8.19.81), (2.48.28), (10.23.78), (9.1.1)]
    Search key (9.1.1) contained in list: false
Map: {(9.1.1)=123, (2.48.28)=54, (8.19.81)=786, (3.49.1)=245, (10.23.78)=1010}
    Hash code for keys in the map:
      (3.49.1): 8451275
     (8.19.81): 4669910
     (2.48.28): 3374351
    (10.23.78): 5737707
       (9.1.1): 31771588
    Search key (9.1.1) has hash code: 31393597
    Map contains search key (9.1.1): false
Exception in thread "main" java.lang.ClassCastException: SimpleVNO cannot be cast
to java.lang.Comparable
    ...
    at TestCaseVNO.test(TestCaseVNO.java:57)
    at TestSimpleVNO.main(TestSimpleVNO.java:15)
```

The output in Example 15.3 demonstrates that all SimpleVNO objects are unique, because the class SimpleVNO does not override the equals() method to provide any other equivalence relation. The result is false for object reference equality and for object value equality. The references refer to distinct objects, although the objects referenced by two of the references have identical states.

Not overriding the equals() method appropriately makes it impossible to search for SimpleVNO objects in arrays, collections, or maps. Since all SimpleVNO objects are distinct, the equals() method in the Object class will always return false, regardless of which object is compared with the search key. As shown by the output from Example 15.3, searching for the version number (9.1.1) in the versions array will always fail. Not surprisingly, the result is the same when searching for a key in a list of SimpleVNO objects. The contains() method of the list relies on the equals() method.

It is possible to create a HashMap with SimpleVNO objects as keys and Integer objects as values, based on the associative arrays versions and downloads. Since the hash-Code() method is not overridden either, the method implementation in the Object class attempts to return distinct integers as hash codes for the objects. Hash codes for all the keys in the map and the search key are all distinct, as the output shows. Searching for a SimpleVNO object in a hash map using hash codes is not successful.

An attempt to create a sorted set results in a ClassCastException. The class SimpleVNO must either implement the compareTo() method of the Comparable interface, or a comparator must be provided, in order for its objects to be maintained in sorted sets or sorted maps (see Section 15.5, p. 802, and Section 15.10, p. 828). However, the result is unpredictable when objects that do not meet the criteria are used in these collections.

Equivalence Relation

An implementation of the `equals()` method must satisfy the properties of an *equivalence relation*:

- *Reflexive*: For any reference `self`, `self.equals(self)` is always `true`.
- *Symmetric*: For any references `x` and `y`, `x.equals(y)` is `true` if and only if `y.equals(x)` is `true`.
- *Transitive*: For any references `x`, `y`, and `z`, if both `x.equals(y)` and `y.equals(z)` are `true`, then `x.equals(z)` is `true`.
- *Consistent*: For any references `x` and `y`, multiple invocations of `x.equals(y)` will always return the same result, provided the objects referenced by these references have not been modified to affect the equals comparison.
- `null` *comparison*: For any non-`null` reference `obj`, the call `obj.equals(null)` always returns `false`.

The general contract of the `equals()` method is defined between *objects of arbitrary classes*. Understanding its criteria is important for providing a proper implementation.

Reflexivity

This rule simply states that an object is equal to itself, regardless of how it is modified. It is easy to satisfy: the object passed as argument and the current object are compared for object reference equality (`==`):

```
if (this == argumentObj)
    return true;
```

Symmetry

The expression `x.equals(y)` invokes the `equals()` method on the object referenced by the reference `x`, whereas the expression `y.equals(x)` invokes the `equals()` method on the object referenced by the reference `y`. Both invocations must return the same result.

If the `equals()` methods invoked are in different classes, the classes must bilaterally agree whether their objects are equal or not. In other words, symmetry can be violated if the `equals()` method of a class makes unilateral decisions about which classes it will interoperate with, while the other classes are not aware of this. Avoiding interoperability with other (non-related) classes when implementing the `equals()` method is strongly recommended.

Transitivity

If two classes, A and B, have a bilateral agreement on their objects being equal, then this rule guarantees that one of them, say B, does not enter into an agreement with a third class C on its own. All classes involved must multilaterally abide by the terms of the contract.

A typical pitfall resulting in broken transitivity is when the equals() method in a subclass calls the equals() method of its superclass, as part of its equals comparison. The equals() method in the subclass usually has code equivalent to the following line:

```
return super.equals(argumentObj) && compareSubclassSpecificAspects();
```

The idea is to compare only the subclass-specific aspects in the subclass equals() method and to use the superclass equals() method for comparing the superclass-specific aspects. However, this approach should be used with extreme caution. The problem lies in getting the equivalence contract fulfilled bilaterally between the superclass and the subclass equals() methods. If the subclass equals() method does not interoperate with superclass objects, symmetry is easily broken. If the subclass equals() method does interoperate with superclass objects, transitivity is easily broken.

If the superclass is abstract, using the superclass equals() method works well. There are no superclass objects for the subclass equals() method to consider. In addition, the superclass equals() method cannot be called directly by any other clients than subclasses. The subclass equals() method then has control of how the superclass equals() method is called. It can safely call the superclass equals() method to compare the superclass-specific aspects of subclass objects.

Consistency

This rule enforces that two objects that are equal (or non-equal) remain equal (or non-equal) as long as they are not modified. For mutable objects, the result of the equals comparison can change if one (or both) are modified between method invocations. However, for immutable objects, the result must always be the same. The equals() method should take into consideration whether the class implements immutable objects, and ensure that the consistency rule is not violated.

null *comparison*

This rule states that no object is equal to null. The contract calls for the equals() method to return false. The method must not throw an exception; that would be violating the contract. A check for this rule is necessary in the implementation. Typically, the reference value passed as argument is explicitly compared with the null value:

```
if (argumentObj == null)
    return false;
```

In many cases, it is preferable to use the `instanceof` operator. It always returns `false` if its left operand is `null`:

```
if (!(argumentObj instanceof MyRefType))
    return false;
```

This test has the added advantage that if the condition fails, the argument reference can be safely downcast.

Example 15.4   *Implementing the* `equals()` *Method*

```
public class UsableVNO {
  // Overrides equals(), but not hashCode().

  private int release;
  private int revision;
  private int patch;

  public UsableVNO(int release, int revision, int patch) {
    this.release  = release;
    this.revision = revision;
    this.patch    = patch;
  }

  public String toString() {
    return "(" + release + "." + revision + "." + patch + ")";
  }

  public boolean equals(Object obj) {            // (1)
    if (obj == this)                             // (2)
      return true;
    if (!(obj instanceof UsableVNO))             // (3)
      return false;
    UsableVNO vno = (UsableVNO) obj;             // (4)
    return vno.patch    == this.patch    &&      // (5)
           vno.revision == this.revision &&
           vno.release  == this.release;
  }
}
```

Example 15.4 shows an implementation of the `equals()` method for version numbers. Next, we provide a checklist for implementing the `equals()` method.

Method Overriding signature

The method header is

```
public boolean equals(Object obj)          // (1)
```

The signature of the method requires that the argument passed is of the type `Object`. The following header will overload the method, not override it:

```
public boolean equals(MyRefType obj)       // Overloaded.
```

The compiler will not complain. Calls to overloaded methods are resolved at compile time, depending on the type of the argument. Calls to overridden methods are resolved at runtime, depending on the type of the actual object referenced by the argument. Comparing the objects of the class MyRefType that overloads the equals() method for equivalence, can give inconsistent results:

```
MyRefType ref1 = new MyRefType();
MyRefType ref2 = new MyRefType();
Object    ref3 = ref2;
boolean b1 = ref1.equals(ref2);    // True. Calls equals() in MyRefType.
boolean b2 = ref1.equals(ref3);    // Always false. Calls equals() in Object.
```

However, if the equals() method is overridden correctly, only the overriding method in MyRefType is called. A class can provide both implementations, but the equals() methods must be consistent.

Reflexivity Test

This is usually the first test performed in the equals() method, avoiding further computation if the test is true. The equals() method in Example 15.4 does this test at (2).

Correct Argument Type

The equals() method in Example 15.4 checks the type of the argument object at (3), using the instanceof operator:

```
if (!(obj instanceof UsableVNO))                    // (3)
  return false;
```

This code also does the null comparison correctly, returning false if the argument obj has the value null.

The instanceof operator will also return true if the argument obj denotes a subclass object of the class UsableVNO. If the class is final, this issue does not arise—there are no subclass objects. The test at (3) can also be replaced by the following code in order to exclude all other objects, including subclass objects:

```
if ((obj == null) || (obj.getClass() != this.getClass()))    // (3a)
  return false;
```

The test in (3a) first performs the null comparison explicitly. The expression (obj.getClass() != this.getClass()) determines whether the classes of the two objects have the same runtime object representing them. If this is the case, the objects are instances of the same class.

Argument Casting

The argument is only cast after checking that the cast will be successful. The instanceof operator ensures the validity of the cast, as done in Example 15.4. The argument is cast at (4) to allow for class-specific field comparisons:

```
UsableVNO vno = (UsableVNO) obj;                    // (4)
```

Field Comparisons

Equivalence comparison involves comparing certain fields from both objects to determine if their logical states match. For fields that are of primitive data types, their primitive values can be compared. Instances of the class UsableVNO in Example 15.4 have fields of primitive data types only. Values of corresponding fields are compared to test for equality between two UsableVNO objects:

```
return vno.patch    == this.patch    &&          // (5)
       vno.revision == this.revision &&
       vno.release  == this.release;
```

If all field comparisons evaluate to true, the equals() method returns true.

For fields that are references, the objects referenced by the references can be compared. For example, if the UsableVNO class declares a field called productInfo, which is a reference, the following code could be used:

```
(vno.productInfo  == this.productInfo ||
(this.productInfo != null && this.productInfo.equals(vno.productInfo)))
```

The expression vno.productInfo == this.productInfo checks for the possibility that the two objects being compared have a common object referenced by both product-Info references. In order to avoid a NullPointerException being thrown, the equals() method is not invoked if the this.productInfo reference is null.

Exact comparison of floating-point values should not be done directly on the values, but on the integer values obtained from their bit patterns (see static methods Float.floatToIntBits() and Double.doubleToLongBits() in the Java Standard Library). This technique eliminates certain anomalies in floating-point comparisons that involve a NaN value or a negative zero (see also the equals() method in Float and Double classes).

Only fields that have significance for the equivalence relation should be considered. Derived fields, whose computation is dependent on other field values in the object, might be redundant to include, including only the derived fields may be prudent. Computing the equivalence relation should be deterministic, therefore, the equals() method should not depend on unreliable resources, such as network access.

The order in which the comparisons of the significant fields are carried out can influence the performance of the equals comparison. Fields that are most likely to differ should be compared as early as possible in order to short-circuit the computation. In our example, patch numbers evolve faster than revision numbers, which, in turn, evolve faster than release numbers. This order is reflected in the return statement at (5) in Example 15.4.

Above all, an implementation of the equals() method must ensure that the equivalence relation is fulfilled.

Example 15.5 is a client that uses the class UsableVNO from Example 15.4. This client runs the same tests as the client in Example 15.3. The difference is that the class UsableVNO overrides the equals() method.

Example 15.5 *Implications of Overriding the* equals() *Method*

```
public class TestUsableVNO {
  public static void main(String[] args) {
    // Three individual version numbers.
    UsableVNO latest  = new UsableVNO(9,1,1);              // (1)
    UsableVNO inShops = new UsableVNO(9,1,1);              // (2)
    UsableVNO older   = new UsableVNO(6,6,6);              // (3)

    // An array of version numbers.
    UsableVNO[] versions =  new UsableVNO[] {              // (4)
        new UsableVNO( 3,49, 1), new UsableVNO( 8,19,81),
        new UsableVNO( 2,48,28), new UsableVNO(10,23,78),
        new UsableVNO( 9, 1, 1)};

    // An array with number of downloads.
    Integer[] downloads = {245, 786, 54,1010, 123};       // (5)

    TestCaseVNO.test(latest, inShops, older, versions, downloads);   // (6)
  }
}
```

Output from the program:

```
class UsableVNO
Test object reference and value equality:
    latest: (9.1.1), inShops: (9.1.1), older: (6.6.6)
    latest == inShops:      false
    latest.equals(inShops): true
    latest == older:        false
    latest.equals(older):   false
Array: [(3.49.1), (8.19.81), (2.48.28), (10.23.78), (9.1.1)]
    Search key (9.1.1) found in array: true
List: [(3.49.1), (8.19.81), (2.48.28), (10.23.78), (9.1.1)]
    Search key (9.1.1) contained in list: true
Map: {(9.1.1)=123, (2.48.28)=54, (8.19.81)=786, (3.49.1)=245, (10.23.78)=1010}
    Hash code for keys in the map:
       (3.49.1): 8451275
       (8.19.81): 4669910
       (2.48.28): 3374351
      (10.23.78): 5737707
        (9.1.1): 31771588
    Search key (9.1.1) has hash code: 31393597
    Map contains search key (9.1.1): false
Exception in thread "main" java.lang.ClassCastException: UsableVNO cannot be cast
to java.lang.Comparable
    ...
    at TestCaseVNO.test(TestCaseVNO.java:59)
    at TestUsableVNO.main(TestUsableVNO.java:18)
```

The output from the program shows that object value equality is compared correctly. Object value equality is now based on identical states, as defined by the equals() method.

The search for a UsableVNO object in an array or a list of UsableVNO objects is now successful, since the equals comparison is based on the states of the objects and not on their reference values.

However, searching in a map or creating sorted collections is still not feasible. For searching in a HashMap, we have to look at the relationship between the equals() and the hashCode() methods. For creating sorted collections or sorted maps, we will provide an implementation of the compareTo() method.

The hashCode() **Method**

Hashing is an efficient technique for storing and retrieving data. A common hashing scheme uses an array where each element is a list of items. The array elements are called *buckets*. Operations in a hashing scheme involve computing an array index from an item. Converting an item to its array index is done by a *hash function*. The array index returned by the hash function is called the *hash value* of the item. The hash value identifies a particular bucket.

Storing an item involves the following steps:

1. Hashing the item to determine the bucket.
2. If the item does not match one already in the bucket, it is stored in the bucket.

Note that no duplicate items are stored. Retrieving an item is based on using a *key*. The key represents the identity of the item. Item retrieval is also a two-step process:

1. Hashing the key to determine the bucket.
2. If the key matches an item in the bucket, this item is retrieved from the bucket.

Different items can hash to the same bucket, meaning that the hash function returns the same hash value for these items. This condition is called a *collision*. The list maintained by a bucket contains the items that hash to the bucket.

The hash value only identifies the bucket. Finding an item in the bucket entails a search and requires an equality function to compare items. The items maintained in a hash-based storage scheme must, therefore, provide two essential functions: a hash function and an equality function.

The performance of a hashing scheme is largely affected by how well the hash function distributes a collection of items over the available buckets. A hash function should not be biased toward any particular hash values. An ideal hash function produces a uniform distribution of hash values for a collection of items across all possible hash values. Such a hash function is not an easy task to design. Fortunately, heuristics exist for constructing adequate hash functions.

A *hash table* contains *key-value entries* as items and the hashing is done on the keys only to provide efficient lookup of values. Matching a given key with a key in an entry, determines the value.

If objects of a class are to be maintained in hash-based collections and maps of the java.util package (see Table 15.2), the class must provide appropriate implementations of the following methods from the Object class:

- a hashCode() method that produces hash values for the objects

- an equals() method that tests objects for equality

As a general rule for implementing these methods, *a class that overrides the* equals() *method must override the* hashCode() *method*. Consequences of not doing so are illustrated by the class UsableVNO in Example 15.4. Elements of this class are used as keys in Example 15.5. The output from the program shows that a map with the following entries is created:

```
Map: {(9.1.1)=123, (2.48.28)=54, (8.19.81)=786, (3.49.1)=245, (10.23.78)=1010}
```

The hashCode() method from the Object class is not overridden by the UsableVNO class and is, therefore, used to compute the hash values of the key objects. This method returns the memory address of the object as the default hash value. The output from the program shows the hash values assigned by this method to the keys in the map:

```
Hash code for keys in the map:
   (3.49.1): 8451275
  (8.19.81): 4669910
  (2.48.28): 3374351
 (10.23.78): 5737707
    (9.1.1): 31771588
```

The attempt to find the search key (9.1.1) in the map is unsuccessful:

```
Search key (9.1.1) has hash code: 31393597
Map contains search key (9.1.1): false
```

The hash values of two objects, which are equal according to the equals() method of the class UsableVNO, are not equal according to the hashCode() method of the Object class. Therefore, the key (9.1.1) of the entry (9.1.1)=123 in the map has a different hash value than the search key (9.1.1). These objects hash to different buckets. The lookup for the search key is done in one bucket and does not find the entry (9.1.1)=123, which is to be found in a completely different bucket. Just overriding the equals() method is not enough. The class UsableVNO violates the key tenet of the hashCode() contract: *equal objects must produce equal hash codes*.

General Contract of the hashCode() *Method*

The general contract of the hashCode() method stipulates:

- *Consistency during execution*: Multiple invocations of the hashCode() method on an object must consistently return the same hash code during the execution of an application, provided the object is not modified to affect the result returned by the equals() method. The hash code need not remain consistent across different executions of the application. This means that using a pseudorandom number generator to produce hash values is not a valid strategy.

- *Object value equality implies hash value equality*: If two objects are equal according to the equals() method, then the hashCode() method must produce the same hash code for these objects. This tenet ties in with the general contract of the equals() method.

- *Object value inequality places no restrictions on the hash value*: If two objects are unequal according to the equals() method, then the hashCode() method need not produce distinct hash codes for these objects. It is strongly recommended that the hashCode() method produce unequal hash codes for unequal objects.

Note that the hash contract does not imply that objects with equal hash codes are equal. Not producing unequal hash codes for unequal objects can have an adverse effect on performance, as unequal objects will hash to the same bucket.

Heuristics for Implementing the hashCode() Method

In Example 15.6, the computation of the hash value in the hashCode() method of the ReliableVNO class embodies heuristics that can produce fairly reasonable hash functions. The hash value is computed according to the following formula:

hashValue = 11 * 31^3 + release * 31^2 + revision * 31^1 + patch

This can be verified by back substitution (see Section G.3, p. 1008). Each significant field is included in the computation. Only the fields that have bearing on the equals() method are included. This ensures that objects that are equal according to the equals() method, also have equal hash values according to the hashCode() method.

Example 15.6 *Implementing the* hashCode() *Method*

```
public class ReliableVNO {
  // Overrides both equals() and hashCode().

  private int release;
  private int revision;
  private int patch;

  public ReliableVNO(int release, int revision, int patch) {
    this.release  = release;
    this.revision = revision;
    this.patch    = patch;
  }

  public String toString() {
    return "(" + release + "." + revision + "." + patch + ")";
```

```
    }

    public boolean equals(Object obj) {              // (1)
      if (obj == this)                               // (2)
        return true;
      if (!(obj instanceof ReliableVNO))             // (3)
        return false;
      ReliableVNO vno = (ReliableVNO) obj;           // (4)
      return vno.patch   == this.patch   &&          // (5)
             vno.revision == this.revision &&
             vno.release  == this.release;
    }

    public int hashCode() {                          // (6)
      int hashValue = 11;
      hashValue = 31 * hashValue + release;
      hashValue = 31 * hashValue + revision;
      hashValue = 31 * hashValue + patch;
      return hashValue;
    }
  }
```

The basic idea is to compute an int hash value sfVal for each significant field sf, and include an assignment of the form shown at (1) in the computation below:

```
  public int hashCode() {
    int sfVal;
    int hashValue = 11;
    ...
    sfVal = ...                     // Compute hash value for each significant field sf.
    hashValue = 31 * hashValue + sfVal;   // (1)
    ...
    return hashValue;
  }
```

This setup ensures that the result from incorporating a field value is used to calculate the contribution from the next field value.

Calculating the hash value sfVal for a significant field sf depends on the type of the field:

- Field sf is boolean:

    sfVal = sf ? 0 : 1;

- Field sf is byte, char, short, or int:

    sfVal = (int)sf;

- Field sf is long:

    sfVal = (int) (sf ^ (sf >>> 32));

- Field sf is float:

    sfVal = Float.floatToInt(sf);

- Field sf is double:

  ```
  long sfValTemp = Double.doubleToLong(sf);
  sfVal = (int) (sfValTemp ^ (sfValTemp >>> 32));
  ```

- Field sf is a reference that denotes an object. Typically, the hashCode() method is invoked recursively if the equals() method is invoked recursively:

  ```
  sfVal = (sf == null ? 0 : sf.hashCode());
  ```

- Field sf is an array. Contribution from each element is calculated similarly to a field.

The order in which the fields are incorporated into the hash code computation will influence the hash value. Fields whose values are derived from other fields can be excluded. There is no point in feeding the hash function with redundant information, since this is unlikely to improve the value distribution. Fields that are not significant for the equals() method must be excluded; otherwise, the hashCode() method might end up contradicting the equals() method. As with the equals() method, data from unreliable resources (e.g., network access) should not be used, and inclusion of transient fields should be avoided.

A legal or correct hash function does not necessarily mean it is appropriate or efficient. The classical example of a legal but inefficient hash function is

```
public int hashCode() {
  return 1949;
}
```

All objects using this method are assigned to the same bucket. The hash table is then no better than a list. For the sake of efficiency, a hash function should strive to produce unequal hash codes for unequal objects.

For numeric wrapper types, the hashCode() implementation returns an int representation of the primitive value, converting the primitive value to an int, if necessary. The Boolean objects for the boolean literals true and false have specific hash values, which are returned by the hashCode() method.

The hashCode() method of the String class returns a hash value that is the value of a polynomial whose variable has the value 31, the coefficients are the characters in the string, and the degree is the string length minus one. For example, the hash value of the string "abc" is computed as follows:

$$\text{hashValue} = \text{'a'} * 31^2 + \text{'b'} * 31^1 + \text{'c'} * 31^0 = 97 * 31 * 31 + 98 * 31 + 99 = 96354$$

For immutable objects, the hash code can be cached, that is, calculated once and returned whenever the hashCode() method is called.

The client in Example 15.7 creates objects of the class ReliableVNO in Example 15.6 and tests them by calling the test() method of class TestCaseVNO in Example 15.1. Output from the program shows that the key (9.1.1) of the entry (9.1.1)= 123 in the map has the same hash value as the search key (9.1.1). The search is successful. These objects hash to the same bucket. Therefore, the search for the key takes place in the right bucket. It finds the entry (9.1.1)= 123 using the equals() method by successfully checking for equality between the search key (9.1.1) and the key (9.1.1) of this entry. However, we still cannot use objects of the class ReliableVNO in sorted sets and maps.

Example 15.7 *Implications of Overriding the* hashCode() *Method*

```
public class TestReliableVNO {
  public static void main(String[] args) {
    // Three individual version numbers.
    ReliableVNO latest  = new ReliableVNO(9,1,1);                      // (1)
    ReliableVNO inShops = new ReliableVNO(9,1,1);                      // (2)
    ReliableVNO older   = new ReliableVNO(6,6,6);                      // (3)

    // An array of version numbers.
    ReliableVNO[] versions = new ReliableVNO[] {                       // (4)
        new ReliableVNO( 3,49, 1), new ReliableVNO( 8,19,81),
        new ReliableVNO( 2,48,28), new ReliableVNO(10,23,78),
        new ReliableVNO( 9, 1, 1)};

    // An array with number of downloads.
    Integer[] downloads = {245, 786, 54,1010, 123};                   // (5)

    TestCaseVNO.test(latest, inShops, older, versions, downloads);    // (6)
  }
}
```

Output from the program:

```
class ReliableVNO
...
Map: {(9.1.1)=123, (2.48.28)=54, (8.19.81)=786, (3.49.1)=245, (10.23.78)=1010}
    Hash code for keys in the map:
      (3.49.1): 332104
      (8.19.81): 336059
      (2.48.28): 331139
     (10.23.78): 338102
       (9.1.1): 336382
    Search key (9.1.1) has hash code: 336382
    Map contains search key (9.1.1): true
Exception in thread "main" java.lang.ClassCastException: ReliableVNO cannot be
cast to java.lang.Comparable
...
```

The Comparable<E> Interface

The *natural ordering* of objects is specified by implementing the generic Comparable interface. A *total ordering* of objects can be specified by implementing a *comparator* that implements the generic Comparator interface.

We will look at the two generic interfaces Comparable and Comparator in turn.

The general contract for the Comparable interface is defined by its only method:

```
int compareTo(E o)
```

It returns a negative integer, zero, or a positive integer if the current object is less than, equal to, or greater than the specified object, based on the natural ordering. It throws a ClassCastException if the reference value passed in the argument cannot be compared to the current object.

Many of the standard classes in the Java API, such as the primitive wrapper classes, String, Date, and File, implement the Comparable interface. Objects implementing this interface can be used as

- elements in a sorted set
- keys in a sorted map
- elements in lists that are sorted manually using the Collections.sort() method

The natural ordering for String objects (and Character objects) is lexicographical ordering, i.e., their comparison is based on the Unicode value of each character in the strings (see Section 10.4, p. 445). Objects of the String and Character classes will be lexicographically maintained as elements in a sorted set, or as keys in a sorted map that uses their natural ordering.

The natural ordering for objects of a numerical wrapper class is in ascending order of the values of the corresponding numerical primitive type (see Section 10.3, p. 428). As elements in a sorted set or as keys in a sorted map that uses their natural ordering, the objects will be maintained in ascending order.

According to the natural ordering for objects of the Boolean class, a Boolean object representing the value false is less than a Boolean object representing the value true.

An implementation of the compareTo() method for the objects of a class should meet the following criteria:

- For any two objects of the class, if the first object is *less than, equal to,* or *greater than* the second object, then the second object must be *greater than, equal to,* or *less than* the first object, respectively, i.e., the comparison is *anti-symmetric.*

- All three comparison relations (*less than, equal to, greater than*) embodied in the compareTo() method must be *transitive.* For example, if obj1.compareTo(obj2) > 0 and obj2.compareTo(obj3) > 0, then obj1.compareTo(obj3) > 0.

- For any two objects of the class, which compare as equal, the compareTo() method must return the same result if these two objects are compared with any other object, i.e., the comparison is *congruent.*

- The compareTo() method must be *consistent with equals*, that is, (obj1.compareTo(obj2) == 0) == (obj1.equals(obj2)). This is recommended if the objects will be maintained in sorted sets or sorted maps.

The magnitude of non-zero values returned by the method is immaterial; the sign indicates the result of the comparison. The general contract of the compareTo() method augments the general contract of the equals() method, providing a natural ordering of the compared objects. The equality test of the compareTo() method has the same provisions as that of the equals() method.

Implementing the compareTo() method is not much different from implementing the equals() method. In fact, given that the functionality of the equals() method is a subset of the functionality of the compareTo() method, the equals() implementation can call the compareTo() method. This guarantees that the two methods are always consistent with one another.

```
public boolean equals(Object other) {
  // ...
  return compareTo(other) == 0;
}
```

- -

Example 15.8   *Implementing the* compareTo() *Method of the* Comparable *Interface*

```
public final class VersionNumber implements Comparable<VersionNumber> {

  private final int release;
  private final int revision;
  private final int patch;

  public VersionNumber(int release, int revision, int patch) {
    this.release  = release;
    this.revision = revision;
    this.patch    = patch;
  }

  public String toString() {
    return "(" + release + "." + revision + "." + patch + ")";
  }

  public boolean equals(Object obj) {              // (1)
    if (obj == this)                                // (2)
      return true;
    if (!(obj instanceof VersionNumber))            // (3)
      return false;
    VersionNumber vno = (VersionNumber) obj;        // (4)
    return vno.patch    == this.patch    &&         // (5)
           vno.revision == this.revision &&
           vno.release  == this.release;
  }

  public int hashCode() {                           // (6)
    int hashValue = 11;
    hashValue = 31 * hashValue + this.release;
    hashValue = 31 * hashValue + this.revision;
    hashValue = 31 * hashValue + this.patch;
    return hashValue;
  }
```

```
   public int compareTo(VersionNumber vno) {              // (7)

      // Compare the release numbers.                     (8)
      if (this.release != vno.release)
        return new Integer(release).compareTo(vno.release);

      // Release numbers are equal,                       (9)
      // must compare revision numbers.
      if (this.revision != vno.revision)
        return new Integer(revision).compareTo(vno.revision);

      // Release and revision numbers are equal,          (10)
      // patch numbers determine the ordering.
      return new Integer(patch).compareTo(vno.patch);
    }
  }
```

A compareTo() method is seldom implemented to interoperate with objects of other classes. For example, this is the case for primitive wrapper classes and the String class. The calls to the compareTo() method in the three assert statements below all result in a compile time error.

```
Integer iRef = 10;
Double dRef = 3.14;
String str = "ten";
StringBuilder sb = new StringBuilder("ten");
assert iRef.compareTo(str) == 0;    // compareTo(Integer) not applicable to
                                    // arguments (String).
assert dRef.compareTo(iRef) > 0;    // compareTo(Double) not applicable to
                                    // arguments (Integer).
assert sb.compareTo(str) == 0;      // No such method in StringBuilder.
```

An implementation of the compareTo() method for version numbers is shown in Example 15.8. Note the specification of the implements clause in the class header. By parameterizing the Comparable interface with the VersionNumber type, the class declaration explicitly excludes comparison with objects of other types. Only VersionNumbers can be compared.

```
public final class VersionNumber implements Comparable<VersionNumber> {
  ...
  public int compareTo(VersionNumber vno) {              // (7)
  ...
  }
  ...
}
```

The signature of the compareTo() method is compareTo(VersionNumber). In order to maintain backward compatibility with non-generic code, the compiler inserts the following *bridge method* with the signature compareTo(Object) into the class.

```
public int compareTo(Object obj) {    // NOT A GOOD IDEA TO RELY ON THIS METHOD!
  return this.compareTo((VersionNumber) obj);
}
```

In an implementation of the compareTo() method, the fields are compared with the most significant field first and the least significant field last. In the case of the version numbers, the release numbers are compared first, followed by the revision numbers, with the patch numbers being compared last. Note that the next least significant fields are only compared if the comparison of the previous higher significant fields yielded equality. Inequality between corresponding significant fields short-circuits the computation. If all significant fields are equal, a zero will be returned. This approach is shown in the implementation of the compareTo() method at (7) through (10) in Example 15.8.

Comparison of integer values in fields can be optimized. In the code for comparing the release numbers at (8) in Example 15.8, we have used the compareTo() method implemented by the Integer class and relied on autoboxing of the vno.release value:

```
if (this.release != vno.release)
  return new Integer(release).compareTo(vno.release);
// Next field comparison
```

The code above can be replaced by the following code for doing the comparison, which relies on the difference between int values:

```
int releaseDiff = release - vno.release;
if (releaseDiff != 0)
  return releaseDiff;
// Next field comparison
```

However, this code can break if the difference is a value not in the range of the int type.

Significant fields with non-boolean primitive values are normally compared using the relational operators < and >. For comparing significant fields denoting constituent objects, the main options are to either invoke the compareTo() method on them or use a comparator.

Example 15.9 is a client that uses the class VersionNumber from Example 15.8. This client also runs the same tests as the clients in Example 15.7, Example 15.5, and Example 15.3. What is different about this implementation is that the class VersionNumber overrides both the equals() and hashCode() methods, and implements the compareTo() method. In addition, the compareTo() method is consistent with equals. Following general class design principles, the class has been declared final so that it cannot be extended. We have already seen the program output in Example 15.1 confirming that all the tests on objects of the VersionNumber class run as expected.

- -

Example 15.9 *Implications of Implementing the* compareTo() *Method*

```
public class TestVersionNumber {
  public static void main(String[] args) {
    // Three individual version numbers.
    VersionNumber latest  = new VersionNumber(9,1,1);           // (1)
```

```
VersionNumber inShops = new VersionNumber(9,1,1);              // (2)
VersionNumber older   = new VersionNumber(6,6,6);              // (3)

// An array of version numbers.
VersionNumber[] versions = new VersionNumber[] {               // (4)
    new VersionNumber( 3,49, 1), new VersionNumber( 8,19,81),
    new VersionNumber( 2,48,28), new VersionNumber(10,23,78),
    new VersionNumber( 9, 1, 1)};

// An array with number of downloads.
Integer[] downloads = {245, 786, 54,1010, 123};               // (5)

TestCaseVNO.test(latest, inShops, older, versions, downloads);  // (6)
  }
}
```

Unlike previous attempts, the following code from Example 15.9 demonstrates that VersionNumber objects can now be maintained in sorted sets and maps:

```
out.println("Sorted set:\n   " + (new TreeSet<N>(vnoList)));     // (22)
out.println("Sorted map:\n   " +
          (new TreeMap<N, Integer>(versionStatistics)));        // (23)
```

The output from executing this code shows that the elements in the set and the map are sorted in the natural ordering for version numbers:

```
Sorted list:
   [(2.48.28), (3.49.1), (8.19.81), (9.1.1), (10.23.78)]
Sorted map:
   {(2.48.28)=54, (3.49.1)=245, (8.19.81)=786, (9.1.1)=123, (10.23.78)=1010}
```

By default, the class TreeSet relies on its elements to implement the compareTo() method. The output from the program in Example 15.9 shows that the TreeSet, created at (22), maintains its elements sorted in the natural ordering dictated by the compareTo() method. Analogously, the output from the program in Example 15.9 shows that the TreeMap, created at (23), maintains its entries sorted on the keys, which are in the natural ordering dictated by the compareTo() method.

We can run generic algorithms on collections of version numbers. Utility methods provided by the Collections and Arrays classes in the java.util package are discussed in Section 15.11, "Working with Collections." The following code sorts the elements in the list that was created at (14) in Example 15.1, and referenced by the reference vnoList:

```
out.println("List before sorting: " + vnoList);
Collections.sort(vnoList, null);                               // (24)
out.println("List after sorting:  " + vnoList);
```

Since the comparator value is null, natural ordering is used. The output from executing this code shows that the elements in the list are indeed sorted in ascending order:

```
List before sorting: [(3.49.1), (8.19.81), (2.48.28), (10.23.78), (9.1.1)]
List after sorting:  [(2.48.28), (3.49.1), (8.19.81), (9.1.1), (10.23.78)]
```

A binary search can be run on this sorted list to find the index of the version number (9.1.1), referenced by the reference searchKey in Example 15.9:

```
int resultIndex = Collections.binarySearch(vnoList, searchKey, null);// (25)
out.println("Binary search in list found key " + searchKey +
            " at index: " + resultIndex);
```

Since the comparator value is null, natural ordering is assumed for the elements in the list. Executing the code prints the correct index of the search key in the sorted list:

```
Binary search in list found key (9.1.1) at index: 3
```

Specifying the comparator with the null value in the test() method in Example 15.9 was necessary to avoid compile time errors. We can readily use VersionNumber objects with the overloaded sort() and binarySearch() methods in the Collections class whose signature explicitly requires that the elements implement the Comparable interface:

```
VersionNumber[] versions =  new VersionNumber[] {
    new VersionNumber( 3,49, 1), new VersionNumber( 8,19,81),
    new VersionNumber( 2,48,28), new VersionNumber(10,23,78),
    new VersionNumber( 9, 1, 1)};

List<VersionNumber> vnList = Arrays.asList(versions);
Collections.sort(vnList); // [(2.48.28), (3.49.1), (8.19.81), (9.1.1), (10.23.78)]
int index1 = Collections.binarySearch(vnList, new VersionNumber(9, 1, 1)); // 3
```

The Comparator<E> Interface

Precise control of ordering can be achieved by creating a customized comparator that imposes a specific total ordering on the elements. All comparators implement the Comparator interface, which has the following single method:

```
int compare(E o1, E o2)
```

The compare() method returns a negative integer, zero, or a positive integer if the first object is less than, equal to, or greater than the second object, according to the total ordering, i.e., it's contract is equivalent to that of the compareTo() method of the Comparable interface. Since this method tests for equality, it is strongly recommended that its implementation does not contradict the semantics of the equals() method.

An alternative ordering to the default natural ordering can be specified by passing a Comparator to the constructor when the sorted set or map is created. The Collections and Arrays classes provide utility methods for sorting, which also take a Comparator (see subsection *Ordering Elements in Lists*, p. 838, and subsection *Sorting Arrays*, p. 842).

Example 15.10 demonstrates the use of different comparators for strings. The program creates an empty sorted set using the TreeSet class. Each program argument is added to the sorted set in the loop at (2). A textual representation of the sorted set is then printed at (3). The output shows the sort ordering in which the elements are maintained in the set. The set is traversed according to the sort ordering.

The String class implements the Comparable interface, providing an implementation of the compareTo() method. The compareTo() method defines the natural ordering for strings, which is lexicographical. The natural ordering is used to maintain the program arguments sorted lexicographically when the sorted set at (1a) is used. If we wish to maintain the strings in a different ordering, we need to provide a customized comparator.

The String class provides a static field (CASE_INSENSITIVE_ORDER) that denotes a comparator object with a compare() method that ignores the case when comparing strings lexicographically. This particular total ordering is used to maintain the program arguments sorted when the sorted set at (1b) is used. The comparator is passed as argument to the set constructor. The output shows how the elements are maintained sorted in the set by this total ordering, which is a *case-insensitive ordering*.

We can create a string comparator that enforces *rhyming ordering* on the strings. In rhyming ordering, two strings are compared by examining their corresponding characters at each position in the two strings, starting with the characters in the *last* position. First the characters in the last position are compared, then those in the last but one position, and so on. For example, given the two strings "report" and "court", the last two characters in both the strings are the same. Continuing backward in the two strings, the character 'o' in the first string is less than the character 'u' in the second string. According to the rhyming ordering, the string "report" is less than the string "court".

Comparing two strings according to the rhyming ordering is equivalent to reversing the strings and comparing the reversed strings lexicographically. If we reverse the two strings, "report" and "court", the reversed string "troper" is lexicographically less than the reversed string "truoc".

A rhyming ordering comparator is implemented by the RhymingStringComparator class in Example 15.10. The compare() method at (4) first creates reversed versions of the strings passed as arguments. A reversed version of a string is created using a string builder, which is first reversed and then converted back to a string, as shown at (5). The compare() method then calls the compareTo() method at (6) to compare the reversed strings, as the lexicographical ordering for the reversed strings is equivalent to the rhyming ordering for the original strings. This particular total ordering is used to maintain the program arguments sorted when the sorted set at (1c) is used. The comparator is again passed as argument to the set constructor. The output shows how the elements are maintained sorted in the set by this total ordering, which is *rhyming ordering*.

Example 15.10 *Natural Ordering and Total Ordering*

```java
import java.util.Comparator;
import java.util.Set;
import java.util.TreeSet;

public class ComparatorUsage {
  public static void main(String[] args) {

    // Choice of comparator.
//  Set<String> strSet = new TreeSet<String>();                              // (1a)
//  Set<String> strSet =
//      new TreeSet<String>(String.CASE_INSENSITIVE_ORDER);                  // (1b)
    Set<String> strSet =
        new TreeSet<String>(new RhymingStringComparator());                  // (1c)

    // Add each command line argument to the set.
    for (String argument : args) {                                           // (2)
      strSet.add(argument);
    }
    System.out.println(strSet);                                              // (3)
  }
}

class RhymingStringComparator implements Comparator<String> {
  public int compare(String obj1, String obj2) {                            // (4)

    // (5) Create reversed versions of the strings:
    String reverseStr1 = new StringBuilder(obj1).reverse().toString();
    String reverseStr2 = new StringBuilder(obj2).reverse().toString();

    // Compare the reversed strings lexicographically.
    return reverseStr1.compareTo(reverseStr2);                              // (6)
  }
}
```

The program is run with the following program arguments on the command line:

```
>java ComparatorUsage court Stuart report Resort assort support transport distort
```

Output from the program using the natural ordering (1a):

```
[Resort, Stuart, assort, court, distort, report, support, transport]
```

Output from the program using the case insensitive ordering (1b):

```
[assort, court, distort, report, Resort, Stuart, support, transport]
```

Output from the program using the rhyming ordering (1c):

```
[Stuart, report, support, transport, Resort, assort, distort, court]
```

Example 15.11 illustrates using a comparator that orders version numbers (Example 15.8) according to their reverse natural ordering. Such a comparator is implemented as an anonymous class by the method reverseComparatorVNO() at (1). The comparator leverages on the compareTo() method implemented by the Version-Number class.

A list of version numbers is created at (3), that is backed by the array created at (2). This list is sorted using the comparator at (4). A binary search is done in this list at (5). We have used the same comparator for the search as we did for the sorting in order to obtain predictable results.

- -

Example 15.11 *Using a Comparator for Version Numbers*

```java
import static java.lang.System.out;

import java.util.Arrays;
import java.util.Collections;
import java.util.Comparator;
import java.util.List;

public class UsingVersionNumberComparator {

  /** Comparator for reverse natural ordering of natural numbers. */
  public static Comparator<VersionNumber> reverseComparatorVNO() {  // (1)
    return new Comparator<VersionNumber>() {
      public int compare(VersionNumber vno1, VersionNumber vno2) {
        return vno2.compareTo(vno1);            // Comparing vno2 with vno1.
      }
    };
  }

  public static void main(String[] args) {
    VersionNumber[] versions = new VersionNumber[] {                  // (2)
        new VersionNumber(3, 49, 1), new VersionNumber(8, 19, 81),
        new VersionNumber(2, 48, 28), new VersionNumber(10, 23, 78),
        new VersionNumber(9, 1, 1) };

    List<VersionNumber> vnList = Arrays.asList(versions);             // (3)
    out.println("List before sorting:\n    " + vnList);
    Collections.sort(vnList, reverseComparatorVNO());                 // (4)
    out.println("List after sorting according to " +
                "reverse natural ordering:\n    " + vnList);
    VersionNumber searchKey = new VersionNumber(9, 1, 1);
    int resultIndex = Collections.binarySearch(vnList, searchKey,
                                reverseComparatorVNO());  // (5)
    out.println("Binary search in list using reverse natural ordering" +
                " found key " + searchKey + " at index: " + resultIndex);
  }
}
```

Program output:

```
List before sorting:
    [(3.49.1), (8.19.81), (2.48.28), (10.23.78), (9.1.1)]
List after sorting according to reverse natural ordering:
    [(10.23.78), (9.1.1), (8.19.81), (3.49.1), (2.48.28)]
Binary search in list using reverse natural ordering found key (9.1.1) at index: 1
```

Review Questions

15.1 Which statements about the hashCode() and equals() methods are true?

Select the two correct answers.

(a) Two objects that are different according to the equals() method, must have different hash values.

(b) Two objects that are equal according to the equals() method, must have the same hash value.

(c) Two objects that have the same hash value, must be equal according to the equals() method.

(d) Two objects that have different hash values, must be unequal according to the equals() method.

15.2 Given that the objects referenced by the parameters override the equals() and the hashCode() methods appropriately, which return values are possible from the following method?

```
String func(Object x, Object y) {
  return (x == y) + " " + x.equals(y) + " " + (x.hashCode() == y.hashCode());
}
```

Select the four correct answers.

(a) "false false false"
(b) "false false true"
(c) "false true false"
(d) "false true true"
(e) "true false false"
(f) "true false true"
(g) "true true false"
(h) "true true true"

15.3 Which code, when inserted at (1), in the equalsImpl() method will provide a correct implementation of the equals() method?

```
public class Pair {
  int a, b;
  public Pair(int a, int b) {
    this.a = a;
    this.b = b;
  }

  public boolean equals(Object o) {
    return (this == o) || (o instanceof Pair) && equalsImpl((Pair) o);
  }

  private boolean equalsImpl(Pair o) {
    // (1) INSERT CODE HERE ...
  }
}
```

Select the three correct answers.

(a) `return a == o.a || b == o.b;`
(b) `return false;`
(c) `return a >= o.a;`
(d) `return a == o.a;`
(e) `return a == o.a && b == o.b;`

15.4 Which code, when inserted at (1), will provide a correct implementation of the hashCode() method in the following program?

```java
import java.util.*;
public class Measurement {
  int count;
  int accumulated;
  public Measurement() {}
  public void record(int v) {
    count++;
    accumulated += v;
  }
  public int average() {
    return accumulated/count;
  }
  public boolean equals(Object other) {
    if (this == other)
      return true;
    if (!(other instanceof Measurement))
      return false;
    Measurement o = (Measurement) other;
    if (count != 0 && o.count != 0)
      return average() == o.average();
    return count == o.count;
  }
  public int hashCode() {
    // (1) INSERT CODE HERE ...
  }
}
```

Select the two correct answers.

(a) `return 31337;`
(b) `return accumulated / count;`
(c) `return (count << 16) ^ accumulated;`
(d) `return ~accumulated;`
(e) `return count == 0 ? 0 : average();`

15.5 What will be the result of compiling and running the following program?

```java
import java.util.Comparator;
class Person implements Comparable<Person> {
  String name;
  int age;
  Person(String name, int age) { this.name = name; this.age = age; }
```

```
        public int compareTo(Person p2) {
          Comparator<String> strCmp = Person.cmp();
          int status = strCmp.compare(this.name, p2.name);
          if (status == 0) {
            Comparator<Integer> intCmp = Person.cmp();
            status = intCmp.compare(this.age, p2.age);
          }
          return status;
        }

        public static <E extends Comparable<E>> Comparator<E> cmp() {
          return  new Comparator<E>() {
            public int compare(E s1, E s2) { return s2.compareTo(s1); }
          };
        }

        public static void main(String[] args) {
          Person p1 = new Person("Tom", 20);
          Person p2 = new Person("Dick", 30);
          Person p3 = new Person("Tom", 40);
          System.out.println((p1.compareTo(p2) < 0) + " " + (p1.compareTo(p3) < 0));
        }
      }
```

Select the one correct answer.

(a) The program will fail to compile.
(b) The program will compile but throw an exception when run.
(c) The program will compile and print true false, when run.
(d) The program will compile and print true true, when run.
(e) The program will compile and print false false, when run.
(f) The program will compile and print false true, when run.

15.2 The Java Collections Framework

A *collection* allows a group of objects to be treated as a single unit. Objects can be stored, retrieved, and manipulated as *elements* of a collection. Arrays are an example of one kind of collection.

Program design often requires the handling of collections of objects. The Java Collections Framework provides a set of standard utility classes for managing various kinds of collections. The core framework is provided in the java.util package and comprises three main parts:

• The core *interfaces* that allow collections to be manipulated independently of their implementation (see Figure 15.1 and Table 15.1). These *generic* interfaces define the common functionality exhibited by collections and facilitate data exchange between collections.

- A set of *implementations* (i.e., concrete classes, listed in Table 15.1) that are specific implementations of the core interfaces, providing data structures that a program can readily use.

- An assortment of static *utility methods* found in the Collections and Arrays *classes* that can be used to perform various operations on collections and arrays, such as sorting and searching, or creating customized collections (see Section 15.11, "Working with Collections").

Figure 15.1   *The Core Interfaces*

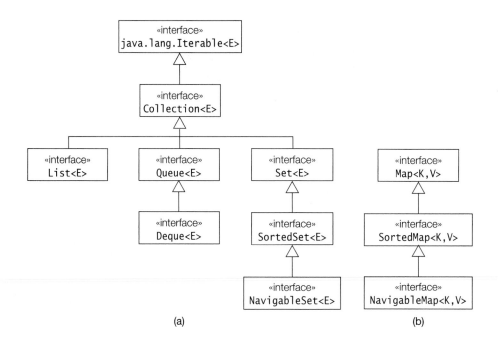

Core Interfaces

The generic Collection interface is a generalized interface for maintaining collections and is the root of the interface inheritance hierarchy for collections shown in Figure 15.1a. These subinterfaces are summarized in Table 15.1. The Collection interface extends the Iterable interface that specifies an *iterator* to sequentially access the elements of an Iterable object (see subsection *Iterators*, p. 785).

Table 15.1 *Core Interfaces in the Collections Framework*

Interface	Description	Concrete Classes
Collection<E>	A basic interface that defines the normal operations that allow a collection of objects to be maintained or handled as a single unit.	
Set<E>	The Set interface extends the Collection interface to represent its mathematical namesake: a *set* of unique elements.	HashSet<E> LinkedHashSet<E>
SortedSet<E>	The SortedSet interface extends the Set interface to provide the required functionality for maintaining a set in which the elements are stored in some sorted order.	TreeSet<E>
NavigableSet<E>	The NavigableSet interface extends and replaces the SortedSet interface to maintain a sorted set, and should be the preferred choice in new code.	TreeSet<E>
List<E>	The List interface extends the Collection interface to maintain a sequence of elements that can contain duplicates.	ArrayList<E> Vector<E> LinkedList<E>
Queue<E>	The Queue interface extends the Collection interface to maintain a collection whose elements need to be processed in some way, i.e., insertion at one end and removal at the other, usually as FIFO (First-In, First-Out).	PriorityQueue<E> LinkedList<E>
Deque<E>	The Deque interface extends the Queue interface to maintain a queue whose elements can be processed at both ends.	ArrayDeque<E> LinkedList<E>
Map<K,V>	A basic interface that defines operations for maintaining mappings of keys to values.	HashMap<K,V> Hashtable<K,V> LinkedHashMap<K,V>
SortedMap<K,V>	The SortedMap interface extends the Map interface for maps that maintain their mappings sorted in key order.	TreeMap<K,V>
NavigableMap<K,V>	The NavigableMap interface extends and replaces the SortedMap interface for sorted maps.	TreeMap<K,V>

The elements in a Set must be unique, that is, no two elements in the set can be equal. The order of elements in a List is *positional*, and individual elements can be accessed according to their position in the list.

Queues and deques, represented respectively by the Queue and the Deque interfaces, define collections whose elements can be processed according to various strategies.

As can be seen from Figure 15.1b, the Map interface does not extend the Collection interface because conceptually, a map is not a collection. A map does not contain elements. It contains *mappings* (also called *entries*) from a set of *key* objects to a set of *value* objects. A key can, at most, be associated with one value, i.e., it must be unique. As the name implies, the SortedMap interface extends the Map interface to maintain its mappings sorted in *key order*. It is superseded by the NavigableMap interface which should be the preferred choice in new code.

Implementations

The java.util package provides implementations of a selection of well-known abstract data types, based on the core interfaces. Figures 15.2 and 15.3 show the inheritance relationship between the core interfaces and the corresponding implementations. None of the concrete implementations inherit directly from the Collection interface. The abstract classes that provide the basis on which concrete classes are implemented, are not shown in Figures 15.2 and 15.3.

By convention, each of the collection implementation classes provides a constructor for creating a collection based on the elements of another Collection object passed as argument. This allows the implementation of a collection to be changed by merely passing the collection to the constructor of the desired implementation. This interchangeability is also true between Map implementations. But collections and maps are not interchangeable. Note that a collection (or a map) only stores reference values of objects, and not the actual objects.

The collections framework is *interface-based*, meaning that collections are manipulated according to their interface types, rather than by the implementation types. By using these interfaces wherever collections of objects are used, various implementations can be used interchangeably.

All the concrete classes shown in Figures 15.2 and 15.3 implement the Serializable and the Cloneable interfaces; therefore, the objects of these classes can be serialized and also cloned.

A summary of collection and map implementations is given in Table 15.2. The contents of this table will be the focus as each core interface and its corresponding implementations are discussed in the subsequent sections.

From Table 15.2, we see that elements in a LinkedHashSet are ordered, in a TreeSet they are sorted, and in a HashSet they have no order (that is, are *unordered*). *Sorting implies ordering* the elements in a collection according to some ranking criteria, usually based on the *values* of the elements. However, elements is an ArrayList are maintained in the order they are inserted in the list, known as the *insertion order*. The elements in such a list are thus *ordered*, but they are *not* sorted, as it is not the values

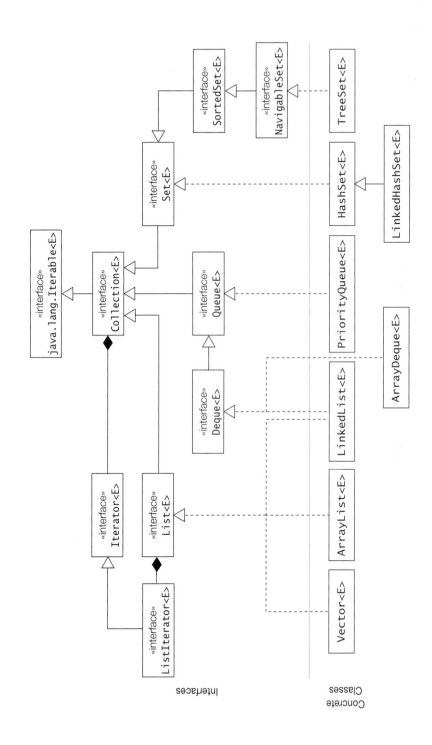

Figure 15.2 *The Core Collection Interfaces and Their Implementations*

Figure 15.3 *The Core Map Interfaces and Their Implementations*

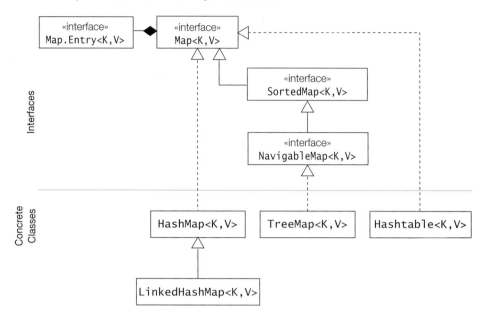

Table 15.2 *Summary of Collection and Map Implementations*

Concrete Collection/ Map	Interface	Dup- licates	Ordered/ Sorted	Methods That Can Be Called On Elements	Data Structures on Which Implementation Is Based
HashSet<E>	Set<E>	Unique elements	No order	equals() hashCode()	Hash table and linked list
LinkedHash- Set<E>	Set<E>	Unique elements	Insertion order	equals() hashCode()	Hash table and doubly-linked list
TreeSet<E>	Sorted- Set<E> Naviga- bleSet<E>	Unique elements	Sorted	compareTo()	Balanced tree
ArrayList<E>	List<E>	Allowed	Insertion order	equals()	Resizable array

Table 15.2 *Summary of Collection and Map Implementations (continued)*

Concrete Collection/ Map	Interface	Dup- licates	Ordered/ Sorted	Methods That Can Be Called On Elements	Data Structures on Which Implementation Is Based
LinkedList<E>	List<E> Queue<E> Deque<E>	Allowed	Insertion/ priority/ deque order	equals() compareTo()	Linked list
Vector<E>	List<E>	Allowed	Insertion order	equals()	Resizable array
Priority- Queue<E>	Queue<E>	Allowed	Access according to priority order	compareTo()	Priority heap (tree-like structure)
ArrayDeque<E>	Queue<E> Deque<E>	Allowed	Access according to either FIFO or LIFO processing order	equals()	Resizable array
HashMap<K,v>	Map<K,V>	Unique keys	No order	equals() hashCode()	Hash table using array
LinkedHash- Map<K,V>	Map<K,V>	Unique keys	Key insertion order/ Access order of entries	equals() hashCode()	Hash table and doubly-linked list
Hash- table<K,V>	Map<K,V>	Unique keys	No order	equals() hashCode()	Hash table
TreeMap<K,V>	Sorted- Map<K,V> Naviga- bleMap<K,V>	Unique keys	Sorted in key order	equals() compareTo()	Balanced tree

of the elements that determine their ranking in the list. Thus, ordering does *not* nec-essarily imply sorting. In a HashSet, the elements are unordered. No ranking of elements is implied in such a set. Whether a collection is sorted, ordered or unordered also has implications when traversing the collection (see subsection *Iterators*, p. 785).

The collection and map implementations discussed in this chapter, except for Vector and Hashtable, are not *thread-safe*, that is, their integrity can be jeopardized by concurrent access. The Java Collections Framework provides a plethora of collections and maps for use in single-threaded and concurrent applications; much more than what is covered in this book.

15.3 Collections

The Collection interface specifies the contract that all collections should implement. Some of the operations in the interface are *optional*, meaning that a collection may choose to provide a stub implementation of such an operation that throws an UnsupportedOperationException when invoked. The implementations of collections from the java.util package support all the optional operations in the Collection interface (see Figure 15.2 and Table 15.2).

Many of the methods return a boolean value to indicate whether the collection was modified as a result of the operation.

Basic Operations

The basic operations are used to query a collection about its contents and allow elements to be added to and removed from a collection. Many examples in this chapter make use of these operations.

```
int size()
boolean isEmpty()
boolean contains(Object element)
boolean add(E element)               Optional
boolean remove(Object element)       Optional
```

The add() and remove() methods return true if the collection was modified as a result of the operation.

By returning the value false, the add() method indicates that the collection excludes duplicates and that the collection already contains an object equal to the argument object.

The contains() method checks for membership of the argument object in the collection, using object value equality.

Note that we can only add an object of a specific type (E). However, a collection allows us to determine whether it has an element equal to any arbitrary object, or remove an element that is equal to any arbitrary object.

Bulk Operations

These operations perform on a collection as a single unit. See Section 15.4 for an example.

```
boolean containsAll(Collection<?> c)
boolean addAll(Collection<? extends E> c)        Optional
boolean removeAll(Collection<?> c)               Optional
boolean retainAll(Collection<?> c)               Optional
void clear()                                     Optional
```

These bulk operations can be used to perform the equivalent of set logic on *arbitrary collections* (i.e., also lists and not just sets). The containsAll() method returns true if all elements of the specified collection are also contained in the current collection.

The addAll(), removeAll(), and retainAll() methods are *destructive* in the sense that the collection on which they are invoked can be modified. The operations performed by these methods are visualized by Venn diagrams in Figure 15.4.

The addAll() requires that the element type of the other collection is the same as, or a subtype of, the element type of the current collection. The removeAll() and retainAll() operations can be performed with collections of any type.

Figure 15.4 *Bulk Operations on Collections*

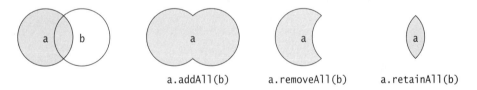

a.addAll(b)   a.removeAll(b)   a.retainAll(b)

Iterators

A collection provides an iterator which allows sequential access to the elements of a collection. An iterator can be obtained by calling the following method of the Collection interface:

```
Iterator<E> iterator()
```

Returns an object which implements the Iterator interface.

The generic interface Iterator is defined as follows:

```
boolean hasNext()
```

Returns true if the underlying collection still has elements left to return. A future call to the next() method will return the next element from the collection.

```
E next()
```

Moves the iterator to the next element in the underlying collection, and returns the current element. If there are no more elements left to return, it throws a NoSuchElementException.

```
void remove()                        Optional
```

Removes the element that was returned by the last call to the next() method from the underlying collection. Invoking this method results in an Illegal-StateException if the next() method has not yet been called or when the remove() method has already been called after the last call to the next() method. This method is optional for an iterator, i.e., it throws an UnsupportedOperation-Exception if the remove operation is not supported.

Using an Iterator to Traverse a Collection

After obtaining the iterator for a collection, the methods provided by the Iterator interface can be used to systematically traverse the elements of the underlying collection one by one. Example 15.12 illustrates the use of an iterator.

Example 15.12 *Using an Iterator*

```java
import java.util.ArrayList;
import java.util.Collection;
import java.util.Iterator;

public class IteratorUsage {
  public static void main(String[] args) {

    // (1) Create a list of Integers.
    Collection<Integer> intList = new ArrayList<Integer>();
    int[] values = { 9, 11, -4, 1, 13, 99, 1, 0 };
    for (int i : values) {
      intList.add(i);
    }
    System.out.println("Before: " + intList);         // (2)

    Iterator<Integer> iterator = intList.iterator();   // (3) Get an iterator.
    while (iterator.hasNext()) {                        // (4) Loop
      int value = iterator.next();                     // (5) The next element
      if (value < 1 || value > 10)                     // (6) Remove the element if
        iterator.remove();                             //        its value is not
                                                       //        between 1 and 10.

    }
```

```
        System.out.println("After:  " + intList);           // (7)
    }
}
```

Output from the program:

```
Before: [9, 11, -4, 1, 13, 99, 1, 0]
After:  [9, 1, 1]
```

- -

Example 15.12 creates a list of integers and then removes from the list all integers that are not between 1 and 10, inclusive. The example uses an ArrayList for the list of integers. First an empty ArrayList is created and elements of an int array are added to the list using a for(:) loop.

In Example 15.12, an iterator is obtained at (3) and used in the loop at (4) to traverse all the elements in the integer list. At (5) the current element is retrieved by the iterator from the list. No casts are necessary, as the compiler guarantees that the iterator will return an Integer object from the underlying list. Its value is automatically unboxed and assigned to an int variable. The call to the remove() method removes the current element from the underlying list if the criteria in the if statement at (6) is satisfied.

Note that the methods are invoked on the iterator, not the underlying collection. The three methods of the iterator should be used *in step* inside a loop, as shown in Example 15.12.

In Example 15.12, we used an iterator in a while loop at (4) for traversing the collection. It is quite common to use an iterator in a for(;;) loop for this purpose, where the iterator is obtained in the initialization part, and the increment part is left empty:

```
for (Iterator<Integer> iterator = intList.iterator(); iterator.hasNext(); /* */) {
  int value = iterator.next();
  if (value < 1 || value > 10)
    iterator.remove();
}
```

The majority of the iterators provided in the java.util package are said to be *fail-fast*. When an iterator has already been obtained, structurally modifying the underlying collection by other means will invalidate the iterator. Subsequent use of this iterator will throw a ConcurrentModificationException, as the iterator checks to see if the collection has been structurally modified every time it accesses the collection. The remove() method of an iterator is the only recommended way to delete elements from the underlying collection during traversal with an iterator.

The order in which the iterator will return the elements from an underlying collection depends on the traversal order supported by the collection. For example, an iterator for a list will traverse the elements in the sequential order they have in the list, whereas the traversal order for the elements in an ordinary set is not predetermined. An iterator for a sorted collection will make the elements available in a given sorted order. Traversal order will be discussed together with the individual concrete classes.

The concrete collection classes override the toString() method to provide a textual representation of their contents. The standard textual representation generated by the toString() method for a collection is

$$[element_1, \ element_2, \ \dots, \ element_n]$$

where each *element$_i$* is the textual representation generated by the toString() method of the individual elements in the collection. In Example 15.12 the toString() method of the collection class is used implicitly at (2) and at (7) to generate a textual representation for the collection.

Using the for(:) Loop to Traverse a Collection

In Section 6.3, p. 220, we showed how to traverse an array using a for(:) loop. A for(:) loop can also be used to traverse any data structure that implements the java.lang.Iterable interface:

```
interface Iterable<E> {
  Iterator<E> iterator();
}
```

The iterator() method returns an iterator that implements the Iterator interface we have seen earlier in this subsection. The Iterable interface implies that if a collection implements an iterator, we can traverse the collection with a for(:) loop.

In the loop construct

```
    for (type variable : expression) statement
```

the value of *expression* can be a reference value that refers to a collection that implements the Iterable interface. From Figure 15.2 we see that the Collection interface extends the Iterable interface, therefore all collections that implement the Collection interface can be traversed using the for(:) loop. A collection that implements the Collection interface and thereby the Iterable interface, has the element type E. This element type E must be assignable to the *type* of the *variable* in the for(:) loop. The *variable* is assigned the reference value of a new element in the collection each time the body of the loop is executed.

The semantics of the for(:) loop discussed in Section 6.3, p. 220, also apply when traversing a collection. In particular, any structural change to the collection (adding or removing elements) in the for(:) loop will result in a ConcurrentModification-Exception.

Example 15.13 illustrates using a for(:) loop to traverse a collection. An empty collection of string builders is created at (1) and populated at (2) using a for(:) loop that traverses over an array of string builders. The collection is traversed in the for(:) loop at (3), reversing and printing the contents of each string builder in the collection. The output verifies that the state of each element in the collection was changed.

Behind the scenes, however, an appropriate iterator is used to traverse the collection, but the for(:) loop simplifies traversing a collection in the source code.

Note that if the collection is ordered or sorted, the iterator will traverse the collection in the ordering used to maintain the elements in the collection. For example, in the case of an ArrayList, the iterator will yield the elements in the same order as the insertion order. In the case of a TreeSet, the iterator will yield the elements in the sort ordering used to maintain the elements in the set. If the collection is unordered, the order in which the iterator will yield the elements is not predictable. Thus, we cannot be sure in which order a Hashset will be traversed.

Example 15.13 *Using a* for(:) *Loop to Iterate Over a Collection*

```java
import java.util.ArrayList;
import java.util.Collection;

public class IterateOverCollection {
  public static void main(String[] args) {

    // Create an empty collection of StringBuilders.
    Collection<StringBuilder> words = new ArrayList<StringBuilder>();    // (1)

    // An array of StringBuilders
    StringBuilder[] strArray = {
        new StringBuilder("t'noD"), new StringBuilder("etareti"),
        new StringBuilder("!em")
    };
    // Add StringBuilders from the array to the collection
    for (StringBuilder str : strArray) {                                 // (2)
      words.add(str);
    }
    System.out.println("Before: " + words);
    //  Iterate over a collection of StringBuilders.
    //  Expression type is Collection<StringBuilder>,
    //  and element type is StringBuilder.
    for (StringBuilder word : words) {                                   // (3)
      System.out.print(word.reverse() + " ");
    }
    System.out.println();
    System.out.println("After: " + words);
  }
}
```

Output from the program:

```
Before: [t'noD, etareti, !em]
Don't iterate me!
After: [Don't, iterate, me!]
```

Array Operations

These operations convert collections to arrays.

```
Object[] toArray()
<T> T[] toArray(T[] a)
```

The first toArray() method returns an array of type Object filled with all the elements of the collection. The second method is a generic method that stores the elements of a collection in an array of type T.

If the given array is big enough, the elements are stored in this array. If there is room to spare in the array, that is, the length of the array is greater than the number of elements in the collection, the spare room is filled with null values before the array is returned. If the array is too small, a new array of type T and appropriate size is created. If T is not a supertype of the runtime type of every element in the collection, an ArrayStoreException is thrown.

Example 15.13 illustrates converting collections to arrays. At (1) the call to the toArray() method returns an array of type Object. Since an array of type Object is not a subtype of an array of type String, the compiler reports an error at (2).

At (3), the call to the toArray() method returns an array of size 3, array type Object[], and element type String, when the method was passed a zero-length array of type Object. In other words, the method created a suitable-size array of type Object since the array passed in the argument was too small. This array was filled with the elements of the set, which are strings. Although the array returned is of type Object, the objects stored in it are of type String. The output from the program confirms these observations.

At (4), the call to the toArray() method returns an array of size 3, array type String[], and element type String, when the method was passed a zero-length array of type String. Now the method creates a new suitable-size array of type String and fills it with the elements of the set, which are strings. The output from the program shows that the array passed in the argument is not the same as the array returned by the method call.

At (5), the call to the toArray() method returns the same array it was passed in the argument, since it is of appropriate size and type. In other words, the array passed in the argument is filled with the elements of the list and returned. This is corroborated by the output from the program.

Lastly, the program throws an ArrayStoreException at (6), because String objects cannot be stored in an array of type Integer.

- -

Example 15.14 *Converting Collections to Arrays*

```
import java.util.Collection;
import java.util.HashSet;
```

```
            public class CollectionToArray {
              public static void main(String[] args) {

                Collection<String> strSet = new HashSet<String>();
                strSet.add("2008"); strSet.add("2009"); strSet.add("2010");
                int n = strSet.size();

                Object[] objects = strSet.toArray();                      // (1)
            //  String[] string = strList.toArray();                      // (2) Compile-time error!

                Object[] objArray = strSet.toArray(new Object[0]);                  // (3)
                System.out.println("Array size: " + objArray.length);
                System.out.println("Array type: " + objArray.getClass().getName());
                System.out.println("Actual element type: " +
                                objArray[0].getClass().getName());

                String[] strArray1 = new String[0];
                String[] strArray2 = strSet.toArray(strArray1);                     // (4)
                System.out.println("strArray1 == strArray2: " + (strArray1 == strArray2));

                String[] strArray3 = new String[n];
                String[] strArray4 = strSet.toArray(strArray3);                     // (5)
                System.out.println("strArray3 == strArray4: " + (strArray3 == strArray4));

                Integer[] intArray = strSet.toArray(new Integer[n]);  // (6) Runtime error!
              }
            }
```

Output from the program:

```
Array size: 3
Array type: [Ljava.lang.Object;
Actual element type: java.lang.String
strArray1 == strArray2: false
strArray3 == strArray4: true
Exception in thread "main" java.lang.ArrayStoreException
    at java.lang.System.arraycopy(Native Method)
    at java.util.ArrayList.toArray(Unknown Source)
    at CollectionToArray.main(CollectionToArray.java:28)
```

Review Questions

15.6   Which of these are core interfaces in the collections framework?

Select the three correct answers.

(a) Set<E>
(b) Bag<E>
(c) LinkedList<E>
(d) Collection<E>
(e) Map<K,V>

15.7   Which of these implementations are provided by the `java.util` package?

Select the two correct answers.

(a) `HashList<E>`
(b) `HashMap<K,V>`
(c) `ArraySet<E>`
(d) `ArrayMap<K,V>`
(e) `TreeMap<K,V>`

15.8   What is the name of the interface used to represent collections that maintain non-unique elements in order?

Select the one correct answer.

(a) `Collection<E>`
(b) `Set<E>`
(c) `SortedSet<E>`
(d) `List<E>`
(e) `Sequence<E>`

15.9   Which methods are specified by the `Iterator<E>` interface?

Select the three correct answers.

(a) `hasNext()`
(b) `hasMore()`
(c) `remove()`
(d) `delete()`
(e) `more()`
(f) `next()`

15.10   Which identifiers, when inserted in appropriate places in the program, will result in the output 911?

```
Collection<_____> myItems = new ArrayList<_____>();
myItems.add(9); myItems.add(1); myItems.add(1);

Iterator<_____> iterator = _____.iterator();
while (_____._____()) {
    System.out.print(_____._____());
}
```

Select the five correct answers.

(a) `hasNext`
(b) `myItems`
(c) `next`
(d) `Integer`
(e) `int`
(f) `Collection`
(g) `iterator`

15.11   What will the program print when it is compiled and run?

```java
import java.util.ArrayList;
import java.util.Collection;

public class RQ400_100 {
  public static void main(String[] args) {
    int sum = 0;
    for (int  i : makeCollection())
      sum += i;
    System.out.println(sum);
  }

  static Collection<Integer> makeCollection() {
    System.out.println("A collection coming up.");
    Collection<Integer> collection = new ArrayList<Integer>();
    collection.add(10); collection.add(20); collection.add(30);
    return collection;
  }
}
```

Select the one correct answer.

(a) `A collection coming up.`
    `60`
(b) `A collection coming up.`
    `A collection coming up.`
    `A collection coming up.`
    `60`
(c) The program does not compile.
(d) None of the above.

15.12   Which statements are true about the for(:) loop:

```
for (type variable : expression) statement
```

Select the three correct answers.

(a) The *variable* is only visible in the for(:) loop body.
(b) The *expression* is only evaluated once.
(c) The type of the expression must be java.lang.Iterable or an array type.
(d) Changing the value of the *variable* in the loop body affects the data structure represented by the *expression*.
(e) The loop runs backwards if the *expression* is negated as follows: !*expression*.
(f) We can iterate over several data structures simultaneously in a for(:) loop.

15.13   What will the program print when compiled and run?

```java
import java.util.ArrayList;
import java.util.Collection;

public class IterateOverCollection2 {
  public static void main(String[] args) {

    Collection<String> words = new ArrayList<String>();
```

```
        words.add("Don't"); words.add("change"); words.add("me!");

        System.out.println("Before: " + words);
        for (String word : words) {
          System.out.print(word.toUpperCase() + "_");
        }
        System.out.println();
        System.out.println("After:  " + words);
    }
  }
```

Select the one correct answer.

(a) `Before: [Don't, change, me!]`
    `DON'T_CHANGE_ME!_`
    `After:  [DON'T, CHANGE, ME!]`

(b) `Before: [Don't, change, me!]`
    `DON'T_CHANGE_ME!_`
    `After:  [Don't, change, me!]`

(c) The program will throw a java.util.ConcurrentModificationException, when run.

(d) The program fails to compile.

15.14 Which code, when inserted at (1), will result in the following output:

```
        Before: [Apple, Orange, Apple]
        After:  [Orange]
```

from the program when compiled and run?

```
import java.util.ArrayList;
import java.util.Iterator;
import java.util.List;

class Fruity {
  private String fName;
  Fruity(String fName) { this.fName = fName; }
  public void setName(String newName) { this.fName = newName; }
  public String toString() { return fName; }
  public boolean equals(Object other) {
    if (this == other) return true;
    if (!(other instanceof Fruity)) return false;
    return fName.equalsIgnoreCase(((Fruity)other).fName);
  }
}

public class RQ400_50 {
  public static void main(String[] args) {
    Fruity apple = new Fruity("Apple");
    Fruity orange = new Fruity("Orange");
    List<Fruity> list = new ArrayList<Fruity>();
    list.add(apple); list.add(orange); list.add(apple);
    System.out.println("Before: " + list);
    // (1) INSERT CODE HERE ...
    System.out.println("After:  " + list);
  }
}
```

Select the two correct answers.

(a)
```
for (Fruity f : list) {
    if (f.equals(apple))
        list.remove(f);
}
```

(b)
```
int i = 0;
for (Fruity f : list) {
    if (f.equals(apple))
        list.remove(i);
    i++;
}
```

(c)
```
for (int j = 0; j < list.size(); j++) {
    Fruity f = list.get(j);
    if (f.equals(apple))
        list.remove(j);
}
```

(d)
```
Iterator<Fruity> itr = list.iterator();
while (itr.hasNext()) {
    Fruity f = itr.next();
    if (f.equals(apple))
        itr.remove();
}
```

15.15 Which statement, when inserted independently at (1), will cause either a compile-time or a runtime error?

```
import java.util.ArrayList;
import java.util.Collection;

public class RQ400_200 {
  public static void main(String[] args) {

    Collection<Integer> intList = new ArrayList<Integer>();
    intList.add(2008); intList.add(2009); intList.add(2010);
    // (1) INSERT STATEMENT HERE!
  }
}
```

Select the four correct answers.

(a) `Object[] objArray1 = intList.toArray();`
(b) `Integer[] intArray1 = intList.toArray();`
(c) `Number[] numArray1 = intList.toArray();`
(d) `Object[] objArray2 = intList.toArray(new Object[0]);`
(e) `Integer[] intArray2 = intList.toArray(new Integer[0]);`
(f) `Integer[] intArray3 = intList.toArray(new Number[0]);`
(g) `Number[] numArray2 = intList.toArray(new Number[0]);`
(h) `Number[] numArray3 = intList.toArray(new Integer[0]);`
(i) `Number[] numArray4 = intList.toArray(new Long[0]);`

15.4 Sets

Unlike other implementations of the Collection interface, implementations of the Set interface do not allow duplicate elements. This also means that a set can contain at most one null value. The Set interface does not define any new methods, and its add() and addAll() methods will not store duplicates. If an element is not currently in the set, two consecutive calls to the add() method to insert the element will first return true, then false. A Set models a mathematical set (see Table 15.3), that is, it is an unordered collection of distinct objects.

Multisets (also called *bags*) that allow duplicate elements cannot be implemented using the Set interface, since this interface requires that elements are unique in the collection.

Table 15.3 *Bulk Operations and Set Logic*

Set Methods (a and b are sets)	Corresponding Mathematical Operations
a.containsAll(b)	$b \subseteq a$ (subset)
a.addAll(b)	$a = a \cup b$ (union)
a.removeAll(b)	$a = a - b$ (difference)
a.retainAll(b)	$a = a \cap b$ (intersection)
a.clear()	$a = \varnothing$ (empty set)

The HashSet<E> and LinkedHashSet<E> Classes

The HashSet class implements the Set interface. Since this implementation uses a hash table, it offers near constant-time performance for most operations. A HashSet does not guarantee any ordering of the elements. However, the LinkedHashSet subclass of HashSet guarantees insertion-order. It is also the implementation of choice if frequent traversal over the set is necessary. The sorted counterpart is Tree-Set, which implements the SortedSet and the NavigableSet interfaces and has logarithmic time complexity (see Section 15.5, p. 800).

A HashSet relies on the implementation of the hashCode() and equals() methods of its elements (see Section 15.1, p. 748). The hashCode() method is used for hashing the elements (p. 760), and the equals() method is needed for comparing elements. In fact, the equality and the hash codes of HashSets are defined in terms of the equality and the hash codes of their elements.

HashSet()

Constructs a new, empty set.

HashSet(Collection c)

Constructs a new set containing the elements in the specified collection. The new set will not contain any duplicates. This offers a convenient way to remove duplicates from a collection.

HashSet(int initialCapacity)

Constructs a new, empty set with the specified initial capacity.

HashSet(int initialCapacity, float loadFactor)

Constructs a new, empty set with the specified initial capacity and the specified load factor.

As mentioned earlier, the LinkedHashSet implementation is a subclass of the HashSet class. It works similarly to a HashSet except for one important detail. Unlike a Hash-Set, a LinkedHashSet guarantees that the iterator will access the elements in *insertion order,* that is, in the order in which they were inserted into the LinkedHashSet.

The LinkedHashSet class offers constructors analogous to the ones in the HashSet class. The initial *capacity* (i.e., the number of buckets in the hash table) and its *load factor* (i.e., the ratio of number of elements stored to its current capacity) can be tuned when the set is created. The default values for these parameters will under most circumstances provide acceptable performance.

Example 15.15 demonstrates traversing a HashSet (see (1)) and a LinkedHashSet (see (2)). Regardless of the order in which elements are inserted into a HashSet, we cannot depend on the order the for(:) loop will traverse the elements in the set, as is evident from the program output. A LinkedHashSet, on the other hand, is always traversed in *insertion order* (i.e., the last element inserted, is the first element retrieved) by the for(:) loop. The program output confirms this behavior, as the meal that was inserted last into the LinkedHashSet, is served first. The same behavior will be exhibited if an iterator is used explicitly.

Example 15.15 *Traversing Over Sets*

```
import java.util.HashSet;
import java.util.LinkedHashSet;
import java.util.Set;
public class TraverseHashSetAndLinkedHashSet {
  public static void main(String[] args) {
    HashSet<String> set1 = new HashSet<String>();                       // (1)
    set1.add("breakfast"); set1.add("lunch"); set1.add("dinner");
    System.out.println("Serving meals from a HashSet (order can vary):");
    for (String meal : set1)
      System.out.println(meal);

    Set<String> set2 = new LinkedHashSet<String>();                     // (2)
    set2.add("breakfast"); set2.add("lunch"); set2.add("dinner");
    System.out.println("Serving meals from a LinkedHashSet" +
                       " (always insertion order):");
```

```
    for (String meal : set2)
      System.out.println(meal);
  }
}
```

Program output:

```
Serving meals from a HashSet (order can vary):
dinner
breakfast
lunch
Serving meals from a LinkedHashSet (always insertion order):
breakfast
lunch
dinner
```

Example 15.16 demonstrates set operations. It determines the following relationships between two sets of characters:

- whether they are disjunct, that is, have no elements in common
- whether they have the same elements, that is, are equivalent
- whether one is a subset of the other
- whether one is a superset of the other
- whether they have a common subset

Given a list of words as program arguments, each argument is turned into a set of characters. This character set is compared with the set of all characters encountered so far in previous arguments.

The set encountered created at (1) accumulates characters as each argument is processed. For each argument, an empty set of characters is created at (2). This characters set is populated with the characters of the current argument at (3). The program first determines if there is a common subset between the two sets at (4), i.e., whether the current argument has any characters that were in previous arguments:

```
// Determine whether a common subset exists.               (4)
Set<Character> commonSubset = new HashSet<Character>(encountered);
commonSubset.retainAll(characters);
boolean areDisjunct = commonSubset.size()==0;
```

Note that the retainAll() operation is destructive. The code at (4) does not affect the encountered and the characters sets. If the size of the common subset is zero, the sets are disjunct; otherwise, the relationship must be narrowed down. The subset and superset relations are determined at (5) using the containsAll() method.

```
// Determine superset and subset relations.               (5)
boolean isSubset = encountered.containsAll(characters);
boolean isSuperset = characters.containsAll(encountered);
```

The sets are equivalent if both the previous relations are true. If the relations are both false, that is, no subset or superset relationship exists, the sets only have the subset computed at (4) in common. The encountered set is updated with the contents of the characters set to accumulate all characters encountered so far. The add-All() method is used for this purpose at (6):

```
encountered.addAll(characters);                          // (6)
```

As we can see from the output, the program prints the contents of the sets in the standard textual representation for collections.

Example 15.16 *Using Sets*

```java
import java.util.HashSet;
import java.util.Set;

public class CharacterSets {
  public static void main(String[] args) {
    int numArgs = args.length;

    // A set keeping track of all characters previously encountered.
    Set<Character> encountered = new HashSet<Character>();        // (1)

    // For each program argument in the command line ...
    for (String argument : args) {

      // Convert the current argument to a set of characters.
      Set<Character> characters = new HashSet<Character>();       // (2)
      int size = argument.length();
      // For each character in the argument...
      for (int j=0; j<size; j++)
        // add character to the characters set.
        characters.add(argument.charAt(j));                      // (3)

      // Determine whether a common subset exists.              (4)
      Set<Character> commonSubset = new HashSet<Character>(encountered);
      commonSubset.retainAll(characters);
      boolean areDisjunct = commonSubset.size()==0;

      if (areDisjunct) {
        System.out.println(characters + " and " + encountered + " are disjunct.");
      } else {
        // Determine superset and subset relations.              (5)
        boolean isSubset = encountered.containsAll(characters);
        boolean isSuperset = characters.containsAll(encountered);
        if (isSubset && isSuperset)
          System.out.println(characters + " is equivalent to " + encountered);
        else if (isSubset)
          System.out.println(characters + " is a subset of " + encountered);
        else if (isSuperset)
          System.out.println(characters + " is a superset of " + encountered);
        else
          System.out.println(characters + " and " + encountered + " have " +
                             commonSubset + " in common.");
      }
```

```
        // Update the set of characters encountered so far.
        encountered.addAll(characters);                        // (6)
      }
    }
  }
```

Running the program with the following arguments:

```
>java CharacterSets i said i am maids
```

results in the following output:

```
[i] and [] are disjunct.
[d, a, s, i] is a superset of [i]
[i] is a subset of [d, a, s, i]
[a, m] and [d, a, s, i] have [a] in common.
[d, a, s, m, i] is equivalent to [d, a, s, m, i]
```

15.5 The SortedSet<E> and NavigableSet<E> Interfaces

Before reading this subsection, it is a good idea to review the subsection *The Comparable<E> Interface*, p. 765, on specifying the natural ordering for objects, and the subsection *The Comparator<E> Interface*, p. 771, on specifying a particular total ordering for objects.

The SortedSet<E> Interface

The SortedSet interface extends the Set interface to provide the functionality for handling sorted sets. Since the elements are sorted, traversing the set either using the for(:) loop or an iterator will access the elements according to the ordering used by the set.

```
// First-last elements
E first()
E last()
```

The first() method returns the first element currently in this sorted set, and the last() method returns the last element currently in this sorted set. The elements are chosen based on the ordering used by the sorted set. Both throw a NoSuchElementException if the sorted set is empty.

```
// Range-view operations
SortedSet<E> headSet(<E> toElement)
SortedSet<E> tailSet(<E> fromElement)
SortedSet<E> subSet(<E> fromElement, <E> toElement)
```

The headSet() method returns a *view* of a portion of this sorted set, whose elements are strictly less than the specified element. Similarly, the tailSet() method returns a view of the portion of this sorted set, whose elements are greater than or equal to the specified element. The subSet() method returns a view of the portion of this sorted set, whose elements range from fromElement, inclusive, to toElement, exclusive (also called *half-open interval*). It throws an IllegalArgumentException if the fromElement is greater than the toElement.

Note that the views present the elements sorted in the same order as the underlying sorted set. Note that changes made through views are also reflected in the underlying sorted set, and vice versa.

```
// Comparator access
Comparator<? super E> comparator()
```

This method returns the comparator associated with this sorted set, or null if it uses the natural ordering of its elements. This comparator, if defined, is used by default when a sorted set is constructed and also used when copying elements into new sorted sets.

The NavigableSet<E> Interface

The NavigableSet interface extends the SortedSet interface with navigation methods to find the closest matches for specific search targets. By navigation, we mean operations that require searching for elements in the navigable set. In the absence of elements, these operations return null rather than throw a NoSuchElementException.

The NavigableSet interface replaces the SortedSet interface and is the preferred choice when a sorted set is required. In addition to the methods of the SortedSet interface, the NavigableSet interface adds the following *new* methods:

```
// First-last elements
E pollFirst()
E pollLast()
```

The pollFirst() method removes and returns the first element and the poll-Last() method removes and returns the last element currently in this navigable set. The element is determined according to some policy employed by the set—for example, queue policy. Both return null if the sorted set is empty.

```
// Range-view operations
NavigableSet<E> headSet(<E> toElement,    boolean inclusive)
NavigableSet<E> tailSet(<E> fromElement, boolean inclusive)
NavigableSet<E> subSet(<E> fromElement, boolean fromInclusive,
                       <E> toElement,    boolean toInclusive)
```

These operations are analogous to the ones in the SortedSet interface (p. 765), returning different views of the underlying navigable set, depending on the bound elements. However, the bound elements can be *excluded or included* by the operation, depending on the value of the boolean argument inclusive.

```
// Closest-matches
E ceiling(E e)
E floor(E e)
E higher(E e)
E lower(E e)
```

The method ceiling() returns the least element in the navigable set greater than or equal to argument e. The method floor() returns the greatest element in the navigable set less than or equal to argument e. The method higher() returns the least element in the navigable set strictly greater than argument e. The method lower() returns the greatest element in the navigable set strictly less than argument e. All methods return null if the required element is not found.

```
// Reverse order
Iterator<E> descendingIterator()
NavigableSet<E> descendingSet()
```

The first method returns a reverse-order view of the elements in the navigable set. The second method returns a reverse-order iterator for the navigable set.

The TreeSet<E> Class

The TreeSet class implements the NavigableSet interface and thereby the SortedSet interface. By default, operations on a sorted set rely on the natural ordering of the elements. However, a total ordering can be specified by passing a customized comparator to the constructor.

The TreeSet implementation uses balanced trees, which deliver excellent (logarithmic) performance for all operations. However, searching in a HashSet can be faster than in a TreeSet because hashing algorithms usually offer better performance than the search algorithms for balanced trees. The TreeSet class is preferred if elements are to be maintained in sorted order and fast insertion and retrieval of individual elements is desired.

The TreeSet class provides four constructors:

```
TreeSet()
```

The default constructor creates a new empty sorted set, according to the natural ordering of the elements.

```
TreeSet(Comparator<? super E> comparator)
```

A constructor that takes an explicit comparator for specific total ordering of the elements.

```
TreeSet(Collection<? extends E> collection)
```

A constructor that creates a sorted set based on a collection, according to the natural ordering of the elements.

> TreeSet(SortedSet<E> set)
>
> A constructor that creates a new set containing the same elements as the specified sorted set, with the same ordering.

Example 15.17 illustrates some selected navigation operations on a TreeSet. The set is created at (1) and populated by calling the Collections.addAll() method at (2). The elements are maintained according to the natural ordering for Strings, i.e., the one defined by the compareTo() method of the Comparable interface implemented by the String class. The subset-view operations at (3) show how the bounds can be inclusive or exclusive. Note also how the closest-match methods at (4) behave. A sorted set with the reverse order corresponding to the natural ordering is created at (5). The methods pollFirst() and pollLast() remove the element that is retrieved, i.e., they change the set structurally.

The following code shows how we can create a sorted set with a specific total ordering by supplying a comparator in the constructor call:

```
NavigableSet<String> strSetB =
            new TreeSet<String>(String.CASE_INSENSITIVE_ORDER);
Collections.addAll(strSetB, "strictly", "dancing", "Java", "Ballroom");
System.out.println(strSetB);          // [Ballroom, dancing, Java, strictly]
```

Example 15.17 *Using Navigable Sets*

```
import java.util.Collections;
import java.util.NavigableSet;
import java.util.TreeSet;
import static java.lang.System.out;

public class SetNavigation {
  public static void main(String[] args) {

    NavigableSet<String> strSetA = new TreeSet<String>();                    // (1)
    Collections.addAll(strSetA, "Strictly", "Java", "dancing", "ballroom");  // (2)
    out.println("Before: " + strSetA);        // [Java, Strictly, ballroom, dancing]

    out.println("\nSubset-views:");                      // (3)
    out.println(strSetA.headSet("ballroom", true));   // [Java, Strictly, ballroom]
    out.println(strSetA.headSet("ballroom", false));  // [Java, Strictly]
    out.println(strSetA.tailSet("Strictly", true));   // [Strictly, ballroom,
                                                       //  dancing]
    out.println(strSetA.tailSet("Strictly", false));  // [ballroom, dancing]
    out.println(strSetA.subSet("A", false, "Z", false )); // [Java, Strictly]
    out.println(strSetA.subSet("a", false, "z", false )); // [ballroom, dancing]

    out.println("\nClosest-matches:");                 // (4)
    out.println(strSetA.ceiling("ball"));              // ballroom
    out.println(strSetA.floor("ball"));                // Strictly
    out.println(strSetA.higher("ballroom"));           // dancing
    out.println(strSetA.lower("ballroom"));            // Strictly
```

```
        out.println("\nReverse order:");                  // (5)
        out.println(strSetA.descendingSet());   // [dancing, ballroom, Strictly, Java]

        out.println("\nFirst-last elements:");             // (6)
        out.println(strSetA.pollFirst());                  // Java
        out.println(strSetA.pollLast());                   // dancing

        out.println("\nAfter: " + strSetA);                // [Strictly, ballroom]
    }
}
```

Program output:

```
Before: [Java, Strictly, ballroom, dancing]

Subset-views:
[Java, Strictly, ballroom]
[Java, Strictly]
[Strictly, ballroom, dancing]
[ballroom, dancing]
[Java, Strictly]
[ballroom, dancing]

Closest-matches:
ballroom
Strictly
dancing
Strictly

Reverse order:
[dancing, ballroom, Strictly, Java]

First-last elements:
Java
dancing

After: [Strictly, ballroom]
```

15.6 Lists

Lists are collections that maintain their elements *in order* and can contain duplicates. The elements in a list are *ordered*. Each element, therefore, has a position in the list. A zero-based index can be used to access the element at the position designated by the index value. The position of an element can change as elements are inserted or deleted from the list, i.e., as the list is changed structurally.

In addition to the operations inherited from the Collection interface, the List interface also defines operations that work specifically on lists: position-based access of the list elements, searching in a list, operations on parts of a list (called *open range-view* operations), and creation of customized iterators. This additional functionality is provided by the following methods in the List interface:

```
// Positional Index
E get(int index)
```

Returns the element at the specified index.

```
E set(int index, E element)                                    Optional
```

Replaces the element at the specified index with the specified element. It returns the previous element at the specified index.

```
void add(int index, E element)                                 Optional
boolean addAll(int index, Collection<? extends E> c)           Optional
```

The first method inserts the specified element at the specified index. If necessary, it shifts the element previously at this index and any subsequent elements one position toward the end of the list. The inherited method add(E) from the Collection interface will append the specified element to the end of the list.

The second method inserts the elements from the specified collection at the specified index, using an iterator of the specified collection, i.e. the method splices the elements of the specified collection into the list at the specified index. The method returns true if any elements were added.

```
E remove(int index)                                            Optional
```

Deletes and returns the element at the specified index, contracting the list accordingly. The inherited method remove(E) from the Collection interface will remove the first occurrence of the element from the list.

In a non-empty list, the first element is at index 0 and the last element is at size()-1. As might be expected, all methods throw an IndexOutOfBoundsException if an illegal index is specified.

```
// Element Search
int indexOf(Object o)
int lastIndexOf(Object o)
```

These methods return the index of the first and the last occurrence of the element that is the same as the specified argument, respectively, if such an element exists in the list; otherwise, the value –1 is returned.

```
// Open Range-View
List<E> subList(int fromIndex, int toIndex)
```

This method returns a *view* of the list, which consists of the sublist of the elements from the index fromIndex to the index toIndex-1, i.e. a half-open interval. A view allows the range it represents in the underlying list to be manipulated. Any changes in the view are reflected in the underlying list, and vice versa. Views can be used to perform operations on specific ranges of a list.

```
// List Iterators
ListIterator<E> listIterator()
ListIterator<E> listIterator(int index)
```

The iterator from the first method traverses the elements consecutively, start-ing with the first element of the list, whereas the iterator from the second method starts traversing the list from the element indicated by the specified index.

```
interface ListIterator<E> extends Iterator<E> {
    boolean hasNext();
    boolean hasPrevious();

    E next();                  // Element after the cursor
    E previous();              // Element before the cursor

    int nextIndex();           // Index of element after the cursor
    int previousIndex();       // Index of element before the cursor

    void remove();             // Optional
    void set(E o);             // Optional
    void add(E o);             // Optional
}
```

The ListIterator interface is a bidirectional iterator for lists. It extends the Iterator interface and allows the list to be traversed in either direction. When traversing lists, it can be helpful to imagine a *cursor* moving forward or back-ward *between* the elements when calls are made to the next() and the previous() methods, respectively. The element that the cursor passes over is returned. When the remove() method is called, the element last passed over is removed from the list.

The ArrayList<E>, LinkedList<E>, and Vector<E> Classes

Three implementations of the List interface are provided in the java.util package: ArrayList, LinkedList, and Vector.

The ArrayList class implements the List interface. The Vector class is a legacy class that has been retrofitted to implement the List interface, and will not be discussed in detail. The Vector and ArrayList classes are implemented using dynamically resizable arrays, providing fast *random access* (i.e., position-based access) and fast list traversal—very much like using an ordinary array. Unlike the ArrayList class, the Vector class is thread-safe, meaning that concurrent calls to the vector will not compromise its integrity. The LinkedList implementation uses a doubly-linked list. Insertions and deletions in a doubly-linked list are very efficient.

The ArrayList and Vector classes offer comparable performance, but Vectors suffer a slight performance penalty due to synchronization. Position-based access has constant-time performance for the ArrayList and Vector classes. However, position-based access is in linear time for a LinkedList owing to traversal in a doubly-linked list. When frequent insertions and deletions occur inside a list, a LinkedList can be worth considering. In most cases, the `ArrayList` implementation is the overall best choice for implementing lists.

In addition to the `List` interface, the `LinkedList` class also implements two other interfaces that allow it to be used for stacks and different kinds of queues (see Section 15.7, p. 809).

The `ArrayList` class provides the following constructors:

```
ArrayList()
ArrayList(Collection<? extends E> c)
```

The default constructor creates a new, empty `ArrayList`.

The second constructor creates a new `ArrayList` containing the elements in the specified collection. The new `ArrayList` will retain any duplicates. The ordering in the `ArrayList` will be determined by the traversal order of the iterator for the collection passed as argument.

The `LinkedList` class provides constructors that are analogous to these two `ArrayList` constructors.

```
ArrayList(int initialCapacity)
```

The third constructor creates a new, empty `ArrayList` with the specified initial capacity.

Example 15.18 illustrates some basic operations on lists. The user gets one shot at guessing a five-digit code. The solution is hard-wired in the example as a list of five `Integer` objects. The `secretSolution` list is created at (1) and populated using the `add()` method. The guess specified at the command line is placed in a separate list, called guess, at (2).

The number of digits that are correctly guessed is determined at (3). The solution is first duplicated and each digit in the guess is removed from the duplicated solution. The number of deletions corresponds to the number of correct digits in the guess list. A digit at a particular index in the guess list is returned by the `get()` method. The `remove()` method returns `true` if the duplicate list was modified, that is, the digit from the guess was found and removed from the duplicated solution. Of course, one could use the `retainAll()` method, as shown below, but the idea in Example 15.18 is to use positional access on the guess list.

```
// Find the number of digits that were correctly included.          (3)
List<Integer> duplicate = new ArrayList<Integer>(secretSolution);
duplicate.retainAll(guess);
numOfDigitsIncluded = duplicate.size();
```

Finding the number of digits that are correctly placed is achieved by using two list iterators at (4), which allow digits in the same position in the guess and the secret-Solution lists to be compared.

Example 15.18 *Using Lists*

```java
import java.util.ArrayList;
import java.util.List;
import java.util.ListIterator;

public class TakeAGuess {
  final static int NUM_DIGITS = 5;

  public static void main(String[] args) {

    // Sanity check on the given data.
    try {
      if (args.length != 1 || args[0].length() != NUM_DIGITS)
        throw new IllegalArgumentException();
      Integer.parseInt(args[0]);
    } catch(IllegalArgumentException nfe) {
      System.err.println("Guess should be " + NUM_DIGITS + " digits.");
      return;
    }
    String guessStr = args[0];
    System.out.println("Guess: " + guessStr);

    /* Initialize the solution list. This program has a fixed solution. */
    List<Integer> secretSolution = new ArrayList<Integer>();            // (1)
    secretSolution.add(5); secretSolution.add(3);
    secretSolution.add(2); secretSolution.add(7);
    secretSolution.add(2);

    // Convert the guess from string to a list of Integers.              (2)
    List<Integer> guess = new ArrayList<Integer>();
    for (int i = 0; i < guessStr.length(); i++)
      guess.add(Character.getNumericValue(guessStr.charAt(i)));

    // Find the number of digits that were correctly included.            (3)
    List<Integer> duplicate = new ArrayList<Integer>(secretSolution);
    int numOfDigitsIncluded = 0;
    for (int i=0; i<NUM_DIGITS; i++)
      if (duplicate.remove(guess.get(i))) numOfDigitsIncluded++;

    /* Find the number of digits correctly placed by comparing the two
       lists, element by element, counting each correct placement. */
    // Need two iterators to traverse through the guess and solution lists.    (4)
    ListIterator<Integer> correct = secretSolution.listIterator();
    ListIterator<Integer> attempt = guess.listIterator();
    int numOfDigitsPlaced = 0;
    while (correct.hasNext())
      if (correct.next().equals(attempt.next())) numOfDigitsPlaced++;

    // Print the results.
    System.out.println(numOfDigitsIncluded + " digit(s) correctly included.");
    System.out.println(numOfDigitsPlaced +   " digit(s) correctly placed.");
  }
}
```

Running the program with the following arguments:

```
>java TakeAGuess 32227
```

gives the following output:

```
Guess: 32227
4 digit(s) correctly included.
1 digit(s) correctly placed.
```

15.7 Queues

In this section we look at the different types of queues provided by the Java collections framework.

The Queue<E> Interface

The Queue interface extends the Collection interface to specify a general contract for queues. A *queue* is a collection that maintains elements in *processing order*. An implementation of the Queue interface provides the queue policy for yielding the next element for processing. A *head* position in the queue specifies where the next element for processing can be obtained. A basic queue usually maintains its elements in *First-In-First-Out* (FIFO) ordering, but other orderings are also quite common: *Last-In-first-Out* (LIFO) ordering (also called *stacks*) or priority ordering (also called *priority queues*). The order in which elements of a queue can be retrieved for processing is dictated either by the natural ordering of the elements or by a comparator.

The Queue interface extends the Collection interface with the following methods:

```
// Insert
boolean add(E element)
boolean offer(E element)
```

Both methods insert the specified element in the queue. The return value indicates the success or failure of the operation. The add() method inherited from the Collection interface throws an IllegalStateException if the queue is full, but the offer() method does not.

```
// Remove
E poll()
E remove()
```

Both methods retrieve the head element and remove it from the queue. If the queue is empty, the poll() method returns null, but the remove() method throws a NoSuchElementException.

```
// Examine
E peek()
E element()
```

Both methods retrieve the head element, but do *not* remove it from the queue. If the queue is empty, the peek() method returns null, but the element() method throws a NoSuchElementException.

The PriorityQueue<E> **and** LinkedList<E> **Classes**

Both the PriorityQueue and LinkedList classes implement the Queue interface. Unless bi-directional traversal is necessary, other queue implementations should be considered, and not the LinkedList class. (The LinkedList class is also eclipsed by the introduction of the ArrayDeque class when it comes to implementing deques, as we will see shortly.)

As the name suggests, the PriorityQueue class is the obvious implementation for a queue with priority ordering. The implementation is based on a *priority heap*, a tree-like structure that yields an element at the head of the queue according to the priority ordering, which is defined either by the natural ordering of its elements or by a comparator. In the case of several elements having the same priority, one of them is chosen arbitrarily.

Elements of a PriorityQueue are *not* sorted. The queue only guarantees that elements can be *removed* in priority order, and any traversal using an iterator does *not* guarantee to abide by the priority order.

The PriorityQueue class provides the following constructors:

```
PriorityQueue()
PriorityQueue(Collection<? extends E> c)
```

The default constructor creates a new, empty PriorityQueue with default initial capacity and natural ordering. The second constructor creates a new PriorityQueue containing the elements in the specified collection. It will have natural ordering of its elements, unless the specified collection is either a SortedSet or another PriorityQueue, in which case, the collection's ordering will be used.

```
PriorityQueue(int initialCapacity)
PriorityQueue(int initialCapacity, Comparator<? super E> comparator)
```

The first constructor creates a new, empty PriorityQueue with the specified initial capacity and natural ordering. The second constructor creates a new, empty PriorityQueue with the specified initial capacity, but the ordering is defined by the specified comparator.

```
PriorityQueue(PriorityQueue<? extends E> pq)
PriorityQueue(SortedSet<? extends E> set)
```

The constructors create a new PriorityQueue with the ordering and the elements from the specified priority queue or sorted set, respectively.

Example 15.19 illustrates using priority queues. The example shows how two priority queues maintain objects of the class Task. The equality of objects in this class is based on the *task number* (Integer), as is the natural ordering of the objects. The natural ordering implemented by the class Task will result in the priority queue yielding its elements in *ascending* order of the task numbers, i.e., tasks with *smaller* task numbers will have *higher* priority. The class Task also defines two comparators at (1) and (2). The first one defines a total ordering of tasks based on *descending* order of the task name (String), and the second one takes both task number and task name into consideration.

The main() method in the class TaskExecutor creates an array with some tasks at (3). Tasks from this array will be loaded into a priority queue. The method testPQ() at (5) uses the priority queue it receives as argument. It loads the queue at (6) from the array, which is also passed as argument. It calls the offer() method to insert a task in the priority queue.

The testPQ() method calls the peek() method at (7) to examine the task at the head of the queue. The tasks are executed by removing them one by one at (8) by calling the poll() method.

The priority queue pq1 at (3) has its priority ordering defined by the natural ordering of the tasks. Note that the textual representation of the queue in the output

```
Queue before executing tasks: [100@breakfast, 200@lunch, 300@dinner, 200@tea]
```

does *not* show the tasks in priority order. It just shows what task there are in the queue. The textual representation of the queue is generated by the print method running an iterator over the queue. The iterator is under no obligation to take the priority order into consideration. The output also shows that the task with the highest priority (i.e., the smallest task number) is at the head of the queue:

```
Task at the head: 100@breakfast
```

The call to the poll() method in the while loop at (8) removes tasks in priority order, as verified by the output:

```
Doing tasks: 100@breakfast 200@tea 200@lunch 300@dinner
```

Since two of the tasks have the same priority, the queue chooses which one should be chosen first. The queue is empty when the peek() method returns null.

We leave it to the reader to verify that the output also conforms to the priority ordering of the pq2 priority queue at (4) that uses the supplied comparator to implement its priority ordering.

- -

Example 15.19 *Using Priority Queues*

```
import java.util.Comparator;

/** Represents a task. */
public class Task implements Comparable<Task> {
  private Integer taskNumber;
```

```java
    private String taskName;

    public Task(Integer tp, String tn) {
      taskNumber = tp;
      taskName = tn;
    }
    public boolean equals(Object obj) { // Equality based on the task number.
      if (obj instanceof Task)
        return this.taskNumber.equals(((Task)obj).taskNumber);
      return false;
    }
    public int compareTo(Task task2) {  // Natural ordering based on the task number.
      return this.taskNumber.compareTo(task2.taskNumber);
    }
    public int hashCode() {              // Hash code based on the task number.
      return this.taskNumber.hashCode();
    }
    public String toString() {
      return taskNumber + "@" + taskName;
    }
    public String getTaskName() {
      return taskName;
    }

    // A total ordering based on *descending* order of task names (String).      (1)
    public static Comparator<Task> comparatorA() {
      return new Comparator<Task>() {
        public int compare(Task task1, Task task2) {
          return task2.getTaskName().compareTo(task1.getTaskName());
        }
      };
    }
    // A total ordering based on task numbers (Integer) and task names (String). (2)
    public static Comparator<Task> comparatorB() {
      return new Comparator<Task>() {
        public int compare(Task task1, Task task2) {
          if (!task1.taskNumber.equals(task2.taskNumber))
            return task1.taskNumber.compareTo(task2.taskNumber);
          if (!task1.taskName.equals(task2.taskName))
            return task1.getTaskName().compareTo(task2.getTaskName());
          return 0;
        }
      };
    }
  }
```

- -

```java
import java.util.Arrays;
import java.util.Comparator;
import java.util.PriorityQueue;

/** Executes tasks. */
public class TaskExecutor {

  public static void main(String[] args) {
```

```
        // Array with some tasks.                                                  (2)
        Task[] taskArray = {
            new Task(200, "lunch"), new Task(200, "tea"),
            new Task(300, "dinner"), new Task(100, "breakfast"),
        };
        System.out.println("Array of tasks: " + Arrays.toString(taskArray));

        // Priority queue using natural ordering                                   (3)
        PriorityQueue<Task> pq1 = new PriorityQueue<Task>();
        testPQ(taskArray, pq1);

        // Priority queue using a total ordering                                   (4)
        Comparator<Task> compA = Task.comparatorB();
        int initCap = 5;
        PriorityQueue<Task> pq2 = new PriorityQueue<Task>(initCap, compA);
        testPQ(taskArray, pq2);
    }

    static void testPQ(Task[] taskArray, PriorityQueue<Task> pq) {          // (5)
        // Load the tasks:                                                         (6)
        for (Task task : taskArray)
          pq.offer(task);
        System.out.println("Queue before executing tasks: " + pq);

        // Peek at the head:                                                       (7)
        System.out.println("Task at the head: " + pq.peek());

        // Do the tasks:                                                           (8)
        System.out.print("Doing tasks: ");
        while (!pq.isEmpty()) {
          Task task = pq.poll();
          System.out.print(task + " ");
        }
    }
}
```

Program output:

```
Array of tasks: [200@lunch, 200@tea, 300@dinner, 100@breakfast]
Queue before executing tasks: [100@breakfast, 200@lunch, 300@dinner, 200@tea]
Task at the head: 100@breakfast
Doing tasks: 100@breakfast 200@tea 200@lunch 300@dinner
Queue after executing tasks: []
Queue before executing tasks: [100@breakfast, 200@lunch, 300@dinner, 200@tea]
Task at the head: 100@breakfast
Doing tasks: 100@breakfast 200@lunch 200@tea 300@dinner
```

The Deque<E> Interface

The Queue interface defines the contract for queues where the head element is
always removed according to a processing order. The processing order is always
defined by the natural ordering or a total ordering of the elements maintained by

the queue. The Deque interface extends the Queue interface to allow *double-ended queues*. Such a queue is called a *deque*. It allows operations not just at its *head*, but also at its *tail*. It is a linear unbounded structure in which elements can be inserted at or removed from *either* end. Various synonyms are used in the literature for the head and tail of a deque: front and back, first and last, start and end.

A deque can be used as *FIFO queue*, where elements added at the tail are presented at the head for inspection or removal in the same order, thus implementing FIFO order. A deque can also be used as a *stack*, where elements are added to and removed from the *same* end, thus implementing LIFO ordering.

The Deque interface defines symmetrical operations at its head and tail. Which end is in question is made evident by the method name. Below, equivalent methods from the Queue are also identified. The push() and pop() methods are convenient for implementing stacks.

```
// Insert
boolean offerFirst(E element)
boolean offerLast(E element)                 Queue equivalent: offer()
void push(E element)                         Synonym: addFirst()
void addFirst(E element)
void addLast(E element)                      Queue equivalent: add()
```

These methods insert the specified element in the deque. They all throw a NullPointerException if the specified element is null. The addFirst() and addLast() methods throw an IllegalStateException if the element cannot be added, but the offerFirst() and offerLast() methods do not.

```
// Remove
E pollFirst()                                Queue equivalent: poll()
E pollLast()
E pop()                                      Synonym: removeFirst()
E removeFirst()                              Queue equivalent: remove()
E removeLast()
boolean removeFirstOccurence(Object obj)
boolean removeLastOccurence(Object obj)
```

These methods remove an element from the deque. The pollFirst() and poll-Last() methods return null if the deque is empty. The removeFirst() and removeLast() methods throw a NoSuchElementException if the deque is empty.

```
// Examine
E peekFirst()                                Queue equivalent: peek()
E peekLast()
E getFirst()                                 Queue equivalent: element()
E getLast()
```

These methods retrieve an element from the deque, but do not remove it from the deque. The peekFirst() and peekLast() methods return null if the deque is empty. The getFirst() and getLast() methods throw a NoSuchElementException if the deque is empty.

```
// Misc.
Iterator<E> descendingIterator()
```

Returns an iterator to traverse the deque in reverse order, i.e., from the tail to the head.

The ArrayDeque<E> and LinkedList<E> Class

The ArrayDeque and LinkedList classes implement the Deque interface. The ArrayDeque class provides better performance than the LinkedList class for implementing FIFO queues, and is also a better choice than the java.util.Stack class for implementing stacks.

An ArrayDeque is also Iterable, and traversal is always from the head to the tail. The class provides the descendingIterator() method for iterating in reverse order. Since deques are not lists, positional access is not possible, nor can they be sorted.

Example 15.20 illustrates using an ArrayDeque both as a stack and as a FIFO queue. Elements from an array are pushed on to the stack at (3), and then popped from the stack at (5). The call to the isEmpty() method in the while loop at (4) determines whether the stack is empty. The output shows that the elements were popped in the reverse order to the order in which they were inserted, i.e., LIFO ordering.

Similarly, elements from an array are inserted at the tail of a FIFO queue at (8), and then removed from the head of the FIFO queue at (10). The call to the isEmpty() method in the while loop at (4) determines whether the FIFO queue is empty. The output shows that the elements were removed in the same order as they were inserted, i.e., FIFO ordering.

Note that in Example 15.20 the stack grows at the head of the deque, but the FIFO queue grows at the tail of the deque.

Example 15.20 *Using Deques as a Stack and as a FIFO Queue*

```
import java.util.ArrayDeque;
import java.util.Arrays;

/** Executes tasks. */
public class TaskExecutor2 {

  public static void main(String[] args) {
    String[] elementArray = {"sway", "and", "twist", "stacks", "tall"};        // (1)
    System.out.println("Array of elements: " + Arrays.toString(elementArray));

    // Using ArrayDeque as a stack:                                            (2)
    ArrayDeque<String> stack = new ArrayDeque<String>();
    for (String string : elementArray)
      stack.push(string);                                  // (3) Push elements.
    System.out.println("Stack before: TOP->" + stack + "<-BOTTOM");
    System.out.print("Popping stack: ");
    while (!stack.isEmpty()) {                              // (4)
```

```
      System.out.print(stack.pop() + " ");              // (5) Pop elements.
    }
    System.out.println("\n");

    // Using ArrayDeque as a FIFO queue:                                (6)
    elementArray = new String[] {"Waiting", "in", "queues", "is", "boring"}; // (7)
    System.out.println("Array of elements: " + Arrays.toString(elementArray));
    ArrayDeque<String> fifoQueue = new ArrayDeque<String>();
    for (String string : elementArray)
      fifoQueue.offerLast(string);                      // (8) Insert at tail.
    System.out.println("Queue before: HEAD->" + fifoQueue  + "<-TAIL");
    System.out.print("Polling queue: ");
    while (!fifoQueue.isEmpty()) {                       // (9)
      String string = fifoQueue.pollFirst();            // (10) Remove from head.
      System.out.print(string.toUpperCase() + " ");
    }
    System.out.println();
  }
}
```

Program output:

```
Array of elements: [sway, and, twist, stacks, tall]
Stack before: TOP->[tall, stacks, twist, and, sway]<-BOTTOM
Popping stack: tall stacks twist and sway

Array of elements: [Waiting, in, queues, is, boring]
Queue before: HEAD->[Waiting, in, queues, is, boring]<-TAIL
Polling queue: WAITING IN QUEUES IS BORING
```

 Review Questions

15.16 Which statements about collections are true?

Select the two correct answers.

(a) Some operations on a collection may throw an UnsupportedOperationException.
(b) Methods calling optional operations in a collection must either catch an UnsupportedOperationException or declare it in their throws clause.
(c) A List can have duplicate elements.
(d) An ArrayList can only accommodate a fixed number of elements.
(e) The Collection interface contains a method named get.

15.17 What will be the result of attempting to compile and run the following program?

```
import java.util.ArrayList;
import java.util.Collection;
import java.util.HashSet;
import java.util.LinkedList;
import java.util.TreeSet;
public class Sets {
```

```
        public static void main(String[] args) {
          HashSet<Integer> set1 = new HashSet<Integer>();
          addRange(set1, 1);
          ArrayList<Integer> list1 = new ArrayList<Integer>();
          addRange(list1, 2);
          TreeSet<Integer> set2 = new TreeSet<Integer>();
          addRange(set2, 3);
          LinkedList<Integer> list2 = new LinkedList<Integer>();
          addRange(list2, 5);
          set1.removeAll(list1);
          list1.addAll(set2);
          list2.addAll(list1);
          set1.removeAll(list2);
          System.out.println(set1);
        }
        static void addRange(Collection<Integer> col, int step) {
          for (int i = step*2; i<=25; i+=step)
            col.add(i);
        }
      }
```

Select the one correct answer.

(a) The program will fail to compile, since operations are performed on incompatible collection implementations.

(b) The program will fail to compile, since the TreeSet referenced by set2 has not been given a Comparator to use when sorting its elements.

(c) The program will compile without error, but will throw an UnsupportedOperation-Exception, when run.

(d) The program will compile without error and will print all primes below 25, when run.

15.18   Which of these methods are defined in the Collection<E> interface?

Select the three correct answers.

(a) add(E o)

(b) retainAll(Collection<?> c)

(c) get(int index)

(d) iterator()

(e) indexOf(Object o)

15.19   What will the following program print?

```
        import java.util.ArrayList;
        import java.util.List;
        import java.util.ListIterator;
        public class Iterate {
          public static void main(String[] args) {
            List<String> l = new ArrayList<String>();
            l.add("A"); l.add("B"); l.add("C"); l.add("D"); l.add("E");
            ListIterator<String> i = l.listIterator();
            i.next(); i.next(); i.next(); i.next();
            i.remove();
```

```
            i.previous(); i.previous();
            i.remove();
            System.out.println(1);
        }
    }
```

Select the one correct answer.

(a) It will print [A, B, C, D, E].
(b) It will print [A, C, E].
(c) It will print [B, D, E].
(d) It will print [A, B, D].
(e) It will print [B, C, E].
(f) It will throw a NoSuchElementException.

15.20   Which sequence of digits will the following program print?

```
import java.util.ArrayList;
import java.util.LinkedList;
import java.util.List;

public class Lists {
    public static void main(String[] args) {
        List<String> list = new ArrayList<String>();
        list.add("1");
        list.add("2");
        list.add(1, "3");
        List<String> list2 = new LinkedList<String>(list);
        list.addAll(list2);
        list2 = list.subList(2, 5);
        list2.clear();
        System.out.println(list);
    }
}
```

Select the one correct answer.

(a) [1, 3, 2]
(b) [1, 3, 3, 2]
(c) [1, 3, 2, 1, 3, 2]
(d) [3, 1, 2]
(e) [3, 1, 1, 2]
(f) None of the above.

15.21   Which of these methods from the Collection interface will return the value true if
the collection was modified during the operation?

Select the two correct answers.

(a) contains()
(b) add()
(c) containsAll()
(d) retainAll()
(e) clear()

15.22   Which statements, when inserted independently at (1), will guarantee that the following program will print [1, 9]?

```
import java.util.*;
public class RightOne {

    public static void main(String[] args) {
        // (1) INSERT DECLARATION HERE.
        collection.add(1); collection.add(9); collection.add(1);
        System.out.println(collection);
    }
}
```

Select the four correct answers.

(a) `Collection<Integer> collection = new HashSet<Integer>();`

(b) `Set<Integer> collection = new HashSet<Integer>();`

(c) `HashSet<Integer> collection = new LinkedHashSet<Integer>();`

(d) `Set<Integer> collection = new LinkedHashSet<Integer>();`

(e) `Collection<Integer> collection = new TreeSet<Integer>();`

(f) `NavigableSet<Integer> collection = new TreeSet<Integer>();`

15.23   What will the program print when it is compiled and run?

```
import static java.lang.System.out;
import java.util.Collections;
import java.util.NavigableSet;
import java.util.TreeSet;

public class RQ400_300 {
    public static void main(String[] args) {
        NavigableSet<String> strSetA = new TreeSet<String>();
        Collections.addAll(strSetA, "set", "shell", "soap");
        out.print(strSetA.ceiling("shell") + " ");
        out.print(strSetA.floor("shell") + " ");
        out.print(strSetA.higher("shell") + " ");
        out.println(strSetA.lower("shell"));
    }
}
```

Select the one correct answer.

(a) `shell soap shell set`

(b) `soap set shell shell`

(c) `shell shell soap set`

(d) `set shell shell soap`

15.24   Which statement, when inserted independently at (1), will result in program output that does not include the word `shell`?

```
import static java.lang.System.out;
import java.util.Collections;
import java.util.NavigableSet;
import java.util.TreeSet;
```

```
public class RQ400_400 {
  public static void main(String[] args) {
    NavigableSet<String> strSetA = new TreeSet<String>();
    Collections.addAll(strSetA, "set", "shell", "soap", "swan");
    // (1) INSERT STATEMENT HERE.
  }
}
```

Select the two correct answers.

(a) out.println(strSetA.headSet("soap", true));
(b) out.println(strSetA.headSet("soap", false));
(c) out.println(strSetA.tailSet("soap", true));
(d) out.println(strSetA.tailSet("soap", false));
(e) out.println(strSetA.subSet("set", false, "soap", true));
(f) out.println(strSetA.subSet("set", true, "soap", false));

15.25 Which collection types, when inserted at (1), will result in a generic method that
       will compile without errors?

```
public static <T> T justDoIt(_____/* (1) INSERT TYPE HERE */_____<T> collection)
{
  return collection.poll();
}
```

Select the three correct answers.

(a) NavigableSet
(b) PriorityQueue
(c) LinkedList
(d) Queue
(e) TreeSet
(f) LinkedHashSet

15.26 Which loop, when inserted independently at (1), will guarantee that the program
       will print sea|sells|she|shells|?

```
import static java.lang.System.out;

import java.util.Collections;
import java.util.PriorityQueue;

public class RQ400_500 {
  public static void main(String[] args) {
    PriorityQueue<String> strPQ = new PriorityQueue<String>();
    Collections.addAll(strPQ, "shells", "she", "sells", "sea");
    // (1) INSERT LOOP HERE
    out.println();
  }
}
```

Select the one correct answer.

(a) for (String word : strPQ) {
        out.print(word + "|");
    }
```
```

```
(b) for (String word : strPQ) {
       out.print(strPQ.peek() + "|");
    }
(c) while (strPQ.peek() != null) {
       out.print(strPQ.poll() + "|");
    }
(d) for (String word : strPQ) {
       out.print(strPQ.poll() + "|");
    }
```

15.8 Maps

A Map defines *mappings* from keys to values. The *<key, value>* pair is called an *entry*. A map does not allow duplicate keys, in other words, the keys are unique. Each key maps to one value at the most, implementing what is called a *single-valued map*. Thus, there is a *many-to-one* relation between keys and values. For example, in a student-grade map, a grade (value) can be awarded to many students (keys), but each student has only one grade.

Both the keys and the values must be objects, with primitive values being wrapped in their respective primitive wrapper objects when they are put in a map.

A map is not a collection and the Map interface does not extend the Collection interface. However, the mappings can be viewed as a collection in various ways: a key set, a value collection, or an entry set. These collection views are the only means of traversing a map.

The Map interface specifies some optional methods. Implementations should throw an UnsupportedOperationException if they do not support such an operation. The implementations of maps from the java.util package support all the optional operations of the Map interface (see Table 15.2 and Figure 15.3).

Basic Operations

These operations constitute the basic functionality provided by a map.

```
Object put(K key, V value)              Optional
Object get(Object key)
Object remove(Object key)               Optional
```

The put() method inserts the <key, value> entry into the map. It returns the old *value* previously associated with the specified key, if any. Otherwise, it returns the null value.

The get() method returns the value to which the specified key is mapped, or null if no entry is found.

The remove() method deletes the entry for the specified key. It returns the *value* previously associated with the specified key, if any. Otherwise, it returns the null value.

```
boolean containsKey(Object key)
boolean containsValue(Object value)
```

The containsKey() method returns true if the specified key is mapped to a value in the map.

The containsValue() method returns true if there exists one or more keys that are mapped to the specified value.

```
int size()
boolean isEmpty()
```

These methods return the number of entries (i.e., number of unique keys in the map) and whether the map is empty or not.

Bulk Operations

Bulk operations can be performed on an entire map.

```
void putAll(Map<? extends K, ? extends V> map)      Optional
void clear()                                         Optional
```

The first method copies all entries from the specified map to the current map, and the second method deletes all entries from the current map.

Collection Views

Views allow information in a map to be represented as collections.

```
Set<K> keySet()
Collection<V> values()
Set<Map, Entry<K, V>> entrySet()
```

These methods provide different views of a map. Changes in the map are reflected in the view, and vice versa. These methods return a set view of keys, a collection view of values, and a set view of *<key, value>* entries, respectively. Note that the Collection returned by the values() method is not a Set, as several keys can map to the same value, that is, duplicate values can be included in the returned collection. Each *<key, value>* in the entry set view is represented by an object implementing the nested Map.Entry interface. An entry in the entry set view can be manipulated by methods defined in this interface, which are self-explanatory:

```
interface Entry<K, V> {
    K getKey();
    V getValue();
    V setValue(V value);
}
```

Elements can be removed from a map via a view, but cannot be added. An iterator over a view will throw an exception if the underlying map is modified concurrently.

15.9 Map Implementations

The HashMap<K,V>, LinkedHashMap<K,V>, and Hashtable<K,V> Classes

Figure 15.3 shows four implementations of the Map interface in the java.util package: HashMap, LinkedHashMap, TreeMap, and Hashtable.

The classes HashMap and Hashtable implement unordered maps. The class LinkedHashMap implements ordered maps, which are discussed below. The class TreeMap implements sorted maps (see Section 15.10, p. 826).

While the HashMap class is not thread-safe and permits one null key, the Hashtable class is thread-safe and permits non-null keys and values only. The thread-safety provided by the Hashtable class comes with a performance penalty. Thread-safe use of maps is also provided by the methods in the Collections class (see Section 15.11, p. 838). Like the Vector class, the Hashtable class is also a legacy class that has been retrofitted to implement the Map interface.

These map implementations are based on a hashing algorithm. Operations on a map thus rely on the hashCode() and equals() methods of the key objects (see Section 15.1, p. 748).

The LinkedHashMap implementation is a subclass of the HashMap class. The relationship between the map classes LinkedHashMap and HashMap is analogous to the relationship between their counterpart set classes LinkedHashSet and HashSet. Elements of a HashMap (and a HashSet) are unordered. The elements of a LinkedHashMap (and a LinkedHashSet) are ordered. By default, the entries of a LinkedHashMap are in *key insertion order*, that is, the order in which the keys are inserted in the map. This order does not change if a key is re-inserted, because no new entry is created if the key's entry already exists. The elements in a LinkedHashSet are in (element) insertion order. However, a LinkedHashMap can also maintain its elements in (element) *access order*, that is, the order in which its entries are accessed, from least-recently accessed to most-recently accessed entries. This *ordering mode* can be specified in one of the constructors of the LinkedHashMap class.

Both the HashMap and the LinkedHashMap classes provide comparable performance, but the HashMap class is the natural choice if ordering is not an issue. Operations such as adding, removing, or finding an entry based on a key are in constant time, as these hash the key. Operations such as finding the entry with a particular value are in linear time, as these involve searching through the entries.

Adding, removing, and finding entries in a `LinkedHashMap` can be slightly slower than in a `HashMap`, as an ordered doubly-linked list has to be maintained. Traversal of a map is through one of its collection-views. For an underlying `LinkedHashMap`, the traversal time is proportional to the size of the map—regardless of its capacity. However, for an underlying `HashMap`, it is proportional to the capacity of the map.

The concrete map implementations override the `toString()` method. The standard textual representation generated by the `toString()` method for a map is

$$\{key_1=value_1,\ key_2=value_2,\ \ldots,\ key_n=value_n\}$$

where each key_i and each $value_i$ is the textual representation generated by the `toString()` method of the individual key and value objects in the map, respectively.

As was the case with collections, implementation classes provide a standard constructor that creates a new empty map, and a constructor that creates a new map based on an existing one. Additional constructors create empty maps with given initial capacities and load factors. The `HashMap` class provides the following constructors:

```
HashMap()
HashMap(int initialCapacity)
HashMap(int initialCapacity, float loadFactor)
```

Constructs a new, empty `HashMap`, using either specified or default initial capacity and load factor.

```
HashMap(Map<? extends K,? extends V> otherMap)
```

Constructs a new map containing the elements in the specified map.

The `LinkedHashMap` and `Hashtable` classes have constructors analogous to the four constructors for the `HashMap` class. In addition, the `LinkedHashMap` class provides a constructor where the ordering mode can also be specified:

```
LinkedHashMap(int initialCapacity, float loadFactor, boolean accessOrder)
```

Constructs a new, empty `LinkedHashMap` with the specified initial capacity, the specified load factor, and the specified ordering mode. The ordering mode is true for *access order* and false for *key insertion order*.

Example 15.21 prints a textual histogram for the frequency of weight measurements in a weight group, where a weight group is defined as an interval of five units. The weight measurements are supplied as program arguments. The example illustrates the use of maps, the creation of key views, and the use of a for(:) loop to traverse a map. The program proceeds as follows:

- An empty `HashMap<Integer, Integer>` is created at (1), where the key is the weight group and the value is the frequency.

- A for(:) loop is used at (2) to read the weights specified as program arguments, converting each weight to its corresponding weight group and updating the frequency of the weight group:

  The weight group is determined at (3). The count is incremented at (4), if necessary, and a new entry is registered at (5). Since keys are unique in a map, any previous entry is overwritten.

  Generic types guarantee that the keys and the values in the map are of the correct type, and autoboxing/unboxing of primitive values guarantees the correct type of an operand in an expression:

  ```
  Integer frequency = groupFreqMap.get(weightGroup);              // (4)
  frequency = (frequency == null) ? 1 : frequency+1;             // (5)
  groupFreqMap.put(weightGroup, frequency);                      // (6)
  ```

- The program creates a sorted set of keys (which are weight groups) from the groupFreqMap at (7). The keySet() method returns a set view of keys, which is passed as argument to a TreeSet.

  ```
  SortedSet<Integer> groupSet
              = new TreeSet<Integer>(groupFreqMap.keySet());     // (7)
  ```

- The histogram is printed by traversing the sorted key set in a for(:) loop at (8), looking up the frequency in the groupFreqMap. A map can only be traversed through one of its views.

  For each key, the corresponding value (i.e., the frequency) is retrieved at (9):

  ```
  int frequency = groupFreqMap.get(group);                       // (9)
  ```

  A *bar* (char[]) for each frequency is created using the Arrays.fill() method at (10), which is converted to string and printed.

- -

Example 15.21 *Using Maps*

```java
import java.util.Arrays;
import java.util.HashMap;
import java.util.Map;
import java.util.SortedSet;
import java.util.TreeSet;

public class WeightGroups {
  public static void main(String[] args) {

    // Create a map to store the frequency for each group.
    Map<Integer, Integer> groupFreqMap = new HashMap<Integer, Integer>();  // (1)

    // Determine the frequencies:
    for (String argument : args) {                               // (2)
      // Get the value from an argument and group into intervals of 5.
      double weight = Double.parseDouble(argument);
      int weightGroup = (int) Math.round(weight/5)*5;            // (3)
      Integer frequency = groupFreqMap.get(weightGroup);         // (4)
      // Increment frequency if necessary.
      frequency = (frequency == null) ? 1 : frequency+1;         // (5)
```

```
      groupFreqMap.put(weightGroup, frequency);                    // (6)
    }

    // Print the histogram:
    // Create a sorted set of groups (keys)
    SortedSet<Integer> groupSet
                    = new TreeSet<Integer>(groupFreqMap.keySet());  // (7)
    // Traverse the keys, looking up the frequency from the map.
    for (int group : groupSet) {                                   // (8)
      int frequency = groupFreqMap.get(group);                    // (9)
      /* Use the Arrays.fill() method to fill a char array with equivalent
       * number of '*' as the frequency value.
       * Convert the char array to string in order to print. */
      char[] bar = new char[frequency];
      Arrays.fill(bar, '*');                                      // (10)
      System.out.println(group + ":\t" + new String(bar));
    }
  }
}
```

Running the program with the following arguments:

```
>java WeightGroups 74 75 93 75 93 82 61 92 10 185
```

gives the following output:

```
10:     *
60:     *
75:     ***
80:     *
90:     *
95:     **
185:    *
```

15.10 The SortedMap<K,V> and NavigableMap<K,V> Interfaces

The SortedMap and NavigableMap interfaces are the analogs of the SortedSet and the NavigableSet interfaces, respectively.

The SortedMap<K,V> Interface

The SortedMap interface extends the Map interface to provide the functionality for implementing maps with *sorted keys*. Its operations are analogous to those of the SortedSet interface (p. 800), applied to maps and keys rather than to sets and elements.

```
// First-last keys
K firstKey()                              Sorted set: first()
K lastKey()                               Sorted set: last()
```

Return the smallest key and the largest key in the sorted map, respectively. They throw a NoSuchElementException if the set is empty.

```
// Range-view operations
SortedMap<K,V> headMap(K toKey)                  Sorted set: headSet()
SortedMap<K,V> tailMap(K fromKey)                Sorted set: tailSet()
SortedMap<K,V> subMap(K fromKey, K toKey)        Sorted set: subSet()
```

Return set views analogous to that of a SortedSet. The set views include the
fromKey if it is present in the map, but the toKey is excluded.

```
// Comparator access
Comparator<? super K> comparator()
```

Returns the key comparator, if the map has one. Otherwise returns null.

The NavigableMap<K,V> Interface

Analogous to the NavigableSet interface extending the SortedSet interface, the
NavigableMap interface extends the SortedMap interface with navigation methods to
find the closest matches for specific search targets. The NavigableMap interface
replaces the SortedMap interface and is the preferred choice when a sorted map is
needed.

In addition to the methods of the SortedMap interface, the NavigableMap interface
adds the *new* methods shown below, where the analogous methods from the
NavigableSet interface are also identified. Note that where a NavigableMap method
returns a Map.Entry object representing a mapping, the corresponding Navigable-
Set method returns an element of the set.

```
// First-last elements
Map.Entry<K, V> pollFirstEntry()                 Navigable set: pollFirst()
Map.Entry<K, V> pollLastEntry()                  Navigable set: pollLast()
Map.Entry<K, V> firstEntry()
Map.Entry<K, V> lastEntry()
```

The pollFirstEntry() method removes and returns the first *entry*, and the poll-
LastEntry() method removes and returns the last *entry* currently in this navigable
map. The entry is determined according to the ordering policy employed by the
map—e.g., natural ordering. Both return null if the navigable set is empty. The
last two methods only retrieve, and do not remove, the value that is returned.

```
// Range-view operations
NavigableMap<K, V> headMap(K toElement,     Navigable set: headSet()
                   boolean inclusive)
NavigableMap<K, V> tailMap(K fromElement,   Navigable set: tailSet()
                   boolean inclusive)
NavigableMap<K, V> subMap(K fromElement,    Navigable set: subSet()
                   boolean fromInclusive,
                           K toElement,
                   boolean toInclusive)
```

These operations are analogous to the ones in the SortedMap interface (p. 826),
returning different views of the underlying navigable map, depending on the
bound elements. However, the bound elements can be *excluded or included* by
the operation, depending on the value of the boolean argument inclusive.

```
// Closest-matches
Map.Entry<K, V> ceilingEntry(K key)         Navigable set: ceiling()
K               ceilingKey(K key)
Map.Entry<K, V> floorEntry(K key)           Navigable set: floor()
K               floorKey(K key)
Map.Entry<K, V> higherEntry(K key)          Navigable set: higher()
K               higherKey(K key)
Map.Entry<K, V> lowerEntry(K key)           Navigable set: lower()
K               lowerKey(K key)
```

The ceiling methods return the least entry (or key) in the navigable map >= to the argument key. The floor methods return the greatest entry (or key) in the navigable map <= to the argument key. The higher methods return the least entry (or key) in the navigable map > the argument key. The lower methods return the greatest entry (or key) in the navigable map < the argument key. All methods return null if there is no such key.

```
// Navigation
NavigableMap<K, V> descendingMap()          Navigable set: descendingSet()
NavigableSet<K> descendingKeySet()
NavigableSet<K> navigableKeySet()
```

The first method returns a reverse-order view of the entries in the navigable map. The second method returns a reverse-order key set for the entries in the navigable map. The last method returns a forward-order key set for the entries in the navigable map.

The TreeMap<K,V> Class

The TreeMap class is the analog of the TreeSet class (p. 802), but in this case for maps. It provides an implementation that sorts its entries in a specific order (see also Figures 15.2 and 15.3).

The TreeMap class implements the NavigableMap interface, and thereby the SortedMap interface. By default, operations on sorted maps rely on the natural ordering of the keys. However, a total ordering can be specified by passing a customized comparator to the constructor.

The TreeMap implementation uses balanced trees, which deliver excellent performance for all operations. However, searching in a HashMap can be faster than in a TreeMap, as hashing algorithms usually offer better performance than the search algorithms for balanced trees.

The TreeMap class provides four constructors, analogous to the ones in the TreeSet class:

```
TreeMap()
```

A standard constructor used to create a new empty sorted map, according to the natural ordering of the keys.

```
TreeMap(Comparator<? super K> c)
```

A constructor that takes an explicit comparator for the keys, that is used to order the entries in the map.

```
TreeMap(Map<? extends K, ? extends V> m)
```

A constructor that can create a sorted map based on a map, according to the natural ordering of the keys.

```
TreeMap(SortedMap<K, ? extends V> m)
```

A constructor that creates a new map containing the same entries as the specified sorted map, with the same ordering for the keys.

Example 15.22 illustrates using navigable maps. It also prints a textual histogram like the one in Example 15.21, but in addition, it prints some statistics about the navigable map.

- An empty NavigableMap<Integer, Integer> is created at (1), where the key is the weight group and the value is the frequency.

- The procedure at (2) reads the weights specified as program arguments, converting each weight to its corresponding weight group, and the updating of the frequency of the weight group is the same as in Example 15.21. Printing the contents of the navigable map at (3), and its size at (4), shows that there are 7 entries ordered in ascending key order:

```
Group frequency map: {10=1, 60=1, 75=3, 80=1, 90=1, 95=2, 185=1}
No. of weight groups: 7
```

- Calls to the methods firstEntry() and lastEntry() at (5) and (6) return the following entries, respectively:

```
First entry: 10=1
Last entry: 185=1
```

- Calls to the methods floorEntry() and higherKey() with the key value 77 at (7) and (8) return the following values, respectively:

```
Greatest entry <= 77: 75=3
Smallest key > 90: 95
```

- Calls to the methods tailMap(75, true) and headMap(75, false) at (9) and (10) return the following map views, respectively:

```
Groups >= 75: {75=3, 80=1, 90=1, 95=2, 185=1}
Groups <  75: {10=1, 60=1}
```

- The method printHistogram() at (13) prints a histogram of the frequencies in a navigable map:

```
public static <K> int printHistogram(NavigableMap<K, Integer> freqMap){ ... }
```

It is a generic method with one type parameter, K, that specifies the type of the keys, and the type of the values (i.e., frequencies) is Integer. The method creates an entry set at (14). Since this entry set is backed by a navigable map, traversal of the entry set is in ascending key order. A for(:) loop is used at (15) to traverse the entry set, printing the histogram for the navigable map. The method also counts the number of values on which the frequencies are based (i.e., it sums the frequencies).

A call to the `printHistogram()` method at (11) with the navigable map of frequencies gives the following results:

```
Histogram:
    10: *
    60: *
    75: ***
    80: *
    90: *
    95: **
   185: *
Number of weights registered: 10
```

It is possible to call the `printHistogram()` method with a *map view* to print partial histograms. Based on the navigable map of frequencies in Example 15.22, the following code:

```
System.out.println("Partial histogram:");
int count = printHistogram(groupFreqMap.subMap(75, true, 185, false));
System.out.println("Number of weights registered: " + count);
```

prints the following partial histogram:

```
Partial histogram:
    75: ***
    80: *
    90: *
    95: **
Number of weights registered: 7
```

- Polling of a navigable map is shown at (12). For each entry, its key and its value is printed.

```
Histogram (by polling):
    10: 1
    60: 1
    75: 3
    80: 1
    90: 1
    95: 2
   185: 1
Number of weights registered: 10
```

Polling is done directly on the navigable map, and the retrieved entry is removed from the map. A map is *not* `Iterable`. However, an iterator or a `for(:)` loop can be used to traverse a *set view* of the map.

Example 15.22 *Using Navigable Maps*

```java
import java.util.Arrays;
import java.util.Map;
import java.util.NavigableMap;
import java.util.Set;
import java.util.TreeMap;

public class WeightGroups2 {
  public static void main(String[] args) {

    // Create a navigable map to store the frequency for each group.
    NavigableMap<Integer, Integer> groupFreqMap =
                        new TreeMap<Integer, Integer>();      // (1)
    // Determine the frequencies:                             // (2)
    for (String argument : args) {
      // Get the value from an argument and group into intervals of 5.
      double weight = Double.parseDouble(argument);
      int weightGroup = (int) Math.round(weight/5)*5;
      Integer frequency = groupFreqMap.get(weightGroup);
      // Increment frequency if necessary.
      frequency = (frequency == null) ? 1 : frequency+1;
      groupFreqMap.put(weightGroup, frequency);
    }

    // Print statistics about the frequency map:
    System.out.println("Group frequency map: " + groupFreqMap);       // (3)
    System.out.println("No. of weight groups: " + groupFreqMap.size());  // (4)

    System.out.println("First entry: " + groupFreqMap.firstEntry());  // (5)
    System.out.println("Last entry: " + groupFreqMap.lastEntry());    // (6)

    System.out.println("Greatest entry <= 77: " +
                       groupFreqMap.floorEntry(77));                  // (7)
    System.out.println("Smallest key > 90: " +
                       groupFreqMap.higherKey(90));                   // (8)

    System.out.println("Groups >= 75: " + groupFreqMap.tailMap(75, true));  // (9)
    System.out.println("Groups <  75: " + groupFreqMap.headMap(75, false)); // (10)

    // Print the histogram for the weight groups:
    System.out.println("Histogram:");
    int numRegistered = printHistogram(groupFreqMap);                 // (11)
    System.out.println("Number of weights registered: " + numRegistered);

    // Poll the navigable map:                                        (12)
    System.out.println("Histogram (by polling):");
    int sumValues = 0;
    while (!groupFreqMap.isEmpty()) {
      Map.Entry<Integer, Integer> entry = groupFreqMap.pollFirstEntry();
      int frequency = entry.getValue();
      sumValues += frequency;
      System.out.printf("%5s: %s%n", entry.getKey(), frequency);
    }
    System.out.println("Number of weights registered: " + sumValues);
  }

  /** Prints histogram from a navigable map containing frequencies.
   *  Returns the sum of frequencies. */
```

```java
    public static <K> int printHistogram(NavigableMap<K, Integer> freqMap) {   // (13)
        // Create a set of entries in ascending key order.
        Set<Map.Entry<K, Integer>> navEntrySet = freqMap.entrySet();           // (14)
        int sumValues= 0;
        // Traverse the set of entries to print the histogram:
        for (Map.Entry<K, Integer> entry : navEntrySet) {                      // (15)
            /* Extract frequency value from entry.
             * Use the Arrays.fill() method to fill a char array with equivalent
             * number of '*' as the frequency value.
             * Convert the char array to string in order to print. */
            int frequency = entry.getValue();
            sumValues += frequency;
            char[] bar = new char[frequency];
            Arrays.fill(bar, '*');
            // Print key and bar.
            System.out.printf("%5s: %s%n", entry.getKey(), new String(bar));
        }
        return sumValues;
    }
}
```

Running the program with the following argument:

```
>java WeightGroups2 74 75 93 75 93 82 61 92 10 185
```

gives the following output:

```
Group frequency map: {10=1, 60=1, 75=3, 80=1, 90=1, 95=2, 185=1}
No. of weight groups: 7
First entry: 10=1
Last entry: 185=1
Greatest entry <= 77: 75=3
Smallest key > 90: 95
Groups >= 75: {75=3, 80=1, 90=1, 95=2, 185=1}
Groups <  75: {10=1, 60=1}
Histogram:
   10: *
   60: *
   75: ***
   80: *
   90: *
   95: **
  185: *
Number of weights registered: 10
Histogram (by polling):
   10: 1
   60: 1
   75: 3
   80: 1
   90: 1
   95: 2
  185: 1
Number of weights registered: 10
```

Review Questions

15.27 Which of these methods can be called on objects implementing the Map<K, V> interface?

Select the two correct answers.
(a) contains(Object o)
(b) addAll(Map<? extends K, ? extends V> m)
(c) remove(Object o)
(d) values()
(e) toArray()

15.28 Which statements are true about maps?

Select the two correct answers.
(a) The return type of the values() method is Set.
(b) Changes made in the set view returned by keySet() will be reflected in the original map.
(c) The Map interface extends the Collection interface.
(d) All keys in a map are unique.
(e) All Map implementations keep the keys sorted.

15.29 Which of these classes have a comparator() method?

Select the two correct answers.
(a) ArrayList
(b) HashMap
(c) TreeSet
(d) HashSet
(e) TreeMap

15.30 Which methods are defined by the java.util.Map.Entry<K, V> interface?

Select the two correct answers.
(a) K getKey()
(b) K setKey(K value)
(c) V getValue()
(d) V setValue(V value)
(e) void set(K key, V value)

15.31 Which statements are true about the following program?

```
import java.util.Collection;
import java.util.Collections;
import java.util.NavigableSet;
import java.util.TreeSet;
public class ConstructingSortedSets {
  public static void main(String[] args) {
```

```
NavigableSet<Integer> navSet
                        = new TreeSet<Integer>(Collections.reverseOrder());
Collections.addAll(navSet, 2010, 3001, 2001);

NavigableSet<Integer> ss1 = new TreeSet<Integer>(navSet);
NavigableSet<Integer> ss2 = new TreeSet<Integer>((Collection<Integer>)navSet);

    for (Integer iRef : navSet)                                    // (1)
      System.out.print(iRef + "|");
    System.out.println();
    for (Integer iRef : ss1)                                       // (2)
      System.out.print(iRef + "|");
    System.out.println();
    for (Integer iRef : ss2)                                       // (3)
      System.out.print(iRef + "|");
    System.out.println();
    while (!ss1.isEmpty())                                         // (4)
      System.out.print(ss1.pollFirst() + "|");
    System.out.println();
    while (!ss2.isEmpty())                                         // (5)
      System.out.print(ss2.pollFirst() + "|");
  }
}
```

Select the three correct answers.

(a) The loop at (1) prints 3001|2010|2001|.

(b) The loops at (1), (2) and (4) print the same output.

(c) The loop at (3) prints 3001|2010|2001|.

(d) All the loops print the same output.

(e) The loops at (3) and (5) print the same output.

15.32   Which code, when inserted independently at (1), will result in the following output from the program: {be=2, not=1, or=1, to=2}?

```
import java.util.Map;
import java.util.TreeMap;
public class FreqMap {
  public static void main(String[] args) {
    Map<String, Integer> freqMap = new TreeMap<String, Integer>();
    for (String key : new String[] {"to", "be", "or", "not", "to", "be"}) {
      // (1) INSERT CODE HERE ...
    }
    System.out.println(freqMap);
  }
}
```

Select the two correct answers.

(a) Integer frequency = freqMap.get(key);
    frequency = (frequency == 0) ? 1 : frequency+1;
    freqMap.put(key, frequency);

(b) Integer frequency = freqMap.get(key);
    frequency = (frequency == null) ? 1 : frequency+1;
    freqMap.put(key, frequency);

(c) ```
    int frequency = freqMap.get(key);
    frequency = (frequency == 0) ? 1 : frequency+1;
    freqMap.put(key, frequency);
    ```

(d) ```
    Integer frequency = (!freqMap.containsKey(key)) ? 1 : freqMap.get(key)+1;
    freqMap.put(key, frequency);
    ```

15.33   What will the program print when compiled and run?

```java
import java.util.Collection;
import java.util.Map;
import java.util.NavigableMap;
import java.util.TreeMap;

public class MapModify {
  public static void main(String[] args) {
    NavigableMap<String, Integer> grades = new TreeMap<String, Integer>();
    grades.put("A",  5); grades.put("B", 10); grades.put("C", 15);
    grades.put("D", 20); grades.put("E", 25);

    System.out.printf("1:%d, ", grades.get(grades.firstKey()));
    System.out.printf("2:%d, ", sumValues(grades.headMap("D")));
    System.out.printf("3:%d, ", sumValues(grades.subMap("B", false, "D", true)));
    grades.subMap(grades.firstKey(), false, grades.lastKey(), false).clear();
    System.out.printf("4:%d%n", sumValues(grades));
  }

  public static <K, M extends Map<K, Integer>> int sumValues(M freqMap) {
    Collection<Integer> values = freqMap.values();
    int sumValues= 0;
    for (int value : values)
      sumValues += value;
    return sumValues;
  }
}
```

Select the one correct answer.

(a) 1:5, 2:50, 3:35, 4:30
(b) 1:5, 2:30, 3:35, 4:30
(c) 1:5, 2:30, 3:25, 4:30
(d) 1:5, 2:30, 3:35, 4:75

15.34   Which code, when inserted independently at (1), will result in the following output from the program: {Soap=10, Salts=10}?

```java
import java.util.*;
public class Mapping {
  public static void main(String[] args) {
    NavigableMap<String, Integer> myMap
                  = new TreeMap<String, Integer>(Collections.reverseOrder());
    myMap.put("Soap", 10); myMap.put("Shampoo", 5); myMap.put("Salts", 10);
    // (1) INSERT CODE HERE ...
    System.out.println(myMap);
  }
}
```

Select the two correct answers.

(a) ```
for (Map.Entry<String, Integer> entry : myMap.entrySet())
    if (entry.getKey().equals("Shampoo"))
      myMap.remove("Shampoo");
```

(b) ```
for (Iterator<String> iterator = myMap.keySet().iterator();
        iterator.hasNext();)
    if (iterator.next().equals("Shampoo"))
      iterator.remove();
```

(c) ```
for (Iterator<String> iterator = myMap.keySet().iterator();
        iterator.hasNext();) {
    if (iterator.next().equals("Shampoo"))
      myMap.remove("Shampoo");
```

(d) ```
for (Map.Entry<String, Integer> entry : myMap.entrySet())
    if (entry.getKey().equals("Shampoo"))
      myMap.remove(entry);
```

(e) ```
myMap.subMap("Shampoo", true, "Shampoo", true).clear();
```

15.35  Which code, when inserted independently at (1), will result in the following output
from the program: {1=Odd, 2=Even, 3=Odd}?

```
import java.util.Map;
import java.util.TreeMap;
public class StringBuilderMap {
  public static void main(String[] args) {
    Map<Integer, StringBuilder> myMap = new TreeMap<Integer, StringBuilder>();
    for (Integer key : new int[] {1, 2, 1, 3, 1, 2, 3, 3}) {
      // (1) INSERT CODE HERE ...
    }
    System.out.println(myMap);
  }

  private static StringBuilder toggle(StringBuilder strBuilder) {
    String value = "Odd";
    if (strBuilder.toString().equals(value))
      value = "Even";
    return strBuilder.replace(0, strBuilder.length(), value);
  }
}
```

Select the one correct answer.

(a) ```
StringBuilder value = myMap.get(key);
myMap.put(key, (value == null) ? new StringBuilder("Odd") :
                 StringBuilderMap.toggle(value));
```

(b) ```
StringBuilder value = myMap.get(key);
if (value == null)
  value = new StringBuilder("Odd");
else
  StringBuilderMap.toggle(value);
myMap.put(key, value);
```
```

(c) ```
    StringBuilder value = myMap.get(key);
    if (!myMap.containsKey(key))
      myMap.put(key, new StringBuilder("Odd"));
    else
      StringBuilderMap.toggle(value);
    ```

(d) All of the above.

**15.36**  Which code, when inserted independently at (1), will result in the following output
from the program: {1=Odd, 2=Even, 3=Odd}?

```
import java.util.Map;
import java.util.TreeMap;
public class StringMap {
  public static void main(String[] args) {
    Map<Integer, String> myMap = new TreeMap<Integer, String>();
    for (Integer key : new int[] {1, 2, 1, 3, 1, 2, 3, 3}) {
      // (1) INSERT CODE HERE ...
    }
    System.out.println(myMap);
  }

  private static String toggle(String str) {
    if (str.equals("Odd"))
      str = str.replace("Odd", "Even");
    else
      str = str.replace("Even", "Odd");
    return str;
  }
}
```

Select the one correct answer.

(a) ```
    String value = myMap.get(key);
    myMap.put(key, (value == null) ? "Odd" : StringMap.toggle(value));
    ```

(b) ```
    String value = myMap.get(key);
    if (value == null)
      value = "Odd";
    else
      StringMap.toggle(value);
    myMap.put(key, value);
    ```

(c) ```
    String value = myMap.get(key);
    if (!myMap.containsKey(key))
      myMap.put(key, "Odd");
    else
      StringMap.toggle(value);
    ```

(d) All of the above.

15.11   Working with Collections

The Java Collections Framework also contains two classes, Collections and Arrays, that provide various operations on collections and arrays, such as sorting and searching, or creating customized collections. Practically any operation on a list can be done using the methods covered in this section.

The methods provided are all public and static, therefore these two keywords will be omitted in their method header declarations in this section.

The methods also throw a NullPointerException if the specified collection or array references passed to them are null.

Ordering Elements in Lists

The Collections class provides two static methods for sorting lists.

```
<E extends Comparable<? super E>> void sort(List<E> list)
<E> void sort(List<E> list, Comparator<? super E> c)
```

The first method sorts the elements in the list according to their natural order-ing. The second method does the sorting according to the total ordering defined by the comparator. In addition, all elements in the list must be *mutually comparable*: the method call e1.compareTo(e2) (or e1.compare(e2) in case of the comparator) must not throw a ClassCastException for any elements e1 and e2 in the list. In other words, it should be possible to compare any two elements in the list. Note that the second method does not require that the type parameter E is Comparable.

```
<E> Comparator<E> reverseOrder()
<E> Comparator<E> reverseOrder(Comparator<E> comparator)
```

The first method returns a comparator that enforces the reverse of the natural ordering. The second one reverses the total ordering defined by the compara-tor. Both are useful for maintaining objects in reverse-natural or reverse-total ordering in sorted collections and arrays.

This code shows how a list of strings is sorted according to different criteria.

```
List<String> strList = new ArrayList<String>();
strList.add("biggest"); strList.add("big");
strList.add("bigger"); strList.add("Bigfoot");

Collections.sort(strList);                                    // Natural order
Collections.sort(strList, Collections.reverseOrder()); // Reverse natural order
Collections.sort(strList, String.CASE_INSENSITIVE_ORDER);// Case insensitive order
Collections.sort(strList,                              // Reverse case insensitive order
            Collections.reverseOrder(String.CASE_INSENSITIVE_ORDER));
```

The output below shows the list before sorting, followed by the results from the calls to the sort() methods above, respectively:

```
Before sorting:                                    [biggest, big, bigger, Bigfoot]
After sorting in natural order:                    [Bigfoot, big, bigger, biggest]
After sorting in reverse natural order:            [biggest, bigger, big, Bigfoot]
After sorting in case insensitive order:           [big, Bigfoot, bigger, biggest]
After sorting in reverse case insensitive order:   [biggest, bigger, Bigfoot, big]
```

It is important to note that the element type of the list must implement the Comparable interface, otherwise the compiler will report an error. The following code shows that a list of StringBuilders cannot be sorted because the class StringBuilder does not implement the Comparable interface.

```
List<StringBuilder> sbList = new ArrayList<StringBuilder>();
sbList.add(new StringBuilder("smallest"));
sbList.add(new StringBuilder("small"));
sbList.add(new StringBuilder("smaller"));
Collections.sort(sbList);                          // Compile-time error!
```

Below is an example of a list whose elements are not mutually comparable. Raw types are used intentionally to create such a list. Predictably the sort() method throws an exception because the primitive wrapper classes do not permit interclass comparison.

```
List freakList = new ArrayList();                  // Raw types.
freakList.add(23); freakList.add(3.14); freakList.add(10L);
Collections.sort(freakList);                       // ClassCastException
```

The comparator returned by the reverseOrder() method can be used with *sorted* collections. The elements in the following sorted set would be maintained in descending order:

```
Set<Integer> intSet = new TreeSet<Integer>(Collections.reverseOrder());
intSet.add(9);   intSet.add(11);
intSet.add(-4);  intSet.add(1);
System.out.println(intSet);          // [11, 9, 1, -4]
```

The following utility methods apply to *any* list, regardless of whether the elements are Comparable or not:

```
void reverse(List<?> list)
```

Reverses the order of the elements in the list.

```
void rotate(List<?> list, int distance)
```

Rotates the elements towards the end of the list by the specified distance. A negative value for the distance will rotate toward the start of the list.

```
void shuffle(List<?> list)
void shuffle(List<?> list, Random rnd)
```

Randomly permutes the list, that is, *shuffles* the elements.

```
void swap(List<?> list, int i, int j)
```

Swaps the elements at indices i and j.

The effect of these utility methods can be limited to a sublist, that is, a segment of the list. The following code illustrates rotation of elements in a list. Note how the rotation in the sublist view is reflected in the original list.

```
// intList refers to the following list:        [9, 11, -4, 1, 7]
Collections.rotate(intList, 2);       // Two to the right.    [1, 7, 9, 11, -4]
Collections.rotate(intList, -2);      // Two to the left.     [9, 11, -4, 1, 7]
List intSublist = intList.subList(1,4);// Sublist:            [11, -4, 1]
Collections.rotate(intSublist, -1);   // One to the left.     [-4, 1, 11]
                                       // intList is now:      [9, -4, 1, 11, 7]
```

Searching in Collections

The Collections class provides two static methods for finding elements in sorted lists.

```
<E> int binarySearch(List<? extends Comparable<? super E>> list, E key)
<E> int binarySearch(List<? extends E> list, E key,
                     Comparator<? super E> c))
```

The methods use a binary search to find the index of the key element in the specified sorted list. The first method requires that the list is sorted according to natural ordering, whereas the second method requires that it is sorted according to the total ordering dictated by the comparator. The elements in the list and the key must also be *mutually comparable*.

Successful searches return the index of the key in the list. A non-negative value indicates a successful search. Unsuccessful searches return a negative value given by the formula -(*insertion point* + 1), where *insertion point* is the index where the key would have been, had it been in the list. In the code below the return value -3 indicates that the key would have been at index 2 had it been in the list.

```
// Sorted String list (natural order): [Bigfoot, big, bigger, biggest]
Collections.sort(strList);
// Search in natural order:
out.println(Collections.binarySearch(strList, "bigger"));   // Successful:  2
out.println(Collections.binarySearch(strList, "bigfeet"));  // Unsuccessful: -3
out.println(Collections.binarySearch(strList, "bigmouth")); // Unsuccessful: -5
```

Proper use of the search methods requires that the list is sorted, and the search is performed according to the same sort ordering. Otherwise, the search results are unpredictable. The example below shows the results of the search when the list strList above was sorted in reverse natural ordering, but was searched assuming natural ordering. Most importantly, the return values reported for unsuccessful searches for the respective keys are incorrect in the list that was sorted in reverse natural ordering.

```
// Sort in reverse natural order: [biggest, bigger, big, Bigfoot]
Collections.sort(strList, Collections.reverseOrder());
// Searching in natural order:
out.println(Collections.binarySearch(strList, "bigger"));   // 1
out.println(Collections.binarySearch(strList, "bigfeet"));  // -1 (INCORRECT)
out.println(Collections.binarySearch(strList, "bigmouth")); // -5 (INCORRECT)
```

Searching the list in reverse natural ordering requires that an appropriate comparator is supplied during the search (as during the sorting), resulting in correct results:

```
// Sort in reverse natural order: [biggest, bigger, big, Bigfoot]
Collections.sort(strList, Collections.reverseOrder());
// Searching in reverse natural order:
out.println(Collections.binarySearch(strList, "bigger",
                                  Collections.reverseOrder())); // 1
out.println(Collections.binarySearch(strList, "bigfeet",
                                  Collections.reverseOrder())); // -3
out.println(Collections.binarySearch(strList, "bigmouth",
                                  Collections.reverseOrder())); // -1
```

The following methods search for *sublists*:

```
int indexOfSubList(List<?> source, List<?> target)
int lastIndexOfSubList(List<?> source, List<?> target)
```

These two methods find the first or last occurrence of the target list in the source list, respectively. They return the starting position of the target list in the source list. The methods are applicable to lists of *any* type.

The following methods find the minimum and maximum elements in a collection:

```
<E extends Object & Comparable<? super E>>
    E max(Collection<? extends E> c)
<E> E max(Collection<? extends E> c, Comparator<? super E> comp)
<E extends Object & Comparable<? super E>>
    E min(Collection<? extends E> c)
<E> E min(Collection<? extends E> cl, Comparator<? super E> comp)
```

The one-argument methods require that the elements have a natural ordering, i.e., are Comparable. The other methods require that the elements have a total ordering enforced by the comparator. Calling any of the methods with an empty collection as parameter results in an NoSuchElementException.

The time for the search is proportional to the size of the collection.

These methods are analogous to the methods first() and last() in the Sorted-Set class and the methods firstKey() and lastKey() in the SortedMap class.

Changing Elements in Collections

The majority of the methods in this category accept a List, while one method operates on arbitrary Collections. They all change the contents of the collection in some way.

```
<E> boolean addAll(Collection<? super E> collection, E... elements)
```

Adds the specified elements to the specified collection. Convenient method for loading a collection with a variable argument list or an array.

```
<E> void copy(List<? super E> destination, List<? extends E> source)
```

Adds the elements from the source list to the destination list.

```
<E> void fill(List<? super E> list, E element)
```

Replaces all of the elements of the list with the specified element.

```
<E> boolean replaceAll(List<E> list, E oldVal, E newVal)
```

Replaces all elements equal to oldVal with newVal in the list; returns true if the list was modified.

```
<E> List<E> nCopies(int n, E element)
```

Creates an immutable list with n copies of the specified element.

The addAll() method is a convenient method for loading a collection with elements from a variable-argument list or an array. Several examples of its usage can be found in this chapter, but more are given below. The array passed should be an array of objects. Note also the autoboxing of the int values specified in (1) and (2). The addAll() method does not allow primitive arrays as vararg arguments, as attempted at (3).

```
List<Integer> intList = new ArrayList<Integer>();
Collections.addAll(intList, 9, 1, 1);                      // (1) A var-arg list
Collections.addAll(intList, new Integer[] {9, 1, 1}); // (2) An array of Integers
Collections.addAll(intList, new int[] {9, 1, 1});     // (3) Compile-time error!
```

Sorting Arrays

The Arrays class provides enough overloaded versions of the sort() method to sort practically any type of array. The discussion on sorting lists (p. 838) is also applicable to sorting arrays.

```
void sort(type[] array)
void sort(type[] array, int fromIndex, int toIndex)
```

These methods sort the elements in the array according to their natural ordering. Permitted *type* for elements include byte, char, double, float, int, long, short and Object. In the case of an array of objects being passed as argument, the *objects* must be mutually comparable according to the natural ordering defined by the Comparable interface.

```
<E> void sort(E[] array, Comparator<? super E> comp)
<E> void sort(E[] array, int fromIndex, int toIndex,
              Comparator<? super E> comp)
```

The two generic methods above sort the array according to the total ordering dictated by the comparator. In particular, the methods require that the elements are mutually comparable according to this comparator.

The bounds, if specified in the methods above, define a half-open interval. Only elements in this interval are then sorted.

The experiment from p. 838 with a list of strings is now repeated with an array of strings, giving identical results. A array of strings is sorted according to different criteria.

```
String[] strArray = {"biggest", "big", "bigger", "Bigfoot"};
Arrays.sort(strArray);                              // Natural order
Arrays.sort(strArray, Collections.reverseOrder());   // Reverse natural order
Arrays.sort(strArray, String.CASE_INSENSITIVE_ORDER);// Case insensitive order
Arrays.sort(strArray,                               // Reverse case insensitive order
            Collections.reverseOrder(String.CASE_INSENSITIVE_ORDER));
```

The output below shows the array before sorting, followed by the results from the calls to the sort() methods above, respectively:

```
Before sorting:                               [biggest, big, bigger, Bigfoot]
After sorting in natural order:               [Bigfoot, big, bigger, biggest]
After sorting in reverse natural order:       [biggest, bigger, big, Bigfoot]
After sorting in case insensitive order:      [big, Bigfoot, bigger, biggest]
After sorting in reverse case insensitive order: [biggest, bigger, Bigfoot, big]
```

The examples below illustrate sorting an array of primitive values (int) at (1), an array of type Object containing mutually comparable elements (String) at (2), and a half-open interval in reverse natural ordering at (3). A ClassCastException is thrown when the elements are not mutually comparable at (4) and (5).

```
int[] intArray = {5, 3, 7, 1};              // int
Arrays.sort(intArray);                      // (1) Natural order: [1, 3, 5, 7]

Object[] objArray1 = {"I", "am", "OK"};     // String
Arrays.sort(objArray1);                     // (2) Natural order: [I, OK, am]

Comparable<Integer>[] comps = new Integer[] {5, 3, 7, 1}; // Integer
Arrays.sort(comps, 1, 4, Collections.reverseOrder());// (3) Reverse natural order:
                                            //       [5, 7, 3, 1]

Object[] objArray2 = {23, 3.14, "ten"};     // Not mutually comparable
// Arrays.sort(objArray2);                  // (4) ClassCastException

Number[] numbers = {23, 3.14, 10L};         // Not mutually comparable
// Arrays.sort(numbers);                    // (5) ClassCastException
```

Searching in Arrays

The Arrays class provides enough overloaded versions of the binarySearch() method to search in practically any type of array that is sorted. The discussion on searching in lists (p. 840) is also applicable to searching in arrays.

The methods below return the index to the key in the sorted array, if the key exists. If not, a negative index is returned, corresponding to (-*insertion point*)-1, where *insertion point* is the index of the element where the key would have been found if it had been in the array. In case there are duplicate elements equal to the key, there is no guarantee which duplicate's index will be returned. The elements and the key must be *mutually comparable*.

The bounds, if specified in the methods below, define a half-open interval. The search is then confined to this interval.

```
int binarySearch(type[] array, type key)
int binarySearch(type[] array, int fromIndex, int toIndex, type key)
```

Permitted *type* for elements include byte, char, double, float, int, long, short, and Object. In the case where an array of objects is passed as argument, the *objects* must be sorted in natural ordering, as defined by the Comparable interface.

```
<E> int binarySearch(E[] array, E key, Comparator<? super E> c)
<E> int binarySearch(E[] array, int fromIndex, int toIndex, E key,
                     Comparator<? super E> c)
```

The two generic methods above require that the array is sorted according to the total ordering dictated by the comparator. In particular, its elements are mutually comparable according to this comparator. The comparator must be equivalent to the one that was used for sorting the array, otherwise the results are unpredictable.

The experiment from p. 840 with a list of strings is now repeated with an array of strings, giving identical results. In the code below the return value -3 indicates that the key would have been found at index 2 had it been in the list.

```
// Sorted String array (natural order): [Bigfoot, big, bigger, biggest]
Arrays.sort(strArray);
// Search in natural order:
out.println(Arrays.binarySearch(strArray, "bigger"));    // Successful:    2
out.println(Arrays.binarySearch(strArray, "bigfeet"));   // Unsuccessful: -3
out.println(Arrays.binarySearch(strArray, "bigmouth"));  // Unsuccessful: -5
```

Results are unpredictable if the array is not sorted or the ordering used in the search is not the same as the sort ordering. Searching in the strArray using reverse natural ordering when the array is sorted in natural ordering gives the wrong result:

```
out.println(Arrays.binarySearch(strArray, "bigger",
                     Collections.reverseOrder()));  // -1 (INCORRECT)
```

A ClassCastException is thrown if the key and the elements are not mutually comparable:

```
out.println(Arrays.binarySearch(strArray, 4)); // Key: 4 => ClassCastException
```

However, this incompatibility is caught at compile time in the case of arrays with primitive values:

```
// Sorted int array (natural order): [1, 3, 5, 7]
out.println(Arrays.binarySearch(intArray, 4.5));// Key: 4.5 => Compile time error!
```

Creating List Views of Arrays

The asList() method in the Arrays class and the toArray() method in the Collection interface provide the bidirectional bridge between arrays and collections. The asList() method of the Arrays class creates List views of arrays.

<E> List<E> asList(E... elements)

Returns a *fixed-size list view* backed by the *array* corresponding to the vararg argument elements.

Changes to the List view reflect in the array, and vice versa. The List is said to be *backed* by the array. The List size is equal to the array length and cannot be changed.

The code below illustrates using the asList() method. The list1 is backed by the array1 at (1). The list2 is backed by an implicit array of Integers at (2). An array of primitive type cannot be passed as argument to this method, as evident by the compile time error at (3).

```
Integer[] array1 = new Integer[] {9, 1, 1};
int[] array2 = new int[] {9, 1, 1};
List<Integer> list1 = Arrays.asList(array1);          // (1) An array of Integers
List<Integer> list2 = Arrays.asList(9, 1, 1);         // (2) A var-arg list
// List<Integer> intList3 = Arrays.asList(array2);    // (3) Compile-time error!
```

Various operations on the list1 show how changes are reflected in the backing array1. Elements cannot be added to the list view (shown at (5)), and elements cannot be removed from a list view (shown at (10)). An UnsupportedOperationException is thrown in both cases. An element at a given position can be changed, as shown at (6). The change is reflected in the list1 and the array1, as shown at (7a) and (7b), respectively. A sublist view is created from the list1 at (8), and sorted at (11). The changes in the sublist1 are reflected in the list1 and the backed array1.

```
System.out.println(list1);                   // (4) [9, 1, 1]
// list1.add(10);                            // (5) UnsupportedOperationException
list1.set(0, 10);                            // (6)
System.out.println(list1);                   // (7a) [10, 1, 1]
System.out.println(Arrays.toString(array1)); // (7b) [10, 1, 1]
List<Integer> sublist1 = list1.subList(0, 2); // (8)
System.out.println(sublist1);                // (9) [10, 1]
// sublist1.clear();                         // (10) UnsupportedOperationException
Collections.sort(sublist1);                  // (11)
System.out.println(sublist1);                // (12a) [1, 10]
System.out.println(list1);                   // (12b) [1, 10, 1]
System.out.println(Arrays.toString(array1)); // (12c) [1, 10, 1]
```

The code below shows how duplicates can be eliminated from an array using these two methods:

```
String[] jiveArray    = new String[] {"java", "jive", "java", "jive"};
Set<String> jiveSet   = new HashSet<String>(Arrays.asList(jivearray));   // (1)
String[] uniqueJiveArray = jiveSet.toArray(new String[0]);               // (2)
```

At (1), the jiveArray is used to create a List, which, in turn, is used to create a Set. At (2) the argument to the toArray() method specifies the type of the array to be created from the set. The final array uniqueJiveArray does not contain duplicates.

Miscellaneous Utility Methods in the Arrays Class

The methods toString() (p. 845) and fill() (Example 15.21, Example 15.22) have previously been used in this chapter. The *type* can be any primitive type or Object in these methods.

```
void fill(type[] a, type val)
void fill(type[] a, int fromIndex, int toIndex, type val)
```

Assigns the specified value to each element of the specified array or specified range.

```
String toString(type[] a)
String deepToString(Object[] a)
```

Returns a text representation of the contents (or "deep contents") of the specified array.

Review Questions

15.37 Which statement is true about the following program?

```
import java.util.ArrayList;
import java.util.Collections;
import java.util.List;

public class WhatIsThis {
  public static void main(String[] args) {
    List<StringBuilder> list = new ArrayList<StringBuilder>();
    list.add(new StringBuilder("B"));
    list.add(new StringBuilder("A"));
    list.add(new StringBuilder("C"));
    Collections.sort(list, Collections.reverseOrder());
    System.out.println(list.subList(1,2));
  }
}
```

Select the one correct answer.

(a) The program will compile and print the following when run: [B].
(b) The program will compile and print the following when run: [B, A].
(c) The program will compile, but throw an exception when run.
(d) The program will not compile.

15.38   Which statement is true about the following program?

```
// NEW RQ
import java.util.ArrayList;
import java.util.Arrays;
import java.util.Collections;
import java.util.List;

public class WhatIsThat {
  public static void main(String[] args) {
    List<StringBuilder> list = new ArrayList<StringBuilder>();
    list.add(new StringBuilder("B"));
    list.add(new StringBuilder("A"));
    list.add(new StringBuilder("D"));
    list.add(new StringBuilder("C"));
    StringBuilder[] sbArray = list.toArray(new StringBuilder[0]);

    Collections.sort(list);
    Collections.sort(list, null);
    Collections.sort(list, Collections.reverseOrder());
    System.out.println("List: " + list);

    Arrays.sort(sbArray);
    Arrays.sort(sbArray, null);
    Arrays.sort(sbArray, Collections.reverseOrder());
    System.out.println("Array: " + Arrays.toString(sbArray));
  }
}
```

Select the one correct answer.

(a) The program will compile and print the following when run: [B].
(b) The program will compile and print the following when run: [B, A].
(c) The program will compile, but throw an exception when run.
(d) The program will not compile.

15.39   Which statements are true about the following program?

```
import java.util.Arrays;

public class GetThatIndex {
  public static void main(String[] args) {
    if (args.length != 1) return;
    printIndex(args[0]);
  }

  public static void printIndex(String key) {
    String[] strings = {"small", "smaller", "smallest", "tiny"};
    System.out.println(Arrays.binarySearch(strings , key));
  }
}
```

Select the two correct answers.

(a) The largest value ever printed by the printIndex() method is 3.
(b) The largest value ever printed by the printIndex() method is 4.

(c) The largest value ever printed by the printIndex() method is 5.
(d) The smallest value ever printed by the printIndex() method is 0.
(e) The smallest value ever printed by the printIndex() method is -4.
(f) The smallest value ever printed by the printIndex() method is -5.
(g) The smallest value ever printed by the printIndex() method is -3.

15.40   Given that the following program compiles and prints the following output when run: 1 1 1.

```java
import java.util.*;

public class SoulSearching {
    public static void main(String[] args) {
        String[] array = {"smallest", "small", "tiny", "smaller"};

        List<String> list1 = Arrays._____(array);
        Collections._____(list1);
        int index1 = Collections._____(list1, "smaller");
        System.out.print(index1 + " ");

        List<String> list2 = Arrays._____(array);
        Collections._____(list2);
        int index2 = list2._____("smaller");
        System.out.print(index2 + " ");

        Arrays._____(array);
        int index3 = Arrays._____(array, "smaller");
        System.out.println(index3);
    }
}
```

Which method names can be used to fill the blanks without violating the behavior of the program?

Select the four correct answers.

(a) asList
(b) contains
(c) sort
(d) findIndex
(e) indexOf
(f) binarySearch
(g) search
(h) toList
(i) toArray
(j) subList

15.41   What will the program print when compiled and run?

```java
import java.util.Arrays;
import java.util.Collections;
import java.util.Comparator;
import java.util.List;
```

```
public class LastOrders {
  public static void main(String[] args) {
    String[] array = {"slurs", "slush", "slurps", "slurry"};
    List<String> list1 = Arrays.asList(array);
    Collections.sort(list1, LastOrders.comparatorX());
    int index1 = Collections.binarySearch(list1, "slurry",
                                      LastOrders.comparatorX());
    System.out.println (list1 + ": slurry at " + index1);
  }

  public static Comparator<String> comparatorX() {
    return new Comparator<String>() {
      public int compare(String str1, String str2) {
        StringBuilder sb1 = new StringBuilder(str1);
        StringBuilder sb2 = new StringBuilder(str2);
        return sb2.reverse().toString().compareTo(sb1.reverse().toString());
      }
    };
  }
}
```

Select the one correct answer.

(a) `[slush, slurs, slurry, slurps]: slurry at 2`
(b) `[slush, slurps, slurs, slurry]: slurry at 3`
(c) `[slurry, slurs, slurps, slush]: slurry at 0`
(d) `[slurps, slurry, slurs, slush]: slurry at 1`

Chapter Summary

The following information was included in this chapter:

- overriding the `equals()` and the `hashCode()` methods from the `Object` class.
- implementing the `Comparable` and the `Comparator` interfaces for ordering of elements.
- an overview of the collections framework in the `java.util` package: core interfaces and their implementations.
- functionality specified by the `Collection` interface and its role in the collections framework.
- sets, and how their functionality is defined by the `Set` interface and implemented by `HashSet` and `LinkedHashSet`.
- sorted and navigable sets, and how their functionality is defined by the `Sorted-Set` and `NavigableSet` interfaces, respectively, and implemented by `TreeSet`.
- lists, and how their functionality is defined by the `List` interface and implemented by `ArrayList`, `Vector`, and `LinkedList`.
- queues and deques, and how their functionality is defined by the `Queue` and `Deque` interfaces, and implemented by `PriorityQueue` and `ArrayDeque`, respectively.

- maps, and how their functionality is defined by the Map interface and implemented by HashMap, LinkedHashMap, and Hashtable.

- sorted and navigable maps, and how their functionality is defined by the SortedMap and NavigableMap interfaces, respectively, and implemented by TreeMap.

- utility methods found in the Collections and Arrays classes, with emphasis on sorting and searching in lists and arrays.

 ## Programming Exercises

15.1 Write a method that takes a string and returns the number of unique characters in the string. It is expected that a string with the same character sequence may be passed several times to the method. Since the counting operation can be time consuming, the method should cache the results so that when the method is given a string previously encountered, it will simply retrieve the stored result. Use collections and maps where appropriate.

15.2 Write a program that creates a concordance of characters occurring in a string (i.e., which characters occur where in a string). Read the string from the command line.
Here is an example of how to run the program:

```
>java Concordance Hello World
{d=[9], o=[4, 6], r=[7], W=[5], H=[0], l=[2, 3, 8], e=[1]}
```

Taking the SCJP 1.6 Exam

··

A.1 Preparing for the Programmer Exam

Sun Educational Services offers many types of certification exams for Java. More information can be found here:

```
http://www.sun.com/training/certification/java/index.xml
```

The focus of this book is on the Sun Certified Programmer for the Java Platform Standard Edition 6 exam (SCJP 1.6), which is a prerequisite for taking many of the certification exams for the Java technology.

The goal of the programmer exam is to test practical knowledge of the Java language. The exam tests for thorough understanding of both the syntax and semantics of the Java programming language.

The exam covers a wide variety of topics, as defined in the objectives for the programmer exam (see Appendix B, p. 857). It covers everything from the basic syntax of the language to detailed knowledge of threading and the core APIs, such as the java.lang package and the collections framework.

The need for real-world experience for this exam cannot be stressed enough. It is next to impossible to pass the test without having some actual experience programming in Java. Simply reading straight through this book is not recommended. Readers should take time to try out what they have learned every step of the way. Readers are encouraged to test their newly acquired knowledge using the review questions provided after every major topic.

Experimenting with the examples and working through the programming exercises in the book will serve to give the reader a much better chance of passing the test. The exam is considered to be difficult, and requires a fair amount of studying on the part of the candidate.

When the reader feels ready for the exam, she should test her skills on the sample exam that is provided in the back of the book (Appendix F). This will give an indication of how well the reader is prepared for the exam, and which topics need further study. The structure of the book should make it easy for the reader to focus on single topics, if necessary.

Even seasoned Java programmers should invest some time in preparing for the exam. Simply having real-world experience is also not enough to pass the exam.

A.2 Registering for the Exam

The exam is administered through *Authorized Worldwide Prometric Testing Centers*. They provide computer-based testing services for a wide variety of clients. Prometric has more than 3,000 testing centers located around the world. The test is paid for through the purchase of vouchers. An exam voucher must be obtained before signing up for the test at a local testing center.

Obtaining an Exam Voucher

Exam vouchers are sold by Sun. Some testing centers may be able to help in obtaining a voucher for the exam.

Be sure to obtain the correct voucher for the programmer exam. The test number for the Sun Certified Programmer for the Java Platform, Standard Edition 6 is *CX-310-065*. Sun will need credit card information to arrange payment. The cost of the voucher vary, depending on the country you live in. For US residents, it costs $300.

Sun will send the voucher as soon as the credit information has been verified. The voucher is sent by FedEx, and will normally arrive within one business day.

It is important to take good care of the voucher, since it is needed to sign up for the test at Prometric. Note that your voucher has an expiration date, usually in 6 to 12 months. Neither Sun nor Prometric will replace lost or expired vouchers, nor will they offer refunds for unused vouchers.

Signing Up for the Test

After obtaining the exam voucher, Prometric can be contacted to sign up for the test by making an appointment at one of the local testing centers.

Contact Information

Both Sun and Prometric have offices and associates around the world that can provide information about the exam. They can be contacted to purchase a voucher or sign up for the test.

The best way to find contact information and local testing centers is to visit their Web sites at:

Sun Java Certification

http://www.sun.com/training/catalog/courses/CX-310-065.xml

Prometric

http://www.prometric.com/Candidates/default.htm

After Taking the Exam

Those passing the exam will immediately receive a temporary certificate. Exam results are sent electronically by the test center to Sun, and Sun will send a permanent certificate by mail, which should arrive within a few weeks.

A.3 How the Examination Is Conducted

Exam type: Multiple choice and drag and drop
Number of questions: 72
Pass score: 65% (47 of 72 questions)
Time limit: 210 minutes

The Testing Locations

When a candidate shows up at the local testing center at the appointed time, she will be escorted to her own little cubicle with a desktop computer. The test will be conducted in this cubicle, using a testing program on the computer. The program will ask questions, record answers, and tabulate scores.

Candidates will not be allowed to bring personal belongings or food with them to the cubicle. During the exam, candidates will be allowed to make notes on a single piece of paper, but they will not be allowed to take these notes with them after the exam. Quite often the exam area is fitted with security cameras.

Utilizing the Allotted Time

The exam consists of 72 questions, which must be answered within 3 hours and 30 minutes. The questions vary in difficulty. Some are easy and some are difficult. With less than 3 minutes to answer each question, the candidate cannot afford to get stuck on the hard questions. If the answer does not become apparent within a reasonable time, it is advisable to move on to the next question. Time permitting, it is possible to return to the unanswered questions later.

An experienced Java programmer used to taking exams should be able to complete the exam well within the allotted time. Any remaining time is best used in reviewing the answers.

The Exam Program

The computer program used to conduct the exam will select a set of questions at random, and present them through a graphical user interface. The interface is designed in such a way that candidates are able to move back and forth through the questions for reviewing purposes. Questions can be temporarily left unanswered, and the candidate can return to them later. Before the exam starts, the candidate is allowed a test run with the computer program. A demo test that has nothing to do with the Java exam is used. Its sole purpose is to allow the candidate to get acquainted with the program being used to conduct the exam.

Immediately after the completion of the exam, the program will present the candidate with the following information:

- An indication of whether the candidate passed or failed. A score of 65% correct (47 of 72, time limit: 210 minutes) is needed to pass the exam.

- The total score. All the questions are weighted equally, and the score is calculated based on the percentage of correct answers. No credit is given for partially correct answers.

- Indications on how well the candidate did on each of the categories of the objectives. Candidates who fail the exam should pay close attention to this information. If the candidate is planning to retake the exam, it may give a good indication of which topics need closer attention.

The program will not divulge which questions were answered correctly.

A.4 The Questions

Types of Questions Asked

Most of the questions follow some common form that requires candidates to apply their knowledge in a special way.

- Analyzing program code.
  The question provides a source code snippet and asks a specific question pertaining to the snippet. Will running the program provide the expected result? What will be written to the standard output when the program is run? Will the code compile? Fill in the missing code in a program in order to make it work.

- Identifying true or false statements.

When analyzing program code, it is useful to try to apply the same rules as the compiler: examining the exact syntax used, rather than making assumptions on what the code tries to accomplish.

The wording of the questions is precise, and expects the responses selected in multiple-choice questions to be precise. This often causes the test to be perceived as fastidious. Close attention should be paid to the wording of the responses in a multiple-choice question.

None of the questions are intentionally meant to be trick questions. Exam questions have been reviewed by both Java experts and language experts to remove as much ambiguity from the wording of the questions as possible.

Since the program used in the exam will select and present the questions in a random fashion, there is no point in trying to guess the form of the questions. The order of the answers in multiple choice questions has been randomized and, thus, has no significance.

Types of Answers Expected

The majority of the questions are multiple choice. The correct number of alternatives to select is designated in the question, and must be selected for the question as a whole to be considered correctly answered.

Another form of question expects the candidate to drag and drop code fragments into appropriate places where the code is missing in a program in order to make the whole program work correctly.

There should be no problem identifying which form of answer each question requires. The wording of the questions will indicate this, and the software used will present the candidate with an input method corresponding to the form of answer expected.

For multiple-choice questions, the program will ask the candidate to select a specific number of answers from a list. Where a single correct answer is expected, radio buttons will allow the selection of only one of the answers. The most appropriate response should be selected.

In questions where all appropriate responses should be selected, checkboxes will allow the selection of each response individually. In this case, all choices should be considered on their own merits. They should not be weighed against each other. It can be helpful to think of each of the choices for the question as an individual true–false question.

Topics Covered by the Questions

Topics covered by the exam are basically derived from the set of objectives defined by Sun for the programmer exam. These objectives are included in Appendix B. All the major topics are covered extensively in the relevant chapters of the book.

The ultimate goal of the exam is to differentiate experienced Java programmers from the rest. Some of the questions are, therefore, aimed at topics that new Java programmers usually find difficult. Such topics include:

- casting and conversion
- polymorphism, overriding, and overloading
- exceptions and `try-catch-finally` blocks
- thread control
- nested classes
- collections and maps

Knowledge obtained from studying other languages such as C++ should be used with care. Some of the questions often seem to lead astray C++ programmers who have not grasped the many differences between C++ and Java. Those with a C++ background should pay special attention to the following Java topics:

- use `null`, not `NULL`
- use `true` and `false`, not 1 and 0.
- widening conversions
- conditional and boolean logic operators
- labeled statements
- accessibility rules
- how polymorphism works

Some of the questions may require intimate knowledge of the core APIs. This book covers the most important classes and methods of the API, but it does not go as far as listing every member of every class. The Java API reference documentation for the JDK should be consulted. It is essential that readers familiarize themselves with the relevant parts of the API documentation. There are API references readily available from many sources.

A.5 Moving on to Other Java Technology Exams

Those passing the programmer exam may want to move on to other exams in Java technology. All exams except the first one in the following list requires the SCJP 1.6 exam as a prerequisite:

- Sun Certified Java Associate (SCJA)
- Sun Certified Java Developer (SCJD)
- Sun Certified Web Component Developer (SCWCD)
- Sun Certified Business Component Developer (SCBCD)
- Sun Certified Developer For Java Web Services (SCDJWS)
- Sun Certified Mobile Application Developer (SCMAD)
- Sun Certified Enterprise Architect (SCEA)

Up-to-date information on the exams can be obtained by following the URL at the beginning of this appendix.

Objectives for the SCJP 1.6 Exam

• •

The objectives for the Sun Certified Programmer for the Java Platform Standard Edition 6 (CX-310-065) exam, also called SCJP 1.6 exam, are defined by Sun, and can be found at

`http://www.sun.com/training/catalog/courses/CX-310-065.xml`

The objectives are organized in *sections*, and each section is *reproduced verbatim* in this appendix. For each section, we have provided references to where in the book the objectives in the section are covered. In addition, the extensive index at the end of the book can also be used to lookup specific topics.

Section 1: Declarations, Initialization, and Scoping

1.1   Develop code that declares classes (including abstract and all forms of nested classes), interfaces, and enums, and includes the appropriate use of package and import statements (including static imports).

    ○   *For class declarations, see Section 3.1, p. 40.*

    ○   *For abstract classes, see Section 4.8, p. 135.*

    ○   *For nested classes, see Chapter 8, p. 351.*

    ○   *For interfaces, see Section 7.6, p. 309.*

    ○   *For enums, see Section 3.5, p. 54.*

    ○   *For package and import statements, see Section 4.2, p. 105.*

1.2   Develop code that declares an interface. Develop code that implements or extends one or more interfaces. Develop code that declares an abstract class. Develop code that extends an abstract class.

    ○   *For interfaces, see Section 7.6, p. 309.*

    ○   *For abstract classes, see Section 4.8, p. 135.*

1.3 Develop code that declares, initializes, and uses primitives, arrays, enums, and objects as static, instance, and local variables. Also, use legal identifiers for variable names.

- *For primitive types, see Section 2.2, p. 28.*
- *For arrays, see Section 3.6, p. 69.*
- *For enums, see Section 3.5, p. 54.*
- *For initialization of static, instance, and local variables, see Section 2.3, p. 31.*
- *For initializers, see Section 9.7, p. 406.*

1.4 Develop code that declares both static and non-static methods, and—if appropriate—use method names that adhere to the JavaBeans naming standards. Also develop code that declares and uses a variable-length argument list.

- *For methods, see Section 3.3, p. 44.*
- *For JavaBeans naming standard, see Section 3.2, p. 41.*
- *For varargs, see Section 3.8, p. 90.*

1.5 Given a code example, determine if a method is correctly overriding or overloading another method, and identify legal return values (including covariant returns), for the method.

- *For overloading methods, see Section 3.3, p. 47.*
- *For overloaded method resolution, see Section 7.10, p. 324.*
- *For overriding methods, see Section 7.2, p. 288.*
- *For return values, see Section 6.4, p. 228.*
- *For covariant return, see Section 7.2, p. 290.*

1.6 Given a set of classes and superclasses, develop constructors for one or more of the classes. Given a class declaration, determine if a default constructor will be created and, if so, determine the behavior of that constructor. Given a nested or non-nested class listing, write code to instantiate the class.

- *For constructors, see Section 3.4, p. 48.*
- *For default constructors, see Section 3.4, p. 49.*
- *For constructor chaining, see Section 7.5, p. 302, and Section 9.11, p. 416.*
- *For instantiating nested classes, see Chapter 8, p. 351.*

Section 2: Flow Control

- *For control flow, see Chapter 6, p. 203.*

2.1 Develop code that implements an `if` or `switch` statement; and identify legal argument types for these statements.

2.2 Develop code that implements all forms of loops and iterators, including the use of `for`, the enhanced `for` loop (for-each), `do`, `while`, labels, `break`, and `continue`; and explain the values taken by loop counter variables during and after loop execution.

2.3 Develop code that makes use of assertions, and distinguish appropriate from inappropriate uses of assertions.

2.4 Develop code that makes use of exceptions and exception handling clauses (`try`, `catch`, `finally`), and declares methods and overriding methods that throw exceptions.

2.5 Recognize the effect of an exception arising at a specified point in a code fragment. Note that the exception may be a runtime exception, a checked exception, or an error.

2.6 Recognize situations that will result in any of the following being thrown: `ArrayIndexOutOfBoundsException`, `ClassCastException`, `IllegalArgumentException`, `IllegalStateException`, `NullPointerException`, `NumberFormatException`, `AssertionError`, `ExceptionInInitializerError`, `StackOverflowError`, or `NoClassDefFoundError`. Understand which of these are thrown by the virtual machine and recognize situations in which others should be thrown programmatically.

Section 3: API Contents

3.1 Develop code that uses the primitive wrapper classes (such as `Boolean`, `Character`, `Double`, `Integer`, etc.), and/or autoboxing & unboxing. Discuss the differences between the `String`, `StringBuilder`, and `StringBuffer` classes.

○ *For boxing and unboxing, see Section 5.1, p. 162.*

○ *For primitive wrapper classes and string handling classes, see Chapter 10, p. 423.*

3.2 Given a scenario involving navigating file systems, reading from files, or writing to files, or interacting with the user, develop the correct solution using the following classes (sometimes in combination), from `java.io`: `BufferedReader`, `BufferedWriter`, `File`, `FileReader`, `FileWriter`, `PrintWriter`, and `Console`.

○ *For file I/O, see Chapter 11, p. 467.*

3.3 Develop code that serializes and/or de-serializes objects using the following APIs from `java.io`: `DataInputStream`, `DataOutputStream`, `FileInputStream`, `FileOutputStream`, `ObjectInputStream`, `ObjectOutputStream` and `Serializable`.

○ *For object serialization, see Section 11.6, p. 510.*

3.4 Use standard J2SE APIs in the `java.text` package to correctly format or parse dates, numbers, and currency values for a specific locale; and, given a scenario, determine the appropriate methods to use if you want to use the default locale or a specific locale. Describe the purpose and use of the `java.util.Locale` class.

○ *For using locales and formatting dates, numbers, and concurrency values, see Chapter 12, p. 531.*

3.5 Write code that uses standard J2SE APIs in the `java.util` and `java.util.regex` packages to format or parse strings or streams. For strings, write code that uses the `Pattern` and `Matcher` classes and the `String.split` method. Recognize and use regular expression patterns for matching (limited to: . (dot), * (star), + (plus), ?, \d, \s,

\w, [], ()). The use of *, +, and ? will be limited to greedy quantifiers, and the parenthesis operator will only be used as a grouping mechanism, not for capturing content during matching. For streams, write code using the `Formatter` and `Scanner` classes and the `PrintWriter.format/printf` methods. Recognize and use formatting parameters (limited to: %b, %c, %d, %f, %s) in format strings.

○ *For string pattern matching using regular expressions, and formatting and tokenizing values, see Chapter 12, p. 531.*

Section 4: Concurrency

○ *For concurrency, see Chapter 13, p. 613.*

4.1 Write code to define, instantiate, and start new threads using both `java.lang.Thread` and `java.lang.Runnable`.

4.2 Recognize the states in which a thread can exist, and identify ways in which a thread can transition from one state to another.

4.3 Given a scenario, write code that makes appropriate use of object locking to protect static or instance variables from concurrent access problems.

4.4 Given a scenario, write code that makes appropriate use of `wait`, `notify`, or `notify-All`.

Section 5: OO Concepts

○ *For OO concepts, see Chapter 7, p. 283.*

5.1 Develop code that implements tight encapsulation, loose coupling, and high cohesion in classes, and describe the benefits.

5.2 Given a scenario, develop code that demonstrates the use of polymorphism. Further, determine when casting will be necessary and recognize compiler versus runtime errors related to object reference casting.

5.3 Explain the effect of modifiers on inheritance with respect to constructors, instance or static variables, and instance or static methods.

○ *For modifiers, see Chapter 4, p. 103.*

5.4 Given a scenario, develop code that declares and/or invokes overridden or overloaded methods and code that declares and/or invokes superclass or overloaded constructors.

○ *For overloaded methods and constructors, see also Chapter 3, p. 39.*

5.5 Develop code that implements "is-a" and/or "has-a" relationships.

Section 6: Collections / Generics

○ *For generics and collections, see Chapter 14, p. 661, and Chapter 15, p. 747, respectively.*

6.1   Given a design scenario, determine which collection classes and/or interfaces should be used to properly implement that design, including the use of the `Comparable` interface.

6.2   Distinguish between correct and incorrect overrides of corresponding `hashCode` and `equals` methods, and explain the difference between `==` and the `equals` method.

6.3   Write code that uses the generic versions of the Collections API, in particular, the `Set`, `List`, and `Map` interfaces and implementation classes. Recognize the limitations of the non-generic Collections API and how to refactor code to use the generic versions. Write code that uses the `NavigableSet` and `NavigableMap` interfaces.

6.4   Develop code that makes proper use of type parameters in class/interface declarations, instance variables, method arguments, and return types; and write generic methods or methods that make use of wildcard types and understand the similarities and differences between these two approaches.

○ *For generics, see Chapter 14, p. 661.*

6.5   Use capabilities in the `java.util` package to write code to manipulate a list by sorting, performing a binary search, or converting the list to an array. Use capabilities in the `java.util` package to write code to manipulate an array by sorting, performing a binary search, or converting the array to a list. Use the `java.util.Comparator` and `java.lang.Comparable` interfaces to affect the sorting of lists and arrays. Furthermore, recognize the effect of the "natural ordering" of primitive wrapper classes and `java.lang.String` on sorting.

Section 7: Fundamentals

7.1   Given a code example and a scenario, write code that uses the appropriate access modifiers, package declarations, and import statements to interact with (through access or inheritance) the code in the example.

○ *For access control, see Chapter 4, p. 103.*

7.2   Given an example of a class and a command-line, determine the expected runtime behavior.

○ *For program arguments, see Section 3.9, p. 95.*

7.3   Determine the effect upon object references and primitive values when they are passed into methods that perform assignments or other modifying operations on the parameters.

○ *For parameter passing, see Section 3.7, p. 81.*

○ *For conversions in assignment and method invocation contexts, see Section 5.2, p. 163.*

○ *For method invocation conversions involving references, see Section 7.10, p. 323.*

7.4   Given a code example, recognize the point at which an object becomes eligible for garbage collection, and determine what is and is not guaranteed by the garbage collection system, and recognize the behaviors of the `Object.finalize()` method.

○ *For garbage collection, see Chapter 9, p. 389.*

7.5   Given the fully-qualified name of a class that is deployed inside and/or outside a JAR file, construct the appropriate directory structure for that class. Given a code example and a classpath, determine whether the classpath will allow the code to compile successfully.

○ *For classpath and JAR files, see Section 4.3, p. 117, and Section 4.4, p. 120, respectively.*

7.6   Write code that correctly applies the appropriate operators including assignment operators (limited to: =, +=, -=), arithmetic operators (limited to: +, -, *, /, %, ++, --), relational operators (limited to: <, <=, >, >=, ==, !=), the instanceof operator, logical operators (limited to: &, |, ^, !, &&, ||), and the conditional operator (? :), to produce a desired result. Write code that determines the equality of two objects or two primitives.

○ *For instanceof operator, see Section 7.11, p. 328.*

○ *For other operators, see Chapter 5, p. 159.*

○ *For object equality, see Section 15.1, p. 751.*

Objectives for the SCJP 1.6 Upgrade Exam

The objectives for the Sun Certified Programmer for the Java Platform, Standard Edition 6 Upgrade Exam (CX-310-066) are defined by Sun, and can be found at:

http://www.sun.com/training/catalog/courses/CX-310-066.xml

This exam can be taken by individuals who have passed a previous version of the programmer exam. The exam consists of 48 multiple-choice questions, which must be answered in 150 minutes. 32 questions (66%) must be answered correctly in order to pass. In the United States, the price of the exam is USD $300.

The objectives are organized in sections, and each section is *reproduced verbatim* in this appendix. The upgrade exam is a subset of the regular programmer exam. For each section, we have provided references to where the relevant material is covered in the book. The extensive index at the end of the book can also be used to lookup specific topics.

The objectives at the beginning of each chapter in the book refer to the SCJP 1.6 exam, and not to the upgrade exam.

Section 1: Declarations, Initialization and Scoping

1.1   Develop code that declares classes (including abstract and all forms of nested classes), interfaces, and enums, and includes the appropriate use of package and import statements (including static imports).

  ○ *For class declarations, see Section 3.1, p. 40.*

  ○ *For abstract classes, see Section 4.8, p. 135.*

  ○ *For nested classes, see Chapter 8, p. 351.*

  ○ *For interfaces, see Section 7.6, p. 309.*

  ○ *For enums, see Section 3.5, p. 54.*

  ○ *For package and import statements, see Section 4.2, p. 105.*

1.2   Develop code that declares, initializes, and uses primitives, arrays, enums, and objects as static, instance, and local variables. Also, use legal identifiers for variable names.

   o *For primitive types, see Section 2.2, p. 28.*

   o *For arrays, see Section 3.6, p. 69.*

   o *For enums, see Section 3.5, p. 54.*

   o *For initialization of static, instance, and local variables, see Section 2.3, p. 31.*

   o *For initializers, see Section 9.7, p. 406*

1.3   Develop code that declares both static and non-static methods and, if appropriate, use method names that adhere to the JavaBeans naming standards. Also develop code that declares and uses a variable-length argument list.

   o *For methods, see Section 3.3, p. 44.*

   o *For JavaBeans naming standard, see Section 3.2, p. 41.*

   o *For varargs, see Section 3.8, p. 90.*

1.4   Given a code example, determine if a method is correctly overriding or overloading another method, and identify legal return values (including covariant returns), for the method.

   o *For overloading methods, see Section 3.3, p. 47.*

   o *For overloaded method resolution, see Section 7.10, p. 324.*

   o *For overriding methods, see Section 7.2, p. 288.*

   o *For return values, see Section 6.4, p. 228.*

   o *For covariant return, see Section 7.2, p. 290.*

1.5   Given a set of classes and superclasses, develop constructors for one or more of the classes. Given a class declaration, determine if a default constructor will be created and, if so, determine the behavior of that constructor. Given a nested or non-nested class listing, write code to instantiate the class.

   o *For constructors, see Section 3.4, p. 48.*

   o *For default constructors, see Section 3.4, p. 49.*

   o *For constructor chaining, see Section 7.5, p. 302, and Section 9.11, p. 416.*

   o *For instantiating nested classes, see Chapter 8, p. 351.*

Section 2: Flow Control

   o *For control flow, see Chapter 6, p. 203.*

2.1   Develop code that implements an `if` or `switch` statement; and identify legal argument types for these statements.

2.2   Develop code that implements all forms of loops and iterators, including the use of `for`, the enhanced `for` loop (for-each), `do`, `while`, labels, `break`, and `continue`; and explain the values taken by loop counter variables during and after loop execution.

2.3   Develop code that makes use of assertions, and distinguish appropriate from inappropriate uses of assertions.

2.4   Develop code that makes use of exceptions and exception handling clauses (try, catch, finally), and declares methods and overriding methods that throw exceptions.

2.5   Recognize situations that will result in any of the following being thrown: ArrayIndexOutOfBoundsException, ClassCastException, IllegalArgumentException, IllegalStateException, NullPointerException, NumberFormatException, AssertionError, ExceptionInInitializerError, StackOverflowError or NoClassDefFoundError. Understand which of these are thrown by the virtual machine and recognize situations in which others should be thrown programmatically.

Section 3: API Contents

3.1   Develop code that uses the primitive wrapper classes (such as Boolean, Character, Double, Integer, and so on), and/or autoboxing & unboxing. Discuss the differences between the String, StringBuilder, and StringBuffer classes.

○ *For boxing and unboxing, see Section 5.1, p. 162.*

○ *For primitive wrapper classes and string handling classes, see Chapter 10, p. 423.*

3.2   Given a scenario involving navigating file systems, reading from files, writing to files, or interacting with the user, develop the correct solution using the following classes (sometimes in combination), from java.io: BufferedReader, BufferedWriter, File, FileReader, FileWriter, PrintWriter, and Console.

○ *For file I/O, see Chapter 11, p. 467.*

3.3   Develop code that serializes and/or de-serializes objects using the following APIs from java.io: DataInputStream, DataOutputStream, FileInputStream, FileOutputStream, ObjectInputStream, ObjectOutputStream and Serializable.

○ *For object serialization, see Section 11.6, p. 510.*

3.4   Use standard J2SE APIs in the java.text package to correctly format or parse dates, numbers, and currency values for a specific locale; and, given a scenario, determine the appropriate methods to use if you want to use the default locale or a specific locale. Describe the purpose and use of the java.util.Locale class.

○ *For using locales, and formatting dates, numbers, and concurrency values, see Chapter 12, p. 531.*

3.5   Write code that uses standard J2SE APIs in the java.util and java.util.regex packages to format or parse strings or streams. For strings, write code that uses the Pattern and Matcher classes and the String.split method. Recognize and use regular expression patterns for matching (limited to: . (dot), * (star), + (plus), ?, \d, \s, \w, [], ()). The use of *, +, and ? will be limited to greedy quantifiers, and the parenthesis operator will only be used as a grouping mechanism, not for capturing content during matching. For streams, write code using the Formatter and

Scanner classes and the `PrintWriter.format/printf` methods. Recognize and use formatting parameters (limited to: %b, %c, %d, %f, %s) in format strings.

○ *For string pattern matching using regular expressions, and formatting and tokenizing values, see Chapter 12, p. 531.*

Section 4: Concurrency

4.1   Recognize the states in which a thread can exist, and identify ways in which a thread can transition from one state to another.

○ *For thread states, see Section 13.6, p. 634.*

4.2   Given a scenario, write code that makes appropriate use of object locking to protect static or instance variables from concurrent access problems.

○ *For object locking, see Section 13.5, p. 626.*

Section 5: OO Concepts

○ *For OO concepts, see Chapter 7, p. 283.*

5.1   Develop code that implements tight encapsulation, loose coupling, and high cohesion in classes, and describe the benefits.

5.2   Given a scenario, develop code that demonstrates the use of polymorphism. Further, determine when casting will be necessary and recognize compiler vs. runtime errors related to object reference casting.

5.3   Explain the effect of modifiers on inheritance with respect to constructors, instance or static variables, and instance or static methods.

5.4   Develop code that implements "is-a" and/or "has-a" relationships.

Section 6: Collections / Generics

○ *For generics and collections, see Chapter 14, p. 661, and Chapter 15, p. 747, respectively.*

6.1   Given a design scenario, determine which collection classes and/or interfaces should be used to properly implement that design, including the use of the `Comparable` interface.

6.2   Write code that uses the generic versions of the Collections API, in particular, the `Set`, `List`, and `Map` interfaces and implementation classes. Recognize the limitations of the non-generic Collections API and how to refactor code to use the generic versions. Write code that uses the `NavigableSet` and `NavigableMap` interfaces.

6.3   Develop code that makes proper use of type parameters in class/interface declarations, instance variables, method arguments, and return types; and write generic methods or methods that make use of wildcard types and understand the similarities and differences between these two approaches.

   ○ *For generics, see Chapter 14, p. 661.*

6.4   Use capabilities in the `java.util` package to write code to manipulate a list by sorting, performing a binary search, or converting the list to an array. Use capabilities in the `java.util` package to write code to manipulate an array by sorting, performing a binary search, or converting the array to a list. Use the `java.util.Comparator` and `java.lang.Comparable` interfaces to affect the sorting of lists and arrays. Furthermore, recognize the effect of the "natural ordering" of primitive wrapper classes and `java.lang.String` on sorting.

Section 7: Fundamentals

7.1   Given an example of a class and a command-line, determine the expected runtime behavior.

   ○ *For program arguments, see Section 3.9, p. 95.*

7.2   Given the fully-qualified name of a class that is deployed inside and/or outside a JAR file, construct the appropriate directory structure for that class. Given a code example and a classpath, determine whether the classpath will allow the code to compile successfully.

   ○ *For classpath and JAR files, see Section 4.3, p. 117, and Section 4.4, p. 120, respectively.*

Annotated Answers
to Review Questions

●●

1 Basics of Java Programming

1.1 *(d)*

A method is an operation defining the behavior for a particular abstraction. Java implements abstractions using classes that have properties and behavior. Behavior is defined by the operations of the abstraction.

1.2 *(b)*

An object is an instance of a class. Objects are created from classes that implement abstractions. The objects that are created are concrete realizations of those abstractions. An object is neither a reference nor a variable.

1.3 *(b)*

(2) is the first line of a constructor declaration. A constructor in Java is declared like a method, except that the name is identical to the class name, and it does not specify a return value. (1) is a header of a class declaration, and (3), (4), and (5) are instance method declarations.

1.4 *(b) and (f)*

Two objects and three reference variables are created by the code. Objects are normally created by using the new operator. The declaration of a reference variable creates a variable regardless of whether a reference value is assigned to it or not.

1.5 *(d)*

An instance member is a field or an instance method. These members belong to an instance of the class rather than the class as a whole. Members which are not explicitly declared static in a class declaration are instance members.

1.6 *(c)*

An object communicates with another object by calling an instance method of the other object.

1.7 *(d) and (f)*

Given the declaration `class B extends A {...}`, we can conclude that class B extends class A, class A is the superclass of class B, class B is a subclass of class A, and class B inherits from class A, which means that objects of class B will inherit the field `value1` from class A.

1.8 *(d)*

The compiler supplied with the JDK is named `javac`. The names of the source files to be compiled are listed on the command line after the command `javac`.

1.9 *(a)*

Java programs are executed by the Java Virtual Machine (JVM). In the JDK, the command `java` is used to start the execution by the JVM. The java command requires the name of a class that has a valid `main()` method. The JVM starts the program execution by calling the `main()` method of the given class. The exact name of the class should be specified, and not the name of the class file, i.e., the `.class` extension in the class file name should not be specified.

2 Language Fundamentals

2.1 *(c)*

`52pickup` is not a legal identifier. The first character of an identifier cannot be a digit.

2.2 *(e)*

In Java, the identifiers `delete`, `thrown`, `exit`, `unsigned`, and `next` are not keywords. Java has a `goto` keyword, but it is reserved and not currently used.

2.3 *(b)*

It is a completely valid comment. Comments do not nest. Everything from the start sequence of a multiple-line comment (`/*`) to the first occurrence of the end sequence of a multiple-line comment (`*/`) is ignored by the compiler.

2.4 *(a) and (d)*

`String` is a class, and `"hello"` and `"t"` denote `String` objects. Java has the following primitive data types: `boolean`, `byte`, `short`, `char`, `int`, `long`, `float`, and `double`.

2.5 *(a), (c), and (e)*

(a) is a boolean data type, while (c) and (e) are floating-point data types.

2.6   *(c)*

The bit representation of int is 32-bits wide and can hold values in the range -2^{31} through $2^{31}-1$.

2.7   *(a), (c), and (d)*

The \u*xxxx* notation can be used anywhere in the source to represent Unicode characters.

2.8   *(c)*

Local variable a is declared but not initialized. The first line of code declares the local variables a and b. The second line of code initializes the local variable b. Local variable a remains uninitialized.

2.9   *(c)*

The local variable of type float will remain uninitialized. Fields and static variables are initialized with a default value. Local variables remain uninitialized unless explicitly initialized. The type of the variable does not affect whether a variable is initialized or not.

2.10   *(e)*

The program will compile. The compiler can figure out that the local variable price will be initialized, since the value of the condition in the if statement is true. The two instance variables and the two static variables are all initialized to the respective default value of their type.

3 Declarations

3.1   *(b)*

Only (b) is a valid method declaration. Methods must specify a return type or must be declared void. This makes (d) and (e) invalid. Methods must specify a list of zero or more comma-separated parameters enclosed by parentheses, ( ). The keyword void cannot be used to specify an empty parameter list. This makes (a) and (c) invalid.

3.2   *(a), (b), and (e)*

Non-static methods have an implicit this object reference. The this reference cannot be changed, as in (c). The this reference can be used in a non-static context to refer to both instance and static members. However, it cannot be used to refer to local variables, as in (d).

3.3   *(a) and (d)*

The first and the third pairs of methods will compile. The second pair of methods will not compile, since their method signatures do not differ. The compiler has no way of differentiating between the two methods. Note that the return type and the names of the parameters are not a part of the method signatures. Both methods in the first pair are named fly and, therefore, overload this method name. The methods in the last pair do not overload the method name glide, since only one method has that name. The method named Glide is distinct from the method named glide, as identifiers are case-sensitive in Java.

3.4   *(a)*

A constructor cannot specify any return type, not even void. A constructor cannot be final, static, or abstract.

3.5   *(b) and (e)*

A constructor can be declared private, but this means that this constructor can only be used within the class. Constructors need not initialize all the fields when a class is instanstiated. A field will be assigned a default value if not explicitly initialized. A constructor is non-static and, as such, it can directly access both the static and non-static members of the class.

3.6   *(c)*

A compilation error will occur at (3), since the class does not have a constructor accepting a single argument of type int. The declaration at (1) declares a method, not a constructor, since it is declared as void. The method happens to have the same name as the class, but that is irrelevant. The class has an implicit default constructor, since the class contains no constructor declarations. This constructor is invoked to create a MyClass object at (2).

3.7   *(a), (b), and (d)*

We cannot instantiate an enum type using the new operator. An enum type is implicitly final. Enum types inherit members from the Object class, as any other reference type.

3.8   *(d)*

An enum type can be run as a standalone application. The constants need not be qualified when referenced inside the enum type declaration. The constants *are* static members. The toString() method always returns the name of the constant, unless it is overridden.

3.9   *(c)*

An enum type can be run as a standalone application. (1), (2), and (3) define *constant-specific class bodies* that override the toString() method. For constants that do not override the toString() method, the name of the constant is returned.

3.10   *(d)*

An enum type cannot be declared as abstract. (b) is not correct, because without the enum type name, it would be a call to an instance method in a static context. Any abstract method must be implemented by each enum constant.

3.11   *(c)*

All enum types override the equals() method from the Object class. The equals() method of an enum type compares its constants for equality according to reference equality (same as with the == operator). This equals() method is final.

3.12   *(a) and (d)*

Declarations in (a) and (d) are overridden in each *constant-specific class body*. Declarations in (b) and (c) are not overridden by the declarations in the constant-specific class bodies, because of the incompatible return type.

3.13   *(c), (e), (f), and (g)*

Note how the nested enum type constants are accessed. Enum constants of an enum type can be compared, and an enum constant is an instance of its enum type.

3.14   *(d)*

Enum constants can be used as case labels and are not qualified with the enum type name in the case label declaration. The switch expression is compatible with the case labels, as the reference this will refer to objects of the enum type Scale5, which is the type of the case labels. The call to the method getGrade() returns a char value, which in this case is 'C'.

3.15   *(d), (f), and (g)*

A nested enum type must be declared inside a static member type, like (2), (3) and (5). Note that a nested enum type is implicitly static, and the keyword static is not mandatory in this case. An enum type cannot be local, as static member types cannot be declared locally.

3.16   *(a), (b), and (d)*

The static method values() returns an array with the enum constants for the specified type. The final method name() always returns the name of the enum constant. There is no names() method for enums in the Java standard library. The loop in (d) only converts the array of enums to a list, and iterates over this list. The argument Direction.class is not an array and, therefore, an illegal argument to the asList() method.

3.17   (b)

A constructor in the enum type is called for each enum constant created, when the enum type is loaded.

3.18   (d)

In Java, arrays are objects. Each array object has a final field named `length` that stores the size of the array.

3.19   (a)

Java allows arrays of length zero. Such an array is passed as argument to the `main()` method when a Java program is run without any program arguments.

3.20   (c)

The [] notation can be placed both after the type name and after the variable name in an array declaration. Multidimensional arrays are created by constructing arrays that can contain references to other arrays. The expression `new int[4][]` will create an array of length 4, which can contain references to arrays of `int` values. The expression `new int[4][4]` will create the same two-dimensional array, but will in addition create four more one-dimensional arrays, each of length 4 and of the type `int[]`. References to each of these arrays are stored in the two-dimensional array. The expression `int[][4]` will not work, because the arrays for the dimensions must be created from left to right.

3.21   (b) and (e)

The size of the array cannot be specified, as in (b) and (e). The size of the array is given implicitly by the initialization code. The size of the array is never specified in the declaration of an array reference. The size of an array is always associated with the array instance (on the right-hand side), not the array reference (on the left-hand side).

3.22   (e)

The array declaration is valid, and will declare and initialize an array of length 20 containing `int` values. All the values of the array are initialized to their default value of 0. The `for(;;)` loop will print all the values in the array, that is, it will print 0 twenty times.

3.23   (d)

The program will print "0 false 0 null" when run. All the instance variables, including the array element, will be initialized to their default values. When concatenated with a string, the values are converted to their string representation. Notice that the `null` pointer is converted to the string "null", rather than throwing a `NullPointerException`.

3.24 *(b)*

Evaluation of the actual parameter i++ yields 0, and increments i to 1 in the process. The value 0 is copied into the formal parameter i of the method addTwo() during method invocation. However, the formal parameter is local to the method, and changing its value does not affect the value in the actual parameter. The value of the variable i in the main() method remains 1.

3.25 *(d)*

The variables a and b are local variables that contain primitive values. When these variables are passed as arguments to another method, the method receives copies of the primitive values in the variables. The actual variables are unaffected by operations performed on the copies of the primitive values within the called method. The variable bArr contains a reference value that denotes an array object containing primitive values. When the variable is passed as a parameter to another method, the method receives a copy of the reference value. Using this reference value, the method can manipulate the object that the reference value denotes. This allows the elements in the array object referenced by bArr to be accessed and modified in the method inc2().

3.26 *(a) and (f)*

A value can only be assigned once to a final variable. A final formal parameter is assigned the value of the actual parameter at method invocation. Within the method body, it is illegal to reassign or modify the value stored in a final parameter. This causes a++ and c = d to fail. Whether the actual parameter is final does not constrain the client that invoked the method, since the actual parameter values are assigned to the formal parameters.

3.27 *(a), (d), and (f)*

The ellipses (. . .) must be specified before the parameter name. Only one varargs parameter is permitted, and it must be the last parameter in the formal parameter list.

3.28 *(c)*

In (a) and (b), the arguments are elements in the array that is passed to the method. In (c), the int array is encapsulated as an element in the array that is passed to the method. Note that int[] is not a subtype of Object[]. In (d), (e), and (f), the argument is a subtype of Object[], and the argument itself is passed without being encapsulated in a new array.

3.29 *(c)*

The method call in (4) calls the method in (2). The method call in (5) calls the method in (1). The method call in (6) calls the method in (3), as does the call in (7). Note the type of the varargs parameter in (3): an array of arrays of int.

3.30   *(d), (f), and (g)*

The main() method must be declared public, static, and void and takes a single array of String objects as argument. The order of the static and public keywords is irrelevant. Also, declaring the method final is irrelevant in this respect.

3.31   *(a), (b), and (c)*

Neither main, String, nor args are reserved keywords, but they are legal identifiers. In the declaration public static void main(String[] args), the identifier main denotes the method that is the entry point of a program. In all other contexts, the identifier main has no predefined meaning.

3.32   *(d)*

The length of the array passed to the main() method is equal to the number of program arguments specified in the command line. Unlike some other programming languages, the element at index 0 does not contain the name of the program. The first argument given is retrieved using args[0], and the last argument given is retrieved using args[args.length-1].

3.33   *(e)*

The program will print "no arguments" and "four arguments" when called with zero and three program arguments, respectively. When the program is called with no program arguments, the args array will be of length zero. The program will in this case print "no arguments". When the program is called with three arguments, the args array will have length 3. Using the index 3 on the numbers array will retrieve the string "four", because the start index is 0.

4   Access Control

4.1   *(c)*

The code will fail to compile, since the package declaration cannot occur after an import statement. The package and import statements, if present, must always precede any type declarations. If a file contains both import statements and a package statement, the package statement must occur before the import statements.

4.2   *(c) and (e)*

The name of the class must be fully qualified. A parameter list after the method name is not permitted. (c) illustrates single static import and (e) illustrates static import on demand.

4.3   *(a) and (b)*

(a) imports all types from the package java.util, including the type java.util.Locale. (b) explicitly imports the type java.util.Locale, which is what is needed.

(c) is syntactically incorrect, as java.util.Locale.UK is not a type. (d) imports types from the package java.util.Locale, but not the type java.util.Locale.

In (e), the static import is specified from a package (java.util), and not from a type, as required. In (f), the static import is incorrectly specified for a type (java.util.Locale) and not for a static member.

Both (g) and (h) with static import do not work, because we are referring to the constant UK using the simple name of the class (Locale) in the main() method.

4.4   (f)

The enum type Signal is not visible outside the package p1. If it were, (b), (c) and (d) would work. No static import is really necessary, since the constants of the enum type Signal are not used in the package p2.

4.5   (a), (b), and (c)

(d) does not statically import p3.Util.print. Note that p3.Util.Format can be imported as a type and as a static member from p3.Util, as in (a) and (b), respectively.

4.6   (b) and (e)

Static import from a class does not automatically import static members of any nested types declared in that class. The order of the import statements is arbitrary as long as it is delcared after any package statement and before any type declaration. Name conflicts must be disambiguated explicitly.

4.7   (b), (d), and (f)

In (a), the file A.class will be placed in the same directory as the file A.java. There is no -D option for the javac command, as in (c). The compiler maps the package structure to the file system, creating the necessary (sub)directories.

4.8   (b) and (d)

In (a) and (c), class A cannot be found. In (e) and (f), class B cannot be found —there is no package under the current directory /top/wrk/pkg to search for class B. Note that specifying pkg in the classpath in (d) is superfluous. The *parent* directory of the package must be specified, i.e., the *location* of the package.

4.9   (d) and (f)

The *parent* directory (or *location*) of the package must be specified. Only (d) and (f) do that. (d) specifies the current directory as well, but the search is from left to right in the specified paths, resulting in the top.sub.A class being found.

4.10   *(a) and (c)*

There is no -d option for the java command, as in (b). There should be no white space between the -D option and the name-value pair, as in (d), and no white space around the = sign either. The value can be quoted, especially if it contains white space.

4.11   *(e)*

4.12   *(c) and (d)*

A class or interface name can be referred to by using either its fully qualified name or its simple name. Using the fully qualified name will always work, but in order to use the simple name it has to be imported. By importing net.basemaster.* all the type names from the package net.basemaster will be imported and can now be referred to using simple names. Importing net.* will not import the subpackage basemaster.

4.13   *(c)*

Any normal class can be declared abstract. A class cannot be instantiated if the class is declared abstract. The declaration of an abstract method cannot provide an implementation. The declaration of a non-abstract method must provide an implementation. If any method in a class is declared abstract, then the class must be declared abstract, so (a) is invalid. The declaration in (b) is not valid, since it omits the keyword abstract in the method declaration. The declaration in (d) is not valid, since it omits the keyword class.

4.14   *(e)*

A class can be extended unless it is declared final. For classes, final means it cannot be extended, while for methods, final means it cannot be overridden in a subclass. A nested static class, (d), can be extended. A private member class, (f), can also be extended. The keyword native can only be used for methods, not for classes and fields.

4.15   *(b) and (d)*

Outside the package, the member j is accessible to any class, whereas the member k is only accessible to subclasses of MyClass.

The field i has package accessibility, and is only accessible by classes inside the package. The field j has public accessibility, and is accessible from anywhere. The field k has protected accessibility, and is accessible from any class inside the package and from subclasses anywhere. The field l has private accessibility, and is only accessible within its own class.

4.16   *(c)*

The default accessibility for members is more restrictive than protected accessibility, but less restrictive than private. Members with default accessibility are only accessible within the class itself and from classes in the same package. Protected members are, in addition, accessible from subclasses anywhere. Members with private accessibility are only accessible within the class itself.

4.17   *(b)*

A private member is only accessible within the class of the member. If no accessibility modifier has been specified for a member, the member has default accessibility, also known as package accessibility. The keyword `default` is not an accessibility modifier, and its only use is as a label in a `switch` statement. A member with package accessibility is only accessible from classes in the same package. Subclasses in other packages cannot access a member with default accessibility.

4.18   *(a), (c), (d), (e), and (h)*

The lines (1), (3), (4), (5), and (8) will compile. Keep in mind that a protected member of a superclass is only accessible in a subclass that is in another package, if the member is inherited by an object of the subclass (or by an object of a subclass of this subclass). This rules out (2), (6), and (7). The class D does not have any inheritance relationship with any of the other classes, and it does not inherit the field pf. This rules out the lines from (9) to (12).

4.19   *(b) and (e)*

You cannot specify accessibility of local variables. They are accessible only within the block in which they are declared.

Objects themselves do not have any accessibility, only references to objects do. If no accessibility modifier (`public`, `protected`, or `private`) is given in the member declaration of a class, the member is only accessible by classes in the same package. A subclass does not have access to members with default accessibility declared in a superclass, unless both classes are in the same package. Local variables cannot be declared `static` or have an accessibility modifier.

4.20   *(c)*

The line `void k() { i++; }` can be re-inserted without introducing errors. Re-inserting line (1) will cause the compilation to fail, since `MyOtherClass` will try to override a `final` method. Re-inserting line (2) will fail, since `MyOtherClass` will no longer have a default constructor. The `main()` method needs to call the default constructor. Re-inserting line (3) will work without any problems, but re-inserting line (4) will fail, since the method will try to access a `private` member of the superclass.

4.21   *(e)*

An object reference is needed to access non-static members. Static methods do not have the implicit object reference `this`, and must always supply an explicit object reference when referring to non-static members. The static method `main()` legally refers to the non-static method `func()`, using the reference variable `ref`. Static members are accessible both from static and non-static methods, using their simple names. No NullPointerException is thrown, as ref refers to an instance of MyClass.

4.22   (c)

Local variables can have the same name as member variables. The local variables will simply shadow the member variables with the same names. Declaration (4) defines a static method that tries to access a variable named a, which is not locally declared. Since the method is static, this access will only be valid if variable a is declared static within the class. Therefore, declarations (1) and (4) cannot occur in the same class declaration, while declarations (2) and (4) can.

4.23   (b)

The keyword this can only be used in instance (non-static) methods. Only one occurrence of each static variable of a class is created, when the class is loaded by the JVM. This occurrence is shared among all the objects of the class (and for that matter, by other clients). Local variables are only accessible within the block scope, regardless of whether the block scope is defined within a static context.

4.24   (c)

A class can be declared abstract even if it does not delcare any abstract methods. The variable k cannot be declared synchronized. Only methods and blocks can be synchronized.

4.25   (c)

The declaration in (c) is not legal, as variables cannot be declared abstract. The keywords static and final are valid modifiers for both field and method declarations. The modifiers abstract and native are valid for methods, but not for fields.

4.26   (a) and (c)

Abstract classes can declare both final methods and non-abstract methods. Non-abstract classes cannot, however, contain abstract methods. Nor can abstract classes be final. Only methods can be declared native.

4.27   (a)

The keyword transient signifies that the fields should not be stored when objects are serialized. Constructors cannot be declared abstract. When an array object is created, as in (c), the elements in the array object are assigned the default value corresponding to the type of the elements. Whether the reference variable denoting the array object is a local or a member variable is irrelevant. Abstract methods from a superclass need not be implemented by a subclass, but the subclass must then be declared abstract.

5 Operators and Expressions

5.1   *(a)*

A value of type char can be assigned to a variable of type int. An widening conversion will convert the value to an int.

5.2   *(d)*

An assignment statement is an expression statement. The value of the expression statement is the value of the expression on the right-hand side. Since the assignment operator is right associative, the statement a = b = c = 20 is evaluated as follows: (a = (b = (c = 20))). This results in the value 20 being assigned to c, then the same value being assigned to b and finally to a. The program will compile, and print 20, when run.

5.3   *(c)*

Strings are objects. The variables a, b, and c are references that can denote such objects. Assigning to a reference only changes the reference value. It does not create a copy of the source object or change the object denoted by the old reference value in the target reference. In other words, assignment to references only affects which object the target reference denotes. The reference value of the "cat" object is first assigned to a, then to b, and later to c. The program prints the string denoted by c, i.e., "cat".

5.4   *(a), (d), and (e)*

A binary expression with any floating-point operand will be evaluated using floating-point arithmetic. Expressions such as 2/3, where both operands are integers, will use integer arithmetic and evaluate to an integer value. In (e), the result of (0x10 * 1L) is promoted to a floating-point value.

5.5   *(b)*

The / operator has higher precedence than the + operator. This means that the expression is evaluated as ((1/2) + (3/2) + 0.1). The associativity of the binary operators is from left to right, giving (((1/2) + (3/2)) + 0.1). Integer division results in ((0 + 1) + 0.1) which evaluates to 1.1.

5.6   *(d)*

0x10 is a hexadecimal literal equivalent to the decimal value 16. 10 is a decimal literal. 010 is an octal literal equivalent to the decimal value 8. The println() method will print the sum of these values, which is 34, in decimal form.

5.7   *(b), (c), and (f)*

The unary + and - operators with right-to-left associativity are used in the valid expressions (b), (c), and (f). Expression (a) tries to use a nonexistent unary - operator with left-to-right associativity, expression (d) tries to use a decrement operator (--) on an expression that does not resolve to a variable, and expression (e) tries to use a nonexistent unary * operator.

5.8   *(b)*

The expression evaluates to –6. The whole expression is evaluated as (((-(-1)) - ((3 * 10) / 5)) - 1) according to the precedence and associativity rules.

5.9   *(a), (b), (d), and (e)*

In (a), the conditions for implicit narrowing conversion are fulfilled: the source is a constant expression of type int, the destination type is of type short, the value of the source (12) is in the range of the destination type. The assignments in (b), (d), and (e) are valid, since the source type is narrower than the target type and an implicit widening conversion will be applied. The expression (c) is not valid. Values of type boolean cannot be converted to other types.

5.10   *(a), (c), and (d)*

The left associativity of the + operator makes the evaluation of (1 + 2 + "3") proceed as follows: (1 + 2) + "3" → 3 + "3" → "33". Evaluation of the expression ("1" + 2 + 3), however, will proceed as follows: ("1" + 2) + 3 → "12" + 3 → "123". (4 + 1.0f) evaluates as 4.0f + 1.0f → 5.0f and (10/9) performs integer division, resulting in the value 1. The operand 'a' in the expression ('a' + 1) will be promoted to int, and the resulting value will be of type int.

5.11   *(d)*

The expression ++k + k++ + + k is evaluated as ((++k) + (k++)) + (+k) → ((2) + (2) + (3)), resulting in the value 7.

5.12   *(d)*

The types char and int are both integral. A char value can be assigned to an int variable since the int type is wider than the char type and an implicit widening conversion will be done. An int type cannot be assigned to a char variable because the char type is narrower than the int type. The compiler will report an error about a possible loss of precision in (4).

5.13   *(c)*

Variables of the type byte can store values in the range –128 to 127. The expression on the right-hand side of the first assignment is the int literal 128. Had this literal been in the range of the byte type, an implicit narrowing conversion would have been applied to convert it to a byte value during assignment. Since 128 is outside the range of the type byte, the program will not compile.

5.14   (a)

First, the expression ++i is evaluated, resulting in the value 2. Now the variable i also has the value 2. The target of the assignment is now determined to be the element array[2]. Evaluation of the right-hand expression, --i, results in the value 1. The variable i now has the value 1. The value of the right-hand expression 1 is then assigned to the array element array[2], resulting in the array contents to become {4, 8, 1}. The program sums these values and prints 13.

5.15   (a) and (c)

The expression (4 <= 4) is true. The null literal can be compared, so (null != null) yields false.

5.16   (c) and (e)

The remainder operator is not limited to integral values, but can also be applied to floating-point operands. Short-circuit evaluation occurs with the conditional operators (&&, ||). The operators *, /, and % have the same level of precedence. The type short has the range -32768 to +32767, inclusive. (+15) is a legal expression using the unary + operator.

5.17   (a), (c), and (e)

The != and ∧ operators, when used on boolean operands, will return true if and only if one operand is true, and false otherwise. This means that d and e in the program will always be assigned the same value, given any combination of truth values in a and b. The program will, therefore, print true four times.

5.18   (b)

The element referenced by a[i] is determined based on the current value of i, which is zero, i.e., the element a[0]. The expression i = 9 will evaluate to the value 9, which will be assigned to the variable i. The value 9 is also assigned to the array element a[0]. After the execution of the statement, the variable i will contain the value 9, and the array a will contain the values 9 and 6. The program will print 9 9 6, when run.

5.19   (c) and (d)

Unlike the & and | operators, the && and || operators short-circuit the evaluation of their operands if the result of the operation can be determined from the value of the first operand. The second operand of the || operator in the program is never evaluated because of short-circuiting. All the operands of the other operators are evaluated. Variable i ends up with the value 3, which is the first digit printed, and j ends up with the value 1, which is the second digit printed.

6 Control Flow

6.1   *(d)*

The program will display the letter b when run. The second if statement is evaluated since the boolean expression of the first if statement is true. The else clause belongs to the second if statement. Since the boolean expression of the second if statement is false, the if block is skipped and the else clause is executed.

6.2   *(a), (b), and (e)*

The conditional expression of an if statement can have any subexpressions, including method calls, as long as the whole expression evaluates to a value of type boolean. The expression (a = b) does not compare the variables a and b, but assigns the value of b to the variable a. The result of the expression is the value being assigned. Since a and b are boolean variables, the value returned by the expression is also boolean. This allows the expression to be used as the condition for an if statement. An if statement must always have an if block, but the else clause is optional. The expression if (false) ; else ; is legal. In this case, both the if block and the else block are simply the empty statement.

6.3   *(f)*

There is nothing wrong with the code. The case and default labels do not have to be specified in any specific order. The use of the break statement is not mandatory, and without it the control flow will simply fall through the labels of the switch statement.

6.4   *(a) and (f)*

The type of the switch expression must be either an enum type or one of the following: byte, char, short, int or the corresponding wrapper type for these primitive types. This excludes (b) and (e). The type of the case labels must be assignable to the type of the switch expression. This excludes (c) and (d). The case label value must be a constant expression, which is not the case in (g) where the case label value is of type Byte.

6.5   *(c)*

The case label value 2 * iLoc is a constant expression whose value is 6, the same as the switch expression. Fall through results in the printout shown in (c).

6.6   *(b)*

The switch expression, when unboxed, has the value 5. The statement associated with the default label is excecuted, and the fall through is stopped by the break statement.

6.7   (a)

The value of the case label iFour is *not* a constant expression and, therefore, the code will not compile.

6.8   (d)

Enum constants can be used as case labels and are not qualified with the enum type name in the case label declaration. The switch expression is compatible with the case labels, as the reference this will refer to objects of the enum type Scale5, which is the type of the case labels. The call to the method getGrade() returns a char value, which in this case is 'C'.

6.9   (e)

The loop body is executed twice and the program will print 3. The first time the loop is executed, the variable i changes from 1 to 2 and the variable b changes from false to true. Then the loop condition is evaluated. Since b is true, the loop body is executed again. This time the variable i changes from 2 to 3 and the variable b changes from true to false. The loop condition is now evaluated again. Since b is now false, the loop terminates and the current value of i is printed.

6.10   (b) and (e)

Both the first and the second number printed will be 10. Both the loop body and the increment expression will be executed exactly 10 times. Each execution of the loop body will be directly followed by an execution of the increment expression. Afterwards, the condition j<10 is evaluated to see whether the loop body should be executed again.

6.11   (c)

Only (c) contains a valid for loop. The initializer in a for statement can contain either declarations or a list of expression statements, but not both as attempted in (a). The loop condition must be of type boolean. (b) tries to use an assignment of an int value (notice the use of = rather than ==) as a loop condition and is, therefore, not valid. The loop condition in the for loop (d) tries to use the uninitialized variable i, and the for loop in (e) is syntactically invalid, as there is only one semicolon.

6.12   (f)

The code will compile without error, but will never terminate when run. All the sections in the for header are optional and can be omitted (but not the semicolons). An omitted loop condition is interpreted as being true. Thus, a for loop with an omitted loop condition will never terminate, unless a break statement is encountered in the loop body. The program will enter an infinite loop at (4).

6.13   *(b), (d), and (e)*

The loop condition in a while statement is not optional. It is not possible to break out of the if statement in (c). Notice that if the if statement had been placed within a labeled block, a switch statement, or a loop, the usage of break would be valid.

6.14   *(a) and (d)*

"i=1, j=0" and "i=2, j=1" are part of the output. The variable i iterates through the values 0, 1, and 2 in the outer loop, while j toggles between the values 0 and 1 in the inner loop. If the values of i and j are equal, the printing of the values is skipped and the execution continues with the next iteration of the outer loop. The following can be deduced when the program is run: variables i and j are both 0 and the execution continues with the next iteration of the outer loop. "i=1, j=0" is printed and the next iteration of the inner loop starts. Variables i and j are both 1 and the execution continues with the next iteration of the outer loop. "i=2, j=0" is printed and the next iteration of the inner loop starts. "i=2, j=1" is printed, j is incremented, j < 2 fails, and the inner loop ends. Variable i is incremented, i < 3 fails, and the outer loop ends.

6.15   *(b)*

The code will fail to compile, since the conditional expression of the if statement is not of type boolean. The conditional expression of an if statement must be of type boolean. The variable i is of type int. There is no conversion between boolean and other primitive types.

6.16   *(d)*

Implementation (4) will correctly return the largest value. The if statement does not return any value and, therefore, cannot be used as in implementations (1) and (2). Implementation (3) is invalid since neither the switch expression nor the case label values can be of type boolean.

6.17   *(c)*

As it stands, the program will compile correctly and will print "3, 2" when run. If the break statement is replaced with a continue statement, the loop will perform all four iterations and will print "4, 3". If the break statement is replaced with a return statement, the whole method will end when i equals 2, before anything is printed. If the break statement is simply removed, leaving the empty statement (;), the loop will complete all four iterations and will print "4, 4".

6.18   *(a) and (c)*

The block construct {} is a compound statement. The compound statement can contain zero or more arbitrary statements. Thus, {{}} is a legal compound statement, containing one statement that is also a compound statement, containing no statement. The block { continue; } by itself is not valid, since the continue statement cannot be used outside the context of a loop. (c) is a valid example of breaking out of a labeled block. (d) is not valid for the same reasons (b) was not valid. The statement at (e) is not true, since the break statement can also be used to break out of labeled blocks, as illustrated by (c).

6.19   *(c) and (d)*

Only the element type in (c), i.e., Integer, can be automatically unboxed to an int as required. The element type in (d) is int.

6.20   *(d) and (e)*

In the header of a for(:) loop, we can only declare a local variable that is compatible with the element type of an Iterable or an array. (The Iterable interface is discussed in Chapter 15). This rules out (a) and (b). The Iterable or array can be specified by an expression that evaluates to a reference type of an Iterable or an array. It is only evaluated once. Expressions that are permissible are found in (a), (d), and (e), but only (d) and (e) specify a legal for(:) header.

6.21   *(d)*

The type of nums is int[][]. The outer loop iterates over the rows, so the type of the loop variable in the outer loop must be int[], and the loop expression is nums. The inner loop iterates over each row, i.e. int[]. The loop variable in the inner loop must be int, and the loop expression in the inner loop is a row given by the loop variable of the outer loop. Only in the loop headers in (d) are both element types compatible.

6.22   *(d)*

There are no problems with automatic unboxing/boxing of the Character variable cRef in the various contexts where it is used in the program.

6.23   *(d)*

The program will only print 1, 4, and 5, in that order. The expression 5/k will throw an ArithmeticException, since k equals 0. Control is transferred to the first catch block, since it is the first block that can handle arithmetic exceptions. This exception handler simply prints 1. The exception has now been caught and normal execution can resume. Before leaving the try statement, the finally block is executed. This block prints 4. The last statement of the main() method prints 5.

6.24   *(b) and (e)*

If run with no arguments, the program will print "The end". If run with one argument, the program will print the given argument followed by "The end". The finally block will always be executed, no matter how control leaves the try block.

6.25   *(d)*

The program will compile without error, but will throw a `NullPointerException` when run. The `throw` statement can only throw `Throwable` objects. A `NullPointerException` will be thrown if the expression of the `throw` statement results in a `null` reference.

6.26   *(c) and (d)*

Normal execution will only resume if the exception is caught by the method. The uncaught exception will propagate up the runtime stack until some method handles it. An overriding method need only declare that it can throw a subset of the checked exceptions the overridden method can throw. The `main()` method can declare that it throws checked exceptions just like any other method. The `finally` block will always be executed, no matter how control leaves the `try` block.

6.27   *(b)*

The program will print 1 and 4, in that order. An `InterruptedException` is handled in the first `catch` block. Inside this block a new `RuntimeException` is thrown. This exception was not thrown inside the `try` block and will not be handled by the `catch` blocks, but will be sent to the caller of the `main()` method. Before this happens, the `finally` block is executed. The code to print 5 is never reached, since the `Runtime-Exception` remains uncaught after the execution of the `finally` block.

6.28   *(a)*

The program will print 2 and throw an `InterruptedException`. An `InterruptedException` is thrown in the `try` block. There is no `catch` block to handle the exception, so it will be sent to the caller of the `main()` method, i.e., to the default exception handler. Before this happens, the `finally` block is executed. The code to print 3 is never reached.

6.29   *(b)*

The only thing that is wrong with the code is the ordering of the `catch` and `finally` blocks. If present, the `finally` block must always appear last in a try-catch-finally construct.

6.30   *(a)*

Overriding methods can specify all, none, or a subset of the checked exceptions the overridden method declares in its `throws` clause. The `InterruptedException` is the only checked exception specified in the `throws` clause of the overridden method. The overriding method `f()` need not specify the `InterruptedException` from the `throws` clause of the overridden method, because the exception is not thrown here.

6.31   *(c)*

The overriding `f()` method in `MyClass` is not permitted to throw the checked `InterruptedException`, since the `f()` method in class `A` does not throw this exception. To avoid compilation errors, either the overriding `f()` method must not throw an InterruptedException or the overridden f() method must declare that it can throw an InterruptedException.

6.32 *(c) and (d)*

Statements (c) and (d) will throw an AssertionError because the first expression is false. Statement (c) will report true as the error message, while (d) will report false as the error message.

6.33 *(b) and (d)*

-ea (enable assertions) is a valid runtime option, not -ae. -source 1.4 is a compile time option. -dsa (disable system assertions) is a valid runtime option, not -dea.

6.34 *(e)*

The class of exceptions thrown by assertion statements is always AssertionError.

6.35 *(c)*

Assertions can be enabled or disabled at runtime, but the assert statements are always compiled into bytecode.

6.36 *(a) and (b)*

Statement (a) will cause the assert statement to throw an AssertionError since (-50 > -50) evaluates to false. Statement (b) will cause the expression 100/value to throw an ArithmeticException since an integer division by zero is attempted.

6.37 *(a) and (d)*

Option (a) enables assertions for all non-system classes, while (d) enables assertions for all classes in the package org and its subpackages. Options (b), (c), and (f) try to enable assertions in specifically named classes: Bottle, org.example, and org.example.ttp. Option (e) is not a valid runtime option.

6.38 *(c)*

The assert statement correctly asserts that 150 is greater than 100 and less than 200.

6.39 *(b) and (d)*

The AssertionError class, like all other error classes, is not a checked exception, and need not be declared in a throws clause. After an AssertionError is thrown, it is propagated exactly the same way as other exceptions, and can be caught by a try-catch construct. It inherits the toString() method from the Throwable class.

6.40 *(d)*

The Object class is the direct superclass of the Throwable class. The Throwable class is the direct superclass of the Error and Exception classes. The Error class is the direct superclass of the AssertionError class. The Exception class is the direct superclass of RuntimeException class.

6.41   *(c) and (d)*

The command line enables assertions for all non-system classes, except for those in the com package or one of its subpackages. (b) and (e) are incorrect because assertions are not enabled for the system classes.

7 Object-Oriented Programming

7.1   *(a) and (b)*

The extends clause is used to specify that a class extends another class. A subclass can be declared abstract regardless of whether the superclass was declared abstract. Private, overridden, and hidden members from the superclass are not inherited by the subclass. A class cannot be declared both abstract and final, since an abstract class needs to be extended to be useful, and a final class cannot be extended. The accessibility of the class is not limited by the accessibility of its members. A class with all the members declared private can still be declared public.

7.2   *(b) and (e)*

The Object class has a public method named equals, but it does not have any method named length. Since all classes are subclasses of the Object class, they all inherit the equals() method. Thus, all Java objects have a public method named equals. In Java, a class can only extend a single superclass, but there is no limit on how many classes can extend a superclass.

7.3   *(b) and (c)*

A subclass need not redefine all the methods defined in the superclass. It is possible for a subclass to define a method with the same name and parameters as a method defined by the superclass, but then the new method must satisfy the criteria for method overriding. A subclass can define a field that can hide a field defined in a superclass. Two classes cannot be the superclass of one another.

7.4   *(a), (b), and (d)*

Bar is a subclass of Foo that overrides the method g(). The statement a.j = 5 is not legal, since the member j in the class Bar cannot be accessed through a Foo reference. The statement b.i = 3 is not legal either, since the private member i cannot be accessed from outside of the class Foo.

7.5   *(a)*

A method can be overridden by defining a method with the same signature (i.e., name and parameter list) and where the return types are the same or covariant. Only instance methods that are accessible by their simple name can be overridden. A private method, therefore, cannot be overridden in subclasses, but the subclasses are allowed to define a new method with exactly the same signature. A final method cannot be overridden. An overriding method cannot exhibit behavior that contradicts the declaration of the original method. An overriding method, therefore, cannot declare that it throws checked exceptions that cannot be thrown by the original method in the superclass.

7.6   *(g)*

It is not possible to invoke the doIt() method in A from an instance method in class C. The method in C needs to call a method in a superclass two levels up in the inheritance hierarchy. The super.super.doIt() strategy will not work, since super is a keyword and cannot be used as an ordinary reference, nor accessed like a field. If the member to be accessed had been a field, the solution would be to cast the this reference to the class of the field and use the resulting reference to access the field. Field access is determined by the declared type of the reference, whereas the instance method to execute is determined by the actual type of the object denoted by the reference.

7.7   *(e)*

The code will compile without errors. None of the calls to a max() method are ambiguous. When the program is run, the main() method will call the max() method in C with the parameters 13 and 29. This method will call the max() method in B with the parameters 23 and 39. The max() method in B will in turn call the max() method in A with the parameters 39 and 23. The max() method in A will return 39 to the max() method in B. The max() method in B will return 29 to the max() method in C. The max() method in C will return 29 to the main() method.

7.8   *(c)*

The simplest way to print the message in the class Message would be to use msg.text. The main() method creates an instance of MyClass, which results in the creation of a Message instance. The field msg denotes this Message object in MySuperclass and is inherited by the MyClass object. Thus, the message in the Message object can be accessed directly by msg.text in the print() method of MyClass.

7.9   *(b) and (g)*

(a) and (1) do not have covariant return types.

(b) overrides (2).

The instance method in (c) cannot override the static method at (4).

The static method in (d) and the static method at (4) do not have compatible return types.

The static method in (e) cannot override the instance method at (3).

The instance method in (f) and the instance method at (5) do not have compatible return types.

The instance method in (g) overrides the instance method at (6), and they have covariant return types.

7.10   *(g)*

In the class Car, the static method getModelName() hides the static method of the same name in the superclass Vehicle. In the class Car, the instance method getRegNo() overrides the instance method of the same name in the superclass Vehicle. The declared type of the reference determines the method to execute when a static method is called, but the actual type of the object at runtime determines the method to execute when an overridden method is called.

7.11   *(d)*

Note that the method equals() in the class Item *overloads* the method with the same name in the Object class. Calls to overloaded methods are resolved at compile-time. Using the reference itemA of the type Item results in the equals() method of the Item to be executed, and using the reference itemC of the type Object results in the equals() method of the Object class to be executed. This is a canonical example where using the @Override annotation in front of the equals() method would be very useful.

7.12   *(e)*

The class MySuper does not have a default constructor. This means that constructors in subclasses must explicitly call the superclass constructor and provide the required parameters. The supplied constructor accomplishes this by calling super(num) in its first statement. Additional constructors can accomplish this either by calling the superclass constructor directly using the super() call, or by calling another constructor in the same class using the this() call which, in turn, calls the superclass constructor. (a) and (b) are not valid, since they do not call the superclass constructor explicitly. (d) fails, since the super() call must always be the first statement in the constructor body. (f) fails, since the super() and this() calls cannot be combined.

7.13   *(b)*

In a subclass without any declared constructors, the implicit default constructor will call super(). The use of the super() and this() statements are not mandatory as long as the superclass has a default constructor. If neither super() nor this() is declared as the first statement in the body of a constructor, then the default super() will implicitly be the first statement. A constructor body cannot have both a super() and a this() statement. Calling super() will not always work, since a superclass might not have a default constructor.

7.14   *(d)*

The program will print 12 followed by Test. When the main() method is executed, it will create a new instance of B by passing "Test" as argument. This results in a call to the constructor of B that has one String parameter. The constructor does not explicitly call any superclass constructor but, instead, the default constructor of the superclass A is called implicitly. The default constructor of A calls the constructor in

A that has two `String` parameters, passing it the argument list ("1", "2"). This constructor calls the constructor with one `String` parameter, passing the argument "12". This constructor prints the argument. Now the execution of all the constructors in A is completed, and execution continues in the constructor of B. This constructor now prints the original argument "Test" and returns to the `main()` method.

7.15   *(b) and (c)*

Interface declarations do not provide any method implementations and only permit multiple interface inheritance. An interface can extend any number of interfaces and can be extended by any number of interfaces. Fields in interfaces are always `static`, and can be declared static explicitly. Abstract method declarations in interfaces are always non-`static`, and cannot be declared static.

7.16   *(a), (c), and (d)*

Fields in interfaces declare named constants, and are always `public`, `static`, and `final`. None of these modifiers are mandatory in a constant declaration. All named constants must be explicitly initialized in the declaration.

7.17   *(a) and (d)*

The keyword `implements` is used when a class implements an interface. The keyword `extends` is used when an interface inherits from another interface or a class inherits from another class.

7.18   *(e)*

The code will compile without errors. The class `MyClass` declares that it implements the interfaces `Interface1` and `Interface2`. Since the class is declared `abstract`, it does not need to implement all abstract method declarations defined in these interfaces. Any non-abstract subclasses of `MyClass` must provide the missing method implementations. The two interfaces share a common abstract method declaration void `g()`. `MyClass` provides an implementation for this abstract method declaration that satisfies both `Interface1` and `Interface2`. Both interfaces provide declarations of constants named `VAL_B`. This can lead to an ambiguity when referring to `VAL_B` by its simple name from `MyClass`. The ambiguity can be resolved by using fully qualified names: `Interface1.VAL_B` and `Interface2.VAL_B`. However, there are no problems with the code as it stands.

7.19   *(a) and (c)*

Declaration (b) fails, since it contains an illegal forward reference to its own named constant. The field type is missing in declaration (d). Declaration (e) tries illegally to use the `protected` modifier, even though named constants always have `public` accessibility. Such constants are implicitly `public`, `static`, and `final`.

7.20 *(c)*

The program will throw a java.lang.ClassCastException in the assignment at (3), when run. The statement at (1) will compile, since the assignment is done from a subclass reference to a superclass reference. The cast at (2) assures the compiler that arrA will refer to an object that can be referenced by arrB. This will work when run, since arrA will refer to an object of type B[]. The cast at (3) will also assure the compiler that arrA will refer to an object that can be referenced by arrB. This will not work when run, since arrA will refer to an object of type A[].

7.21 *(d)*

(4) will cause a compile-time error, since it attempts to assign a reference value of a supertype object to a reference of a subtype. The type of the source reference value is MyClass and the type of the destination reference is MySubclass. (1) and (2) will compile, since the reference is assigned a reference value of the same type. (3) will also compile, since the reference is assigned a reference value of a subtype.

7.22 *(e)*

Only the assignment I1 b = obj3 is valid. The assignment is allowed, since C3 extends C1, which implements I1. The assignment obj2 = obj1 is not legal, since C1 is not a subclass of C2. The assignments obj3 = obj1 and obj3 = obj2 are not legal, since neither C1 nor C2 is a subclass of C3. The assignment I1 a = obj2 is not legal, since C2 does not implement I1. Assignment I2 c = obj1 is not legal, since C1 does not implement I2.

7.23 *(b)*

The statement would be legal at compile time, since the reference x might actually refer to an object of the type Sub. The cast tells the compiler to go ahead and allow the assignment. At runtime, the reference x may turn out to denote an object of the type Super instead. If this happens, the assignment will be aborted and a ClassCast-Exception will be thrown.

7.24 *(c)*

Only A a = d is legal. The reference value in d can be assigned to a, since D implements A. The statements c = d and d = c are illegal, since there is no subtype-supertype relationship between C and D. Even though a cast is provided, the statement d = (D) c is illegal. The object referred to by c cannot possibly be of type D, since D is not a subclass of C. The statement c = b is illegal, since assigning a reference value of a reference of type B to a reference of type C requires a cast.

7.25 *(a), (b), and (c)*

The program will print A, B, and C when run. The object denoted by the reference a is of type C. The object is also an instance of A and B, since C is a subclass of B and B is a subclass of A. The object is not an instance of D.

7.26   *(b)*

The expression (o instanceof B) will return true if the object referred to by o is of type B or a subtype of B. The expression (!(o instanceof C)) will return true unless the object referred to by o is of type C or a subtype of C. Thus, the expression (o instanceof B) && (!(o instanceof C)) will only return true if the object is of type B or a subtype of B that is not C or a subtype of C. Given objects of the classes A, B, and C, this expression will only return true for objects of class B.

7.27   *(a)*

The program will print all the letters I, J, C, and D, when run. The object referred to by the reference x is of class D. Class D extends class C and class C implements interface I. This makes I, J, and C supertypes of class D. The reference value of an object of class D can be assigned to any reference of its supertypes and is, therefore, an instanceof these types.

7.35   *(e)*

The program will print 2 when System.out.println(ref2.f()) is executed. The object referenced by ref2 is of the class C, but the reference is of type B. Since B contains a method f(), the method call will be allowed at compile time. During execution it is determined that the object is of the class C, and dynamic method lookup will cause the overridden method in C to be executed.

7.36   *(c)*

The program will print 1 when run. The f() methods in A and B are private and are not accessible by the subclasses. Because of this, the subclasses cannot overload or override these methods, but simply define new methods with the same signature. The object being called is of the class C. The reference used to access the object is of the type B. Since B contains a method g(), the method call will be allowed at compile time. During execution it is determined that the object is of the class C, and dynamic method lookup will cause the overridden method g() in B to be executed. This method calls a method named f. It can be determined during compilation that this can only refer to the f() method in B, since the method is private and cannot be overridden. This method returns the value 1, which is printed.

7.37   *(c) and (d)*

The code as it stands will compile. The use of inheritance in this code does not define a Planet *has-a* Star relationship. The code will fail if the name of the field starName is changed in the Star class, since the subclass Planet tries to access it using the name starName. An instance of Planet is not an instance of HeavenlyBody. Neither Planet nor Star implements HeavenlyBody.

7.38   *(b)*

The code will compile. The code will not fail to compile if the name of the field starName is changed in the Star class, since the Planet class does not try to access the field by name, but instead uses the public method describe() in the Star class for that purpose. An instance of Planet is not an instance of HeavenlyBody, since it neither implements HeavenlyBody nor extends a class that implements HeavenlyBody.

7.39 *(f)*

(a) to (e) are all true, but (f) is not.

8 Nested Type Declarations

8.1 *(e)*

The code will compile, and print 123, when run. An instance of the Outer class will be created and the field secret will be initialized to 123. A call to the createInner() method will return the reference value of the newly created Inner instance. This object is an instance of a non-static member class and is associated with the outer instance. This means that an object of a non-static member class has access to the members within the outer instance. Since the Inner class is nested in the class containing the field secret, this field is accessible to the Inner instance, even though the field secret is declared private.

8.2 *(b) and (e)*

A static member class is in many respects like a top-level class and can contain non-static fields. Instances of non-static member classes are created in the context of an outer instance. The outer instance is inherently associated with the inner instance. Several non-static member class instances can be created and associated with the same outer instance. Static member classes do not have any inherent outer instance. A static member interface, just like top-level interfaces, cannot contain non-static fields. Nested interfaces are always static.

8.3 *(e)*

The program will fail to compile, since the expression ((State) this).val in the method restore() of the class Memento is invalid. The correct way to access the field val in the class State, which is hidden by the field val in the class Memento, is to use the expression State.this.val. Other than that, there are no problems with the code.

8.4 *(d)*

The program will compile without error, and will print 1, 3, 4, in that order, when run. The expression B.this.val will access the value 1 stored in the field val of the (outer) B instance associated with the (inner) C object referenced by the reference obj. The expression C.this.val will access the value 3 stored in the field val of the C object referenced by the reference obj. The expression super.val will access the field val from A, the superclass of C.

8.5   *(c) and (d)*

The class Inner is a non-static member class of the Outer class and its full name is Outer.Inner. The Inner class does not inherit from the Outer class. The method named doIt is, therefore, neither overridden nor overloaded. Within the scope of the Inner class, the doIt() method of the Outer class is hidden by the doIt() method of the Inner class.

8.6   *(f)*

The nested class Inner is a non-static member class, and can only be instantiated in the context of an outer instance of the class Outer. Each Outer object has its own counter for the number of Inner objects associated with it. The instance method multiply() creates three objects of the class Inner: two in the context of the current Outer instance, and one in the context of a new Outer object.

The counter value printed by the first print statement is returned by the second Inner object which is associated with the current Outer object. And since the current Outer object has two Inner objects associated with it at this point, the value 2 of its counter is printed.

The counter value printed by the second print statement is returned by the third Inner object which is associated with the new Outer object created in the multiply() method. And since the second Outer object has only one Inner object associated with it, the value 1 of its counter is printed.

8.7   *(e)*

Non-static member classes, unlike top-level classes, can have any accessibility modifier. Static member classes can only be declared in top-level or nested static member classes and interfaces. Only static member classes can be declared static. Declaring a class static only means that instances of the class are created without having an outer instance. This has no bearing on whether the members of the class can be static or not.

8.8   *(d) and (e)*

The methods labeled (1) and (3) will not compile, since the non-final parameter i is not accessible from within the inner class. The syntax of the anonymous class in the method labeled (2) is not correct, as the parameter list is missing.

8.9   *(a) and (d)*

No other static members, except final static fields, can be declared within a non-static member class. Members in outer instances are directly accessible using simple names (provided they are not hidden). Fields in nested static member classes need not be final. Anonymous classes cannot have constructors, since they have no names. Nested classes define distinct types from the enclosing class, and the instanceof operator does not take the type of the outer instance into consideration.

8.10   *(d)*

The iterator implemented will traverse the elements of the array in the reverse order, and so will the for(:) loop. The Iterable and the Iterator interfaces are implemented correctly.

8.11   *(b)*

Classes can be declared as members of top-level classes. Such a class is a static member class if it is declared static, otherwise, it is a non-static member class. Top-level classes, local classes, and anonymous classes cannot be declared static.

8.12   *(d)*

Note that the nested classes are locally declared in a static context.

(a) and (b) refer to the field str1 in Inner. (c) refers to the field str1 in Access. (e) requires the Helper class to be in the Inner class in order to compile, but this will not print the right answer. (f), (g), and (h) will not compile, as the Helper local class cannot be accessed using the enclosing class name.

8.13   *(e)*

No statement is executed in the main() method that will print anything. The print statement in the constructor of the Inner class will only be executed if an object of the Inner class is created in the main() method.

8.14   *(b), (c), and (e)*

(b) and (c) because i2 and i3 are instance fields that cannot be accessed from a static context, in this case from a local class in a static method. (f) is not allowed because the local variable i5 is not declared final in the enclosing method.

9 Object Lifetime

9.1   *(e)*

An object is only eligible for garbage collection if all remaining references to the object are from other objects that are also eligible for garbage collection. Therefore, if an object obj2 is eligible for garbage collection and object obj1 contains a reference to it, then object obj1 must also be eligible for garbage collection. Java does not have a keyword delete. An object will not necessarily be garbage collected immediately after it becomes unreachable. However, the object will be eligible for garbage collection. Circular references do not prevent objects from being garbage collected, only reachable references do. An object is not eligible for garbage collection as long as the object can be accessed by any live thread. An object that has been eligible for garbage collection can be made non-eligible. This occurs if the finalize() method of the object creates a reachable reference to the object.

9.2   *(b)*

Before (1), the `String` object initially referenced by `arg1` is denoted by both `msg` and `arg1`. After (1), the `String` object is only denoted by `msg`. At (2), reference `msg` is assigned a new reference value. This reference value denotes a new `String` object created by concatenating contents of several other `String` objects. After (2), there are no references to the `String` object initially referenced by `arg1`. The `String` object is now eligible for garbage collection.

9.7   *(b)*

The `Object` class defines a `protected` `finalize()` method. All classes inherit from `Object`, thus, all objects have a `finalize()` method. Classes can override the `finalize()` method and, as with all overriding, the new method must not reduce the accessibility. The `finalize()` method of an eligible object is called by the garbage collector to allow the object to do any cleaning up before the object is destroyed. When the garbage collector calls the `finalize()` method, it will ignore any exceptions thrown by the `finalize()` method. If the `finalize()` method is called explicitly, normal exception handling occurs when an exception is thrown during the execution of the `finalize()` method, i.e., exceptions are not simply ignored. Calling the `finalize()` method does not in itself destroy the object. Chaining of the `finalize()` method is not enforced by the compiler, and it is not mandatory to call the overridden `finalize()` method.

9.8   *(d)*

The `finalize()` method is like any other method, it can be called explicitly if it is accessible. However, the intended purpose of the method is to be called by the garbage collector in order to clean up before an object is destroyed. Overloading the `finalize()` method name is allowed, but only the method with the original signature will be called by the garbage collector. The `finalize()` method in `Object` is protected. This means that overriding methods must be declared either `protected` or `public`. The `finalize()` method in `Object` can throw any `Throwable` object. An overridden definition of this method can throw any type of `Throwable`. However, overriding methods can limit the range of throwables to *unchecked* exceptions. Further overridden definitions of this method in subclasses will then *not* be able to throw *checked* exceptions.

9.9   *(b)*

The `finalize()` method will never be called more than once on an object, even if the `finalize()` method resurrects the object. An object can be eligible for garbage collection even if there are references denoting the object, as long as the objects owning these references are also eligible for garbage collection. There is no guarantee that the garbage collector will destroy an eligible object before the program terminates. The order in which the objects are destroyed is not guaranteed. The `finalize()` method can make an object that has been eligible for garbage collection accessible again by a live thread.

9.10   *(d) and (g)*

(a), (b), (c), (j), (k), (l): reduce the visibility of the inherited method. (e), (f), (h), (i): the call to the `finalize()` method of the superclass can throw a `Throwable`, which is not handled by the method. The `Throwable` superclass is not assignable to the `Exception` subclass.

9.11   *(e)*

It is not guaranteed if and when the garbage collection will be run, nor in which order the objects will be finalized. However, it is guaranteed that the finalization of an object will only be run once, hence (e) cannot possible be a result from running the program.

9.12   *(c) and (e)*

It is not guaranteed if and when the garbage collection will be run, nor in which order the objects will be finalized. So the program may not print anything. If the garbage collection is run, the `MyString` object created in the program may get finalized before the program terminates. In that case, the `finalize()` method will print A, as the string in the field `str` is not changed by the `concat()` method.

9.13   *(c), (e), and (f)*

The static initializer blocks (a) and (b) are not legal since the fields `alive` and `STEP` are non-static and `final`, respectively. (d) is not a syntactically legal static initializer block.

9.14   *(c)*

The program will compile, and print 50, 70, 0, 20, 0, when run. All fields are given default values unless they are explicitly initialized. Field `i` is assigned the value 50 in the static initializer block that is executed when the class is initialized. This assignment will override the explicit initialization of field `i` in its declaration statement. When the `main()` method is executed, the static field `i` is 50 and the static field `n` is 0. When an instance of the class is created using the `new` operator, the value of static field `n` (i.e., 0) is passed to the constructor. Before the body of the constructor is executed, the instance initializer block is executed, which assigns the values 70 and 20 to the fields `j` and `n`, respectively. When the body of the constructor is executed, the fields `i`, `j`, `k`, and `n`, and the parameter `m`, have the values 50, 70, 0, 20, and 0, respectively.

9.15   *(f)*

This class has a blank final `boolean` variable `active`. This variable must be initialized when an instance is constructed, or else the code will not compile. The keyword `static` is used to signify that a block is a static initializer block. No keyword is used to signify that a block is an instance initializer block. (a) and (b) are not instance initializers blocks, and (c), (d), and (e) fail to initialize the blank final variable `active`.

9.16   *(c)*

The program will compile, and print 2, 3, and 1, when run. When the object is created and initialized, the instance initializer block is executed first, printing 2. Then the instance initializer expression is executed, printing 3. Finally, the constructor body is executed, printing 1. The forward reference in the instance initializer block is legal, as the use of the field m is on the left-hand side of the assignment.

9.17   *(e)*

The program will compile, and print 1, 3, and 2, when run. First, the static initializers are executed when the class is initialized, printing 1 and 3. When the object is created and initialized, the instance initializer block is executed, printing 2.

9.18   *(c) and (e)*

Line A will cause illegal redefinition of the field width. Line B uses an illegal forward reference to the fields width and height. The assignment in line C is legal. Line D is not a legal initializer, since it is neither a declaration nor a block. Line E declares a local variable inside an initializer block, which is legal.

10 Fundamental Classes

10.1   *(b)*

The method hashCode() in the Object class returns a hash code value of type int.

10.2   *(e)*

All arrays are genuine objects and inherit all the methods defined in the Object class, including the clone() method. Neither the hashCode() method nor the equals() method is declared final in the Object() class, and it cannot be guaranteed that implementations of these methods will differentiate between all objects.

10.3   *(a)*

The clone() method of the Object class will throw a CloneNotSupportedException if the class of the object does not implement the Cloneable interface.

10.4   *(a), (c), and (d)*

The class java.lang.Void is considered a wrapper class, although it does not wrap any value. There is no class named java.lang.Int, but there is a wrapper class named java.lang.Integer. A class named java.lang.String also exists, but it is not a wrapper class since all strings in Java are objects.

10.5   *(c) and (d)*

The classes Character and Boolean are non-numeric wrapper classes and they do not extend the Number class. The classes Byte, Short, Integer, Long, Float, and Double are numeric wrapper classes that extend the Number class.

10.6   *(a), (b), and (d)*

All instances of concrete wrapper classes are immutable.

10.7   *(b) and (c)*

All instances of wrapper classes except Void and Character have a constructor that accepts a string parameter. The class Object has only a default constructor.

10.8   *(e)*

While all numeric wrapper classes have the methods byteValue(), doubleValue(), floatValue(), intValue(), longValue(), and shortValue(), only the Boolean class has the booleanValue() method. Likewise, only the Character class has the charValue() method.

10.9   *(b) and (d)*

String is not a wrapper class. All wrapper classes except Boolean and Void have a compareTo() method. Only the numeric wrapper classes have an intValue() method. The Byte class, like all other numeric wrapper classes, extends the Number class.

10.10   *(d)*

Wrapper objects are immutable, but the following values are *interned* when they are wrapped during boxing, i.e., only one wrapper object exists in the program for these primitive values when boxing is applied:
   o boolean values true and false
   o All byte values (-128, 127)
   o short values between -128 and 127
   o int values between -128 and 127
   o char in the range \u0000 to \u007f

10.11   *(a)*

Using the new operator creates a new object. Boxing also creates a new object if one is not already interned from before.

10.12   *(b) and (e)*

The operators - and & cannot be used in conjunction with a String object. The operators + and += perform concatenation on strings, and the dot operator accesses members of the String object.

10.13   *(d)*

The expression str.substring(2,5) will extract the substring "kap". The method extracts the characters from index 2 to index 4, inclusive.

10.14   *(d)*

The program will print str3str1 when run. The concat() method will create and return a new String object, which is the concatenation of the current String object and the String object given as an argument. The expression statement str1.concat(str2) creates a new String object, but its reference value is not stored.

10.15   *(c)*

The trim() method of the String class returns a string where both the leading and the trailing white space of the original string have been removed.

10.16   *(a) and (c)*

The String class and all wrapper classes are declared final and, therefore, cannot be extended. The clone() method is declared protected in the Object class. String objects are immutable and, therefore, cannot be modified. The classes String and StringBuilder are unrelated.

10.17   *(a), (b), (c), and (e)*

The expressions ('c' + 'o' + 'o' + 'l') and ('o' + 'l') are of type int due to numeric promotion. Expression (d) is illegal, since the String class has no constructor taking a single int parameter. Expression (a) is legal, since string literals denote String objects and can be used just like any other object.

10.18   *(d)*

The constant expressions "ab" + "12" and "ab" + 12 will, at compile time, be evaluated to the string-valued constant "ab12". Both variables s and t are assigned a reference to the same interned String object containing "ab12". The variable u is assigned a new String object, created by using the new operator.

10.19   *(a), (c), and (d)*

The String class does not have a constructor that takes a single int as a parameter.

10.20   *(e)*

The String class has no reverse() method.

10.21   *(d)*

The expression "abcdef".charAt(3) evaluates to the character 'd'. The charAt() method takes an int value as an argument and returns a char value. The expression ("abcdef").charAt(3) is legal. It also evaluates to the character 'd'. The index of the first character in a string is 0.

10.22   *(e)*

The expression "Hello there".toLowerCase().equals("hello there") will evaluate to true. The equals() method in the String class will only return true if the two strings have the same sequence of characters.

10.23   *(c)*

The variable middle is assigned the value 6. The variable nt is assigned the string "nt". The substring "nt" occurs three times in the string "Contentment!", starting at indices 2, 5, and 9. The call s.lastIndexOf(nt, middle) returns the start index of the last occurrence of "nt", searching backwards from position 6.

10.24   *(b)*

The reference value in the reference str1 never changes and it refers to the string literal "lower" all the time. The calls to toUpperCase() and replace() return a new String object whose reference value is ignored.

10.25   *(d)*

The call to the putO() method does not change the String object referred to by the s1 reference in the main() method. The reference value returned by the call to the concat() method is ignored.

10.26   *(b)*

The code will fail to compile since the expression (s == sb) is illegal. It compares references of two classes that are not related.

10.27   *(e)*

The program will compile without errors and will print have a when run. The contents of the string buffer are truncated down to 6 characters.

10.28   *(a), (b), and (d)*

The StringBuilder class does not have a constructor that takes an array of char as a parameter.

10.29   *(a)*

The StringBuilder class does not define a trim() method.

10.30   *(d)*

The program will construct an immutable String object containing "eeny" and a StringBuilder object containing " miny". The concat() method returns a reference value to a new immutable String object containing "eeny meeny", but the reference value is not stored. The append() method appends the string " mo" to the string buffer.

10.31   *(b)*

The references sb1 and sb2 are not aliases. The StringBuilder class does not override the equals() method, hence the answer is (b).

10.32 *(a)*

The `StringBuilder` class does not override the `hashCode()` method, but the String class does. The references s1 and s2 refer to a `String` object and a `StringBuilder` object, respectively. The hash values of these objects are computed by the hash-Code() method in the `String` and the `Object` class, respectively—giving different results. The references s1 and s3 refer to two different `String` objects that are equal, hence they have the same hash value.

10.33 *(c)*

The classes `String` and `StringBuilder` are unrelated, therefore the first call to the com-pareTo() method will not compile. The class `StringBuilder` does not implement the `Comparable` interface, therefore the second call to the `compareTo()` method will not compile.

10.34 *(b)*

The call to the putO() method changes the `StringBuilder` object referred to by the s1 reference in the main() method. So does the call to the append() method.

10.35 *(a)*

The type of the return value from the chain of calls is `StringBuilder`, `StringBuilder`, `String`, and int, respectively. The string builder contents are changed to "WOW!" by the two first calls in the chain. The toString() call extracts the character sequence, which is compared with the string literal "WOW". The compareTo() method returns the value 0. The boolean expression evaluates to `false`.

11 **Files and Streams**

11.1 *(a), (b), (c), and (e)*

A string cannot act as the source of an input stream and as the destination of an output stream provided in the java.io package.

11.2 *(b) and (e)*

The separator constant is of type `String` and contains the sequence of characters used as path separators on a given platform. The most common platforms only use a single character as a path separator, but there is no such restriction.

11.3 *(b)*

The method getName() can be used on a `File` object to return the name of the entry excluding the specification of the directory in which the entry resides.

11.4 *(e)*

The length() method can be used on a File object to return the number of bytes in the file. Note that bytes are not the same as characters, and the size of characters in a file depends on the encoding scheme used.

11.5 *(b) and (d)*

Compiling and running the program results in the following output:

```
./documents/../book/../chapter1
/wrk/./documents/../book/../chapter1
/wrk/chapter1
chapter1
./documents/../book/..
```

11.6 *(c)*

The toString() method in the File class produces the same output as the getPath() method. Compiling and running the program results in the following output:

```
ListingFiles.class
.\ListingFiles.class
.\ListingFiles.class
```

11.7 *(b)*

The boolean value false is returned when the method canWrite() is called on a File object representing a file that is not writable on the file system.

11.8 *(a)*

The first parameter of the renameTo() method is of type File. The current file should be renamed to the file name represented by the File object. Note that the File object given does not need to represent an actual entry in the file system. It only represents a valid pathname.

11.9 *(d)*

The write() method writes bytes only. When given an int it only writes the 8 least significant bits.

11.10 *(d)*

The read() method will return -1 when the end of the stream has been reached. Normally an unsigned 8-bit int value is returned (range from 0 to 255). I/O errors result in an IOEXception being thrown.

11.11 *(a) and (c)*

Classes that implement the DataOutput interface, i.e., DataOutputStream and ObjectOutputStream, provide methods for writing binary representations of primitive values. The output stream classes `FileOutputStream`, `PrintStream`, and `Buffered-OutputStream` do not provide such methods.

11.13   *(a), (c), and (d)*

The `Writer` class has no `write()` method with a parameter of type `char`. It has methods with parameters of types `String`, `int`, and `char[]`. The `OutputStream` class has a `write()` method with a parameter of type `int`, but `Writer` is not a subclass of `Output-Stream`.

11.14   *(d)*

The default encoding for `OutputStreamWriter` is the default encoding of the host platform.

11.15   *(a)*

The byte type does not have its own `print()` method in the `PrintWriter` class. There is no natural text representation of a byte.

11.16   *(c)*

The standard error stream is accessed via the static variable named `err` in the `System` class.

11.17   *(d)*

The `print()` methods do not throw an `IOException`.

11.18   *(d)*

The `read()` method of an `InputStreamReader` returns -1 when the end of the stream is reached.

11.19   *(a), (d), and (e)*

(b) There is no stream called `InputStreamWriter`.

(c) The class `FileOutputStream` is not a `Writer`.

11.20   *(b)*

The `readLine()` method of a `BufferedReader` returns `null` when the end of the stream is reached.

11.21   *(c)*

Both the `readLine()` and the `readPassword()` method of the `Console` class return all characters typed on the line. The arguments of the two methods concern the prompt written to the console.

11.22   *(a)*

There are no methods defined in the `Serializable` interface. The interface is a marker interface that is used to signify that the class supports serialization.

11.23   *(c)*

A `ObjectOutputStream` can write both objects and Java primitive types, as it implements the `ObjectInput` and the `DataInput` interfaces. The serialization mechanism will follow object references and can write whole hierarchies of objects.

11.24   *(d)*

During deserialization, the default constructor of the superclass `Person` is called, because this superclass is not `Serializable`.

11.25   *(e)*

During deserialization, the default constructor of the superclass `Person` is called, because the superclass is not `Serializable`. The default constructor initializes the field `name` to the string `"NoName"`.

11.26   *(c)*

During deserialization, the default constructor of the superclass `Person` is not called, because the superclass is `Serializable`.

11.27   *(d)*

The class `Student` is `Serializable`, because its superclass `Person` is `Serializable`. During deserialization, the default constructor of the superclass `Person` is not called because the superclass is `Serializable`. But the field `name` is `transient`, and therefore not serialized.

11.28   *(d)*

During serialization of a `Student` object, the string `"NewName"` is also serialized. During deserialization, this string is read and assigned to the transient field `name` which had not been serialized.

11.29   *(e)*

Note that only `GraduateStudent` is `Serializable`. The field `name` in the `Person` class is `transient`. During serialization of a `GraduateStudent` object, the fields `year` and `studNum` are included as part of the serialization process, but not the field `name`. During deserialization, the private method `readObject()` in the `GraduateStudent` class is called. This method first deserializes the `GraduateStudent` object, but then initializes the fields with new values.

11.30 *(d)*

The field name in the Person class is transient, and the field numOfStudents in the Student class is static. During serialization of a Student object, neither of these fields are serialized. After deserialization, the value of the field name is null, but the value of the static field numOfStudents has been incremented because a second Student object has been created.

12 Localization, Pattern Matching, and Formatting

12.1 *(c)*

It is the information in the current locale which is formatted according to the locale that is passed as argument. Note that the *get* methods are *not* called on the same locale in printLocaleInfo().

12.2 *(b) and (d)*

The Date class does not have any locale-sensitive methods. A negative argument in the non-default constructor indicates a negative offset from the epoch, i.e., a time before the epoch.

12.3 *(d) and (f)*

(d) The roll() method does not recompute and normalize the larger fields.

(f) The first month of the year is 0, and not 1.

12.4 *(e)*

(a), (b) DateFormat is an abstract class and, therefore, cannot be instantiated.

(c), (d) The method getDateTimeInstance() requires either no formatting styles or two formatting styles with an optional locale.

(d) The arguments are not applicable to the format() method.

12.5 *(g)*

(a) The input string "Mar 7, 2008" is not compatible with the formatting style Date-Format.SHORT of the formatter, resulting in an exception.

Leading whitespace and trailing characters are ignored, and values are parsed and normalized in all other cases. The alternatives from (a) to (f) give the following output, respectively:

```
Fri Mar 07 00:00:00 EST 2008
Fri Mar 07 00:00:00 EST 2008
Sun Apr 06 00:00:00 EDT 2008
Wed Jan 07 00:00:00 EST 2009
Fri Mar 07 00:00:00 EST 2008
Fri Mar 07 00:00:00 EST 2008
```

12.6   *(f)*

(f) The method `parseNumber()` does not catch the `ParseException` that can be thrown by the `parse()` method. The `parse()` method returns a `Number`, which is not assignment compatible to a reference of type `Double`. If these errors are corrected, the alternatives from (a) to (e) give the following outputs, respectively:

```
1234.567
0.567
1234
1234.567
1
```

12.7   *(b), (c), and (d)*

The expression *x*+ means one or more occurrences of *x* in the target string. The operator is greedy and, therefore, will match as many contagious occurrences of *x* as possible in the target. The regular expression a+ will match 3 substrings (aa, a, aa) of the target string. The regular expressions aa+ and (aa)+ will match the same 2 substrings of this target string, i.e., (aa, aa). However, these regular expressions would give different results if the target was "aaa". The first one will match the whole target, while the second one will only match the first two as.

12.8   *(a), (c), and (d)*

The expression *x*? means 0 or 1 occurrence of *x* in the target string. The regular expression a? will match 5 non-empty substrings corresponding to the 5 as in the target string. The regular expressions aa? and (aa)? will not match the same substrings of this target string. The regular expression aa? will match the 3 non-empty substrings (aa, a, aa) of the target string, whereas the regular expression (aa)? will match the 2 non-empty substrings (aa, aa) of the target string.

12.9   *(e)*

The expression *x** means 0 or more occurrences of *x* in the target string. The regular expression a* will match the 3 non-empty substrings aa, a, aa in the target string. The regular expression aa* will also match the same 3 non-empty substrings aa, a, aa in the target string. The regular expression (aa)* will only match the 2 non-empty substrings aa and aa in the target string.

12.10   *(e)*

The pattern \d matches a digit, not all integers. The pattern \d will match 0, 5, 7, and 4 in the target string. The pattern \w matches a word character (i.e., letters, digits and _), not a word. The pattern \w will match 0, 5, 7, U, P, _, 4, m, and e in the target string. The pattern \s matches a white space character (i.e., space (' '), tabulator (\t), and newline (\n)), not a string. The pattern \s will match each of the two spaces in the target string. The pattern . will match *any* character in the target string. The operators [] specifies a set of characters to match, not strings to match. The regular expression [meUP] will match the characters U, P, m, and e in the target string.

12.11 *(c) and (e)*

To escape any metacharacter in regexes, we need to specify two backslashes (\\) in Java strings. Note that a backslash (\) is used to escape metacharacters in both Java strings and in regular expressions.

In (1), the compiler reports that \d is an invalid escape sequence in a Java string.

(2) will throw a `java.util.regex.PatternSyntaxException`: dangling metacharacter +, which is the first character in the regex, is missing an operand.

In (3), the compiler reports that \+ is an invalid escape sequence. (4) will match a positive integer with an optional + sign, printing `true`.

The method `Pattern.matches()` returns `true` if the regex matches the *entire* input.

12.12 *(d), (e), (f), and (g)*

(a), (b) A `java.util.regex.PatternSyntaxException` is thrown because the first + in the regex is a dangling metacharacter.

(c) The regex does not match the target "2007", since a sign is required.

The regex (-|\\+)? and [-+]? are equivalent: 0 or 1 occurrence of either - or +. Note that in the [] regex notation, the + sign is an ordinary character as in (e) and (f), and escaping it as in (g) is not necessary. The metacharacter \d is equivalent to [0-9], i.e., any digit.

12.13 *(d)*

The `Pattern` compiles a regular expression and the matcher applies it to the target. Whether the next match exists is given by the method `find()`. The matched input is returned by the method `group()`.

12.14 *(c)*

The no-argument `reset()` method can be used to reset the matcher to the beginning of the current target. That is why the matching against the first target is repeated in the output. The same matcher can be applied to different targets by passing the new target to the `reset()` method.

12.15 *(d)*

Each sequence of white space is replaced by a single space (' '), including the newline (\n) character.

12.16 *(b)*

The application of a* and a+ is greedy in (1) and (2). A *greedy quantifier* reads the whole target string and backtracks to match as much of the input as possible.

The application of a*? and a+? is reluctant in (3) and (4). A *reluctant quantifier* only reads enough of the input to match the regular expression. Note that the substring "Xz" is not matched by X.+?z, as it requires non-empty input between X and z.

12.17 *(b)*

The regular expression [a-zA-Z0-9_]+ will match any permutation of letter, digit, or the '_' character. But only the first character of the match is converted to uppercase. A match that starts with any other character than a lowercase letter is not affected. The appendReplacement() method implements what is called a non-terminal append-and-replace step. The appendTail() method implements what is called a terminal append-and-replace step. The net result is that the buffer contains the modified input after the matcher has exhausted the input.

12.18 *(d)*

Note that the dot (.) does not need escaping, as it loses its metacharacter meaning in a [] pair. On the other hand the - character is a metacharacter for specifying an interval in a [] pair and needs escaping in order to match it in the input.

12.19 *(b), (c), and (d)*

Constructors of the Scanner class accept neither a StringBuffer nor a StringBuilder. A Readable is accepted, and all Readers implement the Readable interface. When the scanner cannot match the next token, it actually throws a InputMismatchException, which is a subtype of NoSuchElementException.

12.20 *(e), (f), and (h)*

The print statement in (e) will print 99.0, as the token is converted to a double value. The method call lexer.nextBoolean() in (f) will throw an InputMismatchException, as the first token cannot be converted to a boolean value. The method call lexer.next-Line() in (h) will read whatever is remaining in the input, in this case, 99 2007 true 786.

Note that the method call lexer.next() in (g) reads the first token as 99, using default delimiters.

12.21 *(c) and (e)*

In (c), the dot (.) is a metacharacter, thus matching any character. Splitting the input on the string pattern in (c) returns the empty string. Splitting the input on the string pattern in (e) returns the following tokens: [A, 2, BCDE, , 6, , F, 8]. Note the empty strings returned which cause input mismatch.

In (a), it is not necessary to escape the dot (.) inside a [] pair. The string pattern "[0.]+" is more general than the string pattern "0+\\.*0*". The regexes (a|b|c) and [abc] are equivalent.

Note that each iteration of the while loop advances the scanner with two tokens in the input, corresponding to the calls of the next methods.

12.22 *(d)*

Note that the dot (.) needs escaping in the string pattern which recognizes a non-empty sequence of word characters that end in a dot (.).

12.23   *(f)*

The regexes will produce the following output, respectively, showing what is matched and not matched by the regex:

```
1234,   567.,X12.34,  X.56,    78.,     X.,
1234, X567.,X12.34,    .56,  X78.,     X.,
X1234, X567., 12.34,  X.56,  X78.,     X.,
1234,   567., 12.34,   .56,    78.,     .,
1234,   567., 12.34,  X.56,    78.,     X.,
1234,   567., 12.34,   .56,    78.,     X.,
```

Note that the regexes in (d) will match a dot (.) as well.

12.24   *(a)*

The delimiters of a scanner can be changed during tokenizing. When setting new delimiters one should take into consideration the delimiter that terminated the previous token, as this must be skipped one way or another in order to find the next token.

12.25   *(f)*

The string pattern of the hasNext() method will only match the tokens "Trick" and "treat", but "Trick!" will be printed on recognizing these tokens. The call to the next() method in the loop will skip the current token in the input. Without this call, the program will go into an infinite loop.

12.26   *(c), (e), and (h)*

The alternatives print the following lines, respectively, when we exclude (c), (e), and (h):

```
|2007| -25.0|mp3 4 u | true| after8|
|2007.0|-25.0|
|2007|25|0|3|4|8|
|mp|u|true|after|
|2007.0|25.0|0.0|mp3|4.0|u|true|after8|
|4|
```

(c) does not skip the input that did not match a double value, in order for the scanner to find the next token, and the program, therefore, goes into an infinite loop.

(e) checks for a boolean value, but tries to read a double instead, resulting in a java.util.InputMismatchException being thrown.

(h) does not skip the input that did not match an int value, in order for the scanner to find the next token, and the program therefore goes into an infinite loop.

12.27   *(a), (c), (d), and (f)*

The classes java.util.StringBuilder and java.util.Scanner do not provide the format() method. The Console class only provides the first form.

12.28   *(c) and (d)*

Only the classes java.util.PrintStream and java.util.PrintWriter provide the printf() method. The Console class only provides the first form.

12.29   *(c) and (d)*

The conversion 'd' cannot be applied to char or Character values. The flag combination '(+-' is also valid.

12.30   *(e)*

In (a) the resulting string is created by String.format() and printed by System.out. A PrintStream (such as System.out) can format and print to its output stream. A Formatter can be connected to an Appendable (which is implemented by the String-Builder) as the destination for the formatted output. The StringBuilder is then printed to the terminal window. A Formatter can also be connected to a Print-Stream (in this case System.out) which is the destination of the formatted output.

12.31   *(e)*

All the three classes PrintStream, PrintWriter, and Formatter have the format() method that writes to the underlying output stream, which is created or provided depending on the constructor argument.

12.32   *(a) and (b)*

First, note that the Object[] array oneDimArray is passed as varargs Object... to the format() method.

(a) In the format %4$-1c, -1 is superfluous if we only want to print 1 character. 4$ here indicates the fourth value in the oneDimArray that represents a row in the twoDimArray. %5s implicitly refers to the first value in the oneDimArray, which is printed with a width of 5 characters right-justified.
In %5$1.1b, %5$ indicates the fifth value (boolean) in the oneDimArray. The precision .1 indicates that only the first character should be printed. The width of 1 is superfluous in 1.1.
%(+8.2f corresponds to the second value (float) in the oneDimArray, indicating that negative values should be enclosed in () and positive values should have the + sign. The width is 8 and the precision is 2 decimals.
%6d corresponds to the third value (int) in the oneDimArray, indicating that the width is 6 characters.

(b) The superfluous -1 in (a) is missing in (b) for formatting a character. The int value is formatted with %6s, giving the same result as %6d in (a).

(c) In the format specification %2$(+-8.2f, the - sign indicates that the value should be printed left-justified, not right-justified as in the output. The format %3$6s in (c) only indicates the third argument (int value) explicitly.

(d) Arguments are made explicit. The format %3$,6d specifies the locale-specific grouping separator (,), which is used for the value 5151, formatting it as 5,151. This is not so in the output.

12.33   (c)

The program will use the following formats %(,+-1.1, %(,+-2.2, and %(,+-3.3 to print the values in the array dArray. The flag '(' results in negative values being enclosed in (). The flag ',' specifies that the locale-specific grouping character should be used. The flag '+' specifies that positive values should be prefixed with the + sign. The flag '-' specifies that values should be printed left-justified. The width is less than the required width, and therefore overridden. The precision can result in rounding, as is the case for the first two values.

12.34   (d)

The respective exceptions thrown by the statements above are:

- java.util.MissingFormatWidthException (requires positive width)

- java.util.UnknownFormatConversionException (because of width 0)

- java.util.IllegalFormatFlagsException (because of the flag combination '(+-')

- java.util.MissingFormatArgumentException (the second format has no matching argument)

- java.util.UnknownFormatConversionException ('!' is an unknown flag)

12.35   (b) and (d)

(b) will throw a java.util.IllegalFormatPrecisionException because of the precision specification. (d) will throw a java.util.FormatFlagsConversionMismatchException because of the + flag.

The other statements will produce the following output, respectively, excluding (b) and (d): |L |, |!|, |h|, |! |, |null|, | V|.

12.36   (h)

The statements will produce the following output, respectively:

    |(123)||+123 ||(00123)||(123) ||-123 ||-123|| 123|

12.37   (i)

(a) will throw a java.util.MissingFormatWidthException. The width is not specified.

(b) will throw a java.util.IllegalFormatPrecisionException. The precision cannot be 0.

The remaining statements will throw a java.util.IllegalFormatConversionException. The conversion d cannot be used with the specified argument.

12.38   *(a), (d), and (e)*

All the loops format the value true.

(a), (d), and (e) use the format strings %2.1b, %4.2b, %6.3b, and %8.4b, resulting in the output:

```
| t|  tr|   tru|    true|
```

(b) uses the format strings %.0b, %2.1b, %4.2b, %6.3b, and %8.4b, resulting in the output:

```
|| t|  tr|   tru|    true|
```

(c) uses the format strings %2.0b, %4.1b, %6.2b, and %8.3b, resulting in the output:

```
|  |  t|   tr|    tru|
```

12.39   *(b)*

(a) will print: |1000| 10|0100|

(b) will print: |1000|+10 | 100|

(c) will print: | +10| 100|1000|

(d) will throw a java.util.IllegalFormatConversionException, as intArray is passed as new Object[] { intArray } to the printf() method. An array is certainly not an int. Remember that int[] is *not* a subtype of Object[], but Integer[] is.

12.40   *(f)*

Rows in the output are printed according to the following formats:

```
%5.0f, %5.1f, %5.2f
%6.0f, %6.1f, %6.2f
%7.0f, %7.1f, %7.2f
%8.0f, %8.1f, %8.2f
%9.0f, %9.1f, %9.2f
```

These formats result in the output shown in (a) to (e), respectively.

13 Threads

13.1   *(c)*

Create a new Thread object and call the method start(). The call to the start() method will return immediately and the thread will start executing the run() method asynchronously.

13.2   *(c)*

When extending the Thread class, the run() method should be overridden to provide the code executed by the thread. This is analogous to implementing the run() method of the Runnable interface.

13.3   *(b) and (e)*

The Thread class implements the Runnable interface and is not abstract. A program terminates when the last user thread finishes. The Runnable interface has a single method named run. Calling the run() method on a Runnable object does not necessarily create a new thread; the run() method is executed by a thread. Instances of the Thread class must be created to spawn new threads.

13.4   *(e)*

The program will compile without errors and will simply terminate without any output when run. Two thread objects will be created, but they will never be started. The start() method must be called on the thread objects to make the threads execute the run() method asynchronously.

13.5   *(b)*

(1) results in the run() method of the Extender class being called, which overrides the method from the Thread class, as does (2). (3) results in the run() method of the Implementer class being called.

Invoking the start() method on a subclass of the Thread class always results in the overridden run() method being called, regardless of whether a Runnable is passed in a constructor of the subclass.

13.6   *(d)*

Note that calling the run() method on a Thread object does not start a thread. However, the run() method of the Thread class will invoke the run() method of the Runnable object that is passed as argument in the constructor call. In other words, the run() method of the R1 class is executed in the R2 thread, i.e., the thread that called the run() method of the Thread class.

13.7   *(c)*

Note that the complete signature of the run() method does not specify a throws clause, meaning it does not throw any *checked* exceptions. However, it can always be implemented with a throws clause containing *unchecked* exceptions, as is the case in the code above.

13.8   *(d)*

The call to the run() method just executes the method in the main thread. Once a thread has terminated, it cannot be started by calling the start() method as shown above. A new thread must be created and started.

13.9   *(a) and (e)*

Because the exact behavior of the scheduler is undefined, the text A, B, and End can be printed in any order. The thread printing B is a daemon thread, which means that the program may terminate before the thread manages to print the letter. Thread A is not a daemon thread, so the letter A will always be printed

13.10   *(b) and (d)*

We cannot synchronize on a primitive value. Synchronizing on a local object is use-less, as each thread will create its own local object and it will not be a shared resource.

13.11   *(b), (c), and (d)*

The lock is also released when an uncaught exception occurs in the block.

13.12   *(a)*

No two threads can concurrently execute synchronized methods on the same object. This does not prevent one thread from executing a non-synchronized method while another thread executes a synchronized method on the same object. The synchronization mechanism in Java acts like recursive semaphores, which means that during the time a thread owns the lock, it may enter and re-enter any region of code associated with the lock, so there is nothing wrong with recursive synchronized calls. Synchronized methods can call other synchronized and non-synchronized methods directly.

13.13   *(b)*

One cannot be certain whether any of the letters i, j, and k will be printed during execution. For each invocation of the doIt() method, each variable pair is incre-mented and their values are always equal when the method returns. The only way a letter could be printed would be if the method check() was executed between the time the first and the second variable were incremented. Since the check() method does not depend on owning any lock, it can be executed at any time, and the method doIt() cannot protect the atomic nature of its operations by acquiring locks.

13.14   *(c) and (d)*

First note that a call to sleep() does not release the lock on the Smiley.class object once a thread has acquired this lock. Even if a thread sleeps, it does not release any locks it might possess.

(a) does not work, as run() is not called directly by the client code.

(b) does not work, as the infinite while loop becomes the critical region and the lock will never be released. Once a thread has the lock, other threads cannot participate in printing smileys.

(c) works, as the lock will be released between each iteration, giving other threads the chance to acquire the lock and print smileys.

(d) works for the same reason as (c), since the three print statements will be exe-cuted as one atomic operation.

(e) may not work, as the three print statements may not be executed as one atomic operation, since the lock will be released after each print statement.

Synchronizing on this does not help, as the printout from each of the three print statements executed by each thread can be interspersed.

13.15 *(d)*

A thread dies when the execution of the run() method ends. The call to the start() method is asynchronous, i.e., it returns immediately, and it moves the thread to the Ready-to-run state. Calling the sleep() or wait() methods will block the thread.

13.16 *(b) and (d)*

The inner createThread() call is evaluated first, and will print 23 as the first number. The last number the main thread prints is 14. After the main thread ends, the thread created by the inner createdThread() completes its join() call and prints 22. After this thread ends, the thread created by the outer createThread() call completes its join() call and prints the number 12 before the program terminates. Note that in the inner call to the createThread() method, the thread t2 can start to execute before this call finishes, resulting in 21 being printed before 24.

13.17 *(b), (c), and (f)*

The wait() and notify() methods of the Object class can only be called on an object whose lock the thread holds, otherwise a java.lang.IllegalMonitorStateException is thrown. The static method yield() of the class Thread does not throw any exceptions. Both the sleep() and join() methods of the Thread class throw an Interrupted-Exception.

13.18 *(d) and (f)*

(a) and (b) result in a java.lang.IllegalMonitorStateException, as the t1 thread does not hold a lock on the current object, i.e., on the thread itself.

(c) The t1 thread will wait forever, as it never gets any notification, and the main thread also waits forever for t1 to complete.

(e) The yield() method does not throw the checked InterruptedException, and the compiler reports an error as the code in the catch block is unreachable.

13.19 *(e)*

The exact behavior of the scheduler is not defined. There is no guarantee that a call to the yield() method will grant other threads use of the CPU.

13.20 *(b)*

The final method notify() is defined in the Object class.

13.21 *(a)*

The priority of a thread is set by calling the setPriority() method in the Thread class. No Thread constructor accepts a priority level as an argument.

13.22 *(a) and (c)*

A thread can hold multiple locks; e.g., by nesting synchronized blocks. Invoking the wait() method on an object whose lock is held by the current thread will relinquish the lock for the duration of the call. The notify() method does not relinquish any locks.

13.23   *(c)*

An IllegalMonitorStateException will be thrown if the wait() method is called when the current thread does not hold the lock of the object.

13.24   *(a), (c), (d), and (e)*

The thread terminates once the run() method completes execution.

13.25   *(d)*

Since the two methods are mutually exclusive, only one operation at a time can take place on the tank that is a shared resource between the two threads.

The method emptying() waits to empty the tank if it is already empty (i.e., isEmpty is true). When the tank becomes full (i.e., isEmpty becomes false), it empties the tank and sets the condition that the tank is empty (i.e., isEmpty is true).

The method filling() waits to fill the tank if it is already full (i.e., isEmpty is false). When the tank becomes empty (i.e., isEmpty becomes true), it fills the tank and sets the condition that the tank is full (i.e., isEmpty is false).

Since the tank is empty to start with (i.e., isEmpty is true), it will be filled first. Once started, the program will continue to print the string "filling" followed by the string "emptying".

Note that the while loop in the pause() method must always check against the field isEmpty.

13.26   *(e)*

The runner thread can only proceed if intArray[0] is not 0. If this element is not 0, it has been initialized to 10 by the main thread. If this element is 0, the runner thread is put into the wait set of the intArray object, and must wait for a notification. The main thread only notifies after initializing both elements of the array to 10. Calling the notify() method on an object with no threads in its wait set does not pose any problems. A thread can only call notify() on an object whose lock it holds. Therefore, the last synchronized block in the main() method is necessary.

14 Generics

14.1   *(b)*

The type of lst is List of Integer and the type of numList is List of Number. The compiler issues an error because List<Integer> is *not* a subtype of List<Number>.

14.2 *(f)*

Assigning bList, a reference of a non-generic list, to oList, a reference of a generic list, in (2) results in an unchecked conversion warning.

14.3 *(c)*

We can only get an Object from a List<? super Integer>. The list could contain Comparable objects, and Number does not implement Comparable.

14.4 *(b)*

The compiler issues an unchecked conversion warning in (1), as we are assigning a raw list to a generic list.

14.5 *(b), (f), and (g)*

We cannot refer to the type parameters of a generic class in a static context, e.g., in static initializer blocks, static field declarations, and as types of local variables in static methods. Also we cannot create an array of a type parameter, as in (2).

14.6 *(e)*

Any generic list can be assigned to a raw list reference. A raw list and an unbounded wildcard list are assignment compatible.

14.7 *(b), (c), (e), and (f)*

In (b), (c), (e), and (f), the parameterized type in the object creation expression is a subtype of the type of the reference. This is not the case in (a): just because HashMap<Integer, String> is a subtype of Map<Integer, String>, it does not follow that HashMap<Integer, HashMap<Integer, String>> is a subtype of Map<Integer, Map<Integer, String>>—there is no subtype covariance relationship between concrete parameterized types. In (d) and (g), wild cards cannot be used to instantiate the class.

14.8 *(b)*

ArrayList<Fruit> is not a subtype of List<? extends Apple>, and ArrayList<Apple> is not a subtype of List<? super Fruit>. Any generic list can be assigned to a raw list reference. A raw list and an unbounded wildcard list are assignment compatible.

14.9 *(a), (b), (c), and (e)*

(a), (b) and (c) The compiler will report unchecked call warnings.

(d) Incompatible types, assigning type Object to type String.

(e) From any list, we are guaranteed to get an Object.

14.10 *(b)*

(a) Primitive types are not permitted as type parameters.

(c) String is not a generic class.

(d) The interface Map cannot be instantiated.

(e) The method call accounts.getNum(name) returns an Object, which cannot be converted to a Long.

14.11 *(d)*

The compiler issues unchecked warnings for calls to the add() method. The TreeSet class orders elements according to their natural ordering. A ClassCastException is thrown at runtime, as Strings are not comparable to Integers.

14.12 *(a) and (b)*

The type of reference g is of raw type Garage. We can put any object in such a garage, but only get Objects out. The type of value returned by the get() method in statements (6) - (8) is Object and, therefore, not compatible for assignment to Vehicle, Car, and Sedan.

14.13 *(b) and (c)*

The type of reference g is of Garage<Car>. We can put a Car (or its subtype) in such a garage and get a Car (or its supertype) out. The type of value returned by the get() method in statement (8) is Car and, therefore, not compatible for assignment to Sedan.

14.14 *(c)*

The type of reference g is of Garage<?>. We cannot put any object in such a garage, and can only get an Object out. The type of value returned by the get() method in statements (6) - (8) is (capture-of ?), i.e., some unknown type and, therefore, not compatible for assignment to Vehicle, Car, and Sedan, as the value might turn out to be of a totally unrelated type. For more details on wildcard capture, see Section 14.9, p. 705.

14.15 *(c)*

The type of reference g is of type Garage<? extends Car>. We cannot put any car in such a garage, and can only get a Car (or its supertype) out. The type of value returned by the get() method in statement (8) is (capture-of ? extends Car), i.e., some unknown subtype of Car and, therefore, not compatible for assignment to Sedan, as the value might turn out be of a type totally unrelated to Sedan. For more details on wildcard capture, see Section 14.9, p. 705.

14.16   *(b) and (c)*

The type of reference g is of type Garage<? super Car>. We can put a Car (or its sub-type) in such a garage, but can only get Objects out. The type of value returned by the get() method in statements (6)-(8) is (capture-of ? super Car), i.e., some super-type of Car and, therefore, not compatible for assignment to Vehicle, Car, and Sedan, as it might be a value of a supertype of Vehicle, Car, or Sedan, respectively. For more details on wildcard capture, see Section 14.9, p. 705.

14.17   *(b), (d), and (e)*

(a) R cannot be resolved.

(b) Ok.

(c) The ClassA is parameterized with only one type parameter.

(d) Ok.

(e) Ok. The declaration says that the parameterized type ClassA<Number> is the supertype of ClassF<U> for any concrete type U that satisfies the constraint U extends Comparable<U> & Serializable. In the code below, String satisfies the constraint. However the target in the first declaration is of the supertype ClassA<Number>, but this is not the case in the second declaration.

```
ClassA<Number> ref1 = new ClassF<String>(); // OK
ClassA<Integer> ref2 = new ClassF<String>();// Not OK
```

(f) The keyword implements cannot be used to specify bounds.

(g) A wildcard cannot be used to specify the type parameter for the superclass.

(h) String is Comparable<String>, therefore, Comparable cannot be implemented more than once with different arguments, i.e., as a bound for U.

(i) From the declaration, superclass ClassA<Integer> implements Comparable<Integer>. Subclass ClassJ thus implements Comparable<Integer>. However, Comparable cannot be implemented more than once with different arguments, i.e., as Comparable<Number> in the declaration.

14.18   *(a) and (e)*

In (b) and (c), we cannot add any object to the list as the list is of an unknown type. From a list of an unknown type, we are only guaranteed to get an Object. In (d) capture-of ? cannot be converted to String.

14.19   *(b)*

It is the fully qualified name of the class after erasure that is printed at runtime. Note that it is the type of the object, not the reference, that is printed. The erasure of all the lists in the program is ArrayList.

14.20   *(b) , (e), and (f)*

(a) and (d) Incompatible types for assignment: cannot convert from List<Integer> to ArrayList<Integer>.

(c) Incompatible types for assignment: cannot convert from List<Integer> to List<Number>.

14.21   *(e)*

(a) Incompatible types for assignment in the main() method: cannot convert from Collection<capture-of ? extends CharSequence> to Collection<String>.

(b) Incompatible return value in the delete4LetterWords() method: cannot convert from Collection<E> to List<E>.

(c) In the for(:) loop, the component type of words (capture-of ? CharSequence) cannot be converted to E.

(d) In the for(:) loop, the component type of words (capture-of ? CharSequence) cannot be converted to E. Incompatible return value in the delete4LetterWords() method: cannot convert from Collection<E> to List<E>.

(e) OK.

(f) Keyword super cannot be used in a constraint. It can only be used with a wildcard (?).

14.22   *(c)*

(a) Cannot instantiate the interface List.

(b) and (d) The method call ds.add(row) expects a list with element type Array-List<Integer>, but row has the type List<Integer>.

(e) Incompatible types for assignment: cannot convert from ArrayList<Array-List<Integer> to List<List<Integer>.

(f) The interface List requires a single type parameter, and it cannot be instantiated.

(g), (h) Both the interface List and the class ArrayList require a single type parameter.

14.23   *(b) and (f)*

After erasure, the method at (1) has the signature overloadMe(List, List). Since all methods are declared void, they must differ in their parameter list after erasure in order to be overloaded with the method at (1). All methods have different parameter lists from that of the method at (1), except for the declarations (b) and (f). In other words, all methods have signatures that are not override-equivalent to the signature of the method at (1), except for (b) and (f).

If one considers the declarations (a) and (e) on their own, these two methods have the same signature overloadMe(Collection, List) after erasure and, therefore, would not be overloaded, i.e., they would be override-equivalent.

14.24   *(c) and (d)*

(a) The method appendAndWrite(Collection<T>, T) cannot be applied to the inferred argument type (List<capture-of#*n* ?>, String). We cannot add to a collection of type Collection<?>.

(b) The method appendAndWrite(Collection<T>, T) cannot be applied to the inferred argument type (List<capture-of#*m* ? extends Object>, String). We cannot add to a collection of type Collection<? extends Object>.

(c) The method appendAndWrite(Collection<T>, T) can be applied to the inferred argument type (List<capture-of#*k* ? super Object>, String). T is Object. We can add any object to a collection of type Collection<? super Object>.

(d) The method appendAndWrite(Collection<T>, T) can be applied to the inferred argument type (List<Object>, String). T is Object. We can add any object to a collection of type Collection<Object>.

14.25   *(b)*

Passing a raw list to either a list of Integers or to a list of type parameter T is not type-safe.

14.26   *(d), (e), and (f)*

(a) The arguments in the call are (List<Number>, List<Integer>). No type inferred from the arguments satisfies the formal parameters (List<? extends T>, List<? super T>).

(b) The arguments in the call are (List<Number>, List<Integer>). The actual type parameter is Number. The arguments do not satisfy the formal parameters (List<? extends Number>, List<? super Number>). List<Number> is a subtype of List<? extends Number>, but List<Integer> is not a subtype of List<? super Number>.

(c) The arguments in the call are (List<Number>, List<Integer>). The actual type parameter is Integer. The arguments do not satisfy the formal parameters (List<? extends Integer>, List<? super Integer>). List<Number> is not a subtype of List<? extends Integer>, although List<Integer> is a subtype of List<? super Integer>.

(d) The arguments in the call are (List<Integer>, List<Number>). The inferred type is Integer. The arguments satisfy the formal parameters (List<? extends Integer>, List<? super Integer>).

(e) The arguments in the call are (List<Integer>, List<Number>). The actual type parameter is Number. The arguments satisfy the formal parameters (List<? extends Number>, List<? super Number>).

(f) Same reasoning as in (d), but the actual type parameter is explicitly specified in the method call.

14.27   (e)

The methods in (1), (2), and (3) are not generic, but the methods in (4) and (5) are. A generic method need not be declared in a generic class. Regardless of what type an object has, it is still an Object.

14.28   (a) and (b)

(a) The class uses the correct syntax to declare the constructors.

(b) The constructors in (2) and (3) have the same erasure and, therefore, only one of them can be declared, i.e., we have a name clash. The compiler reports an error.

(c) A generic class can declare generic constructors, as in (3) and (4).

(d) A type parameter declared by the class can be ignored in the class body.

14.29   (h)

(a) Invokes the default constructor at (1).

(b) Invokes the constructor at (2) with T as String and V as String.

(c) Invokes the constructor at (2) with T as Integer and V as String.

(d) Invokes the constructor at (2) with T as Integer and V as Integer.

(e) Invokes the constructor at (2) with T as String and V as String, same as (b).

(f) Invokes the constructor at (3) with T as Integer and V as String. The constructor requires parameters (Integer, String), which is compatible with the arguments (Integer, String) in the constructor call.

(g) Invokes the constructor at (3) with T as Integer and V as String, same as (f).

(h) T is Integer and V is String. The constructor requires parameters (Integer, String), which is *not* compatible with the arguments (String, Integer) in the constructor call.

14.30   (a), (e), and (i)

The erasure of the signature of (2) is different from the erasure of the signature of (1), i.e., overloaded, since signatures are not override-equivalent. Therefore, of the three alternatives (a), (b), and (c), only (a) is correct.

The signature of (3) is the same as the erasure of the signature of (1), i.e., overridden. Therefore, of the three alternatives (d), (e), and (f), only (e) is correct.

The erasure of the signature of (5) is the same as the signature of (4), and not the other way around, i.e., name clash. Therefore, of the three alternatives (h), (i), and (j), only (i) is correct.

14.31   *(c), (f), (i), and (k)*

The type parameter N in SubC1 does *not* parameterize the supertype SupC. The erasure of the signature of (3) is the same as the erasure of the signature of (1), i.e., name clash. Therefore, of the three alternatives (a), (b), and (c), only (c) is correct.

The type parameter N in SubC1 cannot be guaranteed to be a subtype of the type parameter T in SupC, i.e., incompatible return types for get() methods at (4) and (2). Also, methods cannot be overloaded if only return types are different. Therefore, of the three alternatives (d), (e), and (f), only (f) is correct.

The type parameter N in SubC2 is a subtype of the type parameter M which parameterizes the supertype SupC. The erasure of the signature of (5) is still the same as the erasure of the signature of (1), i.e., name clash. Therefore, of the three alternatives (g), (h), and (i), only (i) is correct.

The type parameter N in SubC1 is a subtype of the type parameter T (through M) in SupC, i.e., covariant return types for the get() methods at (6) and (2), which are overridden. Therefore, of the three alternatives (j), (k), and (l), only (k) is correct.

14.32   *(a), (c), and (e)*

(a) An enum type and its enum values are static. Since type parameters cannot be used in any static context, the parameterization of an enum type would be nonsense.

(c) Generic exceptions or error types are not allowed, because the exception handling mechanism is a runtime mechanism and the JVM is oblivious of generics.

(e) Anonymous classes do not have a name, but a class name is needed for declaring a generic class and specifying its type parameters.

14.33   *(c)*

The type parameter E in the class Tantrum has the upper bound Exception, and the method throwOne() can throw an exception that is a subtype of Exception.

The generic Tantrum class is instantiated correctly in the main() method, as is the non-generic class TantrumException that is a subtype of Exception.

14.34   *(d)*

Casts are permitted, as in (2)-(6), but can result in an unchecked warning. The *assignment* in (5) is from a raw type (List) to a parameterized type (List<Integer>), resulting in an unchecked assignment conversion warning. Note that in (5) the cast does not pose any problem. It is the assignment from generic code to legacy code that can be a potential problem, flagged as an unchecked warning.

In (6), the cast is against the erasure of List<Integer>, that is to say, List. The compiler cannot guarantee that obj is a List<Integer> at runtime, it therefore flags the cast with an unchecked warning.

Only reifiable types in casts do not result in an unchecked warning.

14.35   *(e)*

Instance tests in the scuddle() method use the reified type List<?>. All assignments in the main() method are type-safe.

14.36   *(e), (f), (g), and (h)*

The correct answers all create arrays that have a component type that is reifiable, and the assignment types are compatible.

(a) Cannot instantiate a type parameter.

(b) Cannot create an array whose component type is a type parameter.

(c) Cannot create a generic array of List<T>, as List<T> is not reifiable type..

(d) Cannot create an array of a type parameter.

(i) Unchecked assignment conversion warning, as the assignment is from a non-generic type to a generic type.

14.37   *(c)*

Erasure of E[] in the method copy() is Object[]. The array type Object[] is actually cast to Object[] at runtime, i.e., an identity cast. The method copy() returns an array of Object. In the main() method, the assignment of this array to an array of Strings results in a ClassCastException.

14.38   *(e)*

The method header in (1) is valid. The type of the varargs parameter can be generic. The type of the formal parameter aols is an array of Lists of T. The method prints each list.

The main() method in (2) can be declared as String..., as it is equivalent to String[].

The statement at (3) creates an array of Lists of Strings. The type parameter T is inferred to be String in the method call in (4).

15   Collections and Maps

15.1   *(b) and (d)*

It is recommended that (a) is fulfilled, but it is not a requirement. (c) is also not required, but such objects will lead to collisions in the hash table, as they will map to the same bucket.

15.2   *(a), (b), (d), and (h)*

(c) is eliminated since the hashCode() method cannot claim inequality if the equals() method claims equality. (e) and (f) are eliminated since the equals() method must be reflexive, and (g) is eliminated since the hashCode() method must consistently return the same hash value during the execution.

15.3   *(b), (d), and (e)*

(a) and (c) fail to satisfy the properties of an equivalence relation. (a) is not transitive and (c) is not symmetric.

15.4   *(a) and (e)*

(b) is not correct since it will throw an ArithmeticException when called on a newly created Measurement object. (c) and (d) are not correct since they may return unequal hash values for two objects that are equal according to the equals() method.

15.6   *(a), (d), and (e)*

Set, Collection, and Map are core interfaces in the collections framework. LinkedList is a class that implements the List interface. There is no class or interface named Bag.

15.7   *(b) and (e)*

The java.util package provides map implementations named HashMap and TreeMap. It does not provide any implementations named HashList, ArraySet, and ArrayMap.

15.8   *(d)*

The List interface is implemented by collections that maintain sequences of possibly non-unique elements. Elements retain their insertion ordering in the sequence. Collection classes implementing SortedSet only allow unique elements that are maintained in a sorted order.

15.9   *(a), (c), and (f)*

Only methods in (a), (c), and (f) are in the Iterator<E> interface.

15.10 *(a), (b), (c), (d), and (g)*

With blanks filled in:

```
Collection<Integer> myItems = new ArrayList<Integer>();
myItems.add(9); myItems.add(1); myItems.add(1);

Iterator<Integer> iterator = myItems.iterator();
while (iterator.hasNext()) {
  System.out.print(iterator.next());
}
```

15.11 *(a)*

The expression in the for(:) loop header (in this case, the call to the makeCollection() method) is only evaluated once.

15.12   *(a), (b), and (c)*

Changing the value of the *variable* does not affect the data structure being iterated over. The for(:) loop cannot run backwards. We cannot iterate over several data structures simultaneously in a for(:) loop. The syntax does not allow it.

15.13   *(b)*

A String is immutable. The call to the toUpperCase() method returns a new String object whose text representation is printed. The elements of the collection remain unchanged.

15.14   *(c) and (d)*

The for(:) loop does not allow the list to be modified structurally. In (a) and (b), the code will throw a java.util.ConcurrentModificationException. Note that the iterator in (d) is less restrictive than the for(:) loop, allowing elements to be removed in a controlled way.

15.15   *(b), (c), (f), and (i)*

In (b), (c), and (f), the array type returned by the toArray() method is not a subtype of the array type on the left-hand side, resulting in a compile-time error. The program will throw an ArrayStoreException in (i), because Integer objects cannot be stored in an array of type Long.

15.16   *(a) and (c)*

Some operations on a collection may throw an UnsupportedOperationException. This exception type is unchecked, and the code is not required to explicitly handle unchecked exceptions. A List allows duplicate elements. An ArrayList implements a resizable array. The capacity of the array will be expanded automatically when needed. The List interface defines a get() method, but there is no method by that name in the Collection interface.

15.17   *(d)*

The program will compile without error, and will print all primes below 25 when run. All the collection implementations used in the program implement the Collection interface. The implementation instances are interchangeable when denoted by Collection references. None of the operations performed on the implementations will throw an UnsupportedOperationException. The program finds the primes below 25 by removing all values divisible by 2, 3, and 5 from the set of values from 2 through 25.

15.18   *(a), (b), and (d)*

The methods add(), retainAll(), and iterator() are defined in the Collection interface. The get() and indexOf() methods are defined in the List interface.

15.19   *(b)*

The remove() method removes the last element returned by either next() or previous() method. The four next() calls return A, B, C, and D. D is subsequently removed. The two previous() calls return C and B. B is subsequently removed.

15.20   *(a)*

[1, 3, 2] is printed. First, "1" and "2" are appended to an empty list. Next, "3" is inserted between "1" and "2", and then the list is duplicated. The original list is concatenated with the copy. The sequence of elements in the list is now "1", "3", "2", "1", "3", "2". Then a sublist view allowing access to elements from index 2 to index 5 (exclusive) is created (i.e., the subsequence "2", "1", "3"). The sublist is cleared, thus removing the elements. This is reflected in the original list and the sequence of elements is now "1", "3", "2".

15.21   *(b) and (d)*

The methods add() and retainAll(), return the value true if the collection was modified during the operation. The contains() and containsAll() methods return a boolean value, but these membership operations never modify the current collection, and the return value indicates the result of the membership test. The clear() method does not return a value.

15.22   *(c), (d), (e), and (f)*

Sets cannot have duplicates. HashSet does not guarantee the order of the elements in (a) and (b), therefore there is no guarantee that the program will print [1, 9]. Because LinkedHashSet maintains elements in insertion order in (c) and (d), the program is guaranteed to print [1, 9]. Because TreeSet maintains elements sorted according to the natural ordering in (e) and (f), the program is guaranteed to print [1, 9].

15.23   *(c)*

Note that the methods higher() and lower() are "stricter" than the methods ceiling() and floor().

15.24   *(c) and (d)*

The output from each statement is shown below.

```
(a) [set, shell, soap]
(b) [set, shell]
(c) [soap, swan]
(d) [swan]
(e) [shell, soap]
(f) [set, shell]
```

15.25 *(b), (c), and (d)*

The method poll() is specified in the Queue interface which is implemented by the LinkedList and PriorityQueue classes, thus ruling out (a), (e), and (f). The NavigableSet interface specifies the pollFirst() and pollLast() methods.

15.26 *(c)*

(a) uses an iterator which does not guarantee the order of traversal. (b) traverses the queue, but only peeks at the (same) head element each time. (d) uses an iterator, but tries to change the queue structurally by calling the poll() method at the same time, resulting in a java.util.ConcurrentModificationException. Polling in (c) is done according to the priority ordering, which in this case is natural ordering for strings.

15.27 *(c) and (d)*

The Map<K,V> interface defines the methods remove() and values(). It does not define methods contains(), addAll(), and toArray(). Methods with these names are defined in the Collection interface, but Map does not inherit from Collection.

15.28 *(b) and (d)*

Although all the keys in a map must be unique, multiple identical values may exist. Since values are not unique, the values() method returns a Collection instance and not a Set instance. The collection objects returned by the keySet(), entrySet(), and values() methods are backed by the original Map object. This means that changes made in one are reflected in the other. Although implementations of SortedMap keep the entries sorted on the keys, this is not a requirement for classes that implement Map. For instance, the entries in a HashMap are not sorted.

15.29 *(c) and (e)*

The classes TreeSet and TreeMap implement the comparator() method. The comparator() method is defined in the SortedSet and SortedMap interfaces, and the TreeSet and TreeMap classes implement these interfaces.

15.30 *(a), (c), and (d)*

The key of a Map.Entry cannot be changed since the key is used for locating the entry within the map. There is no set() method. The setValue() method is optional.

15.31 *(a), (b), and (e)*

The output from the program is shown below.

```
3001|2010|2001|
3001|2010|2001|
2001|2010|3001|
3001|2010|2001|
2001|2010|3001|
```

First, the elements in the set navSet are ordered in reverse natural ordering. In the statement

```
NavigableSet<Integer> ss1 = new TreeSet<Integer>(navSet);
```

the signature of the constructor called is

```
TreeSet<Integer>(SortedSet<E> set)
```

resulting in the same ordering for the elements in the set ss1 as in the set navSet, i.e., reverse natural ordering. In the statement

```
NavigableSet<Integer> ss2 = new TreeSet<Integer>((Collection<Integer>)navSet);
```

the signature of the constructor called is

```
TreeSet<Integer>(Collection<? extends E> collection)
```

resulting in the elements in set ss2 having the *same natural ordering* as in the set navSet.

15.32   *(b) and (d)*

Both (a) and (c) result in a NullPointerException: (a) in the expression (frequency == 0) and (b) in the first assignment. In both cases, the reference frequency has the value null, which cannot be boxed or unboxed.

15.33   *(b)*

A map view method creates half-open intervals (i.e., the upper bound is not included), unless the inclusion of the bounds is explicitly specified. Clearing a map view clears the affected entries from the underlying map. The argument to the sumValues() method can be any subtype of Map, where the type of the value is Integer.

15.34   *(b) and (e)*

(a) throws a ConcurrentModificationException. We cannot remove an entry in a for(:) loop. (c) throws a ConcurrentModificationException as well, even though we use an iterator. The remove() method is called on the map, not on the iterator. The argument to the remove() method of the map must implement Comparable, Map.Entry does not, resulting in a ClassCastException in (d).

We can remove an entry from the underlying map when traversing the key set using an iterator, as in (b). (e) creates a map view of one entry and clears it, thereby also clearing it from the underlying map.

15.35   *(d)*

StringBuilders are mutable. A string builder's state can be modified by any of its aliases, in this case by the reference value.

15.36   *(a)*

Strings are immutable. In (b) and (c) the argument value in the call to the method toggle() refers to the old string after completion of the call, so the value in the map is not updated with the new string.

15.37 *(c)*

The class `StringBuilder` does not implement the `Comparable` interface. The `sort()` method that takes a comparator does not place any such requirements on the element type. The program compiles, but throws a `ClassCastException`, as `StringBuilder` objects cannot be compared in reverse natural ordering.

15.38 *(d)*

The class `StringBuilder` does not implement the `Comparable` interface. The `sort()` method (without the comparator) requires that the element type of the list is `Comparable`. The program will not compile.

15.39 *(a) and (f)*

The largest value a match can return is the largest index, i.e., *array.length-1* (==3). The key must be equal to the largest element in the array. If no match is found, a negative value is returned, which is computed as follows: - *(insertion point + 1)*. The smallest value is returned for a key that is greater than the largest element in the array. This key must obviously be placed at the index *array.length* (==4), after the largest element, i.e., the insertion point is 4. The value of the expression - *(insertion point + 1)* is -5, which is the smallest value printed by the method.

15.40 *(a), (c), (e), and (f)*

The `Arrays` class has the following methods: `asList`, `sort`, `binarySearch`. The `Collections` class has the following methods: `sort`, `binarySearch`. The `List` interface has the following methods: `indexOf`, `contains`, `toArray`, `subList`—only `indexOf` is used to look up the index of an element in the list. The method names `findIndex`, `search`, and `toList` are not in any of these classes nor in the `List` interface.

15.41 *(c)*

The comparator orders the strings in descending rhyming ordering: string contents are reversed and then compared in reverse lexicographical ordering. (a) is sorted in reverse natural ordering. (b) is sorted in ascending rhyming ordering. (d) is sorted in natural ordering.

Solutions to Programming Exercises

●●●

1 Basics of Java Programming

1.1 The printStackElements() method of the PrintableCharStack class does not pop the elements.

```java
//Filename: PrintableCharStack.java
public class PrintableCharStack extends CharStack {              // (1)

  // Instance method
  public void printStackElements() {                            // (2)
    for (int i = 0; i <= topOfStack; i++)
      System.out.print(stackArray[i]); // print each char on terminal
    System.out.println();
  }

  // Constructor calls the constructor of the superclass explicitly.
  PrintableCharStack(int capacity) { super(capacity); }         // (3)
}

//Filename: Client.java
public class Client {

  public static void main(String[] args) {

    // Create a printable character stack.
    PrintableCharStack stack = new PrintableCharStack(40);

    // Create a string to push on the stack:
    String str = "!no tis ot nuf era skcatS";
    int length = str.length();

    // Push the string char by char onto the stack:
    for (int i = 0; i < length; i++) {
      stack.push(str.charAt(i));
    }

    System.out.print("Stack contents: ");
```

```
      stack.printStackElements();

      // Pop and print each char from the stack:
      while (!stack.isEmpty()) {
        System.out.print(stack.pop());
      }
      System.out.println();

      System.out.print("Stack contents: ");
      stack.printStackElements();
    }
  }
```

2   Language Fundamentals

2.1   The following program compiles and runs without errors:

```
//Filename: Temperature.java
/* Identifiers and keywords in Java are case-sensitive. Therefore, the
   case of the file name must match the class name, the keywords must
   all be written in lowercase. The name of the String class has a
   capital S. The main method must be static and take an array of
   String objects as an argument. */
public class Temperature {
  public static void main(String[] args) {  // Correct method signature
    double fahrenheit = 62.5;
    // /* identifies the start of a "starred" comment.
    // */ identifies the end.
    /* Convert */
    double celsius = f2c(fahrenheit);
    // '' delimits character literals, "" delimits string literals.
    // Only first character literal is quoted as string to avoid addition.
    // The second char literal is implicitly converted to its string
    // representation, as string concatenation is performed by
    // the last + operator.
    // Java is case-sensitive. The name Celsius should be changed to
    // the variable name celsius.
    System.out.println(fahrenheit + "F" + " = " + celsius + 'C');
  }
  /* Method should be declared static. */
  static double f2c(double fahr) {  // Note parameter type should be double.
    return (fahr - 32) * 5 / 9;
  }
}
```

3 Declarations

3.1

```java
/** A JavaBean for an editing context */
public class EditContext {              // Non-generic version
  private Object selected;
  public void setSelected(Object newSelected) {
    selected = newSelected;
  }
  public Object getSelected() {
    return selected;
  }
}
```

3.2

```java
public class QuizGrader {

  /** Enum type to represent the result of answering a question. */
  enum Result { CORRECT, WRONG, UNANSWERED }

  public static final int PASS_MARK = 5;

  public static void main(String[] args) {

    String[] correctAnswers = { "C", "A", "B", "D", "B", "C", "C", "A" };

    System.out.println("Question  Submitted Ans. Correct Ans.  Result");

    // Counters for misc. statistics:
    int numOfCorrectAnswers = 0;
    int numOfWrongAnswers = 0;
    int numOfUnanswered = 0;

    // Loop through submitted answers and correct answers:
    for (int i = 0; i < args.length; i++) {
      String submittedAnswer = args[i];
      String correctAnswer = correctAnswers[i];
      Result result = determineResult(submittedAnswer, correctAnswer);

      // Print report for current question.
      System.out.printf("%5d%10s%15s%15s%n",
                        i+1, submittedAnswer, correctAnswer, result);
      // Accumulate statistics.
      switch(result) {
        case CORRECT: numOfCorrectAnswers++; break;
        case WRONG: numOfWrongAnswers++; break;
        case UNANSWERED: numOfUnanswered++; break;
      }
    }
    // Print summary of statistics.
    System.out.println("No. of correct answers:      " + numOfCorrectAnswers);
    System.out.println("No. of wrong answers:        " + numOfWrongAnswers);
```

```java
        System.out.println("No. of questions unanswered: " + numOfUnanswered);
        System.out.println("The candidate " +
                    (numOfCorrectAnswers >= PASS_MARK ? "PASSED." : "FAILED."));
    }

    /** Determines the result of answer to a question. */
    public static Result determineResult(String submittedAnswer,
                                         String correctAnswer) {
        Result result = null;
        if (submittedAnswer.equals(correctAnswer))
            result = Result.CORRECT;
        else if (submittedAnswer.equals("X"))
            result = Result.UNANSWERED;
        else
            result = Result.WRONG;
        return result;
    }
}
```

4 Access Control

4.1

```java
//Filename: Account.java
package com.megabankcorp.records;

public class Account { }

//Filename: Database.java
// Specify package
package com.megabankcorp.system;

//Refer to the Account class by using the simple name Account.
import com.megabankcorp.records.Account;

// Class must be abstract since it has abstract methods.
public abstract class Database {

    // Abstract and available from anywhere.
    public abstract void deposit(Account acc, double amount);

    // Abstract and available from anywhere.
    public abstract void withdraw(Account acc, double amount);

    // Abstract and only available from package and subclasses.
    protected abstract double amount(Account acc);

    // Unmodifiable and only available from package.
    final void transfer(Account from, Account to, double amount) {
        withdraw(from, amount);
        deposit(to, amount);
    }
}
```

5 Operators and Expressions

5.1

```java
//Filename: Sunlight.java
public class Sunlight {
  public static void main(String[] args) {
    // Distance from sun (150 million kilometers)
    /* The max value for int is 2147483647, so using int here will
       work. */
    int kmFromSun = 150000000;

    // Again, using int for this value is OK.
    int lightSpeed = 299792458; // Meters per second

    // Convert distance to meters.
    /* The result of this equation will not fit in an int. Let's
       use a long instead. We need to ensure that the values that
       are multiplied really are multiplied using long
       data types, and not multiplied as int data types and later
       converted to long. The L suffix on the 1000L integer
       literal ensures this. The value of kmFromSun will
       implicitly be converted from int to long to match the
       data type of the other factor. The conversion can be done
       implicitly by the compiler since the conversion represents
       a widening of the data type. */
    long mFromSun = kmFromSun * 1000L;

    /* We know that the result value will fit in an int.
       However, the narrowing conversion on assignment from long to int
       in this case requires a cast.*/
    int seconds = (int) (mFromSun / lightSpeed);

    System.out.print("Light will use ");
    printTime(seconds);
    System.out.println(" to travel from the sun to the earth.");
  }

  /* We leave this method alone. */
  public static void printTime(int sec) {
    int min = sec / 60;
    sec = sec - (min * 60);
    System.out.print(min + " minute(s) and " + sec + " second(s)");
  }
}
```

6 Control Flow

6.1   Finding primes using for-loops.

```
//Filename: ForPrimes.java
public class ForPrimes {
  final static int MAX = 100;
  public static void main( String[] args ) {
    numbers:
      for (int num = 1; num < MAX; num++) {
        int divLim = (int) Math.sqrt( num );
        for (int div = 2; div <= divLim; div++)
          if ((num % div) == 0) continue numbers;
        System.out.println( num );
      }
  }
}
```

Finding primes using while-loops.

```
//Filename: WhilePrimes.java
public class WhilePrimes {
  final static int MAX = 100;
  public static void main( String[] args ) {
    int num = 1;
    numbers:
      while (num < MAX) {
        int number = num++;
        int divLim = (int) Math.sqrt( number );
        int div = 2;
        while (div <= divLim)
          if ((number % div++) == 0) continue numbers;
        System.out.println( number );
      }
  }
}
```

6.2

```
package energy;
/** A PowerPlant with a reactor core.
    The solution presented here is provided by Jennie Yip. */
public class PowerPlant {
  /** Each power plant has a reactor core. This has package
      accessibility so that the Control class that is defined in
      the same package can access it. */
  Reactor core;

  /** Initializes the power plant, creates a reactor core. */
  PowerPlant() {
    core = new Reactor();
  }
```

```java
    /** Sound the alarm to evacuate the power plant. */
    public void soundEvacuateAlarm() {
      // ... implementation unspecified ...
    }

    /** Get the level of reactor output that is most desirable at this time.
        (Units are unspecified.) */
    public int getOptimalThroughput() {
      // ... implementation unspecified ...
      return 0;
    }

    /** The main entry point of the program: sets up a PowerPlant
        object and a Control object and lets the Control object run the
        power plant. */
    public static void main(String[] args) {
      PowerPlant plant = new PowerPlant();
      Control ctrl = new Control(plant);
      ctrl.runSystem();
    }
}

/** A reactor core that has a throughput that can be either decreased or
    increased. */
class Reactor {
  /** Get the current throughput of the reactor. (Units are unspecified.) */
  public int getThroughput() {
    // ... implementation unspecified ...
    return 0;
  }

  /** @returns true if the reactor status is critical, false otherwise. */
  public boolean isCritical() {
    // ... implementation unspecified ...
    return false;
  }

  /** Ask the reactor to increase throughput. */
  void increaseThroughput() throws ReactorCritical {
    // ... implementation unspecified ...
  }

  /** Ask the reactor to decrease throughput. */
  void decreaseThroughput() {
    // ... implementation unspecified ...
  }
}

/** This exception class should be used to report that the reactor status is
    critical. */
class ReactorCritical extends Exception {}

/** A controller that will manage the power plant to make sure that the
    reactor runs with optimal throughput.  */
class Control {
  PowerPlant thePlant;
```

```java
  final static int TOLERANCE = 10;

public Control(PowerPlant p) {
  thePlant = p;
}

/** Run the power plant by continuously monitoring the
    optimalThroughput and the actual throughput of the reactor. If
    the throughputs differ by more than 10 units, i.e. tolerance,
    adjust the reactor throughput.
    If the reactor goes critical, the evacuate alarm is
    sounded and the reactor is shut down.
    <p>The runSystem() method does handle the reactor core directly
    but calls methods needAdjustment(), adjustThroughput(), and shutdown
    instead.  */
public void runSystem() {
  try {
    while (true) { // infinite loop
      int optimalThroughput = thePlant.getOptimalThroughput();
      if (needAdjustment(optimalThroughput))
        adjustThroughput(optimalThroughput);
    }
  } catch (ReactorCritical rc) {
    thePlant.soundEvacuateAlarm();
  } finally {
    shutdown();
  }
}

/** Reports whether the throughput of the reactor needs
    adjusting. This method should also monitor and report if the
    reactor goes critical.
    @returns true if the optimal and actual throughput values
    differ by more than 10 units.  */
public boolean needAdjustment(int target) throws ReactorCritical {
  /* We added the throws clause to the method declaration so that
     the method can throw a ReactorCritical exception if the reactor
     goes critical.  */
  if (thePlant.core.isCritical())
    throw new ReactorCritical();
  return Math.abs(thePlant.core.getThroughput() - target) > TOLERANCE;
}

/** Adjust the throughput of the reactor by calling increaseThroughput()
    and decreaseThroughput() until the actual throughput is within 10
    units of the target throughput.  */
public void adjustThroughput(int target) throws ReactorCritical {
  /* We added the throws clause to the method declaration so that
     the method can pass on ReactorCritical exceptions thrown by
     increaseThroughput(). We do this because the adjustThroughput
     does not want to handle the exception.  */
  while (needAdjustment(target)) {
    if ((thePlant.core.getThroughput() - target) > TOLERANCE)
      thePlant.core.increaseThroughput();
    else
```

```
        thePlant.core.decreaseThroughput();
      }
    }

    /** Shut down the reactor by lowering the throughput to 0. */
    public void shutdown() {
      while (thePlant.core.getThroughput() > 0) {
        thePlant.core.decreaseThroughput();
      }
    }
  }
```

7 Object-Oriented Programming

7.1

```
//Filename: Exercise1.java
package chap07_PE1;

interface Function {
  public int evaluate(int arg);
}

class Half implements Function {
  public int evaluate(int arg) {
    return arg/2;
  }
}

public class Exercise1 {

  public static int[] applyFunctionToArray(int[] arrIn) {
    int length = arrIn.length;
    int[] arrOut = new int[length];
    Function func = new Half();
    for (int i = 0; i < length; i++)
      arrOut[i] = func.evaluate(arrIn[i]);
    return arrOut;
  }

  public static void main(String[] args) {
    // Create array with values 1..10
    int length = 10;
    int[] myArr = new int[length];
    for (int i = 0; i < length;) myArr[i] = ++i;
    // Print array
    for (int value : myArr) System.out.println(value);
    // Half values
    myArr = applyFunctionToArray(myArr);
    // Print array again
    for (int value : myArr) System.out.println(value);
  }
}
```

7.2

```java
package chap07_PE2;

//Filename: Exercise2.java
interface Function {
  public int evaluate(int arg);
}

class Half implements Function {
  public int evaluate(int arg) {
    return arg/2;
  }
}

class Print implements Function {
  public int evaluate(int arg) {
    System.out.println(arg);
    return arg;
  }
}

public class Exercise2 {

  public static int[] applyFunctionToArray(int[] arrIn, Function func) {
    int length = arrIn.length;
    int[] arrOut = new int[length];
    for (int i = 0; i < length; i++)
      arrOut[i] = func.evaluate(arrIn[i]);
    return arrOut;
  }

  public static void main(String[] args) {
    // Create array with values 1..10
    int length = 10;
    int[] myArr = new int[length];
    for (int i = 0; i < length;) myArr[i] = ++i;
    // Create a print function
    Function print = new Print();
    // Print array
    applyFunctionToArray(myArr, print);
    // Half values
    myArr = applyFunctionToArray(myArr, new Half());
    // Print array again
    applyFunctionToArray(myArr, print);
  }
}
```

8 Nested Type Declarations

8.1
```java
//Filename: Exercise3.java
interface Function {
  public int evaluate(int arg);
}

class Half implements Function {
  public int evaluate(int arg) {
    return arg/2;
  }
}

class Print implements Function {
  public int evaluate(int arg) {
    System.out.println(arg);
    return arg;
  }
}

public class Exercise3 {
  /* Inner class that applies the function, prints the value, and
       returns the result. */
  static class PrintFunc extends Print {
    PrintFunc(Function f) {
      func = f;
    }
    Function func;
    public int evaluate(int arg) {
      return super.evaluate(func.evaluate(arg));
    }
  }

  // Inner class that just returns the argument unchanged.
  /* Use this when you want a PrintFunc object to print
       the argument as-is. */
  static class NoOpFunc implements Function {
    public int evaluate(int arg) {
      return arg;
    }
  }

  public static void main(String[] args) {
    // Create array with values 1 .. 10
    int[] myArr = new int[10];
    for (int i=0; i<10;) myArr[i] = ++i;
    // Print array without modification
    applyFunctionToArray(myArr, new PrintFunc(new NoOpFunc()));
    // Print halved values
    applyFunctionToArray(myArr, new PrintFunc(new Half()));
  }
```

```java
    public static int[] applyFunctionToArray(int[] arrIn, Function func) {
        int length = arrIn.length;
        int[] arrOut = new int[length];
        for (int i=0; i< length; i++)
            arrOut[i] = func.evaluate(arrIn[i]);
        return arrOut;
    }
}
```

9 Object Lifetime

No programming exercises.

10 Fundamental Classes

10.1

```java
/**
 * Aggregate (non-generic) pairs of arbitrary objects.
 */
public final class Pair {
    private Object first, second;

    /** Construct a Pair object. */
    public Pair(Object one, Object two) {
        first = one;
        second = two;
    }

    /** Provides access to the first aggregated object. */
    public Object getFirst() { return first; }

    /** Provides access to the second aggregated object. */
    public Object getSecond() { return second; }

    /** @return true if the pair of objects are identical. */
    public boolean equals(Object other) {
        if (! (other instanceof Pair)) return false;
        Pair otherPair = (Pair) other;
        return first.equals(otherPair.getFirst()) &&
               second.equals(otherPair.getSecond());
    }

    /** @return a hash code for the aggregate pair. */
    public int hashCode() {
        // XORing the hash codes to create a hash code for the pair.
        return first.hashCode() ^ second.hashCode();
    }
```

```
    /** @return the textual representation of the aggregated objects. */
    public String toString() {
      return "[" + first + "," + second + "]";
    }
  }
```

10.2

```
  /** Determine if a string is a palindrome. */
  public class Palindrome {
    public static void main(String[] args) {
      if (args.length != 1) {
        System.out.println("Usage: java Palindrome <word>");
        return;
      }
      String word = args[0];
      StringBuilder reverseWord = new StringBuilder(word);
      reverseWord.reverse();
      boolean isPalindrome = word.equals(reverseWord.toString());
      System.out.println("The word " + word + " is " +
                         (isPalindrome ? "" : "not ") + "a palindrome");
    }
  }
```

11 Files and Streams

11.1

```
  //Filename: Convert.java
  import java.io.BufferedReader;
  import java.io.BufferedWriter;
  import java.io.FileInputStream;
  import java.io.FileNotFoundException;
  import java.io.FileOutputStream;
  import java.io.IOException;
  import java.io.InputStream;
  import java.io.InputStreamReader;
  import java.io.OutputStream;
  import java.io.OutputStreamWriter;

  public class Convert {
    public static void main(String args[]) {

      String inEncoding  = "8859_1";
      String outEncoding = "UTF8";
      InputStream  inStream  = System.in;
      OutputStream outStream = System.out;

      try {
        try {
          inEncoding  = args[0];
          outEncoding = args[1];
          inStream  = new FileInputStream (args[2]);
          outStream = new FileOutputStream(args[3]);
```

```java
      } catch (ArrayIndexOutOfBoundsException aioobe) {
        // Missing parameters are allowed.
      }
      BufferedReader reader = new BufferedReader(
          new InputStreamReader(inStream, inEncoding)
      );
      BufferedWriter writer = new BufferedWriter(
          new OutputStreamWriter(outStream, outEncoding)
      );
      // Transfer 512 chars at a time.
      char[] cbuf = new char[512];
      while (true) {
        int bytesLastRead = reader.read(cbuf);
        if (bytesLastRead == -1) break;
        writer.write(cbuf, 0, bytesLastRead);
        // Last two args was offset (none) and length.
      }
      reader.close();
      writer.close();
    } catch (FileNotFoundException fnfe) {
      System.err.println("File not found: " + fnfe.getLocalizedMessage());
    } catch (IOException ioe) {
      System.err.println("I/O error: " + ioe.getLocalizedMessage());
    } catch (SecurityException se) {
      System.err.println("Security Error: " + se.getLocalizedMessage());
    }
  }
}
```

12 Localization, Pattern Matching, and Formatting

12.1

```java
import java.io.BufferedReader;
import java.io.FileReader;
import java.io.FileWriter;
import java.io.IOException;
import java.util.ArrayList;
import java.util.List;
import java.util.regex.Matcher;
import java.util.regex.Pattern;

public class VerySimpleGrep {
  public static void main(String[] args) throws IOException {
    // Test file
    FileWriter fw = new FileWriter("test.txt");
    fw.write("To be or not to be.\n");
    fw.write("Only As, no Bs.\n");
    fw.write("A bee movie is not funny.\n");
    fw.write("Bessy was a beautiful beatnik from Bern.\n");
    fw.close();
    String fileName = "test.txt";
    String regexStr = "[bB]e";
    grepFile(fileName, regexStr);
```

```
    // Test on this file:
    fileName = "VerySimpleGrep.java";
    regexStr = "[a-zA-Z_$][a-zA-Z0-9_$]*";
    grepFile(fileName, regexStr);

    // Read file name and regex as program arguments:
    fileName = args[0];
    regexStr = args[1];
    grepFile(fileName, regexStr);
  }

  /**
   * Finds and prints matches for the regex in the text file.
   * @param fileName
   * @param regex
   * @throws IOException
   */
  public static void grepFile(String fileName, String regex)
                              throws IOException {
    Pattern pattern = Pattern.compile(regex);
    BufferedReader source = new BufferedReader(new FileReader(fileName));
    int lineNum = 1;
    String line = source.readLine();
    while (line != null ) {
      if (!line.equals("")) {
        List<String> matchList = grepLine(pattern, line);
        if (matchList.size() != 0)
          System.out.println(lineNum + ": " + matchList);
      }
      lineNum++;
      line = source.readLine();
    }
    source.close();
  }

  /**
   * Finds the matches for the pattern in the target.
   * @param pattern
   * @param target
   * @return List<String> with the matches found in the target
   */
  public static List<String> grepLine(Pattern pattern, String target) {
    Matcher matcher = pattern.matcher(target);
    List<String> matchList = new ArrayList<String>();
    while(matcher.find()) {
      int startCharIndex = matcher.start();
      int lastPlus1Index = matcher.end();
      int lastCharIndex = startCharIndex == lastPlus1Index ?
          lastPlus1Index : lastPlus1Index-1;
      String matchedStr = matcher.group();
      matchList.add("(" + startCharIndex + "," + lastCharIndex + ":" +
          matchedStr + ")");
    }
    return matchList;
  }
}
```

12.2
```java
import static java.lang.System.out;

import java.io.BufferedReader;
import java.io.FileReader;
import java.io.FileWriter;
import java.io.IOException;
import java.util.Arrays;
import java.util.Scanner;
import java.util.regex.Pattern;

public class CSVReader {
  public static void main(String[] args) throws IOException {
    FileWriter fw = new FileWriter("csv.txt");
    fw.write("2.5,25,250\n");
    fw.write("Hi,Hello,Howdy\n");
    fw.write("2008,2009,2010\n");
    fw.write("one,two,three\n");
    fw.close();
    BufferedReader source = new BufferedReader(new FileReader("csv.txt"));
    readCSV(source, 3);
    source.close();
  }
  /**
   * Reads values in CSV format.
   * @param source
   * @param numOfFields
   * @throws IOException
   */
  public static void readCSV(Readable source,
                             int numOfFields)throws IOException {
    Scanner lexer = new Scanner(source);
    Pattern csvPattern = compileCSVPattern(numOfFields);
    out.println("Pattern: " + csvPattern.pattern());
    Pattern splitPattern = Pattern.compile(",");
    while (lexer.hasNextLine()) {
      // Match fields on the line
      String record = lexer.findInLine(csvPattern);
      if (record != null) {
        // Split the record on the split pattern:
        String[] fields = splitPattern.split(record, numOfFields);
        out.println(Arrays.toString(fields));
      }
      lexer.nextLine();            // Clear line separator to continue.
    }
    IOException ioe = lexer.ioException();
    if (ioe != null)
      throw ioe;
  }

  /**
   * Creates a multiline-mode pattern that corresponds to the number of fields
   * specified in CSV format on each line/record:
   * ([^,]+),...,([^,]+)
   * Alternative regular expressions for CSV:
```

```
* ^([^,]+),...,([^,]+)
* ([^,]+),...,([^,]+)$
* ^([^,]+),...,([^,]+)$
* (.+),...,(.+)
*
* @param numOfFields
* @return Pattern to match all the field values.
*/
public static Pattern compileCSVPattern(int numOfFields) {
  assert numOfFields >= 1;
  String fieldPattern = "([^,]+)";
  String patternStr = fieldPattern;
  for (int i = 2; i <= numOfFields; i++) {
    patternStr += "," + fieldPattern;
  }
  return Pattern.compile(patternStr, Pattern.MULTILINE);
}
}
```

13 Threads

13.1

```
//Filename: Counter.java
/*
    Notice that the result of running this program
    may not be what you expect. Since both threads are
    working full throttle it is possible that only one
    of the threads is granted CPU time.
*/

public class Counter implements Runnable {
  public static void main(String[] args) {
    Storage store = new Storage();
    new Counter(store);
    new Printer(store);
  }
  Storage storage;
  Counter(Storage target) {
    storage = target;
    new Thread(this).start();
  }
  public void run() {
    int i=0;
    while (true) {
      storage.setValue(i);
      i++;
    }
  }
}

class Printer implements Runnable {
  Storage storage;
```

```java
  Printer(Storage source) {
    storage = source;
    new Thread(this).start();
  }
  public void run() {
    while (true) {
      System.out.println(storage.getValue());
    }
  }
}

class Storage {
  int value;
  void setValue(int i) { value = i; }
  int getValue() { return value; }
}
```

13.2

```java
//Filename: Counter.java
package pe13_2;
/* Only the Storage class has been altered. */

/* No change to this class */
public class Counter implements Runnable {
  public static void main(String[] args) {
    Storage store = new Storage();
    new Counter(store);
    new Printer(store);
  }
  Storage storage;
  Counter(Storage s) {
    storage = s;
    new Thread(this).start();
  }
  public void run() {
    int i=0;
    while (true) {
      storage.setValue(i);
      i++;
    }
  }
}

/* No changes to this class. */
class Printer implements Runnable {
  Storage storage;
  Printer(Storage s) {
    storage = s;
    new Thread(this).start();
  }
  public void run() {
    while (true) {
      System.out.println(storage.getValue());
    }
  }
}
```

```
/* This class now ensures that getting and setting are done
   in an alternating fashion.
 */
class Storage {
  int value;
  boolean isUnread = false;
  synchronized void setValue(int i) {
    ensureUnread(false);
    value = i;
    setUnread(true);
  }
  synchronized int getValue() {
    ensureUnread(true);
    setUnread(false);
    return value;
  }
  private void ensureUnread(boolean shouldHaveUnread) {
    while (shouldHaveUnread != isUnread)
      try { wait(); }
      catch (InterruptedException ie) {}
  }
  private void setUnread(boolean b) {
    isUnread = b;
    notify();
  }
}
```

14 Generics

14.1

```
import java.util.ArrayList;
import java.util.Collection;
import java.util.HashMap;
import java.util.List;
import java.util.Map;

public class Utilities {

  /** Convert Map to MultiMap */
  public static <K,V> Map<V,List<K>> toMultiMap(Map<K,V> origMap) {
    Map<V, List<K>> multiMap = new HashMap<V,List<K>>();
    Collection<K> keys = origMap.keySet();
    for (K key : keys) {
      V value = origMap.get(key);
      List<K> valueList = multiMap.get(value);
      if (valueList == null) {
        valueList = new ArrayList<K>();
        multiMap.put(value, valueList);
      }
      valueList.add(key);
    }
    return multiMap;
  }
}
```

14.2

```java
import java.util.Arrays;
import java.util.Collection;
import java.util.HashMap;
import java.util.HashSet;
import java.util.Map;
import java.util.Set;

public class GraphTraversal {

  public static void main(String[] args) {
    // (1) Given a directed graph with five vertices:
    Integer[][] neighbors = {
        {1, 3},  // Vertex 0
        {2},     // Vertex 1
        {4},     // Vertex 2
        {1, 2},  // Vertex 3
        {}       // Vertex 4
    };
    Map<Integer, Collection<Integer>> graph
                = new HashMap<Integer, Collection<Integer>>();
    for (int i = 0; i < neighbors.length; i++) {
      graph.put(i, Arrays.asList(neighbors[i]));
    }

    // (2) Get the start vertex.
    int startVertex;
    try {
      startVertex = Integer.parseInt(args[0]);
    } catch (ArrayIndexOutOfBoundsException ive) {
      System.out.println("Usage: java GraphTraversal [0-4]");
      return;
    } catch (NumberFormatException nfe) {
      System.out.println("Usage: java GraphTraversal [0-4]");
      return;
    }

    Set<Integer> visitedSet = GraphTraversal.findVerticesOnPath(graph,
                                                         startVertex);
    System.out.print("Vertex " + startVertex + " is connected to " + visitedSet);
  }

  /**
   * Finds the vertices on a path from a given vertex in a directed graph.
   * In the map, the key is a vertex, and the value is the collection
   * containing its neighbours.
   */
  public static <N> Set<N> findVerticesOnPath(
                Map<N,Collection<N>> graph, N startVertex) {
    // (3) Create a stack for traversing the graph:
    MyStack<N> traversalStack = new MyStack<N>();

    // (4) Create a set for visited vertices:
    Set<N> visitedSet = new HashSet<N>();
```

```
      // (5) Push start vertex on the stack:
      traversalStack.push(startVertex);
      // (6) Handle each vertex found on the stack:
      while (!traversalStack.isEmpty()) {
        N currentVertex = traversalStack.pop();
        // (7) Check if current vertex has been visited.
        if (!visitedSet.contains(currentVertex)) {
          // (8) Add the current vertex to the visited set.
          visitedSet.add(currentVertex);
           // (9) Push neighbors of current vertex on to the stack.
          Collection<N> neighbors = graph.get(currentVertex);
          for (N neighbor : neighbors)
              traversalStack.push(neighbor);
        }
      }
      visitedSet.remove(startVertex);
      return visitedSet;
    }
}
```

15   Collections and Maps

15.1

```
import java.util.HashMap;
import java.util.Map;
import java.util.Set;
import java.util.TreeSet;

public class UniqueCharacterCounter {
  /**
   * A cache, mapping strings to number of unique characters in them.
   */
  static Map<String, Integer> globalCache = new HashMap<String, Integer>();

  public static int countUniqueCharacters(String aString) {
    Integer cachedResult = globalCache.get(aString);
    if (cachedResult != null)
      return cachedResult;
    // Result was not in the cache, calculate it.
    int length = aString.length();
    Set<Character> distinct = new TreeSet<Character>();
    Set<Character> duplicates = new TreeSet<Character>();
    // Determine whether each distinct character in the string is duplicated:
    for (int i = 0; i < length; i++) {
      Character character = aString.charAt(i);
      if (duplicates.contains(character))
        continue;
      boolean isDistinct = distinct.add(character);
      if (!isDistinct)
        duplicates.add(character);
    }
```

```
      // Remove duplicates from the distinct set to obtain unique characters:
      distinct.removeAll(duplicates);
      int result = distinct.size();
      // Put result in cache before returning:
      globalCache.put(aString, result);
      return result;
    }

    /**
     * Demonstrate the cache for mapping strings to number of unique characters
     * in them.
     * Prints the result of applying the operation to each command line argument.
     */
    public static void main(String[] args) {
      int nArgs = args.length;
      for (int i = 0; i < nArgs; i++) {
        String argument = args[i];
        int result = countUniqueCharacters(argument);
        System.out.println(argument + ": " + result);
      }
    }
  }
```

15.2

```
import java.util.ArrayList;
import java.util.HashMap;
import java.util.List;
import java.util.Map;

public class Concordance {

  /** Map for the concordance. */
  public Map<Character, List<Integer>> indexMap =
      new HashMap<Character, List<Integer>>();

  /** Add each character and its index to the concordance */
  public Concordance(StringBuilder input) {
    for (int i = 0; i < input.length(); ++i) {
      addEntry(input.charAt(i), i);
    }
  }

  /** Update the list of indices for a given character */
  void addEntry(char key, int pos) {
    List<Integer> hits = indexMap.get(key);
    if (hits == null) {
      hits = new ArrayList<Integer>();
      indexMap.put(key, hits);
    }
    hits.add(pos);
  }
```

```java
        public static void main(String[] args) {
          StringBuilder input = new StringBuilder();
          for (int i = 0; i < args.length; ++i)
            input.append(args[i]);
          Concordance conc = new Concordance(input);
          System.out.println(conc.indexMap);
        }
      }
```

Mock Exam

●●●

This is a mock exam for Sun Certified Programmer for the Java Platform Standard Edition 6 (SCJP 1.6). It comprises brand new questions, which are similar to the questions that can be expected on the real exam. Working through this exam will give the reader a good indication of how well she is prepared for the real exam, and whether any topics need further study.

Questions

Q1 Given the following class, which statements can be inserted at (1) without causing a compilation error?

```
public class Q6db8 {
  int a;
  int b = 0;
  static int c;

  public void m() {
    int d;
    int e = 0;

    // (1) INSERT CODE HERE.
  }
}
```

Select the four correct answers.

(a) a++;
(b) b++;
(c) c++;
(d) d++;
(e) e++;

Q2 What is wrong with the following code?

```
class MyException extends Exception {}

public class Qb4ab {
  public void foo() {
    try {
```

```
      bar();
    } finally {
      baz();
    } catch (MyException e) {}
  }

  public void bar() throws MyException {
    throw new MyException();
  }

  public void baz() throws RuntimeException {
    throw new RuntimeException();
  }
}
```

Select the one correct answer.

(a) Since the method foo() does not catch the exception generated by the method baz(), it must declare the RuntimeException in a throws clause.

(b) A try block cannot be followed by both a catch and a finally block.

(c) An empty catch block is not allowed.

(d) A catch block cannot follow a finally block.

(e) A finally block must always follow one or more catch blocks.

Q3 What will be written to the standard output when the following program is run?

```
public class Qd803 {
  public static void main(String[] args) {
    String word = "restructure";
    System.out.println(word.substring(2, 3));
  }
}
```

Select the one correct answer.

(a) est
(b) es
(c) str
(d) st
(e) s

Q4 Given that a static method doIt() in the class Work represents work to be done, which block of code will succeed in starting a new thread that will do the work?

Select the one correct answer.

(a)
```
Runnable r = new Runnable() {
    public void run() {
      Work.doIt();
    }
};
Thread t = new Thread(r);
t.start();
```

(b)
```
Thread t = new Thread() {
    public void start() {
      Work.doIt();
    }
};
t.start();
```

```
(c) Runnable r = new Runnable() {
        public void run() {
          Work.doIt();
        }
    };
    r.start();
(d) Thread t = new Thread(new Work());
    t.start();
(e) Runnable t = new Runnable() {
        public void run() {
          Work.doIt();
        }
    };
    t.run();
```

Q5 Which import statements, when inserted at (4) in package p3, will result in a program that can be compiled and run?

```
package p2;
enum March {LEFT, RIGHT;                          // (1)
  public String toString() {
    return "Top-level enum";
  }
}
public class DefenceInDepth {
  public enum March {LEFT, RIGHT;                 // (2)
    public String toString() {
      return "Static enum";
    }
  }
  public enum Military { INFANTRY, AIRFORCE;
    public static enum March {LEFT, RIGHT;        // (3)
      public String toString() {
        return "Statically nested enum";
      }
    }
  }
}
```

```
package p3;
// (4) INSERT IMPORTS HERE
public class MarchingOrders {
  public static void main(String[] args) {
    System.out.println(March.LEFT);
    System.out.println(DefenceInDepth.March.LEFT);
    System.out.println(p2.DefenceInDepth.March.LEFT);
    System.out.println(Military.March.LEFT);
    System.out.println(DefenceInDepth.Military.March.LEFT);
    System.out.println(p2.DefenceInDepth.Military.March.LEFT);
    System.out.println(LEFT);
  }
}
```

Select the three correct answers.

(a) ```
import p2.*;
import p2.DefenceInDepth.*;
import static p2.DefenceInDepth.Military.March.LEFT;
```

(b) ```
import p2.*;
import static p2.DefenceInDepth.*;
import static p2.DefenceInDepth.Military.March.LEFT;
```

(c) ```
import p2.DefenceInDepth;
import static p2.DefenceInDepth.*;
import static p2.DefenceInDepth.Military.March.LEFT;
```

(d) ```
import static p2.DefenceInDepth;
import static p2.DefenceInDepth.*;
import static p2.DefenceInDepth.Military.March.LEFT;
```

(e) ```
import p2.*;
import static p2.DefenceInDepth.*;
import static p2.DefenceInDepth.Military.*;
```

(f) ```
import p2.*;
import static p2.DefenceInDepth.*;
import static p2.DefenceInDepth.Military.March;
```

Q6 What will be printed when the following program is run?

```
public class Q8929 {
  public static void main(String[] args) {
    for (int i = 12; i > 0; i -= 3)
      System.out.print(i);
      System.out.println("");
  }
}
```

Select the one correct answer.

(a) 12
(b) 129630
(c) 12963
(d) 36912
(e) None of the above.

Q7 What will be the result of compiling and running the following program?

```
public class Q275d {
  static int a;
  int b;

  public Q275d() {
    int c;
    c = a;
    a++;
    b += c;
  }

  public static void main(String[] args) {
    new Q275d();
  }
}
```

Select the one correct answer.

(a) The code will fail to compile, since the constructor is trying to access the static members.

(b) The code will fail to compile, since the constructor is trying to use the static field a before it has been initialized.

(c) The code will fail to compile, since the constructor is trying to use the field b before it has been initialized.

(d) The code will fail to compile, since the constructor is trying to use the local variable c before it has been initialized.

(e) The code will compile and run without any problems.

Q8 Which statement is true about the compilation and execution of the following program with assertions enabled?

```
public class Qf1e3 {
  String s1;
  String s2 = "hello";
  String s3;

  Qf1e3() {
    s1 = "hello";
  }

  public static void main(String[] args) {
    (new Qf1e3()).f();
  }

  {
    s3 = "hello";
  }

  void f() {
    String s4 = "hello";
    String s5 = new String("hello");
    assert(s1.equals(s2)); // (1)
    assert(s2.equals(s3)); // (2)
    assert(s3 == s4);      // (3)
    assert(s4 == s5);      // (4)
  }
}
```

Select the one correct answer.

(a) The compilation will fail.

(b) The assertion on the line marked (1) will fail.

(c) The assertion on the line marked (2) will fail.

(d) The assertion on the line marked (3) will fail.

(e) The assertion on the line marked (4) will fail.

(f) The program will run without any errors.

Q9   Under which circumstance will a thread stop?

Select the one correct answer.

(a) The run() method that the thread is executing ends.
(b) When the call to the start() method of the Thread object returns.
(c) The suspend() method is called on the Thread object.
(d) The wait() method is called on the Thread object.

Q10   Which statements are true about the following program?

```
public class Q100_82 {
  public static void main(String[] args) {
    Object o = choose(991, "800");                        // (1)
    Number n1 = choose(991, 3.14);                        // (2)
    Number n2 = Q100_82.<Double>choose((double)991, 3.14); // (3)
    int k = (int) choose(1.3, 3.14);                      // (4)
    int l = (int) (double) choose(1.3, 3.14);            // (5)
  }

  public static <T extends Comparable<T>> T choose(T t1, T t2) {
    return t1.compareTo(t2) >= 0 ? t1 : t2;
  }
}
```

Select the two correct answers.

(a) The class must be declared as a generic type:

```
public class Q100_82<T extends Comparable<T>> { ... }
```

(b) The compiler reports errors in (1).
(c) The compiler reports no errors in (2).
(d) The compiler reports no errors in (3).
(e) The compiler reports no errors in (4).
(f) The compiler reports errors in (5).

Q11   What will be written to the standard output when the following program is run?

```
class Base {
  int i;
  Base() { add(1); }
  void add(int v) { i += v; }
  void print() { System.out.println(i); }
}

class Extension extends Base {
  Extension() { add(2); }
  void add(int v) { i += v*2; }
}

public class Qd073 {
  public static void main(String[] args) {
    bogo(new Extension());
  }

  static void bogo(Base b) {
    b.add(8);
    b.print();
  }
}
```

Select the one correct answer.

(a) 9
(b) 18
(c) 20
(d) 21
(e) 22

Q12   Which collection implementation is suitable for maintaining an ordered sequence
      of objects, when objects are frequently inserted in and removed from the middle of
      the sequence?

Select the one correct answer.

(a) TreeMap
(b) HashSet
(c) Vector
(d) LinkedList
(e) ArrayList

Q13   Which statements, when inserted at (1), will make the program print 1 on the
      standard output when executed?

```
public class Q4a39 {
  int a = 1;
  int b = 1;
  int c = 1;

  class Inner {
    int a = 2;

    int get() {
      int c = 3;
      // (1) INSERT CODE HERE.
      return c;
    }
  }

  Q4a39() {
    Inner i = new Inner();
    System.out.println(i.get());
  }

  public static void main(String[] args) {
    new Q4a39();
  }
}
```

Select the two correct answers.

(a) c = b;
(b) c = this.a;
(c) c = this.b;
(d) c = Q4a39.this.a;
(e) c = c;

Q14 Given the following code:

```
import java.io.*;
public class Q800_110 {

    public static void main(String[] args)
    throws IOException, ClassNotFoundException {
        String[] dirNames = {
            "." + File.separator + "dir1",
            "." + File.separator + "dir2",
            "." + File.separator + "dir1" + File.separator + "dir2"
        };
        for(String dir : dirNames) {
            File file = new File(dir, "myFile.txt");
            System.out.print(/* INSERT EXPRESSION HERE */);  // (1)
        }
    }
}
```

Assume that each directory named in the array dirNames has a file named "myFile.txt".

Which expressions, when inserted at (1), will result in the output "truetruetrue"?

Select the three correct answers.

(a) file.found()

(b) file.isFile()

(c) !file.isDirectory()

(d) file.exists()

(e) file.isAFile()

(f) !file.isADirectory()

Q15 Which is the first line in the following code after which the object created in the line marked (0) will be a candidate for garbage collection, assuming no compiler optimizations are done?

```
public class Q76a9 {
    static String f() {
        String a = "hello";
        String b = "bye";          // (0)
        String c = b + "!";        // (1)
        String d = b;              // (2)

        b = a;                     // (3)
        d = a;                     // (4)
        return c;                  // (5)
    }

    public static void main(String[] args) {
        String msg = f();
        System.out.println(msg);   // (6)
    }
}
```

Select the one correct answer.

(a) The line marked (1).
(b) The line marked (2).
(c) The line marked (3).
(d) The line marked (4).
(e) The line marked (5).
(f) The line marked (6).

Q16 Which string, when inserted at (1), will not result in the same output as the other three strings?

```java
import java.util.regex.Pattern;
import java.util.regex.Matcher;
public class Q500_50 {
  public static void main(String[] args) {
    String index  = "0123456789012345678";
    String target = "JAVA JaVa java jaVA";
    Pattern pattern = Pattern.compile(_____);  // (1)
    Matcher matcher = pattern.matcher(target);
    while(matcher.find()) {
      int startIndex = matcher.start();
      int endIndex = matcher.end();
      int lastIndex = startIndex == endIndex ? endIndex : endIndex-1;
      String matchedStr = matcher.group();
      System.out.print("(" + startIndex + "," + lastIndex + ":" +
                       matchedStr + ")");
    }
    System.out.println();
  }
}
```

Select the one correct answer.

(a) "[A-Za-z]+"
(b) "[a-zA-Z]+"
(c) "[A-Z]+[a-z]+"
(d) "[A-Z[a-z]]+"

Q17 Which method from the String or StringBuilder classes modifies the object on which it is invoked?

Select the one correct answer.

(a) The charAt() method of the String class.
(b) The toUpperCase() method of the String class.
(c) The replace() method of the String class.
(d) The reverse() method of the StringBuilder class.
(e) The length() method of the StringBuilder class.

Q18 Which statements are true, given the code new FileOutputStream("data", true) for creating an object of class FileOutputStream?

Select the two correct answers.

(a) `FileOutputStream` has no constructors matching the given arguments.
(b) An `IOException` will be thrown if a file named "data" already exists.
(c) An `IOException` will be thrown if a file named "data" does not already exist.
(d) If a file named "data" exists, its contents will be reset and overwritten.
(e) If a file named "data" exists, output will be appended to its current contents.

Q19 Which statement, when inserted at (1), will raise a runtime exception?

```
class A {}

class B extends A {}

class C extends A {}

public class Q3ae4 {
  public static void main(String[] args) {
    A x = new A();
    B y = new B();
    C z = new C();

    // (1) INSERT CODE HERE.

  }
}
```

Select the one correct answer.

(a) `x = y;`
(b) `z = x;`
(c) `y = (B) x;`
(d) `z = (C) y;`
(e) `y = (A) y;`

Q20 Given the following program:

```
public class Q400_60 {
  public static void main(String[] args) {
    String str = "loop or not to loop";
    String[] strs = {"loop", "or", "not", "to", "loop"};
    // (1) INSERT LOOP HERE.
  }
}
```

Which code, when inserted at (1), will compile without errors?

Select the four correct answers.

(a) `for (char ch : str)`
       `System.out.print(ch);`
(b) `for (char ch : str.toCharArray())`
       `System.out.print(ch);`
(c) `for (Character ch : str.toCharArray())`
       `System.out.print(ch);`
(d) `for (Character ch : str.toCharArray())`
       `System.out.print(ch.charValue());`

(e) for (String str : strs)
     System.out.print(str);
(f) for (String elt : strs[])
     System.out.print(elt);
(g) for (String elt : strs)
     System.out.print(elt);
(h) for (Character ch : strs[str.length-1].toArray())
     System.out.print(ch);

Q21 A method within a class is only accessible by classes that are defined within the same package as the class of the method. How can such a restriction be enforced?

Select the one correct answer.

(a) Declare the method with the keyword public.
(b) Declare the method with the keyword protected.
(c) Declare the method with the keyword private.
(d) Declare the method with the keyword package.
(e) Do not declare the method with any accessibility modifiers.

Q22 Which code initializes the two-dimensional array matrix so that matrix[3][2] is a valid element?

Select the two correct answers.

```
(a)  int[][] matrix = {
         { 0, 0, 0 },
         { 0, 0, 0 }
     };
(b)  int matrix[][] = new int[4][];
     for (int i = 0; i < matrix.length; i++) matrix[i] = new int[3];
(c)  int matrix[][] = {
         0, 0, 0, 0,
         0, 0, 0, 0,
         0, 0, 0, 0,
         0, 0, 0, 0
     };
(d)  int matrix[3][2];
(e)  int[] matrix[] = { {0, 0, 0}, {0, 0, 0}, {0, 0, 0}, {0, 0, 0} };
```

Q23 Given the following directory structure:

```
/proj
  |--- lib
  |      |--- supercharge.jar
  |
  |--- src
         |--- top
                |--- sub
                       |--- A.java
```

Assume that the current directory is /proj/src, and that the class A declared in the file A.java uses reference types from the JAR file supercharge.jar.

Which commands will succeed without compile-time errors?

Select the two correct answers.

(a) javac -cp ../lib top/sub/A.java
(b) javac -cp ../lib/supercharge top/sub/A.java
(c) javac -cp ../lib/supercharge.jar top/sub/A.java
(d) javac -cp /proj/lib/supercharge.jar top/sub/A.java
(e) javac -cp /proj/lib top/sub/A.java

Q24   What will be the result of attempting to run the following program?

```
public class Qaa75 {
  public static void main(String[] args) {
    String[][][] arr = {
        { {}, null },
        { { "1", "2" }, { "1", null, "3" } },
        {},
        { { "1", null } }
    };

    System.out.println(arr.length + arr[1][2].length);
  }
}
```

Select the one correct answer.

(a) The program will terminate with an ArrayIndexOutOfBoundsException.
(b) The program will terminate with a NullPointerException.
(c) 4 will be written to standard output.
(d) 6 will be written to standard output.
(e) 7 will be written to standard output.

Q25   Which expressions will evaluate to true if preceded by the following code?

```
String a = "hello";
String b = new String(a);
String c = a;
char[] d = { 'h', 'e', 'l', 'l', 'o' };
```

Select the two correct answers.

(a) (a == "Hello")
(b) (a == b)
(c) (a == c)
(d) a.equals(b)
(e) a.equals(d)

Q26   Which statements are true about the following code?

```
class A {
  public A() {}

  public A(int i) { this(); }
}
class B extends A {
  public boolean B(String msg) { return false; }
}
class C extends B {
  private C() { super(); }

  public C(String msg) { this(); }

  public C(int i) {}
}
```

Select the two correct answers.

(a) The code will fail to compile.
(b) The constructor in A that takes an int as an argument will never be called as a result of constructing an object of class B or C.
(c) Class C defines three constructors.
(d) Objects of class B cannot be constructed.
(e) At most one of the constructors of each class is called as a result of constructing an object of class C.

Q27   Given two collection objects referenced by col1 and col2, which statements are true?

Select the two correct answers.

(a) The operation col1.retainAll(col2) will not modify the col1 object.
(b) The operation col1.removeAll(col2) will not modify the col2 object.
(c) The operation col1.addAll(col2) will return a new collection object, containing elements from both col1 and col2.
(d) The operation col1.containsAll(Col2) will not modify the col1 object.

Q28   Which statements are true about the relationships between the following classes?

```
class Foo {
  int num;
  Baz comp = new Baz();
}
class Bar {
  boolean flag;
}
class Baz extends Foo {
  Bar thing = new Bar();
  double limit;
}
```

Select the three correct answers.

(a) A Bar is a Baz.
(b) A Foo has a Bar.
(c) A Baz is a Foo.
(d) A Foo is a Baz.
(e) A Baz has a Bar.

Q29 Which statements are true about the value of a field, when no explicit assignments have been made?

Select the two correct answers.

(a) The value of a field of type `int` is undetermined.
(b) The value of a field of any numeric type is zero.
(c) The compiler may issue an error if the field is used in a method before it is initialized.
(d) A field of type `String` will denote the empty string ("").
(e) The value of all fields which are references is `null`.

Q30 Which statement is not true about the following two statements?

```
FileInputStream inputFile = new FileInputStream("myfile");     // (1)
FileOutputStream outputFile = new FileOutputStream("myfile");   // (2)
```

Select the one correct answer.

(a) Statement (1) throws a `FileNotFoundException` if the file cannot be found, or is a directory or cannot be opened for some reason.
(b) Statement (1) throws an `IOException` if the file cannot be found, or is a directory or cannot be opened for some reason.
(c) Statement (2) throws a `FileNotFoundException` if the file is a directory or cannot be opened for some reason.
(d) Statement (2) throws an `IOException` if the file is a directory or cannot be opened for some reason.
(e) Statement (2) creates a new file if one does not exist and appropriate permissions are granted.
(f) If the file opened by statement (2) already exists, its contents will be overwritten.

Q31 Which statements describe guaranteed behavior of the garbage collection and finalization mechanisms?

Select the two correct answers.

(a) An object is deleted as soon as there are no more references that denote the object.
(b) The `finalize()` method will eventually be called on every object.
(c) The `finalize()` method will never be called more than once on an object.
(d) An object will not be garbage collected as long as it is possible for a live thread to access it through a reference.
(e) The garbage collector will use a mark and sweep algorithm.

Q32   Which `main()` method will succeed in printing the last program argument to the standard output and exit gracefully with no output if no program arguments are specified?

Select the one correct answer.

(a)
```java
public static void main(String[] args) {
    if (args.length != 0)
        System.out.println(args[args.length-1]);
}
```
(b)
```java
public static void main(String[] args) {
    try { System.out.println(args[args.length]); }
    catch (ArrayIndexOutOfBoundsException e) {}
}
```
(c)
```java
public static void main(String[] args) {
    int ix = args.length;
    String last = args[ix];
    if (ix != 0) System.out.println(last);
}
```
(d)
```java
public static void main(String[] args) {
    int ix = args.length-1;
    if (ix > 0) System.out.println(args[ix]);
}
```
(e)
```java
public static void main(String[] args) {
    try { System.out.println(args[args.length-1]); }
    catch (NullPointerException e) {}
}
```

Q33   Which statements are true about the interfaces in the Java Collections Framework?

Select the three correct answers.

(a) Set extends Collection.
(b) All methods defined in Set are also defined in Collection.
(c) List extends Collection.
(d) All methods defined in List are also defined in Collection.
(e) Map extends Collection.

Q34   What will be the result of compiling and running the following code?
```java
public enum FrequentFlyer {
  PLATINUM(20), GOLD(10), SILVER(5), BASIC(0);
  private double extra;

  FrequentFlyer(double extra) {
    this.extra = extra;
  }

  public static void main (String[] args) {
    System.out.println(GOLD.ordinal() > SILVER.ordinal());
    System.out.println(max(GOLD,SILVER));
```

```
    System.out.println(max2(GOLD,SILVER));
}

public static FrequentFlyer max(FrequentFlyer c1, FrequentFlyer c2) {
    FrequentFlyer maxFlyer = c1;
    if (c1.compareTo(c2) < 0)
        maxFlyer = c2;
    return maxFlyer;
}

public static FrequentFlyer max2(FrequentFlyer c1, FrequentFlyer c2) {
    FrequentFlyer maxFlyer = c1;
    if (c1.extra < c2.extra)
        maxFlyer = c2;
    return maxFlyer;
}
}
```

Select the one correct answer.

(a) The program will compile and print:

```
false
SILVER
GOLD
```

(b) The program will compile and print:

```
true
GOLD
SILVER
```

(c) The program will compile and print:

```
true
GOLD
GOLD
```

(d) The program will not compile, since the enum type FrequentFlyer does not implement the Comparable interface.

Q35 Given the following class declarations, which expression identifies whether the object referenced by obj was created by instantiating class B rather than classes A, C, and D?

```
class A {}
class B extends A {}
class C extends B {}
class D extends A {}
```

Select the one correct answer.

(a) obj instanceof B
(b) obj instanceof A && !(obj instanceof C)
(c) obj instanceof B && !(obj instanceof C)
(d) !(obj instanceof C || obj instanceof D)
(e) !(obj instanceof A) && !(obj instanceof C) && !(obj instanceof D)

Q36 What will be written to the standard output when the following program is executed?

```java
public class Qcb90 {
  int a;
  int b;
  public void f() {
    a = 0;
    b = 0;
    int[] c = { 0 };
    g(b, c);
    System.out.println(a + " " + b + " " + c[0] + " ");
  }

  public void g(int b, int[] c) {
    a = 1;
    b = 1;
    c[0] = 1;
  }

  public static void main(String[] args) {
    Qcb90 obj = new Qcb90();

    obj.f();
  }
}
```

Select the one correct answer.

(a) 0 0 0
(b) 0 0 1
(c) 0 1 0
(d) 1 0 0
(e) 1 0 1

Q37 Given the following class, which statements are correct implementations of the hashCode() method?

```java
class ValuePair {
  public int a, b;
  public boolean equals(Object other) {
    try {
      ValuePair o = (ValuePair) other;
      return (a == o.a && b == o.b)
          || (a == o.b && b == o.a);
    } catch (ClassCastException cce) {
      return false;
    }
  }
  public int hashCode() {
    // (1) INSERT CODE HERE.
  }
}
```

Select the three correct answers.

(a) `return 0;`
(b) `return a;`
(c) `return a + b;`
(d) `return a - b;`
(e) `return a ^ b;`

Q38 Given the following code:

```
class Interval<_____> { // (1) INSERT TYPE CONSTRAINT HERE
  private N lower, upper;
  public void update(N value) {
    if (lower == null || value.compareTo(lower) < 0)
      lower = value;
    if (upper == null || value.compareTo(upper) > 0)
      upper = value;
  }
}
```

Which type constraints, when inserted at (1), will allow the class to compile?

Select the four correct answers.

(a) `N extends Object`
(b) `N extends Comparable<N>`
(c) `N extends Object & Comparable<N>`
(d) `N extends Number`
(e) `N extends Number & Comparable<N>`
(f) `N extends Comparable<N> & Number`
(g) `N extends Integer`
(h) `N extends Integer & Comparable<N>`

Q39 Which statements are true regarding the execution of the following code?

```
public class Q3a0a {
  public static void main(String[] args) {
    int j = 5;

    for (int i = 0; i< j; i++) {
      assert i < j-- : i > 0;
      System.out.println(i * j);
    }
  }
}
```

Select the two correct answers.

(a) An `AssertionError` will be thrown if assertions are enabled at runtime.
(b) The last number printed is 4, if assertions are disabled at runtime.
(c) The last number printed is 20, if assertions are disabled at runtime.
(d) The last number printed is 4, if assertions are enabled at runtime.
(e) The last number printed is 20, if assertions are enabled at runtime.

Q40   Which of the following method names are overloaded?

Select the three correct answers.

(a) The method name yield in java.lang.Thread
(b) The method name sleep in java.lang.Thread
(c) The method name wait in java.lang.Object
(d) The method name notify in java.lang.Object

Q41   What will be the result of attempting to compile and run the following program?

```java
public class Q28fd {
  public static void main(String[] args) {
    int counter = 0;
    l1:
    for (int i=0; i<10; i++) {
      l2:
      int j = 0;
      while (j++ < 10) {
        if (j > i) break l2;
        if (j == i) {
          counter++;
          continue l1;
        }
      }
    }
    System.out.println(counter);
  }
}
```

Select the one correct answer.

(a) The program will fail to compile.
(b) The program will not terminate normally.
(c) The program will write 10 to the standard output.
(d) The program will write 0 to the standard output.
(e) The program will write 9 to the standard output.

Q42   Given the following interface declaration, which declaration is valid?

```java
interface I {
  void setValue(int val);
  int getValue();
}
```

Select the one correct answer.

(a) ```java
class A extends I {
    int value;
    void setValue(int val) { value = val; }
    int getValue() { return value; }
}
```
(b) ```java
interface B extends I {
    void increment();
}
```

```
(c) abstract class C implements I {
        int getValue() { return 0; }
        abstract void increment();
    }
(d) interface D implements I {
        void increment();
    }
(e) class E implements I {
        int value;
        public void setValue(int val) { value = val; }
    }
```

Q43 Which statements are true about the methods notify() and notifyAll()?

Select the two correct answers.

(a) An instance of the class Thread has a method named notify that can be invoked.

(b) A call to the method notify() will wake the thread that currently owns the lock of the object.

(c) The method notify() is synchronized.

(d) The method notifyAll() is defined in the class Thread.

(e) When there is more than one thread waiting to obtain the lock of an object, there is no way to be sure which thread will be notified by the notify() method.

Q44 Which statements are true about the correlation between the inner and outer instances of member classes?

Select the two correct answers.

(a) Fields of the outer instance are always accessible to inner instances, regardless of their accessibility modifiers.

(b) Fields of the outer instance can never be accessed using only the variable name within the inner instance.

(c) More than one inner instance can be associated with the same outer instance.

(d) All variables from the outer instance that should be accessible in the inner instance must be declared final.

(e) A class that is declared final cannot have any member classes.

Q45 What will be the result of attempting to compile and run the following code?

```
public class Q6b0c {
    public static void main(String[] args) {
        int i = 4;
        float f = 4.3;
        double d = 1.8;
        int c = 0;
        if (i == f) c++;
        if (((int) (f + d)) == ((int) f + (int) d)) c += 2;
        System.out.println(c);
    }
}
```

Select the one correct answer.

(a) The code will fail to compile.
(b) The value 0 will be written to the standard output.
(c) The value 1 will be written to the standard output.
(d) The value 2 will be written to the standard output.
(e) The value 3 will be written to the standard output.

Q46   Which operators will always evaluate all the operands?

Select the two correct answers.

(a) ||
(b) +
(c) &&
(d) ? :
(e) %

Q47   Which statement concerning the switch construct is true?

Select the one correct answer.

(a) All switch statements must have a default label.
(b) There must be exactly one label for each code segment in a switch statement.
(c) The keyword continue can never occur within the body of a switch statement.
(d) No case label may follow a default label within a single switch statement.
(e) A character literal can be used as a value for a case label.

Q48   Given the following code:

```
public class Q600_90 {
  public static void main(String[] args) {
    Scanner lexer = new Scanner("Treat!");
    if(lexer.hasNext("\\w+")) {
      // (1)
    } else
      lexer.next();
    // (2)
    lexer.close();
    // (3)
  }
}
```

Where in the program can we independently insert the following print statement:

`System.out.print(lexer.next());`

in order for the program to compile and print the following output when run:

`Treat!`

Select the one correct answer.

(a) Insert the print statement at (1) only.
(b) Insert the print statement at (2) only.
(c) Insert the print statement at (3) only.
(d) None of the above.

Q49   Which of the following expressions are valid?

Select the three correct answers.

(a) `System.out.hashCode()`
(b) `"".hashCode()`
(c) `42.hashCode()`
(d) `("4"+2).equals(42)`
(e) `(new java.util.ArrayList<String>()).hashCode()`

Q50   Which statement regarding the following method definition is true?

```
boolean e() {
  try {
    assert false;
  } catch (AssertionError ae) {
    return true;
  }
  return false;      // (1)
}
```

Select the one correct answer.

(a) The code will fail to compile, since catching an `AssertionError` is illegal.
(b) The code will fail to compile, since the `return` statement at (1) is unreachable.
(c) The method will return `true`, regardless of whether assertions are enabled at runtime or not.
(d) The method will return `false`, regardless of whether assertions are enabled at runtime or not.
(e) The method will return `true` if and only if assertions are enabled at runtime.

Q51   Which statement, when inserted at (1), will call the `print()` method in the `Base` class.

```
class Base {
  public void print() {
    System.out.println("base");
  }
}

class Extension extends Base {
  public void print() {
    System.out.println("extension");

    // (1) INSERT CODE HERE.
  }
}

public class Q294d {
  public static void main(String[] args) {
    Extension ext = new Extension();
    ext.print();
  }
}
```

Select the one correct answer.

(a) `Base.print();`
(b) `Base.this.print();`
(c) `print();`
(d) `super.print();`
(e) `this.print();`

Q52 Which statements are true about the following code?

```java
public class Vertical {
  private int alt;
  public synchronized void up() {
    ++alt;
  }
  public void down() {
    --alt;
  }
  public synchronized void jump() {
    int a = alt;
    up();
    down();
    assert(a == alt);
  }
}
```

Select the two correct answers.

(a) The code will fail to compile.
(b) Separate threads can execute the up() method concurrently.
(c) Separate threads can execute the down() method concurrently.
(d) Separate threads can execute both the up() and the down() methods concurrently.
(e) The assertion in the jump() method will not fail under any circumstances.

Q53 Which parameter declarations can be inserted at (1) so that the program compiles without warnings?

```java
interface Wagger{}
class Pet implements Wagger{}
class Dog extends Pet {}
class Cat extends Pet {}

public class Q100_51 {
  public static void main(String[] args) {
    List<Pet> p = new ArrayList<Pet>();
    List<Dog> d = new ArrayList<Dog>();
    List<Cat> c = new ArrayList<Cat>();
    examine(p);
    examine(d);
    examine(c);
  }

  static void examine(_____ pets) {           // (1)
    System.out.print("Your pets need urgent attention.");
  }
}
```

Select the three correct answers.

(a) `List<? extends Pet>`
(b) `List<? super Pet>`
(c) `List<? extends Wagger>`
(d) `List<? super Wagger>`
(e) `List<?>`
(f) All of the above

Q54 What will be written to the standard output when the following program is run?

```
public class Q03e4 {
  public static void main(String[] args) {
    String space = " ";

    String composite = space + "hello" + space + space;
    composite.concat("world");

    String trimmed = composite.trim();

    System.out.println(trimmed.length());
  }
}
```

Select the one correct answer.

(a) 5
(b) 6
(c) 7
(d) 12
(e) 13

Q55 Given the following code, which statements are true about the objects referenced
     by the fields i, j, and k, given that any thread may call the methods a(), b(), and
     c() at any time?

```
class Counter {
  int v = 0;
  synchronized void inc() { v++; }
  synchronized void dec() { v--; }
}
public class Q7ed5 {
  Counter i;
  Counter j;
  Counter k;
  public synchronized void a() {
    i.inc();
    System.out.println("a");
    i.dec();
  }

  public synchronized void b() {
    i.inc(); j.inc(); k.inc();
    System.out.println("b");
    i.dec(); j.dec(); k.dec();
  }
```

```
        public void c() {
          k.inc();
          System.out.println("c");
          k.dec();
        }
      }
```

Select the two correct answers.

(a) i.v is always guaranteed to be 0 or 1.
(b) j.v is always guaranteed to be 0 or 1.
(c) k.v is always guaranteed to be 0 or 1
(d) j.v will always be greater than or equal to k.v at any given time.
(e) k.v will always be greater than or equal to j.v at any given time.

Q56   Which method declarations, when inserted at (1), will not cause the program to fail during compilation?

```
      public class Qdd1f {
        public long sum(long a, long b) { return a + b; }

        // (1) INSERT CODE HERE.

      }
```

Select the two correct answers.

(a) `public int sum(int a, int b) { return a + b; }`
(b) `public int sum(long a, long b) { return 0; }`
(c) `abstract int sum();`
(d) `private long sum(long a, long b) { return a + b; }`
(e) `public long sum(long a, int b) { return a + b; }`

Q57   What will be the result of executing the following program code with assertions enabled?

```
      import java.util.LinkedList;

      public class Q4d3f {
        public static void main(String[] args) {
          LinkedList<String> lla = new LinkedList<String>();
          LinkedList<String> llb = new LinkedList<String>();
          assert lla.size() == llb.size() : "empty";

          lla.add("Hello");
          assert lla.size() == 1 : "size";

          llb.add("Hello");
          assert llb.contains("Hello") : "contains";
          assert lla.get(0).equals(llb.get(0)) : "element";
          assert lla.equals(llb) : "collection";
        }
      }
```

Select the one correct answer.

(a) Execution proceeds normally and produces no output.
(b) An AssertionError with the message "size" is thrown.
(c) An AssertionError with the message "empty" is thrown.
(d) An AssertionError with the message "element" is thrown
(e) An IndexOutOfBoundsException is thrown.
(f) An AssertionError with the message "container" is thrown.

Q58   What will be the result of compiling and running the following code?

```java
public enum FrequentFlyerClass {
  PLATINUM(20), GOLD(10), SILVER(5), BASIC;
  private double extra;
  FrequentFlyerClass(double extra) {
    this.extra = extra;
  }

  public boolean equals(Object other) {
    if (this == other)
      return true;
    if (!(other instanceof FrequentFlyerClass))
      return false;
    return Math.abs(this.extra - ((FrequentFlyerClass) other).extra) < 0.1e-5;
  }

  public static void main (String[] args) {
    GOLD = SILVER;
    System.out.println(GOLD);
    System.out.println(GOLD.equals(SILVER));
  }
}
```

Select the one correct answer.

(a) The program will compile and print:
    GOLD
    false
(b) The program will compile and print:
    SILVER
    true
(c) The program will not compile, because of 3 errors in the program.
(d) The program will not compile, because of 2 errors in the program.
(e) The program will not compile, because of 1 error in the program.

Q59   Which constraint can be inserted at (1) so that the program compiles without warnings?

```java
class NumClass <_____> { // (1)
  T numVal;
}

public class Q100_54 {
  public static void main(String[] args) {
```

```
    NumClass<Number> n1 = new NumClass<Number>();
    NumClass<Integer> n2 = new NumClass<Integer>();
  }
}
```

Select the one correct answer.

(a) `T extends Integer`
(b) `T extends Number`
(c) `? extends Number`
(d) `T super Number`
(e) `T super Integer`
(f) `? super Integer`
(g) None of the above

Q60   What will be the result of compiling and running the following program?

```
public class Varargs {
  public static <E> void print(E e, E...src) {
    System.out.print("|");
    for (E elt : src) {
      System.out.print(elt + "|");
    }
    System.out.println();
  }

  public static void main(String[] args) {
    String[] sa = {"9", "6"};
    print("9", "6");              // (1)
    print(sa);                    // (2)
    print(sa, sa);                // (4)
    print(sa, sa, sa);            // (5)
    print(sa, "9", "6");          // (6)
  }
}
```

Select the one correct answer.

(a) The program does not compile because of errors in one or more calls to the print() method.
(b) The program compiles, but throws a NullPointerException when run.
(c) The program compiles, and prints (where XXXXXX is some hash code for the String class):

    ```
    |9|6|
    |6|
    |
    |[Ljava.lang.String;@XXXXXXX|[Ljava.lang.String;@XXXXXXX|
    |9|6|
    ```

(d) The program compiles, and prints (where XXXXXX is some hash code for the String class):

    ```
    |6|
    |
    |9|6|
    |[Ljava.lang.String;@XXXXXXX|[Ljava.lang.String;@XXXXXXX|
    |9|6|
    ```

Q61   Given the following code:

```
package p1;
public enum Constants {
  ONE, TWO, THREE;
}
```

```
package p2;
// (1) INSERT IMPORT STATEMENTS HERE.
public class Q700_30 {
  public static void main(String[] args) {
    int value = new Random().nextInt(4);
    Constants constant = null;
    switch (value) {
      case 1:
        constant = ONE;
        break;
      case 2:
        constant = TWO;
        break;
      default:
        constant = THREE;
        break;
    }
    out.println(constant);
  }
}
```

Which import statements, when inserted at (1), will result in a program that prints
a constant of the enum type Constants, when compiled and run?

Select the two correct answers.

(a) `import java.util.*;`
     `import p1.Constants;`
     `import static p1.Constants.*;`
     `import static java.lang.System.out;`

(b) `import java.util.*;`
     `import static p1.Constants.*;`
     `import static java.lang.System.out;`

(c) `import java.util.*;`
     `import p1.Constants.*;`
     `import java.lang.System.out;`

(d) `import java.util.*;`
     `import p1.*;`
     `import static p1.Constants.*;`
     `import static java.lang.System.*;`

(e) `import java.util.Random;`
     `import p1.*;`
     `import static p1.Constants.*;`
     `import System.out;`

Q62 Given the following directory structure:

```
/proj
  |--- bin
        |--- top
              |--- sub
```

Assume that the classpath has the value:

```
top:top/sub
```

Which of the following statements are true?

Select the three correct answers.

(a) If the current directory is /proj/bin, the following directories are searched: top
    and sub.
(b) If the current directory is /proj/bin, the following directories are searched:
    bin, top and sub.
(c) If the current directory is /proj, the following directories are searched: bin, top
    and sub.
(d) If the current directory is /proj, no directories are searched.
(e) If the current directory is /proj/top, no directories are searched.

Q63 Given the following code:

```java
package p1;
public enum Format {
  JPEG, GIF, TIFF;
}
```

```java
package p1;
public class Util {
  public enum Format {
    JPEG { public String toString() {return "Jpeggy"; }},
    GIF  { public String toString() {return "Giffy"; }},
    TIFF { public String toString() {return "Tiffy"; }};
  }
  public static <T> void print(T t) {
    System.out.print("|" + t + "|");
  }
}
```

```java
import static p1.Format.*;
import static p1.Util.Format;
import static p1.Util.print;

public class Importing {
  static final int JPEG = 200;
  public static void main(String[] args) {
    final int JPEG = 100;
    print(JPEG);
    print(_____.JPEG);
    print(_____.JPEG);
    print(p1._____.JPEG);
  }
}
```

Which sequence of names, when used top down in the main() method, will print:

|100||200||Jpeggy||JPEG|

Select the one correct answer.

(a) Format, Importing, Format
(b) Format, Format, Format
(c) Importing, Format, Format

Q64 Given the following code:

```
public class Q200_50 {
  public static void main(String[] args) {
    // (1) INSERT METHOD CALL HERE.
  }
  private static void widenAndBox(Long lValue){
    System.out.println("Widen and Box");
  }
}
```

Which method calls, when inserted at (1), will cause the program to print:

Widen and Box

Select the two correct answers.

(a) widenAndBox((byte)10);
(b) widenAndBox(10);
(c) widenAndBox((long)10);
(d) widenAndBox(10L);

Q65 What will the program print when compiled and run?

```
public class Q200_80 {
  public static void main(String[] args) {
    callType(10);
  }

  private static void callType(Number num){
    System.out.println("Number passed");
  }

  private static void callType(Object obj){
    System.out.println("Object passed");
  }
}
```

Select the one correct answer.

(a) The program compiles and prints: Object passed
(b) The program compiles and prints: Number passed
(c) The program fails to compile, because the call to the callType() method is ambiguous.
(d) None of the above.

Q66 What will the program print when compiled and run?

```java
import java.util.ArrayList;
import java.util.List;

public class Q400_70 {
  public static void main(String[] args) {
    List<Integer> list = new ArrayList<Integer>();
    list.add(2007); list.add(2008); list.add(2009);
    System.out.println("Before: " + list);
    for (int i : list) {
      int index = list.indexOf(i);
      list.set(index, ++i);
    }
    System.out.println("After:  " + list);
  }
}
```

Select the one correct answer.

(a) Before: [2007, 2008, 2009]
     After: [2008, 2009, 2010]

(b) Before: [2007, 2008, 2009]
     After: [2010, 2008, 2009]

(c) Before: [2007, 2008, 2009]
     After: [2007, 2008, 2009]

(d) Before: [2007, 2008, 2009]
     After: [2008, 2009, 2007]

(e) The program throws a java.util.ConcurrentModificationException when run.

Q67 Which method implementation will write the given string to a file named "file", using UTF8 encoding?

Select the one correct answer.

(a) ```java
    public void write(String msg) throws IOException {
        FileWriter fw = new FileWriter(new File("file"));
        fw.write(msg);
        fw.close();
    }
    ```

(b) ```java
    public void write(String msg) throws IOException {
        OutputStreamWriter osw = new OutputStreamWriter(
                                    new FileOutputStream("file"), "UTF8");
        osw.write(msg);
        osw.close();
    }
    ```

(c) ```java
    public void write(String msg) throws IOException {
        FileWriter fw = new FileWriter(new File("file"));
        fw.setEncoding("UTF8");
        fw.write(msg);
        fw.close();
    }
    ```
    ```

(d)
```java
public void write(String msg) throws IOException {
    FilterWriter fw = new FilterWriter(
                        new FileWriter("file"), "UTF8");
    fw.write(msg);
    fw.close();
}
```

(e)
```java
public void write(String msg) throws IOException {
    OutputStreamWriter osw = new OutputStreamWriter(
                        new OutputStream(new File("file")), "UTF8");
    osw.write(msg);
    osw.close();
}
```

Q68 Given the following code:

```java
public class Person {
  protected transient String name;
  Person() { this.name = "NoName"; }
  Person(String name) { this.name = name; }
}
```

```java
public class Student extends Person {
  protected long studNum;
  Student() { }
  Student(String name, long studNum) {
    super(name);
    this.studNum = studNum;
  }
}
```

```java
import java.io.Serializable;
public class GraduateStudent extends Student implements Serializable {
  private int year;
  GraduateStudent(String name, long studNum, int year) {
    super(name, studNum);
    this.year = year;
  }

  public String toString() {
    return "(" + name + ", " + studNum + ", " + year + ")";
  }
}
```

```java
import java.io.*;
public class Q800_60 {

  public static void main(String args[])
                    throws IOException, ClassNotFoundException {
    FileOutputStream outputFile = new FileOutputStream("storage.dat");
    ObjectOutputStream outputStream = new ObjectOutputStream(outputFile);
    GraduateStudent stud1 = new GraduateStudent("Aesop", 100, 1);
    System.out.print(stud1);
```

```
      outputStream.writeObject(stud1);
      outputStream.flush();
      outputStream.close();

      FileInputStream inputFile = new FileInputStream("storage.dat");
      ObjectInputStream inputStream = new ObjectInputStream(inputFile);
      GraduateStudent stud2 = (GraduateStudent) inputStream.readObject();
      System.out.println(stud2);
      inputStream.close();
  }
}
```

Which statement is true about the program?

Select the one correct answer.

(a) It fails to compile.
(b) It compiles, but throws an exception at runtime.
(c) It prints (Aesop, 100, 1)(NoName, 0, 1).
(d) It prints (Aesop, 100, 1)(Aesop, 100, 1).
(e) It prints (Aesop, 100, 1)(null, 0, 1).

Q69   The following program formats a double value in the US locale, and prints the
      result 1,234.567. Complete the program using the code snippets given below:

```
import _____;
import _____;

public class FormattingNumbers {
  public static void main(String[] args) {
    double d = 1234.567;
    _____ f = _____(_____);
    System.out.println(_____);
  }
}
```

Any snippet may be used multiple times.

java.text.NumberFormat	NumberFormat
java.util.NumberFormat	DateFormat
java.text.Locale	Format
java.util.Locale	

NumberFormat.getNumberInstance	Locale.US
NumberFormat.getCurrencyInstance	DateFormat.DOUBLE
DateFormat.getInstance	NumberFormat.US
new NumberFormat	

d.format(f)	f.formatNumber(d)
f.format(d)	NumberFormat.format(d)

Q70   Given the following program:

```java
import java.util.Arrays;
public class Q500_100 {
  public static void main(String[] args) {
    String[] tokens = ___(1)___.split(___(2)___);
    System.out.println(Arrays.toString(tokens));
  }
}
```

Which pair of strings, when inserted at (1) and (2), respectively, will result in the following output:

```
[, mybook, mychapter, , mysection]
```

Select the two correct answers.

(a) "\mybook\mychapter\\mysection", "\\"
(b) "\\mybook\\mychapter\\\mysection", "\\\"
(c) "\\mybook\\mychapter\\\\mysection\\", "\\\\"
(d) "\\mybook\\mychapter\\\\mysection\\\\", "\\\\"
(e) "\\mybook\\mychapter\\mysection", "\\"
(f) The program will not compile, regardless of which alternative from (a) to (e) is inserted.
(g) The program will throw an exception when run, regardless of which alternative from (a) to (e) is inserted.

Q71   Given the following code:

```java
public class Q600_30 {
  public static void main(String[] args) {
    // (1) INSERT STATEMENT HERE
  }
}
```

Which statements, when inserted at (1), will print the following:

```
|false|
```

Select the six correct answers.

(a) System.out.printf("|%-4b|", false);
(b) System.out.printf("|%5b|", false);
(c) System.out.printf("|%.5b|", false);
(d) System.out.printf("|%4b|", "false");
(e) System.out.printf("|%3b|", 123);
(f) System.out.printf("|%b|", 123.45);
(g) System.out.printf("|%5b|", new Boolean("911"));
(h) System.out.printf("|%2b|", new Integer(2007));
(i) System.out.printf("|%1b|", (Object[])null);
(j) System.out.printf("|%1b|", (Object)null);
(k) System.out.printf("|%3$b|", null, 123, true);

Q72   Which statements are true about the classes SupA, SubB and SubC?:

```
class SupA<T> {
  public List<?> fuddle() { return null; }
  public List scuddle(T t) { return null; }
}

class SubB<U> extends SupA<U> {
  public List fuddle() { return null;}
  public List<?> scuddle(U t) { return null; }
}

class SubC<V> extends SupA<V> {
  public List<V> fuddle() { return null;}
  public List<? extends Object> scuddle(V t) { return null; }
}
```

Select the four correct answers.

(a) Class SubB will not compile.
(b) Class SubC will not compile.
(c) Class SubB will compile.
(d) Class SubC will compile.
(e) Class SubB overloads the methods in class SupA.
(f) Class SubC overloads the methods in class SupA.
(g) Class SubB overrides the methods in class SupA.
(h) Class SubC overrides the methods in class SupA.

Annotated Answers

Q1   *(a), (b), (c), and (e)*
Only local variables need to be explicitly initialized before use. Fields are assigned a default value if not explicitly initialized.

Q2   *(d)*
A try block must be followed by at least one catch or finally block. No catch blocks can follow a finally block. Methods need not declare that they can throw Runtime Exceptions, as these are unchecked exceptions.

Q3   *(e)*
Giving parameters (2, 3) to the method substring() constructs a string consisting of the characters between positions 2 and 3 of the original string. The positions are indexed in the following manner: position 0 is immediately before the first character of the string, position 1 is between the first and the second character, position 2 is between the second and the third character, and so on.

Q4   *(a)*
A Thread object executes the run() method of a Runnable object on a separate thread when started. A Runnable object can be given when constructing a Thread object. If no Runnable object is supplied, the Thread object (which implements the Runnable

interface) will execute its own `run()` method. A thread is initiated using the `start()` method of the `Thread` object.

Q5   *(a), (b), (c)*

First, note that nested packages or nested static members are not automatically imported.

In (d), `p2.DefenceInDepth` is not a static member and therefore cannot be imported statically.

With (e), `March.LEFT` becomes ambiguous because both the second and the third import statement statically import `March`. The enum constant `LEFT` cannot be resolved either, as its enum type `March` cannot be resolved.

With (f), the enum constant `LEFT` cannot be resolved, as none of the static import statements specify it.

The enum type `p2.March` is also not visible outside the package.

Q6   *(c)*

The loop prints out the values 12, 9, 6, and 3 before terminating.

Q7   *(e)*

The fact that a field is static does not mean that it is not accessible from non-static methods and constructors. All fields are assigned a default value if no initializer is supplied. Local variables must be explicitly initialized before use.

Q8   *(e)*

All the "hello" literals denote the same `String` object. Any `String` object created using the `new` operator will be a distinct new object.

Q9   *(a)*

Calls to the methods `suspend()`, `sleep()`, and `wait()` do not stop a thread. They only cause a thread to move out of its running state. A thread will terminate when the execution of the `run()` method has completed.

Q10   *(b), (d)*

(a) The class need not be declared as a generic type if it defines any generic methods.

(b) The method `choose(T, T)`, where T extends `Comparable<T>`, is not applicable to the arguments (`Integer`, `String`). Note that `Object` is not `Comparable<Object>`.

(c) The method `choose(T, T)`, where T extends `Comparable<T>`, is not applicable to the arguments (`Integer`, `Double`). Note that `Number` is not `Comparable<Number>`.

(d) The actual type parameter `Double` specified in the method call also requires that the `int` argument is cast to a `double` in order for the call to be valid. The method `choose(T, T)`, where T extends `Comparable<T>`, is then applicable to the argument list (`Double`, `Double`).

(e) Cannot convert the `Double` returned by the method to an `int` using a cast.

(f) The method returns a `Double` which is first converted to a `double`, which in turn is converted to an `int`.

Q11   *(e)*

An object of the class Extension is created. The first thing the constructor of Extension does is invoke the constructor of Base, using an implicit super() call. All calls to the method void add(int) are dynamically bound to the add() method in the Extension class, since the actual object is of type Extension. Therefore, this method is called by the constructor of Base, the constructor of Extension, and the bogo() method with the parameters 1, 2, and 8, respectively. The instance field i changes value accordingly: 2, 6, and 22. The final value of 22 is printed.

Q12   *(d)*

TreeMap and HashSet do not maintain an ordered sequence of objects. Vector and ArrayList require shifting of objects on insertion and deletion, while LinkedList does not. When objects are frequently inserted and deleted from the middle of the sequence, LinkedList gives the best performance.

Q13   *(a) and (d)*

Field b of the outer class is not shadowed by any local or inner class variables, therefore, (a) will work. Using this.a will access the field a in the inner class. Using this.b will result in a compilation error, since there is no field b in the inner class. Using Q4a39.this.a will successfully access the field of the outer class. The statement c = c will only reassign the current value of the local variable c to itself.

Q14   *(b), (c), (d)*

The class File does not have methods called found, isAFile, or isADirectory.

Q15   *(d)*

At (1), a new String object is constructed by concatenating the string "bye" in the String object denoted by b and the string "!". After line (2), d and b are aliases. After line (3), b and a are aliases, but d still denotes the String object with "bye" from line (0). After line (4), d and a are aliases. Reference d no longer denotes the String object created in line (0). This String object has no references to it and is, therefore, a candidate for garbage collection.

Q16   *(c)*

The regex in (c) requires a sequence of uppercase letters to be followed by a sequence of lowercase letters. The other regexes are equivalent, as they require a sequence which can consist of upper and/or lower case letters, i.e., any combination of letters.

Running the program with the regex in (c) will produce the following output:

(5,6:Ja)(7,8:Va)

Running the program with the other regexes will produce the following output:

(0,3:JAVA)(5,8:JaVa)(10,13:java)(15,18:jaVA)

Q17   *(d)*

String objects are immutable. None of the methods of the String class modify a String object. Methods toUpperCase() and replace() in the String class will return a new `String` object that contains the modified string. However, `StringBuilder` objects are mutable.

Q18   *(e)*

The second parameter to the constructor specifies whether the file contents should be replaced or appended when the specified file already exists.

Q19   *(c)*
Statement (a) will work just fine, and (b), (d), and (e) will cause compilation errors. Statements (b) and (e) will cause compilation errors because they attempt to assign an incompatible type to the reference. Statement (d) will cause compilation errors, since a cast from B to C is invalid. Being an instance of B excludes the possibility of being an instance of C. Statement (c) will compile, but will throw a runtime exception, since the object that is cast to B is not an instance of B.

Q20   *(b), (c), (d), (g)*

In (a), a `String` is neither an array nor an `Iterable`. In (e), the local variable `str` is redeclared. In (f) the occurrence of the array operator [] is not permissible. In (h), the `String` class does not have a method called `toArray`, but it has a method called `toCharArray`.

Q21   *(e)*
The desired accessibility is package accessibility, which is the default accessibility for members that have no accessibility modifier. The keyword `package` is not an accessibility modifier and cannot be used in this context.

Q22   *(b) and (e)*
For the expression `matrix[3][2]` to access a valid element of a two-dimensional array, the array must have at least four rows and the fourth row must have at least three elements. Fragment (a) produces a 2 × 3 array. Fragment (c) tries to initialize a two-dimensional array as a one-dimensional array. Fragment (d) tries to specify array dimensions in the type of the array reference declaration.

Q23   *(c), (d)*

The pathname of the JAR file, together with the JAR file name, should be specified.

Q24   *(a)*
The expression `arr.length` will evaluate to 4. The expression `arr[1]` will access the element { { "1", "2" }, { "1", null, "3" } }, and `arr[1][2]` will try to access the third sub-element of this element. This produces an `ArrayIndexOutOfBoundsException`, since the element has only two sub-elements.

Q25   *(c) and (d)*
`String` objects can have identical sequences of characters. The `==` operator, when used on `String` object references, will just compare the references and will only return `true` when both references denote the same object (i.e., are aliases). The `equals()` method will return `true` whenever the contents of the `String` objects are identical. An array of char and a `String` are two totally different types and cannot be compared using the `equals()` method of the `String` class.

Q26   *(b) and (c)*

Statement (d) is `false`, since an object of B can be created using the implicit default constructor of the class. B has an implicit default constructor since no constructor has explicitly been defined. Statement (e) is `false`, since the second constructor of C will call the first constructor of C.

Q27   *(b) and (d)*

The `retainAll()`, `removeAll()`, and `addAll()` methods do not return a new collection object, but instead modify the collection object they were called upon. The collection object given as an argument is not affected. The `containsAll()` does not modify either of the collection objects.

Q28   *(b), (c), and (e)*

An instance of the class Baz is also an instance of the class Foo, since the class Baz extends the class Foo. A Baz has a Bar since instances of the class Baz contain an instance of the class Bar by reference. A Foo has a Baz, since instances of the class Foo contain an instance of the class Baz by reference. Since a Foo has a Baz which has a Bar, a Foo has a Bar.

Q29   *(b) and (e)*

Unlike local variables, all fields are initialized with default initial values. All numeric fields are initialized to zero, `boolean` fields to `false`, char fields to `'\u0000'`, and *all* reference fields to `null`.

Q30   *(b), (d)*

Q31   *(c) and (d)*

Very little is guaranteed about the behavior of the garbage collection and finalization mechanisms. The (c) and (d) statements are two of the things that are guaranteed.

Q32   *(a)*

The `main()` method in (b) will always generate and catch an `ArrayIndexOutOfBounds-Exception`, since `args.length` is an illegal index in the args array. The `main()` method in (c) will always throw an `ArrayIndexOutOfBoundsException` since it is also uses `args.length` as an index, but this exception is never caught. The `main()` method in (d) will fail to print the argument if only one program argument is supplied. The `main()` method in (e) will generate an uncaught `ArrayIndexOutOfBoundsException` if no program arguments are specified.

Q33   *(a), (b), and (c)*

Set and List both extend Collection. A map is *not* a collection and Map does not extend Collection. Set does not have any new methods other than those defined in Collection. List defines additional methods to the ones in Collection.

Q34   *(a)*

All enum types implement the Comparable interface. Comparison is based on the natural order, which in this case is the order in which the constants are specified, with the first one being the smallest. The ordinal value of the first enum constant is 0, the next one has the ordinal value 1, and so on.

Q35   *(c)*

The important thing to remember is that if an object is an instance of a class, it is also an instance of all the superclasses of this class.

Q36   *(e)*

Method g() modifies the field a. Method g() modifies the parameter b, not the field b, since the parameter declaration shadows the field. Variables are passed by value, so the change of value in parameter b is confined to the method g(). Method g() modifies the array whose reference value is passed as a parameter. Change to the first element is visible after return from the method g().

Q37   *(a), (c), and (e)*

The equals() method ignores the ordering of a and b when determining if two objects are equivalent. The hashCode() implementation must, therefore, also ignore the ordering of a and b when calculating the hash value, i.e., the implementation must return the same value even after the values of a and b are swapped.

Q38   *(b), (c), (e), (g)*

(a) N is not Comparable.

(b) Ok

(c) Ok. N is Comparable. Specifying Object as a bound is superfluous in this case.

(d) N is not Comparable, as Number is not Comparable.

(e) Ok. N is Number and Comparable.

(f) The class must be specified first in multiple bounds.

(g) Ok. N is Integer and Integer is Comparable, N is Comparable<Integer>.

(h) N is Integer and Integer is Comparable<Integer>, N is Comparable<Integer>. The class cannot implement the same interface, in this case Comparable, more than once.

Q39   *(c) and (d)*

The variable j is only decremented if assertions are enabled. The assertion never fails, since the loop condition ensures that the loop body is only executed as long as i<j is true. With assertions enabled, each iteration decrements j by 1. The last number printed is 20 if assertions are disabled at runtime, and the last number printed is 4 if assertions are enabled at runtime.

Q40   *(b) and (c)*

These names have overloaded methods that allow optional timeout values as parameters.

Q41   *(a)*

The program will fail to compile since the label 12 cannot precede the declaration int j = 0. For a label to be associated with a loop, it must immediately precede the loop construct.

Q42   *(b)*

Classes cannot extend interfaces, they must implement them. Interfaces can extend other interfaces, but cannot implement them. A class must be declared `abstract` if it does not provide an implementation for one of its methods. Methods declared in interfaces are implicitly `public` and `abstract`. Classes that implement these methods must explicitly declare their implementations `public`.

Q43   *(a) and (e)*

The `notify()` and `notifyAll()` methods are declared in the class `Object`. Since all other classes extend `Object`, these methods are also available in instances of all other classes, including `Thread`. The method `notify()` is not synchronized, but will throw an `IllegalMonitorStateException` if the current thread is not the owner of the object lock.

Q44   *(a) and (c)*

Accessing fields of the outer instance using only the variable name works within the inner instance as long as the variable is not shadowed. Fields need not be declared `final` in order to be accessible within the inner instance.

Q45   *(a)*

The code will fail to compile because the literal `4.3` has the type `double`. Assignment of a `double` value to a `float` variable without an explicit cast is not allowed. The code would compile and write `0` to standard output when run, if the literal `4.3` was replaced with `4.3F`.

Q46   *(b) and (e)*

The `&&` and `||` operators exhibit short-circuit behavior. The first operand of the ternary operator (`? :`) is always evaluated. Based on the result of this evaluation, either the second or the third operand is evaluated.

Q47   *(e)*

No labels are mandatory (including the `default` label), and can be placed in any order within the `switch` body. The keyword `continue` may occur within the body of a `switch` statement as long as it pertains to a loop. Any constant non-`long` integral value can be used for `case` labels as long as the type is compatible with the expression in the `switch` expression.

Q48   *(d)*

The condition of the `if` statement will always be `false`, as the string pattern `"\\w+"` will not match the first token `"Treat!"`. No matter what we insert at (1), it will not be executed. The `else` part will always be executed, retrieving the current token with the `next()` method, thereby exhausting the output.

Inserting at (2) will mean attempting to tokenize from an exhausted input, resulting in a `java.util.NoSuchElementException`. Inserting at (3) means calling the `next()` method after closing the scanner, resulting in a `java.lang.IllegalStateException`.

Q49   *(a), (b), and (e)*

Expressions (a), (b), and (e) all call the method `hashCode()` on valid objects. (c) is an illegal expression, as methods cannot be called on primitive values. The call in (d) to the `equals()` method requires an object as argument.

Q50   *(e)*

The method returns `true` if and only if assertions are enabled at runtime. It will only return `false` if assertions are disabled.

Q51   *(d)*

Overridden method implementations are accessed using the `super` keyword. Statements like `print()`, `Base.print()`, and `Base.this.print()` will not work.

Q52   *(c) and (d)*

Executing synchronized code does not guard against executing non-synchronized code concurrently.

Q53   *(a), (c), (e)*

Lists of type `Pet`, `Dog`, and `Cat` are subtypes of `List<? extends Pet>`, `List<? extends Wagger>` and `List<?>`.

`List<? super Pet>` is a supertype for a list of `Pet` itself or a supertype of `Pet`, e.g., `Wagger`, but not `Dog` and `Cat`.

`List<? super Wagger>` is a supertype for a list of `Wagger` itself or a supertype of `Wagger`, e.g., `Object`, but not `Pet`, `Dog`, and `Cat`.

Q54   *(a)*

Strings are immutable, therefore, the `concat()` method has no effect on the original `String` object. The string on which the `trim()` method is called consists of 8 characters, where the first and the two last characters are spaces (`" hello   "`). The `trim()` method returns a new `String` object where the white space characters at each end have been removed. This leaves the 5 characters of the word `"hello"`.

Q55   *(a) and (b)*

If a thread is executing method `b()` on an object, it is guaranteed that no other thread executes methods `a()` and `b()` concurrently. Therefore, the invocation counters `i` and `j` will never show more than one concurrent invocation. Two threads can concurrently be executing methods `b()` and `c()`. Therefore, the invocation counter `k` can easily show more than one concurrent invocation.

Q56   *(a) and (e)*

Declaration (b) fails, since the method signature only differs in the return type. Declaration (c) fails, since it tries to declare an `abstract` method in a non-abstract class. Declaration (d) fails, since its signature is identical to the existing method.

Q57   *(a)*

Execution proceeds normally and produces no output. All assertions are true.

Q58   *(c)*

The program will not compile, because the method equals() cannot be overridden by enum types.

The program will not compile, because the enum constant GOLD cannot be assigned a new value. The constants are final.

The program will not compile, because the enum constant BASIC cannot be created, as no explicit default constructor is defined.

Q59   *(b)*

None of the formal type parameter specifications with a wildcard are permitted. This rules out (c) and (f). The keyword super can only be used with a wildcard, and therefore rules out (d) and (e). NumClass<Number> is not a subtype of NumClass<T extends Integer>, ruling out (a).

Q60   *(d)*

Note that the print() method does not print its first argument. The vararg is passed in the method calls as follows:

```
print("9", "6");          // (1) new String[] {"6"}
print(sa);                // (2) new String[] {}
print(sa, sa);            // (4) sa
print(sa, sa, sa);        // (5) new String[][] {sa, sa}
print(sa, "9", "6");      // (6) new String[] {"9", "6"}
```

Q61   *(a), (d)*

In the program, we need to import the types java.util.Random and the enum type p1.Constants. We also need to statically import the constants of the enum type p1.Constants, and the static field out from the type java.lang.System. All classes must be fully qualified in the import statements. Only (a) and (d) fit the bill.

(b) does not import the enum type p1.Constants. (c) does not import the enum type p1.Constants either. In addition, it does not statically import the constants of the enum type p1.Constants and the static field out from the type java.lang.System. (e) does not statically import the static field out from the type java.lang.System.

Q62   *(a), (d), (e)*

Note that the entries in the classpath are relative paths.

When the current directory is /proj/bin, both entries in the classpath can be found under /proj/bin. The directory bin itself is not searched, as there is no valid path /proj/bin/bin.

When the current directory is /proj, both entries in the classpath cannot be found relative to /proj, i.e., the paths /proj/top and /proj/top/sub are not valid paths.

Q63   *(c)*

We need to access the following:

- `Importing.JPEG` (to print 200)

- `p1.Util.Format.JPEG` (to print `"Jpeggy"`). Since `p1.Util.Format` is statically imported by the second import statement, we need only specify `Format.JPEG`.

- `p1.Format.JPEG` (to print `"JPEG"`), which is explicitly specified to distinguish it from other JPEG declarations. The first import statement is actually superfluous.

Q64   *(c), (d)*

Only primitive types allow automatic widening conversion, wrapper types do not allow automatic widening conversion. A `byte` or an `int` cannot be automatically converted to a `Long`. Automatic boxing and unboxing is only allowed between corresponding primitives types and their wrapper classes.

Q65   *(b)*

The method with the most specific signature is chosen. In this case the `int` argument 10 is converted to an `Integer` which is passed to the `Number` formal parameter, as type `Number` is more specific than `Object`.

Q66   *(b)*

First note that the `indexOf()` method returns the index of the *first* occurrence of its argument in the list. Although the value of variable i is successively changing during the execution of the loop, it is the *first* occurrence of this value that is replaced in each iteration:

```
                   0     1     2
                  [2007, 2008, 2009]
After iteration 1: [2008, 2008, 2009]
After iteration 2: [2009, 2008, 2009]
After iteration 3: [2010, 2008, 2009]
```

Note also that we are not removing or adding elements to the list, only changing the reference values stored in the elements of the list.

Q67   *(b)*

Method implementation (a) will write the string to the file, but will use the native encoding. Method implementation (c) will fail to compile, since a method named `setEncoding` does not exist in class `FileWriter`. Method implementation (d) will fail to compile, since `FilterWriter` is an abstract class that cannot be used to translate encodings. Method implementation (e) will fail to compile, since class `OutputStream` is abstract.

Q68   *(c)*

Note that only `GraduateStudent` is `Serializable`. The field `name` in the `Person` class is `transient`. During serialization of a `GraduateStudent` object, the fields `year` and `studNum` are included as part of the serialization process, but not the field `name`. During deserialization, the default constructors of the superclasses up the inheritance hierarchy of the GraduateStudent class are called, as none of the superclasses are Serializable.

Q69   *The completed program is as follows:*

```java
import java.text.NumberFormat;
import java.util.Locale;

public class FormattingNumbers {
  public static void main(String[] args) {
    double d = 1234.567;
    NumberFormat f = NumberFormat.getNumberInstance(Locale.US);
    System.out.println(f.format(d));
  }
}
```

Q70   *(c), (d)*

The output shows two empty strings (first and third). In order to split on the backslash (\), the required string is "\\\\". Remember that \ is a metacharacter for both Java strings and for regexes. We need to escape \ in the regex specification, which requires \\. In order to escape these two backslashes in a Java string, we need to add a backslash for each backslash we want to escape in the regex, i.e., "\\\\".

In the input string we need to escape each backslash so that it is not interpreted as a metacharacter.

The split() method tokenizes the input on the regex, *but it does not return trailing empty strings.* Therefore, the empty strings matched by the backslashes at the end of the input are not reported. The method call str.split(regex) is equivalent to Pattern.compile(regex).split(str).

Q71   *(a), (b), (c), (g), (i), (j)*

(a) 5 character positions will be used. The width 4 is overridden, and the - sign is superfluous.
(b) 5 character positions will be used. The width 5 is superfluous.
(c) The precision 5 is the same as the length of the resulting string, and therefore superfluous.
(d) The reference value of the string literal "false" is not null, resulting in "true" being printed. Analogous reasoning for (e) and (f).
(g) Since the argument to the Boolean constructor is not "true", the value represented by the wrapper object is false.
(h) Same as (d).
(i) Since the argument is null, the value printed is "false". Width specification is overridden by the length of the string "false". Same for (j).
(k) The third argument is true, therefore "true" is printed.

Q72   *(c), (d), (g), (h)*

The method header signature of the corresponding methods are the same after erasure, i.e. `List fuddle()` and `List scuddle(Object)`. The return type of overriding methods can be a raw type or a parameterized type.

Number Systems and Number Representation

G.1 Number Systems

Binary, Octal, and Hexadecimal Number System

Table G.1 lists the integers from 0 to 16, showing their equivalents in the binary (*base* 2), octal (*base* 8), and hexadecimal (*base* 16) number systems. The shaded cells in each column show the digits in each number system.

Table G.1 *Number Systems*

Decimal (base 10)	Binary (base 2)	Octal (base 8)	Hexadecimal (base 16)
0	0	0	0
1	1	1	1
2	10	2	2
3	11	3	3
4	100	4	4
5	101	5	5
6	110	6	6
7	111	7	7
8	1000	10	8
9	1001	11	9
10	1010	12	a

Continues

Table G.1 *Number Systems (Continued)*

Decimal (base 10)	Binary (base 2)	Octal (base 8)	Hexadecimal (base 16)
11	1011	13	b
12	1100	14	c
13	1101	15	d
14	1110	16	e
15	1111	17	f
16	10000	20	10

In addition to the decimal literals, Java also allows integer literals to be specified in octal and hexadecimal number systems, but not in the binary number system. Octal and hexadecimal numbers are specified with 0 and 0x prefix, respectively. The prefix 0X can also be used for hexadecimal numbers. Note that the leading 0 (zero) digit is not the uppercase letter O. The hexadecimal digits from a to f can also be specified with the corresponding uppercase forms (A to F). Negative integers (e.g., -90) can be specified by prefixing the minus sign (-) to the magnitude, regardless of number system (e.g., -0132 or -0X5A). The actual memory representation of the integer values is discussed in Section G.4.

Converting Binary Numbers to Decimals

A binary number can be converted to its equivalent decimal value by computing the *positional values* of its digits. Each digit in the binary number contributes to the final decimal value by virtue of its position, starting with position 0 (units) for the right-most digit in the number. The positional value of each digit is given by

$$digit \times base^{\,position}$$

The number 101001_2 corresponds to 41_{10} in the decimal number system:

$$101001_2 = 1{\times}2^5 + 0{\times}2^4 + 1{\times}2^3 + 0{\times}2^2 + 0{\times}2^1 + 1{\times}2^0$$
$$= 32 + 0 + 8 + 0 + 0 + 1$$
$$= 41_{10}$$

Converting Octal and Hexadecimal Numbers to Decimals

Similarly, octal (base 8) and hexadecimal (base 16) numbers can be converted to their decimal equivalents:

$$0132 = \mathbf{132_8} = \mathbf{1{\times}8^2 + 3{\times}8^1 + 2{\times}8^0} = 64 + 24 + 2 = 90_{10} \qquad \text{Octal} \rightarrow \text{Decimal}$$

$$0x5a = \mathbf{5a_{16}} = \mathbf{5{\times}16^1 + a{\times}16^0} \qquad = 80 + 10 \qquad = 90_{10} \qquad \text{Hex} \rightarrow \text{Decimal}$$

The same technique can be used to convert a number from any base to its equivalent representation in the decimal number system.

G.2 Relationship between Binary, Octal, and Hexadecimal Numbers

From Table G.1 we see that 3 bits are needed to represent any octal digit, and 4 bits to are needed to represent any hexadecimal digit. We can use this fact to convert between binary, octal, and hexadecimal systems, as shown in Figure G.1.

The procedure for converting an octal to a binary is shown by the arrow marked (a). We can prove that replacing each octal digit by its 3-bit equivalent binary value gives the right result:

$$
\begin{aligned}
\mathbf{173_8} &= \mathbf{1{\times}8^2} & &+\; \mathbf{7{\times}8^1} & &+\; \mathbf{3{\times}8^0} \\
&= \mathbf{1{\times}(2^3)^2} & &+\; \mathbf{7{\times}(2^3)^1} & &+\; \mathbf{3{\times}(2^3)^0} \\
&= \mathbf{1{\times}2^6} & &+\; \mathbf{7{\times}2^3} & &+\; \mathbf{3} \\
&= \mathbf{(001_2){\times}2^6} & &+\; \mathbf{(111_2){\times}2^3} & &+\; \mathbf{(011_2)} \\
&= \mathbf{(0{\times}2^2+0{\times}2^1+1{\times}2^0){\times}2^6} & &+\; \mathbf{(1{\times}2^2+1{\times}2^1+1{\times}2^0){\times}2^3} & &+\; \mathbf{(0{\times}2^2+1{\times}2^1+1{\times}2^0)} \\
&= \mathbf{1{\times}2^6} & &+\; \mathbf{1{\times}2^5+1{\times}2^4+1{\times}2^3} & &+\; \mathbf{0{\times}2^2+1{\times}2^1+1{\times}2^0} \\
&= \mathbf{1{\times}2^6 + 1{\times}2^5 + 1{\times}2^4 + 1{\times}2^3 + 0{\times}2^2 + 1{\times}2^1 + 1{\times}2^0} \\
&= \mathbf{1111011_2}
\end{aligned}
$$

Analogously, we can convert a hexadecimal number to its equivalent binary number by replacing each digit in the hexadecimal number by its 4-bit equivalent binary value, as shown by the arrow marked (b).

Figure G.1   *Converting between Binary, Octal, and Hexadecimal*

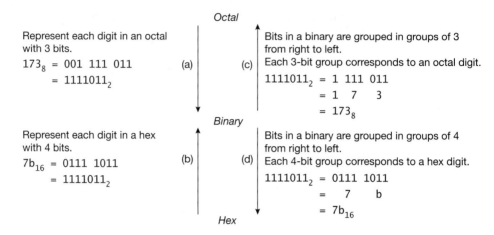

To convert a binary to it octal equivalent, we reverse the procedure outlined earlier (see arrow marked (c) in Figure G.1). The bits in the binary number are grouped into 3-bit groups from right to left. Each such group is replaced by its equivalent octal digit. This corresponds to reversing the computation shown above. Analogously, we can convert a binary to a hexadecimal number by replacing each 4-bit group by its equivalent hex digit (see arrow marked (d) in Figure G.1).

G.3 Converting Decimals

Converting Decimals to Binary Numbers

In order to convert decimals to binaries, we reverse the process outlined in Section G.1 for converting a binary to a decimal.

$41_{10} = 20{\times}2 + \mathbf{1}$	Dividing 41 by 2, gives the quotient 20 and remainder 1.
$20_{10} = 10{\times}2 + \mathbf{0}$	We again divide the current quotient 20 by 2.
$10_{10} = 5{\times}2 + \mathbf{0}$	
$5_{10} = 2{\times}2 + \mathbf{1}$	We repeat this procedure until ...
$2_{10} = 1{\times}2 + \mathbf{0}$	
$1_{10} = 0{\times}2 + \mathbf{1}$	... the quotient is 0.
$\mathbf{41_{10} = 101001_2}$	

The divisor used in the steps above is the base of the target number system (binary, base 2). The binary value, 101001_2, is represented by the remainders, with the last remainder as the left-most bit. Back substitution of the quotient gives the same result:

$$41_{10} = (((((0\times2 + 1)\times2 + 0)\times2 + 1)\times2 + 0)\times2 + 0)\times2 + 1$$
$$= 1\times2^5 + 0\times2^4 + 1\times2^3 + 0\times2^2 + 0\times2^1 + 1\times2^0$$
$$= 101001_2$$

Converting Decimals to Octal and Hexadecimal Numbers

Analogously, we can apply the above procedure for converting an octal to a binary. The conversion for the decimal number 90 can be done as follows:

$$90_{10} = 11\times8 + 2$$
$$11_{10} = 1\times8 + 3$$
$$1_{10} = 0\times8 + 1$$
$$90_{10} = 132_8 = 0132$$

The remainder values represent the digits in the equivalent octal number: 132_8. This can be verified by back substitution, which gives the following result:

$$90_{10} = ((0\times8 + 1)\times8 + 3)\times8 + 2$$
$$= 1\times8^2 + 3\times8^1 + 2\times8^0$$
$$= 132_8 = 0132$$

Conversion to hexadecimal is analogous:

$$90_{10} = 5\times16 + 10$$
$$5_{10} = 0\times16 + 5$$
$$90_{10} = 5a_{16} = 0x5a$$

The remainders represent the digits of the number in the hexadecimal system: 5a. Back substitution gives the same result:

$$90_{10} = (0\times16 + 5)\times16 + 10$$
$$= 5\times16^1 + a\times16^0$$
$$= 5a_{16} = 0x5a$$

G.4 Representing Integers

Integer data types in Java represent *signed* integer values, i.e., both positive and negative integer values. The values of char type can effectively be regarded as *unsigned* 16-bit integers.

Values of type byte are represented as shown in Table G.2. A value of type byte requires 8 bits. With 8 bits, we can represent 2^8 or 256 values. Java uses 2's complement (explained later) to store signed values of integer data types. For the byte data type, this means values are in the range -128 (-2^7) to $+127$ (2^7-1), inclusive.

Bits in an integral value are usually numbered from right to left, starting with the least significant bit 0 (also called the *right-most bit*). When applying bitwise operators, the number of the most significant bit (also called the *left-most bit*) is dependent on the integral type; bit 31 for byte, short, char, and int, and bit 63 for long. The representation of the signed types sets the most significant bit to 1, indicating negative values. Adding 1 to the maximum int value 2147483647 results in the minimum value -2147483648, i.e., the values wrap around for integers and no overflow or underflow is indicated.

Table G.2 *Representing Signed* byte *Values Using 2's Complement*

Decimal Value	Binary Representation (8 bit)	Octal Value with Prefix 0	Hexadecimal Value with Prefix 0x
127	01111111	0177	0x7f
126	01111110	0176	0x7e
...	...	...	...
41	00101001	051	0x29
...	...	...	...
2	00000010	02	0x02
1	00000001	01	0x01
0	00000000	00	0x0
-1	11111111	0377	0xff
-2	11111110	0376	0xfe
...	...	...	...
-41	11010111	0327	0xd7
...	...	...	...
−127	10000001	0201	0x81
−128	10000000	0200	0x80

Calculating 2's Complement

Before we look at 2's complement, we need to understand 1's complement. 1's complement of a binary integer is computed by inverting the bits in the number. Thus, 1's complement of the binary number 00101001 is 11010110. 1's complement of a binary number N_2 is denoted as $\sim N_2$. The following relations hold between a binary integer N_2, its 1's complement $\sim N_2$, and its 2's complement $-N_2$:

$$-N_2 = \sim N_2 + 1$$

$$0 = -N_2 + N_2$$

If N_2 is a positive binary integer, then $-N_2$ denotes its negative binary value, and vice versa. The second relation states that adding a binary integer N_2 to its 2's complement $-N_2$ equals 0.

Given a positive byte value, say 41, the binary representation of -41 can be found as follows:

	Binary Representation	Decimal Value
Given a value, N_2:	00101001	41
Form 1's complement, $\sim N_2$:	11010110	
Add 1:	00000001	
Result is 2's complement, $-N_2$:	11010111	−41

Similarly, given a negative number, say -41, we can find the binary representation of 41:

	Binary Representation	Decimal Value
Given a value, N_2:	11010111	−41
Form 1's complement, $\sim N_2$:	00101000	
Add 1:	00000001	
Result is 2's complement, $-N_2$:	00101001	41

Adding a number N_2 to its 2's complement $-N_2$ gives 0, and the carry bit from the addition of the most significant bits (after any necessary extension of the operands) is ignored:

	Binary representation	Decimal value
Given a value, N_2:	00101001	41
Add 2's complement, $\sim N_2$:	11010111	-41
Sum:	00000000	0

Subtraction between two integers is also computed as addition with 2's complement:

$$N_2 - M_2 = N_2 + (-M_2)$$

For example, calculating $41_{10} - 3_{10}$ (with the correct result 38_{10}) is computed as follows:

	Binary Representation	Decimal Value
Given a value, N_2:	00101001	41
Add $-M_2$ (i.e., subtract M_2):	11111101	-3
Result:	00100110	38

The previous discussion on byte values applies equally to values of other integer types: short, int, and long. These types have their values represented by 2's complement in 16, 32, and 64 bits, respectively.

Index

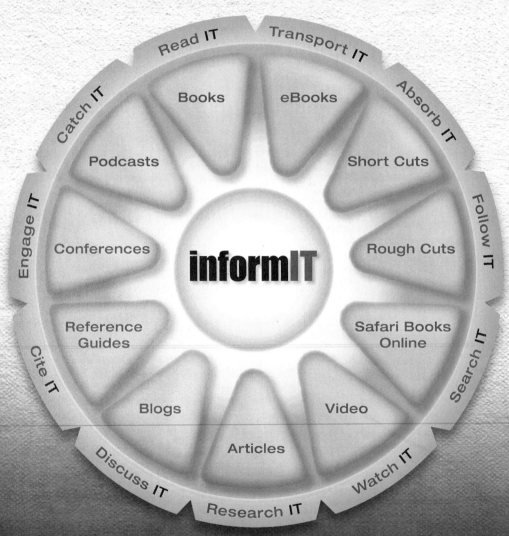